Thailand

a travel survival kit

ประเทศไทย

Joe Cummings

Thailand – a travel survival kit

5th edition

Published by

Lonely Planet Publications
Head Office: PO Box 617, Hawthorn, Vic 3122, Australia
Branches: PO Box 2001A, Berkeley, CA 94702, USA and London, UK

Printed by

Singapore National Printers Ltd, Singapore

Photographs by

Vicki Beale (VB)
Glenn Beanland (GB)
Joe Cummings (JC)
Meredith Hunnibell (MH)
Richard I'Anson (RI)
Ralph Kaminski (RK)
Chris Lee Ack (CLA)
Tracy Maurer (TM)
Peter Morris (PM)
Richard Nebesky (RN)
Joanna O'Brien (JB)
Bill Preston (BP)
Chris Taylor (CT)
Tourism Authority of Thailand (TAT)
Dale Wahren (DW)

Front cover: Temple Mural at Wat Phra Kaew (JC)

First Published

February 1982

This Edition

October 1992

National Library of Australia Cataloguing in Publication Data

Cummings, Joe.
Thailand – a travel survival kit.

5th ed.
Includes index.
ISBN 0 86442 170 2.

1. Thailand – Description and travel – 1976 – Guide-books.
I. Title. (Series : Lonely Planet travel survival kit).

915.930444

Joe Cummings

Joe Cummings has been involved in South-East Asian studies for many years and was a Peace Corps volunteer in Thailand during the '70s. Since then he has been a translator/ interpreter of Thai in San Francisco, a student of Thai language and Asian art history at the University of California, Berkeley (MA 1981), a columnist for *The Asia Record*, an East-West Center Scholar in Hawaii, a university lecturer in Malaysia, and a bilingual studies consultant in the USA and Taiwan.

Fluent in Thai, Joe has travelled through all 73 of the kingdom's provinces by bus, air, train, motorcycle, boat, elephant and on foot. Joe is also the author of Lonely Planet's *Thai Phrasebook* and *Bangkok City Guide*, and a contributor to many other LP titles, including guides on Burma, China, Laos, Malaysia/ Singapore and Indonesia. He occasionally writes for *The San Francisco Examiner, Great Expeditions, Weissman Travel Reports, Condé Nast Traveler* and other periodicals.

From the Author

Thanks to the following people in Thailand and California who assisted along the way: Santichai Euachongprasit, Chalermlap Ganachara Na Ayuthaya, Pradthana Doungmala, Apin Banduwongse, Sapachai Pitaksakorn, Max and Tick, Boonchu Hankham, Suraphon Svetsreni, Suksom Senajai, Ajaan Nirundorn, Thanaphong Boonyarit, Anitra Puangsuwan ('Tuk'), Pradthana Pulperm, Pimol Kalayanasothorn, Darunee Yenjai, Rattana Laongkul, Lamduan Sukhapan, Niyana Angkawut, Nikom Tienchai, Suthep Emsiranunt, Joom & Mary, Uthai Kutrakool, Koliang, Fhu & Ung, Uma and Bunma Kumat, Preecha Thitichon, M L Chainimit Navarat, Adirake, Roger & Doy, Lynne Cummings, Nancy Chandler, Lyn Irvine, David Unkovich, Pierre Vanderhoven, Jeff Nelson, Guido ('Swissie'), Mike Olsen, Don Campbell, George Woodington, Tom Herman, Herb April and Meredith Sue Krashes.

The Tourist Authority of Thailand and its employees throughout Thailand, as usual, were of considerable assistance, as were research assistants David Sheppard and Tom Huhti.

Thanks also to the hundreds of travellers who have taken time to write, especially letter-writers Ian Robinson, Todd Paddock, Bruce Moore, Leon Sebek, Julia Richards, Harold Taw, Ajay Jani, Rebecca Woodgate, Beverly Russell, Glen Hill, Bernie Hodges, Darren Russell, Paul Harris and Guntur Hoffman.

I've tried to name everyone who was of direct help but know I've forgotten a few names along the way. Please forgive me if you're not listed and accept my gratitude.

The fifth edition of this guidebook is dedicated to the memory of Ven Ajaan Chaa (1918-1992).

Author's Note to Readers

When using the information contained in this guide to find your way around Thailand, keep in mind the Buddhist concept of *anicca*, or 'impermanence'. All things in the world of travel especially are in a constant state of flux and Thailand is no exception. What you read here are conceptual snapshots of single moments in time, filtered through one person's perceptions. They represent the very best of my research efforts at the time of writing, but were bound to change the second I turned my attention away from research and began writing it all down, a necessary part of the process in getting this book to you. Don't expect to find things to be exactly as described in the text – stay flexible and you'll enjoy yourself more.

From the Publisher

Miriam Cannell, Jon Murray and Jenny Missen edited this edition of Thailand. Diana Saad helped with the proofing and, along with Tom Smallman and Joe Cummings, saw it through production. Thanks to Michelle Coxall for additional proofing. Ann Jeffree was responsible for the maps, book and cover design. She was given invaluable assistance during production by Tamsin Wilson. Tamsin, Paul Clifton and Trudi Canavan also helped with the maps and illustrations. Thanks to Joe Cummings for supplying the Thai script, to Dan Levin for the Thai script fonts, and to Peter Turner for helping with the conversion of the script. Thanks also to Sharon Wertheim for indexing and to Sue Mitra for her editorial guidance.

Thanks must go to the travellers who used the previous editions of this book and wrote to Lonely Planet with information, comments and suggestions. They are listed at the back of the book.

Warning & Request

Things change – prices go up, schedules change, good places go bad and bad places go bankrupt – nothing stays the same. So if you find things better or worse, recently opened or long since closed, please write and tell us and help make the next edition better. Your letters will be used to help update future editions and, where possible, important changes will also be included in a Stop Press section in reprints.

We greatly appreciate all information that is sent to us by travellers. Back at Lonely Planet we employ a hard-working readers' letters team to sort through the many letters we receive. The best ones will be rewarded with a free copy of the next edition or another Lonely Planet guide if you prefer. We give away lots of books, but, unfortunately, not every letter/postcard does receive one.

Contents

INTRODUCTION 9

FACTS ABOUT THE COUNTRY 10

History 10
Geography 19
Climate 19
Ecology 20
National Parks, Marine Parks & Wildlife Sanctuaries 24
Government 33
Economy 37
Population & People 41
Arts 42
Sport 51
Avoiding Offence 54
Religion 55
Language 60

FACTS FOR THE VISITOR 68

Visas & Embassies 68
Customs 70
Money 70
When to Go 74
What to Bring 74
Tourist Offices 74
Holidays & Festivals 75
Post & Telecommunications 77
Time 80
Electricity 80
Laundry 80
Weights & Measures 81
Books & Maps 81
Media 83
Film & Photography 85
Health 85
Women Travellers 98
Dangers & Annoyances 98
Activities 104
Courses 105
Accommodation 107
Food 108
Drinks 117
Entertainment 120
Things to Buy 122

GETTING THERE & AWAY 126

Air 126
Land 129
Sea 131

GETTING AROUND 132

Air 132
Bus 133
Train 136
Car & Motorbike 140
Bicycle 143
Hitching 143
Boat 143
Local Transport 143

BANGKOK 147

CENTRAL THAILAND 219

Ayuthaya Province 219
Ayuthaya 219
Bang Pa In 226
Lopburi Province 226
Lopburi 226
Ang Thong & Saraburi Provinces 231
Ang Thong 231
Saraburi & Around 231
Suphanburi Province 232
Suphanburi 232
Chachoengsao Province 233
Chachoengsao 233
Nakhon Pathom Province 233
Nakhon Pathom 233
Ratchaburi Province 236
Ratchaburi 236
Around Ratchaburi 236
Kanchanaburi Province 236
Kanchanaburi 237
Around Kanchanaburi 247
Kanchanaburi to Three Pagodas Pass 251
Chonburi Province 255
Si Racha 255
Ko Si Chang 257
Pattaya 258
Around Pattaya 265
Rayong Province 265
Rayong & Around 265
Ko Samet 266
Chanthaburi Province 271
Chanthaburi 271
Trat Province 273
Trat & Around 275
Hat Lek to Cambodia 277
Ko Chang National Marine Park 278

NORTHERN THAILAND 284

Chiang Mai Province 286
Chiang Mai 286
Around Chiang Mai 312
Chom Thong Area 314
North To Fang 316
Fang & Tha Ton 317
Kok River Trip to Chiang Rai .318
Hill-Tribe Treks 319
Lamphun Province 326
Lamphun 326
Pasang 328
Lampang Province 328
Lampang 328
Around Lampang Province 331
Nakhon Sawan Province 333
Nakhon Sawan 333
Kamphaeng Phet Province 333
Kamphaeng Phet 333
Phitsanulok Province 336
Phitsanulok 336
Phu Hin Rong Kla National Park 341
Sukhothai Province 343
Sukhothai 343
Si Satchanalai-Chaliang Historical Park 349
Uttaradit Province 351
Uttaradit 351
Tak Province 352
Tak 354
Mae Sot 354
Around Mae Sot 358
Um Phang 359
Mae Sot to Mae Sariang 360
Mae Hong Son Province 362
Mae Sariang 363
Mae Hong Son 364
Around Mae Hong Son 368
Pai 370
Around Pai 372
Chiang Rai Province 373
Chiang Rai 373
Mae Salong (Santikhiri) 382
Mae Sai 384
Around Mae Sai 387
Chiang Saen 388
Around Chiang Saen 390
Phrae Province 393
Phrae 393
Around Phrae Province 396
Nan Province 399
Nan 400
Around Nan Province 406

NORTH-EAST THAILAND 407

Nakhon Ratchasima Province 409
Nakhon Ratchasima 409
Around Nakhon Ratchasima ... 414
Khao Yai National Park 417
Buriram Province 419
Prasat Hin Khao Phanom Rung Historical Park 419
Buriram 422
Khon Kaen & Roi Et Provinces 424
Khon Kaen 424
Roi Et 426
Udon Thani Province 428
Udon Thani 428
Around Udon Thani Province .432
Nong Khai Province 433
Nong Khai 433
Around Nong Khai Province .. 438
Beung Kan 441
Loei Province 442
Loei 443
Around Loei Province 445
Chiang Khan 446
Tha Li District 449
Lom Sak 450
Nakhon Phanom Province 450
Nakhon Phanom 450
Around Nakhon Phanom Province 452
That Phanom 453
Sakon Nakhon Province 454
Sakon Nakhon 455
Yasothon & Mukdahan Provinces 457
Yasothon 457
Mukdahan 458
Ubon Ratchathani Province 459
Ubon Ratchathani 461
Around Ubon Province 466
Surin & Si Saket Provinces 467
Surin 467
Si Saket 469

SOUTHERN THAILAND 473

Phetburi Province 475
Phetburi 475
Kaeng Krachan National Park 478
Cha-am 479
Around Cha-am 480
Prachuap Khiri Khan Province 481
Hua Hin 481
Khao Sam Roi Yot National Park 488
Prachuap Khiri Khan 488
Around Prachuap Khiri Khan Town 491
Thap Sakae & Bang Saphan ... 491
Chumphon Province 492
Chumphon 492
Around Chumphon Province .. 496
Ranong Province 496
Ranong 496
Around Ranong 500
Laem Son National Park 500
Phang-Nga Province 501
Khuraburi, Takua Pa & Thai Muang 501
Hat Bang Sak & Hat Khao Lak 501
Surin Islands National Park 502
Similan Islands National Park 502
Ao Phang-Nga & Phang-Nga 504
Phuket Province 505
Phuket 507
Phuket Beaches 514
Surat Thani Province 522
Chaiya 522
Surat Thani/Ban Don 523
Khao Sok National Park 527
Ko Samui 529
Ko Pha-Ngan 541
Ko Tao 546
Nakhon Si Thammarat Province 548
Khao Luang National Park 548
Nakhon Si Thammarat 548
Around Nakhon Si Thammarat Province 553
Phattalung Province 554
Phattalung & Around 554
Songkhla Province 557

SOUTHERN THAILAND *cont*

Songkhla.................................557
Ko Yo.......................................561
Khukhut Waterbird Sanctuary 561
Hat Yai.....................................562
Around Hat Yai......................569
Krabi Province 569
Krabi...571
Around Krabi Town...............575
Ko Phi Phi................................579
Ko Jam (Ko Pu) &
Ko Si Boya 583
Ko Lanta...................................583
Trang Province............... 586
Trang..586
Beaches....................................590
Waterfalls.................................592
Caves..593
Khlong Lamchan
Waterbird Park.........................593
Satun Province 593
Satun 593
Ko Tarutao National Marine
Park..596
Ko Bulon Le 600
Thale Ban National Park........ 600
Yala Province 601
Yala 601
Ban Sakai 603
Betong 603
Raman 604
Pattani Province 604
Pattani 604
Narathiwat Province....... 607
Narathiwat...............................607
Sungai Kolok & Ban Taba..... 611

INDEX 616

Map Index..............................615

Map Legend

BOUNDARIES

— · — · — · — · — International Boundary
— · · — · · — · · — Internal Boundary
＋＋＋＋＋＋＋＋＋＋＋ National Park or Reserve
— — — — — — — — The Equator
· · · · · · · · · · · · · · · · The Tropics

SYMBOLS

◉	NEW DELHI National Capital
●	BOMBAY Provincial or State Capital
●	Pune Major Town
●	Barsi Minor Town
■	 Places to Stay
▼	 Places to Eat
⌂	 Post Office
✈		... Airport
i	 Tourist Information
◓	 Bus Station or Terminal
66	 Highway Route Number
☪ ✝ ▓	 Mosque, Church, Cathedral
∴	 Temple or Ruin
✚	 Hospital
✳		.. Lookout
丸	 Camping Area
⼍	 Picnic Area
⌂	 Hut or Chalet
▲	 Mountain or Hill
	 Railway Station
	 Road Bridge
	 Railway Bridge
	 Road Tunnel
	 Railway Tunnel
	 Escarpment or Cliff
		.. Pass
	 Ancient or Historic Wall

ROUTES

———————— Major Road or Highway
— — — — — — Unsealed Major Road
———————— Sealed Road
- - - - - - - - - - Unsealed Road or Track
———————— City Street
＋＋＋＋＋＋＋＋＋＋ Railway
●———●———● Subway
· · · · · · · · · · · · · · Walking Track
— — — — — — Ferry Route
＋＋＋＋＋＋＋ Cable Car or Chair Lift

HYDROGRAPHIC FEATURES

 River or Creek
 Intermittent Stream
 Lake, Intermittent Lake
 Coast Line
	.. Spring
 Waterfall
 Swamp
 Salt Lake or Reef
 Glacier

OTHER FEATURES

	Park, Garden or National Park
 Built Up Area
	... Market or Pedestrian Mall
 Plaza or Town Square
 Cemetery

Note: not all symbols displayed above appear in this book

Introduction

Thailand, or Siam as it was called until the 1940s, has never been colonised by a foreign power, while all of its South-East Asian neighbours have undergone European imperialism (or more recently, ideological domination by Communism – which originated in Europe) at one time or another. True, it has suffered periodic invasions on the part of the Burmese and the Khmers and was briefly occupied by the Japanese in WW II, but the kingdom was never externally controlled long enough to dampen the Thais' serious individualism. Although the Thais are often depicted as fun-loving, happy-go-lucky folk (which they often are), they are also very strong-minded and have struggled for centuries to preserve their independence of spirit.

This is not to say that Thailand has not experienced any Western influence. Like other Asian countries it has both suffered and benefited from contact with foreign cultures. But the ever-changing spirit of Thai culture has remained dominant, even in modern city life.

The end result is that Thailand has much to interest the traveller: historic culture, lively arts, exotic islands, nightlife, a tradition of friendliness and hospitality to strangers, and one of the world's most exciting cuisines.

Travel in this tropical country is fairly comfortable and down-to-earth. The rail, bus and air travel network is extensive and every place worth visiting is easily accessible. There are many places worth visiting, many sights to see, a multi-faceted culture to experience and it is all quite affordable by today's international travel standards.

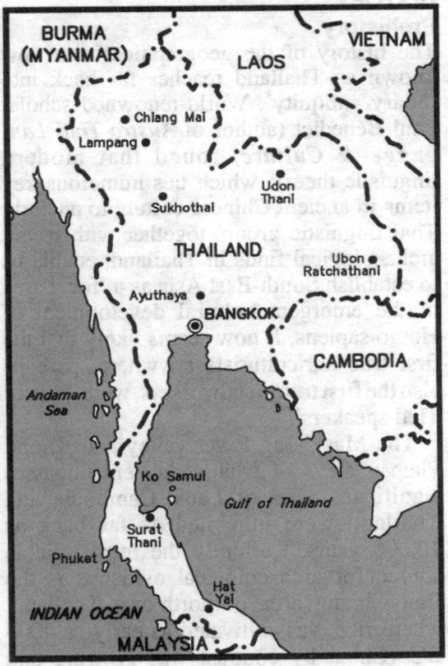

Travellers will, from time to time, notice that the spelling of place names in this book is at variance with other sources. This is because Thai uses a totally different script from our own 'Roman' script. Any Thai name has to be transliterated for those of us who don't read Thai, and transliteration is very often a matter of opinion. For more information on Thai spellings, see the Language section in the Facts about the Country chapter.

Facts about the Country

HISTORY

Prehistory

The history of the geographical area now known as Thailand reaches far back into 'hoary antiquity'. World-renowned scholar Paul Benedict (author of *Austro-Thai Language & Culture)* found that modern linguistic theory, which ties numerous key items in ancient Chinese culture to an early Thai linguistic group, together with recent archaeological finds in Thailand, enable us to establish South-East Asia as a 'focal area in the emergent cultural development of Homo sapiens. It now seems likely that the first true agriculturists anywhere, perhaps also the first true metalworkers, were Austro-Thai speakers'.

The Maekhong River valley and Khorat Plateau areas of what today encompasses significant parts of Laos, Cambodia and Thailand were inhabited as far back as 10,000 years. Currently the most reliable source for archaeological evidence is the Ban Chiang area of north-east Thailand, where rice was cultivated as early as 4000 BC (China by contrast was growing and consuming millet at the time). The Ban Chiang culture had begun bronze metallurgy before 3000 BC; the Middle East's Bronze Age arrived around 2800 BC, China's a thousand years later.

Thai Migration

The ancestors of today's Thais were scattered amidst a vast, nonunified zone of Austro-Thai influence that involved periodic migrations along several different geographic lines. The early Thais proliferated all over South-East Asia, including the islands of Indonesia, and some later settled in south and south-west China, later to 're-migrate' to northern Thailand to establish the first Thai kingdom in the 13th century.

A linguistic map of south China, north-west India and South-East Asia clearly shows that the preferred zones of occupation by the Thai peoples have been river valleys, from the Red River (Hong River) in south China and Vietnam to the Brahmaputra River in Assam. At one time there were two terminals for movement into what is now Thailand – the 'north terminal' in the Yuan Jiang and other river areas in China's Yunnan and Guangxi provinces, and the 'south terminal' along central Thailand's Chao Phraya River. The populations remain quite concentrated in these areas today, while areas between the two were intermediate relay points and as such have always been far less populated.

The Maekhong River valley between Thailand and Laos was one such intermediate migrational zone, as were river valleys along the Nan, Ping, Kok, Yom and Wang rivers in northern Thailand, plus various river areas in Laos and in Burma's Shan states. The migrant Thais established local polities along traditional social schemata according to *muang* (roughly 'principality' or 'district'), under the hereditary rule of chieftains or sovereigns called *châo muang* (muang lord).

Each muang was based in a river valley or section of a valley. Some muang were loosely collected under one chao muang or an alliance of several. One of the largest collections of muang – though not necessarily united – was in south China and was known as Nam Chao (often corrupted as Nan Chao in modern texts) or Lord(s) of the River(s).

In the mid-13th century, the rise to power of the Mongols under Kublai Khan in Sung Dynasty China caused a more dramatic southward migration of Thai peoples. Wherever Thais met indigenous populations of Tibeto-Burmans and Mon-Khmers in the move south (into what is now Burma (Myanmar), Thailand, Laos and Cambodia), they were somehow able to displace, assimilate or co-opt them without force. The most probable explanation for this relatively smooth assimilation is that there were already Thai peoples in the area. Such a supposition finds considerable support in current research on the development of Austro-Thai language and culture.

Early Kingdoms

With no written records or chronologies it is difficult to say with certainty what kind of cultures existed among the muangs of Thailand before the middle of the first millennium. However, by the 6th century AD an important network of agricultural communities was thriving as far south as modern-day Pattani and Yala, and as far north and north-east as Lamphun and Muang Fa Daet (near Khon Kaen). Theravada Buddhism was flourishing and may have entered the region during India's Ashokan period, in the 3rd or 2nd centuries BC, when Indian missionaries were said to have been sent to a land called Suvarnabhumi (Land of Gold). Suvarnabhumi most likely corresponds to a remarkably fertile area stretching from southern Burma, across central Thailand, to eastern Cambodia. Two different cities in the central river basin have long been called Suphanburi (City of Gold) and U Thong (Cradle of Gold).

Dvaravati This loose collection of city-states was given the Sanskrit name Dvaravati (literally, 'place having gates'), the city of Krishna in the Indian epic *Mahabharata*. The French art historian George Coedes discovered the name on some coins excavated in the Nakhon Pathom area, which seems to have been the centre of Dvaravati culture. The Dvaravati period lasted until the 11th or 12th century AD and produced many fine works of art, including distinctive Buddha images (showing Indian Gupta influence), stucco reliefs on temples and in caves, some architecture (little of which remains intact), some exquisite terracotta heads, votive tablets and other miscellaneous sculpture.

Dvaravati may have been a cultural relay point for the pre-Angkor cultures of ancient Cambodia and Champa to the east. The Chinese, through the travels of the famous pilgrim Xuan Zang, knew the area as T'o-lo-po-ti, located between Sriksetra (north Burma) and Tsanapura (Sambor Prei Kuk-Kambuja). The ethnology of the Dvaravati peoples is a controversial subject, though the standard decree is that they were Mons or Mon-Khmers. The Mons themselves seem to have been descended from a group of Indian immigrants from Kalinga, an area overlapping the boundaries of the modern Indian states of Orissa and Andhra Pradesh. The Dvaravati Mons may have been an ethnic mix of these people and people indigenous to the region (the original Thais). In any event, the Dvaravati culture quickly declined in the 11th century under the political domination of the invading Khmers who made their headquarters in Lopburi. The area around Lamphun, then called Hariphunchai, held out until the late 12th or early 13th centuries, as evidenced by the Dvaravati architecture of Wat Kukut in Lamphun.

Khmer Influence The concurrent Khmer conquests of the 7th to 11th centuries brought Khmer cultural influence in the form of art, language and religion. Some of the Sanskrit terms in Mon-Thai vocabulary entered the language during the Khmer or Lopburi period between the 11th and 13th centuries. Monuments from this period located in Kanchanaburi, Lopburi and many locations throughout the north-east were constructed in the Khmer style and compare favourably with architecture in Angkor. Elements of Brahmanism, Theravada Buddhism and Mahayana Buddhism intermixed as Lopburi became a religious centre, and some of each religious Buddhist school – along with Brahmanism – remain to this day in Thai religious and court ceremonies.

Other Kingdoms While all this was taking place, a distinctly Thai state called Nan Chao (650-1250 AD) was flourishing in what later became Yunnan and Sichuan in China. Nan Chao maintained close relations with imperial China and the two neighbours enjoyed much cultural exchange. The Mongols, under Kublai Khan, conquered Nan Chao in

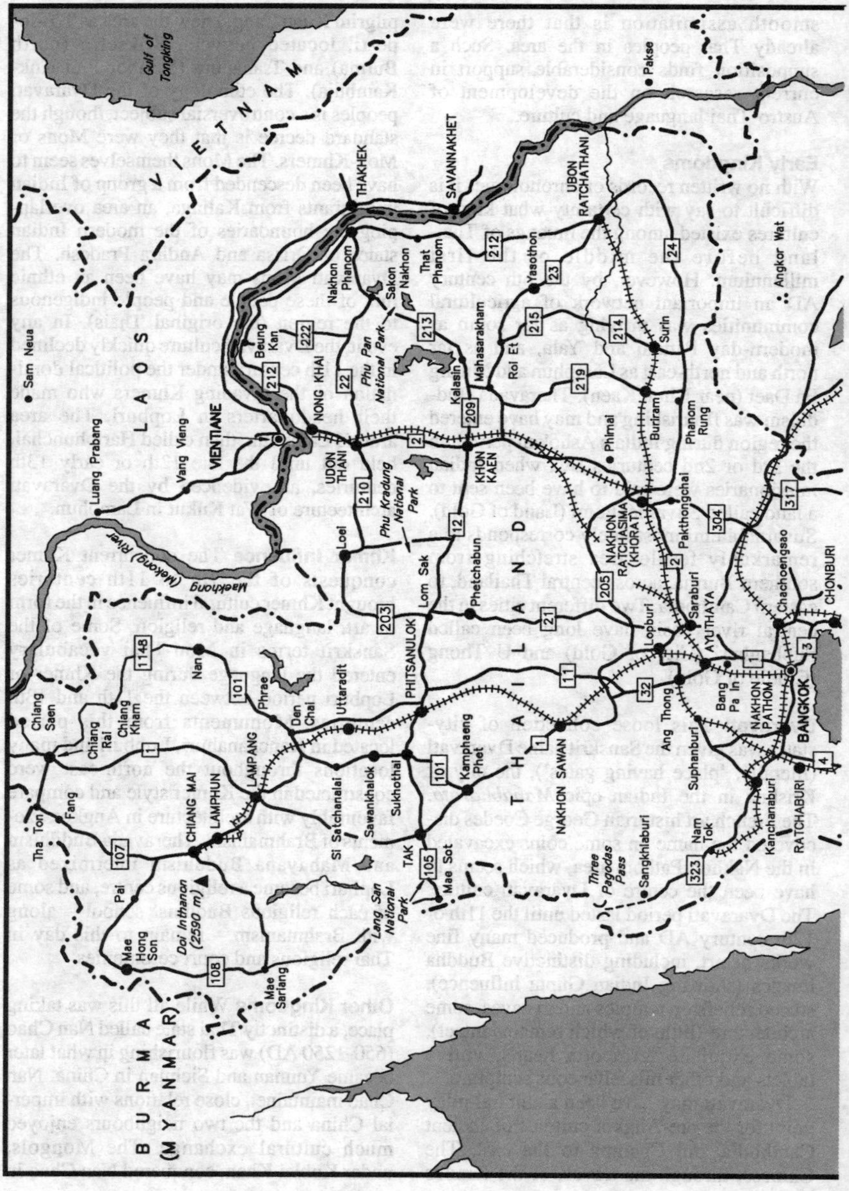
Gulf of Tongking
VIETNAM
LAOS
THAILAND
BURMA
(MYANMAR)
Sam Neua
Luang Prabang
Vang Vieng
VIENTIANE
NONG KHAI
Beung Kan
Nakhon Phanom
THAKHEK
SAVANNAKHET
Pakse
UBON RATCHATHANI
That Phanom
Sakon Nakhon
Phu Pan National Park
UDON THANI
KHON KAEN
Kalasin
Mahasarakham
Roi Et
Yasothon
Surin
Buriram
Phimai
Phanom Rung
Angkor Wat
Loei
Phu Kradung National Park
Lom Sak
Phetchabun
NAKHON RATCHASIMA (KHORAT)
Pakthongchai
Saraburi
Lopburi
AYUTHAYA
Chachoengsao
CHONBURI
BANGKOK
NAKHON PATHOM
Bang Pa In
Ang Thong
Suphanburi
Kanchanaburi
RATCHABURI
Nam Tok
Sangkhlaburi
Three Pagodas Pass
NAKHON SAWAN
Kamphaeng Phet
TAK
Mae Sot
Sukhothai
Si Satchanalai
Sawankhalok
PHITSANULOK
Uttaradit
Den Chai
Phrae
Nan
LAMPANG
LAMPHUN
CHIANG MAI
Doi Inthanon (2590 m)
Lang San National Park
Mae Sarlang
Mae Hong Son
Pai
Tha Ton
Fang
Chiang Rai
Chiang Saen
Chiang Kham
Maekhong (Mekong) River
1
2
3
4
11
12
21
22
23
24
32
101
105
107
108
203
205
209
210
212
213
214
215
219
222
304
317
323
1148

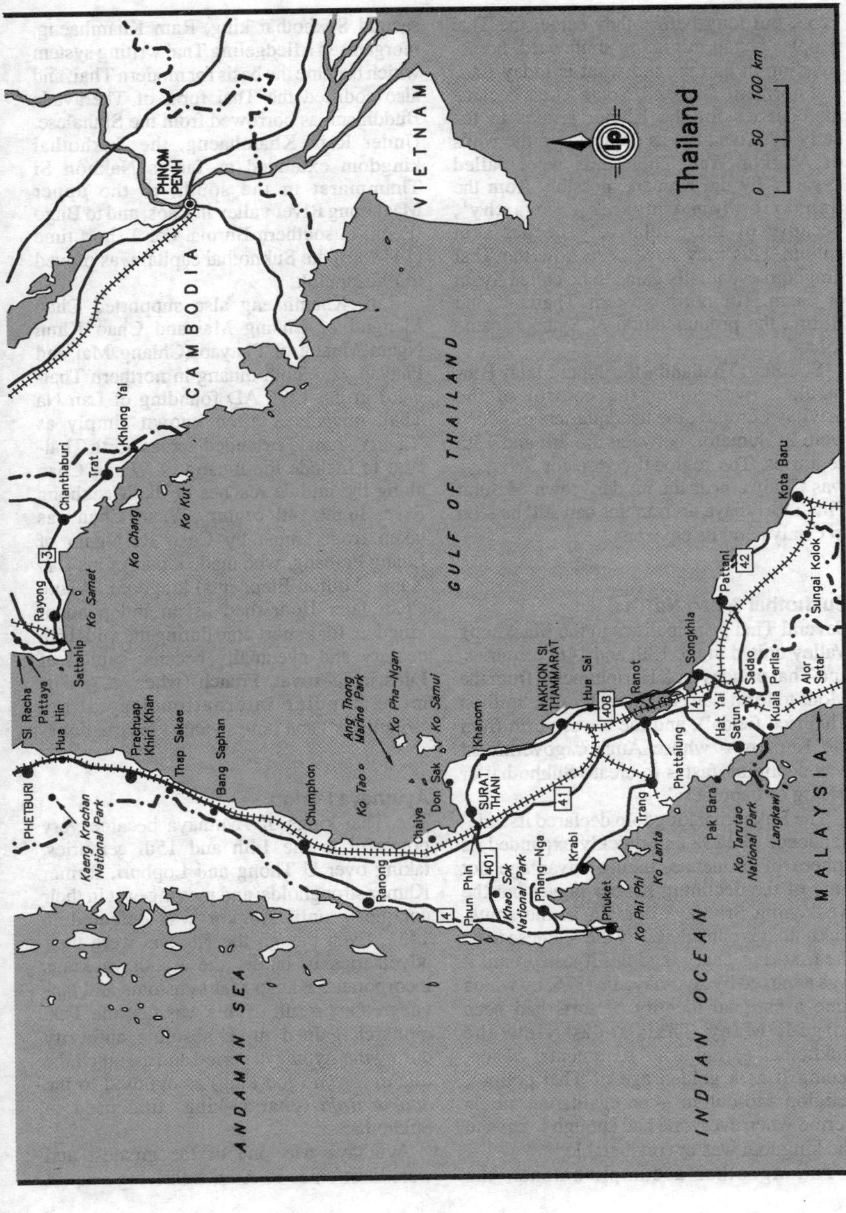
Thailand
0 50 100 km
PHNOM PENH
VIETNAM
CAMBODIA
GULF OF THAILAND
ANDAMAN SEA
INDIAN OCEAN
MALAYSIA
PHETBURI
Kaeng Krachan National Park
Si Racha
Pattaya
Hua Hin
Sattahip
Rayong
Ko Samet
3
Chanthaburi
Trat
Khlong Yai
Ko Chang
Ko Kut
Prachuap Khiri Khan
Thap Sakae
Bang Saphan
Chumphon
Ranong
4
Ko Tao
Ang Thong Marine Park
Ko Pha-Ngan
Ko Samui
Chaiya
Don Sak
Khanom
SURAT THANI
NAKHON SI THAMMARAT
Hua Sai
408
Ranot
41
401
Phun Phin
Khao Sok National Park
Phang-Nga
Krabi
Phuket
Ko Phi Phi
Ko Lanta
Trang
Phattalung
Pak Bara
Ko Tarutao National Park
Satun
Hat Yai
Songkhla
Sadao
Perlis
Kuala Perlis
Langkawi
Alor Setar
Pattani
42
Sungai Kolok
Kota Baru

1253, but long before they came, the Thai peoples began migrating southward, homesteading in and around what is today Laos and northern Thailand. Some Thais became mercenaries for the Khmer armies in the early 12th century, as depicted on the walls of Angkor Wat. The Thais were called 'Syams' by the Khmers, possibly from the Sanskrit *shyama* meaning 'swarthy', because of their relatively deeper skin colour. This may have been how the Thai kingdom eventually came to be called Syam or Siam. (In north-western Thailand and Burma the pronunciation of Syam became 'Shan'.)

Southern Thailand – the upper Malay Peninsula – was under the control of the Srivijaya Empire, the headquarters of which were in Sumatra, between the 8th and 13th centuries. The regional centre for Srivijaya was Chaiya, near the modern town of Surat Thani. Srivijaya art remains can still be seen in Chaiya and its environs.

Sukhothai & Lan Na Thai

Several Thai principalities in the Maekhong Valley united in the 13th and 14th centuries, and Thai princes took Hariphunchai from the Mons to form Lan Na Thai (literally, 'million Thai rice fields'), and the lower north from the Khmers – whose Angkor government was declining fast – to create Sukhothai or 'rising of happiness'.

The Sukhothai kingdom declared its independence in 1238 and quickly expanded its sphere of influence, taking advantage not only of the declining Khmer power but the weakening Srivijaya domain in the south. Sukhothai is considered by the Siamese to be the first true Thai kingdom. It lasted until it was annexed by Ayuthaya in 1376, by which time a national identity of sorts had been forged. Many Thais today view the Sukhothai period with sentimental vision, seeing it as a golden age of Thai politics, religion and culture – an egalitarian, noble period when everyone had enough to eat and the kingdom was unconquerable.

Among other accomplishments, the second Sukhothai king, Ram Khamhaeng, reorganised a fledgeling Thai writing system which became the basis for modern Thai, and also codified the Thai form of Theravada Buddhism, as borrowed from the Sinhalese. Under Ram Khamhaeng, the Sukhothai kingdom extended as far as Nakhon Si Thammarat in the south, to the upper Maekhong River valley in Laos, and to Bago (Pegu) in southern Burma. For a short time (1448-86) the Sukhothai capital was moved to Phitsanulok.

Ram Khamhaeng also supported Chao Mengrai of Chiang Mai and Chao Khun Ngam Muang of Phayao (Chiang Mai and Phayao were both muang in northern Thailand) in the 1296 AD founding of Lan Na Thai, nowadays often known simply as 'Lanna'. Lanna extended across north Thailand to include the muang of Wiang Chan along the middle reaches of the Maekhong River. In the 14th century, Wiang Chan was taken from Lanna by Chao Fa Ngum of Luang Prabang, who made it part of his Lan Xang (Million Elephants) kingdom. Wiang Chan later flourished as an independent kingdom for a short time during the mid-16th century and eventually became capital of Laos in its royal, French (where it got its more popular international spelling, 'Vientiane') and now socialist incarnations.

Ayuthaya Period

The Thai kings of Ayuthaya became very powerful in the 14th and 15th centuries, taking over U Thong and Lopburi, former Khmer strongholds, and moving east in their conquests until Angkor was defeated in 1431. Even though the Khmers were their adversaries in battle, the Ayuthaya kings incorporated Khmer court customs and language. One result of this was that the Thai monarch gained more absolute authority during the Ayuthaya period and assumed the title *devaraja* (god-king) as opposed to the *dhammaraja* (dharma-king) title used in Sukhothai.

Ayuthaya was one of the greatest and wealthiest cities in Asia, a thriving seaport envied not only by the Burmese but by the Europeans who were in great awe of the city. It has been said that London, at the time, was a mere village in comparison.

In the early 16th century Ayuthaya was receiving European visitors, and a Portuguese embassy was established in 1511. The Portuguese were followed by the Dutch in 1605, the English in 1612, the Danes in 1621 and the French in 1662. In the mid-16th century Ayuthaya and the independent kingdom of Lanna came under the control of the Burmese, but the Thais regained rule of both by the end of the century.

A rather peculiar episode unfolded in Ayuthaya when a Greek, Constantine Phaulkon, became a very high official in Siam under King Narai from 1675 to 1688. He kept out the Dutch and the English but allowed the French to station 600 soldiers in the kingdom. The Thais, fearing a takeover, forcefully expelled the French and executed Phaulkon. Ironically, the word for a 'foreigner' (of European descent) in modern Thai is *faràng*, an abbreviated form of *faràngsèt*, meaning 'French'. Siam sealed itself from the West for 150 years following this experience with farangs.

The Burmese again invaded Ayuthaya in 1765 and the capital fell after two years of fierce battle. This time the Burmese destroyed everything sacred to the Thais, including manuscripts, temples and religious sculpture. The Burmese, despite their effectiveness in sacking Ayuthaya, could not maintain a foothold in the kingdom, and Phaya Taksin, a Thai general, made himself king in 1769, ruling from the new capital of Thonburi on the banks of the Chao Phraya River, opposite Bangkok. The Thais regained control of their country and further united the disparate provinces to the north with central Siam.

Taksin eventually came to regard himself as the next Buddha; his ministers, who did not approve of his religious fantasies, deposed and then executed him in the custom reserved for royalty – by beating him to death in a velvet sack so that no royal blood touched the ground.

Chakri Dynasty

Another general, Chao Phaya Chakri, came to power and was crowned in 1782 under the title Rama I. He moved the royal capital across the river to Bangkok and ruled as the first king of the Chakri Dynasty (the present Thai king is Rama IX and it has been prophesied that this dynasty will only have nine kings). In 1809, Rama II (son of Rama I) took the throne and reigned until 1824. Both monarchs assumed the task of restoring the culture so severely damaged by the Burmese decades earlier. Rama III, or Phra Nang Klao (1824-51), went beyond reviving tradition and developed trade with China while increasing domestic agricultural production.

Rama IV, commonly known as King Mongkut (Phra Chom Klao to the Thais), was one of the more colourful and innovative of the early Chakri kings. He originally missed out on the throne in deference to his half-brother Rama III and lived as a Buddhist monk for 27 years. During his long monastic term he became adept in the Sanskrit, Pali, Latin and English languages, studied Western sciences and adopted the strict discipline of local Mon monks. He kept an eye on the outside world and when he took the throne in 1851 he immediately courted diplomatic relations with European nations, while avoiding colonialisation.

In addition, he attempted to align Buddhist cosmology with modern science to the end of demythologising the Thai religion (a process yet to be fully accomplished), and founded the Thammayut monastic sect, based on the strict discipline he had followed as a monk. The Thammayut remains a minority sect in relation to the Mahanikai, who comprise the largest number of Buddhist monks in Thailand.

Thai trade restrictions were loosened by King Mongkut and many Western powers signed trade agreements with the monarch. He also established Siam's first printing press and instituted educational reforms, developing a school system along European lines. Mongkut was the first monarch to show Thai commoners his face in public; he died of malaria in 1868.

His son, King Chulalongkorn (known to the Thais as Chulachomklao or Rama V, 1868-1910), continued Mongkut's tradition of reform, especially in the legal and administrative realm. Educated by European tutors, Chula abolished prostration before the king as well as slavery and corvée. Thailand further benefited from relations with European nations and the USA; railways were built, a civil service established and the legal code restructured. Though Siam still managed to avoid colonialisation, it lost some territory to French Laos and British Burma around this time.

Chula's son King Vajiravudh (also Mongkut Klao or Rama VI, 1910-25) was educated in Britain and during his rather short reign introduced compulsory education and other educational reforms. He further 'Westernised' the nation by making the Thai calendar conform to Western models. His reign was somewhat clouded by a top-down push for Thai nationalism that resulted in strong anti-Chinese sentiment. In 1909 a royal decree required the adoption of Thai surnames for all Thai citizens.

Revolution

While Vajiravudh's brother, King Prajadhipok (Pokklao or Rama VII, 1925-35) ruled, a group of Thai students living in Paris became so enamoured of democratic ideology that they mounted a successful coup d'état against absolute monarchy in Siam. This bloodless revolution led to the development of a constitutional monarchy along British lines, with a mixed military-civilian group in power.

A royalist revolt in 1933 sought to reinstate absolute monarchy, but it failed and left Prajadhipok isolated from both the royalist revolutionaries and the constitution-minded ministers. In 1935 the king abdicated without naming a successor and retired to Britain. The cabinet named his nephew, 10-year-old Ananda Mahidol to the throne as Rama VIII, though Ananda didn't return to Thailand from school in Switzerland until 1945. Phibun (Phibul) Songkhram, a key military leader in the 1932 coup, maintained an effective position of power from 1938 until the end of WW II. Ananda Mahidol (Rama VIII), ascended the throne in 1935 but was shot dead in his bedroom under mysterious circumstances in 1946. His brother, Bhumibol Adulyadej, succeeded him as Rama IX.

Under the influence of Phibun's government, the country's name was officially changed from Siam to Thailand in 1939 – rendered in Thai as 'Prathêt Thai'. ('Prathêt' is derived from the Sanskrit *pradesha* or 'country'; 'thai' is considered to have the connotation of 'free', though in actual usage it simply refers to the Thai, Tai or T'ai peoples, who are found as far east as Tonkin, as far west as Assam, as far north as south China, and as far south as north Malaysia.)

WW II & Postwar Periods

The Japanese outflanked the Allied troops in Malaya and Burma in 1941 and the Phibun government complied with the Japanese in this action by allowing them into the Gulf of Thailand; consequently the Japanese troops occupied a portion of Thailand itself. Phibun then declared war on the USA and Great Britain (in 1942) but Seni Pramoj, the Thai ambassador in Washington, refused to deliver the declaration. Phibun resigned in 1944 under pressure from the Thai underground resistance (Thai Seri), and after V-J Day in 1945, Seni became premier.

In 1946, the year King Ananda was assassinated, Seni and his brother Kukrit were unseated in a general election and a democratic civilian group took power under Pridi Phanomyong, a law professor who had been instrumental in the 1932 revolution. Pridi's civilian government, which changed the country's name back to Siam, ruled for a short time, only to be overthrown by Field Marshal Phibun in 1947. Phibun suspended the constitution and reinstated 'Thailand' as the country's official name in 1949. Under Phibun the government took an extreme anti-Communist stance, refused to recognise the People's Republic of China and became a loyal supporter of French and US foreign policy in South-East Asia.

In 1951 power was wrested from Phibun by General Sarit Thanarat, who continued the tradition of military dictatorship. However, Phibun somehow retained the actual position of premier until 1957 when Sarit finally had him exiled. Elections that same year forced Sarit to resign, go abroad for 'medical treatment' and then return in 1958 to launch another coup. This time he abolished the constitution, dissolved the parliament and banned all political parties, maintaining effective power until his death of cirrhosis in 1963. From 1964 to 1973 the Thai nation was ruled by army officers Thanom Kittikachorn and Praphat Charusathien, during which time Thailand allowed the USA to develop several army bases within its borders in support of the US campaign in Vietnam.

Reacting to political repression, 10,000 Thai students publicly demanded a real constitution in June 1973. In October of the same year the military brutally suppressed a large demonstration at Thammasat University in Bangkok, but General Krit Sivara and King Bhumibol refused to support further bloodshed, forcing Thanom and Praphat to leave Thailand.

Polarisation & Stabilisation

An elected, constitutional government ruled until October 1976 when students demonstrated again, this time protesting Thanom's return to Thailand as a monk. Thammasat University again became a battlefield as border patrol police, along with right-wing, paramilitary civilian groups (Nawaphon, the Red Gaurs and the Village Scouts) assaulted a group of 2000 students holding a sit-in. Hundreds of students were killed and injured in the fracas; more than a thousand were arrested. Using public disorder as an excuse, the military stepped in and installed a new right-wing government with Thanin Kraivichien as premier.

This bloody incident disillusioned many Thai students and older intellectuals not directly involved with the demonstrations, the result being that numerous idealists 'dropped out' of Thai society and joined the People's Liberation Army of Thailand (PLAT) – armed communist insurgents based in the hills who had been active in Thailand since the '30s.

In October 1977 Thanin was replaced by the more moderate General Kriangsak Chomanand in an effort to conciliate with anti-government factions. In 1980 the military-backed position changed hands again, leaving Prem Tinsulanonda at the helm. By this time the PLAT had reached a peak force of around 10,000.

Prem served as prime minister through 1988 and is credited with the political and economic stabilisation of Thailand in the post-Vietnam War years (only one coup attempt in the '80s!). The major accomplishment of the Prem years was a complete dismantling of the Communist Party of Thailand and PLAT through an effective combination of amnesty programmes (which brought the students back from the forests) and military action. His administration is also considered responsible for a gradual democratisation of Thailand which culminated in the 1988 election of his successor, Chatichai Choonhavan.

It may be difficult for new arrivals to Thailand to appreciate the political distance Thailand covered in the '80s. Between 1976 and 1981, freedom of speech and press were rather curtailed in Thailand and a strict curfew was enforced in Bangkok. Anyone caught in the streets past 1 am risked spending the night in one of Bangkok's mosquito-infested 'detention areas'. Under Prem, the curfew was lifted, and dissenting opinions began to be heard again in public.

Traditionally, every leading political figure in Thailand, including Prem, has had to receive the support of the Thai military, who are generally staunch reactionaries. Considering Thailand's geographic position, it's not difficult to understand, to some extent, the fears of this ultra-conservative group. But as the threat of communist takeover (either from within or from nearby Indo-Chinese states) diminished, the military gradually began loosening its hold on national politics. Under Chatichai, Thailand enjoyed a brief period of unprecedented popular participation in government.

Approximately 60% of Chatichai's cabinet were former business executives rather than ex-military officers, as compared to 38% in the previous cabinet. Thailand seemed to be entering a new era in which the country's double-digit economic boom ran concurrently with democratisation. Critics praised the political maturation of Thailand, even if they grumbled that corruption seemed as rife as ever. By the end of the '80s, however, certain high-ranking military officers had become increasingly disappointed with this *coup d'argent*, complaining that Thailand was being run by a plutocracy.

February 1991 Coup

On 23rd February 1991, in a move that shocked Thailand observers around the world, the military overthrew the Chatichai administration in a bloodless coup (Thai: *pàtìwát)* and handed power to the newly formed National Peace-Keeping Council (NPKC), led by General Suchinda Kraprayoon. It was Thailand's 19th coup attempt and one of 10 successful coups since 1932 – but only the second coup to overthrow a democratically elected civilian government. Chatichai lasted longer than any other elected prime minister in Thai history: barely two years and seven months. Charging Chatichai's civilian government with corruption and vote-buying, the NPKC abolished the 1978 constitution and dissolved the parliament. Rights of public assembly were curtailed but the press was closed down for only one day.

Whether or not Chatichai's government was guilty of vote-buying, one of his major mistakes was his appointments of General Chaovalit Yongchaiyuth and former army commander Arthit Kamlang-ek as defence and deputy defence minister respectively. Both were adversaries of the generals who engineered the coup, ie army chief Suchinda and his main ally General Sunthorn Kongsompong (both 'Class 5' officers who graduated from the Chulachomklao Royal Military Academy in 1958, a group that forms the backbone of the NPKC's support). Chatichai was also moving into areas of foreign policy traditionally reserved for the military, especially relations with Burma, Laos and Cambodia, and the generals may have feared that the prime minister would fire them. It was the same old story: a power struggle between military bureaucrats and capitalist politicians.

Following the coup, the NPKC appointed a hand-picked civilian prime minister, Ananda Panyarachun, former ambassador to the USA, Germany, Canada and the UN, to dispel public fears that the junta was planning a return to 100% military rule. Ananda claimed to be his own man, but like his predecessors – elected or not – he was allowed the freedom to make his own decisions only insofar as they didn't affect the military. In spite of obvious constraints, many observers felt Ananda's temporary premiership and cabinet were the best Thailand had ever had.

In December 1991, Thailand's national assembly passed a new constitution that guaranteed an NPKC-biased parliament – 270 appointed senators in the upper house stacked against 360 elected representatives. Under this constitution, regardless of who is chosen as the next prime minister or which political parties fill the lower house, the government will remain largely in the hands of the military unless the public rises up to demand a more democratic charter. The new charter includes a provisional clause allowing for a 'four-year transitional period' to full democracy – a provision which sounds suspiciously close to military subterfuge in neighbouring Myanmar.

Elections & Demonstrations

A general election in March 1992 ushered in a five-party coalition government with Narong Wongwan, whose Samakkhitham (Justice Unity) Party received the most votes, as premier. But amid allegations that Narong was involved in Thailand's drug trade, the military exercised its constitutional prerogative and immediately replaced Narong with (surprise surprise) General Suchinda.

The NPKC promised to eradicate corruption and build democracy, a claim that was difficult to accept since they had done little on either score. In many ways, it was like letting the proverbial fox guard the hen house, as the military is perhaps the most corrupt institution in the country – always claiming to be free of politics and yet forever meddling in them. Thailand's independent political pundits agree there is more oppression under the NPKC than under any administration since pre-1981 days.

In May 1992, several huge demonstrations demanding Suchinda's resignation rocked Bangkok and larger provincial capitals. After street confrontations between the protesters and the military near Bangkok's Democracy Monument resulted in dozens of deaths and hundreds of injuries, Suchinda finally resigned. The military-backed government also agreed to institute a constitutional amendment requiring that Thailand's prime minister come from the ranks of elected MPs. Ananda Panyarachun was reinstated as ad hoc prime minister for a four-month term following which another election will presumably be held.

In most ways, since the events of '91 and '92, Thailand has seen 'business as usual'. Thai cynics will tell you that things *never* change – it depends on how closely you observe politics. The military takeover has undoubtedly hurt Thailand's international image, especially among those observers who had seen Thailand moving toward increased democratisation.

Optimists now see Suchinda's hasty resignation as a sign that the coup was only a minor detour on the country's road toward a more responsive national government. Others say the democratic Chatichai government was merely a short-lived deviation from the norm of military rule. Whatever the immediate outcome of the crisis, it isn't likely the generals will return to their barracks permanently.

GEOGRAPHY

Thailand has an area of 517,000 sq km, making it slightly smaller than the state of Texas in the USA, or about the size of France. Its shape on the map has been compared to the head of an elephant, with its trunk extending down the Malay Peninsula, but it looks to me as if someone has squeezed the lower part of the 'boot' of Italy, forcing the volume into the top portion while reducing the bottom. The centre of Thailand, Bangkok, is at about 14° north latitude, putting it on a level with Madras, Manila, Guatemala and Khartoum.

The country's longest north-to-south distance is about 1860 km, but its shape makes distances in any other direction a thousand km or less. Because the north-south reach spans roughly 16 latitudinal degrees, Thailand has perhaps the most diverse climate in South-East Asia. The topography varies from high mountains in the north – the southernmost extreme of a series of ranges that extend across northern Myanmar and southwest China to the south-eastern edges of the Tibet Plateau – to limestone-encrusted tropical islands in the south that are part of the Malay Archipelago. The rivers and tributaries of northern and central Thailand drain into the Gulf of Thailand via the Chao Phraya Delta near Bangkok; those of the Mun River and other north-eastern waterways exit into the South China Sea via the Maekhong River.

These broad geographic characteristics divide the country into four main zones: the fertile centre region, dominated by the Chao Phraya River; the north-east plateau, the kingdom's poorest region (thanks to 'thin' soil plus occasional droughts and floods), rising some 300 metres above the central plain; northern Thailand, a region of mountains and fertile valleys; and the southern peninsular region, which extends to the Malaysian frontier and is predominantly rainforest. The southern region receives the most annual rainfall and the north-east the least, although the north is less humid.

CLIMATE

Rainfall

Thailand's climate is ruled by monsoons. As a result there are three seasons in northern, north-eastern and central Thailand, and two seasons in southern Thailand. The three-season zone, which extends roughly from Thailand's northernmost reaches to the Phetburi Province on the southern peninsula, experiences a 'dry and wet monsoon climate', with the south-west monsoon arriving between May and July and lasting into November. This is followed by a dry period from November to May, a period that begins with lower relative temperatures (because of the influences of the north-east monsoon, which bypasses this part of Thailand but results in cool breezes) till mid-February, followed by much higher relative temperatures from March to May.

It rains more and longer in the south, which is subject to the north-east monsoon from November to January, as well as the south-west monsoon. Hence most of southern Thailand has only two seasons, a wet and a dry, with smaller temperature differences between the two.

Although the rains 'officially' begin in July (according to the Thai agricultural calendar), they actually depend on the monsoons in any given year. As a rule of thumb, the dry season is shorter the farther south you go. From Chiang Mai north the rains may last six months (mid-November to May); in most of central and north-east Thailand five months (December to May); on the upper peninsula three months (February to May); and below Surat Thani only two months (March and April). Occasional rains in the dry season are know as 'mango showers'.

In central Thailand it rains most during August and September, though there may be floods in October since the ground has reached full saturation by then. If you are in Bangkok in early October don't be surprised if you find yourself in hip-deep water in certain parts of the city. In 1983, when the floods were reputed to be the worst in 30 years, it was hip-deep throughout the city! It rains a little less in the north, August being the peak month. The north-east gets less rain and periodically suffers droughts. In Phuket it rains most in May (an average of 21 out of 30 days) and in October (an average of 22 out of 30 days), as this area undergoes both monsoons. Travelling in the rainy season is generally not unpleasant, but unpaved roads may occasionally be impassable.

Temperature

Most of Thailand is very humid, the mountains in the north being the exception. The temperature can drop to 13°C at night during the cool season in Chiang Mai and even lower in Mae Hong Son – if you're visiting the north during the cooler months, long-sleeved shirts and pullovers would be in order. Because temperatures are more even year-round in the south, when it is 35°C in Bangkok it may be only 32°C in Phuket. The hot part of the dry season reaches its hottest along the north-east plain, and temperatures easily soar to 39°C in the daytime, dropping only a few degrees at night.

ECOLOGY

Flora & Fauna

Thailand is unique in South-East Asia because its north-south axis extends some 1800 km from mainland to peninsular South-East Asia, thus providing potential habitats for an astounding variety of flora & fauna. As in the rest of tropical Asia, most indigenous vegetation in Thailand is associated with two basic types of tropical forest: monsoon forest (with a distinctive dry season of three months or more) and rainforest (where rain falls year-round or nearly year-round).

Monsoon forests are marked by deciduous tree varieties which shed their leaves during the dry season to conserve water; rainforests are typically evergreen. Central, north, eastern and north-eastern Thailand mainly contain monsoon forests while southern Thailand is predominantly a rainforest zone. There is much overlap of the two – some forest zones support a mix of monsoon forest and rainforest vegetation. The country's most famous flora includes an incredible array of fruit trees (see the Food section in the Facts for the Visitor chapter), bamboo (more species than any country outside

China), tropical hardwoods and Thailand's national floral symbol, the orchid.

Wildlife variation is also closely affiliated with geographic and climatic differences. Hence the indigenous fauna of Thailand's northern half is mostly of Indo-Chinese origin while that of the south is generally Sundaic (ie typical of Malaysia, Sumatra, Borneo and Java). The invisible dividing line between the two zoogeographical zones is across the Isthmus of Kra, about halfway down the southern peninsula. The large overlap area between zoogeographical and vegetative zones – extending from around Prachuap Khiri Khan on the southern peninsula to Uthai Thani in the lower north – means that much of Thailand is a potential habitat for plants and animals from both zones.

Thailand is particularly rich in bird life, with over 850 recorded resident and migrating species – approximately 10% of all world species. Coastal and inland waterways of the southern peninsula are especially important habitats for South-East Asian waterfowl. Indigenous mammals of renown – mostly found in dwindling numbers within Thailand's national parks or wildlife sanctuaries – include tigers, leopards, elephants, Asiatic black bears, Malayan sun bears, gaur (Indian bison), banteng (wild cattle), serow (an Asiatic mountain goat), sambar deer, barking deer, mouse deer, tapirs, pangolin, gibbons and macaques.

Herpetofauna include four sea-turtle species along with numerous snake varieties, of which six are venomous: the common cobra (six subspecies), king cobra (hamadryad), banded krait (three species), Malayan viper, green viper and Russell's pit viper. The country's many lizard species include two commonly seen in homes and older hotels or guesthouses, the *tuk-kae* (a large gecko) and the *jing-jok* (a smaller house lizard), as well as larger species like the black jungle monitor.

Environmental Policy

Like all countries with high population densities, Thailand has applied enormous pressure on the ecosystems within its borders. Fifty years ago the countryside was around 70% forest; in 1991 an estimated 20 to 30% of the forest cover remained. Logging and agriculture are mainly to blame for the decline, and the loss of forest cover

---

Thai Environmentalism

It is obvious that only with strong popular participation can Thailand effect a reasonable enforcement of protective laws – which are already plentiful but often ignored. Current examples of 'people power' include the hundreds of forest monasteries that voluntarily protect chunks of forest throughout Thailand. When one such wat was forcibly removed by the military in Buriram Province, thousands of Thais around the country rallied behind the abbot, Phra Prachak, and the wat's protectorship was re-established. On the other side of the coin, wats with less ecologically minded trustees have sold off virgin lands to developers.

One of the greatest recent victories by Thai environmentalists was the 1986 defeat of government plans to construct a hydroelectric facility across the Khwae Yai River. The dam was to be placed over a river section in the middle of the Thung Yai Naresuan and Huay Kha Khaeng wildlife sanctuaries, one of the largest and best preserved monsoon forest areas in South-East Asia. It took four years of organised protest to halt the dam. Social critics fear that under the new government it will be more difficult to mount this type of extended protest because the NPKC has unchecked power to ban all public assembly.

In 1983 Wildlife Fund Thailand (WFT) was created under Queen Sirikit's patronage as an affiliate of the World-Wide Fund for Nature. The main function of the WFT has been to raise public consciousness with regard to the illegal trade in endangered wildlife. Other Thai groups involved in environmental issues include Santi Pracha Dhamma Institute (SPDI), the brainchild of one of Thailand's leading intellectuals, Sulak Sivaraksa (currently exiled from Thailand to avoid NPKC persecution). ■

---

has been accompanied by dwindling wildlife resources. Species notably extinct in Thailand include the kouprey (a type of wild cattle), Schomburgk's deer and the Javan rhino, but innumerable smaller species have also fallen by the wayside.

In response to environmental degradation, the Thai government has created a large number of protected lands (see National Parks & Wildlife Sanctuaries in this chapter) since the 1970s, and has enacted legislation to protect specific plant and animal species. The government hopes to raise total forest cover to 40% by the middle of next century. Thailand has also become a signatory to the UN Convention on International Trade in Endangered Species (CITES).

In 1989, logging was banned in Thailand

Tourism & the Environment

In some instances tourism has had positive effects on environmental conservation in Thailand. Conscious that the country's natural beauty is a major tourist attraction for both residents and foreigners – and that tourism is one of Thailand's major revenue earners – the government has stepped up efforts to protect wilderness areas and to add more acreage to the park system. In Khao Yai National Park, for example, all hotel and golf course facilities are being removed in order to reduce human influences on the park environment and upgrade the wilderness. Under government and private sector pressure on the fishing industry, coral dynamiting has been all but eliminated in the Similan and Surin islands – to preserve the area for tourist visitation.

However, tourism has also made negative contributions. Eager to make fistfuls of cash, hotel developers and tour operators have rushed to provide ecologically inappropriate services for visitors in sensitive areas which are unable to sustain high-profile tourism. Similar concerns are causing the government to look more closely at Ko Phi Phi and Ko Samet – two national park islands notorious for overdevelopment. Part of the problem is that it's not always clear which lands are protected and which are privately owned.

Common problems in marine areas include the anchoring of tour boats on coral reefs and the dumping of rubbish into the sea. Coral and seashells are also illegally collected, and sold in tourist shops. 'Jungle food' restaurants – with endangered species on the menu – flourish near inland national parks. Perhaps the most visible abuses occur in areas without basic garbage and sewage services, where there are piles of rotting garbage, mountains of plastic and open sewage runoff.

One of the saddest sights in Thailand is the piles of discarded plastic water bottles on popular beaches. Worse yet are those seen floating in the sea or in rivers, where they are sometimes ingested by marine or riparian wildlife with fatal results. Many of these bottles started out on a beach only to be washed into the sea during the monsoon season.

What can the average visitor to Thailand do to minimise the impact of tourism on the environment? First off, they can avoid all restaurants serving 'exotic' wildlife species (eg barking deer, pangolin, bear); visitors should also consider taking down the names of any restaurants serving or advertising such fare and filing a letter of complaint with the Tourist Authority of Thailand (TAT), the WFT and the Forestry Department (addresses below). The main patrons of this type of cuisine are the Thais themselves, along with visiting Chinese from Hong Kong and Taiwan. Municipal markets selling endangered species, such as Bangkok's Chatuchak Market, should also be duly noted – consider enclosing photographs to support your complaints. For a list of endangered species in Thailand, contact the WFT.

When using hired boats in the vicinity of coral reefs, insist that boat operators not lower anchor onto coral formations. This is becoming less of a problem with established boating outfits – some of whom mark off sensitive areas with blue-flagged buoys – but is common among small-time pilots. Likewise, volunteer to collect (and later dispose of) rubbish if it's obvious that the usual mode is to throw everything overboard.

Obviously, you should refrain from purchasing coral or items made from coral while in Thailand. Thai law forbids the collection of coral or seashells anywhere in the country – report any observed violations in tourist or marine park areas to the TAT and Forestry Department, or in other places to the WFT.

One of the difficulties in dealing with rubbish and sewage problems in tourist areas is that many following a 1988 disaster in which hundreds of tons of cut timber washed down deforested slopes in Surat Thani Province, killing more than a hundred people and burying a number of villages. It is now illegal to sell timber felled in the country, and all imported timber is theoretically accounted for before going on the market.

These days builders even need government permission to use timber salvaged from old houses. This has helped curb illegal logging operations in the interior (unfortunately Thai timber brokers are now turning their attention to Laos and Burma – neither of which are CITES signatories) but corruption remains a problem.

Corruption also impedes government attempts to shelter 'exotic' species from the

---

Thais don't understand why tourists should expect any different methods of disposal than are used elsewhere in the country. In urban areas or populated rural areas throughout Thailand, piles of rotting rubbish and open sewage lines are frequently the norm – after all, Thailand is still a 'developing' country. Thais sensitive to Western paternalism are fond of pointing out that on a global scale the so-called 'developed' countries contribute far more environmental damage than does Thailand (eg per capita greenhouse emissions for Australia, Canada or the USA average over five tons each while ASEAN countries contribute less than 0.5 tons per capita).

Hence in making complaints or suggestions to Thais employed in the tourist industry it's important to emphasise that you want to work *with* them rather than against them in improving environmental standards.

Whether on land or at sea, refrain from purchasing or accepting drinking water offered in plastic bottles. When there's a choice, request glass water bottles, which are recyclable in Thailand. The 4B deposit is refundable when you return the bottle to any vendor who sells drinking water in glass bottles. For those occasions where only plastic-bottled water is available, you might consider transferring the contents from plastic bottles to your own reusable water container – if the vendor/source of the plastic bottle is a more suitable disposal point than your destination. If not, take the bottle with you and dispose of it at a dumpster or other legitimate collection site so that the bottle doesn't end up blowing in the breeze.

A few guesthouses now offer drinking water from large, reusable plastic water containers as an alternative to the disposable individual containers. This service is available in most areas of Thailand (even relatively remote areas like Ko Chang) and is certainly available wherever the disposable plastic bottles are. Encourage hotel and guesthouse staff to switch from disposable plastic to either glass or reusable plastic.

In outdoor areas where rubbish has accumulated, consider organising an impromptu cleanup crew to collect plastic, styrofoam and other nonbiodegradables for delivery to a regular rubbish pick-up point. If there isn't a pick-up somewhere nearby, enquire about the location of the nearest collection point and deliver the refuse yourself.

By expressing your desire to use environmentally friendly materials – and by taking direct action to avoid the use and indiscriminate disposal of plastic – you can provide an example of environmental consciousness not only for the Thais but for other international visitors.

Write to the following organisations to offer your support for stricter environmental policies or to air specific complaints or suggestions:

Tourist Authority of Thailand
Ratchadamnoen Nok Ave, Bangkok 10100
Wildlife Fund Thailand
251/88090 Phahonyothin Rd, Bangkhen, Bangkok 10220
Office of the National Environment Board
60/1 Soi Prachasumphan 4, Rama IV Rd, Bangkok 10400
The Siam Society
131 Soi Asoke, Sukhumvit Rd, Bangkok 10110
Project for Ecological Recovery
77/3 Soi Nomjit, Naret Rd, Bangkok 10500
Royal Forestry Department
Phahonyothin Rd, Bangkhen, Bangkok 10900
Thailand Information Centre of Environmental Foundation
58/1 Sakol Land, Chaeng Wattana Rd, Pakret, Nonthaburi
Magic Eyes
Bangkok Bank Building, 15th Floor, 333 Silom Rd Bangkok 10400 ■

illicit global wildlife trade and to preserve Thailand's sensitive coastal areas. The Forestry Department is currently under pressure to take immediate action in those areas where preservation laws have gone unenforced, including coastal zones where illegal tourist accommodation has flourished. There has also been a crackdown on restaurants serving 'jungle food' *(aahãan pàa)*, which is exotic and often endangered wildlife species like barking deer, bear, pangolin, civet and gaur.

Forestry Department efforts are limited by lack of personnel and funds. The average ranger is paid only 70B a day to face down armed poachers backed by the rich and powerful godfathers who control illicit timber and wildlife businesses. Some environmentalists claim the 1991 military coup and resultant freedom-restricting constitution will seriously impede environmental progress. The military, on the other hand, claims profit-hungry politicians are most to blame for park encroachment.

Marine resources are also threatened by a lack of long-range conservation goals. The upper portion of the Gulf of Thailand between Rayong and Prachuap Khiri Khan, once one of the most fertile marine areas in the world, is virtually dead due to overfishing and the release of mainland pollutants.

Experts say it's not too late to rehabilitate the upper Gulf by reducing pollution and the number of trawlers, and by restricting commercial fishing to certain zones. An effective ban on the harvest of *plaa tuu* (mackerel) in the spawning stages has brought this fish back from the brink of total depletion. The Bangkok Metropolitan Administration (BMA) is developing a system of sewage treatment plants in the Chao Phraya Delta area with the intention of halting all large-scale dumping of sewage into Gulf waters, but similar action needs to be taken along the entire eastern seaboard, which is fast becoming Thailand's new industrial centre.

Overdevelopment on Ko Phuket is starving the surrounding coral reefs by blocking nutrient-rich runoff from the island's interior, as well as smothering the reefs with pollutants. Ko Samui faces a similar fate if action isn't taken soon to control growth and raise waste-disposal standards.

NATIONAL PARKS, MARINE PARKS & WILDLIFE SANCTUARIES

Despite Thailand's rich diversity of flora & fauna, it has only been in recent years that most of the 66 national parks and 32 wildlife sanctuaries have been established. Together these cover 11.05% of the country's land area, one of the highest ratios of protected to unprotected areas of any nation in the world (compare this figure with India at 4.2%, Malaysia 3.5%, France 8.8% and the USA 10.5%).

A system of wildlife sanctuaries was first provided for in the Wild Animals Reservation and Protection Act of 1960, followed by the National Parks Act of 1961 which established the kingdom's national park programme along with Khao Yai National Park. The majority of the parks, preserves and sanctuaries are well maintained by the Forestry Department, but a few have allowed rampant tourism to threaten the natural environment, most notably on the islands of Ko Samet and Ko Phi Phi. Poaching, illegal logging and shifting cultivation have also taken their toll on protected lands, but since 1990 the government has been cracking down with some success.

Most of the national parks are easily accessible, yet only 5% of the average annual number of visitors is non-Thai. There is usually somewhere to stay, and sometimes meals are provided, but it's a good idea to take your own sleeping bag or mat; basic camping gear is useful for parks without fixed accommodation. You should also take a torch (flashlight), rain gear, insect repellent, a water container and a small medical kit.

Most parks charge a small fee to visit. Advance bookings for accommodation are advisable at the more popular parks, especially on holidays and weekends. Most national park bungalows are around 500 to 1500B a night (unless otherwise noted), and usually sleep five to 10 people. A few parks also have *reuan tháew* (long houses) where

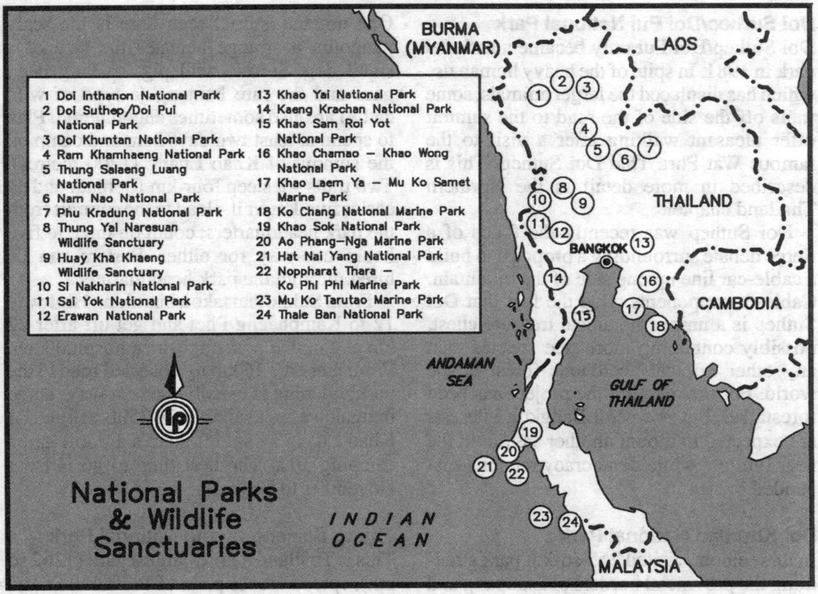

rooms are around 150 to 200B for two. Some have tents for rent at 50 to 60B a night. Finally, if you bring your own tent it's only 5 to 10B per person – almost every park has at least one camping area.

In Bangkok the reservations office is at the national parks division of the Forestry Department (☎ 579-4842/0529), Phahonyothin Rd, Bangkhen (north Bangkok). Bookings from Bangkok must be paid in advance.

Below are overviews of 24 of the more notable national parks, marine parks and sanctuaries. Some are covered in more detail in province chapters. Detailed descriptions of the 63 parks, along with an objective assessment of current park conditions, are available in the recently published *National Parks of Thailand* (Communication Resources, Bangkok, 1991) by Gray, Piprell & Graham. For a true appreciation of Thailand's geography and natural history, a visit to at least one national park is a must.

Doi Inthanon National Park

Doi Inthanon, the centrepiece for this 482-sq-km park, is Thailand's highest mountain at 2565 metres. Off the 47-km, army-built road to the summit are many trails to explore and several impressive waterfalls. Around 4000 Hmong and Karen tribespeople make the mountain slopes their home.

Wildlife in the park includes around 380 bird species as well as Indian civet, barking deer, slow loris, pig-tailed and Assamese macaques and Phayre's leaf-monkey.

From Chiang Mai take a minibus to Chom Tong, then a songthaew. Ask for Doi Inthanon and say you want to get off at Km 31. From the park headquarters there is plenty of traffic for hitching. There are six bungalows (300 to 1000B) and camping areas. Accommodation is also available in hill-tribe villages.

For more information see the Doi Inthanon section in the Northern Thailand chapter.

Doi Suthep/Doi Pui National Park

Doi Suthep/Doi Pui only became a national park in 1981. In spite of the heavy human use which has displaced the larger animals, some trails off the side of the road to the summit offer pleasant walking after a visit to the famous Wat Phra That Doi Suthep. This is described in more detail in the Northern Thailand chapter.

Doi Suthep was recently the focus of a fierce debate surrounding a proposal to build a cable-car line up one side of the mountain. Cable-car opponents cited the fact that Doi Suthep is a unique botanical treasure chest, possibly containing more tree species than any other tropical deciduous forest in the world. For the moment the project has been forestalled, but powerful Bangkok interests are expected to mount another assault in the near future – while democracy remains suspended.

Doi Khuntan National Park

In this seldom-visited 255-sq-km park straddling the provincial borders of Lampang and Lamphun, the trail to the summit of Doi Khuntan (1373 metres) offers great views and the chance to see large mammals, including Asiatic black bear, serow, wild pig, barking deer, tiger and sambar. The summit is 8.3 km from the railway station – an all-day hike. Near the railway station is Khuntan Cave.

The only access is by the Chiang Mai-Lamphun train to tiny Khuntan railway station (one to two hours) at the northern end of Thailand's longest railway tunnel (1.3 km). The train only makes a quick stop, so be careful not to miss it (watch for the tunnel). Weekdays are the best time to go; try to arrive by noon to reach the bungalows (2.5 km above the headquarters) before dark.

The park maintains 12 bungalows ranging from 200 to 1200B; one of the bungalows was built by German engineers in 1917. The best time to go is from November to February.

Ram Khamhaeng National Park

The mountains here are famous as the birthplace of the Thai nation over 700 years ago. One notable animal seen here is the scaly pangolin, a strange anteater the size of a small dog. Serow, wild pig, barking deer, gaur and the rare banteng (a type of wild cattle) are also sometimes encountered. Plan to spend at least two days here and camp on the summit of Khao Luang (1200 metres). Two trails – a steep four-km footpath and an easier five-km trail – lead to the summit from the park headquarters; count on three to five hours one-way for either. Porters can be hired through the park headquarters.

From Sukhothai take a bus along Highway 12 to Kamphaeng Phet and get off after 22 km at a police post opposite a hospital sign. From there it's 16 km by unsealed road to the park; hitching is usually the best way. Three bungalows are available for 250B a night. At Khao Luang's summit there's a dorm and a camping area. The best time to go is from November to February.

Thung Salaeng Luang National Park

This is Thailand's third-largest park (1262 sq km), spread across parts of Phitsanulok and Phetchabun provinces. From the 1960s through the early '80s, the forested mountains of Thung Salaeng Luang were a base for the People's Liberation Army of Thailand (PLAT), the tactical arm of Thailand's illegal Communist Party. Guerrillas were finally routed during a series of battles at Khao Ko in 1981-82.

Park topography is characterised by rugged mountains and grassy valleys and is said to be a habitat for wild elephants, tigers, boars, deer, and over 190 bird species, including the magnificent Siamese fireback pheasant. The park is named for a 10-sq-km savanna in the south-east portion of the park. This meadow rises to 800 metres, making it a comfortable trekking site even in the hot season. Another unique site is Thung Nang Phaya in the park's south-west, a large meadow with pine trees. Most of the park is best visited in the cool season, November to February.

The park is about 50 km from Lom Sak off the Lom Sak to Phetchabun highway. Transport on some park roads requires a

4WD or motorcycle. The park rents six bungalows, long houses and tents; there's a visitors' centre at the park headquarters.

Nam Nao National Park

One of Thailand's most beautiful and valuable parks, Nam Nao covers nearly 1000 sq km in Chaiyaphum and Phetchabun provinces. Although the park was first opened in 1972 it remained a PLAT stronghold until the early '80s. Marked by the sandstone hills of the Phetchabun Mountains, the park features pristine monsoon forest, dense bamboo groves and, at higher elevations, pine forests. A fair system of trails branches out from the park headquarters; the scenic and fairly level Phu Kum Khao trail cuts through pine forests and grass meadow for 24 km. The park also features several waterfalls and caves.

Although it's adjacent to Phu Khiaw Wildlife Sanctuary, a highway bisecting the park has unfortunately made wildlife more accessible to poachers, so many native species are in decline. Elephant and banteng are occasionally spotted, as well as Malayan sun bear, tigers, leopards and Asian jackals. Rumours of rhinoceros persist (last seen in 1971, but tracks were observed in 1979) and the bizarre fur-coated Sumatran rhino may survive here.

The park headquarters is 55 km east of Lom Sak. Daily buses run through the park from Lom Sak or Khon Kaen (103 km). Look for the park office sign on Highway 12 at Km 50; the office is two km from here. The best time to go is from November to February. The Forestry Department operates 10 bungalows (400 to 1200B) and camping areas; tents are available for rent.

Phu Kradung National Park

This 359-sq-km park is centred around Phu Kradung, a bell-shaped mountain (*kràdung* means 'bell') in the north-eastern province of Loei. At the top of the mountain (1360 metres) is a 60-sq-km plateau with a network of marked trails through flower meadows and montane forests of pine, beech and oak. The weather is always cool on top (average year-round temperature 20°C), hence the flora is more like that in a temperate zone. Lower down are mixed deciduous and evergreen monsoon forests as well as sections of cloud forest. Wild elephants and sambar are

among the large mammals living within park boundaries.

The park is best visited between mid-October and mid-June, before the rains set in and flood the trails. Temperatures in December and January can drop as low as 3 to 4°C. Phu Kradung should be avoided during school vacations unless you like crowds.

Daily buses ply the 75-km route between Loei and Phu Kradung district, where it's another seven km by songthaew or motorcycle to the park entrance. Near the park headquarters on the plateau are 15 bungalows and a camping area, along with a number of simple shelters. Porters can be hired at the base of the mountain and bedding can be hired at the park headquarters. See the Phu Kradung section under Loei in the North-East Thailand chapter for more details.

Huay Kha Khaeng & Thung Yai Naresuan Wildlife Sanctuaries

The 2575-sq-km Huay Kha Khaeng sanctuary, together with adjacent 3200-sq-km Thung Yai, form the heart of a 15,000-sq-km indigenous forest centred around the upper Khwae River system in a remote area overlapping Kanchanaburi, Tak and Uthai Thani provinces. Currently the least disturbed riparian habitats in Thailand, these sanctuaries serve as a corridor sheltering a number of rare plant and animal species that have disappeared in other parts of the region. Wildlife inhabiting the sanctuary's lowland deciduous forests are mostly of Indo-Chinese origin along with smaller varieties of Sundaic and Sino-Himalayan species.

This area is the northernmost limit of the Malayan tapir, and at one time was also a habitat for the Javan rhino, now thought to be extinct in Thailand. Other mammalian residents include banteng, gaur, wild elephant, tiger, leopard, clouded leopard and five other wildcat species, plus around 10 primate species including rare Phayre's leaf-monkey and the stump-tailed macaque. Among the 415 bird species found here are the rare green peafowl (a striking relative of the peacock), lesser fish-eagle and nearly extinct white-winged wood duck.

In order to garner more recognition of the sanctuary's uniqueness, Thailand has nominated Huay Kha Khaeng for designation as a UN World Heritage Site. Ironically, Thai conservationist Seub Nakhasathien – who was instrumental in the establishment of both sanctuaries – committed suicide in 1990, despondent over his inability to protect wildlife in the face of corruption.

These sanctuaries offer no visitor facilities and are difficult to reach by road.

Erawan, Si Nakharin & Sai Yok National Parks

These three parks form one main complex of protected lands north-west of Kanchanaburi. Large mammals and many birds can be found in this region.

The 550-sq-km Erawan, Thailand's most visited national park, is best known for its seven-tiered waterfall and the spectacular Phra That Cave. Buses run daily from Kanchanaburi to the market near the park; from there it's two km – hire a minibus, hitch or walk. Try to avoid weekends.

Si Nakharin (1534 sq km) is also noted for its waterfall. To reach the park, continue on the dirt road north from the Erawan headquarters or hire a boat at Tha Kradan, 24 km past the junction to Si Nakharin Dam, for the 1½-hour ride.

Sai Yok (500 sq km) is between Erawan and the Burmese border. Besides waterfalls and limestone caves, it has the world's smallest mammal, Kitti's hog-nosed bat, which weighs just two grams and was discovered in 1973.

Bungalows and dormitories are available at Erawan; at Sai Yok, private house-raft accommodation is offered on the river. From Kanchanaburi, daily buses going north on Highway 323 pass the park entrance, and from there it is about one km.

The falls look their best at the end of the rainy season in November, but visits through February are pleasant. For more detailed information see the Erawan section in the Central Thailand chapter.

Khao Yai National Park
Established in 1961, this is Thailand's oldest national park; it covers 2172 sq km and includes one of the largest intact monsoon forests in mainland Asia. Considered by many park experts to be among the world's best national parks, Khao Yai was recently designated an ASEAN National Heritage Site and has been nominated for similar international status by the UN. The park covers some five vegetational zones and is rich in wildlife, which includes wild elephants, tigers, deer, gaur, gibbons and hornbills. There are more than 50 km of hiking trails, and visitors' facilities are very good.

Recently the Forestry Department decided to expel all tourist accommodation from the park, including TAT hotels and forestry bungalows; overnight camping is still permitted. This was a government response to pressure from resort developers who were encroaching on Khao Yai parklands. Rather than decide who was allowed to build and who wasn't, the government has decided to ban all development, a decision that will undoubtedly have positive effects on park preservation. The Forestry Department has tentative plans to construct simple bungalows near the park entrance; in the meantime, hotel accommodation is available in nearby Pak Chong.

The park is 205 km north-east of Bangkok. Take a bus to Pak Chong from the northern bus terminal (or a train from Bangkok's Hualamphong station or from Ayuthaya). From Pak Chong, *songthaews* (pick-up trucks with bench seats) leave twice a day on weekdays, more frequently on weekends. For more detailed information see the Khao Yai section in the Central Thailand chapter.

Kaeng Krachan National Park
Kaeng Krachan is Thailand's largest national park, spreading over 2900 sq km or nearly half of Phetburi Province. In addition to subtropical rainforest you'll also find areas of savanna-like grasslands, mountains, steep cliffs, caves, waterfalls, long-distance hiking trails and two rivers, the Phetburi and the Pranburi, which are suitable for rafting. The large reservoir above the Kaeng Krachan Dam is stocked with fish.

Wildlife living in Kaeng Krachan include wild elephant, deer, tiger, leopard, clouded leopard, Malayan sun bear, Asiatic black bear, wild pig, gaur, banteng, sambar, mouse deer, barking deer, Asiatic jackal, Malayan porcupine, pangolin, the rare white-handed gibbon, stump-tailed macaque and dusky leaf-monkey. The western portion of the park along the Thai-Burmese border is intersected by the Tenassarim Range, which rises to 1200 metres within park boundaries. Sumatran rhino have been sighted in this area.

More than 250 confirmed bird species inhabit the park, including various hornbills, the woolly necked stork and the extremely rare ratchet-tailed treepie, formerly thought

Great Hornbill

to exist only in remote areas of northern Laos and Vietnam along the Chinese border.

Kaeng Krachan is about 60 km from Phetburi off Route 3175. The turn-off is at Tha Yang on Highway 4. There is no regular transport to the park, but you can hitch or charter a pick-up. There are 11 bungalows for 300 to 1000B, a camping area and a private floating resort. Park rangers will act as guides for 100B per day, plus food costs. The park is best seen from November to June. For more information, see the Kaeng Krachan section in the Southern Thailand chapter.

Khao Sam Roi Yot National Park

This 98-sq-km park on the east coast, north of Prachuap Khiri Khan, offers a large variety of easily accessible attractions, including Thailand's best preserved coastal wetlands. The salt marshes and mud flats are a habitat for more than 30 waterfowl species, including white egret, spotted greenshank, Malaysian plover, painted stork, grey heron, purple heron and the rare white-bellied sea eagle.

The park's name means 'three hundred peaks', a reference to a series of striking limestone hills rising from the sea. Inland wildlife includes the serow (a goat-like antelope that lives on the limestone crags), the crab-eating macaque, Malayan porcupine, leopard and leopard cat and Javan mongoose. Irrawaddy dolphin are occasionally seen offshore.

Another park attraction is Phraya Nakhon Cave, which contains a pavilion built by King Chulalongkorn (Rama V) in 1896. Below the cave are fine beaches.

From Bangkok take a bus to Pranburi, from where you can hitch a ride; trucks go the 35 km to the park headquarters several times daily. The best time to go is from November to February. There are seven bungalows and camping areas. Illegal private accommodation is springing up on Sam Phraya Beach. For more information see the Khao Sam Roi Yot section in the Southern Thailand chapter.

Khao Chamao – Khao Wong National Park

This park in Chanthaburi Province covers only 84 sq km but has an abundance of wildlife which seeks refuge here from the habitat destruction caused by the agriculture and illegal logging in surrounding areas. Mammalian residents include wild elephant, tiger, gaur, sambar and barking deer, serow, banteng, pileated gibbon and the very rare Asiatic black bear. Wreathed and great hornbill, crested serpent-eagle and silver pheasant are among the 53 known bird species that may be spotted. Pools below Khao Chamao Waterfall contain a type of carp that supposedly intoxicates those who eat it; *khão* means hill or mountain; *chamao (jà mao)* means 'to become intoxicated'. Biologists say the effect is actually passed on to humans from a type of fruit fallen from nearby trees, which the carp eat.

Khao Wong features around 80 caves and the waterfalls of Wang Morakot, Hok Sai, Pha Sung and Pha Kluai Mai.

From Rayong or Chanthaburi, take a minibus to Ban Khao Din, where minibuses to the park are available. The best time is from November to February. The park has seven bungalows (costing 500 to 1000B), a dorm and camping areas.

Khao Laem Ya – Mu Ko Samet National Marine Park

Officially declared a national park in 1981, the Ko Samet group and Laem Ya only had a park headquarters installed in 1985. The main islands of the Ko Samet group are Samet, Chan, Makham, Kruai, Plai Tin, Kut and Thalu. Laem Ya is opposite Samet on the mainland, south-west of Ban Phe.

Coral reefs in moderate condition (despite anchor and dynamite damage) are found along the southern tip of Samet and off Ko Thalu. Fine white-sand beaches are strung out along Samet's eastern and parts of its western shore. The interior of the island shelters a few monitor lizards, mouse deer, long-tailed macaques and greater bandicoots. Fruit bats (also called 'flying foxes') live on Ko Thalu.

Tourist accommodation of every level can be found along the mainland sections of the park, as well as on Ko Samet, while the other islands may be visited on day trips from Ko Samet. Strictly speaking, bungalow developments on Ko Samet are illegal, since they're private ventures on public lands. Because many of them were built before the establishment of the park office, the Forestry Department has been unable to take action although a moratorium on new construction is in effect. The most overdeveloped beaches, Ao Wong Deuan and Hat Sai Kaew (White Sand Beach), are undergoing serious environmental damage.

Ko Chang National Marine Park

Ko Chang, 30 km long and eight km wide, is Thailand's second-largest island (after Phuket) and ecologically the most pristine for its size. Sand beaches, mangrove forests and virgin lowland rainforest covering 70% of the island's rugged interior are the main attractions. Hard and soft corals fringe parts of all the islands. Smaller islands in the group – Kut, Kradat and Mak – have at one time or another been heavily planted in rubber or coconut.

About 15% of Ko Chang is privately owned, while parts of Ko Kut and all of Ko Kradat and Ko Mak are in private hands. For the moment, the islands' very remoteness – at the Thai-Cambodian border in Thailand's easternmost province – has served to protect them from the pressures of tourism, but in the future it may be difficult to maintain Ko Chang's current pristine status unless some kind of collective responsibility is recognised. Ko Chang represents an opportunity for a unique and sizable chunk of tropical island habitat to be preserved, if only enough people – including potential visitors – will co-operate to safeguard it.

Private accommodation on the island – beach bungalows ranging from 50 to 900B per day – are mostly found along Ko Chang's west coast. The Forestry Department also maintains a few bungalows on the east coast near its local headquarters at Tha Than Mayom. Camping is permitted on the beaches anywhere on the island.

Ferries carry passengers from Laem Ngop on the mainland to several points around the island. The park headquarters is at Tha Than Mayom on the island's eastern shore but most tourists visit only the sandy western beaches. Laem Ngop can be reached by songthaew from Trat; Trat is five hours by express bus from Bangkok's eastern bus terminal. See the Ko Chang National Marine Park section in the Central Thailand chapter.

Khao Sok National Park

Khao Sok, a 646-sq-km park in Surat Thani Province, features thick rainforest, waterfalls, limestone cliffs and an island-studded lake formed by the Chiaw Lan Dam. Connected to the Khlong Saen Wildlife Sanctuary and three smaller preserves (thus forming the largest contiguous nature preserve on the Thai peninsula), Khao Sok shelters a flux of wildlife, including wild elephant, leopard, serow, banteng, gaur and Malayan sun bear as well as over 175 bird species. In 1986 Slorm's stork – a new species for Thailand – was confirmed.

The park is located 1.5 km off Highway 401 between Takua Pa and Surat Thani at Km 109. Besides the camping area at the park headquarters, there are several private bungalow operations featuring 'tree-house' style accommodation. See the Khao Sok section in the Southern Thailand chapter for details.

Ao Phang-Nga National Marine Park

The forested limestone pillars of Ao Phang-Nga, made famous by the James Bond film *Man with the Golden Gun* are the major attraction of this large bay between Phuket and the mainland. The park is 96 km from Phuket and nine km from Phang-Nga where a minibus can be hired at the market. Alternatively, organise a day tour from Phuket. This park is best seen early in the morning before the hordes of package-tour boats start arriving from Phuket.

There are no bungalows on the islands though camping is allowed; overnight stays in private homes are permitted in Ko Panyi's Muslim village-on-stilts. See the Phang-Nga section in the Southern Thailand chapter for more information.

Hat Nai Yang National Park

This is a marine park protecting 13 km of beach along the north-west portion of Phuket Island. Leatherback turtles nest here from around November to February. The largest coral reef on the island lies in 10 to 20 metres of water around 1500 metres offshore; during low tide you can easily walk to the reef. Despite heavy pressure from passing boats, the coral is in fair condition. There are facilities for day visitors, including snorkelling gear for hire.

The park headquarters is 1.5 km from Phuket Airport. From Phuket minibuses can be hired at the central market for the 32-km ride to Hat Nai Yang. There are several bungalows (150 to 600B) and tents for rent; the new Pearl Village Hotel, at the south end of Hat Nai Yang, offers expensive rooms and bungalows.

Noppharat Thara – Ko Phi Phi National Marine Park

This park consists of several islands in offshore Krabi Province along with a long stretch of beaches from Noppharat Thara to Tham Phra Nang. Wildlife on the islands includes an abundance of corals, reef fish and pelagic birds (eg the Christmas and lesser frigate birds).

The best diving locales are found along Hat Yao (Long Beach) on Ko Phi Phi Don, and between nearby Ko Mai Phai (Bamboo Island) and Ko Yung (Mosquito Island). In recent years tourism on Ko Phi Phi Don, the largest of the island group, has boomed, although rough seas have restricted this to between December and March. Phi Phi Don has suffered a fate similar to that of Ko Samet, wherein neglected law enforcement has allowed unscrupulous bungalow developers and tour-boat operators to place unsustainable environmental pressure on beach and reef areas. Coral is already dying at an alarming rate.

Along the mainland (Krabi) beaches, growth has been more gradual, although a major hotel group has plans to build a resort at the most beautiful of the mainland park areas – Hat Tham Phra Nang. For more details see the section on Krabi in the Southern Thailand chapter.

Mu Ko Tarutao National Marine Park

The 51 islands off Thailand's south-west coast were declared a marine park in 1974, the country's first. The park offers beaches, coral reefs, mangrove swamps and island rainforest. Only one of the islands in the group, Ko Lipe, is inhabited. Sea turtles (green, hawksbill, Pacific Ridley and leatherback) nest on Ko Adang from around September to December. Other sea life occasionally seen includes dolphin, lobster, whale and dugong (sea cow), as well as dozens of tropical reef fish.

Reefs encircling Ko Adang, Ko Rawi and a number of smaller islands offer good diving and snorkelling possibilities. More than a hundred migrant and resident bird species can be sighted on land or over water, including white-bellied sea eagles, reef egrets, herons and hornbills. Crab-eating macaques, dusky langurs, monitor lizards and wild pig are occasionally seen in island interiors.

Ko Tarutao, the largest island, has several beaches, a year-round stream that feeds into a cave, and the remains of a penal colony for political dissidents that operated from 1939 to 1946. The park headquarters, also located on this island, features an outdoor museum, an aquarium and turtle-rearing ponds. There is a store selling basics, and snorkelling gear can be hired.

Share taxis and buses run regularly from Hat Yai to the pier at Pak Bara. Boats to Ko Tarutao and Ko Adang operate daily from November to April, irregularly at other times of the year. Bungalows and camping areas are available on Ko Tarutao and Ko Adang. Camping and private accommodation are available in a sea gypsy *(chao leh)* village on Ko Lipe. For more detailed information see the Ko Tarutao National Marine Park section in the Southern Thailand chapter.

Thale Ban National Park

Located in the province of Satun, Thailand's southernmost park (101 sq km) borders Malaysia. The beautiful, unspoilt forests include the best preserved section of white meranti rainforest (named for a dominant species of dipterocarp trees) in the region – on the Malaysian side this forest is becoming steadily denuded by agricultural development. Most of the wildlife found in Thale Ban is of the Sundaic variety, which includes species generally found in Malaysia, Sumatra, Borneo and Java.

A network of trails offers visitors a chance to view gibbons and macaques, serow and mouse deer, as well as a large number of rare bird species – great argus hornbill, helmeted hornbill, rhinoceros hornbill, masked finfoot, dusky crag martin and black Baza hawk. The park headquarters, situated on a lake in a valley formed by limestone outcroppings, is only two km from the border. Five km north of the office is Yaroi Falls, a nine-tiered waterfall with pools suitable for swimming.

The park entrance is about 37 km east of Satun's provincial capital or 90 km south of Hat Yai via Highway 406 and Route 4184; coming from Malaysia it's about 75 km from Alor Star. The best time to go is from December to March. There are six bungalows and a long house beside the lake with overnight accommodation at 200B per person. For more information see the Thale Ban section in the Southern Thailand chapter.

GOVERNMENT

The 1991 Constitution

The government of the Kingdom of Thailand is nominally a constitutional monarchy inspired by the bicameral British model but with myriad subtle differences. With the recent change of government and new constitution, government hierarchies have been substantially reshuffled.

Thailand's 15th constitution, enacted on 9 December 1991 by the coup regime's National Peace-Keeping Council (NPKC), replaces that promulgated in December of 1978 and allows for limited public participation in the choosing of government officials. National polls elect the 360-member lower house and prime minister, but the 270 senators of the upper house are appointed by the prime minister. The first senate under the current constitution, however, will be chosen by the NPKC and include a large military contingent. The constitution has no provision for the dissolution of the NPKC, who have the power to enact martial law at will.

Candidates for prime minister need not come from the national assembly, and there is no limit on the number of nonelected cabinet members in the prime minister's council of ministers. The upper and lower houses vote jointly on no-confidence motions, which means that a majority senate would need only 46 MPs to oust the government and elect a new prime minister. The military claims that such a system is necessary to guard against the potential for vote-buying, especially in rural areas. However, they have offered no conclusive evidence to show that vote-buying was pervasive in previously elected administrations.

Administrative Divisions

For administrative purposes, Thailand is divided into 73 *jangwàat* or provinces. Each province is subdivided into *amphoe* or districts, which are further subdivided into *kìng-amphoe* (subdistricts), *tambon* (communes or village groups), *mùu-bâan* (villages), *sukhãaphibaan* (sanitation districts) and *thêtsàbaan* (municipalities). Urban areas with more than 50,000 inhabitants and a population density of over 3000 per sq km are designated *nákhon*; those with populations of 10,000 to 50,000 with not less than 3000 per sq km are *muang*.

The capital of a province is an *amphoe muang*. An amphoe muang takes the same name as the province of which it is capital, eg amphoe muang Chiang Mai (often abbreviated as 'muang Chiang Mai') means the city of Chiang Mai, capital of Chiang Mai Province.

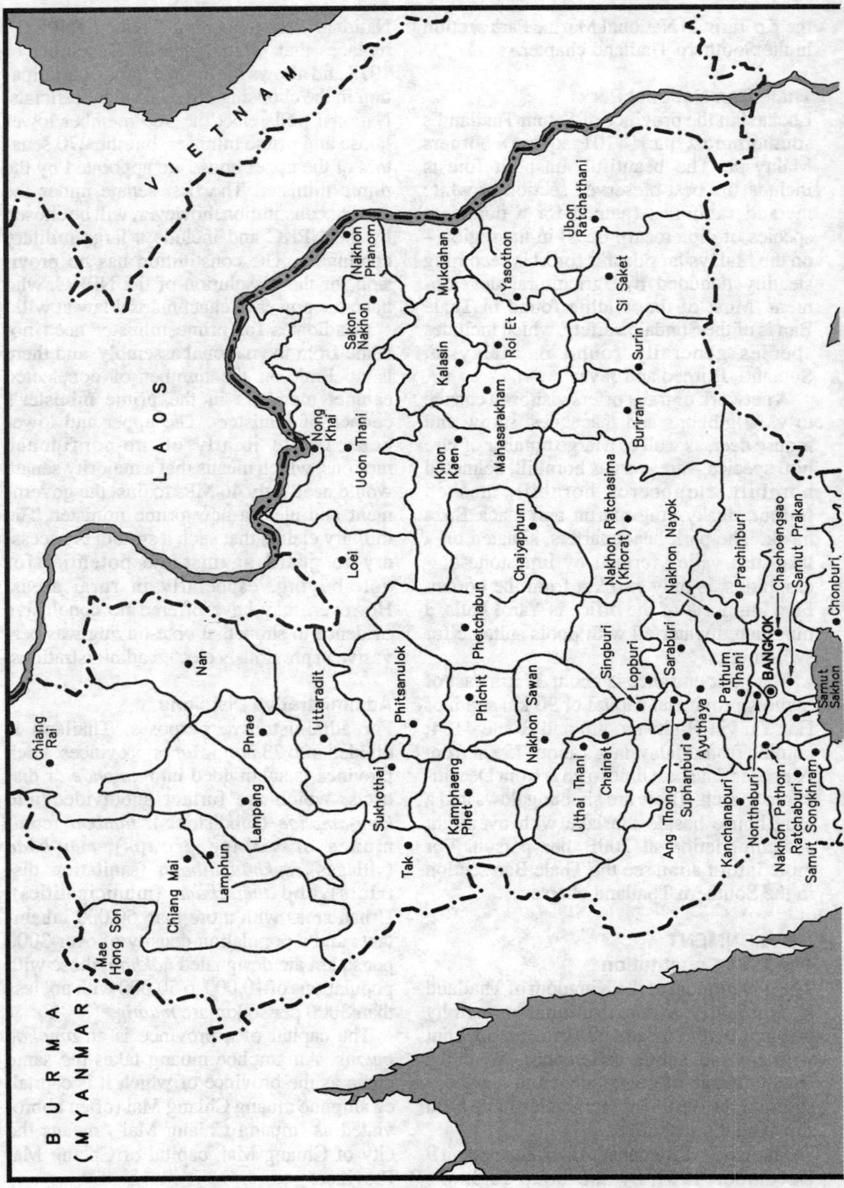
VIETNAM
LAOS
BURMA
(MYANMAR)
Chiang Rai
Mae Hong Son
Chiang Mai
Lamphun
Lampang
Phrae
Nan
Uttaradit
Sukhothai
Tak
Phitsanulok
Kamphaeng Phet
Phichit
Phetchabun
Loei
Udon Thani
Nong Khai
Sakon Nakhon
Nakhon Phanom
Mukdahan
Kalasin
Khon Kaen
Mahasarakham
Roi Et
Yasothon
Ubon Ratchathani
Si Saket
Surin
Buriram
Chaiyaphum
Nakhon Ratchasima (Khorat)
Nakhon Sawan
Uthai Thani
Chainat
Singburi
Lopburi
Saraburi
Ang Thong
Suphanburi
Ayuthaya
Pathum Thani
Nakhon Nayok
Prachinburi
Chachoengsao
Samut Prakan
Chonburi
BANGKOK
Samut Sakhon
Nonthaburi
Nakhon Pathom
Ratchaburi
Samut Songkhram
Kanchanaburi

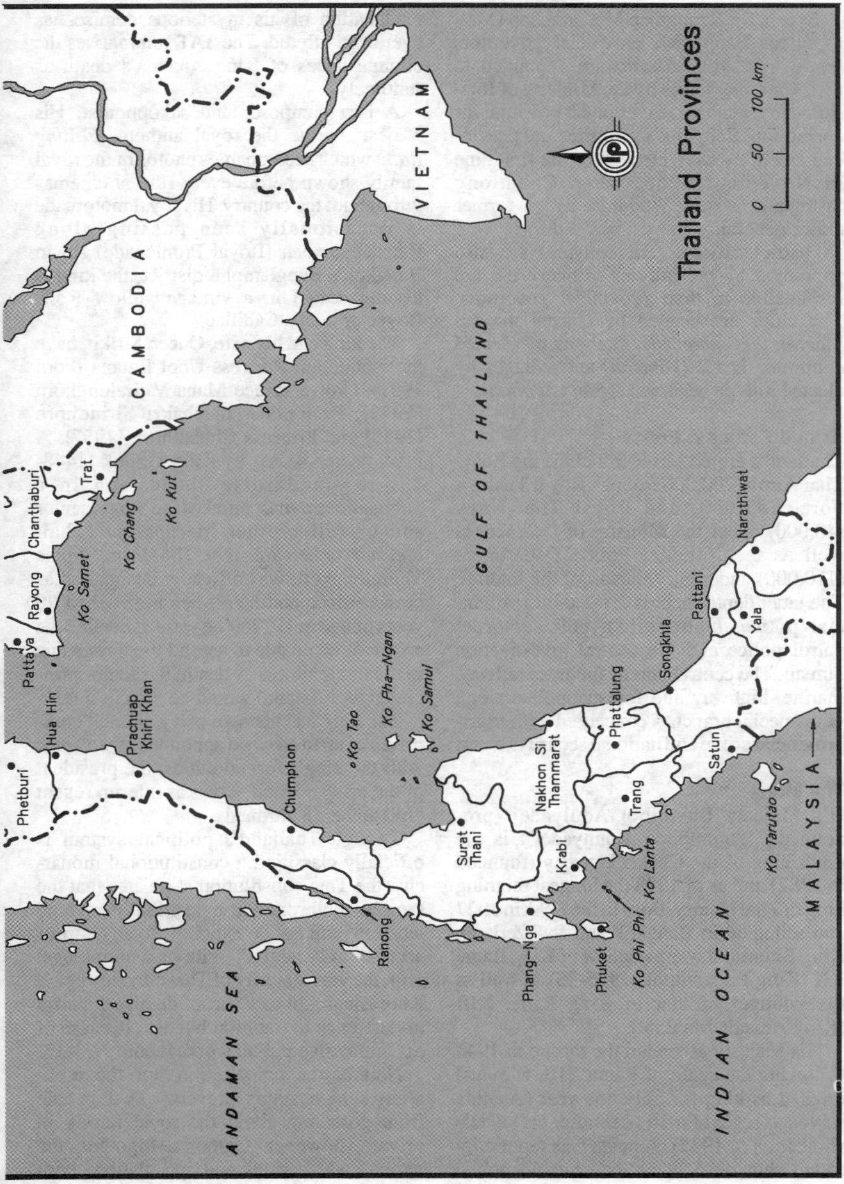
Thailand Provinces
0 50 100 km
CAMBODIA
VIETNAM
GULF OF THAILAND
ANDAMAN SEA
INDIAN OCEAN
MALAYSIA
Phetburi
Hua Hin
Pattaya
Rayong
Chanthaburi
Trat
Ko Samet
Ko Chang
Ko Kut
Prachuap Khiri Khan
Chumphon
Ko Tao
Ko Pha-Ngan
Ko Samui
Ranong
Surat Thani
Nakhon Si Thammarat
Phattalung
Songkhla
Pattani
Yala
Narathiwat
Trang
Satun
Krabi
Phang-Nga
Phuket
Ko Phi Phi
Ko Lanta
Ko Tarutao

Except for Krungthep Mahanakhon (Metropolitan Bangkok), provincial governors *(phûu wâa râatchakaan)* are appointed to their four-year terms by the Ministry of Interior – a system that leaves much potential for corruption. Bangkok's governor and provincial assembly were elected for the first time in November 1985, when Chamlong Srimuang, a strict Buddhist and a former major general, won by a landslide.

District officers *(nai amphoe)* are also appointed by the Interior Ministry but are responsible to their provincial governors. The cities are headed by elected mayors *(naiyók thêtsàmontrii)*, tambons by elected commune heads *(kamnan)* and villages by elected village headmen *(phûu yài bâan)*.

Armed Forces & Police

Thailand's armed services include the Royal Thai Army (200,000 troops), Royal Thai Air Force (43,000) and Royal Thai Navy (40,000) under the Ministry of Defence, as well as the National Police Department (110,000) under the Ministry of the Interior. The latter department is divided into provincial police, metropolitan police, border patrol police and the central investigation bureau. The central bureau includes railway, marine, highway and forestry police along with special branches concerned with trans-provincial crime and national security issues.

The Monarchy

His Majesty Bhumibol Adulyadej (pronounced 'Phumíphon Adunyádèt') is the ninth king of the Chakri Dynasty (founded in 1782) and as of 1988 the longest reigning king in Thai history. Born in the USA in 1927 and schooled in Bangkok and Switzerland, King Bhumibol was a nephew of King Rama XII (King Prajadhipok, 1925-35) as well as the younger brother of King Rama XIII (King Ananda Mahidol).

His Majesty ascended the throne in 1946 following the death of Rama XIII, who had reigned as king for only one year (Ananda served as regent for 10 years after his uncle's abdication in 1935). Ananda was reportedly found shot dead in his bed but no public explanation of his mysterious demise has ever been offered. The TAT summarises the circumstances of King Ananda's death as 'untimely.'

A jazz composer and saxophonist, His Majesty wrote the royal anthem, *Falling Rain*, which accompanies photos of the royal family shown before every film at cinemas throughout the country. His royal motorcade is occasionally seen passing along Ratchadamnoen (Royal Promenade) Rd in Bangkok's Banglamphu district; the king is usually seated in a vintage yellow Rolls Royce or a '50s Cadillac.

The king and his wife, Queen Sirikit, have three children: Princess Ubol Ratana (born 1951), Crown Prince Maha Vajiralongkorn (1952), Princess Mahachakri Sirindhorn (1955) and Princess Chulabhorn (1957). A royal decree issued by King Trailok (1448-88) to standardise succession in a polygamous dynasty makes the king's senior son or full brother his *uparaja* (Thai: *ùpàrâat)* or heir apparent. Thus Prince Maha Vajiralongkorn was officially designated as crown prince and heir when he reached 20 years of age in 1972; if he were to decline the crown or be unable to ascend the throne due to incurable illness or death, the senior princess (Ubol Ratana) would be next in line.

The king has his own privy council comprised of up to 14 royal appointees who assist with the king's formal duties; the president of the privy council serves as interim regent until an heir is throned.

Though Thailand's political system is officially classified a constitutional monarchy, the Thai constitution stipulates that the king be 'enthroned in a position of revered worship' and not be exposed 'to any sort of accusation or action'. With or without legal writ, the vast majority of Thai citizens regard King Bhumibol as a sort of demigod, partly in deference to tradition but also because of his impressive public works record.

Neither the constitution nor the monarchy's high status prevents Thai people from gossiping about the royal family in private, however. Gathered together, the various whisperings and speculations with regard to royal intrigue would make a fine medieval fable. Many Thais, for example, favour Princess Sirindhorn for succession to the Thai throne, though none would say this publicly, nor would this popular sentiment appear in the Thai print or broadcast media.

It is oft repeated that the Thai king has no political power (by law his position is strictly titular and ceremonial) but in times of national political crisis, Thais have often looked to the king for leadership. Two attempted coups d'état in the 1980s may have failed because they received tacit royal disapproval. By implication, the successful military coup of February 1991 must have had palace approval, whether *post facto* or a priori. The 1991 draft constitution drawn up by the NPKC was widely condemned until just a few days before its final reading in the national assembly, when the king spoke out in favour of leaving the draft unchanged during his annual birthday address.

Not surprisingly, the assembly passed the constitution in spite of a few anti-democratic clauses contained therein, even though it would have taken only a few extra days to revise the draft.

Along with nation and religion, the monarchy is very highly regarded in Thai society – negative comments about the king or any member of the royal family is a social as well as legal taboo. See the Avoiding Offence section in this chapter.

ECONOMY

During the '80s, Thailand maintained a steady GNP growth rate which in 1988 reached 13% per annum. Now, Thailand has suddenly found itself on the threshold of attaining the exclusive rank of NIC or 'newly industrialised country', which experts forecast will be fulfilled within the next 10 years. Soon, they say, Thailand will be joining Asia's 'little dragons', also known as the Four Tigers – South Korea, Taiwan, Hong Kong and Singapore – in becoming a leader in the Pacific Rim economic boom.

About 66% of the Thai labour force is currently engaged in agriculture, 10% each in commerce and services, and 8% in manufacturing. Sixty percent of Thailand's exports are agricultural; the country ranks first in the world for rice (a whopping 36.4% of world exports, followed by 20.3% from the USA and 9.3% from Pakistan), second in tapioca (after Brazil) and fifth in coconut (following Indonesia, the Philippines, India and Sri Lanka). In 1991 Thailand became the world's largest producer of natural rubber although it still ranks behind Malaysia in total rubber exports. Other important agricultural exports include sugar, maize, pineapple, cotton, jute, green bean, soybean and palm oil. Processed food and beverages – especially canned shrimp and tuna – also account for significant export earnings.

By the year 2000, it is expected that more than half of Thailand's labour force will be engaged in the manufacturing and industrial sectors. Manufactured goods have become an increasingly important source of foreign exchange revenue and now account for 30% of Thailand's exports. Cement, textiles and electronics lead the way. The country also has substantial natural resources including tin, petroleum and natural gas.

In 1987, tourism became the leading earner of foreign exchange, outdistancing even Thailand's largest single export, textiles. Nearly five million tourists spent 96 billion baht (US$3.8 billion) in 1989. The government's economic strategy remains focused, however, on export-led growth through the development of light industries such as textiles and electronics, backed by rich reserves of natural resources and a large, inexpensive labour force. Observers predict that such a broad-based economy will make Thailand a major economic competitor in Asia in the long term. Thailand also has the lowest foreign debt in South-East Asia, just 26% of the GDP by 1990.

Average per capita income by the beginning of the '90s was 41,000B (US$1640) per year. Regional inequities, however, mean that local averages range from US$300 in the north-east to US$2500 in Bangkok. The minimum wage in Bangkok and surrounding provinces is 115B (US$4.60) per day, as low as 82B a day in the outer provinces.

Opium & the Golden Triangle

The opium poppy, *Papaver somnniferum*, has been cultivated and its resins extracted for use as a narcotic at least since the time of the early Greek Empire. The Chinese were introduced to the drug by Arab traders during the time of Kublai Khan (1279-94). It was so highly valued for its medicinal properties that hill-tribe minorities in southern China began cultivating the opium poppy in order to raise money to pay taxes to their Han Chinese rulers. Easy to grow, opium became a way for the nomadic hill tribes to raise what cash they needed in transactions (willing and unwilling) with the lowland world. Many of the hill tribes that migrated to Thailand and Laos in the post WW II era in order to avoid persecution in Burma and China took with them their one cash crop, the poppy. The poppy is well suited to hillside cultivation as it flourishes on steep slopes and in nutrient-poor soils.

The opium trade became especially lucrative in South- East Asia during the '60s and early '70s when US armed forces were embroiled in Vietnam. Alfred McCoy's *The Politics of Heroin in Southeast Asia* recounts how contact with the GI market not only expanded the immediate Asian market, but provided outlets to world markets. Before this time the source of most of the world's heroin was the Middle East. Soon everybody wanted in and various parties alternately quarrelled over and co-operated in illegal opium commerce. Most notable were the Nationalist Chinese Army refugees living in northern Burma and northern Thailand, and the Burmese anti-government rebels, in particular the Burmese Communist Party, the Shan States Army and the Shan United Army.

The American CIA eventually became involved in a big way, using profits from heroin runs aboard US aircraft to Vietnam and further afield to finance covert operations throughout Indo-China. This of course led to an increase in the availability of heroin throughout the world, which in turn led to increased production in the remote northern areas of Thailand, Burma and Laos, where there was little government interference. This area came to be known as the 'Golden Triangle' because of local fortunes amassed by the 'opium warlords' – Burmese and Chinese military-businesspeople who controlled the movement of opium across three international borders.

As more opium was available, more was consumed and the demand increased along with the profits – so the cycle expanded. As a result, opium cultivation became a full-time job for some hill tribes within the Golden Triangle. Hill economies were destabilised to the point where opium production became a necessary means of survival for thousands of people, including the less nomadic Shan people.

One of the Golden Triangle's most colourful figures is Khun Sa (also known as Chang Chi-Fu, or Sao Mong Khawn) a half-Chinese, half-Shan opium warlord. He got his start in the '50s and '60s working for the Kuomintang (KMT) – Chiang Kai Shek's Nationalist Chinese troops who had fled to Burma. The KMT were continuing military operations against the Chinese Communists along the Burma-China border, financed by the smuggling of opium (with CIA protection). They employed Khun Sa as one of their prime local supporters/advisors. Khun Sa broke with the KMT in the early '60s after establishing his own opium-smuggling business, with heroin refineries in northern Thailand.

From that time on, the history of heroin smuggling in the Golden Triangle has been intertwined with the exploits of Khun Sa. In 1966, the Burmese government deputised Khun Sa as head of 'village defence forces' against the Burmese Communist Party (BCP), which was at maximum strength at this time and fully involved in opium trade. Khun Sa cleverly used his government backing to consolidate power and build up his own militia by developing the Shan United Army (SUA), an anti-government insurgent group heavily involved in opium throughout the Golden Triangle in competition with the BCP and KMT.

When the KMT attempted an 'embargo' on SUA opium trade by blocking caravan routes into Thailand and Laos, Khun Sa initiated what has come to be known as the Opium War of 1967 and thwarted the embargo. However, the KMT managed to chase Khun Sa, along with a contingent of SUA troops running an opium caravan routed for Thailand, into Laos, where Burmese officials arrested Khun Sa and the Laotian government seized the opium. Khun Sa escaped Burmese custody by means of a carefully planned combination of extortion and bribery in 1975 and returned to take command of the SUA. About the same time, the Burmese government broke KMT control of opium trafficking and Khun Sa stepped in to become the prime opium warlord in the Triangle, working from his headquarters in Ban Hin Taek, Chiang Rai Province, Thailand. Coincidentally, US forces pulled out of Indo-China at this time so there was no longer any competition from CIA conduits in Laos. Ironically since then, the primary law-enforcement conflict has been between US-backed Thai forces and the SUA.

Whenever they receive a large financial contribution from the US Drug Enforcement Agency (DEA), Thai army rangers sweep northern Thailand from Tak to Chiang Rai and Mae Hong Son, destroying poppy fields and heroin refineries but rarely making arrests. One recent US$800,000 sweep operation accomplished the destruction of 40 sq km or 25,000 *rai* (one rai is equal to 1600 sq metres) of poppy fields in Chiang Mai, Chiang Rai, Mae Hong Son, Tak and Nan. Hill-tribe and Shan cultivators, at the bottom of the profit scale, stood by helplessly while their primary means of livelihood was hacked to the ground. A crop substitution programme, developed by the Thai royal family in 1959 (a year earlier cultivation of the opium poppy for profit had been made illegal), has generally been recognised as an almost complete failure. Success has only occurred in selected areas where crop substitution is accompanied by a concentrated effort to indoctrinate hill tribes into mainstream Thai culture.

Since the late '70s, the SUA has continued to buy opium from the BCP, Shan and hill-tribe cultivators in Burma and Thailand, transporting and selling the product to Yunnanese-operated heroin refineries in China, Laos and Thailand, who in turn sell to ethnic Chinese (usually Tae Jiu/Chao Zhou) syndicates in Thailand who control access to world markets. SUA strength has been estimated at between 1500 and 8000 regulars, putting it on a par with the BCP and the Karen National Union, Myanmar's two largest insurgent groups (among the 32 different groups operating in 1989). The SUA recently merged with several other Shan armies to form the Muang Tai Army (MTA), led by the Shan State Restoration Council.

A turning point in Khun Sa's fortunes occurred in 1982 and 1983 when the Thais launched a full-scale attack on his Ban Hin Taek stronghold, forcing him to flee to the mountains of the Kok River valley across the border in Myanmar, where he now lives in a fortified network of underground tunnels. This led to the breaking up of opium and heroin production in the Mae Salong-Ban Hin Taek area. In 1991 he announced his 'retirement' but like his Rangoon nemesis Ne Win, Khun Sa has outwitted many international players before and probably still maintains de facto control. Word has it that Khun Sa is a 'marked' man who will soon be sacrificed by corrupt Burmese and Thai generals in order to appease the US government.

Khun Sa's former northern Thailand stronghold is now undergoing heavy 'pacification' or Thai nationalisation. At great expense to the Thai government, tea, coffee, corn and Chinese herbs are now grown where opium once thrived. Whether this particular project is successful or not is another question but the government's strategy seems to be one of isolating and then pushing pockets of the opium trade out of Thailand and into Myanmar and Laos, where it continues uninterrupted. Myanmar remains the largest producer of opium in the world, manufacturing an average of 600 metric tons per annum over the last decade. During a bumper year, the entire Triangle output approaches 2000 tons; Khun Sa recently boasted that the 1992-93 harvest would reach 4000 tons. Only an estimated 1.9 to 2.5% of the opium crop is intercepted by national or international authorities each year.

The Laotian People's Revolutionary Party (LPRP), Laos' ruling group, is currently taking advantage of Thai government action in northern Thailand to encourage an increase in opium production in Laos. They are effectively capturing some share of the market vacated by the SUA in Thailand; north-eastern Laos is dotted with heroin refineries which process Burmese and Laotian opium. If the Burmese government steps up efforts to suppress poppy cultivation in Myanmar, as the Thai government has done in Thailand, Laos may in fact be in a position to corner the market, as it's the only government in the region with an official tolerance towards opium production. Smuggling routes for Laotian opium and heroin cross the Thai border at several points throughout the north and north-east, including the provinces of Chiang Mai, Chiang Rai, Nan, Loei, Nong Khai and Nakhon Phanom.

The cycle continues with power being transferred from warlord to warlord while the hill-tribe and Shan cultivators continue as unwilling pawns in the game. The planting of the poppy and the sale of its collected resins has never been a simple moral issue. Cultivators who have been farming poppies for centuries and heroin addicts who consume the end product have both been exploited by governments and crime syndicates who trade in opium for the advancement of their own power. Because of the complexities involved, opium production in the Golden Triangle must be dealt with as a political, social, cultural and economic problem and not simply as a conventional law-enforcement matter.

So far a one-sided approach has only resulted in the unthinking destruction of minority culture and economy in the Golden Triangle area, rather than an end to the opium and heroin problem. Meanwhile, opium cultivation continues in Thailand in hidden valleys not frequented by the Thai armed forces. Any hill-tribe settlement may legally plant opium poppies for its own consumption. Small plots of land are 'leased' by opium merchants who have allowed production to decentralise in order for poppy resin collection to appear legal. ■

The current inflation rate is about 8% per annum, and travellers should keep this in mind when referring to prices in this edition. As in most other countries, prices continue to rise.

Regional Economies

The north-east of Thailand has the lowest inflation rate and cost of living. This region is poorer than the rest of the country and doesn't get as much tourism; it therefore offers excellent value for the traveller and is in dire need of your travel dollar. Handwoven textiles and farming remain the primary means of livelihood in this area. In the south, fishing, tin mining and rubber production keep the local economy fairly stable.

Central Thailand grows fruit (especially pineapples), sugar cane and rice for export, and supports most of the ever-growing industry (textiles, food processing and cement). North Thailand produces mountain or dry rice (as opposed to water rice, the bulk of the crop produced in Thailand) for domestic use, maize, tea, various fruits and flowers, and is very dependent on tourism. Teak and other lumber were once major products of the north, but since early 1989 all logging has been banned in Thailand in order to prevent further deforestation.

Infrastructure & Growth

Some say that Thailand is growing faster than its infrastructure can handle. Although adequate for most domestic trade, the transport and telecommunications systems are in dire need of upgrading for purposes of international trade. Incoming ships have to wait a week before they can get a berth at busy Klong Toey Port. Access to Klong Toey is limited to ships of less than 10,000 tons or 8.5-metre draft; larger vessels must off-load at the mouth of the Chao Phraya River or offshore near the country's second-largest ports at Si Racha and Sattahip. Thirty smaller ports along the Gulf and Andaman Sea serve fishing fleets and smaller import-export operations.

Engineers are working hard to meet the shipping demands – a new deep-water port has just opened at Laem Chabang, near Si Racha, and is linked to an export-processing zone. Another industrial park and port is under development at Mapthaphut farther east for petrochemical and fertiliser industries.

One of the biggest dilemmas facing the economic planners is whether to acquire a larger foreign debt in order to finance the development of an infrastructure which is capable of handling continued high growth, or whether to allow growth to slow while the infrastructure catches up. Continued rapid growth will probably result in a disproportionate development of the more industrialised central and southern regions, leaving the agricultural north and north-east behind.

Advocates of a slow-growth approach hope for better distribution of wealth around the country through a combination of agribusiness projects and welfare programmes that would bring a higher standard of living to poor rural areas. This makes good sense when one considers the relative differences between Thailand and the Four Tigers (in the proportion of rural to urban dwellers and the high fertility of the land).

The 1990-92 recession has been a blessing in disguise inasmuch as it has allowed Thailand's overheated economy to cool down. The current growth rate has slowed to 7.5% and is not expected to increase more than a half percent or so over the next two years. Even at 8% Thailand will remain one of the world's fastest growing economies.

Indo-China & ASEAN Trade

Aside from its own export-oriented growth, Thailand stands to profit from increased international trade in Laos, Cambodia and Vietnam. At the moment Bangkok is the main launching base for foreign investments in Indo-China, and the Thai baht is second only to the US dollar as the currency of choice for regional commerce. In Laos and Cambodia the only foreign banks are Thai; Vientiane and Phnom Penh have even started building up portions of their national reserves in baht, thus forming a 'baht bloc'.

The proposed ASEAN Free Trade Area (AFTA) will probably be very advantageous for Thailand's economy since Thailand has a highly educated, inexpensive labour pool and a large manufacturing sector. Whether the AFTA is approved by ASEAN members, the Thais will continue to serve as go-betweens for buyers and sellers thwarted by trade embargoes. Officially, Vietnam doesn't have trade relations with either the USA or China, yet Thai joint-venture banks in Hanoi and Ho Chi Minh City finance Vietnamese purchases of Chinese-manufactured tank parts shipped through Thailand while arranging for sales of captured US weaponry, including F-5 jet components, left over from the Vietnam War!

Tourism

According to TAT statistics, the country is currently averaging about five million tourist arrivals per year, a 62-fold increase since 1960 when the government first began keeping statistics.

In 1990 nearly two-thirds of the visitors came from East Asia and the Pacific (3.3 million), with Malaysians leading the way at around 752,000, followed by the Japanese (652,000), Taiwanese (503,000) and Singaporeans (335,000). Europeans as a whole made up approximately 1,230,000 of the total, with Germans at the top (243,000), followed closely by Britons (228,000), French (194,000) and Italians (108,000). The Americas, including Canada and all Latin American countries, totalled about 367,000, of which 285,000 were from the USA and 68,000 from Canada. South Asians chalked up around 267,000 (half from India) while Australians totalled 252,000 and the Middle East sent roughly 94,000. Middle Easterners were the only international group to show a net decline from previous years. As a result of recent Saudi restrictions on tourism to Thailand, Saudi arrivals dropped by 70%; Israeli arrivals on the other hand showed an 11% increase (for a total of 20,000).

The prize for longest average length of stay goes to Germans, Israelis, Belgians and Scandinavians. The average for Germans was 13 nights, followed by the Austrians and Swiss (12.5 each), Israelis (12.4), Belgians (11.7), Danes (11.2), Finns (11.1), Swedes (10.8) and Norwegians (10.6). In contrast, the average stay for Britons was 9.7 nights, Americans 7.9, Australians 7.4 and the Japanese 5.7.

The overall average tourist expenditure for 1989 (the last year for which the TAT has statistics) was 2626B a day. Surprisingly, the biggest spenders were the Koreans, who averaged a daily per capita expenditure of 3165B, followed closely by US visitors at 3100B. The Japanese spent an average of 3005B per day/person, French 2965B, Hong Kongers 2912B, Taiwanese 2902B, Indians 2806B, Canadians 2803B, Australians 2496B, Britons 2432B, Germans 2071 and the frugal Swiss 1759B.

POPULATION & PEOPLE

The population of Thailand is about 57 million and currently growing at a rate of 1.4% per annum (as opposed to 3% in 1970 and 2.5% in 1979), thanks to Khun Mechai's nationwide family-planning campaign. This growth rate does not include the influx of Lao, Cambodian, Vietnamese and Burmese refugees in recent years.

Bangkok is by far the largest city in the kingdom, with a population of nearly seven million (more than 10% of the total population) – too many for the scope of its public services and what little 'city planning' exists. Khon Kaen is the second-largest city but does not have nearly such a big population – just over 200,000. Third and fourth are Hat Yai and Chiang Mai with populations of around 150,000 each. All other towns in Thailand have well below 100,000, with few over 40,000.

The literacy rate of Thailand is approximately 91% and increasing, and the average life expectancy is 66 – in both respects Thailand is a leader in mainland South-East Asia. Infant mortality figures are 24 per 1000 births (figures for neighbouring countries vary from 116 per 1000 in Cambodia to 13 in Malaysia). Thailand as a whole has a relatively youthful population; only about 12% are older than 50.

The Thai Majority

About 75% of the citizenry are ethnic Thais, who can be divided into the central Thais or Siamese of the Chao Phraya Delta (the most densely populated region of the country); the Thai Lao of north-east Thailand; the Thai Pak Tai of southern Thailand; and the northern Thais. Each of these groups speak their own Thai dialect and to a certain extent practice customs unique to their region. Politically and economically the central Thais are the dominant group although they barely outnumber the Thai-Lao of the north-east.

Smaller Thai-speaking groups in Thailand with their own dialects include the Shan (Mae Hong Son), the Thai Lü (Nan, Chiang Rai), the Lao Song (Phetchaburi and Ratchaburi), the Phuan (Chaiyaphum, Phetchaburi, Prachinburi), the Thai Khorat or Sawoei (Nakhon Ratchasima), the Phu Thai (Mukdahan, Sakon Nakhon), the Yaw (Nakhon Phanom, Sakon Nakhon) and the Thai-Malay (Satun, Trang, Krabi).

Minorities

The largest ethnic minority groups living in Thailand are the Chinese (11% of the population, most of whom are second or third generation) and the Malays (3.5%). The remaining 10.5% of the population is divided among smaller non-Thai-speaking groups like the Vietnamese, Khmer, Mon, Semang (Sakai), Moken (*chao leh* or 'sea gypsies'), Htin, Mabri, Khamu and a variety of hill tribes (described more fully in the Northern Thailand chapter).

A small number of Europeans and other non-Asians live in Bangkok and the provinces – their total numbers aren't recorded since very few have immigrant status.

ARTS

Traditional Sculpture & Architecture

The following scheme is the latest one used by Thai art historians to categorise historical styles of Thai art, principally sculpture and architecture (since very little painting prior to the 19th century has survived).

A good way to acquaint yourself with these styles, if you are interested, is to visit the Bangkok National Museum in Bangkok, where works from each of these periods are on display. Then as you travel upcountry and view old monuments and sculpture you'll know what you're seeing, as well as what to look for.

Since 1981, the Thai government made restoration of nine key archaeological sites part of its national economic development plan. As a result, the Fine Arts Department, under the Ministry of Education, has developed nine historical parks (*ùthayaan pràwátìsàat)*: Sukhothai Historical Park in Sukhothai Province; Phra Nakhon Si Ayuthaya Historical Park in Ayuthaya Province; Phanom Rung Historical Park in Buriram Province; Si Thep Historical Park in Phetchabun Province; Phra Nakhon Khiri Historical Park in Phetburi Province; Si Satchanalai Historical Park in Sukhothai

---

Bangkok Primacy

Bangkok has dominated Thailand's urban hierarchy since the late 18th century and is today considered Asia's quintessential 'primate city' by sociologists. A primate city is one that is demographically, politically, economically and culturally dominant over all other cities in the country. Approximately 70% of Thailand's urban population (and 10% of the total population) lives in Bangkok, as compared with 30% in Manila and 27% in Kuala Lumpur (the second and third most primate in the region). More statistics: 79% of the country's university graduates, 78% of its pharmacists and 45% of its physicians live in the capital; 72% of all passenger cars registered in the country (30% of all motor vehicles) are registered in Bangkok. ■

Thai Art Styles

Style	Duration	Centred in	Characteristics
Mon Art (formerly Dvaravati)	6th to 13th C	Central Thailand, also North and North-East	adaptation of Indian styles, principally Gupta
Khmer Art	7th to 13th C	Central and North-East Thailand	post-classic Khmer styles accompanying spread of Khmer empires
Peninsular Art	(formerly Srivijaya period)	Chaiya and Nakhon Si Thammarat	Indian influence 3rd to 5th C, Mon and local influence 5th to 13th C, Khmer influence 11th to 14th C
Lan Na (formerly Chiang Saen)	13th to 14th C	Chiang Mai, Chiang Rai, Phayao, Lamphun, Lampang	Shan/Burmese and Lao traditions mixed with local styles
Sukhothai	13th to 15th C	Sukhothai, Si Satchanalai, Kamphaeng Phet, Phitsanulok	unique to Thailand
Lopburi	10th to 13th C	Central Thailand	mix of Khmer, Pala and local styles
Suphanburi-Sangkhlaburi (formerly U Thong)	13th to 15th C	Central Thailand	mix of Mon, Khmer, and local styles; prototype for Ayuthaya style
Ayuthaya A	1350-1488	Central Thailand	Khmer influences gradually replaced by revived Sukhothai influences
Ayuthaya B	1488-1630	Central Thailand	ornamentation distinctive of Ayuthaya style, eg crowns and jewels on Buddhas, begins
Ayuthaya C	1630-1767	Central Thailand	baroque stage and decline
Ratanakosin	19th C to present	Bangkok	return to simpler designs, beginning of European influences

Art Styles

LOPBURI
10th to 13th centuries

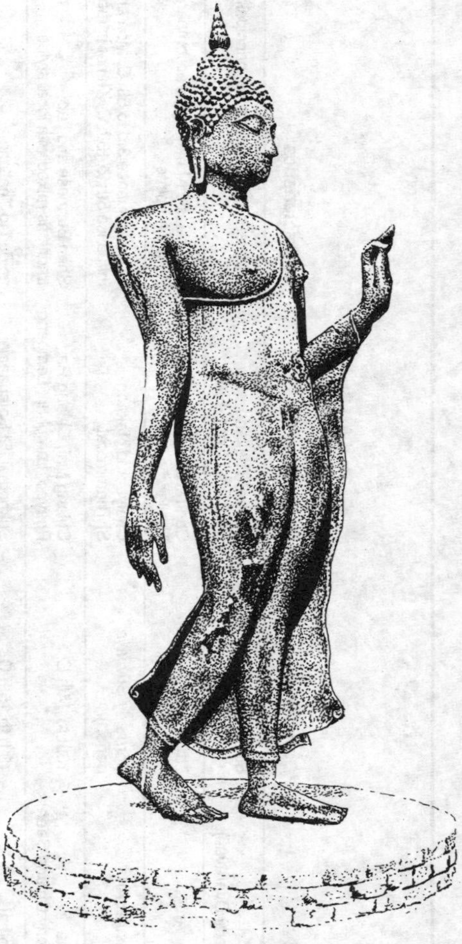

SUKHOTHAI
13th to 15th centuries

MON (Dvaravati)
6th to 11th centuries

MON (Hariphunchai)
11th to 13th centuries

SUPHANBURI-SANGKHLABURI
13th to 15th centuries

LAN NA
13th to 14th centuries

Province; Phimai Historical Park in Nakhon Ratchasima Province; Muang Singh Historical Park in Kanchanaburi Province; and Kamphaeng Phet Historical Park in Kamphaeng Phet Province.

These parks are administered by the Fine Arts Department to guard against theft and vandalism, and to protect tourists from bandits at more remote sites. In 1988 the department even managed to get the famous Phra Narai lintel returned to Prasat Phanom Rung from the Art Institute of Chicago Museum.

Additional areas of historical interest for art and architecture are Thonburi, Lamphun, Nakhon Pathom, Nan, Ratburi, Lopburi, Chaiya, Sawankhalok, Chiang Mai, Phitsanulok, Chiang Saen and Nakhon Si Thammarat. Some of the monuments at these sites have also been restored by the Fine Arts Department and/or by local interests. For more detail on the historical sites, see the relevant regional sections in this book.

Recommended books on Thai art are A B Griswold's classic *Arts of Thailand* (Indiana University Press, 1960), the similarly titled *The Arts of Thailand* (Thames & Hudson, 1991) by Steve Van Beek and *A Concise History of Buddhist Art in Siam* (Tokyo, 1963) by Reginald Le May. Even the newest of these three books is out of date, since research in Thai art history has evolved quickly in recent years, but they make good introductions. There are several decent English-language books on various aspects of Thai art for sale at the national museums around Thailand (particularly at the Bangkok National Museum) and at the Ancient City (Muang Boran) office on Ratchadamnoen Rd in Bangkok.

For information about the export of antiques or objects of art from Thailand, see the Customs section in the Facts for the Visitor chapter.

Modern Architecture

Modern Thai architects are among the most daring in South-East Asia, as even a short visit to Bangkok will confirm. Thais began mixing traditional Thai with European forms in the late 19th and early 20th centuries, as exemplified by Bangkok's Vimanmek Palace, the Author's Wing of the Oriental Hotel, the Chakri Mahaprasat next to Wat Phra Kaew and any number of older residences and shophouses in Bangkok or provincial capitals throughout Thailand. Buildings of mixed heritage in the north and north-east exhibit French and English influences, while those in the south typically show Portuguese influence.

Shophouses throughout the country, whether a 100 years or a 100 days old, share the basic Chinese shophouse *(hâwng tháew* in Thai) design in which the ground floor is reserved for trading purposes while the upper floors contain offices or residences.

During most of the post-WW II era, the trend in modern Thai architecture – inspired by the European Bauhaus movement – was toward a boring functionalism in which the average building looked like a giant egg carton turned on its side. The Thai aesthetic, so vibrant in prewar eras, almost entirely disappeared in this characterless style of architecture.

When Thai architects finally began experimenting again during the building boom of the mid-1980s, it was to provide high-tech designs like Sumet Jumsai's famous robot-shaped Bank of Asia on Sathon Tai Rd. Few people seemed to find the space-age look endearing, but at least it was different. Another trend affixed gaudy Roman and Greek-style columns to rectangular Art Deco boxes in what was almost a parody of Western classical architecture. One of the outcomes of this fashion has been the widespread use of curvilinear banisters on the balconies of almost every new shophouse, apartment or condominium throughout Thailand, often with visually disturbing results.

More recently a handful of rebellious architects have begun reincorporating traditional Thai motifs – mixed with updated Western classics – in new buildings. MIT graduate Rangsan Torsuwan introduced the neoclassic (or neo-Thai) style, the best example of which is the new Grand Hyatt

Erawan in Bangkok. Another architect using traditional Thai architecture in modern functions is Pinyo Suwankiri, who has designed a number of government buildings in Bangkok as well as the Cittaphawan Buddhist School in Chonburi.

A good book for anyone with a general interest in Thai residential design, both interior and exterior, is William Warren's *Thai Style* (Asia Books), a coffee-table tome with excellent photography by Luca Invernizzi Tettoni.

Painting

Except for a few prehistoric cave or rock-wall murals found in Ratburi, Ubon and Udon provinces, not much painting exists in Thailand predating the 18th century. Presumably there were a great number of temple murals in Ayuthaya that were destroyed by the Burmese invasion of 1767. The earliest surviving temple examples are found at Ayuthaya's Wat Ratburana (1424) and Phetburi's Wat Yai Suwannaram (late 17th century).

Nineteenth-century religious painting has fared better; Ratanakosin-style temple art is in fact more highly esteemed for painting then for sculpture or architecture. Typical temple murals feature rich colours and lively detail. Some of the finest are found in Wat Phra Kaew's Wihan Phutthaisawan (Buddhaisawan Chapel) in Bangkok and at Wat Suwannaram in Thonburi.

Modern Painting The beginnings of Thailand's modern art movement are usually attributed to Italian artist Corrado Feroci, who was invited to Thailand by King Rama VI in 1924. Feroci founded the country's first fine arts institute in 1933, a school which eventually developed into Silpakorn University, Thailand's premier training ground for artists and art historians. In gratitude for his contributions, the Thai government gave Feroci the Thai name Silpa Bhirasri.

Today Thailand's most well-known modern-art institute is named after Bhirasri, although modern painting and sculpture are exhibited at a number of Bangkok and Chiang Mai venues. One of the most important modern movements in Thai art was an updating of Buddhist themes, begun in the 1970s by painters Pichai Nirand, Thawan Duchanee and Prateung Emjaroen. The movement has grown stronger since their early efforts combined modern Western schemata with Thai motifs. One Bangkok gallery, the Visual Dhamma Gallery (off Soi Asoke), specialises in the display of modern Thai Buddhist art by a number of different artists.

Another important venue and source of support for modern art is Bangkok's luxury hotels. The largest collection of modern Thai painting anywhere in the world is found in the lobbies and public areas of the Grand Hyatt Erawan; the displays are changed regularly.

Music

Traditional From a Western perspective, traditional Thai music is some of the most bizarre on the planet, but to acquire a taste for it is well worth the effort. The classical, central Thai music is spicy, like Thai food, and features an incredible array of textures and subtleties, hair-raising tempos and pastoral melodies.

The classical orchestra is called the *pìi-phâat* and can include as few as five players or more than 20. Among the more common instruments is the *pìi*, a woodwind instrument which has a reed mouthpiece and is heard prominently at Thai boxing matches. The pii is a relative of a similar Indian instrument, as is the *phin*, a banjo-like stringed instrument descended from the Indian *vina*. A bowed instrument similar to ones played in China and Japan is aptly called the *saw*. The *ranâat èk* is the wooden percussion instrument resembling the Western xylophone, while the *khlui* is a wooden flute. One of the more amazing Thai instruments is the *khawng wong yài*, tuned gongs arranged in a semicircle. There are also several different kinds of drums, some played with the hands, some with sticks.

The pii-phaat ensemble was originally developed to accompany classical dance-drama and shadow theatre but can be heard in straightforward performance these days, in temple fairs as well as concerts. One reason classical Thai music may sound strange to the Western ear is that it does not use a tempered scale as we have been accustomed to hearing since Bach's time. The standard scale does feature an eight-note octave but it is arranged in seven full intervals, with no 'semi-tones'. Thai scales were first transcribed by Peter Feit (Phra Chen Duriyanga) of Thai-German background, who also composed Thailand's national anthem in 1932.

In the north and north-east there are several popular types of reed instruments with multiple bamboo pipes, which function basically like a mouth-organ. Chief among these is the *khaen*, which originated in Laos and when played by an adept musician sounds like a rhythmic, churning calliope. The funky *lûuk thûng*, or 'country' style which originated in the north-east, has become a favourite throughout Thailand.

If you're interested in learning how to play traditional Thai instruments, contact the Bangkok YMCA (☎ 286-1542/2580) to enquire about its weekly classes.

Recommended books on the subject are *The Traditional Music of Thailand* by David Morton, and *Thai Music* by Phra Chen Duriyanga (Peter Feit).

Modern Popular Thai music has borrowed much from Western music, particularly its instruments, but still retains a distinct flavour of its own. Although Bangkok bar bands can play fair imitations of everything from Hank Williams to Olivia Newton-John, there is a growing preference among Thais for a blend of Thai and international styles.

The best example of this is Thailand's famous rock group, Carabao. At the time of writing, Carabao is by far the most popular musical group in Thailand and has even scored hits in Malaysia, Singapore, Indonesia and the Philippines with songs like 'Made in Thailand' (only the chorus is in English). This band and others have crafted an exciting fusion of Thai classical and luuk thung forms with heavy metal. These days almost every other Thai pop group sounds like a Carabao clone, and individual members of the original band are putting out their own albums using the now-classic Carabao sound.

Another inspiring movement in modern Thai music is the fusion of international jazz with Thai classical and folk motifs. The leading exponent of this newer genre is the composer and instrumentalist Tewan Sapsanyakorn (Tong Tewan), whose performances mix Western and Thai instruments. The melodies of his compositions are often Thai-based but the improvisations and rhythms are drawn from such heady sources as Sonny Rollins and Jean-Luc Ponty. Tewan himself plays soprano and alto sax, violin and *khlui*, the Thai flute, with equal virtuosity. When Tewan isn't touring internationally you may catch him and his extremely capable band at the Bangkok clubs Brown Sugar, Trumpet, Round Midnight or Blue Moon.

Cassette tapes of Thai music are readily available throughout the country in department stores, cassette shops and street vendors. The average price for a Thai music cassette is 50 to 60B. Western tapes are cheaper (about 30B each) if bootlegged, but the days of pirate tapes in Thailand are numbered now that the US music industry is enforcing international copyright laws.

Theatre & Dance

Traditionally, Thailand has six kinds of theatre: *khon*, formal masked dance-drama depicting scenes from the *Ramakian* (the Thai version of India's *Ramayana)* and originally performed only for the royal court; *lákhon*, a general term covering several types of dance-dramas (usually for non-royal occasions) as well as Western theatre; *lí-khe* (likay), a partly improvised, often bawdy folk play with dancing and music; *mánohra*, the southern Thai equivalent of li-khe, but based on a 2000-year-old Indian story; *nãng* or shadow plays, limited to southern Thailand; and *hùn lũang* or *lákhon lék* – puppet theatre.

Khon In all khon performances, four types of characters are represented – male humans, female humans, monkeys and demons. Monkey and demon figures are always masked with the elaborate head coverings often seen in tourist promo material. Behind the masks and make-up, all actors are male. Traditional khon is a very expensive production – Ravana's retinue alone (Ravana is the story's principal villain) consists of over a hundred demons, each with a distinctive mask. Perhaps because it was once limited to royal venues and hence never gained a popular following, the khon or *Ramakian* dance-drama tradition has all but died out in Thailand. Bangkok's National Theatre is one of the few places where khon is still performed for the public.

Classical dancer at the royal court

Scenes performed in traditional khon (and lakhon performances) come from the *Ramayana*, India's classic 'epic journey' tale with obvious archetypal parallels in the Greek epic the *Odyssey*, and the Greek myth Jason and the Argonauts. The central story revolves around Prince Rama's search for his beloved Princess Sita, who has been abducted by the evil 10-headed demon Ravana and taken to the island of Lanka. Rama is assisted in his search and in the final battle against Ravana by a host of mythical half-animal, half-human characters including the monkey-god Hanuman. See the later Literature section for some details on the differences between the Indian *Ramayana* and Thai *Ramakian*.

Lakhon The more formal *lákhon nai* (inner lakhon) originally was performed for lower nobility by all-female ensembles; like royal khon it's a dying art. In addition to scenes from the *Ramakian*, lakhon nai performances may include traditional Thai folk tales; whatever the story, text is always sung.

Lákhon nâwk (outer lakhon) deals exclusively with folk tales and features a mix of sung and spoken text, sometimes with improvisation. Both male and female performers are permitted. Like khon and lakhon nai, performances are becoming increasingly rare. More common these days is the less refined *lákhon chatrii*, a fast-paced, costumed dance-drama usually performed at upcountry temple festivals or at shrines (commissioned by a shrine devotee whose wish was granted by the shrine deity). Chatrii stories have been influenced by the older manohra theatre of southern Thailand (see under Manohra later in this section).

Lákhon phûut (speaking lakhon) is the equivalent of Western theatre based on the Greek model – all dialogue is spoken rather than sung. This is the most modern of Thailand's theatre traditions as well as the most popular in cities and larger towns.

Li-khe In rural and small-town Thailand this is the most popular type of live theatre. Most often performed at festivals by troupes of travelling performers, li-khe presents an intriguing mixture of folk and classical music, outrageous costumes, slapstick comedy, sexual innuendo and up-to-date commentary on Thai politics and society. Farangs – even those who speak fluent Thai – are often left behind by the highly idiomatic, culture-specific language and gestures. For true li-khe aficionados, the coming of a renowned troupe is a bigger occasion than the release of a new *Terminator* sequel at the local cinema.

Manohra Also known simply as *nora*, this is southern Thailand's equivalent to li-khe and the oldest surviving Thai dance-drama. The basic story line bears some similarities to the *Ramayana*. In this case the protagonist Prince Suthon (Sudhana in Pali) sets off to rescue the kidnapped Manohra, a *kinnari* or woman-bird princess. As in li-khe, performers add extemporaneous comic rhymed commentary – famed nora masters sometimes compete at local festivals to determine who's the best rapper.

Nang Shadow-puppet theatre – in which two-dimensional figures are manipulated between a cloth screen and light source at night-time performances – has been a South-East Asian tradition for perhaps five centuries. Originally brought to the Malay peninsula by Middle-Eastern traders, the techniques eventually spread to all parts of mainland and peninsula South-East Asia; in Thailand it is mostly found only in the south. As in Malaysia and Indonesia, shadow puppets in Thailand are carved from dried buffalo or cow hides *(nãng* in Thai).

Two distinct shadow-play traditions survive in Thailand. The most common, *nãng thálung*, is named after Phattalung Province where it developed based on Malay models. Like their Malay-Indonesian counterparts, the Thai shadow puppets represent an array of characters from classical and folk drama, principally the *Ramakian* and Phra Aphaimani in Thailand. A single puppet master manipulates the cutouts, which are bound to the ends of buffalo-horn handles. Nang thalung is till occasionally seen at temple fairs in the south, mostly in Songkhla and Nakhon Si Thammarat provinces. Performances are also held periodically for tour groups or visiting dignitaries from Bangkok.

The second tradition, *nãng yài* (literally, 'big hide') uses much larger cutouts, each bound to two wooden poles held by a puppet master; several masters (almost always male) may participate in a single performance. Nang Yai is rarely performed nowadays because of the lack of trained nang masters and the expense of the shadow puppets. Most nang yai made today are sold to interior decorators or tourists – a well-crafted hide puppet may cost as much as 5000B.

Lakhon Lek Like khon, lakhon lek or 'little theatre' (also known as hun luang or 'royal puppets') was once reserved for court performances. Metre-high marionettes made of *koi* paper and wire, wearing elaborate costumes modelled on those of the khon, are used to convey similar themes, music and dance movements. Two Thai puppet masters are required to manipulate each hun luang – including arms, legs, hands, even fingers and eyes – by means of wires attached to long poles. Stories are drawn from Thai folk tales, particularly Phra Aphaimani, and occasionally from the *Ramakian*.

Hun luang is no longer performed, as the performance techniques and puppet-making skills have been lost. The hun luang puppets themselves are highly collectable; the Bangkok National Museum has only one example in its collection. Surviving examples of a smaller, 30-cm court version called *hùn lék* (little puppets) are occasionally used in live performances; only one puppeteer is required for each marionette in hun lek.

Another Thai puppet theatre called *hùn kràbòk* (rod puppets) is based on popular Hainanese puppet shows. It uses 30-cm hand puppets that are carved from wood, and they are viewed from the waist up. Hun krabok

Spirit Houses
Every Thai house or building has to have a spirit house to go with it – a place for the spirits of the site, or *phra phum,* to live in. Without this vital structure you're likely to have the spirits living in the house with you and that can cause all sorts of trouble. Spirit houses look rather like a birdhouse-sized Thai temple mounted on a pedestal. At least your average spirit house does – a big hotel may have a shrine covering a 100 sq metres or more.

How do you ensure that the spirits take up residence in your spirit house rather than in the main house with you? Mainly by making the spirit house a more auspicious place to live in than the main building through daily offerings of food, flowers and incense. The spirit house should also have a prominent location and should not be shaded by the main house. Thus its position has to be planned from the very beginning and installed with due ceremony. If your own house is improved or enlarged then the spirit house should be as well. ■

marionettes are still being crafted and used in performance.

Literature

Of all classical Thai literature, the *Ramakian* is the most pervasive and influential in Thai culture. The Indian source – the *Ramayana* – first came to Thailand with the Khmers 900 years ago, first appearing as stone reliefs on Prasat Hin Phimai and other Angkor-period temples in the north-east. Oral and written versions may also have been available; eventually, though, the Thais developed their own version of the epic, first written down during the reign of Rama I (1782-1809). This version was 60,000 stanzas, about 25% longer than the Sanskrit original.

Although the main theme remains the same, the Thais embroidered on the *Ramayana* by providing much more biographic detail on arch-villain Ravana (Dasakantha, called Thotsakan or '10-headed' in the *Ramakian*) and his wife Montho. Hanuman the monkey-god differs substantially in the Thai version inasmuch as he is very flirtatious with females (in the Hindu version he follows a strict vow of chastity). One of the classic *Ramakian* reliefs at Bangkok's Wat Pho depicts Hanuman holding a maiden's bared breast as if it were an apple.

Also passed on from Indian tradition are the many *jatakas* or life stories of the Buddha (*chaa-tòk* in Thai). Of the 547 jataka tales in the Pali *tripitaka* (Buddhist canon) – each one chronicling a different past life – most appear in Thailand almost word-for-word as they were first written down in Sri Lanka. A group of 50 'extra' stories – based on Thai folk tales of the time – were added by Pali scholars in Chiang Mai 300 to 400 years ago. The most popular jataka in Thailand is one of the Pali originals known as the Mahajati or Mahavessandara (Mahaa-Wetsanthon in Thai), the story of the Buddha's penultimate life. Interior murals in the *bot* or ordination chapel of Thai wats typically depict this jataka and nine others: Temiya, Mahachanaka, Suwannasama, Nemiraja, Mahasotha, Bhuritat, Chantakumara, Nartha and Vithura.

Phra Aphaimani, composed by poet Sunthorn Phu in the late 18th century, is Thailand's most famous classical literary work. Like many of its epic predecessors around the world, it tells the story of an exiled prince who must complete an odyssey of love and war before returning to his kingdom in victory.

SPORT

Thai Boxing (Muay Thai)

Almost anything goes in this martial sport, both in the ring and in the stands. If you don't mind the violence (in the ring) a Thai boxing match is worth attending for the pure spectacle – the wild musical accompaniment, the ceremonial beginning of each match and the frenzied betting around the stadium.

Thai boxing is also telecast on Channel 7 every Sunday afternoon; if you're wondering where everyone is, they're probably inside watching the national sport.

Most of what is known about the early history of Thai boxing comes from Burmese accounts of warfare between Burma and Thailand during the 15th and 16th centuries. The earliest reference (1411 AD) mentions a ferocious style of unarmed combat that decided the fate of Thai kings. A later description tells how Nai Khanom Tom, Thailand's first famous boxer and a prisoner of war in Burma, gained his freedom by roundly defeating a dozen Burmese warriors before the Burmese court. To this day, many martial art aficionados consider the Siamese style the ultimate in hand-to-hand fighting. Hong Kong, China, Singapore, Taiwan, Korea, Japan, the USA, Netherlands, Germany and France have all sent their best and none of the challengers have been able to defeat top-ranked Thai boxers. On one famous occasion, Hong Kong's top five Kung Fu masters were dispatched in less than 6½ minutes cumulative total, all knock-outs.

King Naresuan the Great (1555-1605) was supposed to have been a top-notch boxer himself. He made Muay Thai a required part of military training for all Thai soldiers. Later another Thai king, Phra Chao Seua (the Tiger King) further promoted Thai boxing as a national sport by encouraging prize fights and the development of training camps in the early 18th century. There are accounts of massive wagers and bouts to the death during this time. Phra Chao Seua is said to have been an incognito participant in many of the matches during the early part of his reign. Combatants' fists were wrapped in thick horsehide for maximum impact with minimum knuckle damage. They also used cotton soaked in glue and ground glass and later hemp. Tree bark and seashells were used to protect the groin from lethal kicks.

The high incidence of death and physical injury led the Thai government to institute a ban on Muay Thai in the 1920s, but in the '30s, the sport was revived under a modern set of regulations based on the international Queensberry rules. Bouts were limited to five three-minute rounds separated with two-minute breaks. Contestants had to wear international-style gloves and trunks (always either in red or blue) and their feet were taped but no shoes worn. There are 16 weight divisions in Thai boxing, ranging from mini-flyweight to heavyweight, with the best fighters said to be in the welterweight division (67 kg maximum). As in international-style boxing, matches take place on a 7.3-sq-metre canvas-covered floor with rope retainers supported by four padded posts, rather than the traditional dirt circle.

In spite of these concessions to safety today, all surfaces of the body are still considered fair targets and any part of the body may be used to strike an opponent, except the head. Common blows include high kicks to the neck, elbow thrusts to the face and head, knee hooks to the ribs and low crescent kicks to the calf. A contestant may even grasp an opponent's head between his hands and pull it down to meet an upward knee thrust. Punching is considered the weakest of all blows and kicking merely a way to 'soften up' one's opponent; it is the knee and elbow strikes that are decisive in most matches.

The training of a Thai boxer and particularly the relationship between boxer and trainer is highly ritualised. When a boxer is considered ready for the ring, he is given a new name by his trainer, usually with the name of the training camp as his surname. For the public, the relationship is perhaps best expressed in the *ram muay* (boxing dance) that takes place before every match.

The ram muay ceremony usually lasts about five minutes and expresses obeisance to the fighter's guru *(khruu)*, as well as to the guardian spirit of Thai boxing. This is done through a series of gestures and body movements performed in rhythm to the ringside musical accompaniment of Thai oboe (pii) and percussion. Each boxer works out his own dance, in conjunction with his trainer and in accordance with the style of his particular camp.

The woven headbands and armbands worn into the ring by fighters are sacred ornaments which bestow blessings and divine protection; the headband is removed after the ram muay ceremony, but the armband, which actually contains a small Buddha image, is worn throughout the match. After the bout begins, the fighters continue to bob and weave in rhythm until the action begins to heat up. The musicians continue to play throughout the match and the volume and tempo of the music rise and fall along with the events in the ring.

As Thai boxing has become more popular among Westerners (both spectators and participants) there are increasing numbers of bouts staged for tourists in places like Pattaya, Phuket and Ko Samui. In these, the action may be genuine but the judging below par. Nonetheless, dozens of authentic matches are held every day of the year at the major Bangkok stadiums and in the provinces (there are about 60,000 full-time boxers in Thailand) and these are easily sought out.

Several Thai *nák muay* have gone on to win world championships in international-style boxing. Khaosai Galaxy, the greatest Asian boxer of all time, chalked up 19 WBA bantamweight championships in a row before retiring undefeated in December 1991.

In Thailand an English-language periodical called *Muay Thai: Thai Championship Boxing* appears annually at Bangkok, Chiang Mai and Phuket bookshops that sell English-language material. The annual includes features on muay thai events abroad as well as in Thailand.

Krabi-Krabong

Another traditional Thai martial art still practised in Thailand is *kràbìi-krabong* (literally, 'sword-staff'). As the name implies, this tradition focuses on hand-held weapons techniques, specifically the *kràbìi* (sword), *plông* (quarter-staff), *ngao* (halberd), *dàap sãwng meu* (a pair of swords held in each hand) and *mái sun-sàwk* (a pair of clubs). Although for most Thais krabi-krabong is a ritual artefact to be displayed during festivals or at tourist venues, the art is still solemnly taught according to a 400-year-old tradition handed down from Ayuthaya's Wat Phutthaisawan. The King of Thailand's elite bodyguard are trained in krabi-krabong; many Thai cultural observers perceive it as a 'purer' tradition than muay thai.

Like muay thai of 70 years ago, modern krabi-krabong matches are held within a marked circle, beginning with a *wai khruu* ceremony and accompanied throughout by a musical ensemble. Thai boxing techniques and judo-like throws are employed in conjunction with weapons techniques. Although sharpened weapons are used, the contestants refrain from striking their opponents – the winner is decided on the basis of stamina and technical skill displayed. Although an injured fighter may surrender, injuries do not automatically stop a match.

Takraw

Tàkrâw, sometimes called Siamese football in old English texts, refers to games in which a woven rattan ball about 12 cm in diameter is kicked around. The rattan (or sometimes plastic) ball itself is called a *lûuk tàkrâw*. Takraw is also popular in several neighbouring countries; it was originally introduced to the SEA Games by Thailand but the Malays seem to win the most international championships. The traditional way to play takraw in Thailand is for players to stand in a circle (the size of the circle depends on the number of players) and simply try to keep the ball airborne by kicking it soccer-style. Points are scored for style, difficulty and variety of kicking manoeuvres.

A popular variation on takraw – and the

one used in intramural or international competitions – is played with a volleyball net, using all the same rules as in volleyball except that only the feet and head are permitted to touch the ball. It's amazing to see the Thais perform aerial pirouettes, spiking the ball over the net with their feet. Another variation has players kicking the ball into a hoop 4.5 metres above the ground – basketball with feet, but without a backboard!

For information on muay thai and krabi krabong training courses in Thailand, see the Martial Arts Training section in the Facts for the Visitor chapter.

AVOIDING OFFENCE

Monarchy and religion are the two sacred cows in Thailand. Thais are tolerant of most kinds of behaviour as long as it doesn't insult one of these.

King & Country

The monarchy is held in considerable respect in Thailand and visitors should be respectful too – avoid disparaging remarks about the king, queen or anyone in the royal family. One of Thailand's leading intellectuals, Sulak Sivaraksa, was arrested in the early '80s for *lèse majesté* because of a passing reference to the king's fondness for yachting (Sulak referred to His Majesty as 'the skipper'). Although on that occasion he received a royal pardon, in 1991 Sulak had to flee the country to avoid prosecution again for alleged remarks delivered at Thammasat University about the ruling military junta, with reference to the king. The penalty for lese majesty is seven years' imprisonment.

While it's OK to criticise the Thai government and even Thai culture openly, it's considered a grave insult to Thai nationhood as well as to the monarchy not to stand when you hear the national or royal anthems. Radio and TV stations in Thailand broadcast the national anthem daily at 8 am and 6 pm; in towns and villages (even in some Bangkok neighbourhoods) this can be heard over public loudspeakers in the streets. The Thais stop whatever they're doing to stand during the anthem (except in Bangkok where nobody can hear anything above the street noise) and visitors are expected to do likewise. The royal anthem is played just before films are shown in public cinemas; again, the audience always stands until it's over.

Religion

Correct behaviour in temples entails several guidelines, the most important of which is to dress neatly (no shorts or sleeveless shirts) and to take your shoes off when you enter any building that contains a Buddha image. Buddha images are sacred objects, so don't pose in front of them for pictures and definitely do not clamber upon them.

Monks are not supposed to touch or be touched by women. If a woman wants to hand something to a monk, the object should be placed within reach of the monk, not handed directly to him.

When sitting in a religious edifice, keep your feet pointed away from any Buddha images. The usual way to do this is to sit in the 'mermaid' pose in which your legs are folded to the side, with the feet pointing backwards.

Social Gestures

Traditionally Thais greet each other not with a handshake but with a prayer-like palms-together gesture known as a *wâi*. If someone wais you, you should wai back (unless wai-ed by a child).

The feet are the lowest part of the body (spiritually as well as physically) so don't point your feet at people or point at things with your feet. In the same context, the head is regarded as the highest part of the body, so don't touch Thais on the head either.

Terms of Address

Thais are often addressed by their first name with the honorific *khun* or a title preceding it. Other formal terms of address include *nai* (Mr) and *nang* (Miss or Mrs). Friends often use nicknames or kinship terms like *phîi* (elder sibling) or *náwng* (younger sibling) depending on the age differential.

Dress & Attitude

Beach attire is not considered appropriate for trips into town and it is especially counter-productive if worn to government offices (eg when applying for a visa extension). The attitude of 'This is how I dress at home and no-one is going to stop me' gains nothing but contempt/disrespect from the Thais.

As in most parts of Asia, anger and emotions are rarely displayed and generally get you nowhere. In any argument or dispute, remember the paramount rule is to keep your cool.

Nudity

Regardless of what the Thais may (or may not) have been accustomed to centuries ago, they are quite offended by public nudity today. Bathing nude at beaches in Thailand is illegal. If you are at a truly deserted beach and are sure no Thais may come along, there's nothing stopping you – however, at most beaches travellers should wear suitable attire. Likewise, topless bathing for females is frowned upon in most places except on heavily touristed islands like Phuket, Samui, Samet and Pha-Ngan. Many Thais say that nudity on the beaches is what bothers them most about foreign travellers. These Thais take nudity as a sign of disrespect for the locals, rather than as a libertarian symbol or modern custom. Thais are extremely modest in this respect (despite racy billboards in Bangkok) and it should not be the visitor's intention to 'reform' them.

Message from a Reader

As a final comment on avoiding offence, here is a plea from a female reader who wrote to me following an extended visit she had in Thailand:

> Please do whatever you can to impress on travellers the importance of treating the Thai people, who are so generous and unassuming, with the respect they deserve. If people sunbathe topless, take snapshots of the people like animals in a zoo, and demand Western standards then they are both offending the Thai people and contributing to the opinion many of them have of us being rich, demanding and promiscuous.

RELIGION

Buddhism

About 95% of the Thai citizenry are Theravada Buddhists. The Thais themselves frequently call their religion Lankavamsa (Sinhalese lineage) Buddhism because Siam originally received Buddhism during the Sukhothai period from Sri Lanka. Strictly speaking, Theravada refers to only the earliest forms of Buddhism practised during the Ashokan and immediate post-Ashokan periods in South Asia. The early Dvaravati and pre-Dvaravati forms of Buddhism are not the same as that which has existed in Siamese territories since the 13th century.

Since the Sukhothai period, Thailand has maintained an unbroken canonical tradition and 'pure' ordination lineage, the only country among the Theravadin (using Theravada in its doctrinal sense) countries to do so. Ironically, when the ordination lineage in Sri Lanka broke down during the 18th century under Dutch persecution, it was Siam that restored the Sangha (Buddhist brotherhood) there. To this day the major sect in Sri Lanka is called Siamopalivamsa (Siam-Upali lineage, Upali being the name of the Siamese monk who led the expedition to Ceylon), or simply Siam Nikaya (the Siamese sect).

Basically, the Theravada school of Buddhism is an earlier and, according to its followers, less corrupted form of Buddhism than the Mahayana schools found in East Asia or in the Himalayan lands. The Theravada (literally, 'teaching of the elders') school is also called the 'southern' school since it took the southern route from India, its place of origin, through South-East Asia (Burma, Thailand, Laos and Cambodia in this case), while the 'northern' school proceeded north into Nepal, Tibet, China, Korea, Mongolia, Vietnam and Japan. Because the Theravada school tried to preserve or limit the Buddhist doctrines to only those canons codified in the early Buddhist era, the Mahayana school gave Theravada Buddhism the name Hinayana, or the 'lesser vehicle'. The Mahayana school was the 'great vehicle', because it built upon the

Sculptural Symbolism

Buddha images throughout Thailand are for the most part sculpted according to strict iconographical rules found in traditional Buddhist art texts. The way the monastic robes drape over the body, the direction in which the hair curls, the proportions for each body part – all are to some degree canonised by these texts. The tradition does leave room for innovation, however, allowing the various 'schools' of Buddhist art to distinguish themselves over the centuries.

Aspects of the tradition that almost never vary include the postures and hand positions of Buddha images. Four basic postures (Pali: *asana*) are portrayed: standing, sitting, walking and reclining. The first three are associated with daily activities of the Buddha, ie teaching, meditating and offering refuge to his disciples. These activities are symbolised by each figure's *mudra* or hand position.

Bhumisparsa (Touching the Earth) In this classic mudra the right hand touches the ground while the left rests in the lap. This hand position symbolises the point in the Buddha's life story when he sat in meditation beneath the legendary banyan tree in Bodh Gaya, India and vowed not to budge from the spot until he gained enlightenment. Mara – the Buddhist equivalent of Satan – tried to interrupt the Buddha's meditation by invoking a series of distractions (including tempests, floods, feasts and nubile young maidens). The Buddha's response was to touch the earth, thus calling on nature to witness his resolve. The bhumisparsa mudra is one of the most common mudras seen in Thai Buddhist sculpture; it's also known as the *maravijaya* (victory over Mara) mudra.

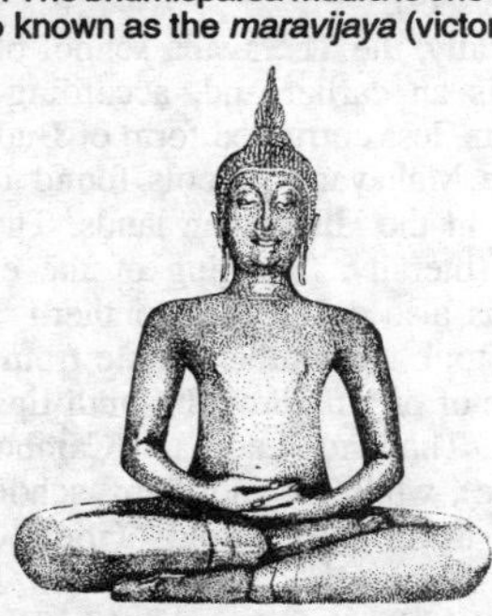

Dhyana (Meditation) Both hands rest palms up on the Buddha's lap, with the right hand on top, signifying meditation.

Vitarka (Turning of the Wheel of Dharma) The thumb and forefinger of one or both hands form a circle with the other fingers curving outward, evoking the first public discourse on Buddhist doctrine.

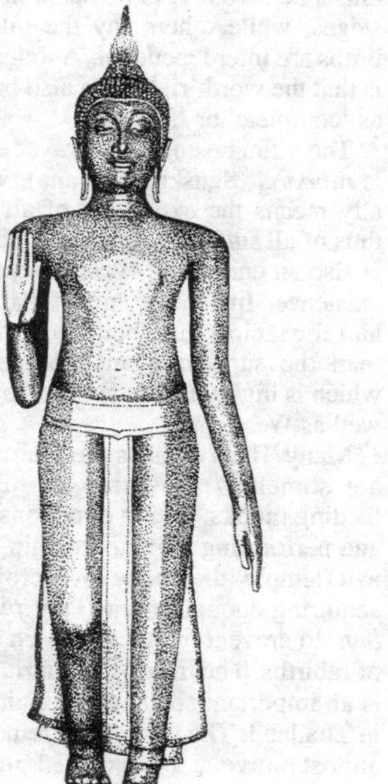

Abhaya (No Fear) One or both hands extend forward, palms out, fingers pointing upward, to symbolise the Buddha's offer of protection or freedom from fear to his followers. This mudra is most commonly seen in conjunction with standing or walking Buddhas.

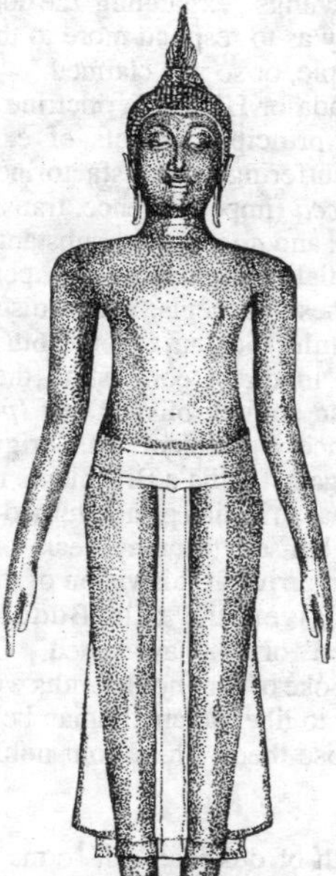

Calling for rain In northern Thailand – especially in Chiang Rai, Nan and Phrae provinces (and across the border in Luang Prabang, Laos) – one occasionally sees a non-canonical mudra in which the arms of a standing image extend straight downward on each side with the palms facing the thighs. Among Thai worshippers this pose symbolises a call for rain to nourish the rice fields.

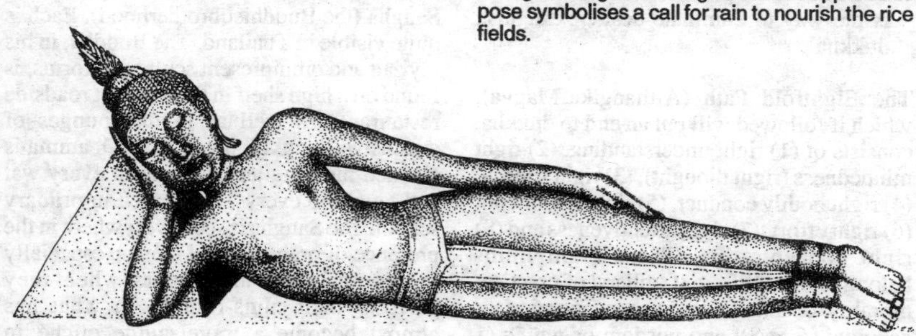

The reclining position represents the Buddha's dying moments when he attained *parinibbana* or ultimate nirvana.

earlier teachings, 'expanding' the doctrine in such a way as to respond more to the needs of lay people, or so it is claimed.

Theravada or Hinayana doctrine stresses the three principal aspects of existence: *dukkha* (suffering, unsatisfactoriness, disease); *anicca* (impermanence, transience of all things); and *anatta* (non-substantiality or non-essentiality of reality – no permanent 'soul'). These concepts, when 'discovered' by Siddhartha Gautama in the 6th century BC, were in direct contrast to the Hindu belief in an eternal, blissful self *(paramatman)*, hence Buddhism was originally a 'heresy' against India's Brahmanic religion.

Gautama, an Indian prince-turned-ascetic, subjected himself to many years of severe austerity to arrive at this vision of the world and was given the title Buddha, 'the enlightened' or 'the awakened'. Gautama Buddha spoke of four noble truths which had the power to liberate any human being who could realise them. These four noble truths are:

1. The truth of dukkha: 'All forms of existence are subject to dukkha (disease, unsatisfactoriness, imperfection)'.
2. The truth of the cause of dukkha – 'Dukkha is caused by *tanha* (desire)'.
3. The truth of the cessation of dukkha – 'Eliminate the cause of dukkha (ie desire) and dukkha will cease to arise'.
4. The truth of the path – 'The Eightfold Path is the way to eliminate desire/extinguish dukkha'.

The Eightfold Path (Atthangika-Magga), which if followed will put an end to dukkha, consists of (1) right understanding, (2) right mindedness (right thought), (3) right speech, (4) right bodily conduct, (5) right livelihood, (6) right effort, (7) right attentiveness and (8) right concentration. These eight limbs belong to three different 'pillars' of practice: morality or *sila* (3 to 5); concentration or *samadhi* (6 to 8); and wisdom or *pañña* (1 and 2). The path is also called the Middle Way, since ideally it avoids both extreme austerity and extreme sensuality. Some Buddhists believe it is to be taken in successive stages, while others say the pillars and/or limbs are interdependent. Another key point is that the word 'right' can also be translated as 'complete' or 'full'.

The ultimate end of Theravada Buddhism is *nibbana* (Sanskrit: nirvana), which literally means the extinction of all desire and thus of all suffering (dukkha). Effectively, it is also an end to the cycle of rebirths that is existence. In reality, most Thai Buddhists aim for rebirth in a 'better' existence rather than the supramundane goal of nibbana, which is highly misunderstood by Asians as well as Westerners.

Many Thais express the feeling that they are somehow unworthy of nibbana. By feeding monks, giving donations to temples and performing regular worship at the local *wat* (temple) they hope to improve their lot, acquiring enough merit (Pali: *puñña*; Thai: *bun)* to prevent or at least lessen the number of rebirths. The making of merit *(tham bun)* is an important social and religious activity in Thailand. The concept of reincarnation is almost universally accepted in Thailand, even by non-Buddhists, and the Buddhist theory of karma is well expressed in the Thai proverb *tham dii, dâi dii; tham chûa, dâi chûa* – 'do good and receive good; do evil and receive evil'.

The Triratna, or Triple Gems, highly respected by Thai Buddhists, include the Buddha, the Dhamma (the teachings) and the Sangha (the Buddhist brotherhood). Each is quite visible in Thailand. The Buddha, in his myriad and omnipresent sculptural forms, is found on a high shelf in the lowliest roadside restaurants as well as in the lounges of expensive Bangkok hotels. The Dhamma is chanted morning and evening in every wat and taught to every Thai citizen in primary school. The Sangha is seen everywhere in the presence of orange-robed monks, especially in the early morning hours when they perform their alms-rounds, in what has almost become a travel-guide cliché in motion.

Socially, every Thai male is expected to become a monk for a short period in his life, optimally between the time he finishes school and the time he starts a career or marries. Men or boys under 20 years of age may enter the Sangha as novices – this is not unusual since a family earns great merit when one of its sons takes robe and bowl. Traditionally, the length of time spent in the wat is three months, during the Buddhist lent *(phansãa)* which begins in July and coincides with the rainy season. However, nowadays men may spend as little as a week or 15 days to accrue merit as monks. There are about 32,000 monasteries in Thailand and 200,000 monks; many of these monks ordain for a lifetime. Of these a large percentage become scholars and teachers, while some specialise in healing and/or folk magic.

The Sangha is divided into two sects, the Mahanikai and the Thammayut. The latter is a minority sect (one Thammayut to 35 Mahanikai) begun by King Mongkut and patterned after an early Mon form of monastic discipline which he had practised as a monk *(bhikkhu)*. Generally, discipline for Thammayut monks is stricter. For example, they eat only once a day – before noon – and must eat only what is in their alms bowl, whereas Mahanikais eat twice before noon and may accept side dishes. Thammayut monks are expected to attain proficiency in meditation as well as Buddhist scholarship or scripture study; the Mahanikai monks typically 'specialise' in one or the other.

An increasing number of foreigners come to Thailand to be ordained as Buddhist monks, especially to study with the famed meditation masters of the forest wats in north-east Thailand (see the Meditation Study section).

There is a Buddhist bookshop selling English-language books across the street from the north entrance to Wat Bovornives (Bowonniwet) in Bangkok.

If you wish to find out more about Buddhism you can contact the World Fellowship of Buddhists (☎ 251-1188), 33 Sukhumvit Rd (between Sois 1 and 3). There's an English meditation class here on the first

---

What's a Wat

Technically speaking a *wát* (a Thai word, from the Pali-Sanskrit *avasatha* or 'dwelling for pupils and ascetics') is a Buddhist compound where men or women can be ordained as monks or nuns. Virtually every village in Thailand has at least one wat, while in towns and cities they're quite numerous. Without an ordination area (designated by *sẽma* or stone ordination markers), a monastic centre where monks or nuns reside is simply a *sãm-nák sõng* (sangha residence). The latter are often established as meditation retreat facilities in forest areas, sometimes in conjunction with larger *wát pàa* or forest monasteries.

The typical wat compound in Thailand will contain: an *uposatha (bòt* in Thai), a consecrated chapel where monastic ordinations are held; a *vihara (wíhãan* in Thai), where important Buddha images are housed; a *sala (sãalaa)* or open-sided shelter for community meetings and dharma talks; a number of *kùtì* or monastic quarters; a *hãw trai* or tripitaka library where Buddhist scriptures are stored; a *hãw klawng* or drum tower (sometimes with a bell tower or *hãw rákhang)*; various *chedis* or stupas (the smaller squarish stupas are *thâat kràdùk* (bone reliquaries), where the ashes of worshippers are interred); plus various ancillary buildings – such as schools or clinics – that differ from wat to wat according to local community needs. Many wats also have a *hãw phĩi khun wát* or spirit house for the temple's reigning earth spirit.

In rural Thailand, the wat often serves as a combination religious centre, grammar school, health clinic, herbal sauna house, community centre, astrology house, transient guesthouse, funeral home and geriatric ward, with monks and nuns serving as staff for one or more of these functions.

The typical wat is also a social centre for Thais and thus a focus for most festival activity. Especially lively are the *ngaan wát* or temple fairs; these take place regularly on certain auspicious dates (eg the advent and end of the Rains Retreat, the anniversary of the Buddha's birth, enlightenment, and death, the anniversary of the first Dhamma (Buddhist teachings) lecture, etc) and usually feature music, feasting, outdoor cinema, and occasional fireworks. Another common type of celebration is the *ngaan sòp* or funeral ceremony. A typical ngaan sop includes a lively procession (with musical accompaniment) from the deceased's home to the wat. ■

Sunday of each month; all are welcome. For more information on meditation study in Thailand, see the Courses section in the Facts for the Visitor chapter, and also the Meditation Study section in the Bangkok chapter.

Recommended books about Buddhism include:

Buddhism in Transition by Donald K Swearer, the Westminster Press, 1970 (Philadelphia)
Buddhism in the Modern World edited by Heinrich Dumoulin, MacMillan Publishing, 1976 (New York)
Buddhism, Imperialism, and War by Trevor Ling, D Reidel Publishing, 1980 (Dordrecht)
World Conqueror and World Renouncer by Stanley Tambiah, Cambridge University Press, 1976 (Cambridge)
Living Buddhist Masters by Jack Kornfield, Buddhist Publication Society, 1989 (Kandy)
Buddhism Explained by Phra Khantipalo, Trasvin Publications, 1991 (Chiang Mai)
Buddhism in Thailand: Its Past and Present by K Kusalasaya, Buddhist Publication Society, 1965 (Kandy)
What the Buddha Taught by Walpola Rahula, Motilal Banarsidass, 1971 (Delhi)
The Central Conception of Buddhism by Th Stcherbatsky, Motilal Banarsidass, 1974 (Delhi)
Buddhist Dictionary by Mahathera Nyanatiloka, Island Hermitage Publications, 1950 (Dodanduwa)

Other Religions

A small percentage of Thais and most of the Malays in the south, amounting to about 4% of the total population, are followers of Islam. Another 1% are Confucianists, Taoists, Mahayana Buddhists, Christians and Hindus. Muslim mosques (in the south) and Chinese temples are both common enough that you will probably come across some in your travels in Thailand. Before entering *any* temple, sanctuary or mosque you must remove your shoes, and in a mosque your head must be covered.

LANGUAGE

During your travels in Thailand, meeting and getting to know Thai people can be a very rewarding experience. I would particularly urge travellers, young and old, to make the effort to meet Thai college and university students. Thai students are, by and large, eager to meet their peers from other countries. They will often know some English, so communication is not as difficult as it may be with merchants, civil servants, etc, plus they are generally willing to teach you useful Thai words and phrases.

Learning some Thai is indispensable for travelling in the kingdom; naturally, the more language you pick up, the closer you get to Thailand's culture and people. Foreigners who speak Thai are so rare in Thailand that it doesn't take much to impress most Thais with a few words in their own language.

Your first attempts to speak the language will probably meet with mixed success, but keep trying. When learning new words or phrases, listen closely to the way the Thais themselves use the various tones – you'll catch on quickly. Don't let laughter at your linguistic attempts discourage you; this amusement is an expression of their appreciation.

For expanding your travel vocabulary, I recommend *Robertson's Practical English-Thai Dictionary* (Charles E Tuttle Co, Tokyo) since it has a phonetic guide to pronunciation with tones and is compact in size. It may be difficult to find, so write to the publisher, Suido 1-chome, 2-6, Bunkyo-ku, Tokyo.

For a more complete selection of phrases and basic vocabulary and grammar for travel in Thailand, see Lonely Planet's *Thai Phrasebook*.

More serious learners of the Thai language should get Mary Haas' *Thai-English Student's Dictionary* (Stanford University Press, Stanford, California) and George McFarland's *Thai-English Dictionary* (also Stanford University Press) – the cream of the crop. For information on Thai-language courses, see the Thai Language Study section under Courses in the Facts for the Visitor chapter.

Script

The Thai script, a fairly recent development in comparison with the spoken language, consists of 44 consonants (but only 21 separate sounds) and 48 vowel and diphthong possibilities (32 separate signs). Experts disagree as to the exact origins of the script, but it was apparently developed around 700 years ago from South Indian, Mon and Khmer models. Like these language models, written Thai proceeds from left to right, though vowel signs may be written before, above, below, 'around' (before, above *and* after), *or* after consonants, depending on the sign.

Though learning the alphabet is not difficult, the writing system itself is fairly complex, so unless you are planning a lengthy stay in Thailand it should perhaps be foregone in favour of learning to actually speak the language. Where possible, place names occurring in headings are given in Thai script as well as in Roman script, so that you can at least 'read' the names of destinations at a pinch, or point to them if necessary.

Tones

In Thai the meaning of a single syllable may be altered by means of five different tones (in standard central Thai): level or mid tone, low tone, falling tone, high tone and rising tone. Consequently, the syllable *mai*, for example, can mean, depending on the tone, 'new', 'burn', 'wood', 'not?' or 'not'. This makes it rather tricky to learn at first, especially for those of us who come from non-tonal-language traditions. Even when we 'know' what the correct tone in Thai should be, our tendency to denote emotion, verbal stress, the interrogative, etc, through tone modulation, often interferes with speaking the correct tone. So the first rule in learning to speak Thai is to divorce emotions from your speech, at least until you have learned the Thai way to express them without changing essential tone value.

The following is a brief attempt to explain the tones. The only way to really understand the differences is by listening to a native or fluent non-native speaker. The range of all five tones is relative to each speaker's vocal range so there is no fixed 'pitch' intrinsic to the language.

The level or mid tone is pronounced 'flat', at the relative middle of the speaker's vocal range. Example: *dii* means good. (No tone mark used.)

The low tone is 'flat' like the mid tone, but pronounced at the relative *bottom* of one's vocal range. It is low, level and with no inflection. Example: *bàat* means baht (the Thai currency).

The falling tone is pronounced as if you were emphasising a word, or calling someone's name from afar. Example: *mâi* means 'no' or 'not'.

The high tone is usually the most difficult for Westerners. It is pronounced near the relative top of the vocal range, as level as possible. Example: *níi* means 'this'.

The rising tone sounds like the inflection English speakers generally give to a question – 'Yes?' Example: *sǎam* means 'three'.

On a visual curve the tones might look like this:

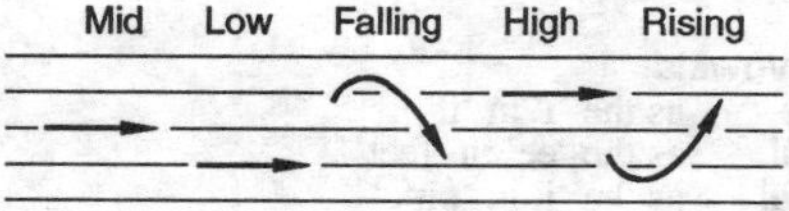

Words in Thai that appear to have more than one syllable are usually compounds made up of two or more word units, each with its own tone. They may be words taken directly from Sanskrit or Pali, in which case each syllable must still have its own tone. Sometimes the tone of the first syllable is not as important as that of the last, so for these I am omitting the tone mark.

Here is a guide to the phonetic system which has been used in the Language, Food and Drink sections, as well as throughout the book when transcribing directly from Thai. It is based on the Royal Thai General System of transcription (RTGS), except that it distinguishes between vowels of short and long duration (eg 'i' and 'ii'; 'a' and 'aa'; 'e' and 'eh'; 'o' and 'oh'), between 'o' and 'aw' (both would be 'o' in the RTGS) and between 'ch' and 'j' (both 'ch' in the RTGS).

Consonants

th as the 't' in 'tea'
ph as the 'p' in 'put' (never as the 'ph' in 'phone')
kh as the 'k' in 'kite'
k as the 'k' in 'skin'; similar to 'g' in 'good', but unaspirated (no accompanying puff of air) and unvoiced
t as the 't' in 'forty', unaspirated; similar to 'd' but unvoiced
p as the 'p' in 'stopper', unvoiced and unaspirated (not like the 'p' in 'put')
ng as the 'ng' in 'sing'; used as an initial consonant in Thai (practice by saying 'sing' without the 'si')
r similar to the 'r' in 'run' but flapped (tongue touches palate); in everyday speech often pronounced like 'l'

All the remaining consonants correspond closely to their English counterparts.

Vowels

i as the 'i' in 'it'
ii as the 'ee' in 'feet'
ai as the 'i' in 'pipe'
aa as the 'a' in 'father'
a half as long as *aa*
ae as the 'a' in 'bat' or 'tab'
e as the 'e' in 'hen'
eh as the 'a' in 'hate'
oe as the 'u' in 'hut' but more closed
u as the 'u' in 'flute'
uu as the 'oo' in 'food', longer than *u*
eu as the 'eu' in French 'deux', or the 'i' in 'sir'
ao as the 'ow' in 'now'
aw as the 'aw' in 'jaw'
o as the 'o' in 'bone'; exception *ko* which is pronounced 'kaw'
oh as the 'o' in 'toe'
eua diphthong, or combination, of *eu* and *a*
ia as 'ee-ya', or as the 'ie' in French *rien*
ua as the 'ou' in 'tour'
uay as the 'ewy' in 'Dewey'
iu as the 'ew' in 'yew'
iaw as the 'io' in 'Rio' or Italian *mio* or *dio*

Here are a few extra hints to help you with the alphabetic tangle:

1. Remember that 'ph' is not meant to be pronounced like the 'ph' in phone but like the 'p' in 'pound' (the 'h' is added to distinguish this consonant sound from the Thai 'p' which is closer to the English 'b'). Can be seen written as 'p', 'ph', and even 'bh'.
2. There is no 'v' sound in Thai; Sukhumvit is pronounced Sukhumwit and Vieng is really Wieng.
3. 'L' or 'r' at the end of a word is always pronounced like an 'n'; hence, Satul is pronounced Satun, Wihar is really Wihan. The exception to this is when 'er' or 'ur' are used to indicate the sound 'oe', as in 'ampher' *(amphoe)*. In the same way 'or' is sometimes used for the sound 'aw' as in 'Porn' *(phawn)*.
4. 'L' and 'r' are often used interchangeably in speech and this shows up in some transliterations. For example, *naliga* (clock) may appear as 'nariga' and *râat nâa* (a type of noodle dish) might be rendered 'laat naa' or 'lat na'.
5. 'U' is often used to represent the short 'a' sound, as in *tam* or *nam*, which may appear as 'tum' and 'num'.
6. Phonetically all Thai words end in a vowel (a, e, i, o, u), a semi-vowel (y, w) or one of three stops: p, t and k. That's it. Words transcribed with 'ch', 'j' or 'd' endings – like Panich, Raj and Had – should be pronounced as if they end in 't', as in Panit, Rat and Hat. Likewise 'g' becomes 'k' (Ralug is actually Raluk) and 'b' becomes 'p' (Thab becomes Thap).
7. Finally, the 'r' in 'sri' is *always* silent, so that word should be pronounced 'sii' (extended 'i' sound, too).

Transliteration

Writing Thai in Roman script is a perennial problem – no truly satisfactory system has yet been devised to assure both consistency and readability. The Thai government uses the Royal Thai General System of Transcription for official government documents in

Thai Consonants

K	ก	KH	ข	KH	ฃ	KH	ค
KH	ฅ	KH	ฆ	NG	ง	J	จ
CH	ฉ	CH	ช	S	ซ	CH	ฌ
Y	ญ	D	ฎ	T	ฏ	TH	ฐ
TH	ฑ	T	ฒ	N	ณ	D	ด
T	ต	TH	ถ	TH	ท	TH	ธ
N	น	B	บ	P	ป	PH	ผ
F	ฝ	PH	พ	F	ฟ	PH	ภ
M	ม	Y	ย	R	ร	L	ล
W	ว	S	ศ	S	ษ	S	ส
H	ห	L	ฬ	–	อ	H	ฮ

English and for most highway signs. However, local variations crop up on hotel signs, city street signs, menus, and so on in such a way that visitors often become confused. Add to this the fact that even the government system has its flaws. For example, 'o' is used for two very different sounds ('o' and the 'aw' in the Language section above), as is 'u' ('u' and 'eu' above). Likewise for 'ch', which is used to represent two different consonant sounds ('ch' and 'j'). The government transcription system also does not distinguish between short and long vowel sounds, which affect the tonal value of every word.

To top it off, many Thai words (especially people and place names) have Sanskrit and Pali spellings but the actual pronunciation bears little relation to that spelling if Romanised strictly according to the original Sanskrit/Pali. Thus Nakhon Si Thammarat, if transliterated literally, becomes 'Nagara Sri Dhammaraja'. If you tried to pronounce it using this Pali transcription, very few Thais would be able to understand you.

Generally, names in this book follow the most common practice or, in the case of hotels for example, simply copy their Roman script name, no matter what devious process was used in its transliteration! When this transliteration is especially distant from actual pronunciation, I've included the pronunciation (following the system given in the Language section) in parentheses after the transliteration. Where no Roman model was available, names were transliterated phonetically directly from Thai. Of course, this will only be helpful to readers who bother to acquaint themselves with the language – I'm constantly amazed at how many people manage to stay great lengths of time in Thailand without learning a word of Thai.

Problems often arise when a name is transliterated differently, even at the same place. 'Thawi', for example, can be Tavi, Thawee, Thavi, Tavee or various other versions. Outside of the International Phonetic Alphabet, there is no 'proper' way to transliterate Thai – only wrong ways. The Thais themselves are incredibly inconsistent in this matter, often using English letters that have no equivalent sound in Thai: Faisal for Phaisan, Bhumiphol for Phumiphon, Vanich for Wanit. Sometimes they even mix literal Sanskrit transcription with Thai pronunciation, as in King Bhumibol (which is pronounced Phumiphon and if transliterated according to the Sanskrit would be Bhumibala).

Greetings & Civilities

When being polite the speaker ends their sentence with *khráp* (for men) or *khâ* (for women). It is the gender of the *speaker* that is being expressed here; it is also the common way to answer 'yes' to a question or show agreement.

greetings/hello
sawàt-dii (khráp/khâ)
สวัสดี (ครับ/ค่ะ)

How are you?
Pen yangai?
เป็นอย่างไร?

I'm fine
Sabàay dii
สบายดี

thank you
khàwp khun
ขอบคุณ

Small Talk

you
khun (for peers)
คุณ
thâan (for elders, people in authority)
ท่าน
phõm (for men) *diichãn* (for women)
ผม (ผู้ชาย) ดิฉัน (ผู้หญิง)

What is your name?
Khun chêu arai?
คุณชื่ออะไร?

My name is ....
Phõm chêu .... (men)

ผมชื่อ......

Diichãn chêu .... (women)

ดิฉันชื่อ......

Do you have ....?
Mii .... *mãi?* (or .... *mii mãi?)*

มี......ไหม? (......มีไหม?)

Do you have noodles?
Mii kũaythĩaw mãi?

มีก๋วยเตี๋ยวไหม?

I/you/he/she/it does not have
mâi mii

ไม่มี

no
mâi châi

ไม่ใช่

no?
mãi? or *châi mãi?*

ไหม?/ใช่ไหม?

when
mêu-arai

เมื่อไหร่?

It doesn't matter.
Mâi pen rai.

ไม่เป็นไร

What is this?
Níi arai?

นี่อะไร?

What do you call this in Thai?
Níi phaasãa thai rîak wâa arai?

นี้ภาษาไทยเรียกว่าอะไร?

I understand.
Khâo jai.

เข้าใจ

Do you understand?
Khâo jai mãi?

เข้าใจไหม?

I don't understand.
Mâi khâo jai.

ไม่เข้าใจ

a little
nít nàwy

นิดหน่อย

Some Verbs

go
pai

ไป

will go
jà pai

จะไป

come
maa

มา

will come
jà maa

จะมา

(I) like ....
châwp ....

ชอบ......

(I) do not like ....
mâi châwp ....

ไม่ชอบ......

(I) would like (+ verb) ....
yàak jà ....

อยากจะ......

(I) would not like ....
mâi yàak jà ....

ไม่อยากจะ......

(I) would like to eat ....
yàak jà thaan ....

อยากจะทาน......

(I) would like ....(+ noun)
yàak dâi ....

อยากได้......

Getting Around

I would like a ticket.
Yàak dâi tũa.

อยากได้ตั๋ว

I would like to go ....
Yàak jà pai ....

อยากจะไป......

Where is (the) ....?
.... *yùu thîi nãi?*

......อยู่ที่ไหนฯ

motorcycle
rót maw-toe-sai

รถมอเตอร์ไซ

train
rót fai

รถไฟ

bus
rót meh or *rót bát*

รถเมล์/รถบัส

car
rót yon

รถยนต์

hotel
rohng raem

โรงแรม

station
sathãanii

สถานี

post office
praisanii

ไปรษณีย์

restaurant
ráan aahãan

ร้านอาหาร

hospital
rohng phayaabaan

โรงพยาบาล

airport
sanãam bin

สนามบิน

market
talàat

ตลาด

beach
hàat

หาด

Accommodation

bathroom
hâwng náam

ห้องน้ำ

toilet
hâwng sûam

ห้องส้วม

room
hâwng

ห้อง

hot
ráwn

ร้อน

cold
não

หนาว

bath/shower
àap náam

อาบน้ำ

towel
phâa chét tua

ผ้าเช็ดตัว

Shopping

How much?
Thâo raí?
เท่าไร?

How much is this?
Níi thâo rai? (or *Kìi bàat?*)
นี่เท่าไร (กี่บาท)

too expensive
phaeng pai
แพงไป

cheap, inexpensive
thùuk
ถูก

Emergencies

(I) need a doctor.
Tâwng-kaan mãw.
ต้องการหมอ

Time

today
wan níi
วันนี้

tomorrow
phrûng níi
พรุ่งนี้

yesterday
mêua waan
เมื่อวาน

Numbers

1	๑	*nèung*	หนึ่ง
2	๒	*sãwng*	สอง
3	๓	*sãam*	สาม
4	๔	*sìi*	สี่
5	๕	*hâa*	ห้า
6	๖	*hòk*	หก
7	๗	*jèt*	เจ็ด
8	๘	*pàet*	แปด
9	๙	*kâo*	เก้า
10	๑๐	*sìp*	สิบ
11		*sìp-èt*	สิบเอ็ด
12		*sìp-sãwng*	สิบสอง
13		*sìp-sãam*	สิบสาม
14		*sìp-sìi*	สิบสี่
20		*yîi-sìp*	ยี่สิบ
21		*yîi-sìp-èt*	ยี่สิบเอ็ด
22		*yîi-sìp-sãwng*	ยี่สิบสอง
23		*yîi-sìp-sãam*	ยี่สิบสาม
30		*sãam-sìp*	สามสิบ
40		*sìi-sìp*	สี่สิบ
50		*hâa-sìp*	ห้าสิบ
100		*ráwy*	ร้อย
200		*sãwng ráwy*	สองร้อย
300		*sãam ráwy*	สามร้อย
1000		*phan*	พัน
10,000		*mèun*	หมื่น
100,000		*sãen*	แสน
1,000,000		*láan*	ล้าน
billion		*phan láan*	พันล้าน

Facts for the Visitor

VISAS & EMBASSIES

Visa Requirements

Transit visas are valid for 30 days and cost around US$10, while tourist visas are good for 60 days and cost US$15. Three passport photos must accompany all applications. The actual fee depends on the country in which you arrange your visa, eg in Penang a tourist visa is M$45.

Most nationalities arriving in Thailand without a visa may be granted a 15-day stay, no extension allowed (unless the visitor comes from a country without a Thai embassy), with proof of onward ticket and sufficient funds. An exception is visitors with New Zealand passports, who may enter Thailand for up to 90 days without a visa! Certain other nationalities – those from smaller European countries like Andorra or Liechtenstein or from Africa, South Asia or Latin America – can obtain 15-day visas upon arrival. Check with a Thai embassy or consulate in advance to be sure if you plan to try arriving without a visa.

'Non-immigrant' visas are good for 90 days, must be applied for in your home country, cost around US$20 and are not difficult to get if you can offer a good reason for your visit.

Visa Extensions

Once a visa is issued, it must be used (ie you must enter Thailand) within 90 days.

If you overstay your visa, the practice at Bangkok International Airport now seems to be to fine you 100B per day of your overstay.

Tourist visas may be extended at the discretion of Thai immigration authorities. The Bangkok office (☎ 286-9176) is on Soi Suan Phlu, Sathon Tai Rd, but you can apply at any immigration office in the country – every provincial capital has one. The usual fee for extension of a tourist visa (up to one month) is 500B. Bring along two photos and two copies each of the photo and visa pages of your passport. Extension of the 15-day transit visa is only allowed if you hold a passport from a country that has no Thai embassy. The 30-day transit visa usually cannot be extended for any reason.

Re-Entry & Multiple-Entry Visas

If you need a re-entry visa for a return trip to Burma or the like, apply at the immigration office on Soi Suan Phlu, Bangkok. The cost is 500B.

Thailand does not issue multiple-entry visas. If you want a visa that enables you to leave the country and then return, the best you can do is to obtain a visa permitting two entries, and this will cost double the single-entry visa. For example, a two-entry three-month non-immigrant visa will cost US$40 and will allow you six months in the country, as long as you cross the Malaysian border (or any other border with immigration facilities) by the end of your first three months. The second half of your visa is validated as soon as you re-cross the Thai border, so there is no need to go to a Thai embassy/consulate abroad. All visas acquired in advance of entry are valid for 90 days from the date of issue.

Working Holidays

If you want to stay longer, a non-immigrant visa is the one to get. Extending it very much depends on how the officials feel about you – if they like you then they will. Money doesn't come into it. An Australian teaching English in Thailand recounted how he had to collect various signatures and go through various interviews which resulted in a 'provisional' extension. Back in his province he then had to report to the local office every 10 days for the next three months until his actual extension came through. 'Extensions needn't be expensive', he reported, 'you just have to say nice things and smile to a lot of people.' Becoming a monk doesn't necessarily mean you'll get a longer visa either – again it depends on whom you see and how they feel about you. See the following section for information on tax clearance for income.

Tax Clearance Anyone who receives income while in Thailand must obtain a tax clearance certificate from the Revenue Department before they'll be permitted to leave the country. The Bangkok office (☎ 281-5777, 282-9899) of the Revenue Department is on Chakkapong Rd not far from the Democracy Monument. There are also Revenue Department offices in every provincial capital.

Old Thai hands note: the tax clearance requirement no longer applies to those who have simply stayed in Thailand beyond a cumulative 90 days within one calendar year – this regulation was abolished in 1991. This makes it much easier for expats or other long-termers who live in Thailand on non-immigrant visas – no more hustling for tax clearance every time you make a visa trip to Penang.

Thai Embassies & Consulates

To apply for a visa, contact one of Thailand's diplomatic missions in any of the following countries. In many cases if you apply in person you may receive a tourist or non-immigrant visa on the day of application; by mail it generally takes anywhere from two to six weeks.

Australia
: Royal Thai Embassy, 111 Empire Circuit, Yarralumla, Canberra, ACT 2600 (☎ 731-149, 732-937)

Burma
: Royal Thai Embassy, 91 Prome Rd, Yangon (☎ 82471, 76555)

Canada
: Royal Thai Embassy, 85 Range Rd, Suite 704, Ottawa, Ontario K1N 8J6 (☎ 237-0476)

China
: Royal Thai Embassy, 40 Guang Hua Lu, Beijing (☎ 521-903, 522-282)

France
: Royal Thai Embassy, 8 Rue Greuze, 75116 Paris (☎ 4704-3222/6892)

Germany
: Royal Thai Embassy, Ubierstrasse 65, 5300 Bonn 2 (☎ 355-065)

Hong Kong
: Royal Thai Embassy, 8th Floor, 8 Cotton Tree Drive, Fairmont House, Central (☎ 216-481)

India
: Royal Thai Embassy, 56-N Nyaya Marg, Chanakyapuri, New Delhi, 110021 (☎ 605-679)
: Royal Thai Consulate, 18-B Mandeville Gardens, Ballygunge, Calcutta 7000019 (☎ 460-836)

Indonesia
: Royal Thai Embassy, Jalan Imam Bonjol 74, Jakarta (☎ 343-762)

Italy
: Royal Thai Embassy, Via Nomentana 132, 00162 Rome (☎ 832-0729)

Japan
: Royal Thai Embassy, 14-6 Kami-Osaki 3-chome, Shinagawa-ku, Tokyo (☎ 441-1386, 442-6750)

Laos
: Royal Thai Embassy, Thanon Phonkheng, Vientiane Poste 128 (☎ 2508, 2543, 2765)

Malaysia
: Royal Thai Embassy, 206 Jalan Ampang 504505 Kuala Lumpur (☎ 488-222/350)

Nepal
: Royal Thai Embassy, Jyoti Kendra Bldg, Thapathali, Kathmandu (☎ 213-910)

Netherlands
: Royal Thai Embassy, Buitenrustweg 1, 2517 KD The Hague (☎ 452-088, 459-703)

New Zealand
: Royal Thai Embassy, 2 Cook St, Wellington 1 (☎ 735-385/391)

Philippines
: Royal Thai Embassy, 107B Rada St, Legaspi Village Makati, Metro Manila (☎ 815-4219/00)

Singapore
: Royal Thai Embassy, 370 Orchard Rd, Singapore 9 (☎ 737-2158/3372)

Sweden
: Royal Thai Embassy, 5th Floor, Sandhamnsgatan 36, 3007 Bern (☎ 462-281/2)

UK
: Royal Thai Embassy, 29-30 Queen's Gate, London SW7 5JB (☎ 589-2834/2944)

USA
: Royal Thai Embassy, 2300 Kalorama Rd NW, Washington, DV 20008 (☎ 667-1446/9)
: Royal Thai Consulate, 801 N LaBrea Ave, Los Angeles, CA 90038 (☎ 937-1894)

Vietnam
: Royal Thai Embassy, So Nha E1, Kho Ngoai Giao Doan, Trung Tu, Hanoi (☎ 56043)

Foreign Embassies & Consulates

Bangkok is a good place to collect visas for westward journeys, and most countries have diplomatic representation in Bangkok. For more information see the Foreign Embassies & Consulates section in the Bangkok chapter.

CUSTOMS

Like most countries, Thailand prohibits the import of illegal drugs, firearms and ammunition (unless registered in advance with the Police Department) and pornographic media. A reasonable amount of clothing for personal use, toiletries and professional instruments are allowed in duty-free, as are one still or one movie/video camera with five rolls of still film or three rolls of movie film or videotape. Up to 200 cigarettes can be brought into the country without paying duty, or for other smoking materials a total of up to 250 grams. One litre of wine or spirits is allowed in duty-free.

Electronic goods like personal stereos, calculators and computers can be a problem if the customs officials have reason to believe you're bringing them in for resale. As long as you don't carry more than one of each, you should be OK. Occasionally, customs will require you to leave a hefty deposit for big-ticket items (eg a lap-top computer or midi-component stereo) which is refunded when you leave the country with the item in question. If you make the mistake of saying you're just passing through and don't plan to use the item while in Thailand, they may ask you to leave it with the Customs Department until you leave the country.

For information on currency import or export, see the Money section.

Antiques & Art

Upon leaving Thailand, you must obtain an export licence for any antiques or objects of art you want to take with you. An antique is any 'archaic movable property whether produced by man or by nature, any part of ancient structure, human skeleton or animal carcass, which by its age or characteristic of production or historical evidence is useful in the field of art, history or archaeology'. An object of art is a 'thing produced by craftsmanship and appreciated as being valuable in the field of art'. Obviously these are very sweeping definitions, so if in doubt go to the Department of Fine Arts for inspection and licensing.

Application can be made by submitting two front-view photos of the object(s) (no more than five objects to a photo) and a photocopy of your passport, along with the object(s) in question, to one of three locations in Thailand: the Bangkok National Museum, the Chiang Mai National Museum or the Songkhla National Museum. You need to allow three to five days for the application and inspection process to be completed.

Thailand has special regulations for taking a Buddha or other deity image (or any part thereof) out of the country. These require not only a licence from the Department of Fine Arts but a permit from the Ministry of Commerce as well. The one exception to this are the small Buddha images *(phrá phim)* that are meant to be worn on a chain around the neck; these may be exported without a licence as long as the reported purpose is religious.

Temporary Vehicle Importation

Passenger vehicles (car, van, truck or motorcycle) can be brought into Thailand for tourist purposes for up to six months. Documents needed for the crossing are: a valid International Driving Licence, passport vehicle registration papers (in the case of a borrowed or hired vehicle, authorisation from the owner) and a cash or bank guarantee equal to the value of the vehicle plus 20%. (For entry through Klong Toey Port or Bangkok Airport, this means a letter of bank credit; for overland crossings via Malaysia a 'self-guarantee' filled in at the border is sufficient.)

MONEY

Currency

The basic unit of Thai currency is the *baht*. There are 100 satang in 1 baht; coins include 25 satang and 50 satang pieces and baht in 1B, 5B and 10B coins. Older coins exhibit Thai numerals only, while newer coins have Thai and Roman numerals. At the time of writing, 1B coins come in three sizes: only the middle size works in public pay phones! Likewise, 5B coins also come in three sizes; a large one with a Thai numeral only and two smaller coins that have Thai and Roman numerals (one of the smaller 5B coins has nine inset edges along the circumference). The new copper-and-silver 10B coin has Thai and Roman-Arabic numerals. Eventually Thailand will phase out the older coins, but in the meantime, counting out change is confusing.

Twenty-five satang equals one *saleng* in colloquial Thai, so if you're quoted a price of six saleng in the market, say, for a small bunch of bananas or a bag of peanuts, this means 1.50B.

Paper currency comes in denominations of 10B (brown), 20B (green), 50B (blue), 100B (red) and 500B (purple) denominations. Fortunately for newcomers to Thailand, numerals are printed in their Western as well as Thai forms. Notes are also scaled according to the amount; the larger the denomination, the larger the note. Large denominations like 500B bills can be hard to change in small towns, but banks will always change them.

Exchange Rates

US$1	=	25.20B
A$1	=	19B
UK£1	=	44.20B
S$1	=	15.30B
DM1	=	5.30B

There is no black-market money exchange for baht, so there's no reason to bring in any Thai currency. Banks or legal moneychangers offer the best exchange rate within the country. The baht is firmly attached to the US dollar and is as stable.

Exchange rates are given in the *Bangkok Post* every day. For buying baht, US dollars are the most readily acceptable currency and travellers' cheques get better rates than cash. Since banks charge 10B commission and duty for each travellers' cheque cashed, you will save on commissions if you use larger cheque denominations (eg a US$50 cheque will only cost 10B while five US$10 cheques will cost 50B). Note that you can't exchange Indonesian rupiah or Nepalese rupees into Thai currency. Bangkok is a good place to buy Indian and Nepalese rupees, however, as well as Burmese kyat, if you're going to any of these countries. Rates are comparable with black-market rates in each of these countries.

Visa credit-card holders can get cash advances of up to US$200 (in baht only) per day through some branches of the Thai Farmers Bank and some Thai Commercial Banks (and also at the night-time exchange windows in well-touristed spots like Banglamphu, Chiang Mai and Ko Samui).

American Express card holders can also get advances, but only in travellers' cheques. The Amex agent is SEA Tours, Suite 414, Siam Center, 965 Rama I Rd.

ATM & Credit Cards

An alternative to carrying around large amounts of cash or travellers' cheques is to open an account at a Thai bank and request an ATM card. Most major banks in Thailand now have automatic teller machines (ATMs) in provincial capitals and in some smaller towns as well. Once you have a card you'll be able to withdraw cash at machines throughout Thailand. Every Thai bank with an ATM programme belongs to one of two systems, Siam Net or Bank Net; hence you can withdraw money from banks that differ from the one holding your account as long as they belong to the same network.

Plastic money is becoming increasingly popular in Thailand and many shops, hotels and restaurants now accept credit cards. The most commonly accepted card is Visa, followed by MasterCard and Diner's Club. American Express and Carte Blanche are of much more limited use.

There are a couple of problems associated with using credit cards in Thailand. Occasionally when you try to use a Visa card at upcountry hotels or shops, the staff may try to tell you that only Visa cards issued by Thai Farmers Bank are acceptable. With a little patience, you should be able to make them understand that the Thai Farmers Bank will pay the merchant and that your bank will pay the Thai Farmers Bank – that any Visa card issued anywhere in the world is indeed acceptable.

The other problem concerns illegal surcharges on credit-card purchases. It's against Thai law to pass on to the customer the 3% merchant fee charged by banks, but almost all merchants in Thailand do it anyway. Some even ask 4 or 5%! The only exception seems to be hotels (although even a few hotels will hit you with a credit-card surcharge). If you don't agree to the surcharge they'll simply refuse to accept your card. Begging and pleading or pointing out the law doesn't seem to help. The best way to get around the illegal surcharge is to politely ask that the credit-card receipt be itemised with cost of product or service and the 3% surcharge listed separately. Then when you pay your bill, photocopy all receipts showing the 3% and request a 'charge back'. If a hotel or shop refuses to itemise the surcharge, take down the vendor's name and address and report them to the TAT tourist police – they may be able to arrange a refund.

See the Dangers & Annoyances section for important warnings on credit-card theft and fraud.

Safety Deposit Boxes

Travellers can rent safety deposit boxes at Bangkok's Safety Deposit Centre, 3rd Floor, Chan Issara Tower, 942/81 Rama IV Rd (near the Silom Rd intersection) for 150B a month plus 2000B for a refundable key deposit. The centre is open from 10 am to 7 pm, Monday to Friday, and from 10 am to 6 pm Saturday, Sunday and public holidays. A few banks will rent safety deposit boxes as well, but generally you need to open an account with them first.

Exchange Control

Legally, any traveller arriving in Thailand must have at least the following amounts of money in cash, travellers' cheques, bank draft, or letter of credit, according to visa category: non-immigrant visa, US$500 per person or US$1000 per family; tourist visa, US$250 per person or US$500 per family; transit visa or no visa, US$125 per person or US$250 per family. This may be checked if you arrive on a one-way ticket or if you look as if you're at 'the end of the road'.

According to new 1991 regulations, there are no limits to the amounts of Thai or foreign currency you may bring into the country. Upon leaving Thailand, you're permitted to take no more than 50,000B per person without special authorisation; exportation of foreign currencies is unrestricted.

It's legal to open a foreign currency account at any commercial bank in Thailand. As long as the funds originate from abroad, there are no restrictions on thier maintenance or withdrawal.

Costs

Food and accommodation outside Bangkok is generally quite inexpensive and even in Bangkok it's fairly low, especially considering the value vis à vis other countries in South and South-East Asia.

Outside Bangkok, budget-squeezers should be able to get by on 200B per day if they really keep watch on their expenses. This estimate includes basic guesthouse accommodation, food, nonalcoholic beverages and local transport, but not film, souvenirs, tours or vehicle hire. Add another 55 to 70B per day for every large beer (30B for small bottles) you drink.

Expenses vary, of course, from place to place; where there are high concentrations of budget travellers, for example, accommodation tends to be cheaper and food more expensive. With experience, you can travel in Thailand for even less if you live like a Thai of modest means and learn to speak the language. Average low-to-middle income Thais certainly don't spend 200B a day when travelling in their own country.

Someone with more money to spend will find that for around 350 or 500B per day, life can be quite comfortable: cleaner and quieter accommodation is easier to find once you pass the 200B-a-night zone in room rates. Of course, a 50B guesthouse room with a mattress on the floor and responsive management is better than a poorly maintained 350B room with air-con that won't turn off and a noisy all-night card game next door.

In Bangkok there's almost no limit to the amount you *could* spend, but if you live frugally, avoid the tourist ghettos and ride the public bus system you could get by on only slightly more than you would spend upcountry. Where you stay in Bangkok is of primary concern, as accommodation there has generally become a good deal more expensive than upcountry accommodation since the tourist boom of 1987. Typically, the visitor spends well over 250B per day in Bangkok just for accommodation – this is generally the absolute minimum for air-con (in a twin room). On the other hand, if you can do without air-con, accommodation can be found in Bangkok for as little as 50B per person. But the noise, heat and pollution in Bangkok may drive many budget travellers to seek more comfort than they might otherwise need upcountry.

Food is somewhat more expensive in Bangkok than in the provinces. However, in Thonburi (Bangkok's 'left bank'), where I lived for some time, many dishes are often *cheaper* than they are upcountry, due to the availability of fresh ingredients. This is also true for the working-class districts on the Bangkok side, like Makkasan. Bangkok is the typical 'primate city' cited by sociologists, meaning that most goods produced by the country as a whole end up in Bangkok. The glaring exception is Western food, which Bangkok has more of than anywhere else in the kingdom but charges the most for it. Eat only Thai and Chinese food if you're trying to spend as little as possible. After all, why go to Thailand to eat steak and potatoes?

Bargaining

Good bargaining, which takes practice, is another way to cut costs. Anything bought in a market should be bargained for; prices in department stores and most non-tourist shops are fixed. Sometimes accommodation rates can be bargained down. One may need to bargain hard in heavily touristed areas since the one-week, all-air-con type of visitor often pays whatever's asked, creating an artificial price zone between the local and tourist market that the budgeteer must deal with.

On the other hand the Thais aren't *always* trying to rip you off, so use some discretion when going for the bone on a price. There's a fine line between bargaining and niggling – getting hot under the collar over 5B makes both seller and buyer lose face. Some more specific suggestions concerning costs can be found in the Accommodation and Things to Buy sections of this chapter.

Transportation between cities and within them is very reasonable; again, bargaining (when hiring a vehicle) can save you a lot of baht. See the Getting Around chapter.

Tipping

Tipping is not a normal practice in Thailand, although they're getting used to it in expensive hotels and restaurants. Elsewhere don't bother. In taxis where you have to bargain the fare, it certainly isn't necessary.

Consumer Taxes

In January 1992 Thailand instituted a 7% value-added tax (VAT) for certain goods and services. Unfortunately no-one seems to know what's subject to VAT and what's not, so the whole situation is rather confusing for the time being. It doesn't mean that products are supposed to increase in retail price by 7% – the increase is to be applied to a retailer's cost for the product. For example, if a merchant's wholesale price is 100B for an item that retails at 200B, the maximum adjusted retail including VAT should be 207B, not 214B. In practice there should be a net decrease in prices for most goods and services since the VAT replaces a graduated business tax that averaged 9%. But this probably won't stop Thai merchants from trying to add 'VAT' surcharges to their sales. Like the credit-card surcharge, a direct VAT surcharge is illegal and should be reported to the TAT tourist police.

Tourist hotels add an 11% hotel tax, and

sometimes an 8 to 10% service charge as well, to your room bill.

WHEN TO GO

The best overall time for visiting most of Thailand vis à vis climate would be between November and February – during these months it rains least and is not so hot. The south is best visited when the rest of Thailand is miserably hot, March to May, while the north is best from mid-November to early December or in February when it begins warming up again. If you're spending time in Bangkok, be prepared to roast in April and do some wading in October – probably the two worst months weather-wise for the capital.

The peak months for tourists are December and August – don't go during these months if you want to avoid crowds of farang vacationers. The least crowded months are June and September.

WHAT TO BRING

Bring as little as possible – one medium-sized shoulder bag or backpack should do it. Pack light, natural-fibre clothes, unless you're going to be in the north in the cool season, in which case you should have a pullover. Pick up a *phâakhamáa* (short Thai-style sarong for men) or a *phâasîn* (a longer sarong for women) to wear in your room, on the beach, or when bathing outdoors. These can be bought at any local market (different patterns/colours in different parts of the country) and the vendors will show you how to tie them.

The sarong is a very handy item; it can be used to sleep on or as a light bedspread, as a makeshift 'shopping bag', as a turban/scarf to keep off the sun and absorb perspiration, as a towel, as a small hammock and as a device with which to climb coconut palms – to name just a few of its many functions. (It is not considered proper street attire, however.)

Sunglasses are a must for most people and can be bought cheaply in Bangkok. Slip-on shoes or sandals are highly recommended – besides being cooler than lace-up shoes, they are easily removed before entering a Thai home or temple. A small torch (flashlight) is a good idea, as it makes it easier to find your way back to your bungalow at night if you are staying at the beach or at a government guesthouse. A couple of other handy things are a compass and a plastic lighter for lighting candles and mosquito coils (lighters, candles and mossie coils are available in Thailand).

Toothpaste, soap and most other toiletries can be purchased anywhere in Thailand. Sun block and mosquito repellent (except 100% DEET – see the Health section) are available, although they're expensive and the quality of both is generally substandard. If you plan to wash your own clothes, bring along a universal sink plug, a few plastic clothespins and three metres of plastic cord or plastic hangers for hanging wet clothes out to dry.

If you plan to spend a great deal of time in one or more of Thailand's beach areas, you might want to bring your own snorkel and mask (see the Diving & Snorkelling section under Activities in this chapter). This would save on having to rent such gear and would also assure a proper fit. Shoes designed for water sports, eg Nike's Aqua Socks, are great for wearing in the water whether you're diving or not. They protect your feet from coral cuts, which easily become infected.

TOURIST OFFICES

The Tourist Authority of Thailand (TAT) is a government-operated tourist information/promotion service with several offices within the country and others overseas. In 1991 the TAT was granted regulatory powers for the monitoring of tourism-related businesses throughout Thailand, including hotels, tour operators, travel agencies and transport companies, in an effort to upgrade the quality of these services and prosecute unscrupulous operators. Whether the TAT will actually be able to achieve anything along these lines remains to be seen.

Local Tourist Offices

In addition to those listed below, the TAT has plans to open new branch offices in Nakhon

Phanom, Udon Thani and Ayuthaya by the end of 1992.

Bangkok
4 Ratchadamnoen Nok Ave, Bangkok 10100 (☎ (02) 282-1143/7)
Cha-am
500/51 Phetkasem Highway, Amphoe Cha-am, Phetburi 76000 (☎ (032) 471502)
Chiang Mai
105/1 Chiang Mai-Lamphun Rd, Chiang Mai 50000 (☎ (053) 248604/7)
Chiang Rai
Singhakai Rd, Chiang Rai 57000
Hat Yai
1/1 Soi 2, Niphat Uthit 3 Rd, Hat Yai, Songkhla 90110 (☎ (074) 243747, 245986)
Kanchanaburi
Saengchuto Rd, Kanchanaburi 71000 (☎ (034) 511200)
Khon Kaen
Sala Phrachakhom, Klang Muang Rd, Khon Kaen 40000 (☎ (043) 244498/9)
Khorat (Nakhon Ratchasima)
2102-2104 Mittaphap Rd, Nakhon Ratchasima 30000 (☎ (044) 243427/751)
Nakhon Si Thammarat
1180 Bowon Bazaar, Ratchadamnoen Rd, Nakhon Si Thammarat 80000 (☎ (075) 345512)
Pattaya
382/1 Chai Hat Rd, Pattaya Beach, Chonburi 20260 (☎ (038) 428750, 429113)
Phitsanulok
209/7-8 Surasi Trade Center, Boromtrailokanat Rd, Phitsanulok 65000 (☎ (055) 252742)
Phuket
73-75 Phuket Rd, Phuket 83000 (☎ (076) 212213, 211036)
Surat Thani
5 Talat Mai Rd, Ban Don, Surat Thani 84000 (☎ (077) 282828)
Ubon Ratchathani
264/1 Khuan Thani Rd, Ubon Ratchathani 34000 (☎ (045) 243770/1)

Overseas Offices

Australia
12th Floor, Exchange Bldg, 56 Pitt St, Sydney NSW 2000 (☎ (02) 247-7549)
France
Office National de Tourisme de Thailande, 90 Ave des Champs Elysées, 75008 Paris, France (☎ 4562-8656)
Germany
4th Floor Bethmann Strasse, 58/IV D-6000 Frankfurt/M 1 (☎ (069) 295704/804)
Hong Kong
Rm 401, Fairmont House, 8 Cotton Tree Drive, Central, Hong Kong (☎ (05) 868-0732)
Italy
Ente Nazionale per il Turismo Thailandese, Via Barberini 50, 00187 Rome (☎ (06) 487-3479)
Japan
Hibiya Mitsui Bldg, 1-2 Yurakucho 1-chome, Chiyoda-ku, Tokyo 100 (☎ (03) 580-6776)
Hiranomachi Yachiyo Bldg, 5F, 1-8-14 Hiranomachi Chuo-ku, Osaka 541 (☎ (06) 231-4434)
Malaysia
c/o Royal Thai Embassy, 206 Jalan Ampang, Kuala Lumpur (☎ 248-0958)
Singapore
c/o Royal Thai Embassy, 370 Orchard Rd 0923 (☎ 235-7694)
UK
49 Albemarle St, London WIX 3FE (☎ (071) 499-7679)
USA
5 World Trade Center, Suite 2449, New York, NY 10048 (☎ (212) 432-0433)
3440 Wilshire Blvd, Suite 1100, Los Angeles, California, 90010 (☎ (213) 382-2353)
303 East Wacker Drive, Suite 400, Chicago, IL 60601

HOLIDAYS & FESTIVALS

The number and frequency of festivals and fairs in Thailand is incredible – there always seems to be something going on, especially during the cool season between November and February.

Exact dates for festivals may vary from year to year, either because of the lunar calendar – which isn't quite in sync with our solar calendar – or because local authorities decide to change festival dates. The TAT publishes an up-to-date *Major Events & Festivals* calendar each year that is useful for anyone planning to attend a particular event.

On dates noted as public holidays, all government offices and banks will be closed.

Note: The official year in Thailand is reckoned from 543 BC, the beginning of the Buddhist Era, so that 1990 AD is 2533 BE.

10 to 12 January
Chaiyaphum Elephant Roundup – a rather recently established event that focuses on re-enactment of medieval elephant-back warfare. It's much smaller and less touristy than the Surin roundup in November.

23 to 29 January
Phra That Phanom Fair – an annual week-long homage to the north-east's most sacred Buddhist stupa in Nakhon Phanom Province. Pilgrims from all over the country attend.

24 to 31 January
Don Chedi Memorial Fair – held at the Don Chedi memorial in Suphanburi Province, this event commemorates the victory of King Naresuan of Ayuthaya over Burmese invaders in 1592. The highlight of the fair is dramatised elephant-back duelling.

February
Magha Puja (Makkha Buchaa) – held on the full moon of the third lunar month to commemorate the preaching of the Buddha to 1250 enlightened monks who came to hear him 'without prior summons'. A public holiday throughout the country culminating in a candle-lit walk around the main chapel at every wat.

1st week of February
Chiang Mai Flower Festival – colourful floats and parades exhibit Chiang Mai's cultivated flora.

1st week of March
ASEAN Barred Ground Dove Fair – large dove-singing contest held in Yala that attracts dove-lovers from all over Thailand, Malaysia, Singapore and Indonesia.

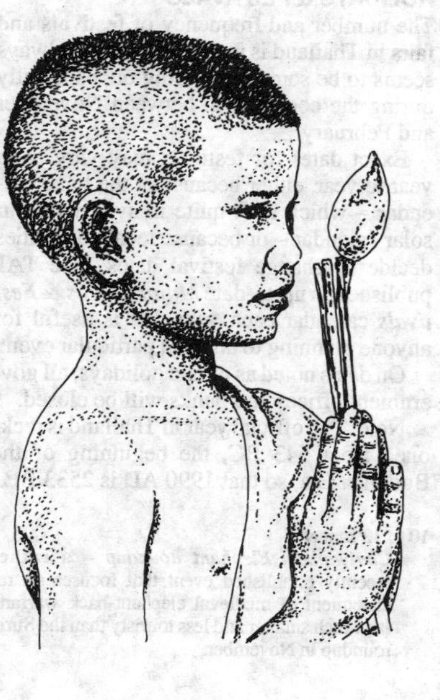

1st or 2nd week of March
Phra Phutthabat Fair – annual pilgrimage to the Temple of the Holy Footprint at Saraburi, 236 km north-east of Bangkok. Quite an affair, with music, outdoor drama and many other festivities. If you're in the area, the shrine is worth visiting even in the 'off season'.

3rd week in March
Bangkok International Jewellery Fair – held in several large Bangkok hotels, this is Thailand's most important annual gem and jewellery trade show. Runs concurrently with the Department of Export Promotion's *Bangkok Gems & Jewellery Fair*.

Last week of March
Prasat Phanom Rung Festival – a newly established festival to commemorate the restoration of this impressive Angkor-style temple complex in Buriram Province. Involves a daytime procession to Khao Phanom Rung and spectacular sound & light shows at night. Be prepared for very hot weather.

6 April
Chakri Day – a public holiday commemorating the founder of the Chakri Dynasty, Rama I.

13 to 15 April
Songkran Festival – the New Year's celebration of the lunar year in Thailand. Buddha images are 'bathed', monks and elders receive the respect of younger Thais by the sprinkling of water over their hands, and a lot of water is tossed about for fun. Songkran generally gives everyone a chance to release their frustrations and literally cool off during the peak of the hot season. Hide out in your room or expect to be soaked; the latter is a lot more fun.

May (Full Moon)
Visakha Puja (Wisakha Buchaa) – a public holiday which falls on the 15th day of the waxing moon in the 6th lunar month. This is considered the date of the Buddha's birth, enlightenment and parinibbana, or passing away. Activities are centred around the wat, with candle-lit processions, much chanting and sermonising, etc.

5 May
Coronation Day – public holiday. The King and Queen preside at a ceremony at Wat Phra Kaew in Bangkok, commemorating their 1946 coronation.

2nd week of May
Royal Ploughing Ceremony – to kick off the official rice-planting season, the king participates in this ancient Brahman ritual at Sanam Luang (the large field across from Wat Phra Kaew) in Bangkok. Thousands of Thais gather to watch, and traffic in this part of the city reaches a standstill.

2nd week of May
Rocket Festival – all over the north-east, villagers craft large skyrockets of bamboo which they then fire into the sky to bring rain for rice fields. This festival is best celebrated in the town of Yasothon, but is also good in Ubon and Nong Khai.

Mid-June
Phii Ta Khon Festival – a unique celebration held in Loei's Dan Sai district in which revellers dress in garish 'spirit' costumes and painted masks of coconut wood. The festival commemorates a Buddhist legend in which a host of spirits *(phĩi)* appeared to greet the Buddha-to-be upon his return to his home town, during his penultimate birth.

Mid-July
Asanha Puja – full moon is a must for this public holiday which commemorates the first sermon preached by the Buddha.

Mid to late July
Khao Phansaa – a public holiday and the beginning of Buddhist 'lent', this is the traditional time of year for young men to enter the monkhood for the rainy season and for all monks to station themselves in a single monastery for the three months. It's a good time to observe a Buddhist ordination.

Mid to late July
Candle Festival – Khao Phansaa is celebrated in the north-east by carving huge candles and parading them on floats in the streets. This festival is best celebrated in Ubon.

12 August
Queen's birthday – this is a public holiday. Ratchadamnoen Ave and the Grand Palace are festooned with coloured lights.

Mid-September
Thailand International Swan-Boat Races – these take place on the Chao Phraya River in Bangkok near the Rama IX Bridge.

Last week of September
Narathiwat Fair – an annual week-long festival celebrating local culture with boat races, dove-singing contests, handicraft displays, traditional southern Thai music and dance. The King and Queen almost always attend.

Late September to early October
Vegetarian Festival – a nine-day celebration in Trang and Phuket during which devout Chinese Buddhists eat only vegetarian food. There are also various ceremonies at Chinese temples and merit-making processions that bring to mind Hindu Thaipusam in its exhibition of self-mortification. Smaller towns in the south such as Krabi and Phang-Nga also celebrate the veggie fest on a smaller scale.

Mid-October to mid-November
Thawt Kathin – a one-month period at the end of the Buddhist 'lent' *(phansãa)* during which new monastic robes and requisites are offered to the Sangha. In Nan Province longboat races are held on the Nan River.

23 October
Chulalongkorn Day – a public holiday in commemoration of King Chulalongkorn (Rama V).

November
Loi Krathong – on the proper full-moon night, small lotus-shaped baskets or boats made of banana leaves containing flowers, incense, candles and a coin are floated on Thai rivers, lakes and canals. This is a peculiarly Thai festival that probably originated in Sukhothai and is best celebrated in the north. In Chiang Mai, where the festival is called Yi Peng, residents also launch hot-air paper balloons into the sky. At the Sukhothai Historical Park there is an impressive sound & light show.

Third weekend in November
Surin Annual Elephant Roundup – Thailand's equivalent to the 'running of the bulls' in Pamplona, Spain, is pretty touristy these days. If you ever wanted to see a lot of elephants in one place, though, here's your chance.

Late November to early December
River Khwae Bridge Week – sound & light shows every night at the Death Railway Bridge in Kanchanaburi, plus historical exhibitions and vintage train rides.

5 December
King's Birthday – this is a public holiday which is celebrated with some fervour in Bangkok. As with the Queen's birthday, it features lots of lights along Ratchadamnoen Ave. Some people erect temporary shrines to the King outside their homes or businesses.

10 December
Constitution Day – public holiday.

31 December to 1 January
New Year's Day – a rather recent public holiday in deference to the Western calendar.

POST & TELECOMMUNICATIONS

Thailand has a very efficient postal service and within the country postage is also very cheap.

The poste restante service is also very reliable, though during high tourist months (December and August) you may have to wait in line at the Bangkok GPO. There is a fee of 1B for every piece of mail collected, 2B for each parcel. As with many Asian countries, confusion at poste restante offices is most likely to arise over given names and surnames. Ask people who are writing to you to print your surname clearly and to underline it. If you're certain a letter should be waiting for you and it cannot be found, it's always wise to check it hasn't been filed under your given name. You can take poste restante at almost any post office in Thailand now.

The American Express office, Suite 414, Siam Center, Rama IV Rd, will also take mail on behalf of Amex card holders. The hours are from 8.30 am to noon and 1 to 4.30 pm, Monday to Friday, and 8.30 to 11.30 am Saturday.

Bangkok's GPO on Charoen Krung (New) Rd is open from 8 am to 8 pm Monday to Friday and from 8 am to 1 pm weekends and holidays. A 24-hour international telecommunications service (including telephone, fax, telex and telegram) is located in a separate building behind and to the right of the main GPO building.

Outside Bangkok the typical provincial GPO is open from 8.30 am to 4.30 pm Monday to Friday, 9 am to noon Saturday. Larger GPOs in provincial capitals may also be open a half day on Sunday.

Postal Rates

Airmail letters weighing 10 grams or less cost 13B to Europe and Australia/New Zealand, 15B to the Americas.

Aerograms cost 8.50B regardless of the destination; postcards are 8B to Europe, Australia and New Zealand, 9B to North America.

Letters sent by registered mail cost 15B in addition to regular airmail postage. International express mail (EMS) fees vary according to country of destination. Sample rates for items weighing 250 grams or less are: Japan 245B; Australia, Germany and the UK 210B; France, Canada and the USA 230B.

The rates for parcels shipped by post vary

Parcel Postage Rates

Destination		1 kg	5 kg	10 kg	20 kg
Australia	*surface*	176B	326B	479B	–
	air	280B	872B	1589B	3029B
Canada	*surface*	152B	278B	400B	717B
	air	339B	1226B	2675B	5229B
France	*surface*	198B	346B	496B	–
	air	396B	1100B	1919B	3693B
Germany	*surface*	137B	266B	393B	654B
	air	264B	908B	1687B	3213B
Japan	*surface*	204B	334B	426B	–
	air	272B	674B	1119B	–
New Zealand	*surface*	180B	332B	522B	–
	air	315B	1032B	1944B	–
UK	*surface*	218B	401B	563B	–
	air	337B	1032B	1850B	3519B
USA	*surface*	135B	454B	824B	1597B
	air	356B	1564B	3035B	6034B

according to weight (rising in one-kg increments), country of destination and whether they're shipped by surface (takes up to two months) or air (one to two weeks). See the Parcel Postage Rates table earlier for sample prices.

Most provincial post offices sell do-it-yourself packing boxes (11 sizes!) costing from 5 to 17B; tape and string are provided at no charge. Some offices even have packing services, which cost from 3 to 5B per parcel depending on size. Private packing services may also be available in the vicinity of large provincial post offices.

You can insure a package's contents for 8.50B for each 1740B of the goods' value.

Telephone

The telephone system in Thailand, operated by the government-subsidised Telephone Organisation of Thailand (TOT), is quite efficient and from Bangkok you can usually direct-dial most major centres with little difficulty.

International Calls A service called Home Country Direct (HCD) is available at Bangkok's GPO (Charoen Krung Rd), at Bangkok International Airport and at larger provincial phone offices; HCD phones offer easy one-button connection with international operators in Japan, Hong Kong, Korea, Italy, Singapore, the UK, the USA, New Zealand, the Netherlands or Taiwan.

Hotels almost always add surcharges (sometimes as much as 30% over and above the TOT rate) for international long-distance calls; it's always cheaper to call abroad from a government telephone office. These offices are almost always attached to a city's GPO; there may also be a separate TOT office down the road, used only for residential or business service (eg billing or installation), not public calls. Often the long-distance phone office is on the GPO's 2nd floor; sometimes it's around the side or just behind the GPO.

Once you've found the proper office and window, the procedure for making an international long-distance call *(thorásàp ráwàang pràthêt)* begins with filling out a bilingual form with your name and details pertaining to the call's destination. Except for collect calls, you must estimate in advance the time you'll be on the phone and pay a deposit equal to the time/distance rate. Usually, only cash or international phone credit cards are acceptable for payment; a few provincial phone offices also accept American Express. If the call doesn't go through you must pay a 30B service charge anyway – unless you're calling collect *(kèp plai-thaang)*. Depending on where you're calling, reimbursing someone later for a collect call to your home country may be less expensive than paying TOT charges – it pays to compare rates at source and destination. For calls between the USA and Thailand, for example, AT&T collect rates are less than TOT's direct rates.

There are also private long-distance telephone offices but these are usually only for calls within Thailand. Private offices with international service always charge more than the government offices, although private office surcharges are usually lower than hotel rates.

Telephone Office Hours GPO phone centres in most provincial capitals are open daily from 7 am to 11 pm; smaller provincial phone offices may be open from 8 am to 8 or 10 pm. Bangkok's international phone office in the GPO is open 24 hours.

Pay Phones There are two kinds of public pay phones in Thailand, 'red' and 'blue'. The red phones are for local city calls and the blue are for long-distance calls (within Thailand). Local calls from pay phones cost 1B. Although there are three different 1B coins in general circulation, only the middle-sized coin fits the coin slots. Some hotels and guesthouses have private pay phones that cost 5B per call; these take only nine-sided 5B coins.

Card phones are now available at most Thai airports as well as the occasional shopping centre, and are spreading to other sites. Telephone cards come in 50B, 100B and

240B denominations; they can be purchased at any TOT office. In airports you can usually buy them at the airport information counter.

Fax, Telex & Telegraph

GPO telephone offices throughout the country offer fax, telegraph and telex services in addition to regular phone service. There's no need to bring your own paper, as the post offices supply their own forms.

Larger hotels with business centres offer the same telecommunication services but always at higher rates.

Area Codes

- 02 Bangkok, Thonburi, Nonthaburi, PathumThani, Samut Prakan
- 32 Phetburi, Cha-am, Prachuap Khiri Khan, Pranburi, Ratchaburi
- 34 Kanchanaburi, Nakhon Pathom, Samut Sakhon, Samut Songkhram
- 35 Ang Thong, Ayuthaya, Suphanburi
- 36 Lopburi, Saraburi, Singburi
- 37 Nakhon Nayok, Prachinburi, Aranya Prathet
- 38 Chachoengsao, Chonburi, Pattaya, Rayong, Si Racha
- 39 Chanthaburi, Trat
- 42 Loei, Chiang Khan, Mukdahan, Nakhon Phanom, Nong Khai, Sakon Nakhon, Udon Thani
- 43 Kalasin, Khon Kaen, Mahasarakham, Roi Et
- 44 Buriram, Chaiyaphum, Nakhon Ratchasima (Khorat)
- 45 Si Saket, Surin, Ubon Ratchathani, Yasothon
- 53 Chiang Mai, Chiang Rai, Lamphun, Mae Hong Song
- 54 Lampang, Nan, Phayao, Phrae
- 55 Kamphaeng Phet, Phitsanulok, Sukhothai, Tak, Mae Sot, Uttaradit
- 56 Nakhon Sawan, Phetchabun, Phichit, Uthai Thani
- 73 Narathiwat, Sungai Kolok, Pattani, Yala
- 74 Hat Yai, Phattalung, Satun, Songkhla
- 75 Krabi, Nakhon Si Thammarat, Trang
- 76 Phang-Nga, Phuket
- 77 Chumphon, Ranong, Surat Thani, Chaiya, Ko Samui

TIME

Thai time is seven hours ahead of GMT (London). Thus noon in Bangkok is 3 pm in Sydney, 1 pm in Perth, 5 am in London, 1 am in New York and 10 pm the previous day in Los Angeles.

The official year in Thailand is reckoned from 543 BC, the beginning of the Buddhist Era, so that 1990 AD is 2533 BE.

Business Hours

Most government offices are open from 8.30 am to 4.30 pm, Monday to Friday, but closed from noon to 1 pm for lunch. Banks are open from 8.30 am to 3.30 pm Monday to Friday, but in Bangkok in particular several banks have special foreign-exchange offices which are open longer hours (generally until 8 pm) and every day of the week.

Businesses usually operate between 8.30 am and 5 pm, Monday to Friday and sometimes Saturday morning as well. Larger shops usually open from 10 am to 6.30 or 7 pm but smaller shops may open earlier and close later.

ELECTRICITY

Electric current is 220 V, 50 cycles.

LAUNDRY

Virtually every hotel and guesthouse in Thailand offers a laundry service. Rates are generally geared to room rates; the cheaper the accommodation, the cheaper the washing and ironing. Cheapest of all are public laundries where you pay by the kg.

Many Thai hotels and guesthouses also have laundry areas where you can wash your clothes at no charge; sometimes there's even a hanging area for drying. For accommodation where a laundry area isn't available, do-it-yourselfers can wash their clothes in the sink and hang clothes out to dry in their rooms – see the What to Bring section in this chapter for useful laundry tools. Laundry detergent is readily available in general mercantile shops and supermarkets.

For dry cleaning, take clothes to a dry cleaner. Laundries that advertise dry cleaning often don't really dry clean (they just boil everything!) or do it badly. Luxury hotels usually have dependable dry cleaning services.

Two reliable dry cleaners in Bangkok are Erawan Dry Cleaners (basement of Landmark Plaza, Sukhumvit Rd) and Sukhumvit Dry Cleaners (929 Sukhumvit Rd near Soi 51). Both of these companies can dry clean large items like sleeping bags as well as clothes.

WEIGHTS & MEASURES

Dimensions and weight are usually expressed using the metric system in Thailand. The exception is land measure, which is often quoted using the traditional Thai system of *waa*, *ngaan* and *râi*. Old-timers in the provinces will occasionally use the traditional Thai system of weights and measures in speech, as will boat-builders, carpenters and other craftspeople when talking about their work. Here are some conversions to use for such occasions:

1 sq *waa*	=	4 sq metres
1 *ngaan* (100 sq waa)	=	400 sq metres
1 *râi* (4 ngaan)	=	1600 sq metres
1 *bàht*	=	15 grams
1 *taleung* or *tamleung* (4 baht)	=	60 grams
1 *chăng* (20 taleung)	=	1.2 kg
1 *hàap* (50 chang)	=	60 kg
1 *níu*	=	about 2 cm (or 1 inch)
1 *khêup* (12 niu)	=	25 cm
1 *sàwk* (2 kheup)	=	50 cm
1 *waa* (4 sawk)	=	2 metres
1 *sén* (20 waa)	=	40 metres
1 *yôht* (400 sen)	=	16 km

BOOKS & MAPS

People, Culture & Society

Culture Shock! Thailand & How to Survive It by Robert & Nanthapa Cooper is an interesting outline on getting along with the Thai way of life. *Letters from Thailand* by Botan (translated by Susan Fulop) and Carol Hollinger's *Mai Pen Rai Means Never Mind* can also be recommended for their insights into traditional Thai culture. *Bangkok Post* reporter Denis Segaller's *Thai Ways* and *More Thai Ways* present yet more expat insights into Thai culture.

For a look at rural life in Thailand, the books of Pira Sudham are unparalleled. Sudham is a Thai author who was born to a poor family in north-east Thailand and has written *Siamese Drama, Monsoon Country* and *People of Esarn (Isaan)*. These books are not translations – Sudham writes in English in order to reach a worldwide audience. These titles are fairly easy to find in Bangkok but can be difficult overseas – the publisher is Siam Media International, GPO Box 1534, Bangkok 10501.

Behind the Smile: Voices of Thailand (Post Publishing, 1990) by Sanitsuda Ekachai is a very enlightening collection of interviews with Thai peasants from all over the country. The Siam Society's *Culture & Environment in Thailand* is a collection of scholarly papers delivered at a 1988 symposium which examined the relationship between Thai culture and the natural world; topics range from the oceanic origins of the Thai race and nature motifs in Thai art to evolving Thai attitudes toward the environment.

For books on Buddhism and Buddhism in Thailand, see the Religion section of the Facts about the Country chapter.

Hill Tribes If you are interested in detailed information on hill tribes, get *The Hill Tribes of Northern Thailand* by Gordon Young (Monograph No 1, The Siam Society). Young was born of third-generation Christian missionaries among Lahu people, speaks several tribal dialects and is even an honorary Lahu chieftain with the highest Lahu title, the Supreme Hunter. The monograph covers 16 tribes, including descriptions, photographs, tables and maps.

From the Hands of the Hills by Margaret Campbell has lots of beautiful pictures. The recently published *Peoples of the Golden Triangle* by Elaine & Paul Lewis is also very good, very photo-oriented and expensive. Lonely Planet's *Thai Hill Tribes Phrasebook* has descriptions of Thailand's major hill tribes, maps, and phrases in several hill-tribe languages.

For short descriptions of Thai hill tribes in this guidebook, see under Hill Tribes in the Northern Thailand chapter.

History & Politics

George Coedes' classic prewar work on South-East Asian history, *The Indianised States of South-East Asia*, contains groundbreaking historical material on early Thai history, as does W A R Wood's *A History of Siam*, published in the same era. One of the best modern accounts is David Wyatt's *Thailand: A Short History* (Trasvin Publications, Chiang Mai). Concentrating on post-revolutionary Thailand, *The Balancing Act: A History of Modern Thailand* (Asia Books) by Joseph Wright Jr, starts with the 1932 revolution and ends with the February 1991 Coup.

The best source of information on Thailand's political scene during the turbulent '60s and '70s is *Political Conflict in Thailand: Reform, Reaction, Revolution* by David Morrell & Chai-anan Samudavanija. *Siam in Crisis* by Sulak Sivaraksa, one of Thailand's leading intellectuals, analyses modern Thai politics from Sulak's unique Buddhist-nationalist perspective.

Thailand's role in the international narcotics trade is covered thoroughly in Alfred McCoy's *The Politics of Heroin in Southeast Asia* and Francis Belanger's *Drugs, the US, and Khun Sa*.

Travel Guides

Two travel guides with some good stuff on history, culture, art, etc are *Nagel's Encyclopaedia-Guide to Thailand*, an expensive little book published in Switzerland, and *Guide to Thailand* by Achille Clarac, edited and translated by Michael Smithies. Clarac's guide originally appeared in English as *Discovering Thailand* in 1971; it hasn't been updated since 1977 but was a pioneering work in its day.

The *Insight Guide to Thailand* (APA Productions, Singapore) is beautifully presented and well written although it's a little hefty to carry around as a travel guide – a worthy item for travel-guide collectors at any rate.

If you can get hold of a copy of *Hudson's Guide to Chiang Mai & the North* you'll learn a lot about this area that is unknown to the average traveller. Much of the information is out of date (since the book is long out of print) but it makes interesting reading and has one of the best Thai phrase sections ever published – 218 phrases *with* tone marks. (Phrase sections without tone marks are next to worthless.) In 1987, Roy Hudson published the minuscule *Hudson's Guide to Mae Hong Son* which you may come across in the north.

Recently, a number of locally produced Thai guidebooks have emerged. *The Shell Guide to Thailand* is basically a directory of hotels, restaurants and service stations but provides many useful addresses and phone numbers and has some good maps. Naturalists should peruse *National Parks of Thailand* by Denis Gray et al, available only in Thailand.

If this is your first trip to Asia, you might also want to have a look at *Before You Go to Asia* (Laurel Publications, San Francisco) by John McCarroll. This book weighs the pros and cons of going on your own versus going with a tour group (the author comes out strongly in favour of going on your own) and lists references for further information on Asian travel.

Food & Shopping

Cooking Thai Food in American Kitchens by Malulee Pinsuvana is useful because it has pictures and diagrams that can help you identify your meals. Another good cookbook is *Thai Cooking* (formerly *The Original Thai Cookbook)* by Jennifer Brennan.

Shopping in Exotic Thailand (Impact Publications, USA) by Ronald and Caryl Rae Krannich is packed with general shopping tips as well as lists of speciality shops and markets throughout Thailand. John Hoskins' *Buyer's Guide to Thai Gems & Jewellery* is a must for anyone contemplating a foray into Thailand's gem market.

Bookshops

Bangkok probably has the largest selection of English-language books and bookshops in South-East Asia. The principal chains are Asia Books (headquarters on Sukhumvit Rd near Soi 15) and DK Book House (Siam

Square); each has branch shops in half a dozen street locations around Bangkok as well as in well-touristed cities like Chiang Mai, Hat Yai and Phuket. Asia and DK offer a wide variety of fiction and periodicals as well as books on Asia. Some of Thailand's larger tourist hotels also have bookshops with English-language books and periodicals.

In Chiang Mai, the independent Suriwong Book Centre on Si Donchai Rd is especially good for books on Thailand and Asia.

Maps

Latest Tour's Guide to Bangkok & Thailand has a bus map of Bangkok on one side and a fair map of Thailand on the other, and is usually priced at around 30B. The bus map is quite necessary if you intend to spend much time in Bangkok and want to use the very economical bus system. It's available at most bookshops in Bangkok which carry English-language materials. A better map of the country is published by APA Productions (also available as a Nelles Maps publication) which costs around US$7 and is available at many Bangkok bookshops as well as overseas.

Even better is the four-map set issued by Thailand's Department of Highways. For 65B you get a very detailed, full-colour road map of the central, northern, north-eastern and southern regions. The maps include information on 'roads not under control by the Highway Department'; for example, many of the roads you may travel on in the Golden Triangle. Bookshops sometimes sell this set for 200B, including a mailing tube, but the Highway Department on Si Ayuthaya Rd and the Bangkok TAT office on Ratchadamnoen Nok Rd offer the set at the lower price. The mailing tube is not worth 135B.

The Roads Association of Thailand publishes a 44-page bilingual road atlas called *Thailand Highway Map*. The atlas has cut the Highway Department maps to a more manageable size and includes dozens of city maps, driving distances and lots of travel and sightseeing information. It costs 90 to 120B depending on the vendor, but beware of inferior knock-offs.

Recently Bartholomew Maps, in conjunction with DK Book House, has come out with the *Handy Map of Thailand*, an ingeniously folded 22 x 13 cm road atlas that can be opened like a book to any section without refolding the map – perfect for the backpacker. Although it's not 100% accurate (neither are the Highway Department maps), the convenience and durable coated paper make it a bargain at 90 to 100B.

The maps from the Highway Department or Bartholomew/DK are more than adequate for most people. At some branches of DK Book House, however, you can also purchase Thai military maps, which focus on areas no larger than the amphoe (local district), complete with elevations and contour lines. These may be of use to the solo trekker, but cost 60B upwards per map. DK also publishes special maps for hill-tribe trekkers. See the section on Hill-Tribe Treks in the Northern Thailand chapter.

There are also Nancy Chandler's very useful city maps of Bangkok and Chiang Mai. These colourful maps serve as up-to-date and informative guides, spotlighting local sights, noting local markets and their wares, outlining local transport and even recommending restaurants.

MEDIA

Newspapers

Thailand's 1991 constitution guarantees freedom of the press, though the National Police Department reserves power to suspend publishing licences for national security reasons. Editors nevertheless exercise self-censorship in certain realms, particularly with regard to the monarchy.

Two English-language newspapers are published daily in Thailand and distributed in most provincial capitals throughout the country: the *Bangkok Post* (morning) and the *Nation* (afternoon). The *Nation* is almost entirely staffed by Thais and presents, obviously, a Thai perspective, while the *Post*, which was Thailand's first English daily (established 1946), has a mixed Thai and international staff and represents a more international view. For regional and international news, the *Post* is the better of the two papers and is in fact regarded by many journalists as the best English daily in South-East Asia. The *Nation*, on the other hand, is to be commended for taking a harder anti-NPKC stance during the 1991 coup.

The Singapore edition of the *International Herald Tribune* is widely available in Bangkok, Chiang Mai and heavily touristed areas like Pattaya and Phuket.

The most popular Thai-language newspapers are *Thai Rath* and *Daily News*, but they're mostly full of blood-and-guts stories. The best Thai journalism is found in the somewhat less popular *Matichon* and *Siam Rath* dailies. Many Thais read the English-language dailies as they consider them better news sources. The *Bangkok Post* has recently announced the publication of a new Thai-language version of the popular English daily.

Radio

Thailand has more than 400 radio stations, with 41 FM and 35 AM stations in Bangkok alone. Bangkok's national public radio station, Radio Thailand (Sathaanii Withayu Haeng Prathet Thai), broadcasts English-language programmes at 97 FM from 6 am to 11 pm. Most of the programmes comprise local, national and international news, sports, business and special news-related features. There is some music on the channel between 9.15 and 11 am, and from 8.30 pm on. For up-to-date news reports this is the station to listen to. An official news bulletin (national news sponsored by the government) is broadcast at 7 am, 12.30 and 7 pm.

Another public radio station is 107 FM, which is affiliated with Radio Thailand and Channel 9 on Thai public television. It broadcasts Radio Thailand news bulletins at the same hours as Radio Thailand (7 am, 12.30 pm and 7 pm). Between 5 pm and 2 am daily, 107 FM features some surprisingly good music programmes with British, Thai and American DJs. Another station with international pop and English-speaking DJs is Radio Bangkok, 95.5 FM.

Chulalongkorn University broadcasts classical music at 101.5 FM from 9.30 to 11.30 pm nightly. A schedule of the evening's programmes can be found in the *Nation* and *Bangkok Post* newspapers.

At 7.30 pm, several FM stations provide English-language soundtracks for local and world satellite news on television Channel 3 (105.5 FM), Channel 7 (103.5 FM), Channel 9 (107 FM) and Channel 11 (8 pm, 88 FM).

The Voice of America, BBC World Service, Radio Canada and Radio Australia all have English and Thai-language broadcasts over short-wave radio from approximately 6 am to midnight. The radio frequencies and schedules, which change hourly, also appear in the *Post* and the *Nation*. Radio listeners without short-wave receivers can listen to VOA on 95.5 FM, and BBC World Service on 105 FM from midnight to 6 am.

Television

Thailand has five TV networks based in Bangkok. Following the 1991 coup the Thai government authorised an extension of telecast time to 24 hours and networks are scrambling to fill air time. As a result, there has been a substantial increase in English-language telecasts – mostly in the morning hours when Thais aren't used to watching TV (wait a year or two!).

Channel 9, the national public television station, broadcasts from 6 am until midnight. At 7 am each weekday morning Channel 9 features a local English news programme (Good Morning Thailand) followed by the NBC Nightly News with Tom Brokaw (from the night before in the USA). Channel 5 is a military network (the only one to operate during coups) and broadcasts from 6 am to midnight; between 6 and 10 am this network presents a mix of ABC, CNN, and English-subtitled Thai news programmes, then CNN headlines again at 11.37 pm.

Channel 3 is privately owned and is on the air from 2 pm until 1.20 am. Channel 7 is military-owned but broadcast time is leased to private companies; hours of operation are from 5.30 to 2.15 am. Channel 11 is run by the Ministry of Education and features educational programmes from 5.30 am until midnight, including TV correspondence classes from Ramkhamhaeng and Sukhothai Thammathirat open universities.

Upcountry cities will generally receive only two networks – Channel 9 and a local private network with restricted hours.

Satellite TV As elsewhere in Asia, satellite television is arriving in Thailand swiftly, and competition for the untapped market is keen. Of the several regional satellite operations aimed at Thailand, the most successful so far is Satellite Television Asian Region (STAR), beamed from Hong Kong via AsiaSat I. STAR offers five free 24-hour channels, including Music TV Asia (a tie-in with America's MTV music-video channel), Prime Sports (international sports coverage), BBC World Service Television (news), and two channels showing movies in Chinese and English. CNN and ESPN are available in Thailand via Indonesia's Palapa satellite, a pay-TV service. Thailand has recently launched its own ThaiSat as an uplink for AsiaSat.

Tourist-class hotels in Thailand often have one or more satellite TV channels (plus in-house video), including a STAR 'sampler' channel that switches from one STAR offering to another.

FILM & PHOTOGRAPHY

Print film is fairly inexpensive and widely available throughout Thailand. Japanese print film costs 60 to 65B per 36 exposures, US print film 75 to 80B. Fujichrome RDP 100 slide film costs around 148B, Kodak Ektachrome 100HC is 140B and Ektachrome 200 about 198B. Slide film, especially Kodachrome, can be hard to find outside Bangkok and Chiang Mai, so be sure to stock up before heading upcountry. Film processing is generally quite good in the larger cities in Thailand and also quite inexpensive. Kodachrome must be sent out of the country for processing, so it can take up to two weeks to get it back.

Pack some silica gel with your camera to prevent mould growing on the inside of your lenses. A polarising filter could be useful to cut down on tropical glare at certain times of day, particularly around water or highly polished glazed-tile work.

Hill-tribe people in some of the regularly visited areas expect money if you photograph them, while certain Karen and Akha will not allow you to point a camera at them. Use discretion when photographing villagers anywhere in Thailand as a camera can be a very intimidating instrument. You may feel better leaving your camera behind when visiting certain areas.

HEALTH

Predeparture Preparations

Travel Insurance As when travelling anywhere in the world a good travel insurance policy is a very wise idea. A motorcycle accident can make an expensive and nasty end to your travels. 'After paying the hospital bills, damage to the bike I hit and goodwill contribution to the local police,' wrote one traveller, 'I wished I had been insured'.

If you undergo medical treatment in Thailand, be sure to collect all receipts and copies of the medical report, in English if possible, for your insurance company.

Medical Kit For basic first aid, I recommend carrying the following:

- Large self-adhesive bandages and Band-aids to help protect ordinary cuts or wounds from infection
- Butterfly closures for cuts that won't close on their own
- Anti-bacterial ointment and powder to treat or prevent infection of wounds
- Immodium, Lomotil, or Pattardium to mitigate the symptoms of diarrhoea
- Antibiotic eye ointment for all-too-common eye infections
- Scissors, tweezers and thermometer

- Aspirin, acetaminophen or paracetamol for headaches and fever
- Rehydration mixture for treatment of severe diarrhoea
- Insect repellent, sun block, suntan lotion and lip balm

The best book I've seen on health maintenance in Asia is Dirk Schroeder's *Staying Healthy in Asia, Africa & Latin America* (Stanford, California: Volunteers in Asia, 1988). In fact, you might want to make this handy little book part of your first-aid kit as it clearly describes symptoms and recommended treatment for illnesses common in Thailand (and elsewhere in Asia).

When seriously ill or injured, you should seek medical attention from a qualified doctor, clinic or hospital if at all possible; employ self-treatment only as a last resort.

Health Preparations Make sure you're healthy before you start travelling, and if you are embarking on a long trip make sure your teeth are OK. If you wear glasses bring a spare pair and your prescription. Losing your glasses can be a real problem, although in many places you can get new spectacles made up quickly, cheaply and competently.

If you require a particular medication, take an adequate supply as it may not be available locally. Take the prescription, with the generic rather than the brand name, which may be unavailable, as it will make getting replacements easier. It's a wise idea to have the prescription with you to show you legally use the medication; it's surprising how often over-the-counter drugs from one place are illegal without a prescription or even banned in another.

Immunisation There are no health requirements for Thailand in terms of required vaccinations unless you are coming from an infected area. Travellers should have a cholera immunisation prior to arriving and a tetanus booster would be a good idea as well in case you injure yourself while travelling. You should also check if vaccinations are required by any countries you are going to after visiting Thailand. A Japanese encephalitis vaccination is a good idea for those who think they may be at moderate or high risk while in Thailand (see the Japanese Encephalitis section for more information). Your doctor may also recommend booster shots against measles or polio.

Plan ahead for getting your vaccinations since some of them require an initial shot followed by a booster, while others should not be given together.

Basic Rules

Care in what you eat and drink is the most important health rule; stomach upsets are the most likely travel health problem, but the majority of these upsets will be relatively minor. Don't become paranoid – after all, trying the local food is part of the experience of travel.

Water The number one rule is *don't drink tap water*. If you don't know for certain that water is safe always assume the worst. Reputable brands of bottled water or soft drinks are generally fine, although in some places refilled bottles are not unknown. Take care with fruit juice, particularly if water may have been added. Tea or coffee should be OK since the water is boiled.

Thai soft drinks are safe to drink, as is the weak Chinese tea served in most restaurants. Ice is produced from purified water under hygienic conditions and is therefore theoretically safe. During transit to the local restaurant, however, conditions are not so hygienic (you may see blocks of ice being dragged along the street), but it's very difficult to resist in the hot season. The rule of thumb is that if it's chipped ice, it probably came from an ice block (which may not have been handled well) but if it's ice cubes or 'tubes', it was delivered from the ice factory in sealed plastic. In rural areas, villagers mostly drink collected rainwater. Most travellers can drink this without problems, but some people can't tolerate it.

In Thailand, virtually no-one bothers with filters, tablets or iodine since bottled water is so cheap and readily available.

Food It is best to buy fruit that you can peel and slice yourself (cheaper, too), but most fare at food stalls is reasonably safe. Salads and fruit should be washed with purified water or peeled where possible. Ice cream is usually OK if it is a reputable brand name, but beware of ice cream from street vendors and ice cream that has melted and been refrozen. Thoroughly cooked food is safest, but not if it has been left to cool or if it has been reheated. Take great care with shellfish or fish and avoid undercooked meat.

If a place looks clean and well run and the vendor also looks clean and healthy then the food is probably safe. In general, places that are packed with travellers or locals will be fine, empty restaurants are questionable.

Nutrition If you're travelling hard and fast and therefore missing meals, or if you simply lose your appetite, you can soon start to lose weight and place your health at risk.

Make sure your diet is well balanced. Eggs, tofu, beans, lentils and nuts are all safe ways to get protein. Fruit you can peel (bananas, oranges or mandarins for example) are always safe and a good source of vitamins. Try to eat plenty of grains (rice) and bread. Remember that although food is generally safer if it is cooked well, overcooked food loses much of its nutritional value. If the food is insufficient it's a good idea to take vitamin and iron pills.

Make sure you drink enough: don't rely on feeling thirsty to indicate when you should drink. Not needing to urinate or very dark yellow urine is a danger sign. Always carry a water bottle with you on long trips. Excessive sweating can lead to loss of salt and therefore muscle cramping. Salt tablets are not a good idea as a preventative but in places where salt is not used much, adding additional salt to food can help.

Vital Signs A normal body temperature is 98.6°F or 37°C, more than 2°C higher is a 'high' fever. A normal adult pulse rate is 60 to 80 beats per minute (children 80 to 100, babies 100 to 140). You should know how to take a temperature and a pulse rate. As a general rule the pulse increases about 20 beats per minute for each 1°C rise in fever.

Respiration rate (breathing) is also an indicator of illness. Count the number of breaths per minute – between 12 and 20 is normal for adults and older children (up to 30 for younger children, 40 for babies). People with a high fever or serious respiratory illness (like pneumonia) breathe more quickly than normal. More than 40 shallow breaths a minute usually means pneumonia.

Hygiene & General Care Many health problems can be avoided by taking care of yourself. Wash your hands frequently – it's quite easy to contaminate your own food. Clean your teeth with purified water rather than straight from the tap. Avoid climatic extremes, keep out of the sun when it's hot. Avoid potential diseases by dressing sensibly. You can get worm infections through bare feet, or dangerous coral cuts by walking over coral without shoes. You can avoid insect bites by covering bare skin when insects are around, by screening windows or beds or by using insect repellents. Seek local advice; if you're told the water is unsafe due to jellyfish, etc, don't go in. In situations were there is no information, discretion is the better part of valour.

Medical Problems & Treatment

Self diagnosis and treatment can be risky; wherever possible seek qualified help. An embassy or consulate can usually advise a good place to go. So can five-star hotels, although they often recommend doctors with five-star prices. This is when that medical insurance really becomes useful! In some places standards of medical attention are so low that for some ailments the best advice is to get on a plane and go somewhere else.

Sunburn In the tropics you can get sunburnt surprisingly quickly even through cloud. Use a sun block and take extra care to cover areas which don't normally see sun – your feet for example. A hat provides added protection and use zinc cream or some other barrier cream for your nose and lips. Calamine lotion is good for mild sunburn.

Prickly Heat Prickly heat is an itchy rash caused by excessive perspiration trapped under the skin. It usually strikes people who have just arrived in a hot climate whose pores have not yet opened sufficiently to cope with greater sweating. Keeping cool by bathing often, using a mild talcum powder, or even by resorting to air-con may help until you acclimatise. One of the best non-prescription medicated powders in Thailand is a brand called Prickly Heat Powder.

Heat Exhaustion Dehydration or salt deficiency can cause heat exhaustion. Take time to acclimatise to high temperatures and make sure you get sufficient liquids. Salt deficiency is characterised by fatigue, lethargy, headaches, giddiness and muscle cramps and in this case salt tablets may help. Vomiting or diarrhoea can deplete your liquid and salt levels. Anhydrotic heat exhaustion, caused by an inability to sweat, is rare and unlike the other forms of heat exhaustion is likely to strike people who have been in a hot climate for some time, rather than newcomers.

Heat Stroke This serious, sometimes fatal, condition can occur if the body's heat regulating mechanism breaks down and the body temperature rises to dangerous levels. Long, continuous periods of exposure to high temperatures can leave you vulnerable to heat stroke and you should avoid excessive alcohol or strenuous activity when you first arrive in a hot climate.

The symptoms are feeling unwell, not sweating very much or at all and a high body temperature (39 to 41°C). Where sweating has ceased, the skin becomes flushed and red. Severe, throbbing headaches and lack of co-ordination will also occur and the sufferer may be confused or aggressive. Eventually the victim will become delirious or convulse. Hospitalisation is essential, but meanwhile get the victim out of the sun, remove clothing and cover them with a wet sheet or towel and then fan them continually.

Fungal Infections Hot-weather fungal infections are most likely to occur on the scalp, between the toes or fingers (athlete's foot) or in the groin (jock itch or crotch rot), or as ringworm on the body. You get ringworm (which is a fungal infection, not a worm) from infected animals or by walking on damp areas, like shower floors.

To prevent fungal infections, wear loose, comfortable clothes, avoid artificial fibres, wash frequently and dry carefully. If you do get an infection, wash the infected area daily with a disinfectant or medicated soap and water and rinse and dry well. Apply an antifungal powder like the widely available Tinaderm. Try to expose the infected area to air or sunlight as much as possible and wash all towels and underwear in hot water and change them often. Public or hotel laundries often wash everything in cold water with very little soap – washing your own underwear will go a long way toward preventing yeast and fungal problems in the crotch area.

Motion Sickness Eating lightly before and during a trip will reduce the chances of motion sickness. If you are prone to motion sickness, try to find a place that minimises disturbance – near the wing on aircraft, close to midships on boats, near the centre on buses. Fresh air usually helps; reading or cigarette smoke doesn't. Commercial anti-motion-sickness preparations, which can cause drowsiness, have to be taken before the trip commences; when you're feeling sick it's too late. Ginger is a natural preventative and is available in capsule form.

Diarrhoea Traveller's diarrhoea, which can be caused by viruses, bacteria, food poisoning, stress, or simply a change in diet, may strike some visitors who stay for any length of time outside Bangkok, but usually subsides within a few days. A few rushed toilet trips with no other symptoms is not indicative of a serious problem. Moderate diarrhoea, involving half a dozen loose movements in a day, is more of a nuisance.

Dehydration is the main danger with any diarrhoea, particularly for children, so fluid replenishment is the number one treatment. Weak black tea with a little sugar, flat soft drinks diluted with water or soda water are all good. With severe diarrhoea a rehydrating solution is necessary to replace minerals and salts. You should stick to a bland diet (rice or noodle soups are good) and cut out all alcohol and caffeine as you recover.

Lomotil or Immodium can be used to bring relief from the symptoms of diarrhoea, although they do not actually cure them. Only use these drugs if absolutely necessary: if you *must* travel for example. For children, Immodium is preferable. Do not use these drugs if you have a high fever or are severely dehydrated. Antibiotics can be very useful in treating severe diarrhoea, especially if it is accompanied by nausea, vomiting, stomach cramps or mild fever. Three days' treatment should be sufficient and an improvement should occur within 24 hours.

If these don't help and/or your stools contain substantial blood and mucus, you may have amoebic dysentery, which can be serious if left untreated – in this case you should see a doctor.

Dysentery This serious illness is caused by contaminated food or water and is characterised by severe diarrhoea, often with blood or mucus in the stool. There are two kinds of dysentery. Bacillary dysentery is characterised by a high fever and rapid development; headache, vomiting and stomach pains are also symptoms. It generally does not last longer than a week, but it is highly contagious.

Amoebic dysentery is more gradual in developing, has no fever or vomiting but is a more serious illness. It is not a self-limiting disease but will persist until treated and can recur and cause long-term damage.

A stool test is necessary with dysentery, but if no medical care is available tetracycline is the prescribed treatment for bacillary dysentery, metronidazole for amoebic dysentery.

Cholera Cholera vaccination is not very effective, but outbreaks of cholera are generally widely reported so you can avoid such areas. The disease is characterised by a sudden onset of acute diarrhoea with 'rice water' stools, vomiting, muscular cramps and extreme weakness. If you contract cholera you need medical help, but in the meantime, treat for dehydration (which can be extreme) and, if there is an appreciable delay in getting to hospital, begin taking tetracycline. This drug should not be given to young children or pregnant women and it should not be used past its expiration date.

Viral Gastroenteritis This is not caused by bacteria but, as the name suggests, by a virus and is characterised by stomach cramps, diarrhoea, sometimes vomiting, sometimes a slight fever. All you can do is rest and drink lots of fluids.

Hepatitis Hepatitis A is the most common form of this disease and is spread by contaminated food or water. The symptoms are fever, chills, headache, fatigue, feelings of weakness and aches and pains, followed by loss of appetite, nausea, vomiting, abdominal pain, dark urine, light coloured faeces, jaundiced skin and the whites of the eyes may turn yellow. You should seek medical advice, but in general there is not much you can do apart from rest, drink lots of fluids, eat lightly and avoid fatty foods. People who have had hepatitis must forego alcohol for six months after the illness, as hepatitis attacks the liver and it needs that amount of time to recover. A preventive injection of immune serum globulin (formerly called gamma globulin) is not 100% effective but may at least mitigate the severity of a hepatitis A infection.

Hepatitis B, which used to be called serum hepatitis, is spread through contact with infected bodily fluids, for example through sexual contact, unsterilised needles and blood transfusions. Avoid having injections, your ears pierced or tattoos done in places where you have doubts about the sanitary conditions. The symptoms of type B are much the same as type A except they are more severe and may lead to irreparable liver damage or even liver cancer. Although there is no treatment for hepatitis B, an effective prophylactic vaccine is readily available in most countries. The immunisation schedule requires two injections at least a month apart followed by a third dose five months after the second. Persons who *should* receive a hepatitis B vaccination include anyone who anticipates contact with blood or other bodily secretions in Thailand – either as health-care workers or through sexual contact with the local population – as well as anyone who will be staying in the country more than six months.

Worms These parasites are most common in rural, tropical areas and a stool test when you return home is not a bad idea. Worms can be present on unwashed vegetables or in undercooked meat and you can pick them up through your skin by walking in bare feet. Infestations may not show up for some time, and although they are generally not serious, if left untreated they can cause severe health problems. A stool test is necessary to pinpoint the problem and medication is often available over the counter.

Schistosomiasis Also known as 'blood flukes', this disease is caused by tiny flatworms that burrow their way through the skin and enter the bloodstream. Humans contact the worms when swimming or bathing in contaminated fresh water (the flukes can't survive in salt water). Symptoms include a rash or skin irritation where the worm larvae have penetrated the skin. The rash/irritation disappears after a few days and there are no symptoms for several weeks until the flukes mature in the bloodstream; then fever, chills, weakness and another rash affect the victim, sometimes along with painful or bloody urination. If left untreated, the disease may result in liver, spleen and lymph-node enlargement, and in advanced cases may lead to irreversible damage to organs and the central nervous system.

The overall risk for this disease is quite low, but it's highest in the southern reaches of the Maekhong River and in the lakes of north-east Thailand – avoid swimming or bathing in these waterways. If submersion is for some reasons unavoidable, vigorous towel-drying reduces the risk of penetration. If schistosomiasis symptoms appear, consult a physician; the usual treatment is a regimen of praziquantel (often sold as Biltricide).

Opisthorchiasis Also called 'liver flukes', these are tiny worms that are occasionally present in freshwater fish. The main risk comes from eating raw or undercooked fish. Travellers should in particular avoid eating *plaa ráa* (sometimes called *paa daek* in north-east Thailand), an unpasteurised fermented fish used as an accompaniment for rice in the north-east. Plaa raa is not commonly served in restaurants, but is common in rural areas of the north-east, where it's considered a great delicacy. The Thai government is currently trying to discourage north-easterners from eating plaa raa or other uncooked fish products. A common roadside billboard in the region these days reads *isăan mâi kin plaa dìp* or 'north-eastern Thailand doesn't eat raw fish'.

Liver flukes *(wiwâat bai tàp* in Thai) are endemic to villages around Sakon Nakhon Province's Nong Han, the largest natural lake in Thailand. Don't swim in this lake! (As with blood flukes, liver flukes can bore into the skin.) A much less common way to contract liver flukes is through swimming in rivers. The only known area where the flukes might be contracted by swimming in contaminated waters is in the southern reaches of the Maekhong River.

The intensity of symptoms depends very much on how many of the flukes get into your body. At low levels, there are virtually no symptoms at all; at higher levels, an overall fatigue, low-grade fever and swollen or tender liver (or general abdominal pain) are the usual symptoms, along with worms or worm eggs in the faeces. Persons suspected of having liver flukes should have a stool sample analysed by a competent doctor or clinic. The usual medication is 750 mg of praziquantel (Biltricide) three times daily for a week.

Tetanus This potentially fatal disease is found in undeveloped tropical areas and is difficult to treat but is preventable with immunisation. Tetanus occurs when a wound becomes infected by a germ which lives in the faeces of animals or people, so clean all cuts, punctures or animal bites. Tetanus is known as lockjaw and the first symptom may be discomfort in swallowing, stiffening of the jaw and neck, then painful convulsions of the jaw and whole body.

Rabies Rabies is found in many countries and is caused by a bite or scratch from an infected animal. Dogs are a noted carrier, as are bats. Any bite, scratch or even lick from a mammal should be cleaned immediately and thoroughly. Scrub with soap and running water, then clean with an alcohol solution. If there is any possibility that the animal is infected, medical help should be sought immediately. Even if the animal is not rabid, all bites should be treated seriously as they can become infected or can result in tetanus. A rabies vaccination is now available and should be considered if you are in a high risk category, eg cave explorers (bat bites) or people working with animals.

Sexually Transmitted Diseases Sexual contact with an infected sexual partner spreads these diseases and while abstinence is the only 100% preventative, use of a latex condom is also effective. In Thailand the most statistically common STD is gonorrhoea, followed by non-specific urethritis (NSU). Typical symptoms for both gonorrhoea and NSU are discharges or pain when urinating. Symptoms may be less marked or not observed at all in women. Syphilis is less common; initial symptoms include sores in the genital area, followed by rash and flu-like symptoms. The symptoms of syphilis eventually disappear completely but the disease continues and can cause severe problems in later years. Treatment of gonorrhoea, NSU and syphilis is by antibiotics.

Two STDs reported in Thailand for which no cure is available are herpes simplex and the human immuno-deficiency virus (HIV), which often (10-35% of the time, according to current estimates) leads to acquired immune deficiency syndrome (AIDS) or AIDS-related complex (ARC), both of which are fatal diseases. In Thailand HIV is most commonly spread through heterosexual activity. The incubation period (time before an infection registers in lab tests) can extend to several years.

HIV can also be spread through infected blood transfusions or by dirty needles – vaccinations, acupuncture and tattooing can be as dangerous as intravenous drug use if the equipment is not clean. In Thailand the second most common source of HIV infection is intravenous injection by drug addicts who share needles. For more information on HIV/AIDS risks, see the AIDS in Thailand section later.

The use of condoms greatly decreases but does not eliminate the risk of STD infection. The Thai phrase for 'condom' is *thũng anaamai*. Latex condoms are more effective than animal-membrane condoms in preventing disease transmission; to specify latex condoms ask for *thũng yaang anaamai*. Good quality latex condoms are distributed free by offices of the Ministry of Public Health throughout the country – they come in numbered sizes, like shoes! Condoms can also be purchased at any pharmacy.

Malaria Ask 10 doctors around the world about malaria prevention and you may get 10 different opinions. Malaria, a mosquito-carried disease, is on the increase all over Asia and unfortunately most of the strains in Thailand are chloroquine-resistant, including the deadly *Plasmodium falciparum*. Hence, taking a malaria prophylactic may have little effect as a preventive and will most certainly contribute to an increase in resistance to these drugs, which are also used in the treatment of the disease.

There is much controversy surrounding the use of certain malarial prophylactics, in particular Fansidar and Lariam (mefloquine). Before leaving, it is wise to contact an infectious diseases hospital or other relevant government health body in your country to find out the latest information regarding malarial prophylactics. Armed with this information, consult a doctor (preferably one with experience in travel medicine) for a prescription if you decide to take chemical suppressants. Factors such as your length of

AIDS in Thailand

Because HIV infections are often associated with sexual contact and Thailand has an international reputation for illicit night-time activities, rumours regarding the status of AIDS in the country vary wildly. Some think the threat is greatly exaggerated while others are convinced the Thai government is involved in a massive coverup of the epidemic. The risks of contracting the disease are very real but should be placed in perspective.

For the record, as of January 1991 the World Health Organisation (WHO) estimated there were approximately 30,000 HIV-positive cases in Thailand (the country's total population is approximately 56 million), a number also supported by the country's Ministry of Health research. To date, full-blown AIDS in the country has been documented in 576 cases but the number will undoubtedly have increased by the time you read this. Thai women and their children are now the highest risk group, as infection has moved from the homosexual population in the early '80s to intravenous drug users mid-decade and then from prostitutes in the late '80s to the general population. In Thailand, homosexual/bisexual males now have the lowest rate of infection next to blood-transfusion recipients, dispelling the myth that AIDS is a 'gay disease'. In 1991, for example, Phrae Province health authorities recorded four HIV-positive male homosexuals and 414 HIV-positive female prostitutes.

Thus the main risk to the casual male visitor is HIV transmission via sexual contact with prostitutes or any Thai female whose HIV infection status in unknown. According to AIDS researchers, the percentage of HIV-positive prostitutes is much higher in rural areas than in Bangkok, especially in northern Thailand (which, for Thai males, is the 'capital' of Thai prostitution). The apparent reason for this is that Bangkok sex workers are much more likely to insist on condom use than their provincial counterparts. Thai male customers, on the other hand, are much less likely to use condoms than farang customers, which explains why even Pattaya – the capital for sex service to foreigners – shows a lower rate of infection than, for example, Chiang Rai. Of the estimated 210,000 sex workers in the country, the vast majority are patronised by Thai customers, and since Thai males visit prostitutes an average of twice a month the virus is now finding its way to their wives and girlfriends.

For female visitors the main statistical risk is having sexual contact with any male – Thai or farang – known to have had intercourse with Thai prostitutes since the mid-80s. For both genders, the second-highest risk activity would be any use of unsterilised needles, especially in illicit intravenous drug use.

The Thai government is not involved in covering up the epidemic and is in fact very keen to make HIV/AIDS statistics public and to educate the public about the disease and how to prevent transmission. Even the TAT is now addressing the issue in their annual reports. WHO officials report that Thailand has done more than any other country in South-East Asia to combat the AIDS threat, including following a WHO-approved national AIDS-prevention campaign since 1988. Radio and TV ads, public billboards and AIDS-awareness marches became everyday occurrences much sooner in Thailand than in Europe or the USA relative to the occurrence of the country's first known AIDS-related death (1984).

On a local level Ministry of Health offices are undertaking intensive public awareness programmes, conducting regular blood tests in brothels, massage parlours and coffee houses and distributing free condoms at their office locations as well as at sex service locations. But health officials don't have the power to close sex service operations; even if they could, officials say this would only force prostitution underground where it would be even more difficult to monitor and educate sex workers.

Although the following fact shouldn't be taken to mean that precautions aren't mandatory, WHO officials estimate Thailand has a much lower per-capita HIV infection rate than Australia, Switzerland or the USA (eg 20,000 among Australia's population of 17 million versus 30,000 among Thailand's 57 million). As elsewhere around the globe, however, it will only worsen with time until/unless a cure is discovered; in the meantime, behaviour modification is the best strategy available.

One of Thailand's chief accomplishments in the war against HIV transmission is that the medical blood supply is now considered safe, thanks to vigorous screening procedures. ■

stay and the areas you plan to visit are relevant in prescribing antimalarials. All commonly prescribed malarial suppressants (eg chloroquine) have the potential to cause side effects – chloroquine is in fact now completely banned in Japan. Mefloquine affects motor skills. In particular, persons allergic to sulphonamides should not take Fansidar.

In fact, the use of Fansidar as a prophylactic has been associated with severe and, in some cases, fatal reactions among travellers who have used the drug in multiple doses (ie two to five doses of Fansidar). For this reason there is now a move by many medical authorities away from the prescription of Fansidar as a malarial prophylactic, even for those travelling in areas where the disease is chloroquine-resistant. Although the incidence of severe reaction is not high, lack of information about the drug suggests that other malarial prophylactics should be used before considering Fansidar.

Recently the Center for Disease Control (CDC) in Atlanta, USA, has reported that various strains of malaria in Thailand are now chloroquine *and* Fansidar-resistant. Instead they are recommending a daily dose of 100 mg doxycycline (doxycycline is also said to prevent or suppress bacillary dysentery), but only if you will be travelling in potentially malarious areas or sleeping outdoors (or in unscreened rooms) in wilderness areas. At the moment Thailand's high-risk areas include northern Kanchanaburi Province (especially Thung Yai Naresuan Wildlife Sanctuary) and parts of Trat Province along the Cambodian border (including Ko Chang).

Rather than load up on drugs that may do you more harm than good, you can take a few other simple precautions that can greatly reduce your chances of contracting any kind of malaria. First of all, apply a good mosquito repellent to skin and clothes whenever and wherever mossies are about. The best repellents are those which contain more than 30% DEET (N,N-diethyl-metatoluamide) – for maximum protection, use a 100% DEET preparation if you can find it. Commercial repellents can be purchased at well-stocked Thai pharmacies but they rarely contain more than 35% DEET.

For those with an allergy or aversion to synthetic repellents, citronella makes a good substitute. Mosquito coils *(yaa kan yung bàep jùt)* do an excellent job of repelling mosquitoes in your room and are readily available in Thailand. Day mosquitoes do not carry malaria, so it is only in the night that you have to worry – peak biting hours are a few hours after dusk and a few hours before dawn.

According to the CDC and to the Region II Malaria Centre in Chiang Mai, there is virtually no risk of malaria in urban areas. Since malaria-carrying mosquitoes (Anopheles) only bite from early evening to early morning, you should sleep under a mosquito net (if possible) when in rural areas, even if you see only a few mosquitoes. If you are outside during the biting hours, use an insect repellent. Even in a malarial area, not every mosquito is carrying the parasite responsible for the disease. Hence, the most important thing is to prevent as many of the critters from biting you as possible, to lessen the odds that you will be 'injected' by one carrying the parasite.

Once the parasites are in your bloodstream, they are carried to your liver where they reproduce. Days, weeks, or even months later (some experts say it can take as long as a year in certain cases), the parasites will enter the bloodstream again from the liver and this is when the symptoms first occur. Symptoms generally begin with chills and headache, followed by a high fever that lasts several hours. This may be accompanied by nausea, diarrhoea and more intense headaches. After a period of sweating the fever may subside and other symptoms go into remission. Of course, a severe flu attack could produce similar symptoms. That is why if you do develop a high fever and think you may have been exposed to the disease, it is imperative you get a blood check for malaria. Virtually any clinic or hospital in Thailand can administer this simple test.

Early treatment is usually successful in

ridding the victim of the disease for good. If untreated or improperly treated, the symptoms will keep returning in cycles as the parasites move from liver to bloodstream and back.

Like many other tropical diseases, malaria is frequently mis-diagnosed in Western countries. If you should develop the symptoms after a return to your home country, be sure to seek medical attention immediately and inform your doctor that you may have been exposed to malaria.

Dengue Fever In some areas of Thailand there is a risk, albeit low, of contracting dengue fever via mosquito transmission. This time it's a day variety (Aedes) you have to worry about. Like malaria, dengue fever seems to be on the increase throughout tropical Asia in recent years. Dengue is found in urban as well as rural areas, especially in areas of human habitation (often indoors) where there is standing water.

Unlike malaria, dengue fever is caused by a virus and there is no chemical prophylactic or vaccination against it. In Thailand there are four strains (serotypes) of dengue and once you've had one you usually develop an immunity specific to that strain. The symptoms come on suddenly and include high fever, severe headache and heavy joint and muscle pain (hence its older name 'breakbone fever'), followed a few days later by a rash that spreads from the torso to the arms, legs and face. Various risk factors such as age, immunity and viral strain may mitigate these symptoms so that they are less severe or last only a few days. Even when the basic symptoms are short-lived, it can take several weeks to fully recover from the resultant weakness.

In rare cases dengue may develop into a more severe condition known as dengue haemorrhagic fever (DHF), or dengue toxic shock syndrome, which is fatal. DHF is most common among Asian children under 15 years who are undergoing a second dengue infection, so the risk of DHF for most international travellers is very low.

Although the latest estimate says you have only a 1 in 10,000 chance of contracting dengue when bitten by the Aedes mosquito (ie only 1 in 10,000 Aedes mosquitoes in Thailand is infectious), I have personally known several travellers (including myself) who have come down with the disease over the years. By contrast I've only ever met one farang who contracted malaria in Thailand. Probably the fact that more people are outdoors in the daytime means exposure is greater. The best way to prevent dengue, as with malaria, is to take care not to be bitten by mosquitoes.

The only treatment for dengue is bed rest, constant rehydration and acetaminophen (Tylenol, Panadol). Avoid aspirin, which increases the risk of haemorrhaging. Hospital supervision is necessary in extreme cases.

Japanese Encephalitis A few years ago this viral disease was practically unheard of. Although long endemic to tropical Asia (as well as China, Korea and Japan), there have been recent rainy-season epidemics in northern Thailand and Vietnam which increase the risk for travellers. A night-biting mosquito (Culex) is the carrier for this disease and the risk is said to be greatest in rural zones near areas where pigs are raised or rice is grown, since pigs and certain wild birds, whose habitat may include rice fields, serve as reservoirs for the virus.

Persons who may be at risk in Thailand are those who will be spending long periods of time in rural areas during the rainy season (July to October). If you belong to this group, you may want to get a Japanese encephalitis vaccination. At the time of writing, the vaccine is only produced in Japan but is available in most Asian capitals. Check with the government health service in your home country before you leave to see if it's available; if not, arrange to be vaccinated in Bangkok, Hong Kong or Singapore, where the vaccine is easy to find.

Timing is important in taking the vaccine; you must receive at least two doses seven to 10 days apart. The Center for Disease Control in Atlanta, USA, recommends a third dose 21 to 30 days after the first for improved immunity. Immunity lasts about a year at which point it's necessary to get a booster shot, then it's every four years after that.

The symptoms of Japanese encephalitis are sudden fever, chills and headache, followed by vomiting and delirium, a strong aversion to bright light, and sore joints and muscles. Advanced cases may result in convulsions and coma. Estimates of the fatality rate for JE range from 5% to 60%.

As with other mosquito-borne diseases, the best way to prevent JE (outside of the vaccine) is to avoid being bitten.

Cuts & Scratches In hot, humid climates like that of Thailand even small wounds can become infected easily. Always keep cuts and scrapes scrupulously clean, especially those on the lower extremities, and you can avoid unnecessary trips to the doctor. If a small wound does become infected, clean it regularly with sterilised water and bandage it with an antibiotic balm or powder. If it's serious, you may have to take a course of antibiotic medication. If the infection is on the legs or feet, stay prone as much as possible until the infection subsides.

Many people who spend lengthy periods of time on the beaches, particularly Ko Samui, end up with infected coral cuts on their feet. Coral formations break the skin and coral particles enter the wound – these cuts are very difficult to keep clean when you're in and out of the water all the time. If a cut becomes infected, stay out of the water until it clears up. Light shoes designed for water sports, eg Nike's Aqua Socks, provide effective protection against coral as well as sea urchins.

Snake Bite To minimise your chances of being bitten always wear boots, socks and long trousers when walking through undergrowth where snakes may be present. Don't put your hands into holes and crevices and be careful when collecting firewood.

Snake bites do not cause instantaneous death and anti-venenes are usually available. Keep the victim calm and still, wrap the bitten limb tightly, as you would for a sprained ankle, and then attach a splint to immobilise it. Then seek medical help, if possible with the dead snake for identification. Don't attempt to catch the snake if there is any remote possibility of being bitten again. Tourniquets and sucking out the poison are now comprehensively discredited.

Jellyfish Local advice (as to the prevalence of jellyfish in specific areas) is the best way of avoiding contact with these sea creatures with their stinging tentacles.

Bedbugs & Lice Bedbugs live in various places, particularly dirty mattresses and bedding. Spots of blood on bedclothes or on the wall around the bed can be read as a suggestion to find another hotel. Bedbugs leave itchy bites in neat rows. Calamine lotion may help.

Lice cause itching and discomfort and make themselves at home in your hair (head lice), your clothing (body lice) or in your pubic hair (crabs). They get to you by direct contact with infected people or through the sharing of combs, clothing and the like. Powder or shampoo treatment will kill the lice, and infected clothing should then be washed in very hot water.

Leeches & Ticks Leeches may be present in damp rainforest and attach themselves to your skin to suck your blood. Trekkers often get them on their legs or in their boots. Salt or a lighted cigarette end will make them fall off. Do not pull them off as the bite is then more likely to become infected. An insect repellent may keep them away.

Vaseline, alcohol or oil will persuade a tick to let go. You should always check your body if you have been walking through a tick-infested area as they can spread typhus.

The best way to prevent leeches from attaching themselves to you is to apply insect repellent to your boots and lower trouser legs. A similarly applied solution of tobacco and water is also effective.

Women's Health

Gynaecological Problems Poor diet, lowered resistance due to overuse of antibiotics, and even contraceptive pills can lead to vaginal infections when travelling in hot climates. Keeping the genital area clean, wearing cotton underwear and skirts or loose-fitting trousers will help to prevent infections.

Yeast infections, characterised by a rash, itch and discharge, can be treated with a vinegar or even lemon juice douche or with yoghurt. Nystatin suppositories are the usual medical prescription. Trichomonas is a more

---

Traditional Thai Medicine

Western medical practices are for the most part restricted to modern hospitals and clinics in Thailand's towns and cities. In villages and rural areas a large number of Thais still practise various forms of traditional healing which were codified in Thailand over 500 years ago. Clinics and healers specialising in traditional Thai medicine can also be found in urban areas; many Thai doctors in fact offer a blend of international medicine – a term ethno-medical scholars prefer to 'Western medicine' – and indigenous medical systems.

Traditional Thai medical theory features many parallels with India's Ayurvedic healing tradition as well as Chinese medicine. In practice, however, Thai diagnostic and therapeutic techniques may differ significantly. Obviously influenced to some degree by these traditions, Thai medicine in turn has been the predominant influence on traditional medicine in Cambodia, Laos and Burma.

Most Thai medicine as practised today is based on two surviving medical texts from the Ayuthaya era, the *Scripture of Diseases* and the *Pharmacopoeia of King Narai*. Presumably many more texts were available before the Burmese sacked Ayuthaya in 1767 and destroyed the kingdom's national archives. A coexisting oral tradition passed down from healer to healer conforms to the surviving texts; other materia medica developed in the Ratanakosin (Bangkok) era are founded on both these texts and the oral tradition.

Like medical practitioners elsewhere in the world, traditional Thai physicians preform diagnoses by evaluating the pulse, heartbeat, skin colour/texture, body temperature, abnormal physical symptoms and bodily excretions (eg blood, urine, faeces) of their patients. Unlike orthodox Western doctors, Thai healers favour a holistic approach that encompasses internal, external, and psycho-spiritual conditions. Thus once diagnosed, patients may be prescribed and issued treatments from among three broad therapeutic categories.

Herbal Medicines Traditional pharmacological therapy employs prescribed herbs, either singly or in combination, from among 700 plant varieties (plus a limited number of animal sources) which are infused, boiled, powdered or otherwise rendered into a consumable form. Common household medicines *(yaa klaang bâan* in Thai) include the root and stem of *baw-ráphét (Tinospora rumphii*, a type of woodclimber) for fever reduction, *râak cha-phluu* (Piper roots) for stomach ailments, and various *yaa hãwm* (fragrant medicines) used as medicinal balms for muscle pain or headaches. Medicines of this type are readily available over the counter at traditional medicine shops and to a lesser extent in modern Thai pharmacies.

More complex remedies called *yaa tamráp luãng* (royally approved/recorded medicine) are prepared and administered only by herbalists skilled in diagnosis, as the mixture and dosage must be adjusted for each patient. One of the most well-known yaa tamrap luang is *chanthá-liilaa*, a powerful remedy for respiratory infections and influenza-induced fevers.

As in the Chinese tradition, many Thai herbs find their way into regional cuisine with the intent of enhancing health as well as taste. *Phrík thai* (black pepper, *Piper nigrum)*, *bai krà-phaw* (stomach leaf) and *bai maeng-lák* (a variety of basil) are common curry ingredients which have proven antacid/carminative properties. Thais eat soups containing *mará* (bitter melon) – a known febrifuge – to bring down a fever.

---

serious infection with a discharge and a burning sensation when urinating. Male sexual partners must also be treated and if a vinegar-water douche is not effective medical attention should be sought. Flagyl is the prescribed drug.

Pregnancy Most miscarriages occur during the first three months of pregnancy so this is the most risky time to travel. The last three months should also be spent within reasonable distance of good medical care. Pregnant women should avoid all unnecessary medication, but vaccinations and malarial prophylactics should still be taken where possible. Additional care should be taken to prevent illness and particular attention should be paid to diet and nutrition.

Hospitals & Clinics

Thailand's most technically advanced hospitals are in Bangkok. In the north, Chiang Mai

---

Massage The second and most internationally famous type of Thai medical therapy is *ráksãa thaang nûat* (massage treatment). The extensive and highly refined Thai massage system combines characteristics of massage (stroking and kneading the muscles), chiropractice (manipulating skeletal parts) and acupressure (applying deep, consistent pressure to specific nerves, tendons, or ligaments) in order to balance the functions of the four body elements *(thâat tháng sìi)*. These four elements are: earth *(din* – solid parts of the body, including nerves, skeleton, muscles, blood vessels, tendons and ligaments); water *(náam* – blood and bodily secretions); fire *(fai* – digestion and metabolism); and air *(lom* – respiration and circulation). Borrowing from India's Ayurvedic tradition, some practitioners employ Pali-Sanskrit terms for the four bodily elements: *pathavidhatu, apodhatu, tecodhatu* and *vayodhatu*.

From the Ayuthaya period until early this century, the Thai government's Department of Health included an official massage division *(phanâek mãw nûat)*. Under the influence of international medicine and modern hospital development, responsibility for the national propagation/maintenance of Thai massage was eventually transferred to Wat Phra Jetuphon (Wat Pho) in Bangkok, where it remains today. Traditional massage therapy has persisted most in the provinces, however, and has recently enjoyed a resurgence of popularity throughout the country.

Within the traditional Thai medical context, a massage therapist *(mãw nûat*, literally, 'massage doctor') usually applies Thai massage together with pharmacological and/or psycho-spiritual treatments as prescribed for a specific medical problem. Nowadays many Thais also use massage as a tool for relaxation and disease prevention, rather than for specific medical problems. Massage associated with Bangkok's Turkish baths *(àap òp nûat* or 'bathe-steam-massage' in Thai) is for the most part performed for recreational or entertainment purposes only (or as an adjunct to prostitution); the techniques used are loosely based on traditional Thai massage.

Psycho-Spiritual Healing A third aspect of traditional Thai medicine called *ráksaã thaang nai* (inner healing) or *kâe kam kaò* (literally, 'old karma repair') includes various types of meditation or visualisation practised by the patient, as well as shamanistic rituals performed by qualified healers. These strategies represent the psycho-spiritual side of Thai medical therapy, and like massage are usually practised in conjunction with other types of treatment. With the increasing acceptance of meditation, hypnosis and biofeedback in Occidental medicine, anthropologists nowadays are less inclined to classify such metaphysical therapy as 'magico-religious', accepting them instead as potentially useful adjunct therapies.

As in the West, psycho-spiritual techniques are most commonly reserved for medical conditions with no apparent physical cause or those for which other therapies have proved unsuccessful. In Thailand they are also occasionally employed as preventive measures, as in the *bai sĩi* ceremony popular in north-eastern Thailand and Laos. This elaborate ceremony, marked by the tying of string loops around a subject's wrists, is intended to bind the 32 *khwãn* or personal guardian spirits – each associated with a specific organ – to the individual. The ritual is often performed before a person departs on a long or distant journey, reasoning that one is more susceptible to illness when away from home. ■

has the best medical care; in the north-east it's Khon Kaen and in the south Hat Yai or Phuket. Elsewhere in the country, every provincial capital has at least one hospital of varying quality as well as several public and private clinics. The best emergency health care, however, can usually be found at military hospitals *(rohng phayaabaan tha-hãan* in Thai); the military hospitals will usually treat foreigners in an emergency. See the respective destination chapters for information on specific health-care facilities.

Should you need urgent dental care, suggested contacts in Bangkok include:

Bumrungrad Medical Centre
  33 Soi 3, Sukhumvit Rd (☎ 253-0250)
Ploenchit Clinic
  Maneeya Bldg, Ploenchit Rd (☎ 251-1567/8902)
Siam Dental Clinic
  412/11-2 Soi 6, Siam Square (☎ 251-6315)

Counselling Services

Qualified professionals at Community Services of Bangkok (☎ 258-5663; 15 Soi 33, Sukhumvit Rd) offer a range of counselling services to foreign residents and newcomers to Thailand.

Members of Alcoholics Anonymous who want to contact the Bangkok group or others who are interested in AA services can call 253-0305 from 7 am to 7 pm or 253-8422 from 7 pm to 7 am for information.

WOMEN TRAVELLERS

Over the past five years, several foreign women have been attacked while travelling alone in remote areas. Everyday incidents of sexual harassment are much less common in Thailand than in India, Indonesia or Malaysia and this may lull women who have recently travelled in these countries into thinking that Thailand travel is safer than it is. If you're a woman travelling alone, try to pair up with other travellers when travelling at night or in remote areas. Urban areas seem relatively safe; the exception is Chiang Mai, where there have been several reports of harassment (oddly, we've had no reports from Bangkok). Make sure hotel and guesthouse rooms are secure at night – if they're not, demand another room or move to another hotel/guesthouse.

Jii-khoh

Small upcountry restaurants are sometimes hang-outs for drunken *jii-khõh*, an all-purpose Thai term that refers to the teenage playboy-hoodlum-cowboy who gets his kicks by violating Thai cultural norms. These oafs sometimes bother foreign women (and men) who are trying to have a quiet meal ('Are you married?' and 'I love you' are common conversation openers). It's best to ignore them rather than try to make snappy comebacks – they won't understand them and will most likely take these responses as encouragement. If the jii-khohs persist, find another restaurant. Unfortunately restaurant proprietors will rarely do anything about such disturbances.

DANGERS & ANNOYANCES

Precautions

Although Thailand is in no way a dangerous country to visit, it's wise to be a little cautious, particularly if you're travelling alone. Solo women travellers should take special care on arrival at Bangkok Airport, particularly at night. Don't take one of Bangkok's often very unofficial taxis (black and white licence tags) by yourself – better the THAI bus, or even the public bus. Both men and women should ensure their rooms are securely locked and bolted at night. Inspect cheap rooms with thin walls for strategic peepholes.

Take caution when leaving valuables in hotel safes. Many travellers have reported unpleasant experiences with leaving valuables in Chiang Mai guesthouses while trekking. Make sure you obtain an itemised receipt for property left with hotels or guesthouses – note the exact quantity of travellers' cheques and all other valuables.

On the road, keep zippered luggage secured with small locks, especially while travelling on buses and trains.

Credit Cards

On return to their home countries, many visitors have received huge credit-card bills for purchases (usually jewellery) charged to their cards in Bangkok while the cards had, supposedly, been secure in the hotel or guest-house safe. It's said that over the two peak months that this first began occurring, credit-card companies lost over US$20 million in Thailand – one major company had 40% of their worldwide losses here! You might consider taking your credit cards with you if you go trekking – if they're stolen on the trail at least the bandits won't be able to use them. Organised gangs in Bangkok specialise in arranging stolen credit-card purchases – in some cases they pay 'down and out' foreigners to fake the signatures.

When making credit-card purchases, don't let vendors take your credit card out of your sight to run it through the machine. Unscrupulous merchants have been known to rub off three or four or more receipts with one credit-card purchase; after the customer leaves the shop, they use the one legitimate receipt as a model to forge your signature on the blanks, then fill in astronomical 'purchases'. Sometimes they wait several weeks – even months – between submitting each charge receipt to the bank, so that you can't remember whether you'd been billed at the same vendor more than once.

Druggings

On trains and buses, particularly in the south, beware of friendly strangers offering cigarettes, drinks or sweets (candy). Several travellers have reported waking up with a headache sometime later to find that their valuables have disappeared. One letter reported how a would-be druggist considerably overdid it with what looked like a machine-wrapped, made-in-England Cadbury's chocolate. His girlfriend spat it out immediately, while he woke up nine hours later in hospital having required emergency resuscitation after his breathing nearly stopped. This happened on the Surat Thani to Phuket bus.

Travellers have also encountered drugged food or drink from friendly strangers in bars and from prostitutes in their own hotel rooms. Thais are also occasional victims, especially at the Moh Chit bus terminal and Chatuchak Park, where young girls are drugged and sold to brothels. Conclusion – don't accept gifts from strangers.

Assault

Robbery of farangs by force is very rare in Thailand, but it does happen. In 1988, two British women were robbed and killed on the island of Ko Chang in Trat Province while hiking across the island at night. Another woman was attacked and killed near Tham Lot in Mae Hong Son Province the previous year while hiking alone and I've heard a similar report from Ko Tarutao. A lone male motorcyclist was shot several times (he survived) on the road to Sangkhlaburi in Kanchanaburi Province in '87 and another man was shot on Ko Samui while walking back to his bungalow at night. Two boats carrying tourists on the Kok River in Chiang Rai were attacked by armed bandits the same year. A male New Zealander lagged behind his trekking group in Mae Hong Son and was shot dead during a robbery attempt.

Approximately eight million people travelled through Thailand in 1987 and 1988 and these are the only incidents of extreme violence I've heard of, so the risk of armed robbery should be considered fairly low. Since 1989 I've received no reports of deadly assault on foreign tourists, so perhaps '87-88 was just a bad couple of years. On the other hand, the clear message here is that the safest practice in remote areas is not to go out alone at night and, if trekking in north Thailand, always walk in groups. More information on hill trekking is given in the Northern Thailand chapter.

Touts

Touting – grabbing newcomers in the street or in railway stations, bus terminals or airports to sell them a service – is a long-time tradition in Asia, and while Thailand doesn't have as many as, say, India, it has its share. In the popular tourist spots it seems like

Scams

Thais are generally so friendly and laid-back that some visitors are lulled into a false sense of security that makes them particularly vulnerable to scams and con schemes of all kinds. Scammers tend to haunt areas where first-time tourists go, such as Bangkok's Grand Palace area. Though you could meet them anywhere in Thailand, the overwhelming majority of scams take place in Bangkok, with Chiang Mai a very distant second.

Most scams begin the same way: a friendly Thai male approaches a lone visitor – usually newly arrived – and strikes up a seemingly innocuous conversation. Sometimes the con man says he's a university student, other times he may claim to work for the World Bank or a similarly distinguished organisation. Eventually the conversation works its way around to the subject of the scam – the better con men can actually make it seem like *you* initiated the topic. That's one of the most bewildering aspects of the con – afterwards victims remember that the whole thing seemed like their idea, not the con artist's.

The scam itself almost always involves either gems or card playing. With gems, the victims find themselves invited to a gem and jewellery shop – your new-found friend is picking up some merchandise for himself and you're just along for the ride. Somewhere along the way he usually claims to have a connection – often a relative – in your home country (what a coincidence!) with whom he has a regular gem export-import business. One way or another, victims are convinced (usually they convince themselves) that they can turn a profit by arranging a gem purchase and reselling the merchandise at home. After all, the jewellery shop just happens to be offering a generous discount today – it's a government or religious holiday, or perhaps it's the shop's 10th anniversary, or maybe they just take a liking to you!

There are a seemingly infinite number of variations on the gem scam, almost all of which end up with the victim making a purchase of small, low-quality sapphires and posting them to their home countries. (If they let you walk out with them, you might return for a refund after realising you'd been taken.) Once you return home, of course, the cheap sapphires turn out to be worth much less than what you paid for them (perhaps one-tenth to one-half). A jeweller in Perth, Australia says he sees about 12 persons a week who have been conned in Thailand. Many have invested and lost virtually all their savings.

Even if you were somehow able to return your purchase to the gem shop in question (I knew one fellow who actually intercepted his parcel at the airport before it left Thailand), chances are slim to none they'd give a full refund. The con artist who brings the mark into the shop gets a commission of 10 to 50% per sale – the shop takes the rest.

---

everyone – young boys waving flyers, tuk-tuk drivers, samlor drivers, schoolgirls – is touting something, usually hotels or guest-houses. For the most part they're completely harmless and sometimes they can be very informative. But take anything a tout says with two large grains of salt. Since touts work on commission and get paid just for delivering you to a guesthouse or hotel (whether you check in or not), they'll say anything to get you to the door.

Often the best (most honest and reliable) hotels and guesthouses refuse to pay tout commissions – so the average tout will try to steer you away from such places. Hence don't believe them if they tell you the hotel or guesthouse you're looking for is 'closed', 'full', 'dirty' or 'bad'. Sometimes (rarely) they're right but most times it's just a ruse to get you to a place that pays more commission. Always have a careful look yourself before checking into a place recommended by a tout. Tuk-tuk and samlor drivers often offer free or low-cost rides to the place they're touting; if you have another place you're interested in, you might agree to go with a driver only if he or she promises to deliver you to your first choice after you've had a look at the place being touted. If drivers refuse, chances are it's because they know your first choice is a better one.

This type of commission work isn't limited to low-budget guesthouses. Taxi drivers and even airline employees at Thailand's major airports – including Bangkok and Chiang Mai – reap commissions from the big hotels as well. At either end of the budget spectrum, the customer

The Thai police are usually of no help whatsoever, believing that merchants are entitled to whatever price they can get. The main victimisers are a handful of shops who get protection from certain high-ranking government officials. These officials put pressure on police not to prosecute or to take as little action as possible. Even the TAT tourist police have never been able to prosecute a Thai jeweller, even in cases of blatant, recurring gem fraud. A Thai police commissioner was recently convicted of fraud in an investigation into a jewellery theft by Thais in Saudi Arabia which resulted in the commissioner's replacing the Saudi gems with fakes!

The card-playing scam starts out much the same – a friendly stranger approaches the lone traveller on the street, strikes up a conversation and then invites you to the house or apartment of his sister (or brother-in-law, etc) for a drink or meal. After a bit of socialising a friend or relative of the con arrives on the scene; it just so happens a little high-stakes card game is planned for later that day. Like the gem scam, the card-game scam has many variations, but eventually the victim is shown some cheating tactics to use with help from the 'dealer', some practice sessions take place and finally the game gets under way with several high rollers at the table. The mark is allowed to win a few hands first, then somehow loses a few, gets bankrolled by one of the friendly Thais, and then loses the Thai's money. Suddenly your new-found buddies aren't so friendly anymore – they want the money you lost. Sometimes the con pretends to be dismayed by it all. Sooner or later you end up cashing in most or all of your travellers' cheques.

Again the police won't take any action – in this case because gambling is illegal in Thailand so you've broken the law by playing cards for money.

The common denominator in all scams of this nature is that the victims' own greed – the desire for an easy score – was their downfall. Other minor scams involve tuk-tuk drivers, hotel employees and bar girls who take new arrivals on city tours; these almost always end up in high-pressure sales situations at silk, jewellery or handicraft shops. In this case greed isn't the ruling motivation – it's simply a matter of weak sales resistance.

Follow TAT's number-one suggestion to tourists: disregard all offers of free shopping or sightseeing help from strangers – they invariably take a commission from your purchases. I would add to this: beware of deals that seem too good to be true – they're usually neither good nor true.

Whether they're able to take any action or not, the TAT now has 'regulatory' powers over shops catering to tourists – you should contact the tourist police if you have any problems with consumer fraud. The tourist police headquarters (☎ 221-6206) is at the Crime Suppression Division, 509 Worachak Rd; you can also contact them through the TAT office on Ratchadamnoen Nok Rd. There is also a new police unit that deals specifically with gem swindles (☎ 254-1067, 235-4017). ■

ends up paying the commission indirectly through raised room rates. Bangkok International Airport employees are notorious for talking newly arrived tourists into staying at badly located, overpriced hotels.

Insurgent Activity

Since the 1920s and 1930s several insurgent groups have operated in Thailand: the Communist Party of Thailand (CPT) with its tactical force; the People's Liberation Army of Thailand (PLAT) in rural areas all over Thailand; and Malay separatists and Muslim revolutionaries in the extreme south. These groups have been mainly involved in propaganda activity, village infiltration and occasional clashes with Thai government troops. Very rarely have they had any encounters with foreign travellers. Aside from sporadic terrorist bombings – mostly in railway stations in the south and sometimes at upcountry festivals – 'innocent' people have not been involved in the insurgent activity. In fact there haven't been any bombings of this nature since the early '80s.

In 1976, the official government estimate of the number of active guerrillas in Thailand was 10,000. By the end of the '70s, however, many CPT followers had surrendered under the government amnesty programme. In the '80s new military strategies, as well as political measures, reduced the number to around two to three thousand.

Only a few dozen CPT guerrillas are still active in Thailand, and these are mainly involved in local extortion rackets under the guise of 'village indoctrination'.

Part of the reason for the CPT's severely

curtailed influence stems from the 1979 split between the CPT and the Chinese Communist Party over policy differences regarding Indo-Chinese revolution – CPT cadres used to receive training in Kunming, China. New highways in previously remote provinces such as Nan and Loei have contributed to improved communications, stability and central (Bangkok) control. This means that most routes in these provinces that were closed to foreigners in the '70s are now open for travel, eg Phitsanulok to Loei via Nakhon Thai. Travellers should also be able to travel from Nan to Loei by bus, and from Chiang Rai to Nan via Chiang Muan. A new road between Phattalung and Hat Yai has cut travel time between those two cities considerably.

In the north and north-east, the government claims that armed resistance has been virtually eliminated and this appears to be verified by independent sources as well as by my own travel experiences through former CPT strongholds. One area that supposedly remains active is a pocket of eastern Nan Province on the Laos border – the Thai government in fact doesn't allow visitors or even its own citizens into this area. Smaller, functionally inactive pockets reportedly still exist in parts of Sakon Nakhon, Tak and Phetburi provinces.

In the south, traditionally a hot spot, communist forces have been all but limited to Camp 508 in a relatively inaccessible area along the Surat Thani-Nakhon Si Thammarat provincial border. The Betong area of Yala Province on the Thai-Malaysian border was until recently the tactical headquarters for the armed Communist Party of Malaya (CPM). Thai and Malaysian government troops occasionally clashed with the insurgents, who from time to time hijacked trucks along the Yala to Betong road. But in December 1989, in exchange for amnesty, the CPM agreed 'to terminate all armed activities' and to respect the laws of Thailand and Malaysia. It appears that this area is now safe for travel.

Cynics note that it's in the Thai army's best interests to claim that communist insurgency still exists, that this notion is used to justify a larger standing army, higher military budgets and continuing political involvements in Bangkok. Most observers do not expect communist guerrilla activity to flare again any time in the foreseeable future. This seems especially true in the light of the great economic strides Thailand has made during the last decade, which have simply made Marxism a less compelling alternative for most of the population. The softening of socialism in adjacent Cambodia and Laos have also greatly reduced the possibility of 'infiltration'.

One continuing thorn in the side of the Thai government is the small but militant Malay-Muslim movement in the south. A group of 111 Muslim separatists belonging to the Pattani United Liberation Organisation (PULO), Barisan Revolusi Nasional (BRN, or National Revolutionary Front) and Barisan Nasional Pembebasan Pattani (BNPP, or National Front for the Freedom of Pattani) surrendered in late '91. PULO formed in 1957, trained in Libya and reached its peak in '81 with a guerrilla strength of around 1800. This was its fourth mass surrender in five years – only a few dozen guerrillas are still active, mainly involved in propaganda activities plus the occasional attack on Thai government vehicles.

Hot Spots Probably the most sensitive areas in Thailand nowadays are the Cambodian and Burmese border areas. Most dangerous is the Thai-Cambodian border area, where Cambodia's former Vietnamese-backed regime sealed the border against the Khmer Rouge with heavy armament, land mines and booby traps. Most but not all of the latter are planted inside Cambodian territory, so it is imperative that you stay away from this border – it will be at least 10 years before the mines are cleared. Armed Khmer bandits are occasionally encountered in the vicinity of Aranyaprathet (but not in Aranyaprathet itself), still considered a risky area for casual travel. The good news is that the Phra Wihaan ruins just inside Cambodia near Ubon are now open to visitors from the Thai side (see the Ubon section in the North-East Thailand chapter for details).

The Burmese border between Mae Sot and Mae Sariang occasionally receives shelling from Burmese troops in pursuit of Karen rebels. The rebels are trying to maintain an independent nation called Kawthoolei along the border with Thailand. If you cross and are captured by the Burmese, you will automatically be suspected of supporting the Karen. If you are captured by the Karen you will probably be released, though they may demand money. The risks of catching a piece of shrapnel are substantially lower if you keep several km between yourself and the Thai-Burmese border in this area – fighting can break out at any time. Mae Sot itself is quite safe these days, though you can still occasionally hear mortar fire in the distance.

In the Three Pagodas Pass area, there is also occasional fighting between Burmese, Karen and Mon armies, who are competing for control over the smuggling trade between Burma and Thailand. Typically, the rebels advance in the rainy season and retreat in the dry; lately this area has been fairly quiet. Along the Burmese-Thai border in northern Mae Hong Son and Chiang Rai provinces, the presence of Shan and Kuomintang armies make this area dangerous if you attempt to travel near opium trade border crossings – obviously these are not signposted, so take care anywhere along the border in this area.

Drugs

Opium, heroin and marijuana are widely used in Thailand, but it is illegal to buy, sell or possess these drugs in any quantity (the exception is opium, possession of which is legal for consumption – but not sale – among hill tribes). A lesser known narcotic, *kratom* (a leaf of the *Mitragyna speciosa* tree), is used by workers and students as a stimulant – similar to Yemen's *qat*. A hundred kratom leaves sell for around 30B, and are sold for 1 to 3B each; the leaf is illegal and said to be addictive.

In the south, especially on the rainy Gulf islands, mushrooms (in Thai *hèt khîi khwai*, 'buffalo-shit mushrooms', or *hèt mao*, 'drunk mushrooms') which contain the hallucinogen psilocybin are sometimes sold to or gathered by foreigners. The legal status of mushroom use or possession is questionable; police have been known to hassle Thais who sell them. Using such mushrooms is a risky proposition as the dosage is always uncertain; I've heard one confirmed story of a farang who swam to his death off Ko Pha-Ngan after a 'special' mushroom omelette.

Although in certain areas of the country drugs seem to be used with some impunity, enforcement is arbitrary – the only way not to risk getting caught is to avoid the scene entirely. Every year perhaps dozens of visiting foreigners are arrested in Thailand for drug use or trafficking and end up doing hard time. A smaller but significant number die of heroin overdoses.

Penalties for drug offences are stiff: if you're caught using marijuana, you face a fine and/or up to one year in prison, while for heroin, the penalty for use can be anywhere from six months to 10 years' imprisonment. In the table below, 'smuggling' refers to any drug possession at a border or airport customs check.

Drug	Quantity	Penalty
Marijuana		
Smuggling	any amount	2 to 15 years imprisonment
Possession	less than 10 kg	up to 5 years imprisonment
Possession	10 kg +	2 to 15 years imprisonment
Heroin		
Smuggling	any amount	life imprisonment
Smuggling with intent to sell	any amount	execution
Possession	10 grams +	imprisonment or execution

ACTIVITIES

Diving & Snorkelling

Thailand's two coastlines and countless islands are popular among divers for their mild waters and colourful marine life. The biggest diving centre is Pattaya, simply because it's less than two hours' drive from Bangkok. There are several islands with reefs within a short boat ride from Pattaya and the little town is packed with dive shops. Phuket is the second biggest jumping-off point and has the advantage of offering the largest variety of places to choose from – small offshore islands less than an hour away, Ao Phang-Nga (a one to two-hour boat ride) with its unusual rock formations and clear green waters, and the world-famous Similan and Surin islands in the Andaman Sea (about four hours away by fast boat).

The up-and-coming area is Chumphon Province, just north of Surat Thani, where there are a dozen or so islands with undisturbed reefs. Most dive shops rent equipment at reasonable rates and some also offer basic instruction and NAUI or PADI qualification for first-timers.

All of these places have areas that are suitable for snorkelling as well as scuba diving, since many reefs are no deeper than two metres. Masks, fins and snorkels are readily available for rent not only at dive centres but also through guesthouses located in beach areas. If you're particular about the quality and condition of the equipment you use, however, you might be better off bringing your own mask and snorkel – some of the stuff for rent is second-rate. And people with large heads may have difficulty finding masks that fit since most of the masks are made or imported for Thai heads.

Some established diving centres are:

Pattaya

Dave's Diver's Den, North Pattaya (☎ (034) 429382)
Max's Dive Shop, Nipa Lodge Hotel, North Pattaya Rd (☎ (034) 428195/321)
Seafari Sports Centre, Royal Garden Beach Resort, South Pattaya (☎ (034) 428126/7)
The Reef Dive Shop, Ocean View Hotel (☎ (034) 428084)
Pattaya International Diving Centre, Siam Bayview Hotel (☎ (034) 428728)
Steve Dive Shop, 579 Soi 4, Beach Rd (☎ (034) 428392)

Phuket

Phuket International Diving Centre, Coral Beach Hotel, Patong Beach (☎ (076) 321106)
Loan Island Resort, Ao Chalong (☎ (076) 211253; 314-5332 in Bangkok)
Sun & Sand Tour Pearl Hotel, Phuket Town (☎ (076) 211901/3; 260-1022/7 in Bangkok)
Andaman Divers 83/8 Thawiwong Rd, Patong Beach (☎ (076) 321155)
Fantasea Divers Patong Beach (☎ (076) 321209)
Marina Sports Marina Cottage, Kata-Karon Beach (☎ (076) 212901/4)
Ocean Divers Patong Beach Hotel (☎ (076) 321166)
Phuket Aquatic Safari 62/0 Rasada Centre, Rasada Rd, Phuket Town (☎ (076) 216562)
Poseidon Memrod Club Phuket Island Resort (☎ (076) 215950/5)
Santana Patong Beach (☎ (076) 321360)
Siam Diving Centre, Kata-Karon Beach (☎ (076) 212901)

Chumphon

Chumphon Cabana Thung Wua Lan Beach (☎ (077) 511885; 224-1884 in Bangkok)
Pornsawan Home Paknam (☎ (077) 521031; 427-1360 in Bangkok)

Bangkok

Thai Diving Centre 44/1 Soi 21, Sukhumvit Rd (☎ 258-3662)
Sea Frog Thai Co 397/1 Soi Siri Chulasewok, Silom Rd (☎ 235-9438)

Several nonprofit diving associations and clubs also exist in Thailand; most of their members are long-term Thai and expat residents. Joining a club trip is an excellent way to meet Thais and farangs with a strong interest in Thailand's dive scene. The country's longest running diving association is the Thailand Sub-Aqua Club (☎ 256-0170, ext 298; ask for Scott Klimo), PO Box 11-1196, Bangkok, 10110. The club offers dive trips and certification year-round.

Golf

Golfing in Thailand? It's not my sport, but golf addicts can get a fix at any of nearly 50 courses in Thailand. Green fees range from 400 to 1000B depending on the day of the week and quality of the course (except for the Navatanee, which is 1100B (!) weekdays, 2200B weekends). Caddy fees are 50 to 150B (caddies are often women) and clubs can be rented for 150 to 300B. Here are a few courses that accept nonmembers:

Bangkok

Krungthep Kretha Golf Course. Closest course to central Bangkok aside from the Royal Dusit. More than 900 caddies work here – Si Nakharin Rd, (☎ 374-6063).

Navatanee Golf Course, 5679 metres, par 72. Top-rated course designed by Robert Trent Jones. Also has gymnasium and swimming pool – 22 Mu 1, Sukhaphiban 2 Rd, Bangkapi, Bangkok (☎ 374-7077)

Railway Training Centre Golf Course, 6052 metres, par 72. Thailand's first 36-hole course, fairly flat, near the airport. Also has swimming pool and tennis courts – Vibhavadi Rangsit Rd, Bangkhen, Bangkok (☎ 271-0130).

Rose Garden Golf Course, 5856 metres, par 72. One of Thailand's most beautiful courses, tight fairways, and usually empty during the week – Rose Garden Resort, Highway 4 (☎ 253-0295).

Royal Dusit Golf Course, 4476 metres, par 66. In the Royal Turf Club in central Bangkok, closed on race days – Phitsanulok Rd (☎ 281-4320).

Outside Bangkok

Phlu Ta Luang Golf Course, 6188 metres, par 72. Thailand's 2nd longest course, part of the Sattahip Royal Navy base. This is a tough course – Sattahip, Chonburi (about 30 km south of Pattaya) (☎ (02) 466-1180).

Khao Yai Golf Course, 9 holes, 2712 metres, par 36. This course has high elevation and cool weather – Khao Yai National Park, Khorat (contact TAT for reservations).

Royal Hua Hin Golf Course, 6055 metres, par 72. Oldest course in Thailand (founded 1924), and features rolling hills – Hua Hin, Prachuap Khiri Khan (☎ (032) 511099).

Phuket Golf & Country Club, 5818 metres, par 72. Newly opened, hilly – off main road between Phuket and Patong Beach (☎ (076) 213388).

Tong Yai Golf Course, 9 holes. Easy course, low fees – Samila Hotel, Songkhla (☎ (074) 311310).

Lanna Golf Course, 6528 metres, par 72. Thailand's longest play, medium difficulty, cool December to January – Highway 107, Chiang Mai (☎ (053) 221-911).

COURSES

Thai Language Study

Several language schools in Bangkok and Chiang Mai offer courses for foreigners in Thai language. Tuition fees average around 250B per hour. Some places will let you trade English lessons for Thai lessons, if not, you can usually teach English on the side to offset tuition costs. There are three recommended schools in Bangkok:

Union Language School
CCT Building, 109 Surawong Rd (☎ 233-4482). Generally recognised as the best and most rigorous course (many missionaries study here). Employs a balance of structure-oriented and communication-oriented methodologies in 80-hour, four-week modules. Private tuition is also available.

AUA Language Center
179 Rajadamri (Ratchadamri) Rd (☎ 252-8170). American University Alumni (AUA) runs one of the largest English-language teaching institutes in the world, so this is a good place to meet Thai students. On the other hand, farangs who study Thai here complain that there's not enough interaction in class because of an emphasis on the so-called 'natural approach', which focuses on teacher input rather than student practice. AUA also has a branch in Chiang Mai.

Nisa Thai Language School
YMCA Collins House, 27 Sathon Tai Rd (☎ 286-9323). This school has a fairly good reputation, though teachers may be less qualified than at Union or AUA language schools. In addition to all the usual levels, Nisa offers a course in preparing for the Baw Hok or Grade 6 examination, a must for anyone wishing to work in the public school system.

Chulalongkorn University in Bangkok, the most prestigious university in Thailand, offers an intensive Thai studies course called 'Perspectives on Thailand'.

The four-week programme includes classes in Thai language, culture, history, politics and economics. Classes meet six hours a day, six days a week (Saturday is usually a field trip) and are offered twice a year: January to February and July to August. Students who have taken the course say they have found the quality of instruction excellent. Tuition is US$1000. Room and board on campus are available though it's much less expensive to live off campus. For further information write to Perspectives on Thailand, 7th Floor, Sasin Graduate Institute of Business Administration, Chulalongkorn University, Bangkok.

The YWCA's Siri Pattana Thai Language School (☎ 286-1936), 13 Sathon Tai Rd, gives Thai language lessons as well as preparation for the Baw Hok exam. Siri Pattana has a second branch at 806 Soi 38, Sukhumvit Rd.

Meditation Study

Thailand has long been a popular place for Western students of Buddhism, particularly those interested in a system of meditation known as *vipassana* (Thai: *wí-pàt-sa-nāa)*, a Pali word which roughly translated means 'insight'. Foreigners who come to Thailand to study vipassana can choose among dozens of temples and study centres which specialise in these teachings. Teaching methods vary from place to place but the general emphasis is on learning to observe mind-body processes from moment to moment. Thai language is usually the medium of instruction but several places also provide instruction in English.

Information on some of the more popular meditation-oriented temples and centres is given in the relevant sections. Instruction and accommodation are free of charge at temples, though donations are expected. Short-term students will find that two-month tourist visas are ample for most courses of study. Long-term students may want to consider a three or six-month non-immigrant visa. A few Westerners are ordained as monks in order to take full advantage of the monastic environment. Monks are generally (but not always) allowed to stay in Thailand as long as they remain in robes. For a detailed look at vipassana study in Thailand, including visa and ordination procedures, read *The Meditation Temples of Thailand: A Guide* (Wayfarer Books, PO Box 5927, Concord, California 94524, USA).

Martial Arts Training

Thai Boxing (Muay Thai) Many Westerners have trained in Thailand (especially since the release of Jean-Claude Van Damme's martial arts flick, *The Kick Boxer*, which was filmed on location in Thailand), but few last more than a week or two in a Thai camp – and fewer still have gone on to compete on Thailand's pro circuit. One farang who went pro in Thailand was Dale Kvalheim, a Dutch once ranked No 10 at Ratchadamnoen Stadium and champion of North-East Thailand from 1972 to 1975. Retired from the ring, Dale now directs muay thai seminars for farangs in Thailand: contact Thai Championship Boxing, (☎ 234-5360; fax 236-7242), Box 1996, Bangkok.

Those interested in training at a traditional muay thai camp might try the PB Boxing Gym on Khao San Rd in Bangkok (behind PB Guest House), the Sityodthong-Payakarun Boxing Camp in Naklua (north of Pattaya) or Fairtex Boxing Camp outside Bangkok (c/o Bunjong Busarakamwongs, Fairtex Garments Factory, 734-742 Trok Kai, Anuwong Rd, Bangkok). Be forewarned, though, that the training is gruelling and features full-contact sparring.

For more information about Thai boxing, see the Sport section in the Facts about the Country chapter.

Krabi-Krabong Krabi-krabong (a traditional Thai martial art; see under Sport in the Facts about the Country chapter for more information) is taught at several Thai colleges and universities, but currently the country's best training venue is the Buddhai

Sawan Fencing School of Thailand (5/1 Phetkasem Rd, Thonburi), where Ajaan Samai Mesamarna carries on the tradition as passed down from Wat Phutthaisawan. Several farangs have trained here, including one American who recently became the first foreigner to attain *ajaan* (master) status.

The *Modern Gladiator Journal* (fax 312-201-9399, PO Box 5619, Chicago, Illinois 60680, USA) is a homespun quarterly devoted to Thai martial arts training and competition.

ACCOMMODATION

Places to stay are abundant, varied and reasonably priced in Thailand.

However, just a word of warning about touts: don't believe them if they say a place is closed, full, dirty or crooked. Sometimes they're right but most times it's just a ruse to get you to a place that pays more commission. (See the earlier Dangers & Annoyances section for more information about touts.)

Guesthouses, Hostels & YMCA/YWCAs

Guesthouses are generally the cheapest accommodation in Thailand and are found in most areas where travellers go in central, north and south Thailand, and are spreading slowly to the east and north-east as well. Guesthouses vary quite a bit in facilities and are particularly popular in Bangkok and Chiang Mai where stiff competition keeps rates low. Some are especially good value, while others are mere flophouses. Many serve food, although there tends to be a bland sameness to meals in guesthouses wherever you are in Thailand.

There is a Thai YHA (25/2 Phitsanulok Rd, Sisao Thewet, Dusit, Bangkok 10300) with member hostels in Bangkok (one), Chiang Mai (three), Chiang Rai (one), Phitsanulok (one), Kanchanaburi (one), Ko Phi Phi (one) and Nan (one). Thai youth hostels range in price from 40B for a dorm bed to 150B for a room. As of 1992, only International Youth Hostel Federation (IYHF) card holders are accepted as guests in Thai hostels; memberships cost 300B per year or 50B for a temporary (one-night) membership.

A YMCA or YWCA costs a bit more than a guesthouse or hostel (an average of 125B and above) and sometimes more than a local hotel, but are generally good value. There are Ys in Bangkok, Chiang Mai and Chiang Rai.

Chinese-Thai Hotels

The standard Thai hotels, often run by Chinese-Thai families, are the easiest accommodation to come by and generally have very reasonable rates (average 60 to 90B for rooms without bath and air-con, or 100 to 200B with bath). They may be located on the main street of town and/or near bus and railway stations.

The most economical hotels to stay in are those without air-con; typical rooms are clean and include a double bed and a ceiling fan. Some have attached Thai-style bathrooms (this will cost a little more). Rates may or may not be posted; if not, they may be increased for the farang, so it is worthwhile bargaining. It is best to have a look around before agreeing to check in, to make sure the room *is* clean, that the fan and lights work and so on. If there is any problem, request another room or a good discount. If possible, always choose a room off the street and away from the front lounge to cut down on ambient noise.

For a room without air-con, ask for a ***hâwng thammádaa*** (ordinary room) or ***hâwng phát lom*** (fan room). A room with air-con is ***hâwng ae***. Sometimes farangs asking for air-con are automatically offered a 'VIP' room, which usually comes with air-con, hot water, fridge and TV at about twice the price of a regular air-con room.

Some Chinese-Thai hotels may double as brothels; the perpetual traffic in and out can be a bit noisy but is generally bearable. Unaccompanied males are often asked if they want female companionship when checking into inexpensive hotels. Even certain middle-class (by Thai standards) hotels are reserved for the 'salesman' crowd, meaning travelling Thai businessmen who frequently expect extra night-time services.

The cheapest hotels may have their names posted in Thai and Chinese only, but you will learn how to find and identify them with experience. Many of these hotels have restaurants downstairs; if they don't, there are usually restaurants and noodle shops nearby.

National Park Accommodation/Camping

Thailand has 66 national parks and nine historical parks. All but 10 of the national parks have bungalows for rent that sleep as many as 10 people for rates of 500 to 1500B, depending on the park and the size of the bungalow.

Camping is allowed in all but four of the national parks (Nam Tok Phliu in Chanthaburi Province, Doi Suthep-Pui in Chiang Mai Province, Hat Chao Mai in Trang Province and Thap Laan in Prachinburi Province) for only 5B per person per night. A few parks also have *reuan tháew* or long houses, where rooms are around 150 to 200B for two, and/or tents on platforms for 50 to 60B a night.

A few of the historical parks have bungalows with rates comparable to those in the national parks, mostly for use by visiting archaeologists.

Universities/Schools

College and university campuses may be able to provide inexpensive accommodation during the summer vacation (March to June). There are universities in Chiang Mai, Nakhon Pathom, Khon Kaen, Mahasarakham and Songkhla. Outside Bangkok there are also teachers' colleges *(wítháyálai khruu)* in every provincial capital which may offer accommodation during the summer vacation.

Tourist Class & Luxury Hotels

These are found only in the main tourist destinations: Bangkok, Chiang Mai, Chiang Rai, Kanchanaburi, Pattaya, Ko Samui, Songkhla, Phuket and Hat Yai. Prices start at around 600B outside Bangkok and Chiang Mai and proceed to 2000B or more – genuine tourist-class hotels in Bangkok start at 1000B or so and go to 2500B for standard rooms, and up to 5000 or 10,000B for a suite. These will all have air-con, TV, Western-style toilets and restaurants. Added to room charges will be an 11% government tax, and most of these hotels will include an additional service charge of 8 to 10%.

The Oriental in Bangkok, rated as the number-one hotel in the world by several executive travel publications, starts at 3100B for a standard single and tops off at 20,000B for a deluxe suite.

Temple Lodgings

If you are a Buddhist or can make a good show of it, you may be able to stay overnight in some temples for a small donation. Facilities are very basic though and early rising is expected. Temple lodgings are usually for men only, unless the wat has a place for lay women to stay. See the section on Meditation Study in the Facts for the Visitor chapter for information on wats in Thailand which will accommodate long-term lay students.

FOOD

Some people take to the food in Thailand immediately while others don't; Thai dishes can be pungent and spicy – a lot of garlic and chillies are used, especially *phrík khîi nũu* (literally, 'mouse-shit peppers') – these are the small torpedo-shaped devils which can

---

Bathing in Thailand

Upcountry, the typical Thai bathroom consists of a tall earthen water jar fed by a spigot and a plastic or metal bowl. You bathe by scooping water out of the water jar and sluicing it over the body. It's very refreshing during the hot and rainy seasons, but takes a little stamina during the cool season if you're not used to it. If the 'bathroom' has no walls, or if you are bathing at a public well or spring in an area where there are no bathrooms, you should bathe while wearing the *phâakhamãa* (sarong for men) or *phâasîn* (sarong for women); bathing nude would offend the Thais. ■

be pushed aside if you are timid about red-hot curries. Almost all Thai food is cooked with fresh ingredients, including vegetables, poultry, pork and some beef. Plenty of lime juice, lemon grass and fresh coriander leaf are added to give the food its characteristic tang, and fish sauce *(náam plaa,* generally made from anchovies) or shrimp paste *(kà-pì)* to make it salty. Rice *khâo* is eaten with most meals.

Other common seasonings include laos or galanga root *(khàa)*, black pepper, three kinds of basil, ground peanuts (more often a condiment), tamarind juice *(náam makhãam)*, ginger *(khĩng)* and coconut milk *(kà-tí)*. The Thais eat a lot of what could be called Chinese food, which is generally, but not always, less spicy. In the north and north-east 'sticky', or glutinous rice *(khâo nĩaw)*, is common and is traditionally eaten with the hands.

Where to Eat

Restaurants or food stalls outside Bangkok usually do not have menus, so it is worth-while memorising a standard 'repertoire' of dishes. Most provinces have their own local specialities in addition to the standards and you might try asking for 'whatever is good', allowing the proprietors to choose for you. Of course, you might get stuck with a large bill this way, but with a little practice in Thai social relations you may get some very pleas-ant results.

The most economical places to eat – and the most dependable – are noodle shops *(ráan kũaytĩaw)*, curry-rice shops *(ráan khâo kaeng)* and night markets *(talàat tôh rûng)*. Most towns and villages have at least one night market and several noodle and/or curry-rice shops. The night markets in Chiang Mai have a slight reputation for over-charging (especially for large parties), but on the other hand I have never been overcharged for food anywhere in Thailand. It helps if you speak Thai as much as possible. Curry shops are generally open for breakfast and lunch only, and are also a very cheap source for nutritious food.

If you're interested in learning how to prepare Thai cuisine, see the section on Thai Cooking Schools in the Bangkok chapter.

What to Eat

Thai food is served with a variety of condi-ments and sauces, including ground red pepper *(phrík bon)*, ground peanuts *(thùa)*, vinegar with sliced chillies *(náam sôm phrík)*, fish sauce with chillies *(náam plaa phrík)*, a spicy red sauce called *náam phrík sĩi raachaa* (from Si Racha, of course) and any number of other dipping sauces *(náam jîm)* for particular dishes. Soy sauce *(náam síi-yú)* can be requested, though this is nor-mally used as a condiment for Chinese food only.

Except for the 'rice plates' and noodle dishes, Thai meals are usually ordered family-style, which is to say that two or more people order together, sharing different dishes. Traditionally, the party orders one of each kind of dish, eg one chicken, one fish, one soup, etc. One dish is generally large enough for two people. One or two extras may be ordered for a large party. If you come to eat at a Thai restaurant alone and order one of these 'entrees', you had better be hungry or know enough Thai to order a small portion. This latter alternative is not really too acceptable socially: Thais generally con-sider eating alone in a restaurant unusual – but then as a farang you're an exception anyway.

A cheaper alternative is to order dishes 'over rice' or *râat khâo*. Curry *(kaeng)* over rice is called *khâo kaeng*; in a standard curry shop khâo kaeng is only 7 to 10B a plate.

Another category of Thai food is called *kàp klâem* – dishes meant to be eaten while drinking alcoholic beverages. On some menus these are translated as 'snacks' or 'appetisers'. Typical kap klaem include *thùa thâwt* (fried peanuts), *kài sãam yàang* (liter-ally 'three kinds of chicken', a plate of chopped ginger, peanuts, mouse-shit peppers and bits of lime – to be mixed and eaten by hand) and various kinds of *yam*, Thai-style salads made with lots of chillies and lime juice.

Note that in Places to Eat sections, tonal

accents have been included for all Thai dishes.

Vegetarian Those visitors who wish to avoid eating all animal food while in Thailand can be accommodated with some effort. Vegetarian restaurants are increasing in number throughout the country, thanks largely to Bangkok's ex-Governor Chamlong Srimuang, who's strict vegetarianism has inspired a nonprofit chain of vegetarian restaurants (Thai: *ráan aahãan mangsàwírát)* in Bangkok and several provincial capitals. Look for the green sign out front with one or two large Thai numerals – each restaurant is numbered according to the order in which it was established. The food at these restaurants is usually served buffet-style and is very inexpensive – 5 to 8B per dish.

Another easy though less widespread venue for vegetarian meals include Indian restaurants, which usually feature a vegetarian section on the menu. Currently these are most prevalent in Bangkok, Chiang Mai, Pattaya and Phuket's Patong Beach. Chinese restaurants are also a good bet since many Chinese Buddhists eat vegetarian food during Buddhist festivals, especially in southern Thailand.

More often than not, however, visiting vegetarians are left to their own devices at the average Thai restaurant. In Thai the magic words are *phõm kin jeh* (for men) or *dii-chãn kin jeh* (women). Like other Thai phrases, getting the tones right makes all the difference – the key word, *jeh*, should rhyme with the English 'jay' without the 'y'. Loosely translated this phrase means 'I eat only vegetarian food'. It might be necessary to follow with the explanation *phõm/dii-chãn kin tàe phàk*, 'I eat only vegetables.' Don't worry – this won't be interpreted to mean no rice, herbs or fruit. For other useful food phrases, see the list later in this section.

Table Etiquette

Using the correct utensils and eating gestures will garner much respect from the Thais, who are of the general opinion that Western table manners are rather coarse.

Thais eat most dishes with a fork and tablespoon except for noodles, which are eaten with chopsticks *(tà-kìap)*; noodle soups are eaten with spoon and chopsticks. Another exception to the fork-and-spoon routine is sticky rice (common in the north and north-east), which is rolled into balls and eaten with the right hand, along with the food accompanying it.

The fork *(sáwm)* is held in the left hand and used as a probe to push food onto the spoon *(cháwn)*; you eat from the spoon. To the Thais, pushing a fork into one's mouth is as uncouth as putting a knife into the mouth would be in Western countries.

When serving yourself from a common platter, put no more than one or two spoonfuls onto your own plate at a time. It's customary at the start of a shared meal to eat a spoonful of plain rice first – a gesture that recognises rice as the most important part of the meal. If you're being hosted by Thais, they'll undoubtedly encourage you to eat less rice and more curries, seafood, etc as a gesture of their generosity (since rice costs comparatively little). The humble guest, however, takes rice with every spoonful.

Always leave some food on the serving platters as well as on your plate. To clean your plate and leave nothing on the serving platters would be a grave insult to your hosts. This is why Thais tend to 'over-order' at social meal occasions – the more food is left on the table, the more generous the host appears.

The following list gives standard dishes in Thai script with a transliterated pronunciation guide, using the system outlined in the Language section and an English translation and description.

Curries *(kaeng)* แกง

hot Thai curry with chicken/beef/pork
kaeng phèt kài/néua/mũu
แกงเผ็ดไก่/เนื้อ/หมู

rich and spicy Muslim-style curry with chicken/beef & potatoes
kaeng mátsàman kài/néua
แกงมัสมั่นไก่/เนื้อ

mild, Indian-style curry with chicken
kaeng kari kài
แกงกะหรี่ไก่

hot & sour fish & vegetable ragout
kaeng sôm
แกงส้ม

'green' curry, made with fish/chicken/beef
kaeng khĩaw-wãan plaa/kài/néua
แกงเขียวหวานปลา/ไก่/เนื้อ

savoury curry with chicken/beef
kaeng phánaeng kài/néua
แกงพะแนงไก่/เนื้อ

chicken curry with bamboo shoots
kaeng kài nàw mái
แกงไก่หน่อไม้

catfish curry
kaeng plaa dùk
แกงปลาดุก

Soups *(súp)* ซุป

mild soup with vegetables & pork
kaeng jèut
แกงจืด

mild soup with vegetables, pork & bean curd
kaeng jèut tâo-hûu
แกงจืดเต้าหู้

soup with chicken, galanga root & coconut
tôm khàa kài
ต้มข่าไก่

prawn & lemon grass soup with mushrooms
tôm yam kûng
ต้มยำกุ้ง

fish ball soup
kaeng jèut lûuk chín
แกงจืดลูกชิ้น

rice soup with fish/chicken/shrimp
khâo tôm plaa/kài/kûng
ข้าวต้มปลา/ไก่/กุ้ง

Egg *(khài)* ไข่

hard-boiled egg
khài tôm
ไข่ต้ม

fried egg
khài dao
ไข่ดาว

plain omelette
khài jiaw
ไข่เจียว

omelette stuffed with vegetables & pork
khài yát sâi
ไข่ยัดไส้

scrambled egg
khài kuan
ไข่กวน

Rice Dishes *(khâo râat nâa)* ข้าวราดหน้า

fried rice with pork/chicken/shrimp
khâo phàt mũu/kài/kûng
ข้าวผัดหมู/ไก่/กุ้ง

boned, sliced Hainan-style chicken with marinated rice
khâo man kài
ข้าวมันไก่

chicken with sauce over rice
khâo nâa kài
ข้าวหน้าไก่

roast duck over rice
khâo nâa pèt
ข้าวหน้าเป็ด

'red' pork (char siu) with rice
khâo mũu daeng
ข้าวหมูแดง

curry over rice
khâo kaeng
ข้าวแกง

Noodles *(kũaytĩaw/bà-mii)* ก๋วยเตี๋ยว/บะหมี่

wide rice noodle soup with vegetables & meat
kũaytĩaw náam
ก๋วยเตี๋ยวน้ำ

wide rice noodles with vegetables & meat
kũaytĩaw hâeng
ก๋วยเตี๋ยวแห้ง

wide rice noodles with gravy
râat nâa
ราดหน้า

thin rice noodles fried with tofu, vegetables, egg & peanuts
phàt thai
ผัดไทย

fried thin noodles with soy sauce
phàt sii-yíw
ผัดซีอิ๊ว

wheat noodles in broth, with vegetables & meat
bà-mii náam
บะหมี่น้ำ

wheat noodles with vegetables & meat
bà-mii hâeng
บะหมี่แห้ง

Seafood *(aahãan tháleh)* อาหารทะเล

steamed crab
puu nêung
ปูนึ่ง

steamed crab claws
kâam puu nêung
ก้ามปูนึ่ง

shark fin soup
hũu chalãam
หูฉลาม

crisp-fried fish
plaa thâwt
ปลาทอด

fried prawns
kûng thâwt
กุ้งทอด

batter-fried prawns
kûng chúp pâeng thâwt
กุ้งชุบแป้งทอด

grilled prawns
kûng phão
กุ้งเผา

steamed fish
plaa nêung
ปลานึ่ง

grilled fish
plaa phão
ปลาเผา

whole fish cooked in ginger, onions, soy sauce
plaa jĩan
ปลาเจี๋ยน

sweet & sour fish
plaa prîaw wãan
ปลาเปรี้ยวหวาน

cellophane noodles baked with crab
wún-sên òp puu
วุ้นเส้นอบปู

spicy fried squid
plaa mèuk phàt phèt
ปลาหมึกผัดเผ็ด

roast squid
plaa mèuk yâang
ปลาหมึกย่าง

oysters fried in egg batter
hãwy thâwt
หอยทอด

squid
plaa mèuk
ปลาหมึก

shrimp
kûng
กุ้ง

fish
plaa
ปลา

catfish
plaa dùk
ปลาดุก

freshwater eel
plaa lãi
ปลาไหล

saltwater eel
plaa lòt
ปลาหลด

tilapia
plaa nin
ปลานิล

spiny lobster
kûng mangkon
กุ้งมังกร

green mussel
hãwy malaeng phùu
หอยแมลงภู่

scallop
hãwy phát
หอยพัด

oyster
hãwy naang rom
หอยนางรม

Miscellaneous

stir-fried mixed vegetables
phàt phàk lãi yàang
ผัดผักหลายอย่าง

spring rolls
pàw-pía
เปาะเปี๊ยะ

beef in oyster sauce
néua phàt náam-man hãwy
เนื้อผัดน้ำมันหอย

duck soup
pèt tũn
เป็ดตุ๋น

roast duck
pèt yâang
เป็ดย่าง

fried chicken
kài thâwt
ไก่ทอด

chicken fried in holy basil
kài phàt bai kà-phrao
ไก่ผัดใบกะเพรา

grilled chicken
kài yâang
ไก่ย่าง

chicken fried with chillies
kài phàt phrík
ไก่ผัดพริก

chicken fried with cashews
kài phàt mét má-mûang
ไก่ผัดเม็ดมะม่วง

morning-glory vine fried in garlic, chilli & bean sauce
phàk bûng fai daeng
ผักบุ้งไฟแดง

'satay' or skewers of barbecued meat, sold on the street
sà-té
สะเต๊ะ

spicy green papaya salad (north-east speciality)
sôm-tam
ส้มตำ

noodles with fish curry
khãnom jiin náam yaa
ขนมจีนน้ำยา

prawns fried with chilies
kûng phàt phrík phão
กุ้งผัดพริกเผา

chicken fried with ginger
kài phàt khĩng
ไก่ผัดขิง

fried wonton
kíaw kràwp
เกี๊ยวกรอบ

cellophane noodle salad
yam wún sên
ยำวุ้นเส้น

spicy chicken or beef salad
lâap kài/néua
ลาบไก่/เนื้อ

hot & sour grilled beef salad
yam néua
ยำเนื้อ

chicken with bean sprouts
kài sàp thùa ngâwk
ไก่สับถั่วงอก

fried fish cakes with cucumber sauce
thâwt man plaa
ทอดมันปลา

Vegetables ***(phàk)*** **ผัก**

angle bean
thùa phuu
ถั่วภู

bitter melon
márá-jiin
มะระจีน

brinjal (round eggplant)
mákhẽua pràw
มะเขือเปราะ

cabbage
phàk kà-làm or *kà-làm plii*
ผะกกะหล่ำ กะหล่ำปลี

cauliflower
dàwk kà-làm
ดอกกะหล่ำ

Chinese radish (daikon)
phàk kàat hũa
ผักกาดหัว

corn
khâo phôht
ข้าวโพด

cucumber
taeng kwaa
แตงกวา

eggplant
mákhẽua mûang
มะเขือม่วง

garlic
kràtiam
กระเทียม

lettuce
phàk kàat
ผักกาด

long bean
thùa fák yao
ถั่วฝักยาว

okra (ladyfingers)
krà-jíap
กระเจี๊ยบ

onion (bulb)
hũa hãwm
หัวหอม

onion (green, 'scallions')
tôn hãwm
ต้นหอม

peanuts (groundnuts)
tùa lísõng
ถั่วลิสง

potato
man faràng
มันฝรั่ง

pumpkin
fák thawng
ฟักทอง

taro
pheùak
เผือก

tomato
mákhẽua thêt
มะเขือเทศ

Fruit *(phõn-lá-mái)* ผลไม้

mandarin orange (year-round)
sôm
ส้ม

watermelon (year-round)
taeng moh
แตงโม

guava (year-round)
fa-ràng
ฝรั่ง

lime (year-round)
má-nao
มะนาว

mangosteen – round, purple fruit with juicy white flesh (April to September)
mang-khút
มังคุด

coconut – grated for cooking when mature, eaten from the shell with a spoon when young; juice is sweetest and most plentiful in young coconuts (year-round)
máphráo
มะพร้าว

rose-apple – small, apple-like texture, very fragrant (April to July)
chom-phûu
ชมพู่

tamarind – comes in sweet as well as tart varieties (year-round)
mákhãam
มะขาม

sapodilla – small, brown, oval, sweet but pungent smelling (July to September)
lámút
ละมุด

pineapple (year-round)
sàp-pàrót
สับปะรด

mango – several varieties & seasons
má-mûang
มะม่วง

custard-apple (July to October)
náwy naa
น้อยหน่า

'rambeh' – small, reddish-brown, sweet, apricot-like (April to May)
máfai
มะไฟ

pomelo – large citrus similar to grapefruit (year-round)
sôm oh
ส้มโอ

papaya (year-round)
málákaw
มะละกอ

durian – held in high esteem by the Thais, but most Westerners dislike this fruit. There are several varieties and seasons, so keep trying
thúrian
ทุเรียน

rambutan – red, hairy-skinned fruit with grape-like interior (July to September)
ngáw
เงาะ

jackfruit – similar in appearance to durian but much easier to take (year-round)
kha-nũn
ขนุน

banana – over 20 varieties (year-round)
klûay
กล้วย

longan – 'dragon's eyes', small, brown, spherical, similar to rambutan (July to October)
lam yài
ลำใย

Sweets *(khãwng wãan)* ของหวาน

Thai custard
sãngkha-yaa
สังขยา

coconut custard
sãngkha-yaa ma-phráo
สังขยามะพร้าว

sweet shredded egg yolk
fãwy thawng
ฝอยทอง

egg custard
mâw kaeng
หม้อแกง

banana in coconut milk
klûay bùat chii
กล้วยบวชชี

'Indian-style' banana, fried
klûay khàek
กล้วยแขก

sweet palm kernels
lûuk taan chêuam
ลูกตาลเชื่อม

Thai jelly with coconut cream
ta-kôh
ตะโก้

sticky rice with coconut cream
khâo nĩaw daeng
ข้าวเหนียวแดง

sticky rice in coconut cream with ripe mango
khâo nĩaw má-mûang
ข้าวเหนียวมะม่วง

Some Useful Food Words

For 'I' men use *phõm*; women use *dii-chãn*

I eat only vegetarian food.
Phõm/dii-chãn kin jeh.
ผม/ดีฉัน กินเจ

I can't eat pork.
Phõm/dii-chãn kin mũu mâi dâi.
ผม/ดีฉัน กินหมูไม่ได้

I can't eat beef.
Phõm/dii-chãn kin néua mâi dâi.
ผม/ดีฉัน กินเนื้อไม่ได้

(I) don't like it hot & spicy.
Mâi châwp phèt.
ไม่ชอบเผ็ด

(I) like it hot & spicy.
Châwp phèt.
ชอบเผ็ด

(I) can eat Thai food.
Kin aahãan thai pen.
กินอาหารไทยเป็น

What do you have that's special?
Mii a-rai phí-sèt?
มีอะไรพิเศษ?

I didn't order this.
Níi phõm/dii-chãn mâi dâi sàng.
นี้ ผม/ดิฉัน ไม่ได้สั่ง

Do you have ....?
Mii .... mãi?
มี...... ไหม?

DRINKS

Nonalcoholic Drinks

Fruit Juices & Shakes The incredible variety of fruits in Thailand means a corresponding availability of nutritious juices and shakes. The all-purpose term for fruit juice is *náam phõn-lá-mái*. Put *náam* (water or juice) together with the name of any fruit and you can get anything from *náam sôm* (orange juice) to *náam taeng moh* (watermelon juice). When a blender or extractor is used, fruit juices may be called *náam khán* or 'squeezed juice' (eg *náam sàppàrót khán*, pineapple juice). When mixed in a blender with ice the result is *náam pon* (literally, 'mixed juice') as in *náam málákaw pon*, a papaya 'smoothie' or 'shake'. Night markets will often have vendors specialising in juices and shakes.

Thais prefer to drink most fruit juices with a little salt mixed in. Unless a vendor is used to serving farangs, your fruit juice or shake will come slightly salted. If you prefer unsalted fruits juices, specify *mâi sài kleua* (without salt).

Sugar cane juice *(náam âwy)* is a Thai favourite and a very refreshing accompaniment to curry-and-rice plates. Many small restaurants or food stalls that don't offer any other juices will have a supply of freshly squeezed naam awy on hand.

Coffee Over the last 10 years or so, Nescafe and other instant coffees have made deep inroads into the Thai coffee culture at the expense of freshly ground coffee. The typical Thai restaurant – especially those in hotels, guesthouses and other tourist-oriented establishments – serves instant coffee with packets of artificial, non-dairy creamer on the side. Up-market hotels and coffee shops sometimes also offer filtered and espresso coffees at premium prices.

Traditionally, coffee in Thailand is locally grown (mostly in northern and southern Thailand), roasted by wholesalers, ground by vendors and filtered just before serving. Thai-grown coffee may not be as full and rich-tasting as gourmet Sumatran, Jamaican or Kona beans but to my palate it's still considerably tastier than Nescafe or other instant coffees.

Sometimes restaurants or vendors with the proper accoutrements for making traditional filtered coffee will keep a supply of Nescafe just for farangs (or moneyed Thais, since instant always costs a few baht more per cup than filtered). To get real Thai coffee ask for *kafae thũng* (literally, 'bag coffee'), which refers to the traditional method of preparing a cup of coffee by filtering hot water through a bag-shaped cloth filter. Thailand's best coffee of this sort is served in Hokkien-style cafes in the southern provinces. Elsewhere in Thailand outdoor morning markets are the best place to find kafae thũng.

The usual kafae thũng is served mixed with sugar and sweetened condensed milk – if you won't want either be sure to specify *kafae dam* (black coffee) followed with *mâi sài náam-taan* (without sugar). Kafae thung is often served in a glass instead of a ceramic cup – to pick a glass of hot coffee up, grasp it along the top rim.

Tea Both Indian-style (black) and Chinese-style (green or semi-cured) teas are commonly served in Thailand. The latter predominates in Chinese restaurants and is the usual ingredient in *náam chaa*, the weak, often lukewarm tea-water traditionally served in Thai restaurants for free. The aluminium teapots seen on every table in the average restaurant are filled with náam chaa; ask for a plain glass *(kâew plào)* and you can drink as much as you'd like at no charge. For iced náam chaa ask for a glass of ice (usually 1B) and pour your own; for fresh, undiluted Chinese tea request *chaa jiin*.

Black tea, both imported and Thai-grown, is usually available in the same restaurants or food stalls that serve real coffee. An order of *chaa ráwn* (hot tea) almost always results in a cup (or glass) of black tea with sugar and condensed milk. As with coffee you must specify as you order if you want black tea without milk and/or sugar.

Water Water purified for drinking purposes is simply called *náam dèum* (drinking water), whether boiled or filtered. *All* water offered to customers in restaurants or to guests in an office or home will be purified, so one needn't fret about the safety of taking a sip (for more information on water safety, see the Health section). In restaurants you can ask for *náam plào* (plain water) which is always either boiled or taken from a purified source; it's served by the glass at no charge or you can order by the bottle. A bottle of carbonated water (soda) costs about the same as a bottle of plain purified water but the bottles are smaller.

Beverages *(khreûang dèum)* เครื่องดื่ม

plain water
náam plào
น้ำเปล่า

hot water
náam ráwn
น้ำร้อน

boiled water
náam tôm
น้ำต้ม

cold water
náam yen
น้ำเย็น

ice
náam khãeng
น้ำแข็ง

Chinese tea
chaa jiin
ชาจีน

weak Chinese tea
náam chaa
น้ำชา

iced Thai tea with milk & sugar
chaa yen
ชาเย็น

iced Thai tea with sugar only
chaa dam yen
ชาดำเย็น

no sugar (command)
mâi sài náam-taan
ไม่ใส่น้ำตาล

hot Thai tea with sugar
chaa dam ráwn
ชาดำร้อน

hot Thai tea with milk & sugar
chaa ráwn
ชาร้อน

hot coffee with milk & sugar
kafae ráwn
กาแฟร้อน

traditional filtered coffee with milk & sugar
kafae thũng (*ko-píi* in southern Thailand)
กาแฟถุง/โกพี้

iced coffee with sugar, no milk
oh-liang
โอเลี้ยง

Ovaltine
oh-wantin
โอวันติน

orange soda
náam sôm
น้ำส้ม

plain milk
nom jèut
นมจืด

iced lime juice with sugar (usually with salt too)
náam manao
น้ำมะนาว

no salt (command)
mâi sài kleua
ไม่ใส่เกลือ

soda water
náam sõh-daa
น้ำโซดา

bottled drinking water
náam dèum khùat
น้ำดื่มขวด

bottle
khùat
ขวด

glass
kâew
แก้ว

Alcoholic Drinks

Drinking in Thailand can be quite expensive in relation to the cost of other consumer activities. The Thai government has placed increasingly heavy taxes on liquor and beer, so that now about 30B out of the 45 to 55B that you pay for a large beer is tax. Whether this is an effort to raise more tax revenue (the result has been a sharp decrease in the consumption of alcoholic beverages for perhaps a net decrease in revenue) or to discourage consumption, drinking can wreak havoc with your budget. One large bottle (630 ml) of Singha beer costs more than half the minimum daily wage of a Bangkok worker.

Beer Three brands of beer are brewed in Thailand: Singha, Amarit and Kloster. Singha (pronounced 'Sĩng' by the Thais) is by far the most common beer in Thailand, with some 88% of the domestic market. The original recipe was formulated in 1934 by nobleman Phya Bhirom Bhakdi and his son Prachuap, who was the first Thai to earn a brewmaster's diploma from Munich's Doemens Institute. Singha is a strong, hoppy-tasting brew thought by many to be the best beer produced in Asia. The barley for Singha is grown in Thailand, the hops are imported from Germany and the rated alcohol content is 4.7%. Singha is sometimes available on tap in pubs and restaurants.

Kloster is quite a bit smoother and lighter than Singha and generally costs 5B more per bottle, but it is a good-tasting brew often favoured by Western visitors, expats and upwardly mobile Thais who view it as somewhat of a status symbol. Boon Rawd Breweries, makers of Singha, have introduced a new lighter beer called Singha Gold in an effort to compete with Kloster, which is becoming increasingly popular in Thailand. At the time of writing, the Gold only comes in small bottles; most people seem to prefer either Kloster or regular Singha to Singha Gold, which is a little on the bland side.

Amarit has a very limited market, though it's basically similar in taste to Singha.

The Thai word for beer is *bia*. Draught beer is *bia sòt* (literally, 'fresh beer').

Spirits Rice whisky is a big favourite in Thailand and somewhat more affordable than beer for the average Thai. It has a sharp, sweet taste not unlike rum, with an alcoholic content of 35%. The two major liquor manufacturers are Suramaharas Co and the Surathip Group. The first produces the famous Mekong (pronounced 'Mâe-khõng') and Kwangthong brands, the second the Hong (swan) labels including Hong Thong, Hong Ngoen, Hong Yok and Hong Tho. Mekong and Kwangthong cost around 100B for a large bottle *(klom)* or 55 to 60B for the flask-sized bottle *(baen)*. An even smaller bottle, the *kòk*, is occasionally available for

30 to 35B. The Hong brands are less expensive.

In March 1986, the two liquor giants met and formed a common board of directors to try to end the fierce competition brought about when a 1985 government tax increase led to a 40% drop in Thai whisky sales. The meeting has resulted in an increase in whisky prices but probably also in better distribution – Mekong and Kwangthong have generally not been available in regions where the Hong labels are marketed and vice versa. A third company, Pramuanphon Distillery in Nakhon Pathom, has recently begun marketing a line of cut-rate rice whisky under three labels: Maew Thong (Gold Cat), Sing Chao Phraya (Chao Phraya Lion) and Singharat (Lion-King).

More expensive Thai whiskies appealing to the pre-Johnnie Walker set include Singharaj blended whisky (240B a bottle) and VO Royal Thai whisky (260B), each with 40% alcohol.

One company in Thailand produces a true rum, that is, a distilled liquor made from sugar cane, called Sang Thip (formerly Sang Som). Alcohol content is 40% and the stock is supposedly aged. Sang Thip costs several baht more than the rice whiskys, but for those who find Mekong and the like unpalatable, it is an alternative worth trying.

Other Liquor A cheaper alternative is *lâo khão*, or 'white liquor', of which there are two broad categories: legal and contraband. The legal kind is generally made from sticky rice and is produced for regional consumption. Like Mekong and its competitors, it is 35% alcohol, but sells for 45 to 50B per klom, or roughly half the price. The taste is sweet and raw and much more aromatic than the amber stuff – no amount of mixer will disguise the distinctive taste.

The illegal kinds are made from various agricultural products including sugar palm, coconut milk, sugar cane, taro and rice. Alcohol content may vary from as little as 10 or 12% to as much as 95%. Generally this *lâo thèuan* (jungle liquor) is weaker in the south and stronger in the north and north-east. This is the choice of the many Thais who can't afford to pay the heavy government liquor taxes; prices vary but 10 to 15B worth of the stronger concoctions will intoxicate three or four people. These types of home-brew or moonshine are generally taken straight with pure water as a chaser. In smaller towns, almost every garage-type restaurant (except, of course, Muslim restaurants) keeps some under the counter for sale. Sometimes roots and herbs are added to jungle liquor to enhance flavour and colour.

Currently, herbal liquors are fashionable throughout the country and can be found at roadside vendors, small pubs and in a few guesthouses. These liquors are made by soaking various herbs, roots, seeds, fruit and bark in lao khao to produce a range of concoctions called *yàa dong*. Many of the yaa dong preparations are purported to have specific health-enhancing qualities. Some of them taste fabulous while others are rank. One well-known herbal liquor pub just outside Bangkok is Pak Kraya Chok (Beggars Union) near Wat Phra Si Mahathat in Bangkhen.

ENTERTAINMENT

Cinema

Movie theatres are found in towns and cities throughout the country. Typical programmes include US and European shoot-em-ups mixed with Thai comedies and romances. Violent action pictures are always a big draw; as a rule of thumb, the smaller the town, the more violent the film offerings are. English-language films are only shown with their original soundtracks in a handful of theatres in Bangkok, Chiang Mai and Hat Yai; elsewhere all foreign films are dubbed in Thai. Ticket prices range from 10 to 50B. Every film in Thailand begins with a playback of the royal anthem, accompanied by projected pictures of the royal family. Viewers are expected to stand during the anthem.

Bars, Coffee Houses & Discos

Urban Thais are night people and every town

Prostitution

Thais generally blame 19th-century Chinese immigrants for bringing prostitution to Thailand, but in reality Thailand was fertile ground because of its longstanding concubinary tradition. In addition, the traditional Thai *mia yài mia nói* (major wife, minor wife) system made it socially permissible for a man to keep several mistresses – all Thai kings through Rama IV had mia nói, as did virtually any Thai male who could afford them until recent times. Even today talk of mia nois hardly raises an eyebrow anywhere in Thailand as the tradition lives on among wealthy businessmen, *jâo phâw* (organised crime 'godfathers') and politicians.

The first brothels in Thailand, however, were indisputably established by Chinese immigrants in Bangkok's Sampeng district in the mid-19th century. In the beginning, only Chinese women worked as prostitutes; when Thai women became involved at the turn of the century, they usually took Chinese names. Prostitution eventually spread from Sampeng to Chinese districts throughout Thailand and is now found in virtually every village, town and city in the kingdom. Ethnic Chinese still control most of the trade, although the prostitutes themselves now come from almost every ethnic background.

Current estimates of the number of Thai citizens directly involved in offering sex services vary from the Ministry of Public Health's conservative 86,000 to wild bar-stool estimates of 500,000. After an intensive two-year study into the prostitution industry, Chulalongkorn University's Population Institute came up with a reasoned estimate of 210,000, a figure now widely considered the most realistic. This number is thought to include around 10,000 male and child prostitutes. The highest per-capita number of sex workers are found in the north; Chiang Mai, for example, has an estimated 3000 service girls in two brothel districts. Brothels are less common in the southern provinces except in Chinese-dominated Phuket, Hat Yai and Yala, and in Thai-Malaysian border towns where the clientele is almost exclusively Malay.

Most of the country's sex industry is invisible to the visiting farang. A typical mid-level coffee house/brothel will offer girls ranked in price according to their beauty or supposed skills; prices are denoted by coloured tags (eg yellow 100B, blue 200B, red 300B, clear 500B.) Back-alley places service low-wage earners for as little as 30B. At the other end of the spectrum, Thai businessmen and government officials entertain in massage parlours and private brothels where services average around 1000B.

Unlike Western prostitution, there are few 'pimps' (people who manage one or more prostitutes) in Thailand. Instead, a network of procurers/suppliers and brothel owners control the trade, taking a high proportion (or all) of the sex service fees. At its worst, the industry takes girls sold or indentured by their families, sometimes even kidnapped, and forces them to work in conditions of virtual slavery. A few years ago a Phuket brothel of the type rarely patronised by farangs caught fire; several young women who were chained to their beds by the management died in the fire. In the Patpong-style bar catering to foreigners, most bar girls and go-go dancers are semi-freelance agents; they earn their income from taking a percentage of drinks bought on their behalf and from sex liaisons arranged outside the premises – usually after closing (if they leave during working hours, a customer usually pays a 'bar fine' on their behalf). Fees for services are then negotiated between customer and prostitute.

Most prostitutes are young, uneducated and from village areas. Researchers estimate they have a maximum working life of 10 to 12 years – if they haven't saved up enough money to retire by then (few do), they're often unemployable due to mental and physical disabilities acquired during their short working life. Various Thai volunteer groups are engaged in counselling Thailand's sex workers – helping them to escape the industry or to educate them to the dangers of STDs, particularly AIDS. Officially prostitution is illegal but the government has been either powerless or unwilling to enforce the laws; in 1992 the Thai cabinet introduced a bill to decriminalise prostitution in the hope that it would make it easier for prostitutes to seek counselling or STD testing without fear of prosecution. ■

of any size has a selection of nightspots. For the most part they are male- dominated, though the situation is changing rapidly in the larger cities where young couples are increasingly seen in bars.

Of the many types of bars, probably the most popular at the moment is the 'old west' style, patterned after Thai fantasies of the 19th-century American west – lots of wood and cowboy paraphernalia. Another up-and-coming style is the 'Thai classic' pub, which is typically decorated with old black & white photos of Thai kings Rama VI and Rama VII, along with Thai antiques from northern and central Thailand. The old west and Thai-classic nightspots are cozy, friendly and popular with couples as well as singles.

More common is the so-called 'coffee house', where Thai men consort with a variety of Thai female hostesses. A variation on this theme is the 'sing-song' bar or coffee house in which a succession of female singers take turns fronting a live band. Small groups of men sit at tables ogling the girls while putting away prodigious amounts of Johnnie Walker, J&B or Mekong whisky. For the price of a few house drinks, the men can invite one of the singers to sit at their table for a while. Some of the singers hire themselves out after closing to the highest bidder.

The 'girlie' bars seen in lurid photos published by the Western media are limited to a few areas in Bangkok, Pattaya and Phuket's Patong Beach. These are the male farang counterpart to the coffee houses described previously, the main difference being that the girls typically wear bathing suits instead of dresses; in some bars they dance to recorded music on a narrow raised stage. To some visitors it's pathetic, to others paradise.

Discotheques are popular in larger cities; outside of Bangkok they're mostly attached to tourist or luxury hotels. The main disco clientele is Thai, though foreigners are welcome. Some provincial discos retain female staff as professional dance partners for male entertainment, but for the most part discos are considered fairly respectable nightspots for couples.

THINGS TO BUY

There are many bargains awaiting you in Thailand if you have the space to carry them back. Always haggle to get the best price, except in department stores. And don't go shopping in the company of touts, tour guides or friendly strangers as they will inevitably – no matter what they say – take a commission on anything you buy, thus driving prices up.

Textiles

Fabric is possibly the best all-round buy in Thailand. Thai silk is considered the best in the world – the coarse weave and soft texture of the silk means it is more easily dyed than harder, smoother silks, resulting in brighter colours and a unique lustre. Silk can be purchased cheaply in the north and north-east where it is made or, more easily, in Bangkok. Excellent and reasonably priced tailor shops can make your choice of fabric into almost any pattern. A silk suit should cost around 3750 to 6250B.

Cottons are also a good deal – common items like the phaakhamaa (reputed to have over a hundred uses in Thailand) and the phaasin (the slightly larger female equivalent) make great tablecloths and curtains. Good ready-made cotton shirts are available, such as the *mâw hâwm* (Thai work shirt) and the *kuay haeng* (Chinese-style shirt) – see the

sections on Pasang in the north and Ko Yo in the south for where to see cotton-weaving.

In recent years, cotton-weaving has become very popular in the north-east and there are fabulous finds in Nong Khai, Roi-Et, Khon Kaen and Mahasarakham. The *mãwn khwãan*, a hard, triangle-shaped pillow made in the north-east, makes a good souvenir and comes in many sizes. The north-east is also famous for its *mát-mii* cloth, thick cotton fabric woven from tie-dyed threads – similar to Indonesia's ikat fabrics.

In the north you can find Lanna-style textiles based on intricate Thai Lü patterns from Nan, Laos and China's Sipsongpanna (Xishuangbanna).

Fairly nice batik *(pa-té)* is available in the south in patterns that are more similar to batik found in Malaysia than in Indonesia.

Clothing

Tailor-made and ready-made clothes are relatively inexpensive. If you're not particular about style you could pick up an entire wardrobe of travelling clothes at one of Bangkok's many street markets (eg Pratunam) for what you'd pay for one designer shirt in New York or Paris.

You're more likely to get a good fit if you resort to a tailor but be wary of the quickie 24-hour tailor shops; the clothing is often made of inferior fabric or the poor tailoring means the arms start falling off after three weeks' wear. It's best to ask Thai or longtime foreign residents for a tailor recommendation and then go for two or three fittings.

Shoulder Bags

Thai shoulder bags *(yâam)* are generally quite well made. They come in many varieties, some woven by hill tribes, others by Thai cottage industry. The best are made by the Lahu hill tribes, whom the Thais call 'Musoe'. The weaving is more skilful and the bags tend to last longer than those made by other tribes. For an extra-large yaam, the Karen-made bag is a good choice, and is easy to find in the Mae Hong Son area. These days many hill tribes are copying patterns from tribes other than their own.

Overall, Chiang Mai has the best selection of standard shoulder bags, but Bangkok has the best prices – try the Indian district, Pahurat, for these as well as anything else made of cloth. Roi-Et and Mahasarakham in the north-east are also good hunting grounds for locally made shoulder bags. Prices range from 45B for a cheaply made bag to 200B for something special.

Antiques

Real antiques cannot be taken out of Thailand without a permit from the Department of Fine Arts. No Buddha image, new or old, may be exported without permission – again, refer to the Fine Arts Department, or, in some cases, the Department of Religious Affairs, under the Ministry of Education. Too many private collectors smuggling and hoarding Siamese art (Buddhas in particular) around the world have led to strict controls. See the section on Customs earlier in this chapter for more information on the export of art objects and antiques.

Chinese and Thai antiques are sold in Chinatown in two areas: Wang Burapha (the streets which have Chinese 'gates' over the entrance) and Nakhon Kasem. Some antiques (and many fakes) are sold at the Weekend Market in Chatuchak Park. Objects for sale in the tourist antique shops are fantastically overpriced, as can be expected. In recent years northern Thailand has become a good source of Thai antiques – prices are about half what you'd typically pay in Bangkok.

Jewellery

Thailand is one of the world's largest exporters of gems and ornaments, rivalled only by India and Sri Lanka. The biggest importers of Thai jewellery are the USA, Japan and Switzerland. One of the results of the remarkable growth of the gem industry – in Thailand the gem trade has increased nearly 10% every year for the last decade – is that the prices are rising rapidly.

If you know what you are doing you can

make some really good buys in both unset gems and finished jewellery. Gold ornaments are sold at a good rate as labour costs are low. The best bargains in gems are jade, rubies and sapphires. Buy from reputable dealers only, unless you're a gemologist. Be wary of special 'deals' that are one-day only or which set you up as a 'courier' in which you're promised big money. Many travellers end up losing big. Shop around and don't be hasty.

The biggest gem centres are Kanchanaburi, Mae Sot and Chanthaburi – these areas are where the Bangkok dealers go to buy their stones. The Asian Institute of Gemological Sciences (☎ 513-2112; fax 236-7803), 484 Ratchadaphisek Rd (off Lat Phrao Rd in the Huay Khwang district, north-east Bangkok), offers short-term courses in gemology as well as tours of gem mines for those interested.

You can bring gems here for inspection but they don't assess value, only authenticity and grading. John Hoskin's book *Buyer's Guide to Thai Gems & Jewellery*, available at Bangkok bookshops, is a useful introduction to Thai gems.

See the Dangers & Annoyances section earlier in this chapter for detailed warnings on gem fraud.

Hill-Tribe Crafts

Interesting embroidery, clothing, bags and jewellery from the north can be bought in Bangkok at Narayan Phand, Lan Luang Rd, at the Queen's Hillcrafts Foundation, in the Sapatum Palace compound behind the Siam Center, and at various tourist shops around town. See Things to Buy in the Bangkok chapter for details.

In Chiang Mai there are shops selling handicrafts all along Thaphae Rd and there is a shop sponsored by missionaries near Prince Royal College. There is a branch of the Queen's Hillcrafts Foundation in Chiang Rai. It's worth shopping around for the best prices and bargaining. The all-round best buys of northern hill-tribe crafts are at the Chiang Mai night bazaar – if you know how to bargain.

Lacquerware

Thailand produces some good Burmese-style lacquerware and sells some Burmese-made stuff along the northern Burmese border. Try Mae Sot, Mae Sariang and Mae Sai for the best buys.

Nielloware

This art came from Europe via Nakhon Si Thammarat and has been cultivated in Thailand for over 700 years. Engraved silver is inlaid with niello – an alloy of lead, silver, copper and sulphur – to form striking black-and-silver jewellery designs. Nielloware is one of Thailand's best buys.

Ceramics

Many kinds of hand-thrown pottery, old and new, are available throughout the kingdom. Most well-known are the greenish Sangkhalok or Thai celadon products from the Sukhothai-Si Satchanalai area and central Thailand's *bencharong* or 'five-colour' style. The latter is based on Chinese patterns while the former is a Thai original that has been imitated throughout China and South-East Asia.

Furniture

Rattan and hardwood furniture items are often good buys and can be made to order. Bangkok and Chiang Mai have the best selection of styles and quality. Teak furniture has become relatively scarce and expensive; rosewood is a more reasonable buy.

Fake or Pirated Goods

In Bangkok, Chiang Mai and all the tourist centres, there is black-market street trade in fake designer goods; particularly Lacoste (crocodile) and Ralph Lauren polo shirts and Rolex, Dunhill and Cartier watches. Tin-tin T-shirts are also big. No one pretends they're the real thing, at least not the vendors themselves. The European manufacturers are applying heavy pressure on the Asian governments involved to get this stuff off the street so it may not be around much longer.

Prerecorded cassette tapes are another illegal bargain in Thailand. The tapes are 'pirated', that is, no royalties are paid to the copyright owners. Average prices are from 25 to 35B per cassette. Word has it that these will disappear from the streets, too, under pressure from the US music industry.

In 1991 four of the major tape piraters (including Peacock and Eagle) agreed to stop producing unlicensed tapes, but only on condition that the police prosecute the myriad smaller companies doing business. Licensed tapes, when available, cost 60 to 80B each; Thai music tapes cost the same.

Other Goods

Bangkok is famous the world over for its street markets – Pratunam, Chatuchak Park, Khlong Toey, Sampeng (Chinatown), Banglamphu and many more – where you'll find things you never imagined you wanted but once you see, you feel you can't possibly do without. Even if you don't want to spend any money, they're great places to wander around.

For top-end shopping, the two main centres in Bangkok are the area around the Oriental Hotel off Charoen Krung (New) Rd and the relatively new River City shopping complex on the river next to the Royal Orchid Sheraton Hotel. Thailand's two big department store chains, Robinson and Central, have several branches in Bangkok as well as in the larger towns.

Getting There & Away

AIR

The expense of getting to Bangkok per air km varies quite a bit depending on your point of departure. However, you can take heart in the fact that Bangkok is one of the cheapest cities in the world to fly out of, due to the Thai government's loose restrictions on airfares and the close competition between airlines and travel agencies. The result is that with a little shopping around, you can come up with some real bargains. If you can find a cheap one-way ticket to Bangkok, take it, because you are virtually guaranteed to find one of equal or lesser cost for the return trip once you get there.

From most places around the world your best bet will be budget, excursion or promotional fares – when enquiring from airlines ask for the various fares in that order. Each carries its own set of restrictions and it's up to you to decide which set works best in your case. Fares fluctuate, but in general they are cheaper from September to April (northern hemisphere) and from March to November (southern hemisphere).

Fares listed here should serve as a guideline – don't count on them staying this way for long (they may go down!).

To/From Australia

These days few people pay the full economy fare from Australia to Bangkok (around A$2000 from Sydney, Melbourne or Brisbane, A$1660 from Perth). Much cheaper are the advance-purchase fares (one-way and return) which must be booked and paid for 21 days in advance, and excursion fares (usually return only) which have no prepay requirements. Two seasons apply to advance-purchase and excursion tickets, the peak is 22 November to 31 January, all the rest of the year is off-peak.

One-way advance-purchase fares are A$1009 from Sydney, Melbourne or Brisbane (A$1194 peak), A$739 from Perth (A$877 peak). The return excursion fares are around A$1453 from Sydney, Melbourne or Brisbane (A$1719 peak), A$1158 from Perth (A$1378 peak). You should be able to knock a bit off these fares if you book through travel agents specialising in discount tickets, but you'll still need to book in advance. At the time of writing, advance-purchase tickets were available for A$1045 from Sydney or Melbourne return (A$1342 peak).

To/From Europe

London 'bucket shops' will have tickets to Bangkok available for around £220 one-way or £400 return. It's also easy to stop over in Bangkok between London and Australia, with return fares for around £650 to the Australian east coast. Good travel agencies to try for these sorts of fares are Trailfinders on Kensington High St and Earls Court Rd, or STA Travel on Old Brompton Rd. Or you can simply check the travel ads in *Time Out* or the *News & Travel Magazine*.

One of the best deals going is on TAROM (Romanian Air Transport), which has Brussels-Bangkok-Brussels fares valid for a year at US$590. Another cheapie is Czechoslovak Airlines, which flies from Prague via London, Frankfurt and Zurich.

To/From North America

If you fly from the West Coast, you can get some great deals through the many bucket shops (who discount tickets by taking a cut in commissions) and consolidators (agencies that buy airline seats in bulk) operating in Los Angeles and San Francisco. One of the oldest and most established of these is Overseas Tours (☎ (800) 227-5988 toll-free outside California; (800) 323-8777, within California) at 475 El Camino Real, Room 206, Millbrae, CA 94030. Overseas Tours (formerly OC Tours) is a Chinese-operated corporation which mainly serves the heavy Asian traffic between San Francisco and the Far East. A return (round-trip) airfare to

Bangkok from any of 12 different West Coast cities starts at around US$700.

While the airlines themselves can rarely match the prices of the discounters, they are worth checking if only to get benchmark prices to use for comparison. Tickets bought directly from the airlines may also have fewer restrictions and/or less strict cancellation policies than those bought from discounters (though this is not always true).

Cheapest from the West Coast are: Thai Airways International (THAI), China Airlines, Korean Airlines and CP Air. Each of these has a budget and/or 'super Apex' fare that costs around US$900 to US$1200 round-trip from Los Angeles, San Francisco or Seattle. THAI is the most overbooked of these airlines from December to March and June to August and hence their flights during these months may entail schedule delays (if you're lucky enough to get a seat at all). Several of these airlines also fly out of New York, Dallas, Chicago and Atlanta – add another US$100 to US$200 to their lowest fares.

To/From Asia

Bangkok Airport There are regular flights to Bangkok from every major city in Asia and it's not so tricky dealing with inter-Asia flights as most airlines offer about the same fares. Here is a sample of current estimated fares:

Singapore to Bangkok	US$150
Hong Kong to Bangkok	US$170-200*
Kuala Lumpur to Bangkok	US$130
Taipei to Bangkok	US$273
Calcutta to Bangkok	US$150
Kathmandu to Bangkok	US$201
Colombo to Bangkok	US$209-250*
New Delhi to Bangkok	US$231
Manila to Bangkok	US$227
Kunming to Bangkok	US$250

*varies according to airline

ASEAN promotional fares (round-trip from any city, eg a Bangkok-Manila-Jakarta fare allows you to go between Manila, Jakarta, Bangkok and Manila; or Jakarta, Bangkok, Manila and Jakarta; or Bangkok, Manila, Jakarta and Bangkok):

Bangkok-Manila-Jakarta	US$505
Bangkok-Singapore-Manila	US$420
Bangkok-Jakarta-Brunei	US$395
Bangkok-Manila-Brunei-Jakarta-Singapore-Kuala Lumpur	US$560

Thailand's Ministry of Transport is finally allowing several new Thailand-based air carriers to provide regional air services to Burma, Vietnam, Laos and Cambodia. Bangkok Airways now flies five times weekly to Phnom Penh on 56-seat Dash 8 turboprops; the airline also plans to offer services between Bangkok, Danang and Hue (Vietnam). SK Air (which was formerly Air Kampuchea, then Air Cambodia) also operates Bangkok-Phnom Penh flights.

For the moment most of these flights can only be booked along with expensive tourist visas, and are usually available only through sanctioned Bangkok travel agencies. Within the next few years, visa restrictions are expected to loosen and booking these flights should get easier.

Hat Yai Airport Both THAI and Malaysian Airline System (MAS) fly from Penang; there are also Tradewind flights from Singapore. See the Hat Yai Getting There & Away section in the Southern Thailand chapter for more details.

Chiang Mai Airport Chiang Mai's Lanna Air Charters has recently begun regular flights between Chiang Mai and Burma's Pagan and Mandalay, and is slated to start service to Luang Prabang (Laos) by the end of 1992. There are also discussions underway for flights between Chiang Mai and Jinghong in the Sipsongpanna (Xishuangbanna) region of south-west China. If the latter service is established, travellers will be able to complete a China route and enter Thailand without having to backtrack to Hong Kong or Beijing (or see most of Thailand without backtracking to Bangkok, then on to China).

Bangkok Airways also plans to offer services between Chiang Mai and Luang Prabang.

Like the regional air services from Bangkok to Burma, Vietnam and Cambodia, most of the flights from Chiang Mai to neighbouring Burma and Laos can still only be booked at certain Bangkok travel agencies.

Arriving in Thailand

Over the last 10 years, the airport facilities at Bangkok International Airport have undergone a US$200 million redevelopment, including a new international terminal that is one of the most modern and convenient in Asia. The old terminal is now used for domestic flights only. However, the very slow immigration lines in the upstairs arrival hall is still a major problem. Despite a long row of impressive-looking immigration counters, there never seem to be enough clerks on duty, even at peak arrival times. Baggage claim, however, is usually quick and efficient (of course they have plenty of time to get it right while you're inching along through immigration).

The customs area has a green lane for passengers with nothing to declare – just walk on through if you're one of these and hand your customs form to one of the clerks by the exit. Baggage trolleys are free for use inside the terminal.

On the 4th floor of the international terminal is the Rajthanee Food Mall, a small cafeteria area where you can choose from Thai, Chinese and European dishes at fairly reasonable prices. Next door is the larger THAI restaurant with more expensive fare. On the 2nd level above the arrival area is a coffee shop, and there is also a small snack bar in the waiting area of the ground floor. The departure lounge has two snack bars which serve beer and liquor.

The foreign currency kiosks on the ground floor of the arrival hall give a good rate of exchange, so there's no need to wait till you're downtown to change money if you need Thai currency. Left-luggage facilities (20B per piece per day, three months maximum) are available in the departure hall (3rd floor) along with currency exchange counters and a 24-hour post/telephone office with a Home Country Direct (HCD) phone service. Another 24-hour post office is located in the departure lounge; a third one in the arrival hall is open from 8.30 am to 4.30 pm. Also on the ground floor of the arrival hall is a tourist information counter and a hotel reservation counter for THA (Thai Hotel Association) members. This doesn't go below the Miami-Malaysia standard of hotel.

If you leave the airport building area and cross the expressway on the pedestrian bridge (just north of the passenger terminal) you'll find yourself in the Don Muang town area where there are all sorts of shops, a market, lots of small restaurants and food stalls, even a wat, all within a hundred metres or so of the airport. The modern and luxurious Airport Hotel (US$100 up) has its own enclosed bridge and 'special mini-stay' daytime rates (8 am to 6 pm) for stays of up to a maximum of three hours for around 400/450B for singles/doubles, including tax and service. Longer daytime rates are available on request (☎ 566-1020/1).

The Thai government has plans to open another international airport about 17 km east of Bangkok at Nong Ngu Hao. This additional airport is expected to be completed by 1996 and will be named Raja Deva (Racha Thewa).

For information on transport from the airport to Bangkok, see under Local Transport in the Getting Around chapter.

Warning Beware of airport touts – anyone trying to steer you away from the city taxi counter or asking where you plan to stay in Bangkok. A legion of touts – some in what appear to be airport or airline uniforms – wait for new arrivals in the arrival area and begin their badgering as soon as you clear customs. Posing as helpful tourist information agents, their main objective is to get commissions from overpriced taxi rides or hotel rooms. If you're foolish enough to mention the hotel or guesthouse you plan to stay at, chances are they'll tell you it's full and that you must go to another hotel (which will pay them a commission, though they may deny it). Sometimes they'll show you a nice collection of photos; don't get suckered in, as these touted hotels are often substandard and badly located.

The THA hotel reservation desk at the back of the arrival hall also takes a commission on every booking, but at least they have a wide selection of accommodation.

Now that the TAT supposedly has regulatory powers, one of its first acts should be to clean the touts out of the airport arrival area, as the present situation gives many visitors a rather negative first impression of Thailand. Then again, some see it as part of the challenge of Asian travel!

Leaving Thailand

Tickets Although other Asian centres are now competitive with Bangkok for buying discounted airline tickets, this is still a good place for shopping around. Note, however, that some Bangkok travel agencies have a shocking reputation. Taking money and then delaying or not coming through with the tickets, providing tickets with limited validity periods or severe use restrictions are all part of the racket. There are a lot of perfectly honest agents, but beware of the rogues.

Some typical discount fares being quoted from Bangkok include:

Around Asia

Calcutta	3750B
Colombo	5225B
Delhi	5775B
Hong Kong	4250B
Jakarta	5875B
Kathmandu	5025B
Kuala Lumpur	3275B
Penang	2575B
Rangoon	2600B
Singapore	3750B

Australia & New Zealand

Sydney/Brisbane/ Melbourne	11,825B
Darwin/Perth	8400B
Auckland	12,000B

Europe

Athens, Amsterdam, Frankfurt, London, Paris, Rome or Zurich: 11,000B

USA

San Francisco/ Los Angeles	11,675B
via Australia	18,200B
New York	12,500B

Booking Problems During the past couple of years the booking of flights in and out of Bangkok during the high season (December to March) has become increasingly difficult. For air travel during these months you should book as far in advance as possible. THAI is finally loosening up its stranglehold on air routes in and out of Thailand, so the situation has improved since the late '80s when the national carrier refused to allow additional airlines permission to add much-needed service through Bangkok.

Also be sure to reconfirm return or ongoing tickets when you arrive in Thailand. Failure to reconfirm can mean losing your reservation.

Departure Tax Airport departure tax is 200B for international flights and 20B for domestic. There is no longer a tax exemption for passengers in transit. See the To/From Bangkok International Airport section in the Getting Around chapter for more details.

LAND

To/From Malaysia

Hat Yai is the major transport hub in southern Thailand. See that section for more details on land transport to Malaysia.

You can cross the west-coast border by taking a bus to one side and another bus from the other side, but don't take the most obvious direct route between Hat Yai and Alor Setar. This is the route used by taxis and buses but there's a long stretch of no-man's-land between the Thai border control at Sadao and the Malaysian one at Changlun. Finding transport across this empty stretch is difficult.

It's much easier to go to Padang Besar,

where the railway line crosses the border. Here you can get a bus right up to the border, walk across and take another bus or taxi on the other side. On either side you'll most likely be mobbed by taxi and motorcycle drivers wanting to take you to immigration. It's better to walk over the railway by bridge into Thailand, and then ignore the touts asking $M until you get to 'official' Thai taxis who will transport you to all the way to Hat Yai, with a stop at the immigration office (2.5 km from the border), for 25B.

There's a daily bus running between Alor Setar, Hat Yai and Kota Baru and reverse.

There's also a road crossing at Keroh (Thai side – Betong), right in the middle between the east and west coasts. This may be used more now that the Penang to Kota Baru road is open. For more information on Betong, see the Yala Province section.

See the Sungai Kolok & Ban Taba sections for crossing the border on the east coast.

The International Express from Singapore to Bangkok via Butterworth, Malaysia, is a great way to travel to Thailand – as long as you don't count on making a smooth change between the Malaysian railway and State Railway of Thailand (SRT) trains. The Thai train almost always leaves on time; the Malaysian train rarely arrives on time. Unfortunately the Thai train leaves from Butterworth even if the Malaysian railway express from Kuala Lumpur is late. To be on the safe side, purchase the Malaysian and Thai portions of your ticket with departures on consecutive days and plan a Butterworth/ Penang stopover.

Bangkok to Butterworth/Penang The daily special express No 11 leaves from Bangkok's Hualamphong station at 3.15 pm, arriving in Hat Yai at 7.04 am the next day, and in Butterworth, Malaysia, at 12.10 pm (Malaysian time, one hour ahead of Thai time). The fare to Butterworth is 980B for 1st class, 451B for 2nd, plus a 50B special express charge. There is no 3rd-class seating on this train.

For a sleeping berth in 2nd class add 100B for an upper berth, 150B for a lower. In 1st class it's 150B per person.

Bangkok to Kuala Lumpur & Singapore For Kuala Lumpur take the Butterworth/ Penang train, changing to the Malaysian day express No 3 in Butterworth, departing there for Kuala Lumpur at 2.15 pm, arriving in Kuala Lumpur at 8.15 pm the same day. The fare from Bangkok is 1432B in 1st class, 659B in 2nd class.

For Singapore, the final leg leaves Kuala Lumpur aboard night express No 61 at 10

Orient Express

A new joint venture between the State Railway of Thailand, the Malaya Siam Royal Mail (Malaysia's state railway) and Singapore's Eastern & Oriental Express (E&O) has purchased the rights from Paris' Venice Simplon to operate an Orient Express between Singapore and Bangkok. Finally, an Orient Express that actually begins and ends in the Orient! The original Orient Express ran between Paris and Constantinople in the 1880s and was considered the grandest rail trip in the world; an updated version along the same route was resurrected around 20 years ago and has been very successful.

The 1943-km Singapore to Bangkok inaugural journey will leave Singapore railway station in November '92 and is expected to reach Bangkok in 41 hours, with stops in Kuala Lumpur, Butterworth, Surat Thani and Hua Hin. As in Europe, this new train is designed to offer cruise-ship luxury on rails; passengers will be accommodated in 13 railway carriages imported from New Zealand and refurbished in 1930s style by the same French designer who remodelled the Venice Simplon Orient Express in Europe. The E&O will also feature three restaurant cars, two bar cars (an observation bar and a piano bar) and a saloon car. All accommodation is in deluxe private cabins with shower and toilet; passengers will be attended by round-the-clock cabin stewards in the true pukkah tradition. Tariffs will start at US$860; a private presidential carriage for two will be available for a mere US$6000.

The train can be booked in Singapore through Eastern & Oriental Express (☎ (65) 227-2068; fax (65) 224-9265), Carlton Bldg No 14-03, 90 Cecil St, Singapore 0106. ■

pm, arriving in Singapore at 6.55 am the next day. The entire two-day journey costs 1965B in 1st class, 899B in 2nd class, not including express surcharge or berth charges if you get a sleeper. If you're going straight through, when you get to Butterworth get off quickly and re-book a sleeping berth to Kuala Lumpur (M$2 to M$3). In Kuala Lumpur you have to get a 2nd-class seat allocation – insist on 2nd or you may be fobbed off with 3rd class on a slower Biasa train.

To/From Burma & Cambodia

There is currently no legal land passage between Burma (Myanmar) and Thailand and the Cambodian border won't be safe for land crossings until mines and booby traps left over from the conflict between the Khmer Rouge and the Vietnamese are removed or detonated.

To/From Laos

Land crossings between Laos and Thailand are permitted at Nong Khai (opposite Laos' Tha Deua, near Vientiane) and at Chong Mek (opposite Pak Se Province). Both crossings are accomplished by short river-ferry rides. See the Getting There & Away sections for Nong Khai and Ubon Ratchathani for more information on these border crossings.

SEA

There are several ways of travelling b… Malaysia and the south of Thailand by … Simplest is to take a long-tail boat betwe… Satun, right down in the south-west corner of Thailand, and Kuala Perlis. The cost is about M$4, or 40B, and boats cross over fairly regularly. You can also take a ferry to the Malaysian island of Langkawi from Satun.

There are immigration posts at both ports so you can make the crossing quite officially, but they're a bit slack at Satun (since they don't get many foreigners arriving this way) so make sure they stamp your passport. See the Satun section for more information.

From Satun you can take a bus to Hat Yai and then arrange transport to other points in the south or further north. It's possible to bypass Hat Yai altogether, by heading directly for Phuket or Krabi via Trang.

You can also take a ferry to Ban Taba on the east coast of Thailand from near Kota Baru as well – see the section on Sungai Kolok & Ban Taba.

See the Phuket section for information on yachts to Penang and other places.

A passenger ferry service between Pulau Langkawi and Phuket, Thailand, began in March '92. It's operated by Syarikat Kuala Perlis-Langkawi Ferry Services.

[...]Around

[...]rvices in Thailand are [...] Airways International (THAI) (following a 1989 merger with the domestic Thai Airways) and cover 23 airports throughout Thailand. On certain southern routes, domestic flights through Hat Yai continue on to Penang, Kuala Lumpur, Singapore and Bandar Seri Begawan.

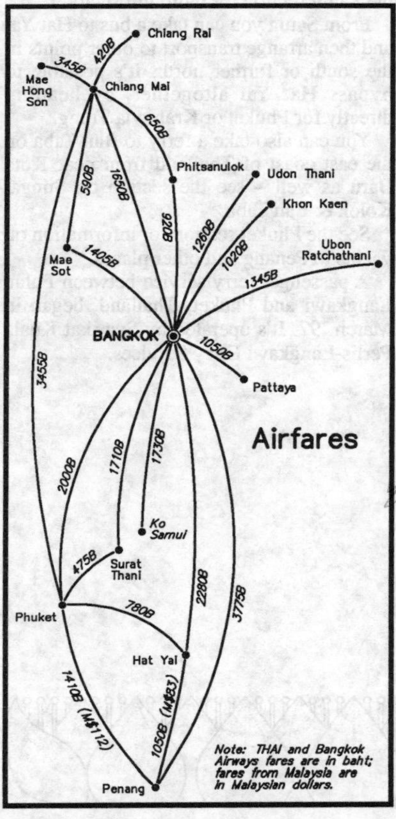

THAI operates Boeing 737s or Airbus 300s on all its main domestic routes, but also has Avro 748s on some smaller routes and to the more remote locations, particularly in the north and north-east, there are small Shorts 330s and 360s. Some of the fares to these remote locations are subsidised.

The accompanying chart shows some of the fares on more popular routes. Where routes are operated by 737s and by Avro 748s or Shorts 330s and 360s, the 737 fares will be higher. Note that through fares are generally less than the combination fares – Chiang Rai to Bangkok, for example, is less than the addition of Chiang Rai to Chiang Mai and Chiang Mai to Bangkok fares. This does not always apply to international fares, however. It's much cheaper to fly from Bangkok to Penang via Phuket or Hat Yai than direct, for example.

THAI Offices

Bangkok

- Head Office, 89 Vibhavadi Rangsit Rd (☎ (02) 513-0121)
- 485 Silom Rd (☎ (02) 234-3100; 233-3810 for reservations)
- 6 Lan Luang Rd (☎ (02) 280-0090; 280-0070/80 for reservations)
- Bangkok International Airport, Don Muang (☎ (02) 523-2081/3, 523-6121)
- 45 Anuwong Rd, Yaowarat (☎ (02) 224-9602/8)
- Asia Hotel, 296 Phayathai Rd (☎ (02) 215-2020/1)
- 4th Floor, Charn Issara Tower (☎ (02) 235-4588)

Chiang Mai

- 240 Prapokklao Rd (☎ (053) 211541/042, 211044/7)
- 183/3 Changklan Rd (☎ (053) 234150, 235462, 233559/60)

Chiang Rai

- 870 Phahonyothin Rd (☎ (054) 711179, 715207)

Hat Yai

- 166/4 Niphat Uthit 2 Rd (☎ (074) 245851, 246165, 243711, 233433)
- 190/6 Niphat Uthit 2 Rd (☎ (074) 231272, 232392)

Khon Kaen

- 183/6 Maliwan Rd (☎ (043) 236523, 239011, 238835)

Lampang
314 Sanambin Rd (☎ (054) 217078, 218199)
Loei
191/1 Charoenrat Rd (☎ (042) 812344, 812355)
Mae Hong Son
71 Singhanatbamrung Rd (☎ (053) 611297, 611194)
Mae Sot
76/1 Prasatwitthi Rd (☎ (055) 531730, 531440)
Nakhon Ratchasima
14 Manat Rd (☎ (044) 257211/5)
Nakhon Si Thammarat
1612 Ratchadamnoen Rd (☎ (075) 342491)
Nan
34 Mahaprom Rd (☎ 710377, 710498)
Narathiwat
322-324 Phuphaphakdi Rd (☎ (073) 511161, 512178)
Nong Khai
453 Prachak Rd (☎ (042) 411530)
Pattani
9 Preeda Rd (☎ (073) 349149)
Pattaya
Royal Cliff Beach Hotel (☎ (038) 419286/7)
Phitsanulok
209/26-28 Bromtrailokanat Rd (☎ (055) 258020, 251671)
Phrae
42-44 Ratsadamnoen Rd (☎ (054) 511123)
Phuket
78 Ranong Rd (☎ (076) 211195, 212499, 212946)
41/33 Montri Rd (☎ (076) 212400, 212644, 212880)
Sakon Nakhon
1446/73 Yuwapattana Rd (☎ (042) 712259)
Songkhla
2 Soi 4, Saiburi Rd (☎ (074) 311012)
Surat Thani
3/27-28 Karoonrat Rd (☎ 273710, 273355)
Tak
485 Taksin Rd (☎ (055) 512164
Trang
199/2 Viseskul Rd (☎ (075) 218066)
Ubon
364 Chayanggoon Rd (☎ (045) 254431, 255894)
Udon
60 Makkang Rd (☎ (☎ 246697, 243222)

Other Domestic Airlines

Bangkok Airways Since January 1989 the Transport Ministry has licensed newcomer Bangkok Airways, owned by Sahakol Air, to fly routes between Bangkok and Hua Hin, Ko Samui and Trang. Planned Bangkok Airways destinations include Trang as well as assorted cities in the north and north-east. For most of its domestic flights (the company also has daily flights to Phnom Penh) Bangkok Airways uses either 37-seat Dash 8-100s or 18-seat Bandeirantes – all turboprops.

Bangkok Airways' fares are competitive with THAI's but the company is small and it remains to be seen whether or not it will survive to become a serious contender. At the moment it's like Mekong and Hong Thong whisky, each concentrating on a different share of the market. The airline's head office (☎ 253-4014/6, 253-8942/8) is at 140 Pacific Place Bldg, Sukhumvit Rd, Bangkok. There are also offices in Hua Hin, Phuket and Ko Samui.

Tropical Sea Air Formerly called Yellowbirds, this fledgling company flies seaplanes between Don Muang Airport and Pattaya (1050B one-way), and is discussing plans to fly to Ko Samet, Ko Samui and other Gulf of Thailand destinations as well. Eventually the company hopes to add Surat to Ko Samui and Phuket to Ko Phi Phi services as well, though the red tape that must be cleared first is probably tremendous.

Tropical Sea Air (☎ 275-6262 in Bangkok) employs Grumman aircraft – the nine-seat Goose and 15-seat Mallard – the type frequently seen in the Caribbean and on the US TV series Fantasy Island. There are rumours of technical problems with this craft and that the company may have to switch to different planes later. With Pattaya tourism on the decline (along with air links to Pattaya's U-Taphao Airport), the odds this operation will survive another two years is only about 50%.

BUS

Government Bus

Several different types of buses ply the roads of Thailand. The cheapest and slowest are the ordinary government-run buses *(rót thamádaa)* that stop in every little town and for every waving hand along the highway. For some destinations – smaller towns – these are your only choice but at least they leave frequently. The faster, more comfortable, less frequent government-run 'tour buses' *(rót thua* or *rót ae)* are usually air-con. If these are available to your destination, they are your very best choice since they don't cost that much more than the ordinary stop-in-every-town buses. The government bus company is called Baw Khaw Saw as an abbreviation of Borisàt Khõn Sòng (literally, 'the transportation company'). Every city and town in Thailand linked by bus transportation has a Baw Khaw Saw terminal, even if it's just a patch of dirt by the roadside.

The service on the government tour buses is usually quite good and includes beverage service and video. On longer routes (eg Bangkok to Chiang Mai, Bangkok to Nong Khai), the air-con tour buses even distribute claim checks for your baggage. Longer routes may also offer two classes of air-con buses, regular and 1st class; the latter buses have toilets. A new innovation are the VIP buses that have fewer seats (34 instead of 44; some routes have Super VIP, with only 24 seats) so that each seat reclines more. Sometimes these are called *rót nawn* or sleepers. For small-to-medium-sized people they are more comfortable, but if you're big you may find yourself squashed when the person in front of you leans back.

Occasionally you'll get a government air bus in which the air-con is broken or the seats are inferior, but in general I've found them more reliable than the private tour buses.

Private Bus

Private buses are available between major tourist and business destinations: Chiang Mai, Surat, Ko Samui, Phuket, Hat Yai, Pattaya, Hua Hin and a number of others. To Chiang Mai, for example, several companies run daily buses out of Bangkok. These can be booked through most hotels or any travel agency, although it's best to book directly through a bus office to be assured that you get what you pay for. Fares may vary from company to company but usually not by more than a few baht. However, fare differences between the government and private bus companies can be substantial. Using Surat Thani as an example, the state-run buses from the southern bus terminals are 125B for ordinary bus, 250B air-con, while the private companies charge up to 300B. On the other hand, air-con buses to Phuket are all the same price, 299B (ordinary bus is 165B), while to Chiang Mai the private buses often cost less than the government buses! Departures for some private companies are more frequent than for the equivalent Baw Khaw Saw route.

There are also private buses running between major destinations within the various regions, eg Nakhon Si Thammarat to Hat Yai in the south, and Chiang Mai to Sukhothai in the north. New companies are cropping up all the time. The numbers seemed to reach a peak in the early '80s, but are now somewhat stabilised because of a crackdown on licensing. Minibuses are used on some routes eg Surat to Krabi and Tak to Mae Sot.

The private air buses are usually no more comfortable than the government air buses and feature similarly narrow seats and a hair-raising ride. The trick the tour companies use to make their buses seem more comfortable is to make you think you're not on a bus, by turning up the air-con until your knees knock, handing out pillows and blankets and serving free soft drinks. On overnight journeys the buses usually stop somewhere en route and passengers are awakened to dismount the bus for a free meal of fried rice or rice soup. A few companies even treat you to a meal before a long overnight trip.

Like their state-run equivalents, the private companies offer VIP (sleeper) buses on long hauls.

Service

Although on average the private companies charge more than the government does on the same routes, the service is not always up to the higher relative cost. In recent years the service on many private lines has in fact declined, especially on the Bangkok to Chiang Mai, Bangkok to Ko Samui, Surat to Phuket and Surat to Krabi routes.

Sometimes the cheaper lines – especially those booked on Khao San Rd in Bangkok –

will switch vehicles at the last moment so that instead of the roomy air bus advertised, you're stuck with a cramped van with broken air-con. One traveller recounted how his Khao San Rd bus stopped for lunch halfway to Chiang Mai and while the passengers were eating, the bus zoomed off – leaving them to finish the journey on their own! For this reason it's always a better idea to book bus tickets directly at a bus office – or at the government Baw Khaw Saw station – rather than through a travel agency.

Another problem with private companies is that they generally spend more time cruising the city for passengers before getting under way than do the government buses.

Safety

Another problem with the private tour buses is that statistically, they meet with more accidents than government air-con buses. Turnovers on tight corners and head-on collisions with trucks are probably due to the inexperience of the drivers on a particular route. This in turn is probably a result of the companies opening and folding so frequently and because of the high priority given to making good time – Thais buy tickets on a company's reputation for speed.

As private bus fares are typically higher than government bus fares, the private bus companies attract a better-heeled clientele among the Thais, as well as foreign tourists. One result is that a tour bus loaded with money or the promise of money is a temptation for upcountry bandits. Hence, private tour buses occasionally get robbed by bands of thieves, but these incidents are diminishing due to increased security under provincial administration.

The most dangerous route now seems to be the road between Surat Thani and Phuket, though this is more so because of the old drugged food/drink/cigarette trick than because of armed robbery. (See the Dangers & Annoyances section in the Facts for the Visitor chapter for details.) In an effort to prevent this menace, which increased rapidly during the early '80s, Thai police now board tour buses plying the southern roads at unannounced intervals, taking photos and videotapes of the passengers and asking for IDs. Reported druggings are now on the decrease.

Large-scale robberies never occur on the ordinary buses, very rarely on the state-run air-con buses and rarely on the trains. The southern train route is the most dangerous. Accidents are not unknown on state-run buses either, so the train still comes out the safest means of transport in Thailand.

Now that you've decided not to go to Thailand after all, I should point out that robberies and accidents are relatively infrequent (though more frequent than they should be) considering the number of buses taken daily, and I've never been on a bus that's suffered either mishap – the odds are

WARNING

While travelling by bus or train, do not accept food, drinks or sweets from strangers no matter how friendly they may seem. You might be drugged or robbed of your belongings.

Tourist Police
509 Vorachak Road
Bangkok
Tel: 221-6206/10

Tourist Assistance Centre
Tourism Authority of Thailand
Ratchadamnoen Nok Avenue, Bangkok
Tel: 282-8129, 281-5051

on your side. Travellers to Thailand should know the risk of tour bus travel against the apparent convenience, especially when there are alternatives. Some travellers really like the tour buses though, so the private companies will continue to do good business.

Keep an eye on your bags when riding buses – thievery by stealth is still the most popular form of robbery in Thailand (eminently preferable to the forceful variety in my opinion), though again the risks are not that great – just be aware. Most pilfering seems to take place on the private bus runs between Bangkok and Chiang Mai, especially on buses booked on Khao San Rd. Keep zippered bags locked and well secured.

TRAIN

The railway network in Thailand, run by the Thai government, is surprisingly good. After travelling several thousand km by train and bus, I have to say that the train wins hands down as the best form of public transport in the kingdom. It is not possible to take the train everywhere in Thailand, but if it were that's how I'd go. If you travel 3rd class, it is often the cheapest way to cover a long distance; by 2nd class it's about the same as a 'tour bus' but much safer and more comfortable. Trains take a bit longer than chartered buses on the same journey but, on overnight trips especially, these are worth the extra travel time.

The trains offer many advantages; there is more space, more room to breathe and stretch out – even in 3rd class – than there is on the best buses. The windows are big and usually open, so that there is no glass between you and the scenery – good for taking photos – and more to see. The scenery itself is always better along the rail routes compared to the scenery along Thai highways – the trains regularly pass small villages, farmland, old temples, etc. Decent, reasonably priced food is available and served at your seat or in the dining car. The pitch-and-roll of the railway cars is much easier on the bones, muscles and nervous system than the quick stops and starts, the harrowing turns and the pot-hole jolts endured on buses. The train is safer in terms of both accidents and robberies. Last, but certainly not least, you meet a lot more interesting people on the trains, or so it seems to me.

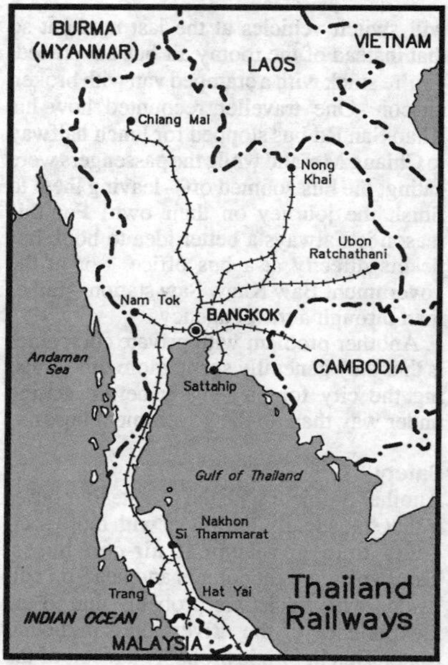

Rail Passes

For those who plan to travel extensively by train in Thailand, the State Railway of Thailand (SRT) offers a Visit Thailand Rail Pass for international passport holders. The Blue Pass allows 20 days of 2nd and 3rd-class travel at 1100B for adults or 550B for children (aged four to 12), supplementary charges not included; the Red Pass (2000B adults, 1100B children) covers all supplementary charges for 2nd and 3rd class. The rates for both passes have dropped 30% since they were first introduced in 1989 – apparently few visitors were buying them at the higher rates.

Are the passes good value? Suppose you were to take a train from Bangkok to Chiang

Mai, spend a week in the north, return to Bangkok and then make a similar excursion to Nong Khai and back; your 2nd-class ticket would cost a total of 1060B by express train, or 1040B by rapid train. In this scenario you'd be paying slightly more per km if you had purchased the Blue Pass. If you were to take even one more lengthy train trip, however, a Blue Pass would more than pay for itself.

If you made the same Chiang Mai and Nong Khai excursions using 'lower berth' sleeper accommodation (ie with a window and a bit more headroom than an 'upper berth' sleeper), you'd pay 1460B by express train, clearly making the 2000B Red Pass less attractive even if you were to take a few shorter side trips. If you had used the 1100B Blue Pass, you'd have had to kick in an extra 400B for the lower berths plus 120B for express surcharges, a total of 1620B and still cheaper than the Red Pass. So for the average visitor who might make four 600 to 700-km train journeys plus a few shorter ones over a 20-day period, it's probably more economical to buy a Blue Pass and pay your own supplementary charges along the way.

On the other hand if you're a real train freak and were to board trains every other day or so for 20 days, then either pass becomes a bargain. The Red Pass has the advantage of not having to deal with the supplementary charges – all you have to do is flash the pass at the booking office and get a seat. Both passes can be used either for making advance reservations or for taking what's available on the day of departure.

Lines

Four main rail lines cover 4000 km along the northern, southern, north-eastern and eastern routes. There are several side routes, notably between Nakhon Pathom and Nam Tok (stopping in Kanchanaburi) in the west central region, and between Tung Song and Kantang (stopping in Trang) in the south. The southern line splits at Hat Yai, one route going to Sungai Kolok in Malaysia, through Yala, and the other route going to Padang Besar in the west, also on the Malaysian border.

A new Bangkok to Pattaya spur was inaugurated in 1991 – whether it will be a successful enough to continue remains to be seen. Within the next few years, a southern spur may be extended from Khiriratnikhom to Phuket, establishing a rail link between Surat Thani and Phuket. A spur from Den Chai to Chiang Rai in the north is also under discussion. The SRT may also renovate the Japanese line that was built with forced POW and coolie labour during WW II between Nam Tok and Sangkhlaburi in Kanchanaburi Province.

Even further afield, the SRT is surveying an unused rail extension between Aranyaprathet in Thailand and Poi Pet in Cambodia with the intention to resume international rail services between the two countries.

Classes

The SRT operates passenger trains in three classes – 1st, 2nd and 3rd – but each class varies considerably depending on whether you're on an ordinary, rapid, or express train.

Third Class A typical 3rd-class car consists of two rows of bench seats divided into facing pairs. Each bench seat is designed to seat two or three passengers, but on a crowded upcountry line nobody seems to care about design considerations. On a rapid train (which carries 2nd and 3rd-class cars only), 3rd-class seats are padded and reasonably comfortable for shorter trips. On ordinary, 3rd-class-only trains in the east and north-east, seats are sometimes made of hard wooden slats, and are not recommended for more than a couple of hours at a time. Express trains do not carry 3rd-class cars at all. Commuter trains in the Bangkok area are all 3rd class and the cars resemble modern subway or rapid transit trains, with plastic seats and ceiling loops for standing passengers.

Second Class In a 2nd-class car, seating arrangements are similar to those on a bus, with pairs of padded seats all facing toward the front of the train. Usually the seats can be adjusted to a reclining angle, and for some people this is good enough for overnight trips. In a 2nd-class sleeper, you'll find two rows of facing seat pairs; each pair is separated from the next by a dividing wall. A table folds down between each pair and at night the seats convert into two fold-down berths, one over the other. Curtains provide a modicum of privacy and the berths are fairly comfortable, with fresh linen for every trip. A toilet stall is located at one end of the car and washing basins at the other. Second-class cars are found only on rapid and express trains; some routes offer air-con 2nd class as well as ordinary 2nd class.

First Class First-class cars provide private cabins for singles or couples. Each private cabin has individually controlled air-con, an electric fan, a fold-down washing basin and mirror, a small table and a long bench seat (or two in a double cabin) that converts into a bed. Drinking water and towels are provided free of charge. First-class cars are available only on express and special express trains.

Sprinter New air-con diesel express trains called 'Sprinters' have recently begun operating on the four trunk lines. Fares are about the same as for regular 1st-class express trains but Sprinter trains have one class only, operate only between 5.35 am and 9.10 pm and make fewer stops than the regular express trains. A Sprinter from Bangkok to Khorat, for example, takes four hours and costs 245B per seat. Departure time from Bangkok is 9.25 am; arrival in Khorat is at 1.31 pm. A 1st-class seat on a regular express train for the same journey would cost 237B; the regular express departs Bangkok at 9 pm and arrives in Khorat at 1.58 am, a trip of about five hours. A 2nd-class seat on the same train would cost 134B.

Sprinter fares include one meal and a snack – served in aeroplane-style styrofoam containers by aeroplane-style attendants – for each journey. If you're not travelling more than 200 km or so you might miss the meal service since serving times are oriented toward passengers who board at the beginning of the route and are riding more than halfway.

Meals

Meal service is available in dining cars and at your seat in 2nd and 1st-class cars. Menus seem to change frequently; for a while there were two menus, a 'special food' menu with prices at 50 to 60B per dish (generally given to tourists) and a cheaper, more extensive menu at 25 to 35B per dish. On my last trip the northern and southern lines had only the more expensive menu. To see if a cheaper menu is available, request the *menuu thamádaa* or ordinary menu. The food is basically the same on both menus but the 'special'-menu items get a fancier presentation.

Train staff sometimes hand out face wipes, then come by later to collect 10B each for them – a racket since there's no indication to passengers that they're not complimentary (on government buses they're free, and they're available in the station for 1B). Drinking water is provided for free, albeit in plastic bottles.

Bookings

The disadvantage of travelling by train, in addition to the time factor mentioned earlier, is that they can be difficult to book. This is especially true around holiday time, eg the middle of April approaching Songkran Festival, since many Thais also prefer the train. Trains out of Bangkok should be booked as far in advance as possible – a minimum of a week for such popular routes as the northern line to Chiang Mai and southern line to Hat Yai, especially if you want a sleeper. For the north-eastern and eastern lines a few days will suffice.

Advance bookings may be made one to 90 days before your intended date of departure. If you want to book tickets in advance go to Hualamphong station in Bangkok, walk through the front of the station house and go straight to the back right-hand corner where a sign says 'Advance Booking' (open 8.30 am to 6 pm Monday to Friday, 8.30 am to noon weekends and holidays). The other ticket windows, on the left-hand side of the station, are for same-day purchases, mostly 3rd class. In the Advance Booking office you will receive a numbered reservation form, white for the southern line, green for north, north-eastern and eastern. Then proceed into the ticketing room, taking the blank reservation form to the appropriate counter. A clerk will fill out the correct forms for you, according to available space on the train you want. This done, you take a seat and wait until your number appears on one of the electronic marquees, at which point the agent at the desk will give you your ticket and collect the money.

Note that buying a return ticket does not necessarily guarantee you a seat on the way back, it only means you do not have to buy a ticket for the return. If you want a guaranteed seat reservation it's best to make that reservation for the return immediately upon arrival at your destination.

Booking trains back to Bangkok is generally not as difficult as booking trains out of Bangkok; however, some stations can be quite difficult, eg buying a ticket from Surat Thani to Bangkok.

Tickets between any stations in Thailand can be purchased at Hualamphong station (☎ 223-3762, 224-7788; fax 225-6068), the main railway station in Bangkok. You can also make advance bookings at Don Muang station, across from Bangkok International Airport. SRT ticket offices are open from 8.30 am to 6 pm on weekdays, 8.30 am to noon on weekends and public holidays.

Train tickets can also be purchased at certain travel agencies in Bangkok, such as Airland on Ploenchit Rd or at the Viengthai

Your Train Tickets

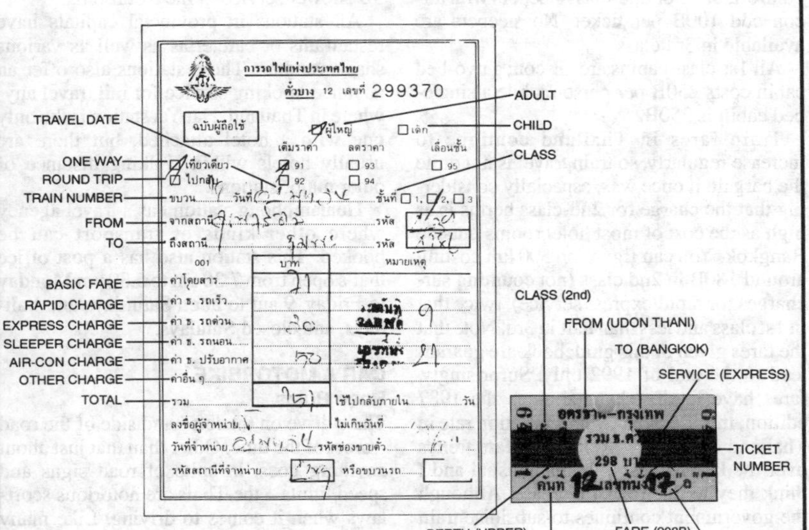

Hotel in Banglamphu (see the Travel Agencies section in the Bangkok chapter). It is much simpler to book trains through these agencies than to book them at the station; however, they usually add a surcharge of 50 to 100B to the ticket price.

Charges & Surcharges

There is a 30B surcharge for express trains *(rót dùan)* and 20B for rapid trains *(rót raew)*. These trains are somewhat faster than the ordinary trains, as they make fewer stops. On the northern line during the daytime there is a 50B surcharge for 2nd-class seats in air-con cars. For the special express *(rót dùan phísèt)* that runs between Bangkok and Singapore there is a 50B surcharge.

The charge for 2nd-class sleeping berths is 70B for an upper berth and 100B for a lower berth (or 100B and 150B respectively on a special express). The difference between upper and lower is that there is a window next to the lower berth and a little more headroom. The upper berth is still quite comfortable. For 2nd-class sleepers with air-con add 100B per ticket. No sleepers are available in 3rd class.

All 1st-class cabins are air-con; a two-bed cabin costs 250B per person while a single-bed cabin is 350B.

Train fares in Thailand continue to increase regularly, so train travel is not quite the bargain it once was, especially considering that the charge for 2nd-class berths is as high as the cost of most hotel rooms outside Bangkok. You can figure on 500 km costing around 180B in 2nd class (not counting surcharges for rapid/express service), twice that in 1st class and less than half in 3rd. Note that the fares given in this guidebook are guaranteed to the end of 1992 only. Surprisingly, fares have hardly changed since the 1987 edition, in spite of an overall inflation rate in Thailand of 5 to 7%. Relative to fare trends over the last 12 years, this is unusual and I think they're due for an increase. Although the government continues to subsidise train travel to a some extent, I predict that fares will be taking a significant jump in the next two to three years, say around 10 to 15%.

Station Services

Accurate up-to-date information on train travel is available at the Rail Travel Aids counter in Hualamphong station. There you can pick up timetables or ask questions about fares and scheduling – one person behind the counter usually speaks a little English. There are two types of timetables available: a condensed English timetable with fares, schedules and routes for rapid and express trains on the four trunk lines (plus schedules for the special and International Express); and complete, separate Thai timetables for each trunk line, with side lines as well. These latter timetables give fares and schedules for all trains, ordinary, rapid and express.

All railway stations in Thailand have baggage storage services (sometimes called the 'cloak room'). The rates and hours of operation vary from station to station. At Hualamphong station the hours are from 4 am to 10.30 pm and left luggage costs 5B per piece the first day, 10B per piece per day thereafter. Hualamphong station also has a 5B shower service in the rest rooms.

All stations in provincial capitals have restaurants or cafeterias as well as various snack vendors. These stations also offer an advance-booking service for rail travel anywhere in Thailand. Hat Yai station is the only one with a hotel attached, but there are usually hotels within walking distance of other major stations.

Hualamphong station has a travel agency where other kinds of transport can be booked. This station also has a post office that's open from 7.30 am to 5.30 pm Monday to Friday, 9 am to noon Saturdays and holidays, and closed Sundays.

CAR & MOTORBIKE

Road Rules

Thais drive on the left-hand side of the road – most of the time. Other than that just about anything goes, in spite of road signs and speed limits – the Thais are notorious scofflaws when it comes to driving. Like many places in Asia, every two-lane road has an invisible third lane in the middle that all drivers feel free to use at any time. Passing on hills and curves is common – as long as you've got the proper Buddhist altar on the dashboard, what could happen?

The main rule to be aware of is that the right of way belongs to the bigger vehicle; this is not what it says in the Thai traffic law, but it's the reality. Maximum speed limits are 60 km/h within city limits, 80 km/h on highways but on any given stretch of highway you'll see vehicles travelling as slowly as 30 km/h or as fast as 150 km/h. Speed traps are becoming more common; they seem especially common along Highway 4 in the south and along provincial highways in the north-east.

The principal hazard to driving in Thailand besides the general disregard for traffic laws is having to contend with so many different types of vehicles on the same road – bullock carts, 18-wheelers, bicycles, tuk-tuks and customised racing bikes. In village areas the vehicular traffic is lighter but you have to contend with stray chickens, dogs, water buffaloes, pigs, cats and goats. Once you get used to the challenge, driving in Thailand is very entertaining but first-time drivers tend to get a bit unnerved.

Rental

Cars, jeeps or vans can be rented in Bangkok, Chiang Mai, Chiang Rai, Mae Hong Son, Pattaya, Phuket, Ko Samui and Hat Yai. A Japanese sedan (eg Toyota Corolla) or minivan typically costs from around 1000 to 1200B per day. The best deals are usually on 4WD Suzuki Caribeans (sic), which can be rented for as low as 700 to 800B per day. Check with travel agencies or large hotels for rental locations. Always verify that a vehicle is insured for liability before signing a rental contract and ask to see the dated insurance documents. If you have an accident while driving an uninsured vehicle you're in for some major hassles.

Motorcycles can be rented in major towns as well as many smaller tourist centres like Krabi, Ko Samui, Ko Pha-Ngan, Mae Sai, Chiang Saen, Nong Khai, etc (see Motorcycle Touring). Rental rates vary considerably from one agency to another and from city to city. Since there is a glut of motorcycles for rent in Chiang Mai and Phuket these days, they can be rented in these towns for as little as 80B per day. A substantial deposit is usually required to rent a car; motorcycle rental usually requires that you leave your passport.

Driving Permits

Foreigners who wish to drive a motor vehicle (including motorcycles) in Thailand need a valid International Driving Permit. If you don't have one, you can apply for a Thai driver's licence at the Police Registration Division (PRD) (☎ 513-0051/5) on Phahonyothin Rd in Bangkok. Provincial capitals also have PRDs. If you present a valid foreign driver's licence at the PRD you'll probably only have to take a written test; other requirements include a medical certificate and three passport-sized colour photos. The forms are in Thai only, so you'll also need an interpreter.

Fuel & Oil

Modern petrol (gasoline) stations with electric pumps are in plentiful supply everywhere in Thailand where there are paved roads. In more remote off-road areas petrol *(ben-sin* or *náam-man rót yon* in Thai) is usually available at small roadside or village stands – typically just a couple of ancient hand-operated pumps fastened to petrol barrels. As we went to press, regular *(thamádaa* in Thai) petrol cost about 10B per litre, super *(phísèt)* a bit more. Diesel *(dii-soen)* fuel is available at most pumps.

The Thai phrase for 'motor oil' is *náam-man khrêuang*.

Motorcycle Touring

Motorcycle travel is becoming a popular way to get around Thailand, especially in the north. Dozens of places along the guesthouse circuit, including many guesthouses themselves, have set up shop with no more than a couple of motorbikes for rent. It is also possible to buy a new or used motorbike and sell it before you leave the country – a good used 125cc bike costs around 20,000B. Daily rentals range from 80B a day for an 80cc or 100cc step-through (eg Honda Dream, Suzuki Crystal) to 300B a day for a 250cc dirt bike. The motorcycle industry in Thailand has stopped assembling dirt bikes, so all the rental bikes of this nature are getting on in years – when they're well maintained they're fine. When they're not well maintained, they can leave you stranded if not worse. The latest trend in Thailand is for small, heavy racing bikes that couldn't be less suitable for the typical farang body.

The legal maximum size for motorcycle manufacture in Thailand is 150cc, though in reality few bikes on the road exceed 125cc. Anything over 150cc must be imported, which means an addition of up to 600% in import duties. The odd rental shop specialises in bigger motorbikes (average 200 to 500cc) – some were imported by foreign residents and later sold on the local market but most came into the country as 'parts' and were discreetly assembled, and licensed under the table.

While motorcycle touring is undoubtedly one of the best ways to see Thailand, it is also undoubtedly one of the easiest ways to cut your travels short, permanently. You can also run up very large repair and/or hospital bills in the blink of an eye. However, with proper safety precautions and driving conduct adapted to local standards, you can see parts of Thailand inaccessible by other modes of transport and still make it home in one piece. Some guidelines to keep in mind:

1. If you've never driven a motorcycle before, stick to the smaller 80 to 100cc step-through bikes with automatic clutches. If you're an experienced rider but have never done off-the-road driving, take it slow the first few days.

2. Always check a machine over thoroughly before you take it out. Look at the tyres to see if they still have tread, look for oil leaks, test the brakes. You may be held liable for any problems that weren't duly noted before your departure. Newer bikes cost more than clunkers, but are generally safer and more reliable. Street bikes are more comfortable and ride more smoothly on paved roads than dirt bikes; it's silly to rent an expensive dirt bike like the Honda MTX 125 if most of your riding is going to be along decent roads. The two-stroke MTX 125 uses twice the fuel of a four-stroke Honda Wing with the same engine size, thus lowering your cruising range in areas where roadside pumps are scarce (the Wing gives you about 300 km per tank while an MTX gets about half that).

3. Wear protective clothing and a helmet (most rental places will provide a helmet with the bike if asked). Without a helmet, a minor slide on gravel can leave you with concussion, cuts or bruises. Long pants, long-sleeved shirts and shoes are highly recommended as protection against sunburn and as a second skin if you fall. If your helmet doesn't have a visor, then wear goggles, glasses or sunglasses to keep bugs, dust and other debris out of your eyes. It is practically suicidal to ride on Thailand's highways without taking these minimum precautions for protecting your body. Gloves are also a good idea – to prevent blisters from holding on to the twist-grips for long periods of time.

4. For distances of over 100 km or so, take along an extra supply of motor oil and, if riding a two-stroke machine like the MTX, two-stroke engine oil. On long trips, oil burns fast.

5. You should never ride alone in remote areas, especially at night. There have been incidents where farang bikers have been shot or harassed while riding alone, mostly in remote rural areas. When riding in pairs or groups, stay spread out so you'll have room to manoeuvre or brake suddenly if necessary.

6. In Thailand the de facto right of way is determined by the size of the vehicle which puts the motorcycle pretty low in the pecking order. Don't fight it and keep clear of trucks and buses.

7. Distribute whatever weight you're carrying on the bike as evenly as possible across the frame. Too much weight at the back of the bike makes the front end less easy to control and prone to rising up suddenly on bumps and inclines.

8. Get insurance with the motorcycle if at all possible. The more reputable motorcycle rental places insure all their bikes; some will do it for an extra charge. Without insurance you're responsible for anything that happens to the bike. If an accident results in a total loss, or if the bike is somehow lost or stolen, you can be out 25,000B plus. Health insurance is also a good idea – get it before you leave home and check the conditions in regard to motorcycle riding.

BICYCLE

Bicycles can also be hired in many locations; guesthouses often have a few for rent at only 20 to 30B per day. Just about anywhere outside Bangkok, bikes are the ideal form of local transport since they're cheap, non-polluting and keep you moving slowly enough to see everything. Carefully note the condition of the bike before hiring; if it breaks down you are responsible and parts can be very expensive.

Many visitors are bringing their own touring bikes to Thailand these days. Grades in most parts of the country are moderate; exceptions include the far north, especially Mae Hong Son and Nan provinces, where you'll need iron thighs. There is plenty of opportunity for dirt-road and off-road pedalling, especially in the north, so a sturdy mountain bike would make a good alternative to a touring rig. Favoured touring routes include the two-lane roads along the Maekhong River in the north and/or the north-east – the terrain is mostly flat and the river scenery is inspiring.

No special permits are needed for bringing a bicycle into the country, although bikes may be registered by customs – which means if you don't leave the country with your bike you'll have to pay a huge customs duty. Most larger cities have bike shops – there are several in Bangkok and Chiang Mai – but they often stock only a few Japanese or locally made parts. All the usual bike trip precautions apply – bring a small repair kit with plenty of spare parts, a helmet, reflective clothing and plenty of insurance.

HITCHING

People have mixed success with hitchhiking in Thailand; sometimes it's great and other times no-one will pick you up. It seems easiest in the more touristed areas of the north and south, most difficult in the central and north-eastern regions where farangs are a relatively rare sight. To stand on a road and try to flag every vehicle that passes by is, to the Thais, something only an uneducated village dweller would do.

If you're prepared to face this perception, the first step is to use the correct gesture used for flagging a ride – the thumb-out gesture isn't recognised by the average Thai. When Thais want a ride they stretch one arm out with the hand open, palm facing down, and move the hand up and down. This is the same gesture used to flag a taxi or bus, which is why some drivers will stop and point to a bus stop if one is nearby.

In general hitching isn't worth the hassle as ordinary buses (no air-con) are frequent and fares are cheap. There's no need to stand at a bus terminal – all you have to do is stand on any road going in your direction and flag down a passing bus or songthaew as described above.

The exception is in areas where there isn't any bus service, though in such places there's not liable to be very much private vehicle traffic either. If you do manage to get a ride it's customary to offer food or cigarettes to the driver if you have any.

BOAT

As any flight over Thailand will reveal, there is plenty of water down there and you'll probably have opportunities to get out on it from time to time. The true Thai river transport is the 'long-tail boat' *(reua hang yao)*, so-called because the propeller is at the end of a long drive shaft extending from the engine. The engine, which varies from a small marine engine to a large car engine, is mounted on gimbals and the whole unit is swivelled to steer the boat. These boats can travel at a phenomenal speed.

Between the mainland and islands in the Gulf of Thailand or Andaman Sea, all sorts of larger ocean-going craft are used. The standard is an all-purpose wooden boat eight to 10 metres long with a large inboard engine, a wheelhouse and a simple roof to shelter passengers and cargo. Faster, more expensive hovercraft or jetfoils are sometimes available in tourist areas.

LOCAL TRANSPORT

The Bangkok Getting Around section has more information on various forms of local transport.

To/From Bangkok International Airport The main international airport is in Don Muang district, approximately 25 km north of Bangkok. You have a choice of transport modes from the airport to city ranging from 3B to 300B in cost.

THAI Bus Thai Airways International has an airport bus that goes to its city terminal at the Asia Hotel for 60B per person. The Asia Hotel is in a good central location on Phayathai Rd between Phetburi and Rama I Rds. From here a tuk-tuk to accommodation in the Siam Square area should be 25B or less. If you're not carrying much, you could also walk there in around 20 minutes. Or walk north to Phetburi Rd and get ordinary bus Nos 2, 45, 60 or air-con bus No 11 to Banglamphu. To other areas of the city, however, you might as well get a direct taxi since the THAI bus fare plus tuk-tuk or taxi fare to, say, Soi Ngam Duphli would approach the 180B direct taxi fare. THAI buses run from 7 am until 9 pm.

THAI also has a minibus service to major hotels (and minor ones if the driver feels like it) for 100B per person. THAI touts in the arrival hall will try to get you into the 300B limo service first, then the 100B minibus, before letting you buy a 60B bus ticket to the Asia Hotel.

There are direct air-con buses to Pattaya from the airport twice daily at 11 am and 9 pm; the fare is 180B one-way. Private sedans cost 1500B per trip. THAI also operates a free shuttle bus between the international and domestic terminals every half hour.

Public Bus Cheapest of all are the public buses to Bangkok which stop on the highway in front of the airport. The ordinary No 29 bus is only 3B, but often crowded – it comes straight down Phahonyothin Rd after entering the city limits. This road soon turns into Phayathai Rd, meanwhile passing Phetburi Rd (where you'll want to get off to change buses if you're going to the Democracy Monument area), Rama I Rd (for buses out to Sukhumvit Rd, or to walk to Soi Kasem San I for Muangphol Lodging, Reno Hotel, etc) and finally turning right on Rama IV Rd to go to the Hualamphong district. You'll want to go the opposite way on Rama IV for the Malaysia, Boston Inn, etc. Bus No 59 goes straight to the Democracy Monument area from the airport.

The air-con public bus No 4 can also be boarded at the airport for 15B to most destinations in Bangkok. It costs less if you're getting off in north Bangkok (say, for the Liberty Hotel in Saphan Khwai district), though this must be established before you pay the fare. Unless you're really strapped for baht, it's worth the extra 12B for the air-con and almost guaranteed seating on the No 4, especially in the hot season, since the trip downtown by bus can take an hour or more.

The No 4 bus does a route which is parallel to the No 29 bus – down Mitthaphap Rd to Ratchaprarop and Ratchadamri Rds, crossing Phetburi, Rama I, Ploenchit and Rama IV Rds, then down Silom, left on Charoen Krung, and across the river to Thonburi. You ought to have some kind of map of Bangkok before attempting the buses so you'll know approximately where to get off. The air-con No 13 also goes to Bangkok from the airport, coming down Phahonyothin Rd (like No 29), turning left at the Victory Monument to Ratchaprarop Rd, then south to Ploenchit Rd, where it goes east out Sukhumvit Rd all the way to Bang Na.

The air-con bus No 10 terminates at the southern bus terminal in Thonburi, where you can get buses direct to Kanchanaburi and points south. There is now an air-con bus No 29 that goes to Hualamphong station along the same basic route as the regular bus No 29.

Air-con buses run from 5 am until 8 or 8.30 pm. Ordinary buses run until 10 pm.

Train You can also get into Bangkok from the airport by train. Just after leaving the passenger terminal, turn right (north), cross the highway via the pedestrian bridge, turn left and walk about 100 metres towards

Top Left: Khaen maker, Roi Et (JC)
Bottom Left: Shadow-puppet carver, Nakhon Si Thammarat (JC)
Top Right: Rice farmers near Ayuthaya (TM)
Bottom Right: Little Buddhists, Bangkok (RI)

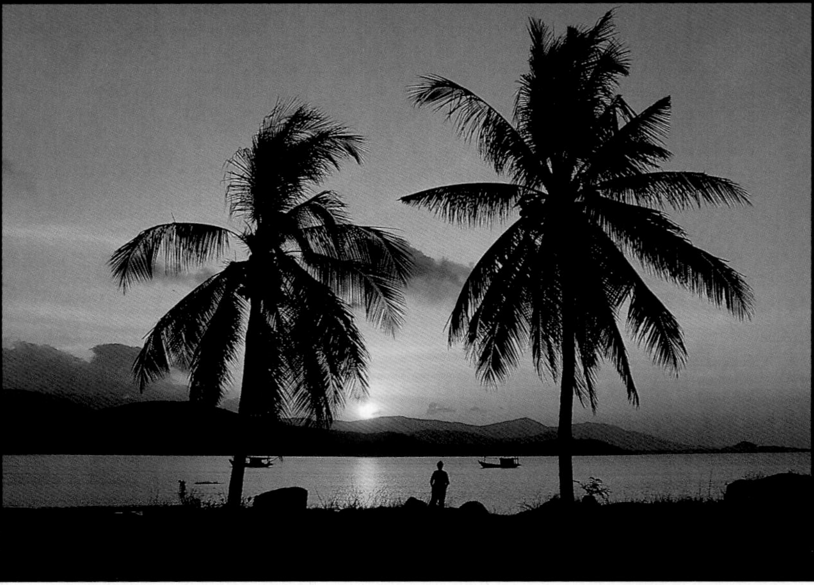

Top: Ko Phi Phi (TAT)
Bottom: Sunset at Big Buddha Beach (RI)

Bangkok. Opposite the big Airport Hotel is the small Don Muang railway station from where trains depart regularly to Bangkok. The 3rd-class fare is only 5B on the ordinary and commuter trains. If you happen to get on a rapid or express train you'll have to pay a 20 or 30B surcharge. There are trains every 15 to 30 minutes between 6.25 am and 10 pm and it take about 45 minutes to reach Hualamphong, the main station in central Bangkok. In the opposite direction trains run frequently between 7.05 am and 10 pm.

You can also ride trains between Hualamphong and Makkasan, which is north of Phetburi Rd near the intersection of Ratchaprarop and Si Ayuthaya Rds, not far from the Indra and Bangkok Palace hotels. There are no direct trains between Don Muang and Makkasan stations; you have to change in Hualamphong. The trip only takes 15 minutes but there are just 11 trains per day, between 6.15 am and 6 pm.

A new air-con Airport Express train has been established especially for the tourist traffic between Don Muang and Hualamphong stations. At the moment the train often leaves the station with few or no passengers, as it's overpriced and a hassle to use. The train ride itself takes about 35 minutes but you must board a shuttle bus from the airport to Don Muang station first since the Airport Hotel won't allow people who aren't hotel guests to use the enclosed pedestrian bridge across the expressway. Since you can't purchase the express tickets at the station (only at the THAI limo desk – yet another THAI scam), you're forced to take the shuttle bus, which has to go 12 km south on the highway and make a U-turn to reach the station, a trip of about 20 minutes.

The total time to reach Hualamphong, not counting bus and train waits (there are only six departures per day), is hence 55 minutes. The fare is 100B each way for air-con, 80B non-air-con (Thais pay only 60B). When you can walk across the open public bridge and take the far more frequent ordinary train – comfortable enough – for 5B (add 20 or 30B for rapid or express trains), why bother with the tourist express?

Taxi The taxis which wait near the arrival area of the airport are supposed to be airport-regulated. Ignore all the touts waiting like sharks near the customs area and buy a taxi ticket from a booth at the southern end of the arrival hall (to the far left as you leave customs). Fares are set according to city destination – no haggling should be necessary; most destinations in central Bangkok are 180B (eg Siam Square) or 200B (eg Banglamphu). Two, three, or even four passengers (if they don't have much luggage) can split the fare. Sometimes unscrupulous drivers will approach you before you reach the desk and try to sell you a ticket for 300B – ignore them and head straight for the desk. A few touts from the old taxi mafia that used to prowl the arrival area are still around and may approach you with fares of around 150B. Their taxis have white and black plates and are not licensed to carry passengers, hence you have less legal recourse in the event of an incident than if you take a licensed taxi (yellow and black plates).

If you really want to save the 30 to 50B, go upstairs to the departure area and get an incoming city taxi, one that has just dropped passengers off. These will usually take you to Bangkok for 120 to 150B. The downstairs taxi mafia frowns on this practice, however, and you may be hassled.

Taxis flagged down on the highway in front of the airport are even cheaper – 80 to 120B for central Bangkok. THAI offers an airport limousine, which is really just a glorified air-con taxi service, for 300B.

Going to the airport from the city, taxis will ask an outrageous amount but will usually go for 150B or so (up to 200B if your bargaining is weak or there aren't many taxis around – but the standard fare is 150B), not too bad if you're looking for the fastest way out, or have a few other travellers with whom to share the fare.

Helicopter The Shangri-La Hotel has its own helicopter service – introduced for the World Bank/IMF meeting in 1991 – from Bangkok Airport to the hotel rooftop for 2700B per person. The flight takes only 10 minutes but is reserved for Shangri-La guests only. If you can afford the copter flight you can certainly afford this hotel, which has one of Bangkok's best river locations.

Bus

In most larger provincial capitals, there are extensive local bus services, generally operating with very low fares (2 to 4B).

Taxi

Many regional centres have taxi services but, as in Bangkok itself, although there may well be meters they're never used. Establishing the fare before departure is essential. Try and get an idea from a third party what the fare should be and be prepared to bargain. In general fares are reasonably low.

Samlor/Tuk-Tuk

Samlor means 'three' *(sãam)* 'wheels' *(láw)*, and that's just what they are – three-wheeled vehicles. There are two types of samlors, motorised and non-motorised. You'll find motorised samlors throughout the country. They're small utility vehicles, powered by a horrendously noisy two-stroke engine – if the noise and vibration doesn't get you the fumes will. These samlors are often known as *tuk-tuks* from the noise they make. The non-motorised version, on the other hand, are bicycle rickshaws, just like you find, in various forms, all over Asia. There are no bicycle samlors in Bangkok but you will find them elsewhere in the country. In either form of samlor the fare must be established, by bargaining if necessary, before departure.

Songthaew

A songthaew *(sãwng tháew*, literally 'two rows') is a small pick-up truck with two rows of bench seats down the sides, very similar to an Indonesian *bemo* and akin to a Filipino *jeepney.* Songthaews sometimes operate fixed routes, just like buses, but they may also run a share-taxi type of service or even be booked individually just like a regular taxi.

Bangkok

The very epitome of the modern, steamy Asian metropolis, Bangkok (population 7,000,000) has a surplus of attractions if you can tolerate the traffic, noise, heat (in the hot season), floods (in the rainy season) and somewhat polluted air. The city is incredibly urbanised, but beneath its modern veneer lies an unmistakable Thai-ness. To say that Bangkok is not Thailand, as has been superciliously claimed by some, is like saying that New York is not the USA, Paris is not France, or London not England.

The capital of Thailand was established at Bangkok in 1782 by the first king of the Chakri Dynasty, Rama I. The name Bangkok comes from *bang makok*, meaning 'place of olives' (not the European variety) and refers to the original site which is only a very small part of what is today called Bangkok by foreigners. The official Thai name is quite a tongue twister:

Krungthep - mahanakhon - bowon - rattanakosin - mahintara - ayuthaya - mahadilok - popnopparat - ratchathani - burirom - udomratchaniwet - mahasathan

Fortunately it is shortened to Krung Thep (City of Angels), in everyday usage. Metropolitan Krung Thep includes Thonburi, the older part of the city (and predecessor to Bangkok as the capital), which is across the Chao Phraya River to the west.

Bangkok caters to diverse interests: there are temples, museums and other historic sites for those interested in traditional Thai culture; an endless variety of good restaurants, clubs, international cultural and social events; movies in several different languages and a modern art institute for those seeking contemporary Krung Thep. As the dean of expat authors in Thailand, William Warren, has said, 'The gift Bangkok offers me is the assurance I will never be bored'.

Orientation

The east side of the river, Bangkok proper, can be divided into two by the main north-south railway line. The portion between the river and the railway is old Bangkok (often called Ko Ratanakosin), where most of the older temples and the original palace are located, as well as the Chinese and Indian districts. That part of the city east of the railway, which covers more than twice as much area as the old districts, is 'new' Bangkok. It can be divided again into the business/tourist district wedged between Charoen Krung (New) Rd and Rama IV Rd, and the sprawling residential/tourist district stretching along Sukhumvit and New Phetburi Rds.

This leaves the hard-to-classify areas below Sathon Tai Rd (which includes Khlong Toey, Bangkok's main port), and the area above Rama IV Rd between the railway and Withayu (Wireless) Rd (which comprises an infinite variety of businesses, several movie theatres, civil service offices, the shopping area of Siam Square, Chulalongkorn University and the National Stadium). The areas along the east bank of the Chao Phraya River are undergoing a surge of redevelopment and many new buildings, particularly hotels, are going up.

On the opposite (west) side of the Chao Phraya River is Thonburi, which was Thailand's capital for 15 years before Bangkok was founded. Few tourists ever set foot on the Thonburi side except to visit Wat Arun, the Temple of the Dawn. Fang Thon (Thon Bank), as it's often called by Thais, seems an age away from the glittering high-rises on the river's east bank, although it is an up-and-coming area for condo development.

Finding Addresses Any city as large and unplanned as Bangkok can be tough to get around. Street names often seem unpronounceable to begin with, compounded by the inconsistency of Romanised Thai spellings. For example, the street often spelt as Rajdamri is pronounced Ratchadamri (with the appropriate tones), or in abbreviated

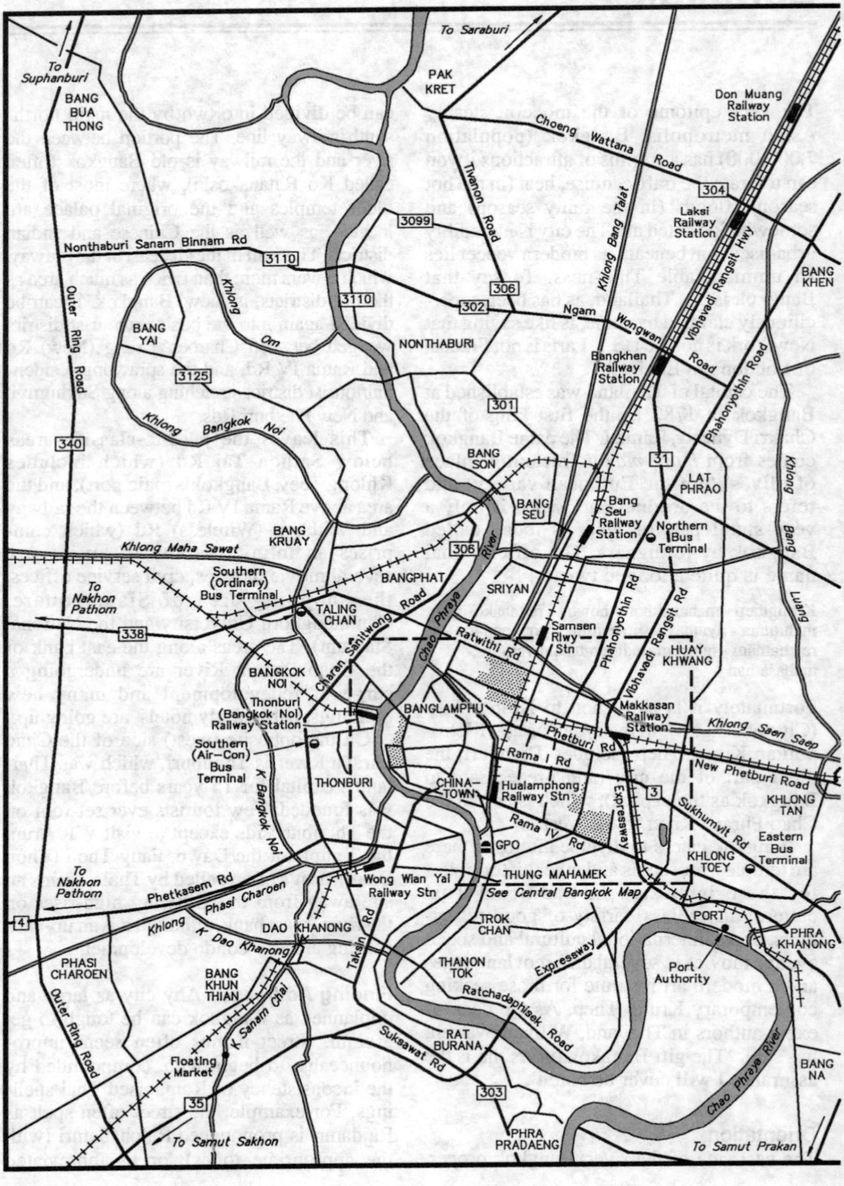
To Saraburi
To Suphanburi
BANG BUA THONG
PAK KRET
Don Muang Railway Station
Choeng Wattana Road
Tiwanon Road
Khlong Bang Talat
304
Laksi Railway Station
3099
Vibhavadi Rangsit Hwy
Nonthaburi Sanam Binnam Rd
3110
3110
Khlong Om
306
BANG KHEN
302
Ngam Wongwan Road
Outer Ring Road
BANG YAI
NONTHABURI
Bangkhen Railway Station
Phahonyothin Road
3125
301
Khlong Bangkok Noi
340
BANG SON
31
LAT PHRAO
Khlong Bang Luang
BANG SEU
Bang Seu Railway Station
Northern Bus Terminal
BANG KRUAY
Khlong Maha Sawat
306
Chao Phraya River
Southern (Ordinary) Bus Terminal
BANGPHAT
To Nakhon Pathom
SRIYAN
TALING CHAN
Sanitwong Road
Ratwithi Rd
Samsen Rlwy Stn
338
Phahonyothin Rd
Vibhavadi Rangsit Rd
HUAY KHWANG
BANGKOK NOI
Charan
Thonburi (Bangkok Noi) Railway Station
BANGLAMPHU
Makkasan Railway Station
Khlong Saen Saep
Southern (Air-Con) Bus Terminal
Phetburi Rd
Rama I Rd
New Phetburi Road
THONBURI
K Bangkok Noi
CHINA-TOWN
Hualamphong Railway Stn
Expressway
3
KHLONG TAN
Rama IV Rd
Sukhumvit Rd
GPO
Eastern Bus Terminal
KHLONG TOEY
To Nakhon Pathom
Wong Wian Yai Railway Stn
THUNG MAHAMEK
See Central Bangkok Map
Phetkasem Rd
Phasi Charoen
PORT
4
Khlong K Dao Khanong
DAO KHANONG
TROK CHAN
PHRA KHANONG
Taksin Rd
PHASI CHAROEN
BANG KHUN THIAN
THANON TOK
Expressway
Port Authority
Outer Ring Road
Ratchadaphisek Road
K Sanam Chai
Suksawat Rd
RAT BURANA
Floating Market
BANG NA
303
35
Chao Phraya River
To Samut Sakhon
PHRA PRADAENG
To Samut Prakan

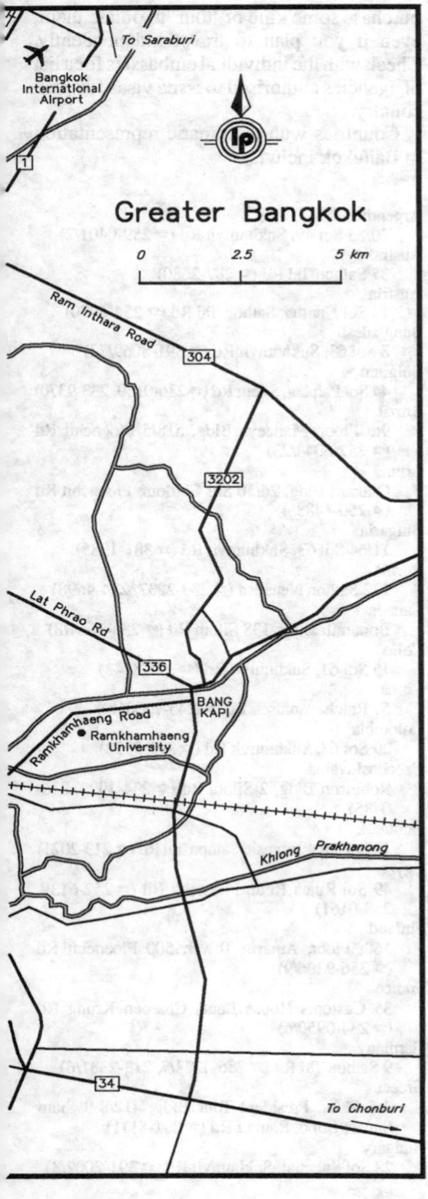

form Rat'damri. The 'v' in Sukhumvit should be pronounced like a 'w'. The most popular location for foreign embassies is known both as Wireless Rd and Withayu Rd (*wítháyú* is Thai for 'radio').

Many street addresses show a string of numbers divided by slashes and hyphens, for example, 48/3-5 Soi 1, Sukhumvit Rd. This is because undeveloped property in Bangkok was originally bought and sold in lots. The number before the slash refers to the original lot number; the numbers following the slash indicate buildings (or entrances to buildings) constructed within that lot. The pre-slash numbers appear in the order in which they were added to city plans, while the post-slash numbers are arbitrarily assigned by developers. As a result numbers along a given street don't always run consecutively.

A *soi* is a small street or lane that runs off a larger street. In our example, the address referred to as 48/3-5 Soi 1, Sukhumvit Rd will be located off Sukhumvit Rd on Soi 1. Alternative ways of writing the same address include 48/3-5 Sukhumvit Rd Soi 1, or even just 48/3-5 Sukhumvit 1.

Information

Tourist Offices The Tourist Authority of Thailand (TAT) has a desk in the arrivals area at Bangkok Airport. Its main office (☎ 282-1143/7) is at Ratchadamnoen Nok Rd. The TAT produces the usual selection of colourful brochures, but they're also one of the best tourist offices in Asia for putting out useful hard facts – on plain but quite invaluable duplicated sheets. The TAT also maintains a Tourist Assistance Centre (☎ 281-5051) for matters relating to theft or other such mishaps; it's open from 8 am to midnight. The paramilitary arm of the TAT, the tourist police, can be quite effective in dealing with such matters, particularly 'unethical' business practices (which sometimes turn out to be cultural misunderstandings).

Money Major Thai banks have currency exchange offices in many areas of Bangkok which are open from 8.30 am to 8 pm every day of the year. You'll find them located in several places along Sukhumvit, Nana Neua, Khao San, Patpong, Surawong, Ratchadamri, Rama IV, Rama I, Silom and Charoen Krung (New) Rds. If you're after currency for other countries in Asia, check with the money changers along Charoen Krung (New) Rd near the GPO.

Post & Telecommunications The GPO is on Charoen Krung (New) Rd. The easiest way to get here is via the Chao Phraya River Express, which stops at Tha Muang Khae at the river end of Soi Charoen Krung 34 just south of the GPO. The poste restante counter opens from 8 am to 8 pm, Monday to Friday and from 8 am to 1 pm on weekends. Each letter you collect costs 1B, parcels 2B, and the staff are very efficient.

There's also a packaging service at the post office where parcels can be wrapped for 3 to 5B plus the cost of materials (up to 20B). Or you can simply buy the materials at the counter and do it yourself. The packaging counter is open Monday to Friday from 8 am to 4.30 pm, Saturday 9 am to noon. When the parcel counter is closed (weekday evenings and Sunday mornings) an informal packing service (using recycled materials) is open behind the service windows.

The international telephone office around the corner from the main GPO building is open 24 hours. If you're calling Japan, Hong Kong, Korea, Italy, Singapore, the UK, the USA, New Zealand, the Netherlands or Taiwan, you can simply enter a vacant HCD (Home Country Direct) booth and get one-button connection with an international operator in any of these countries. For other countries there are IDD phones.

Embassies & Consulates Bangkok is an important place for gathering visas for onward travel. If you're heading on to India you'll definitely need a visa, and if you're going to Nepal it's much better to have a visa although they are granted on entry.

For travel to Burma, Vietnam, Laos or Cambodia you'll also need a visa. All four countries are now issuing 14-day tourist visas, although you will probably have to purchase some kind of 'tour' to obtain them, even if you plan to travel independently. Check with the individual embassies for a list of agencies authorised to issue visas for each country.

Countries with diplomatic representation in Bangkok include:

Argentina
20/85 Soi 49, Sukhumvit Rd (☎ 259-0401/2)
Australia
37 Sathon Tai Rd (☎ 287-2680)
Austria
14 Soi Nantha, Sathon Tai Rd (☎ 254-6970)
Bangladesh
8 Soi 63, Sukhumvit Rd (☎ 391-8069/70)
Belgium
44 Soi Phiphat, Silom Rd (☎ 236-0150, 233-9370)
Brazil
9th Floor, Maneeya Bldg, 518/5 Ploenchit Rd (☎ 252-6043/23)
Brunei
Orakarn Bldg, 26/50 Soi Chitlom, Ploenchit Rd (☎ 250-1483/4)
Bulgaria
11/64 Soi 63, Sukhumvit Rd (☎ 381-1385)
Burma
132 Sathon Neua Rd (☎ 233-2237, 234-4698)
Canada
Boonmitr Bldg, 138 Silom Rd (☎ 234-1561/8)
Chile
15 Soi 61, Sukhumvit Rd (☎ 391-8443)
China
57 Ratchadaphisek Rd (☎ 245-7030/49)
Colombia
29 Soi 63, Sukhumvit Rd (☎ 391-9933)
Czechoslovakia
Robinson Bldg, 2 Silom Rd (☎ 234-1922, 236-0485)
Denmark
10 Soi Attakanprasit, Sathon Tai Rd (☎ 213-2021)
Egypt
49 Soi Ruam Rudi, Ploenchit Rd (☎ 252-6139, 253-0161)
Finland
16th Floor, Amarin Tower, 500 Ploenchit Rd (☎ 256-9306/9)
France
35 Customs House Lane, Charoen Krung Rd (☎ 234-0950/6)
Germany
9 Sathon Tai Rd (☎ 286-4223/7, 213-2331/6)
Greece
3rd Floor, President Tour Bldg, 412/8-9 Siam Square Soi 6, Rama I Rd (☎ 251-5111)
Hungary
28 Soi Sukchai, Sukhumvit Rd (☎ 391-2002/3)

Iceland
59 Soi Navin Chua Ploeng Rd (☎ 249-1300)
India
46 Soi Prasanmit (Soi 23), Sukhumvit Rd (☎ 258-0300/6)
Indonesia
600-602 Phetburi Rd (☎ 252-3135/40)
Iran
602 Sukhumvit Rd (between Sois 22 and 24) (☎ 259-0611/3)
Iraq
47 Pradipat Rd (☎ 278-5335/8)
Ireland
205 United Flour Mill Bldg, Ratchawong Rd (☎ 223-0876)
Israel
31 Soi Lang Suan, Ploenchit Rd (☎ 252-3131/4)
Italy
399 Nang Linchi Rd (☎ 286-4844/6, 287-2054)
Japan
1674 New Phetburi Rd (☎ 252-6151/9)
Jordan
47 Soi 63, Sukhumvit Rd (☎ 391-7142)
Korea (South)
Sathon Thani Bldg, 90 Sathon Neua Rd (☎ 234-0723/6)
Korea (North)
81 Soi Ari 7, Phahonyothin Rd (☎ 278-5118)
Laos
193 Sathon Tai Rd (☎ 254-6963, 213-2573)
Malaysia
35 Sathon Tai Rd (☎ 286-1390/2)
Mexico
Siam Yamaha Bldg, 1 Din Daeng Rd (☎ 245-1415)
Nepal
189 Soi Phuengsuk (Soi 71), Sukhumvit Rd (☎ 391-7240)
Netherlands
106 Wireless (Withayu) Rd (☎ 254-7701, 252-6103/5)
New Zealand
93 Wireless Rd (☎ 251-8165)
Norway
Chokchai Bldg, 690 Sukhumvit Rd (☎ 258-0531/3)
Pakistan
31 Soi Nana Neua, Sukhumvit Rd (☎ 253-0288/9)
Panama
Kaset Rung Ruan Bldg, 122/1 Sathon Neua Rd (☎ 238-2596)
Philippines
760 Sukhumvit Rd (☎ 259-0139)
Peru
Louis T Leonowens Bldg, 723 Si Phaya Rd (☎ 233-5910/7, ext 25)
Poland
61 Soi 23, Sukhumvit Rd (☎ 258-4112/3)
Portugal
26 Captain Bush Lane, Si Phaya Rd (☎ 234-0372, 233-7610)
Romania
105 Soi Charoenpon, Pradipat Rd (☎ 279-7902)
Russia
108 Sathon Neua Rd, (☎ 234-9824, 234-2012, 235-5599)
Saudi Arabia
Sathon Thani Bldg, 90 Sathon Neua Rd (☎ 237-1938, 235-0875/8)
Singapore
129 Sathon Tai Rd (☎ 286-2111, 286-1434)
Spain
93 Wireless (Withayu) Rd (☎ 252-6112)
Sri Lanka
48/3 Soi 1, Sukhumvit Rd (☎ 251-2789)
Sweden
11th Floor, Boonmitr Bldg, 138 Silom Rd (☎ 234-3891, 233-0295)
Switzerland
35 Wireless (Withayu) Rd (☎ 252-8992/4, 253-0156/60)
Taiwan
Far East Trade Office, 10/F Kian Ngwan Bldg, Withayu Rd (☎ 251-9274/6, 251-9393)
Turkey
153/2 Soi Mahadlekluang 1, Ratchadamri Rd (☎ 251-2987/8)
UK
1031 Wireless Rd (☎ 253-0191/9)
USA
95 Wireless Rd (☎ 252-5040/9)
Vietnam
83/1 Wireless Rd (☎ 251-7201/3, 251-5835/8)
Yugoslavia
28 Soi 61, Sukhumvit Rd (☎ 391-9090/1)

Cultural Centres Various Thai and foreign associations organise and support cultural events of a wide-ranging nature. They can be good places to meet Thais with an international outlook as well as Bangkok residents. Some of the more active organisations include:

Alliance Française
French language courses; translation services; monthly bulletin; French films; small library and bookshop; French and Thai cafeteria; music, arts and lecture programmes – 29 Sathon Tai Rd (☎ 286- 3841)
American University Alumni (AUA)
English and Thai language courses; monthly newsletter; American films; TOEFL testing; Thai cafeteria; library; music, art and lecture programmes – 179 Ratchadamri Rd (☎ 252-7067/9)

British Council
: English language classes; monthly calendar of events; British films; music, art and drama programmes – 428 Soi 2, Siam Square, Rama I Rd (☎ 252-6136/8)

Thailand Cultural Centre (TCC)
: Important centre hosting a variety of local and international cultural events, including musical and theatrical performances, art exhibits, cultural workshops and seminars – Ratchadaphisek Rd, Huay Khwang (☎ 247-0028)

The TCC also sponsors the Cultural Information Service Centre, an information clearing house that issues a bimonthly calendar of notable cultural events throughout the country. Many of the events listed are held in Bangkok at foreign culture associations, universities, art galleries, film societies, theatres and music centres. This is the best single source for cultural happenings in Thailand; it even keeps track of obscure provincial festivals like Uttaradit's Langsat Fair or Buriram's Sombat Isan Tai Festival. The calendar is available at the TCC as well as at the TAT office on Ratchadamnoen Nok Rd.

Religious Services More than one reader has written to point out that not everyone who comes to Thailand is either an atheist or a Buddhist. For those seeking houses of worship in the Judaeo-Christian-Muslim tradition:

Catholic
: Assumption Cathedral, 23 Oriental Lane, Charoen Krung (New) Rd(☎ 234-8556)
: Holy Redeemer Church, 123/19 Soi Ruam Rudi (behind US Embassy) (☎ 253-0505)

Jewish
: Jewish Association of Thailand, 121/3 Soi 22, Sukhumvit Rd (☎ 258-2195)

Muslim
: Haroon Mosque, Charoen Krung (New) Rd (near GPO)
: Darool Aman Mosque, Phetburi Rd (near Ratthewi circle)

Protestant
: Calvary Baptist Church, 88 Soi 2, Sukhumvit Rd (☎ 234-3634)
: International Church, 67 Soi 19, Sukhumvit Rd (☎ 252-0353)

Seventh Day Adventist
: Bangkok Ekamai Church, 57 Soi Charoenchai, Ekamai Rd (☎ 391-3593)
: Bangkok Chinese Church, 1325 Rama IV Rd (☎ 215-4529)

Travel Agencies Bangkok is packed with travel agencies of every manner and description, but if you're looking for cheap airline tickets it's wise to be cautious. Some of Bangkok's agencies are quite notorious and should be avoided at all costs. Recently Dusit Travel on Khao San Rd closed up shop and absconded with full airfare payments collected from more than 30 tourists who never received their tickets. The really bad agencies change their names frequently, so ask other travellers for advice. Wherever possible try to see the tickets before you hand over the money. The STA Travel agency in Bangkok is at Tour Centre (☎ 281-5314) in the Thai Hotel, 78 Prachatipatai Rd.

Four agencies permitted to do Thai railway bookings (not all agencies handle rail tickets) are:

Airland
: 866 Ploenchit Rd (☎ 251-9495)

SEA Tours
: Suite 414, 4th Floor, Siam Center, Rama I Rd (☎ 251-4862, 251-2080)

Songserm Travel Center
: 121/7 Soi Chalermla, Phayathai Rd (☎ 250-0768, 252-5190)

Viang Travel
: Viengtai Hotel, 42 Rambutri Rd (☎ 280-1385)

The following agencies specialise in arranging tourist travel to Burma, Laos, Cambodia and Vietnam:

Asian Line Travel
: 755 Silom Rd (☎ 233-1510)

MK Ways
: 57/11 Withayu Rd (☎ 254-5583; fax 254-5583)

Exotissimo Travel
: 21/17 Soi 4, Sukhumvit Rd (☎ 253-5250; fax 254-7683)

Skyline Travel
: Silom Plaza, 491/33 Silom Rd (☎ 236-6586; fax 236-6585)

There are also several brokers on Khao San

Rd who arrange visa packages for Thailand's socialist neighbours, but none are authorised for direct sales – they must work through the other agencies.

Bookshops Bangkok has many good bookshops, possibly the best selection in South-East Asia.

For new books and magazines the two best bookshop chains are Asia Books and Duang Kamol (DK) Book House. Asia Books lives up to its name by having one of the largest selections of English-language titles on Asia in Bangkok. Asia Books's main branch (☎ 252-7277) is at 221 Sukhumvit Rd at Soi 15; large branch shops are at the Landmark Plaza, Sois 3 and 4, Sukhumvit Rd and at the Peninsula Plaza, adjacent to the Regent Bangkok on Ratchadamri Rd. Smaller Asia Books stalls can be found in several of the larger hotels and at Thai airports.

DK Book House is headquartered at Siam Square, off Rama I Rd, with additional branches on Surawong Rd near Patpong, and on Sukhumvit Rd across from the Ambassador City complex (the latter branches are excellent for fiction titles – the Siam Square branch is better for textbooks). There is also a branch in the Mahboonkrong shopping centre opposite Siam Square.

There are several other bookshops with English-language books in the Siam Square complex, including Bangkok Books (Soi 4), the Book Chest (Soi 2) and Odeon Store (Soi 1). In the Silom Rd area, the Bookseller at 81 Patpong 1 has a wide selection.

Suksit Siam, opposite Wat Ratchabophit on Fuang Nakhon Rd, specialises in books on Thai politics, especially those representing the views of Sulak Sivaraksa and the progressive Santi Pracha Dhamma Institute (which has offices next door). The shop also has a number of mainstream titles on Thailand and Asia, both in English and Thai.

If you're looking for second-hand books on Asia, check out Chalermnit Books on Keson (Gaysorn) Rd, near the Le Meridien President Hotel off Ploenchit Rd. There are many titles in French and German as well as English.

Another place with a good selection of used foreign-language titles (English, Chinese, French, German, Swedish) is Elite Used Books, 593/5 Sukhumvit Rd near Villa supermarket. The Weekend Market in Chatuchak Park is also a source of used, often out-of-print books in several languages.

Libraries Besides offering an abundance of reading material, Bangkok's libraries make a peaceful escape from the heat, noise and traffic.

The National Library (☎ 281-5212) on Samsen Rd is an impressive institution with a huge collection of Thai material dating back several centuries as well as smaller numbers of foreign-language books. Membership is free. The Siam Society and National Museum also have collections of English-language materials on the history, art and culture of Thailand.

Both AUA (American University Alumni) and the British Council have lending libraries; the British Council allows only members (residents over 16 years of age only) to borrow books, while AUA has a free public lending service. Both libraries cater primarily to Thai members, hence the emphasis tends to be on English-language teaching rather than, say, the latest fiction. Their main strengths are their up-to-date periodicals sections – the British Council's selection is strictly British of course while AUA's is all-American.

Although you won't be permitted to borrow books unless you're a Chula student, the library in Chulalongkorn University (south of Siam Square) is a good place to hang out – quiet and air-conditioned.

In a class all its own, the Neilson Hays Library (☎ 233-1731), at 193 Surawong Rd next to the British Club, is a historical monument as well as a good, all-purpose lending library. Built in 1921 by Dr Heyward Hays as a memorial to his wife Jennie Neilson Hays, the classic colonial Asian edifice is operated by the 100-year-old Bangkok Library Association and is the oldest English-language library in Thailand. The collection has well over 20,000 volumes,

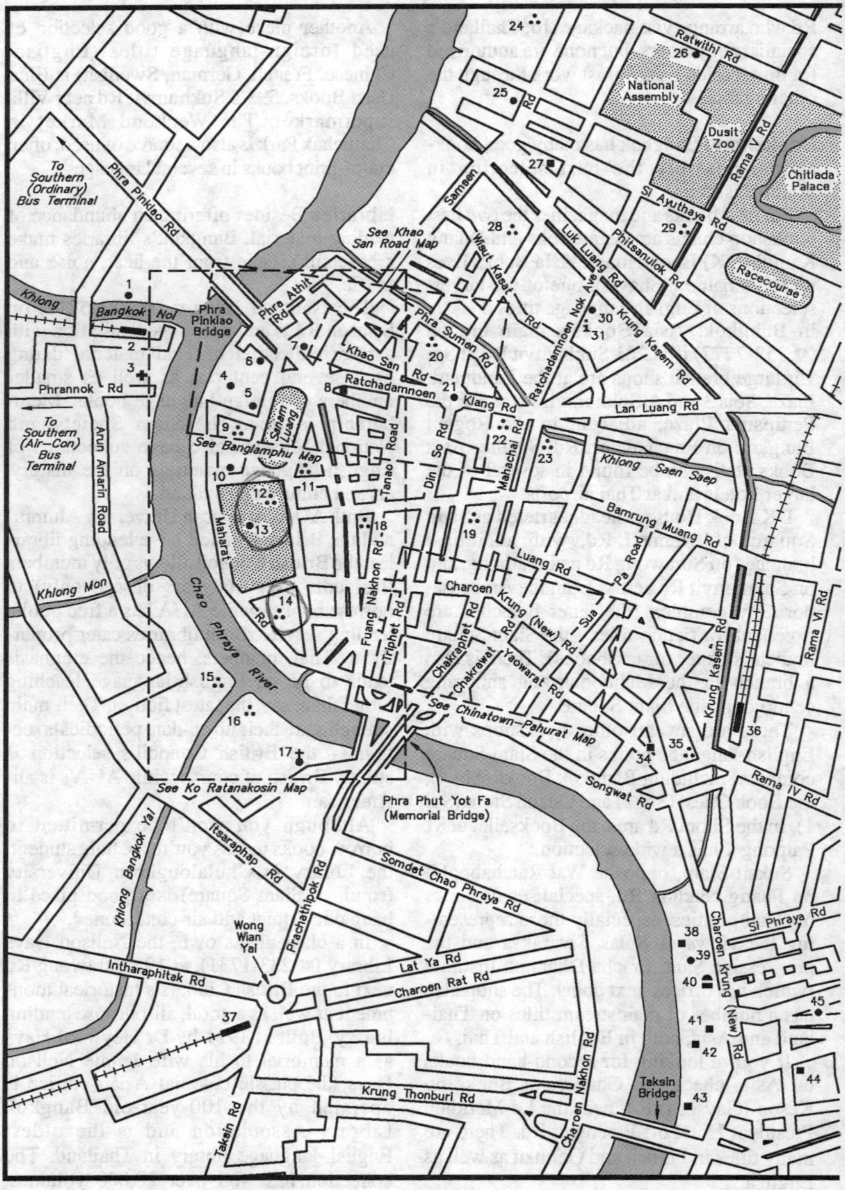
Ratwithi Rd
National Assembly
Dusit Zoo
Rama V Rd
Chitlada Palace
Si Ayuthaya Rd
Racecourse
Samsen Rd
Wisut Kasat
Luk Luang Rd
Phitsanulok Rd
Ratchadamnoen Nok Ave
Krung Kasem Rd
See Khao San Road Map
Phra Athit Rd
Phra Sumen Rd
Khao San Rd
Ratchadamnoen
Klang Rd
Lan Luang Rd
Khlong Saen Saep
Mahachai Rd
Din So Rd
Tanao Road
Sanam Luang
See Banglamphu Map
Bamrung Muang Rd
Luang Rd
Charoen Krung (New) Rd
Sua Pa Road
Chakraphet Rd
Chakrawat Rd
Yaowarat Rd
See Chinatown-Pahurat Map
Fuang Nakhon Rd
Triphet Rd
Maharat Rd
Chao Phraya River
Khlong Mon
Khlong Bangkok Noi
Phra Pinklao Bridge
Phra Pinklao Rd
To Southern (Ordinary) Bus Terminal
Phrannok Rd
To Southern (Air-Con) Bus Terminal
Arun Amarin Road
See Ko Ratanakosin Map
Phra Phut Yot Fa (Memorial Bridge)
Khlong Bangkok Yai
Itsaraphap Rd
Somdet Chao Phraya Rd
Prachathipok Rd
Wong Wian Yai
Intharaphitak Rd
Lat Ya Rd
Charoen Rat Rd
Krung Thonburi Rd
Taksin Rd
Charoen Nakhon Rd
Taksin Bridge
Charoen Krung (New) Rd
Si Phraya Rd
Songwat Rd
Rama IV Rd
Rama VI Rd
Krung Kasem Rd
1 2 3 4 5 6 7 8 9 10 11 12 13 14 15 16 17 18 19 20 21 22 23 24 25 26 27 28 29 30 31 32 33 34 35 36 37 38 39 40 41 42 43 44 45

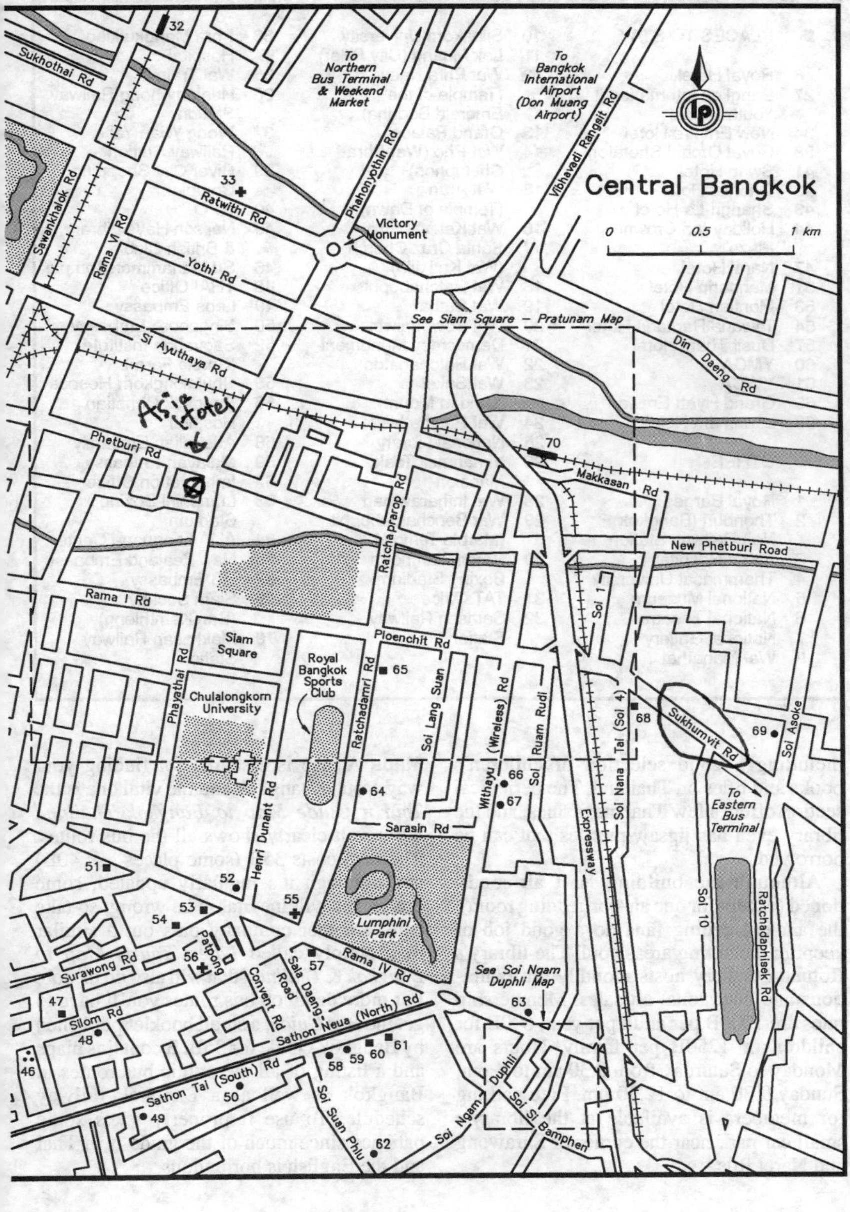
Central Bangkok
0
0.5
1 km
To Northern Bus Terminal & Weekend Market
To Bangkok International Airport (Don Muang Airport)
Sukhothai Rd
Sawankhalok Rd
Rama VI Rd
Ratwithi Rd
Yothi Rd
Phahonyothin Rd
Victory Monument
Vibhavadi Rangsit Rd
See Siam Square – Pratunam Map
Si Ayuthaya Rd
Din Daeng Rd
Asia Hotel
Phetburi Rd
Makkasan Rd
Ratchaprarop Rd
New Phetburi Road
Rama I Rd
Siam Square
Ploenchit Rd
Royal Bangkok Sports Club
Chulalongkorn University
Phayathai Rd
Ratchadamri Rd
Soi Lang Suan
Withayu (Wireless) Rd
Soi Ruam Rudi
Soi 1
Soi Nana Tai (Soi 4)
Expressway
Sukhumvit Rd
Soi Asoke
To Eastern Bus Terminal
Henri Dunant Rd
Sarasin Rd
Lumphini Park
Rama IV Rd
Patpong
Surawong Rd
Convent Rd
Sala Daeng Road
See Soi Ngam Duphli Map
Silom Rd
Sathon Neua (North) Rd
Sathon Tai (South) Rd
Soi Suan Phlu
Soi Ngam Duphli
Soi Si Bamphen
Soi 10
Ratchadaphisek Rd
32
33
46
47
48
49
50
51
52
53
54
55
56
57
58
59
60
61
62
63
64
65
66
67
68
69
70

■ PLACES TO STAY

8 Royal Hotel
27 Bangkok International Youth Hostel
34 New Empire Hotel
38 Royal Orchid Sheraton
41 Swan Hotel
42 Oriental Hotel
43 Shangri-La Hotel
44 Holiday Inn Crowne Plaza
47 Narai Hotel
51 Mandarin Hotel
53 Montien Hotel
54 Tawana Ramada Hotel
57 Dusit Thani Hotel
60 YMCA
61 YWCA
65 Grand Hyatt Erawan
68 Landmark Hotel

OTHER

1 Royal Barges
2 Thonburi (Bangkok Noi) Railway Station
3 Sirirat Hospital
4 Thammasat University
5 National Museum
6 National Theatre
7 National Gallery
9 Wat Mahathat
10 Silpakorn University
11 Lak Muang (City Pillar)
12 Wat Phra Kaew (Temple of the Emerald Buddha)
13 Grand Palace
14 Wat Pho (Wat Phra Chetuphon)
15 Wat Arun (Temple of Dawn)
16 Wat Kalayanamit
17 Santa Cruz Church (Wat Kuti Jiin)
18 Wat Ratchabophit
19 Wat Suthat
20 Wat Bowonniwet
21 Democracy Monument
22 Wat Ratchanatda
23 Wat Saket (Golden Mount)
24 Wat Ratchathiwat
25 National Library
26 Vimanmek Teak Mansion
28 Wat Intharawihan
29 Wat Benchamabophit (Marble Temple)
30 Ratchadamnoen Boxing Stadium
31 TAT Office
32 Samsen Railway Station
33 Phra Mongkutklao Hospital
35 Wat Traimit
36 Hualamphong Railway Station
37 Wong Wian Yai Railway Station
39 River City Shopping Complex
40 GPO
45 Neilson Hays Library & British Club
46 Sri Mariamman Temple
48 THAI Office
49 Laos Embassy
50 Singapore Embassy
52 Saovabha Institute (Snake Farm)
55 Chulalongkorn Hospital
56 Bangkok Christian Hospital
58 Australian Embassy
59 Malayan Embassy
62 Immigration Office
63 Lumphini Boxing Stadium
64 AUA Language Center
66 New Zealand Embassy
67 US Embassy
69 Siam Society (Ban Kamthieng)
70 Makkasan Railway Station

including a good selection of children's books and titles on Thailand. The periodical section offers a few Thai magazines, and the library even has jigsaw puzzles that can be borrowed.

Although the building isn't air-conditioned (except for one air-con reading room), the ancient ceiling fans do a good job of keeping the sitting areas cool. The library's Rotunda Gallery hosts monthly art exhibitions and occasional art sales. Membership rates are 1000B per adult per year, 600B for children or 1250B per family. Hours are Monday to Saturday from 9.30 am to 4 pm, Sunday 9.30 am to 12.30 pm. Free parking for members is available at the library's small car park near the corner of Surawong and Naret Rds.

Maps A map is essential for finding your way around Bangkok and the vital one is the *Tour'n Guide Map to Bangkok Thailand* because it clearly shows all the bus routes. The map costs 35B (some places ask 40B) and although it's regularly updated, some bus routes will inevitably be wrong, so take care. Another company puts out a similar map simply called *Latest Tour's Map to Bangkok & Thailand* that will also do the job. For more detail on bus routes you'll have to get the *Bus Guide*, a small booklet published by Bangkok Guide for 35B. It contains maps and a listing of all the public bus routes in Bangkok as well as a Bangkok railway schedule. To use it properly takes some patience since much of the guide is in Thai and the English is horrendous.

A second map to consider is Nancy Chandler's *Map of Bangkok* which costs 70B. This map has a whole host of information on out-of-the-way places, including lots of stuff on where to buy unusual things around the city. There's a similar companion map to Chiang Mai. The Fine Arts Commission of the Association of Siamese Architects produces a pack of four unusual maps showing temples and important places of cultural interest. The maps are *Bangkok*, *Grand Palace*, *Canals of Thonburi* and *Ayuthaya*. The TAT has recently come out with a *Sightseeing & Shopping Map* of Bangkok that has lively 3-D drawings of popular tourist spots along Ratchadamri, Rama IV, Rama I and Phayathai Rds.

Medical Services Bangkok is Thailand's leading health care centre, with three university research hospitals, 12 public and private hospitals and hundreds of medical clinics. Australian, US and UK embassies usually keep up-to-date lists of doctors who can speak English; for doctors who speak other languages, contact the relevant embassy or consulate.

Several store-front clinics in the Ploenchit Rd area specialise in lab tests for sexually transmitted diseases. Bangkok's better hospitals include:

Bangkok Adventist Hospital
  430 Phitsanulok Rd (☎ 281-1422)
Bangkok Christian Hospital
  124 Silom Rd (☎ 233-6981/9)
Phayathai Hospital
  364/1 Si Ayuthaya Rd (☎ 245-2620)
  or 943 Phahonyothin Rd (☎ 270-0780)
Samitivej Hospital
  133 Soi 49, Sukhumvit Rd (☎ 392-0010/9)
Samrong General Hospital
  Soi 78, Sukhumvit Rd (☎ 393-2131/5)
St Louis Hospital
  215 Sathon Tai Rd (☎ 212-0033/48)

Dangers & Annoyances Bangkok's most heavily touristed areas, especially around Wat Phra Kaew and Khao San Rd, are favourite hunting grounds for Thai con artists of every ilk.

The clever cons will seemingly meet you on the street or in a cafe by accident. More obvious are the tuk-tuk drivers who are out to make a commission by dragging you to a local silk or jewellery shop – even though you've requested an entirely different destination. In either case if you accept an invitation for 'free' sightseeing or shopping, you're quite likely to end up wasting an afternoon or – as happens all too often – losing a lot of money.

For full details on common scams, see the Dangers & Annoyances section in the Facts for the Visitor chapter.

Tourist Police Under the Crime Suppression Division of the National Police Department, the tourist police are a separate force established in 1982 to deal with tourist problems. In Bangkok, some 500 English-speaking officers are stationed in tourist areas – their kiosks, cars and uniforms are clearly marked. If you have any problems related to criminal activity, try contacting the tourist police first. When they can't solve the problem, or if it's out of their jurisdiction, they can act as a bilingual liaison with the regular police. The tourist police headquarters (☎ 221-6206) are at the Crime Suppression Division, 509 Worachak Rd, near the intersection of Worachak and Charoen Krung Rds at the north-eastern edge of Chinatown.

Sightseeing Highlights

If your visit to Bangkok is a short one, you won't begin to be able to see all the city has to offer. For visits of four or five days, must-dos include Wat Phra Kaew and the Grand Palace along with nearby Wat Pho, the National Museum, either the Lak Muang or Erawan shrines, Jim Thompson's House, either Vimanmek Teak Palace or Wang Suan Phakkard, and a river or canal trip.

For a three-day stopover, leave out the National Museum and the shrines. If you have longer – say a week or more – add the Weekend Market, a Thai boxing match and a performance at the National Theatre. Looking for another temple or two? Wat Traimit's Golden Buddha never fails to impress; Wat Arun also makes a pleasant cross-river excursion.

Evenings can be devoted to sampling Bangkok's incredible Thai restaurants – try at least one riverside place to soak up the languid ambience of old Bangkok. You should also seek out at least one Thai musical performance, whether traditional (at a dinner theatre) or modern (at one of the city's many nightclubs).

Wat Phra Kaew & Grand Palace
วัดพระแก้วและพระที่นั่งจักรี

Also called the Temple of the Emerald Buddha, this wat adjoins the Grand Palace on common ground which was consecrated in 1782, the first year of Bangkok rule. Together they have been added to by the different Thai monarchs and consequently feature several different types of architecture. Most of it is in the Bangkok or Ratanakosin style. The wat is a very colourful place, with extensive murals depicting scenes from the *Ramakian* (the Thai version of the Indian epic *Ramayana)* along the inside walls of the compound. Originally painted during Rama III's reign (1824-50), the murals have undergone more than one restoration, including a major one finished in time for the 1982 Bangkok/Chakri Dynasty bicentennial.

Statue in the Grand Palace complex

The so-called Emerald Buddha, 60 cm to 75 cm high (depending on how it is measured), is actually made of a type of jasper or perhaps nephrite (a type of jade), depending on whom you believe. A definite aura of mystery surrounds the image, enhanced by the fact that it cannot be examined closely – it sits in a glass case, on a pedestal high above the heads of worshippers – and photography within the bot is forbidden. Its mystery further adds to the occult significance of the image which is considered the 'talisman' of the Thai kingdom, the legitimator of Thai sovereignty.

It is not known for certain where the image originated or who sculpted it, but it first appeared on record in 15th century Chiang Rai; stylistically it seems to be from the Chiang Saen or Lanna (La Na) period. At that time, the image is said to have been covered with plaster and gold leaf and located in Chiang Rai's own Wat Phra Kaew (literally, 'temple of the jewel holy image'). While being transported elsewhere after a storm had damaged the chedi (in which the image had been kept), the image supposedly lost its plaster covering in a fall. It next appeared in Lampang where it enjoyed a 32-year stay (again at a Wat Phra Kaew) until it was brought to Wat Chedi Luang in Chiang Mai.

Laotian invaders took the image from Chiang Mai in the mid-16th century and brought it to Luang Prabang in Laos. Later it was moved to Wiang Chan (Vientiane). When Thailand's King Taksin waged war against Laos 200 years later, the image was taken back to the Thai capital of Thonburi by General Chakri, who later succeeded Taksin as Rama I, the founder of the Chakri Dynasty. Rama I had the Emerald Buddha moved to the new Thai capital in Bangkok and had two royal robes made for it, one to be worn in the hot season and one for the rainy season. Rama III added another to the wardrobe – to be worn in the cool season. The three robes are still solemnly changed at the beginning of each season by the king himself.

The palace is only used by the king on certain ceremonial occasions, such as Coronation Day, as his residence is now Chitlada Palace in the northern part of the city. The Grand Palace was the headquarters for an attempted coup by General San Chitpatima in April 1981.

Admission to Wat Phra Kaew is 100B, and hours are from 8.30 to 11.30 am and 1 to 3.30 pm. The admission fee includes entry to the Royal Thai Decorations & Coins Pavilion (on the same grounds) and to Vimanmek, 'the world's largest golden teak-wood mansion', near the Dusit Zoo. (See the later Vimanek Teak Mansion section for more details.)

As in any temple compound, shoes should be removed before entering the main chapel *(bòt)* or sanctuaries *(wihãan)* of Wat Phra Kaew. Since wats are a sacred place to Thai Buddhists, visitors should dress and behave decently for their visit. (If you wear shorts you may be refused admission into the Wat Phra Kaew/Grand Palace grounds.)

The most economical way of reaching Wat Phra Kaew and the Grand Palace is by air-con bus Nos 8 or 12. By the Chao Phraya River Express, disembark at Tha Chang.

Wat Pho (Wat Phra Chetuphon)

A long list of superlatives for this one: the oldest and largest wat in Bangkok, it features the largest reclining Buddha and the largest collection of Buddha images in Thailand and was the earliest centre for public education. As a temple site Wat Pho dates back to the 16th century, but its current history really begins in 1781 with the renovation of the original monastery.

Narrow Chetuphon Rd divides the grounds in two, with each section surrounded by huge whitewashed walls. The most interesting part is the northern compound, which includes a very large bot enclosed by a gallery of Buddha images and four wihaans, four large chedis, commemorating the first four Chakri kings, 91 smaller chedis, an old *tripitaka* (Buddhist scriptures) library, a sermon hall, the large wihaan which houses the reclining Buddha, and a school building for classes in Abhidhamma (Buddhist philosophy), plus several less-important structures.

Wat Pho is the national headquarters for the teaching and preservation of traditional Thai medicine, including Thai massage. A massage school convenes in the afternoons at the eastern end of the compound; a massage costs 140B per hour. You can also study massage here in seven to 10-day courses.

The tremendous reclining Buddha, 46 metres long and 15 metres high, illustrates the passing of the Buddha into nirvana. The figure is modelled out of plaster around a brick core and finished in gold leaf. Mother-of-pearl inlay ornaments the eyes and feet of the colossal image, the feet displaying 108 different auspicious *laksanas* or characteristics of a Buddha. The images on display in the four wihaans surrounding the main bot in the eastern part of the compound are interesting. Particularly beautiful are the Phra Jinnarat and Phra Jinachi Buddhas, in the west and south chapels, both from Sukhothai. The galleries extending between the four chapels feature no less than 394 gilded Buddha images.

The temple rubbings for sale at Wat Pho and elsewhere in Thailand come from the reliefs, carved in marble and obtained from the ruins of Ayuthaya, sculpted in the base of the large bot. Many of the reliefs depict scenes from the *Ramakian*. The rubbings are no longer taken directly from the panels but are rubbed from cement casts of the panels made years ago.

The reclining Buddha image can be seen from 8 am to 5 pm daily; admission is 10B. The ticket booth is closed from noon to 1 pm. Air-con bus Nos 6, 8 and 12 stop near Wat Pho. The nearest Chao Phraya Express pier is Tha Thien.

Wat Mahathat

วัดมหาธาตุ

A very old monastery, Wat Mahathat is a national centre for the Mahanikai monastic sect and houses one of Bangkok's two Buddhist universities, Mahathat Rajavidyalaya. On weekends, a large produce market is held on the grounds. Opposite the main entrance on the other side of Maharat Rd is a large religious amulet market.

The temple is officially open to visitors from 9 am to 5 pm every day and on *wan phrá* – Buddhist holy days (the full and new moons every fortnight). Also in the temple grounds is a daily open-air market which features traditional Thai herbal medicine.

Those interested in learning about Buddhist meditation (vipassana), should contact the monks in Section 5 of the temple compound. English-language instruction is usually available.

Wat Mahathat is right across the street from Wat Phra Kaew, on the west side of Sanam Luang. Air-con bus Nos 8 and 12 both pass by it, and the nearest Chao Phraya Express pier is Tha Maharat.

Wat Traimit

วัดไตรมิตร

The attraction at the Temple of the Golden Buddha is, of course, the impressive three-metre tall, 5½-ton, solid-gold Buddha image, which gleams like no other gold artefact I've ever seen.

Sculpted in the graceful Sukhothai style, the image was 'rediscovered' some 30 years ago beneath a stucco or plaster exterior when it fell from a crane while being moved to a new building within the temple compound. It has been theorised that the covering was added to protect it from 'marauding hordes', either during the late Sukhothai period or later in Ayuthaya when the city was under siege by the Burmese. The temple itself is said to date from the early 13th century.

The golden image can be seen every day from 9 am to 5 pm, and admission is 10B. Wat Traimat is near the intersection of Yaowarat and Charoen Krung Rds, near Hualamphong station.

Wat Arun

วัดอรุณ

The 'Temple of Dawn' is named after the Indian god of dawn, Aruna. It appears in all the tourist brochures and is located on the Thonburi side of the Chao Phraya River. The present wat is built on the site of 17th-century Wat Jang, which was the palace and royal temple of King Taksin when Thonburi was the Thai capital; hence, it was the last home of the Emerald Buddha before Rama I brought it across the river to Bangkok.

The tall, 82-metre *prang* (Khmer-style tower) was constructed during the first half of the 19th century by Rama II and Rama III. The unique design elongates the typical Khmer prang into a distinctly Thai shape. Its brick core has a plaster covering embedded with a mosaic of broken, multi-hued Chinese porcelain; the use of broken porcelain for temple ornamentation was common in the early Ratanakosin period when Chinese ships calling at Bangkok used tons of old porcelain as ballast. Steep stairs reach a lookout point about halfway up the prang from where there are fine views of Thonburi and the river. During certain festivals, hundreds of lights illuminate the outline of the prang at night.

Also worth a look is the interior of the bot. The main Buddha image is said to have been designed by Rama II himself. The murals date to the reign of Rama V; particularly impressive is one that depicts Prince Siddhartha encountering examples of birth, old age, sickness and death outside his palace walls.

According to Buddhist legend it was the experience of seeing these phenomena for the first time that led Siddhartha to abandon the worldly life.

The temple looks more impressive from the river than it does from up close, though the peaceful wat grounds make a very nice retreat from the hustle and bustle of Bangkok. Between the prang and the ferry pier is a huge sacred banyan tree.

Wat Arun is open daily from 8.30 am to 5 pm; admission is 5B. To reach Wat Arun from the Bangkok side, catch a cross-river ferry from Tha Tien at Thai Wang Rd (see the Ko Ratanakosin map). Crossings are frequent and only cost 1B.

Wat Benchamabophit
วัดเบญจมบพิตร

This wat of white Carrara marble (hence its tourist name, 'Marble Temple') was built at the turn of the century under Chulalongkorn (Rama V). The large bot is a prime example of modern Thai architecture. The courtyard behind the bot exhibits 53 Buddha images, most of which are copies of famous images and styles from all over Thailand and other Buddhist countries – an education in itself if you're interested in Buddhist iconography.

Wat Ben is at the corner of Si Ayuthaya and Rama V Rds, diagonally opposite the south-west corner of Chitlada Palace; it's open daily and admission is 10B. Air-con bus No 2 and ordinary bus No 72 stop nearby.

Wat Saket
Wat Saket is an undistinguished temple except for the Golden Mount (Phu Khao Thong) on the west side of the grounds which provides a good view of Bangkok rooftops. The artificial hill was created when a large chedi under construction by Rama III collapsed because the soft soil beneath would not support it. The resulting mud-and-brick hill was left to sprout weeds until Rama IV built a small chedi on its crest.

Later his son, Rama V, added to the structure and housed a Buddha relic from India (given to him by the British government) in the chedi. The concrete walls were added during WW II to prevent the hill from eroding. Every November there is a big festival on the grounds of Wat Saket, which includes a candle-lit procession up the Golden Mount.

Admission to Wat Saket is free except for the final approach to the summit of the Golden Mount, which costs 5B. The temple is within walking distance of the Democracy Monument; air-con bus Nos 11 and 12 pass nearby.

Wat Rajanadda (Ratchanatda)
วัดราชนัดดา

Across Mahachai Rd from Wat Saket and behind the old Chalerm Thai movie theatre, this temple dates from the mid-19th century. It was built under Rama III and is an unusual specimen, possibly influenced by Burmese models.

The wat has a well-known market selling Buddhist amulets or magic charms *(phrá phim)* in all sizes, shapes and styles. The amulets not only feature images of the Buddha, but famous Thai monks and Indian deities. Full Buddha images are also for sale. In the Thai language, Buddhas or phra phim are never 'bought' or 'sold', they are 'rented'. The images are purported to protect the wearer from physical harm, though some act as 'love charms'. Amulets that are considered to be particularly powerful tend to cost thousands of baht and are worn by soldiers, taxi drivers and other Thai believers working in high-risk professions. Wat Rajanadda is an expensive place to purchase a charm, but a good place to look.

Wat Bovornives (Bowonniwet)
วัดบวรนิเวศ

Wat Bowon, on Phra Sumen Rd, is the national headquarters for the Thammayut monastic sect, the minority sect in Mahanikai Buddhism. King Mongkut, founder of the Thammayuts, began a royal tradition by residing here as a monk – in fact he was the abbot of Wat Bowon for several years. Since its founding, several Thai kings have temporarily ordained as monks here.

Bangkok's second Buddhist university, Mahamakut University, is housed at Wat Bowon and there is an English-language Buddhist bookshop across the street from the main entrance to the wat.

Lak Muang (City Pillar)
ศาลหลักเมือง

The City Pillar is across the street from the eastern wall of Wat Phra Kaew, at the southern end of Sanam Luang. This shrine encloses a wooden pillar erected by Rama I in 1782 to represent the founding of the new Bangkok capital. Later during the reign of

Rama V five other idols were added to the shrine. The spirit of the pillar is considered the city's guardian deity and receives the daily supplications of countless Thai worshippers, some of whom commission classical Thai dancers to perform lakhon chatrii at the shrine. Some of the offerings include severed pigs' heads with sticks of incense sprouting from their foreheads.

Maha Uma Devi Temple
วัดมหาอุมาเทวี (วัดแขก)

This small Hindu temple is on Silom Rd (near the Pan Rd intersection) in Bangrak, a district with a high concentration of Indian residents. The principal temple structure, built in the 1860s, contains three main deities: Jao Mae Maha Umathewi (Uma Devi) at the centre; Phra Khanthakuman (Khanthakumara) on the right; and Phra Phikhkanesawora (Ganesha) on the left. Along the left interior wall sit rows of Shivas, Vishnus and other Hindu deities, as well as a few Buddhas, so that just about any non-Muslim Asian can worship here – Thai and Chinese devotees come to pray along with Indians.

An interesting ritual takes place in the temple at noon on most days, when a priest brings out a tray carrying an oil lamp, coloured powders and holy water. He sprinkles the water on the hands of worshippers who in turn pass their hands through the lamp flame for purification; then they dip their fingers in the coloured powder and daub prayer marks on their foreheads. On Fridays at around 11.30 am, *prasada* (blessed vegetarian food) is offered to devotees.

Thais call this temple Wat Khaek – *khàek* is a Thai colloquial expression for persons of Indian descent. The literal translation is 'guest', an obvious euphemism for a group of people you don't particularly want as permanent residents; hence most Indians living permanently in Thailand don't appreciate the term.

Wat Phailom

Outside Bangkok, on the east bank of the Chao Phraya River in Pathum Thani Province, this wat is noted for the tens of thousands of open-billed storks that nest in the temple area from December to June. The temple is 51 km from the centre of Bangkok in Pathum Thani's Sam Kok district. Take a Pathum Thani-bound bus (8B) from Bangkok's northern bus terminal and cross the river by ferry to the wat grounds.

Other Temples & Shrines

Marked by its enormous modern-style 32-metre standing Buddha, **Wat Intharawihan** is on Wisut Kasat Rd, just north of Banglamphu (see Central Bangkok map). Check out the hollowed-out air-con stupa with a lifelike image of Luang Paw Toh. Entry to Wat In is by donation.

At **Sao Ching-Cha**, the 'Giant Swing', a spectacular Brahman festival in honour of the Hindu god Shiva used to take place each year until it was stopped during the reign of Rama VII. Participants would swing in ever-heightening arcs in an effort to reach a bag of gold – many died trying. The Giant Swing is a block south of the Democracy Monument. Nearby (see Central Bangkok map) is **Wat Suthat** with interesting Buddha images and panels illustrating incidents in the Buddha's life.

There are also numerous temples on the Thonburi side of the river which are less visited. These include **Wat Kalayanamit** with its towering Buddha statue and, outside, the biggest bronze bell in Thailand; **Wat Pho Bang-O** with its carved gables and Rama III-era murals; **Wat Chaloem Phrakiat**, a temple with tiled gables; and **Wat Thawng Nophakhun** with its Chinese-influenced uposatha (bot). See the Fine Arts Commission *Canals of Thonburi* map for more information on these wats.

East of Bangkok, on Sukhumvit Soi 101, there is the 95-metre high chedi at **Wat Thammamongkhon**, which has a lift so you can ride to the top. The chedi is said to contain a hair of the Buddha presented to Thailand by the Sangharaja (head of a Theravada monastic order) of Bangladesh. The official grand opening ceremonies for the chedi are in 1993.

At the corner of Ratchaprarop Rd and Ploenchit Rd, next to the Grand Hyatt Erawan Hotel, is a large shrine, **San Phra Phrom** (also known as the Erawan Shrine), which was originally built to ward off bad luck during the construction of the first Erawan Hotel (torn down to make way for the Grand Hyatt Erawan some years ago). The four-headed deity at the centre of the shrine is Brahma (Phra Phrom in Thai), the Hindu god of creation. Apparently the developers of the original Erawan first erected a typical Thai spirit house but decided to replace it with the more impressive Brahman shrine after several serious mishaps delayed the hotel construction. Worshippers who have a wish granted may return to the shrine to commission the musicians and dancers who are always on hand to make an impromptu performance.

Since the success of the Erawan Shrine, several other flashy Brahman shrines have been erected around the city next to large hotels and office buildings. Next to the new Zen World Trade Center on Ploenchit Rd is a large shrine containing a standing Shiva.

Another hotel shrine worth seeing is the lingam (phallus) shrine behind the Hilton International in Nai Loet Park off Wireless Rd. Clusters of carved stone and wooden lingam surround a spirit house and shrine built by millionaire businessman Nai Loet to honour **Jao Mae Thapthim**, a female deity thought to reside in the old banyan tree on the site. Someone who made an offering shortly thereafter had a baby, and the shrine has received a steady stream of worshippers – mostly young women seeking fertility – ever since.

Churches

Several Catholic churches were founded in Bangkok in the 17th to 19th centuries. Worth seeing is the **Holy Rosary Church** (known in Thai as Wat Kalawa) in Talat Noi near the River City shopping complex. Built in 1897 by the Portuguese, this old church has a splendid set of stained-glass windows and a very old Christ statue that is carried through the streets during Easter celebrations. The **Church of the Immaculate Conception** near Krungthon Bridge (north of Phra Pinklao Bridge) was founded by the Portuguese and later taken over by Cambodians fleeing civil war. The present building is an 1837 reconstruction on the church's 1674 site. One of the original church buildings survives and is now used as a museum housing holy relics. Another Portuguese-built church is **Santa Cruz** (Wat Kuti Jiin) on the Thonburi side near Phra Phuttha Yot Fa Bridge (Saphan Phut). The architecture shows Chinese influence, hence the Thai name 'Chinese monastic residence'.

Temples & River Walking Tour

This walk covers the area of Ko Ratanakosin (Ratanakosin Island), which rests in a bend of the river in the middle of Bangkok and contains some of the city's most historic architecture – Wat Phra Kaew, the Grand Palace, Wat Pho, Wat Mahathat and Wat Suthat (each described in detail earlier) – and prestigious universities. The river bank in this area is busy with piers and markets, worthwhile attractions in themselves. Despite its name, Ko Ratanakosin is not an island at all, though in the days when Bangkok was known as the 'Venice of the East', Khlong Banglamphu and Khlong Ong Ang – two lengthy adjoining canals to the east that run parallel to the river – were probably large enough that the area seemed like an island.

This circular walk (one to three hours depending on your pace) begins at **Lak Muang** (A), a shrine to Bangkok's city spirit. At the intersection of Ratchadamnoen Nai and Lak Muang Rds (opposite the southern end of Sanam Luang (Royal Field), the shrine can be reached by taxi, by air-con bus No 2, by ordinary bus No 47 or on foot if you're already in the Royal Hotel area. (If the Chao Phraya River Express is more convenient, you can start this walk from Tha Tien – see (E) below). By tradition, every city in Thailand must have a foundation stone which embodies the city spirit *(phĩi*

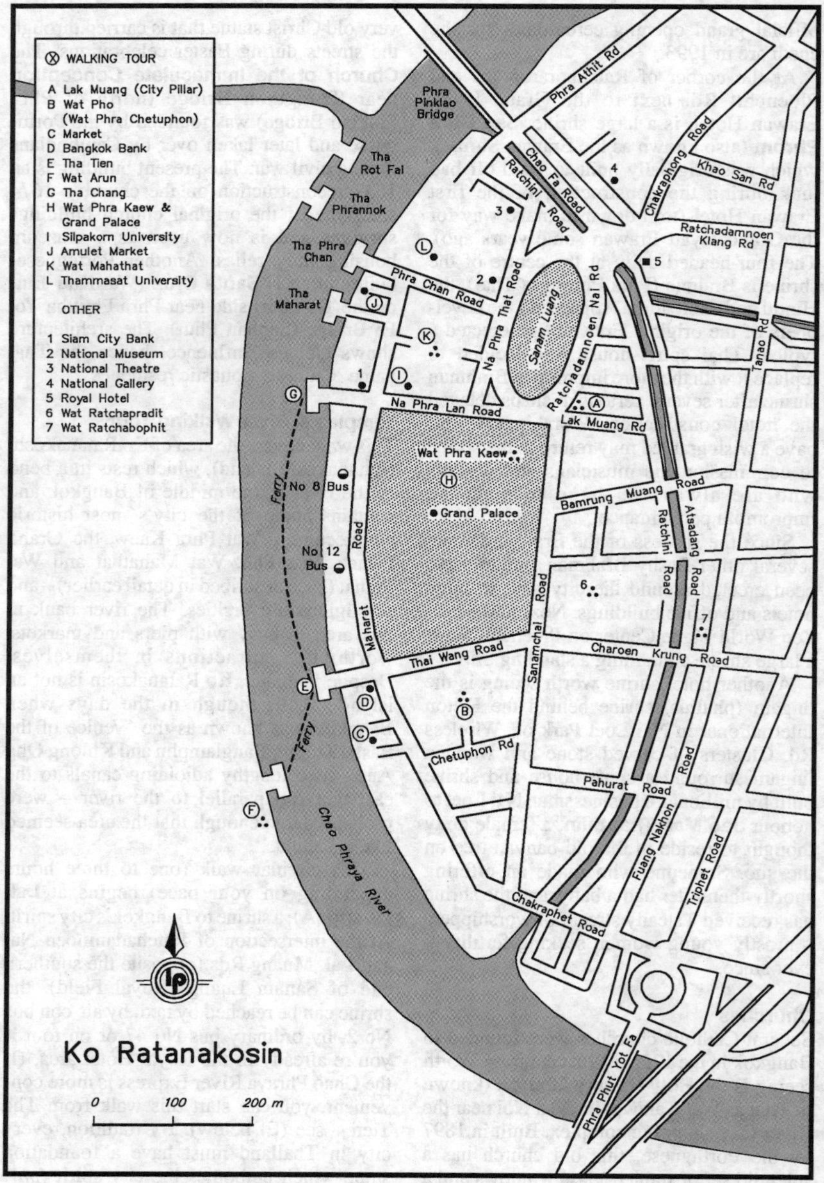

WALKING TOUR
A Lak Muang (City Pillar)
B Wat Pho (Wat Phra Chetuphon)
C Market
D Bangkok Bank
E Tha Tien
F Wat Arun
G Tha Chang
H Wat Phra Kaew & Grand Palace
I Silpakorn University
J Amulet Market
K Wat Mahathat
L Thammasat University
OTHER
1 Siam City Bank
2 National Museum
3 National Theatre
4 National Gallery
5 Royal Hotel
6 Wat Ratchapradit
7 Wat Ratchabophit
Phra Pinklao Bridge
Phra Athit Rd
Chakraphong Road
Khao San Rd
Chao Fa Road
Ratchini Road
Ratchadamnoen Klang Rd
Tha Rot Fai
Tha Phrannok
Tha Phra Chan
Tha Maharat
Phra Chan Road
Na Phra That Road
Sanam Luang
Ratchadamnoen Nai Rd
Tanao Rd
Na Phra Lan Road
Lak Muang Rd
Wat Phra Kaew
Grand Palace
Bamrung Muang Road
Atsadang Road
Ratchini Road
Ferry
No 8 Bus
No 12 Bus
Maharat Road
Sanamchai Road
Thai Wang Road
Charoen Krung Road
Chetuphon Rd
Pahurat Road
Fuang Nakhon Road
Triphet Road
Chakraphet Road
Chao Phraya River
Phra Phut Yot Fa
Ko Ratanakosin
0 100 200 m

muang) and from which inter-city distances are measured. This is Bangkok's most important site of animistic worship; believers throng the area day and night, bringing offerings of flowers, incense, whisky, fruit and even cooked food.

From the Lak Muang, walk south across Lak Muang Rd and along Sanamchai Rd with the Grand Palace/Wat Phra Kaew walls to your right until you come to Chetuphon Rd on the right (the second street after the palace walls end, approximately 500 metres from the pillar). Turn right onto Chetuphon Rd and enter **Wat Pho** (B) through the second portico. Officially named Wat Phra Chetuphon, this is Bangkok's oldest temple and is famous for its huge reclining Buddha (see the earlier Wat Pho section for more details) and for its massage school. The massage school is the oldest in Thailand and is part of a traditional medical college that archives the country's principal texts on Thai medicine. After you've done the rounds of the various sanctuaries within the monastery grounds, exit through the same door and turn right onto Chetuphon Rd, heading toward the river.

Chetuphon Rd ends at Maharat Rd after a hundred metres or so; turn right at Maharat and stroll north, passing the **market** (C) area on your left. At the northern end of this block, Maharat Rd crosses Thai Wang Rd. On the south-western corner is an older branch of the **Bangkok Bank** (D); turn left on Thai Wang to glimpse a row of rare early Ratanakosin-era shophouses. If you continue along Thai Wang Rd to the river you'll arrive at **Tha Tien** (E), one of the pier stops for the Chao Phraya River Express. From an adjacent pier you can catch one of the regular ferries (1B) across the Chao Phraya to **Wat Arun** (F), which features one of Bangkok's most striking prang, a tall Hindu/Khmer-style pagoda (Wat Arun is described in more detail in an earlier section).

Stroll back along Thai Wang Rd to Maharat Rd and turn left to continue the walking tour. On the left along Maharat Rd are two government buildings serving as headquarters for the departments of Internal Trade and Public Welfare. On the right are the whitewhashed west walls of the Grand Palace. Two air-con city buses, Nos 8 and 12, stop along this stretch of Maharat – something to keep in mind when you've had enough walking. About 500 metres from the Thai Wang Rd intersection, Maharat Rd crosses Na Phra Lan Rd; turn left to reach **Tha Chang** (G), another express boat stop; or right to reach the entrance to the Grand Palace and Wat Phra Kaew grounds.

The entrance to the **Grand Palace/Wat Phra Kaew** (H) is on the right (south) side of Na Phra Lan Rd less than a hundred metres from Maharat Rd. All visitors to the palace and temple grounds must be suitably attired, ie no shorts, tank tops or other dress considered unacceptable for temple visits. If you need long pants, a couple of shops opposite the entrance rent baggy pants (which can be worn over your shorts) for 30B. Other shops along this strip offer film, cold drinks, curries and noodles; there is also a small post office. The Grand Palace has been supplanted by Chitlada Palace as the primary residence of the royal family, but it is still used for ceremonial occasions. Wat Phra Kaew is a gleaming example of Bangkok temple architecture at its most baroque – see the earlier Wat Phra Kaew & Grand Palace section for details.

After you've had enough of wandering around the palace and temple grounds, exit via the same doorway and turn left toward the river again. On the right you'll pass the entrance to **Silpakorn University** (I), Thailand's premier university for fine arts studies (a small bookshop inside the gate to the left offers a number of English-language books on Thai art). At Maharat Rd, turn right (past the Siam City Bank on the corner) and almost immediately you'll see vendor tables along the street. On the tables are cheap amulets representing various Hindu and Buddhist deities. Better quality religious amulets *(phrá phim* or *phrá khrêuang* in Thai) are found a bit farther north along Maharat Rd in the large **amulet market** (J) between the road and the river. Walk back into the market area to appreciate how extensive the amulet trade is. Opposite the amulet market on Maharat Rd is **Wat Mahathat** (K), another of Bangkok's older temples and the headquarters for the country's largest monastic sect.

If you're hungry by now, this is a good place on the circuit to take time out for a snack or meal. Head back along Maharat Rd from the amulet market just a few metres and turn right at Trok Thawiphon (the sign reads 'Thawephon'). This alley leads to Tha Maharat, yet another express boat stop; on either side of the pier is a riverside restaurant – *Maharat* to the left and *Lan The* to the right. Although the food at either of these restaurants is quite adequate, most local residents head past the Lan The (no English sign) along the river and into a warren of smaller restaurants and food vendors along the river. The food here is very good and very inexpensive – to order, all you'll need is a pointing index finger.

Renewed and refuelled, start walking north again along Maharat past the amulet market and Wat Mahathat to Phra Chan Rd, around 80 metres from Trok Thawiphon (perhaps 160 metres from Na Phra Lan Rd). Turn left to reach Tha Phra Chan if you want to catch an express boat north or south along the river, or turn right to reach Sanam Luang, the end of the tour. If you take the latter route, you'll pass **Thammasat University** (L) on the left. Thammasat is known for its law and political science faculties; it was also the site of the bloody October '76 demonstrations in which hundreds of Thai students were killed or wounded by military troops. Opposite the university entrance are several very good noodle shops.

National Museum
พิพิธภัณฑ์แห่งชาติ

On Na Phra That Rd, the west side of Sanam Luang, the National Museum is the largest museum in South-East Asia and an excellent place to learn something about Thai art before heading upcountry. All periods and styles are represented from Dvaravati to Ratanakosin, and English-language literature is available.

The museum buildings themselves were originally built in 1782 as the palace of Rama I's viceroy, Prince Wang Na. Rama V (Chulalongkorn) turned it into a museum in 1884.

In addition to the exhibition halls, the museum grounds contain the restored **Buddhaisawan Chapel**. Inside the chapel (built in 1795) are some well-preserved original murals and one of the country's most revered Buddha images, Phra Phut Sihing. Legend says the image came from Ceylon, but art historians attribute its provenance to 13th-century Sukhothai.

Free English tours of the museum are given by the National Museum volunteers on Tuesdays (Thai culture), Wednesdays (Buddhism) and Thursdays (Thai art), starting from the ticket pavilion at 9.30 am. These guided tours are excellent and many people have written to recommend them. The tours are also conducted in German (Thursdays), French and Japanese (Wednesdays). For more information on the tours, contact the volunteers (☎ 215-8173). The museum is open from 9 am to noon and 1 to 4 pm Wednesday to Sunday; admission is 30B.

Royal Barges
เรือพระที่นั่ง

The royal barges are fantastically ornamented boats used in ceremonial processions on the river. The largest is 50 metres long and requires a rowing crew of 50 men, plus seven umbrella bearers, two helmsmen, two navigators, and a flagman, rhythm-keeper and chanter. The barges are kept in sheds on the Thonburi side of the river. They're on Khlong Bangkok Noi, near the Phra Pinklao Bridge. *Suphannahong*, the king's personal barge, is the most important of the boats.

The barge shed is open daily from 8.30 am to 4.30 pm and admission is 10B. To get there, take a ferry to Tha Rot Fai, then walk down the street parallel to the tracks until you come to a bridge over the khlong (canal). Follow the bridge to a wooden walkway that leads to the barge sheds. You can also get there by taking a khlong taxi (5B) up the canal and getting off near the bridge.

Jim Thompson's House

บ้านจิมทอมสัน

Even though it sounds corny when described, this is a great place to visit, because of its authentic Thai residential architecture. Located at the end of an undistinguished soi next to Khlong Saen Saep, the premises once belonged to the American silk entrepreneur Jim Thompson, who deserves most of the credit for the current worldwide popularity of Thai silk. Thompson disappeared in the Cameron Highlands of west Malaysia under quite mysterious circumstances in 1967 and has never been heard from since. On display in the main house is his splendid, small Asian art collection as well as his personal belongings. The Jim Thompson Foundation has a table at the front where you can buy prints of old Siam maps and Siamese horoscopes in postcard and poster form.

The Legendary American – The Remarkable Career & Strange Disappearance of Jim Thompson (Houghton Mifflin, 1970), by William Warren, is an excellent book on Thompson, his career, residence and intriguing disappearance. In Thailand, it has been republished for distribution in Asia as *Jim Thompson: The Legendary American of Thailand* (Jim Thompson Thai Silk Co, Bangkok).

The house, on Soi Kasem San 2, Rama I Rd, is open Monday to Saturday from 8 am to 5 pm. Admission is 100B (proceeds go to Bangkok's School for the Blind) but you may wander around the grounds for free. Students under 25 years get in for 40B. The rather sleazy khlong at the end of the soi is one of Bangkok's most lively.

Wang Suan Phakkard (Phakkat)

วังสวนผักกาด

The 'Lettuce Farm Palace', once the residence of Princess Chumbot of Nakhon Sawan, is a collection of five traditional wooden Thai houses containing varied displays of art, antiques and furnishings. The landscaped grounds are a peaceful oasis complete with ducks and swans and a semi-enclosed garden reminiscent of Japanese gardens. The **Lacquer Pavilion** dates from the Ayuthaya period and features gold-leaf jataka murals. Special exhibitions include seashells and Ban Chiang pottery. In the noise and confusion of Bangkok, the gardens offer a tranquil retreat. The palace is open daily except Sundays from 9 am to 4 pm and admission is 150B (students 30B). It's on Si Ayuthaya Rd, between Phayathai and Ratchaprarop (see Siam Square map); bus No 3 (air-con) passes right in front.

Vimanmek Teak Mansion (Phra Thii Nang Wimanmek)

พระที่นั่งวิมานเมฆ

This beautiful L-shaped, three-storey mansion built of golden teak was the home of King Rama V in the early 1900s. The building contains 81 rooms and is said to be the world's largest golden teak building. Teak was once one of Thailand's greatest natural resources (it has since all but disappeared) and makes an especially good wood for building houses because it's so durable. A special oil contained in the wood makes teak resistant to heavy rain and hot sun and also repels insects. A solid piece of teak can easily last 1000 years.

The interior of the mansion contains various personal effects of the king, and a treasure trove of early Ratanakosin art objects and antiques. There are English-language tours every half hour between 11.15 am and 3 pm. The tours cover around 30 rooms and last an hour.

Vimanmek is open from 9.30 am to 4 pm daily and admission is 50B for adults, 20B for children. It's free if you've already been to the Grand Palace/Wat Phra Kaew and kept the entry ticket for Vimanmek. Note that visitors wearing shorts are refused entry.

Vimanmek is off U-Thong Nai Rd (between Si Ayuthaya and Ratwithi Rds), across from the west side of the Dusit Zoo. An air-con No 3 (Si Ayuthaya Rd) or No 10 (Ratwithi Rd) bus will drop you nearby.

Siam Society & Ban Kamthieng

สยามสมาคมบ้านคำเที่ยง

At 131 Soi Asoke, Sukhumvit Rd, are the publishers of the renowned *Journal of the Siam Society* and valiant preservers of traditional Thai culture. The society headquarters are a good place to visit for those with a serious interest in Thailand – a reference library is open to visitors and Siam Society monographs are for sale. Almost anything you'd want to know about Thailand (outside the political sphere, since the society is sponsored by the royal family) can be researched here. An ethnological museum of sorts exhibiting Thai folk art is located on the Siam Society grounds in the northern-style Kamthieng House. Ban Kamthieng is open Tuesday to Saturday from 9 am to noon and 1 to 5 pm. Admission is 25B.

Art Galleries

Opposite the National Theatre on Chao Fa Rd, the **National Gallery** displays traditional and contemporary art. Most of the art displayed here is by artists who receive government support; the general consensus is that it's not Thailand's best, but the gallery is worth a visit for die-hard art fans or if you're in the vicinity. The gallery is closed Mondays and Tuesdays, and open from 9 am to noon and 1 to 4 pm on other days. Admission is 20B.

At the forefront of the new Buddhist art movement is the **Visual Dhamma Art Gallery** (☎ 258-5879) at 44/28 Soi Asoke (Soi 21, Sukhumvit Rd). Works by some of Thailand's most prominent muralists are sometimes displayed here, along with the occasional foreign exhibition. The gallery is open Monday to Friday from 1 to 6 pm, Saturday from 10 am to 5 pm, or at other times by appointment. Although the address is Soi Asoke, the gallery is actually off Asoke – coming from Sukhumvit Rd, take the second right into a small lane opposite Singha Bier Haus.

Another private gallery specialising in Thai contemporary art is the **Bhirasri Institute** on Soi Attakanprasit, off Soi Ngam Duphli. Named after famous Italian artist Silpa Bhirasri (Italian name Corrado Feroci), this was Thailand's first modern art institute. It's open Monday to Saturday from 9 am to 4 pm; admission is free.

Silpakorn University (near Wat Phra Kaew) is Bangkok's fine arts university and has a gallery of student works. The **Thailand Cultural Centre** on Ratchadaphisek Rd (in the Huay Khwang district, between Soi Tiam Ruammit and Din Daeng Rd) has a small gallery with rotating contemporary art exhibits, as does the **River City** shopping complex next to the Royal Orchid Sheraton on the river. Bangkok's foreign cultural centres hold regular exhibits of foreign and local artists – check the monthly bulletins issued by AUA, Alliance Française, the British Council and the Goethe Institute. For addresses, see under Cultural Centres in this chapter.

Several of Bangkok's luxury hotels display top-quality contemporary art in their lobbies and other public areas. The **Grand Hyatt Erawan** (on the corner of Ratchadamri and Ploenchit Rds) and the **Landmark Hotel** (Sukhumvit Rd) have the best collections of contemporary art in the country. The Erawan alone has over 1900 works exhibited on a rotating basis.

The **Neilson Hays Library** at 195 Surawong Rd occasionally hosts small exhibits in its Rotunda Gallery.

Chinatown (Sampeng)

เยาวราช (สำเพ็ง)

Bangkok's Chinatown, off Yaowarat and Ratchawong Rds, comprises a confusing and crowded array of jewellery, hardware, wholesale food, automotive and fabric shops, as well as dozens of other small businesses. It's a good place to shop since goods here are cheaper than almost anywhere else in Bangkok and the Chinese proprietors like to bargain, especially along Soi Wanit (also known as Sampeng Lane). Chinese and Thai antiques in various grades of age and authenticity are available in the so-called Thieves' Market (Nakhon Kasem), but it's better for browsing than buying these days.

During the annual Vegetarian Festival, celebrated fervently by Thai Chinese for the first nine days of the ninth lunar month (September-October), Bangkok's Chinatown becomes a virtual orgy of vegetarian Thai and Chinese food. The festivities are centred around **Wat Mangkon Kamalawat (Neng Noi Yee)**, one of Chinatown's largest temples, on Charoen Krung Rd. All along Charoen Krung Rd in this vicinity, as well as on Yaowarat Rd to the south, restaurants and noodle shops offer hundreds of different vegetarian dishes.

Pahurat

พาหุรัด

At the edge of Chinatown, around the intersection of Pahurat (Phahurat) and Chakraphet (Chakkaphet) Rds, is a small but thriving Indian district, generally called Pahurat. Here dozens of Indian-owned shops sell all kinds of fabric and clothes. This is the best place in the city to bargain for such items, especially silk. The selection is unbelievable, and Thai shoulder bags (yaams) sold here are the cheapest in Bangkok, perhaps in Thailand.

Behind the more obvious storefronts along these streets, in the 'bowels' of the blocks, is a seemingly endless Indian bazaar selling not only fabric but household items, food and other necessities. There are some good, reasonably priced Indian restaurants in this area, too, and a Sikh temple off Chakraphet Rd.

Chinatown – Pahurat Walking Tour

This route meanders through Bangkok's busy Chinese and Indian market districts – best explored on foot since vehicular traffic in the area is in almost constant gridlock. Depending on your pace and shopping intentions, this lengthy route could take from 1½ to three hours.

Be forewarned that the journey should only be undertaken by those who can withstand extended crowd contact as well as the sometimes unpleasant sights and smells of a traditional fresh market. The reward for tolerating this attack on the senses consists of numerous glimpses into the 'real' day-to-day Bangkok, away from the glittering facade of department stores and office buildings along Bangkok's main avenues – not to mention the opportunity for fabulous bargains. (If you plan to buy anything, you'd better bring along either a phrasebook or an interpreter – very little English is spoken in these areas.)

Start at **Wat Mangkon Kamalawat (Neng Noi Yee)** (A), one of Chinatown's largest and liveliest temples, on Charoen Krung Rd between Mangkon Rd and Soi Itsaranuphap. A taxi direct to the temple is recommended over taking a bus, simply because the district is so congested and street names don't always appear in Roman script. If you're determined to go by bus, Nos 35, 48 and 55 pass the temple going west (the temple entrance will be on the right), or you could take an air-con bus No 8 and get out near the Mangkon Rd intersection on Yaowarat Rd, a block south of Charoen Krung. In either case, to help pinpoint the right area on Charoen Krung Rd look for neighbouring shops selling fruit, cakes, incense and ritual burning paper for offering at the temple. Inscriptions at the entrance are in Chinese and Tibetan, while the labyrinthine interior features a succession of Buddhist, Taoist and Confucianist altars. Virtually at any time of day or night this temple is packed with worshippers lighting incense, filling the ever-burning altar lamps with oil and praying to their ancestors.

Leaving the temple, walk left along Charoen Krung Rd about 20 metres to the nearest crosswalk (a policeman is usually directing traffic here), then cross the street and head down the alley on the other side. You're now heading south-west on **Soi Itsaranuphap** (B), one of Chinatown's main market lanes. This section is lined with

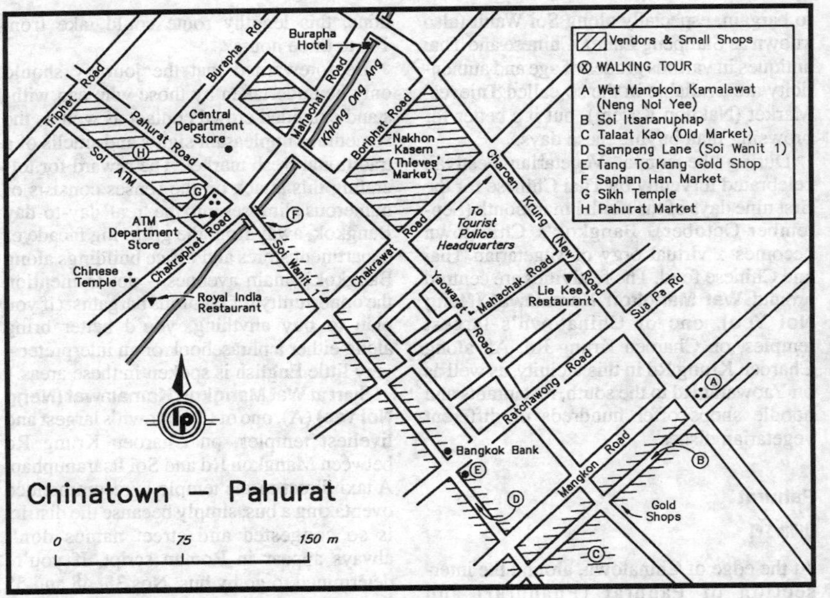

vendors purveying ready-to-eat or preserved foodstuffs, including cleaned chickens, duck and fish; though not for the squeamish, it's one of the cleanest-looking fresh markets in Bangkok.

About a hundred metres down Soi Itsaranuphap you'll cross **Yaowarat Rd**, a main Chinatown thoroughfare. This section of Yaowarat is lined with large and small gold shops; for price and selection, this is probably the best place in Thailand to purchase a gold chain (sold by the *bàht*, a unit of weight equal to 15 grams). From the soi entrance, turn right onto Yaowarat Rd, walk 50 metres to the crosswalk and, using a couple of savvy-looking Chinese crones as screens, navigate your way across the avenue.

Soi Itsaranuphap continues southward on the other side. Down the lane almost immediately on your left is the Chinese-ornamented entrance to **Talaat Kao (Old Market)** (C). This market section off Soi Itsaranuphap has been operating continuously for over 200 years. All manner and size of freshwater and saltwater fin and shellfish are displayed here, alive and filleted – or sometimes half alive and half filleted.

About a hundred metres farther down Itsaranuphap, past rows of vendors selling mostly dried fish, you'll come to a major Chinatown market crossroads. Running perpendicular to Itsaranuphap in either direction is famous **Sampeng Lane (Soi Wanit 1)** (D). Turn right onto Sampeng. This is usually the most crowded of Chinatown's market sois, a traffic jam of pedestrians, pushcarts and the occasional annoying motorbike twisting through the crowds. Shops along this section of Sampeng sell dry goods, especially shoes, clothing, fabric, toys and kitchen ware.

About 25 metres west, Sampeng Lane crosses Mangkon Rd. On either side of the intersection are two of Bangkok's oldest commercial buildings, a Bangkok Bank and the venerable **Tang To Kang** gold shop (E), both over 100 years old. The exteriors of the buildings are classic early Bangkok, showing lots of European influence; the interiors are heavy with hardwood panelling. Continue walking another 60 metres or so to the Ratchawong Rd crossing (a traffic cop is usually stationed here to part the vehicular Red Sea for pedestrians), cross and re-enter Sampeng Lane on the other side.

At this point, fabric shops – many of them operated by Indian (mostly Sikh) merchants – start dominating the selection as the western edge of Chinatown approaches the Indian district of Pahurat. If you're looking for good deals on Thai textiles you're in the right place. But hold off buying until you've had a chance to look through at least a dozen or more shops – they get better the farther you go. After about 65 metres is the small Mahachak Rd crossing and then after another 50 metres or so is the larger Chakrawat (Chakkawat) Rd crossing, where yet another traffic cop assists. Along Chakrawat Rd in this vicinity, as well as farther ahead along Sampeng Lane on the other side of Chakrawat, there are many gem and jewellery shops.

If you were to follow Chakrawat Rd north from Soi Wanit, you could have a look around the Chinese-Thai antique shops of **Nakhon Kasem** (also known as the Thieves' Market since at one time stolen goods were commonly sold here) between Yaowarat and Charoen Krung Rds. After you re-enter Soi Wanit on the other side of Chakrawat Rd the jewellery shops are mixed with an eclectic array of houseware and clothing shops until you arrive, after another 50 metres, at the **Saphan Han** (F) market area, named after a short bridge *(saphãan)* over Khlong Ong Ang. Clustered along the khlong on either side of the bridge is a bevy of vendors selling noodles and snacks. On the other side of the bridge, Sampeng Lane ends at Chakraphet Rd, the eastern edge of the Pahurat district.

Chakraphet Rd is well known for its Indian restaurants and shops selling Indian sweets. One of the best eateries in the area is the Royal India Restaurant, which serves North Indian cuisine and is justly famous for its tasty selection of Indian breads. To get there, turn left onto Chakraphet and walk about 70 metres along the east (left) side of the road; look for the Royal India sign pointing down an alley on the left. On the opposite side of Chakraphet Rd from the Royal India is another Chinese temple. North of this temple, in a back alley on the west side of the road, is a large **Sikh temple** (G) – turn left before the ATM department store to find the entrance. Visitors to the temple – reportedly the second-largest Sikh temple outside of India – are welcome but they must remove their shoes. If you arrive on a Sikh festival day you can partake of the *langar* or communal Sikh meal served in the temple.

Several inexpensive Indian food stalls are found in an alley alongside the department store. Behind the store, stretching westward from Chakraphet Rd to Triphet Rd, is the **Pahurat Market** (H), devoted almost exclusively to textiles and clothing. Pahurat Rd itself runs parallel to and just north of the market.

If you're ready to escape the market hustle and bustle, you can catch city buses on Chakraphet Rd (heading north and then east to the Siam Square and Pratunam areas) or along Pahurat Rd (heading west and then north along Tri Thong Rd to the Banglamphu district).

Dusit Zoo (Khao Dhin Wana)

เขาดิน

The collection of animals at Bangkok's zoo may not be extremely interesting, but there are white elephants and the zoo is a nice place to get away from the noise of the city and observe how the Thais amuse themselves – by eating mainly (food is very good and cheap at the zoo!).

Besides the animal exhibits there's also a botanical garden, a small lake and a children's playground. Entry to the zoo is 10B; hours are from 8 am to 6 pm daily. A small circus performs on weekends and holidays between 11 am and 2 pm. Sundays can be a bit crowded – if you want the zoo mostly to yourself, go on a weekday.

The zoo is in the Dusit district between Chitlada Palace and the National Assembly Hall; the main entrance is off Ratwithi Rd. Bus lines that pass the entrance include the ordinary Nos 8 and 28 and the air-con No 10.

Queen Saovabha Memorial Institute (Snake Farm)

สวนเสาวภา

At this research institute (☎ 252-0161) on Rama IV Rd (near Henri Dunant Rd), venomous snakes are milked daily to make snake-bite antidotes which are distributed throughout the country. The milking sessions – at 11 am and 2.30 pm weekdays, 11 am only on weekends and holidays – have become a major Bangkok tourist attraction; admission is 40B. Feeding time is 3 pm. This will be boring to some, exciting to others. A Thai Red Cross pamphlet entitled 'Health Hints for Travellers' is available for 10B; you can also get common vaccinations such as cholera, typhoid and smallpox here.

Ancient City (Muang Boran)

เมืองโบราณ

Billed as the largest open-air museum in the world, Ancient City (Muang Boran) covers more than 500 sq km and presents outstanding scaled-down facsimiles of many of the kingdom's most famous monuments. The grounds follow Thailand's general geographical outline, with the monuments placed accordingly. The main entrance places visitors at the country's southern tip, from where you work your way to the 'northernmost' monuments. For students of Thai architecture, it's worth a day's visit (it takes an entire day to cover the area). It's also a good place for long undistracted walks, as it's usually quiet and never crowded.

The Ancient City Co (☎ 226-1226/7) also puts out a lavish bilingual periodical devoted to Thai art and architecture called *Muang Boran*. The journal is edited by some of Thailand's leading art historians. The owner of both journal and park is Bangkok's largest Mercedes Benz dealer, who has an avid interest in Thai art.

Ancient City is in Samut Prakan, 33 km from Bangkok along the Old Sukhumvit Highway. Hours are 7 am to 6 pm; admission to the site is 270B. The fare to the Samut Prakan terminal by public bus No 25 is 3B; from there get a songthaew to Muang Boran for 2B. Transport can be also arranged through the Bangkok office at 78 Democracy Monument circle, Ratchadamnoen Rd.

In the same area there is a **Crocodile Farm**, where you can even see crocodile wrestling! The crocodile farm is open from 8 am to 6 pm daily – the reptiles get their

dinner between 5 and 6 pm. Admission is 80B. There are over 30,000 crocs here, as well as elephants, monkeys and snakes.

Monk's Bowl Village

This is the only remaining of three such villages established in Bangkok by King Rama I for the purpose of handcrafting monk's bowls *(bàat)*. The black bowls, used by Thai monks to receive alms-food from faithful Buddhists every morning, are still made here in the traditional manner. The district is known as Ban Baht (Monk's Bowl Village).

To find it, walk south on Boriphat Rd south of Bamrung Muang Rd, then left on Soi Ban Baht. The artisans who fashion the bowls are not always at work, so it's largely a matter of luck whether you'll see them in action. To see monks' robes and bowls for sale, wander down Bamrung Muang Rd in the vicinity of the Giant Swing.

Lumphini Park

สวนลุมพินี

Named after the Buddha's birthplace in Nepal, this is Bangkok's largest and most popular park. The park is bordered by Rama IV Rd to the south, Sarasin Rd to the north, Withayu Rd to the east and Ratchadamri Rd to the west, with entrance gates on all sides. A large artificial lake in the centre is surrounded by broad, well-tended lawns, wooded areas and walking paths – in other words, it's the best outdoor escape from Bangkok without leaving town.

One of the best times to visit the park is in the early morning when the air is fresh (well, relatively so for Bangkok) and legions of Chinese are practising t'ai chi. Also in the morning, vendors set up tables to dispense fresh snake blood and bile, considered health tonics by many Thais and Chinese. Rowboats and paddle boats can be rented at the lake. A weight-lifting area in one section becomes a miniature 'muscle beach' on weekends. Other facilities include a snack bar, several areas with tables and benches for picnics and a couple of tables where ladies serve Chinese tea. Rest rooms are placed at intervals throughout the park.

During kite-flying season, mid-February to April, Lumphini becomes a favoured flight zone; kites *(wâo)* can be purchased in the park in these months.

Sanam Luang

สนามหลวง

Sanam Luang (Royal Field) just north of Wat Phra Kaew is the traditional site for royal cremations, and for the annual Ploughing Ceremony, in which the king officially initiates the rice-growing season. The last ceremonial cremations took place here in 1976, when the king presided over funeral rites for students killed in the demonstrations of that year.

Bangkok's famous Weekend Market was once held at Sanam Luang (it is now held at Chatuchak Park – see the Things to Buy section in this chapter for details). Nowadays the large field is most popularly used as a picnic and recreational area. A large kite competition is held here during the kite-flying season, February to April.

Floating Markets

ตลาดน้ำ

Wat Sai Floating Market In recent years, visitors to the floating market near Wat Sai on Khlong Sanam Chai (off Khlong Dao Khanong) have been divided in their opinions as to whether the trip is worth the early rising to get there by 7 to 7.30 am. There are still plenty of boats out there, selling fresh produce and ready-to-eat foods, but there may be as many boat loads of tourists, not to mention lots of tourist shops.

If you're set on going it might be best to take one of the floating market tours that leave from the Oriental pier (Soi Oriental) or Tha Maharat near Silpakorn University – your only alternative is to charter a whole boat (at the Oriental pier) and that can be quite expensive. Floating market tours cost from 50B, but the cheapest tours probably only give you 20 minutes or so at the market. Be prepared for a very touristy experience.

Khlong Sanam Chai is best accessed via Khlong Dao Khanong, which runs west from the Chao Phraya River opposite the terminus of Charoen Krung Rd, below Krungthep Bridge. (See the Greater Bangkok map.)

Bang Khu Wiang Floating Market At Khlong Bang Khu Wiang in Thonburi there is a small floating market between 4 and 7 am. Boats to the Khu Wiang Market (Talàat Náam Khuu Wiang) leave from the Tha Chang pier near Wat Phra Kaew every morning between 6.15 and 8 am. Other small floating markets (Thai: *talàat náam)* take place in various locations throughout the huge canal system that surrounds Bangkok – hire a long-tail boat for the day and ask around.

Damnoen Saduak Floating Market There is a more lively and less commercial floating market on Khlong Damnoen Saduak in Ratchaburi Province, 104 km south-west of Bangkok, between Nakhon Pathom and Samut Songkhram. You can get buses from the southern bus terminal on Charan Sanitwong Rd in Thonburi to Damnoen Saduak starting at 5 am. This market now sees hordes of tourists as well, and could also be skipped unless you have a burning desire to imitate the classic floating market photography seen in so many tourist brochures. See the Ratchaburi section in the Central Thailand chapter for more details.

Other Attractions

Bangkok has a host of artificial tourist attractions including **Timland** (Thailand in Miniature), an example of the 'see the whole country in half an hour' park which every South-East Asian country seems to have.

The **Rose Garden Country Resort** is south of Bangkok on the Thachin River and includes a Thai cultural village. Admission to the garden area is 10B, another 140B for the 3 pm performances in the cultural village. The garden is open from 8 am to 6 pm daily.

Bangkok also has a **Museum of Science** and a **Planetarium**, both on Sukhumvit Rd between Sois 40 and 42.

At Bang Kapi, **Siam Park** (101 Sukhaphiban 2) is a huge recreational park with pools, water slides, a wave pool and the like. Highly recommended for a splash. Admission is 100B; get there on bus No 27. Another good excursion for kids is **Magic Land**, Thailand's answer to Disneyland, on Phahonyothin Rd just north of Central Plaza.

Military aircraft aficionados shouldn't miss the **Royal Thai Air Force Museum**, on Phahonyothin Rd near Wing 6 of the Don Muang domestic airport terminal. Among the world-class collection of historic aircraft is the only existing Japanese Tachikawa trainer, along with a Spitfire and several Nieuports and Breguets. The museum is open from 8.30 am to 4.30 pm Monday to Friday and on the first weekend of each month; admission is free.

River & Canal Trips

Chao Phraya River Express You can observe urban river life from the water for 1½ hours for only 7B by climbing aboard a Chao Phraya River Express boat at Tha Wat Ratchasingkhon, just north of Krungthep Bridge. If you want to ride the entire length of the express route all the way to Nonthaburi, this is where you must begin. Ordinary bus Nos 1, 22 and 75 and air-con bus No 4 pass Ratchasingkhon pier. Or you could board at any other express boat pier in Bangkok for a shorter ride to Nonthaburi; for example, 20 minutes from Tha Phayap (the first stop north of Krungthon Bridge), or 30 minutes from Tha Phra Athit (near the Phra Pinklao Bridge). Express boats run about every 15 minutes from 6 am to 6 pm daily. See under Boat in the later Getting Around section for more information on the Chao Phraya River Express service.

Khlong Bangkok Noi Taxi Another good boat trip is the Bangkok Noi canal taxi route which leaves from Tha Maharat next to Silpakorn University. The fare is only a few baht and the further up Khlong Bangkok Noi you go, the better the scenery becomes, with teak houses on stilts, old wats and plenty of greenery.

Other Canal Taxis From Tha Tien pier near Wat Pho, get a canal taxi along **Khlong Mon** (leaving every half hour) for more typical canal scenery, including orchid farms (4B). A longer excursion could be made by making a loop along khlongs Bangkok Noi, Chak Phra and Mon, an all-day trip.

From the Tha Phibun Songkram pier in Nonthaburi you can board a boat taxi up picturesque **Khlong Om** and see durian plantations. Boats leave every 15 minutes. From Tha Chang, near Wat Phra Kaew, you can charter long-tail boats for a three-hour tour of Thonburi canals for 150B – you can choose from among eight different canals. It is possible to go as far from Bangkok as Suphanburi and Ratburi (Ratchaburi) by boat, though this may involve many boat connections. Beware of 'agents' who will try to put you on the boat and rake off an extra commission. Before travelling by boat, establish the price – you can't bargain when you're in the middle of the river!

Finally, if you're really a canal freak, look for *50 Trips Through Siam's Canals* (Editions Duang Kamol, 1979) by Geo-Ch Veran (translated from French into English by Sarah Bennett). The book contains 25 detailed maps and clear instructions on how to take the various trips – some of which are very time-consuming. The prolific William Warren has recently written *Bangkok's Waterways*, which may be easier to find.

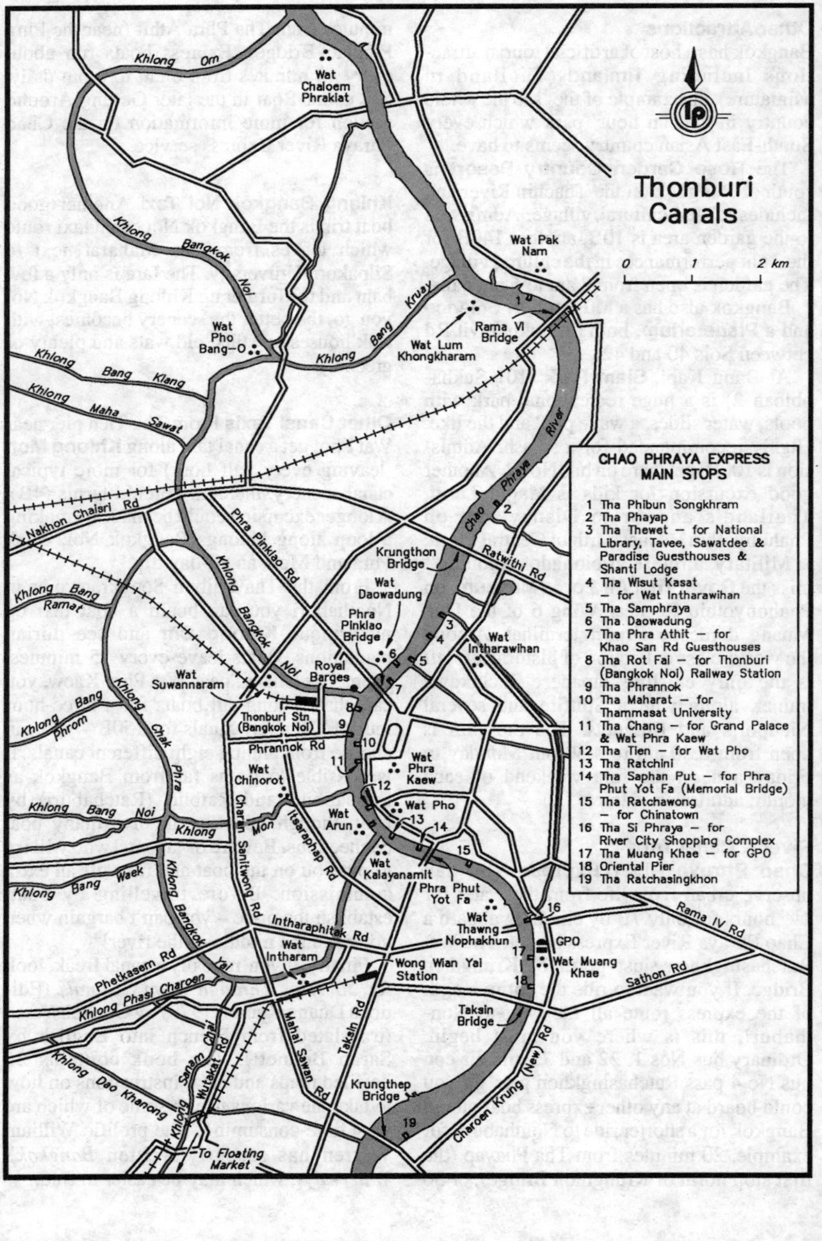

Thonburi Canals
0
1
2 km
CHAO PHRAYA EXPRESS MAIN STOPS
1 Tha Phibun Songkhram
2 Tha Phayap
3 Tha Thewet – for National Library, Tavee, Sawatdee & Paradise Guesthouses & Shanti Lodge
4 Tha Wisut Kasat – for Wat Intharawihan
5 Tha Samphraya
6 Tha Daowadung
7 Tha Phra Athit – for Khao San Rd Guesthouses
8 Tha Rot Fai – for Thonburi (Bangkok Noi) Railway Station
9 Tha Phrannok
10 Tha Maharat – for Thammasat University
11 Tha Chang – for Grand Palace & Wat Phra Kaew
12 Tha Tien – for Wat Pho
13 Tha Ratchini
14 Tha Saphan Put – for Phra Phut Yot Fa (Memorial Bridge)
15 Tha Ratchawong – for Chinatown
16 Tha Si Phraya – for River City Shopping Complex
17 Tha Muang Khae – for GPO
18 Oriental Pier
19 Tha Ratchasingkhon
Khlong Om
Wat Chaloem Phrakiat
Wat Pak Nam
Khlong Bangkok Noi
Khlong Bang Kruay
Rama VI Bridge
Wat Lum Khongkharam
Wat Pho Bang-O
Khlong Bang Klang
Khlong Maha Sawat
Chao Phraya River
Nakhon Chaisri Rd
Phra Pinklao Rd
Ratwithi Rd
Krungthon Bridge
Wat Daowadung
Phra Pinklao Bridge
Khlong Bang Ramat
Wat Intharawihan
Royal Barges
Wat Suwannaram
Khlong Bang Phrom
Thonburi Stn (Bangkok Noi)
Phrannok Rd
Khlong Chak Phra
Wat Chinorot
Wat Phra Kaew
Wat Pho
Khlong Bang Noi
Khlong Mon
Wat Arun
Itsaraphap Rd
Charan Sanitwong Rd
Wat Kalayanamit
Phra Phut Yot Fa
Khlong Bang Waek
Rama IV Rd
Wat Thawng Nophakhun
Intharaphitak Rd
Wat Intharam
GPO
Wat Muang Khae
Phetkasem Rd
Khlong Bangkok Yai
Wong Wian Yai Station
Sathon Rd
Khlong Phasi Charoen
Taksin Bridge
Mahai Sawan Rd
Taksin Rd
Khlong Sanam Chai
Charoen Krung (New) Rd
Khlong Dao Khanong
Krungthep Bridge
Khlong Wutakat Rd
To Floating Market

Top Left: Wat Khaek, Nong Khai (JC)
Bottom Left: Sculptures, Ancient City (JB)
Top Right: Guard, Grand Palace (PM)
Bottom Right: Wat That Phanom, That Phanom (JC)

Top Left: Ko Faan, Big Buddha Beach (RK)
Bottom Left: Wat Phra That Doi Suthep, Chiang Mai (TAT)
Top Right: Kinaree, Grand Palace (PM)
Bottom Right: Fertility shrine, Bangkok (RN)

Dinner Cruises A dozen or more companies in Bangkok run regular cruises along the Chao Phraya for rates ranging from 30 to 500B per person, depending on how far they go and whether dinner is included with the fare. Most require advance phone reservations. The following cruises cost from 400 to 500B per person, including dinner:

Dinner Cruise Co
  River City pier (Tha Si Phraya) to Krungthon Bridge, daily (☎ 234-5599)
Loy Nava Co
  River City pier to Wasukri pier, daily (☎ 437-4932/7329)
Oriental Hotel
  Oriental pier to Nonthaburi, Wednesdays only (☎ 236-0400/9)
Thasaneeya Nava
  River City pier to Wasukri pier, daily (☎ 437-4932)

The following cruises cost from 25 to 40B per person, plus dinner as ordered:

Ban Khun Luang Restaurant
  Ban Khun Luang Restaurant to Oriental pier, Thursday, Friday, Saturday (☎ 243-3235)
Khanap Nam Restaurant
  Krungthon Bridge to Taksin Bridge, daily (☎ 433-6611)
Riverside Company
  Krungthon Bridge to Rama IX Bridge, daily (☎ 424-9848)
River Sight-Seeing Ltd
  River City pier to Nonthaburi, daily (☎ 437-4047)
Yok-Yor Restaurant
  Wisut Kasat pier to Menam Hotel, daily (☎ 281-1829)

Longer Cruises There are also longer day and overnight cruises on the river. The Chao Phraya River Express Boat Co (☎ 222-5330, 225-3002/3) does a tour starting from Tha Maharat at 8 am and returning at 5.30 pm that includes visits to the Thai Folk Arts & Handicrafts Centre, Bang Pa In Palace in Ayuthaya, and the bird sanctuary at Wat Phailom. The price is a very reasonable 140B per person, not including lunch, which you arrange on your own in Bang Pa In.

The Oriental Hotel's luxurious all-air-con *Oriental Queen* (☎ 236-0400/9) also does a cruise to Bang Pa In that leaves at 8 am and returns at 5 pm. The *Oriental Queen* cruise costs 770B including lunch. Note that neither of the above cruises really allows enough time to see Ayuthaya properly, so if that's your primary intention, don't go.

Asia Voyages (☎ 235-4100/4) has recently launched the *Mekhala*, a restored teak rice barge that has been transformed into a six-cabin cruiser. The *Mekhala* leaves Bangkok in the afternoon on Saturday, Monday and Thursday (or from Ayuthaya on Sunday, Tuesday and Friday) and heads upriver toward Ayuthaya (or downriver toward Bangkok). In the evening it anchors at Wat Praket where a candle-lit dinner is served. The next morning passengers offer food to the monks from the wat, and then the barge moves on to Bang Pa In. After a tour of the Summer Palace, a long-tail boat takes passengers on for a tour of the ruins of Ayuthaya. The return to Bangkok is by air-con bus. The cost is 2900B per person double occupancy and includes all meals, accommodation, admission fees in Ayuthaya and hotel transfers.

Sports Clubs

The first and grandest of the city's sports facilities is the **Royal Bangkok Sports Club** (RBSC) between Henri Dunant and Ratchadamri Rds (the green oval marked 'Turf' on the Bangkok bus maps). Facilities include a horse track, polo grounds (located elsewhere off Withayu Rd), swimming pool, sauna, squash and tennis courts (both hard and grass) and 18-hole golf course. There's a waiting list for membership so the only way you're likely to frolic at this prestigious club is to be invited by a lucky RBSC member.

Membership at the **British Club** (☎ 234-0247) is open to citizens of Australia, Canada, New Zealand and the UK or to others by invitation. Among the sports facilities are a pool, squash and tennis courts. The **Mariner Club** (☎ 249-3801) at 27/2 Tha Reua in Khlong Toey has an open membership policy for anyone wanting to use its pool or tennis courts.

Soi Klang Racquet Club (☎ 391-0963), at 8 Soi 49, Sukhumvit Rd has facilities open to the public for squash, tennis, racquetball, swimming and aerobics. Other sports clubs open to the public include:

Asoke Sports Club – 302/81-81 Asoke-Din Daeng Rd; tennis, swimming (☎ 246-2260)
Kanpaibun Tennis Court – 10 Soi 40, Sukhumvit Rd; tennis (☎ 392-1832)
NTT Sports Club – 612/32 Soi Laoladda, Arun Amarin Rd, Thonburi; swimming, weights, aerobics (☎ 433-4623)
Saithip Swimming Pool – 140 Soi 56, Sukhumvit Rd; tennis, badminton, swimming (☎ 331-2037)
Santhikham Court – 217 Soi 109, Sukhumvit Rd; tennis (☎ 393-8480)
Sivalai Tennis Court & Swimming Pool – 168 Soi Anantaphum, Itsaraphap Rd, Thonburi; tennis, swimming
Swim & Slim Family Club – 918 Soi 101/1, Sukhumvit Rd; badminton, swimming, weights (☎ 393-0889)

For a list of golf courses in Bangkok, see the Golf section in the Facts for the Visitor chapter.

Meditation Study

Although at times Bangkok may seem like the most un-Buddhist place on earth, there are several places where interested foreigners can learn about Theravada Buddhist meditation. (See the Religion section in the Facts about the Country chapter for background information on Buddhism in Thailand.)

Wat Mahathat This 18th-century wat opposite Sanam Luang offers meditation instruction several times daily at Section 5, a building near the monks' residences. Some of the Thai monks here speak English and there are often Western monks or long-term residents available to translate. Instruction is based on the Mahasi Sayadaw system of *satipatthana* or mindfulness.

Wat Phleng Vipassana The vice abbot of Wat Phleng, Ajaan Prasert Chantarangsi, teaches vipassana meditation to foreigners in English. Many Westerners have stayed here for varying lengths of time, both as laypersons and as monks or nuns. The teaching methods employed are basically an Abhidhamma-reinforced combination of *samatha* (tranquility), *metta* (loving kindness) and vipassana (insight) techniques. The wat is at Soi Ying Amnuay, Charan Sanitwong Rd, Bangkok Noi, Thonburi.

Wat Pak Nam This very large wat, where hundreds of monks and nuns reside during the Buddhist Rains Retreat, has hosted many foreigners (especially Japanese) over the years. The meditation teacher, Phra Khru Phawana, speaks some English and there are usually people around who can translate. The emphasis is on developing concentration through *nimittas* (acquired mental images) in order to attain trance-absorption states. A small English library is available. Pak Nam is on Thoet Thai Rd, Phasi Charoen, Thonburi.

Wat Rakhang Khositaram Only a few foreigners have studied at this temple, but the meditation teacher, Ajaan Mahathawon from Ubon Province in the north-east, has quite a good reputation. The teaching tradition at Wat Rakhang is strongly Abhidhamma-based, with much emphasis given to Buddhist psychology. Vipassana is considered attainable without strong concentration by means of a dialectic process similar to Krishnamurti's 'choiceless awareness'. To study here, one ought to be able to speak Thai fairly well; otherwise, an interpreter will have to be arranged. Wat Rakhang is on Arun Amarin Rd, Thonburi.

Wat Cholaprathan Rangsarit The teachers here, Ajaan Pañña (the abbot) and Ajaan Khao, employ a modified version of the Mahasi Sayadaw system of *satipatthana* practice. Occasionally there's someone around who can translate; otherwise it will be necessary to arrange in advance for translation. This wat also serves as a Bangkok headquarters for monks from Wat Suanmok (see Chaiya in the Southern Thailand chapter). Wat Cholaprathan is in Pak Kret, Nonthaburi Province; and although not actually part of Bangkok, Nonthaburi is so connected to Bangkok's urban sprawl that you can hardly tell the difference.

World Fellowship of Buddhists The WFB, at 33 Sukhumvit Rd, is a clearing house for information on Theravada Buddhism as well as dialogue between various schools of Buddhism. The centre hosts meditation classes on the first Sunday evening of every month.

Thai Cooking Schools

More and more travellers are coming to Thailand just to learn how to cook. While passing through Mae Sai, I once met a young English chef who was seeking out new cooking secrets. His reputation in England was in part due to his use of Thai ingredients and cooking methods in his own 'nouvelle' cuisine. You, too, can amaze your friends back home after attending a course in Thai cuisine at one of the following places:

Bussaracum Restaurant – 35 Soi Phiphat 2, Convent Rd (☎ 235-8915)
Modern Housewife Centre – 45/6-7 Sethsiri Rd (☎ 279-2831/4)
Mrs Balbir's Cooking School – Mrs Balbir teaches Indian as well as Thai cooking – 1/22 Soi 11, Sukhumvit Rd (☎ 253-2281)
Oriental Hotel Cooking School – features a five-day course under the direction of well-known chef Chali (Charlie) Amatyakul – Soi Oriental, Charoen Krung (New) Rd (☎ 236-0400/39)
UFM Food Centre – most classes offered in Thai; need at least four persons to offer an English-language class – 593/29-39 Soi 33/1, Sukhumvit Rd (☎ 259- 0620/33)

Other Courses

For information about language courses and martial arts training courses in Bangkok, see Activities in the Facts for the Visitor chapter.

Places to Stay – bottom end

Bangkok has perhaps the best variety and quality of budget places to stay of any Asian capital – which is one of the reasons it's such a popular destination for roving world travellers. Because of the wide distribution of places, your choice actually depends on what part of the city you want to be in – the tourist ghettos of Sukhumvit Rd and Silom-Surawong Rds, the backpackers' ghetto of Banglamphu (north of Ratchadamnoen Klang), the centrally located Siam Square area, Chinatown, or the old travellers' centre around Soi Ngam Duphli, off Rama IV Rd.

Chinatown, Hualamphong station and Banglamphu are the best all-round areas for seeing the real Bangkok, and are the cheapest districts for eating and sleeping. The Siam Square area is also well located, in that it's more or less in the centre of Bangkok – this, coupled with the good selection of city buses that pass through the Rama I and Phayathai Rd intersection, makes even more of the city accessible. In addition, Siam Square has good bookshops, several banks, excellent middle-range restaurants, travel agencies and three movie theatres.

For Bangkok, bottom-end accommodation will be taken to mean places costing from 40 to 500B per night; middle-range from 500 to 1500B per night, and top end from 2000B up.

Banglamphu If you're really on a tight budget head for the Khao San Rd area, near the Democracy Monument, parallel to Ratchadamnoen Klang Rd – ordinary bus Nos 2, 15, 17, 44, 56 or 59 will get you there, also air-con bus Nos 11 and 12. This is becoming much more the main travellers' centre these days and new guesthouses are continually springing up.

Rates in Banglamphu are generally the lowest in Bangkok and although some of the places are barely adequate (bedbugs are sometimes a problem), a few are excellent value if you can pay just a bit more. At the bottom end, rooms are quite small and the walls dividing them are thin – in fact most are indistinguishable from one another. Some have small attached cafes with limited menus. Bathrooms are usually down the hall or out the back somewhere; mattresses may be on the floor. The least expensive rooms are 50/80B for singles/doubles, though these are hard to come by due to the hordes of people seeking them out. More common are the 80/100B rooms. During most of the year, it pays to visit several guesthouses before

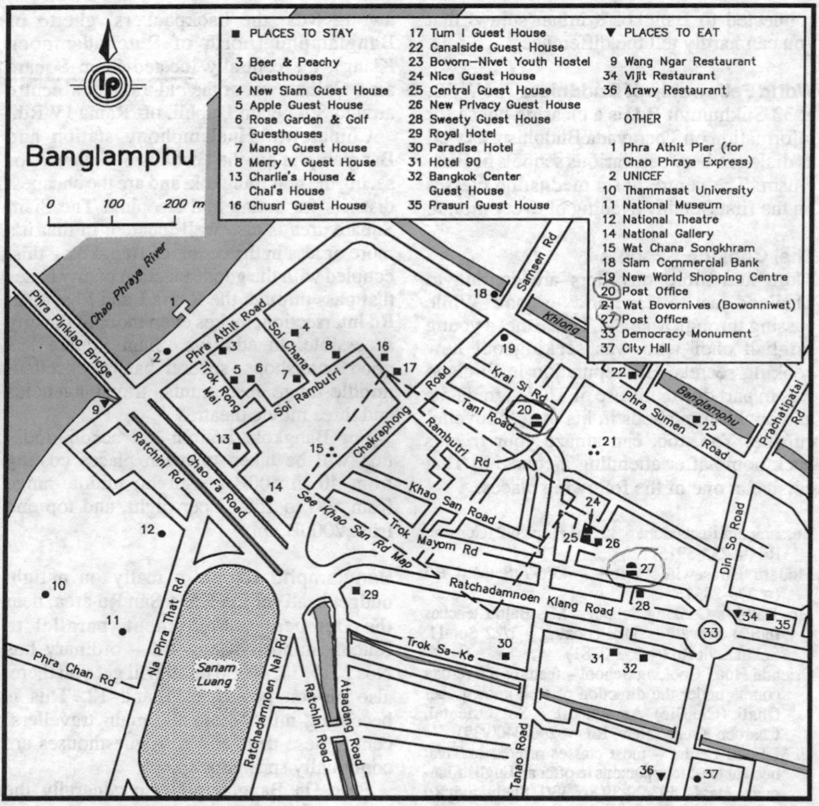

making a decision, but in the high season (December to February), you'd better take the first vacant bed you come across. The best time of day to find a vacancy is from around 9 to 10 am. At night during the peak months (December to March) Khao San Rd is bursting with life.

A decade or so ago there were only two Chinese-Thai hotels on Khao San Rd, the Nith Jaroen Suk (now called New Nith Jaroen Hotel) and the Sri Phranakhon (now the Khao San Palace Hotel). As word got out that these were exceptional and well-located bargains, they filled up with travellers and soon families along the street began turning their shops and homes into guesthouses. Now there are close to a hundred guesthouses in the immediate vicinity, too many to list exhaustively here. If you haven't already arrived with a recommendation in hand, you might best use the Banglamphu and Khao San Rd Area maps and simply pick one at random for your first night; if you're not satisfied you can stow your gear and explore the area till something better turns up. A tip: the guesthouses along Khao San Rd tend to be cubicles in modern shophouses, while those in Banglamphu's quieter lanes and alleys are often housed in old homes, some of them with a lot of character.

Central Banglamphu Entering Khao San Rd from the east, one of the first places you'll come to on the left is *Chada Guest House*, with nice digs for 80 to 100B (see the Khao San Rd map for this guesthouse, as well as for most of the places in this section). Next on the left is *CH Guest House* (they're big on initials here) which is decent value for 50 to 100B. Just beyond CH on the same side of the street is *Siri Guest House* (formerly Grand Guest House) where clean doubles are 100B – there are no singles available. After that is the similar *Ice Guest House*.

Turn left at the first little soi and you'll find three long-running guesthouses: the *Marco Polo Guest House* (also called 160 Guest House) for 40 to 100B; the *Good Luck Guest House* at 50 to 100B; and the best of the three, *VIP Guest House* (☎ 282-5090), where all rooms are 80B. Similar to the above is the newer *Tong Guest House* opposite the Marco Polo. On the right side of Khao San Rd, opposite the VIP soi, are two fair but noisy places that each charge 60 to 100B, the *GTA Guest House* and the *Nat Guest House*.

Continuing west along Khao San, turn right at the next soi and you'll find the old *Charoendee Hotel* where large rooms with character go for 120B. This old favourite had gone sadly downhill but during my last visit was undergoing renovation. It's fairly quiet, since it's off the street.

Across Khao San Rd and down an alley are two of the first guesthouses to appear in Banglamphu. The *Bonny Guest House* (☎ 281-9877) has dorm beds for 40B and singles/doubles for 80/100B, and is fairly clean and friendly. The *Top Guest House* (☎ 281-9954) is next door to the Bonny and owned by the same family. Rates are 60/80/120B for singles/doubles/triples. The newer *Dior Guest House* near the corner of the same soi has small rooms for 80/100B.

Opposite the entrance to the soi on the north side of Khao San is a new incarnation of the *Grand Guest House* with typical 80/100B rooms. The two alleys on either side of the Grand lead to two older Chinese hotels set back off the road. The *Khaosan Palace Hotel* (☎ 282-0578), at 139 Khao San Rd, has seen better days and rooms cost from 150B with ceiling fan and bath. Down the other alley the *New Nith Jaroen Hotel* (☎ 281-9872) has similar rates and rooms to the Khaosan Palace, but slightly better service.

The next alley on the right heading west along Khao San Rd winds through the block toward Rambutri Rd and leads to several cramped places that nonetheless manage to fill up. The names change from time to time; at the time of writing, the guesthouses here were named *Doll, Suneeporn, P, Pro* and *AT*. All feature small luggage-crammed lobbies with staircases leading to rooms layered on several floors and which cost around 60 to 100B. I would avoid this alley altogether unless there's no other choice – it's simply too crowded and closed in.

Back on Khao San Rd, and behind the snooker hall at No 74, is the *PB Guest House*. Mr Lu, the proprietor, speaks English pretty well and is very helpful to travellers. Two-bed rooms cost 80B, and a bed in a 20-bed dorm costs 40B. You can get cheap Thai food here (also Western breakfasts). His wife, Varapin, runs the PB Thai Boxing Gym and some of the boxers stay at the guesthouse. This has a definite 'sporting' atmosphere (with some of the illicit activities Bangkok is known for) – it's not for everybody. Across from PB are two adequate places, the *Buddy Guest House* where singles/doubles are 60/100B, 120B for a larger room with a window overlooking the street, and *Lek Guest House* (☎ 281-2775) which also has fairly good-sized rooms for 80 to 100B.

Next along the same side of Khao San Rd are *Mam's Guest House* and the *Hello Restaurant & Guest House* (☎ 281-8579). Mam's is 80 to 100B, nothing special, but the Hello is well run and has one of the more popular restaurants on Khao San Rd. Good-sized rooms at Hello are 60/100B for singles/doubles, 160B with air-con and windows overlooking the street. Hello has

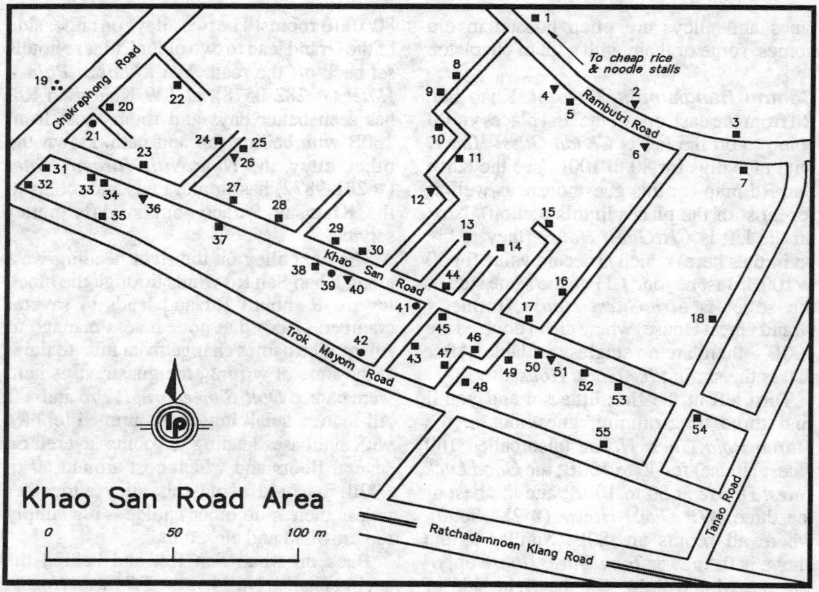

Khao San Road Area

■ PLACES TO STAY

1 Viengtai Hotel
3 Easy Guest House
5 ST Guest House
7 Panee Guest House
8 Green House
9 AT Guest House
10 Suneeporn Guest House
11 Dolls Guest House & Others
13 Khaosan Palace Hotel
14 New Nith Jaroen Hotel
15 Charoendee Hotel (Closed for Renovation)
16 Best Guest House & Restaurant
17 GTA & Nat Guesthouses
18 Harn, VS & Nisa Guesthouses
20 Siam Guest House
22 Chuanpis & Chakrapong Guesthouses
23 Sitdhi Guest House
24 Wally Guest House
25 Chart Guest House
27 Hello Guest House & Restaurant
28 Mam's Guest House
29 Lek Guest House
30 Buddy Guest House
31 Ploy Guest House
32 J Guest House
33 Thai Guest House
34 NS Guest House
35 Joe Guest House
37 Chart Guest House
38 PB Guest House
43 Bonny & Top Guesthouses
44 Grand Guest House
45 Dior Guest House
46 Good Luck Guest House
47 Marco Polo (160 Guest House)
48 Tong Guest House
49 VIP Guest House
50 Ice Guest House
52 Siri Guest House
53 CH Guest House
54 Chada Guest House
55 7-Holder Guest House

▼ PLACES TO EAT

2 Ta-Yai Restaurant
4 Roy's Snacks
6 Aisa Restaurant
12 Buddy Beer Restaurant
26 Royal India Restaurant & No Name Bar
36 Hello Restaurant
40 Khao San Center Restaurant
51 Rit's Cafe

OTHER

19 Wat Chana Songkhram
21 Chana Songkhram Police Station
39 Krung Thai Bank
41 Shops
42 School

another restaurant and guesthouse further down Khao San Rd on the other side with similar conditions and rates.

Opposite the Hello Guest House is the *Chart Guest House* with rooms for 80/100B. On the same side of the street toward the Chakraphong Rd intersection are the *NS* and *Thai* guesthouses. Both have doubles overlooking the street for around 100B. Across the street, the newer *Sitdhi Guest House & Restaurant* is similar to the Hello. The *Ploy Guest House* is right on the corner of Khao San and Chakraphong Rds, above a coffee house/nightclub. Rooms are clean, large and cost 80/120B for singles/doubles, 160B for triples.

Parallel to Khao San Rd but much quieter is Trok Mayom, an alley reserved for mostly pedestrian traffic. *J* and *Joe* (☎ 281-2948) are old teak homes with pleasant rooms for 80 to 150B. Further east toward Tanao Rd is the basic *7-Holder*.

North on Chakraphong Rd you'll find more guesthouses which catch the overflow from Khao San Rd, including an alley with *Siam* and another alley further north with *Chuanpis* and *Chakraphong*, all in the 70 to 100B range. By the time you arrive, book in hand, there'll probably be more guesthouses on and off Chakraphong, as local businesses switch to accommodation.

East Banglamphu There are several guesthouses clustered in the alleys east of Tanao Rd (see Banglamphu map). In general, rooms are bigger here than at places on Khao San Rd. *Central Guest House* (☎ 282-0667) is just off Tanao Rd on Trok Bowonrangsi (*trok* means 'alley') – look for the rather inconspicuous signs. It's a very pleasant guesthouse, with clean, quiet rooms for 50B per person. There are some more spacious doubles for 100B. The *Nice Guest House* nearby is the same price and not bad either. The *New Privacy Guest House* is fair, but perhaps overpriced at 100 to 150B.

Further south off Trok Bowonrangsi is *59 Guest House* which has dorm beds at 40B, and singles/doubles from 60/80B. Around the corner on a small road parallel to Ratchadamnoen Klang is *Sweety Guest House* (☎ 281-6756) with good rooms for 40B per person. Sweety has a roof terrace for lounging and for hanging clothes. Opposite the Sweety and next to the post office is the *Nat II*, which is more like the Khao San Rd standard issue. If you follow Trok Mayom Rd straight through, away from Tanao Rd, you'll reach Din So Rd. Cross Din So, walk away from the traffic circle and you'll see a sign for *Prasuri Guest House* (☎ 280-1428), a place recommended by several readers. It's down Soi Phra Suri on the right and offers pleasant, clean singles/doubles/triples for 120/140/210B; there's a good notice board here. Also down this soi is the *Democratic*, where rooms are a reasonable 80/100B for singles/doubles.

South Banglamphu On the other side of Ratchadamnoen Klang, south of the Khao San Rd area, are a couple of independent hotels and at least one guesthouse worth investigating (see the Banglamphu map). If you walk south along Tanao Rd from Ratchadamnoen Klang, then left at the first soi, you'll come to *Hotel 90* (☎ 224-1843). It's mostly a short-time place but large, clean rooms with fan and private bath are 150/220B, 250B with air-con and TV. A bit further east along the same soi toward Din So Rd is the quiet, sparsely decorated *Bangkok Center Guest House* (☎ 225-1247; fax 224-9149), an old teak home with 100B rooms that are often full.

Return west on this soi to Tanao Rd, turn left and then take the right at Trok Sa-Ke toward the upper mid-range Royal Hotel, and after 50 metres or so you'll come to the *Paradise Hotel* (☎ 224-1876) – an all air-con version of the Hotel 90 with singles/doubles at 250/300B – and the friendly *P Guest House* nearby.

West Banglamphu Several newer guesthouses are on sois between Chakraphong Rd and the Chao Phraya River, putting them within walking distance of the Phra Athit pier where you can catch express boats down or up the river, (see Banglamphu map). This area is also close to the Bangkok Noi (Thonburi) railway station across the river, the Bangkok National Museum and the National Theatre. West of Chakraphong at 61/1 Soi Rambutri are *Chusri Guest House* (☎ 282-9948) and *Tum 1 Guest House*, both of which have adequate rooms for 50B per person but are nothing special. Continuing away from Chakraphong Rd along Soi Rambutri is the newer *Merry V Guest House* (☎ 282-9267) with rooms from 60 to 100B. *My House* (☎ 282-9263) at 37 Soi Rambutri, has rooms with windows for 100B, 80B without. Also in this vicinity are the recently established *Chai's House* (☎ 281-4901) and *Charlie's House* (☎ 282-2092), both off the southern end of Soi Rambutri on Soi Rongmai. Both feature the usual rates and facilities.

Backtracking along Soi Rambutri and turning left into Soi Chana Songkhram, you'll find the *New Siam Guest House* (☎ 282-4554) where good, quiet rooms cost 60 to 100B. Continue on toward the river and you'll reach Phra Athit Rd. On the eastern side of Phra Athit Rd are the *Beer Guest House* and *Peachy Guest House* (☎ 281-6471), which are more like small hotels than family-type guesthouses. The Beer is basic but airy, and rooms cost from 70 to 100B. Peachy (☎ 281-6471) has a pleasant garden restaurant and rooms cost 75/120B for singles/doubles, 250/320B with air-con.

Parallel to Soi Chana on Trok Rong Mai, off Phra Athit Rd, are a few old-timers, most with only two-bed rooms. The *Apple Guest House* (☎ 281-6838), at 10/1 Trok Rong Mai, may not look like much, but it's very popular at 40B per person. Sometimes people sleep in the corridor for 20B if it's really full. The family who run it are helpful, there's a notice board, good food and a garden to sit in. There's also an *Apple Guest House II* out on Trok Kai Chae Rd (off Phra Sumen Rd), for the same price, which one traveller recommended as being better.

The *Rose Garden Guest House* (formerly Roof Garden Guest House) (☎ 281-8366), at 28/6 Trok Rong Mai, has very clean doubles for 80B with fan and shared bath. The rooms are a bit box-like and bare though. On the roof you can get an aerial view of Bangkok and the Chao Phraya River. The *Golf Guest House* next door offers similar accommodation at 40B for a dorm bed, 50/100B for singles/doubles.

North Banglamphu Up on Phra Sumen Rd, opposite the north entrances to Wat Bowon, is the *Canalside Guest House* (☎ 281-7807) which, as its name suggests, overlooks a khlong. Basic rooms are 80/100B – nothing to get excited about – but at least the guesthouse is away from the Khao San ghetto. Near the Phra Sumen intersection where Din So Rd becomes Prachatipatai Rd, the *Bovorn-Nivet Youth Hostel* (☎ 281-6387) had large clean rooms with fan for 70 to 120B, 170B with air-con; the last time I dropped by no-one answered the door, so it may have closed. Or maybe they just lock the doors during the day, like many hostels – better phone first before counting on this one.

Just north of Phra Sumen Rd (across Khlong Banglamphu) is *Noi Guest House* (☎ 282-2898), affiliated with the Noi Guest House of Chiang Mai fame. It's on the 4th floor of an apartment building at 52/9 Soi Ban Phan Thom and gets a breeze most of the time. Rates and facilities are the Banglamphu standard.

Further north-east on a soi off Prachatipatai Rd, near Wat Makut, is a branch of the Bonny Guest House called *James' Guest House* (☎ 280-0362). Clean singles/doubles here are only 50/80B. Another good find is the *River Guest House* (☎ 280-0876), which is at 18/1 Soi Wat Samphraya (Soi 3 Samsen), off Samsen Rd near the river and Tha Samphraya pier; rooms are 70 to 100B. Also on this soi is the *Home & Garden* (☎ 280-1475) with small but clean rooms for 65/100B.

The next river express stop north – and the last in the Banglamphu district – is next to Wisut Kasat Rd, where there are a couple of decent choices. The *C & C Guest House*, near Wat Intharawihan, has very comfortable 80B rooms. Farther along is a comfortable middle-range place, the *Trang Hotel* (☎ 282-2141), at 99/8 Wisut Kasat Rd, where rooms start at 400B. Both of these are located east of Samsen Rd, so they're a few minutes walk from the river.

Thewet & National Library Area The next district north of Banglamphu near the National Library is becoming another little travellers' enclave. Heading north up Samsen Rd (the extension of Chakraphong Rd) from Wisut Kasat Rd, you'll come to *TV Guest House* (☎ 282-7451) at 7 Soi Phra Sawat, just off Samsen Rd to the east. It's clean, modern and good value at 40B for a dorm bed, 80B a double.

Continue another half km or so and cross the canal to the place where Phitsanulok Rd finishes on Samsen Rd and where Si Ayuthaya Rd crosses Samsen Rd. Just beyond this junction is the National Library. On two parallel sois off Si Ayuthaya Rd toward the river (west from Samsen) are five guesthouses run by various members of the same extended family: *Tavee Guest House* (☎ 282-5983), *Sawatdee Guest House* (☎ 282-5349), *Backpacker's Lodge*, *Shanti Lodge* (☎ 281-2497) and the latest addition, *Paradise Guest House* (☎ 282-4094/8673). All are clean, well kept, fairly quiet and cost 40 to 50B for a dorm bed, and from 80/110B for singles/doubles. A fifth, independently run place on the same soi as Paradise is *Little Home Guest House* (☎ 281-3412), which is similar to the others in this area except that it has a busy travel agency in front. There's a good market across the road from both sois, and a few small noodle and rice shops along Krung Kasem Rd, the next parallel street south of Si Ayuthaya (and west of Samsen Rd), which leads to Tha Thewet.

Another way to get to and from the National Library area is by taking advantage of Tha Thewet, a Chao Phraya River Express pier; from the pier you walk east along Krung Kasem Rd to Samsen Rd, turn left, cross the canal and then take another left into Si Ayuthaya Rd. Ordinary bus Nos 3, 6, 9, 16 and 53 pass Si Ayuthaya Rd while going up and down Samsen Rd; No 72 terminates at the corner of Phitsanulok and Samsen Rds, a short walk from Si Ayuthaya. Air-con bus No 10 from the airport also passes close to the area along Ratwithi Rd to the north, before crossing Krungthon Bridge.

East of Samsen Rd, the *Bangkok International Youth Hostel* (☎ 282-0950, 281-0361) is in the same neighbourhood at 25/2 Phitsanulok Rd. A bed in a fan-cooled dorm is 50B, add 10B for the air-con dorm. Rooms with fan and bath are 200B, while air-con singles/doubles with hot water are 250/300B. The fan rooms are larger than the air-con rooms, and there's a cafeteria downstairs. In 1992 the hostel stopped accepting nonmembers as guests. Annual IYHF memberships cost 300B, or you can purchase a temporary membership for 50B. The Bangkok hostel gets mixed reports – the rooms seem nice enough but the staff can be rude.

Soi Ngam Duphli This area off Rama IV Rd is where most budget travellers used to come on their first trip to Bangkok. With a couple of notable exceptions, most of the places to stay here are not cheap or even good value any more, and the whole area has taken on a rather seedy atmosphere ('for junkies and whoremongers' is a description I've heard more than once). Overall, Banglamphu has better accommodation values.

The entrance to Soi Ngam Duphli is on Rama IV Rd, near the Sathon Tai Rd intersection, and within walking distance of the imposing Dusit Thani Hotel and Lumphini Park. Ordinary bus Nos 4, 13, 14, 22, 45, 47, 74, 109 and 115, and air-con bus No 7 all pass by the entrance to Soi Ngam Duphli along Rama IV Rd.

At the northern end of Soi Ngam Duphli near Rama IV Rd is *ETC Guest House* (☎ 286-9424, 287-1478), an efficiently run, multistorey place with a travel agency downstairs. Rooms are small but clean; rates are 120B with shared bath, 160/200B for singles/doubles with private bath. All room rates include a breakfast of cereal, fruit, toast and coffee or tea.

Just south of ETC an alley leads left to the

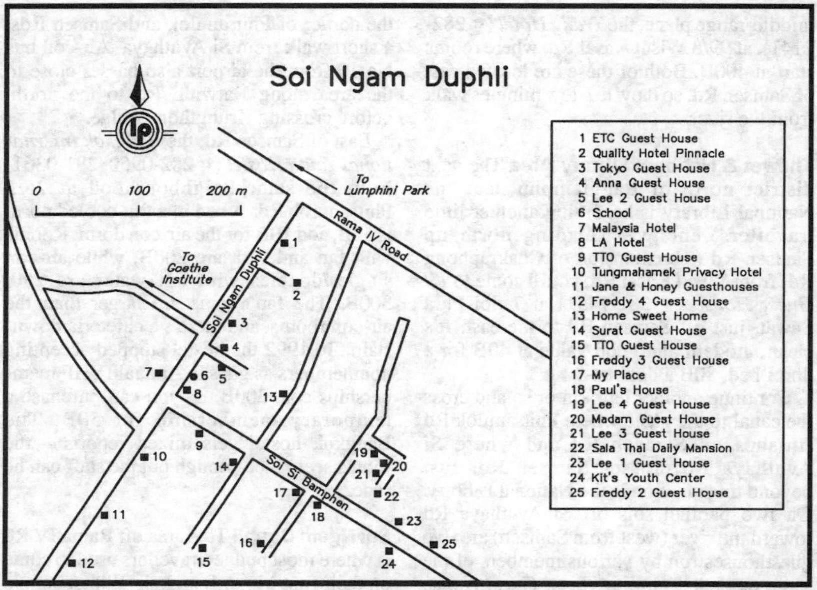

newly constructed *Quality Hotel Pinnacle* (☎ 248-2094), a high-rise business hotel with all the mod cons from 2000B per night – not exactly a budget travellers' choice but one of the city's less expensive places in the top-end (2000B-plus) category. The cheerless *Tokyo Guest House* is further south down Ngam Duphli; rooms are 100/140B for singles/doubles with shared bath – not quite up to the Quality's (or even ETC's) standards.

Next south is an alley on the left that leads to the *Anna* and *Lee 2* guesthouses (there are also Lee 1, Lee 3 and Lee 4 guesthouses nearby). Both have rooms with shared bath starting at 80B; Lee is the better value all round.

Back on Soi Ngam Duphli, the *Malaysia Hotel* (☎ 286-3582/7263), at 54 Soi Ngam Duphli, was once Bangkok's most famous travellers' hotel. Its 120 air-con, hot-water rooms cost 496B for a standard single or double, 546B with a TV and small fridge, and 700B with a TV, larger fridge and carpet. The Malaysia has a swimming pool which may be used by visitors for 50B per day (it's free for guests of course). Since the '70s, the Malaysia has made a conscious effort to distance itself from the backpackers' market; for a while it seemed to be catering directly to the lonely male hired-sex market. The big sign out front advertising 'Day-Off International Club – Paradise for Everyone' has dropped the final phrase 'You'll Never Be Alone Again' and there seem to be fewer hookers around the lobby than in the old days – at least before midnight. After the Patpong bars close, the hotel coffee shop becomes a virtual clearing house for bar girls who didn't pick up an outside customer earlier in the evening.

The *Tungmahamek Privacy Hotel* (☎ 286-2339/8811), across the road to the south of the Malaysia, is also fully air-con and costs 350B for a double. Many 'short-time' residents here give the place a sleazy feel, though it's less of a 'scene' than the Malaysia. In the other direction from the Malaysia is the *LA Hotel* (the English sign just says 'Hotel'), a bit better value if you don't need air-con but also on the short-time circuit – large rooms with bath and fan are 180B, air-con rooms 500B.

Turn left (east) from Ngam Duphli into Soi Si Bamphen and on the right is the seedy *TTO Guest House* with an airless cafe in front. Forgettable rooms are 180B with bath and fan. Further on, before you reach the Boston Inn, is an alley to the right. Around the corner on the right-hand side is the *Surat*, with a spooky spiral staircase leading from floor to tiny floor. Rooms are small but OK; rates are 150B for a fan room, 200B air-con. Near the end of the alley is another branch of the TTO Guest House, this one is quite a bit better as it has clean air-con rooms with private bath for 350 to 390B.

Across Soi Si Bamphen in another alley is the *Home Sweet Home Guest House*. It's a friendly place with rooms at 100/120B for singles/doubles. Further down Si Bamphen is another alley on the right with a guest-house on both corners, *My Place* and *Paul's House*. Both have rooms upstairs that go for 80 to 120B. My Place has the better rooms but the bar can be rather noisy. Down this same alley on the right is *Freddy 3 Guest House* (☎ 287-1665) with basic accommodation for 80 to 100B.

The notorious *Boston Inn* is still a blight on Soi Si Bamphen. Decaying rooms have slid to 60/120B for singles/doubles, but neither the fan nor the water in the attached bath have been functioning for the last couple of years. A suspicious number of drug overdoses in Boston Inn rooms have been reported to the police; among travellers the hotel has a reputation as a Hell's Fawlty Towers. On my last visit I was told that the owner was planning to renovate (at one time the Boston was one of the better places in the Soi Ngam Duphli area), but for now this one's definitely at the very bottom of the list.

If you turn left at the next soi down Si Bamphen, then take the first right, you'll end up in a cul-de-sac with three very good guest-houses. First up on the right as you enter the soi is the clean, secure and well-managed *Lee 4 Guest House* with rooms for 100/120B with shared bath, 150/180B with private bath.

Around the corner, *Madam Guest House* also has a legion of loyal followers for its 80 to 120B rooms and friendly service. Next door, the *Lee 3 Guest House*, the best of the four Lee guesthouses, is also quite pleasant and has large rooms from 100B. The *Sala Thai Daily Mansion* (☎ 287-1436) is at the end of the alley and has large, very clean rooms for 120 to 150B, plus a nice sitting area downstairs.

Back out on Soi Si Bamphen heading south-east are three more guesthouses (last edition there were four – another sign that this area's on the decline). First on the left is the original *Lee 1 Guest House* (from 80B) and on the right the friendly *Kit's Youth Center* (100 to 150B), followed on the left by the nothing-special-but-it'll-do-in-a-pinch *Freddy 2* (formerly Welcome), at 80/100B. All three are very similar and feature medium-size rooms and shared baths.

One last clump of guesthouses in the area is south of the Privacy on Soi Ngam Duphli. First is a new building on the left with tiny, cheap rooms for 120B with fan, 250 to 300B with air-con. The side-by-side guesthouses here change names frequently, but on my last pass they included *Jane*, *Honey* and the incredibly grotty *Freddy 4*, at 80 to 120B with fan. Hookers rent long-term rooms for short-term use in this row. If you're wondering about the original *Freddy Guest House*, it's still down Soi Ngam Duphli past the new building on the left in a building with maze-like passageways – and is more abysmal than ever.

Chinatown & Hualamphong Station This area is central and colourful although rather noisy. There are numerous cheap hotels but it's not a travellers' centre like Soi Ngam Duphli or Banglamphu. Watch your pockets and bag around the Hualamphong area, both on the street and on the bus. The cream of the razor artists operate here as the railway passengers make good pickings.

The *New Empire Hotel* (☎ 234-6990/6) is at 572 Yaowarat Rd, near the Charoen Krung (New) Rd intersection, a short walk from Wat Traimit. Air-con rooms with hot water are 440 to 700B – a bit noisy but a great location if you like Chinatown. The New Empire has a swimming pool and is a favourite among Chinese Thais from the southern region.

Other Chinatown hotels of this calibre, most without English signs out front, can be found along Yaowarat, Chakraphet and Ratchawong Rds. The *Burapha Hotel* (☎ 221-3545/9), at the intersection of Mahachai and Charoen Krung Rds, on the edge of Chinatown, has rates at about the same as the Empire. Likewise for the *Somboon Hotel* (☎ 221-2327), at 415 Yaowarat Rd. The cheapest place in Chinatown is the *Empress* (☎ 221-1251) at 421 Sua Pa Rd, north off Charoen Krung. Basic guesthouse-style rooms here are 100 to 150B.

Several readers have written to recommend the middle-range *River View Guest House* (☎ 234-5429, 235-8501) at 768 Soi Phanurangsi, Songwat Rd in the Talat Noi area – wedged between Silom and Chinatown. The building is behind the Jo Seu Kong Chinese Shrine, about 400 metres from the Royal Orchid Sheraton. To get there, turn right from the corner of Si Phraya Rd (facing the River City shopping complex), take the fourth left, then the first right. Rooms are 400B with fan and private bath, 600B with air-con and hot water; as the name suggests, many rooms have a Chao Phraya River view. If you call from the River City complex, someone from the guesthouse will pick you up.

Along the eastern side of Hualamphong station is Rong Muang Rd which has several dicey Chinese hotels. The *Sri Hualamphong Hotel*, at No 445, is one of the better ones – all rooms are 100B with fan. The *Sahakit (Shakij) Hotel* is a few doors down from the Sri Hualamphong towards Rama IV Rd and is quite OK too. Rooms are 100B up; if you stay here, try to get a room on the 4th floor which has a terrace with a view and the occasional breeze.

The *Jeep Seng* (☎ 214-2808), at 462-64 Rong Muang Rd, is not too clean but it's adequate. Rooms are 100/120B for singles/doubles, and they have good khâo man kài downstairs. Just south of the Jeep Seng is the similar *Toonkee Hotel*.

Out towards the front of the station, after Rong Muang Rd makes a sharp curve, is the *Station Hotel*, a classic Third-World dive. A room with torn curtains, dim sheets and crusty attached bath costs an astounding 120B. What's more astounding is that it seems to be nearly full all the time!

The market area behind the Station Hotel is full of cheap food stalls, and on a small soi parallel to Rong Muang Rd is the *Hoke Aan Hotel*, yet another 100/120B Chinese hole-in-the-wall (but at least it's away from Rong Muang traffic). Also off Rong Muang Rd next to the Chinese market is the noisy but adequate *Nam Ia Hotel* for only 70B.

At least four other cheap Chinese hotels can be found west of the station along Maitrichit Rd, all in the 70 to 100B range.

Many travellers have written to recommend a guesthouse near Hualamphong called *TT Guest House* (☎ 236-3053). From the station, cross Rama IV Rd, walk left down Rama IV, then right on Mahanakhon and look for signs to TT. It's at 138 Soi Wat Mahaphuttharam, off Mahanakhon Rd. Although a 10-minute walk, TT is a bit difficult to find (it's in a little alley) but if you follow the signs it's worth the effort. The owners are friendly and clean singles/doubles cost 60/100B. The 'left-luggage service' here is cheaper than the one at the airport, and there's also a laundry service.

Pahurat There are also several guesthouses in the Indian district of Pahurat, centred around Chakraphet Rd. The *Amarin Guest House*, on Chakraphet has a sign in English, Thai, Hindi and Arabic. Rooms cost from 90B, and are fairly clean. Further down towards the well-known Royal India Restaurant there is a soi (off to the left if you're walking from the pedestrian bridge) on which you'll find *Moon*, *Kamal*, *Bobby's* and *Tony's Fashion*, all offering similar accommodation for 80 to 100B per room. Also in this area are *US Pop*, *Rajin*, *Video* and probably a dozen others. The guesthouses in Pahurat cater to mostly South Asian guests, but are happy to take anyone. It's an economical alternative if you need to be in this part of town or if you want to practise speaking Hindi or Punjabi.

Silom & Surawong Rds Several mid-range guesthouses and hotels can be found in and around the Silom and Surawong Rds area. Another Indian guesthouse is the *Silom Lodge*, on Vaithi Lane off Silom Rd, not far from the Shiva temple. It's quite a walk down Vaithi Lane and rooms are 100B upstairs, somewhat cheaper downstairs, but it does have the advantage of being far removed from heavy street traffic. The proprietor is a very friendly Indian man from Madras (a retired gem dealer) and his kitchen serves delicious south Indian food.

The two hotels nearest Patpong Rd – the *Suriwong* and the *Rose* – are in the 500B range. They can't really be recommended for light sleepers as they suffer from heavy people traffic from the Patpong go-go bars.

On the south side of Silom Rd is Soi Suksavitthaya (Suksa Witthaya), where two good middle-range places are located. First is *Niagara Hotel* (☎ 233-5783/4) at 26 Soi Suksavitthaya, where clean air-con rooms with hot water and telephone are 500B (fan rooms are 250B). Further on at 37 Soi Suksavitthaya is the more up-market *Sathon Inn* (☎ 234-4110) which has all air-con rooms for 890B up.

Also off Silom Rd is *Bangkok Christian Guest House* (☎ 253-3353) at 123 Sala Daeng Soi 2, Convent Rd. It has very nice fan-cooled rooms for 400B including breakfast; air-con rooms cost as much as 700B, also with breakfast. Nearby, at 3 Convent Rd, is the *Swiss Guest House* (☎ 234-1107) where clean, comfortable air-con rooms are 300 to 600B depending on the size of the room.

Opposite the GPO on Charoen Krung Rd are three guesthouses catering mostly to middle-class North Indians, Pakistanis and Bangladeshis – *Mumtaz, Naaz* and *Kabana Inn* – each charging a reasonable 400 to 450B for air-con rooms. Just a bit more expensive but offering better service is the *Woodlands Inn* on the soi that runs along the northern side of the GPO. Clean, air-con rooms with hot water, TV and fridge are 500/600B for singles/doubles. Downstairs is an air-con Indian restaurant, the Cholas.

Siam Square Several good places can be found in this centrally located area (see the Siam Square map), which has the additional advantage of being located near the Asia Hotel terminus for THAI's convenient and inexpensive (60B) airport shuttle bus. There's only one rock-bottom place in the area, the *Scout Hostel* on Rama I Rd, next to the National Stadium. Beds in gender-segregated dorms are still only 30B per night. A locker is provided but that's about it for amenities.

There are several lower middle-range places on or near Soi Kasem San 1, off Rama I Rd near Jim Thompson's house and the National Stadium. The *Muangphol (Muangphon) Building* on the corner of Soi Kasem San 1 and Rama I Rd (931/8 Rama I Rd) has doubles for 480B. It's good value – with air-con, hot water, a restaurant, friendly staff and good service. Behind the Muangphol off this soi is the apartment-style *Pranee Building*, which has one entrance next to the Muangphol and another on Rama I Rd. Fan-cooled rooms with private bath are 250 to 350B; air-con rooms with hot water start at 400B. The Pranee also does some long-term rentals at reasonable rates.

Fans of the surreal US TV series Twin Peaks may feel a twinge when they see the new *White Lodge* (☎ 216-8867, 216-8228), at 36/8 Soi Kasem San 1. Clean rooms are 400/500B for singles/doubles, and there's a pleasant terrace cafe out front. The next one down is the *Star Hotel* at 36/1 Soi Kasem San 1, a classic sort of mid-60s Thai no-tell motel, with fairly clean, comfortable, air-con

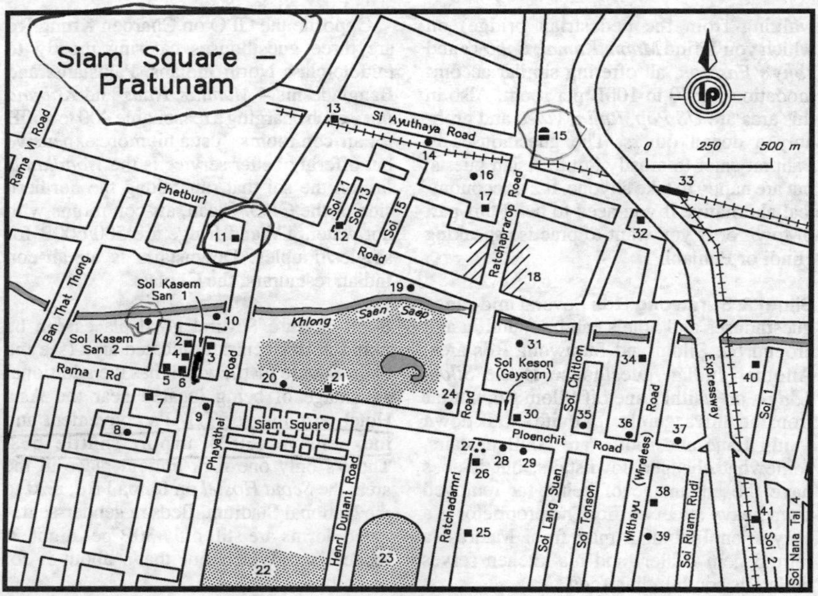

■ PLACES TO STAY

2 Star Hotel
3 A-One Inn
4 Reno Hotel
5 Krit Thai Mansion
6 Pranee & Muongphol Buildings
7 Scout Hostel
11 Asia Hotel
12 First Hotel
13 Florida Hotel
17 Indra Regent Hotel & Aangan Guest House
21 Siam Intercontinental Hotel
25 Regent Bangkok
26 Grand Hyatt Erawan
30 Le Meridien President Hotel
32 Bangkok Palace Hotel
34 Hilton International Hotel
38 Imperial Hotel
40 Golden Palace Hotel
41 Atlanta Hotel

● OTHER

1 Jim Thompson's House
8 National Stadium
9 Mahboonkrong Shopping Centre
10 Tha Ratchathewi
14 Wang Suan Phakkard
15 Post Office
16 Baiyoke Tower
18 Pratunam Market
19 Phanthip Plaza
20 Siam Center
22 Chulalongkorn University
23 Royal Bangkok Sports Club
24 Zen World Trade Center
27 Erawan Shrine (San Phra Phrom)
28 Sogo Department Store
29 Maneeya Center
31 Robinson Department Store
33 Makkasan Railway Station
35 Central Department Store
36 UK Embassy
37 Ploenchit Arcade
39 Vietnam Embassy

rooms with bath and TV for 400 to 500B a double, depending on the room. Some rooms come with their own curtained parking slots so that cars belonging to guests can't be read by passers-by.

Opposite the Star is *A-One Inn* (☎ 215-3029; fax 216-4771) at No 25/12-15, a friendly and pleasant place that gets a lot of return business. Fair-sized air-con doubles with bath and hot water are 400B, spacious triples are 500B. The similar *Bed & Breakfast Inn* diagonally opposite the A-One has similar rates; rooms are substantially smaller than the A-One's but the rates include continental breakfast.

Pratunam Most of the hotels in Pratunam (the area around the Ratchaprarop and Phetburi Rds intersection) have rooms starting at around 1200B (see Places to Stay – middle). However, there are a couple of budget and lower middle-range places in Pratunam (see Siam Square map), so if you want to stay close to the fabulous Pratunam markets you don't necessarily have to spend a lot on a hotel.

Behind the Indra Regent Hotel and shopping mall are several Arab/Pakistani guesthouses with rates of 300 to 500B for air-con rooms, including the pleasant *Aangan Guest House*, which has an Arab/Pakistani/North Indian restaurant downstairs.

Further north in the district is the *AT Guest House* (☎ 245-2963) at 14/1 Soi Ratchatapan (Maw Leng) off Ratchaprarop Rd. It's operated by Alternative Tour Thailand, a travel agency catering to educational tours for NGOs, and offers accommodation in a big house for 150B per person in air-con, gender-segregated dorms, 350B for an air-con double room (one room has a private bath, two rooms share a bath).

Sukhumvit Rd Staying in this area puts you in the newest part of Bangkok and the furthest from the old Bangkok near the river. Buses take longer to get here, and taxis to or from Sukhumvit Rd may cost more since it is known as a residential area for farangs. The majority of the hotels in this area are in the middle price range.

The *Atlanta Hotel* (☎ 252-1650, 252-6069), at 78 Soi 2 (Soi Phasak), Sukhumvit Rd, is an old and reliable stand-by with clean, comfortable rooms in several price categories. Rooms with shared bath and fan cost 150/200B for singles/doubles. A few rooms have private showers for 50B extra. Small singles with fan and shared bath are available for 120B. Air-con rooms are an economical 300/350B for singles/doubles, 400B for triples. There's a swimming pool on the premises.

The *Golden Palace Hotel*, at 15 Soi 1, Sukhumvit Rd, has a swimming pool, is well situated and costs 300 to 400B for a double with air-con and bath. The clientele here are mostly middle-class tourists 'on a budget', but the Golden Palace, too, has seen better days.

A new entry in inner Sukhumvit area is *Thai House Inn* (☎ 255-4698; fax 253-1780), between Sois 5 and 7. Rooms with air-con and hot water are 500B a single or double; facilities include a safety-deposit service and a coffee shop.

The *Miami Hotel* (☎ 252-5140/4759/5036), at Soi 13, Sukhumvit Rd has been taking a slow dive since its '60s and '70s R&R peak. Rooms with fan and bath are now overpriced even at 180B – air-con rooms are apparently no longer available. The *Crown Hotel* (☎ 258-0318), at Soi 29, Sukhumvit, is in similar decline and gets mostly short-time traffic these days.

Further along Sukhumvit Rd, the *Squeeze Inn* at Soi 29 is fairly economical for the area – 100 to 150B for a basic but clean room with fan. *Disra House* (☎ 258-5102), on the access street to Villa Theatre, between Sois 33 and 33/1, has similar rooms for 80 to 120B.

Other Areas One place that's far from any of the usual tourist haunts is *Anne's Travellers' Home* (☎ 377-6793) at 30 Soi Ramkhamhaeng 48, Ramkhamhaeng Rd in the Hua Maak district of eastern Bangkok, near Ramkhamhaeng University. Anne is a well-travelled Thai woman who speaks English well and knows the Thailand travel scene. Her house is furnished with handicrafts from all over Thailand; rooms are 480B a night including a full breakfast served in the garden.

From Banglamphu, Anne's house is a 10B, 40-minute ride by long-tail boat along Khlong Saen Saep; you can board the boat at Tha Phanfa, a canal pier opposite Bangkok Bank on Ratchadamnoen Rd near the Democracy Monument. Or you can board anywhere along the canal, which runs through Pratunam and parallel to Sukhumvit Rd. Once on the boat, ask to get off at the Wat Klang pier (40 minutes from Tha Phanfa), walk to Ramkhamhaeng Rd, and turn left near the bus stop at Soi Ramkhamhaeng 48; the house is on the left-hand side of this soi. Bus No 95 from the airport also goes by this soi (get off at the Hua Maak branch of the Thai Farmer's Bank on Ramkhamhaeng Rd, then walk straight ahead to Soi Ramkhamhaeng 48). Bus Nos 113 and 109 go from the Hualamphong railway station. Anne says she'll pick new arrivals up at the airport if you call. You can write in advance to: Anne Nimcharoen, 30 Soi Ramkhamhaeng 48, Ramkhamhaeng Rd, Bangkok 10240.

If you want to be close to Ratchadamnoen Boxing Stadium or to the head TAT office, have a look at *Venice House* (☎ 281-8262) at 548-546/1 Krung Kasem Rd. This friendly, well-maintained guesthouse is next to Wat Somanat, just around the corner from Ratchadamnoen Nok Rd (walk north on Ratchadamnoen Nok from the stadium, turn right on Krung Kasem and walk about 80 metres till you see a sign for Venice House). Rooms are air-con and cost 250/350B for singles/doubles.

Places to Stay – middle

Bangkok is saturated with small and medium-sized hotels in this category. The clientele at hotels in this range are a very mixed bunch of Asian business travellers, Western journalists on slim expense accounts, economy-class tour groups, along with a smattering of independent tourists who seem to have chosen their hotels at random. Not quite 'international class', these places often offer guests a better sense of being in Thailand than the luxury hotels.

During the late '80s when there was a shortage of tourist accommodation, many mid-range hotels doubled their rates in a grab for short-term profit over long-term goodwill. In the off-season (March to November) you may be able to get a low-occupancy discount off the rates listed below.

Banglamphu Before Khao San Rd was 'discovered' the most popular Banglamphu hotel was the *Viengtai Hotel* (☎ 281-5788) at 42 Rambutri Rd. Over the last decade or so the Viengtai has continually upgraded its facilities until it now sits solidly in the middle price range of Bangkok hotels; singles/doubles are 600 to 1200B.

Besides the Oriental, the oldest continually operating hotel in the city is the *Royal* (☎ 222-9111/20), still going strong at the corner of Ratchadamnoen Klang Ave and Atsadang Rd near the Democracy Monument. The Royal's 24-hour coffee shop is a favourite local rendezvous; this is one of the few upper mid-range places where there are as many Asian as non-Asian guests. Singles/doubles cost 1000/1500B. Incidentally, most of the taxi drivers know this hotel as the 'Ratanakosin' (as the Thai sign on top of the building reads), not as the Royal. (During the bloody May '92 protests against General Suchinda's appointment as prime minister, the Royal served as a makeshift hospital for injured demonstrators.)

Other mid-range places in this area include the *Thai Hotel* (☎ 282-2833), at 78 Prachatipatai Rd, which has singles/doubles at 1300/1500B; and the *Welcome Palace* (☎ 234-5402), at 30 Naret Rd, with 450 rooms at 1000B.

Chinatown A couple of mid-range hotels in the Chinatown area of Bangkok are *Chinatown* (☎ 226-1267), at 526 Yaowarat Rd, which has 80 rooms starting at 1200B; and the *Miramar Hotel* (☎ 222-4191), at 777

Mahachai Rd, where rooms are 1335B for singles or doubles.

Silom & Surawong Rds Bangkok has a YMCA and YWCA, both in the Silom and Surawong Rds area. The *YMCA Collins International House* (☎ 287-1900/2727; fax 287-1996) is at 27 Sathon Tai (South) Rd and has air-con rooms with TV, telephone and private bath from 960 to 1500B. Guests may use the Y's massage room, gym, track and swimming pool. The *YWCA* (☎ 286-1936) is at 13 Sathon Tai Rd and has cheaper fan-cooled singles for 290B, air-con doubles for 600B or 100B for a dorm bed.

Mid-range hotels in Surawong Rd include the *Manohra Hotel* (☎ 234-5070) at No 412 with singles/doubles from 1400 to 1600B; the *New Fuji* (☎ 234-5364) at No 299-310 with rooms from 1166 to 1388B; and the *New Trocadero Hotel* (☎ 234-8920/9) at No 34, where singles or doubles cost from 888 to 1665B.

The *Victory Hotel* (☎ 233-9060), at 322 Silom Rd, has 125 rooms and room rates for singles/doubles are 1000/1700B.

Siam Square In the Siam Square area another old stand-by is the *Reno Hotel* (☎ 215-0026) on Soi Kasem San 1, a veteran from the Vietnam War days when a spate of hotels opened in Bangkok with names of US cities. Air-con singles/doubles cost 600/700B. Nearby *Krit Thai Mansion* (☎ 215-3042) is out on busy Rama I Rd, across from the National Stadium. For 800 to 1000B, facilities include air-con, hot water, private bath, telephone, colour TV/video, fridge and an American-style breakfast. The coffee shop downstairs is open 24 hours.

Pratunam The *Opera Hotel* (☎ 252-4031; fax 253-5360), at 16 Soi Somprasong 1, Phetburi Rd is very near the heart of Pratunam and features air-con doubles with hot water from 500 to 690B. The Opera also has a swimming pool and coffee shop.

The *Siam Hotel* (☎ 252-5081), at 1777 Phetburi Rd, has 120 rooms; singles/doubles cost 833/999B.

Sukhumvit Rd In this area, several readers have recommended the *Mermaids Rest* (☎ 253-3648; fax 253-2401) on Soi 8; air-con rooms are 650 to 850B and there are two swimming pools. Another place that has been recommended is the *Ruamchit Mansion* (☎ 251-6441), at 1-15 Soi 15, Sukhumvit Rd. Air-con rooms range from 450 to 600B and there is hot water, fridge, communal kitchen and a supermarket just below. Monthly rates are available.

The *Federal Hotel* (☎ 253-0175), at 27 Soi 11, Sukhumvit Rd, is a favourite among Vietnam War and Peace Corps vets but I've found the accommodation a bit overpriced at 600 to 1200B, especially for the added-on rooms at ground level; these occasionally flood in the rainy season. The modest pool and coffee shop are the main attractions. The *Golden Gate* at 22/1 Soi 2, Sukhumvit Rd is better value, with large air-con doubles for 550B, including breakfast.

At Soi 24 (by this point even-numbered sois lag behind the odd-numbered ones in distance from the city centre) – in the Washington Cinema area and well off the road – is the quiet *Twenty-Four Inn* (☎ 258-6515; fax 259-9262). Small but well-appointed air-con rooms are 900B. A plus is its location near the Bourbon Street Bar & Restaurant on Soi 22, which has its own *Southern Comfort* (☎ 259-4317) rooms upstairs for 650/850B. Also in this range are two recent entries by the Siam Lodge hotel group: the *City Lodges* on Sois 9 and 19. Rooms at either location are 850B for a single or double, and include air-con, telephone, TV/video and mini-bar. Other mid-range hotels in the Sukhumvit Rd area include:

Federal Hotel, 27 Sukhumvit Rd; 93 rooms, singles/doubles 600 to 1200B (☎ 253-0175)

Fortuna Hotel, 19 Sukhumvit Rd; 110 rooms, singles/doubles 800/1500B (☎ 251-5121)

Grace Hotel, 12 Nana Neua (Soi 3), Sukhumvit Rd; 550 rooms, singles/doubles 675/822B (☎ 252 9170/3)

Grand Inn, 2/7-8 Soi 3, Sukhumvit Rd; 24 rooms, 1090 to 1390B (☎ 254-9021)

Manhattan, Soi 15, Sukhumvit Rd; 206 rooms, singles/doubles 1694B (☎ 252-7141/9)

Nana Hotel, 4 Nana Tai, Sukhumvit Rd; 224 rooms, singles/doubles 770B (☎ 250-1210/9, 250-1380/9)
Park Hotel, 6 Soi 7, Sukhumvit Rd; 128 rooms, singles/doubles 1700B (☎ 252-5110/3)
Rajah Hotel, 18 Soi 4, Sukhumvit Rd; 450 rooms, singles/doubles 1050/1452B (☎ 252-5102/9)
Rex Hotel, 762/1 Soi 32; Sukhumvit Rd; 131 rooms, singles/doubles 1100 to 1500B (☎ 259-0106)

Victory Monument Just north of Siam Square, in the Victory Monument area, are several hotels, including the *Century Hotel* (☎ 245-3271/3) at 9 Rajaprarob (Ratchaprarop) Rd. This hotel has 96 rooms at 800B for singles or doubles. At the *Continental Hotel* (☎ 278-1596/8), 971/16 Phahonyothin Rd, singles cost from 650 to 695B. The *Florida Hotel* (☎ 245-3221/4, 245-1816/9), at 43 Phayathai Square, Phayathai Rd, has singles/doubles at 800/1300B.

Other Areas Hotels in other areas of the city include:

Baron Hotel, 544 Soi Huaykwang, Ratchadaphisek Rd; 155 rooms, singles/doubles 400/600B (☎ 246-4525)
Golden Dragon, 20/21 Ngarm Wongvarn Rd; 114 rooms, singles/doubles 888B (☎ 588-4414/5)
Golden Horse Hotel, 5/1 Damrongrak Rd; 130 rooms, singles/doubles 775/1800B (☎ 281-6909)
Liberty Hotel, 215 Saphan Khwai Pratipat Rd; 209 rooms, singles/doubles from 400/500B to 540/850B (☎ 271-0880)

Places to Stay – top end

Bangkok has all sorts of international standard tourist hotels, from the straightforward package places to some of Asia's classic hotels. Although there's no single area for top-end hotels you'll find quite a few of them around the Siam Square area, along the parallel Surawong and Silom Rds, and along the river, while many of the cheaper 'international standard' places are scattered along Sukhumvit Rd.

A new trend in Bangkok hotels in the past few years has been the appearance of several European-style 'boutique' hotels – small, business-oriented places of around 100 rooms or fewer with rates in the 2000 to 3000B range – like the *Mansion Kempinski* (Soi 11 Sukhumvit Rd), *Princess* (269 Lan Luang Rd), *Somerset* (Soi 15 Sukhumvit Rd), *Swissotel* (Convent Rd) and *Trinity Place* (Soi 5 Silom Rd). Many experienced Bangkok business travellers prefer this type of hotel because they get personal service for about 1000B less than the bigger hotels; also these smaller hotels don't accept tour groups, so regular guests don't have to wade through crowds in the lobby.

In the last couple of years, luxury-class hotels in Bangkok have raised their rates more than any other class of hotel in Thailand, capitalising on the 90%-plus occupancy rates that occurred in the late '80s. When a hotel construction boom collided with the 1990-91 Gulf War and recession, many of the price-gougers were humbled. With lower occupancy rates, you should be able to negotiate discounts on the rates listed. Booking through a travel agency almost always means lower rates – also try asking for a hotel's 'corporate' discount.

All of the hotels in this category will add a 10% service charge plus 8.25% tax to hotel bills on departure.

On the River The 116-year-old *Oriental Bangkok* (☎ 236-0400/39), on the Chao Phraya River, is one of the most famous hotels in Asia, right up there with the Raffles in Singapore. What's more it's also rated as one of the very best hotels in the world, as well as being just about the most expensive in Bangkok. It's worth wandering in if only to see the string quartet playing in the lobby! Nowadays it's looking more modern and less classic – the original Author's Wing is dwarfed by the Tower (built in 1958) and River (1976) wings – though the service is still unsurpassed, with a staff of 1200 for 400 rooms. It's at 48 Oriental Ave, and room rates start from 4400 to 13,500B.

Two other luxury gems along the river are the *Shangri-La* (☎ 236-7777; fax 236-8570) at 89 Soi Wat Suan Phlu, Charoen Krung Rd; and the *Royal Orchid Sheraton* (☎ 234-5599; fax 236-8320), 2 Captain Bush Lane, Si Phraya Rd. The Shangri-La has 694 rooms starting from 5600B, and its own helicopter transport (2700B) from the airport, while the Sheraton (776 rooms, from 4400B) has personal service rivalling the Oriental's (eg the business centre is open 24 hours).

The *Menam* (☎ 289-1148/9; fax 291-9400), also near the river at 2074 Charoen Krung Rd, Yannawa, has 718 rooms from 3993B up. The *Royal River* (☎ 433-0300; fax 433-5880), at 670/805 Charan Sanitwong Rd, Thonburi, has 403 rooms from 2783B.

Silom & Surawong Rds There are many hotels with similar amenities to the Regent, Hilton and Sheraton, but which are a step down in price because of their location or smaller staff-to-guest ratios. In the Silom and Surawong areas these include the *Montien* (☎ 234-8060; fax 234-8060) at 54 Surawong Rd (600 rooms, 3388B up), a very Thai hotel; the *Dusit Thani* (☎ 233-1130; fax 236-6400) at Rama IV Rd (520 rooms, 5445B), a great hotel in a lousy location; the *Narai* (☎ 233-3350; fax 236-7161) at 222 Silom Rd (500 rooms, 3267 to 8470B); and the *Holiday Inn Crowne Plaza* (☎ 238-4300/34; fax 238-5289) at 981 Silom Rd (662 rooms, 4840 to 9680B).

Another new entry in the luxury/executive market is the 222-room *Sukhothai* (☎ 287-0222; fax 287-4980) at 13/3 Sathon Tai Rd. The Sukhothai features an Asian minimalist decor, including an inner courtyard with lily ponds; the same architect and interior designer created Phuket's landmark Amanpuri. Its 222 rooms start at 4300B.

Other top-end hotels in this area include:

Mandarin Hotel, 662 Rama IV Rd; 343 rooms, 2904 to 8000B (☎ 233-4980/9; fax 237-1620)
New Peninsula, 295.3 Surawong Rd; 102 rooms, 2250 to 2553B (☎ 234-3910; fax 236-5526)
Silom Plaza, 320 Silom Rd; 209 rooms, 2420B up (☎ 236-8441/84; fax 236-7566)
Swissotel, 3 Convent Rd; 57 rooms, 2420 to 2766B (☎ 233-5345; fax 236-9425)
Tawana Ramada, 80 Surawong Rd; 265 rooms, 4000B up (☎ 236-0361; fax 236-3738)
Trinity Place, 150 Soi 5, Silom Rd; 109 rooms, 2299 to 2904B (☎ 238-0052, fax 238-3984)

Siam Square & Ploenc
Regent Bangkok (☎ 25
9195), at 155 Ratchada
Oriental in price (though
at the Regent – probably
hotel in the city to offer th... courtesy) and is one of the city's top choices for visiting business travellers because of its efficient business centre. Its 415 rooms start at 5082B.

Another top executive choice is the *Hilton International Bangkok* (☎ 253-0123; fax 253-6509) on Withayu Rd, where you won't find tour groups milling around in the lobby; its 343 rooms start from 5006 to 7570B.

The *Siam Intercontinental* (☎ 253-0355; fax 253-0355), ensconced on spacious grounds at 967 Rama I Rd (near Siam Square), takes in a mix of well-heeled pleasure and business travellers. Its 400 rooms start at 4114B.

The new *Grand Hyatt Erawan*, at the intersection of Ratchadamri and Ploenchit Rds, was raised on the site of the original Erawan Hotel (which came up at the same time as the Royal but was torn down some years ago) and has obvious ambitions to become the city's number-one hotel. The neo-Thai architecture has been well executed; inside is the largest collection of contemporary Thai art in the world. Adding to the elite atmosphere, rooms in the rear of the hotel overlook the Bangkok Royal Sports Club racetrack.

During the 1991 opening, 99 monks ('nine' is considered a lucky number in Thai culture, hence number 99 doubles the good luck) offered Buddhist chants in the lobby and received a sumptuous alms dinner; a Brahman ceremony was performed at the adjacent Erawan Shrine; and at an astrologically auspicious moment 510 balloons and 99 doves were simultaneously freed.

Other top-notch hotels in the Siam Square area include:

Arnoma, 99 Ratchadamri Rd; 400 rooms, 4000B up (☎ 255-6888; fax 255-1824)
Asia Hotel, 296 Phayathai Rd; 640 rooms, 2900 to 3200B; it's in a good location, but often full of tour groups and conventioneers (☎ 215-0808; fax 215-4360)

.: Palace Hotel, 1091/336 New Phetburi Rd; ɔ50 rooms, 2300B up (☎ 253-0500; fax 253-0556)
Imperial Hotel, Wireless Rd; 370 rooms, 4840B up (☎ 254-0023; fax 253-3190)
Indra Regent, Rajaprarob (Ratchaprarop) Rd; 500 rooms, 3388B up (☎ 251-1111; fax 253-3849)
Le Meridien President, 135/26 Gaysorn Rd; 387 rooms, 4500B up (☎ 253-0444; fax 253-7565)

Sukhumvit Rd Top-end hotels in this area include:

Ambassador Hotel, Soi 11, Sukhumvit Rd; 1050 rooms, 2178B up (☎ 254-0444; fax 253-4123)
ANA Grand Pacific Hotel Soi 17-19; Sukhumvit Rd, 4700B up (☎ 233-2922/7; fax 237-5740)
Impala Hotel Soi 24, Sukhumvit Rd; 200 rooms, 2299B up (☎ 258-8612/6; fax 259-2896),
Landmark, 138 Sukhumvit Rd; 415 rooms, 4961 to 9680B ; has a Videotex in every room (☎ 254-0404; fax 253-4259)
Mansion Kempinski, 75/23 Soi 11, Sukhumvit Rd; 127 rooms, 4500 to 4800B (☎ 255-7200; fax 253-2329)
Windsor Hotel, 3 Soi 20, Sukhumvit Rd; 235 rooms, 2420 to 7260B (☎ 258-0160; fax 258-1491)

Other Areas The *Airport Hotel* (☎ 566-1020, fax 566-1941), directly across from the airport, is quite well appointed; its 300 rooms start at 3872B. The only other luxury-class hotel toward the airport is the *Central Plaza Bangkok* (☎ 541-1234; fax 541-1087) at 1695 Phahonyothin Rd. There are 600 rooms, ranging in price from 4356 to 7260B. Other top-end hotels include:

Princess Hotel, 269 Lan Luang Rd; 2600 to 3500B (☎ 281-3088; fax 280-1314)
Quality Hotel Pinnacle, 17 Soi Ngam Duphli, Rama IV Rd; 170 rooms, 2000 to 3200B (☎ 287-3411; fax 287-3420)
Rama Gardens, 9/9 Vibhavadi Rangsit Rd; 364 rooms, 2904 to 6098B (☎ 561-0011; fax 561-1025)
Siam City, 477 Si Ayuthaya Rd; 530 rooms, 4356B up (☎ 247-0120; fax 247-0178)

Places to Eat

No matter where you go in Bangkok you're almost never more than 50 metres away from a restaurant or sidewalk food vendor. The variety of places to eat is simply astounding and defeats all but the most tireless food samplers in their quests to say they've tried everything. As with seeking a place to stay, you can find something in every price range in most districts – with a few obvious exceptions. Chinatown is naturally a good area for Chinese food, while Bangrak and Pahurat (both districts with high concentrations of Indian residents) are good for Indian and Muslim cuisine. Some parts of the city tend to have higher priced restaurants than others (for example, Siam Square, Silom and Surawong Rds and Sukhumvit Rd) while other areas are full of cheap eats (eg Banglamphu and the area around Tha Maharat (Ko Ratanakosin).

Because transport can be such a hassle in Bangkok, most visitors choose a place to eat according to which district is most convenient to reach (rather than seeking out a specific restaurant); this section has therefore been organised by area, rather than cuisine.

Banglamphu & Thewet This area near the river and old part of the city is one of the best for cheap eating establishments. Many of the guesthouses on Khao San Rd have open-air cafes, which are packed out with travellers from November to January. The typical cafe menu here has a few Thai and Chinese standards plus a variety of traveller favourites like fruit salads, muesli and yoghurt. The *Hello* restaurants (there are two on Khao San Rd) are generally reliable. Better is the long-running *Awn*, which has tables on the sidewalk and serves the closest thing to authentic Thai food on this street.

Pahurat's *Royal India* has recently opened a Khao San Rd branch in an alley about 50 metres east of the police station, amid a cluster of Indian tailor shops. The dining room is air-con and the thalis are filling but it's generally not as good as the original on Chakraphet Rd (the Indian bread selection is also smaller).

For more authentic (and cheaper) Thai food check out the next street north of Khao San, Rambutri Rd. Here there are several open-air restaurants serving excellent Thai food at low prices. At the Tanao Rd end of

Rambutri Rd is the small *Ta-Yai Restaurant*, which specialises in southern Thai food – the curries are great. On the opposite side of the street is *Aisa* at No 108, an excellent Thai-Muslim restaurant with several Thai standards but no pork. Another good southern Thai spot is a no-name food shop at 8-10 Chakraphong, south of Khao San and two doors south of the Padung Cheep mask shop. In the mornings this one serves khâo mòk kài (Thai chicken briyani) as well as khâo yam, a kind of rice salad which is a traditional breakfast in southern Thailand. Nearby at No 22 is a cheap and efficient Chinese noodle (bàmìi) and wonton (kíaw) shop; No 28 offers tasty Thai curries.

Farther north of Khao San in the heart of Banglamphu's market are two shopping complexes with food centres, fast-food vendors and supermarkets. At the high-rise *New World shopping centre* the ground floor features donut shops and meatball vendors, the 5th has a supermarket, and on the 8th is a brilliant food centre with city and river views. Centre vendors offer seafood, vegetarian, coffee, noodles, curries and more. The 6th floor of *Banglamphu Department Store* between Krai Si Rd and Rambutri Rd also has a supermarket and small food centre.

Many of the Khao San Rd guesthouse cafes offer vegetarian dishes. For an all-veggie menu at low prices, seek out the *Vegetarian Restaurant* at 85/2 Soi Wat Bowon. To find this out-of-the-way spot, turn left on Tanao Rd at the eastern end of Khao San Rd, then cross the street and turn right down the first narrow alley, then left at Soi Wat Bowon – an English sign reads 'Vegetarian'. Another very good vegetarian place is *Arawy* (no English sign), which is south of Khao San, across Ratchadamnoen Klang at 152 Din So Rd (opposite the City Hall). This was one of Bangkok's first Thai vegetarian restaurants, inspired by ex-Bangkok Governor Chamlong Srimuang. The restaurant also serves a few fish and shrimp dishes.

Good curry and rice is available for around 10B at the outdoor dining hall at *Thammasat University* near the river; it's open for lunch only. Opposite the southern entrance of the university there are several good noodle and rice shops. For north-eastern Thai food, try the restaurants next door to the boxing stadium on Ratchadamnoen Nok Rd, near the TAT office.

At the Tha Wisut Kasat pier in north-western Banglamphu, there's a very good floating restaurant serving seafood called *Yok Yor*. Especially good at Yok Yor is the hàw mòk (fish curry). Nearby is the similar *Chawn Ngoen*; it has no English sign, but there is an English menu.

At the Democracy Monument circle, Ratchadamnoen Klang Ave, are a few air-con Thai restaurants, including the *Vijit* and the *Sorn Daeng*, which have reasonable prices considering the service and facilities. At lunch time on weekdays they're crowded with local government office workers. Both stay open until 11 pm or so.

One of the best restaurants in Bangkok is just off Khao Rd between Ratwithi and Sukhothai Rds, north of Krungthon Bridge and near the river – *Baan Khun Luang*. The lunch buffet (11 am to 2 pm) is especially good value here – 90B for all you can eat from an unbelievable selection of Thai, Chinese, Japanese and seafood.

For those in the mood for continental food, *Kanit's* at 68 Tee Thong Rd is just south of the Sao Ching-Cha (Giant Swing) and is another worthwhile semi-splurge. The lasagna and pizza are probably the best you can find in this part of Bangkok.

Silom & Surawong Rds This area has a few restaurants along the main avenues and a greater number tucked away on sois and alleys. The river end of Silom and Surawong Rds toward Charoen Krung Rd (the Bangrak district) is a good hunting ground for Indian food.

Thai & Other Asian Look for the inexpensive *Charuvan*, near Patpong at 70-72 Silom Rd; it's a glassed-in Thai-Chinese restaurant with two rooms, one with air-con, the other *au naturel* (sweaty in the hot season). This old stand-by has dependable, low-priced

Thai food with discounted beer. The Patpong sois themselves are rather bleak when it comes to Thai food, although the long-running *Thai Room* remains a favourite of local Thai farang couples, Peace Corps volunteers and off-duty bar workers. The decor's not much, but prices are reasonable; the menu features several Mexican, Chinese, European and American dishes, as well as Thai food.

The *Sakura Steak House* on Patpong 1 has a loyal Japanese and Thai following for its inexpensive but good Japanese food. Another very good Japanese place – especially the sushi and sashimi – is *Goro* at 399/1 Soi Siri Chulasewok off Silom; prices are reasonable.

Toward the eastern end of Surawong, near the Montien and Thawana Ramada hotels, is the famous *Somboon* (open from 11 am to midnight), a seafood restaurant known for having the best crab curry in town. Somboon has a second branch further north, across Rama IV Rd near Chulalongkorn University at Soi Chulalongkorn 8.

The area to the east of Silom Rd off Convent and Sala Daeng Rds is a Thai gourmets' enclave. Most of the restaurants tucked away here are very good, but a meal for two will cost 600 to 800B. One that's a bit lower in price, but not in quality, is *Rang Peung* (Honeycomb) at 37 Soi 2, Sala Daeng Rd. The menu combines several different regional Thai cuisines and has especially tasty yam (Thai-style salads). Two can eat well for 150 to 200B. More up-market is *Bussaracum* (pronounced 'boot-sa-ra-kam') at 35 Soi Phipat off Convent Rd. Bussaracum specialises in 'royal Thai' cuisine, that is, recipes that were created for the royal court in days past; these recipes were kept secret from 'commoners' until late this century. Every dish is supposedly prepared only when ordered, from fresh ingredients and freshly ground spices. Live classical Thai music, played at a subdued volume, is also provided. A fancy place, recommended for a splurge. Two can eat for around 600 to 800B.

Moving toward the river, just west of Soi 9 at No 160 Silom Rd, you'll find *Isn't Classic*, a branch of the very popular Siam Square restaurant specialising in north-eastern Thai food. Prices are very reasonable for the good-quality sticky rice, kài yâang (spicy grilled chicken), lâap (meat salad), sôm-tam (spicy green salad) and other isaan delights. Over on Surawong Rd at No 173/8-9, *All Gaengs* is a clean, modern, air-con place specialising in rich Thai curries and spicy Thai-style salads (yam).

A good one-stop eating place with a lot of variety is the Silom Village Trade Centre, an outdoor shopping complex at Soi 24. Though it's basically a tourist spot with higher than average prices, the restaurants are of high quality and plenty of Thais dine here as well. The centrepiece is *Silom Village*, a place with shaded outdoor tables where the emphasis is on fresh Thai seafood – sold by weight. The menu also has extensive Chinese and Japanese sections. For the quick and casual, *Silom Coffee Bar* makes a good choice. At night *Ruen Thep* offers one of the city's better Thai classical dance-and-dinner venues. During the daytime, vendors dressed in traditional Thai clothing sell a variety of traditional snacks like khanõm khrók (steamed coconut pastries) and mîang kham (savoury titbits wrapped in wild tea leaves) – more than a little corny, but again the food quality is high.

The *Soi Prachun (20) night market* which assembles each evening off Silom Rd in front of the municipal market pavilion, is good for eats. During the day there are also a few food vendors in this soi.

Over on Surawong Rd at No 311/2-4 (corner of Soi Pramot), *Maria Bakery & Restaurant* is well known for its fresh Vietnamese and Thai food as well as French pastries, pizza and vegetarian food. A smaller Maria branch can be found next to the GPO on Charoen Krung Rd. Both are clean and air-con, with reasonable prices.

Indian & Muslim Farther toward the western end of Silom and Surawong Rds, Indian eateries begin making appearances one by one. For authentic South Indian food (dosa, idli, vada, etc), try the *Silom Lodge* at 92/1

Vaithy (or Vaithi) Lane, off Silom Rd near the Narai Hotel. It's worth the long walk down Vaithi Lane for the delicious coconut chatni. Another place serving South Indian (in addition to North Indian) food is the basic *Simla Cafe* at 382 Soi Tat Mai (opposite Borneo & Co) off Silom Rd, in an alley behind the Victory Hotel. Across from the Narai Hotel, near the Sri Mariamman temple, street vendors sometimes sell various Indian snacks.

The *Moti Mahal Restaurant* at the old Chartered Bank near the Swan Hotel off Charoen Krung has good Muslim-Indian food, great yoghurt and reasonable prices. *Himali Cha-Cha*, at 1229/11 Charoen Krung Rd, also features good North Indian cuisine, but prices are fairly high.

The *Cholas*, a small air-con place downstairs in the Woodlands Inn on Soi Charoen Krung 32 just north of the GPO, serves decent, no-fuss North Indian food at 40 to 80B a dish. The open-air *Sallim Restaurant* next door to the Woodlands is a cheaper, more working-class place with North Indian, Malay and Thai-Muslim dishes – it's usually packed. Opposite the GPO on Charoen Krung, the *Mumtaz Guest House* has a clean and reasonably priced Muslim restaurant downstairs. Around the corner on Soi Phutthaosot is the very popular but basic-looking *Naaz* (Naat in Thai), often cited as having the richest khâo mòk kài (chicken briyani) in the city. The milk tea is also very good here, and daily specials include chicken masala and mutton kurma. For dessert, the house speciality is firni, a Middle Eastern pudding spiced with coconut, almonds, cardamom and saffron. There are several other Arab/Indian restaurants in this area.

On Soi Prachun (Soi 20) off Silom Rd there's a mosque – Masjid Mirasuddeen – so Muslim food vendors are common.

Western If you crave German or Japanese food, there are plenty of places serving these cuisines on and around Patpong Rd. *Bobby's Arms*, an Aussie Brit pub, has good fish & chips. The *Brown Derby*, also on Patpong 1, is recommended for American-style deli sandwiches.

Wedged between the go-go bars on Patpong 2 are several fast-food chicken joints, including *Kentucky Fried Chicken, Chicken Divine* and *Magic Grill*. Yet another branch of the *Little Home Bakery & Restaurant* does a booming business serving farang and Filipino food on Soi Thaniya (one soi east of Patpong 2).

Opposite the Silom entrance to Patpong, in the CP Tower building, are a cluster of air-con American and Japanese-style fast-food places: *McDonald's, Pizza Hut, Chester's Grilled Chicken, Suzuki Coffee House* and *Toplight Coffee House*. Several are open late to catch the night-time Patpong traffic.

Mexican food in Thailand is always a big risk – usually the flavours are as distant from cocina mexicana as Bangkok is from Mexico City. One of the city's better Mexican food venues is *El Gordo's Cantina* at 130/8 Soi 8, Silom Rd, opposite the Bangkok Bank headquarters. In addition to a good selection of standard Mexican dishes, the restaurant makes a decent margarita.

The tiny *Harmonique* on Soi Charoen Krung 34 around the corner from the GPO is not a full-fledged restaurant but is a refreshing oasis in this extremely busy, smog-filled section of Charoen Krung. European-managed and unobtrusive, the little shop serves a variety of teas, fruit shakes and coffee on Hokkien-style marble-topped tables – a pleasant spot to read poste restante mail while quenching a thirst. The shop also discreetly offers silk and silverwork for sale.

Siam Square This shopping area is interspersed with several low and medium-priced restaurants as well as American fast-food franchises. Chinese food seems to predominate, probably because it's the well-off Chinese Thais that most frequent Siam Square. Soi 1 has three shark-fin places: *Scala, Penang* and *Bangkok*. At the other end of Siam Square, on Henri Dunant Rd, the big noodle restaurant called *Coca Garden* (open from 10.30 am to 10.30 pm) is good for

Chinese-style sukiyaki. The *Uptown* (open 9 am to 11 pm) on Soi 5 offers Thai, Chinese, Japanese and European food at low prices.

Can't decide what kind of Asian or farang food you're in the mood for? Then head for *S&P Restaurant & Bakery* on Soi 12. The extensive menu features Thai, Chinese, Japanese, European and vegetarian specialities, plus a bakery with pies, cakes and pastries – all high-quality fare.

On Soi 11 the *Muslim Food Centre* next to DK Book House serves a mouth-watering selection of inexpensive khâo mòk kài, satay, etc. Also on Soi 11 is the Bangkok branch of London's *Hard Rock Cafe* which serves American and Thai food. Look for the tuk-tuk captioned 'God is my co-pilot' coming out of the building facade. The Hard Rock stays open till 2 am, a bit later than many Siam Square eateries. On the next soi west and south half a block is *Isn't Classic* (an English pun on 'Isaan Classic'), where the north-eastern Thai dishes are always fresh, hot and inexpensive. A whole kài yâang (spicy grilled chicken) is only 55B; beer is also quite reasonable.

On the opposite side of Rama I Rd from Siam Square, the green Siam Center has four floors stacked with coffee shops catering to young Thais, including *UCC City Cafe, Siam Food, Garuda Cafe, Angella Coffeeshop, Dry Fly* and *Highlight Coffeeshop*. Those on the upper floor feature live Thai pop music in the evenings; the UCC (on the ground floor) has a CD jukebox, also the best coffee in the building. Menus are mostly Thai, with smaller selections of Thai, Chinese, Japanese and European. Prices average at around 35 to 75B per dish.

On both sides of Rama I in Siam Square and Siam Center you'll find a battery of American franchises, including *Mister Donut, Dunkin Donuts, Pizza Hut, Shakey's Pizza, McDonald's, A&W Root Beer* and *Kentucky Fried Chicken*. Prices are close to what you would pay in the USA.

If you're staying on or nearby Soi Kasem San I, you don't have to suck motorcycle fumes crossing Rama I and Phayathai Rds to Siam Square, Siam Center or Mahboonkrong to find something to eat. Besides the typical hotel and inn coffee shops found on the soi, there are also two very good, inexpensive curry-and-rice vendors with tables along the east side of the soi. No need to be fluent in Thai, they're used to the 'point-and-serve' system. Right around the corner on Rama I, next to the liquor dealer with the vintage British and US motorcycles out the front, is *Thai Sa Nguan* (no English sign), a fairly clean shop with khâo kaeng (curry and rice) for 10B (two toppings 15B), fried duck with noodles (kŭaytĭaw pèt yâang) and Hainanese-style chicken and rice (khâo man kài).

A bit farther east on Rama I Rd is the sprawling Siam Intercontinental Hotel. One of Bangkok's best restaurant deals is the lunch-time seafood buffet at the hotel's *Talay Thong* (☎ 253-0355) restaurant for 150B (not including tax and service). The buffet is served from noon to 2.30 pm, Monday to Friday only; it's best to book a seat in advance as the restaurant often fills up.

For ice cream, *Pan Pan* at Soi Lang Suan, serves good Italian gelato.

Vegetarian The *Whole Earth Restaurant* is at 93/3 Lang Suan Rd, off Ploenchit Rd and more or less equidistant from the Siam Center, Sukhumvit and Silom Rds. It's a good Thai and Indian vegetarian restaurant, but is a bit pricey if you're on a tight budget. Non-vegetarian dishes are also served.

Mahboonkrong Shopping Centre Another building studded with restaurants, MBK is directly across from Siam Square on Phayathai Rd. A section on the ground floor called Major Plaza contains two cinemas and a good food centre where you don't have to use the typical coupon system. An older food centre is on the 7th floor; both places have vendors serving tasty dishes from all over Thailand, including vegetarian, at prices averaging 20B per plate. Hours are 7 am to 10 pm, but the more popular vendors run out of food as early as 8.30 or 9 pm – come earlier for the best selection. A beer garden on the terrace surrounding two sides of the 7th floor food centre is open in the evening.

Scattered around other floors, especially the 3rd and 4th, are a number of popular medium-priced places, including *Little Home Bakery* (an American-style pancake house with a few Filipino dishes), *13 Coins* (steak, pizza and pasta), *Kobune Japanese Restaurant, Chester's Grilled Chicken, Pizza Hut* and many others.

Zen World Trade Center Not a Buddhist form of commerce, this new office and shopping complex at the corner of Ploenchit and Ratchadamri Rds contains a few up-market restaurants and the city's trendiest food centre. Located on the ground floor of this huge glossy building are *Kroissant House* (coffees, pastries and gelato) and *La Fontana* (swank Italian). *Rocco's Nouvelle Cuisine* is in the Zen Department Store itself and is not 'nouvelle' in the usual sense – menu items include burgers as well as Thai and Chinese standards. The 6th floor of the centre features *Lai-Lai* and *Chao Sua*, two sumptuous Chinese banquet-style places, plus the more casual *Narai Pizzeria*.

The basement of Zen Department Store contains a Thai deli with many curries, a *Mister Isaan* for north-eastern Thai food, a good Japanese sushi-and-noodle bar (a sizable plate of sushi costs 60 to 120B), a bakery, a sandwich/coffee bar and a Western deli. The food centre has very few seats, encouraging takeaways.

Pratunam Pratunam, the market district at the intersection of Phetburi and Ratchaprarop Rds, is a good hunting ground for Thai market food. Check out the night markets behind Ratchaprarop Rd stores (near the Phetburi Rd overpass) and in the little sois near this intersection. These are all great places to eat real Thai food and experience urban Thai culture.

The Pratunam markets are open, with corrugated tin roofs high above the tables and rustic kitchens, all bathed in fluorescent light. The market on the east side of Ratchaprarop Rd is more like a series of connected tents – one speciality here is a tangy fish stomach soup (kaphaw plaa). Four people can eat a large meal, drinking beer or rice whisky and nibbling away for hours and only spend around 150 to 250B (cheaper if it's rice whisky rather than beer). Night markets in Bangkok, as elsewhere in Thailand, have no menus so you had better have your Thai in shape before venturing out for an evening – or better, get a Thai friend to accompany you.

One of the most popular places in Bangkok for Chinese dim sum is *Pantip (Phanthip)* on the ground floor of Phanthip Plaza, Phetburi Rd, opposite colourful Baiyoke Tower. Make sure you arrive before 11 am on Saturdays or you'll have to fight for a table. If it's any enticement, this shopping plaza has among the city's best selections of shops selling computer hardware and software.

For a slightly up-market splurge in the Pratunam area, you might try the *Krua Khunluang* on Soi 33, Phetburi Rd. The restaurant is run by three women from Buriram so there are some north-eastern Thai dishes on the menu like lâap (spicy meat salad with mint leaves) and sôm-tam (spicy green papaya salad), but no English menu.

Sukhumvit Rd This avenue stretching east all the way to the city limits has hundreds of Thai, Chinese and farang restaurants to choose from.

Thai & Other Asian The ground floor of the Ambassador Hotel between Sois 11 and 13 has a good food centre. It offers several varieties of Thai, Chinese, Vietnamese, Japanese, Muslim and vegetarian food at 20 to 40B per dish – you must buy coupons first and exchange them for dishes you order.

Cabbages & Condoms at No 10, Soi 12, is run by the Population & Community Development Association (PDA), the brainchild of Mechai Viravaidya who popularised condoms in Thailand – first for birth control purposes and now as STD prevention. The restaurant offers not only a great selection of condoms, but great Thai food at very reasonable prices as well. The tôm khàa kài (chicken-coconut soup) is particularly tasty here; the restaurant is open from 11 am to 10 pm. The *Mandalay* (☎ 255-2893), at 23/7 Soi Ruam Rudi, is supposedly the only Burmese restaurant in town; it's good but not cheap.

The *Yong Lee Restaurant* at Soi 15, near Asia Books, has excellent Thai and Chinese food at reasonable prices and is a long-time favourite among Thai and farang residents alike. There is a second Yong Lee between Sois 35 and 37.

The famous *Djit Pochana* (☎ 258-1578) has a branch on Soi 20 and is one of the best value restaurants in town for traditional Thai dishes. The all-you-can-eat lunch buffet is 90B. This central section of Sukhumvit Rd is loaded with medium-priced Thai restaurants which feature modern decor but real Thai food. The *Baitarl* (Bai-Taan), at 3 Soi 33, is another very good place for traditional Thai food (though a little more expensive), as is the less expensive *Fuang Fah* across the street.

For nouvelle Thai cuisine, you can try the *Lemongrass* at 5/21 Soi 24, which has an atmospheric setting in an old Thai house decorated with antiques. The food is exceptional; try the yam pèt (Thai-style duck salad). It is open from 11 am to 2 pm and 6 pm to 11 pm.

Another restaurant with an inventive kitchen is *L'Orangery* at 48/11 Soi Ruam Rudi (close to where Ploenchit Rd becomes Sukhumvit Rd). Billed as Pacific Rim cuisine, the food shows the dual influences of Californian and Asian cooking; sometimes it works, sometimes it doesn't.

Another hidden gem down Sukhumvit Rd is *Laicram* (Laikhram) at Soi 33 (☎ 238-2337) and at Soi 49/4 (☎ 392-5864). The food at Laicram is authentic gourmet Thai, but not outrageously priced. One of the house specialities is hàw mòk hãwy, an exquisite thick fish curry steamed with mussels inside the shell. Sôm-tam (spicy green papaya salad) is also excellent here, as is khâo man, rice cooked with coconut milk and bai toei (pandanus leaf). Hours are from 10 am to 9 pm Monday to Saturday, 10 am to 3 pm Sunday.

There are many restaurants around the major hotels on Sukhumvit Rd with mixed Thai, Chinese, European, and American menus – most of average quality and slightly above-average prices, like the *Number One Restaurant*. These are good if you're not used to Thai food. One of the most authentic sources of Thai cuisine on Sukhumvit Rd is the regular *Soi 38 night market* at the junction of Sukhumvit and Soi 38; in addition to a wide variety of Thai foods, market vendors also serve a few Chinese and Malay dishes.

The recently opened *Mrs Balbir's* (☎ 253-2281) at 155/18 Soi 11 (behind the Siam Commercial Bank) has a good variety of vegetarian and non-vegetarian Indian food (mostly North Indian). Mrs Balbir has been teaching Indian cooking for many years and has her own Indian grocery store as well. One of the restaurant's strengths is that it's one of the few in the city which offers Indian breakfasts (served from 7.30 to 11 am). Another good Indian place is *Bangkok Brindawan* (☎ 258-8793) at 15 Soi 35 near the Fuji supermarket. This one specialises in South Indian food. A few medium to expensive restaurants serving Indian, Pakistani and Middle Eastern food are cropping up on and around Soi 3 (Soi Nana Neua), including *Akbar's, Al Hamra, Al Helabi, Nana Fondue* and *Shaharazad*.

Western Homesick Brits need look no farther than *Jool's Bar & Restaurant* at Soi 4 (Soi Nana Tai), past Nana Plaza on the left walking from Sukhumvit Rd. The British-style bar downstairs is a favourite expat hang-out while the dining room upstairs serves decent English food. Several rather expensive West European restaurants (Swiss, French, German, etc) are also found on touristy Sukhumvit Rd. *Crown Pizza*, around the corner from the Crown Hotel, between Sois 29 and 31, has been recommended – it's open fairly late and is air-con. *Bei Otto*, between Sois 12 and 14, is one of the most popular German restaurants in town and has a comfortable bar.

Nostalgic visitors from the States, especially those from southern USA, will appreciate the well-run *Bourbon St Bar & Restaurant* on Soi 22 (behind the Washington Theatre). The menu here emphasises Cajun and Creole cooking; some nights there is also free live music.

One of the top French restaurants in the city, and probably the best not associated with a luxury hotel – is *Le Banyan* (☎ 253-5556) at 59 Soi 8 in a charming early Bangkok-style house. The kitchen is French-managed and the menu covers the territory from ragout d'escargot to canard magret avec foie gras. This is definitely a splurge experience – although the prices are moderate when compared with other elegant French restaurants in the city.

The Italian-owned *Pan Pan* (☎ 252-7501) at 45 Soi Lang Suan is very popular with Western residents for its wood-fired pizza (takeaway orders accepted), pastas, salads, gelato (the best in Thailand) and pastries. A low-cal vegetarian menu is available on request. A second Pan Pan (☎ 258-5071) is located on Soi 33. For American- style pizza, there's a *Pizza Mall* at the corner of Soi 33 and Sukhumvit Rd (the *Uncle Ray's Ice Cream* next door has the best ice cream in Bangkok) and a *Pizza Hut* at Soi 39.

The *Little Home Bakery & Restaurant* (☎ 390-0760), at 413/10-12 Soi 55, has an extensive Western menu along with a few Filipino items – this place has a very loyal Thai following. Unless you're already out this far on Sukhumvit, the Little Home in Mahboonkrong shopping centre would be more convenient to most Bangkok locations.

Chinatown & Pahurat Some of Bangkok's best Chinese and Indian food is found in these adjacent districts but because few tourists stay in this part of town (for good reason – it's simply too congested), they rarely make any eating forays into the area. A few old Chinese restaurants have moved from Chinatown to locations with less traffic, the most famous being Hoi Tien Lao, now called Hoi Tien Lao Rim Nam and located on the Thonburi bank of the Chao Phraya River. But many are still hanging on to their venerable Chinatown addresses – where the atmosphere is still part of the eating experience.

Most of the city's Chinatown restaurants specialise in southern Chinese cuisine, particularly that of coastal Guangdong and Fujian provinces. This means seafood, rice noodles and dumplings are often the best choices. The large, banquet-style Chinese places are mostly found along Yaowarat and Charoen Krung Rds, and include *Lie Kee* (corner of Charoen Krung and Bamrungrat Rds, a block west of Ratchawong Rd), *Laem Thong* (on Soi Bamrungrat just off Charoen Krung Rd) and *Yau Wah Yuen* (near the Yaowarat and Ratchawong Rds intersection). Each of these has an extensive menu, including dim sum before lunch time.

The best noodle and dumpling shops are hidden away on smaller sois and alleys. At No 54 on Soi Bamrungrat is the funky *Chiang Kii*, whose 100B khâ tôm plaa (rice soup with fish) belies the casual surroundings – no place does it better. *Kong Lee*, at 137/141 Ratchawong, has a very loyal clientele for its dry-fried wheat noodles (bàmii hâeng in Thai) – again it's reportedly the best in Bangkok. Another great noodle place, *Pet Tun Jao Thaa*, is on the south-eastern edge of Chinatown in the direction of the GPO, at 945 Soi Wanit 2 opposite the Harbour Department building. The restaurant's name means 'Harbour Department Stewed Duck' – the speciality is rice noodles (kŭaytĭaw) served with duck or goose, either roasted or stewed.

Over in Pahurat, the Indian fabric district, most Indian places serve North Indian cuisine, which is heavily influenced by Moghul or Persian flavours and spices. For many people, the best North Indian restaurant in town is the *Royal India* at 392/1 Chakraphet Rd in Pahurat. It is very crowded at lunch time – almost exclusively with Indian residents – so it might be better to go there after the standard lunch hour or at night. The place has very good curries (both vegetarian and non-vegetarian), dahl, Indian breads (including six kinds of paratha), raita, lassi, etc – all at quite reasonable prices. The *Cha Cha* farther north along Chakraphet is also quite good for North Indian food.

The *ATM department store* on Chakraphet Rd near the pedestrian bridge has a food centre on the top floor that features several Indian vendors – the food is cheap and tasty and there's quite a good selection. Running alongside the ATM building on Soi ATM are several small teahouses with very inexpensive Indian and Nepali food, including lots of fresh chapatis and strong milk tea. For a good choice of inexpensive vegetarian food, try the Sikh-operated *Indrathep* on Soi ATM. In the afternoons, a Sikh man sets up a push-cart on the corner of Soi ATM and Chakraphet Rd and sells vegetarian samosas often cited as the best in Bangkok.

Vegetarian During the annual Vegetarian Festival (centred around Wat Mangkon Kamalawat on Charoen Krung Rd in September-October), Bangkok's Chinatown becomes a virtual orgy of vegetarian Thai and Chinese food. Restaurants and noodle shops in the area offer hundreds of different vegetarian dishes. One of the best spreads is at *Hua Seng Restaurant*, a few doors west of Wat Mangkon on Charoen Krung Rd.

Other Areas *Tum-Nak-Thai (Tamnak Thai)* (☎ 276-7810), 131 Ratchadaphisek Rd, is one of several large outdoor restaurants built over boggy areas of Bangkok's Din Daeng district north of Phetburi. But this one just happens to be billed as the largest outdoor restaurant in the world (verified by the Guiness record book)! It's built on four hectacres of land and water and can serve up to 3000 diners at once. The menu exceeds 250 items and includes Thai, Chinese, Japanese and European food. All orders are computer-coordinated and some of the waiters glide by on roller skates. One section of the restaurant offers while-you-dine Thai classical dance performances. Two can eat here for under 300B including beer.

Dinner Cruises There are a number of companies that run cruises during which you eat dinner. Prices range from 30 to 500B per person depending on how far they go and whether dinner is included in the fare. For more information, see the Dinner Cruises section earlier under River & Canal trips.

Vegetarian The *Bangkok Adventist Hospital cafeteria* (430 Phitsanulok Rd) also serves inexpensive veggie fare. At the south-western corner of Chatuchak Park (where the Weekend Market is held), near the pedestrian bridge and Chinese shrine, look for a sign reading 'Vegetarian' in green letters and you'll find a small Thai veggie restaurant with great food for only 5 to 10B per dish. All the Indian restaurants in town have vegetarian selections on their menus.

Hotel Restaurants For splurge-level food, many of Bangkok's grand luxury hotels provide memorable – if expensive – eating experiences. With Western cuisine, particularly, the quality usually far exceeds anything found in Bangkok's independent restaurants. Some of the city's best Chinese restaurants are also located in hotels. If you're on a budget, check to see if a lunch-time buffet is available on weekdays; usually these are the best deals, ranging from 150 to 250B per person (up to 370B at the Oriental). Also check the *Bangkok Post* and the *Nation* for weekly specials presented by visiting chefs from far-flung corners of the globe – Morocco, Mexico City, Montreal, no matter how obscure, they've probably done the Bangkok hotel circuit.

The Oriental Hotel has six restaurants, all of them managed by world-class chefs – buffet lunches are offered at several. The hotel's relatively new *China House* (☎ 236-0400, ext 3378) has one of the best Chinese kitchens in Bangkok, with an emphasis on Cantonese cooking. The lunch-time dim sum is superb and is a bargain by luxury hotel standards (45B or less per plate). The Oriental's *Lord Jim's* is designed to imitate the interior of a 19th-century Asian steamer, with a view of the river; the menu focuses on seafood (lunch buffet available).

Dusit Thani's *Chinatown* (☎ 236-0450)

was probably the inspiration for the Oriental's China House, though here the menu focuses on Chiu Chau (Chao Zhou) cuisine as well as Cantonese. Dim sum lunch is available, but it's a bit more expensive than the Oriental's. As at the Oriental, service is impeccable. Dusit also has the highly reputed *Mayflower*, with pricey Cantonese cuisine.

For hotel dim sum almost as good as that at the Dusit or Oriental – but at less than a third the price – try the *Jade Garden* (☎ 233-7060) at the Montien Hotel. Though not quite as fancy in presentation, the food is nonetheless impressive.

For French food, the leading hotel contenders are *Ma Maison* (☎ 253-0123) at the Hilton International, *Normandie* (☎ 236-0400, ext 3380) at the Oriental, and *Regent Grill* (☎ 251-6127) at the Regent Bangkok. All are expensive but the meals and service are virtually guaranteed to be of top quality. The Regent Bangkok also offers the slightly less formal *La Brasserie*, specialising in Parisian cuisine.

Finally, if eating at one of the above would mean spending your life savings, try this pauper's version of dining amidst the bright hotel lights of Bangkok. Go to the end of the soi in front of the Shangri-La Hotel and take a ferry (1B) across the river to the wooden pier immediately opposite. Next to this pier is the riverside *Prom*, where you can enjoy an inexpensive Thai seafood meal outdoors with impressive night-time views of the Shangri-La and Oriental hotels opposite. The ferry runs till Prom closes, around 2 am.

Entertainment

In their round-the-clock search for *khwaam sa-nùk* (fun), Bangkokians have made their metropolis one that literally never sleeps. To get an idea of what's available, check the entertainment listings in the daily *Bangkok Post* and the *Nation*, or the tourist-oriented weeklies *This Week* and *Angel City* (the latter two are free at various tourist haunts around town). Possibilities include classical music performances, rock concerts, videotheque dancing, Asian music/theatre ensembles on tour, art shows, international buffets, etc. Boredom should not be a problem in Bangkok, at least not for a short-term visit; however, save some energy and money for your upcountry trip!

Bangkok is loaded with bars, coffee shops, nightclubs and massage parlours left over from the days when the City of Angels was an R&R stop for GIs serving in Vietnam. By and large these throwbacks are seedy, expensive and cater to men only. Then there is the new breed of S&S (sex & sin) bar, some merely refurbished R&R digs, that are more modest, classy and welcome females and couples. Not everybody's cup of tea, but they do a good business. More recently, other places have appeared which are quite chic and suitable for either gender.

All the major hotels have flashy nightclubs too, which are less seedy but more expensive. Many feature live music – rock, country & western, Thai pop music and jazz, the latter usually played by good Filipino bands. Most hotels catering to tourists and businesspeople have up-to-date discos. You'll find the latest recorded music in the smaller neighbourhood bars and mega-discos.

Bars The 'girlie bars' are concentrated along Sukhumvit Rd (east of Soi 21), off Sukhumvit Rd on Soi Nana (including the infamous Grace Hotel, now an all-Arab nightspot); and in the world-famous Patpong Rd area, between Silom and Surawong Rds. Wherever you go prices are about the same; beers are usually 40 to 50B. Patpong (named after the Chinese millionaire, Phat Phong, who owns practically everything on Patpong Rds I and II) has calmed down a bit over the years. These days it has more of an open-air market feel as several of the newer bars are literally on the street, and vendors set up shop in the evening hawking everything from roast squid to fake designer watches. The downstairs clubs with names like King's Castle and Pussy Galore feature go-go dancing while upstairs the real raunch is kept behind closed doors. Don't believe the touts on the street who say the upstairs shows are for free: after the show, a huge bill arrives.

Another holdover from the R&R days is Soi Cowboy (off Sukhumvit between Sois 21 and 23), which still gets pretty wild some nights. Then there's a new bar area located in Nana Plaza off Soi 4 (Soi Nana Tai) Sukhumvit Rd. One bar here, Woodstock, plays some of the better recorded music in town over a decent sound system, and they don't seem to mind if you come and just listen either, ie the girls keep a low profile. Asian Intrigue, in the same complex, has floor shows involving snakes and other interesting scenarios, designed for a wider appeal than the raunchy upstairs shows on Patpong. Nana Plaza comes complete with its own guesthouses in the same complex.

Soi Tantawan and Thaniya Rd, on either side of and parallel to Patpong Rds I and II, feature expensive Japanese-style hostess bars (which non-Japanese are usually barred from entering) as well as a handful of gay bars with names like Mandate and Golden Cock that feature male go-go dancers and 'bar boys'. Transvestite cabarets are big in Bangkok and several are found in this area. Calypso Cabaret has recently moved from its old Soi 24 Sukhumvit Rd location to the Ambassador Hotel at Soi 11. The Calypso has the largest regularly performing transvestite troupe in town, with nightly shows at 8 and 9.45 pm.

Trendy among Bangkok Thais these days is a new kind of bar which strives for a more sophisticated atmosphere, with good service and choice music played at a volume that doesn't discourage conversation. The Thais call them pubs but they bear little resemblance to any traditional English pub. Some are 'theme' bars, conceived around a particular aesthetic. Soi Lang Suan off Ploenchit Rd has several, including the favourites Brown Sugar and Old West. Soi 33 off Sukhumvit Rd has a string of bars named after European artists: Vincent Van Gogh, Ea Manet Club, Renoir Club 1841; you get the idea.

Bangkok is a little short on plain neighbourhood bars without up-market pretensions or down-market sleaze. One that's close to fitting the bill is the Front Page, a journalists' hang-out near the *Bangkok Post* offices on Soi 1, Sala Daeng (off Silom and Rama IV). The Brit-style Jool's on Soi 4 near Nana Plaza is another.

Live Music The three-storey Saxophone Pub Restaurant south-east of the Victory Monument circle at 3/8 Victory Monument, Phayathai Rd, has become a Bangkok institution for musicians of several genres. On the ground floor is a bar/restaurant featuring jazz from 9 pm; the next floor up has a billiards hall with recorded music; the top floor has live bands playing reggae, R&B or blues from 10.30 pm, and on Sundays there's an open jam session. There's never a cover charge at Saxophone and you don't need to dress up.

Along Sarasin Rd, north of Lumphini Park, are a number of live music pubs, including Bangkok's hottest jazz club, Brown Sugar. One of Brown Sugar's top draws has been regular Friday night performances of multi-instrumentalist Tewan, probably Thailand's top jazz performer at the moment. Tewan's fusion of international jazz and Thai folk-classical music results in exciting sounds, and his band is always top rate. The nearby Old West (Thailand's original old west style pub) books good Thai folk groups. Other clubs in the area include Burgundy and Shakin'. To make way for a high-rise development, Brown Sugar is soon moving to Royal City Ave near the Makkasan railway station and Bangkok Palace Hotel; other Sarasin Rd pubs may have to move as well. Check the *Nation's* daily 'Restaurant & Entertainment' page for latest addresses.

Other bars with regular live jazz include the Glass at 22/3-5 Soi 11 Sukhumvit, Round Midnight Pub & Restaurant at 106/2 Soi Lang Suan, Trumpet on Soi 24, and Blue Moon on Ploenchit Rd. The Oriental's famous Bamboo Bar has live jazz nightly in an elegant but relaxed atmosphere; other hotel jazz bars include Entrepreneur at the Asia Hotel (Saturday night only), Cat's Eye at Le Meridien President's (jazz on weeknights) and the Hilton's Music bar (Friday night only).

Rock fans should check out the Co-Bongo Bar on Din So Rd, about 50 metres north of the Democracy Monument in Banglamphu. Decorated with an eclectic mix of pseudo-African artefacts, south-west American Indian pottery, and surf gear, this one-of-a-kind club features a high-calibre rock and reggae group nightly from around 9.30 pm. There's a one-drink minimum but no cover. The Bangkok club most often recommended by my Thai friends is the Som Thong Cafe, at the intersection of Phra Pinklao and Arun Amarin Rds, 200 metres over the Phra Pinklao Bridge in Thonburi. A seasoned Thai band here plays mostly '60s and '70s music from early in the evening till late, though the place doesn't really heat up until after 9 pm.

Discos & Dance Clubs All the major hotels in the city have international-style discotheques but only a few can really be recommended as attractions in themselves. Cover charges are pretty uniform: around 150 to 160B on weekday nights, including one drink, and around 300 to 350B on weekends, including two drinks. Most places don't begin filling up till after 11 pm. Two consistently good hotel discos are the Dusit Thani's newly refurbished videotheque Bubbles (☎ 233-1130), and the Shangri-La's plush Talk of the Town (☎ 236-7777).

Well-heeled Thais and Thai celebrities frequent the exclusive, high-tech Diana's in the Oriental Plaza off Charoen Krung Rd. A younger crowds packs Le Freak at 137 Gaysorn Rd (near Le Meridien President Hotel), which has a live band until 10.30 pm, before switching over to disco. More relaxed is Rome Club (☎ 233-8836) at Soi 4 (Soi Jaruwan), Silom Rd, where DJs play the latest US and UK music video hits over a good sound system and huge video screen. Rome's clientele was once predominantly gay but has become more mixed as word got around about the great dance scene. There's a 100B cover charge from Sunday to Thursday, 200B on weekends (includes one drink).

Bangkok has several huge high-tech discos that hold up to 5000 people each and feature mega-watt sound systems, giant-screen video and the latest in light-show technology. The clientele for these dance palaces is mostly an agro crowd of young, moneyed Thais experimenting with life styles of conspicuous affluence, plus the occasional Bangkok celebrity. The most 'in' discos of this nature are the Paradise on Arun Amarin Rd in Thonburi and the Palace on Vibhavadi Rangsit Highway toward the airport. Another biggie is NASA Spaceadrome at 999 Ramkhamhaeng Rd, which features a sci-fi theme; the cover charge here is only 180B on weekends (140B during the week) and includes two drinks. A mega-disco that gets older as well as younger Thais is the Galaxy on Rama IV Rd, from which WBA world boxing champions Khaosai Galaxy and his brother Khaokor have taken their surname. The Galaxy has also become popular with visiting Japanese. Cover charges at these discos are 150 to 200B and this usually includes a drink or two.

Thai Dance-Drama Thailand's best lakhon and khon performances are held at the National Theatre (☎ 224-1342) on Chao Fa Rd near Phra Pinklao Rd. The theatre's regular public roster schedules performances for the second and last Friday and Saturday of every month as well as on the second Sunday, usually three performances per day. Admission fees are very reasonable, around 50 to 70B depending on the seating. Attendance at a khon performance (masked dance-drama based on stories from the *Ramakian)* is highly recommended.

Occasional classical dance performances are also held at the Thailand Cultural Centre (☎ 245-7711), Ratchadaphisek Rd and at the College of Dramatic Arts, near the National Theatre.

Dinner Theatres Most tourists view performances put on solely for their benefit at one of the several Thai classical dance/dinner theatres in the city (see list). Admission prices at these evening venues average 150 to 500B per person and include a 'typical' Thai dinner (often toned down for farang palates), a couple of selected dance performances and a martial arts display.

The historic Oriental Hotel has its own dinner theatre on the Thonburi side of the Chao Phraya River opposite the hotel (the Sala Rim Nam). The 680B admission is above average but so is the food and the performance; the river ferry between the hotel and restaurant is free. The Oriental also offers a dance/martial art performance called the Kodak Siam Show – no meal included – in the hotel's pool-side garden every Sunday and Thursday at 11 am for 80B. The dinner performance at Silom Village's Ruen Thep restaurant on Silom Rd is also recommended because of the relaxed, semi-outdoor setting.

Baan Thai Restaurant
7 Soi 32, Sukhumvit Rd (☎ 258-5403)
Chao Phraya Restaurant
Phra Pinklao Bridge (☎ 474-2389)
Maneeya's Lotus Room
Ploenchit Rd (☎ 252-6312)
Phiman Restaurant
46 Soi 49, Sukhumvit Rd (☎ 258-7866)
Ruen Thep
Silom Village, Silom Rd (☎ 233-9447)
Sala Norasing
Soi 4, Sukhumvit Rd (☎ 251-5797)
Sala Rim Nam
opposite Oriental Hotel, Charoen Nakhon Rd (☎ 437-6221/3080)
Suwannahong Restaurant
Si Ayuthaya Rd (☎ 245-4448/3747)
Tum-Nak-Thai Restaurant
131 Ratchadaphisek Rd (☎ 277-3828)

Shrine Dancing Free performances of traditional Thai dance can be seen daily at the Lak Muang and Erawan shrines if you happen to arrive when a performance troupe has been commissioned by a worshipper. Although many of the dance movements are the same as those seen in classical lakhon, these relatively crude performances are specially choreographed for ritual purposes and don't represent true classical dance forms. But the dancing is colourful – the dancers wear full costume and are accompanied by live music – so it's worth stopping by to watch a performance if you're in the vicinity. For more information on Thai classical dance see the Arts section in the Facts about the Country chapter.

Thai Boxing *Muay thai* (Thai boxing) can be seen at two boxing stadiums, Lumphini (on Rama IV Rd near Sathon Thai (South) Rd) and Ratchadamnoen (on Ratchadamnoen Nok Rd, next to the TAT office). Admission fees vary according to seating: the cheapest seats in Bangkok are now around 150B and ringside seats cost 500B or more. Monday, Wednesday, Thursday and Sunday, the boxing is at Ratchadamnoen, and Tuesday, Friday and Saturday it's at Lumphini. The Ratchadamnoen matches begin at 6 pm, except for the Sunday shows which start at 5 pm, while the Lumphini matches all begin at 6.20 pm. Aficionados say the best-matched bouts are reserved for Tuesday nights at Lumphini and Thursday nights at Ratchadamnoen. The restaurants on the north side of Ratchadamnoen stadium are well known for their delicious kài yâang and other north-eastern dishes. (For more information on Thai boxing see the Sport section in the Facts about the Country chapter.)

Massage Parlours Massage parlours have been a Bangkok attraction for many years now, though the Tourist Authority of Thailand (TAT) tries to discourage the city's reputation in this respect. Massage as a healing art is a centuries-old tradition in Thailand, and it is possible to get a really legitimate massage in Bangkok – despite the commercialisation of recent years. That many of the modern massage parlours (*àap òp nûat* or 'bathe-steam-massage' in Thai) also deal in prostitution is well known; less well known is the fact that many (but by no means all) of the girls working in the parlours are bonded labour – they are not necessarily there by choice.

It takes a chauvinist male not to be saddened by the sight of 50 girls/women behind a glass wall with numbers pinned to their dresses.

Often the bank of masseuses is divided into sections according to skill and/or appearance. Most expensive is the 'superstar' section, in which the women try to approximate the look of fashion models or actresses. A smaller section is reserved for women who are actually good at giving massages, with no hanky-panky on the side.

Before contemplating anything more than a massage at a modern massage parlour, be sure to read the Health section in the Facts for the Visitor chapter for information on sexually transmitted diseases. There is a definite AIDS presence in Thailand, so condom use is imperative not only in Bangkok but anywhere in Thailand.

Traditional Massage Traditional Thai massage, also called 'ancient' massage, is now widely available in Bangkok as an alternative to the red-light massage parlours. One of the best places to experience a traditional massage is at Wat Pho, Bangkok's oldest temple. Massage here costs 140B per hour or 80B for half an hour. There is also a 30-hour course in Thai massage which can be attended three hours per day for 10 days, or two hours per day for 15 days. Tuition for the course is 3000B. You must also pay the regular 10B per day admission fee for Wat Pho whether you are a student or massagee.

Other places to get traditional Thai massage in Bangkok include Buathip Thai Massage (☎ 255-1045) at 4/13 Soi 5, Sukhumvit Rd; Marble House (☎ 235-3519) at 37/18-19 Soi Surawong Plaza; and Winwan (☎ 251-7467) between Sois 1 and 3. Fees for traditional Thai massage should be no more than 150B per hour, though some places have a 1½-hour minimum. Be aware that not every place advertising traditional or ancient massage offers a really good one; sometimes the only thing 'ancient' about the pommelling is the age of the masseur. Thai massage aficionados say that the best massages are given by blind masseurs (available at Marble House).

Cinema Dozens of movie theatres around town show Thai, Chinese, Indian and occasionally Western movies. The majority of films shown are comedies and shoot-em-ups, with the occasional drama slipping through. These theatres are air-con and quite comfortable, with reasonable rates (20 to 60B). All movies in Thai theatres are preceded by the Thai royal anthem along with projected pictures of King Bhumiphol and other members of the royal family. Everyone in the theatre stands quietly and respectfully for the duration of the anthem (written by the king, incidentally).

The main theatres showing commercial English-language films are Center 1 & 2 at Siam Center; Scala, Lido and Siam at Siam Square; Major 1 & 2 at Mahboonkrong; Century 1 & 2 and Mackenna on Phayathai Rd; and the Washington 1 & 2 at Soi 24 Sukhumvit. Movie ads appear daily in both the *Nation* and the *Bangkok Post*; listings in the *Nation* include addresses and programme times.

Foreign films are often altered before distribution by Thailand's board of censors; usually this involves obscuring nude sequences with Vaseline 'screens'. Some distributors also edit films they consider to be too long; occasionally Thai narration is added to explain the story line (when the *Omen* was released in Thailand, distributors chopped off the ambiguous ending and added a voice-over giving the film a 'new' ending).

Film snobs may prefer the weekly or twice-weekly offerings at Bangkok's foreign cultural clubs. French and German films screened at the cultural clubs are almost always subtitled in English. Admission is sometimes free, sometimes 30 to 40B. For addresses and phone numbers see the Cultural Centres section earlier in this chapter.

Video Video rentals are very popular in Bangkok; not only are videos cheaper than regular film admissions, but many films are available on video that aren't approved for theatre distribution by Thailand's board of censors. For those with access to a TV and VCR, the average rental is around 20B. Sukhumvit Rd has the highest concentration of video shops; the better ones are found in the residential area between Sois 39 and 55.

Things to Buy

Regular visitors to Asia know that in many ways, Bangkok beats Hong Kong and Singapore for deals on handicrafts, textiles, gems, jewellery, art and antiques – nowhere else will you find the same combination of selection, quality and prices. The trouble is finding the good spots, as the city's intense urban tangle makes orientation sometimes difficult. Nancy Chandler's *Map of Bangkok*, which was originally intended as a guide to the city's markets and shopping venues (but includes much more these days), makes a very good buying companion, with annotations on all sorts of small, out-of-the-way shopping venues.

Be sure to re-read the introductory Things to Buy section in the Facts for the Visitor chapter before setting out on a buying spree. Amid all the bargains are a number cleverly disguised rip-off schemes – *caveat emptor*!

Weekend Market This market is at Chatuchak Park, off Phahonyothin Rd and across from the northern bus terminal. Air-con bus Nos 3, 9, 10 and 13 all pass the market – just get off before the northern bus terminal. A dozen other ordinary city buses also pass the market.

Chatuchak's market is the Disneyland of markets. Everything is sold here, from live chickens and snakes to opium pipes and herbal remedies. Thai clothing such as the phaakhamaa (sarong for men) and the phaasin (sarong for women), *kang keng jiin* (Chinese pants) and *sêua mâw hâwm* (blue cotton farmer's shirt) are good buys. You'll also find musical instruments, hill-tribe crafts, religious amulets, flowers, camping gear and military surplus. The best bargains of all are household goods like pots and pans, dishes, drinking glasses, etc. If you're moving to Thailand for an extended period, this is the place to pick up stuff for your kitchen. There is plenty of interesting and tasty food for sale if you're feeling hungry. Don't forget to try out your bargaining skills.

An unfortunate footnote to add is that Chatuchak Park remains an important hub of Thailand's illegal exotic wildlife trade – in spite of occasional police raids – as well as a conduit for endangered species from Burma, Laos and Cambodia. Some species are sold for their exotic food value, eg barking deer, wild boar, crocodiles and pangolins, while some are sold for their supposed medicinal value, eg rare leaf-monkeys. Thai laws protect most of these species, but Thais are notorious scofflaws. Not all wildlife trade here is illicit though; many of the birds sold, including the hill mynah and zebra dove, have been legally raised for sale as pets.

In spite of its name, the Weekend Market is open daily from around 8 am to 8 pm.

Other Markets Just across Kamphaeng Phet Rd from the Weekend Market, **Atok Market** is open every day of the week with a selection similar to the Weekend Market, including flowers and potted plants. **Khlong Toey Market**, under the expressway at the intersection of Rama IV and Narong Rds in the Khlong Toey district, is possibly the cheapest all-purpose market in Bangkok (best on Wednesdays). **Pratunam Market**, at the intersection of Phetburi and Ratchaprarop Rds, runs every day and is very crowded, but has great deals in new, cheap clothing. There is good eating here, too.

Samyan Market is at the north-western corner of the intersection of Rama IV and Phayathai Rds, near Chulalongkorn University. It has all the usual stuff, but is worth a special trip for the tasty and cheap seafood restaurants along the first soi on the right off Phayathai Rd above Rama IV.

A good selection of flowers and plants is available at the **Thewet Market** near the Tha Thewet pier on Krung Kasem Rd. Also in this part of Bangkok you'll find the huge **Banglamphu Market**, which spreads several blocks over Chakraphong, Phra Sumen, Tanao and Rambutri Rds – a short walk from the Khao San Rd guesthouse area. The Banglamphu market area is probably the most comprehensive shopping district in the city as it encompasses everything from street vendors to up-market department stores.

The **Pahurat** and **Chinatown** districts

have interconnected markets selling tons of well-priced fabrics, clothes and household wares, as well as a few places selling gems and jewellery. The **Wong Wian Yai Market** in Thonburi, next to the large traffic circle *(wong wian yài* means 'big circle') directly south-west of Memorial Bridge (Phra Put Yot Pha), is another all-purpose market – but this one rarely gets tourists.

Shopping Centres & Department Stores
The growth of large and small shopping centres has accelerated over the last few years. Central and Robinson department stores, the original stand-bys, have branches in the Sukhumvit and Silom areas with all the usual stuff – designer clothes, Western cosmetics – plus supermarkets and Thai delis, cassette tapes, fabrics and other local products that might be of interest to some travellers.

Oriental Plaza (Soi Oriental, Charoen Krung Rd) and River City shopping complex (near the Royal Orchid Sheraton, off Charoen Krung and Si Phraya Rds) are centres for high-end consumer goods. They're expensive but do have some unique merchandise; River City has two floors specialising in art and antiques. The much smaller Silom Village Trade Centre on Silom Rd has a few antique and handicraft shops with merchandise several rungs lower in price.

Along Ploenchit and Sukhumvit Rds you'll find many newer department stores and shopping centres, including Sogo and Landmark Plaza, but these Tokyo clones tend to be expensive and not that exciting. Peninsula Plaza on Ratchadamri Rd (named after the Bangkok Peninsula Hotel, which has since changed its name to the Regent Bangkok) has a more exclusive selection of shops – many of which have branches at River City and Oriental Plaza – and a good-sized branch of Asia Books. Another high-end shopping complex is the new World Trade Center near the intersection of Ploenchit and Phayathai Rds; its focus is the Zen Department Store, which has clothing shops reminiscent of Hong Kong's high-end boutiques.

Siam Square, on Rama I Rd near Phayathai Rd, is a network of some 12 sois lined with shops selling mid-priced designer clothes, books, sporting goods and antiques. Siam Center, on the opposite side of Rama I, has more up-market clothing shops as well as coffee shops, travel agencies, banks and airline offices.

One of the most varied shopping centres to wander around in is the Mahboonkrong (MBK) centre near Siam Square. It's all air-con, but there are many small, inexpensive vendors and shops in addition to the flashy Tokyu department store. Bargains can be found here if you look.

Antiques & Decorative Items Real Thai antiques are rare and costly. Most Bangkok antique shops keep a few antiques around for collectors, along with lots of pseudo-antiques or traditionally crafted items that look like antiques. The majority of shop operators are quite candid about what's really old and what isn't. As Thai design becomes more popular abroad, many shops are now specialising in Thai home decorative items.

Reliable antique shops (using the word 'antiques' loosely) include Elephant House at 67/12 Soi Phra Phinit, Soi Suan Phlu; Peng Seng, at the corner of Rama IV and Surawong Rds; Asian Heritage, at 57 Soi 23, Sukhumvit Rd; Thai House, 720/6 Sukhumvit Rd, near Soi 28; and Artisan's in the Silom Village Trade Centre, Silom Rd. The River City and Oriental Plaza shopping complexes also have several good, if pricey, antique shops.

Gems & Jewellery Recommending specific shops is tricky since to the average eye one coloured stone looks as good as another, so the risk of a rip-off is much greater than for most other popular shopping items. One shop that's been a long-time favourite with Bangkok expats for service and value in set jewellery is Johnny's Gems (☎ 222-1756) at 199 Fuang Nakhon Rd (off Charoen Krung Rd). Another reputable jewellery place is Merlin et Delauney (☎ 234-3884), with a large showroom and lapidary at 1 Soi Pradit,

Surawong Rd and a smaller shop at the Novotel hotel, Soi 6, Siam Square. Both of the foregoing also have unset stones as well as jewellery; two dependable places that specialise in unset stones are Lambert International (☎ 236-4343) at 807 Silom Rd, and Thai Lapidary (☎ 214-2641), at 277/122 Rama I Rd.

Bronzeware Thailand has the oldest bronze-working tradition in the world and there are several factories in Bangkok producing bronze sculpture and cutlery. Two factories that sell direct to the public (and where you may also be able to observe the bronze-working process) are Siam Bronze Factory (☎ 234-9436), at 1250 Charoen Krung Rd; and SN Thai Bronze Factory (☎ 215-7743), at 157-33 Phetburi Rd. Make sure any items you buy are silicon-coated, otherwise they'll tarnish. To see the casting process for Buddha images, go to the Buddha-Casting Foundry next to Wat Wiset Khan on Phran Nok Rd, Thonburi (take a river ferry from Tha Phra Chan or Tha Maharat on the Bangkok side to reach the foot of Phran Nok Rd).

Many vendors at Wat Mahathat's Sunday market sell old and new bronzeware – haggling is imperative.

Handicrafts Bangkok has excellent buys in Thai handicrafts, though for northern hill-tribe materials you might be able to do better in Chiang Mai. Narayana Phand (☎ 252-4670) on Ratchadamri Rd, is a bit on the touristy side but has a large selection and good marked prices – no haggling is necessary. Central Department Store on Ploenchit Rd has a Thai handicrafts section with marked prices.

Two royally sponsored outlets where profits got directly to hill tribes and villages are the Hill Tribe Foundation (☎ 351-9816) at 195 Phayathai Rd, and the Chitlada Shop, Chitlada Palace. Chitlada also has outlets at Oriental Plaza and the Hilton. Lao Song Handicrafts in the Wattana School compound, 69-71 Soi 19, Sukhumvit Rd, is another self-help project selling village handiwork.

Perhaps the most interesting places to shop for handicrafts are the smaller, independent handicraft shops – each of which has its own style and character. Quality is high and prices reasonable at Rasi Sayam (☎ 258-4195), 32 Soi 23, Sukhumvit Rd; many of the items they carry – including wall-hangings and pottery – are made specifically for this shop. Another good one for pottery as well as lacquerware and fabrics (especially the latter) is Vilai's (☎ 391-6106) at 731/1 Soi 55 (Thong Lor), Sukhumvit Rd. Nandakwang (☎ 258-1962), 108/3 Soi 23 (Soi Prasanmit) is a branch of a factory shop of the same name in Pasang, northern Thailand; high-quality woven cotton clothing and household wares (tablecloths, napkins, etc) are their speciality.

Khon (Thai classical dance-drama) masks of intricately formed wire and papier mache can be purchased at Padung Chiip (no English sign) on Chakraphong Rd just south of the Khao San Rd intersection. For Thai celadon, check Celadon House at 18/7 Soi 21 (Soi Asoke), Sukhumvit Rd. An inexpensive place to pick up new Thai pottery of all shapes and sizes is the Dutch-managed Waraporn Thai Pottery (☎ 375-7746), at 37/1 Sukhaphiban 2 Rd, Bang Kapi.

Getting There & Away

Air Bangkok is a major centre for international flights throughout Asia, and Bangkok's airport is a busy one. Bangkok is also a major centre for buying discounted airline tickets (see the Getting There & Away chapter for details), but be warned that the Bangkok travel agency business has more than a few crooked operators. Domestic flights operated by THAI and Bangkok Airways also fan out from Bangkok all over the country. Addresses of airlines offices in Bangkok are:

Aeroflot
: 183 Mezzanine Floor, Regent House, Ratchadamri Rd (☎ 251-1223; reservations 251-0617)

Air France
: Ground Floor, Chan Issara Tower, 942/51 Rama IV Rd (☎ 234-1330/9; reservations 234-9477)

Air India
Amarin Tower, Ploenchit Rd (☎ 256-9620; reservations 256-9614/8)
Air Lanka
Chan Issara Tower 942/34-5 Rama IV Rd (☎ 236-4981, 235-4982)
Air New Zealand
1053 Charoen Krung Rd (☎ 233-5900/9, 237-1560/2)
Alitalia
Boonmitr Bldg, 138 Silom Rd (☎ 233-4000/4)
All Nippon Airways
2nd Floor, CP Tower, 313 Silom Rd (☎ 238-5121)
Bangkok Airways
Sahakol Air Co, 144 Sukhumvit Rd (☎ 253-4014)
Biman Bangladesh
Chongkolnee Building, 56 Surawong Rd (☎ 235-7643/4, 234-0300/9)
British Airways
Chan Issara Tower, Rama IV Rd (☎ 236-8655/8)
Canadian Airlines International
518/5 Ploenchit Rd (251-4521, 254-8376)
Cathay Pacific Airways
Chan Issara Tower, Rama IV Rd (☎ 235-4330; reservations 233-6105/9)
China Airlines
Peninsula Plaza, Ratchadamri Rd (☎ 253-5733; reservations 253-4438)
China Southern Airlines (formerly CAAC)
134/1-2 Silom Rd (235-6510/1, 235-8159)
Czechoslovak Airlines
2nd Floor Regent House, Ratchadamri Rd (☎ 254-3921/5)
Delta Air Lines
7th Floor, Patpong Bldg, 1 Surawong Rd (☎ 237-6855; reservations 237-6838)
Druk Air (see Thai Airways International)
EgyptAir
3rd Floor, CP Tower, 313 Silom Rd (☎ 231-0505/8)
Finnair
Maneeya Bldg, 518/2 Ploenchit Rd (☎ 251-5445; reservations 251-5012)
Garuda Indonesia
944/19 Rama IV Rd (☎ 233-0981/2; reservations 233-3873)
Gulf Air
Maneeya Bldg, 518/2 Ploenchit Rd (☎ 254-7931/40)
Japan Airlines
33/33-4 Wall Street Tower, Surawong Rd (☎ 234-91111; reservations 233-2440)
KLM Royal Dutch Airlines
2 Patpong Rd (☎ 235-5150/4, 235-5155/9)
Korean Air
Kongboonma Bldg, 699 Silom Rd (☎ 234-0957; reservations 235-9221/6)
Kuwait Airways
159 Ratchadamri Rd (☎ 251-5855)
Lao Aviation
see Thai International Airways
LOT Polish Airlines
485/11-12 Silom Rd (☎ 235-3784/6)
Lufthansa
Bank of America Bldg, 2/2 Wireless Rd (☎ 255-0370)
Malaysian Airlines System
98-102 Surawong Rd (☎ 236-5871; reservations 236-4705/9)
Myanmar Airways
48/5 Pun Rd (☎ 233-3052)
Northwest Airlines
Silom Plaza, 491/39 Silom Rd (☎ 253-4822)
Landmark Plaza, 138 Sukhumvit Rd (253-4822/4423)
Peninsula Plaza, 153 Ratchadamri Rd (☎ 253-4822, 253-4423/5)
Pakistan International Airlines
52 Surawong Rd (☎ 234-2961)
Philippine Airlines
Chongkolnee Bldg, 56 Surawong Rd (☎ 233-2350/2)
Qantas
Chan Issara Tower, 942/51 Rama IV Rd (☎ 236-9193/5, 237-6268)
Royal Brunei Airlines
2nd Floor, Chan Issara Tower, 942/52 Rama IV Rd (☎ 235-4764)
Royal Jordanian Airline
Yada Bldg, 56 Silom Rd (☎ 236-0030)
Royal Nepal Airlines
1/4 Convent Rd (☎ 233-3921/4)
Sabena Belgian World Airlines
109 Surawong Rd (☎ 233-2020)
Scandinavian Airlines System (SAS)
412 Rama I Rd (☎ 252-4181; reservations 253-8333)
Saudi Arabian Airlines
Ground Floor, CCT Bldg, 109 Surawong Rd (☎ 236-9400/3)
Singapore Airlines
12th Floor, Silom Center Bldg, 2 Silom Rd (☎ 236-0303; reservations 236-0440)
Swissair
1 Silom Rd (☎ 233-2930/4; reservations 233-2935/8)
TAROM Romanian Air Transport
89/12 Bangkok Bazaar, Ratchadamri Rd (☎ 253-1681)
Thai Airways International (THAI; also agent for Druk Air, Lao Aviation)
89 Vibhavadi Rangsit Rd (☎ 513-0121; reservations 233-3810)
485 Silom Rd (☎ 234-3100/19)
6 Lan Luang Rd (☎ 288-0070/80/90)
Asia Hotel, 296 Phayathai Rd (☎ (02) 215-2020/4)

Tradewinds Singapore
12th Floor, Silom Centre Bldg, Silom Rd (☎ 236-0303)
Tropical Sea Air
382 Ratchadaphisek Rd (☎ 275-6262/65)
United Airlines
9th Floor, Regent House, 183 Ratchadamri Rd (☎ 253-0558)
Vietnam Airlines
3rd Floor, 572 Ploenchit Rd (☎ 251-4242)

Bus Bangkok is the centre for bus services that fan out all over the kingdom. There are basically three types of long-distance buses. First there are the ordinary public buses, then the air-con public buses. (For the north and eastern bus stations, ordinary and air-con buses leave from separate but adjacent Baw Khaw Saw terminals at each station; the southern station has its air-con and ordinary terminals in different locations.) The third choice is the many private air-con services which leave from various offices and hotels all over the city and provide a deluxe service for those people for whom simple air-con isn't enough!

Public Bus There are three main public bus stations. The northern/north-eastern terminal (☎ 279-4484/7) is on Phahonyothin Rd on the way up to the airport. It's also commonly called the Moh Chit station *(sathāanii māw chít)*. Buses depart here for north and north-eastern destinations like Chiang Mai and Khorat, as well as places closer to Bangkok such as Ayuthaya and Lopburi. Buses to Aranyaprathet also go from here, not from the eastern bus terminal as you might expect.

The eastern bus terminal (☎ 391-2504 ordinary; 391-9829 air-con), the departure point for buses to Pattaya, Rayong, Chanthaburi and other points east, is a long way out along Sukhumvit Rd, at Soi 40 (Soi Ekamai) opposite Soi 63. Most folks call it Ekamai station *(sathāanii èk-amai)*.

The southern bus terminal for buses south to Phuket, Surat Thani and closer centres like Nakhon Pathom and Kanchanaburi, has separate Thonburi locations for ordinary and air-con buses. The air-con terminal (☎ 411-4978/9) is on Charan Sanitwong Rd, near the Bangkok Noi (or Thonburi) railway station; the ordinary bus terminal (☎ 411-0061) has moved to the intersection of Highway 338 and Phra Pinklao Rd.

All stations have left-luggage facilities and small restaurants. When travelling on night buses take care of your belongings. Some of the long-distance buses leaving from Bangkok now issue claim checks for luggage stored under the bus, but valuables are still best kept on your person or within reach.

Private Bus The more reputable private tour buses leave from the public (Baw Khaw Saw) terminals listed above. Some private bus companies arrange pick-ups at Khao San Rd and other guesthouse areas – these pick-ups are illegal since it's against municipal law to carry passengers within the city limits except en route to or from an official terminal. This is why the curtains on these buses are sometimes closed when picking up passengers.

Although fares tend to be lower on private buses, the incidence of reported theft is far greater than on the Baw Khaw Saw buses.

See the Getting Around chapter for more information about bus travel in Thailand. Also, for details on bus fares to/from other towns and cities in Thailand, see the Getting There & Away sections under each place.

Train Bangkok is the terminus for rail services to the south, north and north-east. There are two main railway stations. The big Hualamphong station on Rama IV Rd handles services to the north, north-east and some of the southern services. The Thonburi (or Bangkok Noi) station handles many services to the south. If you're heading south, make certain you know which station your train departs from.

Getting Around

Getting around in Bangkok may be difficult at first for the uninitiated but once you're familiar with the bus system the whole city is accessible. The main obstacle is traffic, which moves at a snail's pace during the day. This means advance planning is a must when you are attending scheduled events or arranging appointments.

If you can travel by river or canal from one point to another, it's always the best choice. Bangkok was once called the 'Venice of the East', but much of the original canal system has been filled in for road construction; with 10% of Thailand's population living in the capital, water transportation, with a few exceptions, has been relegated to a secondary role. Larger canals, especially on the Thonburi side, remain important commercial arteries but many of the smaller canals are hopelessly polluted and would probably have been filled in by now if it weren't for their important drainage function.

Bus You can save a lot of money in Bangkok by sticking to the public buses, which are 3B for any journey under 10 km on the ordinary (non-air-con) blue buses, 2B on the red buses or 5B for the first eight km on the air-con lines. The fare on ordinary buses is 4B for longer trips (eg from Chulalongkorn University to King Mongkut's Institute of Technology in Thonburi on bus No 21) and as high as 15B for air-con buses (eg from Silom Rd to Bangkok Airport on air-con bus No 4). The air-con buses are not only cooler, but are usually less crowded (all bets are off during rush hours).

To do any serious bus riding you'll need a Bangkok bus map – the easiest to read is the *Latest Tour's Guide to Bangkok & Thailand* (put out by Suwannachai), or Thaveepholcharoen's *Bangkok Thailand Tour'n Guide Map*, both of which also have a decent country map of the whole country on the flip sides. The bus numbers are clearly marked in red, air-con buses in larger type. Don't expect the routes to be 100% correct, a few will have changed since the maps last came out, but they'll get you where you're going most of the time. These maps usually retail for 35B or sometimes 40B. A more complete 113-page *Bus Guide* is available in some bookshops and newsstands for 35B, but it's not as easy to use as the bus maps.

Be careful with your belongings while riding Bangkok buses. The place you are most likely to be 'touched' is on the crowded non-air-con buses. Razor artists abound, particularly on buses in the Hualamphong railway station area. These dexterous thieves specialise in slashing your backpack, shoulder bag or even your trousers' pockets with a sharp razor and slipping your valuables out unnoticed. Hold your bag in front of you, under your attention, and carry money in a front shirt pocket, preferably (as the Thais do) maintaining a tactile and visual sensitivity to these areas if the bus is packed shoulder to shoulder. Seasoned travellers don't need this advice as the same precautions are useful all over the world – the trick is to be relaxed but aware (not tense).

Taxi Taxis in Bangkok may have meters but the drivers do not use them. In this respect Bangkok is one of the last hold-outs in South-East Asia; Kuala Lumpur, Singapore and even Jakarta taxis now use meters, but not Bangkok. Thais say this is because both drivers and passengers distrust meters. At any rate, the fare must be decided before you get in the cab unless you really want to 'get taken for a ride'.

During 1991, Bangkok taxi fares rose 20 to 30% over the 1989-90 fares – way beyond the average rate of inflation for other goods and services. Fares to most places within central Bangkok are now 60 to 70B – add 10B or so if it's rush hour or after midnight. Short distances should be under 60B – Siam Square to Silom Rd, for example, should be 50B in relatively light traffic.

To get these fares you must bargain well. There is an over-supply of taxis in Bangkok so just wave a driver on if he won't meet a reasonable fare and flag down another cab. It gets easier with practice and better results are obtained if you speak some Thai. Petrol prices are high in Thailand and they are increasing. About 90% of Bangkok taxis have switched over from gasoline fuel to LP gas in recent years. Most cabs are now air-con, so fares continue to rise. If you are really counting baht, it's better to take a bus – save the taxi for when you're in a genuine hurry. During rush hours taxi drivers can be espe-

Future Traffic Alternatives

At times, the city's traffic situation seems quite hopeless. An estimated 2.3 million vehicles (a figure rising by 1100 per day) crawl through the streets at an average of four km per hour, and nearly half the municipal traffic police are undergoing treatment for respiratory ailments! Several mass transit systems (which are either in the planning or early construction phases) promise much-needed 'decongestion'.

The one most likely to be completed first is the Bangkok Metropolitan Authority's (BMA) light monorail system, which will begin with a six-km Victory Line running north-south through the city (paralleling Ratchaprarop, Ratchadamri and Sathon Tai Rds) and an 8.5-km Sukhumvit Line running east-west (parallel to Ploenchit and Sukhumvit Rds).

However, the system getting the most press these days is the Skytrain network, a more extensive elevated rail project that was proposed in 1986 but only recently assigned to Canada's Lavalin International. Initially, there will be two Skytrain lines, Phrakhanong-Bang Seu (23 km) and Sathon-Lat Phrao (11 km), with two more lines in each direction to follow. If Skytrain gets off the ground as planned, it won't be finished before 1998.

A third contract was recently awarded to Hong Kong developer Hopewell Holdings to construct 60 km of (mostly elevated) railway, and 48 km of highway. In addition, the BMA plans to add several other elevated expressways, including a Din Daeng-Don Muang toll-way system which will connect the airport with downtown Bangkok. The latter is expected to halve the current 30 to 60 minutes travel time between the airport and city.

The investments involved in these projects is enormous, but as current traffic congestion costs the nation over 13 billion baht per year in fuel bills, the potential savings far exceed the outlay. Cheaper alternatives which the government hasn't seriously considered include restricting the ownership of cars (effective in Tokyo), limiting driving frequency (as in Mexico City, where cars with odd-numbered plates are allowed on odd-numbered days, vice versa on even-numbered days) or prohibiting unstickered cars from entering the central business districts (as in Singapore). Ostensibly these latter methods wouldn't work in Bangkok where even enforcement of traffic lights, parking and one-way streets is shaky. ■

cially bad tempered (like everybody else on the road at that time). If they only had working meters, tempers would cool down, as they could relax and let the meter tick away.

At the end of 1991, Bangkok's Land Transport Department, which licenses all taxis, announced a plan to set up experimental taxi stands near shopping centres and major hotels. Supposedly taxis at these stands will be metered – but if the plan turns out anything like the system devised at the airport, drivers will find ways around it.

Tuk-Tuk These three-wheeled taxis, which sound like power saws gone berserk, are only good for very short distances. For longer runs, the fare may be more than the four-wheeled taxi, and there have been some instances of tuk-tuk drivers robbing their passengers at night. Bangkok residents often talk of the tuk-tuks as a nuisance, even a menace, to their already suffering environment. Some have even been trying to enact a ban on tuk-tuks. A few years ago the city supposedly forbade the further production of any new three-wheeled taxis, but every time I go to Bangkok I see hordes of brand new ones. It's a bit of a moral dilemma actually, since the tuk-tuk drivers are usually poor north-easterners who can't afford to rent the quieter, less polluting Japanese auto-taxis.

In heavy traffic, tuk-tuks are faster than taxis since they're able to weave in and out between cars and trucks. This is the main advantage to taking a tuk-tuk for short hops (besides the lower fare; say 40 to 50B against maybe 60 to 70B in a taxi). On the down side, tuk-tuks are not air-con, so you have to breathe all that lead-soaked air (at its thickest in the middle of Bangkok's wide avenues), and they're more dangerous since they easily flip when braking into a fast curve.

Finally, tuk-tuk drivers tend to speak less English than taxi drivers, so many new arrivals have a hard time communicating their destinations. Although some travellers have complained about tuk-tuk drivers deliberately taking them to the wrong destination (to collect commissions from certain restaurants or silk shops), others never seem to have a problem and swear by them.

Motorcycle Taxi As passengers become more desperate in their attempts to beat rush-hour gridlocks, motorcycle taxis have moved from the sois to the main avenues. Fares for a motorcycle taxi are about the same as tuk-tuks except during heavy traffic, when they may cost a bit more.

Riding on the back of a speeding motorcycle taxi is even more of a kamikaze experience than riding in a tuk-tuk. Keep your legs tucked in – the drivers are used to carrying passengers with shorter legs than the those of average farang and they pass perilously close to other vehicles while weaving in and out of traffic.

Boat Although Bangkok's canals (khlongs) are disappearing, there is still plenty of transport along and across the Chao Phraya River and up adjoining canals. River transport is one of the nicest ways of getting around Bangkok as well as, quite often, being much faster than any road-based alternatives. For a start you get a quite different view of the city; secondly, it's much less of a hassle than tangling with the polluted, noisy, traffic-crowded streets. (Just try getting from Banglamphu to the GPO as fast by road.)

Chao Phraya River Express The first step in using river transport successfully is to know your boats. The main ones you'll want to use are the rapid Chao Phraya Express boats *(reua dùan)*, a sort of river bus service. These cost 3, 5 or 7B (depending on the distance) and follow a regular route up and down the river (fares may increase by 1B in '92). They may not necessarily stop at each pier if there are no people waiting, or no-one wants to get off. You buy your tickets on the boat. Chao Phraya Express boats are big, long boats with numbers on their roofs.

Cross-River Ferry From the main Chao Phraya stops and also from almost every other jetty, there are slower cross-river ferries *(reua khâam fâak)* which simply shuttle back and forth across the river. The standard fares are either 50 satang or 1B and you usually pay this at the entrance to the jetty. Be careful, there will probably be a pay window at the jetty and also a straight-through aisle for people taking other boats.

Long-Tail Taxi Finally there are the long-tail boats *(reua hang yao)* which operate a share-taxi system off the main river and up the smaller khlongs. Fares usually start from around 4B – you've really got to know where you're going on these. There are also river taxis where you really do take the whole boat – you'll find them at certain jetties, like the Oriental Hotel, and you can charter them for trips to the floating market, or other attractions. Bargain hard.

A canal taxi service has recently been revived along Khlong Saen Saep, providing a quicker alternative to road transport between the river and eastern Bangkok (ie outer Sukhumvit and Bang Kapi). The boat from Banglamphu to the Ramkhamhaeng University area, for example, costs 10B and

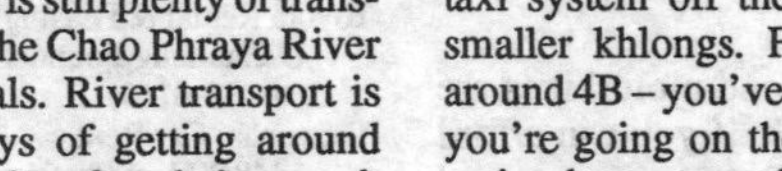

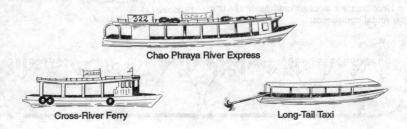

Chao Phraya River Express

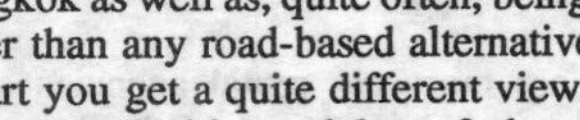
Cross-River Ferry

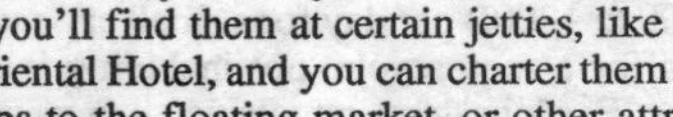
Long-Tail Taxi

takes only 40 minutes. A bus would take at least an hour under normal traffic conditions.

A handy little run along this route is by long-tail boat (5B) from the Siam Square area (from Tha Ratchathewi pier by the bridge next to the Asia Hotel) to the Banglamphu pier near Wat Saket and the Democracy Monument. Although the boats can be crowded, this service is generally much faster than either an auto taxi or bus.

Walking At first glance Bangkok doesn't seem like a great town for walking – its main avenues are so choked with traffic that the noise and thick air tend to drive one indoors. However, quiet spots where walks are rewarding – Lumphini Park, for example, or neighbourhoods off the main streets – do exist. And certain places are much more conveniently seen on foot, particularly the older sections of town along the Chao Phraya River where the roads are so narrow and twisting that bus lines don't go there.

Car & Motorbike Cars and motorbikes are easily rented in Bangkok, if you can afford to and have steel nerves. Rates start at around 1000 to 1200B per day for a small car, much less for a motorcycle, not including insurance. For long-term rentals you can usually arrange a discount of up to 35% off the daily rate. An International Driving Permit and passport are required for all rentals.

For long, cross-country trips, you might consider buying a new or used motorcycle and reselling it when you leave – this can end up being cheaper than renting, especially if you buy a good used bike. See the Getting Around chapter for more details.

Here are the names and addresses of a few car rental companies:

Avis Rent-a-Car
: 2/12 Wireless Rd (☎ 255-5300/4; fax 253-3734); branch offices at the Dusit Thani and Princess hotels

Central Car Rent
: 24 Soi Tonson, Ploenchit Rd (☎ 251-2778)

Grand Car Rent
: 144/3-4 Silom Rd (☎ 234-9956/6867)

Hertz
: 987 Ploenchit Rd (☎ 235-6251/4)
: 1620 New Phetburi Rd (☎ 251-7575)

Highway Car Rent
: 6/2 Rama IV Rd (☎ 235-7746/7, 235-5132)

Inter Car Rent
: 45 Sukhumvit Rd, near Soi 3 (☎ 252-9223)

Klong Toey Car Rent
: 1921 Rama IV Rd (☎ 250-1141/1361/1930)

Krung Thai Car Rent
: 233-5 Asoke-Din Daeng Rd (☎ 246-0089, 246-1525/7)

Petchburee Car Rent
: 23171 New Phetburi Rd (☎ 318-1753/1874)

PTC Tour & Transport
: 22 Soi Tonson, Ploenchit Rd (☎ 251-2356)

Royal Car Rent
: 67 Sathon Tai Rd (☎ 286-3636/6632)

Silver Rent-a-Car
: 402 Sukhumvit Rd (☎ 258-2018/2379)

Toyota Rental & Leasing
: U Chuliang Foundation Bldg, 968 Rama IV Rd (☎ 233-0169)

Thongchai Car Rent
: 1448/1 New Phetburi Rd (☎ 254-5700/1)

There are more car rental agencies along Wireless and New Phetburi Rds. Some also rent motorcycles, but you're better off renting or leasing a bike at a place that specialises in motorcycles. Here are four:

Chusak Yont Shop
: 1400 New Phetburi Rd (☎ 251-9225)

SSK Co
: 35/33 Ladprao Rd (☎ 514-1290)

Visit Laochaiwat
: 1 Soi Prommit, Suthisan Rd (☎ 278-1348)

Hurricane Ltd
: Klong Tan (☎ 314-6087)

Central Thailand

Officially speaking, central Thailand is made up of 25 provinces, stretching as far north as Nakhon Sawan, south to Prachuap Khiri Khan, west to Kanchanaburi and east to Trat. (For the purposes of this guidebook, the north-south boundaries will be narrowed slightly; Nakhon Sawan will be included in the Northern Thailand chapter, and Prachuap Khiri Khan in the Southern Thailand chapter.) Because of the rain-fed network of rivers and canals in the central region, this is the most fertile part of Thailand, supporting vast fields of rice, sugar cane, pineapples and other fruit, and cassava.

Linguistically, the people of central Thailand share a common dialect which is considered 'standard' Thai simply because Bangkok happens to be in the middle of it. High concentrations of Chinese are found throughout the central provinces since this is where a large number of Chinese immigrants started out as farmers and merchants. There are also significant numbers of Mon and Burmese to the west, and Lao and Khmer to the east, for obvious reasons.

Many places in central Thailand can be visited in day trips from Bangkok, but in most cases they make better stepping stones to places further afield. You can, for example, pause in Ayuthaya on the way north to Chiang Mai, or in Nakhon Pathom if you're heading south.

Ayuthaya Province

AYUTHAYA

พระนครศรีอยุธยา

Approximately 86 km north of Bangkok, Ayuthaya (population 60,000) was the Thai capital from 1350 to 1767 and by all accounts it was a splendid city. Prior to 1350, when the capital was moved here from U Thong, it was a Khmer outpost. The city was named after Ayodhya, the home of Rama in the Indian epic *Ramayana*, which is Sanskrit for 'unassailable' or 'undefeatable'. Its full Thai name is Phra Nakhon Si Ayuthaya (Sacred City of Ayodhya).

Thirty-three kings of various Siamese dynasties reigned in Ayuthaya until it was conquered by the Burmese. During its heyday, Thai culture and international commerce flourished in the kingdom – the Ayuthaya period has so far been the apex of Thai history – and Ayuthaya was courted by Dutch, Portuguese, French, English, Chinese and Japanese merchants. All visitors claimed it to be the most illustrious city they had ever seen.

Orientation & Information

The present-day city is located at the confluence of three rivers, the Chao Phraya, the Pa Sak and the smaller Lopburi. A wide canal joins them and makes a complete circle around the town. Long-tail boats can be rented from the boat landing across from Chandra Kasem (Chan Kasem) Palace for a tour around the river/canal; several of the old wat ruins (Wat Phanan Choeng, Wat Phutthaisawan, Wat Kasatthirat and Wat Chai Wattanaram) may be glimpsed from the canal, along with picturesque views of river life. Apart from the historic ruins and museums, Ayuthaya is not particularly inter-

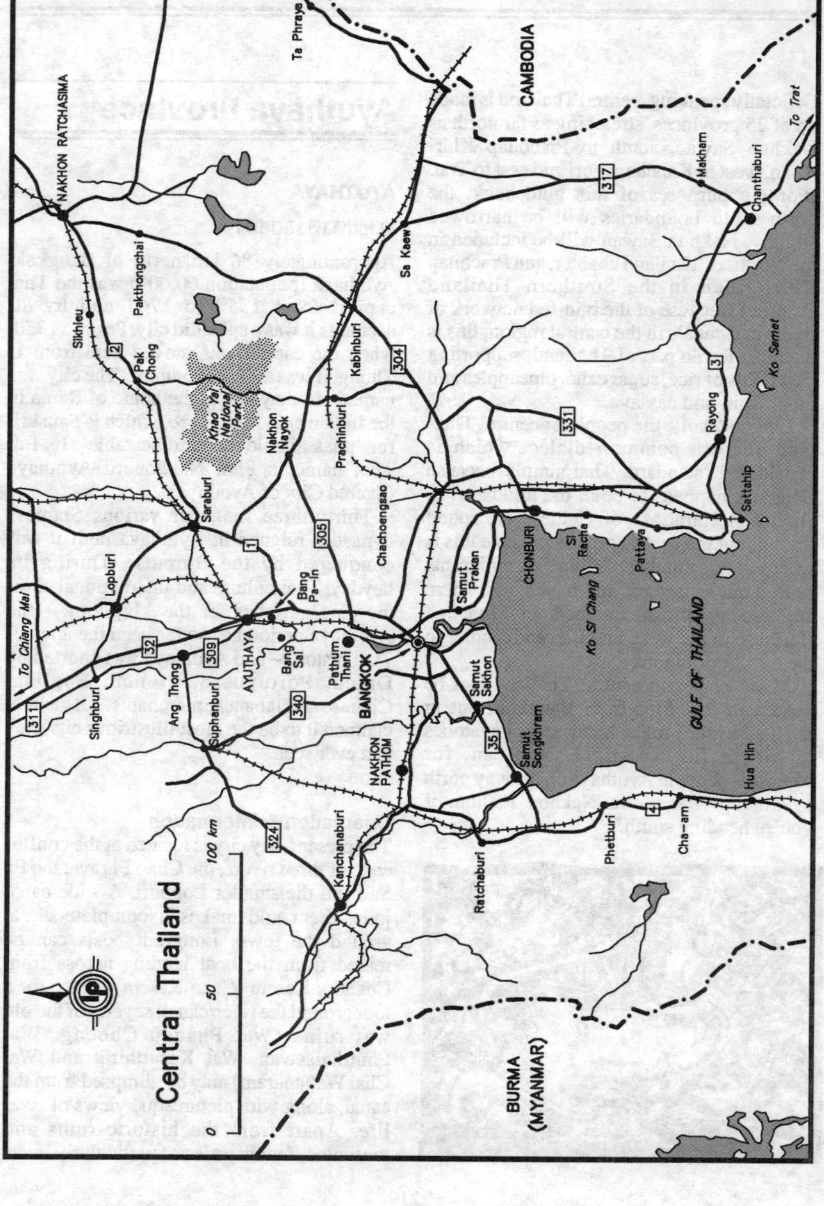
Central Thailand
0
50
100 km
NAKHON RATCHASIMA
Pakthongchai
Sikhleu
Pak Chong
Khao Yai National Park
Saraburi
Lopburi
To Chiang Mai
Singhburi
Ang Thong
AYUTHAYA
Bang Pa-In
Bang Sai
Pathum Thani
BANGKOK
Suphanburi
NAKHON PATHOM
Kanchanaburi
Ratchaburi
Phetburi
Cha-am
Hua Hin
Samut Songkhram
Samut Sakhon
Samut Prakan
Chachoengsao
CHONBURI
Si Racha
Ko Si Chang
Pattaya
Sattahip
Rayong
Ko Samet
Chanthaburi
Makham
To Trat
CAMBODIA
Sa Kaew
Kabinburi
Prachinburi
Nakhon Nayok
Ta Phraya
GULF OF THAILAND
BURMA (MYANMAR)
2
1
305
32
309
311
340
324
35
4
3
331
304
317

esting, but it is one of three cities in Thailand known for their 'gangster' activity.

Many of the ruins now collect a 10 to 20B admission fee during civil service hours (8 am to 4.30 pm). The ruins are most visited on weekends – visit during the week to avoid the crowds. TAT has plans to open a tourist information office in Ayuthaya by the end of 1992; the location is as yet unannounced but it will probably be placed at or near the Chan Kasem National Museum.

National Museum

พิพิธภัณฑ์แห่งชาติ

There are two museums, the main one being the **Chao Sam Phraya Museum**, which is near the intersection of Rotchana Rd (Ayuthaya's main street, connecting with the highway to Bangkok) and Si Sanphet Rd, near the centre of town. It's open from 9 am to noon and 1 to 4 pm, Wednesday to Sunday; entry is 10B.

The second, **Chan Kasem Palace** (Phra Ratchawong Chan Kasem), is a museum piece itself, built by the 17th king of Ayuthaya – Maha Thammarat – for his son Prince Naresuan. Among the exhibits here is a collection of gold treasures from Wat Phra Mahathat and Wat Ratburana. Chan Kasem Palace is in the north-east corner of town, near the river. Hours are the same as at the other museum. Pick up a good map/guide of Ayuthaya at the museum for 25B. Entry here is also 10B.

Ayuthaya Historical Study Centre

ศูนย์ศึกษาประวัติศาสตร์อยุธยา

Funded by the Japanese government, this US$6.8 million historical research institute was recently opened on seven rai near Wat Yai Chai Mongkhon, in a district that housed a Japanese community during Ayuthaya's heyday. The high-tech exhibit area, open to the public, covers five aspects of Ayuthaya's history: city development; port; administration; lifestyles and traditions; and foreign relations. The centre is on Rotchana Rd east of the railway station and is open Monday to Friday from 9 am to 3 pm, Saturday and Sunday from 9 am to 4.30 pm.

Temples & Ruins

Ayuthaya's historic temples are scattered throughout the city and along the encircling rivers. Several of the more central ruins – Wat Phra Si Sanphet, Wat Mongkhon Bophit, Wat Phra Ram, Wat Thammikarat, Wat Ratburana and Wat Mahathat – can easily be visited on foot if you avoid the hottest part of the day from 11 am to 4 pm. Or you could add more temples and ruins to your itinerary by touring the city on rented bicycle. An ideal transport combination for visitors who want to 'do it all' would be bicycle for the central temples, and chartered long-tail boat for the outlying ruins along the river. See the Getting Around section for details on different modes and rates of transport.

Wat Phra Si Sanphet This was the largest temple in Ayuthaya in its time, and was used as the royal temple/palace for several Ayuthaya kings. Built in the 14th century, the compound once contained a 16-metre standing Buddha covered with 250 kg of gold, which was melted down by the Burmese conquerors. It is mainly known for the chedis erected in the quintessential Ayuthaya style, which has come to be identified with Thai art more than any other single style. Admission is 20B.

Wat Mongkhon Bophit This monastery near Si Sanphet contains one of Thailand's largest Buddha images. The present wihaan (Buddhist image sanctuary) was built in 1956.

Wat Phra Mahathat This wat, at the corner of Chee Kun and Naresuan Rds, dates back to the 14th century and was built during the reign of King Ramesuan. Despite extensive damage – not much was left standing after the Burmese hordes – the prang (Khmer-style tower) is still impressive. Admission is 20B.

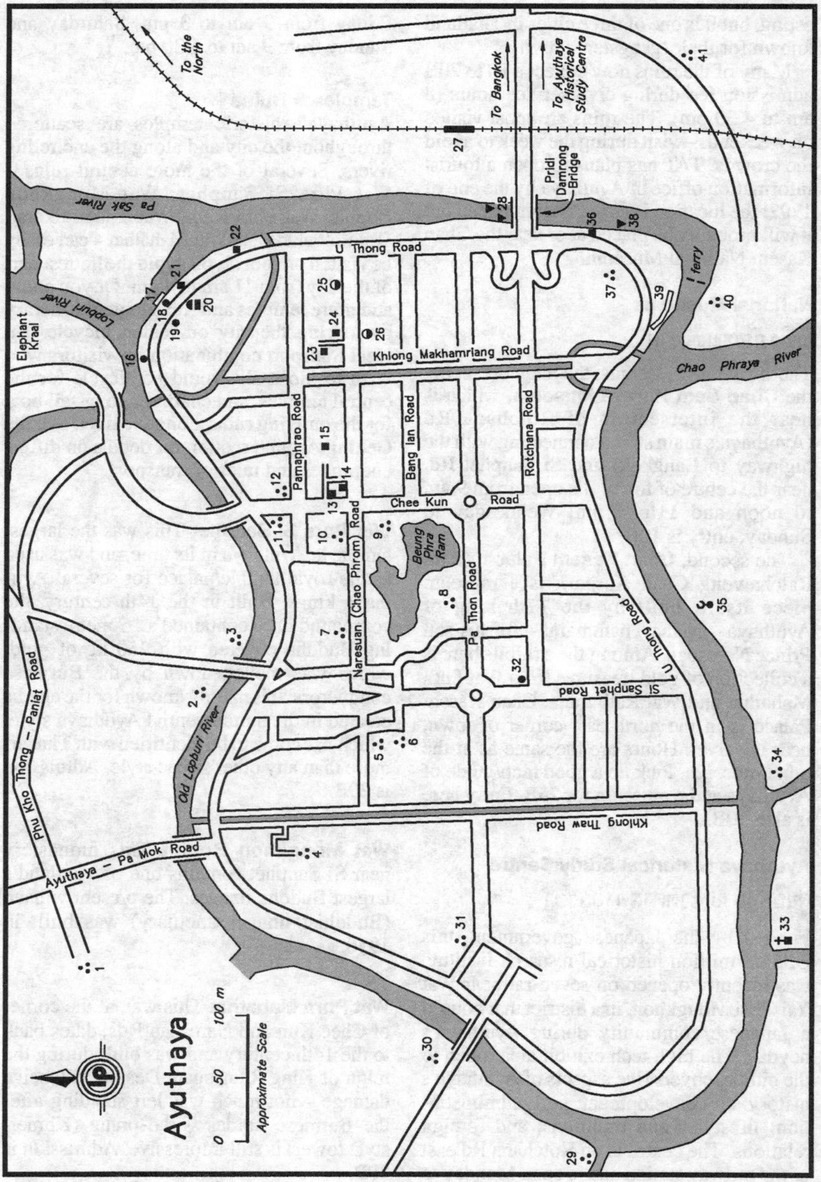
Ayuthaya
0
50
100 m
Approximate Scale
To the North
To Bangkok
To Ayuthaya Historical Study Centre
Pridi Damrong Bridge
Pa Sak River
U Thong Road
Lopburi River
Elephant Kraal
Khlong Makhamriang Road
Chao Phraya River
ferry
Pamaphrao Road
Bang Ian Road
Rotchana Road
Chee Kun Road
Naresuan (Chao Phrom) Road
Beung Phra Ram
Pa Thon Road
U Thong Road
Si Sanphet Road
Phu Kho Thong – Panlat Road
Old Lopburi River
Ayuthaya – Pa Mok Road
Khlong Thaw Road

■ PLACES TO STAY

13 Thongchai Guest House
14 New BJ Guest House
15 Thai Thai Hotel
21 U Thong Inn
22 Cathay Hotel
23 Ayuthaya & Old BJ Guest Houses
24 Si Samai Hotel
36 Pai Thong Guest House

OTHER

1 Phu Khao Thong Temple (Golden Mount Chedi)
2 Wat Na Phra Meru
3 Wat Kuti Thong
4 Wat Lokaya Sutha
5 Wat Phra Si Sanphet (Old Palace)
6 Wat Mongkhon Bophit
7 Wat Thammikarat
8 Wat Phra Ram
9 Wat Phra Mahatat
10 Wat Ratburana
11 Wat Suwannarat
12 Chinese Shrine
16 Hua Raw Market
17 Pier (Boat Landing)
18 Night Market
19 Chan Kasem Palace
20 Post Office
25 Air-con minivans to Bangkok
26 Bus Terminal
27 Railway Station
28 Floating Restaurants
29 Wat Chai Wattanaram
30 Wat Kasatthirat
31 Queen Suriyothai Memorial Pagoda
32 Chao Sam Phraya Museum
33 St Joseph's Cathedral
34 Wat Phutthaisawan
35 Mosque
37 Wat Suwan Dararam
38 Phae Krung Kao
39 Phet Fortress
40 Wat Phanan Choeng
41 Wat Yai Chai Mongkhon

Wat Ratburana The Ratburana ruins are the counterpart to Mahathat across the road; the chedis, however, contain murals and are not quite as dilapidated. Admission is 20B.

Wat Thammikarat To the east of the old palace grounds, inside the river loop, Thammikarat features overgrown chedi ruins and lion sculptures.

Wat Phra Chao Phanan Choeng South-east of town on the Chao Phraya River, this wat was built before Ayuthaya became a Siamese capital. It's not known who built the temple, but it appears to have been constructed in the early 14th century so it's possibly Khmer. The main wihaan contains a highly revered 19-metre sitting Buddha image from which the wat derives its name.

The easiest way to get to Wat Phanan Choeng is by ferry from the pier near Phom Phet fortress, inside the south-east corner of the city centre. For a few extra baht you can take a bicycle with you on the boat.

Wat Na Phra Meru (Phra Mehn/Mane) Across from the old royal palace *(wang lũang)* grounds is a bridge which can be crossed to arrive at Wat Phra Meru. This temple is notable because it escaped destruction in 1767, though it has required restoration over the years. The main bot was built in 1546 and features fortress-like walls and pillars. During the 18th-century Burmese invasion, Burma's Chao Along Phaya chose this site from which to fire cannon at the palace; the cannon exploded and the king was fatally injured, thus ending the sacking of Ayuthaya.

The bot interior contains an impressive carved wooden ceiling and a splendid Ayuthaya-era crowned sitting Buddha, six metres high. Inside a smaller wihaan behind the bot is a green-stone, European-pose (sitting in a chair) Buddha from Ceylon, said to be 1300 years old. The walls of the wihaan show traces of 18th or 19th century murals.

Admission to Wat Phra Meru is 10B.

Wat Yai Chai Mongkhon Wat Yai, as the

locals call it, is south-east of the town proper, but can be reached by minibus for 3 to 4B. It's a quiet old place that was once a famous meditation wat, built in 1357 by King U Thong. The compound contains a very large chedi from which the wat takes its popular name (*yài* means big), and there is a community of *mâe chii*, or Buddhist nuns, residing here. Admission is 10B.

Other Temples Just north of Wat Ratburana, opposite a colourful Chinese shrine, are the smaller ruins of **Wat Suwannarat**. The 400-year-old brick remains of eight chedis, a bot and a wihaan are arranged in a circle, a typical early Ayuthaya layout.

A short boat ride north along the Lopburi River will bring you to modern **Wat Pa Doh**. In front of the bot, a unique Sukhothai-style walking Buddha image strides over a narrow arch, symbolising the crossing from samsara to nirvana.

Festivals

Ayuthaya holds one of the country's largest Loi Krathong festivals on the full moon of the 12th lunar month (usually November). Celebrations are held at several spots in the city; the largest spectacle takes place at **Beung Phra Ram**, the large lake in the centre of city between Wat Phra Ram and Wat Mahathat. Thousands of Thais, many of them from Bangkok, flock to the Beung Phra Ram event to crowd around four or five different outdoor stages offering li-khe, Thai pop, cinema and lakhon chatrii – all at the same time (the din can be deafening)! Fireworks are a big part of the show, and there are lots of food vendors on the site.

More low-key and traditional is the celebration at the **Chan Kasem pier**, where families launch their *krathongs* (small lotus-shaped floats topped with incense and candles) onto the Lopburi-Pa Sak river junction. Although kids throw fireworks here, the overall atmosphere is much closer to the heart of Loi Krathong than at Beung Phra Ram. Krathongs can be purchased at the pier (or you can make your own from materials for sale); for a few baht you can board one of the many waiting canoes at the pier and be paddled out to launch your krathong in the middle of the river. Thai tradition says that any couple who launch a krathong together are destined to be lovers – if not in this lifetime then the next.

Another large Loi Krathong Festival takes place at the **Royal Folk Arts & Crafts Centre** in Bang Sai, about 24 km west of Ayuthaya. At this one the emphasis is on traditional costumes and handmade krathongs. If you can put together a small group, any of the hotels or guesthouses in Ayuthaya can arrange a trip to the Bang Sai Loi Krathong for around 200B or less per person.

During the 10 days leading to the Songkran Festival, in mid-April, there is a sound & light show with fireworks over the ruins. Every day between 10.30 am and 1.30 pm the local government runs boat tours from the U Thong pier for 50B per person.

Places to Stay

Guesthouses For budgeteers, there are five guesthouses in Ayuthaya to choose from. Four of them are located on or off Naresuan Rd, not far from the bus terminal. As elsewhere in Thailand, tuk-tuk and samlor drivers will tell you anything to steer you toward guesthouses that pay commissions (up to 35B per head in this city).

The original BJ Guest House, near the end of a soi off Naresuan Rd (not far from the Si Samai Hotel), has changed its name to *Ayuthaya Guest House* (☎ 251468) but is much the same at 60/80B for singles/doubles in an old house. Next door a branch of the same family runs the *Old BJ Guest House* (☎ 251526) at the same rates. Both offer food service and bike rentals (30B a day).

Yet another BJ relative has opened the *New BJ Guest House* (☎ 251512) at 19/29 Naresuan Rd. Rooms cost 60 to 100B and there's a nice eating area in front. One drawback is that it's right on Naresuan Rd, a main Ayuthaya thoroughfare, so traffic noise may be distracting. Another new place is *Thongchai Guest House* (☎ 252083), on a back road parallel to Naresuan Rd and off

Chee Kun Rd. A choice of rooms is available in bungalows or in a row house for 120B without bath, 200B with fan and bath, or 350B for air-con and bath. This might be better value than either of the Ayuthaya hotels in the same price range (ie U Thong or Cathay).

The bottom of the barrel is *Pai Thong Guest House* (☎ 241830), which is right on the river within walking distance of the railway station but otherwise has little to recommend it. The dog that lives here can be ferocious and has reportedly bitten several guests. Large but very basic rooms are 60B.

Hotels The *Thai Thai* (☎ 251505), at 13/1 Naresuan Rd, set well off the road between the bus terminal and the road to Wat Phra Meru, has large, clean rooms from 120 to 230B with air-con. The *Cathay Hotel* (☎ 251562), near the U Thong towards Hua Raw Market, is 120B for a room with fan, 220B with air-con. 'Clean and friendly,' wrote one traveller, 'they lent us money and refused offers of passports as guarantee'.

Si Samai Hotel (☎ 251104), 12/19 Naresuan Rd, is near the Thai Thai and costs 300B for rooms with fan and bath, 400B with air-con. The *U Thong Hotel* (☎ 251136), on U Thong Rd near Chan Kasem Palace, is similar to the Cathay, with adequate fan rooms for 150B, air-con for 300B.

The top place in town for the moment is *U-Thong Inn* (☎ 242618), where fan rooms start at 180B, air-con rooms go to 480B. It's out on Rotchana Rd past the turn-off for the railway station. An all-new *Holiday Inn* is being built north of the city on the Lopburi River, to open in late '92. Room rates will probably start at around 1500B. Call Holiday Inn's Bangkok office (☎ 539-5153) for the latest information.

Places to Eat

The most dependable and least expensive places to eat are the Hua Raw market, on the river near Chan Kasem Palace, and the Chao Phrom market, on Chao Phrom Rd east of Wat Ratburana. The *Chainam* opposite Chan Kasem Palace next to the Cathay Hotel has tables on the river, a bilingual menu and friendly service; it's also open for breakfast. For something a little fancier, try the air-con *Rodeo Saloon* on U Thong Rd. Despite the name and 'old-west' decor, the food is mostly Thai (English menu available); at night a small band plays Thai and international folk music.

Quite a few restaurants can be found on the main road into Ayuthaya, Rotchana Rd, and there are two floating restaurants on the Pa Sak River, one on either side of the Pridi Damrong Bridge on the west bank, and one on the east bank north of the bridge. Of these, the *Phae Krung Kao* – on the south side of the bridge on the west bank – has the better reputation.

In the evenings a very good night market comes to life near the pier opposite Chan Kasem Palace.

Getting There & Away

Bus Daily buses leave from the northern bus terminal in Bangkok every 10 minutes between 5 am and 7 pm. The fare is 17B and the trip takes around two hours.

Train Trains to Ayuthaya leave Bangkok's Hualamphong station every hour or so between 4.30 am and 10 pm. The 3rd-class fare is 15B for the 1½-hour trip (plus rapid/express charges if it's not an ordinary train); it's hardly worth taking a more expensive seat for this short trip. Train schedules are available from the information booth at Hualamphong station.

Boat There are no longer any scheduled boat services between Bangkok and Ayuthaya. You can charter a boat from Ayuthaya to Bang Pa In for around 300 to 400B, but buses are much faster and nearly 40 times cheaper.

The Oriental and Shangri-La hotels in Bangkok operate luxury cruises to Bang Pa In with side trips by bus to Ayuthaya for around 800 to 1000B per person, including a lavish luncheon. (See the Bangkok River & Canal Trips section for more details.)

Getting Around

Songthaews ply the main city roads for 2B per person. A tuk-tuk from the railway station to any point in Ayuthaya should be around 30B. You can hire a samlor, tuk-tuk or songthaew by the hour or by the day to explore the ruins but the prices are quite high by Thai standards (300B a day for anything with a motor in it). It's better to hire a bicycle or walk.

It's also interesting to hire a boat from the palace pier to do a circular tour of the island and see some of the less accessible ruins. A long-tail boat that will take up to eight people can be hired for 300B for a three-hour trip with stops at Wat Phutthaisawan, Wat Phanan Choeng and Wat Chai Wattanaram.

BANG PA IN

บางปะอิน

Twenty km south of Ayuthaya is Bang Pa In, which has a curious collection of palace buildings in a wide variety of architectural styles. It's a nice boat trip from Ayuthaya, although in itself it's not particularly noteworthy. The palace is open from 8.30 am to noon and 1 to 3 pm daily. Admission is 30B.

Palace Buildings

The postcard stereotype here is a pretty little Thai pavilion in the centre of a small lake by the palace entrance. Inside the palace grounds, the Chinese-style **Wehat Chamrun Palace** is the only building open to visitors. The **Withun Thatsana** building looks like a lighthouse with balconies. It was built to give a fine view over gardens and lakes. There are various other buildings, towers and memorials in the grounds plus an interesting example of topiary where the bushes have been trimmed into the shape of a small herd of elephants.

Wat Niwet Thamaprawat

วัดนิเวศน์ธรรมประวัติ

Across the river and south from the palace grounds, this unusual wat looks much more like a gothic Christian church than anything from Thailand. It was built by Rama V (Chulalongkorn). You get to the wat by crossing the river in a small trolley-like cable car. The crossing is free.

Getting There & Away

Bang Pa In can be reached by minibus (really a large songthaew truck rather than a bus) from Ayuthaya's Chao Phrom Market, Chao Phrom Rd, for 6B. From Bangkok there are buses every half hour or so from the northern bus terminal and the fare is 14B. You can also reach Bang Pa In by train or boat from Bangkok, or by boat from Ayuthaya.

The Chao Phraya River Express Boat Company does a tour every Sunday from the Maharat pier in Bangkok that goes to Wat Phailom in Pathum Thani (November to June) or Wat Chaloem Phrakiat (July to October) as well as Bang Pa In and Bang Sai's Royal Folk Arts & Crafts Centre. The trip leaves from Bangkok at 8 am and returns at 5.30 pm. The price is 180B not including lunch, which you arrange on your own in Bang Pa In.

Lopburi Province

LOPBURI

อ.เมืองลพบุรี

Exactly 154 km north of Bangkok, the town of Lopburi (population 39,000) has been inhabited since at least the Dvaravati period (6th to 11th centuries AD) when it was called Lavo. Nearly all traces of Lavo culture have been erased by Khmer and Thai inhabitants since the 10th century, but many Dvaravati artefacts found in Lopburi can be seen in the Lopburi National Museum. Ruins and statuary in Lopburi span 12 centuries.

The Khmers extended their Angkor empire in the 10th century to include Lavo. It was during this century that they built the Prang Khaek (Hindu Shrine), San Phra Kan (Kala Shrine) and Prang Sam Yot (Three-Spired Shrine) as well as the impressive prang at Wat Phra Sri Ratana Mahathat.

Power over Lopburi was wrested from the Khmers in the 13th century as the Sukhothai

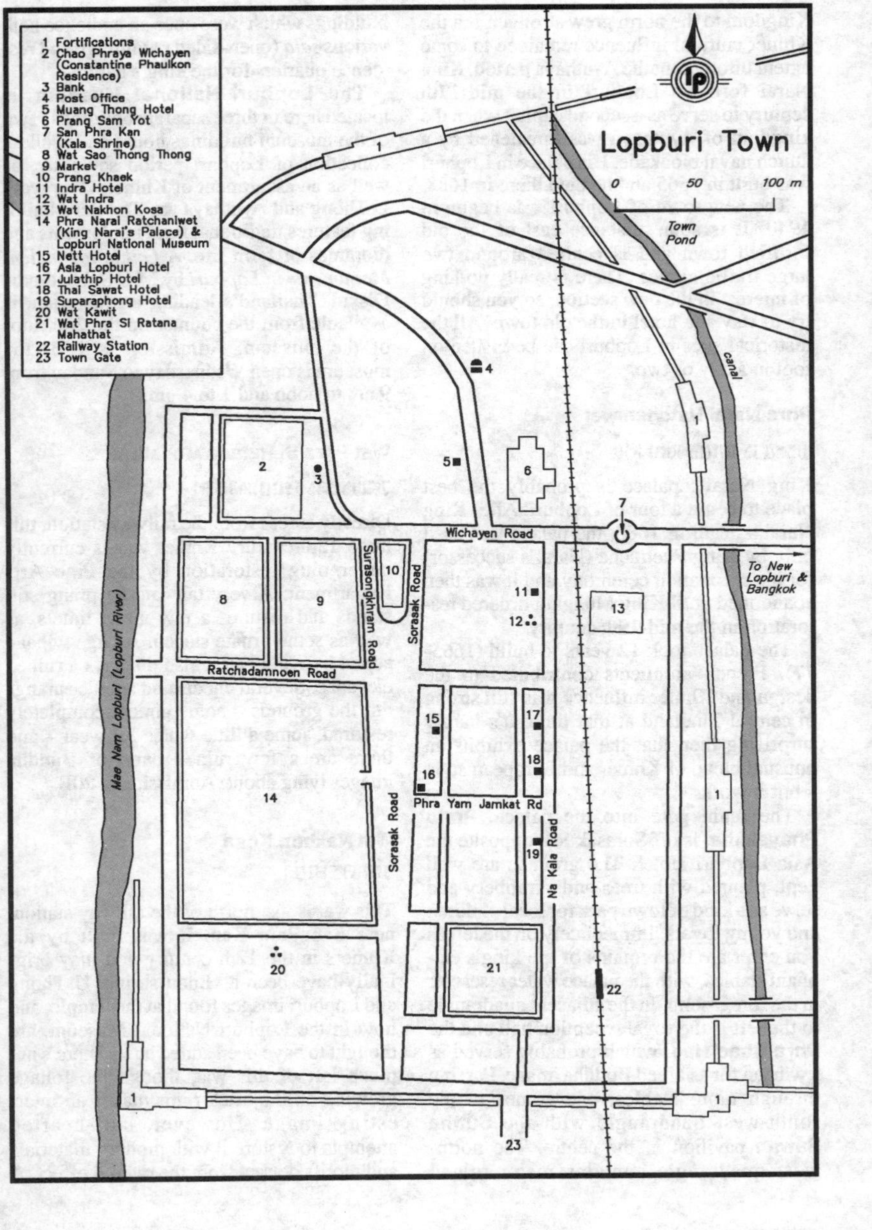
1 Fortifications
2 Chao Phraya Wichayen (Constantine Phaulkon Residence)
3 Bank
4 Post Office
5 Muang Thong Hotel
6 Prang Sam Yot
7 San Phra Kan (Kala Shrine)
8 Wat Sao Thong Thong
9 Market
10 Prang Khaek
11 Indra Hotel
12 Wat Indra
13 Wat Nakhon Kosa
14 Phra Narai Ratchaniwet (King Narai's Palace) & Lopburi National Museum
15 Nett Hotel
16 Asia Lopburi Hotel
17 Julathip Hotel
18 Thai Sawat Hotel
19 Suparaphong Hotel
20 Wat Kawit
21 Wat Phra Si Ratana Mahathat
22 Railway Station
23 Town Gate
Lopburi Town
0 50 100 m
Town Pond
canal
Wichayen Road
To New Lopburi & Bangkok
Surasongkhram Road
Sorasak Road
Ratchadamnoen Road
Phra Yam Jamkat Rd
Na Kala Road
Mae Nam Lopburi (Lopburi River)

Kingdom to the north grew stronger, but the Khmer cultural influence remained to some extent throughout the Ayuthaya period. King Narai fortified Lopburi in the mid-17th century to serve as a second capital when the kingdom of Ayuthaya was threatened by a Dutch naval blockade. His palace in Lopburi was built in 1665 and he died there in 1688.

The new town of Lopburi was begun in 1940. It is some distance east of the old fortified town and is centred around two large traffic circles. There is really nothing of interest in the new section, so you should try to stay at a hotel in the old town. All the historical sites in Lopburi can be visited on foot in a day or two.

Phra Narai Ratchaniwet
พระนารายณ์ราชนิเวศน์

King Narai's palace is probably the best place to begin a tour of Lopburi. After King Narai's death in 1688, the palace was used only by King Phetracha (Narai's successor) for his coronation ceremony and it was then abandoned until King Mongkut ordered restoration in the mid-19th century.

The palace took 12 years to build (1665-77). French architects contributed to the design and Khmer influence was still strong in central Thailand at that time. It's hardly surprising then that the palace exhibits an unusual blend of Khmer and European style – but it works.

The main gate into the palace, **Pratu Phayakkha**, is off Sorasak Rd, opposite the Asia Lopburi Hotel. The grounds are well kept, planted with trees and shrubbery and serve as a kind of town park for local children and young lovers. Immediately on the left as you enter are the remains of the king's elephant stables, with the palace water reservoir in the foreground. In the adjacent quadrangle to the left is the royal reception hall and the **Phra Chao Hao**, which probably served as a wihaan for a valued Buddha image. Passing through more stables, one comes to the south-west quadrangle with the **Suttha Sawan** pavilion in the centre. The north-west quadrangle contains many ruined buildings which were once an audience hall, various *sala* (open-sided pavilions), and residence quarters for the king's harem.

The **Lopburi National Museum** is located here in three separate buildings. Two of the museum buildings house an excellent collection of Lopburi period sculpture, as well as an assortment of Khmer, Dvaravati, U Thong and Ayuthaya art. The third building features traditional farm implements and dioramas of farm life. *A Guide to Ancient Monuments in Lopburi* by M C Subhadradis Diskul, Thailand's leading art historian, is available from the counter on the 2nd floor of the museum. Admission is 10B; the museum is open Wednesday to Sunday from 9 am to noon and 1 to 4 pm.

Wat Phra Si Ratana Mahathat
วัดพระศรีรัตนมหาธาตุ

Directly across from the railway station, this large 12th-century Khmer wat is currently undergoing restoration by the Fine Arts Department. A very tall laterite prang still stands and features a few intact lintels, as well as some ornate stucco. A large wihaan added by King Narai also displays a ruined elegance. Several chedis and smaller prangs dot the grounds – some almost completely restored, some a little worse for wear – and there are a few ruined parts of Buddha images lying about. Admission is 20B.

Wat Nakhon Kosa
วัดนครโกษา

This wat is just north of the railway station, near San Phra Kan. It was built by the Khmers in the 12th century and may originally have been a Hindu shrine. U Thong and Lopburi images found at the temple, and now in the Lopburi National Museum, are thought to have been added later. There's not much left of this wat, though the foliage growing on the brick ruins makes an interesting image. However, half-hearted attempts to restore it with modern materials and motifs detract from the overall effect. A recent excavation has uncovered a larger base below the monument.

Wat Indra & Wat Racha

วัดอินทราและวัดราชา

Wat Indra is across the street from Wat Nakhon Kosa. Practically nothing is known of its history and it's now merely a pile of brick rubble. Wat Racha, off Phra Yam Jamkat Rd, is another pile of bricks with little known history.

Wat Sao Thong Thong

วัดเสาธงทอง

This wat is north-west of the palace centre, behind the central market. The buildings here are in pretty poor shape. The wihaan and large seated Buddha are from the Ayuthaya period; King Narai restored the wihaan (changing its windows to an incongruous but intriguing Gothic style) so the wihaan could be used as a Christian chapel. Niches along the inside walls contain Lopburi-style *naga* Buddhas.

Chao Phraya Wichayen (Constantine Phaulkon Residence)

บ้านวิชาเยนทร์

King Narai built this eclectic Thai-European palace as a residence for foreign ambassadors, of whom the Greek Constantine Phaulkon was the most famous. Phaulkon became one of King Narai's principal advisers and was eventually a royal minister. In 1688, as Narai lay dying, Phaulkon was assassinated by Luang Sorasak, who wanted all the power of Narai's throne for himself. The palace is across the street and north-east of Wat Sao Thong Thong; admission is 20B.

San Phra Kan (Kala Shrine)

ศาลพระกาฬ

Across the railway tracks to the north of Wat Nakhon Kosa, this unimpressive shrine contains a crude gold-leaf-laden image of Kala, the Hindu god of time and death. A virtual sea of monkeys surrounds the shrine, falling out of the tamarind trees and scurrying along the steps leading to the sanctuary. They are getting fat on hand-outs.

Prang Sam Yot

ปรางค์สามยอด

Opposite the Kala Shrine, near the Muang Thong Hotel, this shrine represents classic Khmer-Lopburi style and is another Hindu-turned-Buddhist temple. Originally, the three prangs symbolised the Hindu *trimurti* of Shiva, Vishnu and Brahma. Now two of them contain ruined Lopburi-style Buddha images. Some Khmer lintels can still be made out, and some appear unfinished.

A rather uninteresting U Thong-Ayuthaya imitation Buddha image sits in the brick sanctuary in front of the linked prangs. At the back, facing the Muang Thong Hotel, are a couple of crudely restored images, probably once Lopburi style. The grounds allotted to Prang Sam Yot by the town are rather small and make the structure difficult to photograph. The grounds are virtually surrounded by modern buildings as well. The best view of the monument would probably be from one of the upper floors of the Muang Thong. The monument is lit up at night.

Activities

For those interested in Thai classical music and dance, the **Lopburi Fine Arts College** (Withayalai Kalasilpa Lopburi) is on Phra Yam Jamkat Rd, not far from the palace. Here you can watch young dancers practising the rudiments of classical dance with live musical accompaniment.

You can also pay a visit to the **Travellers Drop in Centre** at 34 Wichayen Rd, Soi 3 Muang, which is part of the Australian Education Placement Centre, an institute for teaching English. Here travellers can meet Thais at the informal English classes held here three times daily. After the class, the students go with travellers and share a meal in a restaurant.

Places to Stay

Lopburi can be visited as a day trip en route to the north, but if you want to stay overnight there are a number of hotels you can try. *Asia Lopburi Hotel* (☎ 411892), on the corner of Sorasak and Phra Yam Jamkat Rds and overlooking King Narai's palace, is clean and comfortable with good service. It has two Chinese restaurants. Rooms are 120B with fan and bath, or up to 280B with air-con.

Muang Thong Hotel (☎ 411036), across from Prang Sam Yot, has noisy but adequate rooms for 100B with fan and bath. Rooms without bath are also available for 80B, or air-con rooms for 200B.

The *Indra* on Na Kala Rd is across from Wat Nakhon Kosa and costs 70B for just-passable rooms with fan and bath. Also on Na Kala Rd, the *Julathip Hotel* is near the Indra but closer to the railway station, and has no English sign. This one is also 70B with fan and bath , but ask to see a room first.

The *Suparaphong Hotel*, also on Na Kala Rd, is not far from Wat Phra Si Ratana Mahathat and the railway station. Rooms at the Suparaphong cost 70B, and are much the same as at the Julathip and Indra hotels.

A few shops from Julathip on the same street is the *Thai Sawat* which, at 60B per room, is Lopburi's cheapest and grungiest.

The *Nett Hotel* (☎ 411738) at 17/1-2 Ratchadamnoen Rd is actually on a soi between Ratchadamnoen and Phra Yam Jamkat Rds, parallel to Sorasak Rd. Clean, quiet rooms with fan and bath cost from 90B.

The *Travellers Drop in Centre* at 34 Wichayen Rd, Soi 3 Muang, also runs a small guesthouse for travellers – there are two double rooms; the cost is 60B for one person or 70 to 80B for two.

Behind the bus station in the new part of town is the *Srisawat*. Rooms here are grubby and cost 90B, but the Chinese owners are friendly. However, it's not recommended unless you have to be in the new town or arrive late at night by bus.

There are so many hotels along Na Kala Rd that bargaining should be possible. Ask if they have a cheaper room: *Mii hâwng tùuk kwàa mãi?*

Places to Eat

Several Chinese restaurants operate along Na Kala Rd, parallel to the railway, especially near the Julathip and Thai Sawat hotels. The food is good but a bit overpriced. Restaurants on the side streets of Ratchadamnoen and Phra Yam Jamkat Rds can be better value. The Chinese-Thai restaurant next to the Asia Lopburi Hotel on Sorasak Rd, across from the main gate to King Narai's palace, makes excellent tôm yam kûng (shrimp and lemon grass soup), kài phàt bai kaphrao (chicken fried in holy basil) and kũaytĩaw râat nâa (fried rice noodles with vegetables and sauce). There are also plenty of cheap curry vendors down the alleys and along the smaller streets in old Lopburi.

The market off Ratchadamnoen and Surasongkhram Rds (just north of the palace) is a great place to pick up food to eat in your hotel room – kài thâwt or kài yâang (fried or roast chicken) with sticky rice, hàw mòk (fish and coconut curry steamed in banana leaves), klûay khàek (Indian-style fried bananas), a wide selection of fruits, satay, khâo krìap (crispy rice cakes), thâwt man plaa (fried fish cakes) and other delights. At 26/47 Soonkangkha Manora, near the Australian Education Placement Centre, is a *Sala Mangsawirat* (Vegetarian Pavilion) with inexpensive Thai veggie food; like most Thai vegetarian restaurants, it's only open from around 10 am to 2 pm.

Getting There & Away

Bus Buses leave for Lopburi every 10 minutes from Ayuthaya, or, if you're coming from Bangkok, about every 20 minutes (5.30 am to 8.30 pm) from the northern terminal. It's a three-hour ride which costs 32B (60B air-con).

Lopburi can also be reached from the west via Kanchanaburi or Suphanburi. If you're coming from Kanchanaburi, you'll have to take a bus first to Suphanburi. The trip lasts two hours, costs 21B, and there's great scenery all the way. In Suphanburi, get off the bus along the town's main street, Malimaen Rd (it has English signs), at the intersection which has an English sign pointing to Sri Prachan. This is also where you catch the bus to Singhburi or Ang Thong, across the river from Lopburi, and a necessary stop.

The Suphanburi to Singhburi leg lasts about 2½ hours for 20B and the scenery gets even better – you'll pass many old, traditional Thai wooden houses (late Ayuthaya style), countless cool rice paddies and small wats of all descriptions. Finally, at the Singhburi bus station, catch one of the frequent buses to Lopburi for 7B (30 minutes). An alternative to the Suphanburi to Singhburi route is to take a bus to Ang Thong (10B) and then a share taxi (15B) or bus (13B) to Lopburi. This is a little faster but not quite as scenic.

From the north-east, Lopburi can be reached via Khorat for 40B.

Train Ordinary trains depart Bangkok's Hualamphong station, heading north, every hour or so between 4.20 am and 8 pm and take only 20 to 30 minutes longer to reach Lopburi than the rapid or express. Only two ordinary trains, the 7.05 am and the 8.30 am, have 2nd-class seats; the rest are 3rd class only. Rapid trains leave at 6.40 am, 3, 8 and 10 pm and take about 2½ hours to reach Lopburi. Only the special express train, which leaves Bangkok every day at 7.40 pm, has 1st-class seats. Fares are 111B in 1st class, 57B in 2nd class and 28B in 3rd, not including surcharges for rapid or express trains.

There are also regular trains from Ayuthaya to Lopburi which take about one hour and cost 13B in 3rd class. It is possible to leave Bangkok or Ayuthaya in the morning, have a look around Lopburi during the day (leaving your bags in the Lopburi railway station) and then carry on to Chiang Mai on one of the night trains (departure times are at 5.27, 8.20 pm and 12.22 am).

Getting Around

Samlors will go anywhere in Lopburi for 10B.

Ang Thong & Saraburi Provinces

ANG THONG

อ.เมืองอ่างทอง

There are some places of interest outside small Ang Thong (population 10,000), between Lopburi and Suphanburi, including **Wat Pa Mok** with its 22-metre-long reclining Buddha. The village of **Ban Phae** is famous for the crafting of Thai drums or *klawng*. Ban Phae is behind the Pa Mok Market on the banks for the Chao Phraya River.

Places to Stay

Rooms cost from 80B in the *Bua Luang* (☎ 611116) on Ayuthaya Rd. The *Ang Thong Hotel & Bungalows* (☎ 611767/8) at 19 Ang Thong Rd is 90B up in the hotel, 100B in the bungalows.

Getting There & Away

A bus from the northern bus terminal in Bangkok costs 25B.

SARABURI & AROUND

อ.เมืองสระบุรี

There's nothing of interest in Saraburi (population 56,000), but between Lopburi and here you can turn off to **Phra Buddhabat** (Phra Phutthabaht). This small and delicately beautiful shrine houses a revered Buddha footprint. Like all genuine Buddha footprints, it is massive and identified by its 108 auspicious distinguishing marks. Twice yearly, in early February and in the middle of March, Phra Buddhabat is the focus of a colourful pilgrimage festival.

Also outside Saraburi is **Krabawk Cave Monastery** (Samnak Song Tham Krabawk), a famous opium and heroin detoxification centre. Originally begun by Mae-chii Mian, a Buddhist nun, the controversial programme has been administered by Luang Phaw Chamrun Panchan since 1959. The programme employs a combination of herbal treatment, counselling, and Dhamma to cure addicts and claims a 70% success rate. Thousands of addicts have come to Tham Krabawk to seek treatment, which begins with a rigorous 10-day session involving the ingestion of emetic herbs to purify the body of intoxicants. In 1975, Phra Chamrun was awarded the Magsaysay Prize for his work. Visitors are welcome at the centre.

Places to Stay

Try the *Thanin* (100B) or the *Suk San* (60 to 120B) at Amphoe Phra Buddhabat. In Saraburi there's the *Kiaw An* (☎ 211656) on Phahonyothin Rd where rooms with fan cost from 100B, or from 200B with air-con. Other hotels include the slightly cheaper *Saraburi* (☎ 211646/500) opposite the bus stop, or the *Saen Suk* (☎ 211104) on Phahonyothin Rd.

Getting There & Away

Ordinary buses from Bangkok's northern bus terminal cost 28B to Saraburi. Songthaews from Saraburi to Phra Buddhabat or Tham Krabawk cost around 5B per person.

Suphanburi Province

SUPHANBURI

อ.เมืองสุพรรณบุรี

Almost 70 km north-east of Kanchanaburi, Suphanburi (population 25,000) is a very old Thai town that may have had some connection with the semi-mythical Suvarnabhumi mentioned in early Buddhist writings. During the Dvaravati period (6th to 10th centuries) it was called Muang Thawarawadi Si Suphannaphumi. Today the town is a prosperous, typical central Thai town with a high proportion of Chinese among the population. There are some noteworthy Ayuthaya-period chedis and one prang (Khmer-style tower). If you're passing through Suphan on a trip from Kanchanaburi to Lopburi, you might want to stop off for a couple of hours, see the sights, eat and rest.

Entering Suphan from the direction of Kanchanaburi, you'll see **Wat Pa Lelai** on the right at the town limits. Several of the buildings, originally built during the U Thong period, are old and the bot is very distinctive because of its extremely high whitewashed walls. Looking inside, you'll realise the building was designed that way in order to house the gigantic late U Thong or early Ayuthaya-style seated Buddha image inside. Exotic-looking goats roam the grounds of this semi-abandoned wat.

Further in towards the town centre, on the left side of Malimaen Rd, is **Wat Phra Si Ratana Mahathat** (this must be the most popular name for wats in Thailand). Set back off the road a bit, this quiet wat features a fine Lopburi-style Khmer prang on which much of the stucco is still intact. There is a staircase inside the prang leading to a small chamber in the top.

Two other wats this side of the new town, **Wat Phra Rup** and **Wat Chum**, have venerable old Ayuthaya chedis.

Don Chedi

อนุสรณ์ดอนเจดีย์

Seven km west of Suphanburi, off Highway 324 on the way to Kanchanaburi, is the road to Don Chedi, a very famous battle site and early war memorial. It was here that King Naresuan, then a prince, defeated the Prince of Burma on elephant back in the late 16th century. In doing so he freed Ayuthaya from domination by the Pegu Kingdom.

The chedi (pagoda) itself was built during Naresuan's lifetime but was neglected in the centuries afterwards. By the reign of King Rama V (Chulalongkorn) at the beginning of this century, its location had been forgotten. Rama V began a search for the site but it wasn't until three years after his death in 1913 that Prince Damrong, an accomplished archaeologist, rediscovered the chedi in Suphanburi Province.

The chedi was restored in 1955 and the area developed as a national historic site. Every year during the week of January 25 (Thai Armed Forces Day), there is a week-long Don Chedi Monument Fair which features a full costume re-enactment of the elephant battle that took place four centuries ago.

During the fair there are regular buses to Don Chedi from Suphanburi, the nearest place to stay. Transport from Bangkok can also be arranged through the bigger travel agencies there.

Places to Stay

The *King Pho Sai* (☎ 511412) at 678 Nen Kaew Rd has rooms from 100B or from 220B with air-con. Other similarly priced hotels are the *KAT* (☎ 511619/639) at 433 Phra Phanwasa, and the *Suk San* (☎ 511668) at 1145 Nang Phim Rd. The *Wanchai*, 309-310 Phra Phanwasa Rd, is a Chinese hotel with rooms from 80B.

Getting There & Away

See the Getting There & Away information for Lopburi. A bus from the northern bus terminal in Bangkok costs 47B.

Chachoengsao Province

CHACHOENGSAO

อ.เมืองฉะเชิงเทรา

This provincial town, divided by the wide Bang Pakong River, is hardly visited by foreign tourists, probably because it's not on any of the major road or rail lines out of Bangkok. As a short day trip, however, it's a good way to escape Bangkok and experience provincial Thai life without encountering the tourists and touts of Ayuthaya or Nakhon Pathom.

The main attraction for Thai visitors to Chachoengsao is **Wat Sothon Wararam Worawihaan**, which houses Phra Phuttha Sothon, one of the most sacred Buddha images in the country. The origins of the 198-cm-high image are shrouded in mystery, but it is associated with a famous monk named Luang Phaw Sothon. Sothon was considered a *phrá sàksìt*, a monk with holy powers, and Buddha amulets modelled on the Phuttha Sothon – if blessed by the monk – are thought to be particularly effective protectors. Luang Phaw Sothon supposedly predicted the exact moment of his own death – thousands gathered at the temple to watch him die while sitting in meditation posture.

In the centre of the city, opposite City Hall, is the 90-rai **Somdet Phra Si Nakharin Park** with shade trees and a large pond.

The **Sorn-Thawee Meditation Centre** (Samnak Vipassana Sonthawi), about 17 km north of the city, offers 20 to 50-day meditation courses in the style of Burma's late Mahasi Sayadaw. Two German monks can provide instruction in English or German. If interested in sitting the course, write in advance to Sorn-Thawee Meditation Centre, Bangkla, Chachoengsao 24110.

Places to Stay

Should you want to stay overnight in Chachoengsao, the *River Inn* (☎ 511921) next to the river on Naruphong Rd has good rooms for 150B up.

Getting There & Away

The best way to visit Chachoengsao by public transport is via the eastern railway line. Ten trains a day leave Bangkok's Hualamphong station between 6 am and 5.25 pm; in the reverse direction trains depart between 6.21 am and 7.16 pm. The fare – 3rd class only – is 13B and the trip takes around an hour and a half each way.

Buses to Chachoengsao leave hourly between 7 am and 4 pm from Bangkok's eastern bus terminal (Soi 40, Sukhumvit Rd) for 18B on the ordinary bus (around two hours) or 25B by air-con bus (an hour and a half).

Nakhon Pathom Province

NAKHON PATHOM

อ.เมืองนครปฐม

Only 56 km west of Bangkok, Nakhon

Pathom (population 48,000) is regarded as the oldest city in Thailand – the name is derived from the Pali 'Nagara Pathama', meaning 'First City'. It was the centre of the Dvaravati Kingdom, a loose collection of city states that flourished between the 6th and 11th centuries AD in the Chao Phraya River valley. The area may have been inhabited before India's Ashokan period (3rd century BC), as it is theorised that Buddhist missionaries from India visited Nakhon Pathom at that time.

Phra Pathom Chedi
พระปฐมเจดีย์

The central attraction in Nakhon Pathom is the famous Phra Pathom Chedi, the tallest Buddhist monument in the world, rising to 127 metres. The original monument, buried within the massive orange-glazed dome, was erected in the early 6th century by Theravada Buddhists of Dvaravati, but in the early 11th century the Khmer King Suryavarman I of Angkor conquered the city and built a Brahman prang over the sanctuary. The pagan Burmese, under King Anuruddha, sacked the city in 1057 and the prang was in ruins until King Mongkut had it restored in 1860. The king had a larger chedi built over the remains according to Buddhist tradition, adding four wihaans, a bot, a replica of the original chedi and assorted salas, prangs and other embellishments. There is even a Chinese temple attached to the outer walls of the Phra Pathom Chedi, next to which outdoor lakhon (classical Thai dance-drama) is sometimes performed.

On the eastern side of the monument, in the bot, is a Dvaravati-style Buddha seated in 'European pose' (in a chair) similar to the one in Wat Phra Meru in Ayuthaya. It may, in fact, have come from Phra Meru.

Opposite the bot is a museum, open Wednesday to Sunday from 9 am to noon and 1 to 4 pm, which contains some interesting Dvaravati sculpture.

Other Attractions

Beside the chedi, the other foci of the town

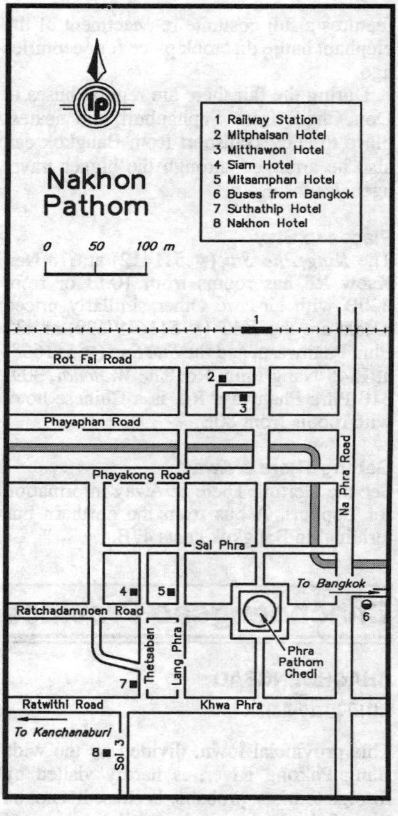

are **Silpakorn University**, west of the chedi off Phetkasem Highway, and **Sanam Chan**, adjacent to the university. Sanam Chan, formerly the grounds for Rama VI's palace, is a pleasant park with a canal passing through it. The somewhat run-down palace still stands in the park but entrance is not permitted.

South-east of the city toward Bangkok, between the districts of Nakhon Chaisi and Sam Phran, is the recently completed **Phra Phutthamonthon** (from the Pali 'Buddhamandala'). This 40.7-metre Sukhothai-style standing Buddha is reportedly the world's tallest; it's surrounded by a 2500-rai landscaped park containing replicas of important Buddhist pilgrimage spots in India and Nepal. Any Bangkok to Nakhon Pathom bus passes the access road to the park (signed in English as well as Thai); from there you can walk, hitch or flag one of the frequent songthaews into the park itself.

Places to Stay – bottom end

The *Mitrthaworn* or Mitthawon (☎ 243115) is on the right as you walk towards the chedi from the railway station. This costs 130/150B for singles/doubles with fan and bath; 180B with air-con. The *Mitphaisan* (☎ 242422) – the English sign reads 'Mitr Paisal' – is further down the alley to the right from Mitthawon. Rooms here are 150/200B for fan and bath; 270/300B with air-con.

Near the west side of Phra Pathom Chedi, next to a furniture store on Lang Phra Rd, is the *Mitsamphan* (☎ 241422). Clean rooms with fan and bath are 120B. All three of the 'Mit' hotels are owned by the same family. Price differences reflect differences in cleanliness and service. This time around my budget vote goes to Mitphaisan.

West of the chedi a few blocks from Mitsamphan on Thetsaban Rd is the *Siam Hotel* (☎ 241754). The staff here are unfriendly and rooms cost 120/160B for singles/doubles with fan and bath or up to 240/260B with air-con. A bit further south at 24/22 to 44/1 Thetsaban Rd, is the *Suthathip Hotel* (☎ 242242), with a boisterous Chinese restaurant downstairs. Rooms seem like an afterthought here and cost 120/160B for singles/doubles with fan and bath.

Places to Stay – top end

The *Nakhon Inn* (☎ 242265, 251152) at 55 Ratwithi Rd is a pleasant 70-room air-con hotel where Thai guests are charged 350/400B for singles/doubles, and farangs are asked to pay 700/800B for the same accommodation! Since this is a private establishment (not government subsidised), this is simple racial discrimination. If you speak Thai well enough, you might be able to get the Thai price.

Places to Eat

Nakhon Pathom has an excellent fruit market along the road between the railway station and the Phra Pathom Chedi; the khâo laam (sticky rice and coconut steamed in a bamboo joint) is reputed to be the best in Thailand. There are many good restaurants in this area, and they are cheap too.

A very good Chinese restaurant, *Ha Seng*, is not far from the chedi; walking north from the chedi on the road to the railway station, turn right onto the first road and walk about 20 metres.

Getting There & Away

Bus Buses for Nakhon Pathom leave the southern bus terminal in Bangkok every 10 minutes from 5 am to 9 pm; the fare is 13B for the one-hour trip. Air-con buses are 24B and leave the air-con southern bus terminal about every 30 minutes between 7 am and 10.30 pm.

Buses to Kanchanaburi leave throughout the day from the left side (coming from the Nakhon Pathom railway station) of the Phra Pathom Chedi – get bus No 81.

Train Ordinary trains (3rd class only) leave the Bangkok Noi (Thonburi) railway station daily at 7.30 and 8 am, 12.30, 1.50, 6.05 and 8 pm, arriving in Nakhon Pathom in about an hour and 10 minutes. The 3rd-class fare is 14B.

There are also ordinary trains to Nakhon Pathom from the Hualamphong station at 9 am and 1.40 pm, plus rapid and express trains roughly hourly between 12.35 and 7.30 pm; the 3rd-class fare is 14B, 2nd class 28B, 1st class 54B (add 20B and 30B respectively for rapid and express service); the ordinary and rapid trains from Hualamphong take an hour and a half, the express is only 10 minutes faster. Second and 1st class are available only on rapid and express trains, but it's not worth taking them since travel time is roughly the same; also, the rapid and express surcharges cost more than the ordinary 3rd-class fares alone.

Ratchaburi Province

RATCHABURI

Ratchaburi (Ratburi) (population 43,000) is the provincial capital of the province of the same name, and is the first major town you reach on the way south from Nakhon Pathom. The town's Chom Bung district is the site for a large 'holding centre' (a Thai Government euphemism for refugee camp) for Burmese and Karens fleeing political persecution in Burma.

Places to Stay

The *Hong Fa Hotel* (☎ 337484) at 89/13 Rat Yindi Rd has rooms with fan and bath for 100 to 140B. Other hotels include the *Araya* (☎ 337781/2) on Kraiphet Rd, with rooms from 100B, or from 240B with air-con.

AROUND RATCHABURI

Damnoen Saduak Floating Market

If the commercialisation of Bangkok's floating market puts you off there is a much more lively and somewhat less touristed floating market (talàat náam) on Khlong Damnoen Saduak in Ratchaburi Province, 104 km south-west of Bangkok, between Nakhon Pathom and Samut Songkhram.

Bus No 78 goes direct from Bangkok's southern bus terminal to Damnoen Saduak every 20 minutes, beginning at 6 am, but you'll have to get one of the first few buses so as to arrive in Damnoen Saduak by 8 or 9 am when the market's at its best. The fare is 40B for air-con or 25B for an ordinary bus. From the pier nearest the bus station, take a 10B water taxi to the talaat naam or simply walk east from the station along the canal until you come to the market area. On either side of Damnoen Saduak Canal are the two most popular markets, **Talaat Ton Khem** and **Talaat Hia Kui**. There is another less crowded market on a smaller canal, a bit south of Damnoen Saduak, called **Talaat Khun Phitak**. To get there, take a water taxi going south from the pier on the south side of Thong Lang Canal, which intersects Damnoen Saduak near the larger floating market and ask for Talaat Khun Phitak.

Another way is to spend the night in Nakhon Pathom and catch an early morning bus out of Nakhon Pathom headed for Samut Songkhram, asking to be let out at Damnoen Saduak. Or spend the night in Damnoen Saduak itself and get up before any tourists arrive.

From the opposite direction, you could get there from Samut Sakhon. To get to Damnoen Saduak from Samut Sakhon, take a local bus to Kratum Baen and then take a songthaew a few km north to the Tha Angton pier on the right bank of the Tha Chin River. From the pier, catch a ferry boat across the river to the Damnoen Saduak Canal, which runs west off the Tha Chin. From the Bang Yang lock, where ferry passengers disembark, take a 30-km trip by hang yao (long-tail boat) to the floating market. The fare is 16B and includes a boat change halfway at Ban Phaew – worth it for what is one of Thailand's most beautiful stretches of waterway.

Kanchanaburi Province

The town of Kanchanaburi was originally established by Rama I as a first line of defence against the Burmese who might use the old invasion route through the Three Pagodas Pass on the Thai-Burmese border. It's still a popular smuggling route into Burma (Myanmar) today.

During WW II, the Japanese occupation in Thailand used Allied prisoners of war to build the infamous Death Railway along this same invasion route, in reverse, along the Khwae Noi River to the pass. Thousands and thousands of prisoners died as a result of brutal treatment by their captors, a story chronicled by Boulle's book *The Bridge Over the River Kwai* and popularised by a movie based on the same. The bridge is still there to be seen (still in use, in fact) and so are the graves of the Allied soldiers. The river

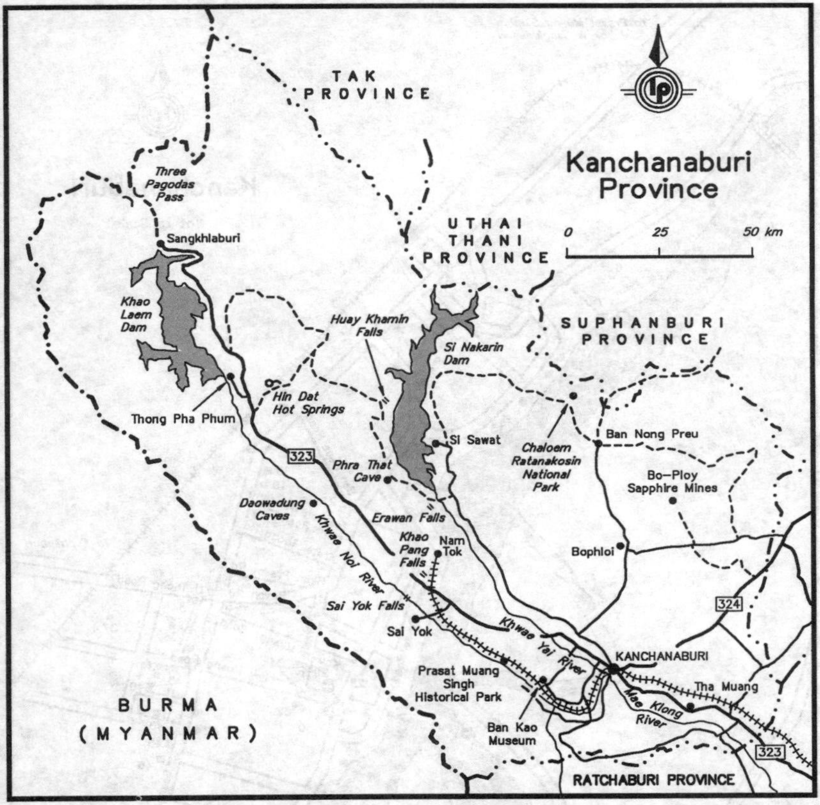

is actually spelled and pronounced Khwae, like 'quack' without the 'ck'.

KANCHANABURI

อ.เมืองกาญจนบุรี

Kanchanaburi (population 33,000) is 130 km west of Bangkok in the slightly elevated valley of the Mae Klong River amidst hills and sugar cane plantations. The town itself has a certain atmosphere and is a fine place to hang out for a while. The weather here is slightly cooler than in Bangkok and the evenings are especially pleasant. Although Kan (as the locals call it; also Kan'buri) gets enough tourists to warrant its own tourist office, not many Western visitors make it here – most tourists are Japanese, or Hong Kong and Singapore Chinese, who blaze through on air-con buses, hitting the River Khwae Bridge, the cemetery on Saengchuto Rd, the Rama River Kwai Hotel, and then hurrying off to the nearby sapphire mines or one of the big waterfalls before heading north to Chiang Mai or back to Bangkok.

Information

The TAT office is on Saengchuto Rd, on the

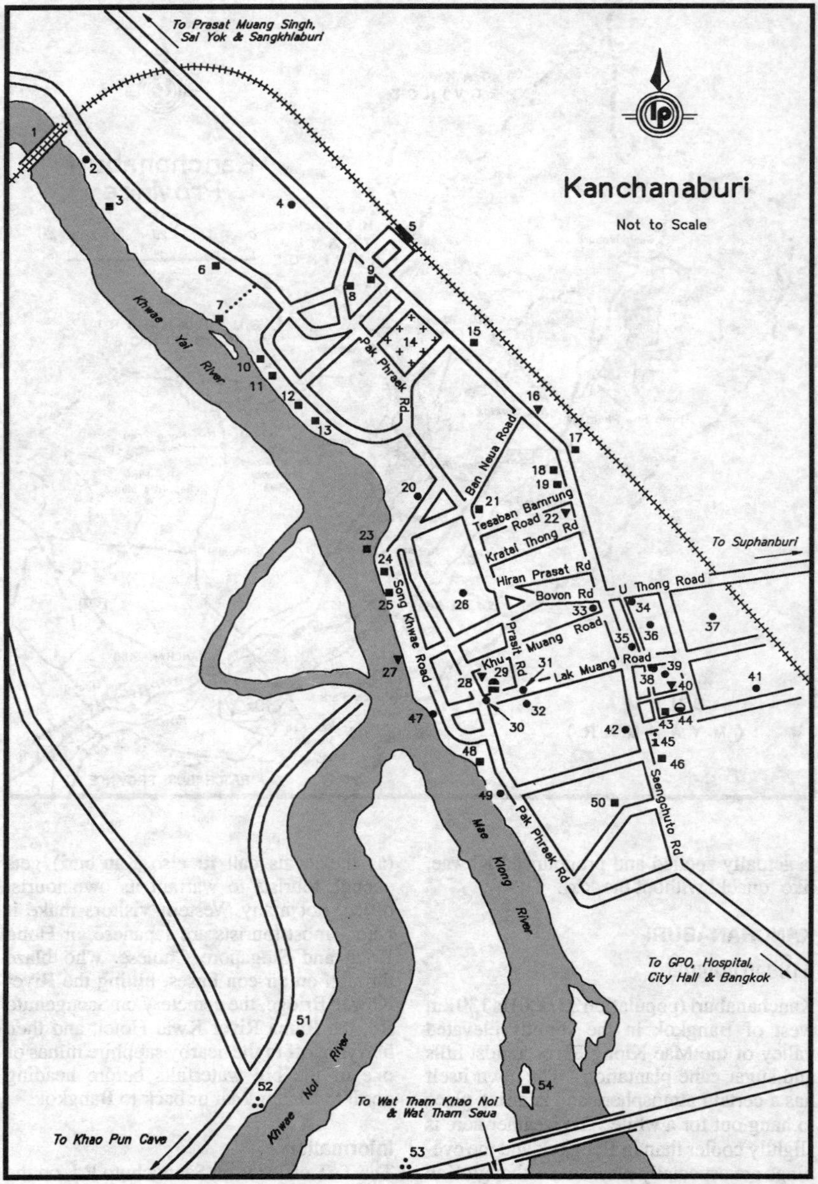
Kanchanaburi
Not to Scale
To Prasat Muang Singh, Sai Yok & Sangkhlaburi
To Suphanburi
To GPO, Hospital, City Hall & Bangkok
To Wat Tham Khao Noi & Wat Tham Seua
To Khao Pun Cave
Khwae Yai River
Mae Klong River
Khwae Noi River
Pak Phraek Rd
Ban Neua Road
Tesaban Bamrung Road
Kratai Thong Rd
Hiran Prasat Rd
Bovon Rd
U Thong Road
Song Khwae Road
Prasit Rd
Muang Road
Lak Muang Road
Khu
Saengchuto Rd
1
2
3
4
5
6
7
8
9
10
11
12
13
14
15
16
17
18
19
20
21
22
23
24
25
26
27
28
29
30
31
32
33
34
35
36
37
38
39
40
41
42
43
44
45
46
47
48
49
50
51
52
53
54

■ PLACES TO STAY

3 Bamboo House
6 UT Guest House
7 Jolly Frog Backpacker's
8 Si Muang Kan Hotel
9 Rung Rung Bungalows
10 PS Guest House
11 Rick's Lodge
12 VN Guest House
13 River Guest House
15 Luxury Hotel
17 River Kwai Hotel
18 Prasopsuk Hotel
19 VL Guest House
21 Ni-Dar Guest House
23 Nitaya Raft House
24 Sam's Place
25 Supakornchai Raft House
43 BT Travel
46 Thai Seri Hotel
48 Nita Raft House
50 Thipvaree Bungalow
54 Kasem Island Resort

▼ PLACES TO EAT

16 Sabai-jit Restaurant
22 New Isaan Restaurant
27 Floating Restaurants
28 Aree Bakery
40 Si Fa Bakery

OTHER

1 Death Railway Bridge
2 Japanese War Memorial
4 Petrol Stations
5 Railway Station
14 Kanchanaburi Allied War Cemetery
20 Songthaews to Khwae River Bridge
26 Markets
29 Lak Muang Rd Post Office
30 Town Gate of Kanchanaburi
31 City Pillar Shrine (Lak Muang)
32 Municipal Office
33 Taxi Stand
34 Bangkok Bank
35 Thai Military Bank
36 Market
37 Cinema
38 Thai Farmers Bank
39 Market
41 Cinema
42 Police Station
44 Bus Station
45 TAT Office
47 Ferry Pier
49 JEATH War Museum
51 Chung Kai Allied War Cemetery
52 Wat Tham Kao Pun
53 Wat Tham Mongkon Thong

right as you enter town before the police station. A free map of the town and province is available, as well as comprehensive information on accommodation and transport. Hours are from 8.30 am to 4.30 pm daily. The office now has a contingent of tourist police, who drive an exceedingly noisy pick-up truck around town. Any problems with theft or other criminal occurrences should be reported to both the tourist police and the regular provincial police.

Post & Telecommunications The GPO on Saengchuto Rd has reopened after renovations (open weekdays 8.30 am to 4.30 pm, weekends 9 am to 2 pm) and has international telephone service daily from 7 am to 11 pm. There is also a small post office on Lak Muang Rd towards the river, close to the Lak Muang Shine.

Death Railway Bridge

สะพานข้ามแม่น้ำแคว

The so-called Bridge Over the River Kwai may be of interest to war historians but really looks quite ordinary. It spans the Khwae Yai River, a tributary of the Mae Klong River, a couple of km north of town – Khwae Yai literally translates as 'large tributary'. It is the story behind the bridge that is dramatic. The materials for the bridge were brought from Java by the Imperial Japanese Army during their occupation of Thailand. In 1945 the bridge was bombed several times and was only rebuilt after the war – the curved portions of the bridge are original. The first version of the bridge, completed in February 1943, was all wood. In April of the same year a second bridge of steel was constructed.

It is estimated that 16,000 POWs died while building the Death Railway to Burma, of which the bridge was only a small part. The strategic objective of the railway was to secure an alternative supply route for the Japanese conquest of Burma and other Asian countries to the west. Construction on the railway began on 16 September 1942 at existing terminals in Thanbyuzayat, Burma and Nong Pladuk, Thailand. Japanese engineers at the time estimated that it would take five years to link Thailand and Burma by rail, but the Japanese army forced the POWs to complete the 415-km railway, of which roughly two-thirds ran through Thailand, in 16 months. The rails were finally joined 37 km south of Three Pagodas Pass. Much of the railway was built in difficult terrain that required high bridges and deep mountain cuttings. The River Khwae Bridge was in use for 20 months before the Allies bombed it in '45.

Although the statistics of the number of POWs who died during the Japanese occupation are horrifying, the figures for the labourers, many from Thailand, Burma, Malaysia and Indonesia, are even worse. It is thought that in total 90,000 to 100,000 coolies died in the area.

Train nuts may enjoy the **railway museum** in front of the bridge, with engines used during WW II on display. Every year during the first week of December there is a nightly sound & light show at the bridge, commemorating the Allied attack on the Death Railway in '45. It's a pretty big scene, with the sounds of bombers and explosions, fantastic bursts of light, etc. The town gets a lot of Thai tourists during this week, so book early if you want to witness this spectacle.

There are a couple of large outdoor restaurants near the bridge, on the river, but these are for tour groups that arrive en masse throughout the day. If you're hungry, better to eat with the tour bus and songthaew drivers in the little noodle places at the northern end of Pak Phraek Rd.

The best way to get to the bridge from town is to catch a songthaew along Pak Phraek Rd (parallel to Saengchuto Rd towards the river) heading north. If you're standing at the River Kwai Hotel, just cross Saengchuto Rd, walk to the right, turn left at the first street and walk until you come to Pak Phraek Rd. Regular songthaews are 3B and stop at the bridge. It's about four km from the centre of town. You can also take a train from the Kanchanaburi railway station to the bridge for 1B.

Allied War Cemeteries

สุสานทหาร

There are two cemeteries containing the remains of Allied POWs who died in captivity during WW II; one is north of town off Saengchuto Rd, just before the railway station, and the other is across the Mae Klong River west of town, a few km down the Khwae Noi (Little Tributary) River.

The **Kanchanaburi War Cemetery** is better cared for, with green lawns and healthy flowers. It's usually a cool spot on a hot Kanchanaburi day. To get there, catch a songthaew anywhere along Saengchuto Rd going north – the fare is 3B. Jump off at the English sign in front of the cemetery on the left, or ask to be let off at the *sùsăan* (Thai for cemetery). Just before the cemetery on the same side of the road is a very colourful Chinese cemetery with burial mounds and inscribed tombstones.

To get to the other cemetery, the **Chung Kai Allied War Cemetery**, take a 2B ferry boat from the pier at the west end of Lak Muang Rd across the Mae Klong, then follow the curving road through picturesque corn and sugar-cane fields until you reach the cemetery on your left. This is a fairly long walk, but the scenery along the way is pleasant. Thai border police frequent this half-paved, half-gravel road and may offer rides to or from the pier.

Like the more visited cemetery north of town, the Chung Kai burial plaques carry names, military insignia and short epitaphs for Dutch, British, French and Australian soldiers.

Very near the Chung Kai Cemetery is a dirt path that leads to **Wat Tham Khao Pun**, one of Kanchanaburi's many cave temples. The path is approximately one km long and passes through thick forest with a few wooden houses along the way.

JEATH War Museum
พิพิธภัณฑ์สงคราม

This odd museum at Wat Chaichumphon is worth visiting just to sit on the cool banks of the Mae Klong. Phra Maha Tomson Tongproh, a Thai monk who devotes much energy to promoting the museum, speaks some English and can answer questions about the exhibits, as well as supply information about what to see around Kanchanaburi and how best to get there. If you show him this book, he'll give you a 5B discount off the usual 20B admission. The museum itself is a replica example of the bamboo-atap huts used to house Allied POWs in the Kanchanaburi area during the Japanese occupation. The long huts contain various photographs taken during the war, drawings and paintings by POWs, maps, weapons and other war memorabilia. According to Phra Tomson, the acronym JEATH represents the fated meeting of Japan, England, Australia/America, Thailand and Holland at Kanchanaburi during WW II.

The War Museum is at the end of Wisuttharangsi (Visutrangsi) Rd, near the TAT office, next to the main compound of Wat Chaichumphon. It's open daily from 8.30 am to 4.30 pm.

Lak Muang Shrine
ศาลหลักเมือง

Like many of the other older Thai cities, Kanchanaburi has a làk muang, or town pillar/phallus, enclosed in a shrine at what was originally the town centre. Kanchanaburi's Lak Muang Shrine is appropriately located on Lak Muang Rd, which intersects Saengchuto Rd two blocks north of the TAT office.

The bulbous-tipped pillar is covered with gold leaf and is much worshipped. Unlike Bangkok's Lak Muang you can get as close to this pillar as you like – no curtain.

Within sight of the pillar, towards the river, stands Kanchanaburi's original city gate.

Wat Tham Mongkon Thong
วัดถ้ำมังกรทอง

The 'Cave Temple of the Golden Dragon' is well known because of the 'Floating Nun' – a 70-plus year-old mae chii who meditates while floating on her back in a pool of water. If you are lucky you might see her, but she seems to be doing this less frequently nowadays (try a Sunday). Thais come from all over Thailand to see her float and to receive her blessings, which she bestows by whistling onto the top of a devotee's head. A sizable contingent of young Thai nuns stay here under the old nun's tutelage.

A long and steep series of steps with dragon-sculpted handrails lead up the craggy mountainside behind the main bot to a complex of limestone caves. Follow the string of light bulbs through the front cave and you'll come out above the wat with a view of the valley and mountains below. One section of the cave requires crawling or duck-walking, so wear appropriate clothing. Bats squeak away above your head and the smell of guano permeates the air.

Another cave wat is off this same road about one or two km from Wat Tham Mongkon Thong towards the pier. It can be seen on a limestone outcropping back from the road some 500 metres or so. The name is **Wat Tham Khao Laem**. The cave is less impressive than that at Wat Tham Mongkon Thong, but there are some interesting old temple buildings on the grounds.

Getting There & Away Heading south-east down Saengchuto Rd from the TAT office, turn right on Chukkadon Rd (marked in English – about halfway between the TAT and GPO), or take a songthaew (2B) from the town centre to the end of Chukkadon Rd. A bridge has replaced the river ferry that used to cross here; wait for any songthaew crossing the bridge and you can be dropped off in front of the temple for 4B.

The road to the wat passes sugar cane fields, karst formations, wooden houses, cattle and rock quarries. Alternatively you could ride a bicycle here from town – the road can be dusty in the dry season but at least it's flat.

Wat Tham Seua & Wat Tham Khao Noi
วัดถ้ำเสือและวัดถ้ำเขาน้อย

These large hilltop monasteries about 15 km south-east of Kanchanaburi are important local pilgrimage spots, especially for Chinese Buddhists. Wat Tham Khao Noi (Little Hill Cave Monastery) is a Chinese temple-monastery similar in size and style to Penang's Kek Lok Si. Adjacent is the half-Thai, half-Chinese-style Wat Tham Seua (Tiger Cave Monastery). Both are built on a ridge over a series of small caves. Wat Tham Khao Noi isn't much of a climb, since it's built onto the side of the slope. Seeing Wat Tham Seua, however, means climbing either a steep set of naga stairs or a meandering set of steps past the cave entrance.

A climb to the top is rewarded with views of the Khwae River on one side, rice fields on the other. Wat Tham Seua features a huge sitting Buddha facing the river, with a conveyor belt that carries money offerings to a huge alms bowl in the image's lap. The easier set of steps to the right of the temple's naga stairs leads to a cave and passes an aviary with peacocks and other exotic birds. The cave itself has the usual assortment of Buddha images.

Getting There & Away By public transport, you can take a bus to Tha Muang (12 km south-east of Kan), then a motorcycle taxi (30B) from near Tha Muang Hospital directly to the temples.

If you're travelling by motorcycle or bicycle, take the right fork of the highway when you reach Tha Muang, turn right past the hospital onto a road along the canal and then across the dam (Muang Dam). From here to Wat Tham Seua and Khao Noi is another four km. Once you cross the dam, turn right down the other side of the river and follow this unpaved road 1.4 km, then turn left toward the pagodas, which can easily be seen in the distance at this point. The network of roads leading to the base of the hill offers several route possibilities – just keep an eye on the pagodas and you'll be able to make the appropriate turns.

By bicycle, you can avoid taking the highway by using back roads along the river. Follow Pak Phraek Rd in Kan south-east and cross the bridge toward Wat Mongkhon Thong, then turn left on the other side and follow the gravel road parallel to river. Eventually (after about 14 km) you'll see the Muang Dam up ahead – at this point you should start looking for the hilltop pagodas on your right. This makes a good day trip by bicycle – the road is flat all the way and avoids the high-speed traffic on the highway. You can break your journey at Ban Tham, a village along the way with its own minor cave wat.

Raft Trips

The number of small-time enterprises offering raft trips up and down the Mae Klong River and its various tributaries in Kanchanaburi Province continues to multiply. The typical raft is a large affair with a two-storey shelter that will carry 15 to 20 people. Average cost for a two-day trip from one of the piers in Kanchanaburi is roughly 400 to 560B per person (more than double what it was two years ago). Such a trip would include stops at Hat Tha Aw, Wat Tham Mongkon Thong, Khao Boon Cave and the Chung Kai Allied War Cemetery, plus all meals and one night's accommodation on the raft. Alcoholic beverages are usually extra. Add more nights and/or go further afield and the cost can escalate quite a bit. It is possible to arrange trips all the way to Sai Yok Falls, for example.

Enquire at any guesthouse, the TAT office, or at the main pier at the end of Lak Muang Rd about raft trips. Perhaps the best trips are arranged by groups of travellers who get together and plan their own raft excursions with one of the raft operators. One way to see the same river sights at a lower cost is to hire a long-tail boat instead of a raft. A 3½-hour tour by long-tail costs around 350B and can take up to five passengers.

Dance-Drama

Across the road from Nitaya Raft House is a place where li-khe, or Thai folk dance-drama, is occasionally performed.

Places to Stay – bottom end

Kanchanaburi has numerous places to stay in every price range but especially in the guesthouse category. The ones along the river can be quite noisy on weekends and holidays due to the floating disco traffic (the worst offender is a multi-raft monstrosity called 'Disco Duck'), so choose your accommodation carefully if an all-night beat keeps you awake.

Samlor drivers get a 25B commission per person for farangs they bring to guesthouses from bus or railway station (on top of what they charge you for the ride), so don't believe everything they say with regard to 'full', 'dirty' or 'closed' – see for yourself.

On the River Down on the riverside, at the junction of the Khwae and Khwae Noi rivers, is the *Nita Raft House* (☎ 514521), where singles/doubles with mosquito net are 40/60B. It's basic but well run, though you should heed the warning on floating discos on weekends and holidays. The manager speaks English and has good info on local sights and activities. Don't confuse Nita with the *Nitaya Raft House* further north along the river near Wat Neua – Nitaya costs 100B up for substandard accommodation and seems particularly noisy.

Spanning the bottom end to middle range is *Sam's Place* (☎ 513971), near the Nitaya Raft House and the floating restaurants. The owner is a local called Sam who spent 10 years in the USA and speaks excellent English. His raft complex is tastefully designed and reasonably priced for what you get. A room with fan and private bath is 100 to 150B for a single or double, 70B with shared bath. For 250B you can get a room with air-con, plus an extra sitting room with a fridge. The raft has a small coffee shop. The only drawback to Sam's is that it's within range of the floating discos.

If you want to stay out near the River Khwae Bridge (and away from the floating discos), the *Bamboo House* (☎ 512532) at 3-5 Soi Vietnam, on the river about a km before the Japanese war memorial off Pattana Rd (continuation of Mae Nam Khwae Rd) costs 100B per room with shared bath, 200B with private bath. The owners are very friendly and the setting is peaceful.

Two popular places a little closer to the city centre (but also distant from Disco Duck) are the *River Guest House* (☎ 512491) and the *VN Guest House* (☎ 514082) where small, basic rooms in bamboo raft houses are

40 to 80B, 100 to 150B with bath. Both are in the same vicinity on the river, not far from the railway station. They tend to get booked out in the high travel season. A bit farther north on the river is the similar *PS Guest House*, also a good choice.

North of the VN, River and PS is the fairly new *Jolly Frog Backpacker's* (☎ 514579), a comparatively huge, 45-room 'bamboo motel' with a popular restaurant. Singles/doubles with shared bath are 40/70B; doubles with private bath are 100B. For samlor transport to any guesthouse in this vicinity, you shouldn't pay more than 10B from the railway station, or 20 to 25B from the bus station.

In Town *BT Travel* (☎ 511967) is near the bus station and TAT on Kanchanaburi Rd and has dorm beds for 30B, as well as adequate rooms for 50 to 80B.

Near Pak Phraek Rd but well off the river is the *Ni-dar Guest House* (☎ 513734), at 11/8 Ban Neua Rd, with basic singles/doubles for 40/70B. The *UT Guest House*, which is near the River Khwae Bridge at 25/25 Mae Nam Khwae Rd, was closed when I last checked; the owners said they had plans to reopen in '92 or '93. If so, they'll charge 50B per person in large two-bed rooms.

One of the best value places in town is the small *Thipvaree Bungalow* (☎ 511063) at 211/1-4 Saengchuto Rd. Basic but clean rooms with fan and private bath are 70B; 120B with air-con. Two rooms are also available without bath for 40B.

Places to Stay – middle

One of the better places in this price range is the new *VL Guest House* across the street from the River Kwai Hotel. A clean, spacious room with fan and hot-water bath is 120B for a single or double. Larger rooms holding four to eight persons go for 50B per person. A double with air-con and hot water is 250B. The VL has a small dining area downstairs, and you can rent bicycles (20B per day) and motorcycles (200B up). Another plus is the generous 2 pm checkout time.

Rick's Lodge (☎ 514831) is along the river between the cheaper VN and PS guesthouses. Tastefully decorated bamboo accommodation with fan and private bath cost 150B on the river, 130B back from the river.

The *Prasopsuk Hotel* (☎ 511777) is at 677 Saengchuto Rd, next door to the VL Guest House. Rooms start at 110B with fan, 200B with air-con and are off the road a bit. The restaurant and nightclub are a Thai scene at night. *Wang Thong Bungalows* (☎ 511046) at 60/3 Saengchuto Rd, and *Boon Yang Bungalows* (☎ 512598) at 139/9 Saengchuto Rd, offer similar rooms for 90B up. In case you haven't figured this out on your own, 'bungalows' (not the beach kind) are the upcountry equivalent of Bangkok's 'short-time' hotels. They're off the road for the same reason that their Bangkok counterparts have heavy curtains over the carports: so that it will be difficult to spot license plate numbers. Still, they function well as tourist hotels too.

Other hotels in town include the *Si Muang Kan* (☎ 511609), at 313/1-3 Saengchuto Rd (the north end) with clean singles/doubles with fan and bath for 90/150B, 150/200B with air-con, and the *Thai Seri Hotel* at the southern end of the same road, near the Visutrangsi Rd intersection and the TAT office, with somewhat dilapidated but adequate rooms for 90B up.

The *Luxury Hotel* (☎ 511168) at 284/1-5 Saengchuto Rd is a couple of blocks north of the River Kwai Hotel, and not as centrally located, but good value. Clean singles/doubles with fan and bath start at 70/150B; 100/200B with air-con.

Very near Sam's Place is *Supakornchai Raft* which is similar in scope but not quite as nice. Rooms with fan and bath are 150B for a large bed, or 200B for two beds.

Perhaps the last word in comfort is *Kasem Island Resort* (☎ 511603; 391-6672 in Bangkok), which is on an island in the middle of the Mae Klong River just a couple of hundred metres from Tha Chukkadon pier. The tastefully designed thatched cottages and house rafts are cool, clean, quiet and go for 650B. Four people can rent a house raft for 900B a night and for eight people it is 1600B. There are facilities for swimming, fishing and rafting as well as an outdoor bar and restaurant. The resort has an office near Tha Chukkadon pier where you can arrange for a free shuttle boat out to the island.

In the vicinity of the bridge are several river resorts of varying quality. On the river before the bridge is the *River Kwai Resort* (☎ 511313), where rustic bungalows on the riverbank are 350B for two, floating bungalows for two are 450B, and two-bedroom floating bungalows for four are 700B. Just above the bridge, two km before the turn-off for Highway 323, are two more river resorts: *Prasopsuk Garden Resort* (☎ 513215; 215-4497 in Bangkok) with air-con town-house doubles for 400B, air-con bungalows for two at 600B, and large bungalows for 10 people at 1000B per night; and *River Kwai Lodge* (☎ 513657; 250-0928 in Bangkok) where a large room for two is 600B with fan and bath or 700B with air-con.

Places to Stay – top end

In Town The closest thing Kanchanaburi has to a 1st-class hotel is the *River Kwai Hotel* (☎ 511184/269) at 284/3-16 Saengchuto Rd. Standard rooms come with air-con, hot water, telephone and TV and cost from 640 to 1200B. Facilities include a coffee shop, disco and swimming pool. Next door is the huge River Paradise massage parlour.

The Sheraton corporation is rumoured to be planning a luxury hotel on the other side of the river just south of town.

Further Out A number of places along the river north-west of town are frequented by Bangkok yuppies who come to clear out their lungs. The *River Kwai Farm*, a resort that attempts to duplicate for tourists the natural simplicity of jungle life, is 38 km south-west of Kanchanaburi at Ban Kao. The bamboo bungalows are without electricity and the daily rate, including three meals a day, is 500B per person. Reservations can be made through River Kwai Farm (☎ 234-7435), 68/2 Sathon Neua Rd, Bangkok, or through the private tour agency in Kanchanaburi on Saengchuto Rd just north of the TAT office.

The *River Kwai Village* is a 60-room air-con resort 70 km from Kanchanaburi, near Nam Tok, on the Khwae Noi River; there are also a few house rafts available. Accommodation (780 to 880B) can be booked through their office in Bangkok (☎ 251-7522/7828), 1054/4 Phetburi Rd, or through any Kanchanaburi travel agency. Other top-end house raft accommodation is in the Sai Yok Falls National Park area: *River Kwai Rafts* (☎ 280-3365 in Bangkok) costs 600B per person including all meals; and *River Kwai Jungle Rafts* (☎ 245-3069/4211 in Bangkok) costs 550 to 650B per person with meals.

On the River Khwae towards Si Sawat and the Si Nakarin Dam are *Kwai Yai River Hut* (☎ Bangkok 392-3286) at 1200B per person including meals and *Kwai Yai Island Resort* (☎ 511261; 521-2389 in Bangkok), at 650 to 700B per person. These can also probably be booked in Kanchanaburi through one of the travel agencies near the bus station. There are several other house raft and bungalow operations along the River Khwae and near Sai Yok Falls on the Khwae Noi River.

Places to Eat

The greatest proliferation of inexpensive restaurants in Kanchanaburi is along the northern end of Saengchuto Rd near the River Kwai Hotel. From here south, to where U Thong Rd crosses Saengchuto, are many good Chinese, Thai and Isaan-style restaurants. As elsewhere in Thailand, the best are generally the most crowded.

For years, one of the most popular has been the *New Isaan* (no English sign), now in a new location at 292/1-2 Saengchuto Rd. The Isaan still serves great kài yâang (whole spicy grilled chicken) for only 50B, khâo niăw (sticky rice), sôm-tam (spicy green papaya salad), etc as well as other Thai and local specialities and inexpensive, ice-cold beer. The kài yâang is grilled right out front and served with two sauces – the usual sweet and sour (náam jîm kài) and a roast red pepper sauce (náam phrík phăo). Grilled fish (plaa phão) is also sometimes available. For some reason sôm-tam doesn't appear on the English menu, though the restaurant makes lots of it for Thai customers. The sound system plays good *lûuk thûng* (north-eastern country) music.

Good, inexpensive eating places can also be found in the markets along Prasit Rd and between U Thong and Lak Muang Rds east of Saengchuto Rd. In the evenings a sizable night market convenes along Saengchuto Rd near the Lak Muang Rd intersection. Two or three doors down from BT Guest House is a noodle shop that's very popular among locals for duck or chicken kũaytĩaw and koi sòi mii (crisp-fried noodles with chicken and mushrooms) – excellent, cheap and fast.

The *Sabai-jit* restaurant, north of the River Kwai Hotel on Saengchuto Rd, has an English menu. Beer and Maekhong whisky are sold here at quite competitive prices and the food is consistently good. Other Thai and Chinese dishes are served apart from those listed on the English menu. If you see someone eating something not listed, point.

A restaurant called *Art & Beer*, across from the railway station, sells large bottles of Singha beer for under 50B. They also feature unusual dishes like beer-marinated beef and phàt thai without the noodles. *Punnee Cafe & Bar* (☎ 513503) on Ban Neua Rd serves Thai and European food according to expat tastes and advertises the coldest beer in town.

Down on the river there are several large floating restaurants where the quality of the food varies but it's hard not to enjoy the atmosphere. Most of them are pretty good according to locals, but if you go, don't expect Western food or large portions – if you know what to order, you could have a very nice meal here. Recommended are the *Thong Nathii* and the *Mae Nam*. Across from the floating restaurants, along the road, are several restaurants that are just as good but less expensive; the best on this row is *Jukkru* (no English sign). This is a festive and prosperous town and people seem to eat out a lot.

Two bakeries handle most of the pastry and bread business in Kan. *Srifa Bakery* on the north side of the bus terminal is the more modern of the two, with everything from French-style pastries to Singapore-style curry puffs. The *Aree Bakery* on Pak Phraek Rd around the corner from the Lak Muang post office is less fancy but it has coffee, tea and sandwiches plus tables and chairs for a sit-down. Aree has great chicken curry puffs and very tasty young coconut pie.

Getting There & Away

Bus Buses leave Bangkok from the southern bus terminal on Charan Sanitwong Rd in Thonburi every 20 minutes daily (beginning at 5 am, last bus at 6.30 pm) for Kanchanaburi. The trip takes about three hours and costs 28B. Buses back to Bangkok leave Kanchanaburi between 5.10 am and 6.30 pm.

Air-con buses leave Bangkok's southern air-con terminal hourly from 6 am to 9.30 pm for 53B. These same buses depart Kanchanaburi for Bangkok from opposite the police station on Saengchuto Rd, not from the bus station. Air-con buses only take about two hours to reach Bangkok. The first bus out is at 5.30 am; the last one to Bangkok leaves at 7 pm.

There are frequent buses throughout the day from nearby Nakhon Pathom. Bus No 81 leaves from the east side of the Phra Pathom Chedi, costs 16B, and takes about 1½ hours.

Train Ordinary trains leave Bangkok Noi (Thonburi) station at 8 am and 1.50 pm, arriving at 10.30 am and 4.26 pm. Only 3rd-class seats are available and the fare is 25B. Trains return to Bangkok from Kanchanaburi at 8.04 am and 2.30 pm, arriving at 10.50 am and 5.10 pm. Ordinary train tickets to Kanchanaburi can be booked on the day of departure.

You can also take the train from the Kanchanaburi station out to the River Khwae Bridge – a three-minute ride for 1B. There is one train only at 10.31 am (No 171).

The same train goes on to the end of the railway line at Nam Tok, which is near Sai Yok Falls. You can catch the train in Kanchanaburi at 10.31 am or at the bridge at 10.36 am; the fare is the same, 17B. Nam Tok is eight km from Khao Pang Falls and 18 km from Hellfire Pass and the River Khwae Village. Two other trains also make the trip to Nam Tok daily, leaving Kanchanaburi at 6 am and 4.28 pm. The trip to Nam Tok takes about two hours. Coming back from Nam Tok, there are trains at 6.05 am, 12.35 pm and 3.15 pm. The early morning trains between Kanchanaburi and Nam Tok (6 and 6.05 am) do not run on weekends and holidays.

Tourist Train There is a special tourist train from Hualamphong station on weekends and holidays which departs Bangkok at 6.15 am and returns at 7.30 pm. The return fare is 250B for adults, 120B for children. It includes an hour-long stop in Nakhon Pathom to see the Phra Pathom Chedi, an hour at the River Khwae Bridge, a minibus to Prasat Muang Singh Historical Park for a short tour, a walk along an elevated 'Death Railway' bridge (no longer in use), a three-hour stop at the river for lunch and a bat-cave visit before returning to Bangkok with a one-hour stopover at the Allied War Cemetery. This ticket should be booked in advance although it's worth trying on the day even if you're told it's full. The State Railway of Thailand (SRT) changes the tour itinerary and price from time to time.

Share Taxi & Minivan You can also take a share taxi from Saengchuto Rd to Bangkok for 50B per person. Taxis leave throughout the day whenever five passengers accumulate at the taxi stand. These taxis will make drops at Khao San Rd or in the Pahurat district. Kanchanaburi guesthouses also arrange daily minivans to Bangkok for 80B per person. Passengers are dropped at Khao San Rd.

Getting Around

Prices are very reasonable in Kanchanaburi, especially for food and accommodation, if you are your own tour guide – don't even consider letting a samlor driver show you around, they want big money. The town is not very big, so getting around on foot or bicycle is easy. A samlor to anywhere in Kanchanaburi should be 10 to 15B for one person. Songthaews run up and down Saengchuto Rd for 2B per passenger.

Bicycles and motorcycles can be rented at some guesthouses, at the Suzuki dealer near the bus station and at the Punnee Cafe. Expect to pay about 150B per day for a motorbike (more for an MTX), 20 to 30B a day for bicycles. Bikes (motor or push) can be taken across the river by ferry for a few baht.

AROUND KANCHANABURI

Most of the interesting places around Kanchanaburi are to the north and west of the town, heading towards Three Pagodas Pass.

Waterfalls

There are seven major waterfalls in Kanchanaburi Province, all north of the capital. They are Erawan, Pha Lan, Traitrung, Khao Pang, Sai Yok, Pha That and Huay Khamin. Of these, the three most worth visiting – if you're looking for grandeur and swimming potential – are Erawan, Sai Yok and Huay Khamin. The Erawan Falls are the easiest to get to from Kanchanaburi, while Sai Yok and Huay Khamin are best visited only if you are able to spend the night in the vicinity of the falls. They are too far for a comfortable day trip from Kanchanaburi.

Any of the waterfalls described here could be visited by motorcycle. Many of the guesthouses in town will rent bikes – offer 150B per day for a 80 to 100cc bike, more for a dirt bike.

Erawan Falls National Park This is the most visited national park in Thailand and one of the most beautiful. The first bus to Erawan leaves the Kanchanaburi bus station at 8 am, takes 1½ to two hours and costs 17B per person. Ask for *rót thammádaa pai náam tòk eh-raawan* (ordinary bus going to Erawan Falls). Take this first bus, as Erawan takes a full day to appreciate and the last bus back to Kanchanaburi leaves Erawan at 4 pm. During the high tourist season (November to January) minibuses go by all the river guesthouses in Kan around 9 am daily to take visitors to the falls (one hour) for 60B per person. The return trip leaves the park at 3.30 pm.

The bus station/market at Erawan is a good 1.5 km from the Erawan National Park, which contains the falls. Once in the park, you'll have to walk two km from the trail entrance to the end of seven levels of waterfalls. The trails weave in and out of the numerous pools and falls, sometimes running alongside the water, sometimes leading across footbridges, splitting in different directions. Wear good walking shoes or sneakers. Also bring a bathing suit as several of the pools beneath the waterfalls are great for swimming. Two limestone caves in the park worth visiting are **Tham Phra That** (12 km north-west of the visitors' centre) and **Tham Wang Badan** (to the west).

There are food stalls near the park entrance and at the bus station/market, outside the park. To cut down on rubbish, food is not allowed beyond the second level of the falls. The waterfalls here, as elsewhere in Kanchanaburi, are best visited during the rainy season or in the first two months of the cool season, when the pools are full and the waterfalls most impressive. The peak crowds at Erawan come in mid-April around the time of the Songkran Festival; weekends can also be crowded. Two-bedroom park bungalows that sleep four can be rented for 250B per night; there is also a bamboo dormitory where you can sleep for 10B a night or a room for 50B.

Huay Khamin Falls These waterfalls are about 25 km north of Erawan. To get there, take a bus to Si Sawat, either from Kanchanaburi or from Erawan. The fare from Erawan should be about 10B; from Kanchanaburi it will be about 27B.

Huay Khamin (Turmeric Stream) has what are probably Kanchanaburi Province's most powerful waterfalls and the pools under the waterfalls are large and deep. This is an excellent place for swimming.

Sai Yok Falls Area About 100 km north-west of Kanchanaburi, Sai Yok is well known for the overnight raft trips that leave from here along the Khwae Noi River; the waterfalls empty directly into the Khwae Noi. The trips are not cheap, but those who have gone say they're worth the money. There is fishing and swimming as well as jungle scenery and wildlife. It was at Sai Yok that the famous Russian roulette scenes in the movie *The Deer Hunter* were filmed.

Forestry Department bungalows are available at Sai Yok for 500 to 1000B per night; they sleep up to six persons. At nearby Sai Yok Noi, outside the park, *Saiyok Noi Bungalows* has huts for 80B with fan, 200B with air-con.

Near Sai Yok are the **Daowadung Caves** (20 minutes north-west by boat) and **Hin Dat Hot Springs** (40 minutes further north by boat). The hot springs *(bàw náam ráwn)* are looked after by a Buddhist monastery, so only men are permitted to bathe there.

Getting There & Away Sai Yok can be reached by direct bus from Kanchanaburi for 25B and the trip takes a little over an hour. You can also get there by boarding a bus bound for Thong Pha Phum. Tell the driver you're going to Sai Yok Yai and he'll let you off at the road to the falls, on the left side of Highway 323. From there you can get local transport to Sai Yok. This method takes about two hours in all and costs about the same as the direct bus. You can also charter boats that can take up to 20 people to Sai Yok for about 400B.

Prasat Muang Singh Historical Park
อุทยานประวัติศาสตร์ปราสาทเมืองสิงห์

About 40 km from Kanchanaburi are the remains of an important 13th-century Khmer outpost of the Angkor Empire called Muang Singh (Lion City). Located on a bend in the Khwae Noi River, the recently restored city ruins cover 460 rai (73.6 hectares) and were declared a historical park under the administration of the Fine Arts Department in 1987.

Originally this location may have been chosen by the Khmers as a relay point for the trade along the Khwae Noi River.

All the Muang Singh shrines are constructed of laterite bricks and are situated in a huge grassy compound surrounded by layers of laterite ramparts. Sections of the ramparts show seven additional layers of earthen walls, suggesting cosmological symbolism in the city plan. Evidence of a sophisticated water system has also been discovered amid the ramparts and moats.

The town encompasses four groups of ruins, though only two groups have been excavated and are visible. In the centre of the complex is the principal shrine, Prasat Muang Singh, which faces east (toward Angkor). Walls surrounding the shrine have gates in each of the cardinal directions. An original sculpture of Avalokitesvara stands on the inside of the northern wall and establishes Muang Singh as a Mahayana Buddhist centre. The shrine was apparently built during the reign of Jayavarman VII in the 12th century.

To the north-east of the main prasat (large temple) are the remains of a smaller shrine whose original contents and purpose are unknown. Near the main entrance to the complex at the north gate is a small outdoor museum, which contains various sculptures of Mahayana Buddhist deities and stucco decorations from the shrines.

Clear evidence that this area was inhabited before the arrival of the Khmers can be seen in another small museum to the south of the complex next to the river. The shed-like building contains a couple of prehistoric human skeletons which were found in the area, and that's it. A more complete exhibit of local neolithic remains is at the Ban Kao Museum (see below).

Entry to the historical park is 20B and it's open daily from 8 am to 4 pm.

Ban Kao Neolithic Museum

พิพิธภัณฑ์บ้านเก่า

During the construction of the Death Railway along the Khwae Noi River, a Dutch POW named Van Heekeren uncovered neolithic remains in the village of Ban Kao (Old Town), which is about seven km south-east of Muang Singh. After the war, a Thai-Danish team retraced Heekeren's discovery and announced that Ban Kao was a major neolithic burial site. Archaeological evidence suggests that this area may have been inhabited as far back as 10,000 years ago.

A small but well-designed museum, displaying 3000 to 4000-year-old artefacts from the excavation of Ban Kao, has been established near the site. Objects are labelled and include a good variety of early pottery and other utensils, as well as human skeletons. Hours are from 8 am to 4.30 pm, Wednesday to Sunday.

Places to Stay & Eat Guest bungalows are available for rent near the south gate of the Prasat Muang Singh Historical Park for 500B. There are a couple of small restaurants at the north gate.

The *River Khwae Farm* is 3.5 km from the Ban Kao (Tha Kilen) railway station. Bungalows and raft houses here start at 450B, including all meals.

Getting There & Away Ban Kao and Muang Singh are best reached by rail from Kanchanaburi via Ban Kao (Tha Kilen) station, which is only one km south of Muang Singh. Walk west towards the river and follow the signs to Muang Singh. Trains leave Kanchanaburi daily at 6 and 10.31 am, arriving in Tha Kilen in about an hour. The fare is 10B. To get to Ban Kao, you may have to walk or hitch six km south along the road that follows the Khwae Noi River, though the occasional songthaew passes along this road, too. It's possible to get from Kanchanaburi to Muang Singh and back in one day by catching the 6 am train there and the 3 pm train back.

If you have your own transport, Ban Kao and/or Muang Singh would make convenient rest stops on the way to Hellfire Pass or Sangkhlaburi.

Chaloem Ratanakosin (Tham Than Lot) National Park

อุทยานแห่งชาติเฉลิมรัตนโกสินทร์

This 59-sq-km park, 97 km north of Kanchanaburi, is of interest to speleologists because of two caves, **Than Lot Yai** and **Than Lot Noi**, and to naturalists for its waterfalls and natural forests. Three waterfalls – **Trai Trang**, **Than Ngun** and **Than Thong** – are within easy hiking distance of the bungalows and camp ground. Bungalows cost from 500 to 1000B per night and sleep 10 to 12 people. Pitch your own tent for 5B per person.

To get to Chaloem Ratanakosin, take a bus from Kanchanaburi to Ban Nong Preu for around 30B (a two to three-hour trip) and then try for a songthaew to the park. Most visitors arrive by car, jeep or motorcycle.

Hellfire Pass/Burma-Thailand Railway Memorial

In 1988, the Australian-Thai Chamber of Commerce completed the first phase of the Hellfire Pass memorial project. The purpose of the project is to honour the Allied prisoners of war and Asian conscripts who died while constructing some of the most difficult stretches of the Burma-Thailand Death Railway, 80 km north-west of Kanchanaburi. 'Hellfire Pass' was the name the POWs gave to the largest of a 1000-metre series of mountain cuttings through soil and solid rock, which were accomplished with minimal equipment (3.5-kg hammers, picks, shovels, steel tap drills, cane baskets for removing dirt and rock, and dynamite for blasting).

The original crew of 400 Australian POWs was later augmented with 600 additional Australian and British prisoners, who worked round the clock in 12 to 18-hour shifts for 12 weeks. The prisoners called it Hellfire Pass because of the way the largest cutting at Konyu looked at night by torch light. By the time the cuttings were finished, 70% of the POW crew had died and were buried in the nearby Konyu Cemetery.

The memorial consists of a trail that follows the railway remains through the Konyu cutting, then winds up and around the pass for an overhead view. At the far end of the cutting is a memorial plaque fastened to solid stone, commemorating the death of the Allied prisoners. There are actually seven cuttings spread over 3.5 km – four smaller cuttings and three larger ones.

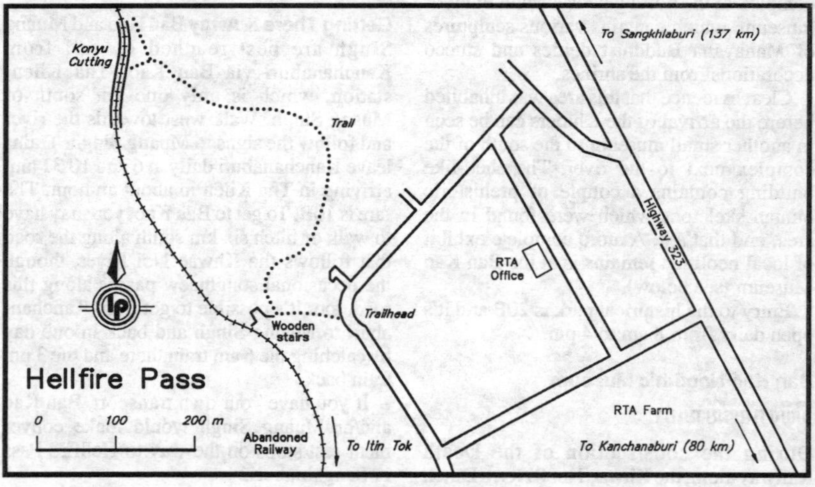

The Australian-Thai Chamber of Commerce also have plans to clear a path to the Hin Tok trestle bridge south-east of the Konyu cutting. This bridge was called the 'Pack of Cards' by the prisoners because it collapsed three times during construction. Eventually some of the track may be restored to exhibit rolling stock from the WW II era.

Access to Hellfire Pass is via the Royal Thai Army (RTA) farm on Highway 323, between Kanchanaburi and Thong Pha Phum. Proceeding north-west along Highway 323, the farm is 80 km from Kanchanaburi, 18 km from the Nam Tok railway terminus, and 11 km from the River Kwai Village Hotel. Once you arrive at the RTA farm, you take one of the dirt roads on either side of the RTA offices about 400 metres around to the posted trailhead. From the trailhead, it's about 340 metres up and down a steep walkway and along the rail bed to the pass.

After walking through the pass and viewing the plaque, you can follow another trail/walkway on the right to get a view of the cutting from above. Then you can either double back the way you came or continue on this trail until it wraps around and meets the trailhead.

Any Kanchanaburi to Thong Pha Phum or Kanchanaburi to Sangkhlaburi bus will pass the RTA farm, but you'll have to let the bus crew know where you want to get off – ask for the *sũan thahãan* (army farm). If you're driving, just remember that the farm is about 80 km from Kanchanaburi and look for the English signs announcing Hellfire Pass on Highway 323.

KANCHANABURI TO THREE PAGODAS PASS

Three Pagodas Pass (Chedi Saam Ong) was one of the terminals of the Death Railway in WW II, and for centuries has been a major relay point for Thai-Burmese trade. Until recently it was a place that the TAT and the Thai government would rather you'd forget about (much like Mae Salong in the north some years ago), but since 1989, when the Burmese government took control of the Burmese side of the border from insurgent armies, it's been promoted as a tourist destination. There's really not much to see at the pass – the attraction lies in the journey itself and the impressive scenery along the way.

It's an all-day journey and will require that you spend at least one night in Sangkhlaburi, which is a somewhat interesting off-the-track destination in itself. The distance between Kanchanaburi and Sangkhlaburi alone is about 200 km, so if you take a motorcycle it is imperative that you fill up before you leave Kanchanaburi and stop for petrol again in Thong Pha Phum, the last town before Sangkhlaburi. By bicycle this would be a very challenging route, but it's been done.

The paved highway used to end in Thong Pha Phum, but now the road from Thong Pha Phum to Sangkhla is paved as well. The road between Sangkhla and Three Pagodas Pass is still unpaved and very dusty (or muddy, if you're foolish enough to go there during the rainy season). The best time to go is during the mid-to-late part of the cool season (January to February). During the rainy season nearly the whole of Sangkhlaburi is under water and travel is difficult.

The road between Kanchanaburi and Thong Pha Phum passes through mostly flat terrain interrupted by the occasional limestone outcropping. This is sugar-cane country, and if you're travelling by bicycle or motorcycle during harvest times you'll have to contend with huge cane trucks, overloaded with cut cane, which strew pieces of cane and dust in their wake – take extra care. Cassava is also cultivated here but the cassava trucks aren't such a nuisance.

The road between Thong Pha Phum and Sangkhlaburi is one of the most beautiful in Thailand, winding through limestone mountains and along the huge lake created by the Khao Laem hydroelectric dam near Thong Pha Phum. In spite of the fact that the road surface is in good condition during the dry season, steep grades and sharp curves make this a fairly dangerous journey.

Between Km 32 and Km 33 (some 42 km before Sangkhlaburi) is the entrance to the

Sunyataram Forest Monastery (Samnak Paa Sunyataram), a forest meditation retreat centre affiliated with one of Thailand's most famous living monks, Ajaan Yantara.

Recently there has been talk in Kanchanaburi of rebuilding the rail connection between Nam Tok and Sangkhlaburi, using the old Japanese rail bed. If it ever happens, this would be a spectacular rail trip. Another pipe dream is the construction of a road between Sangkhlaburi and Um Phang in Tak Province, approximately 120 km to the north.

Sangkhlaburi
สังขละบุรี

This small but important Kanchanaburi outpost is inhabited by a mixture of Burman, Karen, Mon and Thai, but is mostly Karen and Mon. Hundreds of former residents of Burma have moved to the Sangkhla area during the last few years because of the fighting in the Three Pagodas Pass area between the Karen and Mon insurgent armies and between the Burmese government forces and the Karen. These Burmese have fled into Thailand not only to avoid the fighting but to escape being press-ganged as porters for the Burmese army.

The distance between Kanchanaburi and Sangkhlaburi is about 227 km. At the time of writing, Sangkhla has no banks – be sure to bring enough cash from Kanchanaburi for your stay. In a pinch, P Guest House will change travellers' cheques at below the going bank rate.

Things to See & Do Sangkhlaburi sits at the edge of the huge lake formed by Khao Laem Dam. There's not much to do in the town itself except explore the small markets for Burmese handicrafts such as checked cotton blankets, *longyi* (Burmese sarongs) and cheroots. Thailand's longest wooden bridge leads over a section of the lake to a friendly Mon settlement of thatched huts and dirt paths.

The town comes alive on Mon National Day, celebrated during the last week of July. Day trips to nearby waterfalls are a possibility – enquire at P Guest House for details.

Also called Wat Mon since most of the monks here are Mon, **Wat Wang Wiwekaram** is about three km north of the town on the edge of the reservoir. A tall and much revered stupa, Chedi Luang Phaw Utama, is the centrepiece of the wat. Constructed in the style of the Mahabodhi stupa in Bodhgaya, India, the chedi is topped by 400 baht (about six kg) of gold. An earlier chedi is located some distance behind the tall one and is 300 to 400 years old. From the edge of the monastery grounds is a view of the tremendous lake and three rivers that feed into it.

Khao Laem Lake was formed when a dam was erected across the Khwae Noi River near Thong Pha Phum in 1983. The lake submerged an entire village at the confluence of the Khwae Noi, Ranti and Sangkhalia rivers. The spires of the village's Wat Sam Prasop (Three-Junction Temple) can be seen protruding from the lake in the dry season.

Canoes can be rented for exploring the lake, or for longer trips you can hire a longtail boat and pilot. Lake boating is a tranquil pastime, best early in the morning with mist and birdlife – early evening is also good for bird-watching. Two hours across the lake and up the Pikri River by boat from Sangkhla is a huge (population 50,000) Mon refugee camp. On the way to the camp you'll pass through a flooded Ayuthaya-period mountain pass marked by a decrepit Buddha image seated under a small tin-roofed sala. This pass was part of the Thai-Burmese border before the border was moved south-east following WW II.

A branch meditation centre of Kanchanaburi's Sunyataram Forest Monastery is found on the lake's **Ko Kaew Sunyataram** (Sunyataram Jewel Isle). Permission to visit must be obtained from the Sunyataram Forest Monastery first, 42 km before Sangkhlaburi.

Places to Stay Sangkhlaburi has one hotel, the *Sri Daeng Hotel*, which is on the southern edge of town near an army camp and the central market. Rooms are 120B for fan and bath or 300B with air-con. The rooms are fairly clean and comfortable.

Down on the lake behind the town, an enterprising Mon-Karen family operates the *P Guest House* (☎ 71240). Bungalows with verandahs are placed along a slope overlooking the lake; singles/doubles with shared bath are 60/100B; larger doubles with private bath 150B. There's a comfortable dining area with a sunset view of the lake and the chedi at Wat Mon. An information board has maps and suggestions for things to see and do in the area. Canoes can be rented for 10B per hour and there are also bicycles and motorcycles for rent. The staff also arranges long-tail boat tours to the Mon refugee camp when enough people are interested.

A motorcycle taxi from the bus stop in Sangkhla to the P Guest House is 10B; if you come by minivan from Kanchanaburi you can ask the driver to take you to the guesthouse (it's supposed to be door-to-door service). If you want to walk, it's about a km from the market and bus stop – follow the signs.

A couple of km north of Sangkhlaburi on the way to Wat Mon, right on the Sangkhalia River where it meets the lake, is *Songkalia River Huts* (☎ (024) 427-4936). Somewhat run-down floating bungalows that will sleep up to 10 people cost 300 to 600B per night.

Out on the lake are several more expensive raft houses, including the *Runtee Palace* (☎ Bangkok 251-7552) where bungalows are 900 to 1500B with meals. The Runtee, too, has seen better days.

More places are sprouting up on hillsides along the lake. So far all are resorts oriented toward Thai tourists in the 300 to 600B range. For now, Sangkhlaburi is very peaceful – one hopes that local entrepreneurs won't turn it into another Kanchanaburi river scene with all-night floating discos.

If you get stuck in Thong Pha Phum, the best value is *Somjai Neuk Hotel*, on the left side of the town's main street off the highway (an English sign reads 'Hotel'). Rooms are clean, cost 80B with bath, and there's a shaded courtyard in the centre. They also have air-con rooms for 180B. *Si Thong Pha Phum Bungalows* further down the road has large private bungalows for 70B, but is located next to a noisy primary school.

Places to Eat The *Sri Daeng Hotel* in Sangkhlaburi has a decent restaurant downstairs and there are three or four other places to eat down the street. The best food is at the *No-Name Restaurant* (Ráan Aahãan Noh Nehm!) in Sangkhlaburi, opposite the bus terminal.

The *Rung Arun* restaurant, opposite the Sri Daeng Hotel, has an extensive menu and is also good. The day market in the centre of town has a couple of vendor stalls offering Indian nan and curry.

Getting There & Away Buses leave the Kanchanaburi bus terminal for Thong Pha Phum every half hour from 7 am until 6 pm. The fare is 35B and the trip takes about three hours. Buses to Sangkhlaburi leave at 6.45, 9, 10.45 am and 1.15 pm and take four to six hours, depending on how many mishaps occur on the Thong Pha Phum to Sangkhlaburi road. The fare is 60B.

A new *rót tûu* (minivan) service to Sangkhla leaves nine times daily, from 7.30 am to 4.30 pm, from an office on the east side of the Kan bus terminal. The trip takes 3½ hours and costs 90B; if you want to stop off in Thong Pha Phum it's 60B (then from Thong Pha Phum to Sangkhlaburi by van is 50B). Arriving from Kan, the van driver will drop you off at P Guest House or the Sri Daeng Hotel on request. In Sangkhla the vans depart from the No-Name restaurant. From either end it's usually necessary to reserve your seat a day in advance.

If you go by motorcycle, you can count on about five hours to cover the 217 km from Kanchanaburi to Sangkhlaburi, including three or four short rest stops. Alternatively, you can make it an all-day trip and stop off in Ban Kao, Muang Singh, and Hellfire Pass. Be warned, however, that this is not a trip for an inexperienced rider. The Thong Pha Phum to Sangkhlaburi section of the journey (about 70 km) requires sharp reflexes and previous experience on mountain roads. This is also not a motorcycle trip to do alone as stretches of the highway are practically deserted – it's tough to get help if you need it and easy to attract the attention of would-be bandits.

Three Pagodas Pass/Payathonzu
พระเจดีย์สามองค์

The pagodas themselves are rather small, but it is the remote nature of this former black-market outpost that draws a trickle of visitors. Control of the Burmese side of the border once vacillated between the Karen National Union and the Mon Liberation Front, since Three Pagodas was one of several 'toll gates' along the Thai-Burmese border where insurgent armies collected a 5% tax on all merchandise that passed. These ethnic groups used the funds to finance armed resistance against the Burmese government, which has recently increased efforts to regain control of the border area.

The Karen also conduct a huge multimillion dollar business in illegal mining and logging, the products of which are smuggled into Thailand by the truckload under cover of the night – not without the palms-up co-operation of the Thai police, of course. Pressure for control of these border points has increased since the Thai government enacted a ban on all logging in Thailand in 1989, which has of course led to an increase in teak smuggling.

In late 1988, heavy fighting broke out between the Karen and the Mon for control of the 'toll gate' here. Since this is the only place for hundreds of km in either direction where a border crossing is geographically convenient, this is where the Mon army (who traditionally have controlled this area) have customarily collected the 5% tax on smuggling. The Karen insurgents do the same at other points north along the Thai-Burmese border. Burmese government pressure on the Karen further north led to a conflict between the Karen and the Mon over Three Pagodas trade and the village on the Burmese side was virtually burnt to the ground in the 1988 skirmishes.

In 1989 the Rangoon government wrested control of the town from both the Karen and Mon, and the Burmese seem firmly established at the border for the time being. The Burmese have renamed the town Payathonzu and filled it with shops catering to an odd mix of occupation troops and tourists.

Foreigners are now allowed to cross the border here for day trips – the only land crossing permitted for non-Thais along Burma's entire border perimeters. Payathonzu lies 470 km by road from Rangoon but is considered '75% safe' by the Burmese military. Apparently insurgent Karen forces are still in the area and there are occasional firefights.

A true frontier town, Payathonzu has three Burmese teahouses, one with *nam-bya* – the Burmese equivalent to Indian nan bread – one cinema, several mercantile shops with Burmese longyis, cheroots, jade, clothes, and a few souvenir shops with Mon-Karen-Burmese handicrafts. Bargaining is necessary (some English is spoken, also Thai) but in general goods are well priced. About 20 Thai merchants operate in town – the Burmese government offers them free rent to open shops.

Nearby **Kloeng Thaw Falls** takes a couple of hours by motorcycle to reach from Payathonzu. The road to the falls is only open in the dry season – reportedly the Karen control the waterfall area during the rainy season. No-one actually stops you from going to the falls then, though many people will try to wave you back. Even in good weather, the two-rut track is very rugged, not recommended for motorcycle novices.

You'll find very little English spoken out this way and in fact you may hear as much Burmese, Karen and Mon as Thai.

At the border you must check in with Burmese guards and leave all cameras with them – photography is not permitted in Payathonzu. The border is open from 7 am to 6 pm daily.

Places to Stay The only place to stay here is at *Three Pagodas Pass Resort* (☎ 511079; 412-4159 in Bangkok), where large bungalows start at 300B.

Getting There & Away The road to Three Pagodas Pass begins four km before you reach Sangkhla off Highway 323. At this intersection is a Thai police checkpoint where you may have to stop for minor interrogation, depending on recent events in the Three Pagodas Pass area. If the police allow you to proceed, it's 18 km along a very dusty (or very muddy) road to the pass. Along the way you'll pass a couple of villages inhabited entirely by Mon or Karen; you may also notice the Three Pagodas Pass headquarters for the All Burma Students Democratic Front, where self-exiled Rangoon students have set up an opposition movement with the intention of ousting the Ne Win government from Burma.

If you don't have your own wheels, songthaews to Three Pagodas Pass leave about every 40 minutes between 6.30 am and noon from Sangkhlaburi's central market area. The fare is 30B; the last songthaew back to Sangkhlaburi leaves Three Pagodas Pass at around 3.30 pm.

The border is only a short walk from the songthaew stop in Three Pagodas Pass.

Chonburi Province

SI RACHA

ศรีราชา

About 105 km from Bangkok on the east coast of the Gulf of Thailand is the small town of Si Racha (population 23,000), home of the famous spicy sauce *náam phrík sĩi raachaa*. Some of Thailand's best seafood, especially the local oysters, is served here accompanied by this sauce.

The motorised samlors in this fishing town and on Ko Si Chang are unlike those seen anywhere else – huge motorcycles with a side-car at the rear.

On **Ko Loi**, a small rocky island which is connected to the mainland by a long jetty, there is a Thai-Chinese Buddhist temple. Further off shore is a large island called Ko Si Chang, flanked by two smaller islands – Kham Yai to the north and Khang Kao to the south. As this provides a natural shelter from the wind and sea, it is used as a harbour by large incoming freighters. Smaller boats

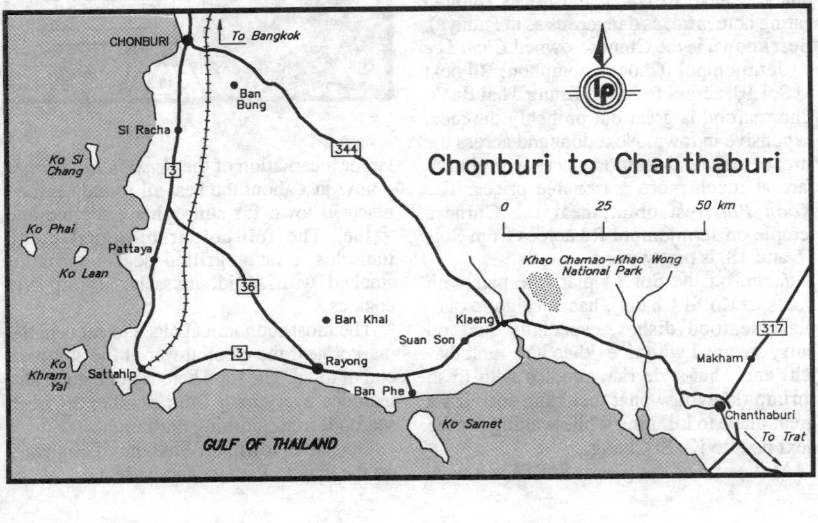

transport goods to the Chao Phraya delta some 50 km away.

A new deep-water port at nearby **Laem Chabang** may eventually erode the huge barge trade in Ko Si Chang's lee.

Places to Stay

The best places to stay in Si Racha are the hotels built on piers over the waterfront. Three of them are very similar in price and quality: *Siriwattana* and *Siwichai*, across from Tessaban 1 Rd and the Bangkok Bank; and *Samchai*, on Soi 10, across from Surasakdi 1 Rd. All have rooms from 100B up and the Samchai has some air-con rooms (250B) as well. The Siriwattana seems to be the cleanest and the service is very good; there are a few rooms out the back for only 80B. All three are open and breezy, with outdoor tables where you can bring food in the evening from nearby markets.

On Soi 18, the *Grand Bungalows* rent bungalows of various sizes, built off the pier, for 400 to 1000B. Each one sleeps several people and they are very popular among holidaying Thais and Chinese.

Places to Eat

There is plenty of good seafood in Si Racha, but you have to watch the prices (though eating here is not as dangerous as in Pattaya). Best known is the Chinese-owned *Chua Lee* on Jermjompol (Choemchomphon) Rd next to Soi 10, across from the Krung Thai Bank. The seafood is great but probably the most expensive in town. Next door and across the street are several seafood places with similar fare at much more reasonable prices. The *Koon Pao* restaurant, near the Chinese temple on Jermjompol Rd across from Sois 16 and 18, is pretty good.

Jarin, on the Soi 14 pier (the pier with boats to Ko Si Chang), has very good one-plate seafood dishes, especially seafood curry steamed with rice (khâo hàw mòk thaleh) and Thai-style rice noodles with fresh shrimp (kũaytĩaw phàt thai kûng sòt). It's a great place to kill time while waiting for the next boat to Ko Si Chang.

At the end of the pier at Soi 18 is a new,

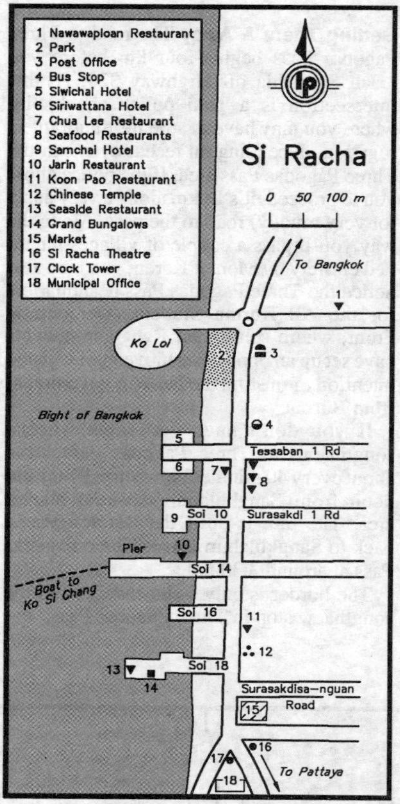

larger incarnation of the *Seaside Restaurant* – now just about the best all-round seafood place in town for atmosphere, service and value. The full-colour bilingual menu includes a tasty grilled seafood platter stacked with squid, mussels, shrimp and cockles.

The most economical place to eat is in the market near the clock tower at the southern end of town. The food here is quite good and includes everything from noodles to fresh seafood, from morning until night.

Outside of town, off Sukhumvit Highway on the way to Pattaya, there are a couple of cheap, but good, fresh seafood places. Locals favour a place near Laem Chabang, about 10 km south of Si Racha, called *Sut Thang Rak* or 'End of Love Rd'. Closer to town is Ao Udom, a small fishing bay where there are several open-air seafood places.

Getting There & Away

Buses to Si Racha leave the eastern bus terminal in Bangkok every 25 minutes or so from 5 am to 7 pm. The ordinary bus is 23B, air-con bus is 42B; travel time is around an hour and 45 minutes. From Pattaya, buses are 5B and take about 30 minutes.

You can also reach Si Racha by 3rd-class train, though not many people come by this method. Train No 239 leaves Hualamphong station at 6.20 am and arrives at Si Racha at 9.05 am (about an hour slower – but more scenic – than the bus). The fare is 28B. A more realistic train trip would be via the No 195 from Chachoengsao – if you happen to be in Chachoengsao – which leaves daily at 2.40 pm and arrives in Si Racha at 3.54 pm. The Chachoengsao to Si Racha fare is 15B.

Getting Around

In Si Racha and on Ko Si Chang there are fleets of huge motorcycle taxis, many powered by Nissan engines, that will take you anywhere in town or on the island for 10 to 20B.

KO SI CHANG

เกาะสีชัง

Ko Si Chang makes a nifty getaway. There is only one town on the island, facing the mainland; the rest of the island is practically deserted and fun to explore. The small population is made up of fisherfolk, retired and working mariners and government workers who are stationed with the customs office or with one of the aquaculture projects on the island. Although there has been talk of building a deep-water port on the island, so far Ko Si Chang has remained free of industry.

Yai Phrik Vipassana Centre, a meditation hermitage, is ensconced in limestone caves and palm huts along the island's centre ridge. The hermit caves make an interesting visit but should be approached with respect – monks and mae chiis from all over Thailand come here to take advantage of the peaceful environment for meditation. Be careful that you don't fall down a limestone shaft; some are nearly covered with vines.

On the opposite side of the island, facing out to sea, are some decent beaches with good snorkelling – take care with the tide and the sea urchins, though. The best, **Hat Tham** (also called Hat Sai), can be reached by following a branch of the ring road on foot to the back of the island. There is also a more public beach at the western end of the island near the old palace grounds, called **Hat Tha Wang**. Thai residents and visitors from the mainland come here for picnics.

The palace was once used by King Chulalongkorn (Rama V) in the summer months, but was abandoned when the French briefly occupied the island in 1893. Little remains of the various palace buildings, but there are a few ruins to see. The main palace building was moved to Bangkok many years ago, but the stairs leading up to it are still there; if you follow these stairs to the crest of the hill overlooking Tha Wang, you'll come to a stone outcropping wrapped in holy cloth. The locals call it 'Bell Rock' because if struck with a rock or heavy stick it rings like a bell. Flanking the rock are what appear to be two ruined chedis. The large chedi on the left actually contains **Wat Atsadangnimit**, a small consecrated chamber where King Rama V used to meditate. The unique Buddha image inside was fashioned 50 years ago by a local monk who now lives in the cave hermitage.

Not far from Wat Atsadangnimit is a large limestone cave called **Tham Saowapha**, which appears to plunge deep into the island. If you have a torch, the cave might be worth exploring.

To the east of town, high on the hill overlooking the sea, is a large **Chinese temple**. During the Chinese New Year in February, the island is overrun with Chinese visitors from the mainland. This is one of Thailand's most interesting Chinese temples, with shrine-caves, several different temple levels and a good view of Si Chang and the ocean. It's a long and steep climb from the road below.

Like most islands along Thailand's eastern seaboard, Ko Si Chang is best visited on weekdays; on weekends and holidays the island can get crowded.

Places to Stay

The easiest places to locate are those near the gate to Hat Tha Wang. *Benz Bungalow* (☎ (038) 216091) offers unique stone bungalows here for 300 to 400B with fan and bath, 600B with air-con. The rather characterless *Tiewpai Guest House* (☎ 216084), also in this area, has a variety of accommodation ranging from 45B for a dorm bed to 450B for an air-con room.

Near Hat Tham at the back of the island is the friendly *Si Phitsanu Bungalow* (☎ (038) 216024). Rooms in a row house cost 200 to 400B per night, or you can get a one-bedroom bungalow overlooking the small bay for 600B, or a two-bedroom one for 1000B.

The *Green House 84* (☎ (038) 216024) is off the ring road towards the Chinese temple and costs 150/200B for basic, but clean singles/doubles in a row house.

In town there are a couple of basic hotels, including the *Ban Ari*, that cost 100B a night but are fairly obvious brothel operations.

You can camp anywhere on the island without any hassle, including in Rama V's abandoned palace at Hat Tha Wang.

Places to Eat

The town has several small restaurants, nothing special, but with all the Thai and Chinese standard dishes.

Getting There & Away

Boats to Ko Si Chang leave regularly from a pier in Si Racha at the end of Soi 14, Jermjompol Rd. The fare is 20B each way; the first boat leaves at about 7 am and the last at 4.30 pm. The last boat back to Si Racha from Si Chang is also at 4.30 pm. As you approach Ko Si Chang by boat, check out the dozens of barges anchored in the island's lee. Their numbers have multiplied from year to year as shipping demands by Thailand's booming import and export business have increased.

Getting Around

There are fleets of huge motorcycle taxis that will take you anywhere in town for 10B. You can also get a complete tour of the island for 70 to 80B.

PATTAYA

พัทยา

On the road through Pattaya (population 50,000), before Pattaya Beach, the bus passes a number of prosperous sign-making businesses. Upon arrival at Pattaya Beach, the reason for their prosperity is immediately apparent – the place is lit up like Hollywood Boulevard at night. Many travellers will find Pattaya lacking in culture as well as good taste, since the whole place seems designed to attract the worst kind of Western tourist. Budget travellers, in particular, would do well to preclude it from their itineraries. Pattaya Beach is not such a great beach to begin with and its biggest businesses, water sports and street sex, have driven prices for food and accommodation beyond Bangkok levels.

Pattaya got its start as a resort when there was a US base at nearby Sattahip during the Vietnam War years – nowadays there are still plenty of sailors about, both Thai and American. Food (especially seafood) is great here, as claimed, but generally way overpriced by national (but not international) standards. That part of South Pattaya known as 'the village' attracts a large number of *ka-toeys*, Thai transvestites, who pose as hookers and ply their trade among the droves of well-heeled European tourists. Germans and Scandinavians lead the pack. Incidentally, the easiest way to tell a ka-toey is by the Adam's apple – a scarf covering the neck is a dead give-away. (Nowadays, though, some ka-toeys have their Adam's apples surgically removed.)

The one thing the Pattaya area has going for it is diving centres (see Diving & Snorkelling in the Facts for the Visitor chapter). There are four or five nice islands off Pattaya's shore, expensive to get to, but if you're a snorkelling or scuba enthusiast, equipment can be booked at any of the several diving shops/schools at Pattaya Beach. Ko Laan, the most popular of the offshore islands, even has places to stay.

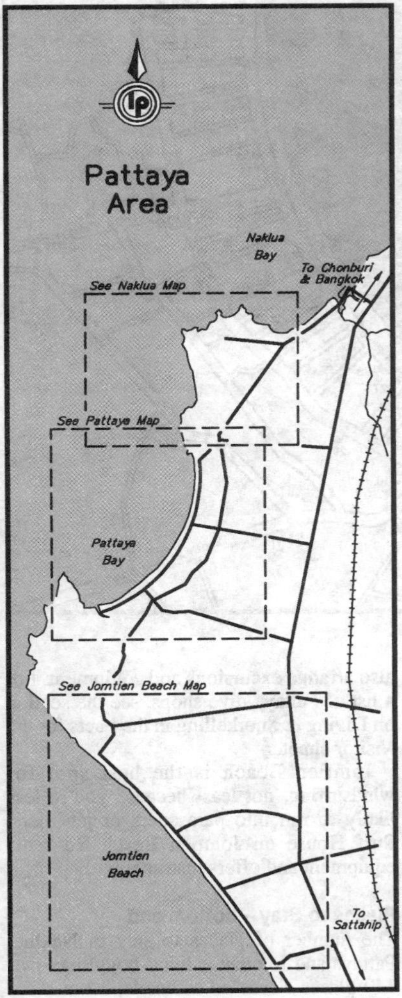

For beach enthusiasts, if you can't get to one of the better beaches in southern Thailand, the best in the Pattaya area is probably Hat Jomtien (Jawmthian), a couple of km south of Pattaya. Here the water is clean and you're well away from the noisy Pattaya bar scene.

Hat Naklua, north of Pattaya, is also quiet and fairly tastefully developed. Jomtien and Naklua are where visiting families tend to stay, as Pattaya/South Pattaya is pretty much given over to single male tourists or couples on package tours. The glitziest digs are in North Pattaya and Cliff beaches (between South Pattaya and Jomtien).

Changing the Image

After garnering a long streak of bad press in both the domestic and international media, Pattaya has recently begun experiencing a steady decline in tourist visitation. In 1992 Pattaya lost the privilege of hosting the annual Siam World Cup – one of Asia's biggest windsurfing competitions – to Phuket. The two principal complaints have been the sidewalk sex scene and Pattaya Bay's water quality.

Local authorities and travel suppliers are now struggling to upgrade Pattaya's image as well as clean the place up. In many ways Pattaya serves as the prime example of what can happen to a beach resort area if no controls are applied to the quality and quantity of tourism development. I'm actually beginning to feel sorry for Pattaya in spite of the fact that local developers have dug their own graves, so to speak. It's too late to turn Pattaya back into the fishing village it once was, but it's not too late to recreate a clean, safe tourist destination if all concerned cooperate.

Information

Tourist Office The Pattaya TAT office, at the midpoint of Pattaya Beach Rd, keeps an up-to-date list of accommodation in the Pattaya area, and is very helpful.

Post & Telecommunications The GPO and international telephone office are together in South Pattaya on Soi 15. There are also several private long-distance phone offices in town, but calls from the government office at the GPO are always less expensive.

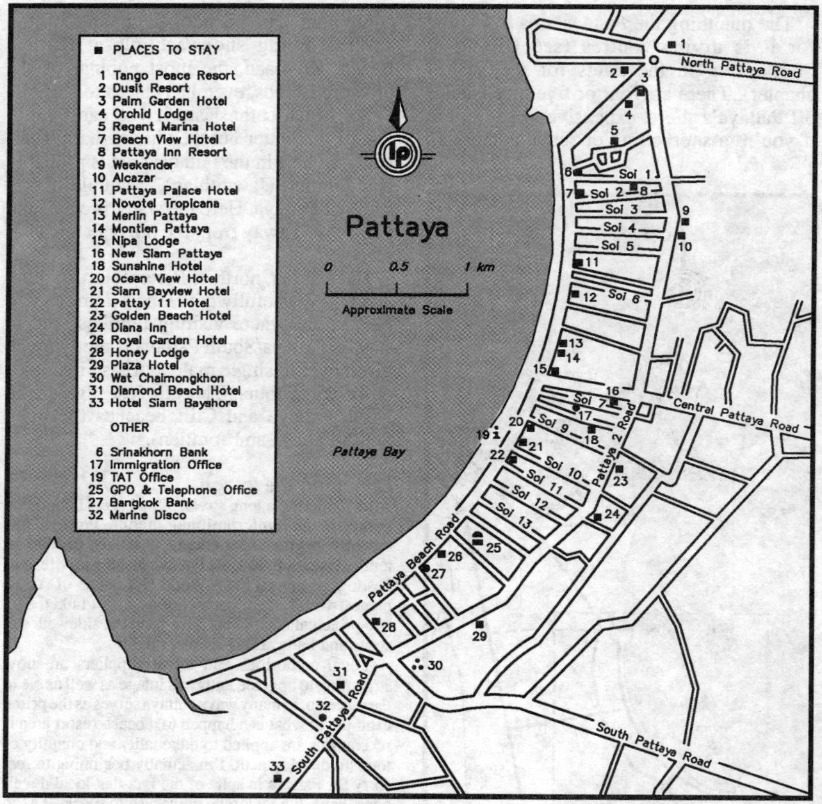

Radio Pattaya has a radio station with English-language broadcasts at FM 107.7 MHz. American and British announcers offer a mix of local news and music.

Water Sports

Waterskiing costs 800 to 1000B per hour including equipment, boat and driver. Parasailing is 250B a shot (about 10 to 15 minutes) and windsurfing 150 to 200B an hour. Diving costs are actually quite reasonable: about 1500B a dive for boat, equipment and underwater guide. Shops along Pattaya Beach Rd advertise; several Pattaya hotels also arrange excursions and equipment. For a list of Pattaya dive shops, see the section on Diving & Snorkelling in the Facts for the Visitor chapter.

Jomtien Beach is the best spot for windsurfing, not least because you're less likely to run into parasailers or jetskiiers. Surf House on Jomtien Beach Rd rents equipment and offers instruction.

Places to Stay – bottom end

The number of places to stay in Naklua, Pattaya and Jomtien is mind-boggling: over 140 places classified as hotels; 80 or more guesthouses; and 32 bungalows. The total number of rooms available is over 13,000! Because of declining occupancy rates, some hotels are now offering special rates; bargaining for a room may also net a lower rate.

The average hotel ranges from 350 to 2000B, and for guesthouses the range is 150 to 300B. The cheapest places in town are the guesthouses in South Pattaya along Pattaya 2 Rd, the street parallel to Pattaya Beach Rd. Most are clustered near Sois 6, 10, 11 and 12. The *Honey Lodge* (☎ 429133) on Soi 10, Pattaya 2 Rd, has rooms in the 200 to 400B range. The *Uthumphorn*, opposite Soi 10 on Pattaya 2, has 150B rooms, as do the nearby *Wangthong*, the *Supin Guest House* on Soi 10, *Winsand Guest House* on Soi 13 and the *Pattaya View Inn* on Soi Post Office.

Also on Pattaya 2 Rd, the *Diana Inn* (☎ 429675) has large rooms with fan and hot-water bath for 200B, plus a pool with bar service – this is still one of Pattaya's best deals. They also have more expensive air-con rooms from 300B.

On Sois 11 and 12, the *Pattaya 11* and the *Pattaya 12* have good air-con rooms for 350B. On Soi 13, the *Malibu Guest House* has 300B air-con rooms that include breakfast. The rest of the many guesthouses on Soi 13 are in the 200 to 300B range, but rooms are usually cramped and without windows.

A German reader wrote to say 'Our impression of Pattaya wasn't as bad as yours' and recommended a place called *Garden Villa* on Naklua Rd (North Pattaya). It costs 300B for an air-con double, is owned by Germans and has 'traditional German food and customs'. Another place that has been recommended is *In de Welkom*; doubles with fan cost 280B and air-con singles cost 300B.

At Jomtien Beach, the bottom end consists of *Sunlight* with 250B air-con rooms at the north end of the beach (next to Surf House).

Places to Stay – middle

Good middle-range places can be found in Naklua, North Pattaya and Jomtien. The *Garden Lodge* (☎ 429109), just off Naklua Rd, has air-con rooms for 350B, a clean pool, good service, and an open-air breakfast buffet. *Pattaya Lodge* (☎ 428014) is further off Naklua Rd, right on the beach. Air-con rooms here are 2000 to 2800B. The *Riviera Pattaya* (☎ 429230) is between the road and the beach and has air-con rooms for 250 to 350B.

Peaceful Jomtien Beach has mostly middle-range 'condotel' places ranging in price from 500 to 700B. The *Jomtien Bayview* (☎ 425889) and *Visit House* (☎ 426331) have air-con rooms for 300 to 400B. The *Silver Sand* (☎ 429717) and *Surf House* (☎ 231158) each have air-con rooms for 400 to 450B. The *Marine Beach* (☎ 231177) and *Sea Breeze* (☎ 231057) are just a bit more expensive at 500 to 750B per air-con room. Jomtien also has several more

---

Water Quality

One of Pattaya's main problems during recent years has been the emptying of raw sewage into the bay, a practice that has posed serious health risks for swimmers. Local officials have finally begun to take notice and are now taking regular bacteria counts along the shoreline and fining hotels or other businesses found to be releasing untreated sewage.

The city is currently expanding its 1986 water-treatment plant and completing a new plant in South Pattaya; together these will eventually handle all sewage produced by the area. Additional plants may soon be constructed at Jomtien Beach and Naklua as well. As a result of these efforts, according to city officials, Pattaya Bay will be returned to its 'pristine' condition by 1993.

In the meantime, according to TAT's recently released pamphlet entitled 'Striving to Resolve Pattaya's Problems', beach areas considered safe for swimming (with a coliform count of less than 1000 MPN per 100 millilitres) include those facing Wong Amat Hotel, Dusit Resort Hotel, Yot Sak shopping centre and the Royal Cliff Hotel. Shoreline areas found to exceed the coliform standard extend from Siam Commercial Bank in South Pattaya to where Khlong Pattaya empties into the sea. Coliform counts here exceeded 1700 MPN per 100 millilitres. ■

expensive places that rent bungalows in the 1000 to 2000B range (see top end – Jomtien Beach). Eventually, the high-rise development of Pattaya and Cliff Beach will most likely spread to Jomtien.

At the time of writing there are only two places to stay on Ko Laan, both in the mid-to-high range. The *Island Inn* (☎ 428444) has fan-cooled rooms with bath for 200 to 500B, while the *Ko Laan Resort* (☎ 428422) has more up-market fan rooms for 700B.

Places to Stay – top end

Pattaya is really a resort for package tourists so the vast majority of its accommodation is in this bracket. The two reigning monarchs of Pattaya luxury hotels are the *Dusit Resort* – at the northern end of Pattaya Beach, with two pools, tennis courts, a health centre and exceptional dim sum in the rooftop restaurant – and the *Royal Cliff Beach Resort* (at the southern end of Pattaya), which is really three hotels in one: a central section for package tours and conventions, a family wing and the very up-scale Royal Wing.

All of the hotels listed below have air-con rooms and swimming pools (unless otherwise noted). Many of the top-end hotels have lowered rates on standard singles and doubles so it's worth asking if anything cheaper is available when requesting a rate quote. Rooms are also often cheaper when booked through a Bangkok travel agency.

Naklua

Prima Villa Hotel, Naklua Soi 18, 91 rooms, 726B up (☎ 429398)
Sea View, Naklua Rd, 159 rooms, 600 to 2200B (☎ 429317)
Wong Amat Hotel, Naklua Rd, 207 rooms, 1300B up (☎ 428118/20)
Woodland Resort, Naklua Rd, 80 rooms, 1000B (☎ 421707)

North Pattaya

Beach View, 104 rooms, 545 to 978B (☎ 422660)
Dusit Resort, Mu 5, Pattaya-Naklua Rd, 408 rooms, 790 to 5400B (☎ 428541; 236-0450 in Bangkok)

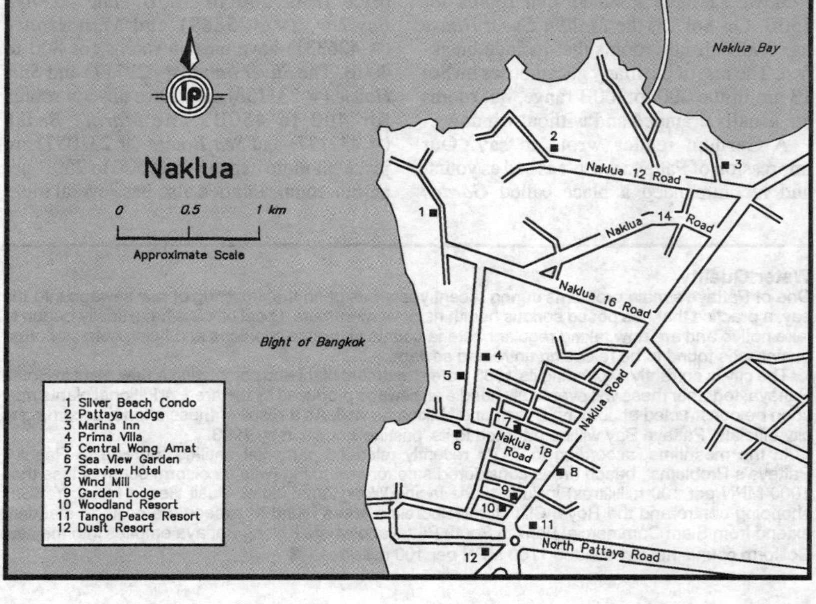

Merlin Pattaya, Beach Rd, 360 rooms, singles/doubles 1694B (☎ 428755/9)
Montien Pattaya Beach Rd, 320 rooms, singles/doubles 1200 to 18,040B (☎ 428155/6)
Orchid Lodge, Beach Rd, 236 rooms, singles/doubles 960 to 2662B (☎ 428175)
Pattaya Palace Hotel, Beach Rd, 261 rooms, 650 to 3000B (☎ 428319)
Regent Marina Hotel, North Pattaya Rd, 208 rooms, 1210 to 2904B (☎ 428015, 429298)

Central & South Pattaya

Diamond Beach Hotel, South Pattaya, 120 rooms, 350 to 1500B (☎ 428071, 429885/6)
Golden Beach Hotel, 519/29 Pattaya 2 Rd, 600 to 900B (☎ 428891)
Nipa Lodge, Beach Rd, 150 rooms, singles/doubles 968 to 2400B (☎ 428321)
Ocean View Hotel, Beach Rd, 111 rooms, 950 to 4000B (☎ 428434)
Royal Garden Resort, Beach Rd, 154 rooms, 900B up (☎ 428122/6/7)
Hotel Siam Bayshore, South Pattaya Rd, 270 rooms, 1200 to 7000B (☎ 428679/80)
Siam Bayview Hotel, Beach Rd, 302 rooms, 1200B up (☎ 428728)

Hat Cliff

Asia Pattaya Beach Hotel, Cliff Rd, 314 rooms, 1690 to 6600B (☎ 428602/6)
Cosy Beach, Cliff Rd, no pool, 62 rooms, 545 to 787B (☎ 429344)
Island View, 150 rooms, 968 to 1452B (☎ 422816)
Royal Cliff Beach Resort, Cliff Rd, 650 rooms, 1452 to 7260B (☎ 428513, 428613/6; 282-0999 in Bangkok)

Hat Jomtien

Amnuaythip Villa, 14 bungalows, 1200 to 1800B (☎ 429220)
Ban Suan, nine bungalows, 1400 (fan) to 2500B (air-con) (☎ 428762)
Coral Inn, 40 rooms, 600 to 800B (☎ 231283)
Golden Beach Resort, 30 apartments, 500 to 1500B (☎ 428205)
Jomtien Chalet, 36 bungalows, 900 to 1400B (☎ 231205)
Jomtien Hill, 16 rooms, 600 to 2600B (☎ 422378)
Jomtien Palace, 140 rooms, 1200 to 1800B (☎ 429149)
Pattaya Park, 240 rooms, 1000 to 3000B (☎ 423000/4)
Sala Jomtien, 12 bungalows, 1300 to 2100B (☎ 231074)

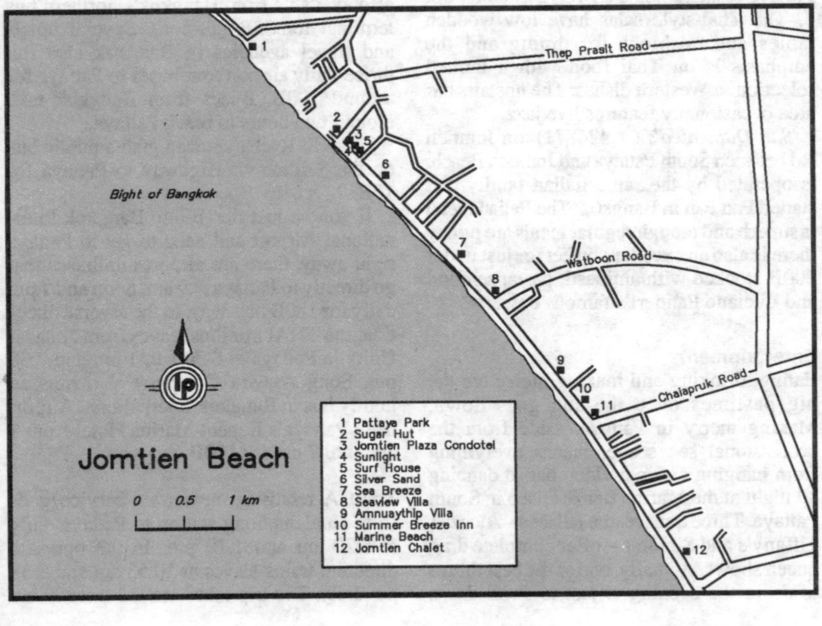

Seaview Villa, seven bungalows, 1000 to 3000B, no air-con (☎ 422766)
Siam Beach Resort, 140 rooms, 1936 to 4840B (☎ 231490)
Suan Nong Nuch, 14 bungalows, six Thai-style houses, 450 to 2500B (☎ Bangkok 252-1786)

Places to Eat

Most food in Pattaya is expensive, but good Thai food is available in shops along Pattaya's back street (Pattaya 2 Rd), away from the beach. Also look for cheap rooms to rent here. The front signs outside the many snack bars reveal that bratwurst mit brot is far more readily available than khâo phàt.

Arabs and South Asians are coming to Pattaya in droves these days, so there is an increasing number of Indian/Pakistani/ Middle Eastern restaurants in town, some with fairly moderate prices.

The best seafood restaurants are in South Pattaya, where you pick out the sea creatures yourself and are charged by weight. Prices are sky-high.

One moderately priced yet well-appointed Pattaya restaurant is the *PIC Kitchen* on Soi 5. The Thai-style salas have low wooden tables and cushions for dining and the emphasis is on Thai food with a limited selection of Western dishes. The upstairs bar area occasionally features live jazz.

San Domenico's (☎ 426871), on Jomtien Rd between South Pattaya and Jomtien Beach, is operated by the same Italian family that started Pan Pan in Bangkok. The Italian menu is superb and though regular meals are pricey there is also an excellent buffet for just under 200B stocked with antipasti, pasta, seafood and Luciano Pantieri's famous desserts.

Entertainment

Eating, drinking and making merry are the big pastimes once the sun goes down. Making merry in Pattaya, aside from the professional sex scene, means everything from hanging out in a video bar to dancing all night at the Marine Bar & Disco in South Pattaya. Three transvestite palaces – Alcazar, Tiffany's and Simon's – offer complete drag queen shows. Actually, one of the best things to do in the evening is just to stroll down Beach Rd and check out the amazing variety of bars – there's one for every proclivity, including a couple of outdoor Thai boxing bars featuring local talent. Truly the Garden of Earthly Delights, in the most Boschean sense.

Getting There & Away

Air Tropical Sea Air (formerly Yellowbird) offers a seaplane service from Bangkok International Airport twice daily on a 15-seat Mallard or 10-seat Goose turboprop. The fare is 1050B one-way. Lately the flights have been on-again, off-again; whether the service will continue on a regular basis depends on whether Pattaya tourism returns to pre-1989 levels.

Bus Ordinary buses from Bangkok's eastern bus terminal cost 29B one-way and leave at 30-minute intervals from 6 am to 8 pm daily. Air-con buses from the same station leave at similar intervals for 50B (or 96B return) between 6 am and 6 pm. Buses to Pattaya are also available from Bangkok's northern bus terminal for 53B (air-con). Several hotels and travel agencies in Bangkok also run thrice-daily air-con tour buses to Pattaya for around 100B. Buses from Bangkok take around two hours to reach Pattaya.

From Si Racha you can grab a public bus on the Sukhumvit Highway to Pattaya for 10B.

If you've just flown into Bangkok International Airport and need to get to Pattaya right away, there are airport minibuses that go directly to Pattaya at 9 am, noon and 7 pm daily for 180B one-way. In the reverse direction, the THAI minibus leaves from Alcazar Unity in Pattaya at 6.30 am, 1 pm and 7.30 pm. Song Asawin Company also runs an hourly bus to Bangkok International Airport from Pattaya's Regent Marina Hotel from 7 am until 7 pm for 100B one-way.

Train A relatively new train service goes from Hualamphong station to Pattaya daily at 6.20 am and 1.10 pm. In the opposite direction trains leaves at 10.53 am and 5.38 pm daily. The trip takes around three hours and costs 31B one way. Although this is an hour longer than the typical bus ride from Bangkok, it beats biting your nails in traffic jams along the highway from Bang Na to Trat.

Getting Around

Songthaew Songthaews cruise up and down Pattaya Beach and Pattaya 2 Rds frequently – just hop on and when you get out pay 5B. If you go to Naklua it's 10B. Don't ask the fare first as the driver may interpret this to mean you want to charter the vehicle. To get to Jomtien you will have to charter a songthaew and the fare should be about 40B.

Boat The ferry to Ko Laan takes 40 minutes and costs a steep 100B. For 250B the ferry service will throw in lunch. Boat charters cost around 700 to 1000B per day depending on the size of the boat.

Car & Jeep Jeeps go for around 500 to 800B per day, and cars start at 800B depending on size and model. All rentals in Pattaya are on a 24-hour basis. Avis has offices at the Dusit Resort (☎ 429901) and Royal Cliff Beach Resort (☎ 422421); Hertz at the Royal Garden Resort (☎ 428122). Pattaya Vehicle Rental Service (☎ 425700) and Pop Eye (☎ 429631), both on Pattaya 2 Rd, have lower rates.

Motorbike Motorbikes cost about 150B per day up to 100cc; a 125cc will cost 200 to 250B and you'll even see a few 750cc to 1000cc machines for hire for 500B. There are several motorcycle hire places along Pattaya Beach Rd and a couple on Pattaya 2 Rd.

AROUND PATTAYA

Further south and then east from Pattaya are more beaches and more resorts. In fact, the more posh places may, in the future, be restructuring themselves in favour of more middle-class tourists and conventioneers.

Bang Saray Villa (☎ 436070) in Bang Saray, has 19 air-con bungalows for 300B, while the *Bang Saray Bay Resort* and *Ban Saray Fishing Lodge* (☎ 436757) are small hotels with air-con rooms for 550B. *Nong Nooch Village* (☎ 429373) has a choice of rooms or bungalows ranging from 300 to 2500B. *Sea Sand Club* (☎ 435163) has 43 air-con bungalows that cost 650B Sunday to Thursday; 750B Friday and Saturday.

There are still some good seafood restaurants for local Thais in Bang Saray – something Pattaya hasn't seen for years.

Still further south is Sattahip, a vacation spot for the Thai military – some of the best beaches in the area are reserved for their use. There are several Thai navy and air force bases in the vicinity.

Rayong Province

RAYONG & AROUND

อ.เมืองระยอง

Rayong (population 42,000) is 220 km from Bangkok by the old highway (Highway 3) or 185 km on Highway 36. The province produces fine fruit (especially durian and pineapple) and *náam plaa* (fish sauce). Rayong itself is not really worth visiting, but nearby beaches are fair and Ko Samet is a favourite island getaway for Bangkokians. Except for Ko Samet, this area has not received many foreign visitors yet, although it has been popular with Thai tourists for several years.

Rayong's beaches are all near **Ban Phe**, a seaside town a few km south-east of the provincial capital (this is also the departure point for Ko Samet). If sun and sand are what you've come to Rayong for, head straight for Ban Phe. Then pick out a beach or board a boat bound for Samet.

Another much smaller island nearby is **Ko Saket**, which is a 20-minute boat ride from the beach of Hat Sai Thong (turn south off Highway 3 at Km 208).

The **Suan Son Pine Park**, five km further down the highway from Ban Phe, is a popular place for Thai picnickers and has white-sand beaches as well.

Suan Wang Kaew is 11 km east of Ban Phe and has more beaches and rather expensive bungalows. **Ko Talu**, across from Wang Kaew, is said to be a good diving area – the proprietors of Suan Wang Kaew, a private park, can arrange boats and gear. Other resort areas along the Rayong coast include **Laem Mae Phim** and **Hat Mae Ram Pheung**.

Khao Chamao-Khao Wong National Park is inland about 17 km north of Km 274 off Highway 3. Though less than 85 sq km, the park is famous for limestone mountains, caves, high cliffs, dense forest, waterfalls, and freshwater swimming and fishing. The park service here rents bungalows, long houses and tents.

Many more resort-type places are popping up along Rayong's coastline. Bangkok developers envisage a string of Thai resorts all the way to Trat along the eastern seaboard, banking on the increasing income and leisure time of Bangkok Thais.

One non-resort development along the coast is the new deep-water port at **Maptaphut** which, along with Chonburi's Laem Chabang Port, is charted to catch the large shipping overflow from Bangkok's Khlong Toey Port.

Places to Stay & Eat

Rayong There are three hotels near the bus station off Sukhumvit Highway. The *Rayong*, at 65/3 Sukhumvit Rd, and the *Otani*, at 69 Sukhumvit, both have rooms from 100B. The latter has some air-con rooms for 300B as well. The *Tawan Ok*, at 52/3 Sukhumvit, has fan-cooled rooms for 90B without bath, 150B with bath.

For cheap food check the market near the Thetsabanteung cinema, or the noodle shop on Taksin Rd next to Wat Lum Mahachaichunphon. There is a very good open-air restaurant along the river belonging to the Fishermen's Association ('Samaakhom Pramong' in Thai).

Ban Phe There are two hotels in Ban Phe, both near the central market. The new *Nuan Napa* has rooms from 150B with fan and bath, while the *Queen* has rooms for 80B (no bath), 120B with bath, and 200B with air-con.

The *Thale Thawng* restaurant, where the tour bus from Bangkok stops, has good Thai seafood dishes – especially recommended is the kũaytĩaw tha-leh, a seafood noodle soup for 10B. The shop across the street is a good place to stock up on food, mosquito coils, etc to take to Ko Samet. You'll most likely be spending some time in this spot, waiting either for the boat to leave the nearby pier for Ko Samet or for the bus to arrive from Bangkok.

Ko Saket *Ko Saket Phet* (☎ 271-2750 in Bangkok) has 15 bungalows and 10 'tourist houses' for 300 to 1500B.

Getting There & Away

See the Getting There & Away section for Ko Samet for details on transport to/from Rayong.

KO SAMET
เกาะเสม็ด

This island earned a permanent place in Thai literature when classical Thai poet Sunthorn Phu set part of his epic *Phra Aphaimani* on the island. The story follows the travails of a prince exiled into an undersea kingdom ruled by a lovesick female giant. A mermaid aids the prince in his escape to Samet where he defeats the giant by playing a magic flute. Formerly Ko Kaew Phitsadan or 'Vast Jewel Isle' – a reference to the abundant white sand, this island became known as Ko Samet or 'Cajeput Isle' after the cajeput tree which grows in abundance here and which is very highly valued as firewood throughout South-East Asia. Locally, the *samet* tree is also used in boat-building.

In the early '80s, the 131-sq-km Ko Samet began receiving its first visitors interested in more than cajeput trees and sand – young Thais in search of a retreat from city life. At that time there were only about 40 houses on the island, built by fisherfolk and Ban Phe locals. Rayong and Bangkok speculators saw the sudden interest in Ko Samet as a chance to cash in on an up-and-coming

Phuket and began buying up land along the beaches. No-one bothered with the fact that Ko Samet, along with Laem Ya and other nearby islands, was part of a national park (one of seven marine parks now in Thailand) and had been since 1981.

When farangs started coming to Ko Samet in greater and greater numbers, spurred on by rumours that Ko Samet was similar to Ko Samui '10 years ago' (one always seems to miss it by a decade, eh?), the National Parks Division stepped in and built a visitors' office on the island, ordered that all bungalows be moved back behind the tree-line and started charging a 5B admission into the park.

Other rather recent changes have included the introduction of several vehicles to the island, more frequent boat services from Ban Phe and a much improved water situation. Ko Samet is a very dry island (which makes it an excellent place to visit during the rainy season). Before they started trucking water to the bungalows you had to bathe at often muddy wells. Now most of the bungalow places have proper Thai-style bathrooms and, as a result, Ko Samet is a much more comfortable and convenient place to visit, though it may be in danger of becoming overcrowded. For now, the bungalows are spread thinly over most of the island with the north-east coast being the most crowded area. The beaches really are lovely, with the whitest, squeakiest sand in Thailand. There is even a little surf occasionally (best months are December to January). However, I still think the accommodation on Samui and Pha-Ngan islands is better value overall, though of course it's much more expensive and time-consuming to reach from Bangkok.

In spite of the fact that the island is supposedly under the protection of the National Parks Division, on recent trips to Ko Samet I was appalled at the runaway growth in the Na Dan and Hat Sai Kaew areas. Piles of rubbish and construction materials have really taken away from the island's charm at the northern end. Once you get away from this end of the island, however, things start looking a bit better.

Ko Samet can be very crowded during Thai public holidays: early November (Loi Krathong Festival); 5 December (King's birthday); 31 December to 1 January (New Year); mid-to-late February (Chinese New Year); mid-April (Songkran Festival). During these times there are people sleeping on the floors of beach restaurants, on the beach, everywhere. September gets the lowest number of visitors (2500 visitors in September 1990), March the most (43,000 visitors – 36,000 of them Thai – in March 1990). Thais in any month are more prevalent than foreigners but many are day visitors; most

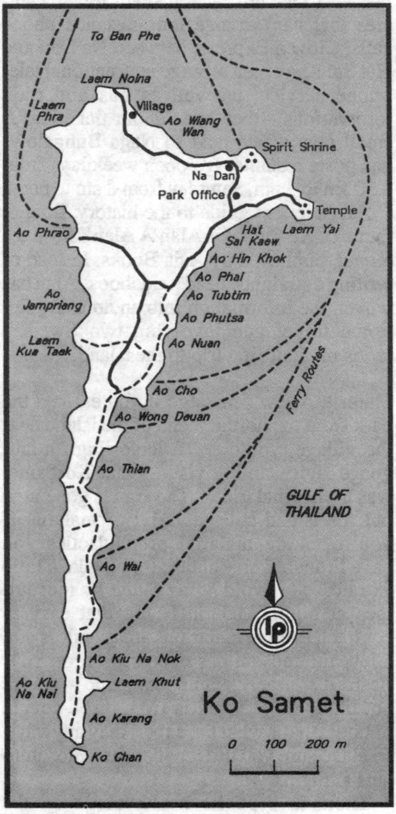

stay at White Sand or Wong Deuan in the more up-market accommodation.

In May 1990 the Forestry Department closed the park to all visitors in an effort to halt encroachment on national park lands, but then reopened the island the next month in response to protests by resort operators. Developers reasonably objected that if Ko Samet is to be closed then so must Ko Phi Phi be. Court hearings continue monthly; the latest word is that there will be a permanent moratorium on new developments in order to preserve the island's forested interior.

Information

Near Na Dan are several small travel agencies that can arrange long-distance phone calls. Citizen Express, between Na Dan and Hat Sai Kaew, can arrange international telephone service, as well as bus and train reservations – they even do air ticketing. A small post office next to Naga Bungalows has poste restante. It's open weekdays from 8.30 am to 3 pm, Saturday from 8 am to noon.

An excellent guide to the history, flora & fauna of Ko Samet is Alan A Alan's 88-page *Samet*, published by Asia Books. Instead of writing a straight-ahead guidebook, Alan has woven the information into an amusing fictional travelogue involving two Swedish twins on their first trip to the island.

Malaria A few years ago if you entered the park from the northern end of the island near the village, you'd see a large English-language sign warning visitors that Ko Samet was highly malarious. The sign is gone now but the island still has a bit of malaria. If you're taking malarial prophylactics you have little to worry about. If not, take a little extra care to avoid being bitten by mosquitoes at night. Malaria is not that easy to contract, even in malarious areas, unless you allow the mosquitoes open season on your flesh. It's largely a numbers game – you're not likely to get malaria from just a couple of bites (that's what the experts say anyway), so make sure you use repellent and mosquito nets at night.

There is a public health clinic on the island, located halfway between the village harbour and the park entrance. Go there for a blood test if you develop a fever while on Ko Samet, or for any other urgent health problems such as attacks from poisonous sea creatures or snakes.

Activities

Several bungalows on the island can arrange boat trips to nearby reefs and uninhabited islands. Ao Phutsa and Naga Beach (Ao Hin Khok) have a couple of windsurfing equipment rental places that do boat trips as well. Chan's Windsurfing, on Naga Beach, puts together day trips to Ko Thalu, Ko Kuti, etc for 150B per person, including food and beverages (minimum of 10 people). They also rent sailboards at reasonable hourly rates with or without instruction.

A Request The Rayong tourist police request that visitors refrain from hiring jet skis on Samet beaches as it is harmful to coral and dangerous to swimmers. The local police won't do anything about it even though it's illegal – either because they're afraid of beach developers or are in their pockets.

Places to Stay

The two most developed (overdeveloped) beaches are Hat Sai Kaew and Ao Wong Deuan. All of the other spots are still rather peaceful. Every bungalow operation on the island has at least one restaurant and most now have running water and electricity.

Since this is a national park, camping is allowed on any of the beaches. In fact, this is a great island to camp on because it hardly ever rains. There is plenty of room; most of the island is uninhabited and so far, tourism is pretty much restricted to the north-eastern beaches.

Places to Stay – east coast

Hat Sai Kaew Samet's prettiest beach, 'Diamond Sand', is a km or so long and 25 to 30 metres wide. The bungalows here happen to be the most commercial on the island, with video in the restaurants at night and lots of lights. They're all very similar and offer a range of accommodation from 50B (in the low season) for simple huts without fan or bath up to 400 to 500B for one with fan, mosquito net and private bath. All face the beach and most have outdoor restaurants serving a variety of seafood. Like elsewhere in Thailand, the daily rate for accommodation can soar suddenly with demand. The more scrupulous places don't hike rates by much, though:

White Sand, 50 to 200B
Ploy Talay, 150 to 500B
VK Villa, 80 to 350B
Saikaew Villa, 50 to 200B
Diamond, 50 to 400B
Seaview, 50 to 200B
Toy, 100 to 200B
Yaka, 100 to 500B
Jit Preecha, 100 to 300B

Ao Hin Khok The beach here is about half the size of Sai Kaew but nearly as pretty – the rocks that give the beach its name add a certain character. Hin Khok is separated from Sai Kaew by a rocky point mounted by a mermaid statue, a representation of the mermaid that carried the mythical Phra Aphaimani to Ko Samet in the Thai epic of the same name. Two of Samet's original bungalow operations still reign here, *Naga* and *Little Hut* (formerly Odd's Little Huts). Naga offers simple bungalows set on a hill overlooking the sea for 80 to 100B. The restaurant at Naga sells great bread (which is distributed to several other bungalows on the island), cookies, cakes and other pastries, baked under the supervision of Englishwoman Sue Wild. The bungalows at Little Hut are a little more solid and go for 100B with shared bath, 150B with private bath; the restaurant here is also quite good.

Further down the beach you may see what looks like a Thai 'gathering of the tribes' – a colourful outpost presided over by Chawalee, a free-spirited Thai woman, who has lived on this beach since long before the bungalows came.

Ao Phai Around the next headland is another shallow bay with *Ao Phai Inn* and *Sea Breeze*, which have bungalows from 150 and 200B, and the *Silver Sand* and *Sunset (Samet) Villa*, with bungalows from 150B.

Ao Phutsa After Ao Phai, the remaining beaches south are separated from one another by steep headlands. To get from one to the next, you have a choice of negotiating rocky paths over the hilly points or walking east to the main road that goes along the centre of the island, then cutting back on side roads to each beach. This is also where the cross-island trail to Ao Phrao starts.

On Ao Phutsa, also known as Ao Thap Thim, you'll find *Phutsa Beach*, where basic huts are 50 to 100B, and the larger *Tub Tim*, where nicer huts are 70 to 300B; the more expensive huts come with fans and bath.

Ao Nuan If you blink, you'll miss this one. Huts at *Ao Nuan* are 70 to 300B.

Ao Cho (Chaw) This bay has its own pier and can be reached directly from Ban Phe on the boat *White Shark*. *Lung Wang* has bungalows starting at 80B. The nicely designed *Tantawan* huts start at 150B.

Ao Wong Deun (Deuan) This area is now mostly given over to more expensive resort-type bungalows. The cheaper bungalows that were here a few years ago have nearly all disappeared and those that remain can't be recommended. It's a little crowded with buildings and people now, but if you want a 300B bungalow, complete with running water and flushing toilet, the best of the lot is *Wong Deun Resort* with huts at 300B. *Wong Deun Villa* is similar but all air-con, ranging from 400 to 2500B. Three boats go back and forth between Ao Wong Deun and Ban Phe – the *Malibu*, *Seahorse*, and *Wong Deun Villa*.

Ao Thian This is better known by its English name, Candlelight Beach. Far removed from the more active beaches to the north, this is the place to come for a little extra solitude, though the bungalow operations here,

Sangthian Beach and *Lung Dam* are no great shakes. Food, I'm told, is a definite minus here too. You can bring your own from the village on the northern tip of the island. Rates are 50B up.

Other Bays You really have to be determined to get away from it all to go further south on the east coast of Samet – not a bad idea. None of the bungalows down here have running water – instead you must rely on rainwater from traditional ceramic water jars. **Ao Wai** is about a km from Ao Thian but can be reached by the boat *Phra Aphai* from Ban Phe. There's only one bungalow operation here, *Sametville*, and rooms are 250 to 500B including all meals. Most bookings are done in Bangkok, but you can try your luck by contacting someone on the *Phra Aphai* at the Ban Phe pier.

Ao Kiu also has only one place to stay at the time of writing, the *Ao Kiu*. Huts are 50 to 500B. The beach here is fairly long and because so few people use it, quite clean. Just a bit further is rocky **Ao Karang**, where rustic *Pakarang* charges 100B per hut (no electricity). Good coral in this area.

Places to Stay – west coast

Hat Ao Phrao (Coconut Bay Beach) is the only beach on the west side of the island. There are nice sunset views. At the northern end of the beach is *Ao Phra Resort* where huts start at 70B and tents go for 50B. Next down is *Rattana* with huts for 50 to 100B. In the middle of the beach is *Dhom* with nice huts built on the hillside for 100 to 500B. At the southern end near the cross-island trail is *SK Hut* where small bungalows are 50B, larger ones up to 500B.

Places to Stay – Na Dan area

To the west of Samet's main pier is a long beach called **Ao Wiang Wan** where several rather characterless bungalows are set up in straight lines facing the mainland. Here you get neither sunrise (maybe a little) nor sunset. The cheapest place is *SK Bungalows* where accommodation is from 50 to 250B. There are several other places with rates in the 150 to 400B range.

All kinds of construction is going on between Na Dan and Hat Sai Kaew, mostly shophouses but possibly new bungalows too.

Getting There & Away

Many Khao San Rd agencies in Bangkok do round-trip transport to Ko Samet including boat for around 220B. This is more expensive than doing it on your own, but for travellers who don't plan to go anywhere else on the east coast it's convenient.

For those who want the flexibility and/or economy of arranging their own travel, the way to go is to bus to Ban Phe in Rayong Province, then catch a boat out to Ko Samet. There are regular buses to Rayong throughout the day from the eastern bus terminal, but if your destination is Ban Phe (for Ko Samet) you'd do better to take one of the direct Ban Phe buses, which only cost 1B more; a songthaew to Ban Phe from Rayong is 10B. The Bangkok to Rayong air-con bus is 69B, Rayong to Ban Phe 70B. You can also get a return (round-trip) ticket to Ban Phe for 120B, a saving of 20B. The company that runs the Ban Phe bus, DD Tours, has a reputation for crummy service, often overbooking on the trip back to Bangkok. They also like to put all the farangs in the back of the bus, regardless of reserved seat numbers. Your only alternative is the ordinary non-air-con bus to Rayong (38B) and then a local bus to Ban Phe.

Boats to Ko Samet leave the Ban Phe pier at regular intervals throughout the day starting at around 8 am. How frequently they depart mostly depends on whether they have enough passengers and/or cargo to make the trip profitable, so there are more frequent boats in the high season, December to March. Still, there are always at least three or four boats a day going to Na Dan and Ao Wong Deuan.

For Hat Sai Kaew, Ao Hin Khok, Ao Phai and Ao Phutsa, take the one of the regular Na Dan boats (operated by Samet Tour, Suriya Tour and Thepmongkonchai) for 30B. From Na Dan you can either walk to these beaches

(10 to 15 minutes) or take one of the trucks that go round the island – if there are several passengers, the fare should be 10B per person to anywhere between Na Dan and Ao Cho. The boat *White Shark* also goes directly to Ao Cho from Ban Phe for 30B – have a look around the Ban Phe pier to see if it's available.

The *Seahorse*, *Malibu* and *Wong Deuan Villa* all go to Ao Wong Deuan for 30B. There's no jetty here, so passengers are pulled to shore on a raft. You can also get a truck-taxi here from Na Dan, but the fare could be as high as 40B if you're alone. For Ao Thian, you should get either the *White Shark* to Ao Cho or one of the Ao Wong Deuan boats.

The *Phra Aphai* makes direct trips to Ao Wai for 30B. For Ao Kiu or Ao Karang, get the *Thep Chonthaleh* (30B).

For Ao Phrao, you can taxi from Na Dan or possibly get a direct boat from Ban Phe for 20B. The boat generally operates from December to May but with the increase in passengers this service may soon go all year.

If you arrive in Ban Phe at night and need a boat to Samet, you can usually charter a one-way trip at the Ban Phe pier for 250 to 300B (to Na Dan).

From Na Dan to Ban Phe Samet Tour seems to run a monopoly on the return trips and they leave only when they're full – a minimum of 18 people for some boats, 25 for others – unless someone contributes more to the passage. The usual fare is 30B.

While waiting for a boat back to the mainland from Na Dan, you may notice a shrine not far from the pier. This *sãan jâo phâw* is a spirit shrine to Puu Dam (Grandfather Black), a sage who once lived on the island. Worshippers offer statues of *reusĩi* (hermit sages), flowers, incense, and fruit.

Getting Around

If you take the boat from Ban Phe to the village harbour (Na Dan), you can easily walk to Hat Sai Kaew, Ao Phai or Ao Cho (Ao Thap Thim). Don't believe the taxi operators who say these beaches are a long distance away. If you're going further down the island, or have a lot of luggage, you can take the taxi (a truck or a three-wheeled affair with a trailer) as far as Ao Wong Deuan. This will cost 20B per person for six to eight people, or 10B each to Ao Cho (or anywhere between Na Dan and Ao Cho). If they don't have enough people to fill the vehicle, they either won't go, or passengers will have to pay more. There are trails from Ao Wong Deuan all the way to the southern tip of the island, and a few cross-island trails as well. Taxis will make trips to Ao Phrao when the road isn't too muddy.

Chanthaburi Province

CHANTHABURI

อ.เมืองจันทบุรี

Situated 330 km from Bangkok, the City of the Moon is a busy gem-mining centre, particularly noted for its sapphires and rubies. Chanthaburi (population 37,000) is also renowned for tropical fruit (rambutan, durian, langsat and mangosteen) and rice noodles – Chanthaburi noodles are in fact exported all over the world.

A significant proportion of the local population are Vietnamese Christians who fled religious or political persecution in Vietnam years ago. The first wave arrived in the 19th century as refugees from anti-Catholic persecution in Cochinchina (southern Vietnam); the second came between the '20s and '40s fleeing French rule; the third wave arrived after the 1975 communist takeover of South Vietnam.

Because of the Vietnamese-French influence, the town has some interesting shophouse architecture, particularly along the river. The French-style cathedral here is the largest in Thailand. Originally, a small missionary chapel was built on this site in 1711. Four reconstructions took place between 1712 and 1906, when the building finally took its current form. The cathedral is 60 metres long and 20 metres wide.

King Taksin Park is a large public park with gazebos and an artificial lake near the centre of town – nice for an evening stroll.

The gem dealers in town are mostly along Trok Kachang off Si Chan Rd in the south-east quarter. All day long buyers and sellers haggle over little piles of blue and red stones. During the first week of June every year there is a gems festival and Chanthaburi can get very crowded.

Two small national parks are within an hour's drive of Chanthaburi. **Khao Khitchakut National Park** is about 28 km north-east of town off Highway 3249 and is known for Krathing Falls, while **Khao Sabap National Park** is only about 14 km south-east off Highway 3 and has Phliu Falls. Khao Sabap has a few park bungalows for rent, while Khao Khitchakut has bungalows as well as a camp ground.

A few km north of town off Highway 3249 is **Khao Phloi Waen**, or 'Sapphire-Ring Mountain', which is only 150 metres high but features a Sri Lankan-style chedi on top, built during the reign of King Mongkut. Tunnels dug into the side of the hill were once gem-mining shafts.

Wat Khao Sukim, quite a well-known

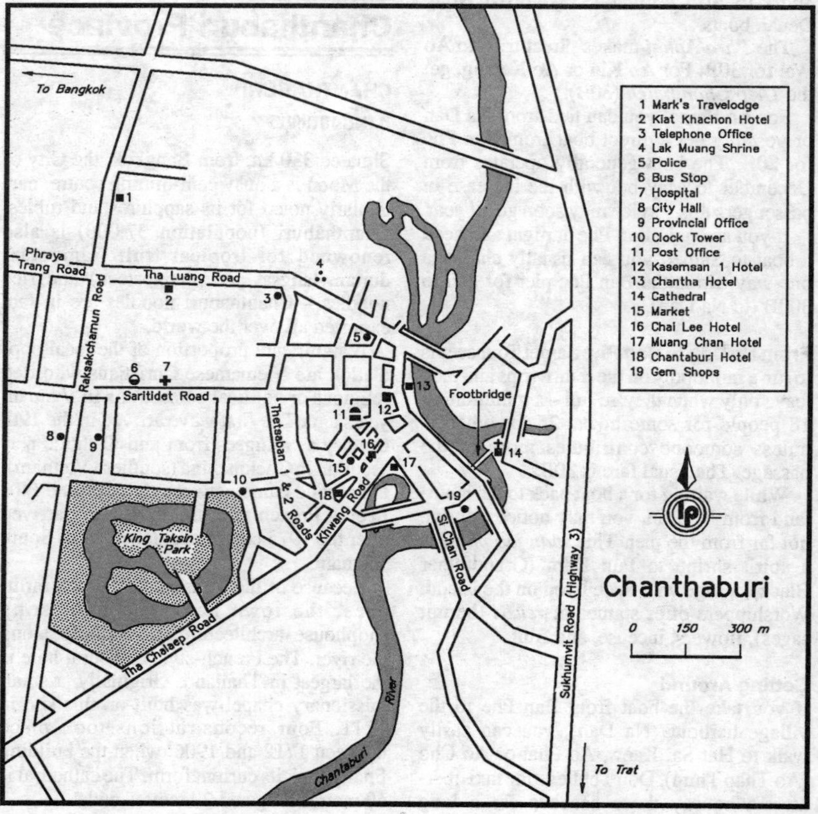

Top Left: Spirit house, Prachinburi (TM)
Bottom Left: Detail of carving, Ancient City (JB)
Top Right: Buddhist shrine, Samut Songkhram (GB)
Bottom Right: Buddha detail, Wat Si Chum, Sukhothai (BP)

Top Left: Monk at festival, Hat Yai (JC)
Top Right: Novice at Phra Pathom Chedi, Nakhon Pathom (RI)
Bottom: Three Pagodas Pass, Kanchanaburi (JC)

meditation centre, is 16 km north of Chanthaburi off Highway 3322. Another meditation centre is at **Wat Sapchan**, 27 km west of Chanthaburi in Tha Mai district; Wat Sapchan is a branch of Ajaan Yantara's Sunyataram Forest Monastery in Kanchanaburi.

Places to Stay

The *Kasemsan I Hotel* (☎ 312340), 98/1 Benchamarachutit Rd has large, clean rooms from 120B or from 200B with air-con. Down by the river on Rim Nam Rd is the cheaper *Chantha Hotel* (☎ 312310) with rooms without bath for 80B, rooms with bath for 100/120B. Some of the rooms have a view of the river – nice spot.

In the municipal market area is the *Kasemsan II* on Rong Muang Rd with the same rates as Kasemsan I but a little noisier due to the location. The nearby *Chai Lee Hotel* on Khwang Rd is similarly priced again, but not as good. In the same area, the *Chanthaburi Hotel* (☎ 311300) on Tha Chala Rd is OK at 120B fan and bath, 200/240B with air-con.

On Si Chan Rd you'll find *Muang Chan Hotel* with adequate rooms in the 120 to 160B range. Out on Tha Luang Rd in the north end of town, away from everything, is the *Kiat Khachon (Kiatkachorn) Hotel* (☎ 311212), with rooms from 120 to 200B.

The top end in town is *Mark's Travelodge* (☎ 311531/647), 14 Raksakchamun Rd. Though not quite 'tourist-class', this is a popular hotel with visiting business travellers. Rooms range from 120B for fan and private bath to 450B for air-con and TV.

Places to Eat

For those famous Chanthaburi noodles, head for the Chinese/Vietnamese part of town along the Chanthaburi River and you'll see variations on the basic rice noodle theme, including delicious crab-fried noodles. On Trok Kachang near the gem stalls is a place serving good khao mok kai, a southern Thai chicken briyani. The *Chanthon Phochana* restaurant beneath the Kasemsan I Hotel has a good variety of Thai and Chinese dishes. At the south-east corner of King Taksin Park are a couple of outdoor ice cream parlours that also serve a few standard Thai dishes.

Getting There & Away

From Bangkok, air-con buses cost 103B; regular buses 56B. From Rayong it's 30B. There are also buses between Khorat and Chanthaburi now via Sa Kaew and Kabinburi. The trip takes four to five hours and passes through good mountain scenery. The total fare is about 55B.

Trat Province

About 400 km from Bangkok, Trat Province borders Cambodia and, as in Chanthaburi, gem-mining is an important occupation. Gem markets *(talàat phloi)* are open daily at the **Hua Thung Market** in Bo Rai district between 7 and 10 am and at the **Khlong Yaw Market** in the same district between 1 and 3 pm. Bo Rai is about 40 km north of Trat on Highway 3389. A smaller market is sometimes open all day in **Khao Saming** district only 20 km north-west of Trat. Sapphires and rubies are good buys if (and only if) you know what you're buying. A sad byproduct of the gem mining is the destruction of vast tracts of land – the topsoil is stripped away, leaving acres of red-orange mud. If the gem business doesn't interest you, another attraction Bo Rai district offers is **Salak Tai Falls** (15 km north-west of Bo Rai).

The other big industry in Trat is the smuggling of consumer goods between Cambodia and Trat. For this reason, travelling alone along the border, or in the offshore islands which serve as conduits for sea smuggling, requires caution. Two farang women (UK and New Zealand citizens) were killed on Ko Chang in 1988 by bandits. More and more people have discovered the beaches and islands of Trat, however, and as the locals and the police have begun to see the benefits of hospitality to outsiders, security has apparently improved.

One relatively safe spot for observing the border trade is at the Thai-Cambodian market in **Khlong Yai**, near the end of Highway 318 south of Trat. An estimated 10 million baht changes hands in the markets of Khlong Yai daily.

As Highway 318 goes east and then south from Trat on the way to Khlong Yai district, the province thins to a narrow sliver between the Gulf of Thailand and Cambodia. Along this sliver are a number of little-known beaches, including **Hat Sai Si Ngoen, Hat Sai Kaew, Hat Thap Thim** and **Hat Ban Cheun**. Ban Cheun has a few bungalows, but there was no accommodation at the other beaches at the time of writing.

At Km 70, off Highway 318, is **Jut Chom Wiw** (View-Admiring Point) where you can get a panorama of the surrounding area. Trat Province's south-easternmost point is reached at **Hat Lek**, which is also a semi-legal jumping-off point for boat trips to the Cambodian coast. Although there are several Thai military checkpoints between Trat and Hat Lek (five at last count), they seem to be getting less strict about allowing foreigners through. For a short time in 1991, the Trat governor had an agreement with his counterpart on the Cambodian side of the border allowing foreigners to cross by boat.

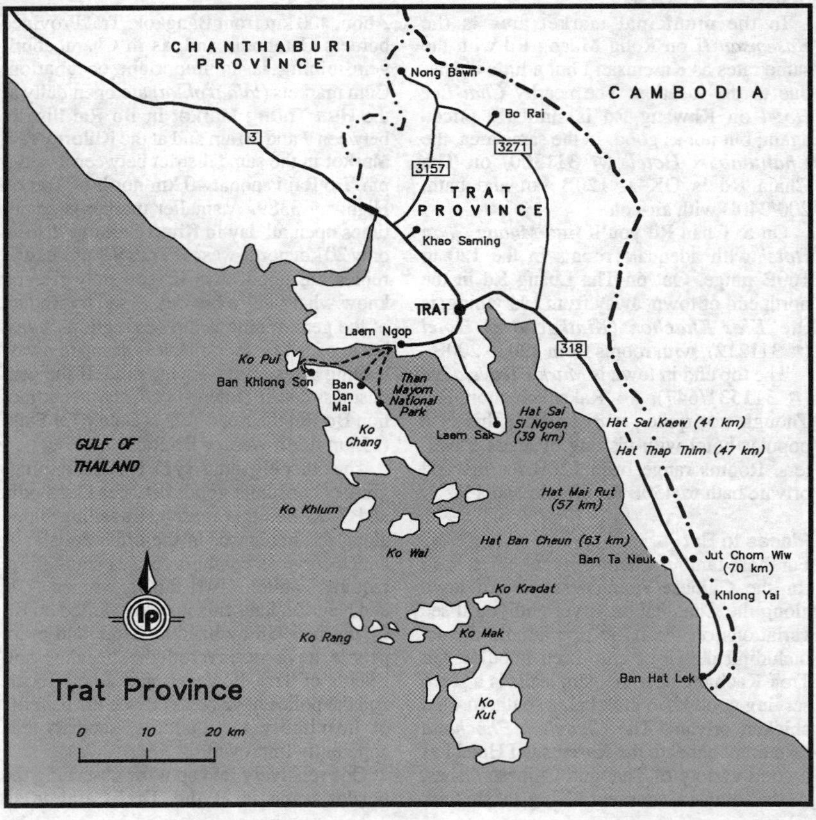

TRAT & AROUND

อ.เมืองตราด

The provincial capital of Trat (population 13,000) has little to offer except as a jumping-off point for the Ko Chang island group or forays into outlying gem and Cambodian markets. The locals are friendly, however, and there are certainly worse places to spend a few days. Market fans will note Trat seems to have more markets for its size than almost any other town in Thailand – probably because it's the closest Thai provincial capital to Cambodian coastal trade.

Information

B&P Travel, on Soi Sukhumvit opposite the municipal market, gives out information on Trat, rents motorcycles, sells and rents a modest selection of backpacking equipment and can arrange local day trips to gem markets or the Trat River estuary. The estuary trips go by boat from the canal in town to the Trat estuary to gather clams (in season) for 100B or less per person for an all-day outing – the exact price depends on the number of people.

Post & Telecommunications The main post office is a long walk from the city centre on Tha Reua Jang Rd. It's open from 8.30 am to 4.30 pm weekdays, 9 am to noon Saturday. The attached international phone office is open daily 7 am till 11 pm.

Information on Ko Chang National Park is available at the park headquarters in Laem Ngop, a small town 20 km south-west of Trat. This is also where you get boats to Ko Chang.

Immigration There is no immigration office in Trat – you must go to the provincial office in Khlong Yai for visa extensions or other immigration matters. If Cambodian border crossings from Trat by land or sea are permitted in the future, this is where you'll have to come to have your passport stamped upon return from Cambodia.

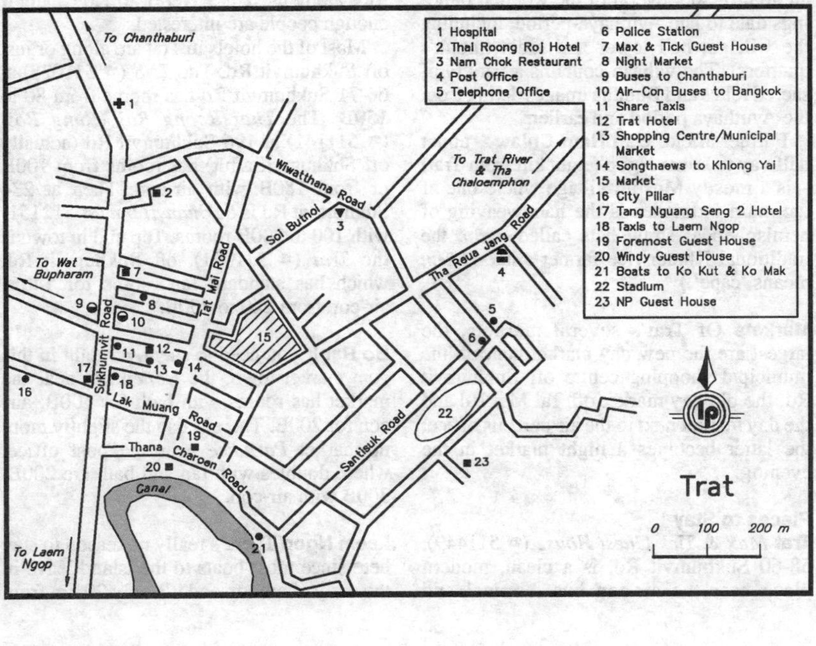

Malaria Rates of infection for malaria are significantly higher for rural Trat (including Ko Chang) than for much of the rest of Thailand, so take the usual precautions. There is a malaria centre on the main road through Laem Ngop (20 km south-west of Trat), opposite Laem Ngop Inn; here you can get the latest information on the disease. This office can also assist with testing and/or treatment for malaria.

Things to See & Do

Trat town's older homes and shophouses are along the canal – you can rent a canoe from one of the guesthouses for a water-level look. During high tide it's possible to boat from the canal to the Trat estuary on the Gulf. This can also be done from the Trat River, north of the city; enquire at **Tha Chaloemphon** (also known simply as *thâa reua* or 'boat pier').

Wat Plai Khlong (Wat Bupharam), two km west of the city centre, is over 200 years old and worth a visit if you're looking to kill an hour or so. Several of the wooden buildings date to late Ayuthaya-period, including the wihaan, bell tower and kutis (monk's quarters). The wihaan contains a variety of sacred relics and Buddha images dating from the Ayuthaya period and earlier.

Further afield, **Ban Nam Chiaw** – about halfway to Laem Ngop (eight km from Trat) – is a mostly Muslim village where one of the main industries is the handweaving of hemispherical straw hats called *ngôp*, the traditional Khmer rice farmer's hat. *(Lãem* means 'cape'.)

Markets Of Trat's several markets, the largest are the new day market beneath the municipal shopping centre off Sukhumvit Rd, the old day market off Tat Mai Rd and the day market next to the air-con bus office; the latter becomes a night market in the evening.

Places to Stay

Trat *Max & Tick Guest House* (☎ 511449), 58-60 Sukhumvit Rd, is a clean, modern place near the air-con bus terminal and market. Rates are 50B per person in a single or double room, 40B per person in a three-bed room. Max and Tick are a friendly young Thai couple who speak excellent English. Their tape collection is one of the best around.

Another friendly spot is the *Foremost Guest House* (☎ 511923), 49 Thana Charoen Rd towards the canal. Rooms are upstairs in an old shophouse; bathrooms are shared but clean, and a hot shower is available. Rates are 50/70B for singles/doubles, 90B a triple, or 30B per person in a dorm. The same family runs the *Windy Guest House* across the road on the canal; here rooms are 60/80B. At either place you can rent canoes for exploring the canal for 20B per day. Bicycles and motorcycles are also available for rent.

A fourth guesthouse has recently opened in a private home in the northern part of town. *NP Guest House* (☎ 512564), at 952 Nerntamuew Rd, has rooms with fan and mosquito netting for 60B per person.

Any of the guesthouses can arrange boat trips along the Trat River or to Ko Chang if enough people are interested.

Most of the hotels in Trat are along or just off Sukhumvit Rd. The *TNS* (☎ 511028) at 66-71 Sukhumvit Rd has rooms from 80 to 150B. The *Thai Roong Roj (Rung Rot)* (☎ 511141) at 196 Sukhumvit Rd (actually off Sukhumvit a bit) has rooms from 100B or from 180B with air-con. Then at 234 Sukhumvit Rd is *Sukhumvit Inn* (☎ 512151) with 100 to 200B rooms. Top end in town is the *Trat* (☎ 511091), off Sukhumvit Rd, which has standard fan rooms for 140B, air-con from 240 to 450B.

Bo Rai If you need to stay overnight in this gem-market town, the *Honey Inn* near the market has rooms with bath for 100B, air-con for 200B. There's also the slightly more up-market *Paradise* near the post office, where doubles with fan and bath are 200B, 300B with air-con.

Laem Ngop There's really no reason to stay here since most boats to the island leave in the early afternoon and it's only 20 km from

Trat. If you must, the *Laem Ngop Inn* and *Paradise* have fan-cooled rooms for 220B, 320B air-con. The *Laem Ngop Guest House* (☎ 512634), also known as Isan Guest House, has rooms in an old house, or bungalows out back, for 70 to 100B; dorm beds are 30B. On the opposite side of the road from Laem Ngop Guest House, the *Chut Kaew Guest House* is run by a nurse, teacher and university student – good for local information (including which Ko Chang boats to avoid). Rooms are 50/100B for singles/doubles.

At the Laem Ngop pier there are two good seafood restaurants.

Khlong Yai There are two hotels to choose from here: *Pavinee* (Pawini), near the share-taxi stand, has rooms for 70 to 100B without bath, 120B with bath; and *Suksamran* has rooms with fan from 120 to 160B, 200B with air-con.

Places to Eat

With all the markets in Trat, you're hardly ever more than 50 metres away from something good to eat. The indoor municipal market beneath the shopping centre has a food section with cheap, good noodle and rice dishes from early morning to early evening. Another good spot for cheap breakfasts is the ancient coffee stand in the old day market on Tat Mai Rd.

In the evenings, there's a good night market next to the Max & Tick Guest House. On the Trat River in the northern part of town is a small but atmospheric night market – a good choice for long, leisurely meals.

The *Nam Chok* outdoor restaurant at the corner of Soi Butnoi and Wiwatthana Rd is one of the better local restaurants. Around lunch-time a good find is *Raan Joh* (no English sign) at 90 Lak Muang Rd. The number is next to impossible to see, just look for the only place making khanõm beũang, a Khmer veggie crepe prepared in a wok. They also do other local specialities – it's very inexpensive but open lunch time only.

Another good find is *Suan Aahaan Puu* (Crab Garden Restaurant) in Ban Laem Hin, on the way to Laem Sok; the owners originally ran the highly acclaimed but now near-defunct *Jiraporn* restaurant next door to the Trat Hotel in town. Ban Laem Hin is about 15 km south-east of town. The menu is in Thai only, so bring along a Thai friend to translate.

Getting There & Away

To/From Bangkok Buses to/from Bangkok cost 128B air-con or 70B ordinary. The trip takes five to six hours one-way by air-con bus, or about eight hours by ordinary bus. Three bus companies operate a Trat to Bangkok service; Sahamit, on Sukhumvit Rd near the Trat Hotel and at Max & Tick Guest House, has the best and most frequent (11 trips a day) air-con buses to Bangkok.

To/From Chanthaburi Ordinary buses between Chanthaburi and Trat are 18B and take about 1½ hours.

You can also take the quicker share taxis between Trat and Chanthaburi for 30B per person, which take around 45 minutes. During the middle of the day, it may take up to an hour to gather the seven passengers necessary for a departure; try to schedule your departure between 7 and 9 am or 4 and 6 pm for the shortest wait.

Getting Around

Samlors around town should cost 5 to 10B per person. Share taxis to Khlong Yai are 25B per person and take about 45 minutes. A door-to-door minibus to Bo Rai is 30B.

HAT LEK TO CAMBODIA

For a few months in 1991 you could take a boat from Hat Lek (100 to 150B) to Ko Kong, an island on the Cambodian side of the border, then another boat to Pak Kong on the mainland, where you could catch a bus all the way to Phnom Penh – legally. At the time of writing the local immigration office at Sao Thong district on the Cambodian mainland is no longer accepting farang visitors; at the beginning of 1992 only Thais were getting in. According to Trat sources, however, farangs can still boat to Ko Kong.

Though not a particularly exciting destination in itself, Ko Kong is an important relay point for goods imported from Singapore into Cambodia, which is now Singapore's largest trade entrepot in Indo-China. You may have to leave your passport and camera behind with the Thai police in Hat Lek.

KO CHANG NATIONAL MARINE PARK

อุทยานแห่งชาติทางทะเลหมู่เกาะช้าง

Forty-seven of the islands off Trat's coastline belong to a national park named for Ko Chang, which is the second-largest island (492 sq km) in Thailand after Phuket. Other major islands in the park include Ko Kut and Ko Mak. Ko Chang itself is about 70% virgin forest, with hills and cliffs reaching as high as the 744-metre Khao Jom Prasat. The island has several small bays and beaches including **Ao Khlong Son**, **Hat Sai Khao**, **Hat Khlong Phrao**, **Hat Kaibae**, **Ao Bang Bao** and **Ao Salak Phet**. Near each of these beaches are small villages, eg Ban Khlong Son, Ban Bang Bao and so on.

So far there's not a single paved road on Ko Chang, only red dirt roads between Khlong Son and Hat Kaibae on the west coast of the island, and between Khlong Son and Ban Salak Phet on the east side, plus walking trails passable by motorcycle from Kaibae to Bang Bao and Salak Kok to Salak Phet. Road crews are working to extend the road on the west side, however, and Trat authorities say the island will have a paved ring road – or at least the beginnings of one – within the next two years. The province has plans to 'civilise' the island further by stringing power lines around the island right behind the paved road.

A series of three waterfalls along the stream of Khlong Mayom in the interior of the island, **Than Mayom** (or Thara Mayom) **Falls**, can be reached via Tha Than Mayom or Ban Dan Mai on the east coast. The waterfall closest to the shore can be climbed in about 45 minutes. The view from the top is quite good and there are two inscribed stones bearing the initials of Rama VI and Rama VII nearby. The second waterfall is about 500 metres further east along Khlong Mayom and the third is about three km from the first. At the third waterfall is another inscribed stone, this one with the initials of Rama V. A smaller waterfall on the west coast can be visited from Ao Phrao or from Hat Kaibae by following Khlong Phrao two km inland.

On **Ko Kut** you'll find beaches mostly along the west side, at Hat Taphao, Hat Khlong Chao and Hat Khlong Yai Kii. The main village on Ko Kut is Ban Khlong Hin Dam.

Ko Mak, the smallest of the three main islands, has a beach along the north-west bay and possibly others as yet undiscovered.

As with other national marine parks in Thailand, park status versus resort development is a hot issue. On Ko Chang, so far, everyone seems to be in agreement about what is park land and what isn't. Any land that was planted before the conferral of park status in 1982 can be privately deeded,

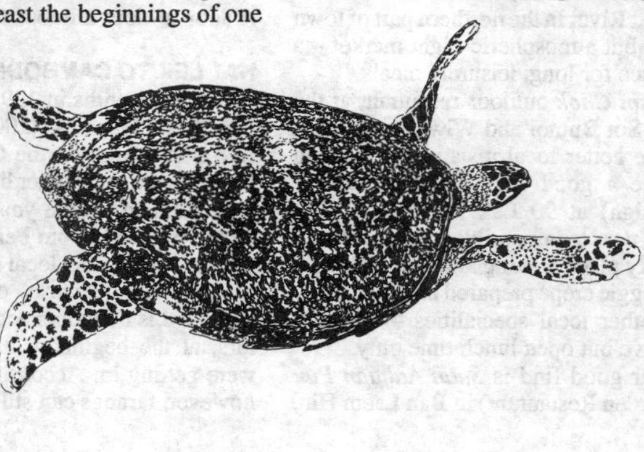

bought, sold and developed – this includes many beach areas used for coconut plantations, or about 15% of the island. The Forestry Department makes regular flights over the island to check for encroachment on the 85% belonging to the national park – mostly in the interior – and they are said to be very strict with interlopers.

Walking on Ko Chang

You can walk from Khlong Son to Hat Sai Khao in about 45 minutes to an hour; from Hat Sai Khao to Hat Khlong Phrao in about two hours; and from Hat Khlong Phrao to Hat Kaibae in about two hours. All three are straightforward walks along the main dirt road. You can also walk from Kaibae to Ao Bang Bao through coconut and rubber plantations – this takes about three to four hours and is a bit more involved (you may have to ask directions from villagers along the way as there are several interconnecting trails).

Bang Bao to Salak Phet? Don't try it unless you're an experienced tropical hiker with moderate orienteering skills – there's a lot of up-and-down and many interconnecting trails. A German who hiked the entire perimeter of the island suggested that for this

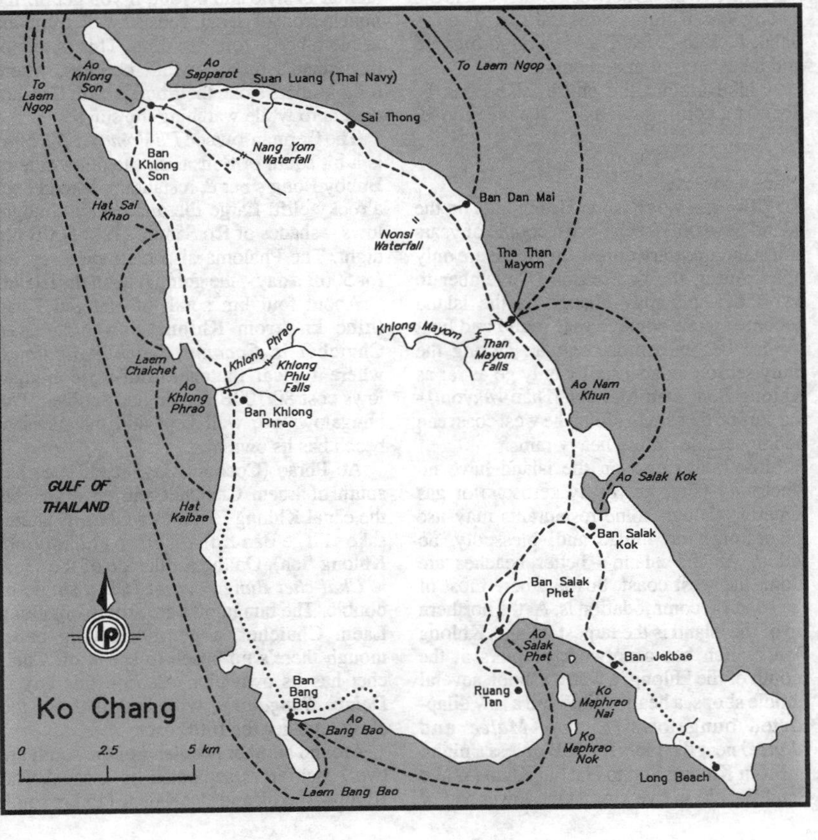

part of the island you carry a note in Thai reading 'I would like to go to Salak Phet. I like very much to walk in the jungle and have done it before. Please show me the start of this trail'. If you don't get lost, this hike will take four to six hours; should you decide to attempt it, carry enough food and water for an overnight, just in case. If you do get lost, climb the nearest hilltop and try to locate the sea or a stream to get a bearing on where you are. Following any stream will usually take you either to a village or to the sea. Then you can either follow the coast or ask directions.

On the east side of the island it's a one-hour walk between Dan Mai and Than Mayom, two hours between Dan Mai and Sai Thong (or Khlong Son and Sai Thong). Salak Kok to Salak Phet is straightforward and takes around three hours.

A hike around the entire island can be done at a comfortable pace in a week to 10 days.

Places to Stay

Ko Chang – west coast Beach huts on the island have only been open a couple of years and standards vary quite a bit. Some are only open during the dry season (November to May) but this may change as the island becomes more popular year round and boat service becomes more regular. During the rainy season, boats usually only go as far as Khlong Son, Dan Mai and Than Mayom – the surf farther south along the west coast can be impassable during heavy rains.

Most bungalows on the island have no electricity (sites are lit by kerosene or gas lanterns, though some restaurants may use generators), no music and, blessedly, no video. As the island's better beaches are along the west coast, this is where most of the beach accommodation is. At the northern tip of the island is the largest village, Khlong Son, which has a network of piers at the mouth of the khlong, a wat, a school, several noodle shops, a health clinic and a few dilapidated bungalows *(Manop, Malee* and *Manee)* near the piers for 50B or less a night.

From Khlong Son to Hat Sai Khao (White Sand Beach) is five km. At the lower end of the beach, well off the road and separated from other Hat Sai Khao bungalow developments by a couple of small rocky points, is the nicely landscaped *White Sand Beach Resort* where solid huts are 100/130B for singles/doubles; roofs are tarped so that they don't leak in the rain.

Next south is a string of cheapies, all costing 50/80B singles/doubles; two people can usually share a hut for 50B per night if they stay more than a couple of days. Starting from the north you'll find an on-again, off-again place with no name first, then *Cookie, Sabai, Tantawan, Bamboo* and, after a small headland, *Honey* and *Sunsai*. All are very similar in style and layout; if you get off the boat in front of Sabai, you can walk from one to the other before deciding. This is one of the island's more 'social' beaches, where long-termers stoke their bongs with Cambodian herb while watching the sun set.

The German-owned *Phaloma Cliff Resort* is a bit south of Sunsai on the other side of Bubby Bong's bar & restaurant, spread over a rocky cliff. Large tile-and-cement bungalows – shades of Ko Samui – cost 500B per night. The Phaloma also rents motorcycles for 500B a day – the going rate on the island!

About four km south of Hat Sai Khao (nine km from Khlong Son) near Ban Chaichet is *Coconut Beach Bungalows*, where typical thatched-roof-style bungalows cost 80/100B for singles/doubles. The bungalows are well kept and the pleasant beach has its own pier.

Ao Phrao (Coconut Bay) itself stretches south of Laem Chaichet and encompasses the canal Khlong Phrao as well as its namesake village Ban Khlong Phrao (12 km from Khlong Son). On the south side of the canal is *Chai-chet Bungalows* at 80B a single or double. The bungalows are strung out along Laem Chaichet, a gently curving cape, though there's no beach to speak of. Chaichet has its own pier. Also on this bay is *Deluxe Bungalows*, with huts that are too close together for 100B each.

Around another headland to the south are two beach areas separated by a canal, Hat Khlong Makok and Hat Kaibae (15 km south of Khlong Son). These beaches tend to disappear during high tide but they're OK – lots of coconut palms. *Magic* has bungalows for 80B but they're none too clean; the owner has a boat monopoly from Laem Ngop so is able to funnel many passengers directly to this beach. Magic's best feature is its restaurant built over the bay. Next door is *Good Luck* (Chokdee), similar to Magic in most respects except that it has no beach.

Next south on Hat Kaibae proper is the secluded *Coral Bungalows*. Huts set amidst a bumper crop of coco palms are 50/80B for singles/doubles. *Nangnuan Bungalows* farther along has similar but better kept (or newer) bungalows for the same rates. *Kaibae Hut*, on the south side of the khlong, has a nicely laid out restaurant and fair bungalows; rates are the usual 50/80B.

Beyond Kaibae Hut more bungalows of similar standard are coming up, including *Kai Bae Beach, Porn*, and *Sea View*, with more doubtless on the way. From here onward all transport is by foot or boat.

Ko Chang – south coast Down along the south coast at Ao Bang Bao is the *Bang Bao Beach Resort* (☎ 511597/604) with average bungalows for 100B, and the cheaper *Bang Bao View* and *Sunset Bungalows* for 70 to 100B. Sunset also has tents for 60B. You may also be able to rent rooms cheaply in the village (Ban Bang Bao).

For now, there's no advertised accommodation at Ao Salak Phet, but a couple of as yet unnamed bungalow places rent huts for 50B a night near the fishing villages of Ruang Tan and Ban Salak Phet. As at Ao Bang Bao, you may be able to rent a room or house in Ban Salak Phet. Bungalows are under construction farther south-east along the bay at Ban Jekbae.

The very secluded *Long Beach Bungalows*, near the end of the long cape to the south-east of Ao Salak Phet, has well-made huts for 100B a night.

Ko Chang – east coast Around on the east coast, starting at the northern end, *Sai Thong Bungalows* has the only beachside accommodation on this side of the island. From here it's a two-hour walk north to Khlong Son or south to Dan Mai. The bungalow owner has his own boat that meets the daily minivan from Khao San Rd at Laem Ngop in the late afternoon. It's a bit of a scam actually, as he takes all new arrivals to his bungalows, charging 50B for the boat ride and 100B to stay at his rather average huts.

At the national park headquarters at Than Mayom you can rent Forestry Department bungalows for 400B a night. A couple of private places, *Thanmayom* and *Maeo*, also rent huts for 60 to 100B a night.

Ko Kut At Hat Taphao on the west coast, the aptly named *First* has basic huts for 50B, with outside bath. If this one's closed when you arrive, try village homes in nearby Ban Hin Dam.

Ko Mak On the north-west bay is *Lazydays Resort* (☎ 281-3412 in Bangkok) at 100B a night.

Ko Kradat The *Ko Kradat* has air-con bungalows for 600B. Mr Chumpon in Bangkok (☎ 311-3668) can arrange accommodation at Ko Kradat and transport to the island in advance.

Places to Eat

Menus at all the bungalows on Ko Chang are pretty similar, with highest marks going to Sabai Bungalows (at Hat Sai Khao) and Kaibae Hut (Hat Kaibae) for well-prepared meals. Just south of Hat Sai Khao's Sunsai Bungalows, on a rocky hillside overlooking the sea, is Ko Chang's first bar/restaurant, *Bubby Bong's*. Run by two ex-California surfers, the open-sided, torch-lit bamboo eatery serves mostly Thai dishes, including grilled seafood. The menu also includes burgers and their famous garlic-chile popcorn. You can get here from bungalows at Hat Sai Khao by walking along the beach or along the road – at night just look for the twinkling lights hovering over the sea.

Getting There & Away

To/From Ko Chang Take a songthaew (10B) from Trat to Laem Ngop on the coast, then a ferry to Ko Chang. From Laem Ngop you have a choice of several different ferries, depending on the destination and time of day. The chart below lists the kinds of departures available; in many cases the same boat makes two or three stops. All times are approximate and depend on weather, number of passengers and any number of other factors. You should check on fares in advance – sometimes the boat crews overcharge farangs.

A couple of things to keep in mind: first, the boat service along the west coast is monopolised by the owners of Magic Bungalows – if Hat Sai Khao is your destination, make sure that you get dropped off there and aren't shanghaied to Magic Bungalows at Hat Kaibae. Kaibae is a fine beach area, but you shouldn't have to go there if you don't want to.

Second, don't take the 200B minivan from Khao San Rd in Bangkok to Laem Ngop in hopes of getting to Ko Chang on the same day – the only way you can make it is if you board the 4 pm boat to Sai Thong, which meets the van in the late afternoon. If you take that boat you'll end up at Sai Thong Bungalows on the north-east coast, at least two hours walk from any other bungalow choices. Some people reckon this is OK, others feel cheated.

No matter what time the Khao San Rd people tell you the minivan is leaving Bangkok, they'll most likely stall so that the Sai Thong boat is the only choice – apparently the van people and the Sai Thong people have an agreement. It's better to spend the night in Trat or Laem Ngop and take your time choosing a boat the next day. Or start out earlier in the day by government tour bus to Trat from Bangkok's eastern bus terminal, then in Trat catch a songthaew to Laem Ngop in time for the noon or 1 pm boats.

If you get enough people together, BJ Travel or the Foremost Guest House in Trat can arrange boat trips from the canal in town

Ferry Timetable

destination	fare	departure	arrival	return
Ban Dan Mai	10B	1 pm	1.30 pm	6 to 6.30 am
Than Mayom	20B	1 pm	1.45 pm	7 am
Khlong Son	20B	1 pm	2 pm	6 & 9 am
Salak Kok	20B	1 pm	2 pm	6.30 to 7 am
Salak Phet	50B	1 pm	3 pm	6 am
Sai Thong	50B	4 pm	4.30 pm	9 am
Hat Sai Khao (White Sand)*	70B	noon & 3 pm	3 & 6 pm	7 to 8 am & 2 pm
Khlong Phrao*	70B	noon & 3 pm	3 & 6 pm	6.30 am & 1.30 pm
Hat Kaibae*	70B	noon & 3 pm	3 & 6 pm	6 am & 1 pm
Ao Bang Bao*	100B	1 & 3 pm	4.30 & 6.30 pm	7 am & 1 pm

* Boats to these beaches may not run in the rainy season.

all the way to Ko Chang (destination of choice, except in high swells when the west coast may be unnavigable) for 100B per person.

To/From Ko Kut Two or three fishing boats a week go to Ko Kut from the pier of Tha Chaloemphon on the Trat River towards the east side of Trat. They'll take passengers for 80B per person. Similar boats leave slightly less frequently (six to eight times a month) from Ban Nam Chiaw, a village about halfway between Trat and Laem Ngop. Departure frequency and times from either pier depend on the weather and the fishing season – it's best to inquire ahead of time. The boats take around six hours to reach Ko Kut.

Coconut boats go to Ko Kut once or twice a month from a pier next to the slaughterhouse in town – same fare and trip duration as the fishing boats.

If you want to charter a boat to Ko Kut, the best place to do so is from Ban Ta Neuk near Km 68 south-east of Trat, about six km before Khlong Yai off Highway 318. A longtail boat, capable of carrying up to 10 people, can be chartered here for 1000B. Travel time is about one hour. During the rainy season these boats may suspend service.

To/From Ko Mak Boats to Ko Mak leave daily (except in high surf) from the Laem Ngop pier at 2.30 pm; the fare is 150B per person. Coconut boats go to Ko Mak from the pier near the slaughterhouse in Trat twice a month. The trip takes five hours and costs 100B per person.

Getting Around

To get from one part of Ko Chang to another you have a choice of motorbike taxi, jeep, boat, and foot (see the earlier Walking on Ko Chang section).

Motorbike The motorcycle taxi mafia on the island charge 20B from Khlong Son to Hat Sai Khao, then from Sai Khao south it's Laem Chaichet 40B, Khlong Phrao 70B and Hat Kaibae 100B. The main motorcycle taxi stand is opposite the north end of Hat Sai Khao; you can also rent one of their motorcycles to drive yourself for 500B a day. The owners claim they have to charge these rates because the island roads are so hard on the bikes.

Jeep Between Ao Salak Kok and Ao Salak Phet there's a daily jeep service that costs 10B per person. The jeep leaves Ao Salak Kok at 4.30 pm, returning from Ao Salak Phet the following day at 6 am.

Boat The regular boat to Ao Phrao and Hat Kaibae usually stops first at Hat Sai Khao and Ao Phrao; you can catch a ride from one area to the other along the west coast for 30B. Boat rides up Khlong Phrao to the falls cost 50B per person and can be arranged through most bungalows.

On the east coast, there is a daily boat service between Than Mayom and Ao Salak Kok further south for 20B per person. On the southern end, you can charter a boat between Salak Phet and Long Beach Bungalows for around 150B.

Charter trips to nearby islands average 500B for a half day. Make sure that the charter includes all user 'fees' for the islands – sometimes the boatmen demand 200B on top of the charter fee for using the beach.

Northern Thailand

The first true Thai kingdoms (Lan Na, Sukhothai, Nan, Chiang Mai and Chiang Saen) arose in what is now northern Thailand, hence this region is bestowed with a wide range of traditional architecture, including great temple ruins. It is also the home of most of the Thai hill tribes, whose cultures are dissolving fast in the face of Thai modernisation and foreign tourism. Yet the scenic beauty of the north has been fairly well preserved, and Chiang Mai is still probably Thailand's most livable city.

The northern Thai people (who call themselves *khon muang)* are known for their relaxed, easy-going manner, which shows up in speech – the northern dialect *(kham muang)* has a rhythm which is slower than that of Thailand's other three main dialects. Northern Thais are very proud of their local customs, considering northern ways to be part of Thailand's 'original' tradition and culture. Symbols expressing cultural solidarity are frequently displayed by northern Thais and include clay water jars placed in front of homes, *kalae* (a carved wooden 'X' motif) which decorate house gables, Shan or hill-tribe style shoulder bags, and the ubiquitous *sêua mâw hâwm* (indigo-dyed rice farmer's shirt) worn on Fridays at many banks, universities and other institutions throughout the north.

Northern Thailand also has its own cuisine, featuring a large variety of vegetables (the region's mountain slopes are well suited to vegetable cultivation). Sticky rice is preferred over the central and southern Thai-style white rice and, as in north-east Thailand and Laos, it is eaten with the hands. Sôm-tam, a tart and spicy salad usually made with green papaya (the northern Thais also use a variety of other fruits and vegetables), is very popular in the north but unlike north-eastern Thais, khon muang tend to eat it as an in-between meal snack rather than as part of a main meal.

The mountainous north also contains the infamous Golden Triangle, the region where Burma, Laos and Thailand meet and where most of the world's illicit opium poppy is grown. Apart from the air of adventure and mystery surrounding the Golden Triangle, it is simply a beautiful area through which to travel.

The Northern Loop

While the straightforward way of travelling north is to head directly from Bangkok to Chiang Mai, there are many interesting alternatives.

The old Laotian Loop – from Bangkok to Vientiane, Luang Prabang and Ban Houei Sai, then back into Thailand to Chiang Rai and eventually Chiang Mai – has been cut short by the Lao government. Still, you can make an interesting northern loop from Bangkok through Chiang Mai and the north-east and back to Bangkok.

Starting north, visit the ancient capitals of Ayuthaya, Lopburi and Sukhothai, or take a longer and less beaten route by heading west to Nakhon Pathom and Kanchanaburi and then travelling north-east by bus to Lopburi via Suphanburi (backtracking to Ayuthaya if desired).

From Lopburi, either head north to Chiang Mai, or stop at Phitsanulok for side trips to Sukhothai, Tak and Mae Sot. It is now possible to travel by road from Mae Sot to Mae Sariang (though the last leg between Tha Song Yang and Mae Sariang isn't paved yet and public transport is scarce), then on to Mae Hong Son or Chiang Mai.

Once you're in Chiang Mai, the usual route is to continue on to Fang for the Kok River boat ride to Chiang Rai, then on into the Golden Triangle towns of Mae Sai and Chiang Saen. Travellers with more time might add to this the Chiang Mai to Pai to Mae Hong Son to Mae Sariang to Chiang Mai circle. A very rough but traversable road between Tha Ton and Doi Mae Salong is an alternative to the Kok River trip once you get to the Fang area.

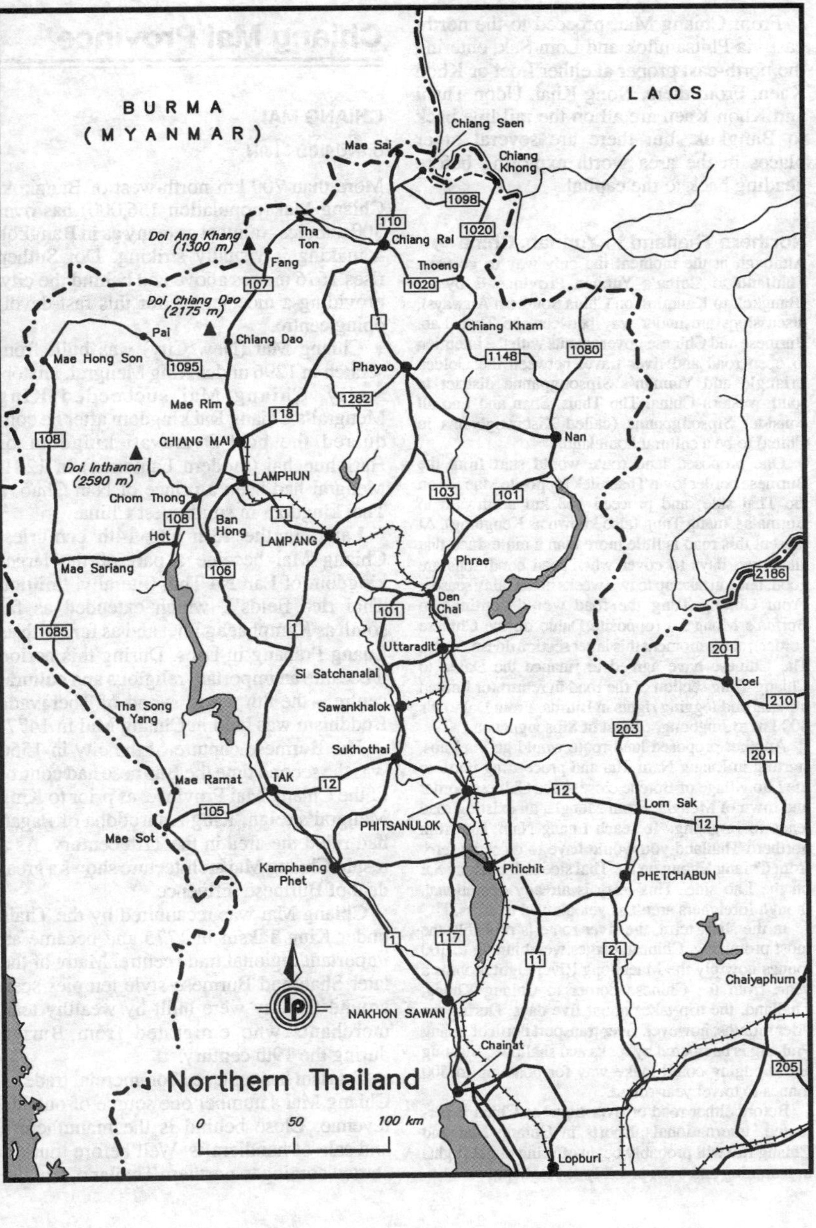
BURMA
(MYANMAR)
LAOS
Chiang Saen
Mae Sai
Chiang Khong
1098
110
1020
Tha Ton
Doi Ang Khang (1300 m)
Chiang Rai
Fang
Thoeng
107
1020
Doi Chiang Dao (2175 m)
1
Pai
Chiang Dao
Chiang Kham
Mae Hong Son
1095
1148
1080
Phayao
Mae Rim
1282
118
108
CHIANG MAI
Nan
Doi Inthanon (2590 m)
LAMPHUN
Chom Thong
103
101
11
108
Ban Hong
Hot
LAMPANG
Mae Sariang
106
Phrae
2186
Den Chai
101
1
1085
Uttaradit
201
Si Satchanalai
Loei
210
Sawankhalok
Tha Song Yang
203
201
Sukhothai
Mae Ramat
TAK
12
12
Lom Sak
12
105
PHITSANULOK
Mae Sot
Kamphaeng Phet
Phichit
PHETCHABUN
117
11
21
Chaiyaphum
1
NAKHON SAWAN
Chainat
205
Northern Thailand
0
50
100 km
Lopburi

From Chiang Mai, proceed to the north-east via Phitsanulok and Lom Sak, entering the north-east proper at either Loei or Khon Kaen. From there, Nong Khai, Udon Thani and Khon Kaen are all on the rail line back to Bangkok, but there are several other places in the area worth exploring before heading back to the capital.

Northern Thailand to Yunnan, China

Although at the moment the only way to go from Thailand to China's Yunnan Province is by air (Bangkok to Kunming on China Southern Airways), discussions are under way between the Thai, Lao, Burmese and Chinese governments with the intention to open road and river travel between the Golden Triangle and Yunnan's Sipsongpanna district in south-western China. The Thais, Shan and Lao all consider Sipsongpanna (called Xishuangbanna in China) to be a cultural homeland.

One proposed land route would start from the Burmese border town Thachilek (opposite Mae Sai on the Thai side) and proceed 168 km northward to Burma's Chiang Tung (also known as Kengtung). At present this road is little more than a mule track that takes two days to cover when road conditions are good, but can take up to two weeks in the rainy season. From Chiang Tung the road would continue to Burma's Mong La (opposite Daluo on the Chinese border); at the moment this latter section doesn't exist. The Chinese have agreed to finance the Daluo to Chiang Tung section of the road in return for limited mineral and logging rights in Burma. From Daluo it's 300 km to Jinghong, capital of Sipsongpanna.

Another proposed land route would go via Laos, starting in Luang Nam Tha and proceeding north to the Lao village of Botene close to the Chinese border and town of Mengla. From Mengla, an existing road leads to Jinghong. To reach Luang Nam Tha from northern Thailand you would have to cross by ferry from Chiang Khong on the Thai side to Ban Huay Sai on the Lao side. This ferry is already operational, though foreigners aren't as yet allowed to cross.

In the short term, the river route is probably the most promising. Chinese barges weighing up to 100 tonnes now ply the Maekhong River eight months a year; from the Chinese border to Chiang Khong, Thailand, the trip takes about five days. During the drier months, however, river transport north of Luang Prabang is hampered by rocks and shallows. Blasting and dredging could make way for boats up to 500 tonnes to travel year-round.

Before either road or river travel to China is perfected, international airports in Chiang Mai and Chiang Rai will probably begin offering direct flights to Kunming and even possibly to Jinghong.

Chiang Mai Province

CHIANG MAI

อ.เมืองเชียงใหม่

More than 700 km north-west of Bangkok, Chiang Mai (population 156,000) has over 300 temples – almost as many as in Bangkok – making it visually striking. Doi Suthep rises 1676 metres above and behind the city, providing a nice setting for this fast-developing centre.

Chiang Mai (New City) was built from scratch in 1296 under King Mengrai. Historically, Chiang Mai succeeded King Mengrai's Chiang Rai kingdom after he conquered the post-Dvaravati kingdom of Hariphunchai (modern Lamphun) in 1281. Mengrai had been a prince of Nan Chao, a Thai kingdom in south-west China.

Later, in the 13th and 14th centuries, Chiang Mai became a part of the larger kingdom of Lan Na Thai (literally, 'million Thai rice fields'), which extended as far south as Kamphaeng Phet and as far north as Luang Prabang in Laos. During this period it became an important religious and cultural centre – the 8th world synod of Theravada Buddhism was held in Chiang Mai in 1477.

The Burmese capture of the city in 1556 was the second time the Burmese had control of the Chiang Mai Province, as prior to King Mengrai's reign, King Anuruddha of Pagan had ruled the area in the 11th century. As a result, Chiang Mai architecture shows a great deal of Burmese influence.

Chiang Mai was recaptured by the Thais under King Taksin in 1775 and became an important regional trade centre. Many of the later Shan and Burmese-style temples seen around the city were built by wealthy teak merchants who emigrated from Burma during the 19th century.

Tourism has replaced commercial trade as Chiang Mai's number one source of outside revenue. Close behind is the manufacture and sale of handicrafts. Well before tourists started coming to northern Thailand, Chiang

Mai was a centre for handcrafted pottery, weaving, umbrellas, silverwork and woodcarving – mainly because it was such a crossroads for travelling artisans from nearby countries. If you visit arts and craft shops anywhere in Thailand today, chances are at least someone working in the shop hails from the Chiang Mai area.

Many visitors stay in Chiang Mai longer than planned because of the high quality of accommodation, food and shopping, the cool nights (in comparison to central Thailand), the international feel of the city and the friendliness of the people. Also, the city is small enough to get around by bicycle.

Not all the foreign faces you see in Chiang Mai are tourists – many live in Chiang Mai part-time or all year round. Chiang Mai residents often comment that living here has all the cultural advantages of being in Bangkok, but fewer of the disadvantages such as traffic jams and air pollution. Lately, however, traffic has increased and the city's main avenues have become noisy and polluted, particularly around the new Tha Phae Gate. This area channels sound and fumes along a 200-metre section of Moon Muang Rd; to restore it in the spirit that motivated the rebuilding of the wall, the city ought to close off all vehicular traffic at the Moon Muang-Ratchadamnoen Rds intersection.

To preserve the city's character, it has been proposed that a 'twin city' be built nearby to channel development away from the old city – possibly at San Kamphaeng to the east. Conservation measures include a 1991 ban on the building of any high-rise construction within 93 metres of a temple, thereby protecting about 87% of all lands within municipal limits. This law is designed to halt any future condo developments along the Ping River – the existing condos have already contributed to water pollution and spoiled the city's skylines. As usual, unscrupulous developers have found a loophole – hotels are exempt from the ban, so many condo-type developments are applying for hotel licences. Others are setting their sights on Chiang Rai further north, where there are no such legal barriers.

Orientation

The old city of Chiang Mai is a neat square bounded by moats. Moon Muang Rd, along the east moat, is the centre for cheap accommodation and places to eat. Tha Phae Rd runs straight from the middle of this side and crosses the Ping River where it changes to Charoen Muang Rd.

The railway station and the GPO are further down Charoen Muang Rd, a fair distance from the centre. There are several bus stations around Chiang Mai, so make certain you're going to the right one.

Several of Chiang Mai's important temples are within the moat area but there are others to the north and west. Doi Suthep rises

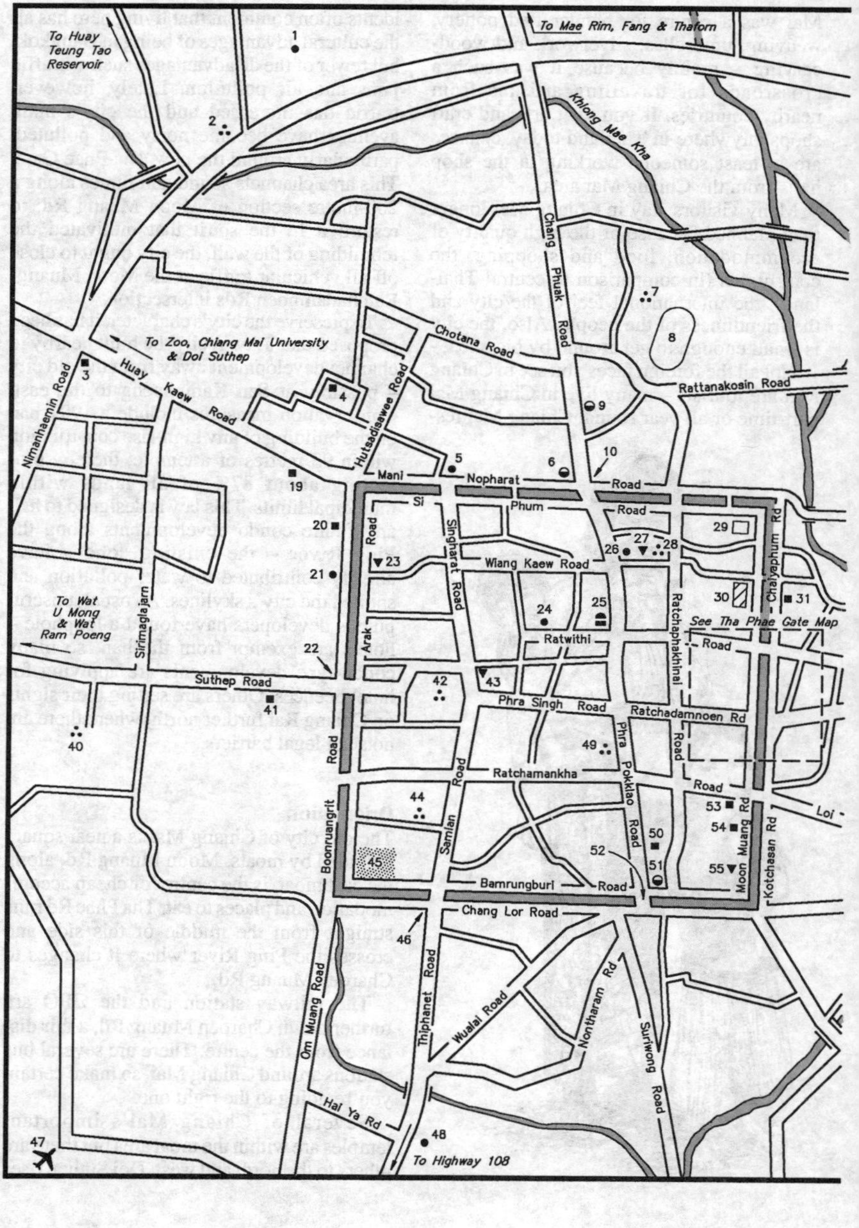
To Huay Teung Tao Reservoir
To Mae Rim, Fang & Thaforn
Khlong Mae Kha
Chang Phuak Road
To Zoo, Chiang Mai University & Doi Suthep
Chotana Road
Huay Kaew Road
Nimanhaemin Road
Hutsadisawee Road
Rattanakosin Road
Mani
Nopharat
Road
Si
Phum
Road
Singharat Road
Arak Road
Wiang Kaew Road
Chaiyaphum Rd
See Tha Phae Gate Map
Ratchaphakhinai Road
Ratwithi
Road
To Wat U Mong & Wat Ram Poeng
Sirimaglajarn
Suthep Road
Phra Singh
Road
Ratchadamnoen Rd
Phra Pokklao Road
Road
Ratchamankha
Road
Loi
Boonruangrit Road
Samlan Road
Moon Muang Rd
Kotchasan Rd
Bamrungburi
Road
Chang Lor Road
Om Muang Road
Thiphanet Road
Wualai Road
Nontharam Rd
Suriwong Road
Hai Ya Rd
To Highway 108
1
2
3
4
5
6
7
8
9
10
19
20
21
22
23
24
25
26
27
28
29
30
31
40
41
42
43
44
45
46
47
48
49
50
51
52
53
54
55

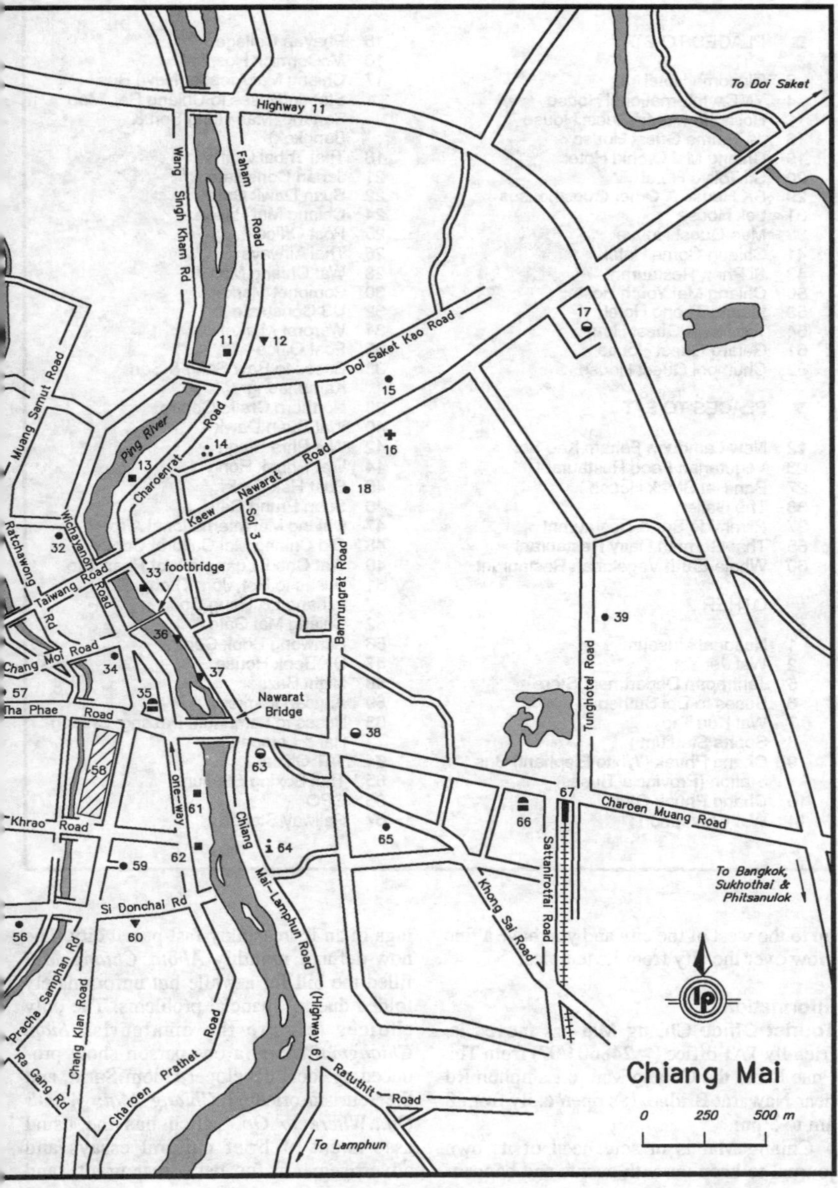
To Doi Saket
Highway 11
Wang Singh Kham Rd
Faham Road
11
12
17
Doi Saket Kao Road
15
Muang Samut Road
Ping River
Charoenrat Road
14
16
13
Kaew Nawarat Road
Sol 3
18
Ratchawong
Wichayanon Road
32
Bamrungrat Road
Taiwang Road
33
footbridge
39
Rd
36
Chang Moi Road
34
37
57
35
Nawarat Bridge
Tungkotel Road
Tha Phae Road
38
63
58
one-way
61
67
Charoen Muang Road
66
Khrao Road
Chiang
65
64
62
59
To Bangkok, Sukhothai & Phitsanulok
Si Donchai Rd
Khong Sai Road
Sattanirotfai Road
Mai–Lamphun Road
56
60
(Highway 6)
Pracha Samphan Rd
Chang Klan Road
Charoen Prathet Road
Ra Gang Rd
Ratuthit Road
To Lamphun
Chiang Mai
0
250
500 m

■ PLACES TO STAY

3 Rincome Hotel
4 YMCA International House
11 Hollanda Montri Guest House
13 Je T'aime Guest House
19 Chiang Mai Orchid Hotel
20 Sri Tokyo Hotel
29 SK House & Other Guesthouses
31 Lek House
33 Mee Guest House
41 Chiang Come Hotel
43 Si Phen Restaurant
50 Chiang Mai Youth Hostel
53 Muang Thong Hotel
54 Top North Guest House
61 Galare Guest House
62 Chumpol Guest House

▼ PLACES TO EAT

12 New Lamduon Faham Kao Soi
23 Vegetarian Food Restaurant
27 Ban Rai Steak House
36 The Gallery
37 Riverside Bar & Restaurant
55 Thai-German Dairy Restaurant
60 Whole Earth Vegetarian Restaurant

OTHER

1 National Museum
2 Wat Jet Yot
5 Tantrapan Department Store
6 Buses to Doi Suthep
7 Wat Kuu Tao
8 Sports Stadium
9 Chang Phuak (White Elephant) Bus Station (Provincial Buses)
10 Chang Phuak Gate
14 Wat Chetuphon
15 Phayap College
16 McCormick Hospital
17 Chiang Mai Arcade (New) Bus Station(Buses to Chiang Rai, Mae Sariang, Mae Hong Son & Bangkok)
18 Thai Tribal Crafts
21 Japan Consulate
22 Suan Dawk Gate
24 Chiang Mai Prison
25 Post Office
26 Thai Airways
28 Wat Chiang Man
30 Somphet Market
32 US Consulate
34 Warorot Market
35 Post Office
38 Buses to Baw Sang & San Kamphaeng
39 Northern Crafts Centre
40 Wat Suan Dawk
42 Wat Phra Singh
44 Wat Phuak Hong
45 Buat Hak Park
46 Suan Prung Gate
47 Chiang Mai International Airport
48 Old Chiang Mai Cultural Centre
49 Wat Chedi Luang & Wat Phan Tao
51 Buses to Hot, Jom Thong, Doi Inthanon & Hang Dong
52 Chiang Mai Gate
56 Suriwong Book Centre
57 DK Book House
58 Night Bazaar
59 Anusan Market
63 Buses to Lamphun, Pasang, Chiang Rai & Lampang
64 TAT Office
65 Thai Boxing Stadium
66 GPO
67 Railway Station

up to the west of the city and you have a fine view over the city from its temples.

Information

Tourist Office Chiang Mai has moved its friendly TAT office (☎ 248604/07) from Tha Phae Rd to the Chiang Mai to Lamphun Rd near Nawarat Bridge. It's open daily from 8 am to 5 pm.

Chiang Mai is in sore need of its own journal to keep up with events and happenings in an increasingly fast-paced city. The now-defunct monthly *About Chiang Mai* filled the bill for a while but unfortunately folded due to financial problems. The only choices left are the amateurish *Siam Chiangmai News*, a one-person show produced by local developer Udom Surin, and the tourism-oriented *Chiang Mai: What's On...Where to Go*, which has the usual assortment of brief cultural essays and advertisements for bars, restaurants and antique shops. Both publications are distributed free and can be picked up at tourist spots throughout the city.

Post & Telecommunications The GPO is on Charoen Muang Rd near the railway station. It's open Monday to Friday from 8.30 am to 4.30 pm, Saturday and Sunday from 9 am to 1 pm. Bus Nos 1 and 3 pass in front of the GPO.

Branch post offices are found at Praisani Rd, Phra Pokklao Rd, Chotana Rd, Chiang Mai University and Chiang Mai International Airport.

Overseas telephone calls, telexes, faxes and telegrams can be arranged 24 hours a day in the telecommunications office around the side and upstairs from the GPO on Charoen Muang Rd. International calls can also be made from larger hotels for a service charge (up to 30%) and at the international telephone office at 44 Si Donchai Rd from 9 am until 10.30 pm.

To phone Bangkok from Chiang Mai, first dial 02, or for Chiang Mai from Bangkok dial 053.

Foreign Consulates Chiang Mai has several foreign consular posts where you may be able to arrange visas or extend passports. The Indian consulate here is a familiar stopping-off point for travellers on their way to India because visas can usually be collected on the same day of application (320B fee).

China
: Canal Rd, opposite Ladda Land (☎ 213710)

India
: 113 Bamrungrat Rd, opposite British Council (☎ 243066, 242491)

Japan
: 12/1 Boonruangrit Rd, near Sri Tokyo Hotel (☎ 214541)

Sweden
: YMCA of Chiang Mai Bldg, Mengrairasmi Rd, Santitham

USA
: 387 Wichayanon Rd (☎ 252629/31)

Cultural Centres Several foreign cultural centres in Chiang Mai host film, music, dance, theatre and other events of a socio-cultural nature.

Alliance Française (☎ 275277) 138 Charoen Prathet Rd. French films (subtitled in English) every Tuesday at 4 pm, Friday at 8 pm; admission is free to members, 10B students, 20B general public. French language courses are also offered.

USIS/AUA (☎ 278407, 211377), 24 Ratchadamnoen Rd. USIS shows US films every second and fourth Saturday at 2 pm and 7 pm; admission is free. AUA offers English and Thai language courses. The basic Thai studies course consists of 50 hours of instruction at three levels; there are also 30-hour classes in 'small talk', reading and writing. Costs range from 1450B for the small talk course to 2050B per level for the 50-hour courses. Private tutoring is also available at 150B per hour.

British Council (☎ 242103), 198 Bamrungrat Rd. Free British movies every Thursday evening at 7 pm.

Tap Root Society (☎ 215860), Soi 3 Huay Kaew Rd. This loose collective of local Thai artists and musicians organises exhibitions and performances. Visiting artists can rent lodgings at the collective.

Books & Maps Chiang Mai harbours several bookshops, the best being DK Book House on Tha Phae Rd and Suriwong Book Centre on Si Donchai Rd. DK has a second branch on Chiang Mai University campus.

The USIS/AUA library on Ratchadamnoen Rd inside the east gate has a large selection of English-language newspapers and magazines. The library is open Monday to Friday from noon to 6 pm. The British Council on Bamrungrat Rd also has a small English-language library. The Chiang Mai University library has a collection of foreign-language titles.

The Library Service at 21/1 Ratchamankha Rd Soi 2, not far from Tha Phae Gate, is a small bookshop-cum-cafe with used paperbacks for sale or trade. The staff also has up-to-date information on motorcycle touring, but there is a fee for this service (20B per person) unless you buy breakfast. The shop is open Monday to Saturday 9 am to 6 pm.

The man who runs the Library Service, David Unkovich, has published a small guidebook entitled *A Pocket Guide for*

Motorcycle Touring in North Thailand which is also available at the Suriwong Book Centre. The book's information is a bit sketchy in places but contains accurate odometer distances between various points throughout the north, which is helpful when navigating by motorcycle, bicycle or 4WD. The author has recently produced a second book, *The Mae Hong Son Loop*, devoted to Mae Hong Son Province.

Finding your way around Chiang Mai is fairly simple although a copy of Nancy Chandler's *Map of Chiang Mai* is a worthwhile investment for 70B. It shows all the main points of interest, bus routes and innumerable oddities which you'd be most unlikely to stumble upon by yourself. Similar in scope are *DK's Chiang Mai Tourist Map* published by DK Book House (this has more emphasis on local transport information but very shaky transliteration) and P&P's *Tourist Map of Chiang Mai*. The latter map can be purchased at the petrol pump next to the TAT office for 40B. TAT also puts out a sketchy city map that's free.

Medical Services The McCormick Hospital (☎ 241107) on Kaew Nawarat Rd is recommended over Chiang Mai Hospital because 'they are more geared up to foreigners, speak better English and won't keep you waiting for so long'. A consultation and treatment for a simple ailment costs about 200B. Other medical facilities include Ariyawongse Clinic on Changmoi Rd, Chiang Mai Hospital on Suan Dawk Rd, Lanna Hospital on Super Highway, and Malaria Centre on 18 Boonruangjit Rd.

Other The tourist police (☎ 248974) have an office next to the TAT on the Chiang Mai to Lamphun Rd. They are open from 6 am until midnight; there's also an after-hours number (☎ 491420).

The immigration office (☎ 213510) is off Route 1141 near the airport (bus No 6 will take you there).

Outside of Bangkok, Chiang Mai has the best supply of quality photographic films in the country. Broadway Photo (☎ 251253), on Tha Phae Rd about 100 metres east of Tha Phae Gate, has a good selection of slide films, including hard-to-find Fujichrome Pro 400 and Velvia 50.

Wat Chiang Man
วัดเชียงมั่น

The oldest wat in the city, Wat Chiang Man was founded by King Mengrai in 1296 and features typical northern Thai architecture with massive teak columns inside the bot (main chapel). Two important Buddha images are kept in the smaller wihaan to the right of the bot. The monks once kept it locked, but now it's open daily from 9 am to 5 pm.

The Buddha Sila is a marble bas-relief standing 20 to 30 cm high. It's supposed to have come from Sri Lanka or India about 2500 years ago. The well-known Crystal Buddha, shuttled back and forth between Siam and Laos like the Emerald Buddha, is kept in the same glass cabinet. It's thought to have come from Lopburi 1800 years ago and stands just 10 cm high.

Wat Chiang Man is off Ratchaphakhinai Rd in the north-west corner of the old city.

Wat Phra Singh
วัดพระสิงห์

Started by King Pa Yo in 1345, the wihaan which houses the Phra Singh image was built between 1385 and 1400 in the classic northern-Thai style found during this period from Chiang Mai to Luang Prabang. The Phra Singh Buddha supposedly comes from Sri Lanka, but it is not particularly Sinhalese in style. As it is identical to two images in Nakhon Si Thammarat and Bangkok, and has quite a travel history (Sukhothai, Ayuthaya, Chiang Rai, Luang Prabang – the usual itinerary for a travelling Buddha image, involving much royal trickery), no-one really knows which image is the real one or can document its provenance. The bot was finished in about 1600.

Wat Phra Singh is at the end of Phra Singh Rd near Suan Dawk Gate.

Wat Chedi Luang

วัดเจดีย์หลวง

This otherwise undistinctive temple complex, at the corner of Phra Pokklao and Phra Singh Rds, contains a very large and venerable chedi dating from 1441. It's now in partial ruins, due to either a 16th century earthquake or the cannon fire of King Taksin in 1775. It's said that the Emerald Buddha was placed in the eastern niche here in 1475. The *lak muang* (guardian deity post) for the city is within the wat compound in the small building to the left of the main entrance.

Thailand's Fine Arts Department is finally getting around to a restoration of the great chedi, with the financial assistance of UNESCO and the Japanese government. Since no-one knows for sure how the original superstructure looked, Thai artisans are designing a new spire for the chedi.

Wat Phan Tao

วัดพันเต้า

Adjacent to Wat Chedi Luang, this wat has a wooden wihaan and some old and interesting monk's quarters. Across Ratchadamnoen Rd from here, at the Phra Pokklao Rd intersection, is an uninteresting monument marking the spot where King Mengrai was struck by lightning!

Wat Jet Yot

วัดเจ็ดยอด

Out of town on the northern highway loop near the Chiang Mai National Museum, this wat was built in the mid-15th century and based on the design of the Mahabodhi Temple in Bodhgaya, India. The seven spires represent the seven weeks Buddha spent in Bodhgaya after his enlightenment. The proportions for the Chiang Mai version are quite different from the Indian original, so it was probably modelled from a small votive tablet depicting the Mahabodhi in distorted perspective.

On the outer walls of the old wihaan is some of the original stucco relief. There's an adjacent stupa of undetermined age and a very glossy wihaan. The entire area is surrounded by well-kept lawns. It's a pleasant, relaxing temple to visit, although curiously it's not a very active temple in terms of worship.

Wat Jet Yot is a bit too far from the city centre to reach on foot; by bicycle it's easy or you can take a No 6 city bus (red).

Wat Suan Dawk

วัดสวนดอก

Built in 1383, the large open wihaan was rebuilt in 1932. The bot contains a 500-year-old bronze Buddha image and vivid jataka (Buddha life-story) murals. Amulets and Buddhist literature printed in English and Thai can be purchased at quite low prices in the wihaan.

There is an interesting group of white-washed stupas, framed by Doi Suthep. The large central stupa contains a Buddha relic which supposedly self-multiplied. One relic was mounted on the back of a white elephant (commemorated by Chiang Mai's White Elephant Gate) which was allowed to wander until it 'chose' a site on which a wat could be built to shelter the relic. The elephant stopped and died at a spot on Doi Suthep, where Wat Phra That Doi Suthep was built.

Wat Kuu Tao

วัดกู่เต้า

North of the moat, near the Sports Stadium, Wat Kuu Tao dates from 1613 and has a unique chedi which looks like a pile of diminishing spheres. Note the amusing sculptures on the outer wall of the wat.

Wat U Mong

วัดอุโมงค์

This forest wat was first used during King Mengrai's rule in the 14th century. Brick-lined tunnels here were supposedly built around 1380 for the clairvoyant monk Thera Jan. The monastery was abandoned at a later date and wasn't reinstated until a local Thai prince sponsored a restoration in the late 1940s. Ajaan Buddhadasa, a well-known monk and teacher at southern Thailand's Wat Suanmok, sent several monks to re-establish a sangha at U Mong. One building contains modern artwork by various monks who have resided at U Mong, including some foreigners. A marvellously grisly image of the fasting Buddha – ribs, veins and all – can be seen on the grounds.

A small library-museum with English-language books on Buddhism is also on the premises. Phra Santi, a German monk, gives talks in English every Sunday from 3 to 6 pm at a sala by the pond.

To get there, travel west on Suthep Rd for about two km and turn left past Wang Nam Kan, then follow the signs for another couple of km to Wat U Mong. Songthaews to Doi Suthep and city bus No 1 also pass the Wang Nam Kan turn-off.

Wat Ram Poeng

วัดร่ำเปิง

Not far from Wat U Mong, this large monastery supports the well-known Northern Insight Meditation Centre (☎ 211620) where many foreigners have studied vipassana. One-month individual courses are taught by a Thai monk (Ajaan Thong and/or Luang Paw Banyat) with Western students or bilingual Thais acting as interpreters.

A large *tripitaka* (Buddhist scriptures) library has recently been completed and houses versions of the Theravada Buddhist canon in Pali, Thai, Chinese, English and other languages. The formal name for this wat is Wat Tapotaram.

To get there, take city bus No 1 or a songthaew west on Suthep Rd to Phayom Market (Talaat Pha-yawm). From here, take a songthaew south to the wat entrance (4B).

Wiang Kum Kam

เวียงกุมกาม

These recently excavated ruins are five km south of the city via Highway 106 (the Chiang Mai to Lamphun road) near the Ping River. Apparently this was the earliest historical settlement in the Chiang Mai area, established by Mons in the 12th or 13th century (well before King Mengrai's reign) as a satellite town for the Hariphunchai kingdom. The city was abandoned in the mid-18th century and visible architectural remains are few – only the layered brick pediments and stupa of Wat Kan Thom (the Mon name; in Thai the temple was known as Wat Chang Kham).

The most important information garnered from the excavation was found on four inscribed stone slabs discovered at the site; the slabs are now in the Chiang Mai National Museum. These inscriptions indicate that the Thai script may actually predate King Ramkhamhaeng's famous Sukhothai inscription (introduced in 1293) by a hundred or more years.

The stones display writing in three scripts of varying ages; the earliest is Mon, the latest is classical Sukhothai script, while the middle-period inscription is proto-Thai. Historical linguists studying the slabs now say that the Thai script was modelled on Mon models, later to be modified by adding Khmer characteristics. This means Ramkhamhaeng was not the 'inventor' of the script as previously thought, but more of a would-be reformer. His reformations appear on only one slab and weren't accepted by contemporaries – his script in fact died with him.

An ideal way of getting to Wiang Kum Kam would be to hire a bicycle; follow the Chiang Mai to Lamphun road south about three km and look for a sign to the ruins on the right. From this junction it's another two km to the ruins. You could also hire a tuk-tuk to take you there for 30 or 40B (one-way). Once you're finished looking around you can walk back to the Chiang Mai to Lamphun Rd and catch a No 2 city bus back into the city.

Other Temples

Temple freaks looking for more wat energy can check out **Wat Phuak Hong** behind

Buak Hat Park off Samlan Rd. The locally revered **Chedi Si Phuak** is over a hundred years old and features the 'stacked spheres' style seen only at Wat Kuu Tao. Another unique local temple is the Burmese-built **Wat Chiang Yuen** on the north side of the moat (across Mani Nopharat Rd) between Chang Phuak Gate and the north-eastern corner of the old city. Besides the large northern-style chedi here, the main attraction is an old Burmese colonial gate and pavilion – on the east side of the school grounds attached to the wat. It looks like it dropped out of the sky from Rangoon or Mandalay.

Three wats along Tha Phae Rd, **Jetawan, Maharam** and **Bupharam** feature highly ornate wihaans and chedis designed by Shan or Burmese artisans; most likely they were originally financed by Burmese teak merchants who immigrated to Chiang Mai a hundred years ago or more.

Chiang Mai National Museum
พิพิธภัณฑ์แห่งชาติ

A good selection of Buddha images, in all styles, are on display, including a very large bronze Buddha downstairs. Pottery is also displayed downstairs (note the 'failed' jar on the stairs), while upstairs there are household and work items. Look for the amusing wooden 'dog' used for spinning thread.

The museum is open from 9 am to 4 pm, Wednesday to Sunday. Admission is 10B. The museum is close to Wat Jet Yot on Highway 11 which curves around the city; city bus No 6 stops nearby.

Chiang Mai Prison
คุกเชียงใหม่

Near the centre of town, off Ratwithi Rd, this is where dozens of farangs have been incarcerated on drug charges. Chiang Mai is notorious for samlor and tuk-tuk drivers who sell dope and then inform the police about their customers. Fines for even the smallest amounts of ganja are very high – 50,000B for a couple of grams is not unusual. Those who cannot afford to buy out of this dangerous game go to jail.

Night Bazaar
An extensive night market sprawls over the area between Loi Khrao and Tha Phae Rds, off Chang Klan Rd, just east of the Khlong Mae Kha, near the Chiang Inn. This market is made up of several different concession areas and dozens of street vendors displaying an incredible variety of Thai and northern Thai goods at very low prices – if you bargain well. Actually, many importers buy here because the prices are so good, especially when buying in quantity.

Good buys include Phrae-style sêua mâw hâwm (blue denim farmers' shirts), northern and north-eastern handwoven fabrics, yaams (shoulder bags), hill-tribe crafts (many tribespeople set up their own concessions here), opium scales, hats, silver jewellery, lacquerware and many other items. Cheap cassette tapes are plentiful too.

If you're in need of new travelling clothes, this is a good place to look. A light cotton dress, trousers or yaams can be bought for between 45 and 60B, and work shirts cost between 50 and 70B, depending on size.

You must bargain patiently but mercilessly. There are so many different concessions selling the same type of items that competition effectively keeps prices low, if you haggle. Look over the whole bazaar before you begin buying. If you're not in the mood or don't have the money to buy, it's still worth a stroll, unless you don't like crowds – most nights it's elbow to elbow. Several restaurants and scores of food trolleys feed the hungry masses.

Tribal Research Institute
ศูนย์ศึกษาชาวเขา

This research institute is on Chiang Mai University campus, five km west of the city. A No 1 bus goes by the university. The institute features a small hill-tribes museum, and literature on hill tribes is available. It's open Monday to Friday, from 8.30 am to 4.30 pm.

Other Attractions

The **Old Chiang Mai Cultural Centre** (☎ 275097) on Highway 108 south of town is a tourist centre where northern Thai and hill-tribe dances are performed nightly from 7 to 10 pm. Performances include a *khan tòk* dinner (northern-style food eaten from small round tables) and cost 200B per person. It's a touristy affair but done well.

Buak Hat Park, in the south-western corner of the moat, is Chiang Mai's miniature counterpart to Bangkok's Lumphini Park, with very pleasant grass expanses, fountains and palms. The **Chiang Mai University** campus is another quiet place to wander around. It's also interesting in the evenings, with a busy night bazaar of its own.

Out towards Doi Suthep, six km from the town centre, are the **Chiang Mai Zoo** (take city bus No 3) and the nearby **Chiang Mai Arboretum**.

Thai Massage Study

Over the years, Chiang Mai has become a centre for Thai massage studies. The oldest and most popular place to study is the Old Medicine Hospital (☎ 275085) on Soi Siwaka Komarat off Wualai Rd, opposite the Old Chiang Mai Cultural Centre. The 11-day course meets daily from 9 am to 4 pm and costs 2270B, including all teaching materials. There are two courses per month year-round except for the first two weeks of April. The curriculum is very traditional, with a northern Thai slant (the Thai name for the institute is actually Northern Traditional Healing Hospital). You can also receive a 1½ hour massage here (a requisite for admission to the course) for 150B.

The rePlace (Das rePlace) (☎ 248838), 1 Chetuphon Rd (off Faham Rd), offers a more modern course based on traditional methods taught by a Thai-Swiss couple (Peng Sarnkam and Lukas Ernst). A variety of study packages are available, costing from 2500B for an 11-day massage workshop only, 2950B with workshop and on-site accommodation, to 3850B for workshop, accommodation, and all meals.

A unique, one-on-one course is available at Baan Nit, Soi 2, Chaiyaphum Rd. The teacher is Nit, a rotund older woman who is a specialist in deep-tissue, nerve and herbal massages. Her methods were handed down to her from a long line of ancestral Chinese healers. Length of study and payment for Nit tutelage is up to the individual – according to what you can afford – but all studies begin with an offering of nine flowers to nine Chinese deities. Nit doesn't speak English so you must know some Thai, though much of the teaching is unspoken. Most students live in and eat meals with Nit and her family while studying. If you want to try Nit's massage talents, you have to pay a minimum of 9B for the same deities; most massagees pay 100B an hour.

Activities

Swimming Landlocked Chiang Mai can get very hot, particularly from March to July. Fortunately local opportunities for a refreshing swim – providing an alternative to the usual tourist solution (vegetating in refrigerated rooms most of the day) – are many.

Huay Teung Tao Reservoir This sizable lake about 12 km north-west of the city is a great place for an all-day swim and picnic, especially during the hotter months. By car or motorcycle you can get there by driving 10 km north on Highway 107 (follow signs towards Mae Rim), then west two km past an army camp to the reservoir. On public transport, you could take a city bus No 2 until it terminates at the army camp, then walk to the reservoir.

Cyclists would do best to pedal to the reservoir via the canal road (Jon Phra Than), head west on Huay Kaew Rd, then turn right just before the canal. Follow the canal road until it ends at the unpaved road between the reservoir and the highway; turn left here and you'll reach the lake after another km or so of pedalling. From the north-west corner of the moat, the bike ride takes about an hour.

If you don't bring your own, food is available from vendors at the lake; fishing is permitted if you'd like to try your luck at hooking lunch.

City Pools Chiang Mai has several swimming pools for public use; you can pay on a per-day basis, or buy an annual membership:

Physical Education College
: Chiang Mai Stadium, Sanam Kila Rd (☎ 211422), 5 to 7 pm weekdays, 8 am to 6 pm weekends, 10B members, 20B nonmembers (annual membership 210B)

Pongpat Swimming Pool
: 73/2 Chotana Rd (☎ 212812), 9 am to 7 pm, 5B members, 15B nonmembers (annual membership 200B)

Rincome Hotel
: Huay Kaew Rd at Nimanhaemin Rd (☎ 221044), 9 am to 7.30 pm, 40B

Chiang Mai University
: Faculty of Education, Huay Kaew Rd (☎ 221699, ext 3050), 10 to 11.45 am and 1 to 5 pm, 15B (annual membership 50B)

Suandok Hospital
: Faculty of Medicine, Suthep Rd (☎ 221699), 9 am to 8 pm (closed Thursdays), 8B

Top North Guest House
: 15 Soi 2, Moon Muang Rd (☎ 213900), 50B

Tennis Anantasiri Tennis Courts, off the expressway and opposite the National Museum, is the best public tennis facility in Chiang Mai. The eight courts are illuminated at night, and you can hire a 'knocker' (tennis opponent) for a reasonable hourly fee in addition to the regular court fee.

Hash House Harriers The Chiang Mai Harriers meet weekly at the Domino Bar, Moon Muang Rd, and organise a weekly 'hash' (foot race) at various locations in the Chiang Mai area (☎ 278503 for details).

Festivals

The week-long Winter Fair in late December and early January is a great occasion, as is the April Songkran Water Festival which is celebrated here with great enthusiasm.

Yet perhaps Chiang Mai's best celebrated festival is the Flower Festival, also called the Flower Carnival, which is held annually in February (actual dates vary from year to year). Events occur over a three-day period and include displays of flower arrangement, a long parade of floats decorated with hundreds and thousands of flowers, folk music, cultural performances and the Queen of the Flower Festival contest. Most activities are centred at Buak Hat Public Park in the south-west corner of the city moats. People from all over the province and the rest of the country turn out for this occasion, so book early if you want a room in town.

Places to Stay – bottom end

At any one time there are about 300 hotels and guesthouses operating in Chiang Mai. Hotels range from 60B (Thai Charoen) to 1600B per single room (Chiang Mai Orchid or Dusit Inn), with an average room costing from 100 to 300B per night. Guesthouses range from 30B per person for a dorm bed to 300B for a room. At the cheaper hotels, 'single' means a room with one large bed (big enough for two) while 'double' means a room with two beds; the number of people staying in the room is irrelevant.

Rip-Offs

Upon arrival in Chiang Mai – whether by bus, plane or train – you'll quite likely be crowded by touts trying to get you to a particular hotel or guesthouse. As elsewhere in Thailand the touts get a commission from every prospective guest they bring to a guest-house/hotel. Even the airport touts get commissions from the large tourist hotels; the commission is often added to your room rate (ie walk-ins get a lower rate than those guests brought by touts).

At the railway station, ignore the official-looking table with uniformed attendants who will try to funnel you into hotels and guesthouses paying commissions – they'll say that anything not on their list is either full, dirty, or closed.

Another scam to be aware of is the bus or minivan services from Khao San Rd in Bangkok, which often advertise a free night's accommodation in Chiang Mai if you buy a Bangkok-Chiang Mai ticket. What usually happens on arrival is that the 'free' guesthouse demands you sign up for one of the hill treks immediately; if you don't, the guesthouse is suddenly 'full'. Sometimes they levy a charge for electricity or hot water. Guesthouses involved in this arrangement may also give you the boot if you don't eat at their restaurant. The savings usually don't justify the hassle; the buses are often late and substandard vehicles may be substituted for the shiny ones shown in photos on the travel agency walls. Better guesthouses don't play this game.

Hotels In Chiang Mai's small Chinatown, the basic *Sri Ratchawongse* (☎ 235864) at 103 Ratchawong Rd, between east moat and the Ping River, has singles/doubles with a fan and bath for 70/150B. Nearby at 94-98 Ratchawong Rd is the nicer *New Mitrapap* (☎ 235436), where rooms are 130 to 200B. Both hotels are close to several good, inexpensive Chinese restaurants, as well as the Warorot Market.

Sri Santitham (☎ 221585) at 15 Soi 4 Chotana Rd, near Chang Puak (White Elephant) bus station, has singles with a fan and bath from 80B, or from 150B with air-con. A better alternative in this area is *Chiang Mai Phu Viang Hotel* (☎ 221632, 21532) at 5-9 Soi 4, Chotana Rd. Clean, spacious rooms are 150B with fan and bath, 250B with air-con.

Thai Charoen (☎ 236640) at 165 Tha Phae Rd, towards the river and between the moat and the TAT office (the Seiko Tour office is out front), has singles with a fan and bath starting from 60B. This location is convenient to the night bazaar but be sure to get a room as far from noisy Tha Phae Rd as possible.

The funky, old Thai-style *Muang Thong* (☎ 278438) at 5 Ratchamankha Rd, a good location inside the city moats, has singles with fan and bath from 120B, two-bed rooms for 170B.

New Chiang Mai (☎ 236561/766) at 22 Chaiyaphum Rd, is pleasant, clean and well located on the east moat. It has spacious rooms with a fan and bath for 130B. Air-con rooms are 200 to 300B. Toward the river, the *Golden Hill Hotel* (☎ 274550) at 112 Chang Klan Rd has middle-range accommodation at budget prices – 150B with fan, 300B with air-con.

Miami (☎ 235240), another reasonable hotel at 119 Chaisiphum Rd, has singles/doubles for 100/130B, and *Nakhorn Ping* (☎ 236024), a long-time favourite at 43 Taiwang Rd, offers similar but cheaper accommodation from 90B per room.

Roong Ruang Hotel (☎ 232017/18), also spelt *Roong Raeng*, has a prime location at 398 Tha Phae Rd, near Tha Phae Gate, on the eastern side of the city moat. The service is good and the rooms, which face an inner courtyard and are thus quiet, have recently been renovated with the addition of pleasant sitting areas. Singles/doubles with a fan and bath are 220/250B or 300/350B with air-con and hot shower. This is a good place to stay for the Flower Festival in early February as the Saturday parade passes right by the entrance. Another entrance is on Chang Moi Kao Rd.

The *Montri Hotel* (☎ 211069/70), on the corner of Moon Muang and Ratchadamnoen Rds, has overpriced singles with a fan and bath for 350B, 450B with air-con. The fan rooms are especially poor value, as they're bombarded by noise from Moon Muang Rd which reflects off Tha Phae wall.

YMCA International House (☎ 221819, 222366) is at 2/4 Mengrairasmi Rd, above the north-west corner of the moat. Singles/doubles in the old wing with a fan and a shared bath are 120/180B, 180/240B with a fan and private bath or 250/300B with air-con. Dorm beds in the old wing are 70B. In the fully air-con new wing, singles/doubles with private bath, telephone and TV are 450/500B. Facilities include a travel agency, handicraft centre and cafeteria.

Guesthouses Guesthouses are clustered in several areas: along Charoenrat Rd east of the Ping River, which is far from the centre of the city but near buses to Chiang Rai, Lamphun and the railway station; along Moon Muang Rd (the inside of the east moat) and on streets off Moon Muang Rd; and along Charoen Prathet Rd, parallel to Charoenrat but west of the Ping River. Several others are scattered elsewhere around the west side of Chiang Mai.

Guesthouses come and go with frequency in Chiang Mai. The best are owned and managed by local families. The worst are those opened by Bangkok Thais who fiddle with your stored belongings while you're off on a trek. There are basically two kinds of budget guesthouse accommodation – old family homes converted into guest rooms (these usually have the best atmosphere though the least privacy) and hotel or apartment-style places with rows of cell-like rooms. In either the furnishings are basic – a bed and few sticks of furniture. Usually you must supply your own towel and soap; rooms are cleaned only after guests leave. You can assume that rooms under 80B will not have a private bath but will probably have a fan.

The cheaper guesthouses make most of their money from food service and hill-tribe trekking rather than from room charges. Many of the guesthouses can arrange bicycle and motorcycle rental. If you phone a guesthouse, most will collect you from the train or bus station for free if they have a room (this saves them having to pay a commission to a driver).

Guesthouses which belong to the Chiang Mai Guest House Association are probably more secure in terms of theft than those which are not. As members pay government taxes, they are generally more interested in long-term operation. The TAT office on the Chiang Mai to Lamphun Rd can provide an up-to-date list of members. The following list is not exhaustive but hits most of the more reliable, long-running places.

Warning Lonely Planet has received many letters from travellers who have left their valuables in a guesthouse safe while they were trekking. Unfortunately, upon their return, they discovered that their property had been removed from the safe and that items such as travellers' cheques, Swiss army pocket knives and sunglasses were missing. One Australian traveller discovered that A$2500 had been spent on her MasterCard which had been left in a safe while she had been trekking. An Irish couple had £6000 worth of goods charged to their credit cards in Bangkok while they were on a three-day trek! If you leave your valuables in a safe, make sure you obtain a fully itemised receipt before departing on a trek.

Inner Moat Area *Chiang Mai Youth Hostel* (☎ 272169) at 31 Phra Pokklao Rd has dorm beds for 40B and rooms from 60 to 100B. An IYH membership is required to stay here; temporary memberships valid for one night cost 50B. It's clean, secure and friendly and its treks get good reviews.

The long-standing *Gemini House* at 22 Ratchadamnoen Rd is an old teak house with a couple of dorms and several rooms. Dorm beds cost 30B per person while rooms with a shared bath cost 50/80B for singles/doubles. Rumour has it that Gemini may be closing soon but it was still in business in late 1991.

The British-run *Kent Guest House* (☎ 217578), 5 Soi 1, Ratchamankha Rd, near Tha Phae Gate, has been recommended by several readers. It has large clean rooms with fan and bath for 110B.

Top North Guest House (☎ 213900) at 15 Soi 2, Moon Muang Rd, is an efficiently run place where rooms cost 200B with fan, 300B with air-con. Facilities include a swimming pool.

Nat Guest House, up from the original youth hostel at 7 Soi 6, Phra Pokklao Rd, is a comfortable place with rooms from 80B.

Manit's Guest House is a one-person show at 81/1 Arak near Suan Dawk Gate, in a large off-the-street house inside the city moat. Large rooms with fan and bath cost 100B in the low season, 150B in the high. Manit handles every aspect of this business himself.

The *Chiangmai Garden Guest House* (☎ 210881) at 82-86 Ratchamankha Rd, formerly Racha Guest House, has clean rooms and good food. Singles/doubles cost 100/120B with fan and bath.

Ban Rai Guest House, behind the well-known Ban Rai Steak House on Soi 13, Phra Pokklao Rd, is a rather noisy apartment-style place with rooms for 120B.

There are plenty of other guesthouses inside the old city, especially down the little side lanes off Moon Muang Rd. Soi 9, off Moon Muang near the north-east corner of the moat, is a particularly good area to look if you're having trouble finding a vacant room during festivals such as Songkran and the Flower Festival. Several tacky, newer buildings here contain cheap guesthouses, including *Libra, SK House, Supreme House, Dear House, Racha* and *Peter*, all very similar with 80 to 100B rooms with shared bath, 150 to 180B with private bath (when available).

Bridging the gap between bottom-end and middle-range places are a couple of comfortable guesthouses in the 175 to 400B range. *Gap House* (☎ 27814), on Soi 4 Ratchadamnoen (behind the USIS/AUA centre) has northern Thai-style houses built around a quiet garden. All rooms have carpet, air-con and private hot showers; rates are 175/350B for singles/doubles and include a filling breakfast. On the other side of Ratchadamnoen at Soi 5, *Rendezvous Guest House* (☎ 213763) is a newish inn costing 80 to 100B for a single with fan, 100 to 130B in a twin room with fan or 280B for an air-con room; add 30B to all rates for hot-water service. Facilities include a video bar.

See under Chang Phuak Gate Area later in this section for places just inside the moat at the northern end of the old city.

Tha Phae Gate Area *Changmoi House* (☎ 251839) at 29 Chang Moi Kao Rd, behind the New Chiang Mai Hotel, is an old favourite. Clean rooms are still only 50, 60 and 70B, depending on the size of the room. Changmoi House also has triples for 100B and may soon be adding a few new 80B rooms. Down an alley off Chang Moi Kao Rd is the basic but adequate *VK Guest House* with singles/ doubles for 50/70B; a three-bed room with bath is available for 35B per person.

Another Chiang Mai original is *Lek House* at 22 Chaiyaphum Rd, near the Chang Moi Kao Rd intersection on the soi to Wat Chompu. It's quiet and has a nice garden. Rooms with fan and bath are 80/100B downstairs, 100/120B in the larger, newer rooms upstairs. The French-supervised restaurant is famous for its buffalo steaks (owner Yves started the trend, now imitated throughout the city). Near Lek House is the equally pleasant standby *Pao Come* at 9 Chang Moi Kao Rd. Singles/doubles cost 50/70B.

A bit further north on this soi is the well-run *Eagle House* (☎ 235387) which has dorm beds for 30B or clean, quiet rooms with private bath for 80 to 100B a double, 70B a single.

In the other direction toward Tha Phae Rd is the hotel-like *Happy House* at 11 Chiang Moi Kao Rd, towards Tha Phae Gate. Big rooms with bathroom range from 100B with fan, 180B with air-con.

The Daret Restaurant has moved from its original Moon Muang Rd location and now operates another restaurant and a rather crowded guesthouse across the moat at 4/5 Chaiyaphum Rd, called *Daret's House*. Rates range from 70 to 100B with a shared bath.

On Soi 6 off Tha Phae Rd, near the gate, is *Times Square Guest House* (☎ 282448), which is similar to Happy House except that it caters to French-speaking guests. Rooms range from 80B (with fan) to 250B (with air-con).

Soi 4, farther east (toward the river) along Tha Phae, has several newer guesthouses: *Thana, Sarah* and *Baan Jongcome*, each with rooms in the 80 to 350B range. *Fang Guest House* (☎ 282940, 272505) is nearby at 46-48 Soi 1 Kamphaeng Din Rd in an all-new building well away from traffic. Clean rooms with fan and bath are 200B a single or double, 250B for triples, and 300B with air-con and carpet. All rooms have hot water; 2nd-floor rooms have windows.

East of the River *Linda Guest House* (☎ 246915), near the railway station at 454/67 Banditpattana Rd, has rooms from 60B. German and English are spoken here. *C&C Teak House* (☎ 246966), at 39 Bamrungrat St, between the railway station and the Ping River, has quiet, comfortable rooms from 60 to 80B.

There are a string of guesthouses along Charoenrat Rd, paralleling the river – a bit far from the centre of town but recommended for those who are seeking a quiet atmosphere. The long-running *Je T'aime* (☎ 241912), 247-9 Charoenrat Rd, has a variety of bungalow-style accommodation on landscaped grounds for 60 to 150B. *Cowboy Guest House* (☎ 241314), at 233 Charoenrat Rd just before Je T'aime, is run by a Thai nicknamed Cowboy (with a son named Banjo and daughter named Guitar!)

who speaks good English – he once ran a Thai restaurant in the Philippines. Bungalows at Cowboy are 100B with private bath, 60/80B with shared bath. The popular *Gold Riverside* at No 282/3 has rooms from only 60 to 80B. On the same road are *Mee Guest House*, at No 193/1, where doubles with bath cost 60B, and *Pun Pun* (☎ 243362), at No 321, where rooms start at a low 40B.

Also off Charoenrat Rd is the almost hidden *Freak Hut* (☎ 244994) at 242 Charoenrat, behind the Thai Samui Life Insurance office. Follow the soi opposite Rimping Condo till it ends, then follow the small footpath to the right. Thatched-wall bungalows cost 70/80B for singles/doubles.

Farther north along Charoenrat (just about where it turns into Faham Rd) at No 365 is the Dutch-run *Hollanda Montri* (☎ 242450), with clean rooms and hot showers from 120 to 140B. The same family owns the Riverside Bar & Restaurant further downriver. In the same vicinity is *The rePlace (Das rePlace)* (☎ 248838), 1 Chetuphon Rd (off Faham Rd), a newish northern-style place that offers residential Thai massage courses. Rooms with fan and shared hot-water bath range from 70 to 350B.

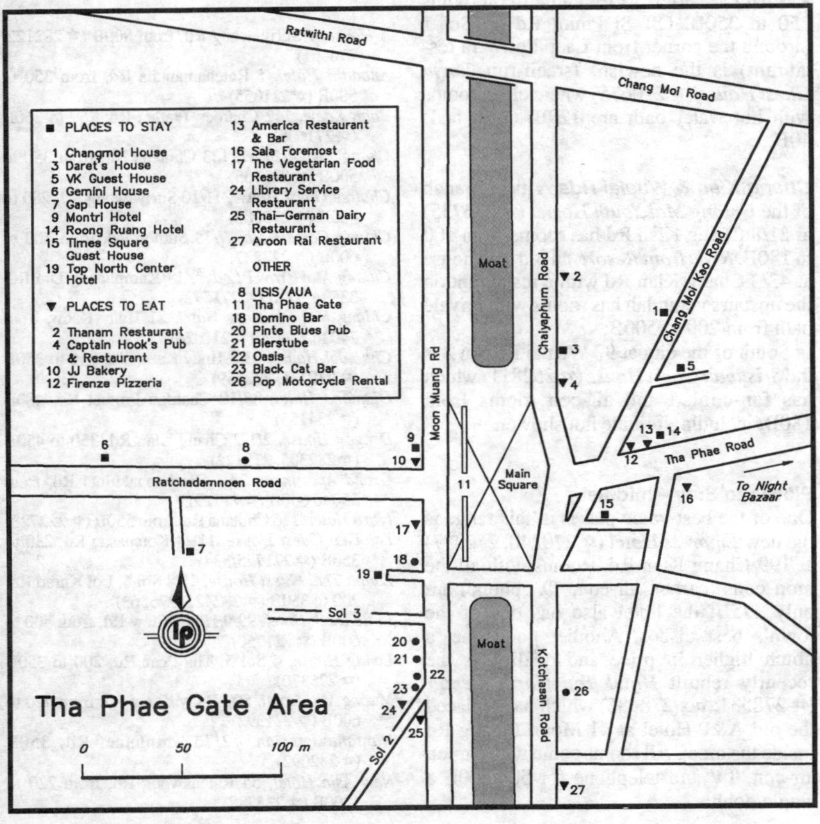

Chang Phuak Gate Area Several guesthouses have sprung up north of the city walls, far from the Tha Phae action but near the Chang Phuak bus station (for Chiang Dao, Fang and Tha Ton). *Camp of Troppo Guest House* (☎ 279360) at 83/2 Ling Kok St, off Chotana Rd, has a relaxed atmosphere and costs from 40 to 80B per room. Further up Chotana Rd at No 129 is *Chawala Guest House* where rooms range between 120 and 220B with a fan and bath. Just inside the moat at this end, *Mountain View Guest House* (☎ 212866), opposite Chang Phuak Gate on Si Phum Rd, has large rooms and hot showers. A dorm bed is 50B, rooms with fan and bath are 80 to 150B, and air-con rooms 250 to 350B. Off Si Phum Rd on Soi 1 (around the corner from Laap Pet Wira restaurant) is the newish, Israeli-run *Tanya Guest House* (☎ 210675) where clean rooms with hot water bath are 120B, dorm beds 40B.

Chang Klan & Wualai Rds A nicer branch of the *Chiang Mai Youth Hostel* (☎ 236735) at 21/8 Chang Klan Rd has rooms from 100 to 180B. *Riverfront Resort*, an old teak house at 43/3 Chang Klan Rd with a restaurant on the upstairs verandah has rooms with private bath from 200 to 500B.

South of the city at 92 Wualai Rd Soi 2 is the *Srisupan Guest House* (☎ 252811) which has fan-cooled and air-con rooms from 180B, including private hot shower.

Places to Stay – middle

One of the best value places in this range is the new *Empress Hotel* (☎ 270240, 272977) at 199 Chang Klan Rd. Rooms with all the mod cons (carpet, air-con, TV, phone) are only 375B; the hotel also has one of the town's best discos. Another good one, a notch higher in price and quality, is the recently rebuilt *Hotel Top North Center* (☎ 278531; fax 278485) which has replaced the old A&P Hotel at 41 Moon Muang Rd inside the moat. All rooms come with carpet, air-con, TV and telephone for 500/600B a single/double.

Some of the places in this price range really blur the line between 'hotel' and 'guesthouse', the difference often being in name only. The popular *Galare Guest House* (☎ 233885), for example, at 7/1 Charoen Prathet Rd Soi 2, is fully air-con and has rooms from 300 to 400B.

In this range you can expect daily room cleaning, the option of air-con (some places have fan rooms also) and – in the hotels – TV and telephone. If anything marks a guesthouse, it's the absence of these latter appliances.

Other guesthouses and hotels in this range, with similar facilities, include:

A House, 7 Suriyawong Rd, from 800B (☎ 282122, 276661)

Anodard Hotel, 5 Ratchamankha Rd, from 350 to 500B (☎ 211055)

Baan Kaew, 142 Charoen Prathet Rd, 260 to 360B (☎ 271606)

Chang Phuak Hotel, 133 Chotana Rd, from 350 to 500B (☎ 221755)

Chatree Guest House, 11/10 Suriyawong Rd, 280 to 400B (☎ 279085)

Chiang Come Hotel, 7/35 Suthep Rd, from 500 to 600B (☎ 222237)

Chiang Mai Travel Lodge, 18 Kamphaeng Din Rd, 335 to 500B (☎ 271572)

Chiang Mai Phucome Hotel, 21 Huay Kaew, from 740 to 1540B (☎ 211026)

Chomdoi House, 33/3 Huay Kaew Rd, 250 to 350B (☎ 210111, 222749)

Diamond Hotel, 33/10 Charoen Prathet Rd, 480B (☎ 234155)

Dragon House, 2/1-2 Chang Klan Rd, 350 to 450B (☎ 282305, 279172)

Grand Apartment, 24/1 Ratchaphakhinai Rd, from 350 to 600B (☎ 217291)

Iyara Hotel, 126 Chotana Rd, from 550B (☎ 222723)

Lai Thai Guest House, 111/4 Kotchasan Rd, 250 to 350B (☎ 271725/534)

Lanna Thai Guest House, 41/8 Soi 6, Loi Khrao Rd, 200 to 350B (☎ 282421, 275563)

Little Duck Hotel, 99/9 Huay Kaew Rd, from 500 to 600B (☎ 221750)

Living House, 4 Soi 5, Tha Phae Rd, 200 to 350B (☎ 275370)

Muang Mai Hotel, 502 Huay Kaew Rd, from 420 to 600B (☎ 221392)

Nantana Pension, 72/76 Thiphanet Rd, 350B (☎ 232092)

New Asia Hotel, 55 Ratchawong Rd, from 220 to 1200B (☎ 235288)

Northern Inn Hotel, 234/12 Mani Nopharat Rd, from 680B (☎ 210002)
Northern Palace, 7/9 Huay Kaew Rd, 270 to 700B (☎ 221549)
Patchara Hotel, 404/8 Santitham Rd, 200 to 500B (☎ 221335)
Porn Ping Tower Hotel, 46-48 Charoen Prathet Rd, from 750B (☎ 270100)
Prince Hotel, 3 Taiwang Rd, from 300 to 1800B (☎ 236396)
The Providence, 99/9 Huay Kaew Rd, 350 to 1200B (☎ 221750, 222122)
Railway Hotel, 47 Charoen Muang Rd, 350 to 700B (☎ 247549)
River Front Resort, 43/3 Chang Klan Rd, 200 to 600B (☎ 275125)
River View Lodge, 25 Charoen Prathet Rd Soi 2, from 500 to 800B, with discounts May to August (☎ 271101, 251109)
Royal Park Hotel, 47 Charoen Muang Rd, from 300 to 750B (☎ 242755)
Sri Tokyo Hotel, 6 Boonruangrit Rd, from 220 to 680B (☎ 213899)
Sumit Hotel, 198 Ratchaphakhinai Rd, from 140 to 290B (☎ 211033)

Places to Stay – top end

Chiang Mai has plenty of more expensive hotels, several of which are along Huay Kaew Rd, towards Doi Suthep. In general hotel rates for luxury hotels are lower in Chiang Mai than in Bangkok. Top properties at the moment are the *Dusit Inn, Rincome* and *Chiang Mai Orchid*. Others include the following, all of which have air-con, TV, telephone and swimming pools:

Chiang Inn Hotel, 100 Chang Klan Rd, from 1000B (☎ 272070)
Chiang Mai Garden Hotel, 330 Super Highway, (Highway 11) 800 to 1200B (☎ 210240)
Chiang Mai Hills, 18 Huay Kaew Rd, from 800B (☎ 211101, 210030)
Chiang Mai Orchid, 100 Huay Kaew Rd, from 1200B (☎ 222099)
Chiang Mai Plaza, 92 Si Donchai Rd, from 950B (☎ 252050)
Chiang Mai President, 226 Wichayanon Rd, from 900B (☎ 253-2166)
Dusit Inn, formerly Chiang Mai Palace, 112 Chang Klan Rd, from 1200B (☎ 281033, 236835)
Holiday Inn Green Hills (opening in 1992), 24 Chiang Mai to Lampang Rd, 200 rooms, from 1200B
Mae Ping, 153 Si Donchai, from 1200B (☎ 270160)
Novotel Suriwong Hotel), 110 Chang Klan Rd, from 1100B (☎ 236789)
Poy Luang Hotel, 146 Super Highway (Highway 11), from 1000B (☎ 242633)
Rincome Hotel, 301 Huay Kaew Rd, from 1331B (☎ 221044)

Places to Eat

Chiang Mai has the best variety of restaurants of any city in Thailand, apart from Bangkok. Most travellers seem to have better luck here than in Bangkok though, simply because it's so much easier to get around and experiment.

Many of Chiang Mai's guesthouses serve a typical menu of Western food and fruit smoothies along with a few pseudo-Thai dishes.

Western Food The *Thai-German Dairy Restaurant* at the corner of Moon Muang Rd and Soi 2 is a long-time favourite for Western breakfasts, although these days its light has been somewhat eclipsed by the amazing *JJ Bakery*, which leases a corner of the Montri Hotel on Moon Muang Rd. In addition to a very diverse menu of Western, Thai and Chinese dishes, JJ has very good coffee, inexpensive cocktails, and a great selection of pies, cakes, croissants and cookies – a personal rave is the toddy palm pie.

Lek House at 22 Chaiyaphum Rd (a short way down a soi), still draws rave reviews from travellers for its buffalo steak and other French grill items as well as breakfast. On New Year's Eve the place is packed and the owner/manager, Yves, sometimes gives away champagne. Another old-time local favourite for steak is the *Ban Rai Steakhouse* on Wiang Kaew Rd near Wat Chiang Man.

English and American-style breakfasts are also good at the *Library Service*, around the corner from the Thai-German Dairy Restaurant on Soi 2. For something continental in the morning, try *Croissant*, next to Wat Jetawan on Tha Phae Rd. Besides its namesake, the cafe has a variety of other breakfast pastries. Yet another hotspot for Western breakfasts is *Kafé* at 127-129 Moon Muang (at Soi 5 near Somphet Market); in addition to breakfasts, the menu here features decent Thai, Chinese and European food at reasonable prices.

The rather new *American Restaurant & Bar* on Tha Phae Rd near the Roong Ruang Hotel, specialises in pizza, burgers and Tex-Mex; for the latter the Yank-supervised cooks grind locally grown corn to make the necessary tortillas.

The Pub, 88 Huay Kaew Rd, is one of the oldest restaurants in Chiang Mai serving continental food. It is not cheap, but *Newsweek* magazine did name it 'one of the world's best bars' in 1986; beer on tap is served. Another place for pub grub is *Heritage-Colonial Pub Restaurant* (☎ 241381) on Soi 2, Kaew Nawarat Rd (first soi just before Prince Royal's College).

La Grillade Restaurant in the Chiang Inn, 100 Chang Klan Rd, serves an international buffet daily from 11 am to 2 pm and 6.30 to 10 pm for 130B per person. The *Roof Garden Restaurant* on the 5th floor (not the 3rd as advertised) of the Times Square Guest House has an extensive menu of French and Thai dishes, candle-lit (at night) tables and a view of Tha Phae Square.

Chiang Mai still doesn't have a Pizza Hut, though rumour says one will open soon on the airport road. McDonald's finally made it, but I'll leave you to find it on your own – if you must.

Thai Food Two good Thai restaurants are the large, open-air *Aroon Rai*, across the moat on Kotchasan Rd, which specialises in northern Thai dishes and has a huge menu, and the smaller but better *Thanam Restaurant* on Chaiyaphum Rd near the New Chiang Mai Hotel and Tha Phae Gate.

Specialities at the super-clean Thanam include phàk náam phrík (fresh vegetables in chilli sauce), plaa dùk phàt phèt (spicy fried catfish), kaeng sôm (hot and sour vegetable ragout with shrimp), as well as local dishes like khâo soi (Burmese chicken curry soup with noodles) and khanõm jiin náam ngiáw (Chinese noodles with spiced chicken curry). Thanam has a small English sign inside. It closes at about 8 pm, doesn't serve alcohol and won't serve people wearing beach clothes (tank tops, etc).

The highly regarded *Si Phen* (no English sign), on Intharawarorot Rd near Wat Phra Singh, specialises in both northern and north-eastern style dishes. The kitchen prepares some of the best sôm-tam in the city, including a variation made with pomelo. The kài yâng-khâo nĩaw combo (grilled chicken and sticky rice) is also very good, as is the khâo sòi and khanõm jiin (with either náam yaa or náam ngíaw) – always incredible. *Loet Rot*, a simple garden restaurant 250 metres north of Wat Phra Singh on Singharat Rd (look for the Thai-script Pepsi sign), also serves many northern Thai dishes, including lâap kài dam (black chicken salad) and pomelo sôm-tam.

East of the Ping River, *Laap Ubon* has two locations at No 37 and No 74-3 Charoenrat Rd (actually Faham Rd, toward the expressway). They serve the best lâap (north-eastern style meat salad with chillies and lime) in town at very low prices. Other *isãan* (north-eastern Thai) dishes are available as well. Another great place for isaan food is *Wira Laap Pet*, in the north-east corner of the old city on Si Phum Rd, inside the moat. The house speciality here is lâap pèt (duck salad).

If you tire of northern Thai cuisines or just want a little coconut in your curry, check out *Khrua Phuket Laikhram* (Classical Phuket Kitchen), a small family-run restaurant at 1/10 Suthep Rd. There's no English sign so far but it's worth hunting down for the delicious, cheap, yet large portions of authentic home-style southern Thai cooking. If there are no seats downstairs, try the upstairs dining room. Specialities include yâwt phráo phàt phèt kûng (spicy stir-fried shrimp with coconut shoots), hèt hũu nũu phàt khài (eggs stir-fried with mouse-ear mushrooms) and yam phukèt laikhram (a delicious salad of cashew nuts and squid). The restaurant has daily specials, too. Ask for Khun Manop, who speaks English.

The *Rincome Hotel* has an excellent all-you-can-eat Thai buffet on Sundays for 140B. The meal charge includes use of the hotel pool for the day.

If you happen to be in the vicinity of the YMCA, there are two small Santitham district places worth trying. *Sa-Nga Choeng*

Top Left: Loi Krathong, Ayuthaya (JC)
Bottom Left: Woodcarver, Ancient City (JB)
Top Right: Drying spring-roll wrappers (JC)
Middle Right: Northern village children (TAT)
Bottom Right: Monk (CT)

Top Left: Rubber plantation, Krabi (JC)
Bottom Left: Orchid, Bang Pa In (JB)

Top Right: Flower festival, Chiang Mai (JC)
Middle Right: Springtime in the north (TAT)
Bottom Right: Palms, Ko Pha-Ngan (MH)

Doi on Charoensuk Rd, a five-minute walk from the Y, has probably the best khâo mòk kài (Thai chicken briyani) and mataba (martabak) in town; it's only open from around 10 am to 2 pm. On the same street, *Noi Muu Bang* has excellent sôm-tam. Neither restaurant has a Roman-script sign – just look for the appropriate dishes on the tables.

Chiang Mai University campus has a very good and inexpensive Thai restaurant called *Than Chom Phue*, open till 10 pm daily.

Several good splurge places for Thai food are found along the Ping River east of the city centre. *Kala Khrang Neung (Once Upon A Time)* (☎ 274932) is set amidst a traditional teak-wood residence and gardens at 385/2 Charoen Prathet Rd. The menu is excellent and includes several northern Thai dishes. Another elegant eatery along the river on Charoen Prathet Rd is *The Gallery*, a converted Chinese temple that's half art gallery, half restaurant; it's owned by Dutch painter Theo Meier's widow.

Over the years, the most consistent riverside place has been the *Riverside Bar & Restaurant*, on Charoenrat Rd, 200 metres north of Nawarat Bridge. The food is almost always superb (try the kài bai hàw toei – chunks of chicken grilled in pandanus leaves). The atmosphere is convivial and there's good live music nightly.

Chinese Food Chiang Mai has a small Chinatown in an area centred around Ratchawong Rd north of Chang Moi Kao Rd. Here you'll find a whole string of Chinese rice and noodle shops, most of them offering variations on Tae Jiu (Chao Zhou or Yunnanese) cooking. Many of the Chinese living in Chiang Mai are Yunnanese immigrants or are direct descendants of Yunnanese immigrants who the Thais call *jiin haw* (literally 'galloping Chinese'). This could be a reference to their migratory ways or to the fact that many brought pack horses from Yunnan.

An old stand-by for Yunnanese food is *Ruam Mit Phochana*, across from the public playground on Sithiwong Rd (one block west of Ratchawong). The food is better than anything you'll find in Kunming, the main capital of China's Yunnan Province; specialities include plaa thâwt náam daeng (whole fried fish in a red sauce, cooked with large, semi-hot Yunnanese red peppers), mũu sãam cham jîm síi-yúu (shredded white pork served with a chilli, garlic and soy sauce), mũu tôm khẽm (salty, boiled pork or 'Yunnanese ham') and tâo hûu phàt phrík daeng (braised bean curd and red peppers). Apart from a rice accompaniment, you can order mantou, which are plain Chinese steamed buns, similar to the Thai salabao, but without stuffing.

Two places flanking the New Mitrapap Hotel on Ratchawong Rd are big on roast duck, pork and goose, as well as dim sum: *Hang Yang Hong Kong* (Hong Kong Roast Goose) and *Buatong*. Both are good for what they do. There are several other inexpensive Chinese restaurants along this street.

For a quick Chinese breakfast, try the *food stall* opposite JJ Bakery on Ratchadamnoen Rd. It has held out against Tha Phae Gate development for many years and still serves cheap jók (rice congee), paa-thông-kõ (Chinese 'doughnuts') and náam tâo-hûu (hot soy milk). This is one of the few places in the Tha Phae Gate area that opens early for breakfast – around 6 am. You can also get great jók from the vendor next to the Bangkok Bank on Chang Moi Rd, with a choice of chicken, fish, shrimp or pork.

Lim Han Nguan (no English sign), east of the river on Charoen Muang Rd near the Bangkok Bank (about midway between the river and the railway station) is famous for its 30 kinds of khâo tôm (rice soup), including the traditional khâo tôm kuay – plain boiled rice soup with side dishes of salted egg, salt pork, etc. Other assets include the 1950s Chinese shophouse decor and the fact that it's open until 3 am.

Market Food Stalls Chiang Mai is full of interesting day and night markets stocked with very inexpensive and very tasty foods. The *Somphet Market* on Moon Muang Rd, north of the Ratwithi Rd intersection, sells cheap takeaway curries, yam, lãap, thâwt man (fish cakes), sweets, seafood, etc. On the opposite side of the moat, along Chaiyaphum Rd north of Lek House, is a small but thriving night market where you can get everything from noodles and seafood to Yunnanese specialities. A lot of farangs eat here, so prices are just a bit higher than average, but the food is usually good.

Another good hunting ground is the very large night market near Chiang Mai Gate along Bamrungburi Rd. People tend to take their time here, making an evening of eating and drinking – there's no hustle to vacate tables for more customers. Over on the east side of the city, a large fruit & vegetable market assembles nightly along Chang Moi Rd near the Charoen Prathet intersection; several rice and noodle vendors are mixed in with the fruit stalls.

In the upstairs section of *Warorot Market* (on the corner of Chang Moi and Wichayanon Rds) are a number of great stalls for khâo tôm, khâo man kài, khâo mũu daeng ('red' pork with rice), jók and khâo sòi (curried chicken and noodle broth), with tables overlooking the market floor. The market is open from 6 am to 5 pm daily.

Anusan Market, near the night bazaar, used to be one of the best places to eat in the city, but many of the stalls have gone downhill during the last few years. If you wander over here, look for the stalls that are crowded – they're usually the best. Several vendors do kũaytĩaw râat nâa thaleh (braised seafood and rice noodles). The large khâo tôm place near the market entrance, *Uan Heh-Haa* still packs in the customers; the most popular dish is the khâo tôm plaa (fish and rice soup). *Sanpakhoi Market*, midway between the river and the railway station on Charoen Muang, has a better selection and lower prices than Anusan.

Noodles Noodles in Chiang Mai are wonderful and the variety astounding. Khâo sòi – a Shan-Burmese concoction of chicken, spicy curried broth and flat, squiggly, wheat noodles which bears a slight resemblance to Malaysian laksa – is one of the most characteristic northern Thai noodle dishes. Most locals say the city's best khâo sòi is found at *New Lamduon Faharm Kao Soi* (formerly Khao Soi Lam Duang) on Charoenrat Rd, just north of Rama IX Bridge opposite Hollanda Montri Guest House. The cook has prepared khâo sòi for no less a person than King Bhumiphol – and it only costs 8B per bowl. Also on the menu are kâo lao (soup without noodles), mũu saté (grilled spiced pork on bamboo skewers), khâo sòi with beef or pork instead of chicken, khanõm rang pheûng (literally, 'beehive pastry', a coconut-flavoured waffle), Maekhong rice whisky and beer.

Another khâo sòi place on the same road is *White House*, across from the Je T'aime guesthouse. Inside the old city, *Khao Soi Suthasinee*, on Soi 1 Intharawarorot opposite the district office, also serves exemplary khâo sòi. Suthasinee has another branch at 164/10 Chang Klan Rd near Lanna Commercial College. Other khâo sòi places can be found around the city – just look for the distinctive noodle shape and orange broth.

If you like khanõm jiin, the thin white noodles served with spicy fish or chicken curry, don't miss the no-name khanom jiin stall off Moon Muang Rd on Soi 5, across from Wat Dawk Euang. It's on the left, about 50 metres from Moon Muang Rd, and serves possibly the best khanõm jiin in town for under 10B a plate, as well as náam âwy (sugar-cane juice) and náam faràng (guava juice).

Vegetarian Food Chiang Mai is blessed with several vegetarian restaurants. One of the most popular is the *Vegetarian Food* (formerly AUM), on Moon Muang Rd near Tha Phae Gate. The all-veggie menu features a varied list of traditional Thai and Chinese dishes, including northern and north-eastern Thai dishes, prepared without meat or eggs. The muesli here is good, too. There is an upstairs eating area with cushions on the floor and low tables. Open from 9 am to 2 pm and 5 to 9 pm.

Less expensive and more traditional is *Sala Mangsawirat 52* on Arak Rd at the west moat, near the Wiang Kaew Rd intersection. Prices are a low 7 to 8B per plate, with some large dishes costing 15B. Run by the strict Dhamma Asoke Buddhist sect associated with ex-Bangkok governor Chamlong Srimuang, it's only open from 10 am to 2 pm and is closed Friday and Saturday.

On Soi 1 Intharawarorot Rd near Suthasinee Khao Soi and Wat Phra Singh is another good Thai vegetarian place. The cooks put out 15 to 20 pots of fresh vegetarian dishes daily between 8 am and early afternoon (till everything's sold). The dishes feature lots of bean curd, squash, peas, pineapples, sprouts and potato, etc and the desserts are good. A reader has also recommended the *Thai Vegetarian Kitchen* on Huay Kaew Rd across from Chiang Mai Phucome Hotel.

Out along Si Donchai Rd, past the Chang Klan Rd intersection, is the *Whole Earth Vegetarian Restaurant* in a transcendental meditation centre. The food is Thai and Indian and the atmosphere is suitably mellow, although the food may be a bit overpriced. Some Indian vegetarian dishes are served at the Indian, Pakistani and Middle Eastern restaurant *Al-Shiraz* at 123 Chang Klan Rd, across from the night bazaar. *The Cafeteria* at 27-29 Chang Klan also serves Arabic and Indian food in vegetarian variations.

Garden Restaurants If you like garden restaurants *(sũan aahãan)*, Chiang Mai has plenty. Several are along Highway 11 near Wat Jet Yot and the National Museum. The food can be very good, but it is the *banyaakàat* (atmosphere) that is most prized by Thais. Inside the moat, one of the city's oldest is *Suan Aahaan Chiang Mai*, on Phra Pokklao Rd between Ratchadamnoen and Ratchamankha Rds.

Entertainment

Live Music Anybody who's anybody makes the scene at the Riverside Rim Ping, a restaurant-cafe on Charoenrat Rd, on the Ping River. It has good food, fruit shakes, cocktails and live music nightly. It's usually packed with both farangs and Thais on weekends, so arrive early to get a table on the outdoor verandah overlooking the river.

Another popular spot for live folk music (and excellent peanut-banana lassis) is the Chiang Mai Tea House on the Chiang Mai to Lamphun Rd just south of Nawarat Bridge. Next to Buak Hat Park on Bamrungburi Rd, the Hill & Bamboo Hut has a large beer garden with live music nightly – a mix of folk and Thai pop. It's worth a visit just to check out this rambling, multilevel wood and thatch complex – it feels like a huge tree house. Old West, near the north-west corner of the old city on Mani Nopharat Rd (west of Tantrapan department store), is decorated in the typical old-west style found in similar pubs throughout Thailand; most nights a live folk or country band plays after 9 pm.

The Arcade, in a former roller rink at the Chiang Mai Arcade bus terminal, is mostly a Thai scene featuring taxi dancing (with paid female dancing partners) to live Thai pop. Couples are welcome – it's not as sleazy as it sounds.

Jazz fans have a choice of two local spots. Captain Hook's on Chaiyaphum Rd (next to Daret's House) has live jazz nightly, as does the Marble Pub, on Huay Kaew Rd above a marble shop (just past the Angus Restaurant and Shell petrol station on the left).

Discos All the flash hotels have discos with high-tech recorded music. Currently the hottest in town are Crystal Cave (Empress Hotel), The Wall (Chiang Inn) and Bubbles (Porn Ping Hotel). The cover charge at each is 90B, which includes one drink. The biggest disco in town is the new Star Wars-style Biosphere Spaceadrome off Charoen Muang Rd near the railway station. Admission is 70B and includes a drink.

All Chiang Mai discos are open till 2 am.

Bars Along Moon Muang Rd, between the Thai-German Dairy Restaurant and Soi 3, are a string of small bars with low-volume music that are good for a quiet drink. The Pinte Blues Pub, at 33/6 Moon Muang Rd, serves espresso and beer, and plays all pre-recorded blues. The Bierstube features

German grub and beer, while the Oasis and Black Cat Bar are pretty featureless except that an inordinate number of Thai women seem to hang about. Domino has good food, draft beer, videos and is the local Hash House Harriers hang-out. The Blues Pub and Domino are the only bars in Tha Phae Gate vicinity where you generally see couples or farang women.

Things to Buy

Hundreds of shops all over Chiang Mai sell hill-tribe and northern Thai craftwork but a lot of it is commercial and touristy junk churned out for the undiscerning. So bargain hard and buy carefully! The nonprofit outlets often have the best quality, and though the prices are sometimes a bit higher than at the night bazaar, a higher percentage of your money goes directly to the hill-tribe artisans. Thai Tribal Crafts (☎ 241043) at 208 Bamrungrat Rd, near the McCormick Hospital, is run by two church groups on a nonprofit basis and has a good selection of quality handicrafts. The YMCA International House also operates a nonprofit handicrafts centre.

The two commercial markets with the widest selections of northern Thai folk crafts are Warorot Market at the eastern end of Chang Moi Kao Rd and the night bazaar off Chang Klan Rd. Warorot (also locally called Kaat Luang) is the oldest market in Chiang Mai. A former royal cremation grounds, it has been a marketplace site since the reign of Chao Inthawarorot (1870-1897). Although the huge enclosure is quite dilapidated (the escalator and lifts don't work anymore), it's an especially good market for fabrics.

In the vicinity of the night bazaar stalls are a couple of dozen permanent shops selling antiques, handicrafts, rattan and hardwood furniture, textiles, jewellery, pottery, basketry, silverwork, woodcarving and other items of local manufacture. One shop that seems to have it all (except jewellery) is the long-running Chiangmai Banyen (☎ 274-007) at 201/1 Wualai Rd, south of the Old Chiang Mai Cultural Centre.

As Chiang Mai is Thailand's main handicraft centre, it's ringed by small cottage factories and workshops where you can watch craftspeople at work. In general, though, merchandise you see at factories outside the city will cost more than it would in Chiang Mai unless you're buying in bulk.

Cotton & Silk Very attractive lengths of material can be made into all sorts of things. Thai silk, with its lush colours and pleasantly rough texture, is a particularly good bargain and is usually cheaper here than in Bangkok. Warorot Market is one of the best and least expensive places to look for fabrics.

Several individual shops in town focus on high-quality traditional (sometimes antique) Thai and Lao fabrics, sold by the metre or made up into original-design clothes. A list of the best places in town would have to include Duang Chitt and Sbun Nga (both opposite the Rincome Hotel), The Loom (Ratchamankha Rd) and Naenna Studio (Soi 9, off Nimanhaemin Rd). Naenna is operated by Patricia Cheeseman, an expert on Thai-Lao textiles who has written extensively on the subject.

If you want to see where and how the cloth is made, go to the nearby town of San Kamphaeng for Thai silk or to Pasang, south of Lamphun, for cotton.

Ceramics Thai Celadon, about six km north of Chiang Mai, turns out ceramics modelled on the Sawankhalok pottery that used to be made hundreds of years ago at Sukhothai and exported all over the region. With their deep, cracked, glazed finish some pieces are very beautiful and prices are often lower than in Bangkok. The factory is closed on Sunday. Other ceramic stores can be found close to the Old Chiang Mai Cultural Centre.

Woodcarving Many types of carvings are available including countless elephants, but who wants a half-size wooden elephant anyway? Teak salad bowls are good and very cheap. Many shops along Tha Phae Rd and in the vicinity of the night bazaar stock wood crafts.

Antiques You'll see lots of these around, including opium weights (the little animal-shaped weights supposedly used to measure opium in the Golden Triangle). Check prices in Bangkok first, as Chiang Mai's shops are not always cheap. Also remember that worldwide there are a lot more instant antiques than authentic ones. The night bazaar area is probably the best place to look for fake antiques. For the real thing, visit the stores along Tha Phae Rd.

Lacquerware Decorated plates, containers, utensils and other items are made by building up layers of lacquer over a wooden or woven bamboo base. Burmese lacquerware, smuggled into the north, can often be seen, especially at Mae Sai.

Silverwork There are several silverwork shops on Wualai Rd close to Chiang Mai Gate. Hill-tribe jewellery, which is heavy, chunky stuff, is very nice.

Clothes All sorts of shirts, blouses and dresses, plain and embroidered, are available at very low prices, but check the quality carefully. The night bazaar and stores along Tha Phae Rd have good selections. See also Cotton & Silk above.

Umbrellas At Baw Sang, the umbrella village, you'll find beautiful hand-painted paper umbrellas. You can also buy very attractive framed, leaf paintings from there.

Department Stores Tantrapan department store is the main shopping centre in town. There are two branches, one on Tha Phae Rd opposite Huang Men Rd and one on Mani Nopharat Rd outside the north-eastern corner of the old city. Tantrapan stocks a wide selection of ready-made clothing, electrical appliances, toiletries, stationery, and other typical department-store items; each store also has a supermarket on one floor.

Another shopping centre is Sri Suan Plaza (also known as Season Plaza) on Chang Klan Rd.

Getting There & Away

Air Chiang Mai International Airport lands regularly scheduled flights from 14 other cities in Thailand as well as Hong Kong and Taipei. Charter flights to Bagan and Mandalay are also possible through travel agencies or tour operators; in the near future, airlines serving Chiang Mai plan to initiate air connections with Kunming (China) and Vientiane (Laos) as well.

The THAI office (☎ 211541) is within the city moat area at 240 Phra Pokklao Rd, behind Wat Chiang Man. THAI has several daily one-hour flights between Bangkok and Chiang Mai. The fare is 1650B coach or 1950B for business class.

Airfares between Chiang Mai and other Thai cities are:

city	fare
Chiang Rai	420B
Mae Hong Son	345B
Nan	510B
Mae Sot	590B
Phitsanulok	650B
Phrae	510B
Tak	765B
Khon Kaen	1115B
Udon Thani	2815B
Ubon Ratchathani	2900B
U Taphao	2075B
Surat Thani	2970B
Phuket	3455B
Hat Yai	3850B

Bus From Bangkok's northern bus terminal there are 14 ordinary buses daily to Chiang Mai, departing from 5.25 am to 10 pm. The nine-hour trip costs 133B via Nakhon Sawan and 140B via Ayuthaya. Four 1st-class air-con buses leave the adjacent air-con terminal between 9.10 and 10.30 am and eight buses leave from 8 to 9.45 pm. These buses take about eight hours and cost 242B one-way. The public buses from the northern bus terminal are generally more reliable and on schedule than the private ones booked in Banglamphu, etc.

Ten or more private tour companies run air-con buses between Bangkok and Chiang

Mai, departing from various points throughout both cities. Round-trip tickets are always somewhat cheaper than one-way tickets. Fares range from 180 to 300B depending on the bus. VIP buses are the most expensive as these have fewer seats per coach to allow for reclining positions. Similar buses can be booked in the Soi Ngam Duphli area of Bangkok and near the Indra Hotel in Pratunam. The more reliable companies include Setthee, Ambassador, Siam Express, Phumin, Chaisit, Thaworn Farm, Poy Luang and Indra.

Several Khao San Rd agencies offer bus tickets to Chiang Mai for as low as 100 to 150B, including a night's free stay at a guesthouse in Chiang Mai. Sometimes this works out well, but the buses can be substandard and the 'free' guesthouse may charge you 40B for electricity or hot water, or apply heavy pressure for you to sign up for one of its treks before you can get a room. Besides, riding in a bus stuffed full of farangs and their bulky backpacks is not the most cultural experience.

The only advantage of the private buses is that they pick you up from where you booked your ticket (supposedly this is legal only for tour operators). If you don't have a lot of baggage it's probably better to leave from the terminal.

Public buses between Chiang Mai and other towns in the north and north-east have frequent departures throughout the day (at least hourly), except for the Mae Sai, Khon Kaen, Udon and Khorat buses which have morning and evening departures only. Here are some fares and trip durations:

city	fare	duration
Chiang Rai	47B	4 hours
(air-con)	65B	3 hours
(1st class)	83B	3 hours
Chiang Saen	60B	4½ hours
(air-con)	107B	3½ hours
Fang*	32B	3½ hours
Khon Kaen	153B	12 hours
(air-con, Highway 12)	214B	12 hours
(air-con, Highway 11)	275B	11 hours
Lampang	25B	1½ hours
Lamphun*	6B	½ hour
(air-con)	50B	1 hour
Mae Hong Son		
(Route 108)	97B	7-8 hours
(air-con)	175B	8 hours
Mae Hong Son		
(Routes 107 & 1095)	100B	8-9 hours
Mae Sai	58B	5 hours
(air-con)	104B	4 hours
Mae Sariang	50B	4-5 hours
Nakhon Ratchasima	145B	12 hours
(air-con)	262B	11 hours
(1st class air-con)	300B	11 hours
Nan	71B	7 hours
(air-con)	100B	6 hours
Pai	50B	4 hours
Pasang*	10B	45 minutes
Phayao		
(Highways 11 & 1)	49B	5 hours
Phayao		
(Routes 1019, 1035 & 1282)	41B	3 hours
Phrae	49B	4 hours
(air-con)	68B	3½ hours
Phetchabun		
(air-con)	235B	8 hours
Phitsanulok	82B	5-6 hours
(air-con)	117B	5 hours
Tak	57B	4 hours
(air-con)	82B	4 hours
Thaton*	37B	4 hours

* Leaves from White Elephant (Chang Phuak) bus station, Chotana Rd. All other buses leave from the Chiang Mai Arcade bus station (also called New Station) off Kaew Nawarat Rd.

For buses to destinations within Chiang Mai Province use the Chang Phuak station, while for buses outside the province use the Chiang Mai Arcade station. City bus No 3 (yellow) goes to the Chiang Mai Arcade station; bus Nos 2 (yellow) and 6 (red) go to the Chang Phuak terminal.

Train Chiang Mai-bound express trains leave Bangkok's Hualamphong station daily at 6 pm (2nd class only) and 7.40 pm (1st and 2nd class), arriving in Chiang Mai at 7.25 and 8.05 am.

Rapid trains leave at 6.40 am, 3 pm (air-con 2nd class) and 10 pm (no air-con), arriving at 7.50 pm, 3.15 am and 11.55 am respectively. Third-class fares (121B) are available only on the No 189, the only ordinary train with daily Chiang Mai service; it leaves Bangkok at 4.20 am and crawls into the Chiang Mai station 16 hours later.

The basic 2nd-class fare is 255B, excluding either the special express (50B), express (30B) or rapid (20B) surcharges. Add 70B for an upper berth and 100B for a lower berth in a 2nd-class sleeping car (100 and 150B respectively on the special express). For air-con 2nd class, add 50B per ticket for ordinary cars and 100B for sleepers. For example, if you take a 2nd-class upper berth on a rapid train, your total fare will be 345B (255+70+20B).

First-class berths are 150B per person in a double cabin, 350B in a single and are available on the special express only.

Trains leave Lopburi for Chiang Mai at 9.03 am (rapid), 5.28 pm (rapid, air-con 2nd class), 8.24 pm (express, air-con 2nd class) and 12.26 am (rapid, no air-con), arriving at the times listed for the same trains from Bangkok. Fares are 245B 2nd class, 130B 3rd class express and 10B less for the rapid.

Berths on sleepers to Chiang Mai are increasingly hard to reserve without booking well in advance. Tour groups sometimes book entire cars. The return trip from Chiang Mai to Bangkok doesn't seem to be as difficult, except during the Songkran (mid-April) and Chinese New Year (February) holiday periods.

The Chiang Mai railway station's cloakroom has a left-luggage facility that is open from 6 am to 6 pm daily. The cost is 5B per piece for the first five days and 10B per piece thereafter. City bus Nos 1, 3 and 6 stop in front of the railway station.

Getting Around

To/From Chiang Mai International Airport

You can get a taxi into the centre of Chiang Mai from the airport for less than 50B, although a songthaew would be less again. From the airport to the city you have a choice of standard airport taxi for 60B or the THAI van for 30B. The airport is only two or three km from the city centre. The red bus No 6 goes to the airport but you must catch it somewhere on the Highway 11 loop.

The tidy little airport has currency exchange counters, a post office, an international (IDD) phone office (open 8.30 am to 8 pm), a tourist information counter, two snack bars (one under the trees by the car park, the other in the arrival area), a bar in an old airforce transport aircraft, a THAI-operated restaurant (departure level) and a duty-free shop (departure level).

Bus City buses operate from 6 am to 6 pm and cost 2B. Nos 1, 2 and 3 (yellow) cover the whole city, No 6 (red) does a loop around the moat and No 4 (red) goes around the highway loop.

Songthaew & Samlor Songthaews go anywhere on their route for 5B. Samlors cost between 10 and 15B for most trips.

Car Rental Cars, jeeps and minivans are readily available at several locations throughout the city. Be sure that the vehicle you rent has insurance (liability) coverage – ask to see the documents and carry a photocopy with you while driving. Some of the more prominent rental agencies are:

Avis
- Chiang Mai Orchid Hotel (☎ 222013)
- Dusit Inn (☎ 273963)
- Chiang Inn Hotel (☎ 272655)

Erawan PUC
- 211/14-15 Chang Klan Rd (☎ 276548)

Hertz
- 12/3 Loi Khrao Rd (☎ 275496)

Bua Toon Car Rent
- 72 Chang Klan Rd (☎ 282906)

PD Express
- 138/4 Phra Pokklao Rd (☎ 216876)

Queen Bee
- 5 Moon Muang Rd (☎ 274349)

Thanompatanakhet
- 105/5 Phra Pokklao Rd (☎ 222607)

Chiang Mai MK
- 370/3 Tha Phae Rd (☎ 234941)

Motorbike These can be rented for 80 to 150B (80 to 100cc Honda step-throughs) or 200 to 250B (Honda MTX 125 or Yamaha 150) per day, depending on the size of the motorbike and the length of rental. Prices are very competitive in Chiang Mai because there's a real glut of motorcycles. For two people, it's cheaper to rent a small motorcycle for the day to visit Doi Suthep than to go up and back on a songthaew. Two of the more reliable places to rent motorcycles for long-distance touring are Pop (☎ 276014) at 51 Kotchasan Rd on the moat and Queen Bee (☎ 274349) at 5 Moon Muang Rd. Both offer motorcycle insurance for 50B per day, not a bad investment considering you could face a 25,000B liability if your bike is stolen. Most policies have a deductible (excess) of 300 to 1000B; so in cases of theft, you're usually responsible for a third to half of the bike's value – even with insurance.

JK Big Bike on Chaiyaphum Rd next to the Soi 2 entrance rents Honda 250XLs for 350B a day; bigger bikes are available as well. Several car rental places also rent motorcycles.

Bicycle This is by far the best way to get around Chiang Mai. The city is small enough so that everywhere is accessible by bike, including Chiang Mai University, Wat U Mong, Wat Suan Dawk and the National Museum on the outskirts of town.

Bicycles can be rented for between 20 and 30B per day from several of the guesthouses or from various places along the east moat.

AROUND CHIANG MAI

Doi Suthep

ดอยสุเทพ

Sixteen km north-west of Chiang Mai is Doi Suthep, an 1601- metre peak named after the hermit Sudeva, who lived on the mountain's slopes for many years. Near its summit is **Wat Phra That Doi Suthep**, first established in 1383 under King Keu Na. A *naga* (dragon-headed serpent) staircase of 300 steps leads to the wat at the end of the winding road up the mountain. At the top, weather permitting, there are some fine aerial views of Chiang Mai. Inside the cloister is an intriguing copper-plated chedi topped by a five-tier gold umbrella.

About five km beyond Wat Phra That is **Phra Tamnak Phu Phing**, a winter palace for the royal family, the gardens of which are open on weekends and holidays. The road that passes Phu Ping Palace splits off to the left, stopping at the peak of Doi Pui. From there a dirt road proceeds for two or three km to a nearby Hmong hill-tribe village. If you won't have an opportunity to visit more remote villages, it's worth visiting this one, even though it is very well touristed. Some Hmong handiwork can be purchased, and traditional homes and costumes can be seen, although these are mostly posed situations. 'Everyone knows some English,' wrote one visitor, such as 'you buy', 'money' and 'I'll have no profit'.

Doi Suthep/Doi Pui National Park Most visitors do a quick tour of the temple, the touristy Hmong village and perhaps the winter palace grounds, altogether missing the surrounding park. This 261-sq-km preserve is home to more than 300 bird species and nearly 2000 species of ferns and flowering plants. Because of its proximity to urban Chiang Mai, development of the park has become a very sensitive issue. The west side of the park has been severely disturbed by poachers and land encroachers, including around 500 hill-tribe families. In 1986 a Bangkok company tried to establish a cable-car system through the park to the temple, but protests petitions and marches by the newly formed Group for Chiang Mai (Chomrom Pheua Chiang Mai) stopped the plan.

There are extensive hiking trails in the park, including one that climbs 1685-metre Doi Pui; the summit is a favourite picnic spot. Other trails pass Hmong villages that rarely get farang visitors. Bungalow and dormitory accommodation is available near the park headquarters (past the temple car park on the right).

Getting There & Away Songthaews to Doi Suthep leave throughout the day from Chang Phuak Gate, along Mani Nopharat Rd. The fare is 30B up and 20B down. To Phu Phing Palace add 10B and to Doi Pui add 20B in each direction.

Baw Sang
บ่อสร้าง

Baw Sang, nine km east of Chiang Mai on Route 1006, is usually called the umbrella village because of its many umbrella manufacturers. Practically the entire village consists of craft shops selling painted umbrellas, fans, silverware, straw handiwork, bamboo and teak, statuary, china, celadon and lacquerware, along with very tacky Chiang Mai and northern Thai souvenirs, as well as quality items.

The larger shops can arrange overseas shipping at reasonable rates. As in Chiang Mai's night bazaar, discounts are offered for quantity purchases. Some of the places will also pack and post parasols, apparently quite reliably.

San Kamphaeng
สันกำแพง

Four or five km further down Route 1006 is San Kamphaeng, which flourishes on cotton and silk weaving. Stores offering finished products line the main street, although the actual weaving is done in small factories down side streets. There are some deals to be had here, especially in silk. For cotton, you'd probably do better in Pasang, a lesser known village near Lamphun, although you may see shirt styles here not available in Pasang. A cotton shirt or blouse can cost between 60 and 250B.

Getting There & Away Buses to Baw Sang (sometimes spelled Bo Sang or Bor Sang) and San Kamphaeng leave Chiang Mai frequently during the day from the north side of Charoen Muang Rd, east of the Ping River. The bus stop is towards the GPO and the railway station and across from San Pa Khoi

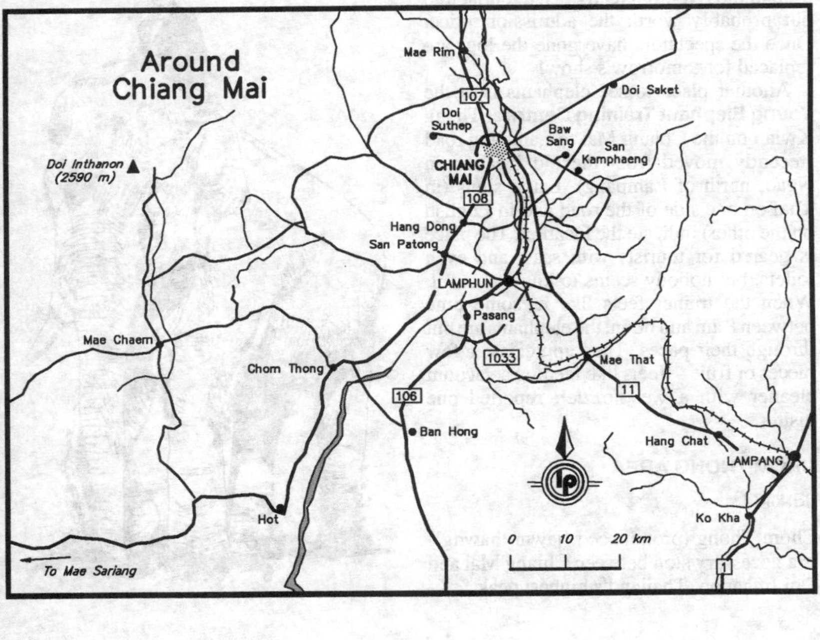

Market. The fare is 4B to Baw Sang and 5B to San Kamphaeng.

Hang Dong

หางดง

Thirteen km south of Chiang Mai on Highway 108 is Hang Dong, which could be called the basket village. Catch a bus from Chiang Mai Gate to Hang Dong (10B fare) where anything made of straw, bamboo or rattan can be found: hats, baskets, furniture, fish traps, rice winnowers, coconut strainers, mats, brooms, rice and fish steamers, fighting-cock cages, bird cages, etc. Most of the shops are actually about two km before Hang Dong.

Elephants

ช้าง

A daily 'elephants at work' show takes place near the Km 58 marker on the Fang road. Arrive at about 9 am or earlier to see bath time in the river. It's really just a tourist trap but probably worth the admission price. Once the spectators have gone the logs are replaced for tomorrow's show!

Another place to see elephants is at the **Young Elephant Training Centre** at Thung Kwian on the Chiang Mai to Lampang road (recently moved from the old location in Ngao, north of Lampang). Large signs (in Thai on one side of the road and in English on the other) indicate the location. The place is geared for tourists with seats and even toilets, but nobody seems to know about it. When the trainer feels like it, some time between 8 am and noon, the elephants are put through their paces. They appreciate a few pieces of fruit – 'feels like feeding a vacuum cleaner with a wet nozzle', reported one visitor.

CHOM THONG AREA

จอมทอง

Chom Thong (pronounced 'jawm thawng') is a necessary stop between Chiang Mai and Doi Inthanon, Thailand's highest peak.

Wat Phra That Si Chom Thong

วัดพระธาตุศรีจอมทอง

If you have time, walk down Chom Thong's main street to Wat Phra That Si Chom Thong. The gilded Burmese chedi in the compound was built in 1451 and the Burmese-style bot, built in 1516, is one of the most beautiful in northern Thailand. Inside and out it is an integrated work of art that deserves admiration; it is well cared for by the local Thais. Fine woodcarving can be seen along the eaves of the roof and inside on the ceiling, which is supported by massive teak columns. The impressive altar is designed like a small prasat (temple) in the typical Lanna style and is said to contain a relic of the right side of the Buddha's skull. The abbot is a very serene old man, soft-spoken and radiant.

Behind the prasat-altar is a room containing religious antiques. More interesting is a

glass case along one wall of the bot which contains ancient Thai weaponry – a little out of place in a wat maybe.

Wat Phra Nawn Yai

วัดพระนอนใหญ่

About halfway between Chiang Mai and Chom Thong you may see Wat Phra Nawn Yai off the highway (on the right heading towards Chom Thong) with its distinctive Disney-like Buddha figures (standing, sitting and reclining), as well as sculptured scenes from selected Jatakas. The statuary is incredibly garish and cartoonish – good for a giggle.

Doi Inthanon National Park

อุทยานแห่งชาติดอยอินทนนท์

Doi Inthanon, Thailand's highest peak (2595 metres), has three impressive waterfalls cascading down its slopes. Starting from the bottom, these are **Mae Klang Falls**, **Wachiratan Falls** and **Siriphum Falls**. The first two have picnic areas and food vendors nearby. Mae Klang is the largest waterfall and easiest to get to, as you must stop there to get a bus to the top of Doi Inthanon. Mae Klang Falls can be climbed nearly to the top, as there is a footbridge leading to massive rock formations over which the water falls. Wachiratan is also very nice and less crowded.

The views from Inthanon are best in the cool dry season from November to February. You can expect the air to be quite chilly towards the top, so bring a jacket or sweater. For most of the year a mist, formed by the condensation of warm humid air below, hangs around the highest peak. Along the 47-km road to the top are many terraced rice fields, tremendous valleys and a few small hill-tribe villages.

The entire mountain is a national park, despite agriculture and human habitation. One of the top destinations for South-East Asia naturalists and bird-watchers, the mist-shrouded upper slopes produce a bumper crops of orchids, lichens, mosses, and epiphytes while supporting nearly 400 bird varieties, more than any other habitat in Thailand. The mountain is also one of the last habitats of the Asiatic black bear, along with Assamese macaque, Phayre's leaf-monkey, and a selection of other rare and not-so-rare monkeys and gibbons, plus the more common Indian civet, barking deer and giant flying squirrel – around 75 mammalian species in all.

Phra Mahathat Naphamethanidon, a chedi built by the Royal Thai Air Force to commemorate the king's 60th birthday in 1989, is off the highway between Km 41 and 42, about four km before reaching the summit. In the base of the octagonal chedi is a hall containing a green stone Buddha image.

Getting There & Away

Buses to Chom Thong leave regularly from just inside the Chiang Mai Gate at the south moat in Chiang Mai. Some buses go directly to Mae Klang Falls and some terminate in Hot, though the latter will let you off in Chom Thong. The fare to Chom Thong, 58 km away, is 11B.

From Chom Thong there are regular songthaews to Mae Klang, about eight km north, for 10B. Songthaews from Mae Klang to Doi Inthanon leave almost hourly until late afternoon and cost 25 to 30B per person. Most of the passengers are locals who get off at various points along the road up, thus allowing a few stationary views of the valleys below. If you're travelling by private vehicle, you'll have to pay a toll of 20B per car or 5B per motorcycle at the park entrance.

For another 10B you can go from Chom Thong to Hot, where you can get buses on to Mae Sariang or Mae Hong Son. However, if you've gone to Doi Inthanon and the waterfalls, you probably won't have time to make it all the way to Mae Sariang or Mae Hong Son in one day, so you may want to stay overnight in the park or in Chom Thong. Forestry Service bungalows near the park headquarters (past the Chom Thong park entrance) cost from 300 to 1000B per night.

In Chom Thong, enquire at the wat for a place to sleep.

NORTH TO FANG

Chiang Dao

เชียงดาว

On the way north to Fang and Tha Ton, you can visit Chiang Dao cave, five km off the road and 72 km north of Chiang Mai. The entrance fee is 5B and the cave is said to extend some 10 to 14 km into 2175-metre Doi Chiang Dao (but the lighting system only runs in about half a km or so).

In Chiang Dao village, there is an old wooden hotel, the *Pieng Dao*, with rooms for 80B. Outside town, the *Chiang Dao Hill Resort* (☎ 236995) has tourist bungalows for 700B up. Buses to Fang from Chiang Mai's Chang Phuak station stop in Chiang Dao (18B).

Doi Ang Khang

ดอยอ่างขาง

About 20 km before Fang is the turn-off for Route 1249 to Doi Ang Khang, Thailand's 'Little Switzerland'. This 1300-metre peak has a cool climate year-round and supports the cultivation of flowers, as well as fruits and vegetables that are usually found only in more temperate climates. A few hill-tribe villages (Lahu, Lisu and Hmong) can be visited on the slopes.

The Yunnanese village of Ban Khum on Doi Ang Khang also has some bungalows for rent.

FANG & THA TON

ฝาง/ท่าตอน

The present city of Fang was founded by King Mengrai in the 13th century, though as a human settlement and trading centre the locale dates back at least 1000 years. North from Chiang Mai along Highway 107, Fang doesn't look particularly inviting, but the town's quiet back streets are lined with interesting little shops in wooden buildings. The Burmese-style **Wat Jong Paen** – near the Wiang Kaew Hotel – has an impressive stacked-roof wihaan. There are also Yao (Mien) and Karen villages nearby which you can visit on your own, but for most people Fang is just a road marker on the way to Tha Ton, the starting point for Kok River trips to Chiang Rai (and other points along the river in between), and for guided or solo treks to the many hill-tribe settlements in the region. However, if you're planning to spend the night before catching the boat, Fang is as good a place to stay as Tha Ton. It's only a half hour or so by songthaew to the river from Fang.

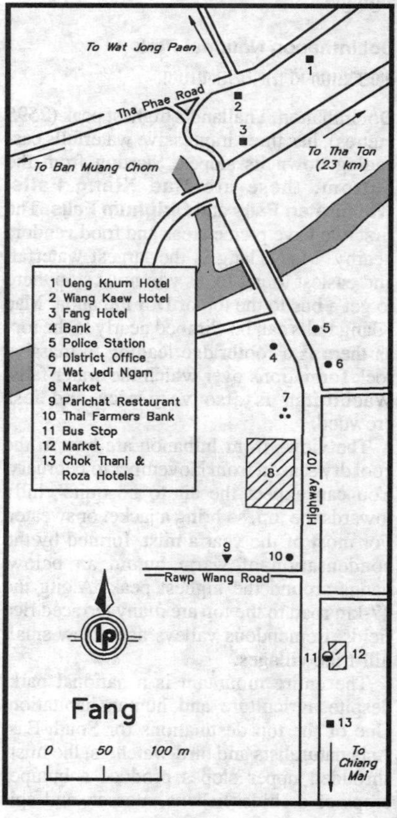

About 10 km west of Fang at Ban Muang Chom, near the agricultural station, is a system of **hot springs**. Just ask for the *bàw náam ráwn* ('baw nam hawn' in northern Thai).

Tha Ton is little more than a collection of riverboats, tourist accommodation, restaurants, souvenir shops and a songthaew stand. For something to do, climb the hill to **Wat Tha Ton** for good views of the surrounding area. There are also some pleasant walks along the river; three-day treks can be arranged through Tip's Travellers House.

Two banks along the main street in Fang offer currency exchange.

Places to Stay & Eat

Fang The oldest hotel in town is the *Fang Hotel (Wiang Fang)*, just off the main road in town on the way to Tha Ton. One-bed rooms in the old wooden wing are 70B, two-bed rooms in the new wing are 100B. A better choice is the friendly *Wiang Kaew Hotel*, behind the Fang Hotel off the main street. Basic but clean rooms with private bath are 100B with hot water, 80B without.

The *Ueng Khum (Euang Kham) Hotel* (☎ 451268) around the corner on Thaw Phae Rd has large bungalow-style accommodation around a courtyard for 120/180B a single/double; all rooms have hot-water showers. More up-market digs near the market on the highway are at the *Chok Thani* and *Roza*, both with fan rooms from 160B, air-con from 280B.

The *Fang Restaurant* (Thai sign reads *Khun Pa)* next to the Fang Hotel entrance has a bilingual menu and quite decent food. The spotless *Parichat Restaurant*, on Rawp Wiang Rd near the highway market, serves an exemplary bowl of khâo sòi with chicken or beef, plus kuăytĭaw, khâo phàt and other standards. Farther down this same road is a row of cheap isaan restaurants and *lao dong* (herbal liquor) bars.

A few food vendors – not quite enough to make a true 'night market' – set up near the bus terminal at night.

Tha Ton If you want to spend the night near the pier in Tha Ton, there are several options. *Phanga's House* (Karen Coffee House) is the old stand-by here and is 30B per person, but it's nearly an hour's walk from the pier.

Thip's Travellers House has expanded to two locations; the older and quieter one is 50 metres west along the river while the new addition, which has a better restaurant, is near the bridge where the road from Fang meets the river. Rates are 40 to 80B for rooms without bath, 80 to 100B with bath.

Chankasem, down near the pier, has a pleasant restaurant on the river and a variety of rooms: 60B with shared bath in the older wooden section; 80B for singles/doubles with fan and bath; 100 to 200B with hot water and 300B for a brick bungalow. Also near the pier is the *Apple Guest House*, with very basic rooms for 40/60B.

Two up-market places in Tha Ton are on the opposite side of the river. The *Maekok River Lodge* (☎ 222172) has landscaped grounds, a pool and deluxe rooms overlooking the river for 825B. Nearby is the similar *Thaton River View Resort*. Also on this side of the river, *Thaton House* has rooms in the 100 to 150B range. There are several restaurants near the pier.

Getting There & Away

Bus & Songthaew Buses to Fang leave from the Chang Phuak bus station north of the White Elephant (Chang Phuak) Gate in Chiang Mai. The three-hour trip costs 32B by ordinary bus and 40B by minibus.

From Fang it's 23 km to Tha Ton. A songthaew does the 40-minute trip for 7B; the larger orange buses from Fang leave less frequently and cost only 5B. Buses leave from near the market, or you can wait in front of the Fang Hotel for a bus or songthaew.

To/From Mae Salong The river isn't the only way to get to Chiang Rai and points north from Tha Ton. Yellow songthaews leave from the north side of the river in Tha Ton to Mae Salong in Chiang Rai Province several times daily between 7 am and 3 pm. The trip takes about 2½ hours and costs 60B per person. Hold tight – the road is pretty rugged.

To/From Pai If you're heading to or coming from Mae Hong Son Province, it's not necessary to dip all the way south to Chiang Mai before continuing westward or eastward. At Ban Mae Malai, the junction of Highway 107 (the Chiang Mai to Fang highway), you can pick up a bus to Pai for 32B; if you're coming from Pai, be sure to get off here to catch a bus north of Fang. Buses between Ban Mae Malai and Fang cost 35B.

Motorbike Motorcycle trekkers can also travel between Tha Ton and Doi Mae Salong, 48 km north-east along a sometimes treacherous, unpaved mountain road. There are a couple of Lisu and Akha villages along the way. The 27 km or so between Doi Mae Salong and the KMT village of Hua Muang Ngam are the most difficult, especially in the rainy season. When conditions are good, the trip can be accomplished in an hour and a half. As this road is improved, the adventure factor will decrease.

For an extra charge, you can take a motorcycle on some boats to Chiang Rai.

KOK RIVER TRIP TO CHIANG RAI

From Tha Ton you can make a half-day long-tail boat trip to Chiang Rai down the Kok River. The regular passenger boat leaves at 12.30 pm and costs 170B per person. You can also charter a boat, which between eight or 10 people works out at much the same cost per person but gives you more room. The trip is a bit of a tourist trap these days as most of the passengers are farangs and the villages along the way sell Coke and there are lots of TV aerials – but it's still fun. The best time to do the trip is at the end of the rainy season in November when the river level is high.

To catch a boat on the same day from Chiang Mai you'd have to leave by 7 or 7.30 am at the latest and make no stops on the way. The 6 am bus is the best bet. The travel time downriver depends on river conditions and the skill of the pilot, taking anywhere from three to five hours. You could actually make the boat trip in a day from Chiang Mai, catching a bus back from Chiang Rai as soon as you arrive, but it's far better to stay in Fang or Tha Ton, take the boat trip, then stay in Chiang Rai or Chiang Saen before travelling on. You may sometimes have to get off and walk or push the boat if it gets stuck on sandbars.

These days some travellers take the boat to Chiang Rai in two or three stages, stopping first in **Mae Salak**, a large Lahu village which is about a third of the distance, or **Ban Ruammit**, a Karen village about two-thirds of the way down. Both villages are well touristed these days (charter boat tours stop for photos and elephant rides), but from here you can trek to other Shan, Thai and hill-tribe villages, or do longer treks south of Ban Salak to **Wawi**, a large multi-ethnic community of jiin haw (Chinese refugees), Lahu, Lisu, Akha, Shan, Karen, Yao and Thai peoples. The Wawi area has dozens of hill-tribe villages of various ethnicities, including the largest Akha community in Thailand (Saen Charoen) and the oldest Lisu settlement (Doi Chang). If this kind of trip appeals to you, pick up the Wawi or Kok River trekking maps at DK Books in Chiang Mai. The maps mark trails and village locations.

Another alternative is to trek south from Mae Salak all the way to the town of **Mae Suai**, where you can catch a bus on to Chiang Rai or back to Chiang Mai. You might also try getting off the boat at one of the smaller villages (see boat fares below) – **Jakheu** looked interesting. It's also possible to make the trip (much more slowly) upriver, despite the rapids, from Chiang Rai.

Several of the guesthouses in Tha Ton now organise raft trips down the river – you pay for a raft to be built and then pole yourself with a guide. This can easily take days, especially when the raft falls apart and has to be rebuilt. A better way is to pull together a small group of travellers and charter one of the house rafts with a guide and cook for a two or three-day journey downriver, stopping off in villages along the way. A house raft generally costs around 300B per person per day including all meals and takes up to six people – so figure on 1000B for a three-day trip with stops at Shan, Lisu and Karen villages along the way. New police regulations require that an experienced boat navigator accompany each raft – the river has lots of tricky spots and there have been some mishaps.

The following table shows boat fares from Tha Thon:

destination	fare
Ban Mai	40B
Mae Salak	50B
Pha Tai	60B
Jakheu	70B
Kok Noi	90B
Pha Khwang	90B
Pha Khiaw	140B
Hat Wua Dam	140B
Ban Ruammit	150B
Chiang Rai	170B

Warning

Whether travelling by raft or long-tail boat, all passengers are required to sign in at police posts three times along the river; once in Tha Ton and once each in Mae Salak and Ban Ruammit. This requirement is part of an overall attempt to improve security along the river following several armed bandit attacks on passing boats during the late '80s. Since 1988 things have been quiet, so the system seems to be effective. Still, don't travel with any valuables you can't afford to lose.

Bring sun block and a hat (one that you can tie down once the boat reaches warp speed) or scarf, as long-tail boats provide no shelter from the sun.

Hill-Tribe Treks

For years Chiang Mai has been a centre for treks into the mountainous northern areas inhabited by hill tribes. It used to be pretty exciting to knock about the dirt roads of rural Chiang Rai Province, do the boat trip between Fang and Chiang Rai and hike into the various villages of the Karen, Hmong, Akha and Yao tribes and the Kuomintang (KMT) settlements. You could spend the night in rustic surroundings and perhaps share some opium with the villagers.

Only a very few Thais living in Chiang Mai had the travel and linguistic knowledge necessary to lead adventurous foreigners through this area. Booking a trip usually meant waiting for optimum conditions and adequate numbers of participants which sometimes took quite a while.

The trips began to gain popularity in the early 1970s and now virtually every hotel and guesthouse in Chiang Mai books hill-tribe tours for countless tour organisations.

Soon the word was out that the area north of the Kok River in the Golden Triangle was being over-trekked, with treks crisscrossing the area in such a fashion that the hill-tribe villages were starting to become human zoos. With their only contact with the outside world coming through a camera lens and a flow of sweets and cigarettes, many villages faced cultural erosion. So the tours moved south of the Kok River, around Chiang Dao and Wiang Papao, then to Mae Hong Son where most of them now operate. It will be only a short time before this area suffers from the heavy traffic as well.

Meanwhile, thousands of foreign travellers each year continue to take these treks. Most come away with a sense of adventure while a few are disillusioned. The primary ingredient in a good trek is having a good leader/organiser, followed by a good group of trekkers. Some travellers finish a tour complaining more about the other trekkers than about the itinerary, food or trek leader.

Before Trekking

Hill-tribe trekking isn't for everyone. Firstly, you must be physically fit to cope with the demands of sustained up and down walking, exposure to the elements and spotty food. Secondly, many people feel awkward walking through hill-tribe villages and playing the role of voyeur.

In cities and villages elsewhere in Thailand, Thais and other lowland groups are quite used to foreign faces and foreign ways (from TV if nothing else), but in the hills of northern Thailand the tribes lead largely insular lives. Hence, hill-tribe tourism has pronounced effects, both positive and negative. On the positive side, travellers have a chance to see how traditional subsistence-oriented societies function. Also, since the Thai government is sensitive about the image projected by their minority groups, tourism may actually have forced it to review and sometimes improve its policies toward hill tribes. On the negative side, trekkers introduce many cultural items and ideas from the outside world that may erode tribal customs to varying degrees.

If you have any qualms about interrupting the traditional patterns of life in hill-tribe areas, you probably should not go trekking. It is undeniable that trekking in northern Thailand is marketed like soap or any other commodity. Anyone who promises you an authentic experience is probably exaggerating at the very least, or at worst contributing to the decline of hill-tribe culture by leading foreigners into unhampered areas.

If you desire to make a trek keep these points in mind: choose your trek operator carefully, try to meet the others in the group (suggest a meeting) and find out exactly what the tour includes and does not include, as usually there are additional expenses beyond the basic rate. If everything works out, even an organised tour can be worthwhile. A useful check list of questions to ask are:

1. How many people will there be in the group? Six is a good maximum, reported one traveller, although others have said that 10 is equally OK.
2. Can the organiser guarantee that no other tourists will visit the same village on the same day, especially overnight?
3. Can the guide speak the language of each village to be visited?
4. Exactly when does the tour begin and end? Some three-day treks turn out to be less than 48 hours.
5. Do they provide transport before and after the trek or is it just by public bus (often with long waits)?

Choosing a Company TAT is making efforts to regulate trekking companies operating out of Chiang Mai and recommend that you trek only with members of the Professional Guide Association of Chiang Mai or the Jungle Tour Club of northern Thailand. Still, with more than 100 companies, it's very difficult to guarantee any kind of control.

These days there are plenty of places apart from Chiang Mai where you can arrange treks. Often these places have better and usually less expensive alternatives which originate closer to the more remote and untrekked areas. Also, they are generally smaller, friendlier operations and the trekkers are usually a more determined bunch since they're not looking for a quick in-and-out trek. The treks are often informally arranged, usually involving discussions of duration, destination, cost, etc (it used to be like that in Chiang Mai).

You can easily arrange treks out of the following northern towns: Chiang Rai, Mae Hong Son, Pai, Mae Sai and Tha Ton. With a little time to seek out the right people, you can also go on organised treks from Mae Sariang, Soppong (near Pai), Mae Sot, the Akha Guest House on the road to Doi Tung and other out-of-the-way guesthouses which are springing up all over northern Thailand.

The down side, of course, is that companies outside of Chiang Mai are generally subject to even less regulation than those in Chiang Mai, and there are fewer guarantees with regard to trekking terms and conditions.

Costs Organised treks out of Chiang Mai average from 1200B for a four-day, three-night trek to 2500B for a deluxe seven-day, six-night trek which includes rafting and/or elephant riding. Rates vary, so it pays to shop around – although these days so many companies are competing for your business that rates have remained pretty stable for the last few years. You can count on an extra 1000B for elephants or other exotic additions to a basic trek. Elephant rides actually become quite boring and even uncomfortable after an hour or two.

Don't choose a trek by price alone. It's better to talk to other travellers in town who have been on treks. Treks out of other towns in the north are usually less expensive – around 200B per person per day.

The Professional Guide Association in Chiang Mai meets monthly to set trek prices and to discuss problems, and issues regular, required reports to TAT about individual treks. All trekking guides and companies are supposed to be government licensed. As a result, a standard for trekking operators has emerged whereby you can expect the price you pay to include: transport to and from the starting/ending points of a trek (if outside Chiang Mai); food (three meals a day) and accommodation in all villages visited; basic first aid; predeparture valuables storage; and sometimes the loan of specific equipment, such as sleeping bags in cool weather or water bottles.

Not included in the price are beverages

Courtesy of *About Chiangmai* magazine (Tim Polt)

other than drinking water or tea, the obligatory opium-smoking with the village headman (how many travellers have I heard say '...and then, oh wow, we actually smoked opium with the village headman!'), lunch on the first and last days and personal porters.

Seasons Probably the best time to trek is November to February when the weather is refreshing with little or no rain and poppies are in bloom everywhere. Between March and May the hills are dry and the weather is quite hot in most northern places. The second-best time to trek is early in the rainy season, between June and July, before the dirt roads become too saturated.

Safety Every year or so there's at least one trekking robbery in northern Thailand. Often the bandits are armed with guns which they will use without hesitation if they meet resistance. Once they collect a load of cameras, watches, money and jewellery, many bandit gangs hightail it across the border into Burma. In spite of this, police have had a good arrest record so far and have created hill-country patrols. Still, gangs can form at any time and anywhere. The problem is that most people living in the rural north believe that all foreigners are very rich (a fair assumption in relation to hill-tribe living standards). Most of these people have never been to Chiang Mai and, from what they have heard about the capital, consider Bangkok to be a virtual paradise of wealth and luxury. So don't take anything with you trekking you can't afford to lose, and don't resist robbery attempts.

Conduct

Once trekking, there are several other guidelines to minimising the negative impact on the local people:

1. Always ask for permission before taking photos of tribal people and/or their dwellings. You can ask through your guide or by using sign language. Because of traditional belief systems, many individuals and even whole tribes may object strongly to being photographed.
2. Show respect for religious symbols and rituals. Don't touch totems at village entrances or any other object of obvious symbolic value without asking permission. Keep your distance from ceremonies being performed unless you're asked to participate.
3. Practise restraint in giving things to tribespeople or bartering with them. Food and medicine are not necessarily appropriate gifts if they result in altering traditional dietary and healing practices. The same goes for clothing. Tribespeople will abandon handwoven tunics for printed T-shirts if they are given a steady supply. If you want to give something to the people you encounter on a trek, the best thing is to make a donation to the village school or other community fund. Your guide can help arrange this.

Opium Smoking Some guides are very strict now about forbidding the smoking of opium on treks. This seems to be a good idea, since one of the problems trekking companies have had in the past is dealing with opium-addicted guides! Volunteers who work in tribal areas also say opium smoking sets a bad example for young people in the villages.

Opium is traditionally a condoned vice of the elderly, yet an increasing number of young people in the villages are now taking opium and heroin. This is possibly due in part to the influence of young trekkers who may smoke once and a few weeks later be hundreds of km away while the villagers continue to face the temptation every day.

Opium overdoses aren't unknown; in 1991 a 23-year-old Brazilian died after smoking 18 pipes of opium while on a trek in northern Thailand.

Independent Trekking

You might consider striking out on your own in a small group of two to five people. Gather as much information as you can about the area you'd like to trek in from the Tribal Research Institute at Chiang Mai University. The institute has an informative pamphlet which is available at its library. Don't bother staff with questions about trekking as they are quite noncommittal, either from fear of liability or fear of retribution from the Chiang Mai trekking companies.

Maps, mostly distributed by guesthouses outside of Chiang Mai, pinpoint various hill-tribe areas in the north. DK Books in Chiang Mai sells two excellent maps on the Wawi area, south of the Kok River, and the Kok River area itself. Both lie in Chiang Rai Province and are considered safe areas for do-it-yourself treks. DK Books plans to produce a series of trekking maps based on research done by the Tribal Research Institute.

Be prepared for language difficulties. Few people you meet will know any English. Usually someone in a village will know some Thai, so a Thai phrasebook can be helpful. Lonely Planet now also publishes a *Thai Hill Tribes Phrasebook* with phrase sections for each of the six major hill-tribe languages.

As in Himalayan trekking in Nepal and India, many people now do short treks on their own at the lower elevations, staying in villages along the way. It is not necessary to bring a lot of food or equipment, just money for food which can be bought along the way in small Thai towns and occasionally in the hill-tribe settlements. However, TAT strongly discourages trekking on your own because of the safety risk. Check in with the police when you arrive in a new district so they can tell you if an area is considered safe or not. A lone trekker is an easy target (see the Safety section).

Trekking Companies

I won't make any specific recommendations for particular trekking companies in Chiang Mai. Many of the trekking guides are freelance and go from one company to the next, so there's no way to predict which companies are going to give the best service at any time. Many guesthouses that advertise their own trekking companies actually act as brokers for off-site operations; they collect a commission for every guest they book onto a trek.

The companies listed here are recognised by TAT and the Professional Guide Association, which means that they should be using licensed guides. Just about every guesthouse in Chiang Mai works through one of these companies. The list represents a mixture of companies which are directly affiliated with hotels/guesthouses and those which are not. Ultimately, the best way to shop for a trek is to talk to travellers who have just returned from treks.

Camp of Troppo, 2 Charoen Prathet Rd (☎ 279360)
Changmoi Trekking (Folkways Tribal Trekking), Changmoi Guest House, 29 Chang Moi Kao Rd (☎ 251839)
Eagle Trekking (Pon & Annette Trekking), Eagle House, 16-18 Chang Moi Kao Rd, Soi 3 (☎ 235387)
DNP Trekking, Welcome Guest House, 37/1 Moon Muang Rd (☎ 210447)
Evergreen, 47 Moon Muang Rd (☎ 276710)
Exotic Travel, 227 Tha Phae Rd (☎ 235515)
Family Tribal Trekking, 9 Soi 7, Moon Muang Rd (☎ 213939)
Inter Travel Agency, 17 Tha Phae Rd (☎ 252512)
Inthanon Tours, 100/19 Huay Kaew Rd (☎ 232722)
Lanna Travel & Tour Service, 94 Charoen Prathet Rd (☎ 251471)
Magic Tour, 59 Moon Muang Rd (☎ 214572)
Markes Travel, 2-4 Tha Phae Rd (☎ 236704)
Mau Tour, 106 Ratchaphakhinai Rd (☎ 211033)
MEI Tour, 261 Tha Phae Rd (☎ 234358)
Northern Thailand Trekking, 59 Moon Muang Rd (☎ 214572)
New Wave Tour, 33/6 Moon Muang Rd (☎ 214040)
Pinan Tour, 235 Tha Phae Rd (☎ 236081)
PS Tours & Travel, New Chiang Mai Hotel, 22 Chaiyaphum Rd (☎ 251721)
Seiko Tour, 164 Tha Phae Rd (☎ 236640)
Singha Travel, 277 Tha Phae Rd (☎ 233198)
Summit Tour & Trekking, 28-30 Tha Phae Rd (☎ 233351)
Top North Trekking, 15 Soi 2, Moon Muang Rd (☎ 213900)
Wattana Tour, 4/4 Chiangmai to Lamphun Rd (☎ 244103)
Youth's Tour, Chiang Mai Youth Hostel, 31 Phra Pokklao Rd (☎ 212863)

Akha (Thai: *I-kaw*)
Population: 38,000
Origin: Tibet
Present locations: Thailand, Laos, Burma, Yunnan
Economy: rice, corn, opium
Belief system: animism, with an emphasis on ancestor worship.
Distinctive characteristics: headdresses of beads, feathers and dangling silver ornaments. Villages are along mountain ridges or on steep slopes from 1000 to 1400 metres in altitude. The well- known Akha Swing Ceremony takes place mid-August to mid-September – between planting and harvest – and is linked to ancestor worship and spirit offerings. The Akha are amongst the poorest of Thailand's ethnic minorities and tend to resist assimilation into the Thai mainstream. Like the Lahu, they often cultivate opium for their own consumption.

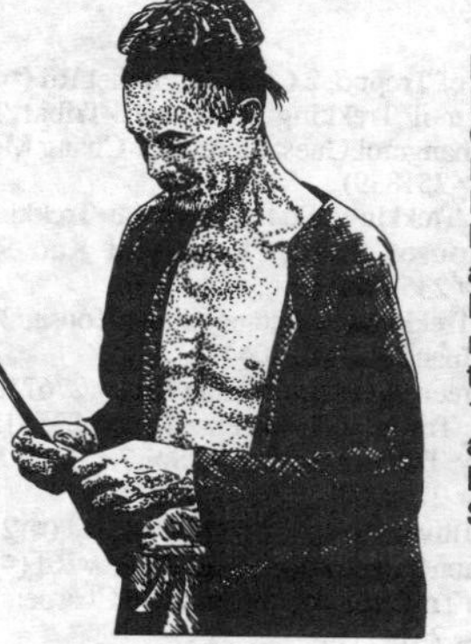

Lahu (Thai: *Musoe*)
Population: 58,700
Origin: Tibet
Present locations: south China, Thailand, Burma
Economy: rice, corn, opium
Belief system: theistic animism (supreme deity is Geusha) and some groups are Christian
Distinctive characteristics: black and red jackets with narrow skirts for women, bright green or blue-green baggy trousers for men. They live in mountainous areas at about 1000 metres. Their intricately woven shoulder bags (yaam) are prized by collectors. There are four main groups – Red Lahu, Black Lahu, White Lahu, Yellow Lahu and Lahu Sheleh.

Lisu (Thai: *Lisaw*)
Population: 25,000
Origin: Tibet
Present locations: Thailand, Yunnan
Economy: rice, opium, corn, livestock
Belief system: animism with ancestor worship and spirit possession.
Distinctive characteristics: the women wear long multi-coloured tunics over trousers and sometimes black turbans with tassels. Men wear baggy green or blue pants pegged in at the ankles. Premarital sex is said to be common, along with freedom in choosing marital partners. Patrilineal clans have pan-tribal jurisdiction, which makes the Lisu unique among hill-tribe groups (most tribes have power centred at the village level with either the shaman or a village headman). Lisu villages are usually in the mountains at about 1000 metres.

Mien (Thai: *Yao*)
Population: 38,000
Origin: central China
Present locations: Thailand, south China, Laos, Burma, Vietnam
Economy: rice, corn, opium
Belief system: animism with ancestor worship and Taoism
Distinctive characteristics: women wear black jackets and trousers decorated with intricately embroidered patches and red fur-like collars, along with large dark blue or black turbans. They have been heavily influenced by Chinese traditions and use Chinese characters to write the Mien language. They tend to settle near mountain springs at between 1000 and 1200 metres. Kinship is patrilineal and marriage ispolygamous. The Mien are highly skilled at embroidery and silversmithing.

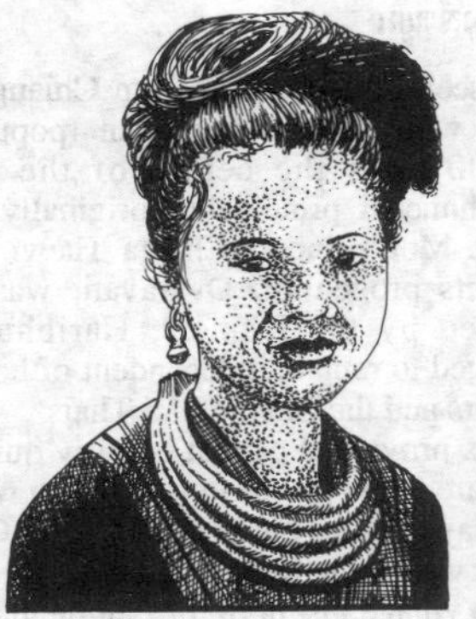

Hmong
(Thai: *Meo* or *Maew*)
Population: 87,000
Origin: south China
Present locations: south China, Thailand, Laos, Vietnam
Economy: rice, corn, opium
Belief system: animism
Distinctive characteristics: simple black jackets and indigo or black baggy trousers with striped borders or indigo skirts, and silver jewellery. Most women wear their hair in a large bun. They usually live on mountain peaks or plateaus above 1000 metres. Kinship is patrilineal and polygamy is permitted. They are Thailand's second-largest hill-tribe group and are especially numerous in Chiang Mai Province.

Karen (Thai: *Yang* or *Kariang*)
Population: 285,000
Origin: Burma
Present locations: Thailand, Burma
Economy: rice, vegetables, livestock
Belief system: animism, Buddhism, Christianity, depending on the group
Distinctive characteristics: thickly woven V-neck tunics of various colours (unmarried women wear white). Kinship is matrilineal and marriage is endogamous. They tend to live in lowland valleys and practice crop rotation rather than swidden (slash-and-burn) agriculture. There are five distinct Karen groups – the White Karen (Skaw Karen), Pwo Karen, Black Karen (Pa-O) and Red Karen (Kayah). These groups combined form the largest hill tribe in Thailand, numbering a quarter of a million people or about half of all hill-tribe people. Many Karen continue to migrate into Thailand from Burma, fleeing Burmese government persecution.

Hill Tribes

The term 'hill tribe' refers to ethnic minorities living in the mountainous regions of north and west Thailand. The Thais refer to them as *chao khão*, literally 'mountain people'. Each hill tribe has its own language, customs, mode of dress and spiritual beliefs.

Most are of seminomadic origin, having migrated to Thailand from Tibet, Burma, China and Laos during the past 200 years or so, although some groups may have been in Thailand much longer. They are 'fourth-world' people in the sense that they belong neither to the main aligned powers nor to the Third-World nations. Rather, they have crossed and continue to cross national borders without regard for recent nationhood. Language and culture constitute the borders of their world – some groups are caught between the 6th and 20th centuries, while others are gradually being assimilated into modern Thai life.

Many tribespeople are moving into lowland areas inhabited by Thais as montane lands become deforested by traditional swidden (slash-and-burn) cultivation methods.

The Tribal Research Institute in Chiang Mai recognises 10 different hill tribes in Thailand, but there may be up to 20. The Institute estimates the total hill-tribe population to be around 550,000.

The earlier descriptions covered the largest tribes, which are also the groups most likely to be encountered on treks. Linguistically, the tribes can be divided into three main groups: the Tibeto-Burman (Lisu, Lahu, Akha); the Karenic (Karen, Kayah); and the Austro-Thai (Hmong, Mien). Comments on ethnic dress refer mostly to the female members of each group as hill-tribe men tend to dress like rural Thais. Population figures are 1989 estimates.

The Shan (Thai Yai) are not included since they are not a hill-tribe group per se – they live in permanent locations, practice Theravada Buddhism and speak a language very similar to Thai. Thai scholars consider the Shan to have been the original inhabitants (Thai Yai means 'larger' or 'majority Thais') of the area. Nevertheless, Shan villages are common stops on hill-tribe trekking itineraries.

For a more complete description of the dress and customs of each tribe, along with a compendium of useful words and phrases in the language of each, plus maps showing areas of habitation, see Lonely Planet's *Thai Hill Tribes Phrasebook.*

Lamphun Province

LAMPHUN

อ.เมืองลำพูน

Best seen on a day trip from Chiang Mai, along with Pasang, Lamphun (population 14,000) was the centre of the small Hariphunchai principality originally ruled by the Mon princess Chama Thewi. Long after its progenitor, Dvaravati, was vanquished by the Khmers, Hariphunchai managed to remain independent of both the Khmers and the Chiang Mai Thais.

This provincial capital is fairly quiet but there are a few places to stay if you want to get away from the hustle and bustle of Chiang Mai or want to study the temples here in depth.

The village just north of Lamphun, Nong Chang Kheun, is known for producing the sweetest lam yai (longan) fruit in the country. During the second week of August, Lamphun hosts the annual Lam Yai Festival, which features floats made of the fruit, and a Miss Lam Yai contest.

Wat Phra That Hariphunchai

วัดพระธาตุหริภุญชัย

On the main road into Lamphun from Chiang Mai on the left is this wat which dates from 1157. It has some interesting post-Dvaravati architecture, a couple of fine Buddha images and two old chedis of the original Hariphunchai style. The tallest chedi is 46 metres high and topped by a nine-tier umbrella made of 6.5 kg of gold.

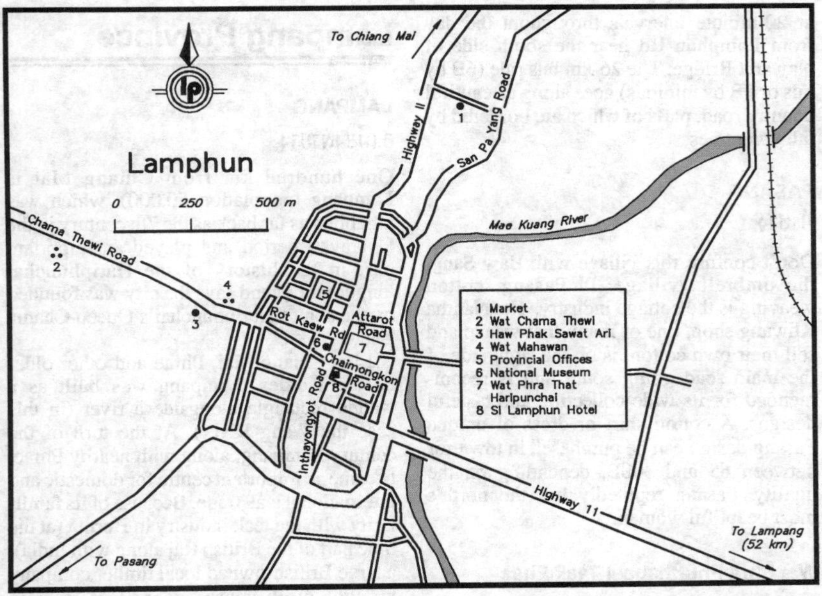

Lamphun National Museum
พิพิธภัณฑ์แห่งชาติลำพูน

Across the street from Wat Phra That Hariphunchai, the museum's small collection includes artefacts from the Dvaravati, Hariphunchai and Lanna kingdoms. Hours are Wednesday to Sunday from 8.30 am to noon and 1 to 4 pm. Entry is 10B.

Wat Chama Thewi (Wat Kukut)
วัดจามเทวี (วัดกู่กุด)

A larger Hariphunchai chedi can be seen at Wat Chama Thewi (popularly called Wat Kukut), which is said to have been erected in the 8th or 9th century as a Dvaravati monument. As it has been restored many times it is now a mixture of several schools.

Each of the four sides of the chedi has five rows of three Buddha figures, diminishing in size on each higher level. The stucco standing Buddhas are definitely of the Dvaravati style, but are probably not the original images.

Wat Kukut is on the opposite side of town from Wat Hariphunchai. To get there, walk west down Mukda Rd, perpendicular to the Chiang Mai to Lamphun road (opposite Wat Hari), passing over the town moat then past the district government offices until you come to the wat on the left.

Places to Stay
Si Lamphun (☎ 511-1760) is on the town's main street, Inthayongyot Rd. Singles/twins without bath are 50/70B, or 80/100B with bath.

Haw Phak Sawat Ari on Chama Thewi Rd near Wat Kukut is where visiting archaeologists stay. For 50B per night or 1000B per month you can have an apartment with a bedroom, bathroom and sitting room.

Getting There & Away
Buses to Lamphun from Chiang Mai leave

at 20-minute intervals throughout the day from Lamphun Rd near the south side of Nawarat Bridge. The 26-km bus ride (6B by bus or 8B by minibus) goes along a beautiful country road, parts of which are bordered by tall *yang* trees.

PASANG

ป่าซาง

Don't confuse this village with Baw Sang, the umbrella village. In Pasang, cotton weaving is the cottage industry. The Nantha Khwang shop, one of many that weave and sell their own cotton, is on the right side of the main road going south and is recommended for its wide collection and tasteful designs. A cotton shirt or dress of unique Pasang design can be purchased in town for between 65 and 300B, depending on the quality. Pasang reputedly has the north's most beautiful women.

Wat Phra Phutthabaat Taak Phaa

วัดพระพุทธบาทตากผ้า

About nine km south of Pasang or 20 km south of Lamphun, off Highway 106 in the subdistrict (tambon) of Ma-Kawk, is this famous Mahanikai wat. A shrine to one of the north's most famous monks, Luang Puu Phromma, it contains a lifelike wax figure of the deceased sitting in meditation.

One of his disciples, Ajaan Thirawattho, teaches meditation to a large contingent of monks who are housed in *kutis* of laterite brick. Behind the spacious grounds is a type of park and a steep hill mounted by a chedi. The wat is named after an unremarkable Buddha footprint (Phra Phutthabaat) shrine in the middle of the lower temple grounds and another spot where Buddha supposedly dried his robes (Taak Phaa) and left an imprint.

Getting There & Away

A songthaew will take you from Lamphun to Pasang for a few baht. From Chiang Mai it costs 10B by regular bus or 12B by minibus.

Lampang Province

LAMPANG

อ.เมืองลำปาง

One hundred km from Chiang Mai is Lampang (population 50,000), which was inhabited as far back as the 7th century in the Dvaravati period and played an important part in the history of the Hariphunchai kingdom. Legend says the city was founded by the son of Hariphunchai's Queen Chama Thewi.

Like Chiang Mai, Phrae and other older northern cities, Lampang was built as a walled rectangle alongside a river (in this case the Wang River). At the turn of the century Lampang, along with nearby Phrae, became an important centre for domestic and international teak trade. Because of its familiarity with the teak industry in Burma (at the time part of the British Raj along with India), a large British-owned local timber company brought in Burmese supervisors to train Burmese and Thai loggers in the area. These well-paid supervisors, along with independent Burmese teak merchants who plied their trade in Lampang, sponsored the construction of more than a dozen impressive temples in the city. Burmese artisans designed and built the temples out of local materials, especially teak. Their legacy lives on in several of Lampang's most well-maintained wats, now among the city's main visitor attractions.

Many Thais visit Lampang for a taste of urban northern Thailand without the crass commercialism of Chiang Mai. Although the downtown area is quite busy, the shophouses have a more traditional feel.

Horsecarts

Lampang is known throughout Thailand as Muang Rot Maa (Horsecart City) because it's the only town in Thailand where horsecarts are still used as public transport. These days, Lampang's horsecarts are mainly for tourists. A 15-minute horsecart tour around town costs a standard 15B; for

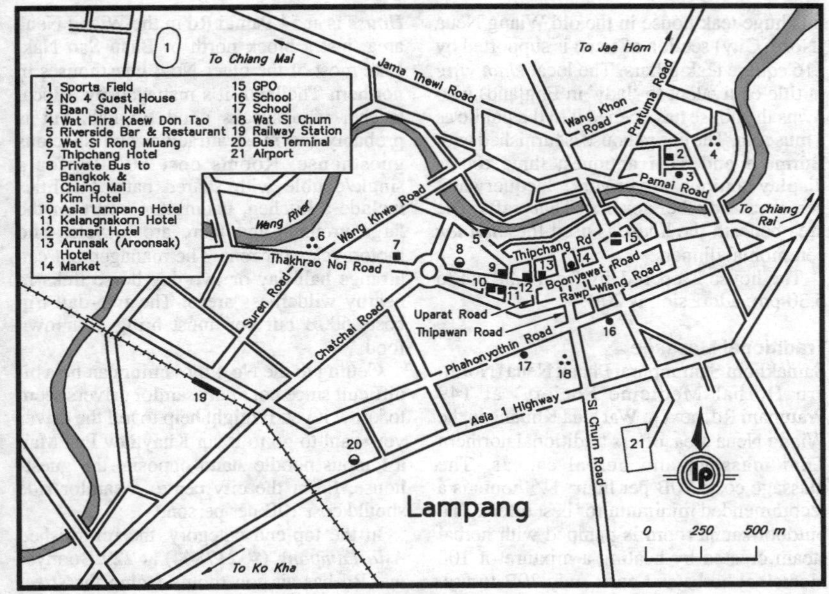

80B you can get a half-hour tour that goes along the Wang River, and for 100B a one-hour tour which stops at Wat Phra Kaew Don Tao and Wat Si Rong Muang. If there's not much business you may be able to negotiate to bring the price down to 50B per half hour or 80B per hour. The main horsecart stands are in front of the City Hall and Thipchang Hotel.

Wat Phra Kaew Don Tao

วัดพระแก้วดอนเต้า

This wat, on the north side of the Wang River, was built during the reign of King Anantayot and housed the Emerald Buddha (know in Bangkok's Wat Phra Kaew) from 1436 to 1468. The main chedi shows Hariphunchai influence, while the adjacent *mondop* (a square building for laypeople) was built in 1909. The mondop, decorated with glass mosaic in typical Burmese style, contains a Mandalay-style Buddha image. A display of Lanna artefacts – mostly religious paraphernalia and woodwork – can be seen in the wat's **Lanna Museum**.

Other Temples

Wat Si Rong Muang and **Wat Si Chum** are two more wats built at the turn of century by Burmese artisans. Both have wihaans and other temple buildings constructed in the Burmese 'layered' style, with tin roofs gabled by intricate woodcarvings.

Besides the wihaan at Wat Phra That Lampang Luang (see the Around Lampang section), the mondop at **Wat Pongsanuk Tai** is one of the few remaining local examples of original Lanna-style temple architecture, which emphasised open-sided wooden buildings.

Baan Sao Nak (Many Pillars House)

บ้านเสานัก

Built in 1896 in the traditional Lanna style,

this huge teak house in the old Wiang Neua (North City) section of town is supported by 116 square teak pillars. The local *khun yĩng* (a title equivalent to 'lady' in England) who owns the house has opened it to the public as a museum. The entire house is furnished with Burmese and Thai antiques; three rooms display antique silverwork, lacquerware, ceramics and other northern Thai crafts. The area beneath the house is used for *khãn tòk* ceremonial dinners.

The house is open daily from 9.30 am to 5.30 pm; admission is 20B.

Traditional Massage

Samakhom Samunphrai Phaak Neua (Northern Herbal Medicine Society) at 149 Pratunam Rd, next to Wat Hua Khuang in the Wiang Neua area, offers traditional northern Thai massage and herbal saunas. The massage costs 70B per hour; 1½ hours is a recommended minimum for best effect. The outdoor sauna room is pumped with herbal steam created by heating a mixture of 108 medicinal herbs and costs only 30B to use. Once you've paid, you can go in and out of the sauna as many times as you want during one visit.

The massage service and sauna are open from 8 am to 8 pm daily.

Places to Stay

There are several economical choices along Boonyawat Rd, which runs through the centre of town. *Sri Sangar (Si Sa-Nga)* (☎ 217070) at No 213-215 has rooms with a fan and bath from 80B and air-con rooms from 200B. *Arunsak (Aroonsak)* (☎ 217344) at No 90/9 is similar but starts at 100B. Cheaper hotels are *Lucky* and *Thap Thim Thong*, both on Kao Mithuna Rd, with basic rooms from 60 to 80B with fan and bath.

More up-market are the *Kim* (☎ 217588) at 168 Boonyawat Rd and the *Kelangnakorn (Khelang Nakhon)* (☎ 217137) across the street, each with clean, comfortable fan rooms from 120 to 170B, air-con from 200 to 260B. The *Romsri* (☎ 217054) at 142 Boonyawat Rd is similar.

The recently established *No 4 Guest House* is at 54 Pamai Rd in the Wiang Neua area, just a block north of Baan Sao Nak. Like most of the other No 4 guesthouses in northern Thailand, it's managed by a local teacher who speaks good English, but is probably the most attractive and spacious guesthouse. Rooms cost 60/80B for a single/double with shared bath. Facilities include a kitchen, badminton court on the large grounds and there are bicycles and motorcycles for rent. The management can arrange half-day or two-day horse treks in nearby wilderness areas. The two-day trip costs 600B but you must bring your own food.

Getting to the No 4 by samlor can be a bit difficult since not many samlor drivers seem to know it yet. It might help to tell the driver you want to go to Raan Kuaytiaw Paa Mai, a famous noodle stand opposite the guesthouse. From the city centre a samlor ride should cost 10B per person.

In the top-end category, the refurbished *Asia Lampang* (☎ 217844) at 229 Boonyawat Rd has air-con rooms facing the street for 290B, and nicer rooms with TV for 400 to 500B. The Asia's pleasant street-level cafe is its best feature.

Rooms at the 130-room *Thip Chang Garnet Lampang* (☎ 218450/337) at 54/22 Thakhrao Noi Rd start at 680B. Facilities include a coffee shop, cafe, supper club and cocktail lounge.

Places to Eat

In the vicinity of the Kim and Asia hotels there are several good rice and noodle shops. *Jakrin*, beneath the Sri Sangar Hotel opposite the Kim Hotel, is a popular, inexpensive Thai-Chinese place with all the standard dishes.

The outdoor *Riverside Bar & Restaurant* is in an old unrestored teak structure at 328 Thipchang Rd on the river. It's a good choice for a sociable drink or meal, with live folk music nightly and reasonable prices considering the high quality of the food and service. The *Black Horse Pub* on Uparat Rd around the corner from the Romsri Hotel is a cosy, tastefully decorated spot with Thai food including kàp klâem (drinking food) and a bar.

Getting There & Away

Buses to Lampang from Phitsanulok's main bus station cost 63B and take four hours. From Chiang Mai, buses for Lampang leave from the Chiang Mai Arcade station and also from next to the Nawarat Bridge in the direction of Lamphun. The fare is 25B and the trip takes 1½ hours.

The bus station in Lampang is some way out of town – 5 to 10B by samlor if you arrive late at night.

To book an air-con bus from Lampang to Bangkok or Chiang Mai there is no need to go out to the bus station as the tour bus companies have offices in town along Boonyawat Rd near the traffic circle. Phaya Yanyon, Thanjit Tour and Thaworn Farm each have VIP buses to Bangkok for 240B that leave nightly around 8 pm.

AROUND LAMPANG PROVINCE

Wat Phra That Lampang Luang

วัดพระธาตุลำปางหลวง

Probably the most magnificent temple in all of northern Thailand, Wat Lampang Luang is also the best compendium of Lanna-style temple architecture. Surrounded by roofed brick cloisters, the centrepiece of the complex is the large, open-sided Wihaan Luang. Thought to have been built in 1476, the impressive building features a triple-tiered wooden roof supported by teak pillars. A huge gilded mondop in the back of the wihaan contains a Buddha image cast in 1563; the faithful leave small gold-coloured Buddha figures close to the mondop and hang Thai Lü weavings behind it.

Early 19th-century jataka murals are painted on wooden panels around the inside upper perimeter of the wihaan. The tall Lanna-style chedi behind the wihaan, raised in 1449 and restored in 1496, measures 24 metres at its base and is 45 metres high. The small, simple Wihaan Ton Kaew to the right of the main wihaan was built in 1476. The oldest structure in the compound is the smaller 13th-century Wihaan Phra Phut to the left (standing with your back to the main gate) of the main chedi; the wihaan to the right of the chedi (Wihaan Naam Taem) was built in the early 16th century and amazingly still contains traces of the original murals.

The Haw Phra Phutthabaat, a small white building behind and to the left of the chedi, has a sign in front that reads 'Women don't step on this place' meaning women are forbidden to climb the steps. You're not missing much, it's just a bare room containing an undistinguished Buddha footprint sculpture. The bot to the left of the Haw Phra dates from 1476.

The lintel over the main entrance to the compound features an impressive intertwined dragon relief – once common in northern Thai temples but rarely seen these days.

Wat Phra That Lampang Luang is 18 km south-west of Lampang in Ko Kha. To get there by public transport, catch a songthaew south on Praisani Rd to the market in Ko Kha (8B), then a Hang Chat-bound songthaew (3B) three km north to the entrance of Wat Phra That Luang.

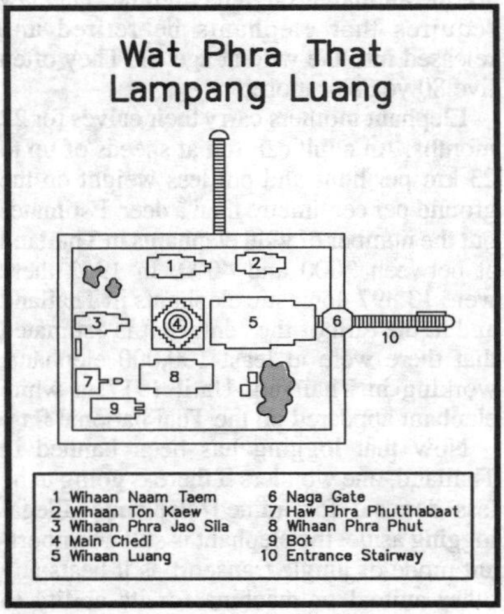

Young Elephant Training Centre
ศูนย์ฝึกลูกช้าง

In Hang Chat district north-west of Lampang, outside Thung Kwian at Km 37, is a camp for the training of young elephants. Also called the Thai Elephant Conservation Centre, this camp has moved from its previous location in Ngao, between Lampang and Chiang Rai; the Ngao centre will remain in use as a care facility for elderly tuskers. In addition to the standard tourist show, the new centre will offer exhibits on the history and culture of Thai elephants as well as elephant rides through the surrounding forest.

Training takes place daily between 7 and 11 am except on public holidays and during the elephants' summer vacation from March to May. Elephants begin training when they're between three and five years old and the training continues for five years. Tasks they learn under the direction of their mahouts include pushing, carrying and piling logs, as well as bathing and walking in procession.

Working elephants have a career of about 50 years, hence when young they are given two mahouts, one older and one younger (sometimes a father and son team) who can see the animal through its lifetime. Thai law requires that elephants be retired and released into the wild at age 61. They often live 80 years or more.

Elephant mothers carry their calves for 22 months. An adult can run at speeds of up to 23 km per hour and put less weight on the ground per centimetre than a deer. Estimates put the number of wild elephants in Thailand at between 3000 and 4000. In 1952 there were 13,397 domestic elephants in Thailand and at the turn of the century it is estimated that there were at least 100,000 elephants working in Thailand. Until 1917, a white elephant appeared on the Thai national flag.

Now that logging has been banned in Thailand, one wonders if there is going to be less demand for trained elephants. Illegal logging aside, the elephant is still an important mode of jungle transport as it beats any other animal or machine for its ability to move through a forest with minimum environmental damage – its large, soft feet distribute the animal's weight without crushing the ground.

To reach the camp, you can take a bus or songthaew from Lampang toward Chiang Mai and get off at Km 37.

Thung Kwian Forest Market
ตลาดป่าทุ่งเกวียน

The famous 'forest market' *(talàat pàa)* at Thung Kwian in Hang Chat district (between Lampang and Chiang Mai off Highway 11) sells all manner of wild flora & fauna from the jungle, including medicinal and culinary herbs, wild mushrooms, bamboo shoots, field rats, beetles, snakes, plus a few rare and endangered species like pangolin. Officials are said to be cracking down on the sale of endangered species. The market meets every Wednesday from around 5 am till noon.

Other Attractions
North and east of Lampang are the cotton-weaving villages of **Jae Hom** and **Mae Tha**. You can wander around and find looms in action; there are also plenty of shops along the main roads.

Pha Thai Cave is 66 km north of Lampang, between Lampang and Chiang Rai about 500 metres off Highway 1. Besides the usual formations – stalagmites and stalactites – the cave has a large Buddha image.

The province is well endowed with waterfalls. Three are found within Wang Neua district, roughly 120 km north of the provincial capital via Highway 1053: **Wang Kaew**, **Wang Thong** and **Than Thong** (Jampa Thong). Wang Kaew is the largest, with 110 tiers from summit to bottom. Near the summit is a Yao (Mien) hill-tribe village. This area became part of the 1172-sq-km **Doi Luang National Park** in 1990; animals protected by the park include serow (Asian mountain goat), barking deer, pangolin and pig-tailed macaque.

In Muang Pan district, about halfway to Wang Neua from Lampang, is another waterfall, **Jae Sawn**, part of the 593-sq-km **Jae**

Sawn National Park. Elevations in the park reach above 2000 metres. Jae Sawn has six drops, each with its own pool; close to the falls are nine hot springs. Camping is permitted in both Jae Sawn and Doi Luang national parks.

Nakhon Sawan Province

NAKHON SAWAN

อ.เมืองนครสวรรค์

A fairly large town on the way north from Bangkok, Nakhon Sawan has an excellent view from the hilltop **Wat Chom Khiri Nak Phrot**. Thais and farangs both agree that Nakhon Sawan is not known for its hospitality. The population (101,000) is largely Chinese and during Chinese New Year celebrations in February every hotel in town is booked.

Places to Stay

Most of the hotels in the city are located along Phahonyothin Rd (the highway from Bangkok) or along Matuli Rd. *Si Phitak* (☎ 221076), at 109/5 Matuli Rd, has decent rooms for between 90 and 120B. Also reasonably priced are the *Asia* (☎ 213752) at 956 Phahonyothin Rd, where rooms range from 80 to 180B, and the *New Thanchit* (☎ 212027) at 110/1 Sawanwithi Rd, where the cost is from 90 to 120B.

Sala Thai (☎ 222938), 217-25 Matuli Rd, has air-con rooms for 200B, and *Airawan (Irawan)* (☎ 221889) at 1-5 Matuli Rd has all air-con rooms from 200 to 450B.

A more expensive hotel is the *Phiman* (☎ 222473), in front of the bus terminal at the Nakhon Sawan shopping centre, where air-con rooms range from 420 to 1500B.

Getting There & Away

The ordinary bus fare from Chiang Mai is 90B (150B air-con). From Bangkok ordinary buses are 48B (87B air-con).

Kamphaeng Phet Province

KAMPHAENG PHET

อ.เมืองกำแพงเพชร

Kamphaeng Phet (population 23,000) was once an important front line of defence for the Sukhothai kingdom but is now mostly known for producing the tastiest *klûay khài* (egg banana) in Thailand.

Old City

เมืองเก่า

Only a couple of km off the Bangkok to Chiang Mai road are some ruins within the old city area of Kamphaeng Phet as well as some very fine remains of the long city wall.

A Kamphaeng Phet Historical Park has been established at the old city site and the area is now cared for by the Department of Fine Arts. There is a 20B entry fee to the ruins within the city wall. Here you'll find **Wat Phra Kaew**, which used to be adjacent to the royal palace. The many weather-corroded Buddha statues here have assumed slender, porous forms which are reminiscent of Giaccobetti sculpture, as many visitors have commented. About 100 metres south-east of Wat Phra Kaew is **Wat Phra That,** distinguished by a large round-based chedi surrounded by laterite columns.

Kamphaeng Phet National Museum

พิพิธภัณฑ์แห่งชาติกำแพงเพชร

Across the road from these temples is a National Museum. Downstairs has the usual survey of Thai art periods while upstairs has a collection of artefacts from the Kamphaeng Phet area, including terracotta ornamentation from ruined temples and Buddha images in the Sukhothai and Ayuthaya styles. The museum is open Wednesday to Sunday from 8.30 am to 4 pm. Admission is 5B.

San Phra Isuan
ศาลพระอิศวร

Near the museum, San Phra Isuan is a shrine with a sandstone base, upon which is a Khmer-style bronze of Shiva (Isvara). This image is actually a replica, as the original is in the Kamphaeng Phet National Museum.

Wat Phra Borom Mathat
วัดพระบรมธาตุ

Across the Ping River are some more neglected ruins in an area that was settled long before Kamphaeng Phet's heyday, although visible remains are post-classical Sukhothai in design. Wat Phra Borom Mathat features a few small chedi and one large chedi of the late Sukhothai period, which is now crowned with a Burmese-style umbrella added early this century.

Other Wats
North-east of the old city walls, **Wat Phra Si Ariyabot** has the shattered remains of standing, sitting, walking and reclining Buddha images sculpted in the classic Sukhothai style.

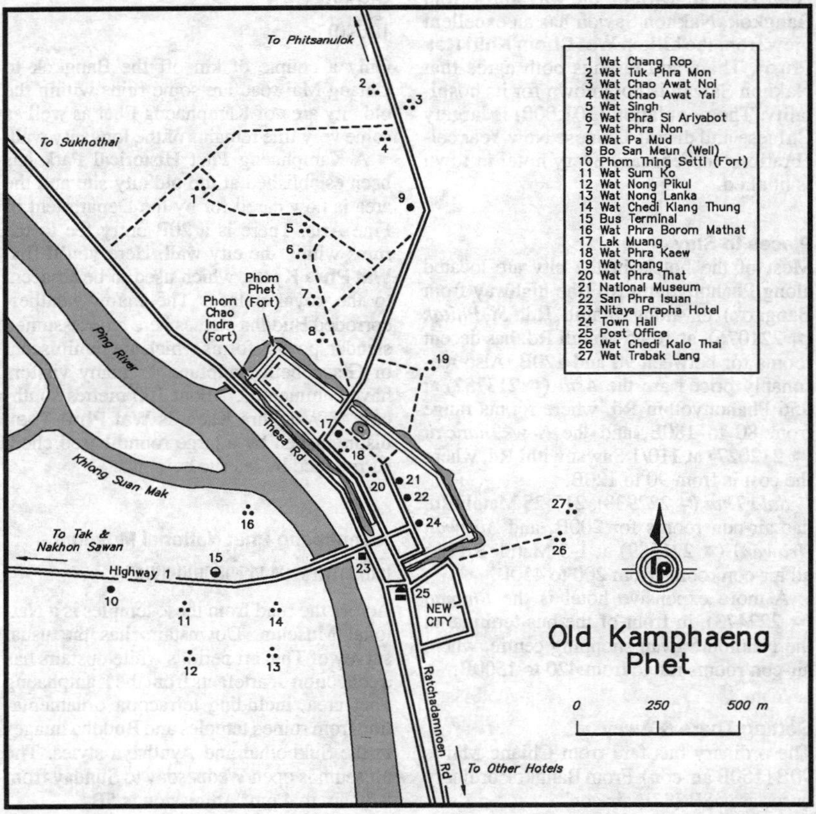

Just north of Ariyabot, **Wat Chang Rop** (literally, 'temple surrounded by elephants') is just that – a temple with an elephant-buttressed wall.

Places to Stay

It can be a little difficult finding accommodation since few signs are in English script. *Nitaya Prapha* (☎ 711381) at 118/1 Thesa Rd is an old wooden hotel with rooms from 60 to 80B. It's on the main road leading to the river bridge (near the roundabout) and is the closest hotel to the old city.

Well into the new part of town on the northern side of Ratchadamnoen Rd is *Ratchadamnoen* (☎ 711029), where fan-cooled rooms range from 80 to 120B (air-con 200B). A bit further down on the left is the town's top-end hotel, *Cha Kang Rao* (☎ 711315), where all rooms are air-con and rates run from 260 to 1500B. The *Phet Hotel* (☎ 712810) near the municipal market at 99 Wijit Rd is also at the top end, with air-con rooms from 250B.

The next street towards the river is Thesa Rd, and down about 200 metres on the right, set off the road, is the *Navarat (Nawarat)* (☎ 711211), with clean, comfortable air-con rooms starting at 250B, and a coffee shop downstairs. In the centre of the new town, not far from the municipal market, is the bustling *Gor Choke Chai (Kaw Chok Chai)* (☎ 711247). Rooms with a fan and bath cost from 80 to 180B, and the staff is friendly.

Places to Eat

A small night market sets up every evening in front of the provincial offices near the old city walls and there are also some cheap restaurants near the roundabout.

In the centre of town is a larger day and night market at the intersection of Wijit and Banthoengjit Rds. Several restaurants can be found along Thesa Rd across from Sirijit Park by the river. The *Malai* (no English sign or menu) at 77 Thesa Rd serves good isaan (north-eastern Thai) food in an outdoor setting. Also on Thesa Rd are a couple of bakeries, *Phayao* and *Tasty*. There are also a few floating restaurants on the river.

Getting There & Away

The bus fare from Bangkok is 69B or 126B air-con. Most visitors arrive from Sukhothai (20B), Phitsanulok (27B) or Tak (14B).

Phitsanulok Province

PHITSANULOK

อ.เมืองพิษณุโลก

Phitsanulok (population 80,000) is often abbreviated as 'Phi-lok'. The town straddles the Nan River about 390 km from Bangkok and makes an excellent base from which to explore the lower north. Besides the venerable temples of Wat Phra Sri Ratana Mahathat and Wat Chulamani in town, you can explore the surrounding attractions of historical Sukhothai, Kamphaeng Phet and Si Satchanalai, as well as the national parks of Thung Salaeng Luang and Phu Hin Rong Kla, the former strategic headquarters of the Communist Party of Thailand. All of these places are within a 150 km radius of Phitsanulok.

Check out the markets by the Nan River for bargains on upcountry crafts.

Information

The TAT office (☎ 252742) at 209/7-8 Borom Trailokanat Rd has knowledgeable and helpful staff (some of TAT's best) whose members give out free maps of the town and a sheet that describes a suggested walking tour.

If you plan to do the trip from Phi-lok to Lom Sak, ask for the sketch map of Highway 12 which marks several waterfalls along the way.

Several banks in town offer foreign-exchange services; only the Bangkok Bank, at 35 Naresuan Rd, has an after-hours exchange window (usually open till 8 pm).

Wat Phra Si

วัดพระศรี

The full name of this temple is Wat Phra Si Ratana Mahathat, but the locals call it Wat

Phra Si or Wat Yai. The main wihaan contains the Chinnarat Buddha (Phra Phuttha Chinnarat), one of Thailand's most revered and copied images. The wat is next to the bridge over the Nan River (on the right as you're heading out of Phi-lok towards Sukhothai). This famous bronze image is probably second in importance only to the Emerald Buddha in Bangkok's Wat Phra Kaew. In terms of total annual donations collected (about 12 million baht per year), Wat Yai follows Wat Sothon in Chachoengsao.

The image was cast in the late Sukhothai style, but what makes it strikingly unique is the flame-like halo around the head and torso that turns up at the bottom to become dragon-serpent heads on either side of the image. The head of this Buddha is a little wider than standard Sukhothai, giving the statue a very solid feel.

The story goes that construction of this wat was commissioned under the reign of King Li Thai in 1357. When it was completed, King Li Thai wanted it to contain three high-quality bronze images, so he sent for well-known sculptors from Si Satchanalai, Chiang Saen and Hariphunchai (Lamphun), as well as five Brahman priests.

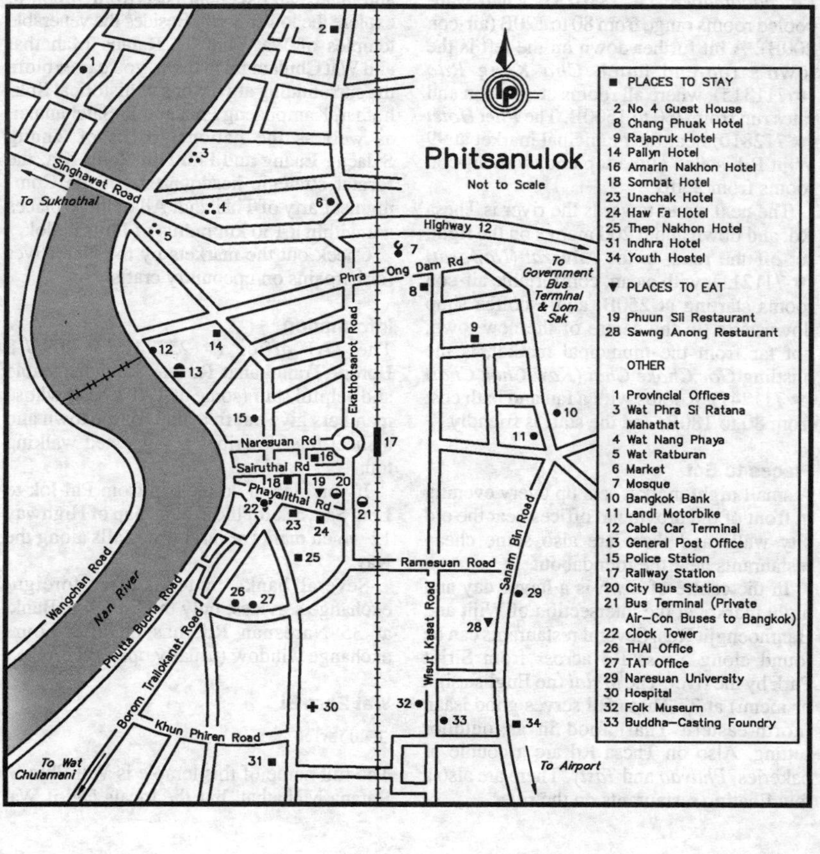

The first two castings worked well, but the third required three attempts before it was decreed the best of all. Legend has it that a white-robed sage appeared from nowhere to assist in the final casting, then disappeared. This last image was named the Chinnarat (Victorious King) Buddha and it became the centrepiece in the wihaan. The other two images, Phra Chinnasi and Phra Si Satsada, were later moved to the royal temple of Wat Bowonniwet in Bangkok. Only the Chinnarat image has the flame-dragon halo.

The walls of the wihaan are low to accommodate the low-swept roof, typical of northern temple architecture, so that the image takes on larger proportions than it might in a central or north-eastern wat. The brilliant interior architecture is such that when you sit on the Italian marble floor in front of the Buddha, the lacquered columns draw your vision toward the image and evoke a strong sense of serenity. The doors of the building are inlaid with mother-of-pearl in a design copied from Bangkok's Wat Phra Kaew.

Another sanctuary to one side has been converted into a museum displaying antique Buddha images, ceramics and other historic artefacts. It's open Wednesday to Sunday, 9 am to 4 pm; admission is free. Dress appropriately when visiting this most sacred of temples – no shorts or revealing tops.

Near Wat Yai, on the same side of the river, are two other temples of the same period – Wat Ratburan and Wat Nang Phaya.

Wat Chulamani

วัดจุฬามณี

Five km south of the city (a 2B trip on bus No 4 down Borom Trailokanat Rd) is Wat Chulamani, the ruins of which date from the Sukhothai period. The original buildings must have been impressive, judging from what remains of the ornate Khmer-style tower (prang). King Borom Trailokanat was ordained as a monk here and there is an old Thai inscription to that effect on the ruined wihaan, dating from the reign of King Narai the Great.

The prang itself has little left of its original height, but Khmer-style door lintels remain, including a very nice one with a Sukhothai walking Buddha and a dhammachakka in the background.

Besides the prang and the wihaan, the only original structures left are the remains of the monastery walls. Still, there is a peaceful, neglected atmosphere about the place.

Buddha-Casting Foundry

โรงหล่อพระ

On Wisut Kasat Rd, not far from the Phitsanulok Youth Hostel, is a small factory where bronze Buddha images of all sizes are cast. Most are copies of the famous Phra Chinnarat Buddha at Wat Yai. Visitors are welcome to watch and there are even detailed photo exhibits describing step by step the 'lost wax' method of metal casting. Some of the larger images take a year or more to complete. The foundry is owned by Dr Thawi, an artisan and nationally renowned expert on northern Thai folklore.

There is a small gift shop at the foundry

where you can purchase bronze images of various sizes.

Folk Museum

พิพิธภัณฑ์พื้นบ้าน

Across the street and a short distance north of the foundry is a folk museum established by Dr Thawi. Exhibits include items from his personal collection of traditional farm implements, cooking utensils, hunting equipment, musical instruments and other folkloric artefacts from throughout the northern region. It's the best collection of its kind in the country and many of the objects on display are virtually nonexistent in modern Thai life. If you're lucky, Dr Thawi may be around to offer you an impromptu demonstration of rustic devices used for calling birds and other animals, including elephants! Entrance to the museum is by donation.

Places to Stay – bottom end

Guesthouses & Hostels The *Phitsanulok Youth Hostel* (☎ 242060) at 38 Sanam Bin Rd is in a 40-year-old house shaded by jasmine vines and is quite comfortable. Sapachai, the owner, worked as a systems analyst in Bangkok for 10 years before giving up the rat race to return to his boyhood home. He has recently built a lofty teak-wood sala behind the main house, using timber from seven old Tak teak houses to create a pleasant, open-air sitting area. Large rooms, each with antique northern-Thai beds, cost 90B a single or 50B per person in two, three and four-bed rooms; dorm beds are 40B. An IYH membership is now mandatory (temporary one-night memberships are 50B; annual membership is 300B). Breakfast costs 25B and includes two eggs, toast, milk and coffee or tea.

From the railway station you can get to the hostel by samlor (5 to 10B) or on a No 3 city bus. From the airport take a samlor (10B) or a No 4 bus which passes by the hostel (on the right). From the bus terminal, take a samlor (10 to 15B) or a No 1 city bus (get off at Ramesuan Rd and walk the last 100 metres or so).

Sukhothai's successful *No 4 Guest House* has opened a branch in Phitsanulok at 11/12 Ekathotsarot Rd, about two km from either the railway or bus stations. As usual, the hallmark here is simple comfort and a casual atmosphere. Rooms with shared bath are 60 to 80B.

The are also a couple of nondescript guest-houses near the government bus terminal, three km from the town centre, with 60B rooms.

Hotels Near the railway station are several inexpensive hotels and places to eat. Two old stand-bys on Phayalithai Rd are the *Haw Fa* (☎ 258425) and the *Unachak* (☎ 258387). Both have adequate rooms with fan and bath for 70 to 100B. Further towards the river on Phayalithai Rd is the similar *Chanprasert.*

If you turn left out of the station and then take the first right turn on to Sairuthai Rd, you'll come to *Sombat Hotel* on the left side of the road. Rooms with shared bath and toilet are 70B, or 80 to 100B with toilet. It's noisy and a bit of a brothel, however. The *Sukkit* (☎ 258876) at 20/1-2 Sairuthai Rd is a bit better at 120 to 150B for a fan room.

Places to Stay – middle

Behind the more up-market Rajapruk Hotel on Phra Ong Dam Rd is the *Rajapruk Guest House Hotel* (☎ 258788), where fan rooms with hot showers go for 180B, air-con 280B. Guests may use the Rajapruk Hotel swimming pool.

Also good is the newish *Indhra Hotel* (☎ 259188, 259638) at 103/8 Sithamatraipidok Rd, south of Phutthachinarat Provincial Hospital (Phitsanulok Teaching Hospital). Clean air-con singles/doubles with TV are 300B.

Places to Stay – top end

Rajapruk Hotel (☎ 258477; fax 251395) at 99/9 Phra Ong Dam Rd offers good upper-range value. All rooms come with air-con, hot showers, carpeting, TV and telephone for 600/700B for singles/doubles.

Others in this range include *Thep Nakhon Hotel* (☎ 258507) at 43/1 Sithammatraipidok Rd, from 500 to 1800B; *Pailyn Hotel* (☎ 252411) at 38 Borom Trailokanat Rd, from 1000B; *Nan Chao Hotel* (☎ 252510; fax 244794), 380 to 1200B; and *Amarin Nakhon Hotel* (☎ 258588), 3/1 Chao Phraya Phitsanulok Rd, 360 to 740B.

Places to Eat

Phitsanulok is a great town for eating. There must be more restaurants per capita here than just about any other town in Thailand.

Excellent, inexpensive Thai food can be had at the *Phuun Sii* opposite the Haw Fa Hotel on Phayalithai Rd. Recommended dishes here include tôm khàa kài (chicken-coconut soup), lâap (minced meat salad), kaeng mátsàman kài (Muslim chicken curry) and thâwt man plaa (fried fish cakes). *Tui Phochana*, opposite Phuun Sii and operated by a cousin from the same family, makes fabulous yam khanũn (curried jackfruit) at the beginning of the cool season, plus many other outstanding Thai curries year-round. There are plenty of other cheap Thai restaurants in this area too.

Butter Home, around the corner from Phuun Sii on Ekathotsarot Rd, has an extensive menu of Thai, Chinese and European dishes at reasonable prices.

Close to the Phitsanulok Youth Hostel are several small noodle and rice shops. Across from the Naresuan (formerly Sinakharinwirot) University campus on Sanam Bin Rd is the very popular and very inexpensive *Sawng Anong* outdoor restaurant, open from 9 am to 3 pm daily. It has a great selection of curries, noodles and Thai desserts, all priced at less than 10B. Try the são náam, a mixture of pineapple, coconut, dried shrimp, ginger and garlic – it's delicious. Also good is the kaeng yûak, a curry made from the heart of a banana palm.

Early risers should try the small but lively morning market next to Naresuan University. Vendors serve inexpensive khâo man kài (Hainanese chicken and rice), salabao (Chinese buns), paa-thông-kõ (Chinese doughnuts) and jók (broken-rice soup) from 6 to 10 am daily.

The cheapest meal in town has got to be kũaytĩaw phàt thai (Thai-style fried rice noodles) at the intersection of Phra Ong Dam Rd and Ekathotsarot Rd. The intersection is called Sii-Yaek Baan Khaek (Indian Village Crossroads) and the vendor on the north-west corner has been serving up 4B dishes of phat thai for many years.

By the mosque on Phra Ong Dam Rd are several Thai-Muslim cafes. One very famous one (no English sign – look for the crowded place near the railroad crossing, with the mosque directly behind it) has thick rotis served with kaeng mátsàman, which is unusual this far north. Ask for roti kaeng to get the set plate. This small cafe also has fresh milk and yoghurt.

A small restaurant next to the Indhra Hotel offers very inexpensive vegetarian food.

On the River Floating restaurants light up the Nan River at night. Good choices include *Song Khwae, Fa Thai, Rim Nam* and *Reuan Phae Riverside*. South of the main string of floating restaurants is a pier where you can board a restaurant-boat owned by Fa Thai that cruises the Nan River every night. You pay 10B to board the boat and then order from a menu as you please – no minimum charge.

Also along the river is a popular night market area with dozens of food vendors, a couple of whom specialise in phàk bûng loi fáa (literally, 'floating-in-the-sky morning glory vine'), which usually translates more simply as 'flying vegetable'. This food fad originated in Chonburi but has somehow taken root in Phi-lok. There are several of these places in town as well as along the river. The dish is basically morning glory vine stir-fried in soy bean sauce and garlic, but with a performance included. The cook fires up a batch in the wok and then flings it through the air to a waiting server who catches it on a plate. The eating places on the river are now so performance-oriented that the server climbs to the top of a van to catch the flying vegetable! Tour companies bring tour groups here and invite tourists to try the catch – it's just as amusing watching the tourists drop phak bung all over the place as it is to watch the cook. During the day this area is a sundries market.

The old and established *Balai* – just back from the river near the fancy Kharana seafood restaurant – is famous for kũaytĩaw hâwy khàa (literally, 'legs-hanging rice noodles'). The name comes from the way customers sit on a bench facing the river, with their legs dangling below. It's only open from 10 am to 4 pm daily.

Entertainment

Along Borom Trailokanat Rd near the Pailyn Hotel is a string of popular Thai pubs. Current local favourites include Country Road (old-west style) and Boran Ban Thoeng (classic Thai).

The very popular Crossroad, at the junction of Highway 12 and Ekathotsarot Rd, features a live band nightly that plays '50s and '60s Thai and international pop. King Kong III, north of the youth hostel on the opposite side of Sanam Bin Rd, is a sing-song club with moderate prices.

Getting There & Away

Air THAI has two daily 45-minute flights to Phitsanulok from Bangkok, at 7.15 am and 3.50 pm. The one-way fare is 920B. There are also regular direct flights between Phitsanulok and Chiang Mai (daily, 650B), Lampang (four times weekly, 485B), Loei (thrice weekly, 465B), Mae Sot (four times weekly, 495B), Nan (thrice weekly, 575B), and Tak (four times weekly, 325B).

Phitsanulok's airport is just out of town. Songthaews leave the airport every 20 minutes or so and go into town for 5B, otherwise you can catch the No 4 city bus for 2B. The big hotels in town run free buses from the airport.

The THAI office (☎ 258020) is at 209/26-28 Borom Trailokanat Rd.

Bus Transport choices out of Phitsanulok are very good, as it's a junction for bus lines running both north and north-east. Bangkok is five hours away by bus and Chiang Mai 5½ hours. Ordinary buses leave Bangkok's northern bus terminal for Phitsanulok several times daily and cost 72B (130B air-con). Be sure to get the *sãi mài* (new route) bus via Nakhon Sawan (Highway 117), as the old route via Tak Fa (Highway 11) takes six hours and costs 6B more.

Direct buses between Phitsanulok and Loei via Dan Sai cost 47B and take four hours. Buses to destinations in other north and north-east provinces leave several times a day from the Baw Saw Khaw (government bus terminal), except for the air-con buses which may depart only once or twice a day:

city	fare	duration
Chiang Mai (via Den Chai)	67B	5½ hours
(air-con)	120B	5½ hours
Chiang Mai (via Tak)	82B	6 hours
(air-con)	117B	6 hours
Chiang Rai (via Sukhothai)	60B	7 hours
(air-con)	131B	7 hours
Chiang Rai (via Uttaradit)	81B	6 hours
(air-con)	110B	6 hours
Khon Kaen	76B	5 hours
(air-con)	106B	5 hours
Khorat (Nakhon Ratchasima)	81B	6 hours
(air-con)	146B	6 hours
Mae Sot	50B	5 hours
Phrae (new route)	37B	3 hours
Phrae (old route)	48B	5 hours
Udon Thani	66B	7 hours
(air-con)	130B	7 hours

Buses to the following nearby points leave on the hour (*), every two hours (**) or every three hours (***) from early morning until 5 or 6 pm (except for Sukhothai buses, which leave every half hour):

city	fare	duration
Sukhothai	14B	1 hour
Kamphaeng Phet*	27B	3 hours
Uttaradit*	35B	3 hours
Phetchabun***	39B	3 hours
Lom Sak*	34B	2 hours
Dan Sai**	32B	3 hours
Tak*	30B	3 hours

Train The 6.40 am and 3 pm rapid trains from Bangkok arrive in Phitsanulok at 12.33 and

9.15 pm. The basic fare is 143B 2nd class or 292B 1st class, plus a 20B surcharge for the rapid service. There is also a new all air-con, 1st-class Sprinter service daily at 8.10 am that arrives at 1.18 pm, an hour shorter than the rapid service. The 285B fare includes a meal and a snack.

Third-class fare (69B) is only available on ordinary trains; the ordinary train with the most convenient arrival time is No 101, which leaves Bangkok at 7.05 am (or Ayuthaya at 8.40 am) and arrives in Phitsanulok at 12.33 pm.

If you're going straight on to Sukhothai from Phitsanulok, a tuk-tuk ride from the station to the bus station four km away is 15B. From there you can get a bus to Sukhothai. Or you can catch a Sukhothai-bound bus anywhere along Singhawat Rd on the west side of the river; a tuk-tuk to Singhawat costs 5B from the railway station.

Boat The Phitsanulok TAT office reports that there are plans for regular river excursions to Phitsanulok from Phetchabun (and presumably in the reverse as well). Enquire at the TAT office for the latest information.

Getting Around

Samlor rides within the town centre should cost 10 to 15B per person. City buses are 2B and there are five lines making the rounds, so you should be able to get just about anywhere by bus. The terminal for city buses is near the railway station off Ekathotsarot Rd. You can cross the river by cable car (2B each way). The cable-car terminal on the east side of the river is near the post office.

Motorcycles can be rented at Landi Motorbike (☎ 252765) at 57/21-22 Phra Ong Dam Rd (near Rajapruk Hotel). Rates are 150B a day for a 100cc and 200B for a 150cc.

PHU HIN RONG KLA NATIONAL PARK

อุทยานแห่งชาติภูหินร่องกล้า

From 1967 to 1982, Phu Hin Rong Kla was the strategic headquarters for the Communist Party of Thailand (CPT) and its tactical arm, the People's Liberation Army of Thailand (PLAT). The location was perfect for an insurgent army, as it was high in the mountains and there were very few roads into CPT territory. Another benefit was that the headquarters were only 50 km from the Lao border, so lines of retreat were well guarded after 1975 when Laos fell to the Pathet Lao. China's Yunnan Province was only 300 km away and it was in the provincial capital, Kunming, that CPT cadres received their training in revolutionary tactics.

The CPT camp at Phu Hin Rong Kla became especially active after the October '76 student uprising in Bangkok in which hundreds of students were killed by the Thai military. Many students fled here to join the CPT and they set up a hospital and a school of political and military tactics. For nearly 20 years the area around Phu Hin Rong Kla served as a battlefield for skirmishes between Thailand's 3rd Army Division, garrisoned in Phitsanulok, and the PLAT.

In 1972, the Thai government launched the 1st, 2nd and 3rd armies, plus the navy, air force, and national guard against the PLAT in an attempt to rout them from Phu Hin Rong Kla, but the action was unsuccessful. In 1980 and 1981, they tried again and were able to recapture some parts of CPT territory. But the decisive blow to the CPT came in 1982 when the government declared amnesty for all the students who had joined the communists after 1976. The departure of most of the students broke the spine of the movement, which had, by this time, become dependent on their membership. A final military push in 1982 effected the surrender of PLAT and Phu Hin Rong Kla was declared a national park.

Information

The park covers about 307 sq km of rugged mountains and forest. The elevation at park headquarters is about 1000 metres, so the park is refreshingly cool even in the hot season. The main attractions are the remains of the CPT stronghold, including a rustic courthouse/meeting hall, the school of military tactics and politics and the CPT administration building. Across the road from the school is a waterwheel designed by exiled engineering students. In another area of the park is a trail that goes to Phaa Chu Thong (Flag Raising Cliff, sometimes called Red Flag Cliff), where the communists would raise the red flag to announce a military victory. Also in this area is an air-raid shelter, a lookout and the remains of the main CPT headquarters – the most inaccessible point in the territory before a road was built by the Thai government. The buildings are bamboo and wood huts with no plumbing or electricity – a testament to how primitive the living conditions were for the insurgents.

At the park headquarters is a small museum which displays relics from CPT days, including medical instruments and weapons. At the end of the road into the park is a small Hmong village. When the CPT were here, the Hmong were their allies. Now they've switched allegiance to the Thai government and are undergoing 'development'. One wonders what would have happened if the CPT had succeeded in its revolutionary goal. Maybe the 3rd Army headquarters in Phitsanulok would now be a museum instead.

If you're not interested in the history of Phu Hin Rong Kla, there are hiking trails, waterfalls and scenic views, plus some interesting rock formations – an area of jutting boulders called Laan Hin Pum (Million Knotty Rocks) and an area of deep rocky crevices where PLAT troops would hide during air raids, called Laan Hin Taek (Million Broken Rocks).

Places to Stay

The Forestry Department rents out two bungalows (sleeping seven each) for 400B, two bungalows that sleep 10 each for 600B and one bungalow which sleeps 15 people for 900B. You can pitch your own tent for 5B a night or sleep in park tents for 30B per person (no bedding provided). If you want to build a fire, you can buy chopped wood for 150B a night.

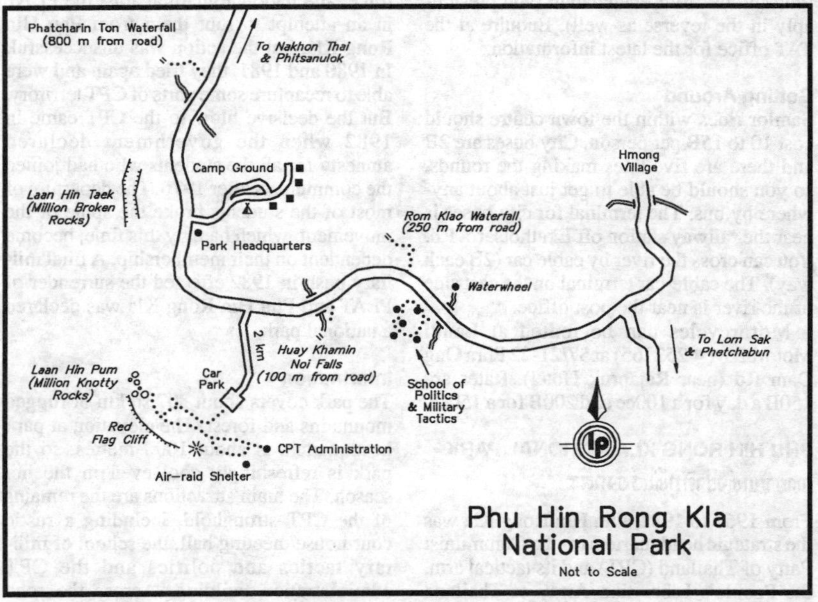

You can book accommodation in advance through the Forestry Department's Bangkok office (☎ 579-0529/4842), or locally by calling their provincial office (☎ 258028) or Golden House Tour Company (☎ 259973, 389002) in Phitsanulok.

Places to Eat

Near the camp ground and bungalows are some food vendors. The best is *Duang Jai Cafeteria* – try its famous carrot sôm-tam.

On the way to or from Phitsanulok, stop at *Kafae Sot* (also called *Queen Coffee)* at the Km 45 marker on Highway 12 (near Ban Kaeng Sawng, close to Kaeng Sawng Waterfall). It has some of the best fresh coffee outside of Bangkok; the beans are all locally grown but have names like Blue Mountain and Brazil. Freshly brewed coffee costs between 15 and 25B per cup, but it's worth it for 100% Arabica or Robusta beans. Ordinarily, Thai coffee is mixed with ground tamarind seed and other additives.

Getting There & Away

The park headquarters are about 125 km from Phitsanulok. To get there, first take an early bus to Nakhon Thai (24B), where you can catch a songthaew to the park (three times daily, 20B).

A small group could also charter a pick-up and driver in Nakhon Thai to visit all the spots for about 550B for the day. The Golden House Tour Company in Phitsanulok, near the TAT, can do all-day tours from Phi-lok (800B) that take up to eight people.

This is a delightful trip if you're on a motorbike as there's not much traffic along the way.

Sukhothai Province

SUKHOTHAI

อ.เมืองสุโขทัย

As Thailand's first capital, Sukhothai (literally, 'rising of happiness') flourished from the mid-13th century to the late-14th century. The new town of Sukhothai (population 25,000) is almost 450 km from Bangkok and is undistinguished except for its very good municipal market in the town centre.

The old city *(muang kao)* of Sukhothai features around 45 sq km of ruins, making an overnight stay in New Sukhothai worthwhile, although you could make a day trip to Old Sukhothai from Phitsanulok.

The Sukhothai kingdom is viewed as the Golden Age of Thai civilisation and the religious art and architecture of the Sukhothai era are considered to be the most classic of Thai styles.

The more remote ruins in the hills west of the old city walls, such as Saphan Hin, used to be considered a dangerous area, but since UNESCO and the Thai government joined in the development of the old city environs, all ruins are safe to visit with or without a guide. The Sukhothai ruins have been declared a historical park and are divided into five zones, each of which has a 20B admission fee. The park's official hours (when admission is collected) are from 6 am to 6 pm.

Ramkhamhaeng National Museum

พิพิธภัณฑ์แห่งชาติรามคำแหง

The museum provides a good starting point for an exploration of the ruins. A replica of the famous Ramkhamhaeng inscription (see Wiang Kum Kam in the Chiang Mai section of this chapter) is kept here amongst a good collection of Sukhothai artefacts.

The museum is open Wednesday to Sunday from 9 am to 4 pm and admission is 20B.

Wat Mahathat

วัดมหาธาตุ

The largest in the city and built in the 13th century, this wat is surrounded by brick walls (206 metres long and 200 metres wide) and a moat. The spires feature the famous lotus bud motif of Sukhothai architecture and some of the original stately Buddha figures still sit among the ruined columns of the old wihaans. There are 198 chedis within the monastery walls – a lot to explore.

Wat Si Sawai
วัดศรีสวาย

Just south of Wat Mahathat, this shrine (dating from the 12th and 13th centuries), features three corn cob-like prangs and a picturesque moat. It was originally built by the Khmers as a Hindu temple.

Wat Sa Si
วัดสระศรี

This wat sits on an island west of the Ramkhamhaeng Monument. It's a simple, classic Sukhothai-style wat with one large Buddha, one chedi and the columns of the ruined wihaan.

Wat Trapang Thong
วัดตระพังทอง

Next to the museum, this small, still-inhabited wat is reached by a footbridge across the large lotus-filled pond which surrounds it. This reservoir, the original site of the Loy Krathong Festival in Thailand, supplies the Sukhothai community with most of its water.

Wat Phra Pai Luang
วัดพระพายหลวง

Outside the city walls to the north, this somewhat isolated wat features three Khmer-style prangs, similar to those at Si Sawai but bigger, dating from the 12th century. This may have been the centre of Sukhothai when it was ruled by the Khmers of Angkor prior to the 13th century.

Wat Si Chum
วัดศรีชุม

This wat is west of the old city and contains an impressive, much-photographed mondop with an 11-metre seated Buddha. A passage in the mondop wall leads to the top. Jataka inscriptions line the ceiling of the passageway, but these can only be seen by candle or torch.

Wat Chang Lom
วัดช้างลม

Off Highway 12, this wat is about a km east of the main park entrance. A large chedi is supported by 36 elephants sculpted into its base.

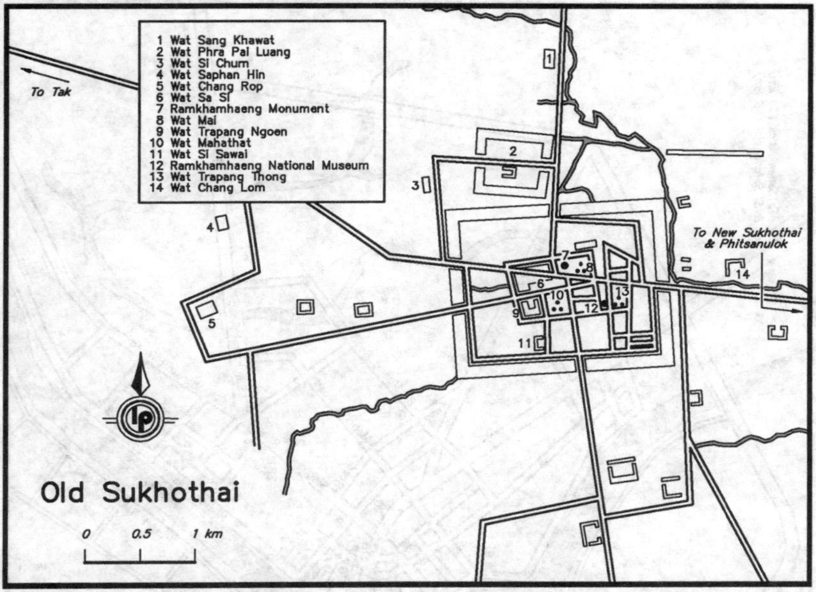

Wat Saphan Hin

วัดสะพานหิน

Saphan Hin is a couple of km to the west of the old city walls, on the crest of a hill that rises about 200 metres above the plain. The name of the wat, which means stone bridge, is a reference to the slate path and staircase leading to the temple, which are still in place. The site affords a good view of the Sukhothai ruins to the south-east and the mountains to the north and south.

All that remains of the original temple are a few chedi and the ruined wihaan, consisting of two rows of laterite columns flanking a 12.5-metre-high standing Buddha image on a brick terrace.

Wat Chang Rop

วัดช้างรอบ

On another hill west of the city, just south of Wat Saphan Hin, this wat features an elephant-base stupa, similar to that at Wat Chang Lom.

Places to Stay

Guesthouses Most of the guesthouses in Sukhothai offer reasonably priced accommodation in family homes (dorms and/or private rooms), and all rent bicycles and motorcycles. The city has experienced something of a guesthouse boom over the last three or four years – the competition keeps rates low.

No 4 Guest House (☎ 611315) is in a large house at 234/6 Charot Withithong Rd, Soi Panitsan, near the Rajthanee Hotel. It's a comfortable place run by four female teachers who speak English well. Dorm beds are 30B and rooms cost from 60 to 90B. Two other branches of this guesthouse can be found at 170 Thani Rd and 62/116 Vichian Chamnong Rd; rates are the same at all three.

Yupa House (☎ 612578) is near the west bank of the Yom River at 44/10 Prawet

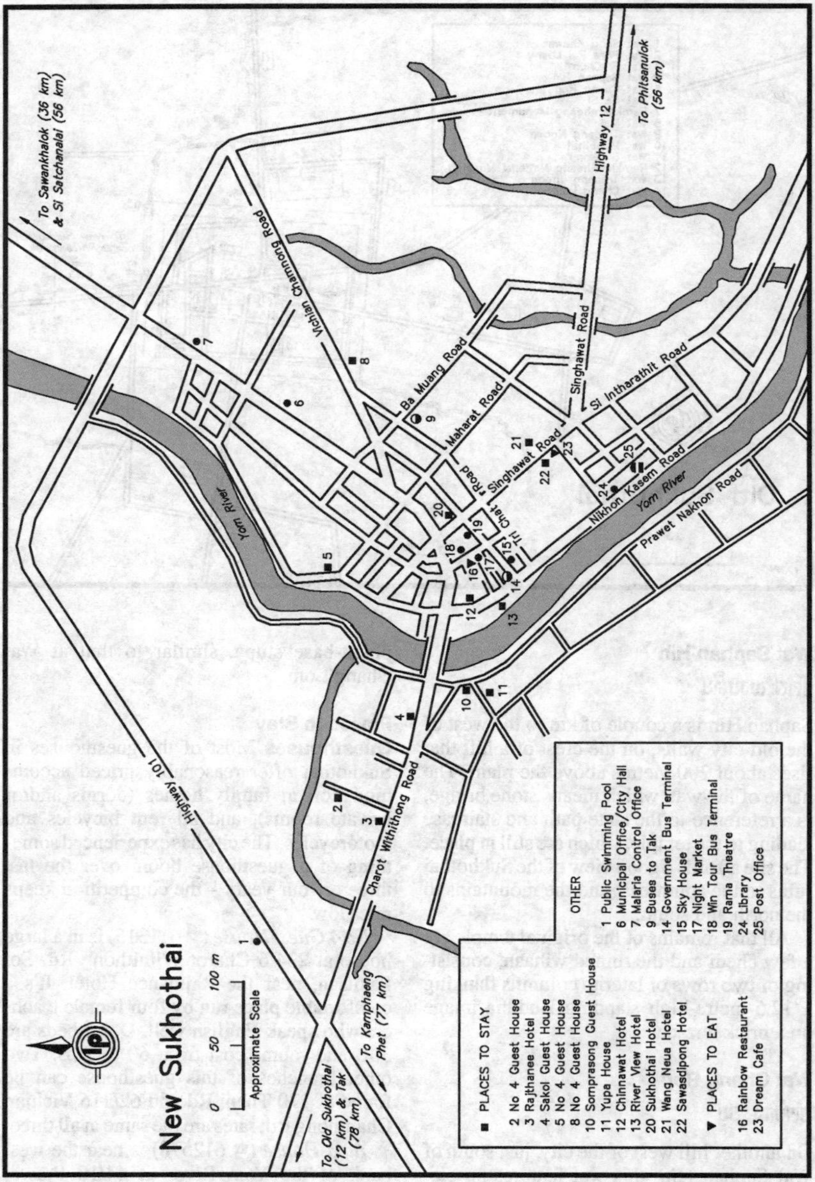
New Sukhothai
Approximate Scale
0
50
100 m
To Old Sukhothai (12 km) & Tak (78 km)
To Kamphaeng Phet (77 km)
To Sawankhalok (36 km) & Si Satchanalai (56 km)
To Phitsanulok (56 km)
Highway 101
Highway 12
Charot Withithong Road
Vichian Chamnong Road
Ba Muang Road
Maharat Road
Singhawat Road
Tri Chat Road
Si Intharathit Road
Nikhon Kasem Road
Prawet Nakhon Road
Yom River
PLACES TO STAY
2 No 4 Guest House
3 Rajthanee Hotel
4 Sakol Guest House
5 No 4 Guest House
8 No 4 Guest House
10 Somprasong Guest House
11 Yupa House
12 Chinnawat Hotel
13 River View Hotel
20 Sukhothai Hotel
21 Wang Neua Hotel
22 Sawasdipong Hotel
PLACES TO EAT
16 Rainbow Restaurant
23 Dream Cafe
OTHER
1 Public Swimming Pool
6 Municipal Office/City Hall
7 Malaria Control Office
9 Buses to Tak
14 Government Bus Terminal
15 Sky House
17 Night Market
18 Win Tour Bus Terminal
19 Rama Theatre
24 Library
25 Post Office

Nakhon Rd, Soi Mekhapatthana. The family that run it are friendly and helpful and often invite guests to share family meals. They have a 30B dorm, plus rooms of various sizes from 60 to 100B. There's a nice view of the city from the roof. *Somprasong Guest House* (☎ 611709) is on the way to Yupa along the same road, at No 32. The rooms are arranged hotel-like on the 2nd floor of a large family house and cost 50/80B for singles/doubles with fan and bath.

The friendly and efficient *Sky House* (☎ 612236), next to the bus terminal, has tourist information, a restaurant and singles/doubles for 60/80B, or four-bed rooms at 40B per person. There is a shared hot-water bath. Sky House has another branch (☎ 612237) two km from town on the road to the historical park. Rooms at this location are 60 to 80B with bath, 190 to 200B with air-con and bath. Both branches lend free bicycles to guests, and motorbikes are also available for rent.

Sakol (Sakon) Rest House (☎ 611487) is on Charot Withithong Rd at No 59-61, near the bridge. The building is rather new and pristine. Dorm beds are 30B; singles/doubles 60/80B. Bicycle rental can be arranged.

Near the bicycle rental places across from the Sukhothai Historical Park are a couple of basic guesthouses with rooms from 80B (probably negotiable since they hardly get any guests). But this area really folds up at night, so unless you like that deserted feeling (or need to be very close to the ruins), it's best to stay in New Sukhothai.

The government plans to allow a company called Ban Boran to build a 1st-class tourist hotel in the historical park.

Hotels There are several good hotels: *Chinnawat* (☎ 611385), at 1-3 Nikhon Kasem Rd, has clean and comfortable rooms, friendly and helpful staff and a cafe downstairs. Rooms with fan and bath cost from 80 to 140B, depending on whether they are in the old or new wing – the old wing is cheaper and a bit quieter. Air-con rooms cost from 170 to 250B, and there are a couple of large rooms with air-con and hot-water bath for 400B. A useful information sheet with bus schedules and maps of the new and old cities is available, and bicycles or motorcycles can be rented.

Wang Neua, formerly Kitimongkol (☎ 611193), at 43 Singhawat Rd, has rooms from 100B (160B air-con). No complaints here. The *Sawasdipong* (☎ 611567), also spelt *Sawatdiphong*, at 56/2-5 Singhawat Rd, across the street from the Wang Neua, is very similar in all respects and costs from 90B (200B with air-con).

Sukhothai (☎ 611133), at 5/5 Singhawat Rd, is an old travellers' favourite with lots of room to sit around downstairs. Fairly clean singles/doubles with fan and bath cost 100/150B and air-con rooms are 200 to 250B. The restaurant is currently being renovated so room rates may rise.

River View Hotel (☎ 611656; fax 613373) is on Nikhon Kasem Rd near the Yom River. It has very clean rooms starting at 150B, air-con rooms from 220B and rooms with all the mod cons from 400 to 650B. There is a large lounge and restaurant downstairs.

Rajthanee (Ratchathani) (☎ 611031), 229 Charot Withithong Rd, is the top hotel in town with a coffee shop, bar and restaurant; all rooms have air-con and hot water. Singles/doubles cost 360/420B in standard rooms and 450/600B in deluxe rooms.

About eight km from the city centre on the road between old and new Sukhothai, the huge, new *Pailyn Sukhothai* (☎ 613311) caters mostly to tour groups and has a disco, health centre and several restaurants. Rooms start at 1000B; occupancy has been quite low since opening (due to the nowhere location), so a little negotiation would probably bring the quoted rates tumbling 20 or 30%.

Places to Eat

The night market across from Win Tour and the municipal market near the town centre are great places to eat. Sukhothai Hotel and Chinnawat Hotel both have restaurants that prepare Thai and Chinese food for Western tastes.

Across from Win Tour is *Rainbow Restaurant & Ice Cream*, owned by the same family that runs the Chinnawat Hotel. It serves a variety of noodle dishes, Thai curries, sandwiches, Western breakfasts and ice cream at very reasonable prices. The downstairs area is in the open air, and the indoor upstairs area is air-con. It is open from 7 am to 10 pm.

On the same side of the street is *Dream Cafe*, an air-con cafe that serves espresso and other 100% coffee drinks, plus Thai herbal liquors and beer. The food is a bit more expensive than at the Rainbow, but the place has character. A larger, nicer version of the Dream Cafe is on Singhawat Rd opposite Bangkok Bank. The extensive menu includes a long list of herbal liquors ('stamina drinks'), ice-cream dishes and very well-prepared Thai and Chinese food. The owner is a long-time antique collector and the place is thickly decorated with 19th-century Thai antiques, a look that is very 'in' with young upper-class Thais these days.

The No 4 guesthouses have information about free dinners put on by the Volunteer English School at Udom Daruni High School. In exchange for helping with one English lesson, travellers are served a large free meal 'to accommodate all tastes including vegetarian'.

Getting There & Away

Sukhothai can be reached by road from Phitsanulok, Tak or Kamphaeng Phet. If you arrive in Phitsanulok by rail or air, take a city bus No 1 (2B) to the air-con bus terminal in the centre, or to the Baw Khaw Saw (government bus) terminal, for buses out of town. The bus to Sukhothai costs 14B, takes about an hour and leaves regularly throughout the day.

From Tak, get a Sukhothai bus at the Baw Khaw Saw terminal just outside of town. The fare is 19B and the trip takes about an hour. Buses from Kamphaeng Phet are 20B and take from one to 1½ hours.

Buses to/from Chiang Mai cost 72B via Tak or 100B via Lampang and take from 4½ to five hours. Buses between Bangkok and Sukhothai are 87B (153B air-con) and take seven hours. Buses to Chiang Rai cost 80 (120B air-con) and take six hours. Buses to Khon Kaen cost 100 (155B air-con) and take from six to seven hours.

Phitsanulok Yan Yon Tour has a daily VIP bus (with reclining seats) to Bangkok for 205B that leaves at 10.45 pm. Ordinary buses to destinations outside Sukhothai Province leave from the government bus terminal; tour buses leave from Win Tour or Phitsanulok Yan Yon Tour near the night market area. Buses to Tak leave from Ban Muang Rd, two streets east of Singhawat Rd.

Buses to Sawankhalok and Si Satchanalai (18B, one hour) leave hourly from the intersection opposite the Sukhothai Hotel, between about 6 am and 6 pm.

Getting Around

Around New Sukhothai, a samlor ride shouldn't cost more than 10 or 15B. Songthaews run frequently between New Sukhothai and the old city (Sukhothai Historical Park), leaving from Charot Withithong Rd near the Yom River; the fare is 5B and it takes 20 to 30 minutes from the river to the park.

The best way to get around Old Sukhothai is by bicycle; these can be rented at shops outside the park entrance for 30B per day or you could borrow or rent one at any guesthouse in the new city.

The park operates a new tram tour service through the old city for 20B per person. Local farmers offer bullock cart rides through the park at the same rate.

SI SATCHANALAI-CHALIANG HISTORICAL PARK

อุทยานประวัติศาสตร์ศรีสัชนาลัย-ชะเลียง

The Sukhothai-period ruins at the old city sites of Si Satchanalai and Chaliang are in the same basic style as those in Old Sukhothai, but with some slightly larger sites. The 13th to 15th-century ruins cover roughly 720 hectares surrounded by a 12-metre wide moat. Chaliang, a km to the south-east, is an older city site (dating to the 11th century) though the two temple remains date to the 14th century.

The ruins at Si Satchanalai are set among

hills and are very attractive in the sense that they're not as heavily visited as the Sukhothai ruins. Recent additions to the park include a coffee shop near the ponds in the middle of the complex. Elephant rides through the park are available for 50 to 100B per person.

Admission to the historical park is 20B.

Wat Chang Lom

วัดช้างล้อม

This temple has the same name and style as the one in Sukhothai – elephants surrounding a stupa – but is somewhat better preserved. A stone inscription says it was built by King Ramkhamhaeng between 1285 and 1291.

Wat Khao Phanom Phloeng

วัดเขาพนมเพลิง

On the hill overlooking Wat Chang Lom to the right are the remains of Wat Khao Phanom Phloeng, including a large seated Buddha, a chedi and stone columns which once supported the roof of the wihaan. From this hill you can make out the general design of the once great city. The slightly higher hill west of Phanom Phloeng is capped by a large Sukhothai chedi, all that remains of **Wat Khao Suwan Khiri**.

Wat Chedi Jet Thaew

วัดเจดีย์เจ็ดแถว

Next to Wat Chang Lom, these ruins contain seven rows of lotus-bud chedi, the largest of which is a copy of one at Wat Mahathat in Old Sukhothai. There is also an interesting brick and plaster wihaan designed to look like a wooden structure (an ancient Indian technique used all over South-East Asia). A prasat and chedi are stacked on the roof.

Wat Nang Phaya

วัดนางพญา

South of Wat Chang Lom and Wat Chedi Jet Thaew, this stupa is Sinhalese in style and was built in the 15th or 16th century, a bit later than other monuments at Si Satchanalai. Stucco reliefs on the large laterite wihaan in front of the stupa date to the Ayuthaya period when Si Satchanalai was known as Sawankhalok.

Wat Phra Si Ratana Mahathat

วัดพระศรีรัตนามหาธาตุ

These ruins at Chaliang consist of a large laterite chedi (dating from 1448-88) between two wihaans. One wihaan contains a large seated Sukhothai Buddha image, a smaller standing image and a bas-relief of the famous walking Buddha, so exemplary of the flowing, boneless Sukhothai style. The other wihaan contains less distinguished images.

Wat Chao Chan

วัดเจ้าจันทร์

These wat ruins are about 500 metres west of Wat Phra Si Ratana Mahathat. The central attraction is a large Khmer-style prang similar to later prangs in Lopburi and probably built during the reign of Khmer King Jayavarman VII (1181-1217). The prang has been restored and is in fairly good shape. The roofless wihaan on the right contains a large, ruined, standing Buddha.

Sawankhalok Kilns

เตาไฟสวรรคโลก

The Sukhothai-Si Satchanalai area was famous for its beautiful pottery, much of which was exported throughout Asia. In China – the biggest importer of Thai pottery during the Sukhothai and Ayuthaya periods – the pieces came to be called 'Sangkalok', a mispronunciation of Sawankhalok (Si Satchanalai's later name). Particularly fine specimens can be seen in the national museums of Jakarta and Pontianak as the Indonesians of the time were keen collectors.

At one time, more than 200 huge pottery kilns lined the Yom River in this area. Several have been carefully excavated and can be viewed at the **Si Satchanalai Centre for Study & Preservation of Sangkalok Kilns**, which opened in 1987. So far the centre has opened two phases to the public, a small museum in Chaliang with excavated pottery samples and one kiln and a larger outdoor kiln site a couple of km north-west of the Si Satchanalai ruins. The exhibits are very well presented although there are no English labels. More phases are planned, including one that will feature a working kiln.

Sawankhalok pottery rejects, buried in the fields, are still being found. Shops in Sukhothai and Sawankhalok sell misfired, broken, warped and fused pieces. The **Sawanwaranayok Museum** near Sawankhalok's Wat Sawankhalam on the west bank of the river exhibits pottery and Buddha images unearthed by local villagers and donated to the wat. Thai Celadon near Chiang Mai is a ceramics centre producing a modern interpretation of the old craft.

Places to Stay & Eat

Wang Yom Resort, just outside the park, has a number of well-appointed bamboo bungalows and a 'handicraft village' among beautifully landscaped grounds. Depending on the location (some are on the river), bungalows here cost from 400B; there are also a few basic huts in the handicraft area that cost 150B a night. Wang Yom's large restaurant is reportedly very good. Food and drink are also available at a coffee shop in the historical park until 6 pm.

Sawankhalok This charming town on the Yom River about 11 km south of the historical park has a couple of other possibilities for visitors wishing to explore the area in more depth. *Muang In* (☎ 642622) at 21 Kasemrat Rd has fan rooms for 160B, air-con for 250B. The newer and more centrally located *Sangsin Hotel* (☎ 641859), at 2 Thetsaban Damri Rd (the main street through town) has fan rooms for 180B, 240 to 320B with air-con. The nearby *Sompasong* has basic but adequate rooms for 60 to 80B.

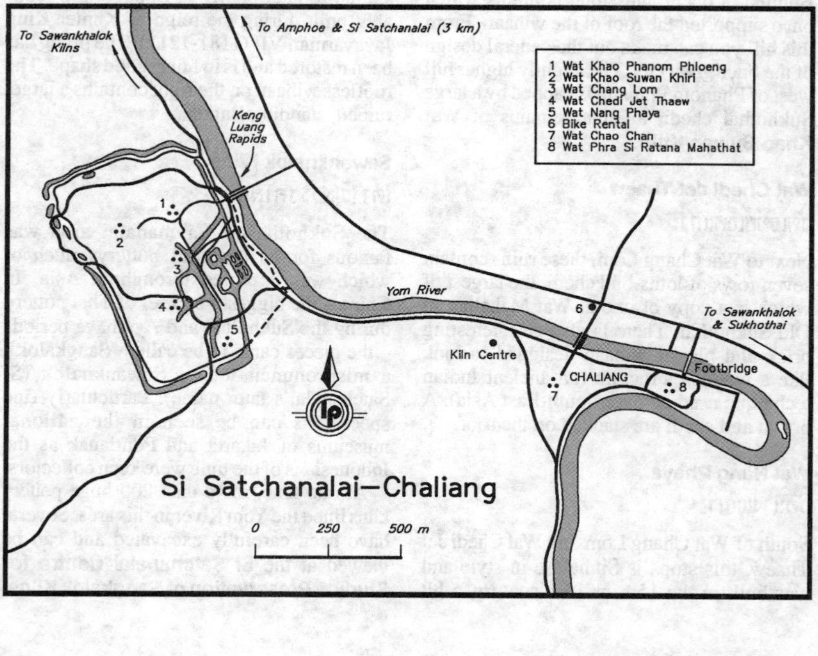

Ko Heng riverside restaurant has great local food and a view of life along the Yom River. *Van Waw*, a noodle shop opposite Sangsin Hotel, is also recommended; it's open from 8 am to 3 pm only. For khâo kaeng (rice and curry), try the shop opposite Thai Farmer's Bank. There is also a night market in town which is bigger than the one is Sukhothai.

Another good eating spot is *Kung Nan*, a Thai and Chinese restaurant on the main road near Muang In Hotel.

Getting There & Away

The Si Satchanalai-Chaliang ruins are off Highway 101 between Sawankhalok and New Si Satchanalai. From Sukhothai, take a Si Satchanalai bus (18B) and ask to get off at the old city (muang kao). There are three places along the left side of the highway where you can get off the bus and reach the ruins; all involve crossing the Yom River. The first leads to a footbridge over the Yom River to Wat Phra Si Ratana Mahathat at Chaliang; the second entrance, about 200 metres past the first, is at a crossroads near the bicycle rental shop and leads over a vehicle bridge to Chaliang's Wat Chao Chan; the third crossing is about two km further north-west just past two hills and leads directly into the Si Satchanalai ruins.

Getting Around

Bicycle is the best way to see the ruins. These can be rented from a shop at the intersection of Highway 101 and the road leading to Wat Chao Chan; rates are a low 20B per day. You can also hire an elephant and mahout to tour Si Satchanalai (but not Chaliang) for 50 to 100B.

Uttaradit Province

UTTARADIT

อ.เมืองอุตรดิถ

Continue north by rail from Si Satchanalai and Sawankhalok to Uttaradit (population 35,000), the capital of Uttaradit Province (population 447,000). Not a big tourist destination, the province is noted for its *langsat* fruit and for the largest earth- filled dam in Thailand, the **Sirikit Dam**, which is 55 km from the town.

Some time in the past, the capital developed a reputation as a city of widows and virgins – perhaps because it served as a battle front during Burmese invasions. Locals are proud that King Taksin, the Thai monarch who finally reunited the Thai kingdom after the Burmese sacked Ayuthaya in the 18th century, was born here. Another local hero, Phraya Phichai Dap Hak, repelled a Burmese invasion in 1772.

The original city formed around Bang Pho Tha It, an important loading point for trade and transport along the Nan River. Teak was once a major local product; the largest teak tree known in the world was found at **Ton Sak Yai (Big Teak Tree) Park**, in Ban Bang Kleua, 92 km north-east of the provincial capital. The 1500-year-old tree was 47 metres high and 9.8 metres in circumference. The remaining teak stands in the park are protected and should live to a ripe old age.

Temples

Behind the railway station toward the river, **Wat Tha Thanon** contains the Luang Phaw Phet, a very sacred, Lanna-style Buddha image considered the focal point of the city's power. More impressive architecturally is **Wat Phra Boromathat**, about five km west of town on the highway to Si Satchanalai. The main wihaan here is built in the Luang Prabang-Lan Xang style, with carved wooden facades over a deep verandah.

Wat Phra Fang is a Sukhothai-period temple ruins in Ban Phra Fang, 25 km south of town along the Nan River.

Places to Stay

P Vanich (Phaw Wanit) 2 (☎ 411499/749) is by the river in the old section of town at 1 Si Uttara Rd, within walking distance of the railway station. Fan rooms cost 100B, or from 200B with air-con. The *Chai Fah* at 131-33 Borom At Rd and the older *Nam Chai* at No 213/4 on the same street are similarly priced. The *P Vanich 1* at 33-5 Phloen Reudi Rd nearby is cheaper at 90 to 130B per room. Top end is the *Seeharaj Hotel* (☎ 411106) at 163 Borom At; all rooms are air-con and cost 480/560B for singles/doubles. Facilities include a coffee shop, restaurant, nightclub and swimming pool.

Getting There & Away

Although it's roughly midway between Phitsanulok and Lampang, few Westerners stop off in Uttaradit (all the more reason to visit!). There is frequent bus transport between the three cities; you can also get there by train. Buses to/from Bangkok cost 102B (ordinary) or 186B (air-con).

Tak Province

Tak, like Loei, Nan, Phetchabun, Krabi and certain other provinces, has traditionally been considered a remote province, that is, one which the central Bangkok government has had little control over. In the 1970s, the mountains of west Tak were a hotbed of communist guerrilla activity. Now the former leader of the local CPT movement is involved in resort hotel development and Tak is open to outsiders, but the area still has an untamed feeling about it. The entire province has a population of only around 328,000.

Western Tak has always presented a distinct contrast with other parts of Thailand because of heavy Karen and Burmese cultural influences. The Thai-Burmese border districts of Mae Ramat, Tha Song Yang and Mae Sot are dotted with Karen refugee camps, a result of recent fighting between the Karen National Union (KNU) and the Burmese government which is driving Karen civilians across the border.

The main source of income for people living on both sides of the border is legal and illegal international trade. Black-market dealings are estimated to account for at least 100 million baht per year in local income. The main smuggling gateways on the Thai side are Tha Song Yang, Mae Sarit, Mae Tan, Wangkha, Mae Sot and Waley. On the Burmese side, all these gateways except Mae Sot and Waley are controlled by the KNU.

One important contraband product is teak, brought into Thailand from Burma on big tractor trailers at night. More than 125,000B in bribes per truckload is distributed among the local Thai authorities responsible for looking the other way. Some of the trade is legal since the Thai and Burmese military leaderships have started cutting deals.

Most of the province is forested and mountainous and is excellent for trekking. Organised trekking occurs, some from out of Chiang Mai further north. There are Hmong (Meo), Musoe (Lahu), Lisu and White and Red Karen settlements throughout the west and north. Many Thais come to Tak to hunt, as the province is known for its abundance of wild animals, especially in the northern section towards Mae Hong Son Province. Much of the hunting is illegal, such as tiger and elephant hunts in national wildlife preserves.

TAK
อ.เมืองตาก

Tak (population 21,000) is not very interesting, except as a point from which to visit Lang Sang National Park to the west or Phumiphon Yanhi Dam to the north.

Places to Stay & Eat

Most of Tak's hotels are lined up on Mahat Thai Bamrung Rd in the town centre. The biggest hotel, *Wiang Tak* (☎ 511910), at 25/3 Mahat Thai Bamrung Rd, has air-con rooms from 330 to 600B. A similar *Wiang Tak 2* has been constructed on the Tak River.

Nearby on the same road, but less expensive, are the *Tak* (☎ 511234), which has rooms with fan and bath from 90B, and the *Mae Ping* (☎ 511807), with similar accommodation for 80B.

On the next street over is the *Sa-nguan Thai* (☎ 511265) at 619 Taksin Rd. Rooms

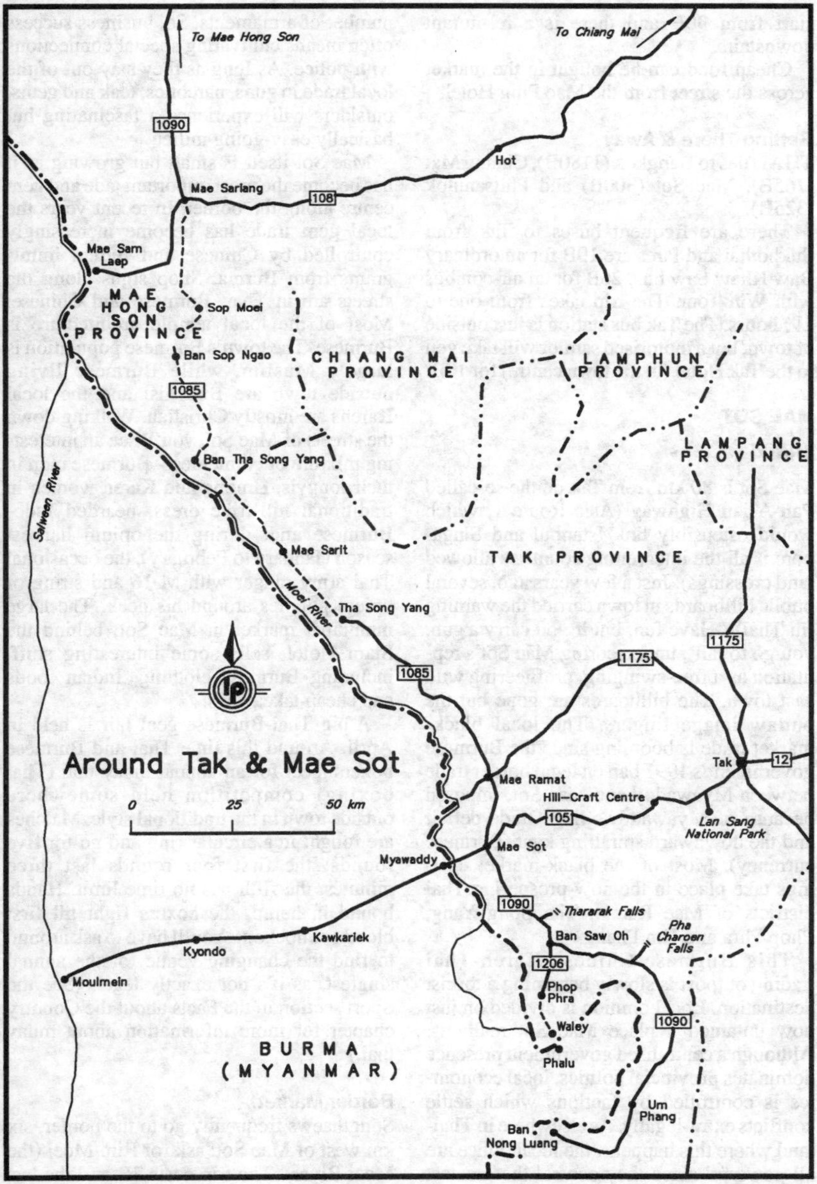
To Mae Hong Son
To Chiang Mai
1090
Hot
Mae Sariang
108
Mae Sam Laep
MAE HONG SON PROVINCE
Sop Moei
Ban Sop Ngao
CHIANG MAI PROVINCE
LAMPHUN PROVINCE
1085
LAMPANG PROVINCE
Ban Tha Song Yang
Salween River
Mae Sarit
TAK PROVINCE
Moei River
Tha Song Yang
1175
1085
1175
Around Tak & Mae Sot
Tak
12
Mae Ramat
0
25
50 km
Hill-Craft Centre
105
Lan Sang National Park
Mae Sot
Myawaddy
1090
Thararak Falls
Pha Charoen Falls
Ban Saw Oh
Kawkariek
Kyondo
1206
Moulmein
Phop Phra
1090
Waley
Phalu
BURMA (MYANMAR)
Um Phang
Ban Nong Luang

start from 90B and there is a restaurant downstairs.

Cheap food can be bought in the market across the street from the Mae Ping Hotel.

Getting There & Away

THAI flies to Bangkok (1180B), Chiang Mai (765B), Mae Sot (300B) and Phitsanulok (325B).

There are frequent buses to Tak from Sukhothai and fares are 19B for an ordinary Baw Khaw Saw bus, 26B for an air-con bus with Win Tour. The trip takes from one to 1½ hours. The Tak bus station is just outside of town, but a motorised samlor will take you to the Tak Hotel (in the town centre) for 10B.

MAE SOT

แม่สอด

Mae Sot is 80 km from Tak on the so-called Pan-Asian Highway (Asia Route 1, which would ostensibly link Istanbul and Singapore if all the intervening countries allowed land crossings). Just a few years ago, several public billboards in town carried the warning (in Thai): 'Have fun, but if you carry a gun, you go to jail', underscoring Mae Sot's reputation as a free-swinging, profiteering wild east town. The billboards are gone but the outlaw image lingers. The local black-market trade is booming since the Burmese government's 1991 ban on legal border trade between Myawaddy and Mae Sot, imposed because of Myawaddy's huge trade deficit and the downward spiralling kyat (Burmese currency). Most of the black-market dealings take place in the now-prospering Thai districts of Mae Ramat, Tha Song Yang, Phop Phra and Um Phang.

This Burmese-Chinese-Karen-Thai trading outpost is slowly becoming a tourist destination. Local opinion is divided on just how untamed a place Mae Sot really is. Although a centralised government presence dominates provincial politics, local economics is controlled by factions which settle conflicts extra-legally. As elsewhere in Thailand where this happens, the local police are all-powerful since they control the greatest number of armaments. So, business success often means cultivating special connections with police. As long as they stay out of the local trade in guns, narcotics, teak and gems, outsiders will experience a fascinating but basically easy-going milieu.

Mae Sot itself is small but growing as it has become the most important jade and gem centre along the border. In recent years the local gem trade has become increasingly controlled by Chinese and Indian immigrants from Burma. Shop signs along the streets are in Thai, Burmese and Chinese. Most of the local temple architecture is Burmese. The town's Burmese population is largely Muslim, while Burmese living outside town are Buddhist and the local Karens are mostly Christian. Walking down the streets of Mae Sot, you'll see an interesting mixture of ethnicities – Burmese men in their longyis, Hmong and Karen women in traditional hill-tribe dress, bearded Indo-Burmese and, during the opium harvest season (January to February), the occasional Thai army ranger with M-16 and string of opium poppies around his neck. The large municipal market in Mae Sot, behind the Siam Hotel, sells some interesting stuff, including Burmese clothing, Indian foods and cheap takeaways.

A big Thai-Burmese gem fair is held in April. Around this time Thai and Burmese boxers meet for an annual muay thai (Thai boxing) competition held somewhere outside town in the traditional style. Matches are fought in a circular ring and go for five rounds; the first four rounds last three minutes, the fifth has no time limit. Hands bound in hemp, the boxers fight till first blood or knockout. You'll have to ask around to find the changing venue for the annual slugfest, as it's not exactly legal. (See the Sport section in the Facts about the Country chapter for more information about muay thai.)

Border Market

Songthaews frequently go to the border, six km west of Mae Sot: ask for Rim Moei (the Moei River). The trip costs 7B and the last

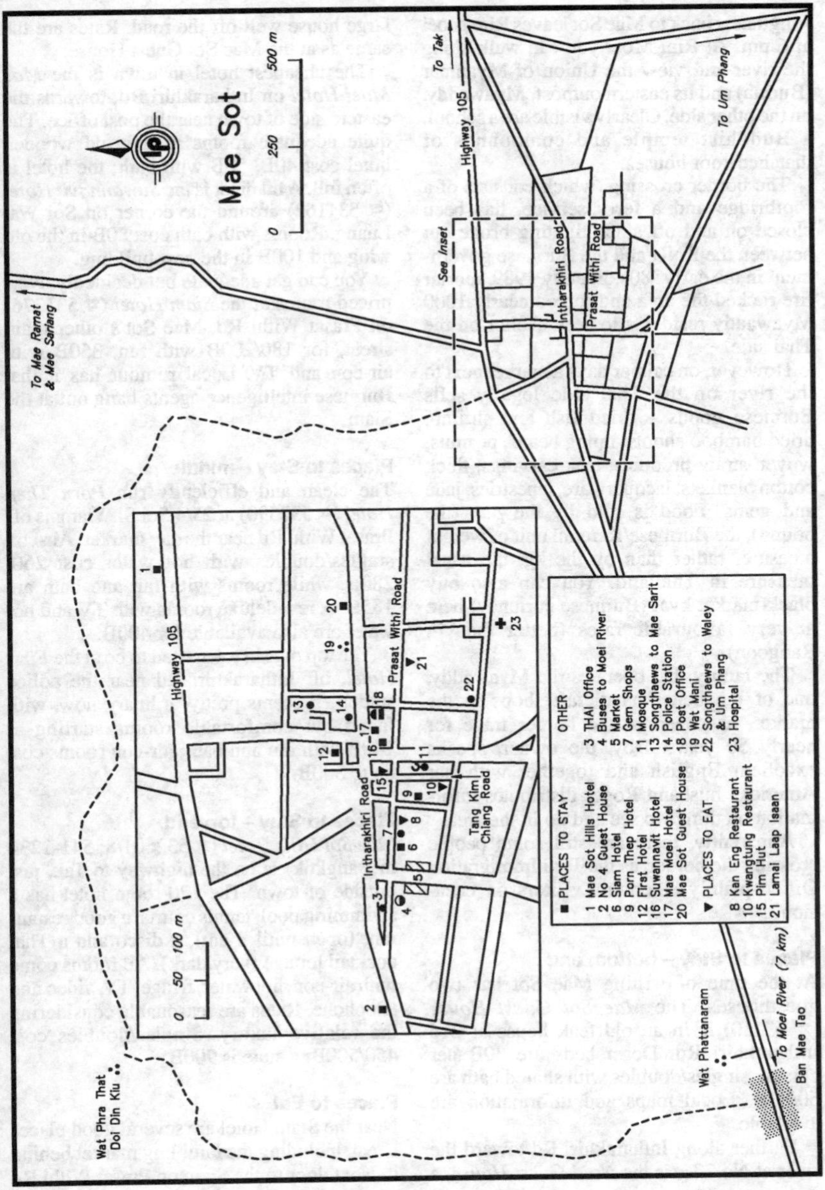
Mae Sot
0 250 500 m
To Mae Ramat & Mae Sariang
To Tak
Highway 105
To Um Phang
See Inset
Intharakhiri Road
Prasat Withi Road
Wat Phra That Doi Din Kiu
Wat Phattanaram
Ban Mae Tao
To Moei River (7 km)
Highway 105
Prasat Withi Road
Intharakhiri Road
Tang Kim Chiang Road
0 50 100 m
■ PLACES TO STAY
1 Mae Sot Hills Hotel
2 No 4 Guest House
6 Siam Hotel
9 Porn Thep Hotel
12 First Hotel
16 Suwannavit Hotel
17 Mae Moei Hotel
20 Mae Sot Guest House
▼ PLACES TO EAT
8 Kan Eng Restaurant
10 Kwangtung Restaurant
15 Pim Hut
21 Lamai Laap Isaan
OTHER
3 THAI Office
4 Buses to Moei River
5 Market
7 Gem Shops
11 Mosque
13 Songthaews to Mae Sarit
14 Police Station
18 Post Office
19 Wat Mani
22 Songthaews to Waley & Um Phang
23 Hospital

songthaew back to Mae Sot leaves Rim Moei at 6 pm. At Rim Moei you can walk along the river and view the Union of Myanmar (Burma) and its eastern outpost, Myawaddy, on the other side. Clearly visible are a school, a Buddhist temple and compounds of thatched-roof houses.

The border crossing, which consists of a footbridge and a ferry service, has been closed on and off since fighting broke out between the KNU and the Burmese government in the early '80s. In early 1989, mortar fire rocked the area and forced nearly 1000 Myawaddy residents to seek shelter on the Thai side.

However, on calmer days a market next to the river on the Thai side legally sells Burmese goods – dried fish and shrimp, dried bamboo shoots, mung beans, peanuts, woven-straw products, teak carvings, thick cotton blankets, lacquerware, tapestries, jade and gems. Food is sold by the *pan* (the pound), the Burmese/Karenni unit of weight measure, rather than by the kg, the usual measure in Thailand. You can also buy black-market kyat (Burmese currency) here at very favourable rates (better than in Rangoon).

The family that operates the Myawaddy, one of the better handicraft shops in the market, has been in the border trade for nearly 50 years. Doy, the owner, speaks excellent English and together with her American husband Roger distributes information on things to see and do in the area.

Apparently, there are still some people crossing the border, as the Thai Immigration Office plainly entertains visitors on occasion.

Places to Stay – bottom end

At the time of writing Mae Sot has two guesthouses. The *Mae Sot Guest House* (☎ 63110) is in an old teak house at 216 Intharakhiri Rd. Dorm beds are 30B per person, singles/doubles with shared bath are 60/80B. Local maps and information are available.

Further along Intharakhiri Rd toward the river at No 736, is the *No 4 Guest House*, a large house well off the road. Rates are the same as at the Mae Sot Guest House.

The cheapest hotel in town is the *Mae Moei Hotel* on Intharakhiri Rd, towards the eastern side of town near the post office. The quite adequate rooms in this old wooden hotel cost 40B, 50B with bath; the hotel is often full. A bit nicer is the *Suwannavit Hotel* (☎ 531162) around the corner on Soi Wat Luang. Rooms with bath cost 80B in the old wing and 100B in the new building.

You can get adequate but decidedly overpriced rooms at the *Siam Hotel* (☎ 531376) on Prasat Withi Rd, Mae Sot's other main street, for 180/200B with fan, 350B with air-con and TV. Local rumour has it that Burmese intelligence agents hang out at the Siam.

Places to Stay – middle

The clean and efficiently run *Porn Thep Hotel* (☎ 532590) at 25/4 Soi Si Wiang is off Prasat Withi Rd near the day market. Air-con singles/doubles with hot water cost 260/280B, while rooms with fan and bath are 185B. A few deluxe rooms with TV and hot water are also available for 400B.

The top digs in town used to be at the *First Hotel*, off Intharakhiri Rd near the police station. It seems pretty ordinary now, with faded but comfortable rooms starting at 140B with fan and bath; air-con rooms cost up to 300B.

Places to Stay – top end

Mae Sot Hills Hotel (☎ 532601/8; 541-1234 in Bangkok) is on the highway to Tak, just outside of town. The 120-room hotel has a swimming pool, tennis courts, a good restaurant (open until 3 am), a disco and a Thai cocktail lounge (very dark). All rooms come with air-con, hot water, fridge, TV, video and telephone. Rates are reasonable considering the relative luxury. Singles/doubles cost 450/500B; a suite is 900B.

Places to Eat

Near the Siam Hotel are several good places to eat, including the rambling market behind it. Next door to the Siam on Prasat Withi Rd is a small food centre with several different vendors serving noodles and curry. A Burmese-run restaurant opposite the mosque has good roti kaeng (curry and flat bread), fresh milk, curries and khâo sòi (spicy chicken broth with flat noodles). There are other Muslim food stalls in the vicinity.

A favourite local snack is kamawng jaw (Burmese for 'fried crispy'), a sort of vegetable tempura. The best place to eat it is at the small vendor stand on Intharakhiri Rd near the Prasat Withi Rd intersection, where the same family has been supplying Mae Sot residents with 'fried crispy' for over 30 years. You can sit on tiny Burmese-style stools around the wok and order fresh chunks of squash, pumpkin or papaya fried in egg batter and dipped in a delicious sauce of peanuts, tamarind, garlic and dried chilli. If you don't want to eat it here they'll wrap for takeaways in two portion sizes, 5B or 10B. The family fires up the wok around 4.30 pm and keeps cooking until 8 pm or until they've run out of ingredients.

Farther east on Prasat Withi Rd, the outdoor *Lamai Laap Isaan* has been serving great isaan food for 15 years. Highlights are súp naw-mái (bamboo-shoot salad), sticky rice, kài yâang, sôm-tam, and several varieties of lâap (minced meat salad) including duck. A bonus is the restaurant's modest cassette collection, which includes tunes by Bing Crosby, Doris Day and Mario Lanza to create just the right atmosphere of cognitive dissonance.

The best Chinese restaurant in town is the unassuming *Kwangtung Restaurant*, which specialises in Cantonese cooking. It's around the corner from the Porn Thep Hotel, south of Prasat Withi Rd.

A little farang restaurant enclave has surfaced along Tang Kim Chiang Rd, where you'll find *Pim Hut* with pizza, steak, Thai and Chinese dishes, ice cream and Western breakfasts at moderate prices. Opposite is the brightly lit *Fah Fah 2 Bakery* with a very similar menu which is slightly less expensive. Both cater to tourists, foreign volunteer workers (from nearby Burmese refugee camps) and upper-middle-class Thais.

Getting There & Away

Air THAI flies to Mae Sot from Bangkok (1405B) four times a week via Phitsanulok (495B) and Tak (300B).

The THAI office in Mae Sot (☎ 531730) is at 76/1 Prasat Withi Rd.

Bus Buses to Mae Sot leave every half hour from the Tak bus station, from 6.30 am until 6 pm. An air-con minibus (rot tuu) costs 25B or you can share a taxi for 35B; in Mae Sot, both depart from the First Hotel car park. The trip takes 1½ hours on a beautiful winding road through forested mountains and passes several hill-tribe villages.

From Bangkok's northern terminal there is one air-con bus per day to Mae Sot, which leaves at 10.15 pm and costs 179B.

Songthaews to destinations north of Mae Sot (eg Mae Sarit, Tha Song Yang) leave from the market north of the police station; those heading south (eg Um Phang) leave from the mosque area.

Getting Around

Most of Mae Sot can be visited on foot. Jit Alai, a motorcycle dealer on Prasat Withi Rd, rents motorcycles for 150B (100cc) to 200B (125cc) a day. Make sure you test-ride a bike before renting; some of Jit Alai's machines are in very poor condition.

AROUND MAE SOT

Ban Mae Tao

บ.แม่เฒ่า

Wat Wattanaram (Phattanaram) is a Burmese temple at Ban Mae Tao, three km west of Mae Sot on the road to the border. A large alabaster sitting Buddha is in a shrine with glass-tile walls, very Burmese in style. In the main wihaan on the 2nd floor is a collection of Burmese musical instruments, including tuned drums and gongs.

Wat Phra That Doi Din Kiu (Ji)

วัดพระธาตุดอยดินกิว(จี)

This is a forest temple 11 km north-west of Mae Sot on a 300-metre hill overlooking the

Moei River and Burma. A small chedi mounted on what looks like a boulder balanced on the edge of a cliff is one of the attractions, and is reminiscent of the Kyaiktiyo Pagoda in Burma.

The trail that winds up the hill provides good views of thick teak forests across the river in Burma. On the Thai side, a scattering of smaller trees is visible. There are a couple of small limestone caves in the side of the hill on the way to the peak. The dirt road that leads to the wat from Mae Tao passes through a couple of Karen villages.

Burmese Refugee Camps

ค่ายผู้หนีภัยพม่า

Several refugee camps have formed along the east bank of the Moei River in either direction from Mae Sot. Most of the refugees in these camps are Karens fleeing battles between Burmese and KNU troops across the border. The camps have been around for nearly a decade but the Thai government has generally kept their existence quiet, fearing the build-up of a huge refugee volunteer industry such as that which developed around the Indo-Chinese camps in eastern Thailand in the 1970s.

Although many Thai and foreign volunteers have come to the refugees' aid, the camps are very much in need of outside assistance. Visitors are always welcome as the refugees are starved for recognition by the international community. Donations of clothes, medicines (to be administered by qualified doctors and nurses) and volunteer English teaching are even more welcome.

Most conveniently visited from Mae Sot are those at **Mawker** (7000 refugees), a couple of hours south of Mae Sot on the road to Waley, and **Huaykalok** (3000 refugees), about an hour north of town on the road to Mae Sarit. If you can't travel to any of the camps yourself, you can leave old clothes or other donations at Mae Sot's No 4 Guest House.

For more information on the plight of the Burmese and Karen refugees, contact the Burma Project (☎ (02) 437-9445; fax 222-5788), 124 Soi Watthongnoppakhun, Somdet Chaophya Rd, Klongsan, Bangkok 10600; or the Santi Pracha Dhamma Institute (☎ (02) 223-4915, fax 222-5188), 117 Fuang Nakhon Rd, Bangkok 10200.

Waley

วะเล่ย์

Thirty-six km from Mae Sot, Route 1206 splits south-west off Route 1090 at Ban Saw Oh and terminates 25 km south at the border town of Waley, an important smuggling point. Until recently, the Burmese side was one of the two main gateways to Kawthoolei, the Karen nation, but in 1989 the Rangoon government ousted the KNU. Burmese teak is the main border trade here now; a huge lumberyard just outside Waley is stacked with piles of teak logs which have crossed at Waley. Visitors may be able to arrange a day crossing by asking nicely at the Thai military post at the Moei River bridge – the guards will radio the Burmese side to see if it's OK.

One can visit hill-tribe villages near **Ban Chedi Kok** as well as the large **Mawker** (Mawkoe) refugee camp, both off Route 1206 on the way to Waley. Opium is cultivated extensively in this area, much to the chagrin of Thai authorities who send rangers in every year to cut down the production. There is a small hotel in Phop Phra with rooms for 50B.

Getting There & Away Songthaews to Waley depart frequently from Mae Sot's main market for 30B per person. If you go by motorcycle or car, follow Route 1090 south-east toward Um Phang and after 36 km take Route 1206 south-west. From this junction it's 25 km to Waley; the last 10 km of the road are unpaved. Your passport may be checked at a police outpost before Waley.

UM PHANG

อุ้มผาง

Route 1090 goes south from Mae Sot to Um Phang, 150 km away. This road used to be called Death Highway because of the guerrilla activity in the area which hindered highway development. Those days are past, but lives are still lost because of brake failure or treacherous turns on this steep, winding road which passes through incredible mountain scenery. Along the way – short hikes off the highway – are two waterfalls, **Thararak Falls** (26 km from Mae Sot) and **Pha Charoen Falls** (41 km). A side road at Km 48 leads to a group of government-sponsored hill-tribe villages.

Near the Burmese border in Um Phang district is the culturally singular village of **Letongkhu** (Leh Tawng Khu). The villagers are for the most part Karen in language and dress, but their spiritual beliefs are unique to this area. They will eat only the meat of wild animals and hence do not raise chickens, ducks, pigs or beef cattle. They do, however, keep buffalo, oxen and elephants as work animals. Some of the men wear their hair in long topknots. The village priests, whom the Thais call *reu-sii* (rishi or sage) have long hair and beards and dress in brown robes. The priests live apart from the village in a temple and practise traditional medicine based on herbal healing and ritual magic. Nobody seems to know where their religion comes from, although there are indications that it may be Hindu-related.

Um Phang itself is an overgrown village populated mostly by Karens at the junction of the Mae Klong and Um Phang rivers. Many Karen villages in this area are very traditional – elephants are used as much as oxen for farm work. Elephant saddles *(yaeng)* and other tack used for elephant wrangling are a common sight on the verandahs of Karen houses outside of town.

Thilasu Falls

น้ำตกทีลอซู

In Um Phang district, you can arrange trips down the Mae Klong River to **Thilasu Falls** and Karen villages for 500B a day (enquire at Um Phang House or nearby BL Tour). The typical three-day excursion includes a raft journey along the river from Um Pang to the falls, then a two-day trek from the falls through the Karen villages of **Khota** and **Palatha**, where a jeep picks trekkers up and returns them to Um Phang. The scenery along the river is stunning, especially after the rainy season (November and December) when the cliffs are streaming with water and Thilasu Falls is at its best. There's a shallow cave behind the falls.

You can also drive to the falls via a rough 47-km road from Um Phang suitable for 4WD or skilled dirt-bike rider only. Or follow the main paved road south of Um Phang to Km 19; the walk to the falls is a stiff four hours from here via **Mo Phado** village. Every two days there's a songthaew for 10 to 15B per person to Km 19; ask for *kii-lôh sìp kâo*.

Places to Stay & Eat

Um Phang House (☎ 513316) in town has pleasant bungalows for 200B with private bath or a few motel-like rooms for 120B.

Your only other choice is *Dream Huts*, a three-km walk from town along the Um Phang River near Samakhii Withaya, a village school for Karen children. It's a peaceful spot, with basic thatched huts for 50B per person; there's no electricity, bathing is done in the river and meals must be arranged in advance. Phirot, the owner, can arrange treks and raft trips.

Um Phang has three or four simple noodle and rice shops plus one morning market and a small sundries shop.

Getting There & Away

Songthaews to Um Phang cost 70B; there's only one trip a day which leaves Mae Sot at about 8 am and takes five or six hours to complete the 164-km journey. Songthaews usually stop for lunch at windy **Ban Rom Klao 4** (original name Um Piam) along the way.

If you decide to try and ride a motorcycle from Mae Sot, be sure it's one with a strong engine as the road has lots of fairly steep grades. You should also carry at least four spare litres of fuel as the only petrol pump along the way is in Ban Rom Klao 4.

MAE SOT TO MAE SARIANG

Route 1085 runs north from Mae Sot all the way to Mae Sariang in Mae Hong Son Province. However, the section of the road north of Tha Song Yang is not yet sealed and the final 75 km was still very rough in late 1991. The government has plans to complete the sealing of the road in the next two years or so, which will make it fairly easy to travel along the Burmese border from Mae Sot to

Mae Sariang (226 km), passing through Mae Ramat, Mae Sarit, Tha Song Yang and Ban Sop Ngao (Mae Ngao).

To date, it has generally only been possible to travel by public transport from Mae Sot as far as Tha Song Yang (137 km) in a day. Your best bet is to spend the night in Mae Sarit (118 km from Mae Sot), then start fresh in the morning to get to Tha Song Yang in time for the lone morning songthaew from Tha Song Yang to Mae Sariang. Songthaews to Mae Sarit are 50B and leave frequently from the market north of the police station in Mae Sot and take four to five hours to reach Mae Sarit. Mae Sarit to Tha Song Yang is 20B and from there to Mae Sariang is 60 to 80B, depending on the songthaew and number of passengers; this last leg takes three or four hours.

If you decide not to stay overnight in Mae Sarit and try for the morning Mae Sariang songthaew, then your only choice will be to continue as far as Tha Song Yang by local songthaew (20B, 19 km further north) in the afternoon. Sometimes there are direct songthaews all the way from Mae Sot to Tha Song Yang for 80B. At this point the traffic really thins out and about the only way you'll make it to Mae Sariang in the afternoon is to hitch (which could be a day's wait or more), or charter a pick-up to Sop Ngao (Mae Ngao) for 300B or, if you're lucky, all the way to Mae Sariang for 500B. You'd then have to hold on tight for the crunchy three to four-hour ride to Mae Sariang along a very bad road. Along the way you'll pass through thick forest, including a few stands of teak, Karen villages, the occasional work elephant and a Thai ranger post called the Black Warrior Kingdom.

During the high tourist season you may be able to book a direct minivan all the way from Mae Sot to Mae Sariang for 150B per person through the Mae Sot or No 4 guesthouses.

Places to Stay

In Mae Sarit, Mr Narong of *Chai Doi House* (☎ 531782 in Mae Sot) meets the first songthaew of the day from Mae Sot and takes prospective guests to his bungalows on a hill overlooking the border area. Rates are 200B a day including all meals. Mr Narong can arrange treks to nearby villages if you'd like to explore the area.

In Mae Sarit there is also a *Mae Salid Guest House*, but we've had reports that women travellers have been hassled there.

There are no guesthouses yet in Tha Song Yang but it would probably be easy to arrange a place to stay by enquiring at the main market (where the songthaews stop) in this prosperous black-market town.

Mae Hong Son Province

Mae Hong Son Province is 368 km from Chiang Mai by the southern route through Mae Sariang (on Highway 108), or 270 km by the northern road through Pai (on Route 1095). Thailand's most north-western province is a crossroads for hill tribes (mostly Karen, with some Hmong, Lisu and Lahu), Shan and Burmese immigrants, and opium traders living in and around the forested Pai River valley.

As the province is so far from the influence of sea winds and is thickly forested and mountainous, the temperature seldom rises above 40°C, while in January the temperature can drop to 2°C. The air is often misty with ground fog in the winter and smoke from slash-and-burn agriculture in the hot season.

MAE SARIANG

แม่สะเรียง

Many of the hill-tribe settlements in Mae Hong Son Province are concentrated in the districts/towns of Khun Yuam, Mae La Noi and Mae Sariang (population 7500), which are good departure points for treks. Of these three small towns, Mae Sariang is the largest and offers the most facilities for use as a base. Nearby **Mae Sam Laep**, west on the Burmese border, can be reached by songthaew or motorcycle, and from there

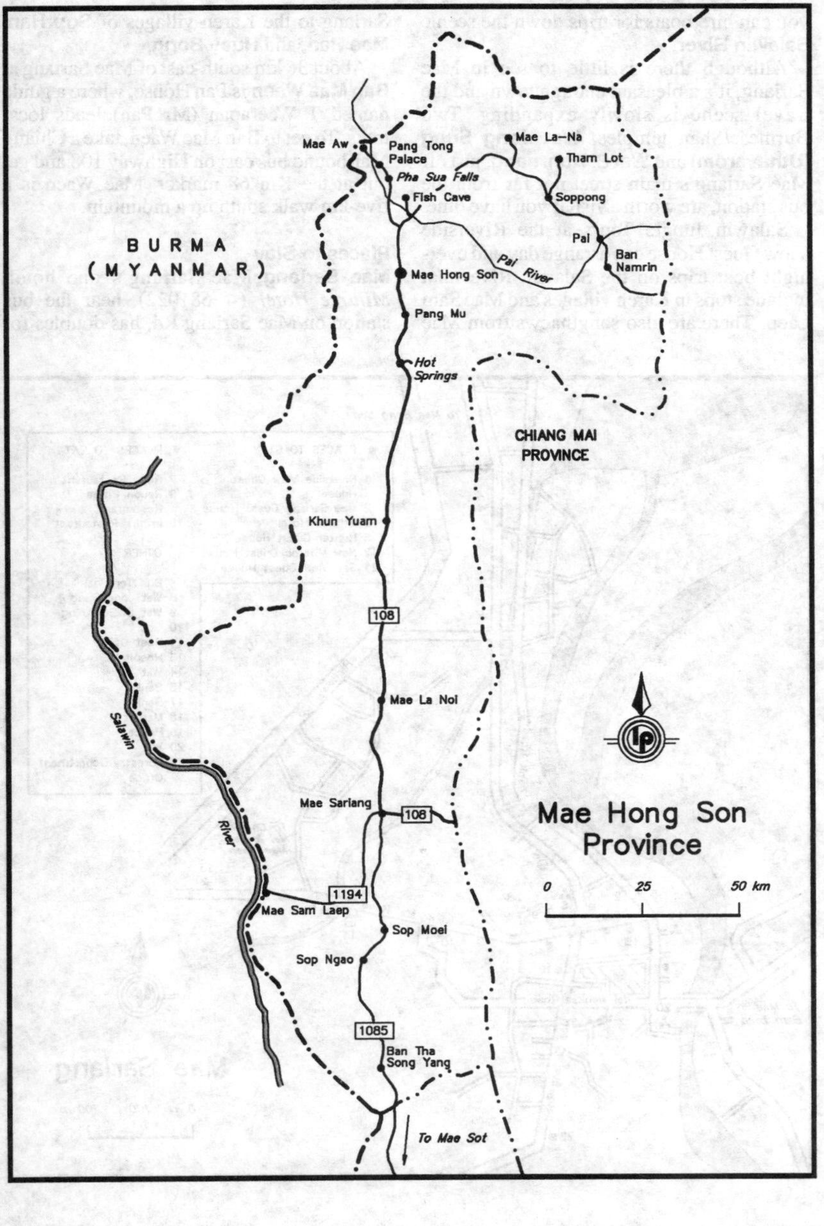
Mae Aw
Pang Tong Palace
Pha Sua Falls
Fish Cave
Mae La-Na
Tham Lot
Soppong
Pai
Ban Namrin
Pai River
BURMA (MYANMAR)
Mae Hong Son
Pang Mu
Hot Springs
CHIANG MAI PROVINCE
Khun Yuam
108
Mae La Noi
Salawin
River
Mae Sariang
108
1194
Mae Sam Laep
Sop Moei
Sop Ngao
1085
Ban Tha Song Yang
To Mae Sot
Mae Hong Son Province
0
25
50 km

you can hire boats for trips down the scenic **Salawin River**.

Although there is little to see in Mae Sariang, it's a pleasant enough town and the travel scene is slowly expanding. Two Burmese/Shan temples, **Wat Jong Sung (Uthayarom)** and **Wat Si Bunruang**, just off Mae Sariang's main street not far from the bus station, are worth a visit if you have time.

Salawin Jungle Tours at the Riverside View Guest House can arrange day and overnight boat trips on the Salawin River that include stops in Karen villages and Mae Sam Laep. There are also songthaews from Mae Sariang to the Karen villages of **Sop Han**, **Mae Han**, and **Huay Bong**.

About 36 km south-east of Mae Sariang at **Ban Mae Waen** is Pan House, where a guide named T Weerapan (Mr Pan) leads local treks. To get to Ban Mae Waen, take a Chiang Mai-bound bus east on Highway 108 and get out at the Km 68 marker. Mae Waen is a five-km walk south up a mountain.

Places to Stay

Mae Sariang Mae Sariang's one hotel, *Mitaree Hotel* (☎ 681022), near the bus station on Mae Sariang Rd, has doubles for

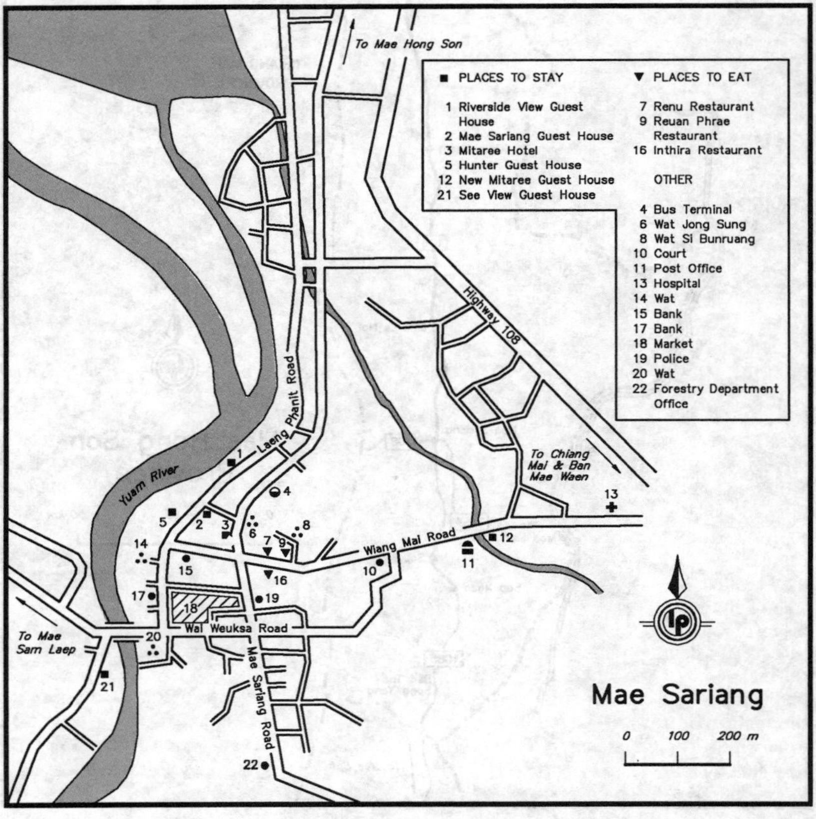

100B in the old wooden wing (called the Mitaree Guest House) or for 200B with hot shower in the new wing. Air-con rooms in the new wing cost 300B.

On Wiang Mai Rd near the post office is *New Mitaree Guest House* run by the same people. Fan rooms with hot showers cost 120 to 150B in the low-rise building, and similar rooms in the new two-storey building are 200 to 250B, 200 to 350B with air-con.

If you turn left out of the bus terminal and then take the first right you'll come to the popular *Mae Sariang Guest House* on Mongkhonchai Rd, opposite the entrance to Wat Uthayarom. Decent rooms are 50B without bath, 80B with one. Around the corner on Laeng Phanit Rd on the Yuam River is the funky *Riverside View Guest House* (☎ 681188) where rooms are 60/100B for singles/doubles, or 120B on the river.

Further south of Laeng Phanit Rd is the recently opened *Hunter House*. Concrete cells with mattress on the floor cost 80B without bath, 100B with private bath. Another new entry is the *See View Guest House* (☎ 681154), which is on the west side of the Yuam River away from the town centre. Rooms in a new row (terrace) house are 100B with fan and bath (120B with hot water). The management claim these rates are negotiable in the low season and that they offer free transport to/from the bus terminal.

Nearby Towns The village headman in Mae Sam Laep lets rooms for 50B per person. In the nearby village of Mae Khong Kha, the *Salween Guest House* also has rooms for 50B per person. There's no public transport to Mae Khong Kha. You can either be dropped off there on a trek or rent a motorcycle.

In Khun Yuam, the *Mit Khun Yuam Hotel* is an old wooden hotel on the main road through the centre of town with rooms from 60B. *Black VIP Guest House* further north on the main road charges 50B per room. Off the main road toward the northern end of town (look for the signs) is *Ban Farang*, operated by a Frenchman and his Thai wife. Dorm beds are 30B, rooms 80B a night; they also rent motorcycles. The nearby *Holiday House* costs a bit more.

Places to Eat

The *Riverside View Guest House* on Laeng Phanit Rd has a pleasant restaurant area downstairs.

The *Inthira Restaurant*, on the left side of Wiang Mai Rd as you enter town from Chiang Mai (not far from the Mae Sariang Rd intersection), serves what is considered some of Thailand's best kài phàt bai kaphrao (chicken fried in holy basil and chillies). The Inthira is also well known for its batter-fried frogs, though you won't see them on the English menu.

Across the street is the *Renu Restaurant*, decorated with photos of the king playing saxophone and offering such menu delights as nut-hatch curry. Both restaurants have English menus, and both are very good. Around the corner on the lane leading to Wat Si Bunruang is *Reuan Phrae Restaurant*, which serves Chinese, Thai, Muslim and vegetarian food. Prices on the bilingual menu are moderate and it's a clean, quiet place.

The food stall next to the bus terminal on Mae Sariang Rd serves excellent khâo sòi and khanõm jiin for less than 10B – it's only open from morning till early afternoon.

Getting There & Around

Buses to Mae Sariang leave Chiang Mai's arcade station about every two hours between 6.30 am and 9 pm. The trip takes about four hours and costs 50B. From Mae Sariang to Khun Yuam it's another 30B, or 52B (and another four to five hours) to Mae Hong Son. There's one daily bus between Tak and Mae Sariang for 77B which takes six hours.

A bus for Bangkok leaves Mae Sariang daily at 5 pm, arriving in Bangkok at 6 am. The fare is 152B.

Local songthaews go from Mae Sariang to the following Karen villages: Sop Han (5B), Mae Han (10B) and Huay Bong (10B). By motorcycle taxis these destinations are 20, 40 and 35B respectively.

Songthaews also ply Route 1085, the road south to Mae Sot, as far as Mae Ngao (Sop Ngao), the closest you can get to Tha Song Yang or Mae Sarit by public transport from Mae Sariang. To Pha Pha it's 10B, to Huay Pho it's 15B, to Mae Kha-Tuan it's 20B and to Mae Ngao (Sop Ngao) it's 35B. At Mae Ngao you can get songthaews southward to Tha Song Yang and Mae Sot.

One songthaew goes to Mae Sam Laep on the Salawin River every morning. The fare is 50B except in the rainy season when it rises to 100B – male passengers may have to get out and push the truck on bad sections of the road.

Next to the service station across from the bus terminal is a small motorcycle rental place.

MAE HONG SON
อ.เมืองแม่ฮ่องสอน

The provincial capital (population 6600) is peaceful (boring to some), despite the intrusion of daily flights from Chiang Mai. Climb the hill west of town, **Doi Kong Mu** (1500 metres), to the Burmese-built **Wat Phra That Doi Kong Mu**, from where there is a nice view of the valley. Much of the capital's prosperity is due to its supply of rice and consumer goods to the drug lords across the border. It's also becoming something of a travellers' scene – there were more than 20 guesthouses at last count. Most of the town's original inhabitants are Shan.

Mae Hong Son is best visited between November and March when the town is at its most beautiful. During the rainy season (June to October) travel in the province can be difficult because there are few paved roads. During the hot season, the Pai River valley fills with smoke from swidden agriculture. The only problem with going in the cool season is that the nights are downright cold – you'll need at least one thick sweater and a good pair of socks for mornings and evenings and a sleeping bag or several blankets. If you're caught short, you might consider buying a blanket at the market (the made-in-China acrylic blankets are cheap) and cutting a hole in the middle for use as a poncho.

Wat Jong Kham & Jong Klang
วัดจองคำและวัดจองกลาง

Next to a large pond in the southern part of town are a couple of semi-interesting Burmese-style wats – Wat Jong Kham and Wat Jong Klang. Jong Kham was built nearly 200 years ago by Thai Yai (Shan) people, who make up about 50% of the population of Mae Hong Son Province. Jong Klang houses 100-year-old glass paintings and woodcarvings from Burma which depict the various lives of the Buddha, but you must ask to see them as they are kept locked away.

Trekking

Trekking out of Mae Hong Son can be arranged at several guesthouses and travel agencies; Mae Hong Son Guest House has some of the most dependable and experienced guides. Don Enterprises, 77/1 Khunlum Praphat Rd, is also recommended. Other trekking agencies are along Khunlum Praphat Rd and Singhanat Bamrung Rd. There is a nearby Karen village which can be visited without a guide by walking one or two hours outside of town.

Festivals

Wat Jong Klang and Wat Jong Kham are the focal point of the Poi Sang Long Festival in March when young Shan boys are ordained as novice monks *(bùat lûuk kâew)* during the school holidays. Like elsewhere in Thailand, the ordinants are carried on the shoulders of friends or relatives and paraded around the wat under festive parasols, but in the Shan custom the boys are dressed in ornate costumes (rather than simple white robes) and wear flower headdresses and facial make-up. Sometimes they ride on ponies.

Another important local event is the Jong Para Festival held at the end of the Buddhist Rains Retreat in October (actually three days before the full moon of the 11th lunar month

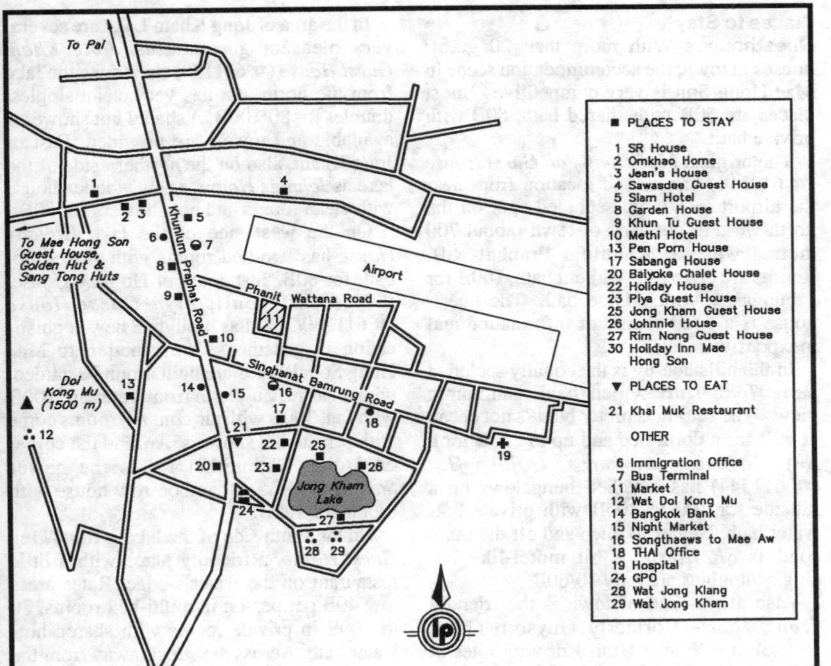

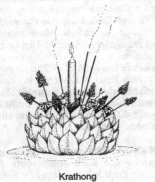

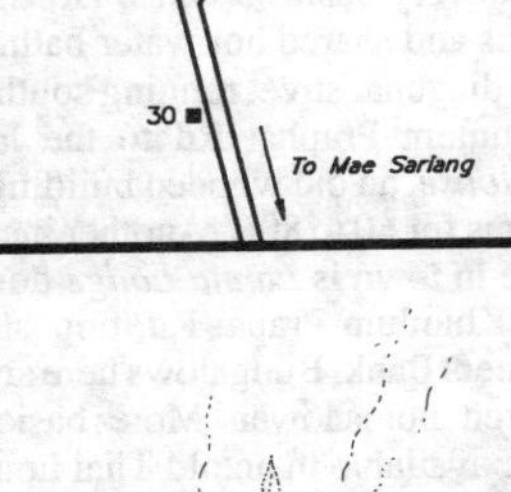
Krathong

– so it varies from year to year). The festival begins with local Shans bringing offerings to monks in the temples in a procession marked by the carrying of castle models on poles. An important part of the festival is the folk theatre and dance performed on the wat grounds, some of which are unique to north-west Thailand.

During Loi Krathong – a national holiday usually celebrated by floating krathongs (small lotus floats) on the nearest pond, lake or river – Mae Hong Son residents launch balloons called *krathong sawān* (heaven krathongs) from Doi Kong Mu.

Places to Stay

Guesthouses With more than 20 guesthouses in town, the accommodation scene in Mae Hong Son is very competitive – most places are 50B with shared bath, 80B with private bath.

The original *Mae Hong Son Guest House* (☎ 612510) has moved location from near the airport to a more secluded spot on the north-western outskirts of town (about 700 metres west of Khunlum Praphat Rd). Rooms are 50 to 80B without bath, 100B for a bungalow with private bath. The guesthouse is a good source of information and inexpensive meals.

In the hills nearby is the equally secluded *Sang Tong Huts* which have panoramic views. The setting is pretty but it's not cheap at 50B for a dorm bed and up to 250B for a hut. In the same area, *Golden Hut* (☎ 611544) has thatched bungalows on a hillside for 100 to 300B with private hot-water bath. Nearer to town and off the same road is *SR House*, a bit motel-like but singles/doubles are only 40/60B.

Also at this end of town is the friendly *Jean's House* (formerly Guysorn Guest House) at 6 Pracha Uthit Rd, with rates at 80B for rooms with bath. Next door to Jean's is *Omkhao Home*, with a very good Thai restaurant and basic bungalow-style rooms for 80B. If you follow this road east across Khunlum Praphat Rd, you'll come to *Sawasdee Guest House* in an old house that was the original Mae Hong Son Guest House premises. Rooms are 40B per person but it's a bit run-down.

Back on Khunlum Praphat Rd, south of the bus terminal on the right and set back off the road a bit, is *Garden House*, where rustic singles/doubles are 50/80B.

Just a bit further down is *Khun Tu Guest House* (Khun Tu Trading) where singles/doubles are 80/160B with shared bath. The one four-bed air-con room with hot bath costs 300B. Khun Tu also sells air tickets and rents motorcycles and bicycles. Khun Tu has another guesthouse north of town called *Khun Tu Tarzan's House Resort*, with similar rates.

In the area of Jong Kham Lake are several very pleasant guesthouses. *Jong Kham Guest House* (☎ 611150) overlooks the lake from the north and has very clean singles/doubles for 80/100B. A shared hot shower is available and towels are provided. East of Jong Kham, also on the northern side of the lake, is *Johnnie House*, a new wooden house with clean rooms and hot showers for 80B.

On the west side of the lake *Holiday House* has two-bed rooms with shared hot bath for 80B. Just south of Holiday House, the recently built *Piya Guest House* (☎ 611260/307) has brought a new sophistication in guesthouse construction to Mae Hong Son. Rooms are built around a garden, with a bar/restaurant in front; rates are 200B with fan, 300B with air-con. All rooms come with private hot showers. Around the corner on Udom Chaonithet Rd is the newer *Sabanga House*, a bamboo row house with rooms for 100B.

On the south side of the lake is *Rim Nong Guest House*, a friendly place with a little restaurant on the water's edge. Rates are a low 40B per person in multi-bed rooms, 70 to 100B in private rooms with shared hot-water bath. Across the street, away from the lake, is the very basic *Jo Guest House* with 80B rooms and shared hot-water bath.

On the diagonal street running south-west from Khunlum Praphat Rd to the lake is *Namrin House*, an old wooden building with basic rooms for 60 to 80B. Another inexpensive place in town is *Lanna Lodge* down an alley off Khunlum Prapat Rd, opposite the Thai Farmers Bank. Bungalows here are 80B with shared hot shower. More basic 50B rooms are available in an old Thai house on the premises.

Pen Porn House (☎ 611577) is on the road to Wat Phra That Doi Kong Mu, in a residential neighbourhood on the west side of town. Rooms in a newly built row house cost 200B a double, 400B in a four-bed room, all with private hot-water bath.

Hotels Most of the hotels in Mae Hong Son are along the main north-south road, Khunlum Praphat. *Siam Hotel* (☎ 611148), next to the bus station, is overpriced at 180/200B for ordinary fan rooms, 350B with air-con. Further down at No 55, *Methi (Mae Tee) Hotel* (☎ 612141) is similarly priced but better; air-con rooms start at 350B.

Sa-nguan Sin Hotel on Singhanat Bamrung Rd, which runs east-west, is an old wooden favourite that was closed in 1991-92 for renovations. When it reopens, rooms will almost certainly be more expensive than the 50 to 70B they cost in 1990.

Toward the southern end of town is *Baiyoke Chalet Hotel* (☎ 611486), formerly the Mitniyom, at 90 Khunlum Praphat. It's got all the typical amenities for 650B in standard rooms, 1200B in VIP ones. The new *Holiday Inn Mae Hong Son* (☎ 611390; 254-2614 in Bangkok) at 114/5-7 Khunlum Praphat is definitely top end. Rooms and bungalows start at 1800B. Holiday Inn facilities include a swimming pool, tennis courts, disco, coffee shop and restaurant.

Places to Eat

Mae Hong Son isn't known for its food, but there are a few decent places to eat besides the guesthouses. *Khai Muk* is one of the better Thai-Chinese restaurants in town; it has recently moved around the corner from its original Khunlum Praphat location to a new outdoor restaurant.

The jók (broken-rice soup) place near the Mae Tee Hotel is still going strong and sells American breakfasts for 20 to 25B. The morning market behind the Mae Tee Hotel is a good place to buy food for trekking. Get there before 8 am.

Across from the Siam Hotel on Khunlum Praphat Rd is the pleasant *Ban Buatong* cafe/restaurant, which has good Thai food and Western breakfasts. Down the road on the left, across from Nong Pam Ice Cream, is the air-con *Sunny Coffee House*, a big night hang-out for young Thais. A better place for an evening drink is the quiet and well-decorated *Lai Phat* at 52/11 Khunlum Praphat Rd, near the Mae Tee Hotel.

Visitors staying at Pen Porn House are close to *Khao Soi Phinnun*, a friendly neighbourhood establishment on the same street which has khâo sòi or kũaytĩaw for 10B, as well as eggs, toast and coffee.

Khunlum Praphat Rd has experienced a minor explosion of farang-food places in the last two years. The *Good Luck Restaurant* offers steak, Italian dishes, hummus, falafel and shishkebab. There are several other tourist-oriented restaurants along this main strip, including the *Fern Pub* and *Old Home*.

Getting There & Away

Air THAI flies to Mae Hong Son from Chiang Mai twice a day at 11.10 am and 5.15 pm. On Monday, Wednesday and Friday there's a third flight at 12.45 pm. The fare is 345B and the flight takes 30 minutes. From Bangkok there's a daily 11.10 flight that costs 1865B and takes two hours and 10 minutes to reach Mae Hong Son (includes a stop in Chiang Mai).

Mae Hong Son's THAI office (☎ 611297, 611194) is at 71 Singhanat Bamrung Rd.

Bus From Chiang Mai there are two bus routes to Mae Hong Son, the northern route through Pai (7 to 8 hours) and the southern route through Mae Sariang (8 to 9 hours). Although it's longer, the southern route through Mae Sariang is much more comfortable because the bus stops every two hours for a 10 to 15-minute break and larger buses – with large seats – are used.

The northern route through Pai, originally built by the Japanese in WW II, is now paved all the way. The road is very winding and offers spectacular views from time to time. Because the buses used on this road are smaller, they're usually more crowded and there's a lot of motion sickness among the younger passengers. Either direction the trip costs around 100B.

The bus to Mae Hong Son via Mae Sariang leaves Chiang Mai's Arcade bus station every two hours between 6.30 am and 9 pm. The fare is 97B. There is also one daily air-con minibus to Mae Hong Son via Mae Sariang at 9 pm for 175B, which takes eight hours. The Pai bus leaves the same station four times a day at 7, 8.30 and 11 am and 2 pm. The fare is 50B (you must change buses in Pai to continue on to Mae Hong Son).

Buses as far as Soppong are 25B or to Pai 40B.

Getting Around

Most of Mae Hong Son is walkable. Motorcycle taxis within town cost 10B, to Doi Kong Mu 30B. Motorcycle drivers will also take passengers further afield but fares out of town are expensive, eg 500B to Soppong.

Several guesthouses in town rent bicycles and motorcycles.

AROUND MAE HONG SON

Rafting

Raft trips on the Pai River to Pai and beyond are gaining in popularity, as are boat trips into the Karen state (or nation, depending on your political alliances) of Burma. The Pai River raft trips can be good if the raft holds up (it's not uncommon for them to fall apart and/or sink), but the Burma trip, which attracts travellers who want to see the Padaung or long-necked people, is a bit of a rip-off, costing about 700B for a four-hour trip through unspectacular scenery to see maybe seven Padaung people who are practically captives of the Karen operators involved.

Mae Aw
แม่ออ

One of the best day trips you can do from the provincial capital is to Mae Aw, north of Mae Hong Son on a mountain peak at the Burmese border. A songthaew there costs 100B return per person during the dry season or 200B in the rainy season and leaves from Singhanat Bamrung Rd near the telephone office – get there at about 8 am. The trip takes two hours and passes Shan, Karen and Hmong villages, the **Pang Tong Summer Palace** and waterfalls.

Mae Aw is a settlement of Hmong (Meo) and Kuomintang peoples, one of the last true KMT outposts in Thailand. Occasionally there is fighting along the border between the KMT and the Shan United Army, led by the infamous opium warlord Khun Sa. When this happens, public transport to these areas is usually suspended and you are advised against going without a guide. (See Opium & the Golden Triangle in the Facts about the Country chapter.)

You can also walk from Mae Hong Son to Chiang Mai if you're up to it. A very high, steep mountain path begins in the mountains on the south-east side of town. The trip is said to take seven days and is supposed to be safe. There are only a few villages along the route, but the scenery is incredible. Food must be carried part of the way (this is a trek for the hardy and experienced). Ask at the Mae Hong Son Guest House for details.

Mae La-Na
แม่ละนา

Between Mae Hong Son and Pai is an area of forests, mountains, streams and limestone caves dotted with Shan and hill-tribe villages. Some of Mae Hong Son's most beautiful scenery is within a day's walk of the Shan villages of Mae La-Na and Soppong, both of which have accommodation.

The Mae La-Na junction is 55 km from Mae Hong Son or 56 km from Pai. The village of Mae La-Na is six km north of the junction and from here you can trek to several Red and Black Lahu villages and a couple of large caves.

Soppong
สบป่อง

Soppong is a small but relatively prosperous market village a couple of hours north-west of Pai and about 70 km from Mae Hong Son.

Close to Soppong are several Lisu, Karen and Lahu hill-tribe villages that can easily be visited on foot. Enquire at the Jungle Guest House or Cave Lodge in Soppong for reliable information. It's important to ask about the current situation as the Burma border area is somewhat sensitive due to the opium trade.

Tham Lot About eight km north of Soppong is Tham Lot, a large limestone cave with a wide stream running through it. It is possible to hike all the way through the cave (approximately 400 metres) by following the stream, though it requires some wading back and forth. Besides the main chamber there are three side chambers that can be reached by ladders – it takes two or three hours to see the whole thing. You can hire a gas lantern (50B) to take into the caverns from the national park caretakers at the park entrance. A guide will cost another 50B.

Tham Lot is one of two local caves which happen to be the longest known caves in mainland South-East Asia, though some as yet unexplored caves in southern Thailand may be even longer. The other is Tham Nam Lang.

Tham Nam Lang Near Ban Nam Khong, 30 km north- west of Soppong, this cave is nine km long and is said to be one of the largest caves in the world in terms of volume. There are many other caves in the area, some of which contain 2000-year-old wooden coffins.

Places to Stay

There is a sprinkling of accommodation in the area, mostly concentrated around Soppong. The *Soppong Guest House* has several simple A-frame huts from 30 to 60B. Better accommodation is at the friendly *Jungle Guest House*, one km west on the road to Mae Hong Son, where well-designed huts are 30B per person and there is also a good restaurant. The nearby *Pangmapa Guest House* is similar.

In the nearby forests and in the vicinity of Tham Lot, several guesthouses have come and gone. Recently, Forestry Department officials have been cracking down on illegal accommodation encroaching on the forest. So far the friendly Lisu Lodge has been closed, along with Tum Lod Bungalows. Accommodation may still be arranged in nearby villages, however.

One place to escape the Forestry Department is the *Cave Lodge* near Tham Lot; it's run by a former trekking guide from Chiang Mai and her Australian husband. They were the first to open regular accommodation in the area, starting the trend. Beds are 30B in a large common room; small meals are 30B each. Follow signs in Soppong to get there – it's about a 1½-hour walk to Ban Tham, the village closest to Tham Lot cave. The village headman rents rooms to travellers, and the Forestry Department has a few bungalows near the cave for 40B per person.

At Ban Nam Khong, the *Wilderness Lodge* is run by the same family that owns the Cave Lodge. Huts are 30B per person.

Just outside Mae La-Na village is the *Mae Lana Guest House* which has four large doubles with mosquito nets for 50B per night and a four-bed dorm for 20B per person. Isabelle and Niwet cook French and Thai food for visitors.

About 12 km north of Mae La-Na in the Black Lahu village of Ban Huay Hea (very close to the Burmese border) is the *Lahu Guest House*, run by a village teacher who speaks English. Simple accommodation is 20B per person and the money goes into a community fund.

Other less convenient guesthouses can be found around Mae Hong Son – the touts will find you at the bus terminal. On the road to Mae Aw, 54 km away and six km before the KMT village, is the *Hill Guest House* where a dorm bed is 20B and singles/doubles are 30/50B.

Places to Eat

In Soppong, try eating at the noodle stand near where the bus stops; there's also a Muslim restaurant across the road which serves khâo sòi and other dishes. An Italian restaurant – looking rather out of place – has opened in front of Soppong Guest House. Aside from these, you're at the mercy of the guesthouse kitchens.

Getting There & Away

Pai to Mae Hong Son buses stop in Soppong and there are two or three each day in either direction. From Mae Hong Son, buses take about 2½ hours and cost 30B. The trip between Pai and Soppong costs 20B and takes from 1½ to two hours.

PAI

ปาย

It first appears that there's not a lot to see in Pai, a peaceful crossroads town about halfway between Chiang Mai and Mae Hong Son on Route 1095. But if you stick around a few days and talk to some of the locals, you may discover some beautiful out-of-town spots in the surrounding hills. Any of the guesthouses in town can provide information on local trekking and a few do guided treks for 200 to 300B per day. Some local trekking guides here specialise in 'hard' treks – one outfit calls itself 'No Mercy Trekking'. Rafting from Pai to Mae Hong Son is also possible – it takes five days when conditions are favourable.

North-west of town are several Shan, Lahu, Lisu and KMT villages and a waterfall that can be visited on foot. The waterfall, **Maw Paeng Falls**, is an eight-km walk from town; you can cut the hike in half by taking a Mae Hong Son-bound bus north about five km and getting off at a signpost for the falls; from the highway it's only four km. A pool at the base of the falls is suitable for swimming.

Wat Phra That Mae Yen

วัดพระธาตุแม่เย็น

Simply known as Wat Mae Yen, this is a newish temple built on a hill with a good view overlooking the valley. Walk one km east from the main intersection in town, across a stream and through a village, to get to the stairs (353 steps) which lead to the top. The monks are vegetarian, uncommon in Thai Buddhist temples. Seven km south of the temple via a dirt road are some hot springs.

Traditional Massage

Pai Traditional Massage (☎ 699121), in a house near the river, has very good northern-Thai massage for 100B an hour. The couple that do the massages are graduates of Chiang Mai's Old Medicine Hospital. They've built their own herbal sauna house where you can steam yourself in *samun phrai* (medicinal herbs) for 30B per visit.

Places to Stay

Across from the bus station is the friendly *Duang Guest House* (☎ 699101), where clean rooms with shared hot-water showers are 60B. A few rooms with private bath are also available at 120B. Further east on this road in an old wooden house is the *Family Guest House,* which charges 30 to 40B per person, but fighting cocks are raised out the back so it's none too quiet. At the far western end of this road, past the hospital, is *Kim Guest House*, which is a bit isolated but quiet. Rooms without bath are 30B, or 50B with one.

Out on the main road through town are a string of guesthouses, some of them quite recently established. Friendly *Nunya's House* (☎ 699051) is in a newer wooden building facing a garden sitting area; rooms with private hot-water bath are 120B, smaller rooms without bath cost 80B. Across the road is *Charlie's House* where rooms around a large courtyard cost 60B with shared bath, 120B with hot-water bath, and 160 to 200B in a bungalow.

Next down the road is *Big Guest House*, a new row house next to a noisy motorcycle garage. Rooms are 80B with shared bath, 120B with private hot-water bath.

A little further down the street in the same direction, the *Wiang Pai Hotel* is a traditional wooden hotel with 15 spacious rooms. Single-bed rooms (sleeping one or two) cost 50B; a two-bed room is 100B. Behind the old hotel is a new wing where a double with a bath is 120B. Hot water is available on request.

Opposite the Wiang Pai is the *Pai City Guest House*, the cheapest accommodation in town. Simple bamboo bungalows are 40B with shared hot-water bath. There is a small eating area in the front where the original Pai Guest House used to be.

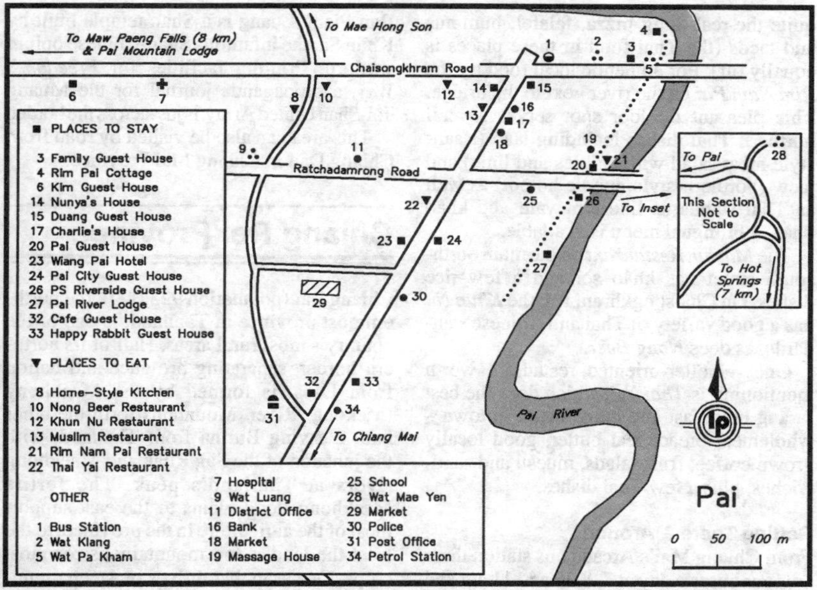

On the southern edge of town, off the road a bit, is the *Happy Rabbit Guest House* (☎ 699162). Formerly the Shan Guest House, it is run by Boonyang, an outgoing Shan who has worked in Bangkok and Saudi Arabia. The atmosphere and food are good and Boonyang tries hard to please. Shan-style bungalows cost 40 to 60B per person, 80B with bath. Newer rooms are 120B with hot-water bath, 200B with bath and fridge.

The *Cafe Guest House* is further south still, on the other side of the road. It caters to budget tour groups and charges 100 to 200B per room.

Along the Pai River east of town are four bungalow operations. The *Pai Guest House* offers basic bungalows near the Rim Nam Pai Restaurant for 40/60B. Just off the road to Wat Mae Yen and next to the bridge is the *PS Riverside Guest House*, which has places to sit along the river, and huts at 40/60B for singles/doubles, 80B with private bath. Further down the river, the *Pai River Lodge* has nice huts arranged in a large circle with a dining/lounge area on stilts in the middle. Rates are 70/80B for singles/doubles. The up-market (for Pai) *Rim Pai Cottage* (☎ 699133, 235931) is further north along the river not far from the bus station. Rim Pai's clean, quiet, A-frames with two beds, a bath, electricity and mosquito net go for 400 to 600B including breakfast. All three places along the river have hot-water showers.

Pai Mountain Lodge (☎ 699068) is seven km north-west of Pai near Maw Paeng Falls and several hill-tribe villages. Spacious A-frames with hot-water baths and stone fireplaces sleep four for 400B – good value. In town you can book a room or arrange transport at 89 Chaisongkhram Rd, near the Northern Green bike shop.

Places to Eat

Most of the places to eat along the main north-south and east-west roads in Pai are farang-oriented cafes with the usual not-quite-the-real-thing pizza, falafel, hummus and tacos (the Thai food in these places is equally off). For authentic local food try the *Rim Nam Pai* on the river next to the bridge. This pleasant outdoor spot serves several northern Thai dishes including lâap (isaan-style meat salad with chillies and lime) and jaew (northern-style noodle hotpot) as well as Thai standards like tôm yam and khâo phàt. A bilingual menu is available.

The *Muslim Restaurant* on the main north-south street has khâo sòi and a few rice dishes. On Chaisongkhram Rd, the *Khun Nu* has a good variety of Thai and Chinese standards, as does *Nong Beer*.

One traveller-oriented restaurant worth mentioning is *Thai Yai*, which does the best farang breakfast and lunch menu in town – wholemeal bread, real butter, good locally grown coffee, fruit salads, muesli and sandwiches, plus a few Thai dishes.

Getting There & Around

From Chiang Mai's Arcade bus station there are four buses a day at 7, 8.30 and 11 am and 2 pm. The distance is only 134 km but the trip takes about three hours due to road conditions in Mae Hong Son Province. The fare is 50B. From Mae Hong Son there are three buses a day at 7 and 11 am and 2 pm. This winding, 111-km stretch takes three to four hours; the fare is also 50B.

All of little Pai is accessible on foot. For local excursions you can rent bicycles or motorcycles at Northern Green on Chaisongkhram Rd. Bicycles cost 50B a day, motorcycles (Honda Dreams) are 150B; you get free maps of the area with every rental.

AROUND PAI

Visitors can use Pai as a base for excursions to nearby hill-tribe villages as described earlier in the Pai section. Further afield, the area north-east of Pai has so far been little explored. A network of unpaved roads – some little more than footpaths – skirt a mountain ridge and the Taeng River valley all the way to the Burmese border near **Wiang Haeng** and **Ban Piang Haeng**, passing several villages along the way. Near Ban Piang Luang is a Shan temple built by Khun Sa, the infamous Shan-Chinese opium warlord. Printing facilities for *Freedom's Way*, a propaganda journal for the Muang Tai-Shan United Army, is just across the border.

This area can also be visited by road from Chiang Dao in Chiang Mai Province.

Chiang Rai Province

Chiang Rai (population 923,000), the northernmost province in Thailand, is one of the country's most rural areas. Half of its northern border, separating province and nation from Laos, is formed by the Maekhong (Mekong) River. Mountains form the other half, cleaving Burma from Thailand, with the junction of the Sai, Ruak and Maekhong rivers at Thailand's peak. The fertile Maekhong flood plains to the east support most of the agriculture in the province; to the west the land is too mountainous for most crops. One crop that thrives on steep mountain slopes is opium, and until very recently Chiang Rai was the centre for most of the poppy cultivated in Thailand.

Crop substitution and other development projects sponsored by the Princess Mother, along with accelerated law enforcement, have pushed much of the opium trade over the border into Burma and Laos. While there are undoubtedly still pockets of the trade here and there, even a few poppy patches, Chiang Rai's Golden Triangle fame is now mostly relegated to history books and museums.

CHIANG RAI

อ.เมืองเชียงราย

A little more than 100 km from Chiang Mai, Chiang Rai (population 45,000) (called 'Chiang Hai' in northern Thai dialect) is known as the gateway to the Golden Triangle. Most visitors to the town are interested in hill-tribe trekking or a boat trip on the Kok River.

Chiang Rai was founded by King Mengrai

in 1262 as part of the Lanna kingdom. It became a Thai territory in 1786 and a province in 1910. Its most historic monument, Wat Phra Kaew, once hosted the Emerald Buddha during its circuitous travels (the image eventually ended up at the wat of the same name in Bangkok). It now houses a replica of Chiang Mai's Wat Phra Singh Buddha image and a new 'Emerald Buddha' all its own.

Lots of wealthy Thais are moving to Chiang Rai and over the last three years or so the area has seen a development boom as local entrepreneurs speculate on the city's future. Golf courses are going up outside the town, and a new international airport is planned to replace the current domestic one. From a tourist point of view, Chiang Rai is becoming an alternative to Chiang Mai, especially for Europeans.

Information

A new Chiang Rai TAT office (☎ 717433) has opened on Singkhlai Rd, north of Wat Phra Singh. Giveaway maps of the city are available, as well as useful brochures on accommodation and transport. It's open daily from 8.30 am to 5 pm.

The GPO is on Utarakit Rd south of Wat Phra Singh and is open from 8.30 am to 4.30 pm weekdays, 9 am to 1 pm weekends and holidays. An office upstairs offers international telephone, telegram, telex and fax services from 7 am to 11 pm daily.

Wat Phra Kaew

วัดพระแก้ว

Originally called Wat Paa Yia (Bamboo Forest Monastery) in local dialect, this is the city's most revered Buddhist temple. Legend says that in 1434 lightning struck the temple's octagonal chedi, which fell apart to reveal the Phra Kaew Morakot or Emerald Buddha (actually made of jade). The image is known to have been created before this date but exactly when and where is open to speculation – supposedly it originally came from Sri Lanka and was once stationed in the Khmer capital of Angkor. In 1436 the image was moved to Wat Phra That Lampang Luang in Lampang, where it stayed for 32 years. From Lampang it was taken to Chiang Mai's Wat Phra Singh for 85 years, then to Luang Prabang and Vientiane in Laos. The Lao rulers kept it for 125 years until the Siamese recaptured it in 1678 and installed it at Wat Phra Kaew in Bangkok.

Chiang Rai recently commissioned a Chinese artist to sculpt a new jade image from Canadian jade. The image was installed at the temple in June 1991. Named the Phra Yok Chiang Rai (Chiang Rai Jade Buddha), it was intentionally made a very close but not exact replica of the Phra Kaew Morakot in Bangkok, with dimensions of 48.3 cm across the base and 65.9 cm in height (the original is 48.3 and 66 cm respectively). At present, the image sits in a gilded box in front of a larger seated image in the main wihaan; eventually it will be moved to the new Lanna-style Haw Phra Kaew (Jewel Buddha Hall) now under construction. The Princess Mother has honoured the image with the royal title of Phra Phuttha Ratanakon Nawutiwat Sanuson Mongkhon, which roughly translates as 'the ultimate blessed jewel-made Buddha image'.

The main wihaan is a medium-sized, nicely preserved wooden structure with unique carved doors. The chedi behind it dates to the late 14th century and is typical Lanna style.

Wat Jet Yot

วัดเจ็ดยอด

The namesake for this wat is a seven-spired chedi similar to the chedi in Chiang Mai's Wat Jet Yot but without stucco ornamentation. Of more aesthetic interest is the wooden ceiling in the front verandah of the main wihaan; the ceiling features a unique Thai astrological fresco.

Wat Phra Singh

วัดพระสิงห์

Yet another temple housing a copy of a famous Buddha image, this one was built in

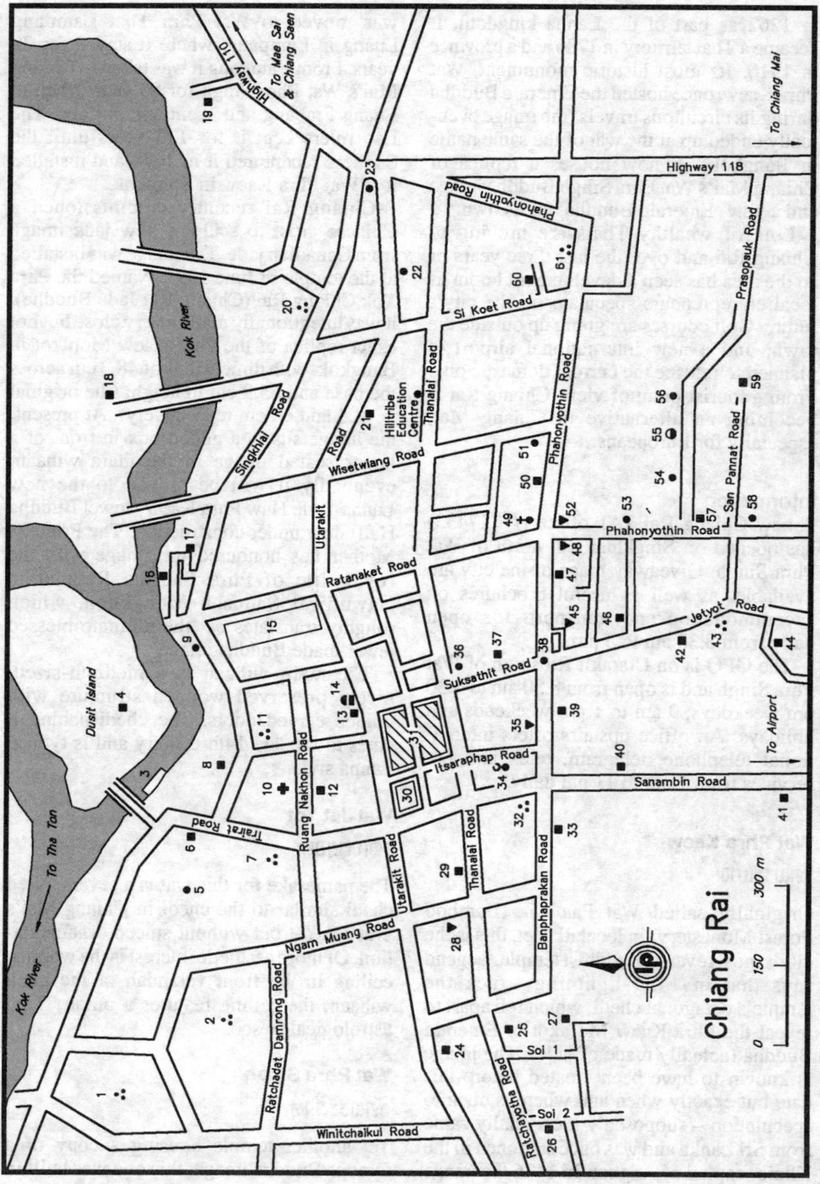
Chiang Rai
Kok River
Dusit Island
To Tha Ton
Highway 110
To Mae Sai & Chiang Saen
Highway 118
To Chiang Mai
Phahonyothin Road
Prasopsuk Road
Si Koet Road
Thanalai Road
Hilltribe Education Centre
Singkhlai Road
Utarakit Road
Wisetwiang Road
Ratanaket Road
San Pannat Road
Jetyot Road
Suksathit Road
To Airport
Itsaraphap Road
Sanambin Road
Banphaprakan Road
Ruang Nakhon Road
Trairat Road
Ngam Muang Road
Ratchadat Damrong Road
Ratchayotha Road
Soi 1
Soi 2
Winitchaikul Road
0 150 300 m

■ PLACES TO STAY

4 Dusit Island Resort
6 Chat House
8 Mae Kok Villa
12 Ruang Nakhon Hotel
13 Siriwattana Hotel
16 Bow Ling Guest House
17 Mae Hong Son Guest House
18 Pintamorn Guest House
19 Joke House
21 Chiangrai Inn
24 Chiang Rai Guest House
25 Lek House
26 Head Guest House
27 Ben Guest House
29 Paowattana Hotel
30 Rama Hotel
33 Saenphu Hotel
37 Chiang Rai (Chiengrai) Hotel
39 Sukniran Hotel
40 Krung Thong Hotel
41 New Boonyoung Guest House
42 Boonbundan Guest House
44 Tourist Inn
46 Wiang Come Hotel
47 Siam Hotel
50 Golden Triangle Inn
57 Wiang Inn Hotel
59 Jira Garden Guest House
60 Seegerd Guest House

▼ PLACES TO EAT

28 Mae Ui Khiaw Restaurant
35 Phetburi Restaurant
45 La Cantina Restaurant
48 Nakhon Pathom Restaurant
52 Napoli Pizza

OTHER

1 Wat Doi Thong
2 Wat Ngam Muang
3 Kok River Pier
5 Government Office & Town Hall
7 Wat Phra Kaew
9 TAT Office
10 Hospital
11 Wat Phra Singh
14 Post Office
15 Police Station
20 Wat
22 Telephone Office
23 King Mengrai Monument
31 Market
32 Wat Ming Muang
34 Mosque
36 Bangkok Bank
38 Clocktower
43 Wat Jet Yot
49 Church
51 Alliance Française & La Terrase Restaurant
53 THAI Office
54 Rama I Cinema
55 Bus Station
56 Rama II Theatre
58 KM Car Rent
61 Wat Si Koet

the late 14th century during the reign of Chiang Rai's King Mahaphrom. A sister temple to Chiang Mai's Wat Phra Singh, the original temple buildings are typical northern-style wooden structures with low, sweeping roofs. The main wihaan houses a copy of Chiang Mai's Phra Singh Buddha.

Other Temples

Wat Phra That Doi Thong is a hilltop wat north-west of Wat Phra Kaew with views of the river and an occasional river breeze. **Wat Paa Kaw**, near the entrance to the current Chiang Rai Airport, is a Shan-built temple with distinctive Burmese designs. Also near the airport is **Wat Phra That Doi Phrabaat**, a northern-style temple perched on a hillside.

Hilltribe Education Centre

ศูนย์การศึกษาชาวเขา

The nonprofit Population & Community Development Association (PDA) operates this combination of museum and handicrafts centre at 620/25 Thanalai Rd (☎ 713410, 711475). Crafts for sale are displayed on the ground floor. The 2nd and 3rd floors of the facility serve as a museum with typical clothing for each tribe, folk implements and other anthropological exhibits. The centre also offers a slide show on Thailand's hill tribes with narration in English, French, German, Japanese and Thai. Admission to the slide show depends on the number of people who want to see it, ranging from 10B per person in a group of 10, to 50B for one person.

If you've already been to the Tribal Research Institute at Chiang Mai University, you'll have seen it all before; otherwise, it's a good place to visit before undertaking any hill-tribe treks. The PDA also organise and lead their own treks which they claim are more respectful of local cultures than the usual commercial trek.

Activities

Trekking More than 20 travel agencies, guesthouses and hotels offer trekking, typically in the Doi Tung and Chiang Khong areas. Chiang Rai's guesthouses were the first places to offer treks in the area and generally have the most experienced guides. Many of the local travel agencies merely act as brokers for guides associated with one of the local guesthouses; hence it may be cheaper to book directly through a guesthouse. The Hilltribe Education Centre also offers guide services. The usual precautions apply: meet with the guide(s) before committing yourself and ask all the pertinent questions. (See the Hill Tribes section earlier in this chapter.)

From the Kok River pier, boats can take you upriver as far as Fang. (See Fang & Tha Thon under Chiang Mai Province in this chapter.) An hour's boat ride from Chiang Rai is **Ban Ruammit**, a fair-sized Karen village. From here you can trek on your own to Lahu, Yao, Akha and Lisu villages – all within a day's walk. Inexpensive room and board (20 to 30B per person, meals 10 to 20B) are available in many villages in the river area. Another popular area for do-it-yourself trekkers is Wawi, south of the river town of Mae Salak near the end of the river route. (See the Kok River Trip to Chiang Rai section earlier.)

Alliance Française The Alliance recently opened a small branch at 585 Wisetwiang Rd, not far from the Golden Triangle Inn on Phahonyothin Rd. Although the centre offers French-language courses, the emphasis is on bringing French culture, particularly food and wine, to Chiang Rai residents. Typical French cuisine is served at a small outdoor cafe situated next to an authentic *pétanque* court and at a few indoor tables. The centre also has a small library of books, magazines and videos from France.

Places to Stay – bottom end & middle

Guesthouses Near the Kok River pier (for boats from Tha Ton) is *Mae Kok Villa* (☎ 711786) at 445 Singkhlai Rd, which has dorm beds for 40B, bungalows with fan and hot bath for 120B, and large singles/doubles with fan and hot bath for 140/160B. IYH card holders get a 10% discount on these rates; nonmembers may be required to purchase a membership. Another nice place near the Kok River pier is *Chat House* (☎ 711481), at 1 Trairat Rd. It's an old Thai house with singles/doubles at 40/60B with shared bath, 60/80B with private bath. There are bicycles for rent and guided treks are available.

A bit east of here in a network of sois off Singkhlai Rd are a couple of small family-run guesthouses. First is the clean and friendly *Bow Ling House* (☎ 712704) which has singles/doubles with shared bath for 40/60B and rooms with private bath for 80B. A hot-water shower is available. Next is the very pleasant *Mae Hong Son Guest House of Chiang Rai*, run by the same family as the original guesthouse in Mae Hong Son. Rooms are 60/80B with shared hot-water showers, 100B with private ones. This guesthouse has a very nice garden cafe, and also rents motorcycles and organises treks.

North of here are a couple of places on a large island separated from the city by a canal. *Chian House* (☎ 713388) at 172 Si Bunruang Rd has simple but nicely done rooms from 60B with cold shower, 80 to 150B for larger rooms with hot shower. Also on the island is *Pintamorn Guest House* (☎ 713317, 714161), where comfortable singles/doubles are 60/120B with hot water. There are also doubles with air-con in a separate house for 250B. A 'sports club' on the premises has work-out rooms open to the public for 50B a day, plus a bar/restaurant and sauna.

The original *Chiang Rai Guest House* (☎ 714305) has moved from its old location at Si Koet Rd to larger premises at 77 Pratu Chiang Mai Rd. Room rates are 40 to 50B a single, 60 to 80B a double with shared bath, and 80 to 120B for doubles with private hot shower. The old house used by the Chiang Rai Guest House at 717/1 Si Koet Rd is now the laid-back *Seegerd Guest House* (☎ 712804), run by knowledgeable trekking guide Adirake. Rooms with shared bath are 50/70B for a single/double.

Lek House (☎ 713337) at 95 Thanalai Rd near the city centre has rooms in an old house for 50B single, 60B double with shared bath, or bungalows with private bath for 80B. If you follow Thanalai further west till it becomes Ratchayotha Rd, you'll find *Head Guest House* at Soi 2. Head's bamboo huts cost from 40 to 60B a single, 70 to 100B a double or triple. Farther down Soi 2, just before it ends at San Khong Noi Rd, is *Chai House* (☎ 716681), a quiet spot away from everything with singles/doubles at 40/50B.

If you follow Soi 1 Ratchayotha south till it ends, then turn left, you'll come to the new *Ben Guest House* (☎ 714653). Clean rooms in a new building made of salvaged teak cost 80B with fan and hot shower, 50 to 60B without bath. The owners speak English very well. About 200 metres past Soi 2 on 21/4 Ratchayotha is *Wisid Guest House* (☎ 713279). Rooms in this old teak and bamboo house are 60B with shared hot bath.

In the southern part of town are *Boonbundan Guest House* (☎ 712914) and *New Boonyoung Guest House* (☎ 712893), both in walled compounds. The Boonbundan is at 1005/13 Jetyot Rd and offers a choice of accommodation – in small rooms off the garden, in huts or in the new air-con building overlooking the garden – something to suit all budgets. Small rooms with shared bath are 40B, slightly larger singles/doubles with hot bath are 50/80B. Singles/doubles in huts are 100/150B with fan and bath, and large singles/doubles with a fan in the new building are 150/200B, 250/350B with air-con. The Boonbundan loans bicycles, rents out motorcycles and runs treks. *New Boonyoung* at 1054/5 Sanambin Rd has a similar arrangement minus the new building. Singles/doubles are 50/70B or 80/100B with hot bath.

Also in this vicinity is the friendly and efficient *Tourist Inn* (☎ 714682) at 1004/5-6 Jetyot Rd. Clean, large rooms are 160B with fan and private bath. Due east of Wat Jet Yot, at the end of San Pannat Rd, *Jira Garden Guest House* (☎ 712556) offers a quiet location and spacious grounds. Large doubles with fan and shared hot-water bath are 100B. Another Jira Garden plus is that it's only a 10-minute walk from the bus station.

Joke House (☎ 716218), at 837/1 Rong Kasat Rd in the north-eastern part of town near the highway to Mae Sai, has dorm beds for 30B, huts for 70B and singles/doubles in a long concrete building for 50/80B with fan and hot shower. Joke House runs treks and rents out motorcycles and cars.

Hotels On Suksathit Rd near the clock tower and district government building is the well-run *Chiengrai Hotel* (☎ 311266), a favourite with Thai truck drivers and travelling salespeople. Clean rooms with fan and bath cost 100 to 150B. Also centrally located is the *Sukniran* (☎ 311055) at 424/1 Banphaprakan Rd, between the clock tower and Wat Ming Muang, and around the corner from the Chiang Rai Hotel. Rooms start at 200B.

Similar to the Sukniran but cheaper is *Siam* (☎ 711077) at 531/6-8 Banphaprakan, where rates start at 120B with a fan and bath, 180B with air-con.

Ruang Nakhon (☎ 711566) at 25 Ruang Nakhon Rd, near the hospital, allows four people to share a room with bath for 200B. Bungalows are 160B, doubles 180B, and air-con doubles from 220 to 420B.

If you favour the old Thai-Chinese type of hotel, check out the *Paowattana* (☎ 711722) at 150 Thanalai Rd, which has rooms for 80B. Another cheap hotel is the *Siriwattana* (☎ 711466) at 485 Utarakit Rd next to the GPO, where singles/doubles cost 80 to 120B and there are a couple of bungalows at 50 to 70B.

The clean and efficient *Krung Thong Hotel* (☎ 711033), at 412 Sanambin Rd, has large rooms with fan and bath from 140B; air-con rooms cost 260B.

The centrally located *Rama Hotel* (☎ 311344) at 331/4 Trairat Rd, a couple of blocks from the clock tower, has added air-con, carpeting and hot-water baths to all its rooms, which cost 420 to 550B. Restaurants, nightclubs and theatres are nearby.

Out of town, at 70 Phahonyothin Rd (the highway to Mae Sai), is the YMCA's *Golden*

Triangle International House (☎ 713785). This is a very modern establishment with dorm beds for 70B, singles/doubles with fan and private bath for 220/260B, or 300/400B with air-con. All rooms come with hot water and a telephone. Guests may use the Y's swimming pool.

Places to Stay – top end

The *Golden Triangle Inn* (☎ 711339; fax 713963), at 590 Phahonyothin Rd, has 39 tastefully designed rooms with tile floors, air-con and hot water for 650B including American breakfast. Also on the landscaped grounds are a cafe, a small Japanese-Thai garden and an efficient travel agency. It's a popular place, so book in advance to ensure you'll get in.

On the same theme, but not quite as successful, is the new *Chiangrai Inn* (☎ 712673; fax 711483) at 661 Utarakit Rd. Large air-con rooms are a bit overpriced at 900/1100B for singles/doubles. Better value in this range is the centrally located *Saenphu Hotel* (☎ 717300/9; fax 711372). Rooms with all the amenities – air-con, TV, phone, fridge – cost 545B for a single or double. The hotel's basement nightclub has live music and is a very popular local rendezvous.

The *Wiang Inn* (☎ 711543) at 893 Phahonyothin Rd has modestly luxurious rooms from 800B. Facilities include a swimming pool, bar, restaurant, coffee shop and disco. Nearing the top of the Chiang Mai room-rate scale is *Wiang Come* (☎ 711800), at 869/90 Premawiphat Rd in the Chiang Rai Trade Centre. International-class rooms start at 1000B (700B for Thais!), complete with TV and fridge. The hotel has a disco, coffee shop, restaurant and nightclub.

A rash of new luxury hotels opened in Chiang Rai just in time for the travel recession of 1990-91. Perched on its own island in the Kok River (you can't miss seeing its stacked white facade if you arrive in Chiang Rai by boat), the 270-room *Dusit Island Resort* (☎ 715777) is an island unto itself, insulating its guests from the rigours of laid-back Chiang Rai. Rooms start at 2200B but since occupancy rates have been running under 25%, the Dusit may consider a discount to attract prospective guests.

Another new white elephant is the 350-room *Little Duck Hotel* (☎ 715620), south of the city past the airport. It's a splendid facility standing mostly empty, with rates starting at 1420B. Apparently the developers believed a rumour that the upcoming international airport would be located near the old airport; the latest plans call for it to be constructed 13 km north of the city.

North on Phahonyothin Rd just before the road crosses the river on the way to Mae Sai, the *Holiday Park Hotel* (☎ 712243) is also new, but better located. Rooms start at 600B; facilities include an attached shopping plaza, restaurant and a garden sitting area.

Places to Eat

Thai There are plenty of restaurants in Chiang Rai, especially along Banphaprakan and Thanalai Rds. Just east of the once-great (now awful) Haw Naliga Restaurant on Banphaprakan Rd are the *Phetburi* and *Ratburi* restaurants. The Phetburi has a particularly good selection of curries and other Thai dishes. One speciality is cha-om thâwt, a type of fried quiche of cha-om greens cut in squares and served with a delicious chilli sauce.

Muang Thong Restaurant, just south of the Wiang Inn, has an extensive Thai and Chinese menu that includes a frog section. The house speciality is kaeng pà pèt, a delicious duck curry made without coconut milk. For northern Thai food, the best place in town is *Mae Ui Khiaw* on Ngam Muang Rd, open from 10 am to 5 pm only.

Nakhon Pathom, yet another local restaurant named after a central Thailand city, is very popular for khâo man kài (Hainanese chicken rice) and kũaytĩaw pèt yaang (roast duck with rice noodles). The restaurant is on Phahonyothin Rd near the Banphaprakan intersection.

Next to the mosque on Itsaraphap Rd is a Thai-Muslim restaurant with delicious khâo mòk kài, a Thai version of chicken briyani.

Near the bus station are the usual food stalls; the night market next to the terminal and Rama I cinema is also good. There's a string of inexpensive rice and noodle restaurants along Jetyot Rd between Thanalai Rd and Wat Jet Yot, near the Chiengrai and Wiang Come hotels.

Western The Clocktower Plaza (also known as Sapkaset Plaza and Soi Sanuk), a recently established L-shaped soi between Banphaprakan and Suksathit Rds, has become something of a farang food and bar centre. *La Cantina* (☎ 716808), operated by an Italian expat, offers an extensive selection of pizza, pasta, Italian regional specialities and wines; Mr Vallicelli even plays Italian opera on the sound system! Next door the American-managed *Cat House Bar & Grille* offers 'burgers, beer, booze, Thai food and rock & roll'.

Bierstube on Phahonyothin Rd south of the Wiang Inn has been recommended for German food, and there are several other Western-style pubs along here and on Suksathit/Jetyot Rd near the Wiang Come Hotel. Further north on Phahonyothin are *Napoli Pizza* and *Magic Grill*, a Thai-owned, fast-food place with burgers and fried chicken.

The Alliance Française de Chiang Rai at 585 Wisetwiang Rd (just off Phahonyothin Rd) serves a prix fixe French lunch at its outdoor *La Terrase* for an inexpensive 200B. An indoor section also offers an à la carte menu in the evenings.

Entertainment

Heuan Kao (Old House), diagonally opposite the Chiengrai Hotel on Suksathit Rd, has live music nightly from 7 pm till midnight. The decor and atmosphere is 'Thai classic' (lots of B&W photos of Rama VII) and there's a reasonable Thai-Chinese menu for munchies, also good ice cream. Clocktower Plaza (Sapkaset Plaza) has a string of bars including the Cat House (mentioned under Places to Eat) and the semi-outdoor Easy Bar. The Easy Bar is for video addicts – English-language videos are shown almost nonstop throughout the afternoon and evening.

The Rama Hotel's Cheers Pub is a lively old-west-style pub with occasional live folk music. Another popular local hang-out is the basement nightclub of the Saenphu Hotel, which has live Thai pop bands nightly.

Getting There & Away

Air THAI flies daily between Chiang Rai and Chiang Mai; the flight takes 40 minutes and costs 420B. Daily flights are also available to/from Bangkok (one hour and 20 minutes, 1855B).

Chiang Rai has plans to open a new international airport at a site 13 km north of the city, with proposed flights from Hong Kong and Kunming. The completion date hasn't yet been announced; word of mouth says it won't be before 1994.

Chiang Rai's THAI office (☎ 711179, 715207) is at 870 Phahonyothin Rd, not far from the Wiang Come Hotel.

Bus There are two bus routes to Chiang Rai from Chiang Mai, an old and a new. The old route *(sãi kào)* heads south from Chiang Mai to Lampang before heading north through Ngao, Phayao, Mae Chai and finally to Chiang Rai. If you want to stop at any of these cities, this is the bus to catch, but the trip will take up to seven hours. In Chiang Mai the bus leaves from the Chiang Mai to Lamphun road, near Nawarat Bridge; the fare is 66B.

The new route *(sãi mài)* heads north-east along Route 1019 to Chiang Rai, stopping in Doi Saket and Wiang Papao, and takes about four hours. The fare is 47B ordinary, 65B air-con or 83B for 1st-class air-con. New-route buses leave from Chiang Mai's Arcade bus station. Chiang Mai to Chiang Rai buses are sometimes stopped for drug searches by police.

Chiang Rai's bus station is on Prasopsuk Rd, several blocks south of Banphaprakan Rd.

Other bus services from Chiang Rai include:

city	fare	duration
Bangkok	157B	12 hours
(air-con)	170B	11 hours
(1st class)	270 to 300B	
(VIP)	420B	
Chiang Saen	14B	1½ hours
Chiang Khong	31B	3 hours
Mae Sai	15B	1¾ hours
Nan	60B	6 hours
Phayao	21B	1¾ hours
Phitsanulok	80B	6 hours
(air-con)	116B	5 hours
Phrae	50B	4 hours

Boat One of the most popular ways of getting to Chiang Rai is the river trip from Tha Ton (see Kok River Trip to Chiang Rai).

For boats heading upriver on the Mae Kok, go to the pier in the north-western corner of town. Regular long boats from Chiang Rai stop at the following villages along the Kok (times are approximate for ideal river conditions):

destination	fare	duration
Ban Ruammit	25B	1 hour
Pong Nam Rawn	30B	1 hour 20 min
Phaa Muup	35B	1¾ hours
Hat Yao	60B	2¼ hours
Phaa Khwang	70B	2½ hours
Kok Noi	90B	3 hours
Phaa Tai 1	20B	3½ hours
Mae Salak	150B	4 hours
Tha Ton	170B	4½ to 5 hours

Getting Around

A samlor ride anywhere in central Chiang Rai should cost 10 to 15B. A city songthaew system (2B fare) circulates along the main city streets.

Several small agencies near the Wiang Come Hotel rent cars, vans and jeeps. KM Car Rent (☎ 715136/054) on Phahonyothin Rd, south of the Wiang Inn, has the best rates and service (including insurance).

Most of the guesthouses in town rent or lend bicycles, which are a good way to get around town. Motorcycles are also easily rented through guesthouses. A reliable motorcycle rental and repair shop is Soon (☎ 714068) on the eastern side of Trairat Rd, between Banphaprakan and Thanalai Rds. Another place that rents motorcycles is next to the Sukniran Hotel.

MAE SALONG (SANTIKHIRI)

แม่สลอง (สันติคีรี)

The village of Mae Salong was originally settled by the renegade KMT 93rd Regiment, which fled to Burma from China after the 1949 Chinese revolution. The renegades were again forced to flee in 1961 when the Burmese government decided they wouldn't allow the KMT to remain legally in northern Burma (some still hide out in the hills).

Ever since the Thai government granted these renegades refugee status in the '60s, the Thais have been trying to incorporate the Yunnanese KMT and their families into the Thai nation. Before now they weren't having much success, as the KMT persisted in involving themselves in the Golden Triangle opium trade, along with opium warlord Khun Sa and the Shan United Army (SUA).

This area is very mountainous and there are few paved roads, so the outside world has always been somewhat cut off from the goings-on in Mae Salong. Hence, for years the KMT were able to ignore attempts by Thai authorities to suppress opium activity and tame the region. Khun Sa, in fact, made his home in nearby Ban Hin Taek (now Ban Theuat Thai) until the early '80s when he was finally routed by the Thai military. Khun Sa's retreat to Burma seemed to signal a change in local attitudes and the Thai government finally began making progress in its pacification of Mae Salong and the surrounding area. (See Opium & the Golden Triangle in the Facts about the Country chapter.)

In a further effort to separate the area from its old image as an opium fiefdom, the Thai government officially changed the name of the village from Mae Salong to Santikhiri (Hill of Peace). The 36-km road from Basang, near Mae Chan, to Santikhiri, is paved (until the early '80s pack horses were used to move goods up the mountain to Mae Salong) and a Thai-language elementary

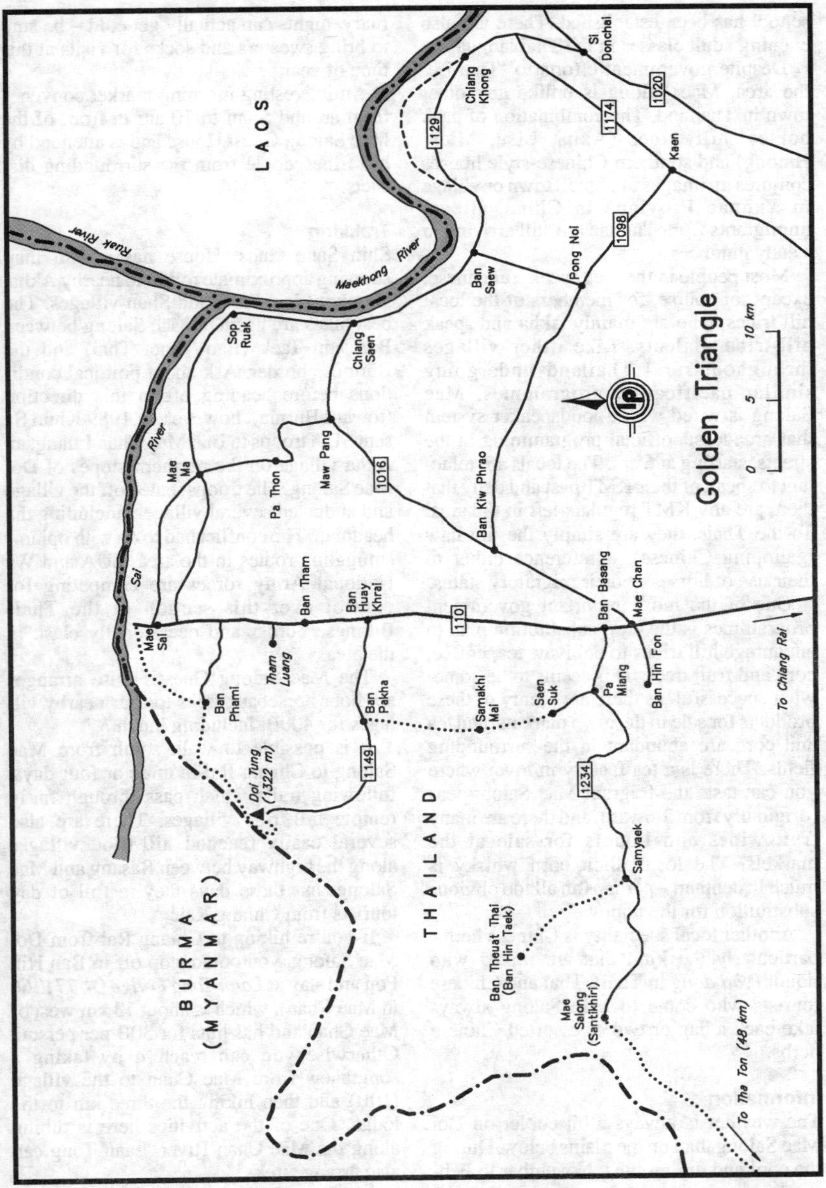
LAOS
BURMA
(MYANMAR)
THAILAND
Golden Triangle
Ruak River
Maekhong River
Sai River
Si Donchai
Chiang Khong
Kaen
Pong Noi
Ban Saew
Sop Ruak
Chiang Saen
Mae Ma
Pa Thon
Maw Pang
Ban Kiw Phrao
Ban Basang
Mae Chan
Ban Hin Fon
Pa Miang
Saen Suk
Samakhi Mai
Ban Pakha
Ban Huay Khrai
Ban Tham
Tham Luang
Mae Sai
Ban Phami
Doi Tung (1322 m)
Samyaek
Ban Theuat Thai (Ban Hin Taek)
Mae Salong (Santikhiri)
To Tha Ton (48 km)
To Chiang Rai
1129
1174
1020
1098
1016
110
1149
1234
0
5
10 km

school has been established. There are also evening adult classes in the Thai language.

Despite government efforts to 'Thai-ise' the area, Mae Salong is unlike any other town in Thailand. The combination of pack horses, hill tribes (Akha, Lisu, Mien, Hmong) and southern Chinese-style houses conjures up images of a small town or village in Yunnan Province in China. Illegal immigrants from Yunnan are still arriving in steady numbers.

Most people in the area speak Yunnanese, except, of course, for members of the local hill tribes, who are mainly Akha and speak hill-tribe dialects. Like other villages throughout rural Thailand undergoing similar pacification programmes, Mae Salong is wired with a loudspeaker system that broadcasts official programming in the streets, starting at 6 am. The locals are reluctant to speak of their KMT past and deny that there are any KMT regulars left in the area. To the Thais, they are simply the jiin haw (galloping Chinese), a reference either to their use of horses or their migratory status.

One of the most important government programmes is the crop-substitution plan to encourage hill tribes to cultivate tea, coffee, corn and fruit trees. This seems to be somewhat successful, as there are plenty of these products for sale in the town markets, and tea and corn are abundant in the surrounding fields. There is a tea factory in town where you can taste the fragrant Mae Salong teas (originally from Taiwan), and there are many fruit wines and liquors for sale at the markets. The local illicit corn whisky is much in demand – perhaps an all too obvious substitution for the poppy.

Another local speciality is Chinese herbs, particularly the kind that are mixed with liquor (*yàa dong* in Thai). Thai and Chinese tourists who come to Mae Salong always take back a bag or two of assorted Chinese herbs.

Information

The weather is always a bit cooler on Doi Mae Salong than on the plains below. During the cool and dry months, November to February, nights can actually get cold – be sure to bring sweaters and socks for visits at this time of year.

An interesting morning market convenes from around 5 am to 10 am in front of the Mae Salong Guest House and is attended by hill tribespeople from the surrounding districts.

Trekking

Shin Sane Guest House has a wall map showing approximate routes to nearby Akha, Hmong, Lisu, Lahu and Shan villages. The best hikes are north of Mae Salong between Ban Hin Taek (Ban Thoet Thai) and the Burmese border. Ask about political conditions before heading off in this direction (toward Burma), however. In 1989 Khun Sa sent SUA troops to Ban Mae Chan Luang, an Akha village on the northern slopes of Doi Mae Salong. The troops sealed off the village and abducted several villagers including the headman. The conflict had to do with opium-smuggling routes in the area. SUA and Wa National Army forces are competing for control over this section of the Thai-Burmese border and occasionally clash in the area.

The Mae Salong Guest House arranges six-hour horseback treks to four nearby villages for 400B, including lunch.

It is possible to walk south from Mae Salong to Chiang Rai in three or four days, following trails which pass through fairly remote hill-tribe villages. There are also several easily reached hill-tribe villages along the highway between Basang and Mae Salong, but these days they're full of day tourists from Chiang Rai.

If you're hiking to Chiang Rai from Doi Mae Salong, you could stop off in Ban Hin Fon and stay at *Laan Tong Lodge* (☎ 771366 in Mae Chan), which is about 13 km west of Mae Chan and has huts for 30B per person. Otherwise you can reach it by taking a songthaew from Mae Chan to the village (10B) and then hiking the three km to the lodge. One of the activities here is tubing along the Mae Chan River. Laan Tong can also arrange treks.

Places to Stay

The *Mae Salong Guest House* is at the high end of town and the Yunnanese couple who run it are very friendly. Clean rooms with shared hot shower are 80B, 100B with private bath. Yunnanese food is served, and several varieties of local fruit spirits, Mae Salong tea and Chinese herbal medicines are also available. The owners can arrange treks on horseback or advise you on making treks on your own. To reach the guesthouse you must pass through the gateway to Mae Salong Resort or through the Shin Sane Guest House.

Shin Sane (Sin Sae) Guest House, Mae Salong's original hotel, is a wooden Chinese affair with a bit more atmosphere than the Mae Salong Guest House. Basic rooms are 50B per person. Information on trekking is available; there is also a nice little eating area and a place for doing laundry. Further along this road is the *Rainbow Guest House* which is nothing special at 50B per person, but the family that run it are friendly.

At the top of the price range is the *Mae Salong Resort* (☎ 714047; 513-9024 in Bangkok) where rooms start at 2000B. Midweek discounts are available. The Yunnanese restaurant here is very good – especially tasty are the fresh mushroom dishes.

Mae Salong Villa (☎ 713444) just below the town centre has bungalow-style accommodation from 500 to 1000B.

Three km from Basang on the road to Mae Salong is a turn-off to *Winnipa Lodge* (☎ 712225) on a hillside overlooking the road. Bungalows are 300 to 1000B; there is also tent accommodation available for 100B a night. From here you can see Doi Tung in the distance.

Places to Eat

Don't miss the many street noodle vendors who sell khanõm jiin náam ngíaw, a delicious Yunnanese rice-noodle concoction topped with spicy chicken curry – Mae Salong's most famous local dish and a gourmet bargain at 5B per bowl.

Around town you'll find a variety of places serving simple Chinese snacks like fluffy mantou (plain steamed Chinese buns) and salabao (pork-stuffed Chinese buns) with delicious pickled vegetables. Many of the Chinese in Santikhiri are Muslims, so you'll find several Chinese-Muslim restaurants serving khâo sòi (curried chicken and noodles).

Getting There & Away

To get to Mae Salong by public transport, take a bus from Mae Sai or Chiang Rai to Ban Basang, which is about two km north of Mae Chan. From Ban Basang, there are songthaews up the mountain to Mae Salong for 40B per person (down again costs 30B). The trip takes about an hour. The bus fare from Chiang Rai to Ban Basang is 10B.

You can also reach Mae Salong by road from Tha Ton. See the earlier Fang & Tha Ton section for details.

MAE SAI

แม่สาย

The northernmost point in Thailand, Mae Sai is a good place from which to explore the Golden Triangle, Doi Tung and Mae Salong. It's also a spot to observe border life, as Mae Sai is one of only two official land crossings open between Burma and Thailand (the other is Three Pagodas Pass). Only Burmese and Thai nationals are allowed to cross the bridge which spans the Sai River border, although there is talk of allowing foreigners to cross the border for the day in the near future. Burmese authorities are sprucing up Thachilek (the town opposite Mae Sai, also spelt Thakhilek) in preparation. Eventually, say local authorities, a paved road will proceed from Thachilek to Chiang Tung (Kengtung) and from there to the Chinese border.

Burmese lacquerware, gems, jade and other goods from Laos and Burma are sold in shops along the main street in Mae Sai, although the trade is mainly a tourist scene now. Many Burmese come over during the day from Thachilek to work or do business, hurrying back by sunset.

Take the steps up the hill near the border to **Wat Phra That Doi Wao**, west of the main street, for superb views over Burma and Mae Sai. There are also some interesting trails in the cliffs and hills overlooking the Mae Sai Guest House and the river.

Motorcycle trekking in the area is quite good due to plenty of challenging back roads and trails. Chad Guest House in Mae Sai has good information on motorcycle treks.

Mai Sai is a base for exploring the nearby caves of Tham Luang (Great Cave), Tham Pum, and Tham Pla, as well as the trip to Doi Tung (see Around Mai Sai).

Places to Stay

Guesthouses Near the town entrance and the bus terminal is *Chad House*, off the main street a bit in a residential neighbourhood. The Thai-Shan family that run it are friendly and helpful, and the food is particularly good. There's a garden with tables for evening repasts and a talking *nók wiang phao* bird from Burma that speaks the Shan dialect. Chad has a few motorcycles for rent and has a wealth of information on motorcycle trekking in the area. Chad himself leads small motorcycle treks on little-known trails, having travelled back and forth between Mae Sai and Shan State for several years. Rooms are 80B with shared bath. There are a couple of more expensive bungalows with private bath, and a 10-bed dorm for 40B per person. A hot-water shower is available.

Mae Sai Guest House (☎ 732021) is often full due to its scenic and restful location on the river across from Burma. It's about a km walk from the end of Mae Sai's main road and thus very quiet. Bungalows cost from 40 to 50B a single, 70 to 90B a double; rooms with private bath are 120B. A hot shower is available, there's a good restaurant, motorcycles are for rent and treks can be arranged. The only drawback is that it's a long dark walk into town if you want to eat out or stroll the main drag at night.

Closer to town and just back from the river is *Mae Sai Plaza Guest House* (☎ 732230). This huge hillside bamboo and wood complex has a laid-back atmosphere and a cafe overlooking the road – good for people-watching. Singles/doubles with shared bath cost from 50/80B to 60/100B, doubles with private bath are 120B and there are larger rooms at 200B with hot bath; most rooms have a view of the river. Between Mae Sai Plaza and Mae Sai Guest House, next to the river landing for local Thai-Burmese trade, is the relatively new *Sai Riverside*. Nice, secure rooms are 120B with fan and private bath, 200B with hot water.

Also on the river is *Northern Guest House* (☎ 731537) where a variety of rooms and huts are available from 60B for a basic double with shared bath, or you can pay up to 200B for a double with hot shower. It has places to sit along the river.

Piya Phon Guest House, in the market area, costs 100 to 200B for a concrete cell used mostly for short-time business. West of the market area off the back road to Doi Tung are the newer *Tom* (60 to 100B for quiet rooms; motorcycles for rent) and *Doi Wao* (fancier bungalows on a hillside for 100 to 200B).

Hotels *Mae Sai Hotel* (☎ 721462), off Phahonyothin Rd in the centre of town, isn't a bad budget choice. Singles/doubles with fan and private bath are 100/150B, air-con rooms with hot bath are 280B.

Sin Wattana (☎ 731950) is on the same side of Phahonyothin Rd across from the market; fairly well-kept rooms cost from 120B. A few rooms without bath are also available for under 100B.

Top North Hotel (☎ 731955), further up Phahonyothin Rd on the opposite side, has comfortable singles/doubles for 250B, 450B with air-con. All rooms have private hot-water showers. The new *Leo Hotel* (☎ 732064), opposite the bus terminal, has rooms for 480B including air-con, hot water, TV and fridge – good mid-range value.

Tai Tong (Thai Thong) Hotel (☎ 731975) at 6 Phahonyothin Rd has standard rooms at 500B, and somewhat larger rooms for 600B.

All come with air-con and hot water, but considering the rooms, these rates are perhaps a tad high.

The nine-storey, 150-room *Wang Thong Hotel* was under construction in the centre of town as we went to press. Rates at this tourist-oriented luxury hotel will probably be in the 800 to 1500B range.

Places to Eat

The night market is rather small but the Chinese vendors do excellent kũaytĩaw phàt sĩi-yúu (rice noodles stir-fried in soy sauce) and other noodle dishes. You can also get fresh paa-thông-kõ (Chinese doughnuts) and hot soy milk.

Jojo Coffeeshop on Phahonyothin Rd serves very good Thai curries and Thai vegetarian dishes, plus ice cream and Western snacks. You'll eat well while contemplating the collection of Lanna-style wooden Buddhas along the walls. Down near the bridge on the river is a floating restaurant that's OK.

The Frontier Saloon, down near the Chad Guest House, is still the 'in' night spot where draft beer and Maekhong whisky are served in an old-west setting.

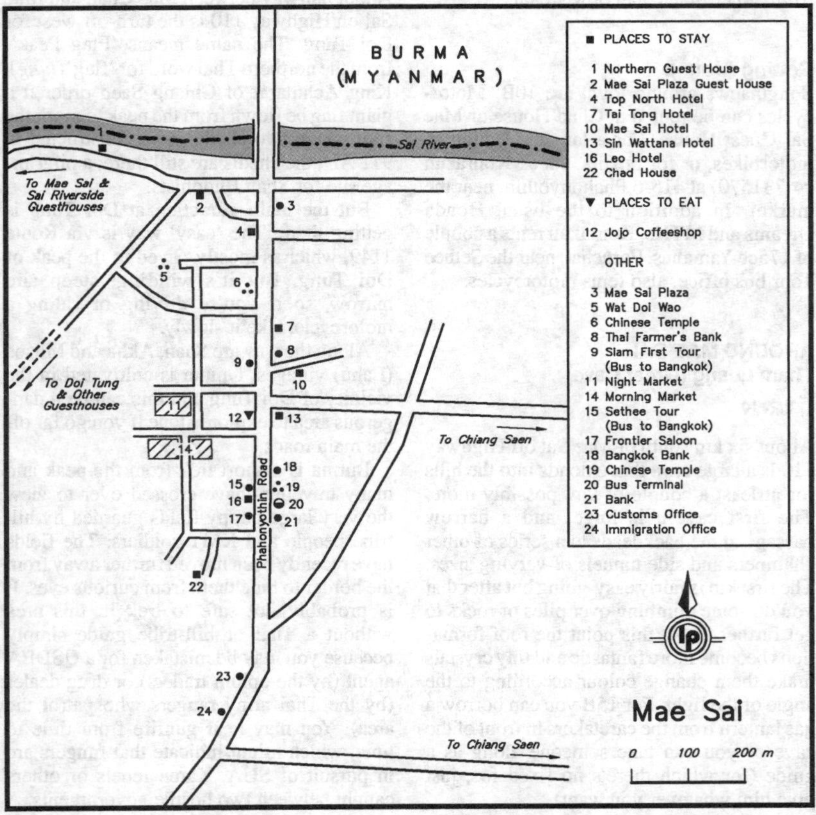

Getting There & Away

Buses to Mae Sai leave frequently from Chiang Rai and cost 15B for the 1½-hour trip. From Chiang Saen by bus costs 14B via Mae Chan. (See Getting There & Away in the Chiang Saen section for details on different routes between Mae Sai and Chiang Saen.)

Sethee Tour and Siam First Tour each have VIP 'sleeper' buses from Mae Sai to Bangkok that leave at about 5.30 or 6 pm daily for 445B; the journey takes between 13 and 14 hours. Ordinary buses to Bangkok cost 159B (air-con 305B) and take 16 to 18 hours.

Buses to the turn-off for Doi Tung are 7B from either Mae Chan or Mae Sai.

Getting Around

Songthaews around town are 10B. Motorcycles can be rented at Chad House or Mae Sai Guest House. For a larger selection of motorbikes, or for repairs, check Konrakan (☎ 731570) at 415-6 Phahonyothin, near the market. In addition to the usual Honda Dreams and MTXs, Konrakan rents a couple of 175cc Yamahas. Pornchai, near the Sethee Tour bus office, also rents motorcycles.

AROUND MAE SAI

Tham Luang (Great Cave)

ถ้ำหลวง

About six km south of Mae Sai off Highway 110 is a large cave that extends into the hills for at least a couple of km, possibly more. The first cavern is huge, and a narrow passage at the back leads to a series of other chambers and side tunnels of varying sizes. The first km is fairly easy-going but after that you do some climbing over piles of rocks to get further in. At this point the roof formations become more fantastic and tiny crystals make them change colour according to the angle of the light. For 15B you can borrow a gas lantern from the caretakers in front of the cave or you can take someone along as a guide (for which there's no fixed fee; just give him whatever you want).

Tham Pum/Tham Pla

ถ้ำปุ่มและถ้ำปลา

Only 13 km south of Mae Sai, just off Highway 110 at Ban Tham, are a couple of caves with freshwater lakes inside. Bring a torch to explore the caves as there are no lights. The real attraction here, though, is the unique Khmer-style chedi in front of the cave entrance. It's a very large, multi-tiered structure that is unlike any other in Thailand.

Doi Tung

ดอยตุง

About halfway between Mae Chan and Mae Sai on Highway 110 is the turn-off west for Doi Tung. The name means 'Flag Peak', from the northern Thai word for 'flag' *(tung)*. King Achutarat of Chiang Saen ordered a giant flag be flown from the peak to mark the spot where two chedis were constructed in 911 AD; the chedis are still there, a pilgrimage site for Shan Buddhists.

But the main attraction at Doi Tung is getting there. The 'easy' way is via Route 1149, which is mostly paved to the peak of Doi Tung. But it's winding, steep and narrow, so if you're driving or riding a motorcycle, take it slowly.

Along the way are Shan, Akha and Musoe (Lahu) villages. Opium is cultivated in the vicinity of Doi Tung and this can be a dangerous area to explore alone if you go far off the main roads.

Burma is a short trek from the peak and many travellers have crossed over to view the very large poppy fields guarded by hill tribespeople and KMT soldiers. The fields have recently been moved further away from the border to hide them from curious eyes. It is probably not safe to trek in this area without a Thai or hill-tribe guide simply because you may be mistaken for a USDEA agent (by the opium traders) or drug dealer (by the Thai army rangers who patrol the area). You may hear gunfire from time to time, which might indicate that rangers are in pursuit of SUA, Karen rebels or others caught between two hostile governments. A few years ago a lone farang motorcyclist was shot and killed near the Burmese fields. Since then the villagers have moved the poppy fields back three km from the border.

At the peak, 1800 metres above sea level, is **Wat Phra That Doi Tung**, which is nothing special as wats go, but you can't beat the setting. From here you can get an aerial view of the snaky road you have just climbed. The TAT has plans to build a tourist information centre on Route 1149 about three km before the peak.

You can also travel by motorcycle between Doi Tung and Mae Sai along a challenging 15-km dirt track that starts in the Akha village of Ban Phami, eight km south of Mae Sai (four km south along Highway 110, then four km west), and ends about two-thirds of the way up Doi Tung. You can also pick this road up by following the dirt road that starts in front of Mae Sai's Wat Doi Wao. This route has lots of tight curves, mud, rocks, precipitous drops, passing lorries and bulldozers – figure on two to 2½ hours by motorbike from Mae Sai. Eventually this road will be paved but for now it's a road for experienced bikers only. The road also runs high in the mountains along the Burmese border and should not be travelled alone. Ask first in Mae Sai about border conditions.

Places to Stay Out on Route 1149, the road to Doi Tung, is the *Akha Guest House* in the Akha village of Ban Pakha. This is the place to stay if you want to trek in the Doi Tung area. There is no electricity or running water and the food is not that good, but there are nice views of the valley below. Bungalows are 50B per night and guides can be hired for as little as 50B per person for a day trek.

About three to four hours' walk south-west of Ban Pakha is *Chiang Rai Mountain Guest House* on the Mae Kham River near Samakhi Mai village, from where you can trek to Mae Salong.

Getting There & Away From Ban Huay Khrai, at the Doi Tung turn-off, a songthaew to the Akha Guest House at Ban Pakha is 10B or 30B all the way to Doi Tung, 18 km away. The road to Doi Tung has seriously deteriorated above Pakha in the last few years and this section is becoming more of a challenge to climb, whether you're in a truck, jeep or motorcycle. Meanwhile, the Highway Department is busy building a new road parallel to, but several km away from, the present one.

CHIANG SAEN
เชียงแสน

A little more than 60 km from Chiang Rai, Chiang Saen is a small crossroads town on the banks of the Maekhong River. Scattered throughout the town are the ruins of the Chiang Saen kingdom, founded in 1325, including chedis, images of the Buddha and earthen city ramparts. A few of the old monuments still standing predate Chiang Saen by a couple of hundred years.

The sleepy town hasn't changed much in spite of 'Golden Triangle' commercialisation, which is concentrated in nearby Sop Ruak. Practically everything in Chiang Saen closes down by 9 pm.

Bicycles can be rented at the guesthouses in town for interesting side trips in the vicinity.

National Museum
พิพิธภัณฑ์แห่งชาติ

Near the town entrance, a small national museum displays artefacts from the Lanna period as well as prehistoric stone tools from the area, and hill-tribe crafts, dress and musical instruments. It's open Wednesday to Sunday from 9 am to 4 pm and admission is 10B. The archaeological station behind the museum has a large, detailed wall map of Chiang Saen and the surrounding area.

Wat Chedi Luang
วัดเจดีย์หลวง

Behind the museum to the east, this wat has a remarkable eight-sided chedi. It's 58 metres tall and was built in the 12th century.

Wat Pa Sak
วัดป่าสัก

About 200 metres from the Chiang Saen Gate are the remains of Wat Pa Sak, which is undergoing restoration by the Fine Arts Department. The ruins of seven monuments are visible. The main mid-14th century stupa combines elements of the Hariphunchai and Sukhothai styles with a possible pagan Burmese influence. Since these ruins are a historical park, there is a 20B admission fee.

Wat Phra That Chom Kitti
วัดพระธาตุจอมกิตติ

About 2.5 km north of Wat Pa Sak on a hilltop are the remains of Wat Phra That Chom Kitti and Wat Chom Chang. The round chedi of Wat Phra That is thought to have been constructed before the founding of the kingdom. The smaller chedi below it belonged to Wat Chom Chang. These chedis aren't really much to see, but there's a good view of Chiang Saen and the river from the top of the hill.

The Lao side of the mighty Maekhong looks deserted, but Lao boats flying Pathet Lao flags do occasionally float by. Hill-tribe crafts can be bought in a few shops along the river. Some of the townspeople, Lao immigrants, speak French.

Places to Stay

Most budget travellers stay in Chiang Saen these days. The *Chiang Saen Guest House* is the cheapest, with small singles/doubles for 30/50B, and larger rooms with private bath for 80/100B. It's on the road to Sop Ruak, opposite the river.

A bit further along this road on the same side is the newer *Siam Guest House*. Singles/doubles in huts with mosquito nets cost 50/60B without bath, 70/80B with one. This guesthouse also has a pleasant cafe, and rents out bicycles and motorcycles.

Further north on the edge of town (about 1.5 km from the bus terminal) is the secluded *Gin Guest House* with a variety of overnight possibilities. Rooms in the main house cost 200 to 500B with private hot bath, 100B without; dorm beds are 40B. Bamboo huts behind the house are 60/80B for singles/doubles; nicer bungalows are 200/300B. Gin lends bicycles for up to an hour at no charge; after that they're 15B per half day, 30B the whole day.

Inside the town is the *Suree Guest House* (☎ 714762), about 100 metres off the main road near the post office. A big house run by friendly folk, the cost is 50B a double with shared bath, 80/100B for singles/doubles with private bath.

If all these places are full, the only other choice is the *Poonsuk Hotel*, a ramshackle building near the end of Chiang Saen's main street, towards the river. Double rooms are from 40 to 70B, and mosquito nets are provided.

About five km out of town near Chiang Saen Lake, *Yonok* (a garden restaurant) has a few 500B bungalows with fridge and hot showers.

Places to Eat

The long-standing *Sala Thai Restaurant* overlooks the Maekhong River and is still the best eating place in Chiang Saen. Two special dishes worth trying that are not on English menu are yam kài, a fiery soup with chicken, fresh mushrooms and plenty of lemon grass and lime leaves, and thúa lantao phát kûng, prawns stir-fried with snow peas.

Cheap eats are available in and near the market on the river road.

Yonok, a good garden restaurant five km out of town towards Mae Chan, is one km off the highway next to Chiang Saen Lake. The kitchen specialises in freshwater fish – try the plaa nin thâwt (fresh fried Nile fish). There's no English menu, so bring your eating guide if your Thai isn't up to it.

Getting There & Away

There are frequent buses from Chiang Rai to Chiang Saen for 15B. The trip takes between 40 minutes and 1½ hours.

Returning from Chiang Saen, don't take a Chiang Mai bus (out of Chiang Saen directly) unless you want to travel along the old road (sãi kào). The old road passes through Pham, Phayao, Ngao, Lampang and Lamphun before arriving in Chiang Mai, a trip that takes from seven to nine hours. To take the new road (sãi mài), first go to Chiang Rai (on a Chiang Rai bus of course) then change to a Chiang Mai bus, a trip of about 4½ hours.

Getting Around

A good way to see the Chiang Saen-Mae Sai area is on two wheels – bicycles and motorcycles can be rented in either town, though there's usually a better choice of machines in Mae Sai.

From Mae Sai to Chiang Saen there's a choice of two partly paved roads (one from the centre of Mae Sai and one near the town entrance – see the Mae Sai map), or a fully paved road via Highway 110 to Mae Chan and then Route 1016 to Chiang Saen.

The roads out of Mae Sai are considerably more direct but there are several forks where you have to make educated guesses on which way to go (there are occasional signs). The two roads join near the village of Mae Ma where you have a choice of going east through Sop Ruak or south through Pa Thon. The eastern route is more scenic.

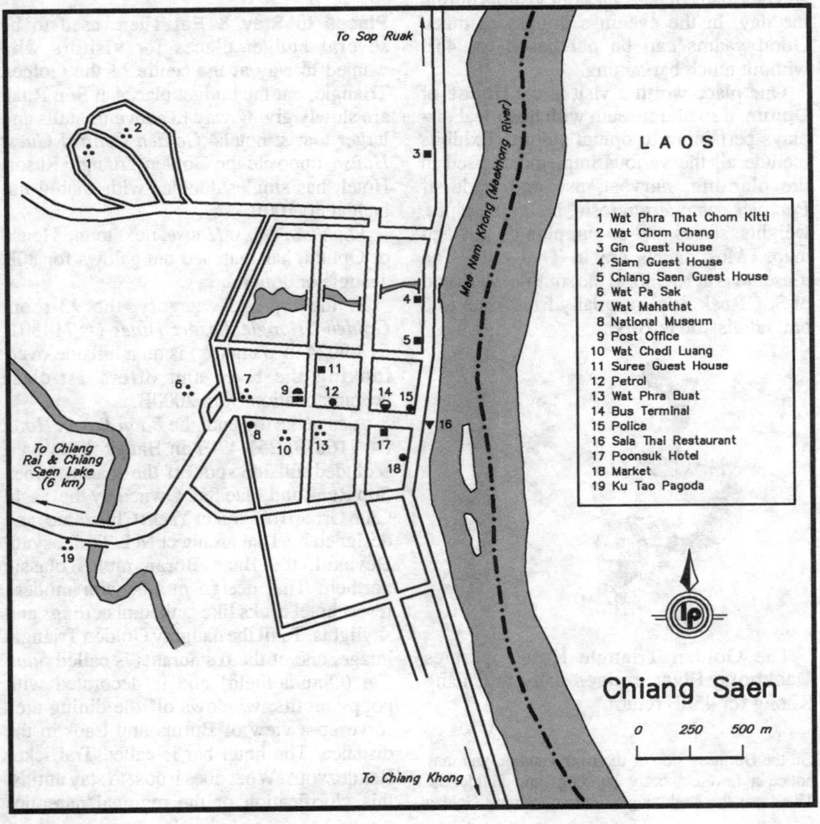

AROUND CHIANG SAEN

Sop Ruak

สบรวก

Fourteen km north of Chiang Saen is Sop Ruak, the official centre of the Golden Triangle. This is where the borders of Burma, Thailand and Laos meet, at the confluence of the Ruak and Maekhong rivers. In historical terms, 'Golden Triangle' actually refers to a much larger area, stretching thousands of sq km into Burma, Laos and Thailand, within which the opium trade is prevalent.

Sop Ruak has become something of a tourist trap, with souvenir stalls, restaurants and bus loads of package-tour visitors during the day. In the evenings things are quiet. Good yaams can be purchased for 45B without much bargaining.

One place worth a visit is the **House of Opium**, a small museum with historical displays pertaining to opium culture. Exhibits include all the various implements used in the planting, harvest, use and trade of *Papaver somniferum* resin, including pipes, weights, scales and so on, plus photos and maps. Most labels are in Thai only. The museum is at Km 30, at the south-eastern end of Sop Ruak. It's open daily from 7 am to 6 pm; admission is 10B.

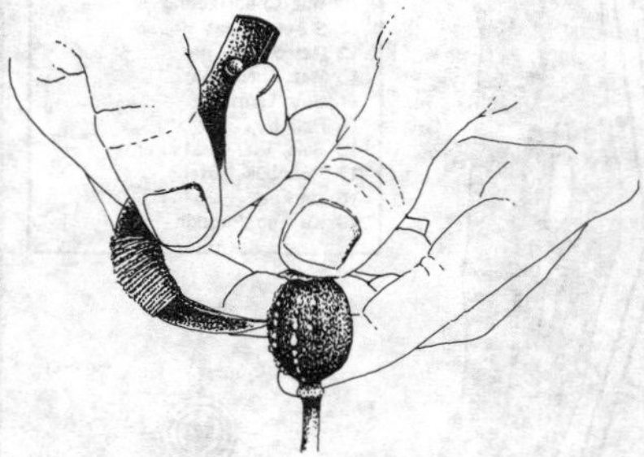

The Golden Triangle Hotel operates **Maekhong River cruises** daily to Chiang Khong for 450B return.

On the Burmese side of the river junction you may notice a few temporary buildings and bulldozers. These are the beginnings of the upcoming Golden Triangle Paradise Resort, a huge hotel-and-trade project financed by a wealthy Thai businessman from Suphanburi who has leased nearly 3000 rai from the Burmese government. The site has become the man's private fiefdom – no-one enters or leaves the area without his permission (visas are superfluous).

In addition to 300 hotel rooms and a trade centre, plans for the complex include an 18-hole golf course, helipad, hospital and hovercraft pier. Rumours persist that the hotel will eventually add a casino, which will not only draw business from Thailand, Laos and Burma but will also play host to visiting riverboats from China. Ironically, the proposed casino is supposedly backed by Macau gambling kingpins who are worried about the return of the Portuguese colonial enclave to China in 1999. Only two currencies – baht and dollars – will be accepted at the hotel.

Places to Stay & Eat There used to be several budget places for visitors who wanted to stay at the centre of the Golden Triangle, but the budget places at Sop Ruak are slowly giving way to souvenir stalls and larger tourist hotels. *Golden Central Guest House*, opposite the Golden Triangle Resort Hotel, has singles/doubles with shared hot bath at 80/100B.

Phukham Guest House, next to the House of Opium, has thatched bungalows for 80B a single or double.

In the top-end category, the 73-room *Golden Triangle Resort Hotel* (☎ 714801; 513-9024 in Bangkok) is on a hillside overlooking the river and offers 1st-class accommodation from 2000B.

Also at the top end, the *Baan Boran Hotel* (☎ 716678; 251-4707 in Bangkok) is on a secluded hillside spot off the road between Sop Ruak and Mae Sai. Owned by the Yacht Club Group (of Phuket Yacht Club fame) and designed by Thai architect M L Tridhosyuth Devakul, the Baan Boran melds classic northern Thai design motifs with modern resort hotel tricks like cathedral ceilings and skylights. To fit the naughty Golden Triangle image, one of the restaurants is called *Suan Fin* (Opium Field) and is decorated with poppy motifs; windows off the dining area serve up a view of Burma and Laos in the distance. The hotel bar is called Trafficker Rendezvous. What does it cost to stay amidst this glorification of the regional narcotics trade? Singles are 2400B, doubles 2700B, and one-bedroom suites 5500B.

Getting There & Away From Chiang Saen to Sop Ruak, a songthaew/share taxi costs 10B; these leave several times a day.

The road between Mae Sai and Sop Ruak is slowly being paved. When last I travelled this road it was a mess – part mud, part paved, and very slow going due to the presence of road construction vehicles. Once the paving is completed it should be a breeze.

Chiang Khong
เชียงของ

Across the river from Ban Huay (Houei) Sai in Laos, this used to be the place where you began or finished the old 'Laotian Loop'. More remote yet more lively than Chiang Saen, Chiang Khong is an important market town for local hill tribes and for trade – legal and illegal – with northern Laos.

Chiang Khong has several northern-style wats of minor interest. **Wat Luang**, on the main road, was once one of the most important temples in Chiang Rai Province and features a chedi dating to the 13th century (restored in 1881).

The village of **Ban Hat Khrai**, about a km south of Chiang Khong, is famous as being one of the few places where *plaa bèuk* (giant Maekhong catfish) are still caught.

On occasion, farangs have been permitted to cross into Laos by ferry for the day; eventually the Lao government may make Ban Huay Sai an official point of entry.

Places to Stay & Eat *Fang Khong Hotel* (☎ 791063) is on the main road in the centre of town and has adequate rooms with fan and shower for 150B, better rooms with air-con and hot-water shower for 350B. The friendly *Damrong Phunsuk* (☎ 791036) nearby has very basic rooms for 70 to 100B with shared bath.

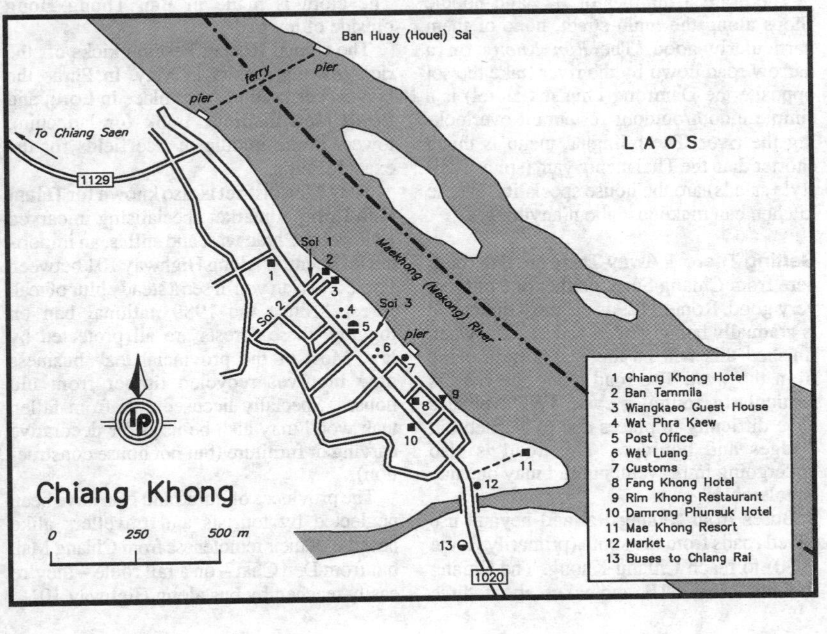

There are two guesthouses at the northern end of town in a neighbourhood called Ban Wiang Kaew. The *Wiangkaeo Guest House* (☎ 791140) is an old house with a terrace overlooking the river and Ban Huay Sai. Clean rooms are 100B with shared bath, 250B with breakfast and bath; if the latter deal seems a bit steep, you might try asking for a room without breakfast. *Ban Tammila (Riverside)* (☎ 791234), just north of the Wiangkaeo Guest House, has rooms in a new, wooden hotel-like building for 100B with shared bath, 150B with hot-water shower. The owners have a restaurant across the street with very good Thai food.

Further north and toward the river road from Chiang Saen is the *Chiang Khong Hotel* (☎ 791182). Plain but nicely kept singles/doubles with hot shower and fan are 120/150B.

Out of town on the river and toward the bus terminal, the *Mae Khong Resort* has up-market bungalows for 250B with fan and bath, 500B with air-con.

There are a number of rice and noodle shops along the main street, none of them particularly good. The *Rim Khong* on a narrow road down by the river (take the soi opposite the Damrong Phunsuk Hotel) is a simple indoor/outdoor restaurant overlooking the river. The bilingual menu is much shorter than the Thai menu; yam (spicy Thai-style salads) are the house speciality, but the kitchen can make just about anything.

Getting There & Away There are two roads here from Chiang Saen, neither one of them very good. Route 1129 is the most direct and is gradually being graded and paved – when finished this will be the best way to come from the west. The road along the river is particularly rough – even 4WD vehicles have difficulty in places due to washed-out bridges and boulders. This road is also undergoing improvements and may one day be tolerable.

Buses from Chiang Rai and beyond use paved roads from the south (primarily Route 1020) to reach Chiang Khong. The Chiang Rai bus costs 31B and takes about three hours. Air-con buses to/from Bangkok cost 320B and take around 13 hours.

Boats taking up to 10 passengers can be chartered up the Maekhong River from Chiang Khong to Chiang Saen for 800B. Boat crews can be contacted near the customs pier behind Wat Luang, or farther north at the pier for ferries to Laos.

Ferries across to Ban Huay Sai in Laos leave frequently from the ferry pier at the northern end of town for 20B each way.

Phrae Province

Phrae Province is probably most famous for the distinctive sêua mâw hâwm, the indigo-dyed cotton farmer's shirt seen all over Thailand. 'Made in Phrae' has always been a sign of distinction for these staples of rural Thai life and since the student-worker-farmer political solidarity of the 1970s, even Thai university professors like to wear them. The cloth is made in Ban Thung Hong outside of town.

The annual Rocket Festival kicks off the rice-growing season in May. In Phrae the biggest celebrations take place in **Long** and **Sung Men** districts. Look for launching towers in the middle of rice fields for the exact location.

Sung Men district is also known for **Talaat Hua Dong**, a market specialising in carved teak wood. Phrae was, and still is, an important teak centre. Along Highway 101 between Phrae and Nan you'll see a steady blur of teak forests. Since the 1989 national ban on logging, these forests are all protected by law. Most of the provincial teak business now involves recycled timber from old houses. Specially licensed cuts from fallen teak wood may also be used for decorative carving or furniture (but not house construction).

The provinces of Phrae and Nan have been neglected by tourists and travellers alike because of their remoteness from Chiang Mai, but from Den Chai – on a rail route – they're easily reached by bus along Highway 101.

PHRAE

อ.เมืองแพร่

This provincial capital (population 21,000) is only 23 km from the Den Chai railway station on the Chiang Mai line. Like Chiang Mai and Lampang, Phrae has an old city surrounded by a moat alongside a river (here, the Yom River). Unlike Chiang Mai, Phrae's old city still has lots of quiet lanes and old teak houses – if you're a fan of traditional Thai teak architecture, you'll find more of it here than in any other city of similar size anywhere in Thailand. The local temple architecture has successfully resisted central Thai influence over the centuries as well. It's a bit unusual since you'll find a mix of Burmese, northern Thai (Nan and Lanna) and Lao styles.

South-east of the old city, the newer, more modern Phrae looks like any other medium-sized town in Thailand.

Wat Luang

วัดหลวง

This is the oldest wat in the city, probably dating to the founding of the city in the 12th or 13th centuries. **Phra That Luang Chang Kham**, the large octagonal Lanna-style chedi, sits on a square base with elephants coming out of all four sides, surrounded by kutis and coconut palms. As is sometimes seen in Phrae and Nan, the chedi is swathed in Thai Lü silk.

The verandah of the main wihaan is in the classic Luang Prabang-Lan Xang style but has unfortunately been bricked in with laterite. Opposite the front of the wihaan is **Pratu Khong**, part of the city's original entrance gate. No longer used as a gate, it now contains a statue of Jao Pu, an early Lanna ruler. The image is very sacred to local residents, who leave offerings of fruit, flowers, candles and incense.

Also on the wat grounds is a museum displaying temple antiques, ceramics and religious art from the Lanna, Nan, Pegu and Mon periods. A 16th-century, Phrae-made sitting Buddha on the 2nd floor is particularly exquisite. There are also some 19th-century photos with English labels on display, including some gruesome shots of a beheading.

Wat Phra Non

วัดพระนอน

South-west a few hundred metres from Wat Luang is a 300-year-old wat named for its highly revered reclining Buddha image. The bot was built around 200 years ago and has a very impressive three-tiered roof with a separate two-tiered portico and gilded carved wooden facade with *Ramayana* scenes. The wihaan behind the bot contains the Phra Non (a reclining Buddha), swathed in Thai Lü cloth with bead and foil decoration.

Wat Jom Sawan

วัดจอมสวรรค์

Outside the old city on Ban Mai Rd, this temple was built by local Shans early this century, and shows Shan and Burmese influence throughout. The well-preserved wooden wihaans and bot have high, tiered, tower-like roofs like those found in Mandalay. A large copper-crowned chedi has lost most of its stucco to reveal the artful brickwork beneath. A prized temple possession in the main wihaan is a tripitaka (Buddhist scriptures) section consisting of 16 ivory pages engraved in Burmese. As in Lampang, temples like this were originally sponsored by Burmese teak merchants who immigrated to northern Thailand at the turn of the century.

Other Temples

Wat Sa Baw Kaew, just outside the north-eastern corner of the moat, is a Shan-Burmese-style temple similar to Wat Jom Sawan. **Wat Phra Ruang**, inside the old city, is typical of Phrae's many old city wats, with a Nan-style, cruciform-plan bot, a Lao-style wihaan and a Lanna chedi.

One day an art historian is going to have to sort out this temple mix – I suspect there's

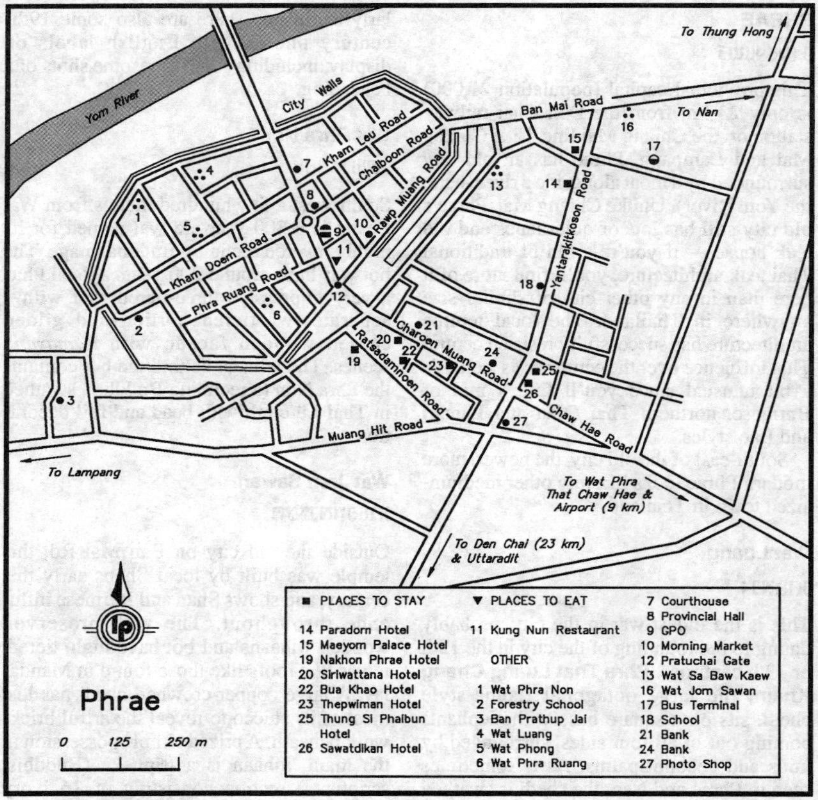

a uniform design of local (Nan-Phrae) provenance that hasn't yet been identified.

Ban Prathup Jai (Prathapjai)

บ้านประทับใจ

You can see lots of good woodcarving in Phrae. On the western outskirts of town is Ban Prathup Jai (Impressive House), also called Ban Sao Roi Tan (Hundred Pillar-Filled House), a large northern-style teak house which was built using more than 130 teak logs, each over 3000 years old. Opened in 1985, the house took four years to build, using timber taken from nine old rural houses. The interior pillars are ornately carved.

Places to Stay

Several inexpensive hotels can be found along Charoen Muang Rd, including *Ho Fa*, *Siriwattana* and *Thepwiman*, all of which have rooms for around 100B; Thepwiman is the best of the bunch.

The friendly *Thung Si Phaibun* (☎ 511011), at 84 Yantarakitkoson Rd, has clean rooms with fan and bath for 90 to 130B, air-con for just 200B. *Sawatdikan* at

No 76-8 is similar to the Thung Si Phaibun but not as well kept; rooms start at 70B.

Nakhon Phrae Hotel (☎ 511969) at 29 Ratsadamnoen Rd is a short walk from the old city. Large singles/doubles with fan and hot water cost 250B in the old wing; across the street in the new wing standard air-con rooms are 350B or 500B with TV and fridge. Local tourist information is available in the lobbies of both wings.

Boukawe (Bua Khao) Hotel (☎ 511372), at 8/1 Soi 1 Ratsadamnoen Rd, has fan rooms for 70B, air-con for 160B – it's mostly a brothel, however, with girls haunting the doorways. The only hotel in the old city, *Neramit* on Wichairacha Rd, is also a brothel, quoting 60B rate for short-time use, 120B for an all-night stay.

Paradorn (Pharadon) (☎ 511177), at 177 Yantarakitkoson Rd, has moderately priced singles/doubles with fan and bath for 140/160B, air-con rooms from 350B. Information on local attractions is available in the lobby. At the top of the scale in Phrae is the *Maeyom Palace Hotel* (☎ 522906; fax 522904) on Yantarakitkoson Rd a hundred metres north-east of the Paradorn. Rooms with air-con, carpet, TV, phone and fridge cost from 1000 to 1200B. Hotel facilities include a pool and two restaurants; the hotel also provides free transport to/from the bus terminal and airport.

A new luxury hotel, *Nakhon Phrae Tower*, is under construction on Muang Hit Rd – to be completed by 1993.

For much of 1991 you could stay at a comfortable branch of Sukhothai's No 4 Guest House in Phrae. Alas, a lack of paying guests forced the house to close down before we went to press. If Phrae tourism picks ups, perhaps it will re-open.

Places to Eat

Yantarakitkoson Rd, the main road through Phrae's modern half, is dotted with small restaurants. *Ban Fai*, a large indoor/outdoor restaurant catering to Thai tourists, is at the southern end of Yantarakitkoson. Attached to the restaurant are a folklore museum and craft shop; there's even an auto service so you can have your car worked on while you eat! The menu is Thai-Chinese-farang, with a few northern-Thai dishes, too. Prices are moderately high.

Phrae Phochana on Ratsadamnoen Rd near the Phrae Hotel has good standard Thai food and is inexpensive. Inside the old city near the Pratuchai intersection (Charoen Muang and Rawp Muang Rd), the humble *Kung Nun* serves excellent curry and rice dishes. There's no English sign – it's directly opposite a shop selling maw hawm clothes.

A good night market convenes just outside the Pratuchai intersection every evening. There's another night market behind the Paradorn Hotel on weekday evenings only.

Getting There & Away

Bus Ordinary buses from Bangkok's northern bus terminal depart hourly between 5 and 9.30 pm (120B). Air-con buses cost 213B and leave at 8.30 and 8.50 pm; VIP (sleeper) buses cost 395B and leave at 8.30 and 9 pm.

From Chiang Mai's Arcade bus station, ordinary buses leave at 8 and 11 am, and 3 and 5 pm (49B, four hours). An air-con bus leaves from the same station at 10 am and 10 pm (74B). From Sukhothai, ordinary buses are 40B, air-con 55B.

Train Trains to Den Chai railway station from Bangkok are 90B 3rd class, 188B 2nd class or 389B 1st class, plus supplementary charges as they apply. The only trains that arrive at a decent hour are the No 101 ordinary (3rd class only, departs Bangkok at 7.05 am and arrives in Den Chai at 5.50 pm); the No 901 special express (1st and 2nd class only, leaves at 8.10 am and arrives at 3.08 pm); and the No 59 rapid (2nd class only, leaves at 10 pm and arrives at 7.14 am). On the No 59 you can get a 2nd-class sleeper.

Buses and songthaews leave Den Chai frequently for Phrae and cost 10B.

AROUND PHRAE PROVINCE

Wat Phra That Chaw Hae

วัดพระธาตุช่อแฮ

On a hill about nine km south-east of town

off Route 1022, this wat is famous for its 33-metre-high gilded chedi. Chaw Hae is the name of the cloth that worshippers wrap around the chedi – it's a type of satin said to have originated in Xishuangbanna (Sipsongpanna, literally '12,000 fields' in northern Thai). Like Chiang Mai's Wat Doi Suthep, this is an important pilgrimage site for northern Thais. The **Phra Jao Than Jai** Buddha image here – similar in appearance to Phra Jinnarat in Phitsanulok – is reputed to impart fertility to women who make offerings to it.

The bot has a gilded wooden ceiling, rococo pillars and walls with lotus-bud mosaics. The temple is approached by tiered naga stairs; the hilltop is surrounded by mature teak trees, protected from cutting because they are on monastic grounds.

Songthaews between the city and Phra That Chaw Hae are frequent and cost 7B.

Phae Muang Phii
แพะเมืองผี

The name means 'Ghost-Land', a reference to this strange geological phenomenon about 18 km north-east of Phrae off Highway 101. Erosion has created bizarre pillars of soil and rock that look like giant fungi. The area has recently been made a provincial park; there are shaded tables and food vendors near the entrance – you may need a drink after wandering around the baked surfaces between the eroded pillars.

Getting there by public transport entails a bus ride nine km toward Nan, getting off at the signed turn-off for Phae Muang Phii, and then catching a songthaew another six km to a second right-hand turn-off to the park. From this point you must walk or hitch about 2.5 km to reach the entrance.

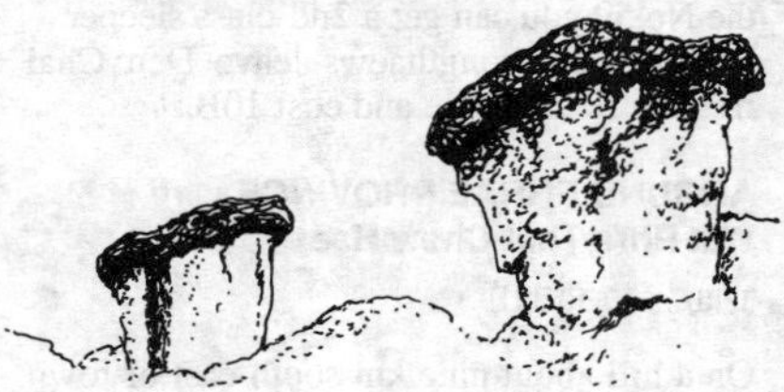

Mabri Hill Tribe
ชนเผ่ามาบรี

Along the border of Phrae and Nan provinces live the remaining members of the Mabri (sometimes spelt Mrabri or Mlabri) hill tribe, whom the Thais call *phĩi thong leũang* (spirits of the yellow leaves). The most nomadic of all the tribes in Thailand, the Mabri customarily move on when the leaves of their temporary huts turn yellow, hence their Thai name. Now, however, their numbers have been greatly reduced (to possibly as few as 150) and experts suspect that few of the Mabri still migrate in the traditional way.

Traditionally, the Mabri are strict hunter-gatherers but many now work as field labourers for Thais or other hill-tribe groups such as the Hmong, in exchange for pigs and cloth. Little is known about the tribe's belief system, but it is said that the Mabri believe they are not entitled to cultivate the land for themselves. A Mabri woman typically changes mates every five or six years, taking any children from the previous union with her. The Mabris' knowledge of medicinal plants is said to be enormous, encompassing the effective use of herbs for fertility and contraception, and for the treatment of snake or centipede poisoning. When a member of the tribe dies, the body is put in a tree top to be eaten by birds.

In Phrae Province there is a small settlement of around 40 Mabri living in Rong Khwang district (north-east of the capital, near Phae Muang Phii) under the protection/control of American missionary Eugene Long. Long calls himself 'Boonyuen Suksaneh' and the Mabris' village 'Ban Boonyuen' – a classic scenario right out of Peter Mathiessen's *At Play in the Fields of the Lord.* Ban Boonyuen can only be reached on foot or by elephant; the nearest village linked by road is 12 km away.

The remaining 150 or so Mabri live across the provincial border in Nan. The Thai government has recently initiated the 'Pre-Agricultural Development of Mabri Society Project' in both provinces to ease the

Mabri into modern rural society without an accompanying loss of culture. According to project leaders, the effort is necessary to protect the Mabri from becoming a slave society within northern Thailand's increasingly capitalist rural economy. Because of their anti-materialist beliefs, the Mabri perform menial labour for the Hmong and other hill tribes for little or no compensation.

Nan Province

One of Thailand's remote provinces (an official Thai government designation), Nan was formerly so choked with bandits and PLAT insurgents that travellers were discouraged from visiting. The Thai government couldn't get any roads built in the province because guerrillas would periodically destroy highway building equipment at night.

With the successes of the Thai army and a more stable political machine in Bangkok during the last few decades, Nan is opening up and more roads are being built. The roads that link the provincial capital with the nearby provinces of Chiang Rai, Phrae, Uttaradit, etc pass through exquisite scenery of rich river valleys and rice fields. Like Loei in the north-east, this is a province to be explored for its natural beauty and its likable people, who live close to traditional rural rhythms.

Nan remains a largely rural province with not a factory or condo in sight. Most of the inhabitants are agriculturally employed, growing sticky rice, beans, corn, tobacco and vegetables in the fertile river plains. Nan is also famous for two fruits: *fai jiin* (a Chinese version of Thailand's indigenous *má-fai)* and *sôm sĩi thong*, golden-skinned oranges. The latter are Nan's most famous export, commanding high prices in Bangkok and Malaysia. Apparently the cooler winter weather in Nan turns the skin orange (lowland Thai oranges are mostly green) and imparts a unique sweet-tart flavour. **Thung Chang district** supposedly grows the best som sii thong in the province. Nan is also famous for its *phrík yài hâeng*, long hot chillies similar to those grown in China's Sichuan Province. During the hot season, you'll see lots of highly photographic chillies drying by the roadside.

Geography

Nan shares a 227-km border with Sayaburi Province in Laos.

Only 25% of the land is arable (and only half of that actively cultivated), as most of the province is covered by heavily forested mountains; **Doi Phu Kha**, at 2000 metres, is the highest peak. Half of the forests in the province are virgin upland monsoon forest. Most of the province's population of 364,000 live in the Nan River valley, a bowl-shaped depression ringed by mountains on all sides. Major river systems in the province include the Nan, Sam Wa, Samun, Haeng, Lae and Pua.

People

Nan is a sparsely populated province but the ethnic groups found here differ significantly from those in other northern provinces. Outside the Nan River valley, the predominant hill tribes are Mien (around 8000), with smaller numbers of Hmong. Along the south-western provincial border with Phrae are a few small Mabri settlements as well. What makes Nan unique, however, is the presence of three lesser known groups seldom seen outside this province: the Thai Lü, Htin and Khamu.

Thai Lü This ethnic minority, often called Lua or Lawa by the Thais, began migrating to Nan from China's Xishuangbanna (Sipsongpanna) around 200 years ago and now reside mostly in Pua, Thung Chang, Tha Wang Pha and Mae Jarim districts. Their influence on Nan (and to a lesser extent, Phrae) culture has been very important. The temple architecture at Wat Phra That Chae Haeng, Wat Phumin and Wat Nong Bua – typified by thick walls with small windows, two or three-tiered roofs, curved pediments and naga lintels – is a Thai Lü (who are Theravada Buddhists) inheritance. Thai Lü

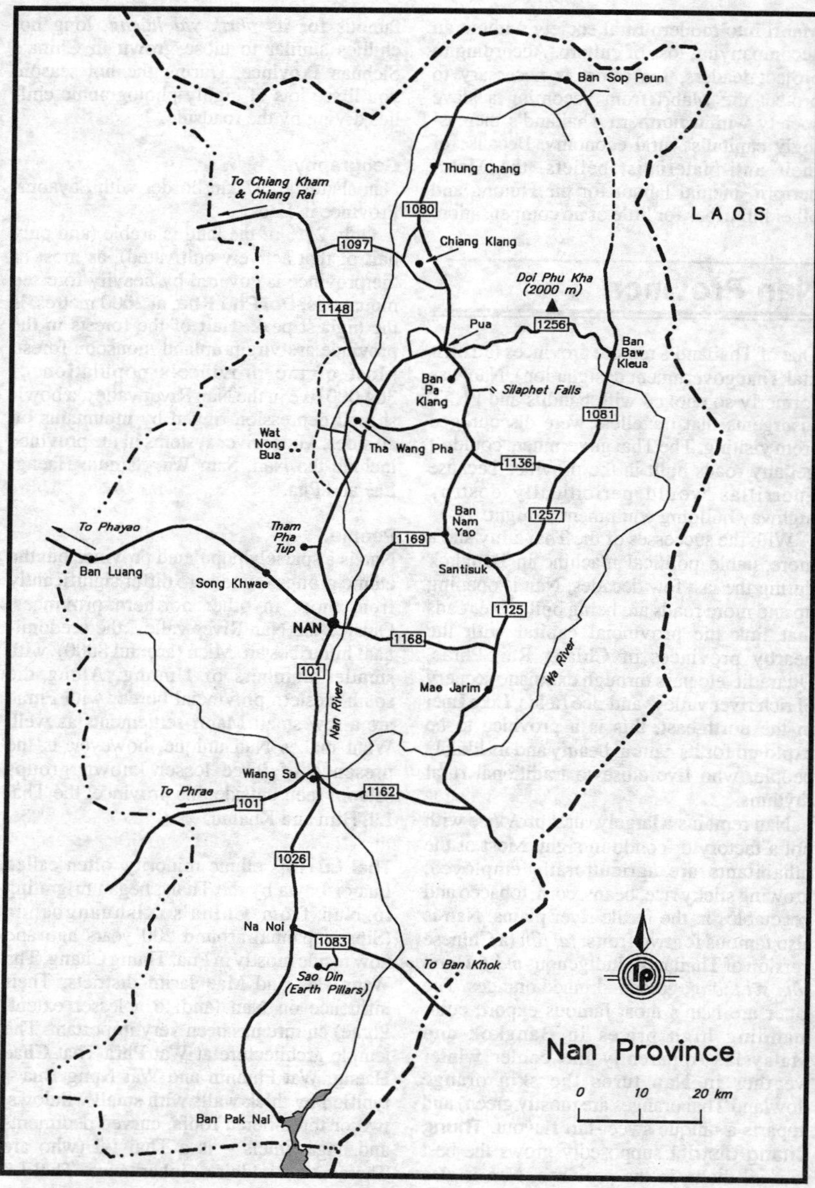
Ban Sop Peun
Thung Chang
To Chiang Kham & Chiang Rai
1080
LAOS
1097
Chiang Klang
Doi Phu Kha (2000 m)
1148
Pua
1256
Ban Baw Kleua
Ban Pa Klang
Silaphet Falls
1081
Wat Nong Bua
Tha Wang Pha
1136
Ban Nam Yao
1257
To Phayao
Tham Pha Tup
1169
Ban Luang
Song Khwae
Santisuk
NAN
1125
1168
101
Nan River
Mae Jarim
Wa River
Wiang Sa
1162
To Phrae
101
1026
Na Noi
1083
To Ban Khok
Sao Din (Earth Pillars)
Nan Province
0 10 20 km
Ban Pak Nai

fabrics are considered among the most prized in northern Thailand and the weaving motifs show up in many Nan handicrafts.

The Thai Lü build traditional wooden or bamboo-thatched houses on thick wooden stilts, beneath which they place their kitchens and weaving looms. Many still make all their own clothes, typically sewn from dark blue cotton fabrics. Many Thai Lü villages support themselves by growing rice and vegetables.

Thai Lü-style temple

Htin Pronounced 'Tin', this Mon-Khmer group of about 3000 lives in villages of 50 or so families in remote mountain valleys of Chiang Klang, Pua and Thung Chang districts. A substantial number also live across the border in Sayaburi Province, Laos. They typically subsist by hunting for wild game, breeding domestic animals, farming small plots of land and, in Ban Baw Kleua, by extracting salt from salt wells.

Htin houses are typically made of thatched bamboo and raised on bamboo or wood stilts. No metal – including nails – is used in house construction because of a Htin taboo. The Htin are particularly skilled at manipulating bamboo to make everything needed around the house; for floor mats and baskets they interweave pared bamboo with a black-coloured grass to create bold geometric patterns. They also use bamboo to fashion a musical instrument of stepped pipes – similar to the *angkalung* of central Thailand and Indonesia – which is shaken to produce musical tones. The Htin don't weave their own fabrics, often buying clothes from neighbouring Miens.

Htin house

Khamu Like the Thai Lü, the Khamu migrated to Nan around 150 years ago from Sipsongpanna. There are now around 5000 in Nan (more than anywhere else in Thailand), mostly in Wiang Sa, Thung Chang, Chiang Klang and Pua districts. Their villages are established near streams; their houses have dirt floors like those of the Hmong but roofs sport crossed roof beams similar to the northern Thai *kalae* (locally called *kapkri-aak)*. The Khamu are skilled at metalwork and perform regular rituals to placate Salok, the spirit of the forge. Khamu villages are usually very self-sufficient; villagers hold fast to tradition and are known to value thrift and hard work. Ban Huay Sataeng in Thung Chang district is one of the largest and easiest Khamu villages to visit in the province.

NAN

อ.เมืองน่าน

Just over 668 km from Bangkok, little-known Nan (population 25,000) is steeped in history. For centuries Muang Nan was an isolated, independent kingdom with few ties to the outside world. Ample evidence of prehistoric habitation exists, but it wasn't until several small muangs (ancient Thai river-valley states) consolidated to form Nanthaburi on the Nan River in the mid-1300s – concurrent with the founding of Luang Prabang and the Lan Xang (Million Elephants) kingdom in Laos – that the city became a power to contend with. Associated with the powerful Sukhothai kingdom, the city-state took the title Waranakhon (Sanskrit: Varanagara or 'Excellent City') and played a significant role in the development of early Thai nationalism.

Toward the end of the 14th century Nan became one of the nine northern Thai-Lao principalities that comprised Lan Na Thai (Million Thai Fields, now known as Lanna) and the city-state flourished throughout the 15th century. The Burmese, however, took control of the kingdom in 1558 and transferred many inhabitants to Burma as slaves; the city was all but abandoned until western Thailand was wrested from the Burmese in 1786. The local dynasty then regained local sovereignty and remained semi-autonomous until 1931 when Nan finally accepted full Bangkok sponsorship.

Parts of the old city wall and several early wats dating from the Lanna period can be seen in present-day Nan. Muang Nan's wats are quite distinctive. Some temple structures show Lanna influence, while others belong to the Thai Lü legacy brought from Sipsongpanna, the Thai Lü's historical homeland.

Wat Phumin
วัดภูมินทร์

Nan's most famous temple is celebrated for its cruciform bot which was constructed in 1596 and restored during the reign of Chao Anantavorapitthidet (1867-74). Murals on the walls depicting the Khatta Kumara and Nimi Jatakas were executed during the restoration by Thai Lü artists; the bot exterior exemplifies the work of Thai Lü architects as well. The murals are considered of historic as well as aesthetic importance since they incorporate scenes of local life from the era in which they were painted.

The ornate altar in the centre of the bot has four sides with four Sukhothai-style sitting Buddhas in *marawichai* (victory over Mara, one hand touching the ground) pose facing each direction.

Wat Phra That Chae Haeng
วัดพระธาตุแช่แห้ง

Two km past the bridge which spans the Nan River, heading west out of town, this very old temple dating from 1355 is the most sacred wat in Nan Province. It is set in a square, walled enclosure on a hill with a view of Nan and the valley. The Lü-influenced bot features a triple-tiered roof with carved wooden eaves, and dragon reliefs over the doors. A gilded Lanna-style chedi sits on a large square base next to the bot with sides measuring 22.5 metres long; the entire chedi is 55.5 metres high.

Wat Phra That Chang Kham
วัดพระธาตุช้างค้ำ

This is the second most important temple in the city after Wat Phumin; the founding date is unknown. The main wihaan, reconstructed in 1458, has a huge seated Buddha image and faint murals in the process of being painstakingly uncovered. (Earlier this century an abbot reportedly ordered the murals to be whitewashed because he thought they were distracting worshippers from concentrating on his sermons.)

Also in the wihaan is a collection of Lanna-period scrolls inscribed (in Lanna script) not only with the usual Buddhist scriptures but with the history, law and astrology of the times. A Nan-style *thammat* – a throne once used by abbots during sermons – sits to one side.

The magnificent chedi behind the wihaan dates to the 14th century, probably around the same time the temple was founded. It features elephant supports similar to those seen in Sukhothai and Si Satchanalai.

Next to the chedi is a small, undistinguished bot from the same era. Wat Chang Kham's current abbot told me an interesting story involving the bot and a Buddha image that was once kept inside.

According to his holiness, in 1955 art historian A B Griswold offered to purchase the 145-cm-tall Buddha inside the small bot. The image appeared to be a crude Sukhothai-style walking Buddha moulded of plaster. After agreeing to pay the abbot 25,000B for the image, Griswold began removing the image from the bot – but as he did it fell and the plaster around the statue broke away to reveal an original Sukhothai

Buddha of pure gold underneath. Needless to say, the abbot made Griswold give it back, much to the latter's chagrin. The image is now kept behind a glass partition, along with other valuable Buddhist images from the area, in the abbot's kuti. Did Griswold suspect what lay beneath the plaster? The abbot refuses to speculate, at least on record.

Wat Chang Kham is also distinguished by having the largest *hǎw trai* or tripitaka (Buddhist scripture) library in Thailand. It's as big as or bigger than the average wihaan, but now lies empty.

The wat is opposite the Nan National Museum on Pha Kong Rd.

Wat Hua Khuang

วัดหัวข่วง

Largely ignored by art historians, this small wat diagonally opposite Wat Chang Kham features a distinctive Lanna/Lan Xang-style chedi with four Buddha niches, a wooden tripitaka library (now used as a kuti) and a noteworthy bot with a Luang Prabang-style carved wooden verandah. Inside are a carved wooden ceiling and a huge naga altar. The temple's founding date is unknown but stylistic cues suggest this may be one of the city's oldest wats.

Wat Suan Tan

วัดสวนตาล

Reportedly established in 1456, Wat Suan Tan (Palm Grove Monastery) features an interesting 15th-century chedi (40 metres high) that combines prang and lotus-bud motifs of obvious Sukhothai influence. The heavily restored wihaan contains an early Sukhothai-style bronze sitting Buddha.

Wat Suan Tan is on Suan Tan Rd, near the north-eastern end of Pha Kong Rd.

Nan National Museum

พิพิธภัณฑ์แห่งชาติน่าน

Housed in the 1903-vintage palace of Nan's last two feudal lords (Phra Chao Suriyapongpalidet and Chao Mahaphrom Surathada), this museum first opened its doors in 1973. Recent renovations have made it one of the most up-to-date provincial museums in Thailand. Unlike most provincial museums in the country, this one also has English labels for many items on display.

The ground floor is divided into six exhibition rooms with ethnological exhibits covering the various ethnic groups found in the province, including the northern Thais, Thai Lü, Htin, Khamu, Mabri, Hmong and Mien. Among the items on display are silverwork, textiles, folk utensils and tribal costumes. On the 2nd floor of the museum are exhibits on Nan history, archaeology, local architecture, royal regalia, weapons, ceramics and religious art.

The museum's collection of Buddha images includes rare Lanna styles as well as the floppy-eared local styles, usually wooden standing images in the 'calling for rain' pose (with hands at the sides, pointing down) which show a marked Luang Prabang influence. The astute museum curators posit a Nan style of art in Buddhist sculpture; some examples on display seem very imitative of other Thai styles, while others are quite distinctive – the ears cure outwards. Also on display on the 2nd floor is a rare 'black' (actually reddish-brown) elephant tusk said to have been presented to a Nan lord over 300 years ago. The tusk is held aloft by a wooden Garuda sculpture.

The museum is open Wednesday to Sunday from 9 am to noon and 1 to 4 pm. Admission is 10B. A building adjacent to the museum has a few books on Thai art and archaeology for sale.

Festivals

The Golden Orange Festival (Thetsakaan Som Sii Thong) is held during December-January – the peak harvest time for the oranges. Among the festival events are a parade of floats decorated with Nan oranges and the coronation of an Orange Queen. During the hot season (March to May), in years when there's a bumper crop of phrik yai and the chilli-growers have extra income to spend, Nan occasionally celebrates a

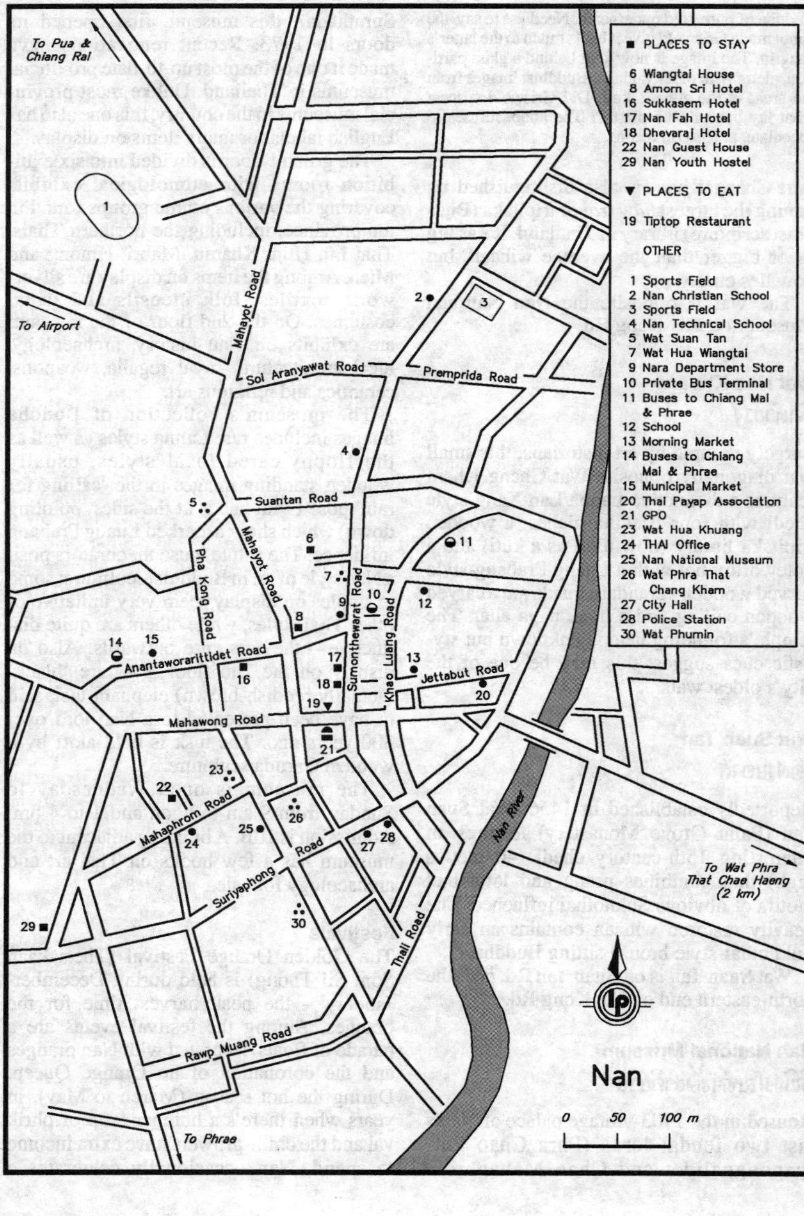

PLACES TO STAY
6 Wiangtai House
8 Amorn Sri Hotel
16 Sukkasem Hotel
17 Nan Fah Hotel
18 Dhevaraj Hotel
22 Nan Guest House
29 Nan Youth Hostel
PLACES TO EAT
19 Tiptop Restaurant
OTHER
1 Sports Field
2 Nan Christian School
3 Sports Field
4 Nan Technical School
5 Wat Suan Tan
7 Wat Hua Wiangtai
9 Nara Department Store
10 Private Bus Terminal
11 Buses to Chiang Mai & Phrae
12 School
13 Morning Market
14 Buses to Chiang Mai & Phrae
15 Municipal Market
20 Thai Payap Association
21 GPO
23 Wat Hua Khuang
24 THAI Office
25 Nan National Museum
26 Wat Phra That Chang Kham
27 City Hall
28 Police Station
30 Wat Phumin
To Pua & Chiang Rai
To Airport
Mahayot Road
Soi Aranyawat Road
Prempida Road
Suantan Road
Pha Kong Road
Sumonthewarat Road
Khao Luang Road
Anantaworarittidet Road
Jettabut Road
Mahawong Road
Mahaphrom Road
Suriyaphong Road
Thali Road
Rawp Muang Road
Nan River
To Wat Phra That Chae Haeng (2 km)
To Phrae
Nan
0 50 100 m

Chilli Festival (Ngaan Phrik) with pepper-festooned floats, chilli-eating contests and the coronation of, what else, a Chilli Queen.

Between mid-September and mid-October, Muang Nan celebrates Thaan Kuay Salaak, a holiday unique to Nan in which special offerings dedicated to one's ancestors are presented to monks in the local temples.

At the end of the Buddhist Rains Retreat (mid-October to mid-November), during the *thâwt kathin* (robes-offering) for Wat Phra That Chang Kham, impressive long-boat races are held on the Nan River. The all-wooden 30-metre-long boats display sculpted naga heads and tails and hold up to 50 rowers.

Although not a festival per se, one local rite unique to Nan that's worth observing (if you have the opportunity) is the Seup Chataa or 'Extend Life' ceremony. Although at one time the ritual was performed annually, it is now most often held when someone is seriously ill or other bad fortune is deemed to have occurred. In the ceremony, the supplicant sits beneath a pyramid-like structure of reeds and flowers while monks and a shaman skilled at Seup Chataa execute a prescribed series of offerings (usually eggs and fruits) and sacred chants.

Places to Stay

Guesthouses The *Nan Guest House* (☎ 771148) is in a large house at 57/16 Mahaphrom Rd (actually at the end of a soi off Mahaphrom Rd) near the THAI office. Singles/doubles with shared bath cost 40/60B; rooms with private bath, 80B. The guesthouse is run by a couple of Bangkok-educated local Thais who dispense tourist information about the area.

Wiangtai House (☎ 710247), at 21/1 Soi Wat Hua Wiang Tai (off Sumonthewarat Rd near the Nara department store) has upstairs rooms in a large modern house for 100B (one large bed), 120B (two beds) and 150B (three beds). Bathrooms are shared but very clean. Mr Tu, the owner, knows the area well and leads treks.

The *Nan Youth Hostel* (☎ 710322) is in a large, old house near the junction of Mahaphrom and Suriyaphong Rds. For IYH members, dorm accommodation is 30B per person and singles/doubles are 50/70B; non-members pay 40B and 60/80B respectively. The hostel staff hadn't decided yet whether they would follow Bangkok's new IYH regulation permitting only members only to stay – presumably they're remote enough that they can establish their own policy. Travel information is available, as are guided treks.

Hotels *Amorn Si* (☎ 710510) at 97 Mahayot Rd has very basic rooms for 100B; it's at a very busy intersection so may not be the quietest choice. *Sukkasem* (☎ 710141) at 29/31 Anantaworarittidet Rd has better rooms from 130B with fan and bath, 160B with air-con.

The recently renovated, all-wood *Nan Fah* (☎ 710284) at 438-440 Sumonthewarat (next to the Dhevaraj Hotel) has a bit of atmosphere; one of the teak pillars supporting the hotel extends for three storeys, and there's an antique shop on the ground floor. All rooms come with air-con and cost from 350 to 370B.

The all air-con *Dhevaraj (Thewarat) Hotel* (☎ 710094) at 466 Sumonthewarat Rd is a four-storey place built around a tiled courtyard with a fountain. It's not really fancy but it's a pleasant place and is the best hotel Nan has to offer. Large, clean rooms on the 2nd floor, with fan and private bath, are 300B – a bit steep due to the lack of competition, but the rooms are a cut above the usual fan room. Rooms toward the back of the hotel are quieter than those toward the front. Rooms on the 3rd floor are all air-con and cost 450 to 700B. On the top floor are 'VIP' rooms with double-paned windows; these cost from 800 to 1200B.

Places to Eat

A night market assembles at the corner of Pha Kong and Anantaworarittidet Rds every night; it's not that spectacular, but the vendors along the sidewalks nearby have fairly good food. Another group of food vendors sets up along the soi opposite the Dhevaraj Hotel.

The most dependable restaurant in the vicinity of the Nam Fah and Dhevaraj hotels is the popular *Siam Phochana*. It's a very popular morning spot for jók with a choice of fish, shrimp, chicken or pork; the menu has all the other Thai and Chinese standards as well, and is open late. If you turn left at the soi next to Siam Phochana and follow it a couple of hundred metres you'll come to the semi-outdoor *Suan Isan*, the best choice in town for isaan food – it's clean and the service is good.

The *Bandu Restaurant*, behind the craft and antique shop on the ground floor of the Nan Fah Hotel, is very popular on weekend nights when there's live folk music. It's decorated with northern Thai antiques; when the weather is dry a few tables are put outdoors. The house speciality is not to be missed – shrimp curry steamed inside a young coconut *(hàw mòk kûng ma-phráo àwn)*. It's delicious but doesn't appear on the English menu.

The only farang place in Nan so far is the Swiss-run, air-con *Tiptop Restaurant*, around the corner from the Dhevaraj Hotel on Mahawong Rd. The menu includes Italian, Swiss and Thai dishes; prices are moderate. It's open from 8 am to 2 pm and 6 to 10 pm daily.

Things to Buy

Good buys include local textiles, especially the Thai Lü weaving styles from Sipsongpanna. Typical Thai Lü fabrics feature red and black designs on white cotton in floral, geometric and animal designs; indigo and red on white is also common. A favourite is the 'flowing-water design' *(lai náam lãi)* showing stepped patterns representing streams, rivers and waterfalls.

Local Mien embroidery and Hmong appliqué are of excellent quality – not as mass-produced as that typically found in Chiang Mai. Htin grass-and-bamboo baskets and mats are worth a look, too.

The nonprofit Thai-Payap Association, one of Thailand's most successful village self-help projects, has a shop at 24 Jettabut Rd near the morning market and bus terminal. Supported by Britain's Ockenden Venture from 1979-90, the association now involves 21 villages and has become totally self-sufficient. The handiwork offered through Thai Payap is among the highest quality available, often including more intricate, time-consuming designs. All proceeds go directly to the participating villages – even the administrative staff consists of trained village representatives.

The arts and antique shop on the ground floor of the Nan Fah Hotel has a wide selection of local crafts, including silverwork and jewellery. There are also several small artisan-operated shops in the same vicinity along Sumonthewarat Rd and along Mahawong and Anantaworarittidet Rds.

Getting There & Away

You can fly to Nan from Chiang Mai (510B), Phitsanulok (575B), Phrae (300B) or Bangkok (1530B).

Buses run from Chiang Mai, Chiang Rai and Phrae to Nan. The fare from Chiang Mai's Arcade bus station is 71B (99B air-con, 127B 1st-class air-con) and the trip takes from six to seven hours. From Chiang Rai there's one daily bus at 9.30 am (60B) which takes seven gruelling hours via treacherous mountain roads – get a window seat as there's usually lots of motion sickness. The most direct way to Nan is from Den Chai via Phrae. (See Getting There & Away for Phrae.) Buses from Phrae to Nan leave frequently, cost 27B and take from two to 2½ hours.

From Nan, buses to Chiang Mai, Chiang Rai and Phrae leave from a terminal west of the large market on Anantaworarittidet Rd.

Ordinary buses to Uttaradit, Phitsanulok, Sukhothai and other points south as far as Bangkok leave from the Baw Khaw Saw terminal off Kha Luang Rd. Regular government-run air-con buses to Bangkok cost 178B, 1st-class air-con is 229B and VIP buses are 350B.

Private VIP Bangkok buses leave from offices along the eastern end of

Anantaworarittidet Rd, not far from the Baw Khaw Saw terminal. New Phrae Tour, one of the private companies, has VIP buses to Bangkok for only 260B – check the number of seats before booking, though.

As provincial roads improve, eventually you should be able to bus from Nan to Nakhon Thai and connect with the Phitsanulok to Loei route.

Getting Around

Fhu Travel Service on Sumonthewarat Rd rents Honda Dreams for 150B per day, bicycles for 30B. Oversea Shop (☎ 710258) at 488 Sumonthewarat Rd (a few doors down from the Dhevaraj Hotel) rents bicycles and motorbikes at similar rates and can also handle repairs.

Samlors around town cost 10B.

AROUND NAN PROVINCE

Trekking

Nan has nothing like the organised trekking industry found in Chiang Rai and Chiang Mai, but several local individuals in Nan lead two or three-day excursions into the mountains.

Fhu Travel Service (☎ 710636) at 453/4 Sumonthewarat Rd offers treks to Mabri, Hmong, Mien, Thai Lü and Htin villages combined with raft trips on the Nan River. A one-day 'soft' trek costs 500B per person; two nights (three days) is 1300B to 1600B per person (depending on the number of people) and three nights (four days) is 2800B. Fhu tends to concentrate on the northern areas of the province.

Wiangtai House (☎ 710247) at 2/1 Soi Wat Hua Wian Tai, does two-night (three-day) treks for 2500B per person, four-day (five-night) trips for 3500B. Nan Youth Hostel (☎ 710322) is another place that organises treks. Wiangtai focuses on the southern areas of the province, including trips to the 'fog sea' on a mountain ridge at the Phrae border.

Fees should include guide services, transport and all meals and accommodation.

Doi Phu Kha National Park

อุทยานแห่งชาติดอยภูคา

This very recently established national park is centred around 2000-metre Do Phu Kha in the Pua and Baw Kleua districts of north-eastern Nan (about 75 km from Nan). There are several Htin, Mien, Hmong and Thai Lü villages in the park and vicinity, as well as a couple of caves and waterfalls and endless opportunities for forest walks. As yet there is no established visitor accommodation in the park; in the meantime rangers will allow visitors to stay in park buildings at no charge. This area gets quite cool in the winter months – evening temperatures of 5 to 10° C are not uncommon – so dress accordingly.

To reach the park by public transport you must first take a bus north of Nan to Pua (12B), and then pick up one of the infrequent songthaews to the park headquarters (15B). A songthaew to the summit of Doi Phu Kha costs 35B. If you come by motorcycle, be forewarned that Route 1256 from Pua deteriorates as you get closer to the summit. Beyond the summit the stretch to Ban Baw Kleua is very rough in spots.

Ban Baw Kleua is a Htin village south-east of the park whose main occupation is the extraction of salt from local salt wells (Baw Kleua means 'salt well'). Route 1256 meets Route 1081 near Baw Kleua; Route 1081 can be followed south back to Nan via a network of paved and unpaved roads.

Wat Nong Bua

วัดหนองบัว

This historic Thai Lü temple is in a Lü village near **Tha Wang Pha**, approximately 30 km north of Nan. Featuring a typical two-tiered roof and carved wooden portico, the design is simple yet striking – note the carved naga heads at the roof corners.

You can also see Thai Lü weaving in action in this village. The home of Khun Janthasom Phrompanya near the wat serves as a local weaving centre – check there for the locations of looms, or to look at fabrics for purchase.

Songthaews to Tha Wang Pha (12B) leave from opposite Nan's Sukkasem Hotel. Get off at Samyaek Longbom, a three-way intersection before Tha Wang Pha, and walk two km over a river bridge to Nong Bua.

Tham Pha Tup

ถ้ำผาตูบ

This limestone cave complex is about 10 km north of Nan and is part of a new wildlife reserve. Songthaews from opposite the Sukkasem Hotel cost 5B to the turn-off to the cave.

Sao Din

เสาดิน

Literally 'Earth Pillars', Sao Din is an erosionary phenomena similar to that found at Phae Muang Phii in Phrae Province – tall columns of earth protruding from a barren depression. The area covers nearly 20 rai (32 sq km) off Route 1026 in Na Noi district about 30 km south of Nan.

Sao Din is best visited by bicycle or motorcycle since it's time-consuming to reach by public transport. If you don't have your own wheels, take a songthaew to Wiang Sa, then change to another to Na Noi. From Na Noi you must get yet another songthaew bound for Fak Tha or Ban Khok, getting off at the entrance to Sao Din after five km or so. From here you'll have to walk or hitch four km to Sao Din itself. There are also occasional direct songthaews from Na Noi.

Other Attractions

There are a couple of interesting destinations near Pua, roughly 50 km north of Nan. **Silaphet Falls** is south-east of Pua just off the road between Pua and Ban Nam Yao. The water falls in a wide swath over a cliff and is best seen at the end of the monsoon season in November. On the way to the falls and west of the road, is the Mien village of **Ban Pa Klang**, worth a visit to see silversmiths at work. This village supplies many silver shops in Chiang Mai and Bangkok.

Other Mien villages that specialise in silverwork can be found along Highway 101 between Nan and Phrae in the vicinity of Song Khwae.

The **Thale Sap Neua** (Northern Lake) formed by the Sirikit Dam is an important freshwater fishery for Nan, as well as a recreational attraction for Nan residents. **Ban Pak Nai** on its northern shore is the main fishing village.

North-East Thailand

In many ways, the north-eastern region of Thailand is the kingdom's heartland. Partly due to the area's general non-development, the older Thai customs remain more intact here than elsewhere in the country. The region also hosts fewer tourists – in 1990, for example, only 2% of the country's annual international arrivals ventured into north-east Thailand.

Isaan (the collective term for the region) officially consists of 17 provinces: Buriram, Chaiyaphum, Kalasin, Khon Kaen, Loei, Mahasarakham, Mukdahan, Nakhon Ratchasima (Khorat), Nakhon Phanom, Nong Khai, Roi Et, Sakon Nakhon, Si Saket, Surin, Ubon Ratchathani, Udon Thani and Yasothon.

Sites of historical and archaeological significance abound in the north-east, several of which have been restored or excavated. The term *isăan* is used to classify the region, the people *(khon isăan)* and the food *(aahăan isăan)* of north-east Thailand. The name comes from Isana, the Sanskrit name for the Mon-Khmer kingdom which flourished in (what is now) north-east Thailand and pre-Angkor Cambodia. Later the Angkor Empire extended well into this region too.

A mixture of Lao and Khmer influence is a mark of isaan culture and language. The Khmers have left behind several Angkor Wat-like monuments near Surin, Khorat, Buriram and other north-eastern towns. Near the Maekhong River/Lao border in Nakhon Phanom Province is the famous Lao-style temple, Wat That Phanom. Many of the people living in this area speak Lao or a Thai dialect which is very close to Lao – in fact there are more people of Lao heritage in north-east Thailand than in all of Laos. In certain areas of the lower north-east, Khmer is the most common language.

Isaan food is famous for its pungency and choice of ingredients. Well-known dishes include *kài yâang* (grilled spiced chicken) and *sôm-tam* (spicy salad made with grated unripe papaya, lime juice, garlic, fish sauce and fresh hot pepper). North-easterners eat glutinous rice with their meals, rolling the almost translucent grains into balls with their hands.

The music of the north-east is also highly distinctive in its folk tradition, using instruments such as the *khaen*, a reed instrument with two long rows of bamboo pipes strung together, the *ponglang*, a xylophone-like instrument made of short wooden logs and the *pin*, a type of small three-stringed lute played with a large plectrum. The most popular song forms are of the *lûuk thûng* (literally, 'children of the fields') type, a very rhythmic style in comparison to the classical music of central Thailand.

The best silk in Thailand is said to come from the north-east, around Khorat (Nakhon Ratchasima), Khon Kaen and Roi Et. A visit to north-eastern silk-weaving towns can uncover bargains, as well as provide an education in Thai weaving techniques.

For real antiquity, Udon Province offers prehistoric cave drawings at Ban Pheu, north of Udon Thani, and a look at the ancient ceramic and bronze culture at Ban Chiang to the east. This latter site, excavated by the late Chester Gorman and his team of anthropologists from the University of Pennsylvania, may prove to be the remains of the world's oldest agricultural society and first bronze metallurgy, predating by centuries developments in the Tigris/Euphrates Valley and in China.

Travellers who want to know more about north-east Thailand should read the works of Pira Sudham, a Thai author born in Buriram. His autobiographical *People of Esarn (Isaan)* is especially recommended.

Compared to the rest of Thailand, the pace is slower, the people friendlier and inflation is less effective in the isaan provinces, and although fewer people speak or understand English, travel in the north-east is easy. Main train and bus lines in the north-east are

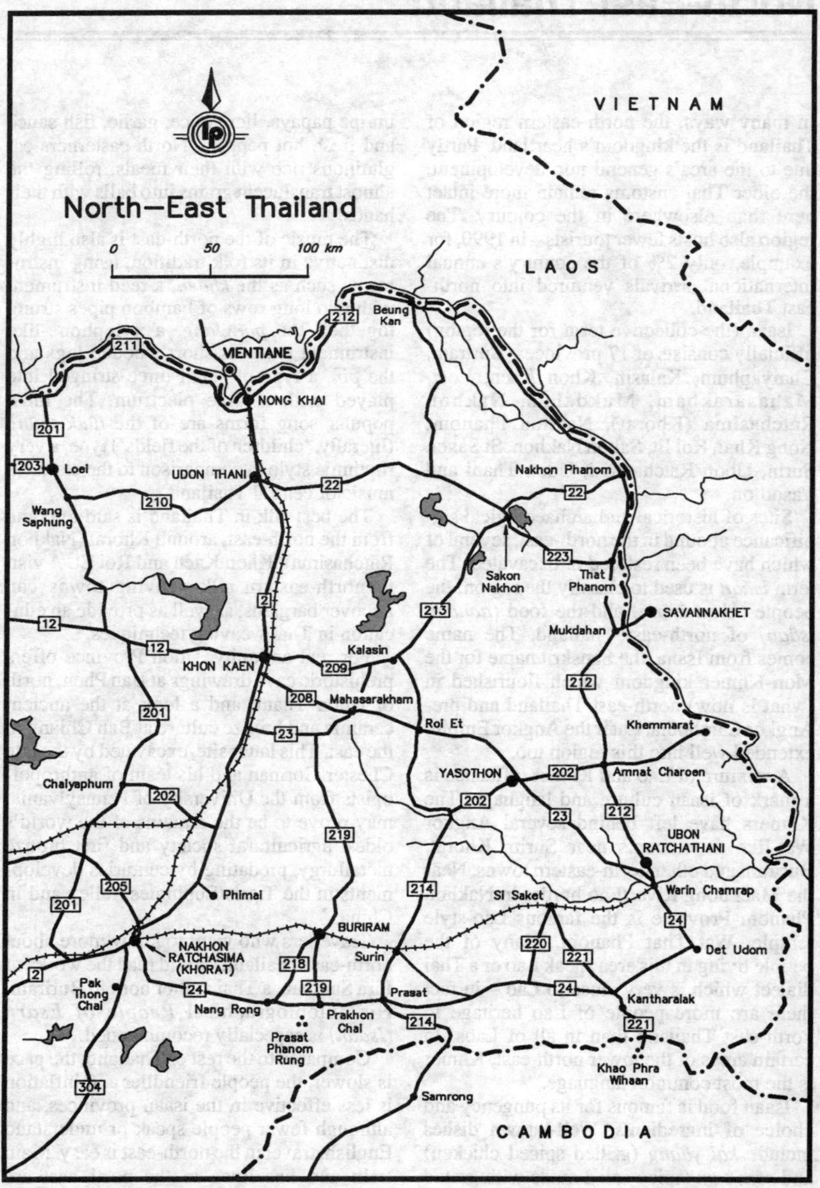
North-East Thailand
0
50
100 km
VIETNAM
LAOS
CAMBODIA
VIENTIANE
NONG KHAI
Beung Kan
212
211
201
203
Loei
UDON THANI
22
210
Wang Saphung
Nakhon Phanom
223
Sakon Nakhon
That Phanom
213
SAVANNAKHET
Mukdahan
12
2
KHON KAEN
Kalasin
209
208
Mahasarakham
23
Roi Et
Khemmarat
YASOTHON
202
Amnat Charoen
Chaiyaphum
219
UBON RATCHATHANI
214
Warin Chamrap
Si Saket
205
Phimai
24
BURIRAM
220
221
Det Udom
NAKHON RATCHASIMA (KHORAT)
218
Surin
Pak Thong Chai
Prasat
Kantharalak
Nang Rong
Prakhon Chai
Prasat Phanom Rung
Khao Phra Wihaan
304
Samrong

between Bangkok and Nong Khai, and between Bangkok and Ubon Ratchathani. The north-east can also be reached from northern Thailand by bus or plane from Phitsanulok, with Khon Kaen as the 'gateway'.

Nakhon Ratchasima Province

Thailand's largest province (20,500 sq km) is most well known for silk weaving. Some of Thailand's best silk is made in the village of Pak Thong Chai, 30 km south-west of Khorat on Highway 304. Many of the Bangkok silk houses have their cloth made there, so don't expect to get any special bargains just because you went all that way. There are also a couple of silk shops in Khorat (Ratri Thai Silk on Ratchadamnoen Rd near the Thao Suranari Shrine, and Thusnee (Thatsani) Thai Silk on Buarong Rd), which are just as good for their selection and price. Still, Pak Thong Chai is worth a trip if you're interested in observing Thai silk-weaving methods.

Khorat's other big attraction is Angkor-period Khmer ruins scattered about the province. Most are little more than a jumble of stones or a single prang, but the restorations at Prasat Phimai and Wat Phanomwan are worth a visit.

NAKHON RATCHASIMA

นครราชสีมา

Exactly 250 km from Bangkok, Nakhon Ratchasima (population 205,000) is also known as Khorat. No longer the quaint isaan town it once was, Khorat has become an important transportation hub and a burgeoning industrial centre – since 1988 new factory registrations have averaged 1300 per year. Yet only in 1992 did the city get its first international-class hotel.

Khorat is often cited as only a train or bus stop from the nearby Phimai ruins, but is a fairly interesting place in itself. Up until the mid-Ayuthaya period it was actually two towns, Sema and Khorakpura, which merged under the reign of King Narai. To this day, Khorat has a split personality of sorts, with the older less commercial half to the west, and the newer downtown half inside the city moats to the east, although neither town was originally here.

One of the seven air bases in Thailand used by US armed forces to launch air strikes on Laos and Vietnam in the '60s and '70s was in Khorat. A few retired GIs still live in the area with their Thai families, and the Veterans of Foreign Wars Cafeteria is still open on Phoklang Rd. But the heavy US influence that was obvious in the late '70s after the base was closed has all but faded away. Yes, the big massage parlours are still there but the clientele is almost exclusively Thai.

Local city boosters have their hopes for glory pinned on Thai Expo '94, to be held at Khorat's Suranari Technological University from January to March 1994. The highway from Bangkok is being widened and a new Sheraton is being built just for the occasion.

Information

The TAT office (☎ 2243751, 255243) on Mittaphap Rd (western edge of town) is worth a visit since it has plenty of information on the north-east and a good map of Khorat. To get there, walk straight across from the entrance to the Nakhon Ratchasima railway station to Mukkhamontri Rd, turn left and walk (or catch a No 2 bus) west until you reach the highway to Bangkok – Mittaphap Rd. TAT is just across the road, on the south-west corner. The office is open daily from 8.30 am to 4.30 pm.

Mahawirawong National Museum

พิพิธภัณฑ์แห่งชาติมหาวีรวงศ์

In the grounds of Wat Sutchinda, directly across from the government buildings off Ratchadamnoen Rd and just outside the city moat, this museum has a good collection of Khmer art objects, especially door lintels, as well as objects from other periods. It's open from 9 am to noon and 1 to 4 pm, Wednesday to Sunday. Admission is 10B.

Thao Suranari Memorial
อนุสาวรีย์ท้าวสุรนารี

At the Chumphon Gate to downtown Khorat, on the west side, is this much-worshipped memorial shrine to Khun Ying Mo, a courageous Thai woman who led the local citizens in a battle against Lao invaders from Vientiane during the rule of Rama III. There is a curious miniature model of a bus at the shrine, donated by local bus drivers perhaps in the hope that they will be protected from danger by Khun Ying Mo's spirit.

Khorat Song In the evenings you can see performances of *phlaeng khorâat*, the traditional Khorat folk song, in an area opposite the shrine near some shops selling preserved pork. It's usually performed by groups of four singers hired by people whose supplications to Thao Suranari have been honoured. To show gratitude to the spirit, they pay for the performance. Over 100 groups are for hire, usually for 400B per performance.

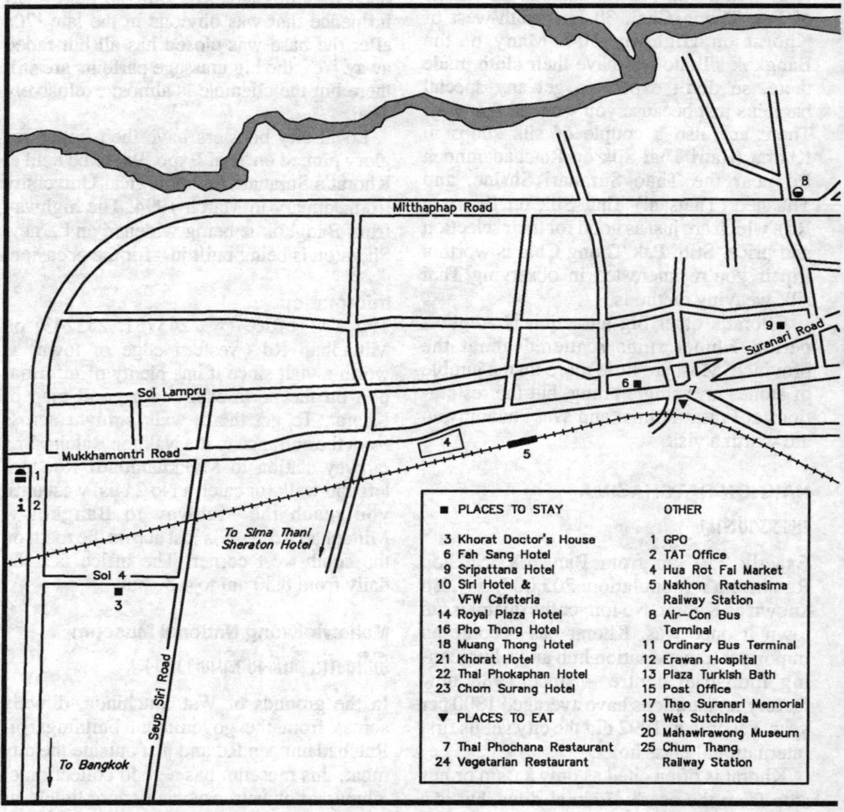

Wat Sala Loi

วัดศาลาลอย

This distinctive modern 'Temple of the Floating Pavilion' is 400 metres east of the north-eastern corner of the city moat and has a bot shaped like a Chinese junk.

Wat Paa Salawan

วัดป่าสาละวัน

This Thammayut 'forest monastery', once surrounded by jungle, has been engulfed by the city, but it's still a quiet escape. The abbot, Luang Phaw Phut, is quite well known as a meditation teacher and has developed a strong lay following in the area. A few relics belonging to the legendary Ajaan Man are on display in the main wihaan, a large but simple wooden affair. A cemetery on the grounds has a couple of markers with photos of US veterans who lived their remaining years in Khorat. Wat Paa Salawan is in the south-west sector of town behind Chum Thang railway station.

Swimming Pools

Landlocked Khorat is quite warm most of the

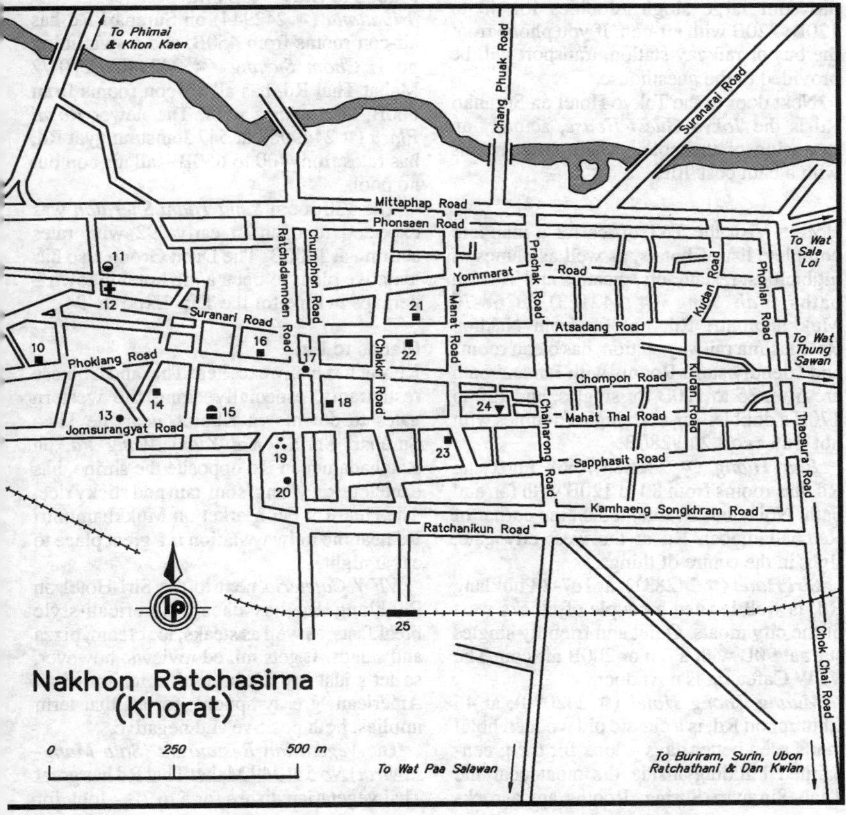

year – a swim at one of the several local public pools will revive all but the most wilted. Each of the following charges 20B per day per person: Chanya Swimming Pool (☎ 252305) on Seup Siri Rd, Rama Swimming Pool (☎ 242019) on Mittaphap Rd and Sripattana Hotel (☎ 242944) on Suranari Rd. The pool at the Sripattana Hotel on Suranari Rd has a good poolside snack bar.

Places to Stay – bottom end

Guesthouses Khorat's first guesthouse, *Khorat Doctor's House* (☎ 255846), is at 78 Soi 4, Seup Siri Rd in the western area of the city. The house is quiet and comfortable and has four large singles/doubles for 40 to 120B; 220B with air-con. If you phone from the bus or railway station, transport will be provided to the guesthouse.

Next door to the Tokyo Hotel on Suranari Rd is the *Tokyo Guest House*, actually an extension of the hotel, where large rooms with a bath cost 70B.

Hotels Visit the TAT office for a map and complete list of hotels, as well as names of nightclubs, restaurants, theatres and Turkish baths. *Fah Sang* (☎ 242123), at 68-70 Mukkhamontri Rd, not far from Nakhon Ratchasima railway station, has clean rooms and friendly staff. Rooms with fan and bath are from 85 to 120B for singles, and 130 to 170B a double. Air-con singles/doubles with hot water cost 240/280B.

Pho Thong (☎ 242084), 658 Phoklang Rd, has rooms from 80 to 120B with fan and bath. Noisy but livable, it's on the corner of Ratchadamnoen Rd at the west city gate, right in the centre of things.

Siri Hotel (☎ 242831), at 167-8 Phoklang Rd, is well located a couple of blocks west of the city moats. Quiet and friendly singles start at 90B with a fan or 200B air-con. The VFW Cafeteria is next door.

Muang Thong Hotel (☎ 242090), at 46 Chumphon Rd, is a classic old wooden hotel that's seen better days – look for the green-painted building inside the moat near the Thao Suranari Shrine. Rooms are a rock-bottom 60B a night – be sure to get a room off the street.

Thai Phokaphan (☎ 242454), 104-6 Atsadang Rd, is inside the city moats, across the street from the more expensive Khorat Hotel and the CP Turkish Bath. Good singles/doubles are 120/190B; 240B with air-con.

Cathay (☎ 242889), at 3692/5-6 Ratchadamnoen Rd, has reasonable rates (100 to 130B), but is a bit out of the way.

Khorat Hotel (☎ 242260), 191 Atsadang Rd, has singles/doubles for 180/250B; or from 200B with air-con.

Places to Stay – top end

Sripattana (☎ 242944) on Suranari Rd has air-con rooms from 450B, and a swimming pool. *Chom Surang* (☎ 242940), 2701/2 Mahat Thai Rd, has all air-con rooms from 600B, also with a pool. The newer *Royal Plaza* (☎ 244906), at 547 Jomsurangyat Rd, has rates from 400 to 650B – all air-con but no pool.

The 130-room *Sima Thani Sheraton* was expected to open in early '92 with rates starting at 1300B. The Dusit Group also has tentative plans to open a big hotel in town – perhaps in time for the Thai Expo in '94.

Places to Eat

Khorat has many excellent Thai and Chinese restaurants, especially along the western gates to downtown Khorat, near the Thao Suranari Shrine. *Kai Yaang Wang Fa*, on Ratchadamnoen Rd opposite the shrine, has excellent kài yâang, sôm-tam and sticky rice. The Hua Rot Fai Market on Mukkhamontri Rd near the railway station is a great place to eat at night.

VFW Cafeteria next to the Siri Hotel on Phoklang Rd has cheap American-style breakfasts, as well as steaks, ice cream, pizza and salads. It gets mixed reviews, however, so let's just say it's a good imitation of an American 'greasy spoon', for all that term implies, both positive and negative.

The *Vegetarian Restaurant (Sala Mangsawirat) No 5* at 249 Mahat Thai Rd has great Thai vegetarian dishes for 5 to 7B – look for the large green sign with a Thai numeral 5. It's open from around 10 am to 3 pm. Another good place for price and selection is the food centre on the top floor of the *Grand Plaza* shopping centre.

The well-known *Thai Phochana* at 142 Jomsurangyat Rd has a mix of standard Thai and local specialities, including mìi khorâat (Khorat-style noodles) and yam kòp yâang (roast frog salad). Also good here is kaeng phèt pèt (duck curry).

Farm Platoothong Restaurant on Seup Siri Rd close to the Doctor's House is a good place for a slow Thai splurge – great service and food. You can also fish for your own food in the farm's ponds for 20B per hour (a rod & reel costs 30B per day).

Thale Thai, opposite the Chom Surang Hotel on Mahat Thai Rd, is a very good outdoor seafood restaurant. *The Spider* on Jomphon Rd is an air-con restaurant/pub with the best farang food in town, plus a list of Thai dishes.

Getting There & Away

Air THAI flies to Khorat from Bangkok daily; the fare is 540B one-way. There is also one weekly flight (Saturday) from Khorat to Ubon Ratchathani for 730B.

The THAI office (☎ 257211) is at 14 Manat Rd, off Mahat Thai Rd inside the city moat.

The privately owned Bangkok Airways once had frequent flights to Khorat, but these were suspended a couple of years ago along with all its other routes. Now that Bangkok Airways is flying to southern Thailand again, there's a possibility it will re-establish the north-eastern flights.

Bus Ordinary buses leave the northern bus terminal in Bangkok every 15 or 20 minutes from 5 am to 9.30 pm. The fare is 51B and the trip takes four hours. Air-con buses cost 92B.

Buses between Khorat and Khon Kaen cost 39B. Direct buses between Khorat and Chanthaburi on the south-east coast run hourly between 4.30 am and 4 pm. The fare is 69B and the journey takes about eight hours.

Between Khorat and Phitsanulok there are three air-con buses a day, one in the morning at about 8 am, another at 5 pm and another at 8 pm. The fare is 146B and the trip takes from three to four hours. Buses without air-con leave Khorat four times a day, at 4.30, 6 and 10 am and 3.30 pm. The fare is 82B.

Air-con buses arrive and depart from the air-con bus terminal on Mittaphap Rd. Regular buses leave from next to the Erawan Hospital.

Train An express train bound for Ubon Ratchathani departs Bangkok's Hualamphong station at 9 pm, arriving in Khorat at 1.58 am – hardly the best time to look for a hotel.

Rapid trains on the Ubon line depart at 6.50 am and 6.45 pm, arriving in Khorat at 11.36 am and 11.56 pm respectively. These are much more convenient arrival times, especially the morning arrival which leaves plenty of daylight time to explore the town.

There are also ordinary diesel trains on this line at 7.15 am (3rd class only), 9.10 am (3rd class only), 11.05 am (2nd and 3rd class), 11.45 am (3rd class only), 3.25 pm (3rd class only), 9.50 pm (2nd and 3rd class) and 11.25 pm (3rd class only) which all arrive in Khorat about 5½ to six hours after departure. The 1st-class fare (express train only) is 207B, 2nd class is 104B and 3rd class 50B. Add 20B for the rapid trains and 30B for the express. The train passes through some great scenery on the Khorat Plateau, including a view of the enormous white Buddha figure at Wat Theppitak on a thickly forested hillside.

The new four-hour Sprinter service leaves Bangkok at 9.25 and 10.15 am, arriving in Khorat at 1.31 and 2.18 pm respectively. The fare is 245B.

Getting Around

Samlors around town cost 5 to 10B; tuk-tuks cost 15 to 20B. The city also has a fairly extensive bus system. From the railway station, bus No 1 heads east along Phoklang

Rd; No 2 heads west along Mukkhamontri Rd and No 3 goes east along Jomsurangyat Rd. The fare is 2B.

Motorcycles can be rented (150B per day for 80 to 100cc, 200B for 125cc) from Wirot Yan Yon (☎ 245521) at 554-556 Phoklang Rd.

AROUND NAKHON RATCHASIMA

Pak Thong Chai

ปักธงชัย

Thirty-two km south of Nakhon Ratchasima, on Highway 304, is Pak Thong Chai, Thailand's most famous silk-weaving village. Several varieties and prices of silk are available and most weavers sell directly to the public. However, prices are not necessarily lower than in Khorat or Bangkok. Around 70 silk factories are located in the district. Pak Thong Chai Silk & Cultural Centre opened in 1991 to offer demonstrations of the silk-weaving process as well as the opportunity to purchase silks at reasonable prices.

A bus to Pak Thong Chai leaves the bus station in Khorat every 30 minutes, the last at 4 pm. The fare is 10B.

Achaan Pan and *Pak Thong Chai* hotels are both on the main road through town and have rooms from 60B.

Dan Kwian

ด่านเกวียน

Travellers interested in Thai ceramics might pay a visit to Dan Kwian, a village 15 km south-east of Khorat. This village has been producing pottery for hundreds of years; originally this was a bullock-cart stop for traders on their way to markets in old Khorat (Dan Kwian means 'bullock cart checkpoint'). Dan Kwian pottery is famous for its rough texture and rust-like hue – only kaolin from this district produces such results.

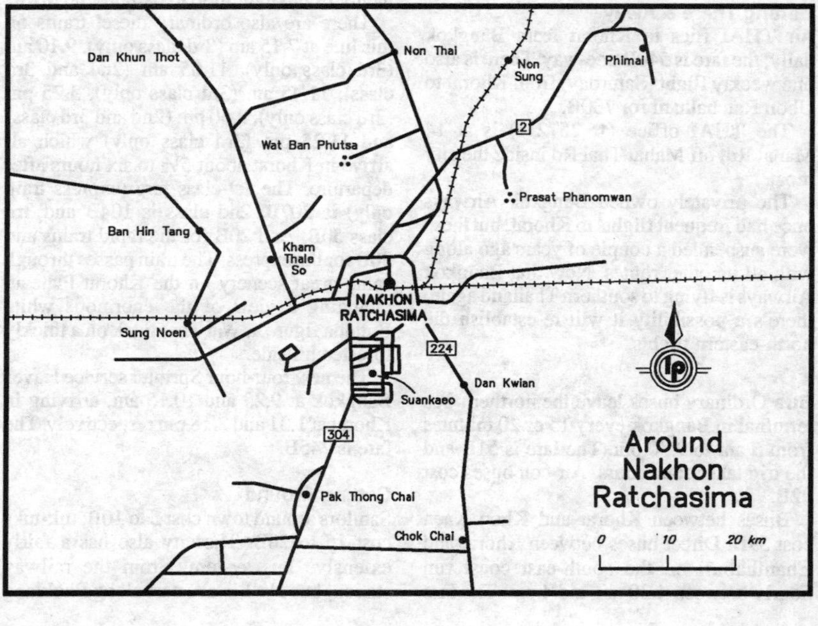

Several more or less permanent shops line the highway. Prices are very good – many exporters shop for Thai pottery here. It's not all pottery either – clay is shaped and fired into all kinds of art objects, including jewellery.

To get here from Khorat by public transport, hop a songthaew from the east city gate; the fare to Dan Kwian is 6B.

Phimai
พิมาย

The small town of Phimai is nothing much, but staying the night is pleasant enough if you're here to visit Prasat Hin Phimai. (If you want to visit the ruins as a day trip from Khorat, an 8 am bus would give you plenty of wandering time at the ruins with time to spare for the return bus trip in the late afternoon.)

Outside the town entrance, a couple of km down Highway 206, is Thailand's largest banyan tree, a mega-florum spread over an island in a large pond (actually a state irrigation reservoir). The locals call it **Sai Ngam**, meaning 'beautiful banyan'; you can walk through the banyan branches via wooden

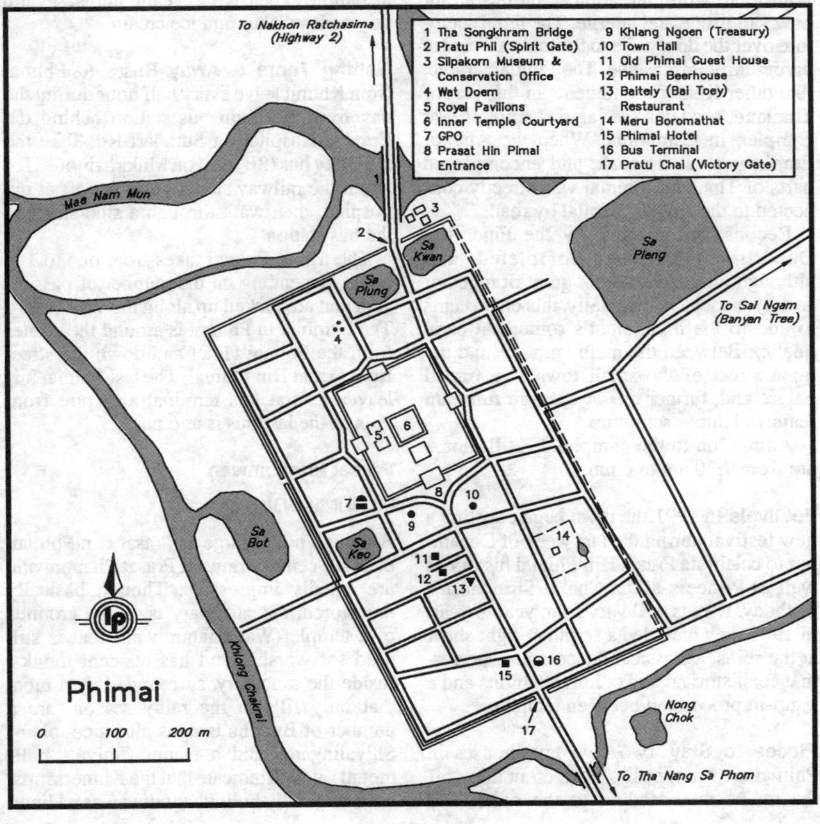

walkways built over the pond. Food vendors and astrologers offer their services to picnickers in the vicinity.

Bicycles can be rented for 30B per day at a shop at 246/1-3 Chomsudasadet Rd.

Prasat Hin Phimai This Angkor-period Khmer shrine, 60 km north-east of Khorat, makes Phimai worth a visit. Originally started by Khmer King Jayavarman V in the late 10th century and finished by King Suriyavarman I in the early 11th century, this Mahayana Buddhist temple projects a majesty that transcends its size. The main shrine, of cruciform design, is made of white sandstone, while the adjunct shrines are of pink sandstone and laterite. The lintel sculpture over the doorways to the main shrine are particularly impressive. The Phimai temple, like other Khmer monuments in this part of Thailand, predates the famous Angkor Wat complex in Cambodia. When the Angkor Empire was at its peak, and encompassed parts of Thailand, Phimai was directly connected to the Angkor capital by road.

Reconstruction work by the Fine Arts Department has been completed, and although the pieces do not quite fit together as they must have originally, this only seems to add to the monument's somewhat eerie quality. Between the main entrance and the main street of the small town is a ruined palace and, further on, an open-air museum features Khmer sculpture.

Admission to the complex is 20B; hours are from 7.30 am to 6 pm.

Festivals In 1991 the town began hosting a new festival during the last week of December to celebrate Prasat Hin Phimai history as well as Princess Maha Chakri Sirindhorn's birthday. Events will vary from year to year; in 1991 they included a sound & light show at the ruins, a classical dance-drama performance, historical and cultural exhibits and a lamp-lit procession between temples.

Places to Stay Two new guesthouses in Phimai are on opposite sides of an alley off the main street leading to the ruins. *Old Phimai Guest House* (☎ 471725) has dorm beds for 60B, plus singles/doubles/triples for 80/100/140B in a large house. *Phimai Beerhouse* opposite is mostly a pub, but takes the overflow from the Old Phimai.

The town's one hotel, *Phimai Hotel*, is around the corner from the bus terminal and has very clean and comfortable rooms from 80 to 130B without bath, 120 to 180B with a bath, and from 200 to 300B with air-con.

Places to Eat Good Thai and Chinese food is available at the *Baiteiy (Bai Toey)* restaurant near the hotel and guesthouses. Daily lunch specials are just 15 to 20B; there are also more expensive a la carte items, several vegetarian dishes and ice cream.

Getting There & Away Buses to Phimai from Khorat leave every half hour during the day from the main bus station behind the Erawan Hospital on Suranari Rd. Take the No 2 city bus (2B) east on Mukkhamontri Rd (from the railway station) and get off at the hospital, then walk through a side street to the bus station.

The trip to Phimai takes from one to 1½ hours, depending on the number of passengers that are picked up along the way (14B). The terminal in Phimai is around the corner from the Phimai Hotel and down the street from Prasat Hin Phimai. The last Phimai bus leaves Khorat bus terminal at 8 pm; from Phimai the last bus is at 6 pm.

Prasat Phanomwan

ปราสาทพนมวัน

Although not as large as Prasat Hin Phimai, the 11th-century ruins at Prasat Phanomwan are equally impressive. Though basically unrestored, the sanctuary is on the grounds of a temple (Wat Phanomwan) that is still used for worship and has resident monks. Inside the sanctuary, surrounded by a moat that only fills in the rainy season, are a number of Buddha images plus a couple of Shivalingams and a Nandi (Shiva's bull-mount), which indicate that the Khmers must have originally built Phanomwan as a Hindu temple. Fifty metres south-west of the main sanctuary is a building that houses other sculpture and artefacts.

A French team has recently begun working on a restoration of Phanomwan.

Getting There Prasat Phanomwan is off Highway 2 about 15 km north-east of Khorat on the way to Phimai – ask to be let off at Ban Saen Muang (4B), then hop on a local songthaew, hitchhike or walk the six km through Ban Saen Muang, Ban Nong Bua and Ban Makham to get to Prasat Phanomwan.

There are also three direct buses a day to Phanomwan from Khorat's Phosaen Gate at 7 am, 10 am and noon. The fare is 5B.

KHAO YAI NATIONAL PARK

อุทยานแห่งชาติเขาใหญ่

Founded as Thailand's first national park in 1961, 2168-sq-km Khao Yai is considered by many park experts to be among the world's top five national parks. The terrain covers five vegetation zones: semi-evergreen rainforest (400 to 900 metres), evergreen rainforest (100 to 400 metres), hill evergreen forest (over 1000 metres) and mixed deciduous forest (northern slopes at 400 to 600 metres), plus savanna and secondary-growth forest in areas where agriculture and logging occurred before the area was protected.

Some 200 to 300 wild elephants reside within park boundaries; other recorded mammals include sambar deer, barking deer, gaur, wild pig, Malayan sun bear, Asiatic black bear, tiger, leopard, serow, and various gibbons and macaques. In general these animals are most easily spotted during the rainy season from June to October. Khao Yai also has Thailand's largest population of hornbills, including the great hornbill *(nók kòk* or *nók kaahang* in Thai), king of the bird kingdom, as well as wreathed hornbill *(nók ngaa cháang*, literally 'elephant-tusk bird'), Indian pied hornbill *(nók khàek)*, and rhinoceros hornbill *(nók râet)*. Hornbills breed from January to May, the best time to see them. They also feed on figs, so ficus trees are good places to find them.

The park has over 40 km of hiking trails, many of them formed by wildlife movement. Elevations range from 250 to 1400 metres where the western edge of Cambodia's Dongrek mountain range meets the southern edge of the Khorat Plateau. You can get a rather inaccurate trail map from the park headquarters. It's easy to get lost on the longer trails so it's advisable to hire a guide. The charge will be 100B per day no matter how many people go. The guide is liable to ask for a tip. If you do plan to go walking, it is a good idea to take boots as leeches can be a problem – although apparently mosquito repellent does help to keep leeches away.

In nearby Pak Chong you can also arrange a 1½ day tour with Tom (Swedish) and Maew (Thai) from the Jungle Guest House. Their tour begins with a half-day jaunt to a bat cave outside park boundaries, followed by an all-day trip through the park, including evening wildlife-spotting. The tour costs 500B per person. Several other would-be guides wait at the bus terminals to snare new arrivals.

Places to Stay

In years past, the TAT's *Khao Yai Hotel* offered bungalow, motel and dormitory accommodation at the park, but all permanent visitor accommodation was scheduled for removal by the end of 1992. Forestry Department bungalows were also slated for removal, but overnight camping is still allowed in camping areas where you can pitch a tent for 5B per person per night. There are also platforms in the park where rangers will allow you to sleep for 10B per night.

In nearby Pak Chong, the *Jungle Guest House* (☎ 312877, 311989), off Soi 3 at 752/11 Kongwaksin Rd, offers basic rooms for 70B per night including a substantial breakfast. The guesthouse is a 10 to 15-minute walk from the bus terminals on Friendship Highway; turn right from the Khorat terminal (or left from the Bangkok terminal), then left at the traffic light, left again at Soi 3 (at the Bamboo Restaurant)

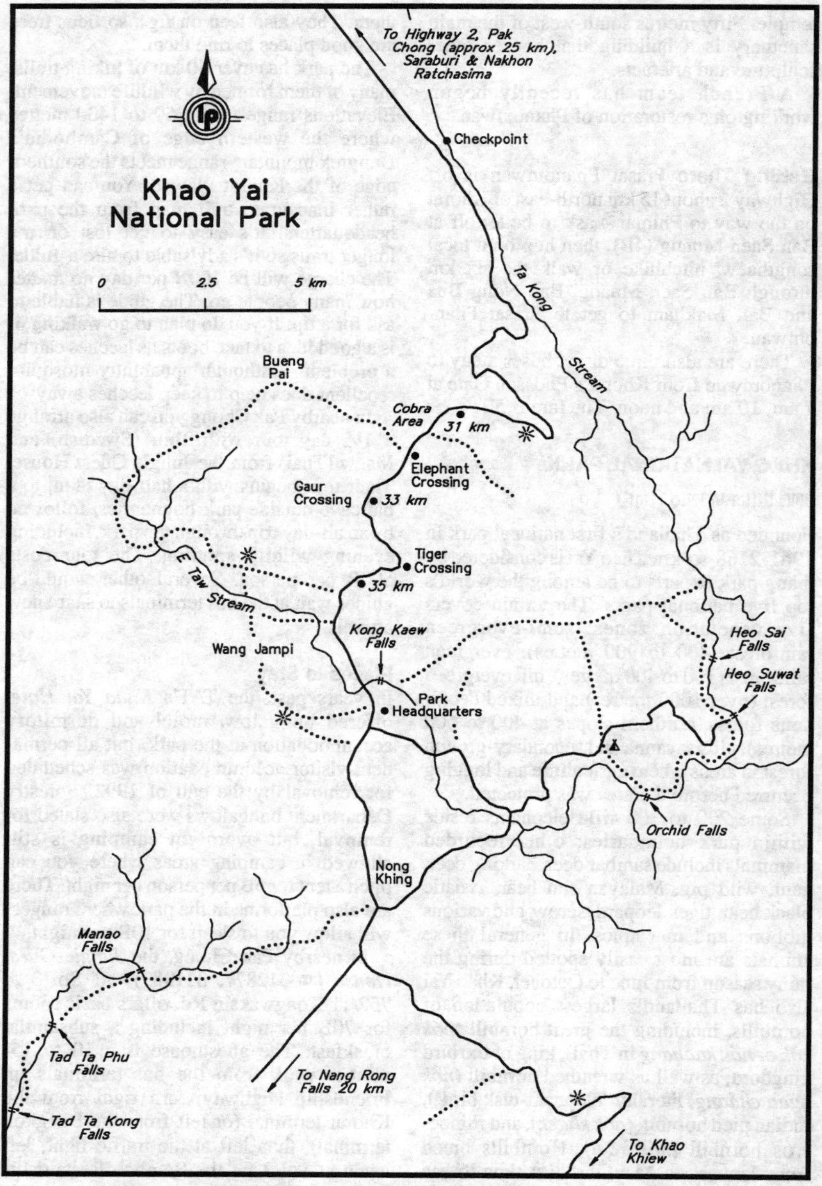
Khao Yai National Park
0
2.5
5 km
To Highway 2, Pak Chong (approx 25 km), Saraburi & Nakhon Ratchasima
Checkpoint
Ta Kong Stream
Bueng Pai
Cobra Area
31 km
Elephant Crossing
Gaur Crossing
33 km
Tiger Crossing
35 km
E Taw Stream
Kong Kaew Falls
Wang Jampi
Park Headquarters
Heo Sai Falls
Heo Suwat Falls
Orchid Falls
Nong Khing
Manao Falls
Tad Ta Phu Falls
Tad Ta Kong Falls
To Nang Rong Falls 20 km
To Khao Khiew

and then after about 200 metres left again, just before an open field.

Getting There & Away
From Bangkok take a bus (every 15 minutes 5 am to 10 pm; 35B ordinary, 65B air-con) from the northern bus station to Pak Chong, from where you can hitch or take a songthaew to the park gates. The fare is 10B from opposite the air-con bus terminal in Pak Chong. You may also be able to take a direct bus from Bangkok at certain times of year – enquire at the northern bus station.

You can also easily get to Pak Chong from Ayuthaya by ordinary train for 23B 3rd class, 47B 2nd class; the trip takes around three hours. From Bangkok the train costs 36B 3rd class, 73B 2nd class, not including the surcharge (20B) for rapid trains; the ordinary train takes around four hours from Bangkok, the rapid is half an hour shorter.

Hitchhiking in the park is usually easy.

Buriram Province

Buriram is a large province (number 18 out of 73) with a small capital and a long history. During the Angkor period this area was an important part of the Khmer Empire. The restored ruins at Prasat Hin Khao Phanom Rung are the most impressive of all Angkor monuments in Thailand; other lesser known ruins in the province include Prasat Hin Muang Tham, Ku Rasi, Prasat Ban Khok Ngiu, Prasat Nong Hong, Prasat Ban Thai Charoen, Prasat Nong Kong, Prang Ku Samathom, Prang Ku Khao Plaibat, Prang Ku Suwan Taeng, Prang Ku Khao Kadong and many others.

Generally speaking, prasat (from the Sanskrit architectural term *prasada)* refers to large temple sanctuaries with a cruciform floor plan, while ku and prang ku are smaller Khmer-style chedis or stupas. However, many Thais use these terms interchangeably. Prasat is sometimes translated in Thai tourist literature as 'castle' or 'palace', but these Khmer monuments were never used as royal residences.

Most of the ruins in Buriram are little more than piles of bricks by the side of a road or out in a field. As the Fine Arts Department and/or the local community continue restoration in the province, more of the Khmer monuments mentioned here may become worth seeing.

Buriram Province is currently notorious among Thais for the 320-hectare **Dong Yai Forest** protected by monk Prajak Kuttajitto, who 'ordained' trees with monastic robes and sacred thread so people wouldn't cut them. In 1991 he and his followers were finally run out of the forest by the Thai military but not without the sustained protests of thousands of sympathetic Thai citizens.

PRASAT HIN KHAO PHANOM RUNG HISTORICAL PARK
ปราสาทหินเขาพนมรุ้ง

Phanom Rung is Khmer for Big Hill, but the Thais have added their own word for hill *(khāo)* to the name as well as the word for stone *(hĩn)* to describe the prasat.

Orientation & Information
Prasat Phanom Rung is on an extinct volcanic cone, 383 metres above sea level, that dominates the flat countryside for some distance in all directions. To the south-east you can clearly see Cambodia's Dongrek Mountains, and it's in this direction that the capital of the Angkor Empire once lay. The prasat's temple complex is the largest and best restored of all the Khmer monuments in Thailand (it took 17 years to complete the restoration) and although it's not the easiest place to reach, it's well worth the effort.

The temple was constructed between the 10th and 13th centuries with the bulk of the work being done during the reign of King Suriyavarman II (1113 to 1150 AD), which by all accounts was the apex of Angkor architecture. The complex faces east, towards the original Angkor capital. Of the

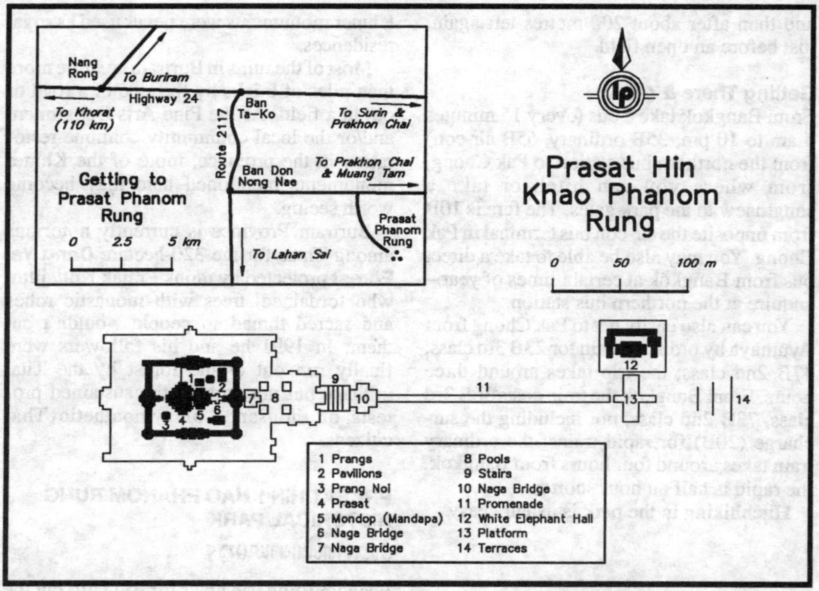

three other great Khmer monuments of South-East Asia, Angkor Wat faces west, Prasat Khao Viharn faces north and Prasat Hin Phimai faces south-east. Nobody knows for sure whether these orientations have any special significance, especially as most smaller Khmer monuments in Thailand face east (towards the dawn – typical of Hindu temple orientation).

A small museum on the grounds contains some sculpture from the complex and photographs of the 17-year restoration process.

There is a 20B admission fee to the Phanom Rung Historical Park during daylight hours. *The Sanctuary Phanomrung*, by Dr Sorajet Woragamvijya is an informative booklet put out by the Lower North-East Study Association (LNESA). It is sold near the entrance to the complex for 20B (vendors may ask 50B, but the LNESA says visitors shouldn't pay more than 20B). Several English-speaking guides also offer their services at the complex – fee negotiable.

Design

One of the most remarkable design aspects of Phanom Rung is the promenade leading to the main gate. This is the best surviving example in Thailand. It begins on a slope 400 metres east of the main tower with three earthen terraces. Next comes a cruciform base for what may have been a wooden pavilion. To the right of this is a stone hall known locally as the White Elephant Hall. On the north side of this hall are two pools that were probably once used for ritual ablutions before entering the temple complex. Flower garlands to be used as offerings in the temple may also have been handed out here. After you step down from the pavilion area, you'll come to a 160-metre avenue paved with laterite and sandstone blocks and flanked by sandstone pillars with lotus-bud tops, said to be early Angkor style (1100 to 1180 AD). The avenue ends at the first and largest of three naga bridges.

These naga bridges are the only three

which have survived in Thailand. The first is flanked by 16 five-headed nagas (cobra deities) in the classic Angkor style. After passing this bridge and climbing the stairway you come to the magnificent east gallery leading into the main sanctuary. The central prasat has a gallery on each of four sides and the entrance to each gallery is itself a smaller version of the main tower. The galleries have curvilinear roofs and false balustraded windows. Once inside the temple walls, look at each of the galleries and the *gopura* entrances, paying particular attention to the lintels over the porticoes. The craftwork at Phanom Rung represents the pinnacle of Khmer artistic achievement, on a par with the reliefs at Angkor Wat in Cambodia.

Sculpture

The Phanom Rung complex was originally built as a Hindu monument and exhibits iconography related to the worship of Vishnu and Shiva. Excellent sculptures of both Vaishnava and Shaiva deities can be seen in the lintels or pediments over the doorways to the central monuments and in various other key points on the sanctuary exterior.

On the east portico of the mondop (antechamber to the prasat or main sanctuary) is a Nataraja (Dancing Shiva), in the late Baphuan or early Angkor style, while on the south entrance are the remains of Shiva and Uma riding their bull mount, Nandi. The central cell of the prasat contains a Shivalingam or phallus image.

Several sculptured images of Vishnu and his incarnations Rama and Krishna can be found on various other lintels and cornices. Probably the most beautiful is the **Pra Narai Lintel**, a relief depicting Lord Narayana, a reclining Vishnu in the midst of the Hindu creation myth. Growing from his navel is a lotus that branches into several blossoms, on one of which sits the creator god Brahma. On either side of Vishnu are heads of Kala, the god of Time and Death. He is asleep on the milky sea of eternity, here represented by a naga snake. This lintel sits above the eastern gate (the main entrance) beneath the Shiva Nataraja relief.

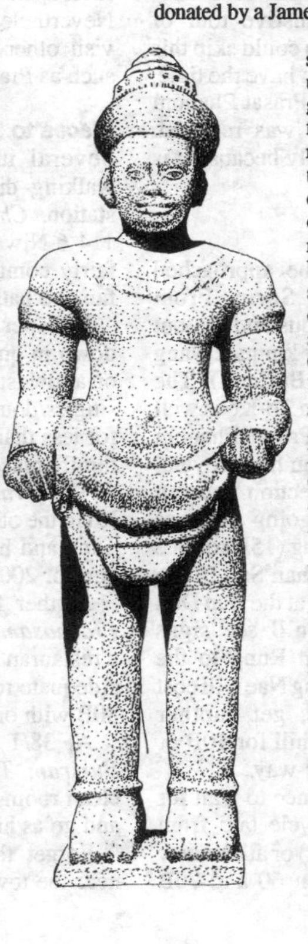

An interesting story goes with the Phra Narai (Thai for Lord Narayana) lintel. In the 1960s it was noticed that the lintel was missing from the sanctuary and an investigation determined that it must have disappeared between 1961 and 1965. A mysterious helicopter was reportedly seen in the vicinity during this period. The Thais later discovered the lintel on display at the Art Institute of Chicago; the lintel had been donated by a James Alsdorf.

The Thai government as well as several private foundations tried unsuccessfully for many years to get the artwork returned to its rightful place. As the complex was reaching the final stages of restoration in preparation for the official opening in May 1988, a public outcry in Thailand demanded the return of the missing lintel. In the USA, Thai residents and American sympathisers demonstrated in front of the Chicago museum. The socially conscious Thai pop group Carabao recorded an album entitled *Thap Lang (Lintel)* that featured an album cover with a picture of the Statue of Liberty cradling the Phra Narai lintel in her left arm! The chorus of the title song went: *Take back Michael Jackson – Give us back Phra Narai.*

In December 1988 the Alsdorf Foundation returned the Phra Narai lintel to Thailand in exchange for US$250,000 (paid by private sources in the USA) and an arrangement whereby Thailand's Fine Arts Department would make temporary loans of various Thai art objects to the Art Institute of Chicago on a continuing basis. Rumour in Thailand has it that of the seven Thais involved in the original theft and sale of the lintel, only one is still alive. The other six are supposed to have met unnatural deaths.

Phanom Rung Festival
During the week of the nationwide Songkran Festival in April, the local people have their own special celebration that commemorates the restoration of Prasat Phanom Rung. During the day there is a procession up Phanom Rung Hill and at night sound & light shows and dance-dramas are performed in the temple complex.

Prasat Muang Tam
ปราสาทเมืองต่ำ
About five km south of Phanom Rung, this Khmer site dates to the late 10th century and was sponsored by King Jayavarman V. The laterite wall is still in fair condition, but most of the prasat has tumbled down. Unless you're attempting an exhaustive tour of Khmer ruins in Thailand, you could skip this one. On the other hand, if you have the time, it gives a good idea of what Prasat Phanom Rung looked like before it was restored. Admission is 20B, presumably because it is undergoing restoration.

Getting There & Away
Prasat Phanom Rung can be approached from Khorat, Buriram or Surin. From Khorat, take a Surin-bound bus and get out at Ban Ta-Ko, which is a few km past Nang Rong (the turn-off north to Buriram). The fare should be about 20B; Ban To-Ko is well marked as the turn-off for Prasat Phanom Rung. Once in Ban Ta-Ko you have several options. At the Ta-Ko intersection you can wait for a songthaew that's going as far as the foot of Khao Phanom Rung (15B) or one that's on the way south to Lahan Sai. If you take a Lahan Sai truck, get off at the Ban Don Nong Nae intersection (you'll see signs pointing the way to Phanom Rung to the east). From Ta-Ko to Don Nong Nae will cost 3B. From Don Nong Nae, get another songthaew to the foot of the hill for 10B or charter a pick-up for 40B one-way.

If you don't have the patience to wait for a songthaew, take a motorcycle taxi from Ta-Ko to Don Nong Nae (30B) or all the way to Phanom Rung for between 60 and 70B each way. A round trip will cost 120 to 150B; for an extra 50B the drivers will add Muang Tam. These rates include waiting for you while you tour the ruins.

There are also a couple of morning songthaews from Buriram Market that go directly to Ban Don Nong Nae; these are met by songthaews that go straight to the ruins.

From Surin, take a Khorat-bound bus and get off at the same place on Highway 24, Ban Ta-Ko, then follow the directions as from Khorat.

BURIRAM
อ.เมืองบุรีรัมย์
Buriram is a small provincial capital (population 29,000) with not a lot to do. Nevertheless it is a good base from which to visit other attractions around the province such as Prasat Phanom Rung.

Places to Stay
Several inexpensive hotels are within walking distance of the Buriram railway station. *Chai Jaroen Hotel* (☎ 601559) at 114-6 Niwat Rd, in front of the station, has fairly comfortable rooms from 80B with a fan and bath.

Cheaper but definitely a step or three down in quality is the *Nivas (Niwat) Hotel*, on a soi just off Niwat Rd. Its barely adequate singles/doubles are 60/70B (50B a double for less than three hours) – it's not exactly a family place.

The *Grand Hotel* (☎ 611089), up Niwat Rd in the other direction, has fair rooms with a fan and bath starting at 100B or with aircon for 200B.

Further from the railway station is the *Prachasamakhi Hotel*, a Chinese hotel with a restaurant downstairs on Sunthonthep Rd. Adequate rooms cost 50B without a bath or 80B with one.

At 38/1 Romburi Rd is the fairly nice *Buriram Thai Hotel* (☎ 611112), where clean rooms start at 100B with fan and bath and go as high as 500B for a deluxe room.

Forget the dirty, desolate *Krung Rome* near the town entrance from Highway 218.

It's a large multistorey place that serves as a short-time outlet for the 'coffee shop' next door. From a distance it doesn't look that bad but they don't keep the power running during the day.

Buriram will soon be getting its first tourist-class hotel, the 229-room *Buriram Plaza*; the rates haven't been announced yet but I'd predict 500 to 800B per night for air-con rooms.

You can also stay closer to Prasat Phanom Rung by spending the night at the nondescript hotel in Nang Rong. It's cheap, friendly and noisy, and there's an attached restaurant.

Places to Eat

In front of the railway station is a small night market with good, inexpensive food. This area also has a few restaurants that are open during the day for breakfast and lunch. The one on the corner of the clock tower opens early in the morning and sells coffee, tea and paa-thông-kõ (light Chinese pastries).

At the Samatakan and Thani Rds intersection is a larger night market that has mostly Chinese as well as a few isaan vendors.

The *Maitrichit Restaurant* on Sunthonthep Rd near the Prachasamakhi Hotel has a large selection of Thai and Chinese standards

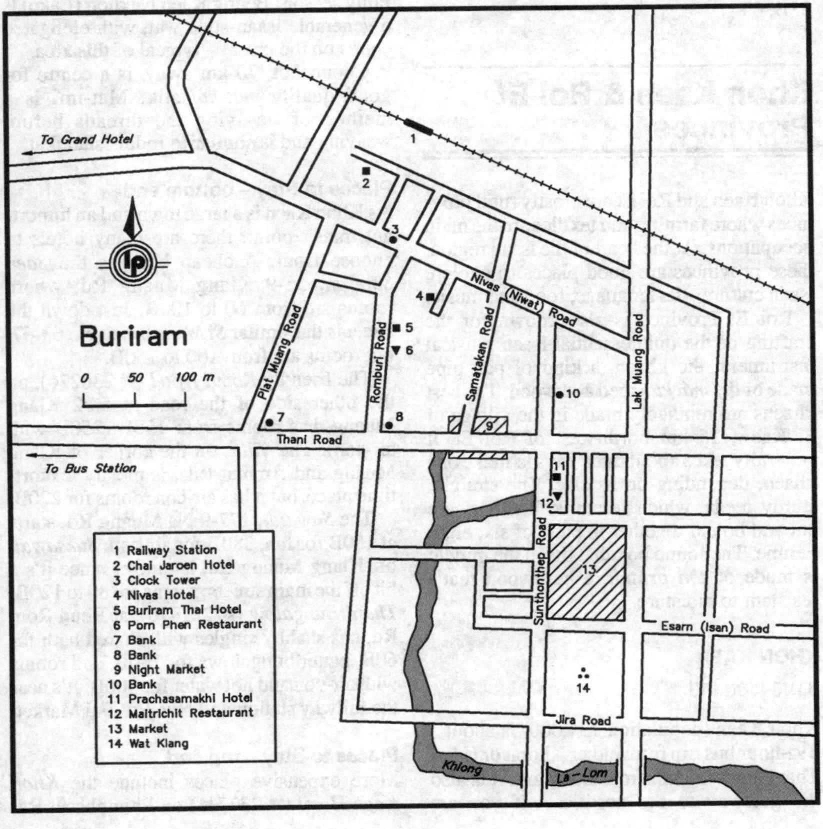

which are served from morning until night. Also good is the *Porn Phen (Phawn Phen)* near the Buriram Thai Hotel on Romburi Rd.

Just after you turn left (east) from Ban Don Nong Nae on the way to Phanom Rung there is a nice little family-owned place called *Baan Nit (Nit's House)* where you can get good home-cooked local food. Nit only has a few tables, but out in this area there's not a lot of choice.

Getting There & Away

Buses from Khorat to Buriram leave about every half hour between 4.30 am and 7.30 pm. The trip takes about 2½ hours and costs 33B.

Khon Kaen & Roi Et Provinces

Khon Kaen and Roi Et are mostly rural provinces where farming and textiles are the main occupations. At the heart of the isaan region, these provinces are good places to explore isaan culture – its language, food and music.

Roi Et Province is also known for the crafting of the quintessential isaan musical instrument, the khaen, a kind of pan pipe made of the *mái kuu* reed and wood. The best khaens are reputedly made in the village of Si Kaew, 15 km north-west of Roi Et. It generally takes about three days to make one khaen, depending on its size. The straight, sturdy reeds, which resemble bamboo, are cut and bound together in pairs of six, eight or nine. The sound box that fits in the middle is made of *tôn pràtuu*, a hardwood that's resistant to moisture.

KHON KAEN

อ.เมืองขอนแก่น

Khon Kaen (population 134,000) is about a 2½-hour bus trip from either Khorat or Udon Thani, and 450 km from Bangkok. It is also the gateway to the north-east if you are coming from Phitsanulok in northern Thailand by bus or plane.

Khon Kaen is one of Thailand's largest cities outside Bangkok and is an important commercial, financial, educational and communications centre for isaan. For visitors, about the only thing of interest is a very good provincial branch of the **National Museum**, which features Dvaravati objects, *sẽma* (ordination marker) stones from Kalasin and Muang Fa Daet, and bronze and ceramic artefacts from Ban Chiang. It's open Wednesday to Sunday from 9 am to noon and 1 to 5 pm. Admission is 10B.

On the banks of Khon Kaen's large (in the rainy season) Beung Kaen Nakhon (Lake) is a venerable isaan-style wat, with elongated spires on the prasat – typical of this area.

Chonnabot, 70 km away, is a centre for good quality *mát-mii* silk. Mat-mii is a method of tie-dying the threads before weaving and is similar to Indonesian ikat.

Places to Stay – bottom end

As Khon Kaen is a large town and an important transit point, there are many hotels to choose from. A cheap hotel is the *Saen Samran*, 55-9 Klang Muang Rd, where rooms are from 60 to 100B. Just down the street is the similar *Si Mongkon* at No 61-67, but rooms are from 100 to 150B.

The friendly *Roma Hotel* (☎ 236276), on the other side of the road at 50/2 Klang Muang, has rooms from 150B (250B with air-con). The *Villa*, on the corner of Klang Muang and Ammat Rds, is mostly a short-time place, but it has air-con rooms for 220B.

The *Sawatdi*, 177-9 Na Muang Rd, starts at 150B for fan, 380B for air-con. *Suksawat*, off Klang Muang Rd, is quieter since it's a bit off the main streets; rooms are 80 to 120B. *Thani Bungalow* (☎ 221470), at Reun Rom Rd, has shabby singles with shared bath for 60B, better bungalows for 150B, and rooms with air-con and hot water for 300B. It's near the railway station and Hua Rot Fai Market.

Places to Stay – top end

More expensive places include the *Khon Kaen Hotel* (☎ 237711) on Phimphasut Rd, which has air-con rooms from 300B, the *Khosa Khon Kaen* (☎ 225014) on Si Chan Rd where rooms are from 375 to 700B, and the *Rot Sukhon Hotel* (☎ 238576), near the Khon Kaen Hotel on Klang Muang Rd, where rooms start at 363B. Top end is the *Kaen Inn* (☎ 237744), 56 Klang Muang Rd; doubles cost 700 to 1200B with air-con, TV, telephone and fridge.

Places to Eat

The *Jerat Restaurant* across from the municipal market on Klang Muang Rd has good isaan food. Khon Kaen has a lively night market with plenty of good food stalls, next to the air-con bus terminal. Next to the Roma Hotel is *Kai Yang Thiparot*, a good place for kài yâang and other isaan food.

A couple of places serving farang food have opened recently, including the local Peace Corps favourite *The Parrot* on Si Chan Rd near Fairy Plaza. Pizza is among the Western delicacies on the menu. Around the corner on Yimsiri Rd are a few more spots catering to farangs, like *Harry's Wine Bar*.

Things to Buy

Khon Kaen is a good place to buy hand-

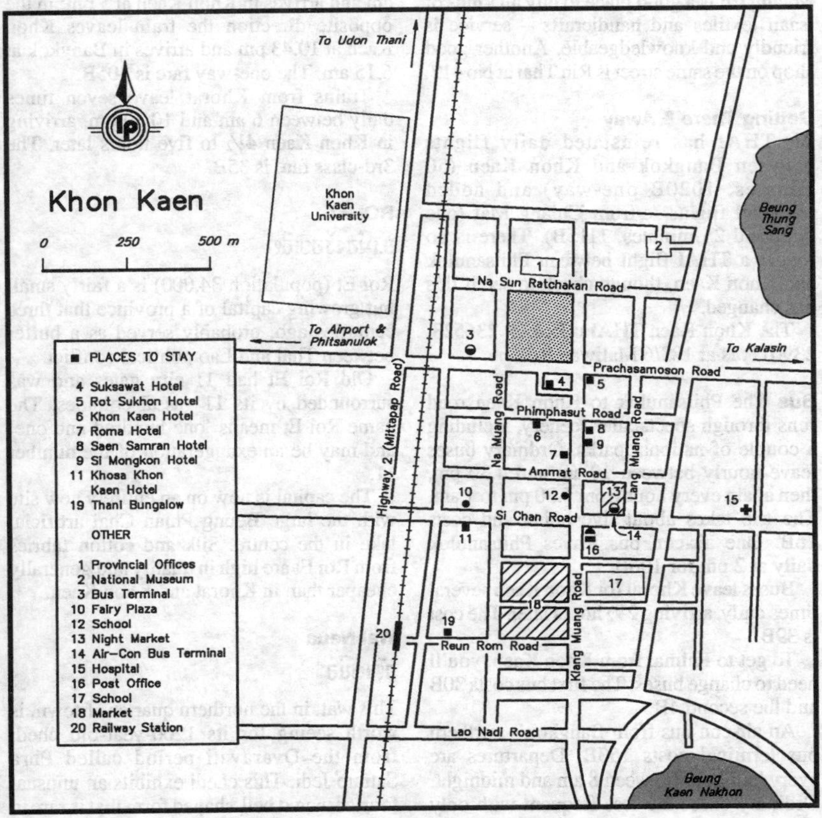

crafted isaan goods such as silk and cotton fabrics (you can get mat-mii cotton as well as silk), silver and basketry. A speciality of the north-east is the *mãwn khwãan* (axe pillow), a stiff triangle-shaped pillow used as a support while sitting on the floor. These come in many sizes, from small enough to carry in a handbag to large enough to fill your entire backpack. Perhaps the most practical way to acquire axe pillows while on the road is to buy them unstuffed *(mâi sài nûn*, 'no kapok inserted') – the covers are easily carried and you can stuff them when you get home.

Mongkonstarn (☎ 221229) at 526-430 Na Muang Rd is a good place to buy all kinds of isaan textiles and handicrafts – service is friendly and knowledgeable. Another good shop on the same street is Rin Thai at No 412.

Getting There & Away

Air THAI has reinstated daily flights between Bangkok and Khon Kaen (50 minutes, 1020B one-way) and added weekend flights to/from Chiang Mai (one hour and 25 minutes, 1115B). There is no longer a THAI flight between Phitsanulok and Khon Kaen, though check to see if this has changed.

The Khon Kaen THAI office (☎ 236523, 239011) is at 183/6 Maliwan Rd.

Bus The Phitsanulok to Khon Kaen road runs through spectacular scenery, including a couple of national parks. Ordinary buses leave hourly between 10 am and 4.30 pm, then again every hour from 6.30 pm to 1 am. The trip takes about five hours and costs 76B. One air-con bus leaves Phitsanulok daily at 2 pm for 106B.

Buses leave Khorat for Khon Kaen several times daily, arriving 2½ hours later. The cost is 39B.

To get to Phimai from Khon Kaen, you'll need to change buses. The first bus costs 30B and the second 4B.

An air-con bus from Bangkok's northern bus terminal costs 153B. Departures are every half hour between 8 am and midnight. Ordinary buses are less frequent with only five departures a day between 9.30 am and 11.10 pm. The fare is 85B.

Air-con night buses to Chiang Mai are available for 247B.

Train The departure times for trains to Khon Kaen from Bangkok are the same as those noted for the Nong Khai line to Khorat (see Khorat section). The trip takes about eight hours regardless of which train you catch. Only the express has 1st-class service. The basic fare is 333B 1st class, 162B 2nd class and 77B 3rd class, plus appropriate charges for rapid or express service.

The new Sprinter leaves Bangkok at 10.15 am and arrives in Khon Kaen at 5 pm; in the opposite direction the train leaves Khon Kaen at 10.43 pm and arrives in Bangkok at 6.15 am. The one-way fare is 305B.

Trains from Khorat leave seven times daily between 6 am and 10.30 pm, arriving in Khon Kaen 4½ to five hours later. The 3rd-class fare is 35B.

ROI ET
อ.เมืองร้อยเอ็ด

Roi Et (population 34,000) is a fairly small but growing capital of a province that three centuries ago, probably served as a buffer between Thai and Lao political conflict.

Old Roi Et had 11 city gates and was surrounded by its 11 vassal colonies. The name Roi Et means 'one hundred and one' and may be an exaggeration of the number 11.

The capital is now on an entirely new site with the large Beung Phlan Chai artificial lake in the centre. Silk and cotton fabrics from Roi Et are high in quality and generally cheaper than in Khorat and Khon Kaen.

Wat Neua
วัดเหนือ

This wat, in the northern quarter of town, is worth seeing for its 1200-year-old chedi from the Dvaravati period called Phra Satuup Jedi. This chedi exhibits an unusual four-cornered bell-shaped form that is rare in

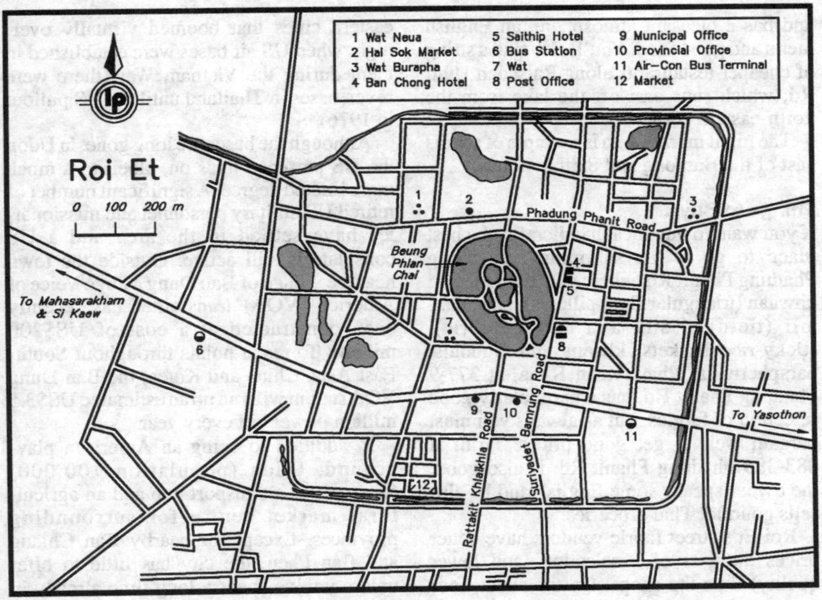

Thailand. Around the bot are a few old Dvaravati sema stones and to one side of the wat is an inscribed pillar, erected by the Khmers when they controlled this area during the 11th and 12th centuries.

Wat Burapha

วัดบูรพา

The tall, standing Buddha that towers above Roi Et's minimal skyline is the Phra Phuttharatana-mongkon-mahamuni (Phra Sung Yai for short) at Wat Burapha. Despite being of little artistic significance, it's hard to ignore. From the ground to the tip of the *ùtsànìt* (flame-top head ornament), it's 67.8 metres high, including the base. You can climb a staircase through a building which supports the figure to about as high as the Buddha's knees and get a view of the town.

Places to Stay

Ban Chong (Banjong) (☎ 511235) at 99-101 Suriyadet Bamrung Rd has adequate rooms with fan and bath from 90 to 150B. On the same street at No 133 is the *Saithip* where fan-cooled rooms start at 150B, air-con from 170B. *Niyom Hotel* (☎ 511170) is near textile shops at 315-7 Phadung Phanit Rd; adequate rooms cost 60 to 120B. There are cheaper hotels along Rattakit Khlaikhla Rd, including the *Thian Di* at No 52-62, where basic rooms start at 60B.

Mai Thai (☎ 511136) at 99 Haisok Rd has all air-con rooms for 300 to 1000B. The newer *Phetcharat Hotel* (☎ 511741, 514058; fax 511837) opposite the Mai Thai has clean rooms with fan and bath for 120 to 150B or nicely appointed air-con rooms with hot water for 200 to 360B. Ask for a room off the road.

Places to Eat

Around the edge of Beung Phalan Chai are several medium-priced garden restaurants. The *Khao Laeng* is on the north-eastern side and has a pleasant atmosphere, an English menu and good food. You'll also find a string of cheaper restaurants along Ratsadan Uthit Rd, which runs east off the lake from the north-eastern corner.

The night market area is a couple of streets east of the Banjong and Saithip hotels.

Things to Buy

If you want to buy local handicrafts, the best place to go is the shopping area along Phadung Phanit Rd, where you'll find mawn khwaan (triangular floor pillows), phaa mat-mii (tie-dyed silk and cotton fabric), sticky-rice baskets, khaens and Buddhist paraphernalia. Phaw Kaan Khaa, at 377-9 Phadung Phanit Rd, has a particularly good selection of fabrics, but as always you must bargain well to get good prices. Jarin, at 383-385 Phadung Phanit Rd, is also good; the owner speaks some English and he also sells gourmet Thai groceries.

Roi Et's street fabric vendors have better prices but less of a selection (and lower quality) than the shops. On the street, four metres of yeoman-quality cotton mat-mii costs as low as 100B.

Getting There & Away

Buses from Udon Thani to Roi Et are 23B (air-con 50B), and from Khon Kaen 20B (air-con 45B). If you're coming straight from Bangkok's northern bus terminal, you can catch an air-con bus for 175B at 8.30 am or 10 am, or every half hour from 8.30 to 11.30 pm. The trip takes about eight hours.

Getting Around

Samlors around town are 10B; motorised samlors cost 15 to 20B.

Udon Thani Province

UDON THANI

อ.เมืองอุดรธานี

Just over 560 km from Bangkok, Udon (often spelt Udorn) is one of several north-eastern cities that boomed virtually overnight when US air bases were established in them during the Vietnam War (there were seven bases in Thailand until the US pullout in 1976).

Although the bases are long gone, in Udon the US presence lives on, albeit to a much more limited degree. A significant number of retired US military personnel and missionaries have settled in the area and a US consulate is still active. Outside the town near the village of Ban Dung a huge Voice of America (VOA) transmitter has recently been constructed at a cost of US$200 million. To reach points throughout South-East Asia, China and Korea, the Ban Dung VOA station will run up an estimated US$3.5 million power bill every year.

In addition to being an American playground, Udon (population 100,000) functions as a transport hub and an agricultural market centre for surrounding provinces. Except for nearby Ban Chiang and Ban Pheu, the city has little to offer unless you've spent a long time already in the north-east and seek Western amenities like air-con coffee houses, flashy ice-cream and massage parlours or farang food. To get away from the busy downtown area, go for a walk around Nong Prajak, a reservoir/park in the north-western part of town.

The parking lot in Charoensi Plaza shopping centre turns into an all-night farmers market after 10 pm.

Information

Several banks along the main avenues provide foreign exchange services. Only the Bangkok Bank on Prajak Rd has an after-hours exchange window – usually open till 8 pm.

The GPO on Wattana Rd is open 8.30 am to 4.30 pm Monday to Friday and 9 am to noon weekends and holidays. The upstairs telephone office is open 7 am to 10 pm daily.

There's a small US consulate (☎ 244270) in the north-western section of the city at 35/6 Suphakit Janya Rd, near Nong Prajak park. The staff can assist US citizens with the extension or replacement of their passports

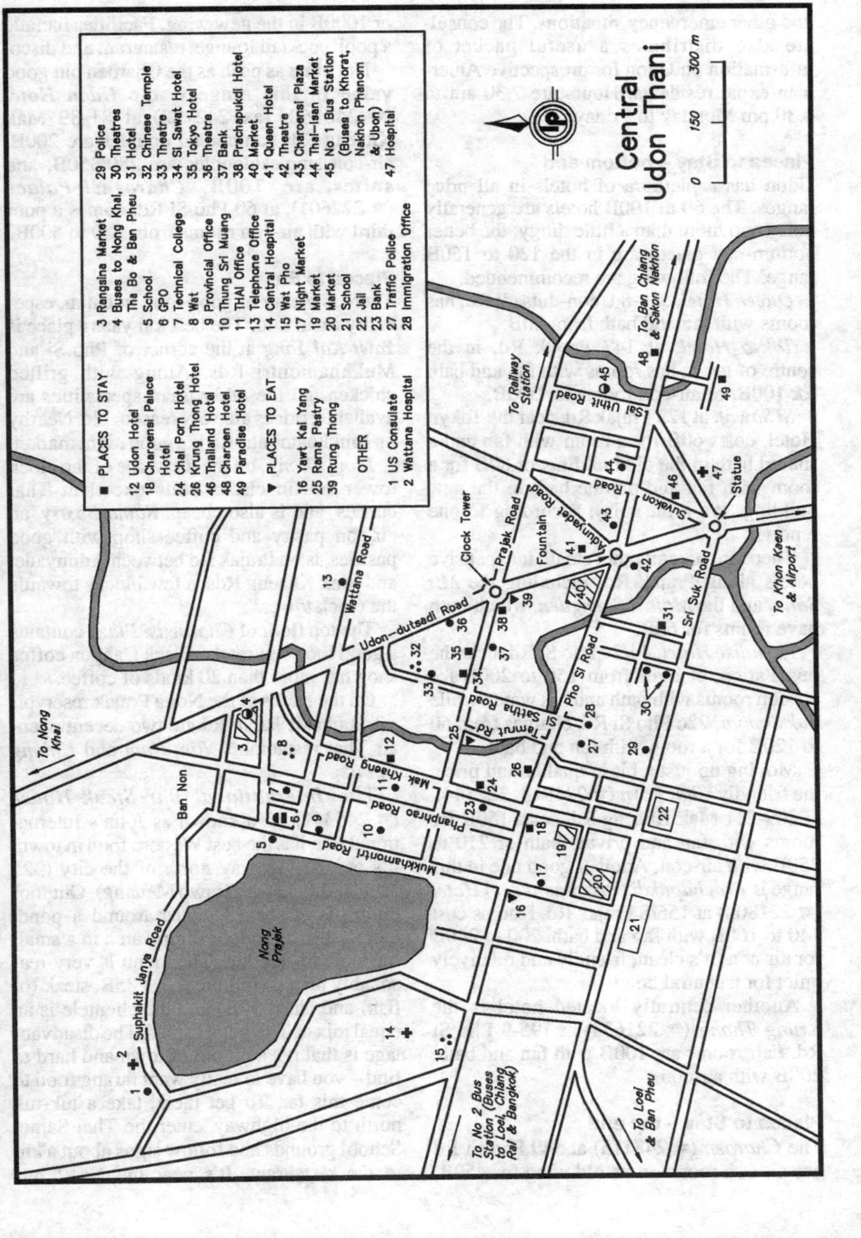
Central Udon Thani
0 150 300 m
PLACES TO STAY
12 Udon Hotel
18 Charoensi Palace Hotel
24 Chai Porn Hotel
26 Krung Thong Hotel
46 Thailand Hotel
48 Charoen Hotel
49 Paradise Hotel
PLACES TO EAT
16 Yawt Kai Yang
25 Rama Pastry
39 Rung Thong
OTHER
1 US Consulate
2 Wattana Hospital
3 Rangsina Market
4 Buses to Nong Khai, Tha Bo & Ban Pheu
5 School
6 GPO
7 Technical College
8 Wat
9 Provincial Office
10 Thung Sri Muang
11 THAI Office
13 Telephone Office
14 Central Hospital
15 Wat Pho
17 Night Market
19 Market
20 Market
21 School
22 Jail
23 Bank
27 Traffic Police
28 Immigration Office
29 Police
30 Theatres
31 Hotel
32 Chinese Temple
33 Theatre
34 Si Sawat Hotel
35 Tokyo Hotel
36 Theatre
37 Bank
38 Prachapukdi Hotel
40 Market
41 Queen Hotel
42 Theatre
43 Charoensi Plaza
44 Thai–Isan Market
45 No 1 Bus Station (Buses to Khorat, Nakhon Phanom & Ubon)
47 Hospital
To Nong Khai
Ban Non
Nong Prajak
Suphakit Janya Road
Mukkhamontri Road
Phanphrao Road
Mak Khaeng Road
Wattana Road
Udon-dutsadi Road
Prajak Road
Clock Tower
Fountain
Adunyadet Road
Sai Uthit Road
Suakon Road
Sri Suk Road
Pho Si Road
Sattha Road
Tamrut Rd
Statue
To Railway Station
To Ban Chiang & Sakon Nakhon
To Khon Kaen & Airport
To Loei & Ban Pheu
To No 2 Bus Station (Buses to Loei, Chiang Rai & Bangkok)

and other emergency situations. The consulate also distributes a useful packet of information on Udon for prospective American expat residents. Hours are 7.30 am to 4.30 pm Monday to Friday.

Places to Stay – bottom end

Udon has a plethora of hotels in all price ranges. The 60 to 100B hotels are generally noisy and more than a little dingy; the better bottom-end places are in the 120 to 150B range. The following are recommended.

Queen Hotel, at 6-8 Udon-dutsadi Rd, has rooms with fan and bath from 80B.

Tokyo Hotel, at 147 Prajak Rd, in the centre of town, has rooms with fan and bath for 100B, or air-con rooms for 300B.

Si Sawat, at 123 Prajak Rd, near the Tokyo Hotel, costs 60B for a room with fan and a shared bath in the old building, or 80B for a room with fan and private bath in the new building. It's a bit noisy, according to one report.

There are several other small, inexpensive hotels along Prajak Rd, including the *Mit Sahai* and the *Malasi Saengden*, which both have rooms for 60B.

Paradise Hotel, 44/29 Pho Si Rd, near the bus station, charges from 150 to 200B for air-con rooms with bath and hot water, while *Suk Somjai*, 226 Pho Si Rd, charges from 60 to 120B for a room with fan and bath.

Moving up just a bit in quality and price, the friendly *Chai Porn* (☎ 221913, 222144), at 209-211 Mak Khaeng Rd, costs 150B for rooms with fan and private bath or 210 to 250B with air-con. Another good one in this range is *Prachapukdi (Prachapakdee) Hotel* (☎ 221804) at 156/8 Prajak Rd. Rooms cost 140 to 160B with fan and bath, 200 to 240B for air-con; it's clean, friendly and relatively quiet for a central hotel.

Another centrally located hotel is the *Krung Thong* (☎ 221634) at 195-9 Pho Si Rd. Fair rooms are 100B with fan and bath, 200B with air-con.

Places to Stay – top end

The *Charoen* (☎ 248115) at 549 Pho Si Rd has air-con rooms in its old wing for 450B, or 1000B in the new wing. Facilities include a pool, cocktail lounge, restaurant and disco.

Not quite as posh as the Charoen but good value in this range is the *Udon Hotel* (☎ 248160; fax 242782) at 81-89 Mak Khaeng Rd. Fan-cooled doubles are 200B, air-con singles/doubles are 280/350B, and suites are 700B. *Charoensi Palace* (☎ 222601), at 60 Pho Si Rd, comes a poor third with air-con rooms from 250 to 500B.

Places to Eat

There is plenty of good food in Udon, especially isaan fare. The best kài yâang place is *Yawt Kai Yang* at the corner of Pho Si and Mukkhamontri Rds. Along with grilled chicken, all the other isaan specialities are available; prices are very reasonable. Nearby on Mukkhamontri Rd is a good night market.

Rung Thong, on the west side of the clock tower traffic circle, sells excellent Thai curries and is also cheap. *Rama Pastry*, an air-con pastry and coffee shop with good pastries, is on Prajak Rd between Adunyadet and Mak Khaeng Rds, a few blocks towards the clock tower.

The top floor of *Charoensi Plaza* contains a good food centre; the Black Canyon coffee shop has more than 20 kinds of coffee.

On the banks of the Nong Prajak reservoir off Suphakit Janya Rd are two decent open-air Thai restaurants, *Rim Nam* and *Khiang Chon*.

The *International Bar Steak House* (☎ 245341), also known as John's International Bar, has the best Western food in town; it's off the highway north of the city (325 Muu 4, Ban Leuam Rawp Meuang). Outdoor dining is at shaded tables around a pond; there's also an indoor dining area in a small tin-roofed brick hut. The menu is very reasonably priced (full breakfast 35B, steak (or fish) and chips 50B) and the clientele is an equal mix of Thais and expats. The disadvantage is that it's a bit out of town and hard to find – you have to really want farang food to come this far. To get there, take a tuk-tuk north to the highway, enter the Thai Samet School grounds and follow signs about a km to the restaurant. It's near the No 2 bus station, which is about a 150-metre walk from the school.

Two other places with farang food are the *Pizza House* at 63/1 Naresuan Rd and *TJ's Restaurant*, 337 Nong Sam Rong Rd.

Entertainment

The Chao Phraya Theatre, at 150 Ratchaphatsadu Rd, has a sound room that plays the original soundtracks for English-language films – probably the only such theatre in north-east Thailand. For somewhere to go at night, the Charoen Hotel has a comfortable bar and also a disco. La Reine at the Udon Hotel is a popular cabaret-style club.

Things to Buy

Udon's main shopping district is centred around Pho Si Rd between the fountain circle and Mak Khaeng Rd. Charoensi Plaza is just east of the fountain circle and has all the typical department-store merchandise.

Mae Lamun is a good local craft shop on Prajak Rd just east of Mak Khaeng Rd; it's on the 2nd floor of a store selling Buddhist paraphernalia. Mae Lamun has a selection of quality silks and cottons, silver, jewellery, Buddha images and ready-made clothes tailored from local fabrics. Prices start high but are negotiable. Another good craft shop – especially for pillows – is Thi Non Michai at 208 Pho Si Rd.

Getting There & Away

Air THAI flies to Udon from Bangkok daily. The flight takes an hour and costs 1260B. The Udon office (☎ 246697, 243222) is at 60 Mak Khaeng Rd.

Bus Buses for Udon leave Bangkok's northern bus terminal throughout the day from 9 am to 11.30 pm. The trip takes 11 to 12 hours and the fare is 106B (191B air-con).

Buses leave the main bus station in Khorat every half hour during the day and arrive five hours later. The cost is 60B (110B air-con).

Getting out of Udon by bus, you must first sort out the tangle of departure points scattered around the city. Ordinary buses to Nong Khai (15 buses a day, 5.30 am to 3.30 pm, 11B) leave from Rangsina Market on the northern outskirts of town; take city bus No 6 or a songthaew north along Udon-dutsadi Rd to get to Talaat Rangsina. You can also get buses to Tha Bo, Si Chiangmai and Ban Pheu from here. The No 2 bus station is on the north-western outskirts of the city next to the highway and has buses to Loei, Nakhon Phanom, Chiang Rai, Si Chiangmai, Nong Khai and Bangkok.

The No 1 bus station is off Sai Uthit Rd near the Charoen Hotel in the south-eastern end of town. Buses from here go mostly to points south and east of Udon, including Khorat, Sakon Nakhon, Nakhon Phanom, Ubon, Khon Kaen, Roi Et and Bangkok, but also go to Beung Kan.

There are also private air-con buses to Bangkok. The company with the best local reputation is 407 Co (☎ 221121) at 125/3 Prajak Rd.

Train The 8.30 pm Nong Khai express from Bangkok arrives in Udon at 6.38 am the next day. The 1st-class fare is 413B, 2nd class is 198B and 3rd class is 95B, plus applicable charges for sleeper and express service.

The all air-con, 1st-class Sprinter leaves Bangkok daily at 10.15 am and arrives in Udon at 6.34 pm; in the reverse direction the Sprinter leaves Udon at 9.06 pm and arrives in Bangkok at 6.15 am. The one-way fare is 340B, which includes a couple of meals.

Rapid trains leave Bangkok on the Nong Khai line at 6.15 am and 7 pm, arriving in Udon at 4 pm and 5.25 am. A special, all-inclusive 3rd-class fare (110B) applies on rapid trains to Udon.

Getting Around

Samlor drivers in Udon practically doubled their rates overnight when 50 Yanks were brought in to work on the VOA station outside the town in 1990-91; apparently the engineers were throwing their dollars around with abandon. With a permanent contingent of VOA employees in the area, just about any farang who happens through Udon will have to deal with this two-tier price system (which exists to some extent everywhere in Thailand

– it's just grossly exaggerated in Udon). Reasonable fares are 5 to 10B on short sprints (eg the No 1 bus station to the Paradise Hotel), 10 to 15B for a medium-length trip (eg No 1 bus station to the Prachapukdi Hotel) or up to 20B for a longer jaunt (eg Charoensi Plaza to Nong Prajak Park).

A more hassle-free way to get around is by city bus. The most useful city bus for visitors is the yellow No 2, which plies a route from the No 2 bus station, south along Suphakit Janya Rd, and then along Pho Si Rd past the Charoen Hotel. The fare is only 2B.

AROUND UDON THANI PROVINCE

Ban Chiang

บ้านเชียง

Ban Chiang, 50 km east of Udon Thani, now plays host to a steady trickle of tourists from all over Thailand and a few from beyond. As well as the original excavation at **Wat Pho Si Nai** at the village edge (open to the public), there is a recently constructed museum with extensive Ban Chiang exhibits. This is worth a trip if you're at all interested in the historic Ban Chiang culture, which goes back at least 5000 years and quite possibly 7000. The museum is closed Monday and Tuesday. A map of the area is available at the museum.

The Bang Chiang culture, an agricultural society which once thrived in north-eastern Thailand, is known for its early bronze metallurgy and clay pottery, especially pots and vases with distinctive burnt-ochre swirl designs, most of which were associated with burial sites. The locals attempt to sell Ban Chiang artefacts, real and fake, but neither type will be allowed out of the country, so don't buy them. Some of the local handicrafts, such as thick handwoven cotton fabric, are good buys.

Getting There & Away There is a regular bus between Udon and Ban Chiang for 20B.

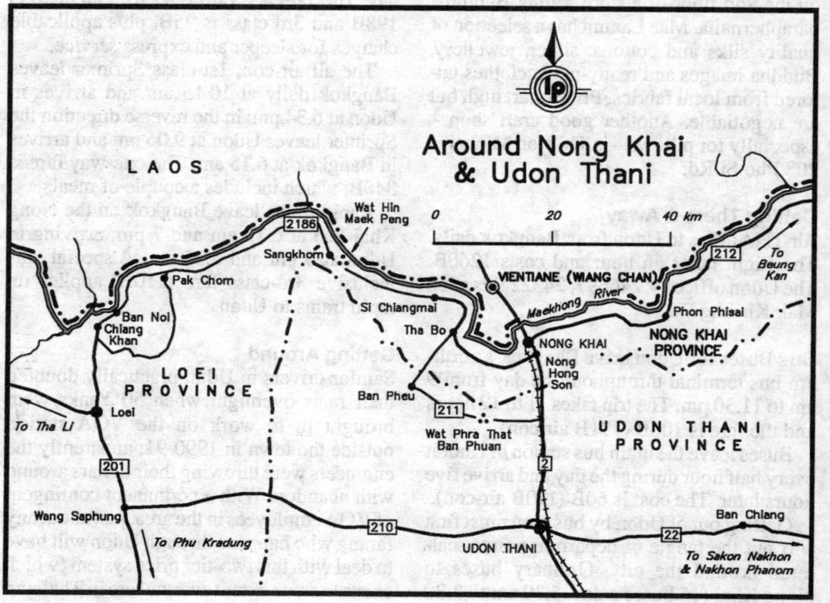

Top Left: Monkeys (JC)
Bottom Left: Elephant (CLA)
Top Right: Water buffalo (TAT)
Bottom Right: Elephant riding (TAT)

Top Left: Wat Phra That Choeng Chum, Sakon Nakhon (JC)
Bottom Left: Ceramic detail, Wat Arun (GB)
Top Right: Mosaic, Wat Chiang Man, Chiang Mai (JC)
Bottom Right: Temple ruins, Ayuthaya (RI)

Buses leave in either direction several times a day, but the last leaves Ban Chiang in the late afternoon.

Ban Pheu
บ้านผือ

Ban Pheu district, 42 km north-west of Udon Thani, has a peculiar mix of prehistoric cave paintings, bizarre geological formations and Buddhist shrines, the bulk of which are at Phra Phutthabat Bua Bok, 12 km outside Ban Pheu on Phra Bat hill. The area has recently been declared **Phu Phra Bat Historical Park**.

The formations are a madhouse of balanced rocks, spires and whale-sized boulders, with several shrines and three wats built in and around the formations. A trail meandering through the park takes around two hours to negotiate at a normal pace.

At the entrance to the area is the largest temple in the historical park, **Wat Phra That Phra Phutthabat Bua Bok**. Prehistoric paintings are in several caves and feature wild animals, humans and cryptic symbols. To the south-east of the main wat are the caves of **Tham Lai Meu** and **Tham Non Sao Eh** and to the west are **Tham Khon** and **Tham Wua Daeng**. For isaan residents, this is an important place of pilgrimage. For visitors, the side-by-side progression from rock art to Buddhist temples represents a localised evolution of thought and aesthetics.

A crude trail map is available at the park entrance, although it doesn't include all the caves nor all the trail branches.

Getting There & Away Ban Pheu has one hotel (70B with shared bath) if you want to spend some time here. Otherwise, it can be visited as a long day trip from either Udon or Nong Khai. From Udon it's a 14B songthaew ride to Ban Pheu or 20B from Nong Khai. From Ban Pheu, take a songthaew for 4B to the village nearest the site, Ban Tiu, then walk or hitch the three km to Wat Phra Phutthabat. You could also charter a motorcycle in the Ban Pheu market to take you all the way to Phra Phutthabat.

Easiest of all would be to visit the park by bicycle or motorbike from Nong Khai.

Nong Khai Province

Nong Khai Province is long and narrow, with 300 km of its length along the Maekhong River. Yet at its widest point, the province is only 50 km across. Even if you can't cross into Laos, Nong Khai is a fascinating province to explore. It has long, open views of the Maekhong River and Laos on the other side. There are touches of Lao-French influence on local culture which has made for good food and interesting wats.

The Thai name for the river is Mae Nam Khong. Mae Nam means river (literally, 'mother water') and Khong is its name, hence the term 'Maekhong River' is a bit redundant. Westerners have called it the 'Mekong River' for decades and the Thais themselves sometimes call it 'Maekhong' for short, so I'm compromising and calling it the 'Maekhong River'. By agreement between the Thai and Lao governments, all islands in the Maekhong River – including sandbars that appear only in the dry season – belong to Laos.

NONG KHAI
อ.เมืองหนองคาย

More than 620 km from Bangkok and 55 km from Udon Thani, Nong Khai (population 30,000) is where Highway 2, the Friendship Highway, ends at the Maekhong River. Across the river is Laos.

Nong Khai has a row of old buildings of French-Chinese architecture along Meechai Rd, east of Soi Si Khun Muang parallel to the river. Unfortunately, local developers are razing some of the most historic buildings in Nong Khai and replacing them with the ugly egg-carton architecture common all over urban Asia. Let's hope Nong Khai residents make a plea for historical preservation or there'll soon be no historic buildings left in Nong Khai.

The restaurant next to the immigration office and pier is a good place to sit and watch the small ferry boats (flying Pathet Lao flags) cross back and forth between Thailand and the Lao People's Democratic Republic. Obviously a great deal of travel is allowed between shores, as the boats always have passengers.

In the river is **Phra That Nong Khai**, a Lao chedi which can be seen in the dry season when the Maekhong lowers about 30 metres. The chedi slipped into the river in 1847 and continues to slide – it's near the middle now.

Sunset **boat rides** are available daily at around 5 pm from next to the floating restaurant behind Wat Hai Sok.

In the second week of March the Nong Khai Show is held with lots of festivities.

Nong Khai is one of five crossings open along the Thai-Lao border (the other three are Chiang Khong, Nakhon Phanom, That Phanom and Mukdahan) and citizens of the two countries are allowed to cross at will for day trips. Thais can fairly easily get visas for longer trips.

For foreign visitors, visas to Laos are now readily available through travel agencies in Bangkok. Also try the immigration office in Nong Khai in case they've decided to let foreigners across for day trips too, though this is probably not likely yet.

Several visa brokers in Nong Khai can arrange the necessary paperwork for visits of up to two weeks. Current prices vary from 2000 to 3125B; waiting periods of four to 10 days are typical, depending on the broker. You'll need four passport photos for the visa.

If your visit is approved, take a ferry across to Tha Deua in Laos and catch a bus or taxi to Vientiane. The Thai and Lao governments are currently building the Australian-financed **Friendship Bridge** (Saphan Mittaphap) over the river from Ban Chommani (3 km west of Nong Khai) to Tha Na Laeng (19 km south-east of Vientiane) on the Lao side. The 1190-metre bridge is expected to be completed by the beginning of 1993; eventually both rail and road links between Nong Khai and Vientiane will cross the bridge.

Wat Pho Chai
วัดโพธิ์ชัย

This temple off Prajak Rd in the south-eastern part of town is renowned for its large Lan Xang-era sitting Buddha. The head of the image is pure gold, the body is bronze, and the utsanit (flame-top head ornament) is set with rubies.

Murals in the bot depict the image's travels from the interior of Laos to the banks of the Maekhong, where it was put on a raft. A storm capsized the raft and the image sat at the bottom of the river from 1550 to 1575, when it was salvaged and placed in Wat Haw Kawng (now called Wat Pradit Thammakun) on the Thai side of the river. The image was moved to Wat Pho Chai during the reign of King Mongkut (1852-1868).

Sala Kaew Ku
ศาลาแก้วกู่

Also called Wat Khaek (Indian Temple) by locals, this strange Hindu-Buddhist temple, established in 1978, is a tribute to the wild imagination of Luang Pu Bunleua Surirat. Luang Pu (Venerable Grandfather) is a Brahmanic yogi-priest-shaman who merges Hindu and Buddhist philosophy, mythology and iconography into a cryptic whole. He has developed a large following in north-eastern Thailand and Laos, where he lived for many years before moving to Nong Khai (he still maintains a temple in Laos). He is supposed to have studied under a Hindu *rishi* in Vietnam.

The focus of the temple is the many bizarre cement statues of Shiva, Vishnu, Buddha and every other Hindu or Buddhist deity imaginable, as well as numerous secular figures, all supposedly cast by unskilled artists under Luang Pu's direction. The style of the figures is remarkably uniform, with faces which look like benign Polynesian masks. A sound system wired into the park sometimes plays a bizarre mixture of avant-garde electronic and pop musical selections – Luang Pu's favourite artist is Donna Summer!

In the shrine building there are two large rooms, upstairs and down, full of framed pictures of Hindu or Buddhist deities, temple donors, Luang Pu at various ages, plus smaller bronze and wooden figures of every description and provenance, guaranteed to throw an art historian into a state of disorientation.

If the building is locked, you can ask one of the attendants to open it for you; there are two stairways to the second level, one for males and one for females.

In Nong Khai, it is said that any person who drinks water offered by Luang Pu will turn all his possessions over to the temple, so bring your own canteen.

Getting There & Away To get to Sala Kaew Ku, board a songthaew heading south-east towards Beung Kan and ask to get off at Wat Khaek, which is four or five km outside of town, near St Paul Nong Khai School. The fare should be about 7B.

If you have your own wheels, look for a sign on the right about two turn-offs past St Paul's that reads 'Salakeokoo' referring to the official name, Sala Kaew Ku (Jewel Grotto Shelter).

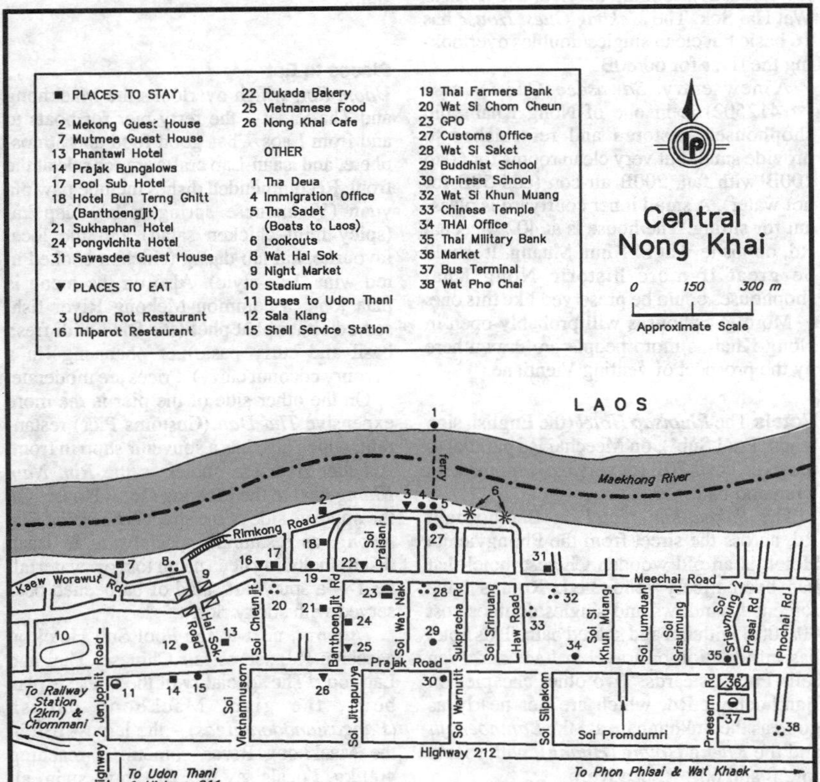

Festivals

Like many other cities in the north-east, Nong Khai has a large Rocket Festival (Ngaan Bun Bâng Fai) during the full moon of May, and a Candle Festival (Ngaan Hàe Thian) at the beginning of Phansãa, or the Buddhist Rains Retreat, in late July.

Places to Stay

Guesthouses *Mutmee (Mat-mii) Guest House* is on the river and has rooms in an old house at 60B for singles, 80B for medium-sized doubles and 100B for large doubles. Extra beds are 30B. It has a pleasant garden restaurant overlooking the river and it's near Wat Hai Sok. The *Mekong Guest House* has 16 basic but clean singles/doubles overlooking the river for 60/80B.

A new entry, *Sawasdee Guest House* (☎ 412502) is in one of Nong Khai's old shophouses, restored and refurbished to provide small but very clean rooms for 60 to 100B with fan, 200B air-con (add 50B for hot water). A small inner courtyard is pleasant for sitting. The house is at 402 Meechai Rd, opposite Wat Si Khun Muang. It would be great if more historic Nong Khai shophouses could be preserved like this one.

More guesthouses will probably open in Nong Khai as more people are drawn here by the prospect of visiting Vientiane.

Hotels The *Phunsap Hotel* (the English sign reads 'Pool Sub'), on Meechai Rd parallel to the river, costs 70B for very basic rooms with a fan and bath.

The *Sukhaphan Hotel* on Banthoengjit Rd, across the street from the Phongvichita Hotel, is an old wooden Chinese hotel that has been nicely renovated. Rooms have screened windows and singles/doubles cost 80/100B with fan and shared bath. This hotel has information on travel in Laos and even sells Lao postcards. Two other cheapies on Banthoengjit Rd, which are not nearly as good as the Sukhaphan, are the *Banthoengjit* and the *Kheng Houng (Huang)*, with rooms for 50 and 60B respectively.

Pongvichita (Phongwichit) at 723 Banthoengjit Rd, across the street from the Sukhaphan, is fairly clean and businesslike and costs 110B for a room with fan and bath, 250 to 400B with air-con.

Prajak Bungalows (☎ 411116), at 1178 Prajak Rd, has quiet rooms off-street singles/doubles with fan for 120/160B, or 260/300B with air-con.

At the top end in Nong Khai is the *Phanthavy (Phantawi)* (☎ 411568), at 1241 Hai Sok Rd, where very tidy rooms with fan and bath are 150B; 300 to 450B with air-con. Across the street is *Phantawi Bungalows* under the same management and at the same rates. There's a decent coffee shop downstairs.

Places to Eat

Udom Rot, which overlooks the Maekhong and Tha Sadet – the ferry pier for boats to and from Laos – has good food and atmosphere, and isaan-Lao crafts are for sale at the front. Recommended dishes include pàw pía yuan (Vietnamese spring rolls), lâap kài (spicy mint chicken salad) and the local favourite, kài lâo daeng (chicken cooked in red wine, Lao-style). Also on the menu is plaa jòhk, a common Mekong River fish, served either phàt phèt (stir-fried with fresh basil and curry paste) or phanaeng (in a savoury coconut curry). Prices are moderate.

On the other side of the pier is the more expensive *Tha Dan* (Customs Pier) restaurant, which also has a souvenir shop in front. A better riverside choice is the *Rim Nam Khong* next to the Mekong Guest House. On the opposite side of the street is *Nam Tok Rim Khong*, as restaurant specialising in isaan dishes including neúa náam tòk, or 'waterfall beef' – a spicy/tart salad of barbecued beef served with sticky rice.

Thiparot, next to the Pool Sub Hotel on Meechai Rd, serves fair Chinese, Thai and Lao food. The speciality of the house is plaa bèuk, the giant Maekhong catfish *(Pangasianodon gigas)* – the largest fish in the Maekhong River, sometimes reaching 400 kg. Locals say this fish must swim all the way from Qinghai Province in China where the Maekhong originates. The texture is very meaty but it has a delicate flavour, similar to tuna or swordfish, only whiter in colour. It's best prepared as plaa bèuk phàt phèt in which chunks of plaa beuk are fried in fresh basil-laced curry paste. The giant catfish is not listed on the English part of the menu, only on the Thai specials list on the first page. Also good at Thiparot are the plaa sa-nguang sa-nguan (tender freshwater fish fried in garlic and black pepper). The menu is reasonably priced; a bar has recently been added.

The *Dukada Bakery* on Meechai Rd has a variety of pastries, Western breakfasts and Thai food and is one of the few places in Thailand that gives you a choice of Nescafe or Thai coffee (I'll take the real thing over Nescafe any day, even when mixed with tamarind seed).

For Chinese food, *Nong Khai Phochana* at the corner of Banthoengjit and Prajak Rds is good – selections include Chinese roast duck, red pork, kũaytĩaw (fried noodles) and bà-mìi (Chinese noodles).

Near Wat Hai Sok off Meechai Rd is a small night market and along Meechai Rd between Hai Sok Rd and Wat Si Saket are several small restaurants. In the early morning two vendors opposite Hai Sok market sell jók kài (chicken rice congee), khâo jii (Lao-French bread) and paa-thông-kõ (Chinese 'doughnuts'); along a soi inside Wat Hai Sok is *Coffee Haisoke*, a small vendor stall with good Lao-style coffee for a few baht. These vendors offer a much tastier and atmospheric breakfast alternative to the expensive *Espresso Corner* on the same corner.

Next door to the Espresso Corner is another tourist trap, *Otto Family Restaurant*. Both restaurants cater to farangs with bland Thai/Lao/Chinese/farang menus of spaghetti, sandwiches, pizza and so on. The Thai food is better elsewhere.

Along the southern end of Banthoengjit Rd, there are several no-name restaurants specialising in Vietnamese food, mainly rice noodles, spring rolls and dumplings – very cheap and good.

Things to Buy

A shop called Village Weaver Handicrafts at 786/1 Prajak Rd, sells high quality, moderately priced woven fabrics and ready-made clothes. The staff can also tailor clothing in a day or two from fabric purchased. The shop was established by the Good Shepherd Sisters as part of a project to encourage local girls to stay in the villages and earn money by weaving rather than leaving home to seek work in urban centres. The hand-dyed mat-mii cotton is particularly good here, and visitors are welcome to observe the methods in the weaving workshop behind the shop. It's down Prajak Rd past the bus terminal – 5 to 10B by samlor from the centre of town. The Thai name of the project is Hattakam Sing Thaw.

Getting There & Away

Bus Buses to Nong Khai leave Udon approximately every 30 minutes throughout the day from the Udon bus station. The trip takes about 1¼ hours and costs 12B.

Buses to Nong Khai from Bangkok's northern bus terminal leave between 5 and 8.30 am, and 8.10 and 8.54 pm. The trip is a long nine to 10 hours and costs 120B for an ordinary bus. Air-con buses are 209B and leave three times a day at 9 am, and 9 and 9.30 pm. Most people take the train.

Buses from Khorat start running in the afternoon and continue into the early evening. The fare is 75B and the trip takes six to seven hours.

If you're coming from Loei Province you can get buses from Chiang Khan or Pak Chom, without having to double back to Udon. It's 65B from Chiang Khan and 50B from Pak Chom.

Nong Khai's main bus station off Prajak Rd has buses to Si Chiangmai, Beung Kan, Loei, Udon, Ubon, Tha Bo, Bangkok and Rayong.

Train From Bangkok, the Nong Khai express leaves Hualamphong station daily at 8.30 pm, arriving in Nong Khai at 7.30 am. Two rapid trains leave daily at 6.15 am and 7 pm, arriving at 4.50 pm and 6.15 am. Basic one-way fares are 450B 1st class and 215B 2nd class, not including surcharges for express or rapid service (30B and 20B) or sleeping berths. The state railway runs a 3rd-class special on rapid trains for 115B inclusive, a saving of 8B on the regular 3rd-class fare plus rapid charge.

Boat to Laos Ferry boats from Tha Deua on the Laos side of the Maekhong cost 30B each way. At the present time you must have a visa to board the boat to Laos; in the reverse direction you'll need a visa if you plan to spend more than 15 days in Thailand. There is also a vehicle ferry between Chommani (3 km west of Nong Khai) on the Thai side and Tha Na Laeng on the Lao side.

By 1993 the new Friendship Bridge will replace the Chommani ferry for vehicular traffic between the two countries. The US$31 million bridge will feature two traffic lanes with space for a railway between, and a new railhead is planned on the Thai side to serve the crossing. On the Lao side a new rail line (the country's first!) will skirt Vientiane to the south-east and terminate in the vicinity of That Luang.

Getting Around

Samlors around the town centre cost 5 to 10B; tuk-tuks are 10 to 20B.

Nana Motor (☎ 411998) at 1160 Meechai Rd rents motorbikes at reasonable rates.

AROUND NONG KHAI PROVINCE

Wat Phra That Bang Phuan

วัดพระธาตุบังพวน

Twelve km south of Nong Khai, on Highway 2 and then 11 km west on Highway 211, Wat Bang Phuan is one of the most sacred sites in the north-east because of the old Indian-style stupa found here. It's similar to the original chedi beneath the Phra Pathom Chedi in Nakhon Pathom, but no-one knows when either chedi was built. Speculation has it that it must have been in the early centuries AD or possibly even earlier.

In 1559 King Jayachettha of Chanthaburi (not the present Chanthaburi in Thailand, but Wiang Chan – known as Vientiane – in Laos) extended his capital across the Maekhong and built a newer, taller, Lao-style chedi over the original as a demonstration of faith (just as King Mongkut did in Nakhon Pathom). Vientiane is the French spelling of the Lao name Wiang Chan which, like the Thai Chanthaburi, means City of the Moon. Rain caused the chedi to lean precariously and in 1970 it fell over. The Fine Arts Department restored it in 1978 with the Sangharaja, Thailand's Supreme Buddhist Patriarch, presiding over the rededication.

Actually, it is the remaining 16th-century Lao chedis in the compound (two contain semi-intact Buddha images in their niches) that give the wat its charm. There is also a roofless wihaan with a large Buddha image, and a massive round brick base that must have supported another large chedi at one time. Recently, a small museum displaying site relics has opened to the public.

Getting There & Away To get to Wat Phra That Bang Phuan, get a Si Chiangmai or Sangkhom-bound songthaew or bus in Nong Khai and ask for Ban Bang Phuan (12B). Otherwise get any bus south on Highway 2 and get off in Ban Nong Hong Song, the junction for Highway 211. From there you can grab the next bus (from either Udon or Nong Khai) that's going to Si Chiangmai and get off near the wat. The fare should be about 10B to the road leading off Highway 211, an easy walk to the wat from that point.

Tha Bo

ท่าบ่อ

Along the Maekhong River and Highway 211 between Nong Khai and the Loei Province line are several smaller towns and villages where life revolves around farming and minimal trade between Laos and Thailand.

Surrounded by banana plantations and vegetable fields flourishing in the fertile Maekhong floodplains, Tha Bo (population 16,000) is the most important market centre between Nong Khai and Loei. An open-air market along the main street probably offers more wild plants and herbs than any market along the Maekhong, along with Tha Bo's most famous local product – tomatoes. Irrigation is provided by the **Huay Mong Dam**, which crosses the Maekhong at the western edge of town. There is a pleasant public park next to the dam.

Aside from the market and dam, the town's only other claim to fame is **Wat Ong Teu**, an old Lao-style temple sheltering a 'crying Buddha'. According to local legend, the left hand of the bronze image was once cut off by art thieves; tears streamed from the Buddha's eyes until the hand was returned.

Places to Stay & Eat *Suksan Hotel* on the main street through town has basic rooms for 60B. Out on the road from Nong Khai at the town's eastern entrance is *SP Guest House*, a former dive hotel with rooms for 80B.

Quieter and more unusual accommodation is available at *Isan Orchid Guest Lodge* (☎ 431665), 87/9 Kaowarawut Rd, a large modern house in the middle of village-like surroundings near the river. Owned by a retired American businessman but managed by Thais, the house has large comfortable air-con rooms from 500 to 750B including breakfast. A smaller bungalow next to the main house is available for 700 to 850B. The manager can arrange Udon airport pick-up as well as trips to Phra Phutthabat Bua Bok; bicycles can be borrowed at no charge.

There are several modest noodle and rice shops on the main street plus a couple of kài yâang places. Near the river at the north-eastern end of town is *Suan Aahaan Taling Naam*, a garden restaurant specialising in 'mountain chicken', which denotes a method of grilling whole chickens standing on end rather than horizontal.

Getting There & Away All songthaews and buses from Nong Khai (25 km east) bound for Si Chiangmai will drop passengers in Tha Bo. If you're biking it from Nong Khai, you have a choice of the scenic but unpaved river road or paved and fast – but less scenic – Highway 211. Eventually the river road will be paved, in which case it will become the fastest and most direct route to Tha Bo and further west.

Si Chiangmai
ศรีเชียงใหม่

Just across the river from Vientiane, Si Chiangmai has a large number of Lao and Vietnamese who make their living from the manufacture of rice-paper spring-roll wrappers. You can see the translucent disks drying in the sun on bamboo racks all over town. Si Chiangmai is one of the leading exporters of spring-roll wrappers in the world! Many of the Vietnamese and Lao residents are Roman Catholic and there is a small cathedral in town. A local bakery bakes fresh French rolls every morning.

Ferries now cross regularly to Vientiane; there are immigration and customs offices in town. However, foreigners (non-Thais) are usually referred to Nong Khai for river crossings.

Places to Stay There is only one guesthouse in town but more will surely start up. *Tim Guest House* is run by a friendly young Swiss-French man (who speaks English, French, German and Thai). Rooms start at 40B for a small single to 100B for a large double with a river view (but over the street). Simple Thai and farang food is served in a dining area downstairs. The guesthouse arranges Maekhong boat trips to Nong Khai and Sangkhom and rents out bicycles and motorcycles. It's on Rim Khong Rd near the river in the centre of town – walk west from the bus terminal and turn right at Soi 17, then turn left at the end of the road and you'll find Tim Guest House on the left.

Adjacent to Tim is the basic *Hotel Suwan*, with rooms for 50 to 90B.

Getting There & Away Probably because of its importance as a spring-roll wrapper capital, Si Chiangmai has an abundance of public transport in and out. Bus fares to/from Si Chiangmai are:

to/from	fare
Nong Khai	12B
Sangkhom	10B
Udon Thani	20B
Khon Kaen	41B
(air-con)	80B
Khorat	75B
(air-con)	120B
Bangkok	
(air-con)	160B

Wat Hin Maak Peng

วัดหินหมากเป้ง

Sixty km north-west of Nong Khai between Si Chiangmai and Sangkhom, Wat Hin is worth a trip just for the scenery along Highway 211 from Nong Khai. This monastery is locally known for its *thutong* (Pali: *dhutanga)* monks – men who have taken ascetic vows in addition to the standard 227 precepts. These vows include eating only once a day, wearing only forest robes made from discarded cloth and having a strong emphasis on meditation. There are also several *mâe chii* (Buddhist nuns) living here.

The place is very quiet and peaceful, set in a cool forest with lots of bamboo groves, overlooking the Maekhong. The monastic kutis are built among giant boulders that form a cliff high above the river; casual visitors aren't allowed into this area however. Below the cliff is a sandy beach and more rock formations. Directly across the river a Lao forest temple can be seen. Fisherfolk occasionally drift by on house rafts.

The abbot at Wat Hin Maak Peng requests that visitors to the wat dress politely – no shorts or sleeveless tops. Those that don't observe the code will be denied entrance.

Getting There & Away To get there take a songthaew from Nong Khai to Si Chiangmai (12B) and ask for a songthaew directly to Wat Hin (there are a few) or to Sangkhom, which is just past the entrance to Wat Hin – the other passengers will let you know when the truck passes it. The second songthaew is 10B. On the way to Wat Hin you might notice a large topiary at Ban Phran Phrao on the right side of the highway.

Sangkhom

สังคม

The tiny town of Sangkhom could be used as a rest stop on a slow journey along the Maekhong River between Loei and Nong Khai. Wat Hin Maak Peng is nearby and there are some good hikes to caves and waterfalls in the area. The guesthouses hand out maps of the area.

One of the most accessible and largest local waterfalls is **Than Thip Falls** a few km west of Sangkhom. The waterfall has two major levels; the upper level is cleaner and has a deep pool (during or just after the rainy season) which is good for a dip. The falls are a long walk from the road – this is a trip best accomplished by motorcycle.

Places to Stay & Eat The town's four guesthouses are off the main road through town near the river.

Most popular at the moment is the friendly and efficient *River Huts Guest House*, where thatched huts overlooking the river are 60/80B for singles/doubles. The food is good here, too, and the staff offer motorcycles and bicycles for rent. Nearby is the *Bouy Guest House*, also a pleasant place with huts on the river. Singles/doubles next to the river are 50/70B, or 40/60B nearer the road. Next door is the *DD Guest House* with similar rates.

TXK Guest House had two locations, one near the market and bus station and one further west, but it has closed the former. It looked a bit shabby during my last visit but was as welcoming as ever; huts are only 50B.

A restaurant next to River Huts has a pleasant sitting area over the river and is the number-one nightspot in tiny Sangkhom. Ask around and you may be able to locate a taste of náam yân, the sweetest moonshine from Laos.

Getting There & Away Buses from Nong Khai are 25B and the trip takes about two hours. From Loei it's 45B and three or four hours. Pak Chom is 1½ hours away and the fare is 20B. From nearby Si Chiangmai, it's 10B. Westward beyond Pak Chom, songthaews are less frequent because the road worsens; the fare to Chiang Khan is 15B.

BEUNG KAN

บึงกาฬ

This is a small dusty town on the Maekhong River, 185 km east of Nong Khai by Highway 212. You may want to break your journey here if you are working your way around the north-eastern border from Nong Khai to Nakhon Phanom (as opposed to the easier but less interesting Udon to Sakon Nakhon to Nakhon Phanom route).

The closer you get to Nakhon Phanom Province, the more Vietnamese you will see working in the rice fields or herding cows along the road. Nearly all the farmers in this area, whether ethnic Vietnamese or Thai, wear a simple Vietnamese-style straw hat to fend off the sun and rain.

Wat Phu Thawk (Wat Chedi Khiri Wihaan)

วัดภูทอก (วัดเจดีย์คีรีวิหาร)

Travellers interested in north-eastern forest wats can visit this nearby wat, a massive sandstone outcropping in the middle of a rather arid plain – a real hermit's delight. The entire outcropping, with its amazing network of caves and breathtaking views, belongs to the wat. The wat mountain is climbed by a seven-level series of stairs representing the seven levels of enlightenment in Buddhist psychology. Monastic kutis are scattered around the mountain, in caves and on cliffs. As you make the strenuous climb, each level is cooler than the one before. It is the cool and quiet isolation of this wat that entices monks and mae chiis from all over the north-east to come and meditate here.

This wat used to be the domain of the famous meditation master Ajaan Juan – a disciple of the fierce Ajaan Man who disappeared many years ago. Ajaan Juan died in a plane crash a few years ago, along with several other monks who were flying to Bangkok for Queen Sirikhit's birthday celebration. The plane went down just outside Don Muang Airport. Many north-easterners have taken this incident as proof that the present queen is a source of misfortune.

To get to Wat Phu Thawk, you'll have to take an early morning songthaew south on Highway 222 to Ban Siwilai (25 km, 7B), then another songthaew east (left) on a dirt road, 20 km to the wat (10B). This songthaew carries merit-makers. Hitching might be possible if you miss the truck. A reader reported getting a type of local tuk-tuk to the wat in the afternoon from Siwilai for 10B.

Places to Stay

Hotels in Beung Kan are all in the 40 to 80B price range (forget air-con). The *Samanmit*, *Neramit* and *Santisuk* are on Prasatchai Rd while the *Chantha* is on Chansin Rd.

Getting There & Away

The bus from Nong Khai to Beung Kan is 40B. Nakhon Phanom to Beung Kan buses are 45B.

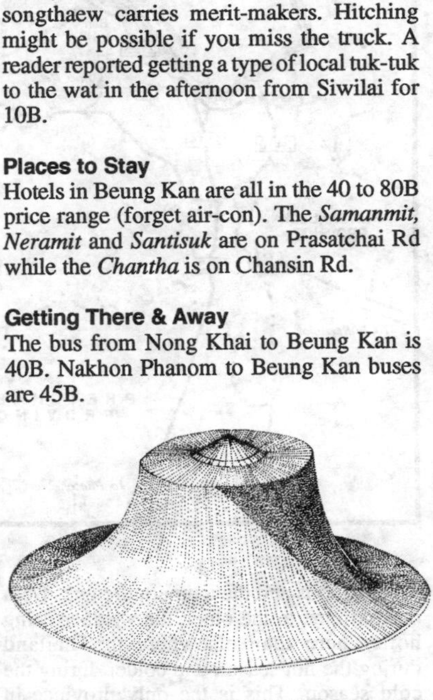

Loei Province

Nearly 520 km from Bangkok, 150 km from Udon, 269 km from Phitsanulok via Lom Sak and 200 km via Nakhon Thai, Loei is one of Thailand's most beautiful and unspoiled provinces. The geography is

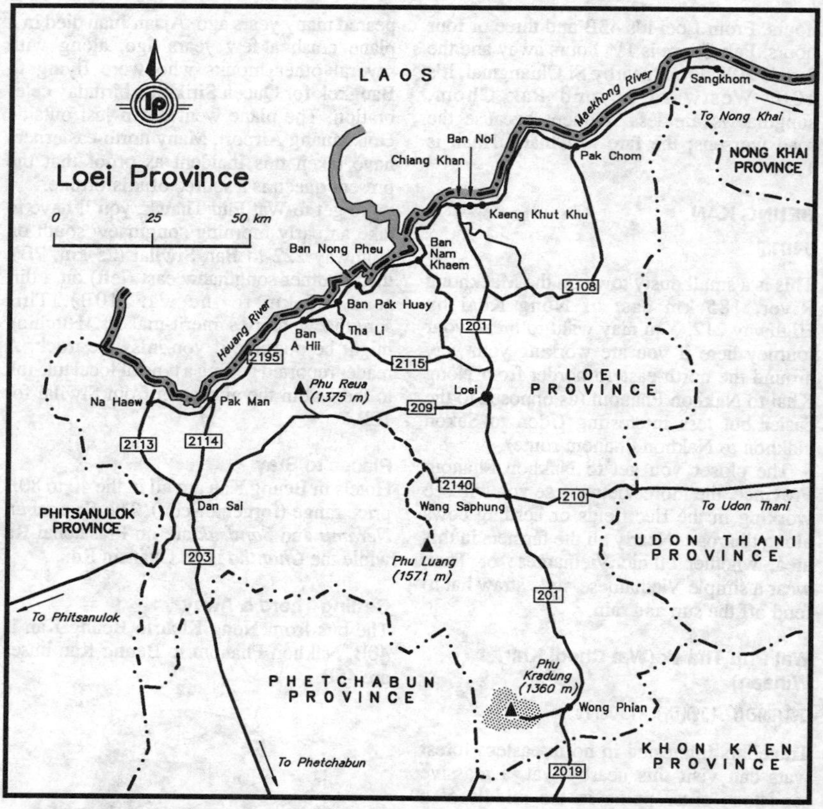

mountainous and the temperature goes from one extreme to the other, the weather being hotter here than elsewhere in Thailand during the hot season and colder during the cold season. This is the only province in Thailand where temperatures occasionally drop to 0°C.

The culture is an unusual mix of northern and north-eastern influences, which has produced many local dialects. The rural life of Loei outside the provincial capital has retained more of a traditional village flavour than elsewhere in Thailand, with the possible exceptions of Nan and Phetchabun, also once classified as remote or closed provinces.

Within the province, Phu Kradung, Phu Luang and Phu Reua national parks, as well as the districts of Tha Li and Chiang Khan, are good places to explore for natural attractions.

LOEI

อ.เมืองเลย

In the provincial capital of Loei (population 24,000) there is little to see or do. Cotton is one of Loei's big crops, so it's a pretty good place to buy cotton goods, especially the heavy cotton quilts (quite necessary in the cool months) made in Chiang Khan district – they're priced by the kg. During the first week of February, Loei holds a Cotton Blossom Festival which culminates in a parade of cotton-decorated floats and, naturally, a Cotton Blossom Queen beauty contest.

About three km north of Loei is a water recreation park with a large swimming pool called **Loei Land**. The admission is a reasonable 30B per day.

Places to Stay

Guesthouses *Muang Loei Guest House* has two locations, both within walking distance of the bus terminal. Neither offer anything great, just basic and not particularly clean rooms for 50B per person. The English-speaking management distributes travel information.

The recently established *Friendship Guest House* (☎ 812399) at 257/12 Soi Boon Charoen, has pleasant rooms in a quiet section of town near the river for 50/80B. To get there from the centre of town, hop on a samlor for 15B or walk south on Charoen Rat Rd past the post office until you reach Wat Si Bunruang on your left. Turn left on Soi Boon Charoen and follow the sign to the guesthouse.

Hotels *Sarai Thong Hotel,* off Ruamjit Rd, has 56 rooms in three buildings, costing from 60 to 150B. All rooms have a fan and bath. Service isn't great, but it's off the street so is usually quiet.

Phu Luang Hotel (☎ 811532/570) at 55 Charoen Rat Rd near the market costs 150/200B for singles/doubles with fan and bath, or 250/300B with air-con. It has a restaurant and nightclub.

At 122/1 Charoen Rat Rd, across from the Bangkok Bank, is the friendly *Thai Udom Hotel* (☎ 811763), with exactly the same

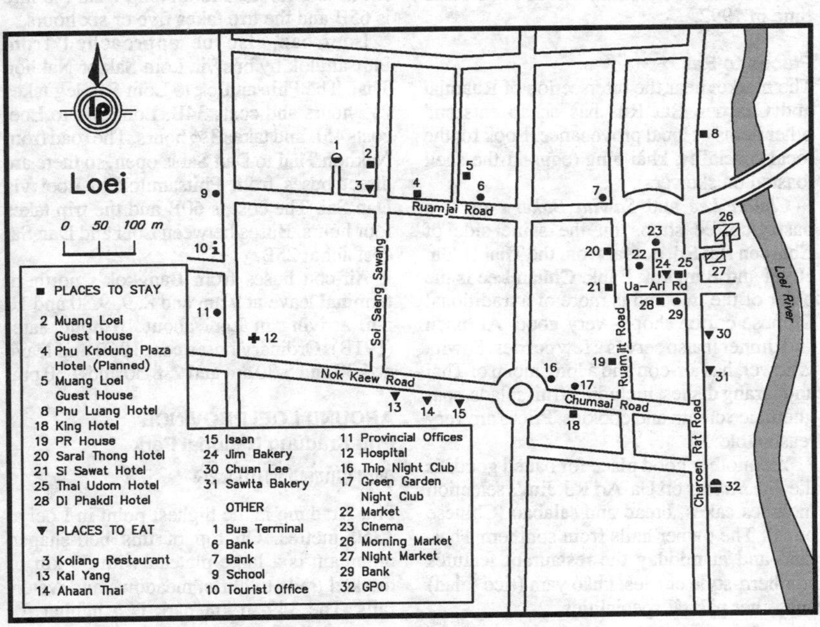

rates as the Phu Luang. Overall it's a better choice, especially if you take a room away from the street.

Srisawat (Si Sawat) on Ruamjit Rd near Sarai Thong, has singles/doubles for 60/100B and similar facilities to Sarai Thong.

The *Di Phakdi* (☎ 811294) on Ua Ari Rd, around the corner from Thai Udom and opposite the cinema, has fair rooms from 60B with fan and bath.

Over on Chumsai Rd near the Green Garden and Thip nightclubs is the well-run *King* (☎ 811701), where rooms cost from 150 to 200B with fan and bath, or 300 to 450B with air-con and hot water. Also in this vicinity, just off Chumsai Rd, is the new *PR House* (☎ 811416) with modest apartments for rent with fan and solar-heated shower for 120 to 200B per night, less for long-term stays.

Construction of the new *Phu Kradung Plaza*, a business-oriented hotel on Ruamjai Rd near the bus terminal, should begin some time in 1992.

Places to Eat

The market near the intersection of Ruamjai and Charoen Rat Rds has cheap eats and other items of local provenance. Look for the local speciality, khài pîng (eggs-in-the-shell toasted on skewers).

Chuan Lee and *Sawita Bakery* are two pastry/coffee shops on the same side of Charoen Rat Rd, not far from the Thai Udom Hotel and Bangkok Bank. Chuan Lee is the older of the two and is more of a traditional Chinese coffee shop – very good. At lunch and dinner it also serves a few curries. Sawita is newer, has air-con and a long menu of Thai and farang dishes, including fruit salads, spaghetti, ice cream and cookies. Prices are very reasonable.

Yet another good place for baked goods is the *Jim Bakery* on Ua-Ari Rd. Jim's selection includes cakes, bread and salabao (Chinese buns). The owner hails from southern Thailand and at midday the restaurant features southern-style curries, khâo yam (rice salad) and other pàk tâi specialities.

Koliang Restaurant, on the north side of Ruamjai Rd around the corner from the bus station, has great boat noodles and kũaytĩaw.

Along Nok Kaew Rd between Soi Saeng Sawang and the traffic circle are two moderately priced Thai restaurants. The *Isaan* specialises in north-eastern food and *Saw Aahaan Thai* serves all kinds of Thai dishes. A simpler place on Nok Kaew Rd near Soi Saeng Sawang does kài yâang and sôm-tam.

Entertainment

Further up Nok Kaew Rd from the isaan restaurant and across from the King Hotel are two Thai nightclubs with live music: the Thip and the Green Garden. Younger Thais go dancing at clubs near the Phu Luang Hotel and the night market, such as the Rim Nam and the Tharn Thong.

Getting There & Away

Buses to Loei leave Udon regularly until late afternoon for 31B. The 150-km trip takes about four hours. From Nong Khai the fare is 65B and the trip takes five or six hours.

Loei can also be approached from Phitsanulok by bus via Lom Sak or Nakhon Thai. The Phitsanulok to Lom Sak leg takes 2½ hours and costs 34B. Lom Sak to Loei costs 45B and takes 3½ hours. The road from Nakhon Thai to Dan Sai is open, so there are direct buses from Phitsanulok to Loei via Dan Sai. The cost is 60B and the trip takes four hours. Buses between Loei and Dan Sai cost about 25B.

Air-con buses from Bangkok's northern terminal leave at 9 am and 8, 9, 9.30 and 10 pm, arriving in Loei about 10 hours later (191B). Ordinary buses cost 106B and leave at 4.30 and 5.30 am and 2, 8.30 and 9.30 pm.

AROUND LOEI PROVINCE

Phu Kradung National Park

อุทยานแห่งชาติภูกระดึง

Phu Kradung is the highest point in Loei at 1360 metres. On top of this bell-shaped mountain is a large plateau with 50 km of marked trails to cliffs, meadows and waterfalls. The 349-sq-km park is a habitat for various forest animals, including elephants, Asian jackal, Asiatic black bear, barking deer, sambar, serow, white-handed gibbon and the occasional tiger. A Buddhist shrine near the park headquarters is a favourite local pilgrimage site.

The main trail scaling Phu Kradung is six km long and takes about four hours to climb (or rather walk – it's not that challenging since the most difficult parts have bamboo ladders and stairs for support). The climb is quite scenic. It's a further three km to the park headquarters. You can hire porters to carry your gear for 10B per kg.

During the hottest months, from March to June, it's best to start the climb about dawn to avoid the heat. It can get quite cold at night in February and March (5°C), when blankets are available for hire. Phu Kradung is closed to visitors during the rainy season from mid-July to early October because it is considered too hazardous, being very slippery and subject to mud slides. The park can get crowded during school holidays (especially March to May when Thai schools are closed).

Buses to Phu Kradung leave the Loei bus station in the morning for the 75-km trip.

Places to Stay Lots of young Thais, mainly friendly college students, camp here. Tents already set up cost 40B a night and boards for the bottom of the tents are available. Blankets and pillows cost extra. Set up your own tent for 5B per person. Cabins cost from 400 to 1200B depending on size, but will sleep five or more people. The cabins have water and electricity, but food must be brought with you from the villages below. The park gates open at 8 am. There are several small restaurants on the plateau.

Phu Reua National Park
อุทยานแห่งชาติภูเรือ

This relatively small park of 121 sq km surrounds Phu Reua (Boat Mountain), so named because a cliff jutting from the peak is shaped like a Chinese junk. The easy 2½-hour hike to the summit (1375 metres) passes from tropical to broad-leaf evergreen forest to pine forest. In December, temperatures near the summit approach freezing at night.

The park entrance is about 50 km west of the provincial capital on Highway 203. Although there is public transport from Loei to the town of Phu Reua, it is difficult to find songthaews all the way to the park except on weekends and holidays. Forestry Department bungalows cost from 250 to 500B a night for up to five people. Tents can be pitched for 5B. On weekends and holidays, food is sometimes available from vendors in the park; at other times you may be able to arrange food through the park rangers.

Phu Luang National Park
อุทยานแห่งชาติภูหลวง

Yet another mountain retreat, Phu Luang (1550 metres) is less visited than either Phu Kradung or Phu Reua. Wildlife is reportedly abundant in the park's higher elevations. To get there you'll need your own wheels (hitchhiking is also a possibility); take Highway 201 south from Loei for around 30 km and then take Route 2250 south-west another 20 km. Rustic accommodation is available for 100B per person per night, or you can camp for 5B a night. Bring your own food or make arrangements with the park staff.

Dan Sai
ด่านซ้าย

About 80 km west of Loei is the small town of Dan Sai which is famous for its unique Bun Prawet Festival. The three-day festival is part of the larger Rocket Festival that takes place throughout the north-east in May. Nobody seems to know how or when the distinctive festival in Dai Sai first began.

The first day is celebrated in the procession of Phi Ta Khon, a type of masked parade. Participants wear huge masks which are made from carved coconut-tree trunks, topped with a wicker sticky-rice steamer! The procession is marked by a lot of music and dancing. On the second day, Dan Sai residents fire off the usual bamboo rockets and on the third day they retire to **Wat Pon Chai** to listen to Buddhist sermons.

Pak Chom
ปากชม

Pak Chom is the first town of any size you come to in Loei Province if travelling west along the Maekhong River from Nong Khai. There is nothing much to do here but take walks along the river or to nearby villages. **Ban Winai**, a large Lao and Hmong refugee camp, is nearby but is not open to casual visitors. Some 30,000 Hmong tribespeople at the camp may voluntarily participate in a Laos repatriation programme in the near future, in which case the camp will probably close.

After Pak Chom, travelling west, you come to Chiang Khan.

Places to Stay *Pak Chom Guest House* (formerly Mae Khong Bungalows), on the western edge of town next to the river, has four quiet bungalows for 50B. Coming from Nong Khai, walk straight across the intersection where the road makes a 90° turn left toward Chiang Khan, and walk about 500 metres till you see the sign pointing right to the Pak Chom Guest House. The huts are another 300 metres toward the river. *Chumpee (Jampi) Guest House*, which is more or less in the centre, but also on the river, charges the same rates but is not as quiet and secluded.

Getting There & Away From Chiang Khan, buses to Pak Chom are 14B. Buses from Sangkhom or Loei cost 25B. Songthaews between Pak Chom and Ban Winai (11 km) are 5B and leave Pak Chom every half hour in the morning, less frequently in the afternoon.

CHIANG KHAN
เชียงคาน

Chiang Khan is about 50 km from Loei, on the Maekhong River in a large valley surrounded by mountains. The wooden shophouses along the back streets give the place a bit of a frontier atmosphere and there are some nice views of the Maekhong River.

Visas can be extended at the immigration office, next to the GPO, in Chiang Khan.

Wats

The town's wats feature a style of architecture rarely seen in Thailand – wihaans with colonnaded fronts and painted shutters that seem to indicate a French (via Laos) influence. A good example in the centre of town is **Wat Paa Klang** (Wat Machatimaram), which is about 100 years old and features a new glittery superstructure; in the grounds of this wat is a small Chinese garden with pond, waterfall and Chinese-style sculptures of Buddha and Kuan Yin.

Wat Mahathat in the centre of town is Chiang Khan's oldest temple; the bot, constructed in 1654, has a new roof over old walls, with faded murals on the front.

Temple structures at **Wat Santi** and **Wat Thakhok** are similar to those at Wat Paa Klang (minus the Chinese garden). The walls of the temple buildings are stained red from all the red dust and mud that builds up in the dry and rainy seasons.

Wat Tha Khaek is a 600 to 700-year-old temple, two km outside Chiang Khan, on the way to Ban Noi and Kaeng Khut Khu. The seated Buddha image in the bot is very sacred and it is said that holy water prepared in front of the image has the power to cure any ailing person who drinks it or bathes in it.

Other well-known monastic centres in the area include **Phu Pha Baen**, 10 km east of Chiang Khan, where monks meditate in caves and on tree platforms, and **Wat Si Song Nong**, west of Kaeng Khut Ku (within easy walking distance) on the river. This is a small forest wat where the highly respected Ajaan Maha Bun Nak resides.

Kaeng Khut Khu
แก่งคุดคู้

About four km downstream from Chiang Khan is the Kaeng Khut Khu, a stretch of rapids (best in the dry, hot season) with a park on the Thai side and a village on the Laos side. You can hire a boat to reach the rapids. The park has roofed picnic areas; recently a river retaining wall was added, spoiling the riverside effect to a large degree. Vendors sell delicious isaan food – kài yâang (grilled chicken), sôm-tam (spicy green papaya salad) and khâo niãw (sticky rice) – as well as kûng tên (literally 'dancing shrimp' – fresh, river prawns served live in a light sauce of lime juice and chillies), and kûng thâwt (the same fried whole in batter) and drinks. This is a nice place to spend a few hours.

Festivals
Chiang Khan comes alive during *àwk phansãa*, the end of the Buddhist Rains Retreat in October. At that time there's a week-long festival which features displays of large carved wax prasat at each of the temples in town as well as boat races on the river. At night there are performances of *mãw lam* (isaan musical comedy), in the field facing the GPO.

Places to Stay
In Town The *Chiang Khan Guest House* (☎ 821023) has fair rooms for 60B, or 80B with two beds and a shared bath. The dining area overlooks the river and good, inexpensive food is served. At night it's a bit of a Thai hang-out. It's between Sois 19 and 20 on Chai Khong Rd, which runs along the Maekhong.

Down between Sois 12 and 13 is the easy-going *Nong Sam Guest House* which is run by an Englishman and his Thai wife. Large, comfortable, screened singles/doubles in this old wooden house on the river are 60/80B with fan and shared bath. The couple have just finished building some bungalows on the river on one edge of town; rates are the same as in town.

Also on Chai Khong Rd, opposite Soi 17, is the *Nong Ball Guest House*. It's owned by the Nong Sam's former landlords who decided to cash in on their success. Singles/doubles are 50/100B. Turn away from the river altogether on Soi 12 and you'll find *Zen Guest House*, which is basic but has the largest fleet of rental bicycles in town. Rooms are only 40B a night.

Out on Chiang Khan Rd opposite Soi 20 is *Ong Guest House* with simple rooms for 60/80B.

For a hotel, there's the atmospheric *Souksomboon (Suksombun)* on Chai Khong Rd just past Soi 9 – look for the entranceway sign that says 'In – Out Hotel'. Rooms are 60B with fan and shared bath or 80 to 100B with a private bath. Around the corner of Soi 9 is the *Phoonsawad (Phunsawat)*, which has similar facilities and rates.

Kaeng Khut Khu No-name brick bungalows near the rapids cost from 150 to 500B depending on size and amenities. *Seeview Huts*, near Ban Noi on the road between the rapids and the highway, cost 200B. The quiet huts are well off the road and next to the river, with a pleasant dining area.

Places to Eat
Most of the better eating places in Chiang Khan are clustered on Soi 9 and around the intersection of Soi 9 and Chiang Khan Rd. The most popular dish in town seems to be the local version of phàt thai, which here contains thin rice noodles fried with bean sprouts, eggs, and pork (rather than egg, tofu, sprouts, peanuts and dried shrimp). Practi-

cally every restaurant in town lists this dish first on its menu! A few places serve khãnom jiin (thin white wheat noodles with chilli sauce), which the locals call khâo pun.

For cheap breakfasts, head for the morning market off Soi 9 near Wat Santi. Between 5 and 7.30 am there are a couple of stalls selling kafae thũng (Thai coffee), curries and paa-thông-kõ (Chinese pastries). The simple riverside restaurant at the Suksambun Hotel serves good Thai and Chinese standards.

The nearest thing to a local splurge is the *Pui Fai Restaurant* on Chai Khong Rd between Sois 20 and 21. The food is good and in the evening a succession of Thai singers provide entertainment.

Getting There & Away

Songthaews to Chiang Khan leave almost hourly from the Loei bus station for 14B (one hour). There is no regular transport between Tha Li and Chiang Khan, although a dirt road does run along the border.

For transport between Chiang Khan and Nong Khai, see the Pak Chom, Sangkhom and Si Chiangmai sections.

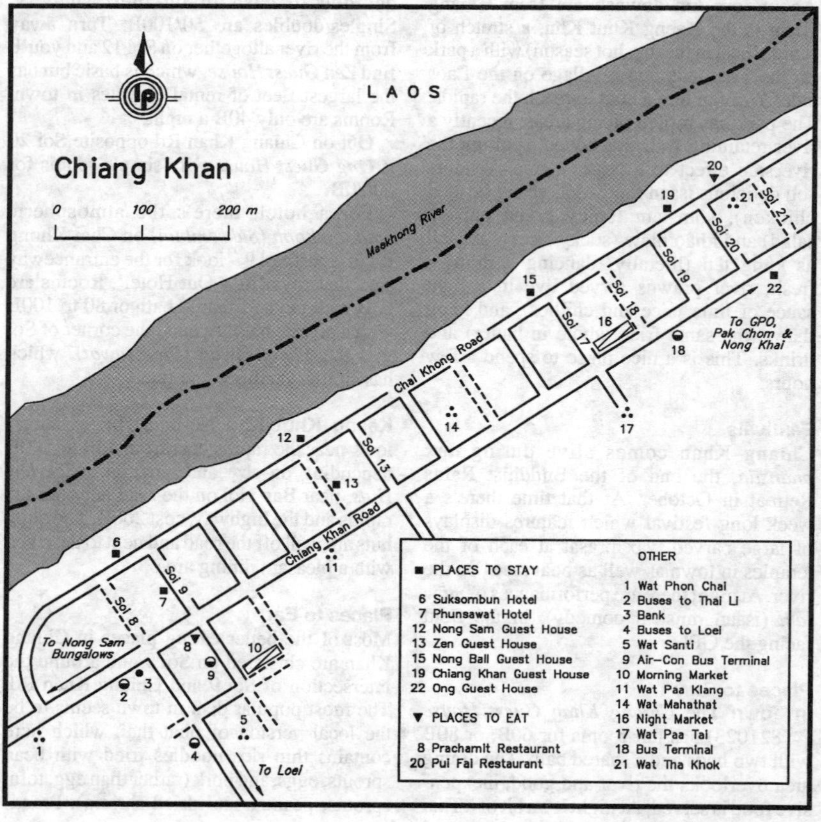

THA LI DISTRICT
อ.ท่าลี่

Perhaps the most beautiful part of Loei is the area which borders Laos from Dan Sai district in the west to Pak Chom in the east, including the district of Tha Li. Much of the district is the Thai half of a valley surrounded by the Khao Noi, Khao Laem and Khao Ngu mountains on the Thai side, and Phu Lane, Phu Hat Sone and Phu Nam Kieng on the Lao side. The small town of Tha Li itself is 50 km from Loei, on Route 2115, only about eight km from the Lao border, formed here by the Heuang River, a tributary of the Maekhong (which joins the border east of here towards Chiang Khan).

Now that relations between Laos and Thailand have normalised, local commerce back and forth across the Heuang River seems to be growing daily. Ban Nong Pheu, perched on the border, is bustling with a mixture of legal and black-market trade. Handmade products such as cotton fabrics and straw mats, and contraband goods such as ganja and lâo khão (white liquor), come across from Laos in exchange for finished goods such as medicine and machine parts. These are 'wild west' villages where travellers go at their own risk – mostly they're easygoing and safe but a lot goes on beneath the apparently calm surface. The local border police have been known to go fishing in the Heuang River using hand grenades; village brothels indenture young Lao refugees.

The village men are prodigious drinkers but rarely touch beer or Maekhong whiskey. Instead they drink lâo khão, a clear, colourless, fiery liquid with a very high alcohol content, distilled from glutinous rice. In a pun referring to Thailand's famous Maekhong whisky, they call it 'Mae Heuang' after the local tributary. Inside nearly every bottle (20B per litre) is inserted a thick black medicinal root called *yaa dong*, which is said to dissolve away the aches and pains of the day's work and prevent hangovers. It does seem to mellow the flavour of the lâo khão, which has a taste somewhere in between high-proof rum and tequila.

In vivid contrast to these villages are several model villages *(mùu bâan tua yàang)* organised by government officials as showcases for counter-insurgency in Loei Province. You'll know if you've stumbled upon one of these by the fenced-in houses with name tags on the doors. They also seem to be mostly empty of people – all hard at work in the fields, say officials. Some model villages even have model families (only one per village) which you are invited to visit. Walk right in and see model dad and model mum. Though Thai citizens as near as Loei and Chiang Khan still seem to be ignorant of their existence, I encountered model villages in Loei again during a 1991 visit.

Near Ban Pak Huay is one of the best places for swimming in the Heuang River, between January and May when the water is clear. None of these villages, including Tha Li, has a hotel or guesthouse, but you can usually spend the night at a village temple for a small donation. The wat with the Lao-style chedi off Route 2115 between Tha Li and Pak Huay has hosted several overnight farang visitors.

Ban Nong Pheu & Beyond
บ้านหนองผือ

Fifty km from Chiang Khan along rugged Route 2195 (only the first 13 km are paved), Ban Nong Pheu is a market village for local Thai-Lao trade across the Heuang River, where dozens of ferries flit back and forth all day long. Sit by the border post for an hour or two and you'll be amazed at all the merchandise that comes on and off the narrow boats – cases of Fab detergent, bags of cement, chickens and pigs, lumber, roots, rice. At a wat compound a short walk from the river is an outdoor market where a lot of the goods change hands; there are also a few noodle stalls and cold drink vendors to re-energise visitors who have made it to this little corner of the world. This market doesn't meet every day of the week – enquire in Loei or Chiang Khan for the current schedule. The river traffic is busiest on market days.

About 10 km further west along Route

2195 is **Ban A Hii**, another market village on the river that's similar to Ban Nong Pheu but usually less lively. The road continues past Ban A Hii to nondescript Pak Man and ends after about 45 km at Na Haew. Some highway maps optimistically show a road link between Na Haew and eastern Phitsanulok Province, but when I last visited the area, Na Haew was the end of the line unless you took Route 2113 south to Dan Sai and then went on to Phitsanulok via Nakhon Thai. In the future a road will probably go directly from Na Haew along the Lao border to Rom Klao in Phitsanulok, and from there north to Nan Province.

Getting There & Away

Songthaews from Loei leave almost hourly for Tha Li. The trip takes an hour and costs 14B. Songthaews between Tha Li and Ban A Hi or Ban Pak Huay cost 7B.

LOM SAK
หล่มสัก

It's a scenic trip to/from Phitsanulok via this small town in Phetchabun Province on the way to/from Loei and Khon Kaen. There are several places to stay near the bus stop, including the *Sawang Hotel* for 70 to 100B.

Nakhon Phanom Province

Nakhon Phanom Province has a large Lao and Vietnamese presence, although the capital is in the hands of ethnic Chinese. If you've come to this province to visit That Phanom, you'll probably have to stop here first to change buses, unless you go directly to That Phanom from Sakon Nakhon via Highway 223.

NAKHON PHANOM
อ.เมืองนครพนม

Nakhon Phanom (population 33,000) is 242 km from Udon and 296 km from Nong Khai. It's a dull town which just happens to have a really panoramic view of the Maekhong River and the craggy mountains of Laos beyond – in fact the Sanskrit-Khmer name means 'City of Hills'.

The interior murals of the bot at **Wat Si Thep**, in town on the street of the same name, show jatakas (life stories of the Buddha) along the upper part, and kings of the Chakri Dynasty along the lower part. On the back of the bot is a colourful triptych done in modern style.

The Lao town on the other side of the Maekhong River is **Tha Khaek**; the large white building visible at the southern end of Tha Khaek is a new hotel – at present it receives only Lao and Thai guests, as farangs aren't allowed to cross here yet.

Festivals

On the full moon of the 11th lunar month (usually mid-November), Nakhon Phanom residents celebrate Wan Phra Jao Prot Lok – a holiday in honour of Buddha's ascent to the Devaloka (deity world) to offer the residing devas a Dhamma sermon. Besides the usual wat offering, festival activities include the launching of *reua fai* or 'fire boats' on the Maekhong. Originally these eight to 10-metre boats were made of banana logs or bamboo but modern versions can be fashioned of wood or synthetic materials. The boats carry offerings of cakes, rice and flowers; at night the boats are launched on the river and illuminated in a spectacular display.

At the end of the Buddhist Rains Retreat (Awk Phansaa) in October, Nakhon Phanom hosts longboat races similar to those seen in many towns along the Maekhong.

Places to Stay

The *River Inn* on the Maekhong River used to be one of the nicest places in town but has taken a definite downturn in recent years. Rooms with a fan and bath cost from 100B, with some air-con rooms available.

A good budget bet is the *First Hotel* at 370 Si Thep Rd, which has somewhat run-down but clean rooms with fan and bath for 80B. A bit better is the *Windsor Hotel* (no English sign), 692/19 Bamrung Muang Rd, which has very nice singles/doubles for 140/160B with fan and bath, and air-con rooms for 300B. Behind the Windsor, on the corner of Si Thep and Ruamjit Rds, is the *Grand Hotel* which has similar rooms for 120/150B or 300B with air-con.

The *Si Thep Hotel* (☎ 511036), at 708/11 Si Thep Rd, costs 180/200B for rooms with fan and bath in the old wing, or 300/350B for air-con rooms in the new wing. VIP rooms with fridge and TV are available for 500B.

The top-end place in town is the *Nakhon Phanom Hotel* (☎ 511455) at 403 Aphiban Bancha Rd, where rooms with fan and bath cost 150B and air-con rooms are 250B, 300B with hot water or 500B VIP (add fridge and TV).

Places to Eat

Most of the town's better Thai and Chinese restaurants are along the river on Sunthon Wichit Rd and include *Plaa Beuk Thong (Golden Giant Catfish), Ban Suan* and *New Suan Mai*. I found New Suan Mai to be the best of the three; not only does it have the

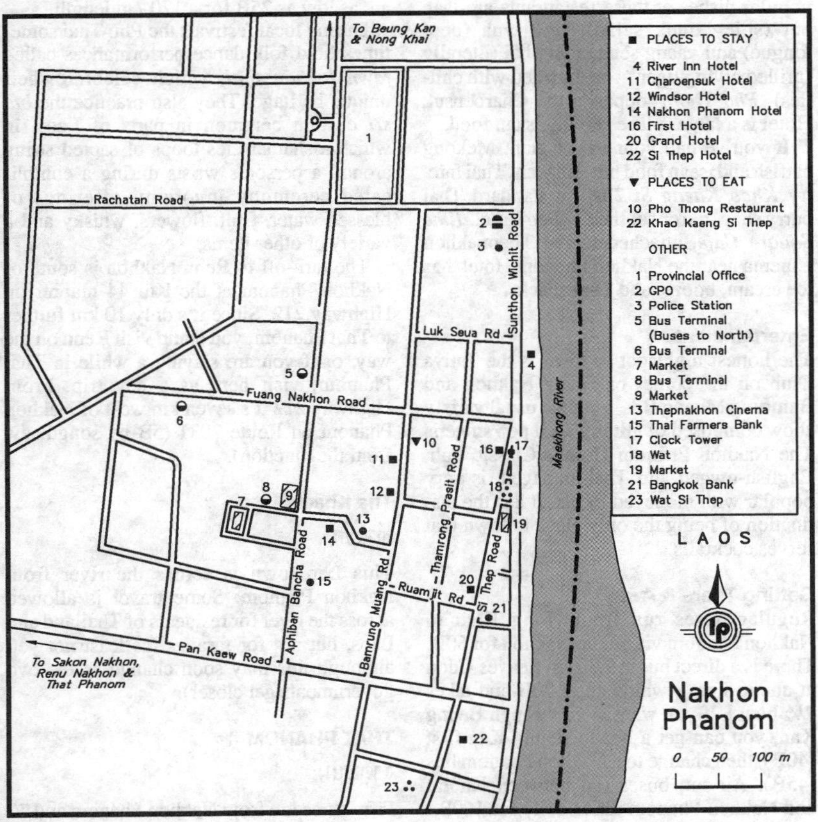

best food and river view, it's also got a city map on the wall. Giant Mekong catfish is served phàt phèt (stir-fried with basil and curry paste), tôm yam (in a spicy lemon-grass broth), phàt kratiam (garlic-fried) or òp mâw din (baked in a clay pot).

There are several good, inexpensive restaurants serving dishes like noodles and curry and rice along Bamrung Muang Rd north of the Windsor and Charoensuk hotels. Two small rice shops between the Charoensuk Hotel and Honey Massage, *Rot Mai* and *Rot Isaan*, serve local specialities, including jàew háwn, a sukiyaki-style soup with noodles, beef and vegetables. Other popular dishes at these restaurants are lâap pèt (spicy duck salad), ling wua (beef tongue) and yâang sěua ráwng hâi (literally 'grilled crying tiger' – beef grilled with chillies). *Pho Thong* opposite the Charoensuk Hotel is a larger place serving isaan food.

If you've had your fill of giant Mekong catfish and isaan food but still want Thai fare, try *Khao Kaeng Si Thep*, a standard Thai curry shop in front of the Si Thep Hotel. *Time Square Cafe*, attached to the Thepnakhon Cinema near the Nakhon Phanom Hotel, has ice cream, booze, and Thai snacks.

Entertainment

The hottest nightspot in town is the Tatiya Club on the corner of Fuang Nakhon and Bamrung Muang Rds, with the usual variety show composed of glittery Thai pop singers. The Nakhon Phanom Hotel's Classic Pub, English-owned and Thai-managed, is very popular with moneyed locals. It has the distinction of being the only place in town that serves cocktails.

Getting There & Away

Regular buses run from Nong Khai to Nakhon Phanom via Sakon Nakhon for 50B. There is a direct bus at 9.30 am (leaves Udon at about 8 am), which costs 70B and takes 7½ hours. If you want to go through Beung Kan, you can get a bus to Beung Kan first (40B), then change to a Nakhon Phanom bus (45B). Air-con buses run between Khorat and Nakhon Phanom thrice daily for 160B.

AROUND NAKHON PHANOM PROVINCE

Renu Nakhon

เรณูนคร

The village of Renu Nakhon is known for the weaving of cotton and silk fabrics, especially mat-mii designs. The local Phu Thai, a Thai tribe separate from mainstream Siamese and Lao, also market their designs here. Each Wednesday there's a big handicraft market near Wat Phra That Renu Nakhon. On other days you can buy from a few vendors near the temple or directly from weavers in the village. Prices for rough grades of mat-mii are as low as 25B for a 170-cm length.

During local festivals the Phu Thai sometimes hold folk dance performances called *fáwn lakhon thai*, which celebrate their unique heritage. They also practice the *bai sĩi* custom common in parts of Laos, in which a shaman ties loops of sacred string around a person's wrists during a complicated ceremony involving offerings of blessed water, fruit, flowers, whisky and a variety of other items.

The turn-off to Renu Nakhon is south of Nakhon Phanom at the Km 44 marker on Highway 212. Since it's only 10 km further to That Phanom, you could visit Renu on the way, or if you are staying a while in That Phanom, visit here as a day trip. From Highway 212 it's seven km west of Nakhon Phanom on Route 2031 (5B by songthaew from the junction).

Tha Khaek

ท่าแขก

This Lao town is across the river from Nakhon Phanom. Some travel is allowed across the river for residents of Thailand and Laos, but not for farangs (as least not yet, although this may soon change as the two governments get closer).

THAT PHANOM

ธาตุพนม

Fifty-three km from Nakhon Phanom and 70

km from Sakon Nakhon, the centre of activity in this small town is Wat That Phanom.

The short road between Wat That Phanom and the old town on the Maekhong River passes under a large Lao arch of victory which is similar to the arch at the end of Lan Xang Rd in Vientiane (which also leads to Vientiane's Wat That). This section of That Phanom is interesting, with French-Chinese architecture reminiscent of old Vientiane or Saigon.

In mid-February, the annual Phra That Phanom fair attracts quite a crowd to the town.

If you need to change money, go to the Thai Military Bank which is on the road to Nakhon Phanom.

Hundreds of Lao merchants cross the river for the market on Monday and Thursday from around 8.30 am to noon. There are two market locations in town, one on the highway near the wat and one on the river north of the pier. The latter is where the Lao congregate on their twice-weekly visits. Exotic offerings include Lao herbal medicines, forest roots, Vietnamese pigs, and animal skins; the maddest haggling occurs just before the market closes, when Thai buyers try to take advantage of the Lao reluctance to carry unsold merchandise back to Laos.

About 16 km south of town is a wooded park next to **Kaeng Kabao**, a set of rapids in the Maekhong River. Nearby hills afford views over the river and Laos on the other side. The usual food vendors make this a good spot for an impromptu picnic – it's an easy bicycle ride from That Phanom.

Wat That Phanom

The centrepiece of this wat is a huge *thâat* or Lao-style chedi, more impressive than any chedi in present-day Laos. The monument, which caved in during heavy rains in 1975 and was restored in 1978, is a talismanic symbol of isaan and is highly revered by

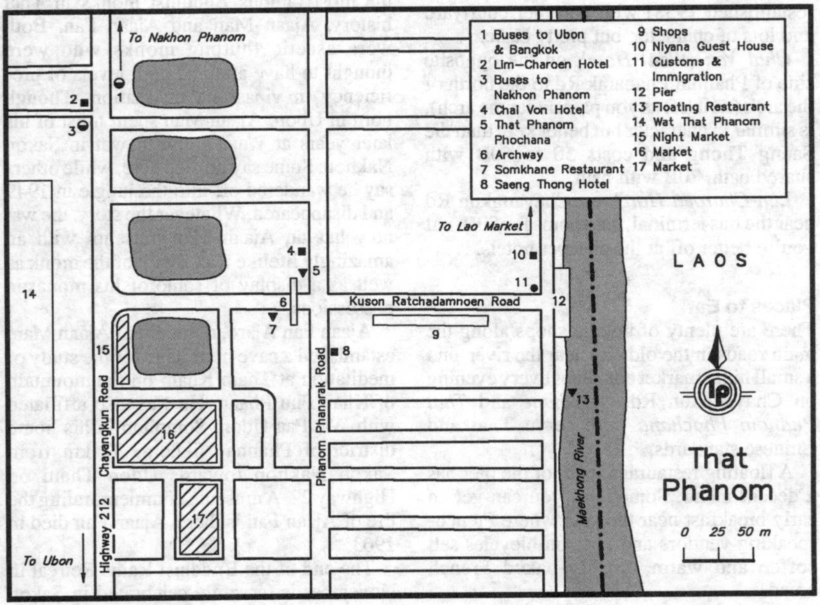

Buddhists all over Thailand. The dating of the wat is disputed, but some archaeologists set its age at about 1500 years. The chedi is 57 (or 52, depending on whom you believe) metres high and the spire is decorated with 110 kg of gold. Surrounding the famous chedi is a cloister filled with Buddha images and behind the wat is a shady park.

Places to Stay

That Phanom's first guesthouse has recently opened. The owner of *Niyana Guest House* moved here from Nong Khai and has a place on the river near the That Phanom pier. Dorm beds are 30B, singles are 50 to 60B and a double room is 80B. Niyana can arrange bicycle rentals and short boat trips on the river.

The old town has three hotels. To reach *Saeng Thong Hotel*, turn right on to Phanom Phanarak Rd as you pass under the arch and it's on the left side of the street 30 metres down. An adequate room with a fan and shared bath costs 60B. It's a funky place (established 1958) with an inner courtyard and lots of character, but pretty basic.

Chai Von (Wan) Hotel, on the opposite side of Phanom Phanarak Rd to the north of the arch (turn left as you pass under the arch), is similar in character but better kept than the Saeng Thong and costs 50 to 60B with shared bath, 70B with bath.

Lim-Charoen Hotel, on Chayangkun Rd near the bus terminal, has rooms for 80B, but you're better off at the cheaper hotels.

Places to Eat

There are plenty of noodle shops along the main roads in the old city near the river, and a small night market convenes every evening on Chayangkun Rd. *Somkhane* and *That Phanom Phochana* both serve Thai and Chinese standards.

A floating restaurant south of the pier has a decent menu. Sometimes you can get an early breakfast near the pier, where French-speaking vendors and girls on bicycles sell coffee and warm, freshly baked French bread.

Getting There & Away

Bus From the bus terminal on Chayangkun Rd there are regular buses to Mukdahan (12B), Ubon (44B, air-con 80B), Sakon Nakhon (17B, air-con 30B), Nakhon Phanom (22B air-con) and Udon Thani (47B). The air-con Khorat to Nakhon Phanom bus stops at That Phanom. The fare (160B) is the same as all the way to Nakhon Phanom.

Songthaew Songthaews to That Phanom leave regularly from the intersection near the Nakhon Phanom Hotel in Nakhon Phanom and cost 12B. Stay on until you see the chedi on the right. The trip takes about 1½ hours.

Sakon Nakhon Province

Sakon Nakhon Province is well known among Thais as the one-time home of two of the most famous Buddhist monks in Thai history, Ajaan Man and Ajaan Fan. Both were ascetic thutong monks who were thought to have attained high levels of proficiency in vipassana meditation. Though born in Ubon, Ajaan Man spent most of his later years at Wat Paa Sutthawat in Sakon Nakhon. Some say he died here, while others say he wandered off into the jungle in 1949 and disappeared. Whatever the story, the wat now has an Ajaan Man museum with an amazingly lifelike wax figure of the monk as well as a display of some of his monastic possessions.

Ajaan Fan Ajaro, a student of Ajaan Man, established a cave hermitage for the study of meditation at Tham Kham on the mountain of Khao Phu Phaan. He was also affiliated with Wat Paa Udom Somphon in his home district of Phanna Nikhom, 37 km from Sakon Nakhon towards Udon Thani on Highway 22. A museum commemorating the life of Ajaan Fan is there. Ajaan Fan died in 1963.

The end of the Buddhist Rains Retreat in November is fervently celebrated in Sakon with the carving and display of wax prasats, as well as parades.

SAKON NAKHON

สกลนคร

The name for this town (and the province of course) can be translated as either 'Universal City' (as intended) or 'Part City' (more appropriate). As a secondary agricultural market centre (after Udon Thani) for the upper isaan, it's mostly a conglomeration of shops selling farm equipment. For most visitors, the only reason to stay in the city is to visit Wat Choeng Chum and Wat Narai Jeng Weng.

Along the eastern edge of town is **Nong Han**, Thailand's largest natural lake. Don't swim in the lake as it's infested with liver flukes (opisthorchiasis). The villages around the lake have recorded among the highest incidences of opisthorchiasis in the world, since many of the villagers eat snails gathered from water plants in the lake. These snails play host to the flukes, which bore through human or animal skin and breed in the internal organs. (See the Health section in the Facts for the Visitor chapter.)

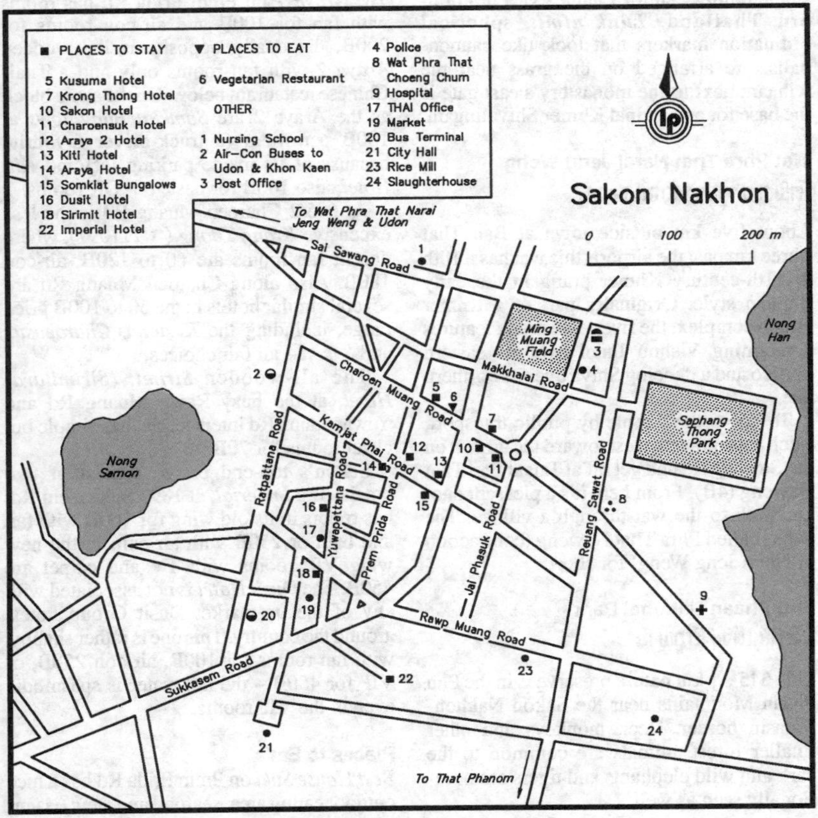

Wat Phra That Choeng Chum

วัดพระธาตุเชิงชุม

Next to the Nong Han Lake in town, this wat features a 25-metre-high Lao-style chedi which was erected during the Ayuthaya period over a smaller 11th-century Khmer prang. To view the prang you must enter through the adjacent wihaan. If the door to the chedi is locked, ask one of the monks to open it – they're used to having visitors. Around the base of the prang is a collection of Lao and Khmer Buddha images.

Also on the grounds is a small Lan Xang-era bot and a wihaan built in the cruciform shape reminiscent of Lanna styles in northern Thailand. *Lûuk nímít*, spherical ordination markers that look like cannonballs, are arranged on the grass near the wihaan; next to the monastery's east gate is the base for an original Khmer Shivalingam.

Wat Phra That Narai Jeng Weng

วัดพระธาตุนารายณ์เจงเวง

About five km outside town at Ban That (three km past the airport) this wat has a 10th to 11th-century Khmer prang in the early Bapuan style. Originally part of a Khmer Hindu complex, the five-level prang features a reclining Vishnu lintel over its eastern portico and a dancing Shiva over its northern one.

To get to the temple by public transport, catch a songthaew west toward the airport on Sai Sawang Rd and get off at Talaat Ban That Naweng (4B). From here it's a pleasant one-km walk to the wat through a village. The wat is called Phra That Naweng (contraction of Narai Jeng Weng) for short.

Phu Phaan National Park

อุทยานแห่งชาติภูพาน

This 645-sq-km nature preserve is in the Phu Phaan Mountains near the Sakon Nakhon-Kalasin border. Deer, monkeys and other smaller forest animals are common to the park and wild elephants and tigers are occasionally seen as well.

The mountain forests are thick and the area is fairly undeveloped. It has been used as a hiding spot by two guerrilla forces – the Thai resistance against the Japanese in WW II and later the PLAT guerrillas in the '70s.

The park has few hiking trails but there are good views along Highway 213 between Sakon Nakhon and Kalasin. Three waterfalls – Tat Ton, Hew Sin Chai and Kham Hom – can be visited fairly easily.

The **Tham Seri Thai** cave was used by the Thai Seri during WW II as an arsenal and mess hall.

Places to Stay

The *Araya 1* on Prem Prida Rd has rooms with fan for 100B and air-con rooms for 200B; diagonally opposite is the wooden *Araya 2* with fan rooms only and a Thai-Chinese restaurant below. On the same block as the Araya 2 are *Somkiat Bungalows* at 100B per room (a truck-driver favourite because of its inside parking lot) and *Kiti Hotel*, also 100B for basic but OK rooms.

At 645/2 Charoen Muang Rd is the less expensive *Krong Thong* (☎ 711097), where decent fan rooms are 60 to 120B, air-con 180B. Also along Charoen Muang Rd are several similar hotels in the 60 to 100B price range, including the *Kusuma, Charoensuk* and *Sakon* – all fair choices.

The all-wooden *Sirimit (Sirimitara) Hotel*, at the busy Rawp Muang Rd and Yuwapattana Rd intersection, has simple but clean rooms for 70B.

Sakon's top-end places consist of two hotels. The *Imperial*, at 1892 Sukkasem Rd, has rooms in its old wing for 160B with fan and bath or 250B with air-con; in the new wing VIP rooms with TV and carpet are 450B. The *Dusit Hotel* is not associated with any of the up-market Dusit Group hotels around the country. This one is rather shabby, with fan rooms for 100B, air-con 250B, or VIP for 450B – the hot water is spasmodic even in the VIP rooms.

Places to Eat

Best House Suki on Prem Prida Rd has a nice outdoor eating area, seafood and jàew (isaan-style sukiyaki – a noodle hot-pot). Night markets are open each evening near the traffic circle at Charoen Muang and Jai Phasuk Rds, and also at the intersection of Charoen Muang and Sukkasem Rds. Both are very popular nightspots, open till late.

Along Prem Prida Rd are three inexpensive Thai-Chinese restaurants that seem to do half the restaurant business in the city. They're apparent clones of one another; the offerings at all three are similar (buffet-style curries and stir-fries) and all sport names that end in *-rak* (love): *Mitrak* (Friend Love), *Yawt Rak* (Peak of Love) and *Na Rak* (Lovable). All serve passable food at cheap prices.

Laap fans shouldn't miss *Phen Laap Pet*, an inexpensive Sakon institution on Prem Prida Rd with a choice of lâap pèt khão or lâap pèt daeng – white duck salad and red duck salad ('red' means with duck blood). Other house specialities are yam (another kind of isaan salad, usually with vegetables or seafood), khài yát sâi (ground pork and vegetable omelette), and plaa sãam rót or 'three-flavour fish', a whole fish fried with onions, chillies and garlic.

If duck blood or other animal food isn't your thing, move on over to the *Vegetarian Restaurant* on Charoen Muang Rd between Sukkasem Rd and Prem Prida Rd. All dishes are between 5 and 10B, but it's only open from 6 am to 1 pm.

Getting There & Away

Air Should you wish to fly in or out of Sakon Nakhon, THAI has one flight a day from Bangkok (1465B one-way). The office (☎ 712259) in Sakon is at 1446 Yuwapattana Rd, near the Dusit Hotel.

Bus Direct buses to Sakon are available from Ubon (55B), Nakhon Phanom (20B), Kalasin (35B), That Phanom (17B) and Udon (48B). Buses from Sakon to Bangkok are 119B (three departures a day) or 215B air-con (there is one evening departure a day). Buses between Khorat and Sakon (air-con only) are 138B and leave six times daily.

Private air-con buses to Udon and Khon Kaen leave three times daily from the Udon-Sakhon Doen Rot bus office, next to the Esso station on Sukkasem Rd.

Yasothon & Mukdahan Provinces

Once part of Ubon Ratchathani Province, these adjacent provinces in the lower north-east are Thailand's two newest and isaan's smallest provinces. Both are mostly rural in character, with small capital cities serving as market centres for surrounding farms.

YASOTHON

อ.เมืองยโสธร

Yasothon (population 21,000) is difficult to get to, but if you happen to be in the area (say, in Ubon, which is about 100 km away) during May, it might be worth a two-hour bus trip (from Ubon) to catch the annual Rocket Festival which takes place from 8 May to 10 May. The festival (Bun Bâng Fai in Thai) is prevalent throughout the north-east as a rain and fertility rite, and is celebrated most fervently in Yasothon, where it involves parades and a fantastic fireworks display. The name of the town, which has the largest Muslim population in the north-east, comes from the Sanskrit 'Yasodhara' which means preserver or maintainer of glory, and is also the name of one of Krishna's sons by Rukmini in the *Mahabharata*.

The village of **Si Than** in Pa Tiu district, about 20 km east of Yasothon off Highway 202, is renowned for the crafting of firm, triangle-shaped mawn khwaan (axe pillows), which are said to rival those of Roi Et.

Places to Stay

Udomphon at 80/1-2 Uthairamrit Rd costs from 70 to 80B for rooms with fan and bath, while the *Surawet Wattana*, at 128/1 Changsanit Rd, costs from 80 to 100B. If you can't get into either of these try the *Yot Nakhon*

(☎ 711122), 141-143/1-3 Uthairamrit Rd, where rooms are from 100B, or from 200B with air-con.

Getting There & Away

A bus to Yasothon from Ubon costs 23B and from Khorat it's 56B ordinary or 114B air-con.

MUKDAHAN

อ.เมืองมุกดาหาร

Exactly 55 km south of That Phanom and 170 km north of Ubon Ratchathani, Mukdahan (population 23,000) was formerly part of Nakhon Phanom and Ubon provinces, but since September 1982 Mukdahan has been Thailand's newest province.

Mukdahan is known for its beautiful Maekhong scenery and as a Thai-Lao trade centre. It's directly opposite the city of Savannakhet in Laos. There's a daily Lao-Vietnamese market on the grounds of **Wat Si Mongkon Tai** near the Mukdahan pier.

Mukdahan might make a nice stopover between Nakhon Phanom or That Phanom and Ubon. For a view of the town, climb the 500-metre **Phu Narom** hill, three km south of town.

The Bangkok Bank of Commerce on Samut Sakdarak Rd in town has a currency exchange service.

Phu Pha Thoep National Park

อุทยานแห่งชาติภูผาเทิบ

Sixteen km south of Mukdahan off Route 2034 is a hilly area of caves and unusual mushroom-shaped rock formations. Besides the rock formations, the park is a habitat for barking deer, wild boar, monkeys and civets. The main entrance to the park is actually 25 km from town, just south of the Ubon pro-

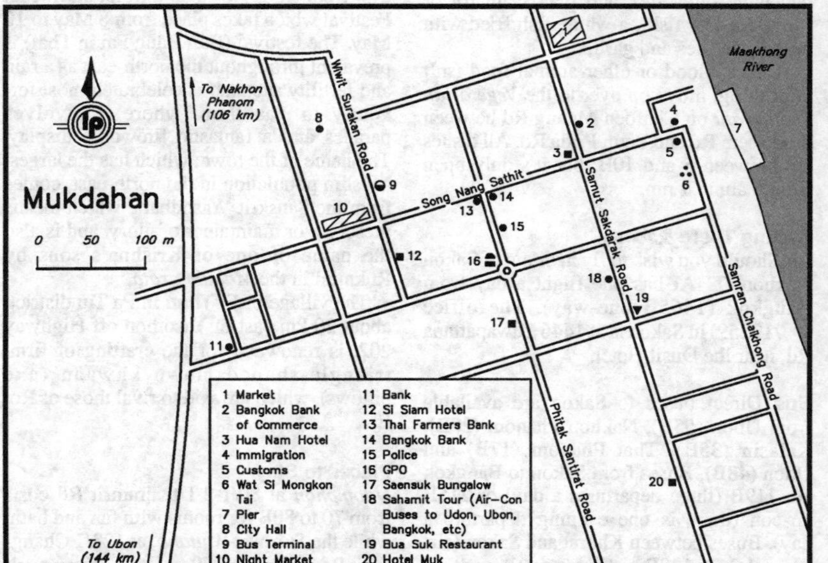

vincial line. About two km south-west into the park, next to a waterfall, is a collection of dozens of small Buddha images.

Places to Stay

None of the hotels in Mukdahan are any great deals but they're adequate. The *Hua Nam Hotel* (☎ 611137) at 20 Samut Sakdarak Rd quoted 100B for rooms with fan and shared bath – a little high – or 220B with air-con and private bath. On the same road is the cheaper *Banthom Kasem Hotel*, but it's a real dive. Better is *Saensuk Bungalow* at 2 Phitak Santirat, which offers clean, quiet rooms for 100 to 200B fan, 300B air-con.

There is also the *Hong Kong Hotel* at 161/1-2 Phitak Santirat Rd where rooms are 80B with fan and bath, and the *Si Siam Hotel* on Wiwit Surakan Rd which has rooms for 100B with fan and bath; 200B with air-con.

Mukdahan Hotel (Hotel Muk) is probably the best deal in town – it's a little away from the centre of town on Samut Sakdarak Rd and rooms cost 100B with fan and shared bath; 250B with air-con.

Places to Eat

The night market along Song Nang Sathit Rd has kài yâang, sôm-tam, khâo jii (Lao baguette sandwiches), and páw-pía (Vietnamese spring rolls, either fresh (sòt) or fried (thâwt)). The *Bua Suk* on Samut Sakdarak Rd near Sahamit Tour has good curries and khanŏm jiin. *Khao Tom Suanrak*, next to Hua Nam Hotel, is a Chinese rice-soup place that's open all night. Another place that's open in the wee hours is the *Suwa Blend Restaurant/Pub* next to the Hotel Muk. House specialities are American-style breakfast and khâo tôm. On the river about a km south of the pier, the *Riverside* has a shady outdoor area with a view of Savannakhet. The menu covers mostly Thai and Chinese dishes, but lâap is also served. Prices are moderate and the beer is cold.

Getting There & Away

There are regular buses from either direction – 40B from Nakhon Phanom (and half that from That Phanom) or 34B from Ubon.

VIP (sleeper) buses to Bangkok and ordinary buses to Nakhon Phanom leave from the intersection of Wiwit Surakan and Song Nang Sathit Rds near the government bus office. Sahamit Tour on Samut Sakdarak Rd has air-con buses to Bangkok, Nakhon Phanom, Udon, Ubon and Sakon Nakhon.

Ubon Ratchathani Province

Ubon is the north-east's largest province and the provincial capital is one of the largest towns in Thailand. About 300 km of the province borders on Laos and around 60 km borders Cambodia. The local TAT office is trying to promote the area where the three countries meet as the 'Emerald Triangle' in counterpart to northern Thailand's Golden Triangle. The 'emerald' in the title ostensibly refers to the many acres of intact monsoon forest in this part of the province – largely due to the fact that it has been sparsely populated because of war tensions. Now that the Khmer Rouge have stopped military activities in the area, travel in the tri-border zone is considered safe.

Many centuries ago Ubon was a Khmer settlement, although little visible evidence remains of the Khmer era. Following the decline of the Khmer empires, the area was settled by groups of Lao in 1773 and 1792 and today the Lao influence in the province predominates over the Khmer.

UBON RATCHATHANI

อ.เมืองอุบลราชธานี

Ubon (sometimes spelt Ubol, though the 'l' is pronounced like an 'n') is 557 km from Bangkok, 271 km from Nakhon Phanom and 311 km from Khorat. One of Thailand's largest towns (population 200,000), it's a financial, educational, communications and agricultural market centre for eastern isaan. Like Udon and Khorat, it served as a US air base in the Vietnam War days. The city's

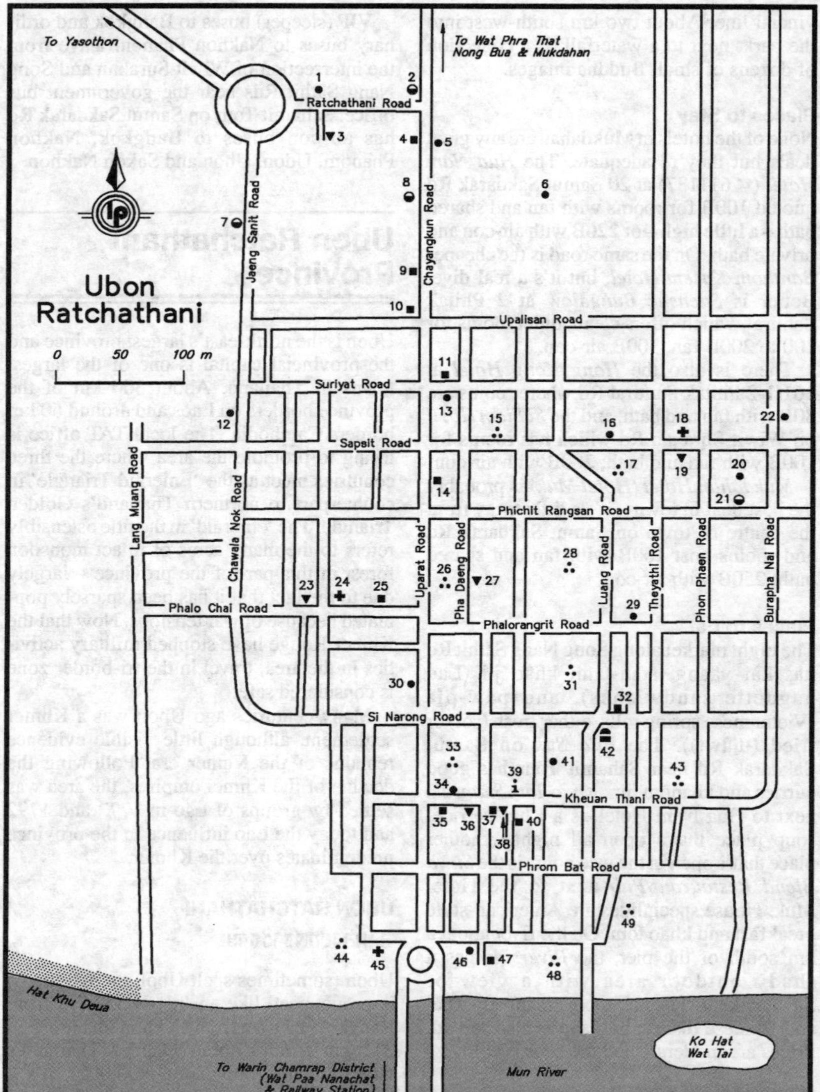
Ubon Ratchathani
0 50 100 m
To Yasothon
To Wat Phra That Nong Bua & Mukdahan
Ratchathani Road
Jaeng Sanit Road
Chayangkun Road
Upalisan Road
Suriyat Road
Sapsit Road
Phichit Rangsan Road
Lang Muang Road
Chawala Nok Road
Uparat Road
Pha Daeng Road
Luang Road
Theyathi Road
Phon Phaen Road
Burapha Nai Road
Phalo Chai Road
Phalorangrit Road
Si Narong Road
Kheuan Thani Road
Phrom Bat Road
Hat Khu Deua
To Warin Chamrap District (Wat Paa Nanachat & Railway Station)
Mun River
Ko Hat Wat Tai

■ PLACES TO STAY

4 Pathumrat Hotel
9 Regent Palace Hotel
10 Racha Hotel
11 Suriyat Hotel
14 Tokyo Hotel
25 Bodin Hotel
32 Krung Thong Hotel
35 Ubon Hotel
37 Ratchathani Hotel
40 Sri Kamol Hotel
47 Si Isaan Hotel

▼ PLACES TO EAT

3 Fern Hut
19 Vegetarian Restaurant
23 Sala Mangsawirat
27 Sakon Restaurant
36 Jiaw Kii (Chiokee) Restaurant
38 Hong Thong Restaurant

OTHER

1 Ubon Teachers' College
2 Buses for Mukdahan, Udon & Sakon Nakhon
5 THAI Office
6 Airfield
7 Buses to Yasothon
8 Bus Terminal
12 Highway Department Office
13 C Wattana Motorcycles
15 Wat Jaeng
16 Police
17 Wat Paa Yai
18 Sapsit Prasong Hospital
20 Market No 5
21 Buses to Phibun Mangsahan & Khong Jiam
22 Market
24 Central Memorial Hospital
26 Wat Suthatsanaram
28 Wat Paa Noi
29 Cinema
30 Province & District Offices
31 Wat Thung Si Muang
33 City Shrine
34 Ubon National Museum
39 TAT Office
41 Municipal Office
42 GPO
43 Wat Liap
44 Wat Supatanaram
45 Rom Kao Hospital
46 Market
48 Wat Luang
49 Wat Klang

main attractions are the October candle festival, a few wats and a National Museum.

Information

Tourist Office The TAT (☎ 243770) has a very helpful branch office at 264/1 Kheuan Thani Rd, opposite the Sri Kamol Hotel. The office distributes free maps of Ubon and other information handouts; it's open daily from 8.30 am to 4.30 pm.

Post & Telecommunications Ubon's GPO is near the intersection of Luang and Si Narong Rds. It's open from 8.30 am to 4.30 pm Monday to Friday, 9 am to noon on weekends. The telephone office is next door and is open daily from 7 am to 11 pm.

Medical Services The new Rom Kao Hospital on Uparat Rd near the bridge is the best medical facility in the lower north-east.

Ubon National Museum

พิพิธภัณฑ์แห่งชาติอุบล

Housed in a former palace of the Rama VI era, west of the TAT office on Kheuan Thani Rd, the National Museum is a good place to learn about Ubon's history and culture before exploring the city or province. Most of the exhibits have bilingual labels.

Flanking the main entrance are a large Dvaravati-period sema (ordination stone) and Pallava-inscribed pillars from the Khmer era. The room to the left of the entrance has general information on Ubon history and geography. This is followed by a prehistory room with displays of stone and bronze implements, burial urns and pottery resembling that found in Ban Chiang, plus reproductions of the Phaa Taem rock paintings. The next rooms cover the historical era and contain many real treasures of mainland South-East Asian art, including Hindu-Khmer sculpture from the Chenla, Bapuan and Angkor eras; Lao Buddhas; Ubon textiles; local musical instruments; and folk utensils (rice containers, fish traps, betel-nut holders).

The museum is open from 9 am to noon and 1 to 4 pm, Wednesday to Sunday. Admission is 10B.

Wat Thung Si Muang
วัดทุ่งศรีเมือง

Off Luang Rd, near the centre of town, this wat was originally built during the reign of Rama III (1824-51) and has a *hãw trai* (tripitaka library) in good shape. It rests on high-angled stilts in the middle of a small pond. Nearby is an old mondop with a Buddha footprint symbol. The interior of the bot is painted with 150-year-old jataka murals.

Wat Phra That Nong Bua
วัดพระธาตุหนองบัว

This wat is on the road to Nakhon Phanom on the outskirts of town (catch a white city bus for 2B) and is based almost exactly on the Mahabodhi stupa in Bodhgaya, India. It is much better than Wat Jet Yot in Chiang Mai, which is purported to be a Mahabodhi reproduction, but was designed by people who never saw the real thing. The jataka reliefs on the outside of the chedi are very good. There are two groups of four niches on each side of the four-sided chedi which contain Buddhas in different standing postures. The stances look like stylised Gupta or Dvaravati closed-robe poses.

Wat Supatanaram
วัดสุปัฏนาราม

Called Wat Supat for short, the unique bot at this temple features a mix of Khmer, European and Thai styles. In contrast to the usual Thai-or Lao-style temple structures of the region, the bot is made entirely of stone, like the early Khmer stone prasats; the roof corners display dragons instead of the usual *jâo fáa* or sky spirits.

In front of the bot is the largest wooden bell in Thailand.

Wat Jaeng
วัดแจ้ง

This wat, on Sapsit Rd, has a typical Lao-style bot (known locally by the Lao term, *sim*). The carved wooden verandah depicts a *kotchasi*, a mythical cross between an elephant and a horse; above that is Erawan, Indra's three-headed elephant mount.

Warin Chamrap District Temples

Ubon city district is separated from Warin Chamrap to the south by the Mun River. Two well-known wats in this district are forest monasteries (wát pàa) founded by the famous monk and meditation master Ajaan Chaa. The venerable ajaan passed away in January 1992 after a productive and inspirational life, but his teachings live on at these two hermitages.

Wat Nong Paa Phong About 10 km past the railway station and in Warin Chamrap district is Wat Nong Paa Phong. This very famous forest wat was founded by Ajaan Chaa, who also founded many other branch temples in Ubon Province and one in Sussex, England. All of these temples are known for their quiet discipline and daily routine of work and meditation.

Dozens of Westerners have studied here during the past 20 years and many live here or at branch temples as ordained monks.

Ajaan Chaa, a former disciple of the most famous north-eastern teacher of them all, Ajaan Man (who disappeared from sight some years ago), was known for his simple and direct teaching method which seemed to cross all international barriers.

The wat features a small museum and a chedi where Ajaan Chaa's ashes are interred. To get to the wat from Ubon, take a pink city bus No 3 to the Baw Khaw Saw terminal, then catch a songthaew going to the wat.

Wat Paa Nanachat Beung Wai The abbot at Wat Paa Nanachat Beung Wai is Canadian, the vice-abbot is English and most of the monks are European or Japanese. As English is the main language spoken here, Wat Paa Nanachat is a better place to visit than Wat Nong Paa Phong if you are interested in more than sightseeing. The wat is very clean, cool and quiet. Both men and women are welcome, but men are required to shave their heads if they want to stay beyond three days.

From Ubon, take a white, city bus No 1 south down Uparat Rd, cross the bridge over the Mun River and get off as the bus turns right in Warin Chamrap for the railway station. From there, catch any songthaew heading south (though heading west eventually, towards Si Saket) and ask to be let off at Wat Nanachat – everybody knows it.

You can also get there by catching a Si Saket bus from Ubon for 3B to Beung Wai, the village across the road from Wat Nanachat. There is a sign in English at the edge of the road – the wat is in the forest behind the rice fields.

You can also hire a tuk-tuk direct to the wat from town for about 50B.

Ko Hat Wat Tai
เกาะหาดวัดใต้

This is a small island in the Mun River on the southern edge of town. During the hot and dry months, from March to May, it is a favourite picnic spot and there are 'beaches' on the island where you can swim. You can get there by boat from the northern shore of the river.

Hat Khu Deua
หาดคูเดือ

Hat Khu Deua is a 'beach' area on the northern bank of the river west of town, off Lang Muang Rd. Several thatched salas offer shade for picnicking or napping by the river; you can even stay overnight in simple raft houses at no charge.

Festivals

The Candle Festival (Ngaan Hae Thian) is most grandly celebrated in Ubon, with music, parades, floats, beauty contests and enormous carved candles of all shapes – human, animal, divine and abstract. The evening processions are impressive. The festival begins around Khao Phansaa, the first day of the Buddhist Rains Retreat in late July, and lasts five days. Spirits are high and hotels are full. It's worth a trip this time of year just to see the festival.

Places to Stay – bottom end

There are plenty of places to choose from in Ubon. Several cheaper hotels are along Suriyat Rd: *Suriyat Hotel*, 47/1-4 Suriyat Rd, where a basic room with fan costs 80B or 160B with air-con; the *Dollar*, 39/5 Suriyat Rd, which has the same rates as the Suriyat; and *Homsa-ad (Hawm Sa-at)*, 80/10 Suriyat Rd, which has bare, dingy rooms from 80 to 100B.

Another cheapie is the *Decha* on Kheuan Thani Rd where rooms are 80B with fan, 160B with air-con. A better choice in this range is the *Si Isaan (Far East)* (☎ 253204) at 220/6 Ratchabut Rd; singles/doubles are 80/140B with fan and private bath.

The friendly *Racha Hotel* at 149/21 Chayangkun Rd, north of the town centre, starts at 90B for clean rooms with fan and bath or 200B with air-con.

Places to Stay – middle

At 24 Si Narong Rd is the *Krung Thong* (☎ 241609) with air-con rooms for a reasonable 200 to 380B, fan-cooled doubles for 150B. The *Tokyo Hotel* is at 178 Uparat Rd where it meets Chayangkun Rd, near the town centre. It's very nice and well kept; singles/doubles with fan and bath cost 90/140B or 120/220B with air-con.

The *Bodin (Badin)*, near the Sala Mangsawirat vegetarian restaurant on Phalo Chai Rd, has singles/doubles with fan for 200B and air-con rooms for 320B. It's a bit overpriced for the hotel's shabby condition though it's a favourite with the 'salespeople' crowd.

Ubon Hotel (Kao Chan) at 333 Kheuan Thani Rd has gone steadily downhill over the years. Dank singles/doubles with fan and bath are 160/220B or 240/330B with air-con. Similar in price but in better condition is the *Ratchathani Hotel* (☎ 254599), at 229 Kheuan Thani Rd, where decent singles/doubles are 180/240B with fan or 290/370B air-con.

Places to Stay – top end

The flashy 168-room *Pathumrat Hotel* (☎ 241501; fax 243792) at 173 Chayangkun Rd, once the top hotel in Ubon, has 'deluxe' air-con rooms for 600B, rooms with video for 1850B. Facilities include a coffee shop, restaurant and massage parlour.

Best value over 500B is the new 116-room *Regent Palace Hotel* (☎ 244031; fax 255489) at 265-271 Chayangkun Rd. Clean quiet carpeted rooms with TV and phone are 500/600B singles/doubles including tax and service. Facilities include a lobby coffee shop, a cocktail lounge and a snooker club. These may be promotional 'soft opening' rates – if reception quotes 800/900B (as listed at the TAT) a discount may be available.

Another good top-end place is the refurbished and efficient *Sri Kamol (Si Kamon) Hotel* (☎ 241136, fax 243792) at 22/2 Ubonsak Rd near the Ratchathani Hotel. Room rates are the same as at the Regent Palace.

Places to Eat

On Si Narong Rd the *Choeng Ubon* (opposite Ritayakhom School) and *Song Rot* (opposite the telephone office) make good kũaytĩaw. *Raan Khao Tom Hong Thong*, a Chinese-Thai restaurant on Kheuan Thani Rd (not far from the Ratchathani Hotel and on the same side of the street) has the largest selection of dishes on display that I have ever seen in a restaurant of its size. Goose and duck dishes are house specials. Try khâo nâa pèt or khâo nâa hàan – roast duck or goose on rice – cheap and delicious. Also good are the crab claw curry, fried crab rolls and kài phàt khĩng (chicken fried in ginger). It's open for lunch and dinner only but doesn't close until the early-morning hours. The *Mae Mun 2* and *Thiang Rak* on the same street are similar late-night khâo tôm places.

Ubon is famous for its isaan food – many Thai gourmets claim it has the best in all of isaan. Lâap pèt (spicy duck salad) is the local speciality, often eaten with tôm fák (squash soup) and Chinese mushrooms. Good places for laap pet include *Laap Luk Thung* on Suriyat Rd (behind the hospital), *Piak* on Jaeng Sanit Rd (next to a radio relay station), *Suan Maphrao,* also on Jaeng Sanit Rd (next to Si Maha Pho Hospital) and *Laap Kan Aeng* on Kheuan Thani (next to Wat Liap). Ubon is also big on kài yâang (grilled Lao-style chicken) and everyone in town agrees that the best is at *Kai Yaang Wat Jaeng*, which is opposite Wat Jaeng and is open from 10 am to 1 pm only.

Ubon has two vegetarian restaurants. At 108/4 Phalo Chai Rd near the Central Memorial Hospital and the Bodin Hotel is *Sala Mangsawirat.* Look for a small English sign reading 'Vegetarian Food'. It's practically next door to the big Muang Thong massage parlour. The food is cheap (5 to 10B) and delicious, very Thai but 100% vegetarian. The walls are covered with Buddhist slogans in Thai, many of them quotes from Ajaan Buddhadasa. The other vegetarian place is across from Sapsit Prasong Hospital on Sapsit Rd and has similar Thai vegetarian cuisine at about the same prices. Another possible source of vegetarian food is the *Hong Fa Restaurant* opposite the Pathumrat Hotel on Chayangkun Rd. The cooks at Hong Fa will prepare vegetarian Chinese dishes on request; this is where Chinese Buddhists eat when taking vegetarian vows.

Fern Hut, down a soi opposite the teacher's college *(wítháyalai khruu* in Thai) sells good cakes and other baked items.

Ubon has two night markets which are open from dusk to dawn, one by the river near the bridge *(talàat yài* or big market), and the other near the bus terminal on Chayangkun Rd – convenient to hotels on Chayangkun and Suriyat Rds.

For breakfast, *Chiokee (Jiaw Kii)* on Kheuan Thani Rd is very popular among local office workers. Prices are good and it has everything from khâo tôm to ham and eggs. One of their specialities is jók (broken-rice soup or congee).

Entertainment

Folk Music The Pathuma Coffeeshop in the Pathumrat Hotel features a traditional music ensemble that plays such isaan instruments as the khaen (stepped reed pipes), ponglang (log xylophone) and *hai song* (water jars with bands strung across the openings, played with graceful hand movements). There's no cover charge, but a bottle of beer is 90B – worth it for the excellent performances. The ensemble plays nightly.

Nightclubs Also in the Pathumrat Hotel is The Champ, a disco-style club. Chikki, in the Sinratchabut Cinema on Ratchabut Rd, is a smoky Thai-style nightclub.

Massage Thai Massage Clinic (☎ 254746) at 369-371 Sapsit Rd offers traditional massage from 9 am to 9 pm daily. Rates are 100B per hour.

Ubon also has several *àap òp nûat* (bathe-steam-massage) places that probably got their start during the days when a US air base was located outside town.

Things to Buy

One of the major local specialities is silver betel-nut containers moulded using the lost-wax process. The Ubon National Museum on Kheuan Thani Rd has a good exhibit of locally produced betel boxes; to see them being made, visit **Ban Pa-Ao**, a silversmithing village between Ubon and Yasothon off Highway 23.

Several shops on Ratchabut Rd – Phanchat, Khampun, Mit Ying, Den Fa and Ket Kaew – carry Ubon handicrafts, including fabrics and silverwork.

Getting There & Away

Air THAI has one daily flight from Bangkok to Ubon at 6 pm, except on Monday and Saturday when flights leave at 9.25 am. The fare is 1345B and the flight takes an hour.

Bus Two tour buses a day go to Ubon from Nakhon Phanom at 7 am and 2 pm, leaving from the intersection of Bamrung Muang and Ratsadorn Uthit Rds near the Windsor Hotel. The fare is 98B. Ordinary buses from the Baw Khaw Saw station leave regularly from morning until late afternoon for 53B. The trip takes 5½ hours on the tour bus and six to seven hours on the rot thammada (ordinary bus).

Buses for Ubon leave the northern bus terminal in Bangkok up to 15 times a day from 4.30 am through to nearly midnight. These cost 126B or 227B with air-con, but the air-con buses only run between 7.30 and 9.30 pm. Other fares to/from Ubon are:

destination	fare
Khong Jiam	30B
Phibun Mangsahan	10B
Yasothon	23B
Si Saket	14B
Surin	34B
Buriram	44B
Kantharalak (for Khao Phra Wihaan)	23B
Prakhon Chai (for Prasat Phanom Rung)	56B
Mukdahan	34B
Sakon Nakhon	55B
(air-con)	100B
Udon Thani	80B
(air-con)	140B
Khon Kaen	56B
(air-con)	101B
Mahasarakham	43B
(air-con)	78B
Roi Et	36B
(air-con)	65B
Khorat	80B
(air-con)	146B
That Phanom	45B
(air-con)	80B

Train The Ubon Ratchathani express leaves Bangkok daily at 9 pm, arriving in Ubon at 7.05 am the next morning. The basic 1st-class fare is 416B, 2nd class is 200B and 3rd class is 95B, not including surcharges for express service or a sleeping berth. Rapid trains leave at 6.50 am, 6.45 and 10.45 pm, arriving in Ubon about 11 hours later. There is no 1st class on the rapid trains. Ordinary trains take only about an hour longer to reach Ubon; there are five departures daily in either direction between 5.20 am 11.25 pm.

Rapid trains from Khorat leave at 11.44 am and 12.08 am, arriving in Ubon at 4.45 pm and 5.20 am. The basic fares are 121B 2nd class and 58B 3rd class.

The new all-air-con Sprinter leaves Bangkok at 9.25 am and arrives in Ubon at

5.50 pm; the fare is 345B, including a couple of aeroplane-style meals.

Ubon's railway station is in Warin Chamrap; take a white No 2 city bus to reach Chayangkun Rd in the city centre.

Getting Around

A city bus system runs large buses along the main avenues, very convenient for getting from one end of town to the other cheaply (fare is 2B). Samlors around town are 5 to 15B depending on distance.

Motorcycles can be rented at C Wattana (☎ 241906), 269 Suriyat Rd. This agency also rents cars, as does Chi Chi Tour (☎ 241464) and Asia (☎ 241321), both on Chayangkun Rd.

AROUND UBON PROVINCE

Phibun Mangsahan & Khong Jiam

The small riverside district of Khong Jiam is 75 km east of Ubon via Highway 217 to Phibun Mangsahan and then over the Mun River by bridge at the end of Route 2222. Visitors often stop in Phibun to see a set of rapids called **Kaeng Sapheu** next to the river crossing.

On the way along Route 2222 you can stop at **Sae Hua Maew Falls** and **Wat Tham Hehw Sin Chai**. The latter is a cave temple with a waterfall cascading over the front of the cave. Also in the vicinity are two other waterfalls, **Pak Taew Falls** in Nam Yuen district – a tall vertical drop – and the low but wide **Taton Falls.**

There's not much to see in the town of Khong Jiam itself except for the huge conical fish traps that are made here for local use – they look very much like the fish traps that appear in the 3000-year-old prehistoric murals at Pha Taem (see later in this section). Thais visit Khong Jiam to see the junction of the Mun and Maekhong rivers, a confluence that results in Mae Nam Song Sii (Two-Colour River). A pier in front of the riverside restaurant has ferries across to Laos for 5B – sometimes they let foreigners across, sometimes not. Provincial officials on both sides of the border are trying to arrange permanent permission for day crossings by foreigners.

You can charter local long-tail boats to tour sites along the river – 200B will hire a boat holding up to 15 people all day.

Places to Stay & Eat – Khong Jiam *Apple Guest House* (☎ 351160) in Khong Jiam has rooms in a two-storey building off the main road through town. There are two large, clean rooms upstairs and six smaller rooms downstairs. Rates are 90B per room; soap and towels provided.

Near the river, the friendly *Khong Jiam Guest House* (☎ /fax 351074) has fan rooms with bath for 90B, air-con for 170B.

Along the riverside are two restaurants. *Araya* is very popular on weekends and serves a variety of freshwater fish, Thai-Lao standards, river turtle (ta-phâap náam) and wild pig.

Places to Stay & Eat – Phibun Mangsahan *Sanamchai Guest House* (☎ 441289) in Phibun has modern bungalows for 100 to 150B with fan, 200B with air-con. There's a pub and garden restaurant opposite the guesthouse. Near the bridge to Route 2222 is a simple restaurant famous for salabao (Chinese buns) and nãng kòp (frog skin, usually fried). Thais visiting Pha Taem always stop here on the way to stock up on salabao and frog skin.

Getting There & Away Buses from Ubon to Phibun (45 km) cost 10B and leave from near the Warin Chamrap railway station between 5 am and 5.30 pm. Direct buses to Khong Jiam (74 km) cost 30B and leave from Market No 5 between 9 am and 1 pm. When direct buses aren't running to Khong Jiam, catch a Phibun bus from Warin and change to a Khong Jiam bus (10B) in Phibun.

Chong Mek
ช่องเม็ก

South of Khong Jiam via Highway 217 is the small trading town of Chong Mek on the Thai-Lao border. Chong Mek has the distinction of being the only town in Thailand where you can cross into Laos by land. At the time of writing you must have a Laos visa valid for Pakse entry to cross here; and you must specify that you want to cross at Chong Mek when applying for the visa. The southern Laos capital of Pakse is three hours by road from Ban Mai Sing Amphon, the village on the Laos side of the border.

Thai visitors come to Chong Mek to drink *oliang* (Chinese-style iced coffee) and shop for Lao and Vietnamese souvenirs.

Pha Taem

ผาแต้ม

In Khong Jiam district, 94 km north-east of Ubon, near the confluence of the Mun and Maekhong rivers, is a tall stone cliff called Pha Taem. The cliff is about 200 metres long and features prehistoric colour paintings that are 3000 or more years old. Mural subjects include fish traps, plaa beuk (giant Mekong catfish), turtles, elephants, human hands and a few geometric designs – all very reminiscent of prehistoric rock art found at widely separated sites around the world.

A 500-metre trail descends from the cliff edge to the base past two platforms where visitors can view the rock paintings; from the top of the cliff you get a bird's eye view of Laos. Vendors sell snacks and beverages near the top of the cliff. A cliff-top visitors' centre is planned for future construction and will contain exhibits pertaining to the paintings and local geology.

On the road to Pha Taem is **Sao Chaliang**, an area of unusual stone formations similar to Phu Thoep in Mukdahan.

Getting There & Away Pha Taem is 20 km beyond Khong Jiam via Route 2112, but there's no direct public transport there. The bus from Ubon to Khong Jiam will pass the final turn-off to Pha Taem on request; then you can walk or hitch five km to the cliff.

By car, bike or motorcycle, go east on Highway 217 to Phibun Mangsahan, then turn left (north) across the Mun River on Route 2222 and follow this road to Khong Jiam. From Khong Jiam, take Route 2134 north-west to Ban Huay Phai and then go north-east at the first turn-off to Pha Taem.

Surin & Si Saket Provinces

These adjacent provinces between Buriram and Ubon border Cambodia and are dotted with ancient Khmer ruins built during the 11th and 12th-century Angkor Empire. Other than the ruins, the only other major attraction in the area is the Surin Annual Elephant Roundup.

SURIN

สุรินทร์

Surin (population 40,000), 452 km from Bangkok, is a quiet provincial capital except during the Elephant Roundup in late November. At that time a carnival atmosphere reigns with elephants providing the entertainment. If ever you wanted to see a lot of elephants in one place (there are more elephants now in Thailand than in India), this is your chance.

Culturally, Surin represents an intersection of Lao, Central Thai, Khmer and Suay peoples, resulting in an interesting mix of dialects and customs. A fifth group contributing to the blend has been the many volunteers and UN employees working with local refugee camps; though with the huge refugee industry winding down, their influence is beginning to wane.

To see Surin's elephants during the off season, visit **Ban Tha Klang** in Tha Tum district, about 40 km north of Surin. Many of the performers at the annual festival are trained here.

Silk-weaving can be observed at several local villages, including **Khwaosinarin** and **Ban Janrom**.

Khmer Temple Ruins

The southern reach of Surin Province along the Cambodian border harbours several

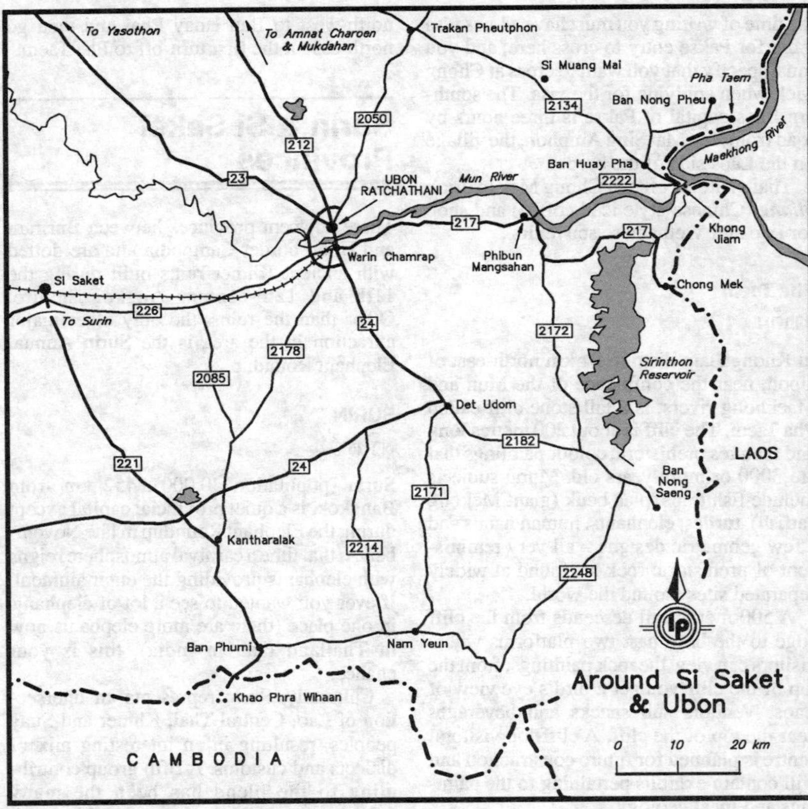

minor Angkor-period ruins, including **Prasat Hin Ban Phluang** (30 km south of Surin). The solitary sandstone sanctuary, mounted on a laterite platform, exhibits well-sculpted stone lintels.

A larger Khmer site can be seen 30 km north-east of town at **Prasat Sikhoraphum**. Sikhoraphum (or Si Khonphum) features five Khmer prangs, the tallest of which reaches 32 metres. The doorways to the central prang are decorated with stone carvings of Hindu deities in the Angkor Wat style.

Surin can also be used as a base for visiting the Khmer ruins at **Prasat Phanom Rung** and **Muang Tam**, about 75 km south-west of Surin in Buriram Province (see the Buriram Province section for details).

Places to Stay

The recently opened *Pirom Guest House* (☎ 515140) at 242 Krung Si Nai Rd has dorm beds for 40B per person and singles/doubles for 60/100B. Pirom knows the area well and can suggest ideas for day trips around Surin, including excursions to lesser known Khmer temple sites.

Hotel rates may increase during the Elephant Roundup and hotels may fill up, but otherwise, *Krung Si* (☎ 511037), at 15/11-4 Krung Si Nai Rd, charges from 90 to 100B, and *New Hotel* (☎ 511341/322), 22 Thanasan Rd, charges from 100 to 150B and has some air-con rooms from 200B. Also on Thanasan Rd at No 155-61 is *Saeng Thong*, which has rooms from 150 to 220B.

The *Amarin* (☎ 511407), at Thetsaban 1 Rd, costs from 95 to 150B or from 160B with air-con. Not far from it is a similar place, the *Thanachai* at No 14.

The top-end *Phetkasem Hotel* (☎ 511274, 511576), is at 104 Jit Bamrung Rd. All rooms are air-con, and rates are from 300 to 1000B.

Getting There & Away

Bus Surin buses leave several times a day from Bangkok's northern bus terminal between 6 am and 10.15 pm (86B one-way). During the Elephant Roundup, there are many special air-con buses to Surin, organised by major hotels and tour companies. The regular government-run air-con bus costs 155B and leaves the air-con northern terminal daily at 11 am, 9.30, 10 and 10.10 pm.

Buses from Khorat take about four hours and cost 40B.

Train Most people travel to Surin by rapid train No 31, which leaves Bangkok at 6.50 am, arriving in Surin at 2.07 pm. The fares are 173B 2nd class and 93B 3rd class, including the rapid surcharge. Book your seats at least two weeks in advance for travel during November. A faster train is the air-con diesel No 931 to Surin at 11.05 am, arriving at 5.35 pm for 20B less (no surcharges for 3rd class; 50B surcharge in air-con 2nd class). If you prefer night train travel, the rapid No 51 leaves Bangkok at 10.45 pm and arrives in Surin at 6.44 am

SI SAKET

ศรีสะเกษ

Si Saket's provincial capital (population 22,000) is only about half the size of Surin's; with nothing like Surin's elephant festival to provide support, the town has less of a tourist infrastructure – a boon for visitors in search of laid-back, authentic isaan ways. Also, Si Saket Province has more Khmer ruins of significance within its borders than Surin.

With the recent opening of Khao Phra Wihaan, a major Angkor site just over the provincial border in Cambodia, the town's fortunes may change as it becomes the gateway for visitors to the ruins. The vast majority of visitors to Khao Phra Wihaan so far have been Thais.

Khao Phra Wihaan

เขาพระวิหาร

After a year of negotiations between the Cambodian and Thai governments, the Khmer ruins of Khao Phra Wihaan (other common spellings include Kao Prea Vihar and Khao Phra Viharn) have finally been opened to the public. Lying just across the Cambodian border opposite Si Saket Province's Kantharalak, the ruins are virtually inaccessible from the Cambodian side and until the recent Khmer Rouge ceasefire in Cambodia they were also off-limits from the Thai side. Now that it's safe to travel in the area, an agreement has been worked out wherein both sides of the border benefit from tourist visitation.

Khao Phra Wihaan was built over two centuries under a succession of Khmer kings, beginning with Rajendravarman II in the mid-10th century and ending with Suryavarman II in the early 12th century – it was the latter who also commanded the construction of Angkor Wat. The hill itself was sacred to Khmer Hindus for at least 500 years before the completion of the temple complex, however, and there were smaller brick monuments on the site prior to the reign of Rajendravarman II.

Phra Wihaan sits atop a 600-metre hill at the edge of the Dangrek Mountain Range, commanding a view of the Thai plains to the west. Built originally as a Hindu temple in the classic Bapuan and early Angkor styles, the complex extends a linear 850 metres, encompassing three *gopuras* (entrance pavilions), and a large prasat or sanctuary surrounded by a courtyard and galleries. A stepped naga approach ascends approximately 120 metres from the foot of the hill to the sanctuary.

The temple complex is semi-restored – the general condition is somewhere between that of Prasat Phanomwan in Khorat and Prasat Phanom Rung in Buriram. One naga balustrade of around 30 metres is still intact; the first two gopuras have all but fallen down and many of the temple buildings are roofless, but abundant examples of stone carving are intact and visible. The doorways to the third gopura have been nicely preserved and one (the inner door facing south) is surmounted by a well-executed carved stone lintel depicting Shiva and consort Uma sitting on Nandi (Shiva's bull), under the shade of a symmetrised tree. A Vishnu creation lintel is also visible on the second gopura; in contrast to the famous Phanom Rung lintel depicting the same subject, this one shows Vishnu climbing the churning stick rather than reclining on the ocean below.

The main prasat tower in the final court at the summit is in need of major restoration before the viewer can get a true idea of its

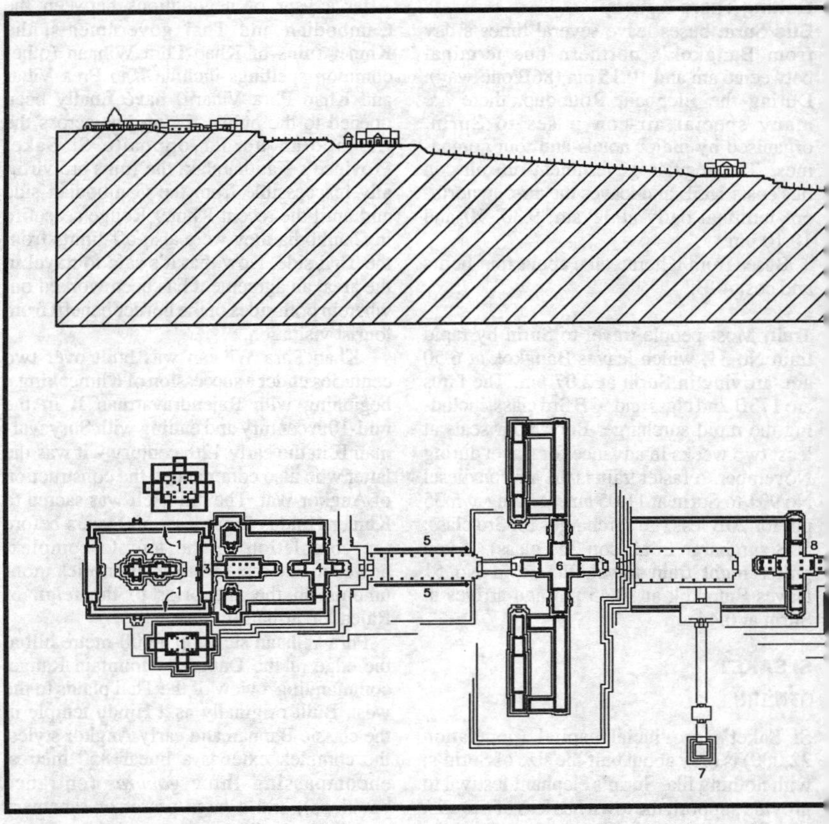

former magnificence. Many of the stone carvings from the prasat are either missing or lie buried in nearby rubble. The galleries leading to the prasat have fared better and have even kept their arched roofs. Eventually the complex may undergo a total restoration but at the moment the money from entrance fees is supposedly going toward the improvement of the road to Phra Wihaan from the Cambodian side (currently Cambodian officials must walk six to eight hours to reach the Thai border).

Getting There & Away Highway 221 leads 95 km south from Si Saket all the way to the temple access road via Kantharalak – catch a songthaew from near the main day market in Si Saket for 15B. If you miss the infrequent direct songthaew service, you may have to bus first to Kantharalak and pick up another songthaew to Khao Phra Wihaan there.

At the Thai army checkpoint you must complete an entry form (so far these are available in Thai only – you'll have to appeal for assistance if you don't read Thai) and present a passport or other picture ID. The announced admission fees for Thais are 5B

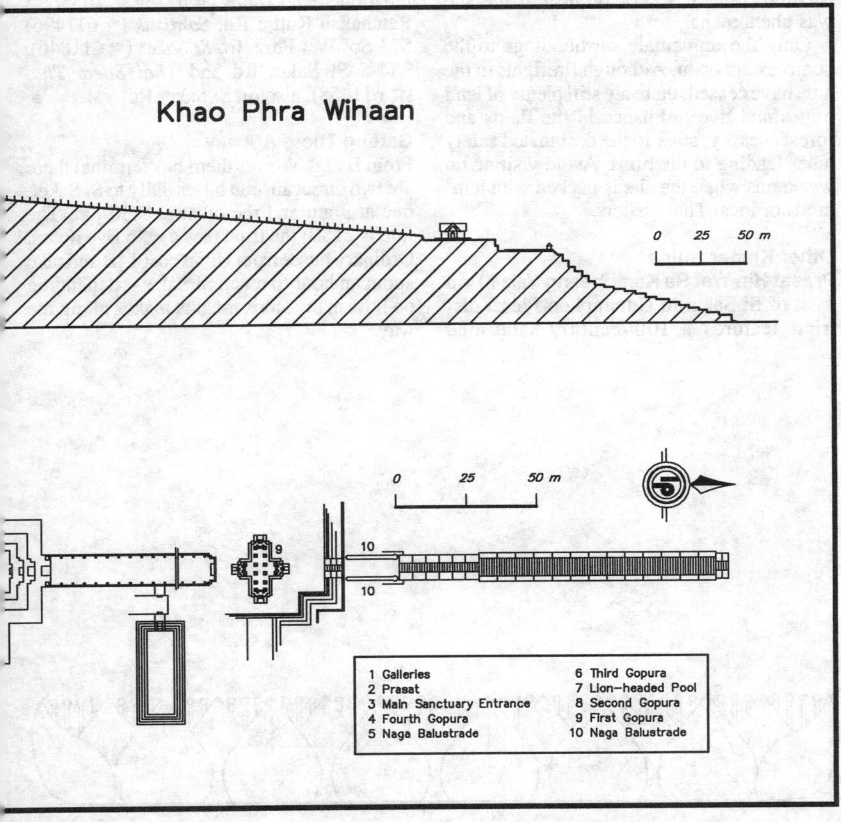

for students, 60B for adults; and for foreign visitors 100B for children, 200B for adults. When the site first opened in January 1992, half the farang fee was collected on either side of the border to ensure that the Thais and Cambodians each got their share of the loot.

At the Cambodian checkpoint you must leave your ID as a security deposit. These procedures – the two-instalment fee, filling-in of forms – seems a bit cumbersome and I would be surprised if the whole process weren't eventually streamlined. Another aspect of the experience that needs attention is rubbish collection – during the first few months of Khao Phra Wihaan's opening, the accumulation of visitor rubbish at the site was phenomenal.

Only the immediate surroundings to the complex are open. Although firefights in the area have ceased, there are still plenty of land mines and live ordinance in the fields and forests nearby; stick to the designated safety lanes leading to the ruins. Avoid visiting on weekends when the site is packed with hundreds of local Thai visitors.

Other Khmer Ruins

Prasat Hin Wat Sa Kamphaeng Yai, 40 km west of Si Saket in Uthumphon Phisai district, features a 10th-century sandstone prang with carved doorways. The ruined sanctuary is on the grounds of Wat Sa Kamphaeng Yai's modern successor. About eight km west of town via Route 2084 is the similar but smaller **Prasat Hin Wat Sa Kamphaeng Noi**.

Other minor Khmer sites in the province include Prasat Prang Ku, Prasat Ban Prasat and Prasat Phu Fai.

Places to Stay

Phrom Phiman (☎ 611141), at 849/1 Lak Muang Rd, has fan rooms for 100B, air-con rooms from 250 to 350B. Everything else in town is in the 60 to 120B range for simple fan rooms: *Pho Thong* (☎ 611542), 1055/2-5 Ratchakan Rotfai Rd, *Santisuk* (☎ 611496) 573 Soi Wat Phra To, *Si Saket* (☎ 611846), 384-5 Si Saket Rd and *Thai Soem Thai* (☎ 611458), also on Si Saket Rd.

Getting There & Away

From Bangkok's northern bus terminal there are two direct air-con buses daily to Si Saket, one at 9 am and the other at 9.30 pm. The fare is 215B; the trip takes 4½ to five hours. Ordinary buses from Ubon cost 14B and take about an hour to reach Si Saket – depending on how many stops the bus makes along the way.

Southern Thailand

History

Although under Thai political domination for several centuries, the south has always remained culturally apart from the other regions of Thailand. Historically, the peninsula has been linked to cultures in ancient Indonesia, particularly the Srivijaya Empire, which ruled a string of principalities in what is today Malaysia, southern Thailand and Indonesia. The Srivijaya Dynasty was based in Sumatra and lasted nearly 500 years (8th to 13th centuries). The influence of Malay-Indonesian culture is still apparent in the ethnicity, religion, art and language of the *Thai pàk tâi*, the southern Thais.

Culture & Language

The Thai pak tai dress differently, build their houses differently and eat differently from Thais in the north. Many are followers of Islam, so there are quite a few mosques in southern cities; men often cover their heads and the long sarong is favoured over the shorter phâakhamãa worn in the northern, central and north-eastern regions. There are also a good many Chinese living in the south – the influence of whom can be seen in the old architecture and in the baggy Chinese pants worn by non-Muslims.

All speak a dialect common among southern Thais that confounds even visitors from other Thai regions – diction is short and fast: *pai nãi* (Where are you going?) becomes *p'nái*; and *tham arai* (What are you doing?) becomes *'rái*. The clipped tones fly into the outer regions of intelligibility, giving the aural impression of a tape played at the wrong speed. In the provinces nearest Malaysia – Yala, Pattani, Narathiwat and Satun – many Thai Muslims speak Yawi, an old Malay dialect with some similarities to modern Bahasa Malaysia and Bahasa Indonesia.

You'll notice that 'Ao', 'Hat' and 'Ban' sometimes precede place names; *ao* means bay, *hàat* is beach and *bâan* is village.

Southern Thais are stereotypically regarded as rebellious folk, considering themselves reluctant subjects of Bangkok rule and Thai (central Thai) custom. Indeed, Thai Muslims (ethnic Malays) living in the provinces bordering on Malaysia complain of persecution by Thai government troops who police the area for insurgent activity. There has even been some talk of these provinces seceding from Thailand, an event that is unlikely to occur in the near future.

Geography & Economy

Bounded by water on two sides, the people of southern Thailand are by and large a seafaring lot. One consequence of this natural affinity with the ocean is the abundance of delectable seafood, prepared southern-style. Brightly painted fishing boats, hanging nets and neat thatched huts add to the pak tai setting; travellers who do a stint in southern Thailand are likely to come face to face with more than a few visions of 'tropical paradise', whatever their expectations might be.

Three of Thailand's most important exports – rubber, tin and coconut – are produced in the south so that the standard of living is a bit higher than in other provincial regions. However, southern Thais claim that most of the wealth is in the hands of ethnic Chinese. In any of the truly southern-Thai provinces (from Chumphon south), it is obvious that the Chinese are concentrated in the urban provincial capitals while the poorer Muslims live in the rural areas. Actually, the urban concentration of Chinese is a fact of life throughout South-East Asia which becomes more noticeable in southern Thailand and the Islamic state of Malaysia because of religious-cultural differences.

In official government terms, southern Thailand is made up of 14 provinces: Chumphon, Krabi, Nakhon Si Thammarat, Narathiwat, Pattani, Phang-Nga, Phattalung, Phuket, Ranong, Satun, Songkhla, Surat

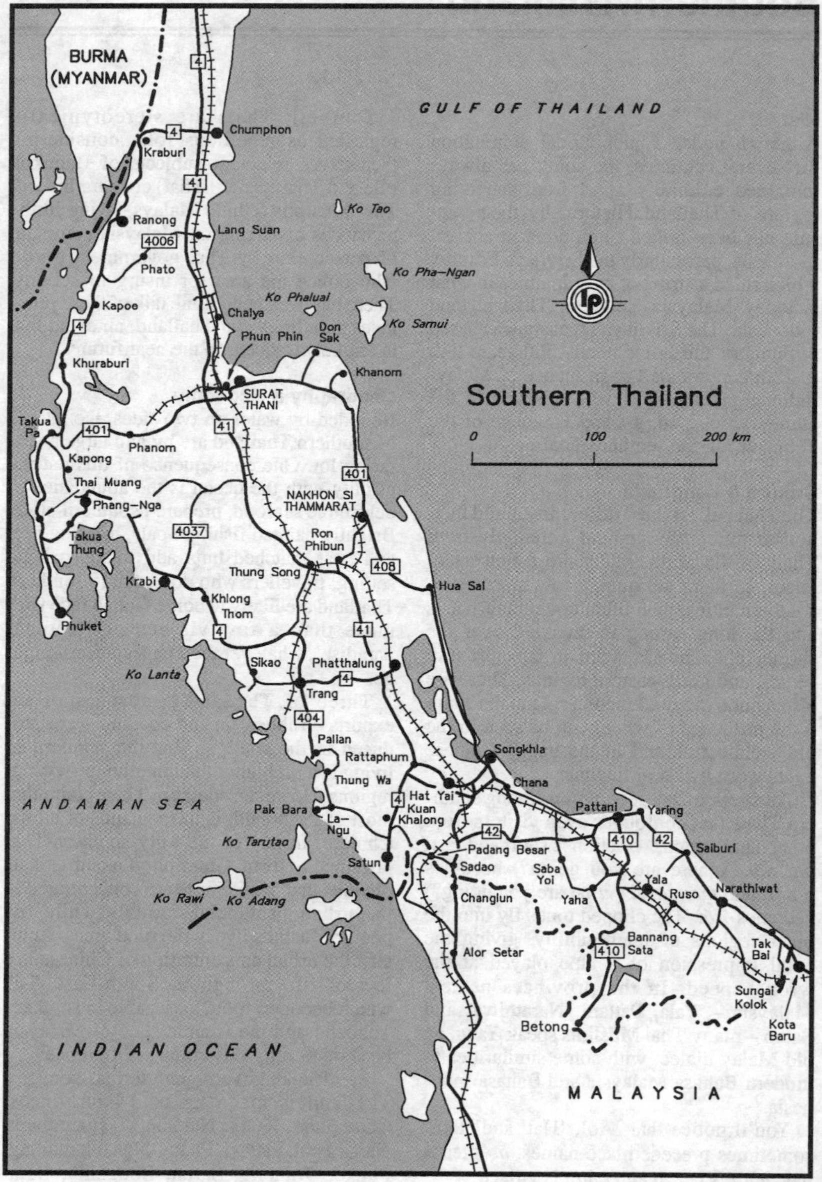

Southern Thailand
0
100
200 km
BURMA (MYANMAR)
GULF OF THAILAND
ANDAMAN SEA
INDIAN OCEAN
MALAYSIA
Chumphon
Kraburi
Ranong
Lang Suan
Phato
Kapoe
Khuraburi
Chaiya
Phun Phin
Don Sak
Khanom
SURAT THANI
Takua Pa
Phanom
Kapong
Thai Muang
Phang-Nga
Takua Thung
NAKHON SI THAMMARAT
Ron Phibun
Thung Song
Hua Sai
Krabi
Khlong Thom
Phuket
Sikao
Phatthalung
Trang
Ko Lanta
Palian
Rattaphum
Songkhla
Thung Wa
Hat Yai
Chana
Kuan Khalong
Pak Bara
La-Ngu
Ko Tarutao
Satun
Padang Besar
Sadao
Saba Yoi
Changlun
Yaha
Ko Rawi
Ko Adang
Alor Setar
Pattani
Yaring
Saiburi
Yala
Ruso
Narathiwat
Bannang Sata
Tak Bai
Sungai Kolok
Kota Baru
Betong
Ko Tao
Ko Pha-Ngan
Ko Phaluai
Ko Samui
4
41
4006
401
4037
408
404
42
410

Thani, Trang and Yala. For the purposes of this guide, we've included all provinces on the southern peninsula, taking Phetburi and Prachuap Khiri Khan from central Thailand and putting them alongside the others on the official list.

Phetburi Province

PHETBURI

อ.เมืองเพชรบุรี

Situated 160 km south of Bangkok, Phetburi (or Phetchaburi; also known as Muang Phet) (population 35,000) is worth a stopover for its many old temples spanning several centuries. Six or seven temples can be seen while taking a circular walk of two or three hours through the city: Wat Yai Suwannaram, Wat Trailok, Wat Kamphaeng Laeng, Wat Phra Suang, Wat Ko Kaew Sutharam and Wat Mahathat. These temples have made very few concessions to the 20th century and thus provide a glimpse of the traditional Siamese urban wat (temple).

Also noteworthy is Khao Wang, just west of the city, which has the remains of a King Mongkut palace and several wats, plus a good aerial view of the city. The underground Buddhist shrine at the Khao Luang Caves is also worth seeing.

Orientation & Information

If you arrive at the railway station, follow the road south-east of the tracks until you come to Ratchadamnoen Rd, then turn right. Follow Ratchadamnoen Rd south to the second major intersection and turn left towards downtown Phetburi to begin the walk. Or take a samlor from the railway station to Chomrut Bridge (Saphan Chomrut), for 8B. If you've come by bus, you'll be getting off very near the Chomrut Bridge. This is the centre of Phetburi, more or less – from here you can check out hotels if you're spending the night, or, if you're not, stow your gear at the Anglican church next to the bus station.

Wat Yai Suwannaram

วัดใหญ่สุวรรณาราม

After you've crossed the Phetburi River by Chomrut Bridge (the second northernmost bridge in Phetburi) and passed the Nam Chai Hotel on the left, walk about 300 metres further until you see a big temple on the right. This is Wat Yai, dating from the reign of King Chulalongkorn (1851-68). The main bot (main chapel) is surrounded by a cloister filled with sober Buddha images. The murals inside the bot are in good condition. Next to the bot is a beautifully designed old *hàw trai* or tripitaka (Buddhist scripture) library.

Wat Borom & Wat Trailok

วัดบรมและวัดไตรโลก

These two wats are next to one another on the opposite side of the road from Wat Yai, a little east. They are distinctive for their monastic halls and long, graceful wooden 'dormitories' on stilts.

Turn right onto the road heading south from Wat Trailok and follow this road down past a bamboo fence on the right to the entrance for Wat Kamphaeng Laeng.

Wat Kamphaeng Laeng

วัดกำแพงแลง

This is a very old (13th century) Khmer site with five prangs (Khmer-style chedis) and part of the original wall still standing. The prang in front contains a Buddha footprint. Of the other four, two contain images dedicated to famous luang phaw (venerable elderly monks), one was in ruins (but is being restored) and the fifth has recently been uncovered from a mound of dirt. The Khmers built these as Hindu monuments, so the Buddhist symbols are late additions.

Wat Phra Suang & Wat Lat

วัดพระสวงและวัดลาด

Follow the road next to Wat Kamphaeng Laeng, heading west back towards the river until you pass Wat Phra Suang on the left,

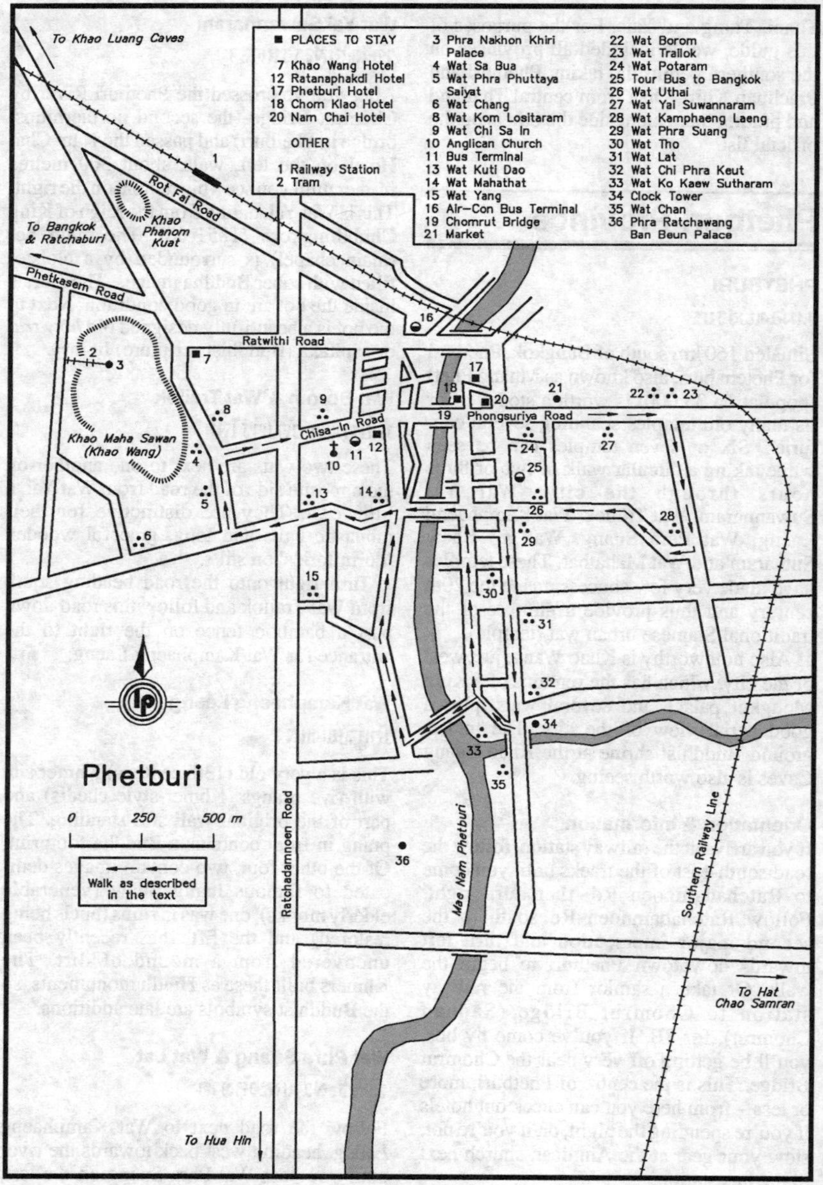

■ PLACES TO STAY
7 Khao Wang Hotel
12 Ratanaphakdi Hotel
17 Phetburi Hotel
18 Chom Klao Hotel
20 Nam Chai Hotel
OTHER
1 Railway Station
2 Tram
3 Phra Nakhon Khiri Palace
4 Wat Sa Bua
5 Wat Phra Phuttaya Saiyat
6 Wat Chang
8 Wat Kom Lositaram
9 Wat Chi Sa In
10 Anglican Church
11 Bus Terminal
13 Wat Kuti Dao
14 Wat Mahathat
15 Wat Yang
16 Air-Con Bus Terminal
19 Chomrut Bridge
21 Market
22 Wat Borom
23 Wat Trailok
24 Wat Potaram
25 Tour Bus to Bangkok
26 Wat Uthai
27 Wat Yai Suwannaram
28 Wat Kamphaeng Laeng
29 Wat Phra Suang
30 Wat Tho
31 Wat Lat
32 Wat Chi Phra Keut
33 Wat Ko Kaew Sutharam
34 Clock Tower
35 Wat Chan
36 Phra Ratchawang Ban Beun Palace
To Khao Luang Caves
Rot Fai Road
Khao Phanom Kuat
To Bangkok & Ratchaburi
Phetkasem Road
Ratwithi Road
Chisa-In Road
Phongsuriya Road
Khao Maha Sawan (Khao Wang)
Ratchadamnoen Road
Mae Nam Phetburi
Southern Railway Line
To Hat Chao Samran
To Hua Hin
Phetburi
0 250 500 m
Walk as described in the text

undistinguished except for one very nice Ayuthaya-style prasat. Turn left immediately after this wat, heading south again until you come to the clock tower at the southern edge of town. You'll have passed Wat Lat on the left side of the street along the way, but it's not worth breaking your momentum for; this is a long walk.

Wat Ko Kaew Sutharam

วัดแก้วสุทธาราม

Turn right at the clock tower and look for signs leading to Wat Ko. Two different sois on the left lead to the wat, which is behind the shops along the curving street. The bot features early 18th-century murals that are among the best conceived in Thailand. There is also a large wooden monastic hall on stilts similar to the ones at Wat Borom and Wat Trailok, but in much better condition.

Wat Mahathat

วัดมหาธาตุ

Follow the street in front of Wat Ko north (back towards downtown Phetburi), and walk over the first bridge you come to on the left, which leads to Wat Mahathat. Alternatively, you can cross the river at Wat Ko, near the clock tower and take the street on the other side of the river around to Wat Mahathat. The large white prang of Wat Mahathat can be seen from a distance – a typical late-Ayuthaya early-Ratanakosin adaptation of the Khmer prangs of Lopburi and Phimai. This is obviously an important temple in Phetburi, judging from all the activity here.

Khao Wang & Phra Nakhon Khiri Historical Park

เขาวัง/อุทยานประวัติศาสตร์พระนครคีรี

Just west of the city, a 5B samlor ride from the bus station, is Khao Wang. Cobblestone paths lead up and around the hill, which is studded with wats and various components of King Mongkut's palace on Phra Nakhon Khiri (Holy City Hill). The views are great, especially at sunset. The walk up looks easy but is fairly strenuous. Fat monkeys loll about in the trees and on the walls along the main paths. In 1988, Phra Nakhon Khiri was declared a national historical park so there is now an entry fee of 20B. A tram has been installed to save you walking up to the peak (5B per person one-way).

Khao Luang Caves

ถ้ำเขาหลวง

Five km north of Phetburi is the cave sanctuary of Khao Luang (Great Hill). Concrete steps lead down into an anteroom then into the main cavern, which is filled with old Buddha images, many of them put in place by King Mongkut (Rama IV). Sunlight from two holes in the chamber ceiling spray light on the images, a favourite subject for photographers. To the rear of the main cavern is an entrance to a third, smaller chamber. On the right of the entrance is Wat Bunthawi, with a sala (open-sided shelter) designed by the abbot himself.

Admission to the caves is free (donations accepted). A samlor from the city centre to Khao Luang costs 50B.

Places to Stay

Of the variety of places to stay in Phetburi, the following are recommended. On the eastern side of Chomrut Bridge, on the right bank of Phetburi River, is the *Chom Klao Hotel*, an ordinary, fairly clean Chinese hotel with friendly staff. It costs 70B for rooms with fan and shared bath, or 100B with private bath.

The *Nam Chai Hotel* is a block further east from Chomrut Bridge and the Chom Klao Hotel, and has rooms for 70 to 120B, but is not as good value as the Chom Klao. Cheaper still is the *Ratanaphakdi Hotel* next to the bus terminal, with rooms for 70 to 90B.

Behind the Chom Klao is the *Phetburi Hotel*, another divey sort of place, with rooms for 90B with fan and bath.

The *Khao Wang Hotel* (☎ 425167), opposite Khao Wang (the Hill Palace) used to be my favourite in Phet, but reports indicate the rooms may have gone downhill recently. A fairly clean room with fan and bath cost 90/130B for a single/double. Air-con rooms are 150/200B.

The best hotel in town is the friendly and clean *Phetkasem Hotel*, 86/1 Phetkasem Rd, which is on the highway north to Bangkok on the edge of town. Rooms are 100 to 150B with fan and bath, 200 to 300B with air-con.

Places to Eat

There are several good restaurants in the Khao Wang area, with a variety of standard Thai and Chinese dishes.

Between 6 pm and midnight, look for Boon Plamcho, a vendor who sets up on the corner by the Chom Klao Hotel and fries the best kũaytĩaw phàt thai noodles in town.

Other good eating can be found downtown along the main street to the clock tower. Across from Wat Mahathat, *Lamiet* sells really good khanõm mâw kaeng (egg custard) and fãwy thawng (sweet shredded egg yolk) – which they ship to Bangkok. A shop across the street from Wat Lat called *Saw Rung Huang* also has great khanõm, including a delicious kind of khâo krìap (rice crisps) made with coconut and sesame. Both shops also have branches near Khao Wang, where a whole group of egg custard places serve tourists.

Getting There & Away

Bus From Bangkok, buses leave regularly from the southern bus terminals on Charan Sanitwong Rd in Thonburi for 30B ordinary on the new road, 25B on the old road (via Ratchaburi and Nakhon Pathom), or 54B air-con. The bus takes about 2½ hours.

Buses to Phetburi from Cha-am and Hua Hin are 10 and 15B. Other ordinary bus fares are Ratchaburi 13B and Nakhon Pathom 25B.

Train Trains leave Bangkok's Hualamphong station at 9 am, 12.35 pm (rapid), 2 pm (special express), 3.15 pm (special express), 4 pm (rapid), 5.30 pm (rapid), 6.30 pm (rapid) and 7.20 pm (express). All trains take about 3½ hours to reach Phetburi so it's not really worth the surcharges for rapid or express service – take an ordinary train. A 3rd-class fare is 34B.

Getting Around

Samlors go anywhere in the town centre for 10B; or you can charter one for the whole day for 100B.

KAENG KRACHAN NATIONAL PARK

อุทยานแห่งชาติแก่งกระจาน

This 3000-sq-km park is Thailand's largest, covering nearly half of Phetburi Province along the Burmese border. In spite of its size and proximity to Bangkok, Kaeng Krachan doesn't seem to get many visitors (or perhaps its huge size just swallows them up). Because this part of Phetburi receives some of the heaviest rainfall in Thailand, the rainforest here is particularly thick and abundant in places. There are also areas of savanna-like grasslands, mountains, steep cliffs, caves, waterfalls, long-distance hiking trails and two rivers, the Phetburi and the Pranburi, which are suitable for rafting. Above the **Kaeng Krachan Dam** is a large reservoir stocked with fish. Animals living in Kaeng Krachan include wild elephants, deer, tigers, bears, boars, gaurs and wild cattle. There are small Karen settlements here as well.

Forestry officials at the park headquarters can sometimes be hired as guides for overnight trekking in the park.

Places to Stay

The six bungalows near the park headquarters have rates ranging from 300 to 700B, depending on their size. You can also set up your own tent for 5B per person per night. *Kaeng Krachan Resorts* (☎ 513-3238 in Bangkok) offers expensive 'floatel' accommodation at the reservoir.

Getting There & Away

Kaeng Krachan is about 60 km from Phetburi, off Route 3175. The turn-off for Route 3175 is at Tha Yang on Highway 4, about 18 km south of Phetburi. The park headquarters is eight km past the dam where the road ends. There is no regular transport to the park, but you can hitch or charter a pick-up.

CHA-AM

ชะอำ

A tiny town 178 km from Bangkok, 18 km from Phetburi and 25 km from Hua Hin, Cha-am is known for its long, casuarina-lined beach, good seafood and, on weekends and school holidays, its party atmosphere – sort of a Palm Beach or Fort Lauderdale for Thai students. During the week the beach is virtually deserted.

Beach umbrellas and sling chairs are available for hire. The jet skis are a definite minus; if the local tourism promoters want to lure visitors away from fast-developing Hua Hin, the first thing they should do is get rid of the jet skis. There are public bath-houses where you can bathe in freshwater for 5B.

Near the beach there's not much of a town to speak of – the old centre is on the opposite side of Phetkasem Highway, where you'll find the post office, market and government offices. Inland from the beach (follow the signs) at **Wat Neranchararama** is a fat, white, six-armed Buddha statue; the six hands cover the nine bodily orifices in a symbolic gesture denying the senses.

Information

A new TAT office (☎ 471502) has been established on Phetkasem Highway just south of town. The staff is very helpful; they distribute information on Cha-am, Phetburi and Hua Hin.

Places to Stay – bottom end & middle

Cha-am Beach has three basic types of accommodation: charming old-style, spacious, wooden beach bungalows on stilts, set back from the road; tacky apartment-style hotels built of cheap materials and faulty plumbing right on the beach road; and more expensive 'condotel' developments. New places are going up all the time at the northern and southern ends of town. Expect a 20 to 50% discount on posted rates for weekday stays.

One main road leads to the beach area from the highway; if you turn right you'll find the places listed under 'South' below; turn left and you'll see those listed under 'North'.

South Near the air-con bus terminal, *Jack* and *Donut* guesthouses are in a row of modern shophouses similar to the scourge of Pattaya, Hua Hin and Phuket's Patong Beach – they all look the same. Rooms are 150B with shared bath. *Andaman*, a better apartment-style place facing the beach, costs 250B with bath.

Santisuk Bungalows & Beach Resort (☎ 571211) is a long-time favourite, with both the early Cha-am style wooden cottages and a newer, equally tasteful section. A one-room cottage with bath and fan is 300B; larger two-bedroom cottages with bath and sitting area are 600B, and it's 1000B for a three-bedroom, two-bath place. The *Nirandorn Resort* (☎ 471038) has similar cottages for 600B.

Saeng Thong Condominiums (☎ 471466) costs 500 to 800B per night, less in the rainy season. The *White Hotel*, an apartment-style place, costs 300 to 800B. *Arunthip* has tacky but cheap two-bedroom bungalows for 150B on weekdays, 300B on weekends.

North *JJ Hotel* and *Somkheat Villa* are adjacent apartment-style hotels with rooms in the 400 to 500B and 700 to 800B range. *Rua Makam Villa* (☎ 471073) has the old-style wooden cottages, spacious and off the road, for 500 to 800B. *Happy Home* is newer but similar.

Many places in Cha-am call themselves 'resorts' but the only place in the central area that comes close to the term is *Cha-am Methavalai Hotel* (☎ 471480), which has well-kept, modern rooms with flowers spilling from every balcony, plus a pool and a small beach area of its own in front. Rack rates are 1800B but during the week an automatic 30 to 40% discount is subtracted.

The *Kaen-Chan Hotel* (☎ 471314) has a variety of accommodation: bungalows are 150 to 250B with fan, 200 to 350B with air-con; air-con rooms in the hotel are 1200 to 1500B, with a 20% discount on weekdays.

The next cheapest places are *Jitravee Resort* and *Cha-am Villa* (☎ 471010/241), which will let you have rooms for 200B mid-week (300B on weekends), and *Cha-Am Inn* (☎ 471154), which has rooms for 250B mid-week. *Santikham Bungalows* (☎ 471329) are a reasonable 200B weekdays, 300B weekends; all rooms have air-con. *Cha-am Holiday Lodge* has similar bungalows from 200B.

Inthira Plaza This new complex off the main road (Narathip Rd) running to the beach from the highway is striving to become a Pattaya-style bar centre ('entertainment centre' in the jargon of the moment). A couple of the bars have apartment-style rooms upstairs, eg *Kiwi Apartments* above the Midnite Magic Bar for 250B with fan and bath, 350B with air-con. Could be noisy at night.

Places to Stay – top end

North of town a bit, the *Regent Cha-am Beach Resort* (☎ 47180/91) has rooms starting at 1800B; they advertise a 30 to 40% discount weekdays. Facilities include a swimming pool, squash and tennis courts and a fitness centre.

Also on the beach north of town is the posh *Dusit Resort & Polo Club* (☎ 520009) where rates start at 3630B. The Dusit offers a fitness centre, mini-golf, horseback riding, pool, tennis and squash courts and, of course, polo.

Vendors on the beach sell fair chow. Opposite the beach are several good seafood restaurants which, unlike the bungalows, are reasonably priced.

Getting There & Away

Buses from Phetburi and Hua Hin are 10B (from Hua Hin, take a Phetburi-bound bus). Ask to be let off at Hat Cha-am (Cha-am Beach).

Ordinary buses from Bangkok to Cha-am cost 38B (55B air-con). Buses leave from the southern bus terminals.

AROUND CHA-AM

Hat Peuktian

หาดปึกเตียน

This sandy beach between Cha-am and Phetburi has the usual casuarina trees and food vendors favoured by Thai beach-goers, and hardly a farang in sight. Three rocky islets are within wading distance of shore, one with a sala for shade. Also standing knee-deep just offshore is a six-metre statue of Phi Seua Samut, the undersea female deity that terrorised the protagonist of the Thai classical epic Phra Aphaimani. A statue of the prince himself sits on a nearby rock playing flute.

A tasteless two-storey townhouse-style development has recently been built off the beach. Designed in the pseudo-classical style prevalent in modern city blocks all over Thailand, it looks rather incongruous with the natural beach surroundings.

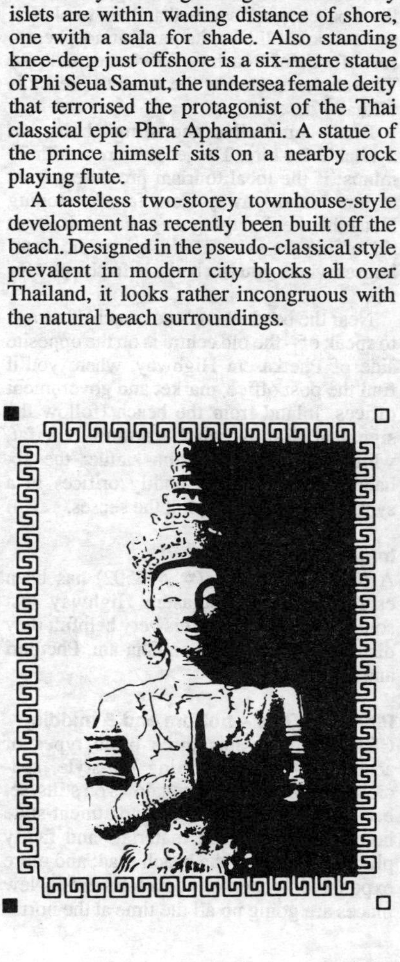

Prachuap Khiri Khan Province

Pineapples and fishing are the main livelihoods of the Thais living in this narrow province along the upper part of the peninsula. Along the Gulf coast are a variety of small seaside resorts, most of them very low-key.

HUA HIN
หัวหิน

Traditionally a favourite beach resort for Thais, Hua Hin (population 31,000) has been undergoing rapid change during the last three years or so. The secret is out: Hua Hin is a quiet and fairly economical place to get away from it all, and yet it's less than four hours by train from Bangkok. The private sector in Hua Hin have been promoting Hua Hin tourism, and developers are moving in. The resort now attracts a mix of Thais and older farang tourists who are seeking a comfortable beach holiday near Bangkok but who don't want the sleaziness of Pattaya.

Unfortunately Hua Hin may go the way of Pattaya unless the local community and the interlopers start planning now, before the sleaze and environmental destruction sets in. Already appearing are a lot of the same kind of cheap, unsightly shophouse-apartment buildings with plumbing problems seen in Pattaya and Phuket's Patong Beach. One good sign – so far – is that the girlie bar invasion has been restricted to nearby Cha-am. A new sewage treatment plant and municipal sewer system are also under construction and the beach is cleaner than ever. On the other hand, Hua Hin is gradually losing its fishing village atmosphere – the fishing fleet is being moved out of Hua Hin and the squid-drying piers have been replaced by hotels.

Thailand's royal family still uses the Klai Kangwon Palace, a summer residence built near the beach by Rama VII. The main swimming beach still has thatched umbrellas and

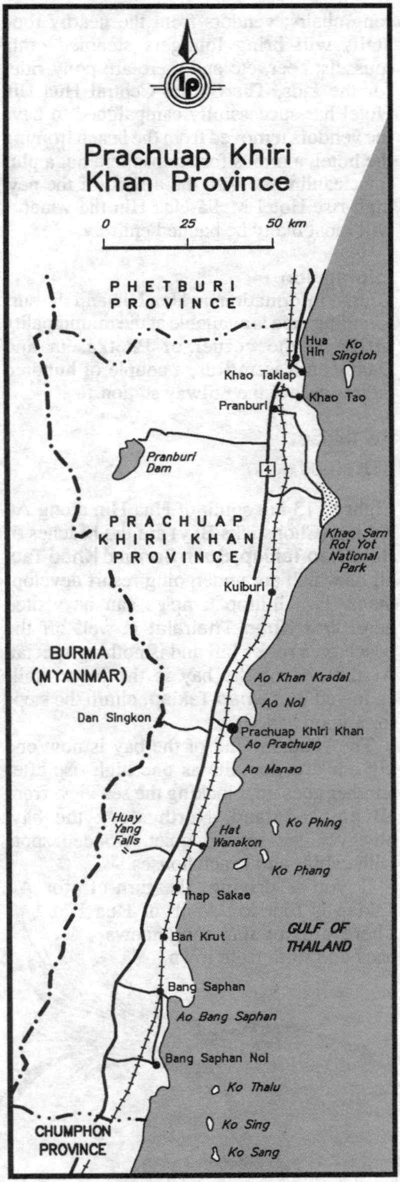

long chairs; vendors from the nearby food stalls will bring loungers steamed crab, mussels, beer, etc and there are pony rides for the kids. The Sofitel Central Hua Hin Hotel has successfully campaigned to have the vendors removed from the beach fronting the hotel, a minus for atmosphere but a plus for cleanliness. With the arrival of the new high-rise Hotel Meliá Hua Hin the vendors will most likely be banned entirely.

Information

Tourist information on Hua Hin and the surrounding area is available at the municipality office at the corner of Phetkasem and Damnoen Kasem Rds, a couple of hundred metres east of the railway station.

Ao Takiap

อาวตะเกียบ

Eight to 13 km south of Hua Hin along Ao Takiap (Chopsticks Bay) are the beaches of **Hat Khao Takiap**, **Suan Son** and **Khao Tao**, all of which are undergoing resort development. Two hilltop temples can be visited here. **Wat Khao Thairalat** is well off the beach on a rocky hill and is nothing special. At the end of the bay is the more well-endowed **Wat Khao Takiap**; climb the steps for a good bay view.

The southern end of the bay is now one big construction site as one high-rise after another goes up, blocking the sea view from all points inland. North along the bay, however, are several quiet, wooded spots with cabins and beach houses.

If you're driving, the turn-off for Ao Takiap is four km south of Hua Hin. There are regular songthaews back and forth from town.

Places to Stay – bottom end

Prices are moving up quickly for places near the beach. Hotels in town are still reasonable and it's only a five or 10-minute walk to the beach from most of them.

Guesthouses Near – but not on – the beach, the cheapest places are found along or just off Naretdamri Rd. Several small hotels and guesthouses in this area have rooms for 100 to 300B a night. Rooms at *Dang's House* on Naretdamri Rd cost 80 to 100B with shared bath, 120 to 150B with private bath. On the next block north, *Sriosraupsin Guest House* at 152/1 Naretdamri costs 200B for a small room with bath and fan, 250B for larger rooms. Also on this block, the *Europa* at No 158 has rooms for 120 to 150B with bath, and a European restaurant downstairs. *Sunee Guest House*, next door, is an old wooden building with rooms for 100 to 150B with shared bath.

Along a soi off Naretdamri Rd just north of Damnoen Kasem Rd is the comfortable-looking *Forum Guest House*. Rooms cost 150 to 200B, some rooms with bath, some without. On same soi are the similar *MP* and *SM* guesthouses.

Parichart Guest House, next to Dang's House, is a more up-market place with rooms for 300B with fan and private bath, 400 to 450B with air-con.

Along the next soi north off Naretdamri are a couple of charming old wooden guesthouses. Above the *Crocodile Bar* are several basic 120B rooms with shared bath. Next door, *Phuen Guest House* is a fairly quiet place with a nice atmosphere and the same rates as the Crocodile. *Baan Klang Soi* on the opposite side of the soi has similar charm and rates. Also on this soi is the modern, apartment-style *Ban Pak Hua Hin*; it's quiet, exceptionally clean, and costs 150 to 200B with fan and bath, 300B with air-con.

Further up Naretdamri Rd where the old squid piers used to be are two wooden motel-like places built on piers over the edge of the sea. *Mod (Mot) Guest House* has rather small rooms for 250B with fan, 400B with air-con, while the *Seabreeze (Sirima)* costs 250B for

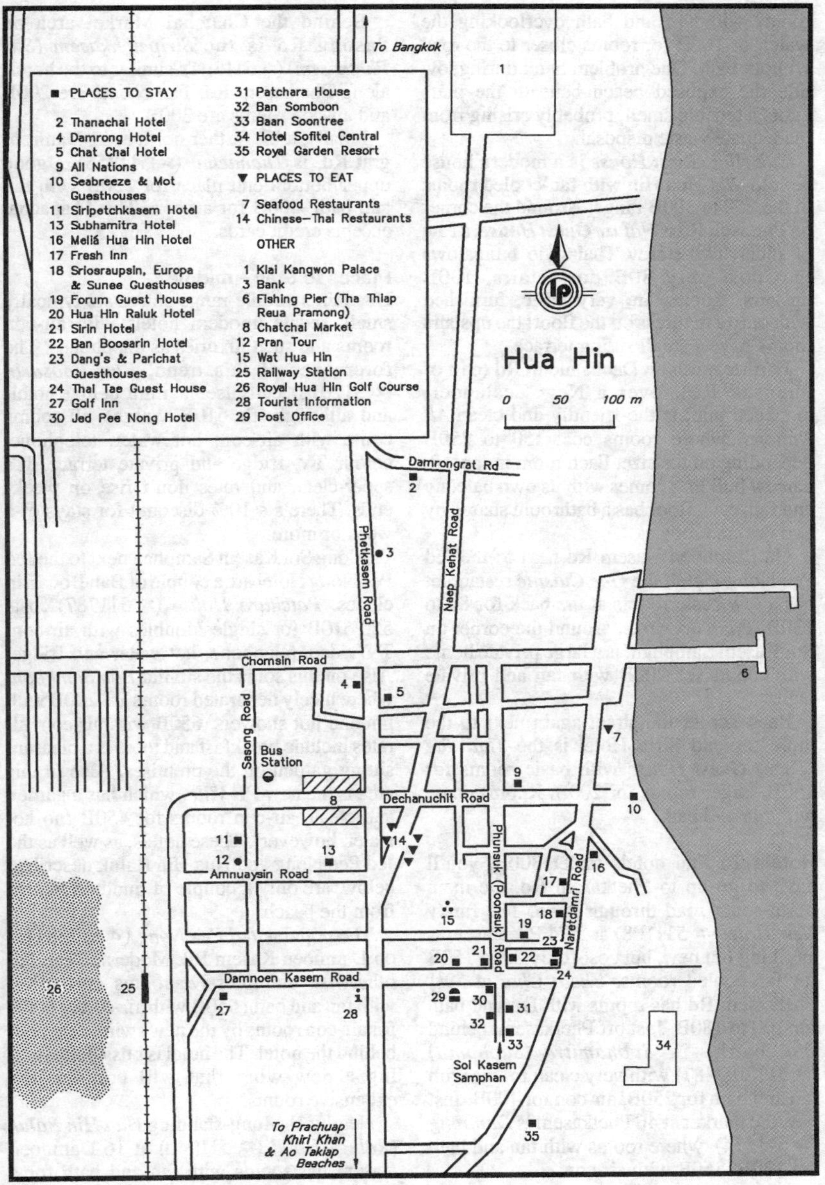
To Bangkok
PLACES TO STAY
2 Thanachai Hotel
4 Damrong Hotel
5 Chat Chai Hotel
9 All Nations
10 Seabreeze & Mot Guesthouses
11 Siripetchkasem Hotel
13 Subhamitra Hotel
16 Meliá Hua Hin Hotel
17 Fresh Inn
18 Sriosraupsin, Europa & Sunee Guesthouses
19 Forum Guest House
20 Hua Hin Raluk Hotel
21 Sirin Hotel
22 Ban Boosarin Hotel
23 Dang's & Parichat Guesthouses
24 Thai Tae Guest House
27 Golf Inn
30 Jed Pee Nong Hotel
31 Patchara House
32 Ban Somboon
33 Baan Soontree
34 Hotel Sofitel Central
35 Royal Garden Resort
PLACES TO EAT
7 Seafood Restaurants
14 Chinese–Thai Restaurants
OTHER
1 Klai Kangwon Palace
3 Bank
6 Fishing Pier (Tha Thiap Reua Pramong)
8 Chatchai Market
12 Pran Tour
15 Wat Hua Hin
25 Railway Station
26 Royal Hua Hin Golf Course
28 Tourist Information
29 Post Office
Hua Hin
0 50 100 m
Damrongrat Rd
Phetkasem Road
Naep Kehat Road
Chomsin Road
Sasong Road
Bus Station
Dechanuchit Road
Amnuaysin Road
Phunsuk (Poonsuk) Road
Naretdamri Road
Damnoen Kasem Road
Soi Kasem Samphan
To Prachuap Khiri Khan & Ao Takiap Beaches

rooms with fan and bath overlooking the water, or 160B for rooms closer to the road without bath. One problem here: during low tide the exposed beach beneath the piers emits a terrible smell, probably arising from inadequate waste disposal.

Sukwilai Guest House is a modern house next to Wat Hua Hin with fan-cooled rooms in the 250 to 300B range. Around the corner on Phunsuk Rd is *Nature Guest House*, a row of older, two-storey Thai-style bungalows that cost only 80B downstairs, 100B upstairs. Rooms are very basic, furnished with only a mattress on the floor; the upstairs rooms have a small sitting terrace.

Further north on Dechanuchit Rd (east of Phunsuk Rd), over a New Zealander-managed pub, is the friendly and clean *All Nations*, where rooms cost 150 to 250B depending on the size. Each room in the tall, narrow building comes with its own balcony and fan; each floor has a bathroom shared by two or three rooms.

On Damnoen Kasem Rd next to the Jed Pee Nong Hotel, the *Gee Cuisine* restaurant has a few basic rooms at the back for 80 to 130B. *Baan Soontree*, around the corner on Soi Kasem Samphan, is a large private home with rooms for 200B with fan and private bath.

Back across the street again next to the more top-end Sirin Hotel is the *Thai Tae (Thae) Guest House* with basic rooms for 150B, larger rooms for 200B. Rooms come with fan and bath.

Hotels To find hotels under 300B, you'll have to go up to Phetkasem Rd, the main north-south road through town. The funky *New Hotel* (☎ 511108) at 39/4 Phetkasem is anything but new, but costs only 80 to 150B for fan-cooled rooms. *Chaat Chai* at 59/1 Phetkasem Rd has rooms with fan and bath for 100 to 180B. Just off Phetkasem, behind the bank, is *Subhamitra (Suphamit)* (☎ 511208/487) with very clean rooms with fan and bath for 250B, air-con for 400B. Just past the market at 46 Phetkasem is *Damrong* (☎ 511574), where rooms with fan and bath are 120B, 350B with air-con.

Behind the Chatchai Market area on Sasong Rd is the *Siripetchkasem (Siri Phetkasem)* (☎ 511394), similar to the hotels along Phetkasem Rd. Fan rooms are 200B and air-con rooms are 300B.

Finally, a bit further north at 11 Damrongrat Rd, is *Thanachai* (☎ 511755), a good upper bottom-end place for 250B with fan and bath, 400B for air-con. The Thanachai accepts credit cards.

Places to Stay – middle

Hua Hin's middle-range places are typically small, sedate, modern hotels with air-con rooms and such luxuries as telephones. The forerunner of this trend, *Ban Boosarin* (☎ 512076), calls itself a 'mini-deluxe hotel' and although it's 610B a night, all rooms come with air-con, hot water, telephone, colour TV, fridge and private terrace. It's super-clean and rates don't rise on week-ends. There's a 10% discount for stays of a week or more.

Along Soi Kasem Samphan next to the Jed Pee Nong Hotel are a couple of Ban Boosarin clones. *Patchara House* (☎ 511787) costs 550/610B for singles/doubles with air-con, TV/video, telephone, hot water and fridge. Also on this soi is the similar *Ban Somboon*, where nicely decorated rooms are 200B with fan and hot showers, 650B with air-con; all rates include breakfast and there is a pleasant sitting garden on the premises. Also in this area is the new *PP Villa*, which has a garden and clean, air-con rooms for 450B (no hot water, however). These hotels, as well as the Jed Pee Nong and Hua Hin Raluk described below, are only a couple of hundred metres from the beach.

The popular *Jed Pee Nong* (☎ 512381) is on Damnoen Kasem Rd. Modern, clean but otherwise unimpressive rooms cost 400B with fan and bath, 550B with air-con or 600B for air-con rooms by the new swimming pool behind the hotel. The hotel is busy constructing a new wing that will contain less expensive rooms.

Nearby, the long-standing *Hua Hin Raluk (Ralug) Hotel* (☎ 511940) at 16 Damnoen Kasem has rooms with fan and bath for a reasonable 200B, air-con for 500B. There are also some large bungalows for 350B with fan, 450B with air-con. The Raluk is adding a high-rise wing which may be operated under a separate name – rates will probably be in the 600 to 800B range.

On Naretdamri Rd, the modern *Fresh Inn* (☎ 511389) has all air-con rooms for 500B; this pleasant tourist-class hotel would have had a sea view if not for the construction of the high-rise Meliá Hua Hin between it and the sea.

Running north-east from Chomsin Rd (the road leading to the main pier) is Naep Khehat Rd. At No 73/5-7, the *Phananchai Hotel* (☎ 511707) has air-con rooms for 400 to 750B. It's a bit of a walk from the swimming beaches but all rooms come with air-con, hot water, TV and telephone.

Places to Stay – top end

The air-con *Sirin Hotel* (☎ 511150) is on Damnoen Kasem Rd toward the beach, down from the Raluk. The rooms here are well kept and come with hot water and a fridge. The semi-outdoor restaurant area is pleasant. Double rooms are 750B during the week and 990B on weekends and holidays.

Near the railway station, off Damnoen Kasem Rd near the Hua Hin golf course, is the new *Golf Inn* (☎ 512473), where air-con rooms are 605 to 726B.

Hua Hin has two other top-end hotels. *Hotel Sofitel Central Hua Hin* (☎ 512021, 512040; 233-0974/0980 in Bangkok), formerly the Hua Hin Railway Hotel, is a magnificent two-storey colonial-style place on the beach at the end of Damnoen Kasem Rd. Rooms in the original L-shaped colonial wing cost 2178B; rooms in the new wing are more expensive but there is also a Villa Wing across the road with original one and two-bedroom beach bungalows for 1800 to 2500B. From December 20 to February 20 there's a 400B peak-season supplement on all room charges.

The all-new *Meliá Hua Hin* (☎ 511053) off Naretdamri Rd is part of the Spanish-owned Meliá hotel chain and is Hua Hin's first high-rise hotel (also the first to mar the skyline, unfortunately). Rooms with all the

---

Hua Hin Railway Hotel

In 1922 the State Railway of Thailand (then the Royal Thai Railway) extended the national rail network to Hua Hin to allow easier access to the Hua Hin summer palace. The area proved to be a popular vacation spot among non-royals too, so in the following year they built the Hua Hin Railway Hotel, a graceful colonial-style inn on the sea, with sweeping teak stairways and high-ceilinged rooms. When I researched the first edition of this guide in 1981, a double room was still only 90B and the service was just as unhurried as it had been when I first stayed here in 1977. It probably hadn't changed much since 1923, except for the addition of electric lighting and screened doors and windows. Big-bladed ceiling fans stirred the humid sea air and in the dining room one ate using State Railway silverware and thick china from the '20s. Unfortunately, when Bangkok's Central Department Store took over the management of the hotel they floundered in their attempt to upgrade the facilities, failing to take advantage of the hotel's original ambience.

In 1986 the French hotel chain Sofitel became part of a joint venture with Central and together they restored the hotel to most of its former glory. It now bears the awkward name *Hotel Sofitel Central Hua Hin*, but if you've been looking for an historic South-East Asian hotel to spend some money on, this might be it. All of the wood panelling and brass fixtures throughout the rooms and open hallways have been restored. While the old railway silverware and china have been resigned to antique cabinet displays, the spacious, lazy ambience of a previous age remains. Even if you don't want to spend the money to stay here, it's worth a stroll through the grounds and open sitting areas for a little history. It's more interesting in terms of atmosphere than either the Raffles in Singapore or the Oriental in Bangkok (neither of which have eight-hectare grounds), and somewhere in-between in terms of luxury. Latest reports, however, say standards have slipped since the lay-off of all European management.

Incidentally, in 1983 this hotel was used as Hotel Le Phnom for the filming of *The Killing Fields*. Also, the State Railway of Thailand still owns the hotel; Sofitel/Central are just leasing it. ■

---

amenities are scheduled to cost from 1600 to 3000B depending on the time of year.

There are also a few top-end places on beaches just north and south of town:

Royal Garden Resort 107/1 Phetkasem Rd, from 3000B, plus 300B peak-season supplement November to April (☎ 511881; 251-8659 in Bangkok)
Royal Garden Village, 45 Phetkasem Rd, from 3500B, plus 300B peak-season supplement November to April (☎ 512412/5; 251-8659 in Bangkok)
Sailom Hotel, from 750B Sunday to Thursday, add 700B on weekends (☎ 511890/1; 258-0652 in Bangkok)
Hua Hin Highland Resort, from 4600B; it's on a hill north of town, and is a favourite of golfers who frequent the nearby Royal Hua Hin Golf Course (☎ 211-2579 in Bangkok)
Hua Hin Palace Hotel, 500 to 700B (☎ 511151)

Places to Stay – out of town

In Hat Takiap, the *Chom Deuan Guest House* (☎ 512463) has four fan-cooled rooms ranging in price from 500B upwards. The *Fangkhlun Guest House* (☎ 512402) has five fan-cooled rooms from 400 to 500B. The *Khao Takiap Resort* (☎ 512405) has fan-cooled rooms sleeping up to eight people for 700B a night, air-con rooms sleeping up to 10 for 1000B. The cheaper *Sri Pathum Guest House* (☎ 512339) has 11 rooms from 250B with fan, 350B air-con; and the *Vegas Guest House* (☎ 512290) has 32 rooms priced from 390B.

One new discovery this time around was *Nong Khae Cabin Hua Hin* (☎ 511291), a former Christian retreat centre with quiet, secluded cabins in the woods along the northern part of the bay. Spacious cabins with two large, clean bedrooms, ceiling fans and bath are 650B on weekdays, 1100B on weekends and holidays. Rates include breakfast; free transport to/from the railway station is available if you call. Also in this area of Ao Takiap (called Nong Khae) are *Rung Arun Guest House* (☎ 511291) with cabins ranging from 150 to 700B and *Chaihat Noen Chale* (☎ 511288) with 14 air-con rooms for 1500B each.

In Hat Khao Tao, the *Nanthasuda Guesthouse (Nanthasuda Restaurant)* has rooms from 300B, while Hat Suan Son has the modern *Suan Son Padiphat* (☎ 511239) with fan-cooled rooms for 250B (600B on the sea) or air-con rooms for 500 to 1000B.

In Pranburi, the *Pranburi Beach Resort* (☎ 233-3871 in Bangkok) has rooms priced from 1400B; the *Pransiri Hotel* (☎ 621061), at 283 Phetkasem Rd, has rooms starting from 140B.

Places to Eat

The best seafood in Hua Hin is found in three main areas. Firstly, along Damnoen Kasem Rd near the Jed Pee Nong and Raluk hotels, and off Damnoen Kasem, on Phunsuk Rd and Naretdamri Rd, there are some medium-priced restaurants. Secondly, there's excellent and inexpensive food in the Chatchai night market, off Phetkasem on Dechanuchit Rd, and in nearby Chinese-Thai restaurants. The third area is next to Tha Thiap Reua Pramong, the big fishing pier at the end of Chomsin Rd. The fish is, of course, fresh off the boats but not necessarily the cheapest in town. One of the places near the pier, *Saeng Thai*, is the oldest seafood restaurant in Hua Hin and quite reliable if you know how to order. The best value for money can be found in the smaller eating places on and off Chomsin Rd and in the Chatchai night market. There is also a night market on Chomsin Rd.

The best seafood to order in Hua Hin is plaa sãmlii (cotton fish or kingfish), plaa kapõng (perch), plaa mèuk (squid), hãwy malaeng phùu (mussels) and puu (crab). The various forms of preparation include:

dìp	raw
nêung	steamed
phão	grilled
phàt	sliced, filleted and fried
râat phrík	smothered in garlic and chillies
thâwt	fried whole
tôm yam	in a hot and tangy broth
yâang	roast (squid only)

Chatchai Market is excellent for Thai breakfast – they sell very good jók and khâo tôm (rice soups). Fresh-fried paa-thông-kõ Hua Hin-style (small and crispy, not oily), are 1B for three. A few vendors also serve hot soy milk in bowls (4B) – break a few paa-thông-kõ into the soy milk and drink free náam chaa – a very tasty and filling breakfast for 7B if you can eat nine paa-thông-kõ.

Gee Cuisine next to the Jed Pee Nong caters mostly to farangs but the Thai food is generally good. The nonstop video in the evenings, however, is a curse one hopes won't spread to other restaurants in town.

Phunsuk and Naretdamri roads are becoming centres for farang-oriented eateries. The *Tan Thong* does good seafood and also has a bar. The *Beergarden* is just what it sounds like – an outdoor pub with Western food. The *Headrock Cafe* (not a mis-spelling but a pun on the name Hua Hin – 'head rock') is more of a drinking place, but also has Thai and Western food. On the next street up, Phunsuk Rd, is the Italian *La Villa* with pizza, spaghetti, lasagna and so on. Under French management, the new *La Bodega* restaurant at the Forum Guest House features French and Spanish cuisine. The Europa Guest House also has a continental restaurant. *Kiwi Corner* at 21 Chomsin serves Western breakfasts.

Entertainment

Several farang bars under German, Swiss, Italian, French and New Zealand management can be found in and around Naretdamri and Phunsuk Rds. All Nations Bar at 10-10/1 Dechanuchit successfully recreates a pub atmosphere and has quite a collection of flags and other memorabilia from around the world.

Stone Town, an old-west style pub next to Jed Pee Nong Hotel on Damnoen Kasem Rd, features live folk and country music nightly. For Thai rock 'n' roll, check out the Rock Walk Pub off Chomsin Rd, where live Thai bands – many from Bangkok – appear nightly. The room and sound system are well designed for listening; there's no cover charge and drinks are no more expensive than at any of the town's farang bars.

Getting There & Away

Air Bangkok Airways flies to Hua Hin daily for 825B one-way; the flight takes 25 minutes.

Bus Buses from Bangkok's southern bus terminal are 74B air-con, 41B ordinary. The trip takes about four hours. Pran Tour on Sasong Rd near the Siripetchkasem Hotel in Hua Hin runs air-con buses to Bangkok every half hour from 3 am to 9 pm, for 55B 2nd class air-con or 74B 1st class air-con. Pran Tour air-con buses to Phetburi are 50B.

Ordinary buses for Hua Hin leave Phetburi regularly for 15B. The same bus can be picked up in Cha-am for 10B. From Nakhon Pathom an ordinary bus is 32B.

For local buses from Hua Hin to the beaches of Khao Takiap (5B), Khao Tam (4B) and Suan Son (4B), go to the ordinary bus terminal on Sasong Rd. These buses run from around 6 am until 5 pm. Buses to Pranburi are 7B.

Train The same trains south apply here as those described under Phetburi's Getting There & Away section. The train trip takes three hours and 45 minutes; 1st-class fare is 182B (express only), 2nd class 92B (rapid and express only), 3rd class is 44B.

You can also come by train from any other station on the southern railway line, including Phetburi (3rd class, 13B), Nakhon Pathom (2nd/3rd class 52/33B), Prachuap (3rd class, 19B), Surat Thani (2nd/3rd class, 116/74B) and Hat Yai (2nd/3rd class, 183/116B).

Getting Around

Samlor fares in Hua Hin have been set by the municipal authorities so there shouldn't be any haggling. Here are some sample fares: the railway station to the beach, 10B; the bus terminal to the Sofitel Central Hotel, 15B; Chatchai Market to the fishing pier, 10B; the railway station to the Royal Garden Resort, 20B.

Motorcycles and bicycles can be rented from a couple of places on Damnoen Kasem Rd near the Jed Pee Nong Hotel. Motorcycle rates are reasonable: 100 to 150B per day for 100cc, 150 to 250B for 125cc. Occasionally larger bikes – 400 to 750cc – are available for 500 to 600B a day. Bicycles are 20 to 40B per day.

At the fishing pier in Hua Hin you can hire boats out to Ko Singtoh for 600B a day. On Hat Takiap you can get boats for 500B.

KHAO SAM ROI YOT NATIONAL PARK
อุทยานแห่งชาติเขาสามร้อยยอด

This 98-sq-km park has magnificent views of the Prachuap coastline if you can stand a little climbing. Khao Daeng is only about half an hour's walk from the park headquarters, and from here you can see the ocean as well as some freshwater lagoons. If you have the time and energy, climb the 605-metre **Khao Krachom** for even better views. If you're lucky, you may come across a serow (Asian mountain goat) while hiking. The lagoons and coastal marshes are great places for bird-watching; along the coast you may see the occasional pod of Irrawaddy dolphins passing by.

The other big attraction at Sam Roi Yot (Three Hundred Peaks) are the three caves of **Tham Kaew, Tham Sai** and **Tham Phraya Nakhon**. Tham Phraya Nakhon is the most interesting and can be reached by boat or on foot. The boat trip only takes about half an hour there and back, while it's half an hour each way on foot along a steep trail. There are actually two large caverns, both with sinkholes that allow light in. In one cave is a royal sala built for King Chulalongkorn, who would stop off here when travelling back and forth between Bangkok and Nakhon Si Thammarat.

English-speaking guides can be hired at the park office for 50B per hike.

Places to Stay

The Forestry Department hires out two-person tents for 30B per night and large bungalows for 500 to 1000B per night; they sleep 10 to 20 people. You can also pitch your own tent for 5B per person on Laem Sala or Hat Sam Phraya, which are just beyond the visitors' centre. There is a restaurant on Hat Laem Sala. Bring repellent along as the park is rife with mosquitoes.

Getting There & Away

Catch a bus to Pranburi (7B from Hua Hin) and then another to the park for 10B. Sometimes it's necessary to change buses in Bang Phu. If you're coming by car or motorcycle from Hua Hin, it's about 25 km to the park turn-off, then another 38 km to park headquarters.

PRACHUAP KHIRI KHAN
อ.เมืองประจวบคีรีขันธ์

Roughly 80 km south of Hua Hin, Prachuap Khiri Khan (population 14,000) is the provincial capital, though it is somewhat smaller than Hua Hin. There are no real swimming beaches in town, though the eight-km-long bay of Ao Prachuap is pretty enough. The seafood here is fantastic, however, and cheaper than in Hua Hin. Fishing is still the mainstay of the local economy.

Orientation & Information

South of Ao Prachuap, around a small headland, is the scenic **Ao Manao**, a bay ringed by a clean white-sand beach with small islands offshore. Because a Thai air-force base is near the bay, the beach was closed to the public until 1990, when the local authorities decided to open the area to day visitors. The beach is two or three km from the base entrance; you must leave your passport at the gate and sign in. There are several salas along the beach, one restaurant, toilets and a shower.

At the northern end of Ao Prachuap is **Khao Chong Krajok** (Mirror Tunnel Mountain – named after the hole through the side of the mountain which appears to reflect the sky). At the top is **Wat Thammikaram,** established by King Rama VI. You can climb the hill for a view of the town and bay – and entertain the hordes of monkeys who live here.

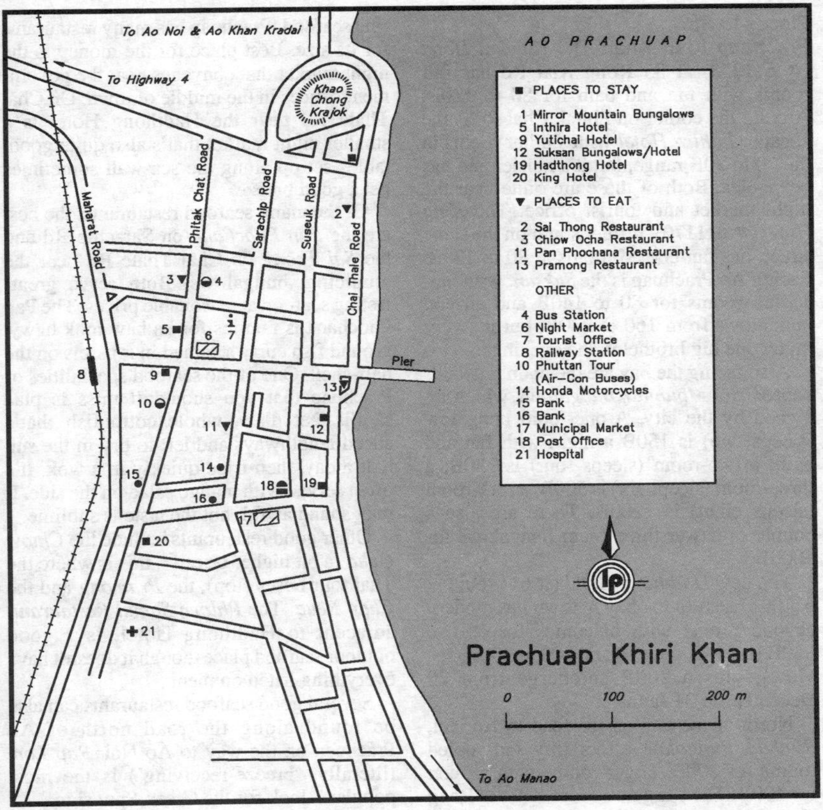

If you continue north from Prachuap Khiri Khan around Ao Prachuap to the headland you'll come to a small boat-building village on **Ao Bang Nang Lom** where they still make wooden fishing vessels using traditional Thai methods. It takes about two months to finish a 12-metre boat, which will sell for 300,000 to 400,000B without an engine. West of the beach at Ao Bang Nang Lom is a canal, **Khlong Bang Nang Lom**, lined with picturesque mangroves.

A few km north of Ao Prachuap is another bay, **Ao Noi**, the site of a small fishing village with a few rooms to let.

Prachuap has its own city-run tourist office in the centre of town. The staff is very friendly and they have maps and photos of all the attractions in the area.

Pinit Ounope, a local postal worker, has been recommended for his inexpensive day tours to Khao Sam Roi Yot, Dan Singkhon and to nearby beaches, national parks and waterfalls. He lives at 265 Susuak Rd near the beach in town and invites travellers to visit him. His house is rather difficult to find; you can also ask for him at the post office. The typical day tour is 200B for two people, plus 50B for each extra person.

Places to Stay

Prachuap Khiri Khan The *Yutichai Hotel* (☎ 611055) at 35 Kong Kiat Rd has fair rooms with fan and bath for 80 to 120B. Around the corner on Phitak Chat Rd is the cheaper *Inthira Hotel* with similar rooms in the 70 to 80B range, but it's noisier and has peepholes. Both of these are quite near the night market and tourist office. The *King Hotel* (☎ 611170), further south on the same street, has fan-cooled rooms at 80 to 120B. Facing Ao Prachuap is the *Suksan*, with fan-cooled rooms for 80 to 140B and air-con bungalows from 160 to 220B, but it's very much one big brothel in the evenings.

Also facing the bay are the plain but well-kept *Mirror Mountain Bungalows*, which are owned by the city. A one-room bungalow (sleeps two) is 150B a night with fan and bath; a two-room (sleeps four) is 350B; a three-room (sleeps six) is 500B; a four-room (sleeps eight) is 1200B. There are also a couple of newer three-room bungalows for 1000B.

The new *Hadthong Hotel* (☎ 611960; fax 611003) next to the bay in town has modern air-con rooms with balconies for 650 to 850B (mountain view) and 800 to 950B (sea view), plus a 200B surcharge from 20 December to 31 January.

North of the city on the road to Ao Noi, *Rimhad Bungalow* offers tiny fan-cooled rooms for 200B, larger rooms with air-con for 400B. The bungalows face Khlong Bang Nang Lom and mangroves. *Happy Inn* nearby has the same prices and similar accommodation.

Ao Noi In Ao Noi there are several rooms and small 'weekend inns', most catering to Thais. *Aow Noi Beach Bungalows* (☎ 510-9790 in Bangkok) offers well-kept cottages for 450 to 600B a night with breakfast. Run by a former German volunteer worker and his Thai wife, facilities include a small bar and restaurant with Thai and Western food, plus a clean, secluded beach.

Places to Eat

Because of its well-deserved reputation for fine seafood, Prachuap has many restaurants for its size. Best place for the money is the night market that convenes near the government offices in the middle of town. On Chai Thale Rd near the Hadthong Hotel is a smaller night market that's also quite good; tables set up along the sea wall sometimes get a good breeze.

Of the many seafood restaurants, the best are the *Pan Phochana* on Sarachip Rd and the *Sai Thong* on Chai Thale Rd near the municipal bungalows. Both serve great-tasting seafood at reasonable prices. The Pan Phochana is famous for its hàw mòk hãwy, ground fish curry steamed in mussels on the half-shell. One of the seafood specialities of Prachuap that you shouldn't miss is plaa sãmlii tàet dìaw, whole cottonfish that's sliced lengthways and left to dry in the sun half a day, then fried quickly in a wok. It's often served with mango salad on the side. It may sound awful, but the taste is sublime.

Other good restaurants include the *Chiow Ocha* (a bit higher priced – this is where the Thai tour buses stop), the *Pramong* and the *Chao Reua*. The *Phloen Samut Restaurant*, adjacent to Hadthong Hotel, is a good outdoor seafood place though it doesn't have everything listed on menu.

Several good seafood restaurants can also be found along the road north of Ao Prachuap on the way to Ao Noi. *Rap Lom* (literally, 'breeze-receiving') is the most popular – look for the Green Spot sign.

Across from the Inthira Hotel is a small morning market with tea stalls that serve cheap curries and noodles.

Getting There & Away

Bus From Bangkok, ordinary buses are 63B and they leave the southern bus terminal frequently between 4.30 and 5.20 pm. Air-con buses cost 105B from the southern air-con terminal. In the opposite direction, air-con buses to Bangkok cost 100B and leave from Phuttan Tour (☎ 611411) on Phitak Chat Rd at 8.30 am, noon, 3.30 pm and 1 am. In either direction the trip takes four to five hours.

From Hua Hin buses are 21B and they

leave from the bus station on Sasong Rd every 20 minutes from 7 am to 3 pm.

From Prachuap you can catch ordinary buses to Chumphon (40B), Surat Thani (72B), Nakhon Si Thammarat (98B), Krabi (110B) and Phuket (113B). The air-con bus from Bangkok to Samui stops on the highway in Prachuap at 12.30 am – if seats are available you can buy a through ticket to Samui for 160B.

Train For departure details from Bangkok, see the earlier Phetburi Getting There & Away section: the same services apply. Fares from Bangkok are 122B for 2nd class and 58B for 3rd class. Ordinary trains between Hua Hin and Prachuap are 19B; from Hua Hin they leave at 10.30 am, 11.47 am, and 6.25 pm, arriving in Prachuap an hour and a half later. There are also a couple of rapid trains between the two towns, but the time saved is only about 20 minutes.

Getting Around

Prachuap is small enough to get around on foot. You can hire a tuk-tuk to Ao Noi for 20B. The Honda dealer on Sarachip Rd rents motorcycles, as does the Suzuki dealer on Phitak Chat Rd.

AROUND PRACHUAP KHIRI KHAN TOWN

Wat Khao Tham Khan Kradai

วัดเขาถ้ำคันกระได

About eight km north of town, following the same road beyond Ao Noi, is this small cave wat at one end of lengthy **Ao Khan Kradai**. A trail at the base of the limestone hill leads up and around the side to a small cavern and then a larger one which contains a reclining Buddha. If you have a torch you can proceed to a larger second chamber also containing Buddha images. From this trail you get a good view of Ao Khan Kradai (also known as Ao Khan Bandai), a long, beautiful bay that stretches out below. The beach here is suitable for swimming and is virtually deserted. It's not far from Ao Noi, so you could stay in Ao Noi and walk to this beach. Or you could stay in town, rent a motorcycle and make a day trip to Ao Khan Kradai.

Dan Singkhon

ด่านสิงขร

Just south of Prachuap is a road leading west to Dan Singkhon on the Burmese border. This is the narrowest point in Thailand between the Gulf of Thailand and Burma – only 12 km across. The Burmese side changed from Karen to Burmese control following skirmishes in 1988-89. The border is closed; on the Thai side is a small frontier village and a Thai police camp with wooden semi-underground bunkers built in a circle.

Off the road on the way to the Dan Singkhon are a couple of small cave hermitages. The more famous one at **Khao Hin Thoen**, surrounded by a park of the same name, has some interesting rock formations and sculptures – but watch out for the dogs. The road to Khao Hin Thoen starts where the paved road to Dan Singkhon breaks left. **Khao Khan Hawk** (also known as Phutthakan Bang Kao) is a less well-known cave nearby where elderly monk Luang Phaw Buaphan Chatimetho lives. Devotees from a local village bring him food each morning.

THAP SAKAE & BANG SAPHAN

ทับสะแกและบางสะพาน

These two districts lie south of Prachuap Khiri Khan and together they offer a string of fairly good beaches that hardly get any tourists.

The town of Thap Sakae is set back from the coast and isn't much, but along the seashore there are a few places to stay (see below). The beach opposite Thap Sakae isn't anything special either but north and south of town are the beaches of **Hat Wanakon** and **Hat Laem Kum**. There is no private accommodation at these beaches at the moment, but you could ask permission to camp at Wat Laem Kum, which is on a prime spot right in the middle of Hat Laem Kum. Laem Kum is only 3.5 km from Thap Sakae and at the northern end is the fishing village of Ban Don Sai, where you can buy food.

Bang Saphan (Bang Saphan Yai) is no great shakes as a town either, but the long beaches here are beginning to attract some speculative development. In the vicinity of Bang Saphan you'll find the beaches of **Hat Sai Kaew, Hat Ban Krut, Hat Khiriwong, Hat Ban Nong Mongkon, Hat (Ao) Baw Thawng Lang, Hat Pha Daeng** and **Hat Bang Boet**, all of which are worth looking up. Getting around can be a problem since there isn't much public transport between these beaches.

Places to Stay & Eat

Thap Sakae In Thap Sakae, there are three hotels to choose from: the *Chawalit*, right off the highway with rooms for 100 to 200B with fan and bath; the *Sukkasem*, near the centre of town with rooms for 100 to 180B; and the *Thiparot*, with rooms for 100 to 200B. On the coast opposite Thap Sakae are a couple of concrete block-style bungalows for 150 to 300B, eg *Chan Reua*. Much more congenial and economical is the *Talay Inn* (☎ 671417), a cluster of nine bamboo huts on a lake fed by the Huay Yang Waterfall, but back from the beach a bit in the fishing village. Accommodation is 50B per person. The owner-manager, Khun Yo, was a nurse in England for 12 years and he takes good care of his guests. His place is about one km east of the Thap Sakae railway station, which is about 1.5 km from Thap Sakae. Talay Inn is within easy walking distance of the sea, and there is fishing and swimming in the lake.

Hat Sai Kaew Between Thap Sakae and Bang Saphan on the beach of Hat Kaew (Km 372, Highway 4) is *Haad Kaeo Beach Resort* (☎ 611035). It's actually just 200 metres from the Ban Koktahom railway station, which can only be reached by ordinary train from the Hua Hin, Prachuap, Thap Sakae, Bang Saphan Yai or Chumphon terminals. Pretty white bungalows with green roofs are 200B per day.

Hat Khiriwong *Tawee Beach Resort* (also *Tawees*, *Tawee Sea*) has bungalows with private bath for 70 to 150B. Take a train or bus to the nearby town of Ban Krut, then a motorcycle taxi (30B) to Hat Khiriwong.

Bang Saphan Along the bay of Ao Bang Saphan are several beach hotels and bungalows. The *Hat Somboon Sea View* is 250B per room with private bath. For 150B a night you could stay at any of the following: *Sarika Villa*, *Sung Haeng Hotel*, *Hat Sai Kaew Resort* or *Wanwina Bungalows*.

Karol L's (☎ 032-691058), operated by an American and his Thai wife, has 80B bungalows in the old Samui style six km south of Bang Saphan Yai. If you call from the railway or bus terminal, they'll provide free transport.

The *Krua Klang Ao* restaurant is a good place for seafood, right near the centre of Ao Bang Saphan.

Getting There & Away

Buses from Prachuap to Thap Sakae are 6B and from Thap Sakae to Bang Saphan Yai 8B. If you're coming from further south, buses from Chumphon to Bang Saphan Yai are 25B.

You can also get 3rd-class trains between Hua Hin, Prachuap, Thap Sakae, Ban Koktahom, Ban Krut and Bang Saphan Yai for a few baht on each leg, as all of them have railway stations (the rapid and express lines do not stop in Thap Sakae, Ban Krut or Bang Saphan).

Chumphon Province

CHUMPHON

อ.เมืองชุมพร

About 500 km south of Bangkok, Chumphon (population 15,000) is the junction town where you turn west to Ranong and Phuket or continue south on the newer road to Surat Thani, Nakhon Si Thammarat and Songkhla. The name is derived from *chumnumphon*,

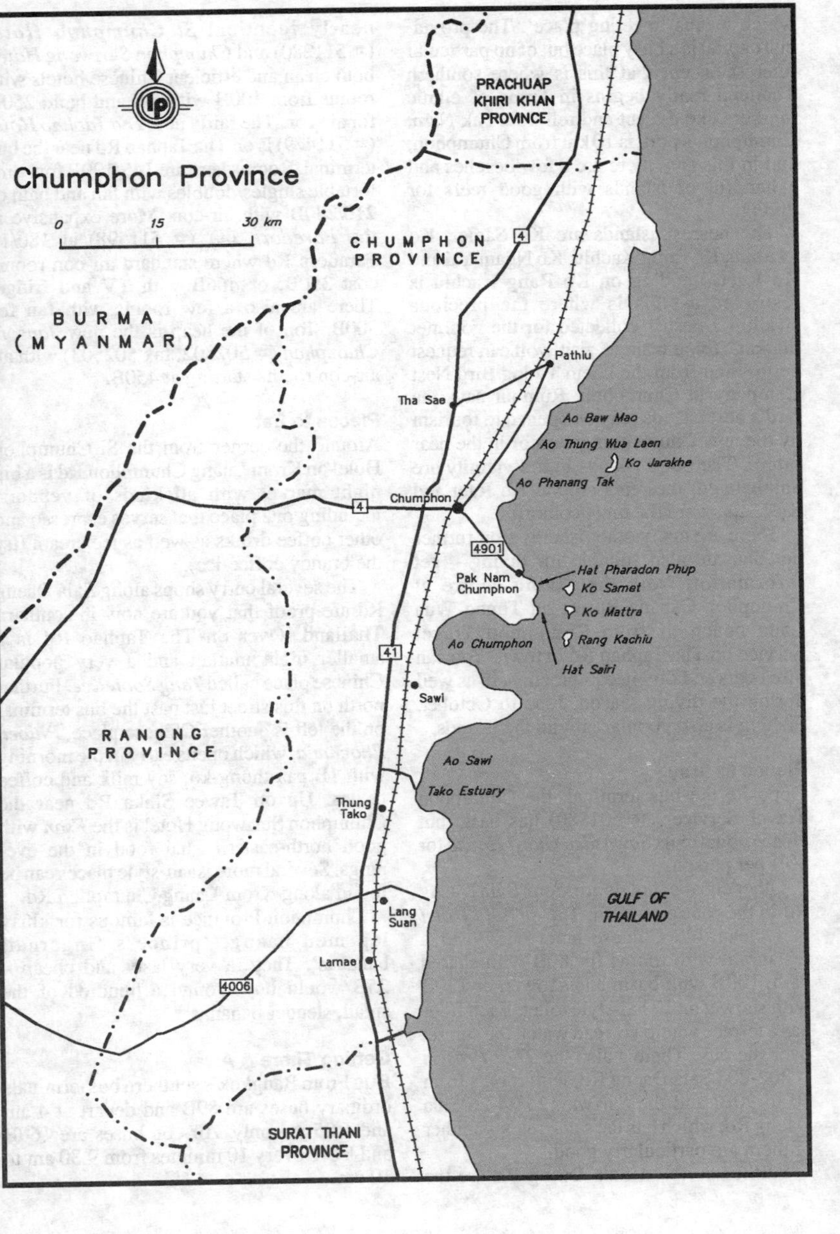
Chumphon Province
0 15 30 km
PRACHUAP KHIRI KHAN PROVINCE
CHUMPHON PROVINCE
BURMA (MYANMAR)
RANONG PROVINCE
SURAT THANI PROVINCE
GULF OF THAILAND
4
4
4901
41
4006
Pathiu
Tha Sae
Ao Baw Mao
Ao Thung Wua Laen
Ko Jarakhe
Ao Phanang Tak
Chumphon
Hat Pharadon Phup
Pak Nam Chumphon
Ko Samet
Ko Mattra
Rang Kachiu
Ao Chumphon
Hat Sairi
Sawi
Ao Sawi
Tako Estuary
Thung Tako
Lang Suan
Lamae

which means 'meeting place'. The provincial capital is a busy place but of no particular interest except that this is where southern Thailand really begins in terms of ethnic markers like dialect and religion. Pak Nam, Chumphon's port, is 10 km from Chumphon, and in this area there are a few beaches and a handful of islands with good reefs for diving.

The nearest islands are Ko Samet, Ko Mattara, Ko Rang Kachiu, Ko Ngam Yai and Ko Raet. Landing on Ko Rang Kachiu is restricted as this is where the precious swallow's nest is collected for the gourmet market. If you want to visit, you can request permission from the Laem Thong Bird Nest Company in Chumphon. Rumour says the bird's nest islands may be opened to tourism by the new Chumphon governor in the near future. The other islands in the vicinity are uninhabited; the reefs around Ko Raet and Ko Mattara are the most colourful.

There are many other islands a bit further out that are also suitable for diving – get information from the diving centre at Chumphon Cabana Resort on Thung Wua Laen beach or from Chumphon Travel Service on Tha Taphao Rd in town. You can hire boats and diving equipment here as well during the diving season, June to October. Fishing is also popular around the islands.

Places to Stay

Opposite the bus terminal, the Chumphon Travel Service, (☎ 501880) has basic but clean rooms in its *Sawasdee Guest House* for 50B per person.

Other cheaper hotels are along Sala Daeng Rd in the centre of town. The *Si Taifa Hotel* is a clean, old Chinese hotel built over a restaurant with rooms for 80B with shared bath, 100B with basin and shower, or 120B with shower and Thai-style toilet. Each floor has a terrace where you can watch the sun set over the city. There's also the *Thai Prasert* at 202-204 Sala Daeng Rd, with rooms from 70 to 90B; and the *Suriya*, 125/24-26 Sala Daeng Rd, which has the same rates – neither of them are particularly good.

Further north on Sala Daeng Rd are the nearly identical *Si Chumphon Hotel* (☎ 511280) and *Chumphon Suriwong Hotel*, both clean and efficient Chinese hotels with rooms from 100B with fan and bath, 250B for air-con. The fairly new *Tha Taphao Hotel* (☎ 511479) is on Tha Taphao Rd near the bus terminal. Rooms here are 145/190B for comfortable singles/doubles with fan and bath or 210/280B with air-con. More expensive is the *Paradorn Inn* (☎ 511598) at 180/12 Paradorn Rd where standard air-con rooms cost 350B, or 466B with TV and fridge. There are also a few rooms with fan for 300B. Top of the heap is the new *Jansom Chumphon* (☎ 502502; fax 502503) with all air-con rooms starting at 450B.

Places to Eat

Around the corner from the Si Chumphon Hotel on Krom Luang Chumphon Rd is a big night market with all kinds of vendors, including one place that serves espresso and other coffee drinks as well as ice cream (try the brandy coffee-ice).

The several curry shops along Sala Daeng Rd are proof that you are now in southern Thailand. Over on Tha Taphao Rd is a smaller night market and a very popular Chinese place called *Tang Soon Kee*. Further north on this street just past the bus terminal on the left is another Chinese place, *Phloen Phochana*, which opens early in the morning with 1B paa-thông-kõ, soy milk and coffee or tea. Up on Tawee Sinka Rd near the Chumphon Suriwong Hotel is the *Esan* with good north-eastern Thai food in the evenings. Several more isaan-style places can be found along Krom Luang Chumphon Rd.

Chumphon Province is famous for klûay lép meu naang, 'princess fingernail bananas'. They're very tasty and cheap – 25B would buy around a hundred of the small, slender bananas.

Getting There & Away

Bus From Bangkok's southern bus terminals ordinary buses are 89B and depart at 4 am and 6.05 am only. Air-con buses are 160B and leave every 10 minutes from 9.30 am to 10 pm.

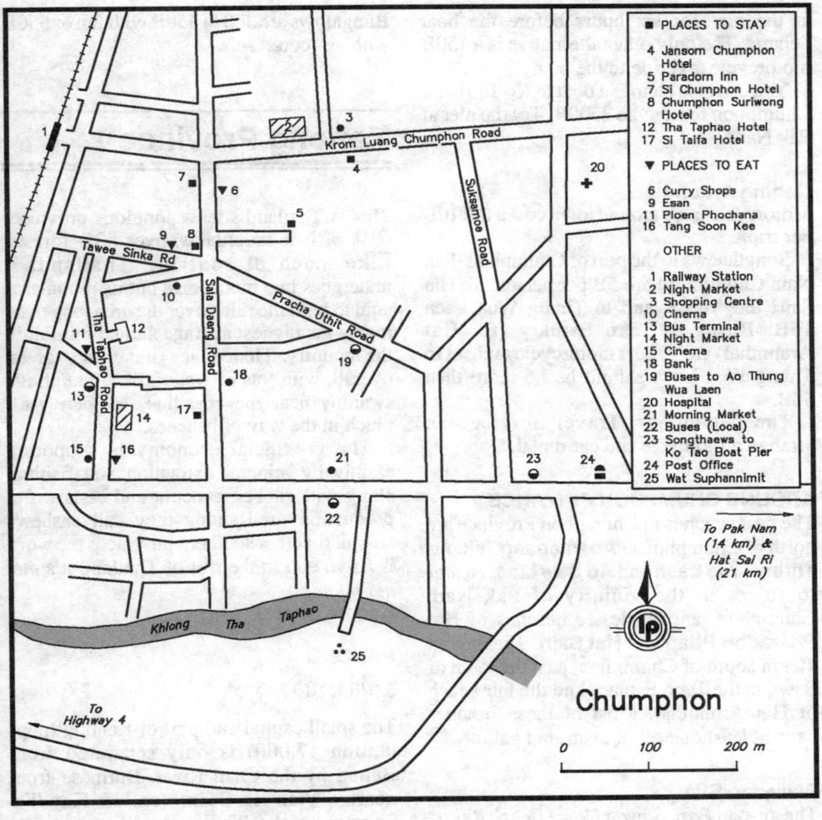

Buses run regularly between Surat Thani and Chumphon for 45B, and to/from Ranong for 27B. Bang Saphan to Chumphon is 25B, Prachuap to Chumphon 40B.

Train Rapid and express trains from Bangkok (Bangkok Noi station in Thonburi) take about 7½ hours to reach Chumphon and cost 82B 3rd class, 172B 2nd class, or 356B 1st class (express only). See the Phetburi Getting There & Away section for departure times.

Boat to Ko Tao This small island north of Ko Samui and Ko Pha-Ngan (covered in a later section) can be reached by boat from Tha Reua Ko Tao (Ko Tao boat pier), 10 km south-east of town. The regular daily boat leaves at midnight, costs 200B and takes about six hours to reach Ko Tao. From Ko Tao the boat usually leaves at 10 am and arrives at Tha Reua Ko Tao around 3.30 pm.

Songthaews run to Tha Reua Ko Tao frequently between 6 am and 6 pm for 10B. After 6 pm, Chumphon Travel Service (Sawasdee Guesthouse) has a van to the pier around 9.30 pm for 30B per person. Going by CTS van means you won't have to wait at the pier for six hours before the boat departs. The only other alternative is a 150B motorcycle taxi ride to the pier.

You can also charter a boat to Ko Tao from Chumphon for maybe 2500B. Try the pier at Pak Nam.

Getting Around

Motorcycle taxis around town cost a flat 10B per trip.

Songthaews to the port of Chumphon (Pak Nam Chumphon) are 5B per person. To Hat Sairi they're 8B and to Thung Wua Laen 15B. Buses to Tako Estuary (for Hat Arunothai) are 13B. A motorcycle taxi out to Thung Wua Laen should be no more than 50B.

The Chumphon Travel Service can arrange motorcycle and car rental.

AROUND CHUMPHON PROVINCE

The best beaches in Chumphon Province are north of Chumphon at **Ao Phanang Tak, Ao Thung Wua Laen** and **Ao Baw Mao**. Nearer to town, in the vicinity of Pak Nam Chumphon, are the lesser beaches of **Hat Pharadon Phap** and **Hat Sairi**. Then about 40 km south of Chumphon, past the town of Sawi, is the Tako Estuary and the fair beach of Hat Arunothai. Most of these beaches have at least one set of resort bungalows.

Places to Stay

The air-con *Porn Sawan Home Beach Resort* (☎ 521031) is at Pak Nam Chumphon on Pharadon Phap beach and has rooms starting at 550B. *Sai Ree Lodge* (☎ 502023; fax 502479) at nearby Hat Sari has concrete bungalows with thatched roofs for 600 to 800B with fan, 1000B with air-con.

Chumphon Cabana Resort (☎ 501990; 224-1994 in Bangkok) on Hat Thung Wua Laen (12 km north of Chumphon) has 26 well-appointed bungalows and 20 sets of diving equipment. The nightly tariff ranges from 300 to 1000B.

Chumphon Sunny Beach (☎ 511-3746 in Bangkok) is at the Tako Estuary on Hat Arunothai, about 50 km south of Chumphon. Bungalows are 300 to 450B with fan or 550B with air- con.

Ranong Province

This is Thailand's least populous province; 67% of it is mountains, over 80% forests. Like much of southern Thailand, it undergoes two monsoons, but its mountains tend to hold the rains over the area longer, so it gets the highest average annual rainfall in the country. Hence, it's incredibly green overall, with lots of waterfalls although it's swampy near the coastline, so there isn't much in the way of beaches.

The provincial economy is supported mainly by mineral extraction and fishing, along with rubber, coconut and cashew nut production. In Ranong they call cashews *ka-yuu* (in other southern provinces the word is *ka-yii* and in the rest of Thailand it's *mét má-mûang)*.

RANONG

อ.เมืองระนอง

The small capital and port of Ranong (population 17,000) is only separated from Burma by the Chan River. Burmese from nearby Victoria Point (called Kaw/Ko Sawng by the Thais, meaning 'second island', or Kaw Thaung in the Burmese pronunciation) hop across to trade in Thailand or work on fishing boats. Although there is nothing of great cultural interest in the town, the buildings are architecturally interesting since this area was originally settled by Hokkien Chinese.

Information

Ranong is about 600 km south of Bangkok, 300 km north of Phuket. Most of Ranong's banks are on Tha Muang Rd, the road to the fishing pier. There is a post office on Ruangrat Rd in the old town district.

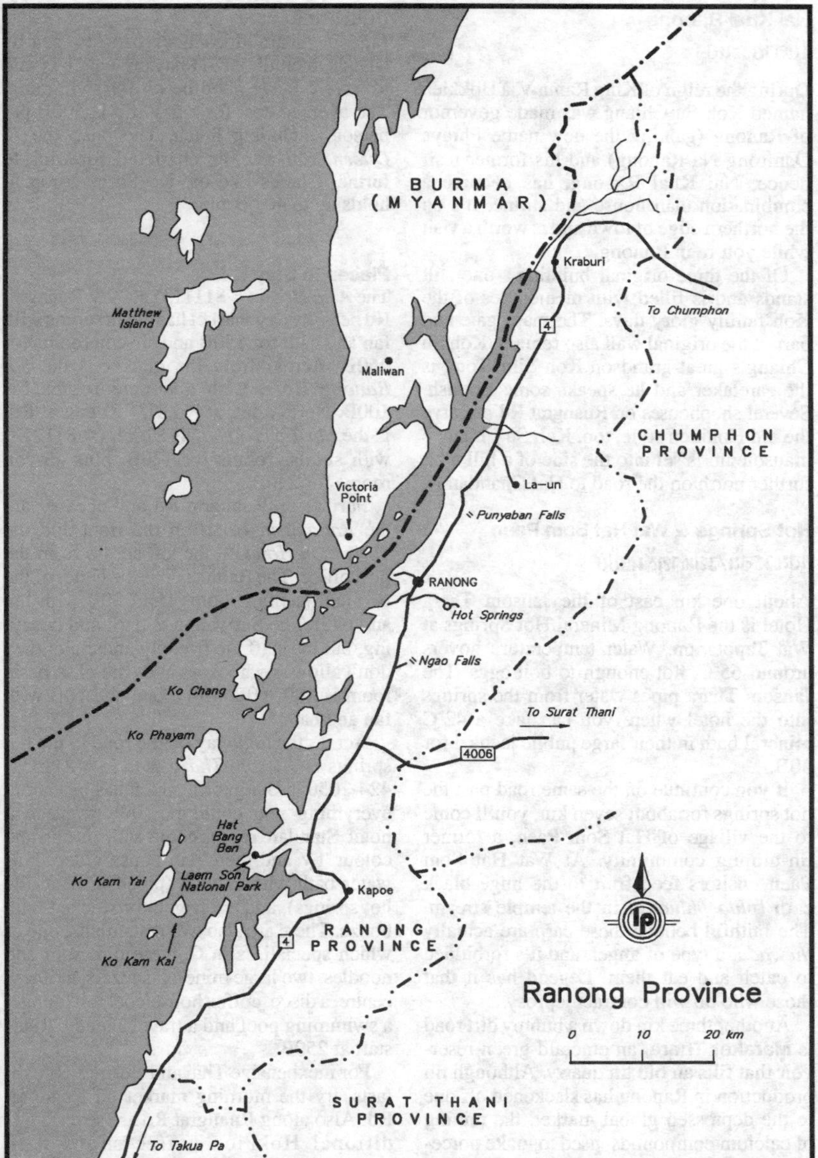
BURMA
(MYANMAR)
Matthew Island
Maliwan
Kraburi
To Chumphon
4
CHUMPHON
PROVINCE
La-un
Victoria Point
Punyaban Falls
RANONG
Hot Springs
Ngao Falls
Ko Chang
To Surat Thani
Ko Phayam
4006
Hat Bang Ben
Ko Kam Yai
Laem Son National Park
Kapoe
RANONG
PROVINCE
4
Ko Kam Kai
Ranong Province
0 10 20 km
SURAT THANI
PROVINCE
To Takua Pa

Nai Khai Ranong

ไนค่ายระนอง

During the reign of King Rama V, a Hokkien named Koh Su Chiang was made governor of Ranong (gaining the new name Phraya Damrong Na Ranong) and his former residence, Nai Khai Ranong, has become a combination clan house and shrine. It's on the northern edge of town and is worth a visit while you're in Ranong.

Of the three original buildings, one still stands and is filled with mementoes of the Koh family glory days. The main gate and part of the original wall also remain. Koh Su Chiang's great-grandson Koh Sim Kong is the caretaker and he speaks some English. Several shophouses on Ruangrat Rd preserve the old Hokkien style, too. Koh Su Chiang's mausoleum is set into the side of a hill a bit further north on the road to Hat Chandamri.

Hot Springs & Wat Hat Som Paen

บ่อน้ำร้อน/วัดหาดส้มแป้น

About one km east of the Jansom Thara Hotel is the Ranong Mineral Hot Springs at Wat Tapotaram. Water temperature hovers around 65°C, hot enough to boil eggs. The Jansom Thara pipes water from the springs into the hotel where you can take a 42°C mineral bath in their large public jacuzzi for 50B.

If you continue on the same road past the hot springs for about seven km, you'll come to the village of Hat Som Paen, a former tin-mining community. At Wat Hat Som Paen, visitors feed fruit to the huge black carp *(plaa phluang)* in the temple stream. The faithful believe these carp are actually *thewada*, a type of angel, and it's forbidden to catch and eat them. Legend has it that those who do will contract leprosy.

Another three km down a bumpy dirt road is **Marakot Thara**, an emerald-green reservoir that fills an old tin quarry. Although tin production in Ranong has slackened off due to the depressed global market, the mining of calcium compounds, used to make porcelain, is still profitable.

Boat Trips

Jansom Thara does boat trips to nearby islands, including Ko Phayam, which is said to have a fairly good beach for swimming. The average cost for a day trip is 300B per person, including lunch. The boat, the *JS Queen*, can also be chartered for trips to further islands like the Ko Surin group. It holds up to 40 people.

Places to Stay & Eat

The *Asia Hotel* (☎ 811113) at 39/9 Ruangrat Rd near the day market has clean rooms with fan and bath for 150B and air-con rooms for 250B. Across from the market is the *Sin Ranong Hotel* with adequate rooms for 100B. North a bit, at No 81/1 Ruangrat Rd, is the *Sin Tavee (Thawi) Hotel* (☎ 811213) with similar rooms for 120B, plus air-con rooms for 240B.

Further up Ruangrat Rd and cheaper are the *Rattanasin Hotel* on the right and the *Suriyanon Hotel* on the left across from the post office. The Rattanasin is the better of the two and has fair rooms from 80B with fan and bath. The Suriyanon is dark and decaying, but the staff are friendly and claim they don't allow any hookers in the hotel. A basic room is 50B, 60B with a fan, and 70B with fan and bath.

Across the highway on the road to the hot springs is *Jansom Thara Hotel* (☎ 811511; 424-2050 in Bangkok), which has just about everything you could possibly want in a hotel. Standard rooms come with air-con and colour TV and there's in-house video, hot-water bath with jacuzzi (piped in from the hot springs), and a refrigerator stocked with booze. There are also two restaurants, one of which specialises in Chinese dim sum and noodles, two large mineral jacuzzis, a fitness centre, a disco, coffee house/cocktail lounge, a swimming pool and a travel agency. Rates start at 250B.

For inexpensive Thai and Burmese breakfasts, try the morning market on Ruangrat Rd. Also along Ruangrat Rd are several traditional Hokkien coffee shops with marble-topped tables and enamelled metal teapots. One of the best restaurants in town is the *Sombun Restaurant*, across from the Rattanasin Hotel, with great seafood and standard Thai-Chinese dishes.

Getting There & Away

You can get to Ranong via Chumphon (27B), Surat Thani (60B, 80B air-con), Takua Pa (32B) and Phuket (60B). The bus terminal in Ranong is out of town near the Jansom Thara Hotel, but buses stop in town on Ruangrat Rd before proceeding on to the terminal.

Air-con minivans run between Phuket (opposite the Imperial Hotel) and the Jansom Thara Hotel in Ranong for 180B. The van leaves Ranong at around 8 am and arrives in Phuket at 12.30 am; in the opposite direction it leaves Phuket at 2 pm and arrives in Ranong at 6.30 pm. In either direction the van stops in Takua Pa for a meal (not included in the fare). They also have a minivan that runs between Surat Thani (Muang Tai Hotel) and Ranong for 150B. Departure from Ranong is at 8 am, arriving in Surat at 11.30 am. From Surat the van leaves at 12.10 pm and arrives in Ranong at 3.40 pm.

Getting Around

Songthaews ply the roads around Ranong and out to the hot springs and Hat Som Paen (No 2), Hat Chandamri (No 3) and Saphan Pla (No 2). The fare is 4 to 5B to any of these places. See the Around Ranong section for details. Motorcycle taxis (look for the orange vests) will take you anywhere in town for 5B, or for 10 to 15B to the other places.

AROUND RANONG

Hat Chandamri

หาดชาญดำริ

Touted as the nearest beach to Ranong, Hat Chandamri is really more of a mud flat. A sister hotel to the Jansom Thara in Ranong, the *Jansom Thara Resort* has similarly equipped bungalows (but no jacuzzis) for 1000B. From the dining terrace overlooking the bay, you can eat seafood and watch the sun set over Burma's Victoria Point.

The beach is 10 km north-west of Ranong, about 15B by motorcycle taxi or 4 to 5B by songthaew.

Fishermen's Pier

สะพานปลา

The provincial fishing port, Tha Thiap Reua Pramong, is eight km south-west of Ranong. It's called **Saphan Pla** (Fish Bridge) for short and is always bustling with activity as fishing boats are loaded and unloaded with great cargoes of flapping fish. About half the boats are Burmese, as the fish traders buy from anyone who lands fish here. Boats can be chartered here for day trips to nearby islands. Unless you want to see heaps of fish or charter a fishing boat, there's really no reason to go out to the port.

Isthmus of Kra

คอคอดกระ

About 60 km north of Ranong, in Kraburi district, is the Isthmus of Kra, the narrowest point in Thailand. Barely 22 km separates the Gulf of Thailand from the Indian Ocean at this point. Just off Highway 4 is a monument commemorating this geographical wonder. At one time the Thai government had plans to construct the so-called Kra Canal here, but the latest word is that the canal will run east from Satun Province through Songkhla, about 500 km further south.

Waterfalls

น้ำตก

Of the several well-known waterfalls in Ranong Province, **Ngao Falls** and **Punyaban Falls** are within walking distance of Highway 4. Ngao is 13 km south of Ranong while Punyaban is 15 km north. Just ride a songthaew in either direction and ask to be let off at the *náam tòk* (waterfall).

LAEM SON NATIONAL PARK

อุทยานแห่งชาติแหลมสน

The Laem Son (Pine Cape) Wildlife & Forest Preserve, stretches 315 sq km over the Kapoe district of Ranong and Khuraburi district in Phang-Nga. This area includes about 100 km of Andaman Sea coastline as well as over 20 islands. Much of the coast here is covered with mangrove swamps, home to various species of birds, fish, deer and monkeys, including the crab-eating macaques which are easily seen while driving along the road to the park headquarters.

The best known and most accessible beach is **Hat Bang Ben**, where the main park offices, restaurant and bungalows are. This is a long, sandy beach backed by shady casuarina trees and it is said to be safe for swimming year-round. From Hat Bang Ben you can see several islands, including the nearby Ko Kam Yai, Ko Kam Nui, Mu Ko Yipun, Ko Kang Kao and, to the north, Ko Phayam. The park staff can arrange boat trips out to any of these islands. During low tide you can walk to a nearby island just a couple of hundred metres away from Hat Bang Ben.

Ko Phayam is inhabited by around 100 Thais, who mostly make their living by fishing or growing cashews. There is a good swimming beach on Phayam and on the western side of some of the Kam islands, as well as some live coral. The beach on **Ko Kam Nui** has particularly clear water for swimming and snorkelling plus the added bonus of fresh water year-round and plenty of grassy areas for camping. One island on the other side of Ko Kam Yai which can't be seen from the beach is **Ko Kam Tok** (also called Ko Ao Khao Khwai). It's only about 200 metres from Ko Kam Yai, and, like Ko Kam Nui, has a good beach, coral, fresh water and a camping area. **Ko Kam Yai** is 14 km south-west of Hat Bang Ben.

About three km north of Hat Bang Ben, across the canal, is another beach, **Hat Laem Son**, which is almost always deserted and is 'undeveloped' according to park authorities (which means they won't guarantee your safety). The only way to get there is to hike from Bang Ben. In the opposite direction, about 50 km south of Hat Bang Ben, is **Hat Praphat**, very similar to Bang Ben with casuarina trees and a long beach. A second park office is located here and this one can be reached by road via the Phetkasem Highway.

In the canals you ford coming into the park, you may notice large wooden racks which are used for raising oysters.

Places to Stay & Eat

According to park authorities at Laem Son, the cost for accommodation in any of the park bungalows is 'by donation', which means you should be able to stay there for about 100B per person. Camping is allowed anywhere amongst the casuarina trees for 5B per person. Just outside the park entrance is the private *Komain Villa* where small bungalows are 100B per night. The food at the park cafe is rather pricey, but considering it has to be brought over 10 km of rough road, the prices are understandable. Slightly cheaper places can be found near Komain Villa.

Getting There & Away

The turn-off for Laem Son is about 58 km down the Phetkasem Highway (No 4) from Ranong, between Km 657 and 658. Any bus heading south from Ranong can drop you off here or you could hitch fairly easily as there is plenty of traffic along Highway 4. Once you're off the highway, however, you'll have to wait a bit to flag down pick-up trucks going to the village near Laem Son. If you can't get a ride all the way, it's a two-km walk from the village to the park. If you have your own vehicle, don't attempt this road when it's wet unless you have 4WD or a good off-road bike.

Phang-Nga Province

KHURABURI, TAKUA PA & THAI MUANG

คุระบุรี,ตะกั่วป่าและท้ายเมือง

These districts of Phang-Nga Province are of little interest in themselves but are departure points for other destinations. From Khuraburi you can reach the remote Surin and Similan Islands, or from Takua Pa you can head east to Khao Sok National Park and Surat Thani.

Takua Pa is also about halfway between Ranong and Phuket so buses often make rest stops here. Just off the highway is the *Extra Hotel* with rooms from 120B if you want to stop for the night.

In the district of Thai Muang is **Thai Muang Beach National Park**, where sea turtles come to lay eggs between November and February. **Thap Lamu**, about 23 km north of Thai Muang, has a pier with boats to the Similan Islands. *Poseidon Bungalows* here has huts for 60 to 200B; the owners also arrange three-day Similan trips for 1600B, including food and accommodation. To get to Poseidon, take a motorcycle taxi (20B) from the Thap Lamu highway intersection.

HAT BANG SAK & HAT KHAO LAK

หาดบางสัก/หาดเขาหลัก

South of Takua Pa, 13 and 25 km respectively, are the beaches of Bang Sak and Khao Lak. The beach at Khao Lak is pretty, but somewhat stoney. Accommodation is available at *Khao Lak Bungalows* from 60B.

Bang Sak is a long sandy beach backed by casuarina trees. Thais claim the roasted fish sold by vendors in Bang Sak is the best in Thailand. Both beaches are just a km or two off Highway 4.

SURIN ISLANDS NATIONAL PARK
อุทยานแห่งชาติหมู่เกาะสุรินทร์

A national park since 1981, the Surin Islands are famous for excellent diving and sport-fishing. The two main islands (there are five in all) of Ko Surin Neua and Ko Surin Tai (North Surin Island and South Surin Island) are about 60 km from Khuraburi. The park office and visitors' centre is on the south-west side of the north island at Ao Mae Yai where boats anchor. Admission to the park is 5B.

On the southern island is a village of sea gypsies *(chao le* or *chao náam)* and this is also where the official camp ground is located. The best diving is said to be in the channel between these two islands. The chao naam hold a large ceremony, involving ancestral worship, on Ko Surin Tai during the full moon in March. The island may be off-limits during that time, so ask at the park office.

Places to Stay
Accommodation at the park bungalows is 100B per person. At the camp ground, two-person tents are 60B a night or you can use you own (or camp without a tent) for 5B per night per person.

Getting There & Away
The mainland office of Surin Islands National Park is in Khuraburi, about 70 km south of Ranong. You can charter a boat out to the Surin Islands from Khuraburi either through the park officers (who will merely serve as brokers/interpreters) or from the Phae Pla Chumphon pier at Ban Hin Lat. The road to Ban Hin Lat runs off Highway 4 at Km 110, just north of the Khuraburi turn-off. A 15-metre boat that takes up to eight persons can be chartered for around 2000B for a round trip – it takes four to five hours each way. Ordinarily boat travel is only considered safe between December and early May, between the two monsoons.

You can also get boats to the Surin Islands from Hat Patong or Hat Rawai in Phuket. A regular charter boat from Phuket takes 10 hours, or you can get a Songserm express boat during the diving season (December to April) that takes only three hours 15 minutes. However, the fare for the express boat is 1500B per person – if you have more than a couple of people it's cheaper to go from Khuraburi. Group tours sometimes go from Khuraburi for 500B per person.

SIMILAN ISLANDS NATIONAL PARK
อุทยานแห่งชาติหมู่เกาะสิมิลัน

The Similan Islands are world-renowned among diving enthusiasts for incredible underwater sightseeing at depths ranging from two to 30 metres. As elsewhere in the Andaman Sea, the best diving months are December to May when the weather is good and the sea is at its clearest (and boat trips are much safer). West of the islands is a reef zone known among divers as 'Burmese Banks', a favourite among shark enthusiasts because of the swirling schools of sharks (mostly harmless leopard sharks) that frequent the area.

The Similans are also sometimes called Ko Kao, or Nine Islands, because there are nine of them – each has a number as well as a name. The word 'Similan' in fact comes from the Malay word 'sembilan' for 'nine'. Counting in order from the north, they are Ko Bon, Ko Ba Ngu, Ko Similan, Ko Payu, Ko Miang (which is actually two islands close together), Ko Payan, Ko Payang and Ko Hu Yong. Sometimes you see these listed in the reverse order. They're relatively small islands and uninhabited except for park officials and occasional tourist groups from Phuket. The park office is on the largest island, Ko Similan, and admission is 5B.

Boat Trips
Overnight diving excursions from Patong are fairly reasonable in cost – about 1500B a day including food, accommodation and

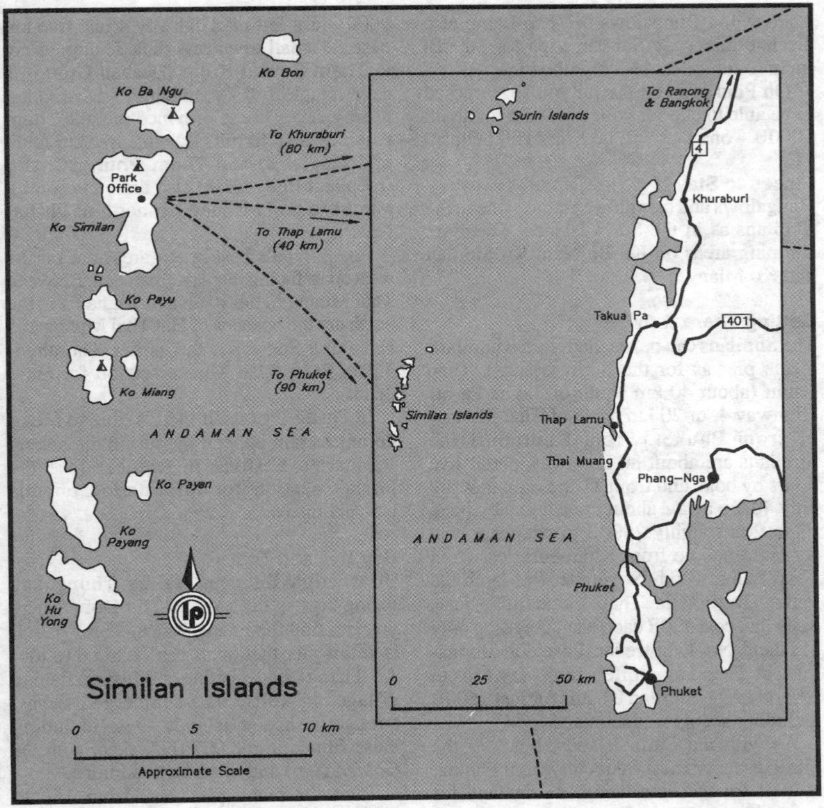

underwater guides. Equipment is extra. Non-divers can join these trips for around half the cost – snorkellers are welcome.

Seatran Travel (☎ 211809; fax 213510), 65 Phang-Nga Rd, Phuket, runs their new Jet Cat – a high-speed, Norwegian-built, catamaran jetfoil – from Phuket to the Similans between November and April. The Jet Cat leaves Phuket at 8.30 am, takes 2½ hours to reach the islands, and returns to Phuket at 6 pm. Rates are 1900B per adult, 1450B for children 2-12, and include hotel-pier-hotel transport, snorkelling equipment, lunch, soft drinks and snacks. A companion surface submarine, the *Pakarang*, offers reef-viewing excursions for non-divers.

You can also spend the night offshore aboard the company's *Seatran Queen*, which remains at sea Wednesday to Friday for most of the season (the boat keeps all waste on board until it is collected and disposed of in Phuket). Overnight rates are 1200B for a two-berth cabin, 1800B for a three-berth, 2400B four-berth or 3600B six-berth. Breakfast is complimentary.

Phuket's Songserm Travel (☎ 214272), 64/2 Rasada Center offers a less luxurious package at slightly lower rates.

Poseidon Bungalows in Thap Lamu also arrange three-day Similan trips for 1600B, including food and accommodation.

On Phuket's Hat Rawai you're supposed to be able to charter your own boat for about 5000B – one that will take up to 30 people.

Places to Stay

Bungalows and camping cost the same in the Similans as in the Surin Islands. There are camping areas on Ko Ba Ngu, Ko Similan and Ko Miang.

Getting There & Away

The Similans can be reached from Khuraburi (same pier as for the Surin Islands), Thap Lamu (about 40 km south of Takua Pa off Highway 4, or 20 km north of Thai Muang) or from Phuket. From Khuraburi the Similans are about 80 km away, about five hours by boat, and from Thap Lamu they are only 40 km away, about three hours by boat. Figure on roughly 2500B to charter a boat for eight people from Khuraburi, less from Thap Lamu. From November to March the Parks Division in Thap Lamu runs boats daily that cost 500B each way; they stop only at Island No 4, however. Poseidon Bungalows in Thap Lamu offers three-day trips to several of the Similan Islands for just 1600B including accommodation and food.

As with the Surin Islands, boats to the Similans leave most frequently from Phuket, at least for the time being. As demand for boats from Khuraburi and Takua Pa increases, a regularly scheduled boat service from these points is bound to start.

AO PHANG-NGA & PHANG-NGA

อ่าวพังงา/อ.เมืองพังงา

Over 95 km from Phuket, the area around Ao Phang-Nga is quite scenic – lots of limestone cliffs, odd rock formations, islands that rise out of the sea like inverted mountains, not to mention caves and quaint fishing villages. Phang-Nga would make a good motorcycle trip from Phuket, or, if you have time, you could spend a few days there.

On the way to Phang-Nga (population 9000), turn left off Highway 4 just five km past the small town of Takua Thung, to get to **Tham Suwan Kuha** (Heaven Grotto), a cave temple full of Buddha images. Other nearby caves in the province include **Tham Rusisawan** (Hermit Heaven; three km south of Phang-Nga) and **Tham Phung Chang** (Elephant Belly Cave; also three km south). **Manohra Falls** is nine km north of Phang-Nga.

Phang-Nga's best beach areas are on the west coast facing the Andaman Sea. Between Thai Muang in the south and Takua Pa in the north are the beaches of Hat Thai Muang and Hat Bang Sak – see the earlier Khuraburi, Takua Pa & Thai Muang section for more details.

In Phang-Nga itself there's little to see or do unless you happen by during the annual Vegetarian Festival in October (see the Phuket section for information on this unusual festival).

Bay & Island Tours

Boat Trips Between Takua Thung and Phang-Nga is the road to **Tha Don**, where you can find the Phang-Nga customs pier. It is at this pier that boats can be hired to tour Ao Phang-Nga, visiting a Muslim fishing village on stilts, half-submerged caves, strangely shaped islands (yes, including those filmed in the 007 flick, *Man with the Golden Gun)* and other local oddities.

Tours from the pier vary from 150 to 400B; from Phuket they cost at least 300B per person. A postman from Ko Panyi (one of Ao Phang-Nga's islands) named Sayan has been doing overnight tours of Ao Phang-Nga for several years now which continue to receive good reviews from travellers. The tour costs 250B per person and includes a boat tour of **Tham Lawt** (a large water cave), **Ko Phing Kan** (Leaning Island), **Ko Khao Tapu** (Nail Mountain Island), **Ko Maju**, **Tham Naga**, a former mangrove charcoal factory and **Ko Panyi**, plus dinner, breakfast and accommodation in a Muslim fishing village on Ko Panyi. Sayan also leads early morning trips for 150B that include a seafood lunch and return in the afternoon. He can be contacted at the Thawisuk Hotel (and only the Thawisuk Hotel – beware of impostors at Tha Don) in Phang-Nga. You can also take a ferry to Ko Panyi on your own for 20B.

Whatever you do, try to avoid touring the bay in the middle of the day (10 am to 4 pm) when hundreds of package tourists crowd the islands. On Ko Panyi always ask the price before eating as the restaurants often overcharge.

Canoe Tours A new Phuket outfit called Sea Canoeing (☎ 076-212172) offers inflatable canoe excursions of the bay. The canoes are able to enter semi-submerged caves inaccessible by the long-tail boats. Reviews so far have been good. Other information on the tours wasn't available as we went to press but it might be worth checking out.

Places to Stay

Phang-Nga has several small hotels. The *Thawisuk* is right in the middle of town, a bright blue building with the English sign 'Hotel'. Fairly clean, quiet rooms upstairs go for 80B, with fan, bath, towel, soap and boiled water – the best value in Phang-Nga. On the rooftop of Thawisuk you can sit and have a beer while watching the sun set over Phang-Nga's rooftops and the limestone cliffs surrounding the town.

The *Lak Muang* (☎ 411125/1288), on Phetkasem Rd, just outside town, towards Krabi, has rooms from 100B and a restaurant. The *Rak Phang-Nga*, across the street from Thawisuk toward Phuket, is 80B but somewhat dirty and noisy. Opposite the Rak Phang-Nga is the noisy *Ratanapong Hotel*, overpriced at 120 to 350B. Further down the road towards Phuket is the *Muang Thong*, with clean, quiet singles/doubles for 100/150B with fan, 200 to 300B with air-con. Outside town even further towards Phuket is *Lak Muang II* with all air-con rooms from 230B.

Tha Don The *Phang-Nga Bay Resort Hotel* (☎ 411067/70) near the customs pier out of town cost 726 to 847B. Facilities include a swimming pool and a decent restaurant. All rooms come with TV, telephone and fridge.

Places to Eat

Duang Restaurant next to Bangkok Bank on the main road has a bilingual menu and a good selection of Thai and Chinese dishes, including southern-Thai specialities.

Several food stalls on the main street of Phang-Nga sell cheap and delicious khanõm jiin with chicken curry, náam yaa (spicy ground-fish curry) or náam phrík (sweet and spicy peanut sauce). One vendor in front of the market (opposite Bangkok Bank) serves khanõm jiin with an amazing 12 varieties of free vegetable accompaniments. Roti kaeng (flatbread and curry) is available in the morning market from around 5 am to 10 am. There are also the usual Chinese khâo man kài places around town.

Getting There & Away

Buses for Phang-Nga leave from the Phuket bus terminal on Phang-Nga Rd, near the Thepkasatri Rd intersection, hourly between 6.20 am and 6 pm. The trip to Phang-Nga takes 1¾ hours and the one-way fare is 22B. Alternatively you can rent a motorcycle from Phuket.

From Krabi a bus is 25B and takes 1½ hours. Songthaews between Phang-Nga and Tha Don (the Phang-Nga customs pier) are 7B.

Getting Around

Most of the town is easily accessible on foot. The Fuji photo shop on the main road rents motorcycles.

Phuket Province

Exactly 885 km from Bangkok, the 'Pearl of the South', as the tourist industry has dubbed it, Phuket (pronounced 'Poo-get') is Thailand's largest island (810 sq km) and a province in itself. While tourism and tin are Phuket's major moneymakers, the island is still big enough to accommodate escapists of

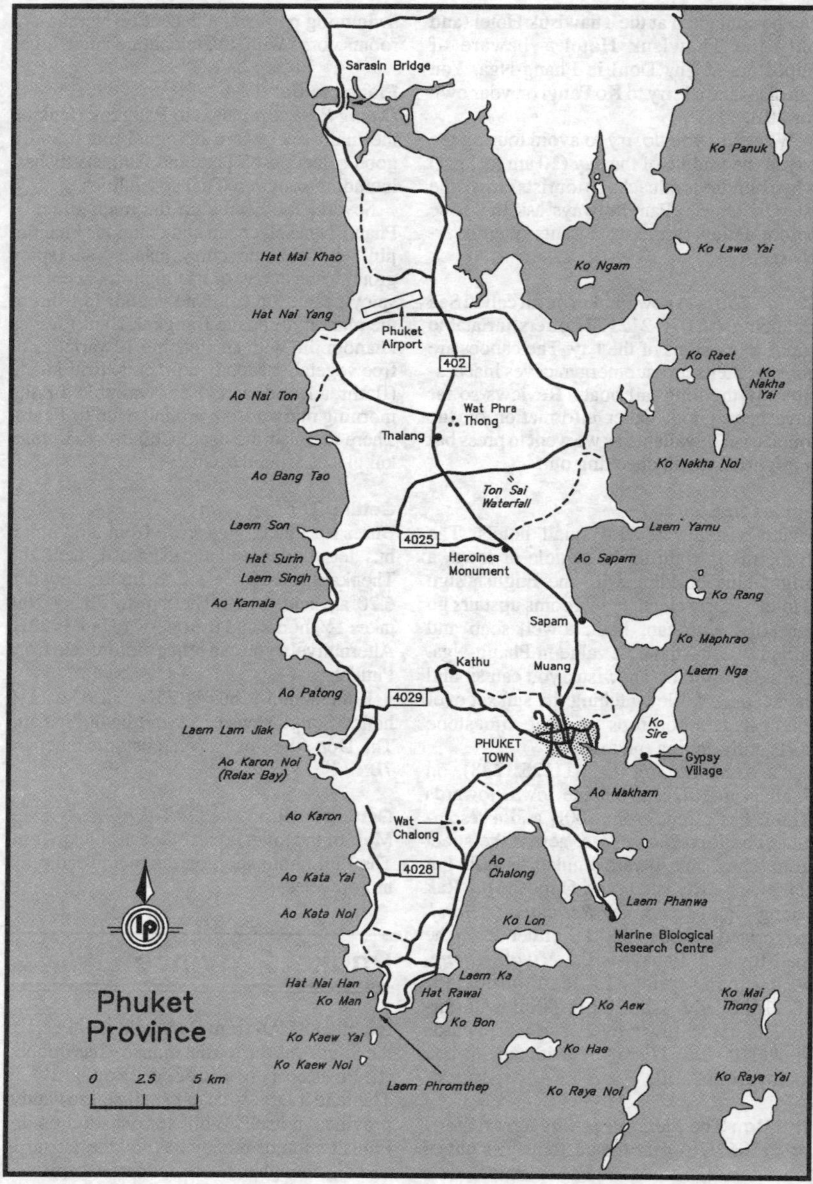
Sarasin Bridge
Ko Panuk
Ko Lawa Yai
Ko Ngam
Hat Mai Khao
Hat Nai Yang
Phuket Airport
402
Ko Raet
Ko Nakha Yai
Ao Nai Ton
Wat Phra Thong
Thalang
Ko Nakha Noi
Ao Bang Tao
Ton Sai Waterfall
Laem Son
Laem Yamu
4025
Hat Surin
Heroines Monument
Ao Sapam
Laem Singh
Ko Rang
Ao Kamala
Sapam
Ko Maphrao
Kathu
Muang
Laem Nga
Ao Patong
4029
Ko Sire
Laem Lam Jiak
PHUKET TOWN
Gypsy Village
Ao Karon Noi (Relax Bay)
Ao Makham
Ao Karon
Wat Chalong
Ao Chalong
4028
Ao Kata Yai
Laem Phanwa
Ao Kata Noi
Ko Lon
Marine Biological Research Centre
Laem Ka
Hat Nai Han
Hat Rawai
Ko Man
Ko Aew
Ko Mai Thong
Ko Bon
Phuket Province
Ko Kaew Yai
Ko Hae
Ko Kaew Noi
0 2.5 5 km
Laem Phromthep
Ko Raya Noi
Ko Raya Yai

nearly all budget levels. Formerly called Ko Thalang ('Phuket' and 'Thalang' are both Malay names), Phuket has a culture all of its own, combining Chinese and Portuguese influences, like Songkhla, with that of the Chao Le, the indigenous ocean-going people. About 35% of the island's population are Thai Muslims.

In the Andaman Sea off southern Thailand's west coast, the island's terrain is incredibly varied, with rocky beaches, long, broad, sandy beaches, limestone cliffs, forested hills and tropical vegetation of all kinds. Great seafood is available all over the island and several offshore islands are known for good snorkelling and scuba-diving.

Comparisons with Ko Samui, off the east coast, as well as with other Thai islands, are inevitable of course. All in all, there is more to do in Phuket, but that means more to spend your money on, too. There are more tourists in Phuket but they are concentrated at certain beaches – Patong and Kata, for example. Beaches like Nai Han and Karon are relatively quiet, in spite of major tourist development at both. Ko Samui is gradually starting to develop along Phuket lines but the feel of the two islands is different – Samui is much further out in the sea and as such gives one more a feeling of adventure than Phuket, which is connected to the mainland by a bridge.

Development on Phuket has been influenced by the fact that Phuket is Thailand's richest province (on a per capita basis), with plenty of money available for investment. The turning point was probably reached when a Club Méditerranée was established at Hat Kata, followed by the construction of the more lavish Phuket Yacht Club on Nai Han and Le Meridien on Karon Noi (Relax Bay). This marked an end to the era of cheap bungalows which started in the early '70s and lasted a decade. Now the cheapies have just about all been bought out. However, Phuket still has a few secluded and undeveloped beaches, at least for the time being.

The geography of Phuket is more varied than any other island in Thailand. One reason for this is its size, which has allowed micro-climates to develop in different areas of the island. Try them all if you have time. Don't ignore the interior of the island, which offers rice paddies, plantations of rubber, cashew nut, cacao, pineapple and coconut, as well as Phuket's last bit of island rainforest.

PHUKET
อ.เมืองภูเก็ต

At the south-eastern end of the island is Phuket (population 50,000).

Information

The TAT office (☎ 212213, 211036) on Phuket Rd has a list of the standard songthaew charges out to the various beaches and also the recommended charter costs for a complete vehicle.

The tourist police can be reached on 212046 or 212213.

The post office is on Montri Rd; it's open Monday to Friday from 8.30 am to 4.30 pm, Saturday and Sunday 9 am to noon. The overseas telephone office is around the corner on Phang-Nga Rd and is open 24 hours.

The Mission Hospital (☎ 212386) on Thepkasatri Rd is the best medical centre on the island.

Things to See & Do

Besides wandering down the narrow streets lined with historic Sino-Portuguese architecture, you can visit some interesting markets (good places to buy baggy Chinese pants and sarongs), many decent restaurants and several cinemas.

Walk up **Khao Rang**, sometimes called Phuket Hill, north-west of town, for a nice view of the city, jungle and sea.

The island of **Ko Sire**, four km east of Phuket and separated from the bigger island by a canal, has a sea-gypsy village and a hill-top reclining Buddha.

In the grounds of the Cape Panwa Sheraton Resort on Laem Phanwa is **Phanwa House**, a classic Sino-Portuguese mansion that's open to the public. The mansion has a

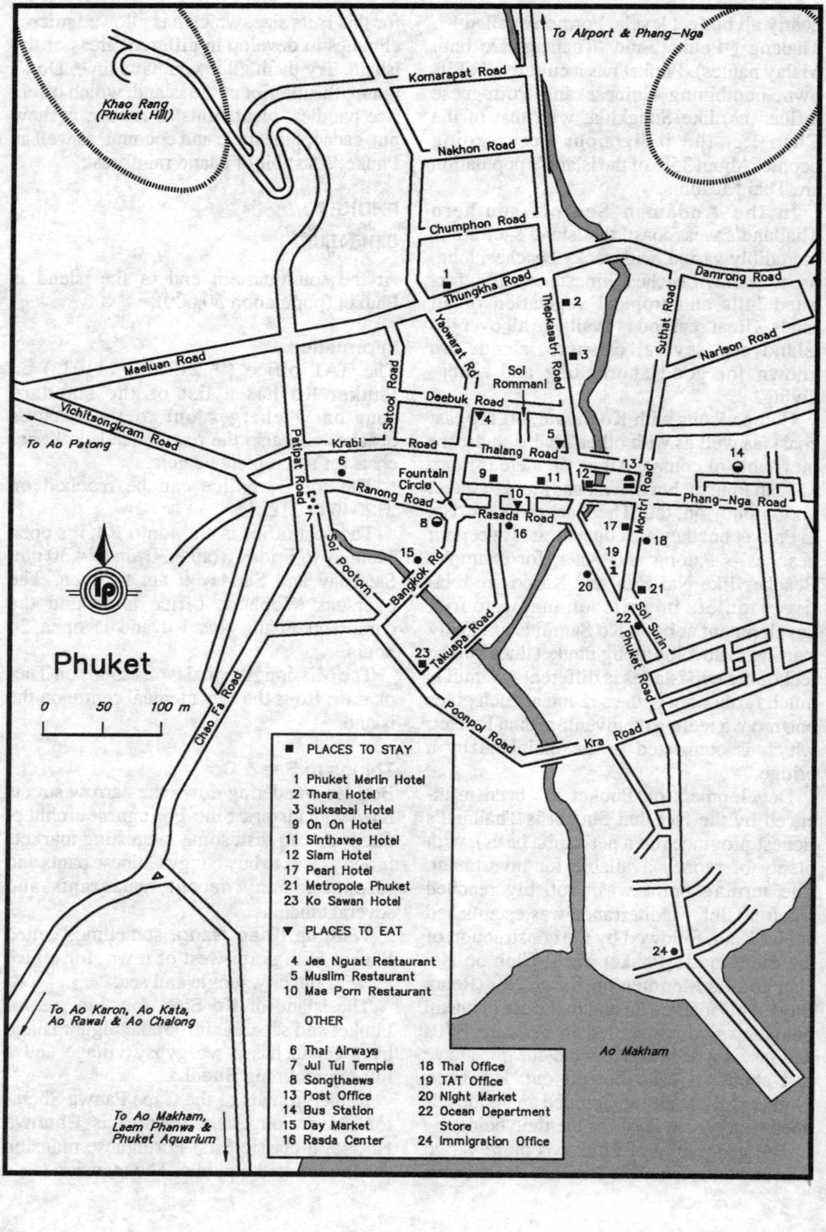
To Airport & Phang-Nga
Komarapat Road
Khao Rang (Phuket Hill)
Nakhon Road
Chumphon Road
Damrong Road
Thungkha Road
Yaowarat Rd
Thepkasatri Road
Suthat Road
Narison Road
Maeluan Road
Satool Road
Soi Rommani
Deebuk Road
Vichitsongkram Road
To Ao Patong
Krabi Road
Thalang Road
Patipat Road
Fountain Circle
Ranong Road
Phang-Nga Road
Rasada Road
Montri Road
Soi Pootorn
Bangkok Rd
Takuapa Road
Soi Surin
Phuket Road
Phuket
0 50 100 m
Chao Fa Road
Poonpol Road
Kra Road
Ao Makham
To Ao Karon, Ao Kata, Ao Rawai & Ao Chalong
To Ao Makham, Laem Phanwa & Phuket Aquarium
PLACES TO STAY
1 Phuket Merlin Hotel
2 Thara Hotel
3 Suksabai Hotel
9 On On Hotel
11 Sinthavee Hotel
12 Siam Hotel
17 Pearl Hotel
21 Metropole Phuket
23 Ko Sawan Hotel
PLACES TO EAT
4 Jee Nguat Restaurant
5 Muslim Restaurant
10 Mae Porn Restaurant
OTHER
6 Thai Airways
7 Jui Tui Temple
8 Songthaews
13 Post Office
14 Bus Station
15 Day Market
16 Rasda Center
18 Thai Office
19 TAT Office
20 Night Market
22 Ocean Department Store
24 Immigration Office

library and a collection of antique furniture and art; high tea is served daily on the verandah.

Phuket's **Shooting Range** (☎ 381667) on the road between Ao Chalong and Hat Kata is open to the public for target practice. Guns on hand include .45 automatic pistols, M-16s and AK-47s; you're charged by the rounds of ammunition you use, eg 10 .22 bullets cost 350B, 50 .45 bullets go for 1750B. Ear protectors are available. If blasting away at human-shaped paper targets doesn't excite you, the same owners offer horseback riding at the nearby Phuket Riding Club.

Twenty km north of town is the **Khao Phra Taew National Park**. To get there, take Thepkasatri Rd to the district of Thalang, and turn right at the intersection for Ton Sai Waterfall three km down the road. There are some nice jungle hikes in this park, which features the last of the island's virgin rainforest. The waterfall is best in the rainy season, between June and November.

Also in Thalang district, just north of the crossroads near Thalang village, is **Wat Phra Thong**, Phuket's 'Temple of the Gold Buddha'. The image is half buried – those who have tried to excavate it have met with unfortunate consequences. Parts of the movie *Good Morning Vietnam* were filmed in Thalang.

Diving Phuket is ringed by good dive sites. Among the more popular are the small islands to the south-east for coral, and Shark Point (a habitat for harmless leopard sharks) at the southern tip of the island.

The centre for most Phuket diving operations is Patong Beach. In Phuket, there are four dive shops that rent equipment and lead dives: Andaman Sea Sports (☎ 211752); Phuket Aquatic Safaris (☎ 216562); PFC Diving Centre (☎ 215527); and Phuket Divers (☎ 215738).

Vegetarian Festival

Phuket's most important festival is the Vegetarian Festival, which takes place during the first nine days of the ninth lunar month of the Chinese calendar. This is usually late September or October. Basically, the festival celebrates the beginning of the month of 'Taoist Lent', when devout Chinese abstain from eating all meat and meat products. In Phuket, the festival activities are centred around five Chinese temples, with the Jui Tui temple on Ranong Rd the most important, followed by Bang Niaw and Sui Boon Tong

Participants in the Vegetarian Festival

temples. Events are also celebrated at temples in the nearby towns of Kathu (where the festival originated) and Ban Tha Reua.

The TAT office in Phuket prints a helpful schedule of events for the Vegetarian Festival each year. If you plan to attend the street processions, consider bringing earplugs to make the noise of the firecrackers more tolerable. The festival also takes place in Trang and other southern-Thai towns.

Besides abstention from meat, the Vegetarian Festival involves various processions, temple offerings and cultural performances and culminates with incredible acts of self-mortification – walking on hot coals, climbing knife-blade ladders, piercing the skin with sharp objects and so on. Shopowners along Phuket's downtown streets set up altars in front of their shopfronts offering nine tiny cups of tea, incense, fruit, candles and flowers to the nine Emperor Gods invoked by the festival. Those participating as mediums bring the nine deities to earth for the festival by entering into a trance state and piercing their cheeks with all manner of objects – sharpened tree branches (with leaves still attached!), spears, trombones, daggers; some even eviscerate their tongues with saw or axe blades. During street procession these mediums stop at the shopfront altars, where they pick up the offered fruit and either add it to the objects piercing their cheeks or pass it on to bystanders as a blessing. They also drink one of the nine cups of tea and grab some flowers to stick in their waistbands. The shopowners and their family stand by with their hands together in a *wai* gesture, out of respect for the mediums and the deities by whom they are temporarily possessed.

The entire atmosphere is one of religious frenzy, with deafening firecrackers, ritual dancing, bloody shirt fronts and so on. Oddly enough, there is no record of this kind of activity associated with Taoist Lent in China. Some historians assume that the Chinese here were somehow influenced by the Hindu festival of Thaipusam in nearby Malaysia, which features similar acts of self-mortification. The local Chinese claim, however, that the festival was started by a theatre troupe from China who stopped off in nearby Kathu around 150 years ago. The story goes that the troupe was struck seriously ill and that they decided the illness had befallen them because they had failed to propitiate the nine 'Emperor Gods' of Taoism. The nine-day penance they performed included self-piercing, meditation and a strict vegetarian diet.

The TAT office in Phuket prints a helpful schedule of events for the Vegetarian Festival each year. If you plan to attend the street processions, consider bringing earplugs to make the noise of the firecrackers more tolerable. The festival also takes place in Trang and other towns in southern Thailand.

Places to Stay – bottom end

Near the centre of town, and close to the songthaew terminal for most outlying beaches, is the *On On Hotel* at 19 Phang-Nga Rd. This hotel's old Sino-Portuguese architecture (established 1929) gives it real character – rates range from 80 to 150B with fan, 300B with air-con. The *Pengman* nearby at 69 Phang-Nga Rd, above a Chinese restaurant, costs 80 to 100B with fan and bath, but is not too special. Another rock-bottom place is the Chinese *Laem Thong* on funky Soi Rommani, where rooms are 50 to 80B.

The *Ko Sawan Hotel*, 19/8 Poonpol Rd, out towards the waterfront in a red-light district, is 80B and over but deals mostly in short-time trade. The *Thara Hotel* on Thepkasatri Rd is 80B with fan and bath; the nearby *Suksabai Hotel* (☎ 212287) is a bit better at 100 to 120B for similar but cleaner rooms. The *Siam Hotel*, 13-15 Phuket Rd has clean rooms with fan and bath for 150B.

A notch higher are *Sukchai*, 17/1 Komarapat Rd, at 100 to 120B with fan and bath, 160B with air-con, and *Taweekit* at 7/3 Chao Fa Rd which costs about the same. The *Thawon Hotel* (☎ 211333) at 74 Rasada Rd has also been recommended – it has good rooms for 180B with fan and bath (380B with air-con) and has a swimming pool. Similar is the *Montri* (☎ 212936), 12/6 Montri Rd, without a swimming pool; rooms are 150B.

The newly established *Wasana Guest House* (☎ 211754, 213385), at 159 Ranong Rd (next to the fresh market) has clean rooms for 150B with fan and bath or 250B with air-con.

Places to Stay – middle

The clean and friendly *Imperial Hotel 1* (☎ 212311), at 51 Phuket Rd, has good rooms for 250B with fan, 360B with air-con.

In the centre of town, at 81 Phang-Nga Rd,

is the entirely renovated *Sinthavee Hotel* (☎ 212153) with comfortable air-con rooms for 400/500B a single/double or 850/950B for deluxe rooms. All rooms come with carpeting, hot-water bath and refrigerators (add TV/video for deluxe); other facilities include a 24-hour coffee shop, business centre, spa and disco.

Places to Stay – top end

The *Pearl Hotel* (☎ 211044) at 42 Montri Rd has 221 rooms from 800B, a rooftop restaurant, swimming pool and so on. The *Phuket Merlin* (☎ 211618) at 158/1 Yaowarat Rd has 185 rooms from 860B; again there's a swimming pool.

The *Phuket Garden Hotel* (☎ 216900/8) on Bangkok Rd costs from 900B with a pool and all the usual facilities.

Topping off all the top-enders is the plush *Metropole Phuket* (☎ 215050; fax 215990) on Montri Rd. 'Superior' singles/doubles cost 1936/2178B; 2178/2420B for deluxe. Facilities include two Chinese restaurants, a coffee shop, three bars, swimming pool, fitness centre, business centre and airport shuttle service.

Places to Eat

If there's one thing the town of Phuket is known for, it's good food. One long-running local institution is *Raan Jee Nguat*, a Phuket-style restaurant run by Hokkien Chinese, across the street from the now defunct Siam Cinema on the corner of historic Yaowarat and Deebuk Rds. Jee Nguat serves Phuket's most famous dish – delicious khanõm jiin náam yaa phukèt – Chinese noodles in a pureed fish and curry sauce, Phuket-style, with fresh cucumbers, long green beans and other fresh vegetables on the side – for under 10B. Also good are khài plaa mòk, a Phuket version of hàw mòk (eggs, fish and curry paste steamed in banana leaves) and the kari mai fan, similar to Malaysian laksa, but using rice noodles. The curries are highly esteemed as well. This is one of many Phuket restaurants to have won the Chuan Chim (Invitation to Taste), a designation by a panel of Thai connoisseurs sponsored by Shell Oil Thailand (similar to the Michelin rating in France). Look for the yellow Shell symbol over the doorway. Don't tarry, though; they open early in the morning but close down around 2 pm.

Very popular with Thais and farangs alike and deservedly so, is the *Mae Porn*, a restaurant at the corner of Phang-Nga Rd and Soi Pradit, close to the On On and Sinthavee Hotels. There's an air-con room as well as outdoor tables and they sell curries, seafood, fruit shakes, you name it and Mae Porn has it, all at very reasonable prices. Another popular spot in town is *Kanda Bakery* on Rasada Rd. It's open early in the morning with fresh-baked whole-wheat bread, baguettes, croissants and real brewed coffee.

Kaw Yam (Khao Yam), on Thungkha Rd in front of the Phuket Merlin, has a middle-class, indoor-outdoor atmosphere enjoyed by local office workers for breakfast and lunch. The kitchen serves very well-prepared khâo yam, the southern-Thai rice salad, as well as khanõm jiin and many other Phuket specialities. Just as good for khanõm jiin but cheaper is *Khwan Khanom Jiin* (no English sign) next door.

Another good local discovery is the simple Muslim restaurant at the corner Thepkasatri and Thalang Rds – look for the star and crescent. This friendly family-run place serves delicious and inexpensive mátsaman kài (chicken-potato curry), roti kaeng (flatbread and curry – in the morning only) and khâo mòk kài (chicken briyani – usually gone by 1 pm).

Fried rice and pastry fans shouldn't miss *Kaew Jai* (no English sign), at 151 Phang-Nga between Phuket and Montri Rds. More basic than Kanda Bakery, this is the Thai idea of pastry heaven – especially the custard cake, cashew cake and creme caramel – even if the service is a bit surly. Among the fried rice dishes on hand are khâo phàt náam phrík phão (fried rice with roasted chilli paste), khâo phàt khreûang kaeng (rice fried in curry paste) and khâo phàt bai kà-phrao (with holy basil), each with a choice of chicken, pork, crab, shrimp or squid.

The 24-hour coffee shop at the *Sinthavee*

Hotel has cheap lunch specials and late night khâo tôm service. For a splurge, the dim sum service (11 am to 2 pm) at the Hotel Metropole's *Fortuna Pavilion* is an excellent choice.

The newish tourist-oriented Rasda Center, a shopping complex around the Phuket Department Store off Rasada Rd, has several small, up-market eating places like *Le Glacier* (ice cream), *Krua Thai* (fancy Thai cuisine), *Rasada Cafe* and *Le Cafe* (good coffees).

Finally, there's the ever-dependable and ever-tasty night market on Phuket Rd, which is fast and cheap. *Nai Yao*, two doors south of the night market and open only at night, has an excellent, inexpensive seafood menu (bilingual), cold beer and tables on the sidewalk. The house speciality is the unique and highly recommended tôm yam haeng (dry tôm yam) which can be ordered with chicken, shrimp or squid.

Khao Rang (Phuket Hill) *Thungkha Kafae* is an outdoor restaurant at the top of the hill with a very pleasant atmosphere and good food. Try the tôm khàa kài (chicken coconut soup) or khài jiaw hãwy naang rom (oyster omelette). It's open from 11 am to 11 pm daily.

Ao Chalong Just past Wat Chalong (on the left past the five-road intersection, *hâa yâek* Wat Chalong) is *Kan Aeng*, a good fresh seafood place. You order by weight, choosing from squid, oysters, cockles, crab, mussels and several kinds of fish, and then specify the method of cooking, whether grilled (phão), steamed (nêung), fried (thâwt), parboiled (luak – for squid), or in soup (tôm yam). Large grilled crabs are about 50 to 60B apiece. It used to be out on a pier over the bay itself, but is now housed in a new enclosed restaurant, not as cheap as the old location.

Entertainment

The Pearl cinema on the corner of Ranong and Montri Rds near the Pearl Hotel has a sound room where the original soundtracks for English-language films are played. The Alliance Française (☎ 212429), at 3 Soi 1, Pattana Rd, shows French films weekly.

The major hotels have discos and/or karaoke clubs. The Timber Hut, on the eastern side of Yaowarat Rd just south of Thungkha Rd, is a well-run pub with an attractive woodsy decor, lots of Phuket and Thai food and live music after 9 pm. This is perhaps the only non-hotel bar in town with cocktails (60B).

Municipal law allows only one modern massage parlour to operate – in the Pearl Hotel.

Phuket has four traditional *ram wong* (circle dance) clubs along Montri and Thalang Rds. Ram wong is a standard Thai couples' dance, and like most couples' dancing around the world, it's really a sort of courtship ritual. At these clubs, however, it's more like Chinese tea-dancing, where men pay hostesses to dance with them. The clientele is mostly older Thais.

Getting There & Away

Air THAI has several daily flights from Bangkok for 2000B each way. The flight takes just over an hour, except for departures which have a half-hour stopover in Surat Thani.

There are also regular flights to and from Hat Yai (780B), Trang (435B), Nakhon Si Thammarat (340B) and Surat Thani (475B).

THAI flies to Penang (Malaysia) daily; the trip takes an hour and costs 1410B. Other international destinations from Phuket include Langkawi, Kuala Lumpur, Singapore, Hong Kong, Taipei and Sydney.

THAI has two offices: one at 78 Ranong Rd (☎ 211195) and the other at 41/33 Montri Rd (☎ 212880).

Bus From Bangkok, one air-con bus leaves the southern bus terminal at 8 am, and then nine buses leave at 15-minute intervals between 6.30 and 8.30 pm. The trip takes 13 to 14 hours and the one-way fare is 299B. Ordinary buses leave seven times a day from 7.30 am until 10.30 pm for 166B. Advance bookings are not possible.

Several private tour buses run from Bangkok to Phuket regularly with fares of 299B one-way or 540B return. Most have one bus a day which leaves at 6 or 7 pm. Try Thai Transport on Ratchadamnoen Klang near the Benz showroom. The ride along the west coast between Ranong and Phuket can be hair-raising if you are awake, so it is fortunate that this part of the trip takes place during the wee hours of the morning.

From Phuket, most tour buses to Bangkok leave at 3 pm. Several agencies have their offices on Ratsada and Phang-Nga Rds downtown.

Fares and trip durations for local bus trips to and from Phuket include:

destination	fare	hours
Surat Thani	61B	6
Trang	62B	6
Hat Yai	91B	8
(air-con)	154B	6
Nakhon Si Thammarat	75B	8
Krabi	38B	4½
Phang-Nga	22B	2½
Takua Pa	31B	3

Taxi & Minivan There are also share taxis between Phuket and other provincial capitals in the south; taxi fares are generally double the fare of an ordinary bus (Krabi 120B, Surat 150B, Trang 120B). The taxi stand for Nakhon Si Thammarat, Surat Thani, Krabi, Trang and Hat Yai is on Phang-Nga Rd, near the Pearl Cinema.

Some companies run air-con minivans *(rót tuu)* with through tickets to Ko Samui from Phuket – part of a minivan circuit that goes Phuket, Surat, Krabi and Ranong. As in share taxis, fares are about double the public bus fares. You can also get vans to Hat Yai (250B), Krabi (150B), Penang (550B), Kuala Lumpur (650B) and Singapore (700B). Vans can be booked at the same intersection as the share taxis.

Boat You can often travel by yacht between Phuket and Penang. Ask around at Patong Beach to see what's available. The *Szygie* usually sails from Phuket to Penang periodically between 1 December and 30 April. Contact the operators at Restaurant Number Four, Hat Patong, Phuket or J Travel, Chulia St, Georgetown, Penang. They sail Phuket, Ko Phi Phi, Langkawi and Penang.

You can also find yachts going further afield, particularly to Sri Lanka. December and early January is the best month to look for them. The crossing takes about 10 to 15 days.

Getting Around

To/From the Airport THAI operates a shuttle bus between the town and airport (11 km from town) for 50B per person. There's a similar service to Patong, Kata or Karon beaches for 80B.

You can also take one of the rather infrequent songthaews for 15B. By taxi the trip costs 120B.

Songthaew Songthaews run regularly from Phuket to the various Phuket beaches for 10 to 20B – see the following Phuket Beaches section for details. Beware of tales about the tourist office being five km away, or that the only way to reach the beaches is by taxi, or even that you'll need a taxi to get from the bus station to the town centre.

Songthaews or tuk-tuks around town cost a standard 7B. Songthaews to the beaches depart from close to the town centre and the tourist office. Officially, songthaews stop running at 5 pm so after that time you must charter your own songthaew to the beaches.

Motorcycle Motorcycle taxis around town are 10B. You can hire motorcycles (usually 80 to 125cc Japanese bikes) from various places at the beaches or in Phuket. Costs are in the 150 to 250B per day range. Take care when riding a bike – if you have an accident you're unlikely to find that medical attention is as good as you get back home. People who ride around in shorts and T-shirt and a pair of thongs are asking for trouble. A minor spill whilst wearing reasonable clothes would leave you bruised and shaken, but for somebody clad in shorts it could result in enough skin loss to end their travels right there.

Bigger bikes (over 150cc) can be rented at a couple of shops at Patong and Karon.

Car Rental Several agencies in town rent Suzuki jeeps for 800B per day, including insurance. If you rent for a week or more you can get the price down to 700B per day. Avis charges a bit more (around 1000B a day) but has outlets around the island at Le Meridien, Holiday Inn, Phuket Acadia, Dusit Laguna, Phuket Cabana, Club Med, Phuket Island Resort and the airport.

PHUKET BEACHES

Phuket beach accommodation has come a long way since 1977 when I first stayed at Kata and Nai Han in thatched-roof huts for 10B a night – in fact that was the going rate anywhere on the island. Until the late '80s you could still find simple beach places for around 50B but nowadays 80 or 100B is rock-bottom. Any remaining accommodation costing under 300B will probably be upgraded within the next couple of years to a minimum of 500B as Phuket completes the final stages of moving from rustic beach hideaway to full-fledged international resort.

Patong

ป่าตอง

Directly west of Phuket, Patong is a large curved beach around Ao Patong. In the last few years, Hat Patong has been rapidly turning into another Pattaya in all respects. It is now a strip of hotels, up-market bungalows, German restaurants, expensive seafood places, beer bars, nightclubs and coffee houses. Ironically, though this began as Phuket's most expensive beach the prices are stabilising as the local accommodation market has become saturated with over 70 places to stay. Eventually this will probably become one of the cheapest beaches on the island to stay at, as it becomes funkier and rowdier.

Dive Shops Patong is the diving centre of the island and these shops rent equipment and lead dive tours: Andaman Divers (☎ 321155); Ocean Divers at the Patong Beach Hotel (☎ 321166); Santana International Diving (☎ 321360); South-East Asia Yacht Charter (☎ 321292); and Fantasea Divers (☎ 321309).

Boat Trips Several different companies on Patong do one-day cruises to nearby islands. For excursions to the Similan and Surin Islands off the Andaman coast of Phang-Nga Province, see the sections on these islands in the Ranong Province section.

Hash House Harriers Phuket's chapter of the running-and-drinking HHH meets regularly at the Expat Bar on Soi Bangla. Hashes (foot races) are held on Saturday afternoons; all are welcome to participate.

Boat Charter Motor yachts, sailboats and catamarans can be chartered with or without crew at Rawai Beach and Patong Beach. A fully crewed, air-con, 47-foot catamaran can be chartered from the Moorings, a French outfit on Patong Beach, for around US$1800 per person per week.

Places to Stay Rates on Patong really vary

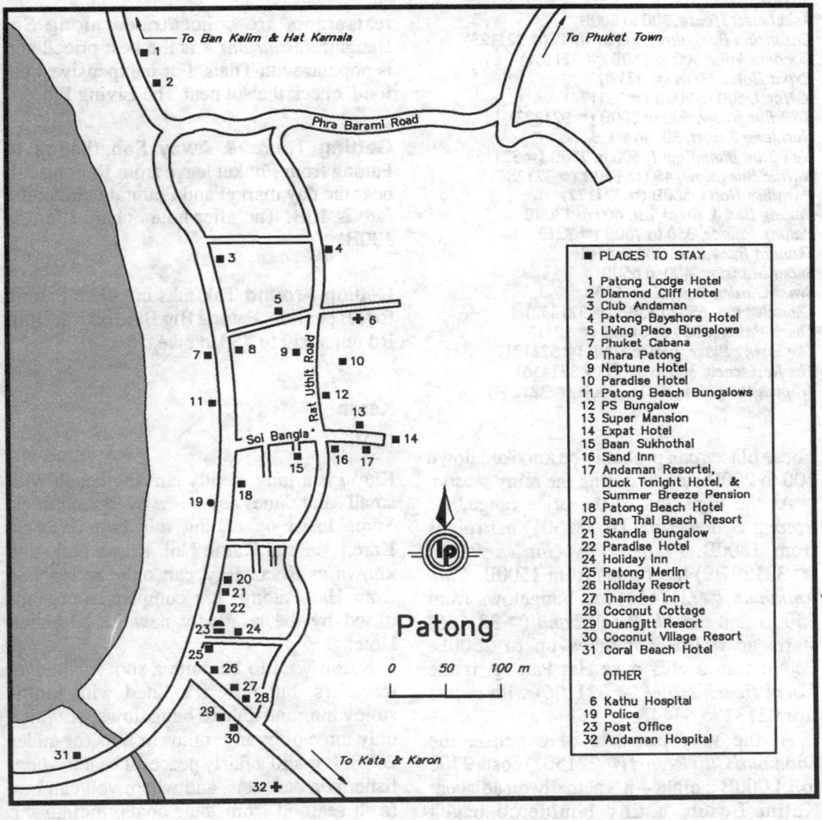

according to season. In the high season (December to March, and August) you'll be doing very well to find something under 400B a night. During off-months some of the 400B places will drop as low as 200B or even 100B but that's about it. Most of the bungalows of yore have been replaced by tacky modern apartment buildings, often with faulty plumbing. Bottom-end places usually come with fan and shared bath; more expensive rooms in this category will have a private bath. During the rainy season, May to November, you may be able to knock 100B off the following rates:

Capricorn Bungalow, 200 to 400B
Golden Fields, 200B
Golden Inn, 250B
Club Oasis, 350 to 450B
Jeep Bungalow, 250B
Shamrock Park Inn, 100 to 350B
Duck Tonight, 250 to 300B
Baan Koson, 250B
PS 1, 200 to 300B
PS II, 350B
Seven Seas Bungalow, 400B
Suksan Mansion, 350B

The middle range of Patong Beach is 400 to 900B, which usually includes air-con and private bath. In this range are:

Asia Guest House, 300 to 800B
Casuarina Bungalow, 400 to 400B (☎ 321123)
Coconut Villa, 500 to 750B (☎ 321161)
Expat Hotel, 500B (☎ 321300)
K Hotel, 500 to 700B (☎ 321124)
KSR Bungalow, 500 to 800B (☎ 321322)
Nerntong Resort, 300 to 600B
New Tum Bungalow 1, 500 to 750B (☎ 321159)
Nordic Bungalow, 450 to 850B (☎ 321284)
Paradise Hotel, 500B (☎ 321172)
Patong Bed & Breakfast, 600 to 1300B
Patong Palace, 350 to 700B (☎ 321359)
Skandia Bungalow, 200 to 650B
Super Mansion, 400 to 650B
Swiss Garden Bungalow, 650B
Thamdee Inn, 650 to 850B (☎ 321452)
Thara Patong, 500 to 1400B (☎ 321135)
The Living Place, 650 to 800B (☎ 321121)
The Residence, 300 to 800B (☎ 321456)
Tropica Bungalow, 600 to 900B (☎ 321204)

These places can probably be knocked down 100 to 200B a night during the rainy season.

At the high end of the price range, the *Patong Beach Hotel* (☎ 321301) has rooms from 1800B. *Patong Bay Garden Resort* (☎ 321297/9) has rooms from 1500B, *Club Andaman* (☎ 211451) has bungalows from 3500B and the *Phuket Cabana* (☎ 321135) starts at 1936B and goes up to 2500B. Perched on a cliff over Hat Patong, is the *Coral Beach Hotel* (☎ 321106) with rooms from 2733 to 5344B.

At the very pinnacle of expense, the *Diamond Cliff Resort* (☎ 321501) costs 2700 to 14,000B a night – it's actually on adjacent Kalim Beach, a tiny bouldered beach between Patong and Kamala. A couple of other places at Kalim Beach, next to the village of Ban Kalim, include the modern *Kalim Residence* (☎ 321353) at 1800 to 2200B, and the *Patong Lodge Hotel* (☎ 321286) at 2500 to 1800B. At the northern end of Patong, not quite as far north as Ban Kalim, is the *Thavorn Palm Beach Hotel* (☎ 381034), with 250 rooms for 3000B and up; the Thavorn has its own beach area.

The Holiday Inn international hotel chain has plans to build on Patong Beach.

Places to Eat Patong has stacks of restaurants, some of them quite good. The seafood restaurants are concentrated along Soi Bangla; *Restaurant 4* is the best priced and is popular with Thais. For inexpensive Thai food, check the soi near The Living Place.

Getting There & Away Songthaews to Patong from Phuket leave from Ranong Rd, near the day market and Fountain circle; the fare is 10B. The after-hours charter fare is 130B.

Getting Around Tuk-tuks circulate Patong for 5B per ride. Patong Big Bike on Rat Uthit Rd rents 250 to 750cc bikes.

Karon

กะรน

Karon is a long, gently curving beach with small sand dunes and a few evergreen trees. Some insist on calling this two beaches: Karon Yai and Karon Noi. Karon Noi, also known as Relax Bay, can only be reached from Hat Patong. It's completely monopolised by the relatively new Le Meridien Hotel.

Karon used to be quite a spot for budget travellers, but now it's lined with multistorey inns and deluxe bungalows, of which only three offer any rooms or huts for under 200B. It is still a fairly peaceful beach where fishermen cast nets, and where you can buy fresh seafood from their boats, though the rice fields between the beach and the surrounding hills have been abandoned. A few bars are moving in, too – signs of a Patong-like growth. See Kata – Getting There & Away for details on transport to Karon.

Places to Stay On the north of the headland straddling Karon and Kata is the old-style *Kata Tropicana*, still hanging on with bungalows for 80 to 100B. *Happy Hut* next door has 100B bungalows; both of these are well off the beach though. At the northern end of the beach is *Dream Hut* with rooms for 100 to 200B; the nearby *Coco Cabana* and *Lume & Yai* cost 300 to 500B.

In the mid-range (averaging 500B and up) are the *Karon Village* (☎ 381431) 400 to 700B, *Kampong Karon* (☎ 212901 ext 103) 700B, *Karon Guest House* (☎ 381860) 300 to 600B, *Thepsomboon Inn* 300 to 600B, *Phuket Ocean Resort* (☎ 381599) 600 to 1200B and *Ruam Thep Inn*, 8 rooms, 500B.

The remaining places on Karon are new resort-type hotels – which have more than doubled in number over the last two years – with rooms starting at 1000B or above, with air-con, swimming pools, etc.

The top end is:

Green Valley, 40 rooms, 1000B (☎ 381468)

Islandia Park Resort, 128 rooms, 1400 to 6000B (☎ 381491)

Karon Bay Inn, 30 rooms, 100 to 1100B

Karon Inn, 100 rooms, 1450 to 1650B (☎ 381519)

Karon View Point, 2000 to 3800B (☎ 381853)

Karon Villa-Karon Royal Wing, 152 rooms, from 2420B (☎ 381139)

Le Meridien Hotel, 464 rooms, from 3630B (☎ 321480)

Phuket Arcadia Hotel, 225 rooms, from 3802B (☎ 381038)

Phuket Golden Sand Inn, 95 rooms, 600 to 1200B (☎ 381493)

Phuket Island View, 81 rooms, 1500B (☎ 381919)

Sand Resort, 32 rooms, 1500B (☎ 212901)

South Sea Resort, 100 rooms, from 2904B (☎ 381611)

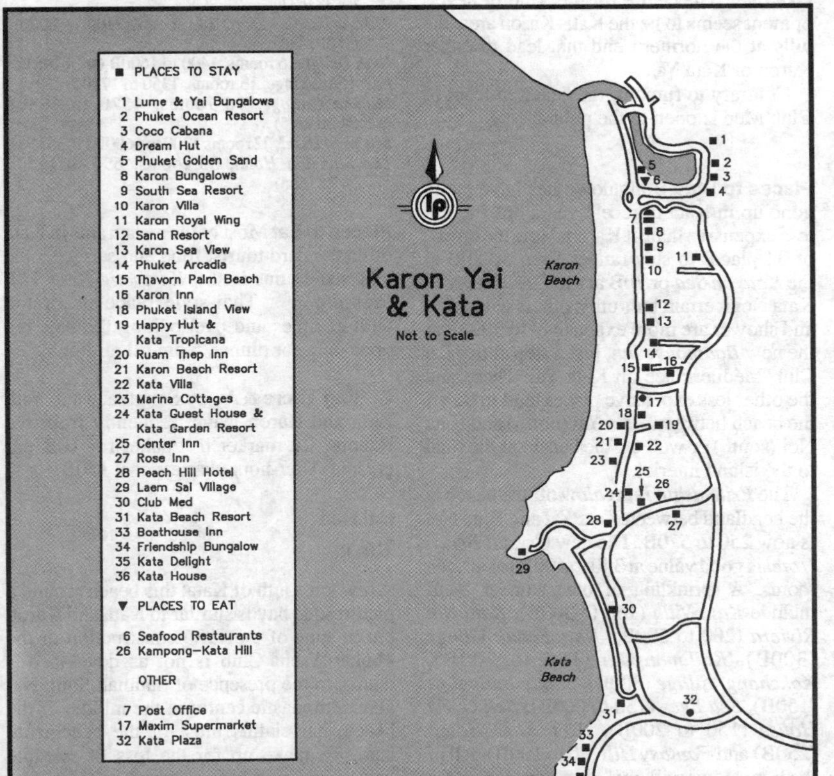

Kata

กะตะ

Just around a headland south from Karon, Kata is more interesting as a beach than Karon, and is divided into two – Ao Kata Yai (Big Kata Bay) and Ao Kata Noi (Little Kata Bay). The small island of Ko Pu is within swimming distance of the shore and on the way are some pretty nice coral reefs. The water here is usually very clear and snorkelling gear can be rented from several of the bungalow groups. With a dozen sets of bungalows and a Club Med it can get a bit crowded, and the video bars are starting to take over. The centre for this kind of development seems to be the Kata-Karon area, the hills at the northern end that lead to either Karon or Kata Yai.

Contrary to rumour, the beach in front of Club Med is open to the public.

Places to Stay Bungalow rates have really gone up in Kata in recent years but are still less expensive than at Karon. Now the crowd of 34 places to stay ranges from 50/80B at the *Kata on Sea* or 70B at the *Cool Breeze* at Kata Noi (certain huts only, others with toilet and shower are more expensive) to 3993B at the new *Boathouse Inn*, just a step above the Club Méditerranée on Kata Yai. These and the other less expensive places tend to be off the beach between Kata Yai (north) and Kata Noi (south) or well off the beach on the road to the island interior.

The *Friendship Bungalow* off the beach at the headland between Kata Yai and Kata Noi is now 250 to 520B. The new *Crystal Beach Hotel* is good value at 300 to 400B for air-con rooms. A sprinkling of others under 500B include *Kata Villa* (150 to 300B), *Kata Noi Riviera* (200 to 500B), *Kata Sanuk Village* (300B), *Kullapang-ha* (150 to 200B), *Kokchang Village* (300B), *Shady Bungalow* (150B), *Sea Bees* (150 to 200B), *Bell Guest House* (150 to 200B), *P&T Kata House* (250B) and *Fantasy Hill* (80 to 100B). All of the bungalows will give discounts during the low season, from May to October.

Medium-range places (all air-con) in Kata include *Bougainville Terrace House* (☎ 381060) at 500 to 600B, *Pop Cottage* (☎ 381060) from 350B, *Peach Hill Hotel* (☎ 212807) from 400B and *Hallo Guest House* (☎ 381631) from 400 to 600B.

The *Kata Thani Hotel* (☎ 381417) on the beach at Kata Noi has up-market rooms and bungalows for 2662 to 12,000B. Other top-enders include:

Boat House Inn, 36 rooms, 3509 to 3993B (☎ 381557)
Club Méditerranée, 300 rooms, 2650 to 3750B (☎ 381455)
Hayashi Thai House, 50 rooms, 2057 to 2299B (☎ 381631)
Kakata Beach Resort, 280 rooms, 2100 to 8000B, (☎ 381530)
Kata Delight, 6 rooms, 1400 to 1600B (☎ 381481)
Laem Sai Village, 13 rooms, 1350 to 1720B
Marina Cottage, 96 rooms, 1320 to 1980B (☎ 381625)
Sea Wind Hotel, 22 rooms 1200 to 1600B (☎ 381564)
The Mansion Hotel, 33 rooms, 650 to 1250B (☎ 381565)

Places to Eat Most of the restaurants in Kata offer standard tourist food and service. One that stands out is the *Kampong-Kata Hill Restaurant*, a Thai-style place decorated with antiques and overlooking the bay. It's open only for dinner, 5 pm till midnight.

Getting There & Away Songthaews to both Kata and Karon leave frequently from the Ranong Rd market in Phuket for 10B per person. After-hour charters cost 130B.

Nai Han

ในหาน

A few km south of Kata, this beach around a picturesque bay is similar to Kata and Karon but in spite of the 1986 construction of the Phuket Yacht Club is not as developed – thanks to the presence of Samnak Song Nai Han, a monastic centre in the middle of the beach that claims most of the beachfront land. To make up for the loss of saleable beachfront, developers started cutting away the forests on the hillsides overlooking the

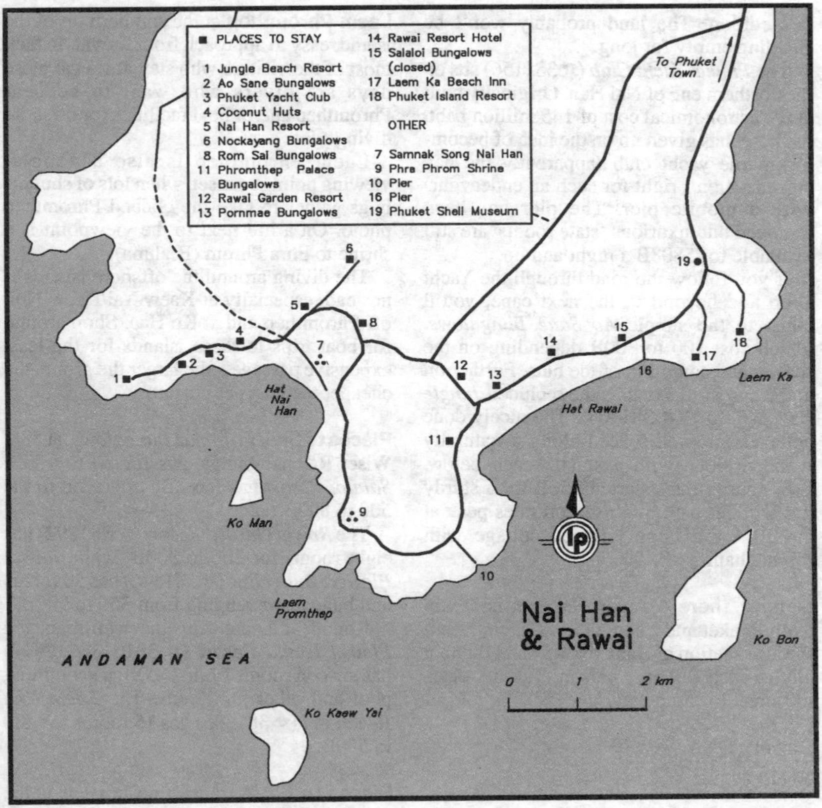

beach but recently the development seems to have reached a halt. This means that Nai Han is usually one of the least crowded beaches on the southern part of the island.

The TAT says Nai Han beach is a dangerous place to swim during the monsoon season (May to October) but it really varies according to daily or weekly weather changes – look for the red flag, which means dangerous swimming conditions.

Places to Stay Except for the Yacht Club there's really not much accommodation available on or even near the beach. *Coconut Huts* is still surviving on the slope behind the Coconut Cafe, near the Phuket Yacht Club entrance. Simple huts are 100B a night. Well back from the beach, in a rubber plantation opposite rice paddies, is the quiet *Nockayang Bungalows* for 140B with bath. You should be able to talk them down to 100B since the huts really aren't very well maintained. On the way to Nockayang is the motel-like *Nai Han Resort* (☎ 381810) with decent rooms for 500 to 800B.

Sunset Bungalows, which used to be a economical place to stay along the opposite end of the bay, have been torn down since last edition. The land probably won't be standing empty for long.

The *Phuket Yacht Club* (☎ 381156) sits on the northern end of Nai Han. Originally built at the astronomical cost of 145 million baht, the hotel has given up on the idea of becoming a true yacht club (apparently the bay currents aren't right for such an endeavour) with a mobile pier. The pier has been removed but luxurious 'state rooms' are still available for 5808B a night and up.

If you follow the road through the Yacht Club and beyond to the next cape, you'll come to the simple *Ao Sane Bungalows*, which cost 100 to 300B depending on the season and condition of the huts. Further on at the end of this road is the secluded *Jungle Beach Resort* (☎ 381108). The nicely done cottages are well-spaced along a naturally wooded slope with a small beach below. Low-season rates start at 250B for a sturdy hut without bath; high-season rates peak at 1200B for a large terraced cottage with private bath.

Getting There & Away Nai Han is 18 km from Phuket and a songthaew (leaving from the intersection of Bangkok Rd and Fountain circle) costs 20B per person. Tuk-tuk charters are 130B one-way.

Rawai
ราไวย์

Rawai was one of the first coastal areas on Phuket to be developed, simply because it was near Phuket and there was already a rather large fishing community there. Once other nicer beach areas like Patong and Karon were 'discovered', Rawai began to lose popularity gradually (the big 88-room Rawai Resort Hotel recently went out of business) and today it is a rather spiritless place – but at least it's not crowded.

The beach is not so great, but there is a lot happening in or near Rawai: a local sea gypsy village; Hat Laem Kha (better than Rawai) to the north; boats to the nearby islands of Ko Lon, Ko Hae, Ko Hew, Ko Phi Phi and others; and good snorkelling off **Laem Phromthep** at the southern tip of the island, easy to approach from Rawai. In fact, most of the visitors who stay at Rawai these days are divers who want to be near Phromthep and/or boat facilities for offshore diving trips.

Laem Phromthep is also a popular viewing point at sunset, when lots of shutterbugs gather to take the cliched Phromthep photo. On a hill next to the viewpoint is a shrine to Phra Phrom (Brahma).

The diving around the offshore islands is not bad, especially at Kaew Yai/Kaew Noi, off Phromthep and at Ko Hae. Shop around for boat trips to these islands for the least expensive passage – the larger the group, the cheaper the cost per person.

Places to Stay *Pornmae Bungalows*, at 58/1 Wiset Rd, has bungalows for 80 to 100B. *Salaloi Resort* has recently upgraded to the 500 to 800B range.

The *Rawai Garden Resort* (☎ 381292) has eight rooms for 200 to 300B, while *Rawai Plaza & Bungalow* (☎ 381346) has 50 rooms and bungalows ranging from 350 to 900B.

Round at Laem Kha the well-managed *Phuket Island Resort* (☎ 381018, 212910) has air-con rooms from 2500B, a swimming pool and other mod cons. The *Laem Kha Beach Inn* (☎ 381305) has 15 rooms for 400 to 550B.

Places to Eat An attraction in itself is the *Jambalaya Cafe* near Rawai on the road to Phuket. The food is Thai – sorry, no jambalaya – but the Restless Cowboys band play Hank Williams nightly except Sunday.

Getting There & Away Rawai is about 16 km from Phuket and getting there costs 10B by songthaew from the circle at Bangkok Rd. Tuk-tuk charters cost 90B from Phuket.

Laem Singh & Kamala
แหลมสิงห์/หาดกมลา

North of Ao Patong, 24 km from Phuket, Laem Singh (Cape Singh) is a beautiful little rock-dominated beach. You could camp here and eat on Surin beach or in Ban Kamala, a village further south. If you're renting a motorbike, this is a nice little trip down Highway 402 and then over dirt roads from Surin to Kamala. Just before Surin, in Ban Thao village No 2, is one of southern Thailand's most beautiful mosques, a large whitewashed, immaculate structure with lacquered wooden doors.

Hat Kamala is a lovely stretch of sand and sea south of Surin and Laem Singh. So far the only beach accommodation is the up-market *Phuket Kamala Resort* (☎ 212901), where rooms cost 1700 to 1900B a night. In the village are several small houses for rent starting at around 500B a night. At the southern end of the bay, overlooking but not on the beach is *Kamala Beach Estate*, where fully equipped, modern apartments go for 4800 to 8000B a night.

Warning All of the western Phuket beaches, including Surin, Laem Singh and Kamala, have strong riptides during the monsoons. Take care when swimming, or don't go in the water at all if you're not a strong swimmer.

Surin

สุรินทร์

A little north of Laem Singh, Surin has a long beach and sometimes fairly heavy surf. When the water is calm, there's fair snorkelling here. The beach has long been a popular place for local Thais to come and nibble at seafood snacks and *miang kham* sold by vendors along the beach.

So far the southern stretches of Surin have been spared hotel development. The northern end has been dubbed 'Pansea Beach' by developers and is claimed by the exclusive Amanpuri and Pansea resorts. *Amanpuri Resort* (☎ 311394) plays host to Thailand's celebrity traffic, each of whom gets a 133-sq-metre pavilion and a personal attendant; the staff to guest ratio is in fact 3½ to one. It's owned by Indonesian Adrian Zecha and designed by the architect who designed the former Shah of Iran's Winter Palace. You can expect to pay US$250 to US$500 a day for a room here. The older *Pansea* (☎ 212901) has rooms for 2400 to 4600B including breakfast and dinner. The Pansea has its own golf course.

Ao Bang Tao

บางเทา

North of Surin around a cape is Ao Bang Tao, a long sandy beach. In 1992, the Siam World Cup windsurfing championships moved from Pattaya's Jomtien Beach to Bang Tao.

There are several good middle-range and up-market places to stay. Least expensive is the quiet and secluded *Bangtao Lagoon Bungalow*, with small cottages for 350B, medium-size ones for 450B, or 600B for the largest. *Bangtao Cottage* is built on a hillside over the southern end of the bay and costs 550B a night.

Rooms at the recently completed *Dusit Laguna Resort* (☎ 311320) are 4100B, suites considerably more, not including tax. From 20 December to 20 February there is a 400B peak-season surcharge. Another top-end place at the northern end of the bay is the *Royal Park Beach Resort* (☎ 311453), where rooms start at 2500B. The Grande Sheraton hotel is on its way to Bang Tao.

Getting There & Away A songthaew from Phuket's Ranong Rd to Surin, Kamala or Bang Tao costs 20B. Tuk-tuk charters are 200B to Surin and Kamala, 170B to Bang Tao.

Nai Yang & Mai Khao

ในยาง/ไม้ขาว

Both of these beaches are near Phuket Airport, about 30 km from Phuket. Nai Yang, a fairly secluded beach favoured by Thais, is actually a national park, with one set of government-run bungalows. It's about five km further north along Highway 402 (Thepkasatri Rd) to Phuket's longest beach, Hat Mai Khao, where sea turtles lay their eggs between November and February each year. About a km off Nai Yang is a decent reef at a depth of 10 to 20 metres.

Camping is allowed on both Nai Yang and Mai Khao beaches. The park accommodation on Nai Yang cost 200B in a dorm-like long house, 300B in a four-bed bungalow, 600B in one with 12 beds. Two-person tents can be rented for 60B a night.

Although this is a national park, somehow the fancy *Pearl Village Beach Hotel* (☎ 311338) managed to slip in on 20 acres at the southern end of the beach. Air-con rooms and cottages start at 2900B. Another apparent encroacher is the 4000B-a-night *Crown Nai Yang Condotel.*

Getting There & Away A songthaew from Phuket to Nai Yang costs 20B. A tuk-tuk charter costs 250B.

Other Beaches

Out on Laem Phanwa by itself is the *Cape Phanwa Sheraton* (☎ 391123), where luxury digs start at 3025B.

There are a couple of places to stay on Ko Sire, including *Madam Puye Bungalow* for 200B and *Siray Seaview Bungalow* for 300 to 500B.

Surat Thani Province

CHAIYA

ไชยา

About 640 km from Bangkok, Chaiya is just north of Surat Thani and is best visited as a day trip from there. Chaiya is one of the oldest cities in Thailand, dating back to the Srivijaya Empire. In fact, the name may be a contraction of Siwichaiya, the Thai pronunciation of the city that was a regional capital between the 8th and 10th centuries. Previous to this time the area was on the Indian trade route in South-East Asia. Many Srivijaya artefacts in the National Museum in Bangkok were found in Chaiya, including the Avalokitesvara Bodhisattva bronze, considered to be a masterpiece of Buddhist art.

The restored Borom That Chaiya stupa at **Wat Phra Mahathat**, just outside of town, is a fine example of Srivijaya architecture and strongly resembles the *candis* of central Java. A ruined stupa at nearby Wat Kaew, also from the Srivijaya period, again shows central Javanese influence (or perhaps vice versa) as well as Cham (9th-century South Vietnam) characteristics.

Wat Suan Mokkhaphalaram

วัดสวนโมกขพลาราม

Wat Suanmok (short for Wat Suan Mokkhaphalaram – literally, 'garden of liberation'), west of Wat Kaew, is a modern forest wat founded by Buddhadasa Bhikkhu (Thai: Phutthathat), Thailand's most famous monk. Buddhadasa, a rotund octogenarian, ordained as a monk when he was 21 years old, spent many years studying the Pali scriptures and then retired to the forest for six years of solitary meditation. Returning to ecclesiastical society, he was made abbot of Wat Phra Mahathat, a high distinction, but conceived of Suanmok as an alternative to orthodox Thai temples.

The philosophy that has guided Buddhadasa is ecumenical in nature, comprising Zen, Taoist and Christian elements, as well as the traditional Theravada schemata. Today the hermitage is spread over 60 hectares of wooded hillside and features huts for 40 monks, a museum/library, and a 'spiritual theatre'. This latter building has bas-reliefs on the outer walls which are facsimiles of sculpture at Sanchi, Bharhut and Amaravati in India. The interior walls feature modern Buddhist painting, eclectic to say the least, executed by the resident monks.

Resident farang monks here hold meditation retreats the first 10 days of every month. Anyone is welcome to participate; a 50B donation per day is requested to cover food costs.

Places to Stay

Stay in Surat Thani for visits to Chaiya or request permission to stay in the guest quarters at Wat Suanmok. There is also an old Chinese-Thai hotel in Chaiya for 60B.

Getting There & Away

If you're going to Surat Thani by train, you can get off at the small Chaiya railway station, then later catch another train to Phun Phin, Surat's railway station. From Surat you can either hire a taxi or get a train going north from Phun Phin. Taxis are best hired from Phun Phin, too. The trains between Phun Phin and Chaiya may be full but you can always stand or squat in a 3rd-class car for the short trip. The ordinary train costs 8B in 3rd class to Chaiya and takes about an hour to get there.

Suanmok is about seven km outside of town on the highway to Surat and Chumphon. Until late afternoon there are songthaews from the Chaiya railway station to Wat Suanmok for 6B per passenger. There are also buses (bound for Surat) from the front of the movie theatre on Chaiya's main street. Turn right on the road in front of the railway station. The fare to Wat Suanmok is 3B. If buses aren't running you can hire a motorcycle (and driver) for 10 to 15B anywhere along Chaiya's main street.

Coming from Surat it isn't necessary to go to Chaiya at all if you're heading for Wat Suanmok. Buses run there frequently and directly from the Talaat Kaset bus station. The trip takes about 45 minutes and costs 10B.

SURAT THANI/BAN DON

อ.เมืองสุราษฎร์ธานี/บ้านดอน

There is little of particular historical interest at Surat Thani (population 41,000), a busy commercial centre and port dealing in rubber and coconut, but the town has character nonetheless. It's 651 km from Bangkok and the first point in a southbound journey towards Malaysia that really feels and looks like southern Thailand. For most people Surat Thani (often known as Surat) is only a stop on the way to Ko Samui or Ko Pha-Ngan, luscious islands 32 km off the coast, so the Talaat Kaset bus station in Ban Don and the ferry piers to the east become the centres of attention.

Boats to Ko Samui

Your boat to Ko Samui could leave from one of four places in Surat Province, depending on the time of day, time of year, and mode of transport by which you arrive in Surat: from Tha Thong, on the Tapi River north-east of Surat, it's a 2½-hour boat trip to Samui on the day express; from Ban Don the night ferry takes four hours to Samui or five hours to Ko Pha-Ngan; from Don Sak, 60 km from Surat, the vehicle ferry takes 1½ hours; and from Khanom, 80 km away, it's a one-hour trip to Samui.

It's not so much your decision as what's next available when you arrive at the bus terminal in Surat or railway station in Phun Phin – touts working for the two ferry companies will lead you to one or the other. Don Sak and Khanom have the only vehicle-ferry facilities (Ban Don and Tha Thong are for passengers only), so if you're bringing along a car or motorcycle, you'd best go straight to Don Sak. When the sea is rough, the vehicle ferries leave from Khanom instead. For more details on the ferries see the Ko Samui Getting There & Away section.

Ban Don is a great place to wander about while waiting for a night boat to Samui. There is a fabulous fruit market along the waterfront, and several all-purpose 'general stores' and pharmacies on the streets opposite the pier where you can get good deals on phaakhamaas and Thai work shirts, as well pick up some supplies for the islands.

During the low season (ie any time except December to February or August), Thai girls may throng the piers around departure time for the Ko Samui boats, inviting farangs to stay at this or that bungalow. This same tactic is employed at the Na Thon or Thong Yang piers upon arrival at Ko Samui. During the high tourist season, however, this isn't necessary as every place is just about booked out.

Places to Stay – bottom end

For many of Surat Thani's cheaper hotels, business consists largely of 'short-time' trade. This doesn't make them any less suitable as regular hotels, it's just that there's likely to be rather more noise as guests arrive and depart with some frequency. In fact, in many ways it's better to zip straight through Surat Thani since there's nothing of interest to hold you. You're quite likely to sleep better on the night boat than in a noisy hotel.

Another alternative is to stay near the railway station in Phun Phin (see under Places to Stay – Phun Phin).

All of the following are within walking (or samlor) distance of the Ban Don boat pier.

Off Ban Don Rd, near the municipal pier, on a fairly quiet street off Si Chaiya Rd, is the *Seree (Seri) Hotel*. You get clean rooms with fan and bath for 120B, air-con rooms cost 220B.

The *Surat Hotel* (☎ 272243) on Na Muang Rd, between the Grand City Hotel and bus station, costs 80 to 100B for rooms with fan and bath. One traveller has reported that there are some quiet, renovated rooms. Opposite the Surat are the similar *Phanfa* and *Premsook*.

The *Grand City Hotel* (formerly *Muang Thong)* (☎ 272560), at 428 Na Muang Rd has rather shabby rooms with fan and bath for 140B; it's undergoing renovation so perhaps improvements are in store.

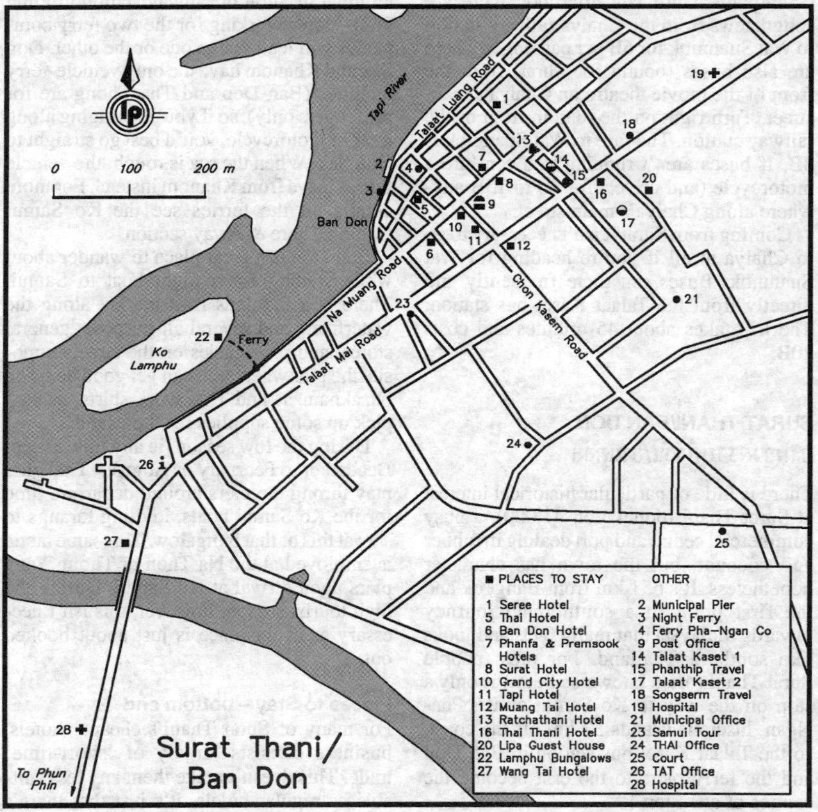

One block from the night boat pier on Si Chaiya Rd is the *Thai Hotel*, which is 120/170B for adequate singles/doubles with fan and bath.

The best budget value in Surat is the *Ban Don Hotel* on Na Muang Rd towards the morning market, with clean singles/doubles with fan and bath for 100/150B. Enter through a Chinese restaurant. The *Thai Rung Ruang Hotel* (☎ 273249), 191/199 Mitkasem Rd is also good with rooms from 120B.

On the corner of Si Chaiya Rd and the road between the river and bus station is the *Ratchathani Hotel* (☎ 272972/143), which starts at 120B for rooms with fan and bath. The *Lipa Guest House* is a brand new place at the Talaat Kaset II bus station with rooms for 80B.

On Lamphu Island, in the Tapi River, is *Lamphu Bungalows* (☎ 272495) with bungalows from 150 to 200B with fan and bath, 240B with air-con. The free ferry to Ko Lamphu leaves from opposite the police station on the river front. The attendant raises a red flag to hail a boat from the island; the boat is in service till 2 am from the Surat side, though you can wake the boatman on the island side later than that for trips in the reverse direction.

Places to Stay – middle

The *Tapi Hotel* (☎ 272575), at 100 Chon Kasem Rd, has air-con rooms from 300B, fan-cooled rooms from 180B. The *Muang Tai* (☎ 272367), at 390-392 Talaat Mai Rd, has fan-cooled rooms from 150B and air-con rooms from 300B.

Places to Stay – top end

Surat Thani also has a number of more expensive hotels including the *Wang Tai* (☎ 273410/1) at 1 Talaat Mai Rd. It's a big hotel with nearly 300 rooms, a swimming pool and prices from 450B. The *Siam Thani* (☎ 391-0280), at 180 Surat Thani-Phun Phin Rd, costs 480B but during the low season offers a 50% discount. There's a good restaurant. The *Siam Thara*, on Don Nok Rd near the Talaat Mai Rd intersection, has air-con rooms for 480 to 560B.

Places to Eat

In Surat, the Talaat Kaset market area next to the bus terminal, and the morning market between Na Muang and Si Chaiya are good food-hunting places. Many stalls near the bus station specialise in khâo kài òp, a marinated baked chicken on rice which is very tasty. During mango season, a lot of street vendors in Surat sell incredible khâo niãw má-mûang, coconut-sweetened sticky rice with sliced ripe mango.

J Home Bakery, around the corner from the Grand City Hotel, is a dark, poorly ventilated air-con place, but it has inexpensive Western breakfasts, a few baked goods, plus Thai and Chinese dishes on a bilingual menu. Better bakery choices are the *Valaisak Bakery* next to the Tapi Hotel or the *Home Bakery* next to the Phanfa Hotel. Next door to J Home is the inexpensive and popular *Yong Hua Long*, a decent Chinese restaurant with roast duck and a large buffet table.

Places to Stay & Eat – Phun Phin

You may find yourself needing accommodation in Phun Phin, either because you've become stranded there due to booked-out trains or because you've come in from Samui in the evening and plan to get an early-morning train out of Surat before the Surat to Phun Phin bus service starts. If so, there are several cheap but adequate hotels just across from the railway station. The *Tai Fah* has rooms for 80B without bath. Slightly better at the same location is the *Sri Thani*, also with 80B rooms.

Around the corner on the road to Surat, but still quite close to the railway station, are the *Kaew Fah* for 80B and the nicer *Queen* for 120 to 170B with fan, 250 to 300B with air-con.

Across from the Queen and Kaew Fah is a good night market with cheap eats. The Tai Fah and Sri Thani do Thai, Chinese and farang food at reasonable prices.

Getting There & Away

Air THAI flies to Surat Thani from Bangkok (daily, 1710B), Chiang Mai (twice a week, 2970B), Nakhon Si Thammarat (three times a week, 340B), Hat Yai (via Phuket, 1200B), Phuket (daily, 475B) and Trang (three times a week, 495B).

The THAI office (☎ 272610) is at 3/27-28 Karunarat Rd (☎ 272610, 273/355). A THAI shuttle between Surat Thani and the airport costs 35B per person.

Bus, Share Taxi & Minivan Air-con buses leave Bangkok's southern air-con bus terminal in Thonburi daily at 8 and 8.30 pm, arriving in Surat 11 hours later; the fare is 225B. Ordinary buses leave the ordinary southern bus terminal at 8 am, 8 and 9.30 pm for 125B. Special VIP buses for overnight trips to Ban Don from Bangkok with only 30 seats (more reclining room) cost 300B; super VIP (24 seats) buses are available for 350B.

Public buses and share taxis run from the Talaat Kaset I or II markets. Muang Tai bus company books air-con bus tickets to several destinations in southern Thailand from its desk in the lobby of the Surat Hotel, including VIP buses to Bangkok. Phanthip (Phuntip) Travel handles minivan bookings.

Several private tour companies run buses to Surat from Bangkok for 200 to 300B. Other fares to/from Surat are:

destination	fare	hours
Narathiwat	100B	6
Trang	53B	3
(share taxi)	100B	3
Nakhon Si Thammarat	30B	2½
(air-con)	40B	2
(share taxi)	60B	2
Yala	92B	6
Krabi	50B	4
(air-con)	80B	3
(share taxi or van)	150B	2
Satun	76B	4
Hat Yai	68B	5
(air-con)	120B	4
(share taxi or van)	150B	3½
Phuket	61B	6
(air-con)	100B	5
(share taxi or van)	150B	4
Ranong	60B	5
(air-con)	80B	4
(share taxi or van)	150B	3½
Phang-Nga	50B	4
(air-con)	70B	3
(share taxi)	80B	2½

Train Trains for Surat, which don't really stop in Surat but in Phun Phin, 14 km west of town, leave Bangkok's Hualamphong terminal at 12.35 pm (rapid), 2 pm (special express), 3.15 pm (special express), 4 pm (rapid), 5.30 pm (rapid), 6.30 pm (rapid) and 7.20 pm (express) arriving 10½ to 11 hours later.

The 6.30 pm train (rapid No 41) is the most convenient, arriving at 6.03 am and giving you plenty of time to catch a boat to Samui, if that's your destination. Fares are 470B in 1st class (available only on the 2 and 3.15 pm special express), 224B in 2nd class and 107B in 3rd class, not including the rapid/express/special express surcharges or berths.

The Sprinter (all 1st class) leaves Bangkok daily at 9.10 pm and arrives in Phun Phin at 6.15 am for 370B. There is also a new 9.55 pm diesel express that only takes nine hours to reach Phun Phin for the usual 2nd or 3rd class fare. Neither of these trains has sleeping berths.

The Phun Phin railway station has a 24-hour left-luggage room that costs 5B for the first five days, 10B thereafter. The advance ticket office is open daily from 6 to 11 am and noon to 6 pm.

It can be difficult to book long-distance trains out of Phun Phin – for long-distance travel, it may be easier to book a bus, especially if heading south. The trains are very often full and it's a drag to take the bus 14 km from town to the Phun Phin railway station and be turned away. You could buy a 'standing room only' 3rd-class ticket and stand for an hour or two until someone vacates a seat down the line.

Advance train reservations can be made without going all the way out to Phun Phin station, at Phanthip travel agency on Talaat Mai Rd in Ban Don, near the market/bus station. You might try making a reservation *before* boarding a boat for Samui. The Songserm Travel Service on Samui also does reservations.

Here is a list of other train fares out of Surat (not including surcharges on rapid, express or air-con coaches):

destination	1st class	2nd class	3rd class
Chaiya	8B		
Chumphon	71B	34B	
Hat Yai	228B	114B	55B
Nakhon Si Thammarat (Thung Song)	103B	54B	26B
Prachuap Khiri Khan	255B	127B	61B
Bangkok	470B	224B	107B

Train/Bus/Boat Combinations These days many travellers are buying tickets from the State Railway that go straight through to Ko Samui or Ko Pha-Ngan from Bangkok on a train, bus and boat combination. For example, a 2nd-class air-con sleeper that includes bus to boat transfers through to Samui costs 529B. See the Getting There & Away sections under each island for more details.

Getting Around

Buses to Ban Don from Phun Phin railway station leave every 10 minutes or so from 6 am to 8 pm for 5B per person. Some of the buses drive straight to the pier (if they have enough tourists on the bus), while others will terminate at the Ban Don bus station, from where you must get another bus to Tha Thong (or to Ban Don if you're taking the night ferry).

If you arrive in Phun Phin on one of the night trains, you can get a free bus from the railway station to the pier, courtesy of the boat service, for the morning boat departures. If your train arrives in Phun Phin when the buses aren't running (which includes all trains except No 41 trains), then you're out of luck and will have to hire a taxi to Ban Don, for about 60 to 70B, or hang out in one of the Phun Phin street cafes until buses start running.

Orange buses from Ban Don bus station to Phun Phin railway station run every five minutes from 5 am to 7.30 pm for 5B per person. Empty buses also wait at the Tha Thong pier for passengers arriving from Ko Samui on the express boat, ready to drive them directly to the railway station or destinations further afield.

KHAO SOK NATIONAL PARK

อุทยานแห่งชาติเขาสก

This 646-sq-km park is in the western part of Surat Thani Province, off Highway 401 about a third of the way from Takua Pa to Surat Thani. The park features 65,000 hectares of thick native rainforest with waterfalls, limestone cliffs, numerous streams, a lake formed by the Chiaw Lan Dam and many trails, mostly along rivers. Entrance to the park is 30B; the rangers also take jungle tours and/or rafting trips for 150B per day.

Places to Stay

Khao Sok has a camping area and several places to stay. The national park has a house with rooms for 350B. Tents can be rented for 50B per person. A small restaurant near the entrance serves inexpensive meals.

Accommodation is also available just outside the park at *Tree Tops River Huts* (radio ☎ 076-421155/613, both ext 107), which offers six rooms with bath for 150/200B a single/double, or a tree house with bath for 300B, and meals for 30 to 60B. *Bamboo House*, off the main road to the park, has seven rooms for 80/100B with shared bath, 150/200B with private bath, plus 100B extra for three meals a day.

AITS Jungle House off the same road beyond the Bamboo House, about a km from the park, has seven rooms for 100 to 200B, plus tree houses for 300B and two large houses with rooms and private bath and deck for 500B; meals cost 200B a day or you order à la carte at breakfast and lunch, 80B for a set Thai dinner. Contact Lost Horizon Travel (☎ 279-4967) in Bangkok, or the Jungle House itself (radio ☎ 076-421155, ext 205). All places have guides for jungle trips. Meals are available for 30 to 50B.

Tree Tops Guest House started the Khao Sok experience several years ago but these days the guesthouse accepts only package tours booked through Vieng Travel (☎ 280-3537) in Bangkok. A typical package for four nights (two nights at Treetops, two nights at their raft house) with meals is 3900B.

Getting There & Away

From Phun Phin or Surat there are frequent buses to Km 109 (the park's entrance) for 50B air-con, 26B ordinary. You can also come from the Phuket side of the peninsula by bus.

KO SAMUI

เกาะสมุย

Ko Samui (population 32,000) long ago attained a somewhat legendary status among Asian travellers, yet until recently it never really escalated to the touristic proportions of other similar getaways found between Goa and Bali. With the advent of the Don Sak auto/bus ferry and the opening of the airport, things have been changing fast. During the high seasons, January to February and July to August, it can be difficult to find a place to stay, even though most beaches are

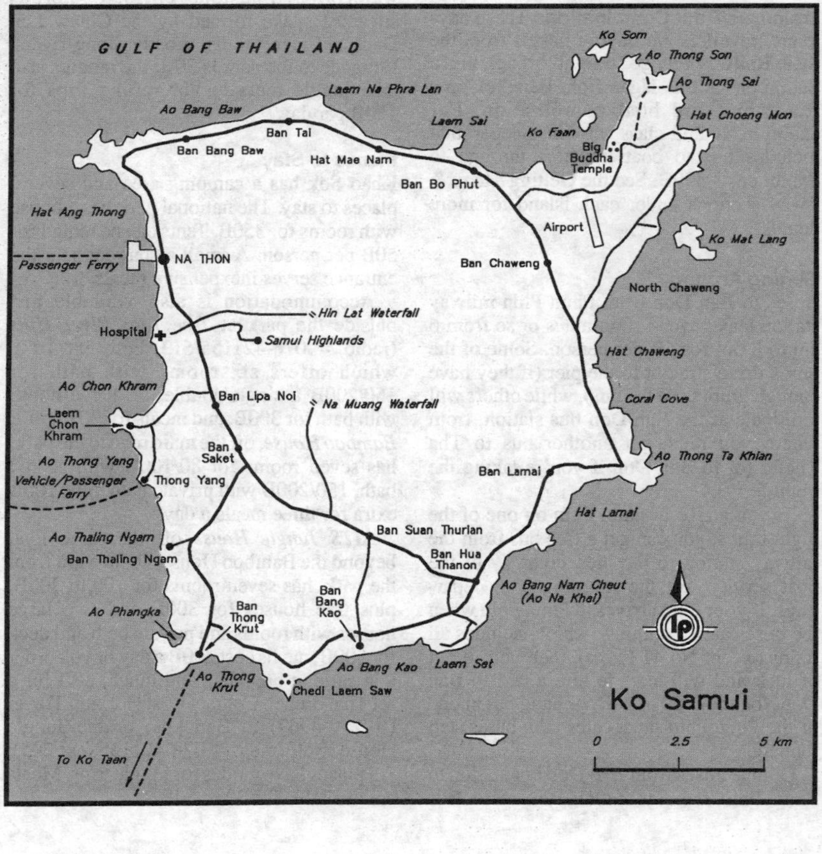

Top Left: Rooftops, Chiang Mai (CT)
Bottom Left: Wat Phumin, Nan (JC)
Top Right: Wat Chao Chan, Chaliang, Sukhothai (JC)
Bottom Right: Grand Palace, Bangkok (RI)

Top Left: Umbrellas (RI)
Middle Left: Southern market (TAT)
Bottom Left: Fruit vendor (JC)

Top Right: Sorting mushrooms (JB)
Bottom Right: Pottery, Dan Kwian (JC)

crowded with bungalows. The port town teems with farangs getting on and off the ferry boats, booking tickets onward, collecting mail at the post office. Now that Bangkok Airways has daily flights to Samui, the island is rushing headlong into top-end development.

Airport or no airport, Samui is still an enjoyable place to spend some time. It still has some of the best accommodation values in Thailand and a laid-back atmosphere that makes it quite relaxing. Even with an airport, it still has the advantage of being off the mainland and far away from Bangkok. Coconuts are still the mainstay of the local economy – up to two million are shipped to Bangkok each month. But there's no going back to 1971, when the first two tourists arrived on a coconut boat from Bangkok (much to the surprise of a friend of mine who had been living on the island for four years as a Peace Corps volunteer).

Samui is different from other islands in southern Thailand and its inhabitants refer to themselves as *chao samũi* (Samui folk) rather than Thais. They are even friendlier than the average upcountry Thai, in my opinion, and have a great sense of humour, although those who are in constant contact with tourists may be a bit jaded.

The island also has a distinctive cuisine, influenced by the omnipresent coconut, the main source of income for chao samui. Coconut palms blanket the island, from the hillocks right up to the beaches. The durian, rambutan and langsat fruits are also cultivated on Samui.

Ko Samui is part of an island group that used to be called Mu Ko Samui, though you rarely hear that term these days. It's Thailand's third-largest island, at 247 sq km, and is surrounded by 80 smaller islands. Six of these, Pha-Ngan, Ta Loy, Tao, Taen, Ma Ko and Ta Pao, are inhabited as well.

The population of Ko Samui is for the most part concentrated in the port town of Na Thon, on the western side of the island facing the mainland and in 10 or 11 small villages scattered around the island. One road encircles the island with several side roads poking into the interior; this main road is now paved all the way around.

One of my main complaints about Samui today is that the Reggae Pub (a large, commercial dance club at Chaweng Beach) has nailed too many signs to palms around the island – not only does it get quite monotonous, it spoils the natural scenery. Truer to the reggae message, someone should start a campaign to get these removed.

Information

When to Go The best time to visit the Samui group of islands is during the hot and dry season, February to late June. From July to October it can be raining on and off, and from October to January there are sometimes heavy winds. However, many travellers have reported fine weather (and fewer crowds) in September and October. November tends to get some of the rain which also affects the east coast of Malaysia at this time. Prices tend to soar from December to July, whatever the weather.

Immigration Travellers have been able to extend their tourist visas at the Ko Samui immigration office in Na Thon for 500B.

Maps In Surat or on Ko Samui, you can pick up TAT's helpful Surat Thani map, which has maps of Surat Thani, the province, Ang Thong National Marine Park and Ko Samui, along with travel info. A couple of private companies now do good maps of Ko Samui, Pha-Ngan and Tao, which are available in tourist areas of Surat and on the islands for 35B.

Warning Several travellers have written to say take care with local agents for train and bus bookings. Bookings sometimes don't get made at all, the bus turns out to be far inferior to what was expected or other hassles develop. Take care with local boat trips to nearby islands reported another visitor. His boat was nearly swamped on a windy day and he eventually had to spend the night stranded on an uninhabited island.

Massage

Great 45-minute massages by male masseurs are often available for 40B at the sala opposite the post office in Na Thon. Several traditional massage houses are opening around the island as well, and the usual massage ladies tramp the more popular beaches looking for muscles to pummel.

Muay Thai

At the northern end of Na Thon there's a Thai boxing ring with regularly scheduled matches. Admission is 100B to most fights.

Diving

Many small dive operations have opened around the island. Gear hired for beach dives costs around 350B per day. A four-day, three-night dive trip to Ko Tao, including food and accommodation, costs around 4500B.

Waterfalls

Besides the beaches and rustic, thatched-roof bungalows, Samui has a couple of waterfalls. **Hin Lat Falls** is about three km from Na Thon and is a worthwhile visit if you're waiting in town for a boat back to the mainland. You can get there on foot – walk 100 metres or so south of town on the main road, turning left at the road by the hospital. Go straight along this road about two km to arrive at the entrance to the waterfall. From here, it's about a half-hour walk along a trail to the top of the waterfall.

Na Muang Falls, in the centre of the island 10 km from Na Thon, is more scenic and less frequented. A songthaew from Na Thon should be about 20B. Songthaews can also be hired at Chaweng and Lamai beaches.

Temples

For temple enthusiasts, at the southern end of the island, near the village of Bang Kao, there is **Wat Laem Saw** with an interesting old chedi. At the northern end, on a small rocky island joined to Samui by a causeway, is the so-called **Temple of the Big Buddha**, Phra Yai. The modern image, about 12 metres in height, makes a nice silhouette against the tropical sky and sea behind it. The image is surrounded by *kutis* (meditation huts), mostly unoccupied. The monks like receiving visitors there, though a sign in English requests that proper attire (no shorts) be worn on the temple premises. There is also an old semi-abandoned temple, **Wat Pang Ba**, near the northern end of Hat Chaweng where 10-day vipassana courses are occasionally held for farangs; the courses are led by farang monks from Wat Suanmok in Chaiya.

Near the car park at the entrance to Hin Laet Falls is another trail left to **Suan Dharmapala**, a meditation temple.

Ang Thong National Marine Park

อุทยานแห่งชาติทางทะเลอ่างทอง

From Ko Samui, a couple of tour operators run day trips out to the Ang Thong archipelago, 31 km north-west. A typical tour costs 250B per person, leaves Na Thon at 8.30 am and returns at 5.30 pm. Lunch is included, along with snorkelling in a sort of lagoon formed by one of the islands, from which Ang Thong gets its name (Golden Jar), and a climb to the top of a 240-metre hill to view the whole island group. Tours depart daily in the high season, less frequently in the rainy season. The tours are still getting rave reviews.

At least once a month there's also an overnight tour, as there are bungalows on Ko Wua Ta Lap. These cost 400B per person and include three meals and accommodation at the bungalows. You may be able to book a passage alone to the Ang Thong islands; enquire at Songserm Travel Service or Ko Samui Travel Centre in Na Thon.

Na Thon

หน้าทอน

On the upper west side of the island, Na Thon (pronounced 'Naa Thawn') is where express and night passenger ferries from the piers in Surat disembark. Car ferries from Don Sak or Khanom land at Ao Thong Yang about 10 km south of Na Thon (see the Beaches

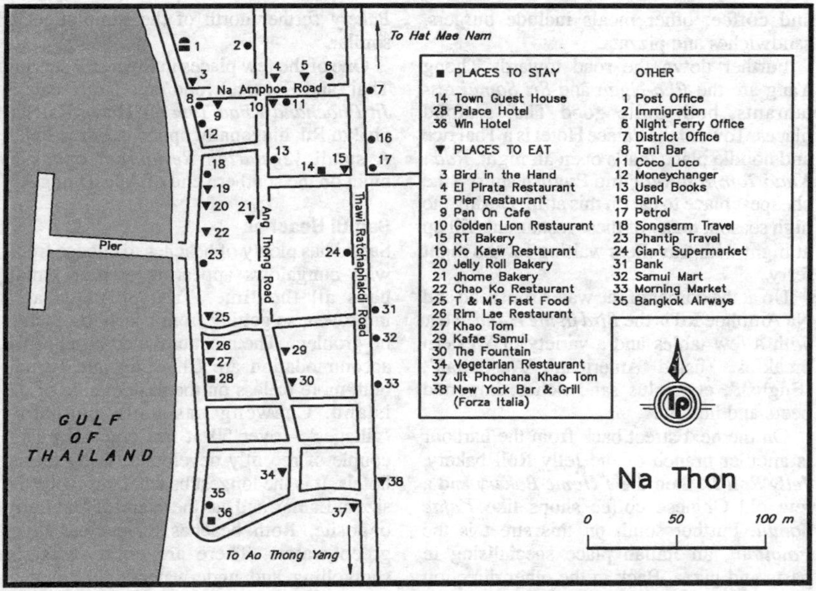

section). If you're not travelling on a combination ticket you'll probably end up spending some time in Na Thon on your way in and/or out, waiting for the next ferry. Or if you're a long-term beachcomber, it makes a nice change to come into Na Thon once in a while for a little town life.

Although it's basically a tourist town now, Na Thon still sports a few old teak Chinese shophouses and cafes.

Places to Stay If you want or need to stay in Ko Samui's largest settlement there are seven places to choose from at the time of writing.

The *Palace Hotel* (Thai name *Chai Thale)* has clean, spacious rooms starting at 200B with fan or 450B with air-con. Next door to the Palace is a dark wooden building with no sign that happens to be Na Thon's cheapest hotel (and a notorious brothel) at 50 to 70B per room. If you're looking for something cheap, a better choice would to share a room at the *Town Guest House* on Wattana Rd, which has Khao San-style rooms with fan and bath for 150 to 180B.

The new *Win Hotel* further down the road has all air-con rooms with TV and telephone for 420B, plus a nice coffee shop downstairs.

Chao Koh Bungalow, just north of town, is 250 to 600B. *Samui Bungalow*, near the post office, charges from 120B for rather small rooms with fan and bath. South of town are the *Chokana*, at 200B a single or double, 250B for a room that sleeps four, and the *Jinta*, with singles/doubles for 100/150B.

Places to Eat There are several good restaurants and watering holes in Na Thon. On the road facing the harbour, the *Chao Koh Restaurant* is one of the few place still around since the last edition of this guide – still serving good seafood and Thai standards at reasonable prices. *Ko Kaew* is a similar standby. A good place for breakfast is the *Jelly Roll*, a bakery with homemade pastries and coffee; other meals include burgers, sandwiches and pizzata.

Further down the road towards Thong Yang are the *Pha-Ngan* and *Sri Samui* restaurants, both quite good Thai seafood places. Toward the Palace Hotel is a Thai rice and noodle place that's open all night, *Raan Khao Tom Toh Rung* (no English sign) – the cheapest place to eat on this strip. During the high season, many of these restaurants fill up at night with travellers waiting for the night ferry.

Up at the corner of the waterfront road and Na Amphoe Rd is the *Bird in the Hand*, a bar with a few tables and a variety of Western breakfasts (listed 'American', 'Australian', 'English', etc), plus sandwiches, imported beers and liquors.

On the next street back from the harbour is another branch of the Jelly Roll bakery, *Jelly Roll II*, then the *J Home Bakery* and a few old Chinese coffee shops like *Kafae Samui*. Further south on this street is the *Fountain*, an Italian place specialising in pasta and pizza. Back in the other direction (north) on an intersection is *El Pirata*, a small Spanish garden restaurant with pizza and paella. Across the street from El Pirata is the *Golden Lion*, a medium-priced seafood place. Down the street a bit from El Pirata is the *Pier Restaurant*, a popular bar/restaurant with video to keep everyone seated and glassy-eyed. Other bars in the vicinity include the *Tani Bar* and the *Golden Lion Pub*, open only at night from around 6 pm to midnight. After midnight the only places open are the *Khao Tom Toh Rung* and the flashy Thai nightclub *Pan On Cafe*, which is rather expensive, dark and well chilled.

The third street back from the harbour is mostly travel agencies, photo shops and other small businesses. Two small supermarkets, Samui Mart and Giant Supermarket are also back here. The Charoen Laap morning market is still in operation on this street as well. Down at the southern end is the *New York Bar & Grill (Forza Italia)* with Italian and American-style deli food. The nearby *Tang's Restaurant & Bakery* is yet another place catering to farang tastes. The *RT Bakery* further north of the same street is similar.

One of the few places in town still serving Thai (and Chinese) food on a large scale is *Jit Phochana Khao Tom* on Thawi Ratchaphakdi Rd, diagonally opposite Forza Italia. A small *Vegetarian Restaurant* opens at night on the southern end of Ang Thong Rd.

Samui Beaches

Samui has plenty of beaches to choose from, with bungalows appearing at more small bays all the time. Transport has also improved, so getting from beach to beach is no problem. The most crowded beaches for accommodation are Chaweng and Lamai, both more or less on the eastern side of the island. Chaweng has more bungalow 'villages' – over 50 at last count – plus a couple of recently developed flashy tourist hotels. It is the longest beach, over twice the size of Lamai, and has the island of **Mat Lang** opposite. Both beaches have clear blue-green waters. There are coral reefs for snorkelling and underwater sightseeing at both. Perhaps there's a bit more to do in Hat Lamai because of its proximity to two villages – Ban Lamai and Ban Hua Thanon. At the wat in Ban Lamai is the **Ban Lamai Cultural Hall**, a sort of folk museum displaying local ceramics, household utensils, hunting weapons and musical instruments.

Chaweng is definitely the target of current up-market development because of its long beach. Another factor is that only Chaweng Beach (and the northern part of Lamai) has water deep enough for swimming from October to April; most other beaches on the island become very shallow during these months.

For more peace and quiet, try the beaches along the north, south and west coasts. Mae Nam, Bo Phut and Big Buddha are along the northern end; Bo Phut and Big Buddha are part of a bay that holds **Ko Faan** (the island with the 'big Buddha'), separated by a small headland. The water here is not quite as clear as at Chaweng or Lamai, but the feeling of seclusion is greater, and accommodation is cheaper.

Hat Thong Yang is on the western side of the island and is even more secluded (only a few sets of bungalows there), but the beach isn't that great by Samui standards. There is also Hat Ang Thong, just north of Na Thon, very rocky but with more local colour (eg fishing boats) than the others. The southern end of the island now has many bungalows as well, set in little out-of-the-way coves – worth seeking out. And then there's everywhere in-between – every bay, cove or cape with a strip of sand gets a bungalow nowadays, right around the island.

Accommodation & Food Prices vary considerably according to the time of year and occupancy rates. Some of the bungalow operators on Samui have a nasty habit of tripling room rates when rooms are scarce, so a hut that's 80B in June could be 250B in August. Rates given in this section can only serve as a guideline – they could go lower if you bargain or higher if space is tight.

Everyone has his or her own idea of what the perfect beach bungalow is. At Ko Samui, the search could take a month or two, with over 150 operations to choose from. Most offer roughly the same services and accommodation for 50 to 150B, though some are quite a bit more. The best thing to do is to go to the beach you think you want to stay at and pick one you like – look inside the huts, check out the restaurant, the menu, the guests. You can always move if you're not satisfied.

Beach accommodation around Samui now falls into four basic categories chronicling the evolution of places to stay on the island. The first phase included simple bungalows with thatched roofs and walls of local, easily replaceable materials; the next phase brought concrete bathrooms attached to the old-style huts, a transition to the third phase of cement walls and tile roofs – the predominant style now, with more advanced facilities like fans and sometimes air-con. The latest wave is luxury rooms and bungalows indistinguishable from mainland inns and hotels.

Generally anything that costs less than 100B a night will mean a shared bath, which may be preferable when you remember that mosquitoes breed in standing water. For a pretty basic bungalow with private bath, 100 to 150B is the minimum on Ko Samui.

Food is touch and go at all the beaches – one meal can be great, the next at the very same place not so great. Fresh seafood is usually what they do best and the cheapest way to eat it is to catch it yourself and have the bungalow cooks prepare it for you, or buy it in one of the many fishing villages around the island, direct from the fishermen themselves, or in the village markets. Good places to buy are in the relatively large Muslim fishing villages of Mae Nam, Bo Phut and Hua Thanon.

The island has changed so much in the years between editions of this book (not to mention the way it has changed since 1971, when the first tourists arrived), that I hesitate to name favourites. Cooks come and go, bungalows flourish and go bankrupt, owners are assassinated by competitors – you never can tell from season to season. Prices have remained fairly stable here in recent years, unlike at Phuket, but they are creeping up. It's easy to get from one beach to another, so you can always change bungalows. The jet-set seem to be discovering Samui but, thank goodness, Club Med and Amanpuri decided to build on Phuket rather than here. Finally, if Samui isn't to your liking, move islands! Think about Ko Pha-Ngan or Ko Tao.

What follows are some general comments on staying at Samui's various beaches, moving clockwise around the island from Na Thon.

Ban Tai (Ao Bang Baw)
บ้านใต้ (อ่าวบางบ่อ)

Ban Tai is the first beach area north of Na Thon; so far there are only three places to stay here. The beach here has fair snorkelling and swimming. The new *Axolotl Village*, run by an Italian-German partnership, caters to Europeans (the staff speaks English, Italian, German and French) with tastefully designed, mid-range rooms for 300B or bungalows for 400 to 600B. Meditation and massage rooms were under construction when I visited; a very pleasant restaurant area overlooking the beach was complete.

Next door is the similar-looking and similar-priced *Blue River* under Thai management. Also at Ban Tai is *Sunbeam*, a set of bungalows in a very nice setting. Huts are 250 to 300B, all with private bath.

Hat Mae Nam

หาดแม่น้ำ

Hat Mae Nam is 14 km from Na Thon and expanding rapidly in terms of budget bungalow development – definitely the cheapest area on the island at this writing.

At the headland (Laem Na Phra Lan) where Ao Bang Baw ends and Mae Nam begins is the *Plant Inn*, also spelled *Phalarn*, with bungalows from 50 to 200B. A second branch, the *Phalarn Inn II*, has recently opened with rooms ranging from 150 to 300B.

Also in this area are *Coco Palm Village*, *Home Bay Bungalows*, *Naplarn Villa*, *Harry's OK Village* and *Nahlan Rest House* – all in the 50 to 150B range. The beach in front of Wat Na Phalaan is undeveloped and the locals hope it will stay that way – topless bathing is strongly discouraged here.

The next group of places east includes *Shangrilah Bungalows*, *Anong Villa*, *Maenam Resort*, *Palm Point Village* and *Shady Shack Bungalows*, where prices vary from 40 to 100B at Shady Shack to 200 to 300B at Maenam Resort.

The huge *Santiburi Resort Hotel* is being built next to Ban Mae Nam – with tennis courts and all, it will probably run to around 650B.

Right in Ban Mae Nam are *Lolita Bungalows* (50 to 100B) and the new *Maenam Inn*, a hotel on the circuit road with air-con rooms for 330B in the low season, 550B in the high, or 680B with TV.

Down on Hat Mae Nam proper is *Friendly*, which has clean, well-kept huts for 40B per person, and good food too. Also good are *LaPaz Villa* (50 to 80B), and *Silent* (70 to 150B).

Moving toward Bo Phut are *Moon Hut Bungalows*, *Rose Bungalows*, *Laem Sai Bungalows*, *Maenam Villa* and *Rainbow Bungalows*.

There are at least 10 or 15 other bungalow operations between Laem Na Phra Lan and Laem Sai, where Ao Mae Nam ends. The *Ubon Villa* (30 to 80B) has been recommended by a few readers.

Hat Bo Phut

หาดบ่อผุด

This beach has a reputation for peace and quiet; there are about 18 places to stay here in total. Before you arrive at Bo Phut village is a string of 80 to 200B places, including *Bo Phut Guesthouse*, *Sandy Resort*, *World Resort*, *Samui Palm Beach*, *Palm Garden*, *Calm Beach Resort*, *Peace*, plus the *Samui Euphoria* a semi-luxury place in the 700 to 1000B range. World and Calm each have more expensive 500B bungalows as well.

Proceeding east, a road off the main round-island road runs to the left and along the bay towards the village. Here you'll find the original *Boon Bungalows*, a small operation with 40 to 50B huts, as well as the *New Boon Privacy*, owned by the same family. At New Boon large, comfortable bungalows with two beds, fan and fridge go for 400 to 500B. The restaurants at both Boons are good. West of Boon's is *Ziggy Stardust*, a clean and popular place with huts for 150 to 250B. Next to Ziggy's is the new *Siam Sea Lodge*, a small hotel with rooms for 300B with fan, hot water and fridge, or 400B with ocean view. You'll find several more cheapies along this strip, including *Smile House*, *Miami* and *Oasis*, all with huts in the 50 to 100B range.

If you continue through the village along the water, you'll find *Sky Blue*, a place off by itself with huts for 40 to 60B. This area is sometimes called Hat Bang Rak.

The village has a couple of cheap local-style restaurants as well as a couple of farang places with French names.

Big Buddha Beach (Hat Phra Yai)

หาดพระใหญ่

This now has nearly a dozen bungalow operations, including the moderately expensive air-con *Nara Bungalows* (☎ 421364) with rooms for 380 to 600B and a swimming pool. *Family Village* gets good reviews and costs 100 to 200B. *Big Buddha Bungalows* (150 to 200B) is still OK. *Ocean View* and *Sun Set* are about the cheapest places here now, with simple huts at 30 to 100B. The rest – *Niphon*, *Como's*, *Champ Resort*, *Beach House*, *Kinnaree* and *Number One* – are in the 100 to 200B range.

Ao Thong Son & Ao Thong Sai

อ่าวท้องสน/อ่าวท้องไทร

The big cape between Big Buddha and Chaweng is actually a series of four capes and coves, the first of which is Ao Thong Son. The road to Thong Son is a bit on the hellish side, but that keeps this area quiet and secluded. *Samui Thongson Resort* has its own cove and bungalows for 200B with fan, 850 to 1200B with air-con. *Thongson Bay Bungalows* next door has old-style bungalows for 80 to 100B; further on is the similar *Golden Pine*.

The next cove over is as yet undeveloped and there isn't even a dirt road there yet. The third, Ao Thong Sai, has *Tongsai Bay Hotel & Cottages* (☎ 421451), a heavily guarded resort with a private beach, swimming pool and tennis courts. Rates are 3800 to 4200B.

Hat Choeng Mon

หาดเชิงมน

The largest cove following Ao Thong Sai has been called by several names, but the beach is generally known as Hat Choeng Mon. Here find *PS Villa* (50 to 200B), *Choeng Mon Palace* (500 to 800B), *Chat Kaew Resort* (50 to 200B), *Island View* (40 to 100B) and the well laid out *Sun Sand Resort* (950B), which has sturdy thatched-roof bungalows connected by wooden walkways on a breezy hillside. Across from the beach is **Ko Faan Yai**, an island that can be reached on foot in low tide.

Next is the smaller bay called Ao Yai Noi, just before north Chaweng. This little bay is quite picturesque, with large boulders framing the beach. The secluded *IKK* bungalows are 150 to 200B and the *Coral Bay Resort* has larger bungalows that range from 450B with fan to 800B with air-con.

Hat Chaweng

หาดเฉวง

Hat Chaweng, Samui's longest beach, also has the island's highest concentration of bungalows and is even getting a few tourist hotels. Prices are moving up-market fast; accommodation is now perhaps 50B at the lowest in the off season, and up to 2600B at the Imperial Samui. There is now a little commercial 'strip' behind the central beach with restaurants, souvenir shops and discos. If there are a lot of vacant huts (there usually are during the low season) you can sometimes talk prices down to 50B for a basic hut. The beach is beautiful here, and local developers are finally cleaning up some of the trashy areas behind the bungalows that were becoming a problem in the early '80s.

Chaweng has km after km of beach and bungalows – perhaps 50 or more in all – so have a look around before deciding on a place. There are basically three sections: North Chaweng, Hat Chaweng proper and Chaweng Noi.

North Chaweng places are mostly in the 80 to 200B range, with simple bungalows with private bath at the northernmost end. These include the *Matlang Resort*, *Samui Island Resort*, *Marine*, *Moon*, *Family* and *K John Resort*. Then at the end nearest to central Chaweng are a group of places starting at 500B: *Samui Village*, *Palm Reef Hotel*, *The Island*, *Blue Lagoon Hotel* and *Samui Palace*.

The central area, Hat Chaweng proper, is the longest and has the most bungalows and hotels. This is also where the strip behind the hotels and huts is centred, with restaurants, bars, discos, video parlours, tourist police and even a mobile currency exchange. The *Manohra* restaurant here features classical southern-Thai dancing performances with dinner. Water sports are big here, too, so you can rent sailboards, go diving, sail a catamaran, charter a junk and so on. This area also has the highest average prices on the island, not only because accommodation is more up-market but simply because this is/was the prettiest beach on the island. In general, the places get more expensive as you move from north to south; many of these are owned by the same families as owned them under different names 10 years ago, some have just added the word 'Resort' to the name. The *Reggae Pub* is building a huge zoo-like complex off the beach with accommodation – the din will probably be incredible. Rather than list all the places on Chaweng Central, I'll just give examples across the spectrum, starting at the north:

Chaweng Villa, 80 to 200B
Lucky Mother, 80 to 200B
Coconut Grove, 60 to 200B
Chaweng Garden, 150 to 400B
Malibu Resort, 50 to 250B
Long Beach, 50 to 300B
Thai House, 80 to 200B
The Village, 700 to 800B
Samui Pansea, 950 to 2000B
Joy Resort, 400 to 800B
Munchies Resort, 400 to 700B

If you're getting the idea that this isn't the beach for backpackers, you're right. To save money, it's better to stay at the cheaper places at North Chaweng or Chaweng Noi and make use of all three beach areas, or go to another beach entirely.

Chaweng Noi is off by itself around a headland at the southern end of central Hat Chaweng. One place that straddles the headland on both bays is the aptly named *First Bungalows* (they were the first to build on this beach 12 years ago), with old-style Samui bungalows for 200B, concrete-and-tile types for 500B. The *New Star* is reasonably priced at 80 to 350B. Nearby *Fair House* has fan-cooled rooms for 150B, air-con up to 800B.

Samui's top property at the moment, the *Imperial Samui*, is built on a slope in the middle of Chaweng Noi proper and costs 1600 to 2600B for air-con accommodation with telephone and colour TV. The Imperial's 56 cottages and 24-room hotel are built in a pseudo-Mediterranean style with a 700-sq-metre saltwater swimming pool and a terrace restaurant with a view. Not very far from the Imperial is the upgraded *Sunshine*, where huts are now 900B up. The *Maew* is a pre-Imperial hold-out where huts are still 40 to 100B – if it hasn't disappeared. The *Thawee* is another oldie for 80 to 150B and the *Chaweng Noi* is similarly priced. Finally there's the *Tropicana Beach Resort* with all air-con rooms at 800 to 1500B.

Coral Cove (Ao Thong Yang)
อ่าวท้องยาง

Another series of capes and coves starts at the end of Chaweng Noi, beginning with scenic Coral Cove. Somehow the Thais have managed to squeeze three places around the cove, plus one across the road. The only one with immediate beach access is *Coral Cove*, where basic huts are 70 to 200B. The *Hi Coral Cove* above is 100 to 200B. The *Hillside Hut* on the hill opposite the road and the *Coral Cove Resort* are in the same price range.

Ao Thong Ta Khian
อ่าวท้องตะเคียน

This is another small, steep-sided cove, similar to Coral Cove and banked by huge boulders. At the time of writing there is one small set of bungalows here, *Thong Ta Khian Kata Garden*. The huts overlook the bay and cost 80 to 100B. There are a couple of good seafood restaurants down on the bay, and this is a good place for fishing.

Hat Lamai
หาดละไม

After Chaweng, this is Samui's most popular beach for farangs. Hat Lamai rates are just a bit lower than at Chaweng overall, without the larger places like the Pansea or Imperial (yet) and fewer of the 500B-plus places. As at Chaweng, the bay has developed in sections, with a long central beach flanked by hilly areas. Recently there have been reports of burglaries and muggings at Lamai. These could be isolated incidents or could signal a trend; take care with valuables – have them locked away in a guesthouse or hotel office if possible.

Cheaper huts at the north-eastern end are at *Comfort* (50 to 150B), *Thong Gaid Garden* (50 to 100B), *Blue Lagoon* (60 to 300B), and, back from the beach, *My Friend* (50B). More expensive are the newer places, including *Island Resort* (200 to 500B), *Rose Garden* (50 to 200B) and *Spanish Eyes* (100 to 150B). There are a sprinkling of others here that seem to come and go with the seasons.

Down into the main section of Lamai is a string of places for 100 to 400B including *Mui*, *Fantasy Villa*, *Magic*, *Coconut Villa* and the *Weekender*. The Weekender has a wide variety of bungalows and activities to choose from, including a bit of a nightlife. Moving into the centre of Ao Lamai, you'll come across *Coconut Beach* (40 to 500B), *Animal House* (skip this one, it's received several complaints), *Lamai Inn* (150 to 300B) and the *Best Resort* (150 to 500B). This is the part of the bay closest to Ban Lamai village and the beginning of the Lamai 'scene' – lots of bars and low-rent discos.

Next comes a string of slightly up-market 100 to 350B places: *Marina Villa*, *Sawatdi*, *Mira Mare*, *Sea Breeze*, *Aloha*, *Varinda Resort* and *Thai House Inn*. All of these have fairly elaborate dining areas; the Aloha (☎ 421418) is said to have a good Italian restaurant. The *Golden Sand* and *Moonlight* are 200 to 300B.

Finishing up central Hat Lamai is a mixture of 50 to 80B and 100 to 200B places. The *White Sand* is one of the Lamai originals and huts are still 40B. A farang flea market is held here on Sundays – many travellers sell handmade jewellery. The long-standing *Palm* is still here as well, but they've upgraded the bungalows to the 150 to 250B price-range. The *Nice Resort* has huts for 150B up but they're really too close together. Finally, there's the *Sun Rise* with acceptable 50 to 150B huts.

At this point a headland interrupts Ao Lamai and the bay beyond is known as **Ao Bang Nam Cheut**, named after the freshwater stream that runs into the bay here. During the dry months the sea is too shallow for swimming here, but in the late rainy season when the surf is too high elsewhere on the island's beaches, south Lamai is one of the best for swimming. Way out on the rocky point is *Rock* with simple huts interspersed between boulders for 40 to 60B. Down farther is *Anika, Noi* and *Best Wishes*, all with huts for 50 to 60B. The *Swiss Chalet* has large bungalows overlooking the sea for 150 to 200B and the restaurant does Swiss as well as Thai food. Then comes the old-timer *Rocky* with the same rates.

Ao Na Khai & Laem Set

Just beyond the village of Ban Hua Thanon at the southern end of Ao Na Khai is an area sometimes called Hat Na Thian. As at Lanai, the places along the southern end of the island are pretty rocky, which means good snorkelling (there's a long reef here), but perhaps not such good swimming. Prices in this area seem fairly reasonable – 100B here gets you what 200B might in Chaweng. The hard part is finding these places, since they're off the round-island road, down dirt tracks, and most don't have phones. You might try exploring this area on a motorcycle first. The *Cosy Resort* has 11 well-spaced huts for 100 to 200B. Down a different road in the same area is the *Samui Orchid Resort* (☎ 421079), which, with huts and a swimming pool for 450 to 750B, is slightly up-market. Turn right here, follow the coast and you'll come to the basic *Sonny View* (50B) and the nicely designed *Na Thian* (100 to 150B). At the end of the road is the secluded *Laem Set Inn* (radio ☎ (01) 212-2762). Rates vary from 1250B for a standard bungalow that wouldn't cost more than 500B elsewhere on the island to 2000B for a larger bungalow – priced at least 1000B above market.

Ao Bang Kao

This bay is at the very south end of the island between Laem Set and Laem So (Saw). Again, you have to go off the round-island road a couple of km to find these places: *River Garden* (50 to 100B), *Diamond Villa* (50 to 100B), *Samui Coral Beach* (100 to 300B) and *Waikiki* (300 to 400B).

Ao Thong Krut & Ko Taen

Next to the village of Ban Thong Krut on Ao Thong Krut is, what else, *Thong Krut*, where huts with private bath are only 80B.

Ban Thong Krut is also the jumping-off point for boat trips to four offshore islands: **Ko Taen, Ko Raap, Ko Mat Daeng** (best coral) and **Ko Mat Sun**. Ko Taen has two bungalow villages along the east-coast beach at Ao Awk; *Tan Village* and *Coral Beach*, both for 200B a night. Ko Mat Sum has good beaches – some travellers have camped here.

Boats to Ko Taen cost 150B each way. If you want to have a good look at the islands, you can charter a boat at the *Sunset Restaurant* in Thong Krut from 9 am to 4 pm for 700 to 800B; the boats carry up to 10 persons. The Sunset Restaurant has good seafood – best to arrange in advance – and delicious coconut shakes.

West Coast

Several bays along Samui's western side have places to stay, including Thong Yang, where the Don Sak ferry docks. The beaches here turn to mud flats during low tide, however, so they're more or less for people seeking to get away from the east coast scene, not for beach fanatics.

Ao Phangka Around Laem Hin Khom on the bottom of Samui's western side is this little bay, sometimes called Emerald Cove. The secluded *Emerald Cove* and *Sea Gull* have huts with rates from 50 to 100B – it's a nice setting and perfectly quiet.

Ao Thong Yang The car ferry jetty is here in Ao Thong Yang. Near the pier are *Sunflower* (30 to 400B), *Coco Cabana Beach Club* (80 to 250B) and the motel-like *Samui Ferry Inn* (400 to 600B). The Coco Cabana is the best of the lot.

Ao Chon Khram On the way to Na Thon is sweeping Ao Chon Khram with the *Lipa Lodge* and *International*. The Lipa Lodge is especially nice, with a good site on the bay. Rates start at 60B, most huts are about 80 to 100B, with a few as high as 450B. There is a good restaurant and bar here, not bad for the money. On the other hand, the International is nothing special at 150 to 400B.

Getting There & Away

Air Bangkok Airways (☎ 253-4014), 144 Sukhumvit Rd, Bangkok, now flies daily to Ko Samui. The fare is 1730B one-way – no discount for a return ticket. The flight duration is one hour and 10 minutes, with flights departing Bangkok five times daily. Bangkok Airways has plans to offer Samui-Phuket flights in the future.

The Samui Airport departure tax is 100B. Bangkok Airways has a limo for 60B per person to/from its Na Thon office; the limo also departs from JR Bungalow on Chaweng Beach and Best Resort in Lamai. Chartered taxis cost 120B to anywhere on the island.

Bus Most private buses from Bangkok cost around 300B including the ferry to Samui. The government bus/ferry fare from the Bangkok's northern air-con bus terminal is 280B. From Khao San Rd in Bangkok it's possible to get bus-ferry combination tickets for as low as 180B, but service is substandard and theft is more frequent than on the more expensive buses.

Train The SRT also does rail/bus/ferry tickets straight through to Samui from Bangkok. The fares are 399B for a 2nd-class upper berth, 429B for a 2nd-class lower berth, 284B for a 2nd-class seat and 210B for a 3rd-class seat. This includes rapid service and berth charges; add 100B for air-con. This only comes out cheaper (10B less) than doing the connections yourself if you buy the 2nd-class seat. For all other tickets it's 30 to 50B more expensive.

Boat To sort out the ferry situation you have to first understand that there are two ferry companies, one hovercraft company and three ferry piers (actually four but only three are in use at one time) on the Surat Thani coast and two on Ko Samui. Neither ferry company is going to tell you about the other. Songserm Travel runs the express ferry boats from the Tha Thong pier, six km north-east of downtown Surat, and the slow night boats from the Ban Don pier in town. These take passengers only. The express boats used to leave from the same pier in Ban Don as the night ferry – when the river is unusually high they may use this pier again.

Samui Ferry Co runs the vehicle ferries from Don Sak (or Khanom when the sea is high). This is the company that gets most of the bus/boat and some of the train/bus/boat combination business.

The hovercraft is a new operation and service so far has been irregular.

Express Boat from Tha Thong From November to May three express boats go to Samui (Na Thon) daily from Tha Thong and each takes two to 2½ hours to reach the island. From November to May the departure times are usually 7.30, 11.30 am and 2 pm, though these change from time to time. From June to October there are only two express boats a day at 7.30 am and 12.30 pm – the seas usually are too high in the late afternoon for a third sailing in this direction during the rainy season. Passage is 100B one-way, 190B return. The express ferry boats have two decks, one with seats below and an upper deck that is really just a big luggage rack – good for sunbathing.

From Na Thon back to Surat, there are departures at 7.15 am, noon and 3 pm from November to May, or 7.30 am and 3 pm June to October. The 7.15 or 7.30 am boat includes a bus ride to the railway station in Phun Phin; the afternoon boats include a bus to the railway station and to the Talaat Kaset bus station in Ban Don.

Night Ferry from Ban Don There is also a slow boat for Samui that leaves the Ban Don pier each night at 11 pm, reaching Na Thon around 5 am. This one costs 60B for the upper deck (includes pillows and mattresses), or 40B down below (straw mats only). This trip is not particularly recommended unless you arrive in Surat Thani too late for the fast boat and don't want to stay in Ban Don. Some travellers have reported, however, that a night on the boat is preferable to a night in a noisy Surat Thani short-time hotel. And it does give you more sun time on Samui, after all. The night ferry back to Samui leaves Na Thon at 9 pm, arriving at 3 am.

Don't leave your bags unattended on the night ferry, as thefts have been a problem recently. The thefts usually occur after you drop your bags on the ferry well before departure and then go for a walk around the pier area. Most victims don't notice anything's missing until they unpack after arrival on Samui.

Hovercraft from Tha Thon The new hovercraft service takes 1½ hours from Tha Thong to Na Thon and costs 350B each way. Phanthip Travel can book the hovercraft in Surat; on Samui you'll have to go the hovercraft office, near the Win Hotel in Na Thon. Considering the hovercraft fare is more than triple the express boat fare, it's not really worth the half-hour time saving. This service probably won't last more than a year unless the fare is lowered.

Vehicle Ferry from Don Sak Tour buses run directly from Bangkok to Ko Samui, via the car ferry from Don Sak in Surat Thani Province, for around 230B. Check with the big tour bus companies or any travel agency.

From Talaat Mai Rd in Surat Thani you can also get bus/ferry combination tickets straight through to Na Thon. These cost 60B on an ordinary bus, 80B for an air-con bus. Pedestrians or people in private vehicles can also take the ferry directly from Don Sak, which leaves at 8, 10 am, noon, 2 and 5 pm, and takes one hour to reach the Thong Yang pier on Samui. In the opposite direction, ferries leave Thong Yang at the same times except for the first ferry, which leaves at 7.30 am instead of 8 am.

The fare for pedestrians is 40B, for a motorcycle and driver 70B, and for a car and driver 180B. Passengers on private vehicles pay the pedestrian fare. Don Sak is about 60 km from Surat Thani. A bus from the Surat Thani bus station is 10B and takes 45 minutes to an hour to arrive at the Don Sak Ferry. If you're coming north from Nakhon Si Thammarat, this might be the ferry to take, though from Surat Thani the Tha Thong ferry is definitely more convenient.

From Ko Samui, air-con buses to Bangkok leave from near the pier in Na Thon at 1.30 and 3.30 pm daily, both arriving at 5 am due to the stopover in Surat. Through buses to Hat Yai from Samui cost 230B and leave Na Thon at 7.30 am, 3 and 9 pm, arriving six hours later. Check with the several travel agencies in Na Thon for the latest routes.

Getting Around

It is quite possible to hitch around the island, despite the fact that anyone on the island with a car is likely to want to boost their income by charging for rides.

The official songthaew fares are 10B from Na Thon to Lamai, Mae Nam or Bo Phut, 15B to Big Buddha or Chaweng, 20B to Choeng Mon. From the car-ferry landing in Thong Yang, rates are 15B for Lamai, Mae Nam and Bo Phut/Big Buddha, 20B for Chaweng, 25B for Choeng Mon. These minibuses run regularly during daylight hours only. A bus between Thong Yang and Na Thon is 5B. Note that if you're arriving in Thong Yang on a bus (via the vehicle ferry), your bus/boat fare includes a ride into Na Thon.

Several places rent motorcycles in Na Thon and at various bungalows around the island. The going rate is 150B per day, but on longer periods you can get the price down (say 280B for two days, 400B for three days, etc). Rates are generally lower in Na Thon and it makes more sense to rent them there if you're going back that way. Take it easy on the bikes; several farangs die or are seriously injured in motorcycle accidents every year on Samui, and, besides, the locals really don't like seeing their roads become race tracks.

KO PHA-NGAN
เกาะพะงัน

Ko Pha-Ngan, about a half-hour boat ride north of Ko Samui, has become the island of choice for those who find Samui too crowded. It started out as sort of a 'back-door escape' from Samui but is pretty well established now, with a regular boat service and nearly 90 places to stay around the 190-sq-km island. It's definitely worth a visit for its remaining deserted beaches (they haven't all been built upon) and, if you like snorkelling, for its live-coral formations.

In the interior of this somewhat smaller island are the **Than Sadet** and **Phaeng** waterfalls.

Although hordes of backpackers have discovered Ko Pha-Ngan, a lack of roads has so far spared it from tourist hotel and package tour development. Compared to Samui, Ko Pha-Ngan has a lower concentration of bungalows, less-crowded beaches and coves, and an overall less 'spoiled' atmosphere. Pha-Ngan aficionados say the seafood is fresher and cheaper than on Samui's beaches, but it really varies from place to place. As Samui becomes more expensive for both travellers and investors, more and more people will be drawn to Pha-Ngan. But for the time being, overall living costs are about half what you'd pay on Samui.

Another bonus is that the island hasn't yet been cursed with video; unlike Samui, travellers actually interact instead of staring over one another's shoulders at a video screen. Nor are there blaring stereos (except at the island's party capital, Hat Rin).

Wat Khao Tham

วัดเขาถ้ำ

This cave temple is beautifully situated on top of a hill near the little village of Ban Khai. An American monk lived here for over a decade and his ashes are interred on a cliff overlooking a field of palms below the wat. It's not a true wat since there are only two monks and a nun in residence (a quorum of five monks is necessary for wat status).

Ten-day meditation retreats taught by an American-Australian couple are held here during the latter half of most months. The cost is 900B; write in advance for information or preregister in person. A bulletin board at the temple also has information.

Thong Sala

ท้องศาลา

Ko Pha-Ngan has a total population of roughly 7500 and about half of them live in and around the small port town of Thong Sala. This is where the ferry boats from Surat and Samui (Na Thon) dock although there are also smaller boats from Mae Nam and Bo Phut on Samui.

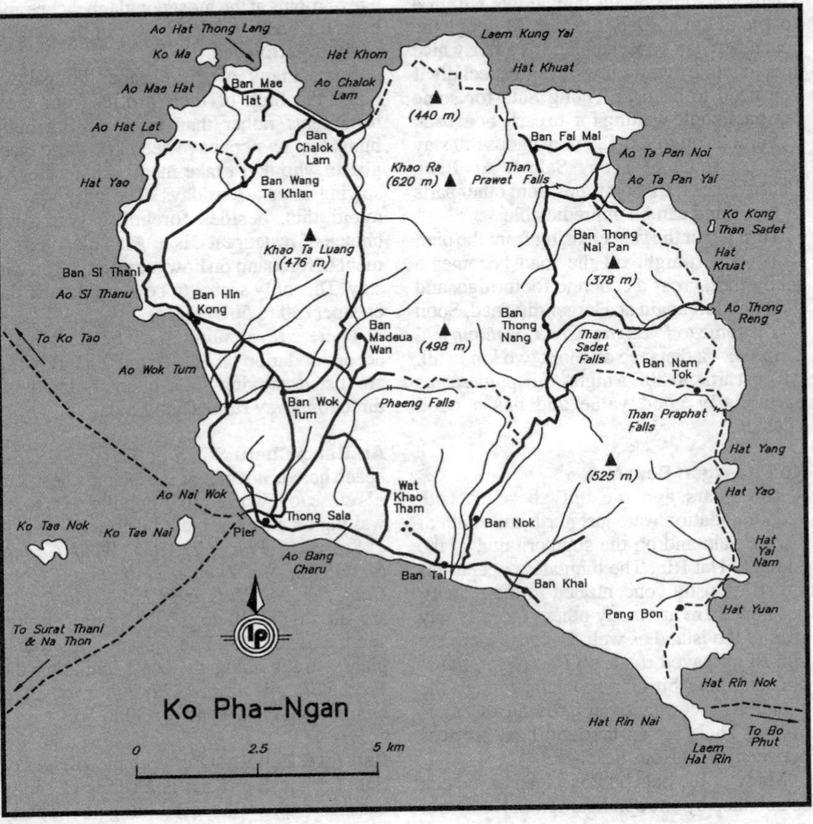

Thong Sala is the only place on the island where you can change money at regular bank rates and post or receive mail. You can also rent motorcycles here for 150 to 250B per day.

Although it is possible to rent rooms in Thong Sala, most people of course choose to stay at one of Pha-Ngan's beaches.

In town the *Shady Nook Guest House* and *Vantana Guest House* offer adequate rooms for 100B a night. There is also a small no-name hotel that's mostly used as the town brothel for 80 to 100B a night.

Ao Nai Wok

There are some beach bungalows within a couple of km north of the pier. Although the beach here isn't spectacular, it's a fairly nice area to while away a few days – especially if you need to be near Thong Sala for some reason. People waiting for an early boat back to Surat or on to Ko Tao may choose to stay here (or south of Thong Sala at Ao Bang Charu) since transport times from other parts of the island can be unpredictable.

Turn left at the first crossing from the pier, then walk straight till the road becomes a sandy trail, cross a concrete footbridge, and then turn left again at a larger dirt road. Soon you'll come to *Phangan*, *Chan*, *Wattana* and *Siriphun* – a distance of about two km in all. All cost around 80B a night – Siriphun seems particularly good value and has a good kitchen.

Ko Pha-Ngan Beaches

A few years ago the only beaches with accommodation were just north and south of Thong Sala and on the southern end of the island at Hat Rin. The bungalow operations are still mostly concentrated in these areas, but now there are many other places to stay around the island as well. Because there are almost no paved roads on Pha-Ngan, transport can be a bit of a problem, though the situation is constantly improving as enterprising Thais set up taxi and boat services between the various beaches.

Many of the huts on Pha-Ngan have been established by entrepreneurs from Ko Samui with several years experience in the bungalow business. Huts go for 40 to 80B a night on average; many do not have electricity or running water. Some have generators which are only on for limited hours in the evening – the lights dim when they make a fruit shake. For many people, of course, this adds to Pha-Ngan's appeal. Other places are moving into the 80 to 150B range, which almost always includes a private bath. As travel to Pha-Ngan seems particularly seasonal, you should be able to talk bungalow rates down when occupancy is low. During the peak months, December to February and July and August, there can be an acute shortage of rooms at the most popular beaches and even the boats coming here can be dangerously overcrowded.

Since many of the cheaper bungalows make the bulk of their profits from their restaurants rather than from renting huts, bungalow owners have been known to eject guests who don't take meals where they're staying after a few days. The only way to avoid this, besides foregoing your own choice of restaurants, is to get a clear agreement beforehand on how many days you can stay. This only seems to be a problem at the cheaper (30 to 50B) places.

There are a number of beaches with accommodation on Pha-Ngan; the following are listed moving in a counter-clockwise direction away from Thong Sala.

Ao Bang Charu South of Thong Sala, the beach here is not one of the island's best, but it's close to town and so is popular with folks waiting for boats or bank business.

Sea Surf, *Phangan Villa*, *Wind Chime*, *Moonlight*, *Sun Dance*, *Half Moon*, *Coco Club*, *Bamboo Huts* and *Chokkhana Resort* are all in the 40 to 100B range. Further south-east towards Ban Tai are a few other places strung along the coast including the *First Villa*, *Windward*, *First Resort*, *Bunbandan* and *P Park*, all for 30 to 50B.

Ban Tai & Ban Khai Between the villages of Ban Tai and Ban Khai is a series of sandy beaches with well-spaced bungalow operations, all in the 30 to 60B range. Here you can find *Pink*, *Liberty*, *Jup*, *Lucky*, *Lee's Garden*, *Sun*, *Copa*, *Pan Beach*, *Pha-Ngan Rainbow*, *Golden Beach*, *Windy Huts*, *Green Peace*, *Laem Thong*, *Thong Yang*, *Banja Beach*, *Booms Cafe*, *CK's Chalet* and *Silvery Moon*.

In Ban Khai the locals also rent rooms to travellers, especially from December to February when just about everything is filled up. You can get a hut for a month at very low rates here.

Laem Hat Rin This long cape juts south-east and has beaches along both its westward and eastward sides. The eastward side has the best beach, Hat Rin Nok, a long sandy strip lined with coconut palms. The snorkelling here is pretty good, but between October and March the surf can be a little hairy.

Along the western side, sometimes called Hat Rin Nai (Inner Rin Beach), you'll find long-runners *Palm Beach* and *Sunset*, both for 30 to 50B. Newer places that offer similarly priced accommodation are *Sun Beach*, *Bang Son Villa*, *Sandy*, *Sea Side*, *Rainbow*, *Sooksom*, *Coral*, *Neptune's*, *Dolphin*, *Charung*, *Family House*, *K*, *Rainbow*, *Coral*, *Chok Chai* and, down near the tip of the cape, *Lighthouse*. The *Rin Beach Resort* has a few larger huts with private bath for 150B as well as the 30B cheapies.

Across the ridge on the east side is Hat Rin Nok (Outer Rin Beach), famous for its monthly 'full moon parties' featuring all-night beach dancing and the ingestion of various illicit substances – forget about sleeping on these nights. The bungalows here are stacked rather closely together and include *Seaview*, *Tommy*, *Sunrise*, *Hat Rin*, *Chinese Rose*, *Phangan Bayshore Resort* and *Paradise*. These are all in the 40 to 80B range. The *Palita Lodge* has huts with private bath for 100 to 150B, plus cheaper 50B huts.

On both sides of Hat Rin, hammers and saws are busy putting together new huts, so there may be quite a few more places by now. Hat Rin beach huts now have electricity from 6 pm till midnight.

East Coast Beaches Above Hat Rin Nok around a headland, at the north-eastern end of the bay (sometimes called Kontee Beach), are the secluded *Mountain Sea*, *Serenity* and *Bovy* all rock-bottom places for 30B. Further north along the coast there is no accommodation (except at Ao Thong Reng), at this writing, until you reach Ao Ta Pan Yai, about 17 km north. But a dirt track (traversable on foot but only partially by motorcycle) does run along the coast from Hat Rin about half that distance before heading inland to Ban Nam Tok and Than Sadet Falls.

Between Hat Rin and the village of Ban Nam Tok are several little coves with the white-sand beaches of Hat Yuan (2.5 km north of Hat Rin), Hat Yai Nam (3.5 km), Hat Yao (five km) and Hat Yang (six km), all virtually deserted. Then 2.5 km north of Ban Nam Tok by dirt track is the pretty, double bay of Ao Thong Reng, where *No Name* bungalows are 30B.

Ao Thong Nai Pan This bay is really made up of two bays, **Ao Ta Pan Yai** and **Ao Ta Pan Noi**. On the beach at Ta Pan Yai, near Ban Thong Nai Pan village, are the *White Sand* and the *Nice Beach*, both with 10 or 11 huts for 30 to 50B each. Up on Thong Ta Pan Noi are the very nicely situated *Panviman Resort* and the *Thong Nai Pan Resort*. The Panviman overlooks the bay and is run by a retired Thai boxer. Huts are 60B up, all with private bath. The more basic *Thong Nai Pan Resort* costs 50 to 60B.

Hat Khuat & Chalok Lam These are two pretty bays with beaches on the northern end of Pha-Ngan, still largely undeveloped because of the distances involved from major transport points to Samui and the mainland. Hat Khuat (Bottle Beach) is the smaller of the two and currently has three sets of bungalows, all in the 30 to 60B range – *Bottle Beach*, *OD* and *Sea Love*. West of Hat Khuat, 2.5 km across Laem Kung Yai, is **Hat Khom**, where the *Coral Bay* and *Buddy* go for 30 to 40B. You can walk to Hat Khuat from Ban Chalok Lam but until they build a better bridge over Khlong Ok, no jeeps or motorcycles can access it – all the better for quiet days and nights.

East of the fishing village of Ban Chalok Lam, where the drying of squid seems to be the main activity, are *Fanta*, *Try Tong Resort* and *Thai Life*, all with simple huts for 30 to 50B. At the other end of long Chalok Lam beach, west of the village, is the slightly nicer *Wattana* with huts for 60 to 150B. The beach is better here, too.

In friendly Ban Chalok Lam you can rent bikes and diving equipment. There are also several restaurants – none of them very good.

Ao Hat Thong Lang & Ao Mae Hat As you move west on Pha-Ngan, as on Samui, the sand gets browner and coarser. The secluded beach and cove at Ao Hat Thong Lang has only *Hat Thong Lang* so far with huts at the usual 30 to 40B rate.

The beach at Ao Mae Hat is no great shakes, but there is a bit of coral offshore. The *Mae Hat Bay Resort* and *Island View Cabana* have simple huts for 40B plus huts with private bath for up to 150B. The Island View also has a good restaurant. The village of Ban Mae Hat is nearby.

Hat Lat & Hat Yao These coral-fringed beaches are fairly difficult to reach – the road from Ban Si Thanu to the south is very bad in spots, even for experienced dirt-bikers – come by boat if possible. Hat Lat has two 30B places, *My Way* and *Had Lad*. Down at Hat Yao are the basic *Benjawan*, *Hat Yao*, *Sandy Bay*, *Ibiza*, *Dream Hill*, *Blue Coral Beach*, *Malibu* and *Hat Thian*, all with basic 30 to 50B huts.

Ao Si Thanu In this area you begin to see the occasional mangrove along the coast. There are four places to stay along the beach here, perhaps too many for the attractions this part of the island holds. The 30B *Laem Son* is at the southern end of the bay, right on the cape. The popular *Sea Flower, Seetanu*, and *Great Bay* all have bungalows with private bath for 60 to 150B. *Loy Fah*, at the southern end of the bay on the cape, has good 150B huts with bath and mosquito net, plus simpler huts for 50B. A handful of others here seem to come and go with the seasons.

Ao Wok Tum This long bay is just a few km north of Thong Sala but so far has hardly any development. At the northern end of Wok Tum, not far from the village of Ban Si Thanu, is the basic *Lipstick* for the usual 30 to 40B. Down at the southern end of Ao Wok Tum on the cape between this bay and Ao Nai Wok are the similar *Tuk* and *Kiat*. A little further down around the cape of Hin Nok are *OK*, *Chuenjitt*, *Darin*, *Sea Scene*, *Porn Sawan*, *Cookies* and *Beach*, all with simple 30 to 40B huts.

See the earlier Tong Sala section for accommodation just north of Thong Sala at Ao Nai Wok.

Ko Tae Nai This little island is right across the bay from the Thong Sala pier and the *Koh Tae Nai* rents huts for 100 to 200B with shared bath. A new up-market place, *Sea Fan Resort* has 20 rooms that start at 1000B. The island is not really worth the short trip.

Getting There & Away

To/From Ko Samui – express boat Songserm Co express boats to Ko Pha-Ngan leave from the Na Thon pier on Ko Samui every day at 10 am and 3 pm from November to May or 10 am and 4 pm from June to October. The trip takes 40 minutes and costs 60B one-way. Boats back to Samui leave Pha-Ngan's Thong Sala pier at 6.15 and 12.30 am daily from November to May, or 6.30 am and 1 pm from June to October. The express-boat routes to Pha-Ngan are extensions of the Surat to Ko Samui routes, so you can go straight to Pha-Ngan from Surat with a short stopover in Na Thon (see the Ko Samui Getting There & Away section for express boat times from Surat) for 120B one-way or 210B return.

To/From Ko Samui – other boats A small boat goes direct from Samui's Bo Phut village to Hat Rin on Ko Pha-Ngan for 50B. The boat leaves just about every day at 9 am, depending on the weather and number of prospective passengers, and takes 40 to 45 minutes to reach the bay at Hat Rin. Sometimes there is also an afternoon boat at 3.30 pm. As more and more people choose this route to Ko Pha-Ngan, services will probably become more regular. In the reverse direction it usually leaves at 9 am and 2.30 pm.

From April to September there is also one boat a day between Hat Mae Nam on Samui and Ao Thong Nai Pan on Pha-Ngan. The fare is 60B and the boat usually leaves around 9 am.

To/From Surat Thani – express boat Ferry Pha-Ngan Co (☎ 286461) at 10 Chon Kasem Rd (near the Ban Don pier) has one direct boat daily to Ko Pha-Ngan. The company's bus meets the night train from Bangkok at Phun Phin station at 6.40 am, then there's another pick-up at the ferry office in Ban Don at 7.45 am. The ferry leaves from Don Sak pier at 9 am and arrives in Ko Pha-Ngan at 11.30 am. On the return trip the ferry leaves Ko Pha-Ngan at 1 pm; connecting buses arrive at the railway station at 5.15 pm in time for the evening rapid and express trains north or south. The ferry fare is 95B each way.

To/From Surat Thani – night ferry You can also take the slow night ferry direct to Pha-Ngan from the Ban Don pier in Surat. It leaves nightly at midnight, takes five hours to arrive at Thong Sala, and costs 80B on the upper deck, 40B on the lower. The same ferry continues on to Ko Tao for 50B lower deck, 100B upper.

As with the night ferry to Samui, don't leave your bags unattended on the boat – there have been several reports of theft.

To/From Ko Tao During the high travel season, January to March, there are daily boats between Thong Sala and Ko Tao, 47 km north. The trip takes 4½ hours and costs 100B one-way. From April to December the boats to/from Ko Tao only leave two or three times a week, depending on the weather.

Train/Bus/Boat Combinations At Bangkok's Hualamphong railway station you can purchase train tickets that include a bus from the Surat Thani railway station (Phun Phin) to the Ban Don pier and then a ferry to Ko Pha-Ngan. A 2nd-class seat costs 309B inclusive, while a 3rd-class seat is 235B. Second-class sleeper combinations cost 424B for an upper berth, 459B for a lower. Add 100B for an air-con coach.

Getting Around

A couple of roads branch out from Thong Sala, primarily to the north and the south. One road goes north-west from Thong Sala a few km along the shoreline to the villages of Ban Hin Kong and Ban Si Thanu. From Ban Si Thanu the road travels north-east across the island to Ban Chalok Lam. Another road goes straight north from Thong Sala to Chalok Lam. There is also a very poor dirt road along the west coast from Ban Si Thanu to Ao Hat Yao and Ao Hat Lat.

Hat Khuat (Bottle Beach) can be reached on foot from Ban Fai Mai (two km) or Ban Chalok Lam (four km) or there are boats.

The road south from Thong Sala to Ban Khai passes an intersection where another road goes north to Ban Thong Nang and Ban Thong Nai Pan. Songthaews and motorcycle taxis handle all the public transport along island roads. Some places can only be reached by motorcycle; some places only by boat or foot.

You can rent motorcycles in Thong Sala for 150 to 250B a day.

Songthaew & Motorcycle Taxi From Thong Sala, a songthaew to Ban Hin Kong (for Ao Si Thanu and Hat Yao) is 20B per person, a motorcycle taxi 25B. To Wat Khao Tham, Ban Tai or Ban Khai, it's 15B by songthaew, 20B by motorcycle.

A songthaew from Thong Sala to Ban Chalok Lam is 25B, a motorcycle taxi 30B.

To get to Hat Rin from Thong Sala, you have to take a taxi to Ban Khai and then walk three km. You can also get there by boat; see the following Boat section.

Thong Nai Pan can be reached by motorcycle from Thong Sala (130B) or Ban Tai (120B). See the following Boat section for water transport to Thong Nai Pan.

Boat There are daily boats from Ao Chalok Lam to Hat Khuat in the late afternoon for 20B. The boats leave Hat Khuat around 9 am.

Thong Nai Pan can be reached by boat from Hat Rin on south Pha-Ngan at 7 am for 40B, but these boats generally run only between April and September. When the express boat arrives at the Thong Sala pier from Surat or Samui, there are usually boats waiting to take passengers on to Hat Rin for 30B – it takes about 45 minutes. Passengers already on Pha-Ngan can take these boats, too – they go in each direction two or three times daily.

KO TAO

เกาะเต่า

Ko Tao translates as 'Turtle Island', named for its shape. It's only about 21 sq km in area and the population of 750 are mostly involved in fishing and growing coconuts. If you want to enjoy palm-studded Samui-style geography without the crowds, this might be the place. Since it takes at least five hours to get there from the mainland (from either Chumphon or Surat Thani via Ko Pha-Ngan), Ko Tao doesn't get people coming over for day trips or for quick overnighters.

Ban Mae Hat on the western side of the island is where inter-island boats land. The only other villages on the island are **Ban Hat Sai Ri** in the centre of the northern part and **Ban Chalok Ban Kao** to the south. Just a km off the north-west shore of the island is **Ko Nang Yuan**, which is really three islands joined by a sand bar.

The granite promontory of **Laem Tato** at the southern tip of Ko Tao makes a nice hike from Ban Chalok Ban Kao.

Places to Stay

Huts are very simple and inexpensive on Ko Tao as local materials have only been used up to now – at last count there were about 440 huts in 36 locations around the island. All bungalows on the island are without electricity and cost from 30 to 50B per night for one or two persons.

On Ao Mae beach just north of Ban Mae Hat are *Nuan Nang*, with basic huts for 30 to 50B and huts with bath for 60 to 80B, then *Dam* for 30 to 50B. A bit further north on this beach at Laem Cho Po Ro (Jaw Paw Raw) is *Khao* for 50B.

Around this headland, to the north, is the long Hat Sai Ri with only two bungalow operations at this writing, the *O-Chai* and *Sai Ri* for 30 to 50B. Nearby is Ban Hat Sai Ri, about 2.5 km from Ban Mae Hat. Further north facing Ko Nang Yuan on Laem Nam Tok are the similar *Shopping*, *Mahana Bay*, *CFT* and *R Seena*.

On the northern end of the island at Ao Ma-Muang (Mango Bay) are the newer *Mango Bay* and *Ao Muang*, which are only accessible by boat from Mae Hat. At Ao Hin Wong two km east of Ban Hat Sai Ri are a handful of huts called *Sahat*, for 30B.

Continuing clockwise around the island to Ao Mao, connected by a two-km dirt trail with Ban Hat Sai Ri, are three newer places, *Tanote Bay*, *Diamond* and *Sunrise*. The next two coves south, Ao Tanot and Ao Leuk, have one bungalow operation each – *Amity* (about three km from Ban Mae Hat) and *Ao Leuk Resort* (one km from Ban Chalok Ban Kao).

A couple of km south of Ban Mae Hat at Laem Hin Sam Kon is the nicely situated *Neptune* for 30 to 40B. Below this promontory is Hat Sai Nuan, where you can find the *Sai Thong*, *Sabay* and *Cha*, for 50B. The only way to get there is to walk two km along the dirt track from Mae Hat.

About two km east of Sai Nuan (or two km south of Ban Mae Hat) are two small beaches on Ao Chalok Ban Kao. On the first is *Taraporn* (30 to 40B) and on the second *Laem Khlong* (50B). The village of Chalok Ban Kao is quite close and there's a road between here and Ban Mae Hat. On the other side of Ban Chalok Lam on the same bay are the *K See*, *Koh Tao Cottage* and *Ta To Lagoon*, all 30 to 50B.

On the other side of the impressive Laem

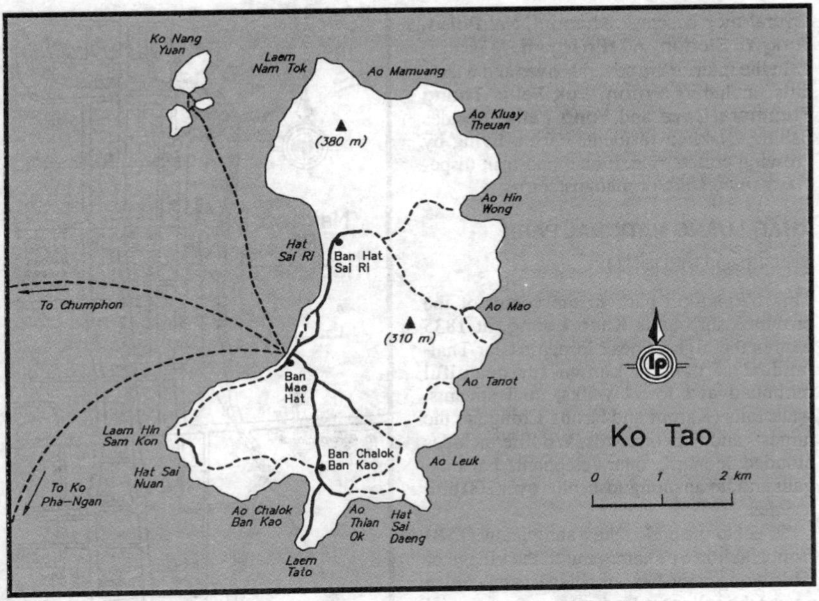

Tato to the east is pretty Ao Thian Ok with *Hope*, *Rocky* and *Niyom*, all 30 to 50B. Another km or so east is Hat Sai Daeng where *Kiat* offers simple huts for 50B.

Finally, on Ko Nang Yuan are the *Nang Yuan* bungalows for 80 to 170B. One problem in staying on Ko Nang Yuan might be putting up with diving groups that occasionally take over the island. Another is their tendency to kick out impecunious guests who don't order enough food at the restaurant. Regular twice-daily boats to Nang Yuan from the Ban Mae Hat pier are 15B per person. You can charter a ride there for 50B.

Getting There & Away

To/From Ko Pha-Ngan Depending on weather conditions, anywhere from two to seven boats a week go between the Thong Sala pier on Ko Pha-Ngan and Ban Mae Hat on Ko Tao. The trip takes anywhere from three to 4½ hours and costs 100B per person. Boats leave Thong Sala around 10 am.

To/From Chumphon From the mainland there are usually four to five boats a week from Chumphon to Ko Tao – some weeks fewer if the swells are high. These scheduled boats are 150 to 200B per person, leave Chumphon at midnight and take five to six hours to reach Ko Tao. See the Chumphon section for more details.

Nakhon Si Thammarat Province

Much of this large southern province is covered with rugged mountains and forests, which were, until very recently, the last refuge of Thailand's communist insurgents. The province's eastern border is formed by the Gulf of Thailand and much of the provincial economy is dependent on fishing and shrimp raising. Along the north coast are several nice beaches: **Khanom, Nai Phlao, Tong Yi, Sichon** and **Hin Ngam**.

In the interior are several caves and waterfalls, including **Phrom Lok Falls, Thong Phannara Cave** and **Yong Falls**. Besides fishing, Nakhon residents earn a living by growing coffee, rice, rubber and fruit (especially *mongkhút*, or mangosteen).

KHAO LUANG NATIONAL PARK
อุทยานแห่งชาติเขาหลวง

This 570-sq-km park in the centre of the province surrounds **Khao Luang**, at 1835 metres the highest peak in peninsular Thailand. The park is known for beautiful mountain and forest walks, cool streams, waterfalls (Karom and Krung Ching are the largest) and fruit orchards. Wildlife includes clouded leopard, tiger, elephant, banteng, gaur and Javan mongoose, plus over 200 bird species.

To get to the park, take a songthaew (15B) from Nakhon Si Thammarat to the village of Khiriwong at the base of Khao Luang. Twice a year the villagers lead groups on a special climb up the mountain – ask at the TAT office in Nakhon Si Thammarat for details.

NAKHON SI THAMMARAT
อ.เมืองนครศรีธรรมราช

Nakhon Si Thammarat (population 72,000) is 780 km from Bangkok. Centuries before the 8th-century Srivijaya Empire subjugated the peninsula, there was a city-state here called Ligor or Lagor, capital of the Tambralinga kingdom, which was well known throughout Oceania. Later, when Ceylonese-ordained Buddhist monks established a cloister at the city, the name was changed to the Pali-Sanskrit *Nagara Sri Dhammaraja* (City of the Sacred Dharma-King), rendered in Thai phonetics as Nakhon Si Thammarat. During the early development of the various Thai kingdoms, Nakhon Si Thammarat was a very important centre of religion and culture. Thai shadow play *(nãng thalung)* and classical dance-drama *(lakhon* – Thai pronunciation of Lagor) are

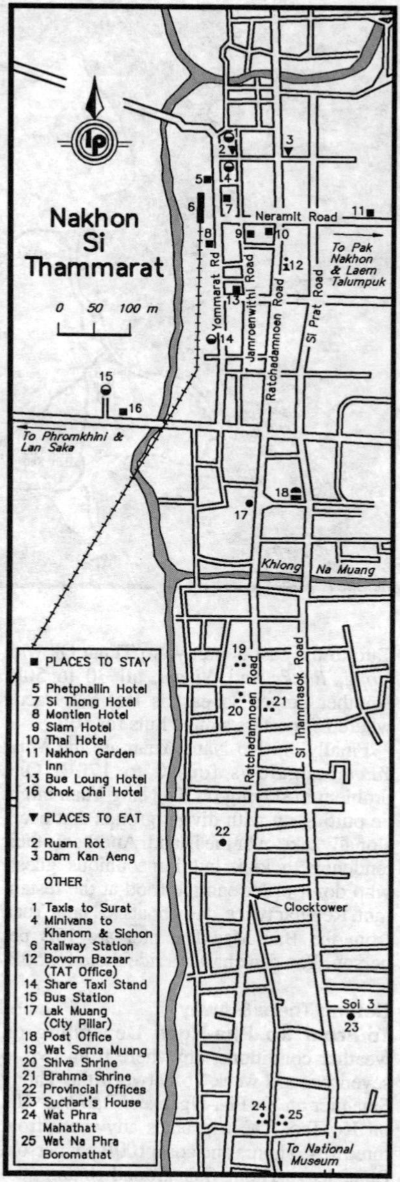

supposed to have been developed in Nakhon Si Thammarat; buffalo-hide shadow puppets and dance masks are still made here.

Today Nakhon Si Thammarat is also known for its nielloware, a silver and black alloy/enamel jewellery technique borrowed from China many centuries ago. Until recently it was also known for its higher-than-average crime rate but lately the city has been trying to change Nakhon's image by cracking down on gangster activity. A new civic pride has developed in recent years and the natives are now quite fond of being called *khon khawn* (Nakhon people).

Orientation & Information

Nakhon Si Thammarat can be divided into two sections, the historic half south of the clock tower and the new city centre north of the clock tower and Khlong Na Muang. The new city has all the hotels and most of the restaurants, as well as more movie theatres per sq km than any other city in Thailand.

Bovorn (Bowon) Bazaar is a cluster of restaurants, handicraft shops and a new TAT office (☎ 345512) on Ratchadamnoen Rd that are participating in the city's attempted revitalisation process.

Suan Nang Seu Nakhon Bowonrat

The Suan Nang Seu or 'Book Garden', at 116 Ratchadamnoen Rd next to Bovorn Bazaar and Siam Commercial Bank, is Nakhon's intellectual centre (look for the traditional water jar on a platform in front). Housed in an 80-year-old building that once served variously as a *sinsae* (Chinese doctor) clinic, opium den and hotel, this nonprofit bookshop specialises in books (mostly in Thai) on local history as well as national politics and religion. It also co-ordinates Dhamma lectures and sponsors local arts and craft exhibits.

Wat Phra Mahathat

วัดพระมหาธาตุ

This is the city's oldest site, reputed to be over 1000 years old. Reconstructed in the mid-13th century, it features a 78-metre chedi, crowned by a solid gold spire weighing several hundred kg. The temple's bot contains one of Thailand's three identical Phra Singh Buddhas, one of which is supposed to have been originally cast in Ceylon before being brought to Sukhothai (through Nakhon Si Thammarat), Chiang Mai and later, Ayuthaya. The other images are at Wat Phra Singh in Chiang Mai and the National Museum in Bangkok – each is claimed to be the original.

Besides the distinctive bot and chedi there are many intricately designed wihaans surrounding the chedi, several of which contain crowned Nakhon Si Thammarat/Ayuthaya-style Buddhas in glass cabinets. One wihaan houses a funky museum (admission by donation) with carved wooden kruts (garudas, Vishnu's mythical bird-mount), old Siwichai votive tablets, Buddha figures of every description including a standing Dvaravati figure and a Siwichai *naga* Buddha, pearl-inlaid alms bowls and other oddities. It would be really good if the artefacts were labelled – at present many are not identified in either Thai or English. This is the biggest wat in the south, comparable to Wat Pho and other large Bangkok wats. If you like wats, this one is well worth a trip.

Wat Phra Mahathat's full name, Wat Phra Mahathat Woramahawihaan, is sometimes abbreviated as Wat Phra Boromathat. It's about two km from the new town centre – hop on any bus or songthaew going down Ratchadamnoen Rd for 2B.

Wat Na Phra Boromathat

วัดหน้าพระบรมธาตุ

Across the road from Wat Mahathat, this is the residence for monks serving at Mahathat. There is a nice Gandhara-style fasting Buddha in front of the bot here.

Nakhon Si Thammarat National Museum

พิพิธภัณฑ์แห่งชาตินครศรีธรรมราช

This is past the principal wats on Ratchadamnoen Rd heading south, across from Wat Thao Khot and Wat Phet Jarik, on the left –

2B by city bus or 3B by songthaew. Since the Tampaling (or Tambralinga) kingdom traded with Indian, Arabic, Dvaravati and Champa states, much art from these places found its way to the Nakhon Si Thammarat area, and some is now on display in the National Museum here. Notable are Dong-Son bronze drums, Dvaravati Buddha images and Pallava (south Indian) Hindu sculpture. Locally produced art is also on display.

If you've already had your fill of the usual Thai art history surveys from Ban Chiang to Ayuthaya, go straight to the Art of Southern Thailand exhibit in a room on the left of the foyer. Here you'll find many fine images of Nakhon Si Thammarat provenance, including Phutthasihing, U Thong and late Ayuthaya styles. The Nakhon Si Thammarat-produced Ayuthaya style seems to be the most common, with distinctive, almost comical, crowned faces. The so-called Phutthasihing-style Buddha looks a little like the Palla-influenced Chiang Saen Buddha, but is shorter and more 'pneumatic'.

Admission to the museum is 10B and hours are Wednesday to Sunday, from 9 am to 4 pm.

Hindu Temples

There are also three Hindu temples in Nakhon Si Thammarat, along Ratchadamnoen Rd inside the city walls. Brahmin priests from these temples take part each year in the Royal Ploughing Ceremony in Bangkok. One temple houses a locally famous Shivalingam (phallic shrine) which is worshipped, among others, by women hoping to bear children.

Shadow Puppet Workshop

Traditionally, there are two styles of shadow puppets, *nãng thalung* and *nãng yài*; the former are similar in size to the typical Malay-Indonesian style puppets while the latter are nearly life-size and unique to Thailand. Both are intricately carved from buffalo-hide. Performances of Thai shadow theatre are rare nowadays (usually only during festivals) but there are two places in town where you can see the puppets being made.

The acknowledged master of shadow puppet craft – both manufacture and performance – is Suchart Subsin (Suchaat Sapsin), a Nakhon resident with a workshop at 110/18 Si Thammasok Soi 3, not far from Wat Phra Mahathat. Khun Suchart has received several awards for his mastery and preservation of the craft and has performed for the king. His workshop is open to the public; if enough people are assembled he may even be talked into providing a performance at his small outdoor studio. Puppets can be purchased here at reasonable prices – and here only, as he refuses to sell them through distributors. On some puppets the fur is left on the hide for additional effect – these cost a bit more as special care must be taken in tanning them.

Another craftsperson, Mesa Chotiphan, welcomes visitors to her workshop in the northern part of town. Mesa sells to distributors but will also sell direct at lower prices. Her house is at 558/4 Soi Rong Jeh, Ratchadamnoen Rd (☎ 343979). If you call she will pick you up from anywhere in the city. To get there on your own, go north from the city centre on Ratchadamnoen Rd and after about a half km north of the sports field, take the soi opposite the Chinese cemetery (before reaching the golf course and military base).

Festivals

Every year in mid-October there is a southern-Thai festival called **Chak Phra Pak Tai** held in Songkhla, Surat Thani and Nakhon Si Thammarat. In Nakhon Si Thammarat the festival is centred around Wat Mahathat and includes performances of nang thalung and lakhon as well as the parading of Buddha images around the city to collection donations for local temples.

In the third lunar month (February to March) the city holds the colourful **Hae Phaa Khun That** in which a lengthy cloth jataka painting is wrapped around the main chedi at Wat Phra Mahathat.

Places to Stay – bottom end

Most of Nakhon Si Thammarat's hotels are near the train and bus stations.

On Yommarat (Yammaraj) Rd, across from the railway station, is the *Si Thong Hotel*, with adequate rooms for 100B with fan and bath. Also on Yommarat Rd are the *Nakhon Hotel* and *Yaowarat*, with the same rates and facilities as Si Thong.

On Jamroenwithi Rd (walk straight down Neramit Rd opposite the railway station two blocks and make a right on Jamroenwithi Rd) is the large *Siam Hotel*; rooms with fan and bath cost from 100 and 180B. Across the street is the *Muang Thong Hotel*, where 100B will get you a clean room with fan and bath. Near the Siam, on the same side of the street, is the *Thai Fa Hotel*, which, at 70B, has better rooms than either the Nakhon or the Si Thong.

Others are the newer *Thai Lee* at 1130 Ratchadamnoen Rd where rooms with fan and bath cost 80 to 150B, and the similarly priced *Laem Thong* at 1213/5-6 Yommarat.

Places to Stay – middle & top end

Nakhon Si Thammarat's flashiest hotels are the *Thai Hotel* (☎ 356505/451) on Ratchadamnoen Rd, two blocks from the railway station, and the *Taksin* (☎ 356788/90) on Si Prat Rd. The Thai Hotel has fan-cooled singles/doubles for 180/265B, and air-con rooms ranging from 557 to 605B. At the Taksin air-con rooms start at 250B. The newer *Bue Loung (Bua Luang) Hotel* (☎ 341518), on Soi Luang Muang off Jamroenwithi Rd, has large, clean singles/doubles with fan and bath for 120/180B, and air-con doubles for 260B.

On Yommarat Rd near the railway station, the *Montien* (☎ 341908) and *Phetpailin* (☎ 341896; fax 343943) each have rooms starting at 150B (air-con from 280B).

The best top-end choice is the quiet *Nakhon Garden Inn* (☎ 344831) at 1/4 Pak Nakhon Rd east of the centre. All 50 rooms with air-con and TV and cost 450 to 500B.

Places to Eat

There are lots of funky old Chinese restaurants along Yommarat and Jamroenwithi Rds. The latter street is the city's main culinary centre – at night it's lined with inexpensive food vendors and by day there are plenty of rice and noodle shops. *Yong Seng* (no English sign) is a very good, inexpensive Chinese restaurant on Jamroenwithi Rd.

To try some of Nakhon's excellent Thai coffee, stop by *Hao Coffee* at Bovorn Bazaar. Basically an update of an original Hokkien-style coffee shop once run by the owner's family in Nakhon, Hao Coffee serves international coffees as well as southern-Thai-Hokkien-style coffee (listed as 'Hao coffee' on the menu) served with a tea chaser. Ask for fresh milk (nom sòt) if you abhor powdered non-dairy creamer.

Adjacent to Hao Coffee is *Khrua Nakhon*, a large open-air restaurant serving real Nakhon cuisine, including khâo yam (southern-style rice salad), kaeng tai plaa (spicy fish curry) khanõm jiin (curry noodles served with a huge tray of veggies) and seafood. The restaurant also has egg-and-toast breakfasts; you can order Hao coffee from next door if you'd like. With a banyan tree in front and a modest display of southern-Thai folk art, the atmosphere is hard to beat. Next to Khrua Nakhon is *Ban Lakhon*, in an old house, which is also very good for Thai food.

At the corner of the alley leading into Bovorn Bazaar, Nakhon's most famous roti vendors set up nightly. In Nakhon, roti klûay (banana roti) is a tradition – the vendors here use only fresh mashed bananas, no banana preserves or the like. Other offerings here include roti with curry (roti kaeng), with egg (roti khài) or as mataba (stuffed with meat and vegetables). They also do great khanõm jìip, dumplings stuffed with a chicken-shrimp mixture, along with Nakhon coffee and better-than-average milk tea.

Among a cluster of restaurants near the intersection of Jamroenwithi and Watkhit Rd is *Ruam Rot*, which serves very good curries and khanõm jiin. They claim they use no preservatives or artificial flavours; the emphasis is on southern-Thai curries like kaeng mátsàman and kaeng tai plaa. East of this intersection at the corner of Ratchadamnoen and Watkhit is the very popular Thai-Chinese *Dam Kan Aeng*, which is packed with hungry customers every night.

Entertainment

Beyond the cinemas in town, there's not a lot of nightlife. The Dallas Cowboy, a pub in Bovorn Bazaar, is a small, convincingly decorated old-west bar with a long list of cocktails from Tom Collins to Señor Playboy.

Getting There & Away

Air THAI has four flights a week to/from Bangkok (1770B), three flights a week to/from Phuket (690B) via Hat Yai and four flights weekly to/from Trang (500B). The THAI office (☎ 342491) in Nakhon is at 1612 Ratchadamnoen Rd.

Bus Air-con buses bound for Nakhon Si Thammarat leave Bangkok's southern air-con bus terminal daily at 9 am and every 20 minutes from 6.30 to 7.50 pm, arriving 12 hours later, for 270B. Air-con buses in the reverse direction leave at about the same times. Ordinary buses leave Bangkok at 6.50 and 8 am, 5 and 9.30 pm for 150B.

From Surat Thani there are daily buses to Nakhon; check with the tour-bus companies on Na Muang Rd. A tour bus from Surat to Nakhon should cost 60 to 65B one-way. Direct buses now run from Songkhla via a bridge over the entrance to Thale Noi (the inland sea). Check with one of the tour-bus companies on Niphat Uthit 2 Rd in Hat Yai. Muang Tai Tours, on Jamroenwithi Rd in Nakhon Si Thammarat, does a 60B trip to Surat that includes a good meal and a video movie.

Hourly buses to Nakhon Si Thammarat leave Krabi's Talaat Kao for 50B per person and take about four hours.

Train Most southbound trains stop at the junction of Thung Song, about 40 km west of Nakhon Si Thammarat, from where you must take a bus or taxi to the coast. However, two trains actually go all the way to Nakhon Si Thammarat (there is a branch line from Khao Chum Thong to Nakhon Si Thammarat): the rapid No 47, which leaves Bangkok's Hualamphong station at 5.30 pm, arriving in Nakhon Si Thammarat at 8.35 am, and the express No 15, which leaves Bangkok at 7.20 pm and arrives in Nakhon Si Thammarat at 10 am. Most travellers will not be booking a train directly to Nakhon Si Thammarat, but if you want to, a 1st-class fare is 590B, 2nd class 279B, 3rd class 133B, not including surcharges for rapid/express service or sleeping berths.

Share Taxis This seems to be the most popular form for inter-city travel out of Nakhon. The huge share-taxi terminal on Yommarat Rd has taxis to Thung Song (25B), Khanom (40B), Sichon (30B), Krabi (80B), Trang (60B), Phuket (150B) and Phattalung (50B). A second smaller stand on Thewarat Rd has taxis to Surat (60B), Chumphon (130B) and Ranong (180B).

Getting Around

City buses run north-south along Ratchadamnoen and Si Thammasok Rds for 2B. Songthaews do similar routes for 3B during the day, 4B at night.

AROUND NAKHON SI THAMMARAT PROVINCE

Laem Talumpuk

แหลมตะลุมพุก

This is a small scenic cape not far from Nakhon Si Thammarat. Take a bus from Neramit Rd going east to Pak Nakhon for 8B, then cross the inlet by ferry to Laem Talumpuk.

Hat Sa Bua

หาดสระบัว

Sixteen km north of Nakhon Si Thammarat in the Tha Sala district, about 9B by songthaew, off Highway 401 to Surat, are some semi-deserted white-sand beaches with few tourists. As yet accommodation isn't available, but there are some very reasonably priced restaurants here.

Hat Sichon & Hin Ngam
หาดสิชล/หาดหินงาม

Hat Sichon and Hat Hin Ngam are stunning beaches 37 km north of Nakhon Si Thammarat in Sichon district. Another good beach, **Hat Tong Yi**, is accessible only by boat and is hence almost always deserted – it's between Sichon and Hin Ngam (a chartered boat to Tong Yi from either beach costs 100 to 200B).

Get the bus for Hat Hin Ngam or Sichon from the Nakhon Si Thammarat bus station for 15B or take a share taxi for 30B. Hat Sichon comes first; Hin Ngam is another 1.5 km. *Prasansuk Villa* has 30 bungalows for rent at 200 to 300B. At Hin Ngam, *Hin Ngam Bungalow & Restaurant* (☎ 536299) costs 150B.

Ao Khanom
อ่าวขนอม

About 25 km from Sichon, 70 km from Surat or 80 km from Nakhon Si Thammarat is the bay of Ao Khanom. Not far from the vehicle-ferry landing for Ko Samui in Khanom is a string of three white-sand beaches, Hat Nai Praet, Hat Nai Phlao, Hat Na Dan and Hat Pak Nam. *Khanom Hills Resort* (☎ 529403) at Nai Phlao has six rooms for 400B and up. Also at Nai Phlao are *Fern Bay Resort* 300B, the *Nai Phlao Bay Resort* (☎ 529039) 400 to 650B, *Supa Villa* (☎ 529237) 400 to 600B and the new *Khanab Nam Diamond Cliff Resort* (☎ 529000/111) with 25 rooms for 500 to 1000B.

Hat Na Dan has the *Watanyoo Villa* (☎ 529224) for 120 to 400B.

Phattalung Province

Over 840 km from Bangkok and 95 km from Hat Yai, Phattalung is one of the south's only rice-growing provinces and it has prospered as a result.

PHATTALUNG & AROUND
อ.เมืองพัทลุง

The provincial capital (population 33,000) is fairly small (you can walk around the perimeter of downtown Phattalung in an hour, even stopping for rice), but it is unique among southern-Thai towns. Judging from the number of *hang thong* (gold dealers) on Poh Saat Rd, there must be a large Chinese population.

Phattalung is also famous for the original nãng thalung (shadow play) which was probably named after Phattalung – *nãng* means hide (untanned leather), and *thalung* is taken from Phattalung. The Thai shadow-play tradition remains only in Nakhon Si Thammarat and Phattalung, though the best performances are seen in the former. A typical performance begins at midnight and lasts four to five hours. Usually they take place during *ngaan wát* (temple fairs).

The town is situated between two picturesque, foliage-trimmed limestone peaks, **Khao Ok Thalu** (literally, 'punctured-chest mountain') and **Khao Hua Taek** (or 'broken-head mountain'). Local myth has it that these two mountains were the wife and mistress of a third mountain to the north, **Khao Muang**, who fought a fierce battle over the adulterous husband, leaving them with their 'wounds'. The names refer to their geographic peculiarities – Ok Thalu has a tunnel through its upper peak, while Hua Taek is sort of split at the top.

Like most Thai towns, Phattalung's street plan is laid out in a grid pattern. Most of the local sights are nearby. To change money it's best to go to the Thai Farmer's Bank on Ramet Rd.

Wat Kuhasawan
วัดคูหาสวรรค์

On the western side of town – from the railway station Kuhasawan Rd leads right to it – Wat Kuhasawan comprises one large cave with rather ugly statues, but the cave is high and cool. A tall passageway leads deeper into the cave – lights can be switched on by the monks. Steps lead around the cave to the top of the mountain for a nice view of rice fields and mountains further west.

To the right of the main cave is an old hermit's cave – the monk died in 1973 and his form is commemorated by a statue at the second level of stairs. Good views of Khao Ok Thalu and most of Phattalung City can be had from certain points around this cave.

Wat Wang

วัดวัง

Over 100 years old, this is the oldest wat in Phattalung. The palace of a Thai prince was originally located just east of the wat *(wang* means palace), but only the wall remains. The original chedi is in front of the wat. A closed bot has a decaying set of murals with Buddhist and *Ramayana* themes. You have to open the doors and windows to see them. Wat Wang is about four km east of Phattalung on the road to Lam Pam. Take a songthaew from next to the post office (3B).

Lam Pam

ลำปำ

If you follow Phattalung's main street, Ramet Rd, east over the railway tracks past Wat Wang, you'll come to Lam Pam on the banks of the Thale Luang, the upper part of the south's inland sea (Thale Noi). For 5B you can ride a songthaew from next to the post office out to Lam Pam in 15 minutes, or hire a motorcycle for 10B.

Under shady trees next to the freshwater 'sea', are beach chairs and tables where you can relax, enjoy the breeze and order food – crab, mussels, other shellfish, squid, plus beer, soda, etc. Although the inland sea itself is not at all spectacular, this is a nice spot to while away a few hours drinking beer and eating the fabulous speciality plaa mèuk klûay yâang (literally, 'banana squid' – an egg-carrying squid, roasted over charcoal), along with miang kham, the unique do-it-yourself concoction of dried shrimp, peanuts, lime, garlic, ginger, chilli, toasted coconut and salty-sweet sauce wrapped in wild tea leaves.

Tham Malai

ถ้ำมาลัย

Three km north of Phattalung near the railway line is a hill with a large cave, Tham Malai, at its base. On top of the hill are some Chinese shrines, though a Thai Theravada monk resides there. There are excellent views of Phattalung and surrounding mountains from the top.

The cave itself is more interesting than the shrines. Bring a torch (flashlight) and you can explore the various rooms within the cavern. The cave is more or less in its natural state, with its stalagmites and stalactites still intact. Even without a light, it's worth exploring a bit – when the cave reaches its darkest point, you'll come upon an opening leading back around to daylight.

If the canal running parallel to the railway has enough water, you can get a boat for 5B as far as Tham Malai – easiest in December and January. If the water is too low, walk along the tracks until you come to a footbridge which will take you over the canal onto a path leading to the cave.

Thale Noi Waterbird Sanctuary

อุทยานนกน้ำทะเลน้อย

Thale Noi is a small inland sea or lake, 32 km north-east of Phattalung, which is a waterbird sanctuary protected by the Forestry Department. Among the 182 species of waterbird here, the most prominent is the *nók i kong*, with its long funny feet which quiver like malfunctioning landing gear as the bird takes flight, and the *nók pèt daeng*, a small, red-headed 'duck bird', related to the whistling teal, that skitters along the water. The best time for bird sightings is November and December; the least number of birds is seen from May to August.

The sea itself is sort of a large swamp similar to the Everglades in the southern

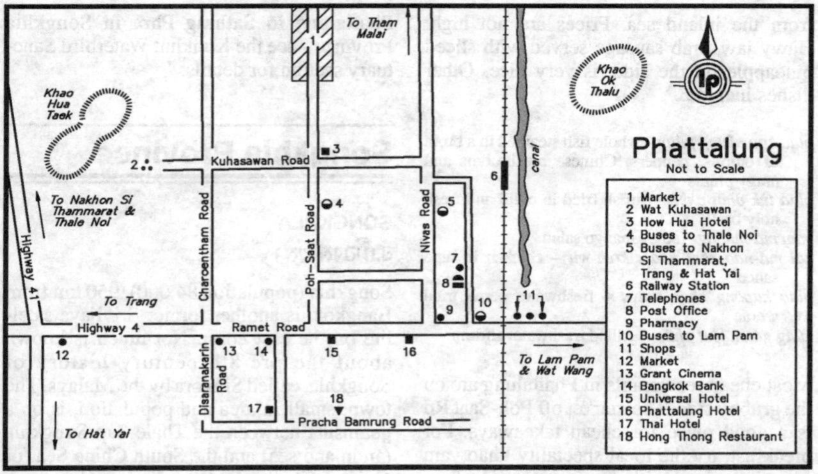

USA. The major forms of vegetation are water vines and *dôn kòk*, a reed which the nok i kong use to build large 'platforms' over the water for nesting purposes. The local Thais also use these same reeds, after drying them in the sun, to make woven floor mats which are sold throughout Phattalung. The village near the park entrance to Thale Noi is a good place to observe the reed-weaving methods.

To get there, take a Thale Noi bus from the local bus stop on Poh Saat Rd in Phattalung. The bus stops at the sanctuary after about an hour's journey and costs 8B. Long-tail boats can be hired at the pier to take passengers out and around the Thale Noi for two hours for 150B. The last bus back to Phattalung leaves around 5 pm.

Places to Stay

Phattalung Ramet Rd is the main drag where you will find two of Phattalung's four principal hotels.

At 43 Ramet Rd, the *Phattalung Hotel 1* is dingy but adequate and costs 80 to 120B with fan and bath. The newer *Phattalung 2* at No 34/1 costs 100 to 180B for better rooms. The *Thai Sakon* (the English sign reads 'Universal Hotel') is a short distance west of the Phattalung Hotel on Ramet Rd, at the intersection with Poh-Saat Rd. It's clean and has adequate rooms with fan and bath for 80B.

The *Thai Hotel* is a large hotel on Disara-Nakarin Rd, off Ramet Rd near the Rama Cafe and Bangkok Bank. Rooms are 150B with fan and bath, up to 250B with air-con.

The *How Hua Hotel* (Haw Fa), on the corner of Poh-Saat and Kuhasawan Rds, has rooms with fan and bath for 130B, air-con rooms for 260B. It's also very clean.

Lam Pam The *Lampam Resort* (☎ 611486) has bungalows for 200B.

Thale Noi Out at the waterbird sanctuary, the Forestry Department has a few bungalows for rent for 300B.

Places to Eat

The best restaurant in Phattalung is the well-known *Hong Thong Restaurant* on Pracha Bamrung Rd – turn left off Disara-Nakarin Rd just past the new Thai Hotel. This is a family-run Chinese place and the seafood is excellent since Phattalung is only a few km from the inland sea. Prices are not high. Hàwy jaw, crab sausage served with sliced pineapple on the side, is very nice. Other dishes include:

plaa kao nêung púay – whole fish steamed in a broth of onions, peppers, Chinese mushrooms and tangy plums
plaa tùk phàt phèt – catfish fried in chilli and fresh holy basil
yam má-mûang – spicy mango salad
kài má-nao râat náam kreh-wii – chicken in lime sauce
plaa kapõng khão thâwt – freshwater perch fried whole
kûng náam jèut phão – grilled freshwater shrimp

Most cheap restaurants in Phattalung are on the grubby side. The market off Poh-Saat Rd is a good place for cheap takeaways. For breakfast, try the local speciality khâo yam (dry rice mixed with coconut, peanuts, lime leaves and shrimp), it's delicious. About three km west of town where Highway 4 meets Highway 41 is a *Muslim market.* Several food stalls here sell Muslim food like khâo mòk kài (chicken briyani) and the southern-Thai version of kài yâang.

Getting There & Away

Bus & Share Taxi Buses from the Baw Khaw Saw station in Nakhon Si Thammarat take two hours and cost 30B; share taxis are 50B. Buses from Hat Yai and Songkhla are 24B and 30B respectively and take about the same time.

Buses from Trang are 15B and take 1½ hours. Phattalung to Phuket buses are 75B and take seven hours.

Train Special express trains from Bangkok leave Hualamphong station at 2 and 3.15 pm, arriving in Phattalung at 4.26 and 5.41 am. The cheaper rapid No 43 leaves Bangkok at 4 pm and arrives in Phattalung at 7 am. Basic fares are 611B 1st class (express only), 288B 2nd class, 137B 3rd class, plus appropriate surcharges.

Boat It's possible to travel across the inland sea by regularly scheduled ferry boat from Phattalung to Sathing Phra in Songkhla Province – see the Khukhut Waterbird Sanctuary section for details.

Songkhla Province

SONGKHLA

อ.เมืองสงขลา

Songkhla (population 84,000), 950 km from Bangkok, is another former Srivijaya satellite on the east coast. Not much is known about the pre-8th century history of Songkhla, called Singora by the Malays. The town, small in area and population, is on a peninsula between the Thale Sap Songkhla (an inland sea) and the South China Sea (or Gulf of Thailand, depending on how you look at it). The inhabitants are a colourful mixture of Thais, Chinese and Muslims (ethnic Malays), and the local architecture and cuisine reflect the combination. Older southern Thais still refer to the city as Singora or Singkhon.

The seafood served along the white Hat Samila is excellent, though the beach itself is not that great for swimming, especially if you've just come from Ko Samui. However, beaches are not Songkhla's main attraction, even if the TAT promotes them as such – the town has plenty of other curiosities to offer, though the evergreen trees along Hat Samila give it a rather nice visual effect.

In recent years Songkhla has become increasingly Westernised due to the influx of multinational oil company employees – particularly British and American. A short string of bars with names like Anytime and Offshore has opened up along Sadao Rd to serve oil workers.

Orientation & Information

The town has a split personality, with the charming older town west of Ramwithi Rd toward the waterfront, and the new town east of Ramwithi Rd – a modern mix of business and suburbia.

Consulates Next to the governor's residence on Sadao Rd is the US Consulate (☎ 321441). An AUA branch opposite offers 10-week Thai language courses for 1500B.

The Malaysian Consulate (☎ 311062, 311104) is next to Khao Noi a 4 Sukhum Rd, near Hat Samila.

Hash House Harriers With all the expats living in Songkhla, there would have to be an HHH chapter. Songkhla's HHH, founded in 1981, usually holds hashes on Saturday at 4.30 pm at different locations around the city. Information is available in the lobbies of the Pavilion and Royal Crown hotels.

Thale Sap Songkhla

ทะเลสาบสงขลา

Stretching north-west of the city is the huge brackish lake or 'inland sea' of Thale Sap Songkhla. Parts of the Thale Sap are heavily fished, the most sought-after catch being the famous black tiger prawn. Illegal gill-net trawling for the prawn is now threatening the overall fish population; legal fishermen have begun organising against gill-net use.

The city's waterfront on the inland sea is buzzing with activity: ice is loaded onto fishing boats on their way out to sea, baskets and baskets of fish are unloaded onto the pier from boats just arrived, fish markets are setting up and disassembling, long-tail boats doing taxi business between islands and mainland are tooling about. The fish smell along the piers is pretty powerful though, so be warned.

Around Town

For interesting Songkhla architecture, walk along the back streets parallel to the inland sea waterfront – Nang Ngam, Nakhon Nai and Nakhon Nawk Rds all have some older Songkhla architecture showing Chinese, Portuguese and Malay influence, but it's disappearing fast. A few km south of Hat Samila is **Kao Saen**, a quaint Muslim fishing village – this is where the tourist photos of gaily painted fishing vessels are taken.

National Museum

พิพิธภัณฑ์แห่งชาติ

This is in a 100-year-old building of southern Sino-Portuguese architecture, between Rong Muang and Jana Rds (off Vichianchom Rd). The museum contains exhibits from all national art-style periods, particularly the Srivijaya. Hours are the usual 9 am to noon and 1 to 4 pm, Wednesday to Sunday; admission is 10B.

Wat Matchimawat

วัดมัชฌิมาวาส

On Saiburi Rd towards Hat Yai, this wat has an old marble Buddha image and a small museum. There is also an old Sinhalese-style chedi and royal pavilion at the top of Khao Tang Kuan, a hill rising up at the northern end of the peninsula.

Beaches

Besides the strip of white sand along **Hat Samila**, there's the less frequented **Hat Son Awn** on a slender cape jutting out between the Gulf of Thailand and Thale Sap, north of Samila.

Other Attractions

Songkhla is southern Thailand's educational centre; there is one university, several colleges, technical schools and research institutes, a nursing college and a military training camp, all in or near the town.

Suan Tun, a topiary park across from the Samila Hotel, has yew hedges trimmed into animal shapes.

Places to Stay – bottom end

The best deal in Songkhla is the *Narai Hotel* (☎ 311078), at 14 Chai Khao Rd, near the foot of Khao Tang Kuan. It's an older wooden hotel with clean quiet singles/doubles with fan and shared bath for 80/90B. A huge double with bath is 150B.

Another place with character is the *Nang Ngam Hotel*, a small Chinese Hotel on Nang Ngam Rd near Yaring Rd. Rather basic rooms are 70 to 90B, but for anyone who

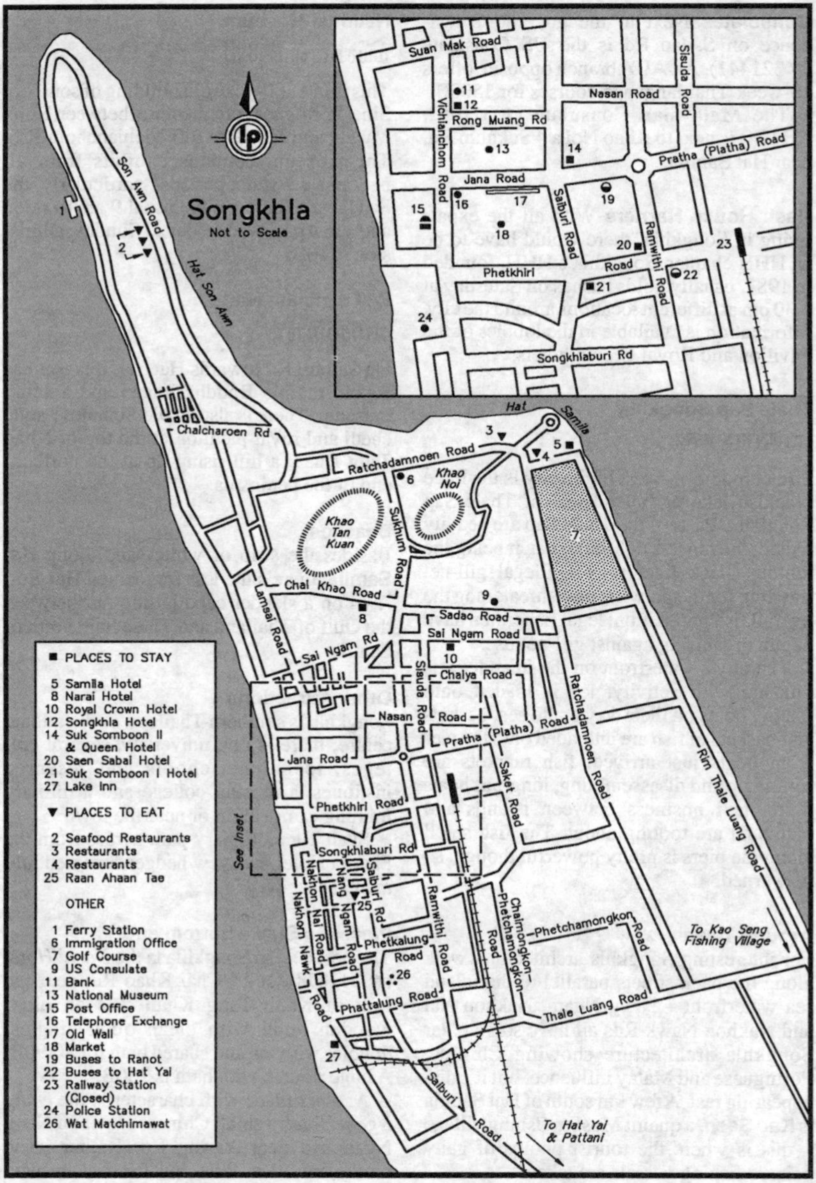
Songkhla
Not to Scale
Son Awn Road
Hat Son Awn
Chalcharoen Rd
Ratchadamnoen Road
Hat Samila
Khao Noi
Khao Tan Kuan
Sukhum Road
Chai Khao Road
Lamsai Road
Sadao Road
Sai Ngam Road
Sai Ngam Rd
Chalya Road
Sisuda Road
Nasan Road
Pratha (Platha) Road
Jana Road
Phetkhiri Road
Saket Road
Ratchadamnoen Road
Rim Thale Luang Road
Songkhlaburi Rd
Saiburi Rd
Nang Ngam Road
Nakhon Nai Road
Nakhorn Nawk Road
Ramwithi Road
Phetkalung Road
Phattalung Road
Chaimongkon–Phetchamongkon Road
Phetchamongkon Road
Thale Luang Road
Saiburi Road
To Kao Seng Fishing Village
To Hat Yai & Pattani
See Inset
Suan Mak Road
Vichianchom Road
Rong Muang Rd
Ramwithi Road
Phetkhiri Road
Saiburi Road
■ PLACES TO STAY
5 Samila Hotel
8 Narai Hotel
10 Royal Crown Hotel
12 Songkhla Hotel
14 Suk Somboon II & Queen Hotel
20 Saen Sabai Hotel
21 Suk Somboon I Hotel
27 Lake Inn
▼ PLACES TO EAT
2 Seafood Restaurants
3 Restaurants
4 Restaurants
25 Raan Ahaan Tae
OTHER
1 Ferry Station
6 Immigration Office
7 Golf Course
9 US Consulate
11 Bank
13 National Museum
15 Post Office
16 Telephone Exchange
17 Old Wall
18 Market
19 Buses to Ranot
22 Buses to Hat Yai
23 Railway Station (Closed)
24 Police Station
26 Wat Matchimawat

wants to be in the heart of the old Chinese district this is the place.

The refurbished *Songkhla Hotel*, on Vichianchom Rd, across from the Fishing Station, has good 100B rooms with shared bath, 150B with private bath.

The *Suk Somboon II* on Saiburi Rd, near the museum, is not bad for 120B a double, although they're just wooden rooms, off a large central area, and you have to ask for that price – posted rates start at 140B. Rooms in the air-con room next door are 300B.

The *Wiang Sawan*, in the middle of the block between Saiburi and Ramwithi Rds not far from Wat Matchimawat, has rooms from 140B, which is a bit overpriced for what you get.

Places to Stay – middle

The *Saen Sabai* (☎ 311090) at 1 Phetkhiri Rd is well located and has clean, if small, rooms in an early Bangkok-style building for 150/270B with fan or 300B with air-con. Nearby is a more expensive branch of the *Suk Somboon* on Saiburi Rd with fan-cooled singles/doubles for 140/220B. Next door is a new all-air-con wing with rooms for 300B or 450B with TV, bathtub and fridge.

The *Queen* (☎ 311138) at 20 Saiburi Rd, next door to the Suk Somboon 2, has decent air-con rooms from 280B. The similarly priced *Charn (Chan)* (☎ 311903) is on the same road but on the outskirts of the downtown area on the way to Hat Yai.

Places to Stay – top end

The *Samila Hotel* (☎ 311310/4) on the beachfront has air-con singles/doubles for 486/567B; it 's the only hotel in town with a swimming pool. The popular *Lake Inn* (☎ 314240) is a rambling multi-storey place with great views right on the Thale Sap. Rooms are 280B with air-con and hot water, 390B with TV and a bathtub, or 480B with a lake view.

Two places in town cater mostly to visiting oil company employees and their families. *The Pavilion* (☎ 311355, 312733) on Platha Rd costs 440B a single or double for rooms with air-con, TV with in-house video, fridge and carpet. The *Royal Crown* (☎ 312174) on Sai Ngam Rd has similar rooms for 450B.

Places to Eat

There are lots of good restaurants in Songkhla but a few tend to overcharge foreign tourists. The best seafood place, according to locals, is the *Raan Aahaan Tae* on Nang Ngam Rd (off Songkhlaburi Rd and parallel to Saiburi Rd). Look for a brightly lit place just south of the cinema. The seafood on the beach is pretty good too – try the curried crab claws or spicy fried squid.

Competing with Tae for the best seafood title is *Buakaew* on Samila Beach – there are several other seafood places in this vicinity. Fancier seafood places are found along Son Awn Rd near the beach – but these also tend to have the hordes of young Thai hostesses kept on to satisfy the Thai male penchant for chatting up *aw-aw* (young girls).

Along Nang Ngam Rd in the Chinese section are several cheap Chinese noodle and congee shops. At the end of Nang Ngam Rd along Phattalung Rd (near the mosque) are several modest Thai-Muslim restaurants; roti kaeng is available at an old worn coffee shop at the corner of Nang Ngam and Phattalung – it's open only from early morning till lunch time.

Khao Noi Phochana on Vichianchom Rd near the Songkhla Hotel, has a good lunch-time selection of Thai and Chinese rice dishes. Several food stalls on Sisuda Rd, near the Sai Ngam Rd intersection, do isaan (north-eastern Thai) food.

There are several fast-food spots at the intersection of Sisuda and Pratha Rd, including *Jam Quik* and *Fresh Baker* plus a few popular Thai and Chinese restaurants. Further south along Sisuda near the Chalerm Thong cinema and the old railway station is a hawker's centre and night market. The former railway station is now a casual cafe bar. *Ou-en* nearby is a very popular Chinese restaurant with outdoor tables; the house speciality is Peking duck. The very clean *Khun Ying*, next door to the Jazzy Blue Pub on Sisuda near the Platha intersection, has inexpensive curries and khanõm jiin.

Entertainment

The Smile Bar and Cheeky Pub on Saket Rd next to Wat Saket cater to oil workers and other expats in town with imported liquors, air-con and cable TV. The Offshore and Anytime on Sadao are similar.

Thais tend to congregate at bars with live music in the vicinity of the Sisuda-Platha Rd intersection.

Getting There & Away

Bus Air-con public buses leave Bangkok's southern bus terminal daily at 6.30, 7 and 7.35 pm, arriving in Songkhla 19 hours later, (319B). Ordinary buses are 182B, or 187B to Hat Yai from Bangkok. The privately owned tour buses out of Bangkok (and there are several available) are quicker but cost around 350B. A VIP (sleeper) bus costs 400B.

Air-con buses from Surat to Songkhla and Hat Yai cost 130B one-way. From Songkhla to Hat Yai, big green buses leave every 15 minutes (7B) from Rong Muang Rd, across from the Songkhla National Museum, around the corner from the Songkhla Hotel, or they can be flagged down anywhere along Vichianchom or Saiburi Rds, towards Hat Yai.

Air-con minivans to Hat Yai are 10B. Share taxis are 12B to Hat Yai, 40B to Pattani and 50B to Yala.

Train The old railway spur to Songkhla no longer has a passenger service. See Hat Yai's Getting There & Away section for trains to nearby Hat Yai.

Getting Around

For getting around in town, songthaews circulate Songkhla and take passengers, for 3B, to any point on their route. Motorcycle taxis anywhere in town are 5B.

KO YO

เกาะยอ

An island on the inland sea, Ko Yo (pronounced Kaw Yaw) is worth visiting just to see the cotton-weaving cottage industry there. The good-quality, distinctive phâa kàw yaw is hand-woven on rustic looms and available on the spot at 'wholesale' prices – meaning you still have to bargain but have a chance of undercutting the usual city price.

Many different households around this thickly forested, sultry island are engaged in cotton-weaving, but there is now a central market off the highway so it's no longer necessary to go from place to place comparing prices and fabric quality. At the market, prices for cloth and ready-made clothes are excellent if you bargain, and especially if you speak Thai. If you're more interested in observing the weaving process, take a walk down the road behind the market where virtually every other house has a loom or two – listen for the clacking sound made by the hand-operated wooden looms.

There are also a couple of semi-interesting wats, Khao Bo and Thai Yaw, to visit. Along the main road through Ko Yo are several large seafood restaurants overlooking Thale Sap. *Pornthip* (about a half km before the market) is reportedly the best.

Folklore Museum

At the northern end of the island at Ban Ao Sai, about two km past the Ko Yo cloth market, is a large folklore museum run by the Institute of Southern-Thai Studies, a division of Sinakharinwirot University. Opened in 1991, the complex of Thai-style pavilions overlooking the Thale Sap Songkhla contain well-curated collections (but unfortunately no English labels) of folk art as well as a library and souvenir shop. Displays include pottery, beads, shadow puppets, basketry, textiles, musical instruments, boats, religious art, weapons and various household, agricultural and fishing implements.

In the institute grounds are a series of small gardens, including one occasionally used for traditional shadow theatre performances, a medicinal herb garden and a bamboo culture garden.

Admission to the museum is 10B.

Getting There & Away

From Hat Yai, direct Ko Yo buses – actually

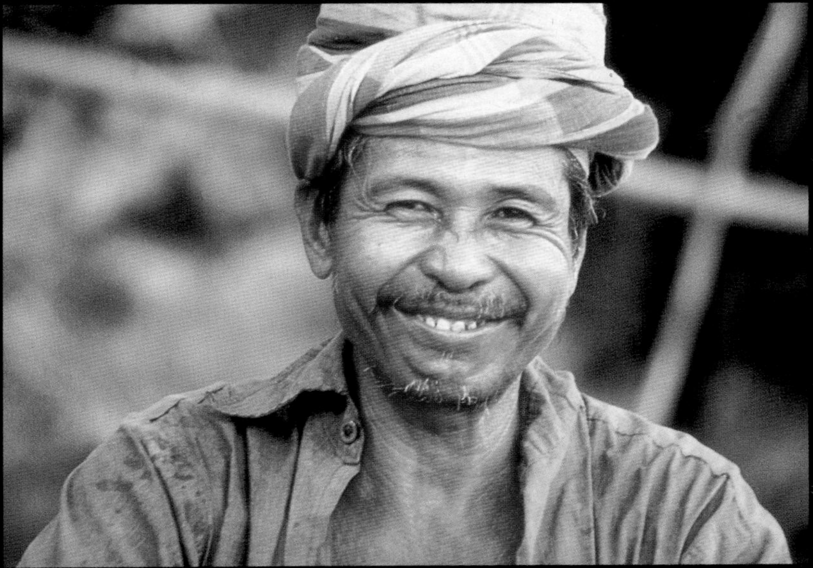

Top: 'Papa Taraporn', Ko Tao (MH)
Bottom: Practising traditional dancing (TAT)

Top Left: Waterfall near Sangkhom (JC)
Bottom Left: Sunset on Phuket (VB)
Top Right: Ko Phi Phi (TAT)
Bottom Left: Pattaya Beach (TAT)

large wooden songthaews – leave from near the clock tower on Phetkasem Rd frequently throughout the day. The fare to Ko Yo is 7B; although the bus terminates on Ko Yai further on it will stop in front of the cloth market on Ko Yo (ask for *nâa talàat*, 'in front of the market'). To get off at the museum, about two km past the market, ask for *phíphítaphan*. From Songkhla, buses to Ranot pass through Ko Yo for the same fare.

Nakhon Si Thammarat or Ranot-bound buses from Hat Yai also pass through Ko Yo via the new bridge system and will stop at the market or museum. Another way to get here is to take a Hat Yai to Songkhla bus to the junction for Ko Yo (5B), then catch the Songkhla-Ranot bus for 3B to the market or museum.

KHUKHUT WATERBIRD SANCTUARY

อุทยานนกน้ำคูขุด

On the eastern shore of the Songkhla inland sea, near Sathing Phra, about 80 km north of Songkhla, is a 520-sq-km sanctuary for waterbirds. Together with the similar Thale Noi Waterbird Sanctuary in Phattalung, the wetlands are a habitat for over 200 resident and migrant bird species over the entire Thale Sap, including bitterns, egrets and herons (these three are called *nók yang* in Thai), rare Javanese pond heron, fishing eagles *(nók yiaw)*, cormorants *(nók kaa)*, storks, kites, hawks, falcons, plovers, sand-pipers, terns *(nók nang)* and kingfishers.

A book available at the park office has very detailed information on the waterbirds and maps showing habitats. The best birding months are November and December, the worst are May to August.

You can arrange boat trips through the park service – it's 150B for an hour birding excursion, or 300B for a three-hour trip to see birds and stop at two islands.

Places to Stay & Eat

The *Khukhon Guest House* is an old wooden house on Thale Sap with a terrace restaurant overlooking the lake. Rooms here usually cost 100B but the last time I visited it was closed. It may reopen, but meanwhile it's easy to find rooms in the village – the house next door to the old Khukhon Guesthouse (the sign is still up) rents rooms for 100B a night.

A rustic eating area over the lake next to the office serves good Thai food.

Getting There & Away

Buses to Sathing Phra are 12B from Songkhla – take a red Ranot-bound bus. From the bus stop in front of the Sathing Phra district office you can walk the three km to the park or get a motorcycle taxi for 7B.

You can also get boats to Khukhut from Phattalung. An express boat (30B) leaves Lam Pam five times a day and takes two hours. Slower boats (17B) leave twice a day and take three hours.

HAT YAI

หาดใหญ่

Hat Yai (population 130,000), 933 km from Bangkok, is southern Thailand's commercial centre and one of the kingdom's largest cities, though it is only a district of Songkhla Province. A steady stream of customers from Malaysia keep Hat Yai's downtown business district booming. Everything from dried fruit to stereos are sold in the shops along Niphat Uthit Rds Nos 1, 2 and 3, not far from the railway station. Many travellers stay in Hat Yai on their way to and from Malaysia.

Culturally, Hat Yai is very much a Chinese town at its centre, with loads of gold shops and Chinese restaurants. A substantial Muslim minority is concentrated in certain sections of the city, eg near the mosque off Niphat Songkhrao Rd.

Information

Tourist Office The TAT Office (☎ 243747) is at 1/1 Soi 2 Niphat Uthit 3 Rd and is open daily from 8.30 am to 4.30 pm. The tourist police (☎ 246733) can also be found here.

Post & Telephone Hat Yai's GPO is on Niphat Songkhrao 1 Rd just south of the stadium and is open from 8.30 am to 4.30 pm weekdays, 9 am to noon weekends. The adjacent telephone office is open 7 am to 11 pm daily. There is also a more convenient branch post office on Rattakan Rd, just north of the railway station. A private packing service is available next door to the Rattakan post office.

Immigration The immigration office is near the U Taphao Bridge on Nasathanee Rd. The nearest Malaysian Consulate is in Songkhla.

Money Hat Yai is loaded with banks. Several after-hours exchange windows are along Niphat Uthit 2 and 3 Rds near the Thamnoonvithi Rd (pronounced Thammanun Withi) intersection.

Photography The Chia Colour Lab at 58-60 Suphasan Rangsan Rd, next to the Singapore Hotel, offers a good selection of films and quality processing.

Wat Hat Yai Nai

วัดหาดใหญ่ใน

A few km west of town, off Phetkasem Rd towards the airport, is Wat Hat Yai Nai. A very large (35 metres) reclining Buddha on the premises (Phra Phut Mahatamongkon) is currently being restored along with the wihaan to house it. Inside the image's gigantic base is a curious little museum/souvenir shop/mausoleum. The old abbot likes receiving visitors. To get there, hop on a songthaew near the intersection of Niphat Uthit 1 Rd and Phetkasem Rds and get off after crossing the U Taphao Bridge.

Bullfights

Bullfighting, involving two bulls in opposition rather than person and bull, takes place as a spectator sport twice monthly in Hat Yai. On the first Sunday of each month it's at an arena next to the Nora Hotel off Thamnoonvithi Rd, and on the second Sunday it is at the Hat Yai Arena on Highway 4, near the airport. Matches take place continuously all day from 10.30 am until 6 pm and admission is 30B – although many hundred times that amount changes hands during the nonstop betting by Thai spectators.

Places to Stay – bottom end

Hat Yai has dozens of hotels within walking distance of the railway station.

Cheaper places nearby include the *Cathay Guest House* (☎ 243815), on the corner of Thamnoonvithi and Niphat Uthit 2, three blocks from the station, with rooms ranging from 120 to 180B; there is also a 60B dorm. The Cathay has become a travellers' centre in Hat Yai because of its good location, helpful staff and plentiful travel info for trips onward, including tips on travel in Malaysia. They serve food (and also don't mind if you bring takeaways in and eat in the lounge). There is a reliable bus ticket agency downstairs.

Cheaper still are some of the older Chinese Hotels in the downtown area. Rooms are very basic but they're usually secure and service is quite OK – you can get towels and soap on request. The *Tong Nam Hotel* at 118-120 Niphat Uthit 3 Rd is a basic Chinese hotel with rooms for 80B with shared bath, 100B with private bath. *Kim Hua*, opposite and further south on the same road is 130 to 150B for fan and bath.

The *Savoy Hotel*, 3½ blocks from the station on Niphat Uthit 2 Rd, has fair 80B rooms, although doubles are often 120B or more. The name's been changed to New Savoy, but it's as rundown as ever.

On Niphat Uthit 1 Rd is the *Mandarin Hotel*, with rather overpriced rooms for 130B a double with fan and bath, 250B triple. The *Grand Hotel*, at 257-9 Thamnoonvithi Rd, is better, with fairly clean rooms with fan and bath for 120 to 150B.

The *Weng Aun* is an old Chinese Hotel across from King's Hotel on Niphat Uthit 1 Rd, four doors down from the Muslim Ocha restaurant. Basic singles start at 70B.

The friendly *Thin Aek Hotel* at 16 Duangchan Rd (behind Diana Department Store on Niphat Uthit 3 Rd) is another old Chinese relic; it's mostly a holding place for Bangladeshis trying to immigrate to Malaysia, but the owner caters to farang travellers

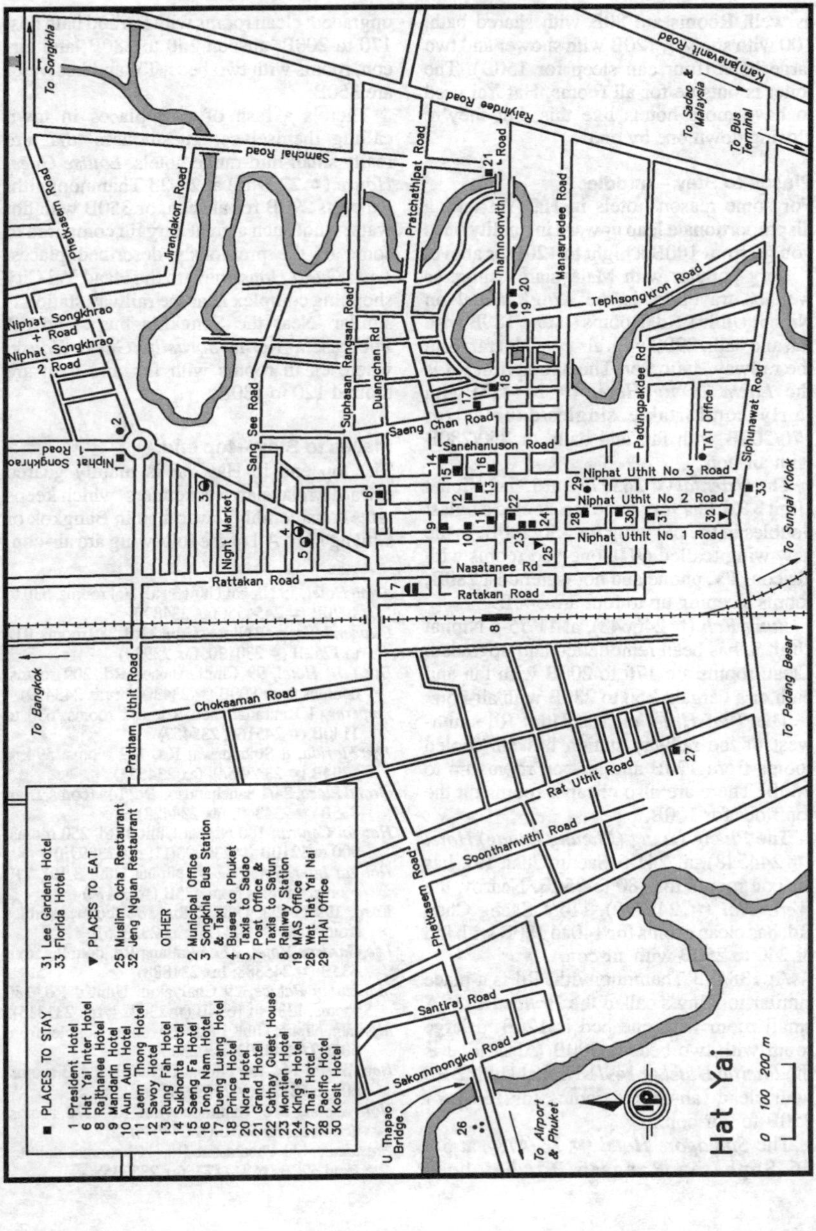

Hat Yai
0 100 200 m
To Songkhla
Kanjanavanit Road
Ratyindee Road
To Sadao & Malaysia
To Bus Terminal
Samchai Road
Phetkasem Road
Jirandakorn Road
Pratchathipat Road
Thamnoonvithi Road
Manasruedee Road
Tephsongkron Road
Niphat Songkhrao 3 Road
Niphat Songkhrao 2 Road
Niphat Songkhrao 1 Road
Suphasan Rangsan Road
Duangchan Rd
Sang See Road
Saeng Chan Road
Sanehanuson Road
Padungpakdee Rd
Siphunawat Road
TAT Office
Niphat Uthit No 3 Road
Niphat Uthit No 2 Road
Niphat Uthit No 1 Road
Night Market
Nasatanee Rd
Rattakan Road
Ratakan Road
To Sungai Kolok
To Padang Besar
To Bangkok
Pratham Uthit Road
Choksaman Road
Rat Uthit Road
Soonthamvithi Road
Phetkasem Road
Santiraj Road
Sakornmongkol Road
U Thapao Bridge
To Airport & Phuket
PLACES TO STAY
1 President Hotel
6 Hat Yai Inter Hotel
8 Rajthanee Hotel
9 Mandarin Hotel
10 Aun Aun Hotel
11 Laem Thong Hotel
12 Savoy Hotel
13 Rung Fah Hotel
14 Sukhonta Hotel
15 Saeng Fa Hotel
16 Tong Nam Hotel
17 Pueng Luang Hotel
18 Prince Hotel
20 Nora Hotel
21 Grand Hotel
22 Cathay Guest House
23 Montien Hotel
24 King's Hotel
27 Thai Hotel
28 Pacific Hotel
30 Kosit Hotel
31 Lee Gardens Hotel
33 Florida Hotel
PLACES TO EAT
25 Muslim Ocha Restaurant
32 Jeng Nguan Restaurant
OTHER
2 Municipal Office
3 Songkhla Bus Station
4 Buses to Phuket & Taxi
5 Taxis to Sadao
7 Post Office & Taxis to Satun
8 Railway Station
19 MAS Office
26 Wat Hat Yai Nai
29 THAI Office

as well. Rooms are 80B with shared bath, 100 with shower, 120B with shower and two large beds (four can sleep for 150B). The toilet is outside for all rooms. Hat Yai used to have more hotels like this, but they're closing down one by one.

Places to Stay – middle

For some reason hotels in Hat Yai take a disproportionate leap upward in quality once you go from 100B a night to 120B or above.

Very popular with Malaysian visitors as well as travellers is the *King's Hotel* on Niphat Uthit 1 Rd. Rooms start at 180B with fan and bath, 290B with air-con. Not far from the railway station on Thamnoonvithi Rd is the *Laem Thong Hotel* (☎ 244433) with fairly comfortable singles/doubles for 170/200B with fan and bath, or 250/280B with air-con.

The *Oriental* (☎ 245977), at 137-9 Niphat Uthit 3 Rd, has very good fan-cooled singles/doubles in the old wing for 150/200B. In the new wing (called *OH),* one-bed rooms with air-con, TV, phone and hot water cost 280B; rooms sleeping up to four are 340B.

Rung Fah (☎ 246643), at 117/5-6 Niphat Uthit 3, has been remodelled and upgraded. Clean rooms are 170 to 200B with fan and bath or a bargain 250 to 280B with air-con.

The *Thai Hotel* on Rat Uthit Rd southwest of the railway station has fan-cooled rooms from 120B and air-con rooms up to 260B. There are also cheaper rooms on the top floor for 100B.

The *Pueng Luang (Pheung Luang) Hotel* (☎ 244548), at 241-5 Saeng Chan Rd, has air-con rooms for 180 to 250B. Nearby, the *Wang Noi* (☎ 245729), 114/1 Saeng Chan Rd, has clean rooms for 140 to 180B with fan or 240 to 250B with air-con.

At 138/2-3 Thamnoonvithi Rd is a place similar to King's called the *Prince Hotel.* A small room with one bed is 120B; a large room with two beds is 200B. Also good is the *Pacific Hotel* at 149/1 Niphat Uthit 2 Rd with clean fan-cooled rooms for 150B, or 250B for air-con.

The *Singapore Hotel* (☎ 237478), at 62-66 Suphasan Rangsan Rd, has been upgraded: clean rooms with fan and bath cost 170 to 200B, air-con 250 to 280B, and air-con, rooms with two beds, TV and hot water are 350B.

There's a rash of new places in town calling themselves 'guesthouses' that are really small mid-range hotels. *Louise Guest House* (☎ 220966) at 21-23 Thamnoonvithi Rd costs 290B for air-con, or 350B with hot water – not such a great bargain compared to some of the previously described places. *Lada Guest House* next to the Haad Yai City shopping complex near the railway station is similar. Near the Songkhla bus stand off Phetkasem Rd is *Sorasilp Guest House*, where clean rooms with fan and bath are around 120 to 180B.

Places to Stay – top end

The top end in Hat Yai is mainly geared toward Malaysian weekenders, which keeps rates considerably lower than in Bangkok or Chiang Mai. All of the following are air-con:

Asian Hotel, 55 Niphat Uthit 3 Rd, 104 rooms, 530 to 1020B (☎ 245455; fax 234890)

Diamond Plaza, 62 Niphat Uthit 3 Rd, 280 rooms, 912 to 1252B (☎ 230130; fax 23924)

Dusit JB Hotel, 99 Chuti Anuson Rd, 209 rooms, doubles from 800B (☎ 234300/8; fax 243499)

Emperor, 1 Ranrattankhon Rd, 108 rooms, 630 to 1140B (☎ 245166, 235457)

The Florida, 8 Siphunawat Rd, 119 rooms, 594 to 1794B (☎ 234555/9; fax 234553)

Grand Plaza, 24/1 Sanehanuson Rd, 145 rooms, from 835B (☎ 234340; fax 234428)

Hat Yai Central, 180 Niphat Uthit 3 Rd, 250 rooms, 900 to 1210B (☎ 230000/11; fax 230990)

Hat Yai Inter Hotel, 42-44 Niphat Uthit 3 Rd, 210 rooms, doubles from 475B (☎ 24474)

Kosit, 199 Niphat Uthit 2 Rd, 182 rooms, doubles from 506B (☎ 244711; fax 232365)

Lee Gardens Hotel, 1 Lee Pattana Rd, doubles from 835B (☎ 245888; fax 231888)

Manhattan Palace, 29 Chaiyakun Uthit 4 Rd, 180 rooms, 1331 to 1694B (☎ 230724; fax 231315)

Montien, Niphat Uthit 1 Rd, 180 rooms, doubles from 506B (☎ 245593; fax 230043)

New World, 144-158 Niphat Uthit 2 Rd, 133 rooms, 605 to 1212B (☎ 246993)

Nora Hotel, 216 Thamnoonvithi Rd, 170 rooms, doubles from 515B (☎ 244944/82)

President, 420 Phetkasem Rd, 110 rooms, doubles from 620B (☎ 244477; fax 235355)

Rajthanee, Railway Station, doubles from 550B (☎ 232288)
The Regency, 23 Prachathipat Rd, 189 rooms, doubles from 750B (☎ 245454, 231021)
The Royal Hotel, 106 Prachathipat Rd, 136 rooms, 780 to 1560B (☎ 232162)
Scala Hotel, 43/42-43 Tanrattanakhon Rd, 84 rooms, 480 to 700B (☎ 246983)
Sukhonta, Sanehanuson Rd, 204 rooms, doubles from 700B (☎ 243999)
Thep Nakhon, 37 Pracharak Rd, 125 rooms, 400 to 1200B (☎ 245161)

Places to Eat

Hat Yai is southern Thailand's gourmet mecca, offering fresh seafood from both the Gulf of Thailand and the Andaman Sea, bird's nests, shark fins, Muslim roti and curries, Chinese noodles and dim sum. Lots of good, cheap restaurants can be found along the three Niphat Uthit Rds, in the markets off side streets between them, and also near the railway station.

Chinese Start the day with inexpensive dim sum at *Shangrila* on Thamnoonvithi Rd near the Cathay Guesthouse. Specialities include khanõm jìip (dumplings), salabao (Chinese buns) and khâo nâa pèt (roast duck on rice). In the evenings the Chinese food action moves to *Hua Lee* at the corner of Niphat Uthit 3 and Thamnoonvithi Rds; it's open till the wee hours.

Jeng Nguan is an old feasting stand-by near the end of end of Niphat Uthit 1 Rd (turn right from the station, it's on a corner on the left-hand side). Try the tâo hûu thâwt kràwp (fried bean curd), hũu chalãam (shark-fin soup), bàmìi plaa phàt (fried noodles with fish), or kíaw plaa (fish wonton). It's open from 9 am until late at night.

On Thamnoonvithi Rd between Niphat Uthit Rds 1 and 2 are the *Thanad Sri Number 1* and *Thanad Sri Number 2* noodle shops, which serve very tasty and inexpensive noodle and rice dishes. They close at about 6 pm.

Noodle Garden, opposite the Odean shopping mall on Sanehanuson Rd, is a more up-market noodle restaurant; there's a second branch on the ground floor of Diana Department Store (Niphat Uthit 3 Rd). Several hotels in town also have good splurge-style Chinese restaurants, including *China Town* (Scala Hotel), *Hong Kong* (Lee Gardens Hotel) and *Dynasty* (Dusit JB Hotel).

Malay & Indian The *Muslim-O-Cha*, across from the King's Hotel, is still going strong, with roti kaeng (roti chanai in Malay) in the mornings and curries all day. This is one of the few Muslim cafes in town where women – even non-Muslim – seem welcome. There are a couple of other Muslim restaurants near this one.

On Niyomrat Rd between Niphat Uthit 1 and 2 are *Ruby*, *Abedeen* and *Mustafa* restaurants, all specialising in Muslim food. Ruby has the best selection of dishes, including Indian paratha, dal, chapati, briyani, and various mutton chicken, fish and veggie dishes. Abedeen is good for tôm yam kûng (spicy shrimp lemon-grass soup).

Sumatera Restaurant, next to the Pakistan Mosque near the Holiday Plaza Hotel, does Malay dishes like rojak (peanut-sauce salad) and nasi briyani (spiced rice plate).

Thai Although Chinese and Malay food rules in Hat Yai, there are a few Thai places as well. *Noppakao*, a Chinese-owned place on Thamnoonvithi Rd, has an inexpensive and tasty Thai food buffet in the middle of the day and an a la carte menu at other times. Another good Thai restaurant is *Niyom Rot* (the English sign says 'Niyom Rosh') in front of the Nora Hotel on Thamnoonvithi Rd. The plaa krabàwk thâwt, whole sea mullet fried with eggs intact, is particularly prized here.

Although the name is Lao, the *Viang Chan* at 12 Niphat Uthit 2 Rd serves Thai and north-eastern Thai dishes along with Chinese. The food centre below the Tong Nam Hotel has both Thai and Chinese dishes.

Night Markets The extensive night market along Montri 1 Rd specialises in fresh seafood; you can dine on three seafood dishes and one vegetable dish for less than 150B here if you speak Thai. There are smaller night markets along Suphasan Rangsan Rd and Si Phuwanat Rd.

Other Food The *Satellite Restaurant* on Thamnoonvithi Rd next door to Noppakao Restaurant, has a great selection of ice creams, sundaes, shakes, banana splits and Western breakfasts. The menu features colour photos of all the ice cream dishes; prices are reasonable. *Royal Bakery*, at 41 Thamnoonvithi (between Niphat Uthit 1 & 2), has assorted Chinese and Western pastries.

For something very different, cruise down Thanon Nguu (Snake Street – Soi 2, Channiwet Rd), Hat Yai's most popular spot for snake fetishists. After a live snake is slit lengthwise with a scalpel, the blood is drained and drunk with honey, Chinese rice wine or herbal liquor. Besides the blood, the heart, gall bladder and penis are also highly regarded. Skins are sold to manufacturers of wallets, belts and other accessories, while the meat is given away to customers for soup. Rates range from 100B for the evisceration of a small-to-medium cobra to 2000B for a king cobra three or four metres in length.

Entertainment

Most of the many clubs and coffee shops in town cater to Malaysian clientele. The bigger hotels have discos; among the most popular discos are the Zodiac (Sukhontha Hotel), the Metro (JB Hotel) and the New York (Manhattan Palace Hotel). Cover-charges are only 50 to 80B.

The Post Laserdisc on Thamnoonvithi Rd, a block east of the Cathay Guest House, is a music video/laserdisc bar with an excellent sound system and well-placed monitors. It has mostly Western movies, and programmes change nightly – the fairly up-to-date music videos are a filler between the films. The daily schedule starts at 10 am and goes until 1 am – mostly Thais and farangs come here. The only charge is a 7B added to your drink bill.

Opposite the Post Laserdisc, Sugar Rock is one of the more durable Hat Yai pubs, with good food, good prices and a low-key atmosphere.

Four of Hat Yai's six cinemas have sound rooms where the original English soundtrack of English-language films can be heard while watching films that have been dubbed in Thai for the rest of the theatre: Siam (Phetkasem Rd), Coliseum (Pratchathipat Rd), Chalerm Thai (Suphasan Rangsan Rd) and the Hat Yai Rama (Phetkasem Rd).

Things to Buy

Shopping is Hat Yai's number-one draw, with most of the market action taking place along Niphat Uthit 2 and 3 Rds. Here you'll find Thai and Malaysian batik, cheap electronics and inexpensive clothing.

SMS Muslim Store, 17 Niphat Uthit 1, has an excellent selection of south Indian sarongs, plus Thai, Malay and Indonesian batiks; although the markets are cheaper they can't compare with SMS in terms of quality and selection.

DK Book House, about 50 metres from the railway station on Thamnoonvithi Rd, carries English-language books and maps.

Hat Yai has three major department stores on Niphat Uthit 3 Rd (Diana, Ocean and Yongdee) and two on Thamnoonvithi Rd (World and the new Haad Yai City).

Getting There & Away – Thailand

Air THAI flies between Hat Yai and Bangkok five to six times daily. Flights take an hour and 20 minutes; the fare is 2280B one-way.

There are also THAI flights to Hat Yai from Narathiwat (three times weekly, 420B), Pattani (twice weekly, 300B) and Phuket (daily, 780B).

Bus To Songkhla the green buses leave from outside the small clock tower on Phetkasem Rd. Share taxis leave from around the corner near the President Hotel.

Tour buses from Bangkok are 338B (VIP 400B) and leave the southern air-con bus terminal every 15 minutes from 5.30 to 8.15 pm. The trip takes 13 hours. Private companies sometimes have fares as low as 319B. Ordinary government buses cost 187B and leave Bangkok at 9.45 and 10.50 pm.

There are also buses running between Phuket and Hat Yai; ordinary buses are 91B (eight hours) and air-con 154B (six hours). Air-con minivans to Nakhon Si Thammarat are available for 80B from the Rado Hotel on Sanehanuson Rd.

Magic Tour (☎ 234535), a travel agency downstairs from the Cathay Guesthouse, does express air-con buses and minivans to Phuket, Krabi, Ko Samui and Bangkok. Other buses from Hat Yai include:

destination	fare	hours
Ko Samui	165B	6
Narathiwat	50B	3
(air-con)	60B	3
Pattani	26B	2½
(air-con)	35B	1½
Phattalung	24B	2
Satun	22B	1½
(air-con)	35B	1
Surat Thani	68B	5
(air-con)	120B	4
Trang	35B	2
Yala	35B	2½

Private tour-bus companies include:

Golden Way Travel, 124/8 Thamnoonvithi Rd (☎ 233917)
Magic Tour, bottom floor Cathay Guesthouse (☎ 234535)
Hat Yai Swanthai Tours, 108 Thamnoonvithi Rd (☎ 246706)
Sunny Tour, Niphat Uthit 2 Rd (☎ 244156)
Pan Siam, 99 Niphat Uthit 2 Rd (☎ 237440)

Share Taxi Share taxis are an important way of getting from one province to another quickly in the south. There are seven share-taxi stands in Hat Yai, each specialising in certain destinations.

In general, share-taxi fares cost about the same as an air-con bus, but the taxis are about 30% faster. Share taxis also offer door-to-door drop-offs at the destination. The downside is that the drivers wait around for enough passengers (usually five minimum) for a departure. If you hit it right the taxi may leave immediately; otherwise you may have to wait a half hour or more. The drivers also drive at hair-raising speeds – not a pleasant experience for high-strung passengers.

Train Trains from Bangkok to Hat Yai leave Hualamphong station daily at 2 pm (special express No 19), 3.15 pm (special express No

Share Taxi Fares

destination	fare	hours	taxi stand
Songkhla	15B	1/2	near the President Hotel off Phetkasem Rd
Phattalung	40B	1¼	Suphasan Rangsan Rd near Wat Cheu Chang
Trang	60B	2½	Suphasan Rangsan Rd near Wat Cheu Chang
Sungai Kolok	120B	3½	Suphasan Rangsan Rd near Wat Cheu Chang
Betong	100B	3½	Suphasan Rangsan Rd near Wat Cheu Chang
Nakhon Si Thammarat	70B	2½	Suphasan Rangsan Rd near Wat Cheu Chang
Phuket	220B	6	Duangchan Rd
Surat Thani	150B	5	Duangchan Rd
Krabi	150B	5	Duangchan Rd
Narathiwat	80B	3	Niphat Uthit 1 Rd
Sadao	25B	1	Siam Nakarin Department Store, Phetkasem Rd
Khukhut	25B	1	Siam Nakarin Department Store, Phetkasem Rd
Ranot	30B	2	Siam Nakarin Department Store, Phetkasem Rd
Yala	60B	2	Niphat Uthit 2 Rd, near Cathay Guesthouse
Satun	35B	1½	Rattakan Rd, near the post office
La-Ngu	50B	1½	Rattakan Rd, near the post office

11) and 4 pm (rapid No 43), arriving in Hat Yai at 5.47 am, 7.04 am and 8.50 am. The basic fare is 664B 1st class (express only), 313B 2nd class or 149B 3rd class. Surat Thani to Hat Yai costs 55B, 3rd class.

The Advance Booking office at the station is open 8.30 am to 5 pm daily. The station's Rajthanee Restaurant is open from 6 am to midnight; there's also a cheaper eating area on platform. A left-luggage office (the sign reads 'Cloak Room') is open daily from 4.30 to 11 am and noon to 6 pm. The cost is 5B per piece for the first five days, 10B thereafter.

Getting There & Away – international

Hat Yai is a very important travel junction – almost any Thailand-Malaysia overland trip involves a stop here.

Air Both THAI and MAS fly from Penang; there are also Tradewind flights from Singapore.

THAI (☎ 243711) has offices in the centre of town at 166/4 Niphat Uthit 2 Rd (☎ 245851) and 190/6 Niphat Uthit 2 Rd (☎ 231272). Malaysian Airlines System (☎ 243729, 245443) is on Thamnoonvithi Rd near the Nora Hotel.

Hat Yai International Airport has a post office with an IDD telephone in the arrival area; it's open from 8.30 am to 4.30 pm weekdays, 9 am to noon Saturday, closed Sunday. Other airport facilities include the Sky Lounge Cafe & Restaurant on the ground floor near the domestic check-in, a less expensive coffee shop on the 2nd-floor departure level and foreign exchange kiosks.

Bus From Padang Besar at the Malaysian border, buses are 15B and take an hour to reach Hat Yai. Bus services operate between 6 am and 8 pm.

Magic Tour (☎ 234535), a travel agency downstairs from the Cathay Guesthouse, does express air-con buses and minivans to Penang (200B and five hours by bus), Kuala Lumpur, Singapore, and destinations within Thailand. Golden Way Travel (☎ 233917), 124/8 Thamnoonvithi Rd, runs VIP (30 reclining seats) buses to Singapore for 430B including all meals; super VIP (22 seats) costs 530B.

Other bus information out of Hat Yai:

destination	fare	hours
Butterworth (for Penang)	200B	6
Kuala Lumpur*	250 to 300B	12
Singapore*	300 to 350B	15

*denotes private tour-bus companies; see the earlier list

Warning Care should be taken in selecting travel agencies for bus trips into Malaysia. Recently there have been reports of bus companies demanding 'visa fees' before crossing the border – since visas aren't required for most nationalities, this is a blatant rip-off. The offending company collects your passport on the bus and then asks for the fee – holding your passport hostage. Refuse all requests for visa or border-crossing fees – all services are supposed to be included in the ticket price. One Hat Yai company that has reportedly perpetrated this scam is Chaw Weng Tours.

Share Taxis Share taxis are a popular way of travelling between Hat Yai and Penang in Malaysia. They're faster than the tour buses, although less comfortable and more expensive. Big old Thai-registered Chevys or Mercedes depart from Hat Yai around 9 am every morning. You'll find them at the railway station or along Niphat Uthit 2. In Penang you can find them around the cheap travellers' hotels in Georgetown. The cost is about M$22 – this is probably the fastest way of travelling between the two countries, and you cross the border with a minimum of fuss.

From Hat Yai the fare to Padang Besar is 35B for the one-hour trip; taxis are on Duangchan Rd. For Penang the stand is on Niphat Uthit 1 Rd and the three-hour trip costs 220B.

Getting Around

To/From the Airport The THAI van costs 40B per person for transport to the city;

there's also a private 150B THAI limo service. A regular taxi costs 100B from the airport, about half that from the city.

Local Transport The innumerable songthaews around Hat Yai cost 5B per person. Watch out when you cross the street or they'll mow you down.

AROUND HAT YAI

Ton Nga Chang Falls

น้ำตกโตนงาช้าง

'Elephant Tusk' Falls, 24 km west of Hat Yai via Highway 4 in Rattaphum district, is a seven-tier cascade that falls in two streams (thus resembling two tusks). If you're staying over in Hat Yai, the falls make a nice break from the hustle and bustle of the city. The waterfall looks its best at the end of the rainy season, October to December.

To get to the falls take a Rattaphum-bound songthaew (10B) and ask to get off at the *náam tòk* (waterfall).

Krabi Province

Krabi Province has scenic *karst* formations near the coast, similar to those in Phang-Nga Province, even in the middle of the Krabi River. Krabi itself sits on the banks of the river right before it empties into the Andaman. Near town you can see Bird, Cat and Mouse Islands, named for their shapes.

Offshore are over 150 islands offering excellent recreational opportunities; many of the islands belong to the **Hat Noppharat Thara – Ko Phi Phi National Marine Park**. Hundreds of years ago, Krabi's waters were a favourite hide-out for Asian pirates because of all the islands and water caves. Latter-day pirates now steal islands or parts of islands for development – land encroachment is reportedly taking place on Phi Phi Don, Poda, Pu, Bubu, Jam, Po, Bilek (Hong), Kamyai and Kluang.

The interior of the province, noted for its tropical forests and the Phanom Bencha mountain range, has barely been explored.

Krabi has a nearly new, but hardly used, deep-sea port financed by local speculators in tin, rubber and palm oil, Krabi's most important sources of income. The occasional ship from Singapore (sometimes even a Singapore or Penang junk) anchors here and if you know the right people you can buy tax-free cigarettes and other luxury items while one of these boats is in port.

Beach accommodation is inexpensive (though not as cheap as Ko Pha-Ngan) and there are regular boats to Ko Phi Phi, 42 km west. From December to March, the hotels and bungalows along Krabi's beaches can fill up. The beaches of Krabi are nearly deserted in the rainy season, so this is a good time to go. This part of Krabi has been 'discovered' by world travellers and beach bungalows are expanding operations to accommodate them.

KRABI

อ.เมืองกระบี่

Nearly 1000 km from Bangkok and 180 km from Phuket, the fast-developing provincial capital, Krabi (population 16,000), has friendly townspeople, good food and some good beaches nearby.

A joint venture between THAI and the Thailand Cultural Centre is currently planning to renovate the Krabi customs house on Jao Fa Rd and transform the building into a southern-Thai cultural museum. When the project is completed, the museum will contain a collection of 30,000-year-old artefacts of local provenance, a seashell collection, and various folk items from southern-Thai culture, such as chao naam (sea gypsies) folkcraft and costumes from *likhe pàa* (jungle theatre) and other local performing arts.

Information

The post and telephone office is on Utarakit Rd past the turn-off for the Jao Fa pier. Visas can easily be extended at the immigration

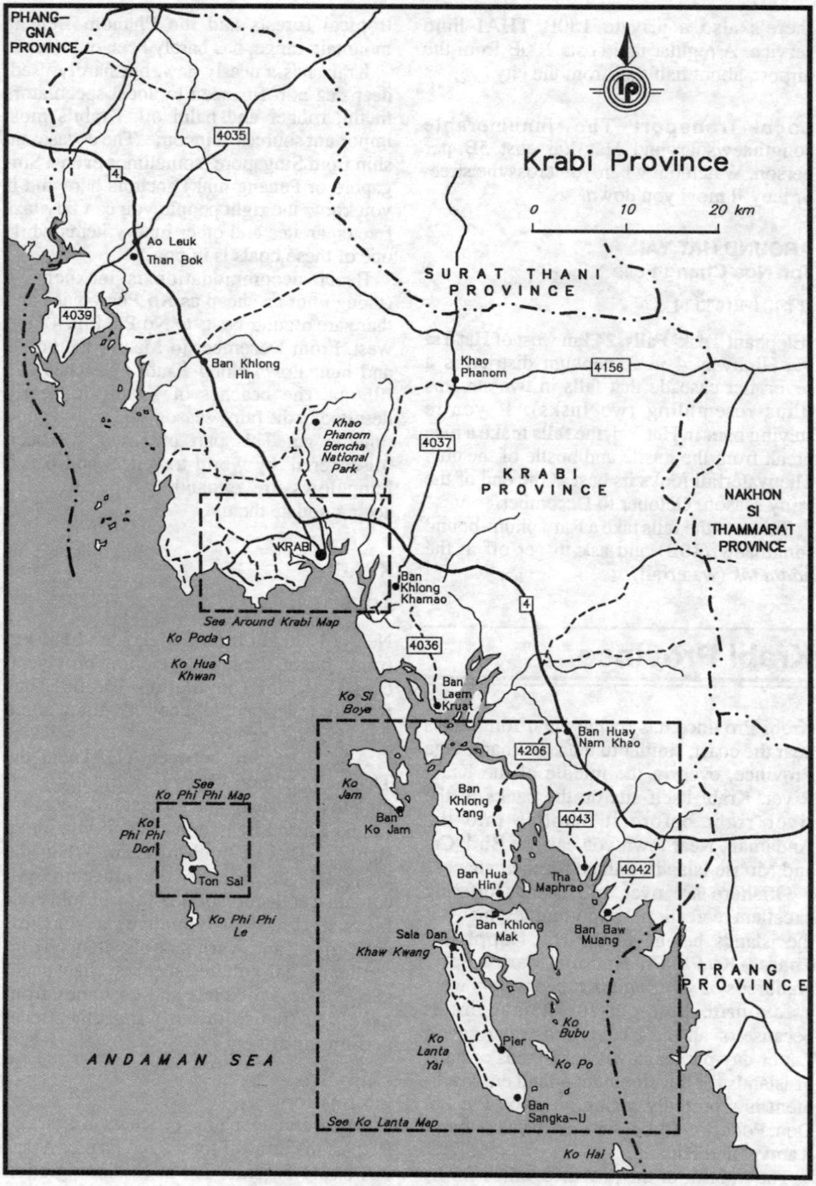
Krabi Province
0
10
20 km
PHANG–GNA PROVINCE
SURAT THANI PROVINCE
KRABI PROVINCE
NAKHON SI THAMMARAT PROVINCE
TRANG PROVINCE
ANDAMAN SEA
4035
4
4039
4156
4037
4036
4206
4043
4042
Ao Leuk
Than Bok
Ban Khlong Hin
Khao Phanom
Khao Phanom Bencha National Park
KRABI
Ban Khlong Khanao
See Around Krabi Map
Ko Poda
Ko Hua Khwan
Ko Si Boye
Ban Laem Kruat
Ban Huay Nam Khao
Ko Jam
Ban Ko Jam
Ban Khlong Yang
See Ko Phi Phi Map
Ko Phi Phi Don
Ton Sai
Ko Phi Phi Le
Ban Hua Hin
Tha Maphrao
Ban Khlong Mak
Ban Baw Muang
Sala Dan
Khaw Kwang
Ko Bubu
Ko Lanta Yai
Pier
Ko Po
Ban Sangka–U
See Ko Lanta Map
Ko Hai

office, which is a bit further along the same road.

Maps Bangkok Guide has a *Guide Map of Krabi* (35B) that contains several mini-maps of areas of interest throughout the province. If it's kept up to date it should prove to be very useful for travel in the area. The locally produced *Krabi Tourist Map* is also quite good.

Travel Agencies Krabi has dozens of fly-by-night travel agencies that will book accommodation at beaches and islands as well as tour-bus and boat tickets. Jungle Book and Chan Phen, both on Utarakit Rd, have been the most reliable over the years.

Su-Saan Hawy (Shell Cemetery)
สุสานหอย

Nineteen km west of town, on Laem Pho, is the so-called Shell Fossil Cemetery, a shell 'graveyard', where 75-million-year-old shell fossils have formed giant slabs jutting into the sea. To get there, take a songthaew from the Krabi waterfront for 15B – ask for 'Su-Saan hawy'.

Wat Tham Seua
วัดถ้ำเสือ

In the other direction, about six km north and then eight km east of town, is Wat Tham Seua (Tiger Cave Temple), one of southern Thailand's most famous forest wats. The main bot is built into a long, shallow limestone cave, on either side of which dozens of *kutis* (monastic cells) are built into various cliffs and caves.

The abbot is Ajaan Jamnien, a Thai monk in his forties who has allowed a rather obvious personality cult to develop around him. The usual pictures of split cadavers and decaying corpses on the walls (useful meditation objects for countering lust) are interspersed with large portraits of Ajaan Jamnien, who is well known as a teacher of vipassana and *metta* (loving-kindness). It is said that he was apprenticed at an early age to a blind lay priest and astrologer who practised folk medicine and that he has been a celibate his entire life. Many young women come here to practise as eight-precept nuns.

The best part of the temple grounds can be found in a little valley behind the ridge where the bot is located. Follow the path past the main wat buildings, through a little village with nuns' quarters, until you come to some steep stairways on the left. The first leads to an arduous climb to the top of a karst hill with a good view of the area. The second stairway, next to a large statue of Kuan Yin, leads over a gap in the ridge and into a valley of tall trees and limestone caves. Enter the caves on your left and look for light switches on the walls – the network of caves is wired so that you can light your way chamber by chamber through the labyrinth until you rejoin the path on the other side. There are several kutis in and around the caves, and it's interesting to see the differences in interior decorating – some are very spartan and others are outfitted like oriental bachelor pads. A path winds through a grove of trees surrounded by tall limestone cliffs covered with a patchwork of foliage. If you continue to follow the path you'll eventually end up where you started, at the bottom of the staircase.

To get to Wat Tham Seua, take a songthaew from Utarakit Rd to the Talaat Kao junction for 3B, then change to any bus or songthaew east on Highway 4 towards Trang and Hat Yai and get off at the road on the left just after Km 108 – if you tell the bus operators 'Wat Tham Seua' they'll let you off in the right place. It's a two-km walk straight up this road to the wat.

In the mornings there are a few songthaews from Phattana Rd in town that pass the turn-off for Wat Tham Seua (10B) on their way to Ban Hua Hin. Also in the morning there is usually a songthaew or two going direct to Wat Tham Seua from Talaat Kao for around 5B.

Places to Stay
Guesthouses The cheapest places in Krabi are the many guesthouses which seem to be

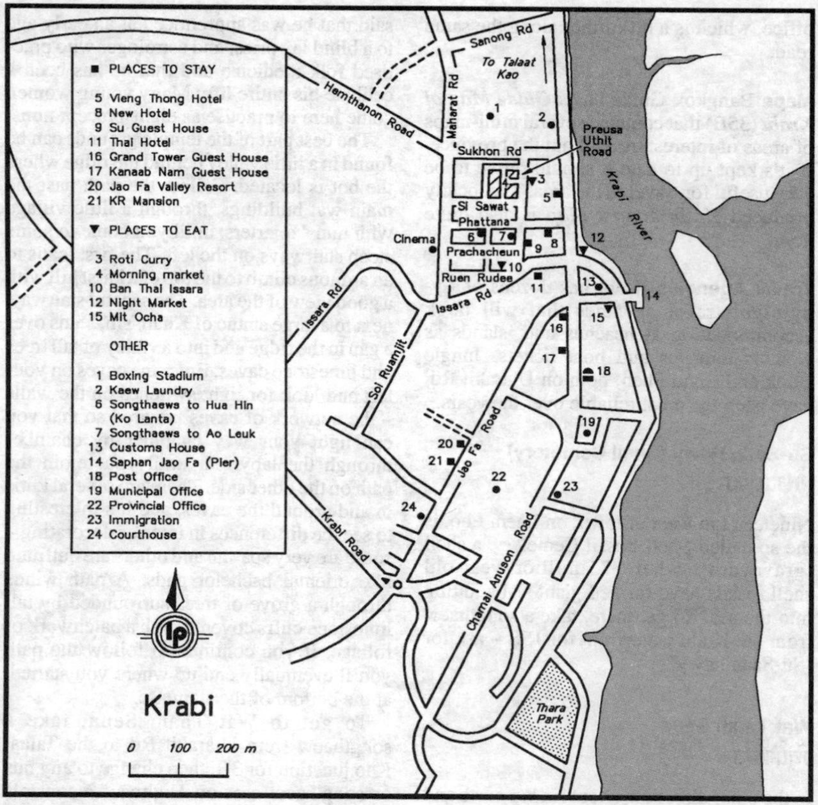

springing up everywhere. Some only stay around a season or two, others seem fairly stable. The ones in the business district feature closet-like rooms above modern shop buildings, often with faulty plumbing – OK for one night before heading to a nearby beach or island but not very suitable for long-term stays.

Downtown you'll find the *Su Guest House* on Preusa Uthit Rd, with 60 to 70B rooms with shared bath. Similar to Su Guesthouse are the *Krabi Guest House* and *B&B Guest House* on the same street.

Over on Ruen Rudee Rd are several other places with the usual upstairs rooms and slow plumbing, including *Walker, Coconut Home* and *KL*, all with rooms for 50/80B a single/double with shared bath. Around the corner on Maharat Rd is the *Seaside*, of similar ilk. Better than any of these are the large, fairly clean rooms with private bath at *Grand Tower Guest House* (☎ 612948), over Grand Travel Center on Utarakit Rd. Rates here are 150/200B for singles/doubles.

Quieter and more comfortable are the guesthouses just south-west of town near the courthouse. Top of the heap is the new *KR Mansion & Guest House* (☎ 612761; fax

612545) on Jao Fa Rd, which has immaculate rooms for 100 to 120B with fan and shared bath, or for 180B a single or double with fan and private bath. The KR will also rent rooms by the month (2700B). Several local civil servants room here; another bonus is the Tamarind Tree restaurant downstairs. The rooftop provides a 360° view of Krabi – great for sunsets. The friendly staff can arrange motorcycle rentals and boat tickets as well.

Also on Jao Fa Rd is *Chao Fa Valley Guesthouse & Resort*, which has OK rooms and bungalows for 80 to 300B.

On the southern extension of Issara Rd, which is more or less parallel to Jao Fa Rd, are the *V&S Guest House* and *Lek's House*, both with pleasant rooms in old wooden houses for 60 to 80B. Lek's also has dorm beds for 30B.

Along Utarakit Rd in the vicinity of the post office are the *Kanaab Nam* and *Cha* guesthouses, older houses with rooms for 60 to 80B.

Hotels Hotels in Krabi have always been lacking in quality and the situation has not improved. Travellers seeking mid-range comfort would do better to lodge at the *KR Mansion* or one of the other guesthouses.

The *New Hotel* (☎ 611318) on Phattana Rd has adequate rooms for 120B with fan and bath, from 140B with air-con. The old wing of the *Thai Hotel* on Issara Rd has disappeared, leaving only the new building with overpriced rooms. This used to be good value, but they seem to have raised the rates and lowered the standards. Rooms with fan start at 250B, air-con from 360B.

Vieng (Wiang) Thong (☎ 611188/288), at 155 Utarakit Rd, is better. Large doubles with fan and bath are 250B or 360B with air-con; add hot water and TV for 480B and a fridge for 600B.

Outside town near the Talaat Kao bus terminal are the sleazy *Kittisuk*, on Si Phang-Nga Rd, and *Naowarat* on Utarakit Rd. The Kittisuk has a few 80B rooms, while the Naowarat starts at 180B.

Places to Eat

What Krabi lacks in hotels it more than makes up for in good eating places. The *Reuan Phae*, a floating restaurant on the river in front of town, isn't all that great for a meal but it's fine for a beer or rice whisky while watching the river rise and fall with the tide; the fried shrimp cakes (thâwt man kûng) are worth trying. Further south down Utarakit Rd is a night market near the big pier (called Saphan Jao Fa) with great seafood at low prices and a host of Thai dessert vendors.

Panan (no English sign), at the corner of Ruen Rudee and Maharat, has khâo mòk kài (chicken briyani) in the mornings, inexpensive curries and kŭaytĭaw the rest of day. The Roman script sign reads Makanan Islam (Malay for 'Muslim Food').

The KR Mansion's *Tamarind Tree* on Jao Fa Rd is a small family-run restaurant with good southern-style curries (only 10B per plate with rice) or you can get khanŏm jiin náam yaa (thin, white, wheat noodles with ground fish curry) for 5B. In the mornings they also serve khâo yam, the southern-Thai breakfast of rice mixed with dried shrimp, toasted coconut, ginger and lime – sort of the Thai equivalent of Swiss muesli – for 8B. The Tamarind Tree also serves a few farang dishes.

Two places on Ruen Rudee specialising in Western breakfasts and a mixed menu of Thai and farang food are the nicely decorated *Ban Thai Issara* and *May & Mark* next door.

One of the best restaurants in town for standard Thai dishes and local cuisine is the *Kotung* near Saphan Jao Fa pier. The tôm yam kûng is especially good, as is anything else made with fresh seafood. One of the specialities of the house is hăwy lâwt, a tube-like shellfish that looks something like 'squid-in-a-shell', quickly steamed/stir-fried in a sauce of basil and garlic – delectable. Prices are reasonable.

For cheap Thai breakfasts, the morning market off Si Sawat Rd in the middle of town is good. Not far from the morning market on Preusa Uthit Rd is a Muslim place that serves roti chanai, the Malaysian-style breakfast of flat bread and curry. Look for a sign that says

'Hot Roti Curry Service'. Another cheap and tasty breakfast spot is *Mit Ocha*, a funky coffee shop on the corner of Utarakit and Jao Fa Rds, opposite the customs house. Besides Thai-style coffee and tea, the old Chinese couple here serves khanõm jiin (served with chunks of pineapple as well as the usual assorted veggies), and custard and sticky rice wrapped in banana leaves (khâo nĩaw sãngkha-yaa) – help yourself from the plates on the tables. A good place to hang out if waiting for morning boat to Phi Phi.

Getting There & Away

Air Bangkok Airways plans regular flights to Krabi when it gets government clearance to use Krabi Airport.

Bus, Share Taxi & Minivan Government buses to/from Bangkok cost 161B ordinary, 290B air-con or 350B VIP (425B for super VIP – 24 seats). Ordinary buses to/from Phuket cost 38B and take four hours. Share taxis to/from Phuket cost 70B, air-con minivans 150B.

Buses for Krabi leave Phang-Nga several times a day for 25B. Direct Krabi to Surat buses take 4 hours for 50B (150B air-con). From Hat Yai it's 60B and four hours; from Trang, 30B, 2½ hours. There are also share taxis to/from Trang, Hat Yai and Satun. The share taxi fare is roughly twice the ordinary bus fare.

Out-of-province buses to/from Krabi arrive at and depart from Talaat Kao, a junction about four km north of Krabi on the highway between Phang-Nga and Trang. To get to the centre of Krabi, catch a songthaew for 3B. Private air-con buses leaves from Songserm Travel Center on Utarakit Rd.

Songthaews to Ban Hua Hin (for Ko Lanta) leave from Phattana Rd near the New Hotel in town – 25B to Ban Hua Hin. They leave about every half hour from 10 am to 2 pm. There are also more expensive air-con minivans.

When the current renovation of the Krabi Airport is finished, Bangkok Airways will begin regular flights from Bangkok.

Boat Krabi can be reached by sea from Ko Phi Phi and Ko Lanta. See the respective Phi Phi and Lanta sections for details.

Getting Around

Any place in town can easily be reached on foot, but if you plan to do a lot of exploring out of town, renting a motorcycle might be a good idea. The Suzuki dealer on Preusa Uthit Rd rents bikes for 150 to 200B a day. A couple of other places do motorcycle rental as well, including the Grand Travel Center on the corner of Jao Fa and Utarakit Rds.

Songthaews to Ao Leuk (for Than Bokkharani Park) leave from the intersection of Phattana and Preusa Uthit Rds for 15B. To Ao Nang (15B) they leave from Utarakit Rd near the New Hotel. Boats to the islands and beaches mostly leave from Jao Fa pier. See the Ao Nang & Laem Phra Nang section for boat details.

AROUND KRABI TOWN

Hat Noppharat Thara

หาดนพรัตน์ธารา

Eighteen km north-west of Krabi, this beach used to be called Hat Khlong Haeng (Dry Canal Beach) because the canal that flows into the Andaman Sea here is dry except during, and just after, the monsoon season. Field Marshal Sarit gave the beach its current Pali-Sanskrit name, which means 'Beach of the Nine-Gemmed Stream', as a tribute to its beauty. Recently the forest backing the beach has been cleared for some as yet unannounced project.

The two-km-long beach is part of Hat Noppharat Thara – Ko Phi Phi National Marine Park, and is a favourite spot for Thai picnickers. There are some government bungalows for rent and a visitors' centre of sorts, with wall maps of the marine park.

The park pier at the northern end of Noppharat Thara has boats across the canal to Hat Khlong Muang, where the *Andaman Inn, Emerald Bungalows* and *Bamboo Bungalows* offer beach accommodation.

Ao Nang Area

อ่าวนาง

South of Noppharat Thara is a series of bays where limestone cliffs and caves drop right into the sea. The water is quite clear and there are some coral reefs in the shallows. The longest beach is along Ao Nang, a lovely spot easily reached by road from Krabi.

Over the headlands to the south are the beaches of **Phai Phlong, Ton Sai, Rai Leh**, and then the cape of Laem Phra Nang which encompasses **Hat Tham Phra Nang** (Princess Cave Beach) on the western side, and a beach facing east usually called East Rai Leh (or **Hat Nam Mao**).

All these beaches are accessible either by hiking over the headland cliffs, or by taking a boat from either Ao Nang or Krabi, although word has it that a tunnel road will be built to Hat Phai Phlong to provide access for a new resort hotel that is being constructed there.

Hat Tham Phra Nang This is perhaps the most beautiful beach in this area. At one end is a tall limestone cliff that contains **Tham Phra Nang Nok** (Outer Princess Cave), a cave that is said to be the home of a mythical sea princess. Local fishermen place carved wooden phalli in the cave as offerings to the princess so that she will provide plenty of fish for them. Inside the cliff is a hidden lagoon called **Sa Phra Nang** (Princess Pool) that can be reached by following a cave trail into the side of the mountain. A rope guides hikers along the way and it takes about 40 minutes to reach the lagoon. If you break left off the trail after 50 metres from the start, you can reach a 'window' in the cliff that affords a view of Rai Leh West and East beaches. It's also possible to climb to the top of the mountain from here (some rock-climbing is involved) and get an aerial view of the entire cape and the islands of **Ko Poda** and **Ko Hua Khwan** (also known as Chicken Island) in the distance.

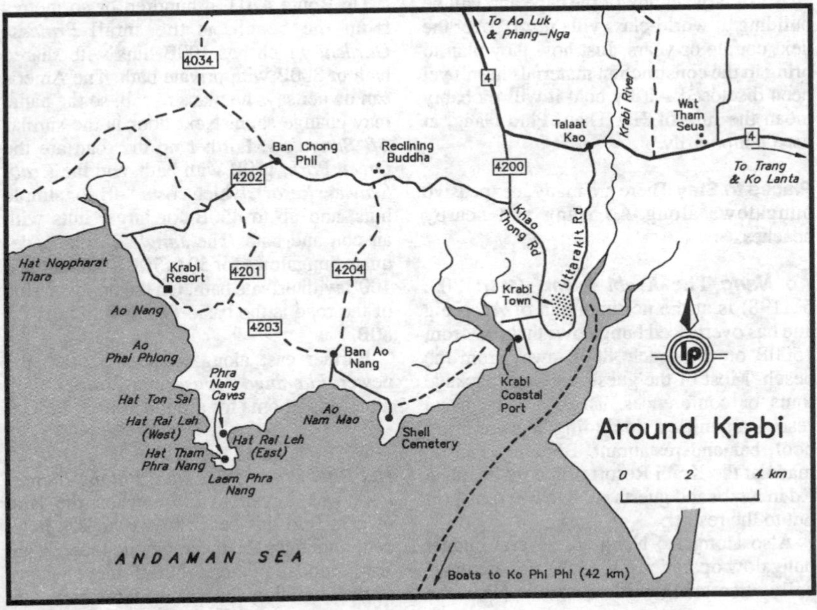

A second, larger cave was recently discovered on Laem Phra Nang. The entrance is in the middle of the peninsula not far from Hillside Huts. This one is called **Tham Phra Nang Nai** (Inner Princess Cave) and consists of three caverns. All three contain some of the most beautiful limestone formations in the country, including a golden 'stone waterfall' of sparkling quartz. Local mythology now says that this cave is the 'grand palace' of the sea princess while Tham Phra Nang on the beach is her 'summer palace'.

The islands off Laem Phra Nang are good areas for snorkelling. Besides Ko Poda and Ko Hua Khwan is the nearer island of **Ko Rang Nok** (Bird Nest Island) and, next to that, a larger unnamed island (possibly the same island at low tide) with an undersea cave. One fairly interesting dive site is the sunken boat just south of Ko Rang Nok, a favoured fish habitat. Some of the bungalows do reasonably priced day trips to these as well as other islands in the area.

The Dusit hotel chain has recently purchased a large chunk of the cape and will be building a 'world-class villa resort' over the next couple or years. Just how they plan to bring in the construction materials hasn't yet been disclosed – if by boat it will probably mean the ruin of Hat Tham Phra Nang, at least temporarily.

Places to Stay There are many inexpensive bungalows along Ao Nang and nearby beaches.

Ao Nang The *Krabi Resort* (☎ 611300, 611198) is at the northern end of Ao Nang and has overpriced bungalows that cost from 1500B on the beach, 880B away from the beach. Most of the guests are with package tours or conferences. There are the usual resort amenities, including a swimming pool, bar and restaurant. Bookings can be made at the Krabi Resort office on Phattana Rd in Krabi and guests receive free transport out to the resort.

Also along Ao Nang are several budget bungalow operations, though rates are gradually increasing with demand. Near the turn-off for the Krabi Resort but not on the beach are *Ao Nang Ban Leh* with 70B huts (shared bath), and the *Ao Nang Hill* for 40 to 60B. On the water is *PS Cottage* with huts for 100B with private bath – a nice spot. Going south along the beach you'll come to *Wanna's Place* and *Gift's*, both 50B for simple huts or 150B for larger huts with bath. After that is a long undeveloped stretch where the *Ao Nang Plaza* is under construction.

The beach road intersects with Route 4203 to Krabi just before you arrive at *Phra-Nang Inn* (☎ 612173/4), a tastefully designed 'tropical hotel' with sweeping views of the bay and a small pool. Large air-con rooms are 1000B a night in the high season (usually December to February), 750B the remainder of the year. They have a good restaurant.

Next door is the *Ao Nang Villa*, also a good place, with roomy cottages for 200B (300B in high season) with fan, 400B (650B) with air-con or 550B (850B) with air-con and hot water.

Up Route 4203, a hundred or so metres from the beach, is the small *Princess Garden*, which has 100B huts with shared bath or 300B with private bath. The American owner says he plans to sell, so the name may change soon. Next door is the similar *BB Bungalow*. Further up the road are the *Green Park*, 150B with bath, and the *Krabi Seaview Resort*, which costs 80B for simple huts, and up to 450B for larger huts with air-con and bath. The *Jungle Hut* has adequate bungalows for 50 to 70B without bath, 100B with private bath. On the opposite side of the road is the basic *Peace* with huts for 80B.

Further east along Route 4203 are the newer *Flamingo House* and *Hillock* with motel-like rooms for around 100B.

Hat Phai Phlong The *Phai Phlong Bungalows* was forced to close when the land owners sold this beach to a Bangkok hotel conglomerate. At the moment there is no accommodation here, but if they haven't started building the planned resort yet, it might be worth boating over for the day – nice beach.

Ao Ton Sai This beach can only be reached by boat from Ao Nang, Ao Nam Mao or Krabi. Until very recently, *Andaman Bungalows* provided accommodation which was highly praised, but a new owner has moved in and at this writing there's no word on prospective development, though it will probably be something up-market.

Hat Rai Leh (West) There are four places to choose from here. *Railay Village* has 150B huts with bath, and the *Railae Beach* and *Sand Sea* have the same plus 50B huts without bath. *Sunset* has larger bungalows, all with private bath, for 200 to 300B for three to four people. All have dining areas. At the northern end of the beach is a private beach condominium development. It's possible to rent vacant bungalows from the caretakers for 400 to 1000B a night.

Hat Rai Leh can be reached by boat from Ao Nang, Ao Nam Mao or Krabi, or on foot from Hat Phra Nang and Hat Rai Leh (east) (but these must be approached by boat as well).

Hat Tham Phra Nang While the Dusit is busy building its exclusive resort there is no accommodation on this beach. Barbed wire has been strung around most of the area, though a wooden walkway has been left around the perimeter of the limestone bluff so that you can walk to and from the beach.

As at West Rai Leh and Hat Ton Sai, Phra Nang is accessible by boat only.

Hat Rai Leh (East) The beach along here tends toward mud flats during low tide; most people who stay here walk over to Hat Tham Phra Nang for beach activities.

Queen, *Sunrise*, *Ya-Ya* and *Coco Bungalows* all offer fair bungalows for 80 to 100B in December and January, half that the rest of the year. Ya-Ya is the best maintained.

At the northern end of the beach is *Hill Side Huts* for 70B with shared bath, 150B with private bath, negotiable in the off season. A bit further near the Phra Nang Nai caves is the *Diamond Cave Bungalows* with huts in a rubber grove for 30B. The Diamond Cave Blue Bar, against a rock cliff next to the cave and the bungalows, is atmospheric but the night-time din carries some distance – light sleepers beware.

Getting There & Away Hat Noppharat Thara and Ao Nang can be reached by songthaews that leave about every 15 minutes from 7 am to 5 pm from Utarakit Rd in Krabi, near the New Hotel. The fare is 15B and the trip takes 30 to 40 minutes.

You can get boats to Ton Sai, West Rai Leh and Laem Phra Nang at several places. For Ton Sai, the best thing to do is get a songthaew out to Ao Nang, then a boat from Ao Nang to Ton Sai. It's 15B per person for two people or more, 30B if you don't want to wait for a second passenger to show up.

For West Rai Leh or anywhere on Laem Phra Nang, you can get a boat direct from Krabi's Jao Fa pier for 30B. It takes about 45 minutes to reach Phra Nang. However, boats will only go all the way round the cape to West Rai Leh and Hat Phra Nang from October to April when the sea is tame enough. During the other half of the year they only go as far as East Rai Leh but you can easily walk from here to West Rai Leh or Hat Phra Nang. You can also get boats from Ao Nang for 20B all year round, but in this case they only go as far as West Rai Leh and Hat Phra Nang (again, you can walk to East Rai Leh from here).

Another alternative is to take a songthaew as far as Ao Nam Mao, a small fishing bay near the Shell Cemetery, for 15B and then a boat to Laem Phra Nang for 20B (three or more people required).

Some of the beach bungalows have agents in town who can help arrange boats – but there's still a charge.

Than Bokkharani National Park

อุทยานแห่งชาติธารโบกขรณี

Than Bokkharani National Park was established in 1991 and encompasses nine caves throughout the Ao Leuk area in northern Krabi Province as well as the former botanical gardens for which the park was named.

The park is best visited just after the monsoons – when it has been dry a long time the water levels go down and in the midst of the rains it can be a bit murky. In December Than Bokkharani looks like something cooked up by Disney, but it's real and entirely natural. Emerald green waters flow out of a narrow cave in a tall cliff and into a large lotus pool, which overflows steadily into a wide stream, itself dividing into many smaller streams in several stages. At each stage there's a pool and a little waterfall. Tall trees spread over 40 rai (6.4 sq km) provide plenty of cool shade. Thais from Ao Leuk come to bathe here on weekends and then it's full of laughing people playing in the streams and pools. During the week there are only a few people about, mostly kids doing a little fishing. Vendors sell noodles, roast chicken, delicious batter-fried squid and sôm-tam under a roofed area to one side.

Caves Among the park-protected caves scattered around the Ao Leuk district, one of the most interesting is **Tham Hua Kalok**, set in a limestone hill in a seldom-visited bend of mangrove-lined Khlong Baw Thaw. Besides impressive stalactite formations, the high-ceilinged cave features 2000 to 3000-year-old cave paintings of human and animal figures and geometric designs.

Nearby **Tham Lawt** (literally, 'tube cave') is distinguished by a navigable stream flowing through it – it's longer than Phang-Nga's Tham Lawt but shorter than Mae Hong Son's.

Places to Stay *Ao Leuk Bungalow*, on the highway a half km before Than Bok, offers decent if overpriced cottages for 200B with private bath; you should be able to bargain for a lower rate if there are empty rooms.

In nearby Ao Leuk Tai, the wooden *Thai Wiwat Hotel* next to the district office has plain rooms for 60B.

Getting There & Away Than Bok, as the locals call it, is off Highway 4 between Krabi and Phang-Nga, near the town of Ao Leuk, one km south-west toward Laem Sak. To get there, take a songthaew from the intersection of Phattana and Preusa Uthit Rds in Krabi to Ao Leuk for 15B; get off just before town and it's an easy walk to the park entrance on the left.

To visit Tham Lawt and Tham Hua Kalok you must charter a boat from Tha Baw Thaw, around 6.5 km south-west of Than Bok. The tours are run exclusively by Ao Leuk native Uma Kumat and his son Bunma. They'll take one or two people for 100B; up to 10 can charter a boat for 250B. The boats run along secluded Khlong Baw Thaw and through Tham Lawt before stopping at Tham Hua Kalok. The pier at Tha Baw Thaw is 4.3 km from Than Bok via Route 4039, then two km by dirt road through an oil palm plantation. You must provide your own transport to Tha Baw Thaw.

Khao Phanom Bencha National Park
อุทยานแห่งชาติเขาพนมเบญจา

This 50-sq-km park is in the middle of virgin rainforest along the Phanom Bencha mountain range. The main scenic attractions are the three-level **Huay To Falls, Khao Pheung Cave** and **Huay Sadeh Falls**, all within three km of the park office. Other less well-known streams and waterfalls can be discovered here as well. Clouded leopards, black panthers, Asiatic black bears, deer, leaf monkeys, gibbons and various tropical birds make their home here. The park has a camp ground where you are welcome to pitch your own tent for 5B per person per night.

Getting There & Away Public transport direct to Khao Phanom Bencha National Park from Krabi or Talaat Kao is rare. Two roads run to the park off Highway 4. One is only about half a km from Talaat Kao – you could walk to this junction and hitch, or hire a truck in Talaat Kao all the way for 100B or so. The other road is about 10 km north of Krabi off Highway 4. You could get to this junction via a songthaew or a bus heading north to Ao Leuk.

It would be cheaper to rent a motorcycle in Krabi for a day trip to Phanom Bencha than to charter a pick-up. Try to have someone at the park watch your bike while hiking to nearby falls – motorcycle theft at Phanom Bencha has been a real problem lately.

KO PHI PHI

เกาะพีพี

Ko Phi Phi actually consists of two islands about 40 km from Krabi, Phi Phi Le and Phi Phi Don. Both are part of Hat Noppharat Thara – Ko Phi Phi National Marine Park, though this means little in the face of the blatant land encroachment now taking place on Phi Phi Don.

Only parts of Phi Phi Don are actually under the administration of the Park Division of the Royal Thai Forestry Department. Phi Phi Le and the western cliffs of Phi Phi Don are left to the nest collectors and the part of Phi Phi Don where the chao naam live is also not included in the park.

Phi Phi Don

พีพีดอน

Phi Phi Don is the larger of the two islands, sort of a dumb-bell shaped island with scenic hills, awesome cliffs, long beaches, emerald waters and remarkable bird and sea life. The 'handle' in the middle has long, white-sand beaches on either side, only a few hundred metres apart. The beach on the southern side curves around **Ao Ton Sai**, where boats from Phuket and Krabi dock. There is also a Thai-Muslim village here. On the northern side of the handle is **Ao Lo Dalam**.

The uninhabited (except for beach huts) western section of the island is called Ko Nawk (Outer Island), and the eastern section, which is much larger, is Ko Nai (Inner Island). At the north of the eastern end is Laem Tong, where the island's chao naam (sea gypsies) population lives. The number of chao naam here varies from time to time, as they are still a somewhat nomadic people, sailing from island to island, stopping off to repair their boats or fishing nets, but there are generally about 100. Like Pacific islanders of perhaps a hundred years ago, they tend to be very warm and friendly horizon-gazers. Of late, resort developers have been buying up their land.

Hat Yao (Long Beach) faces south and has some of Phi Phi Don's best coral reefs. Ton Sai, Lo Dalam and Hat Yao all have beach bungalows. Over a ridge, north-west from Hat Yao, is another very beautiful beach, **Hat Lanti**, with good surf, but so far the locals haven't allowed any bungalows here out of respect for the large village mosque situated in a coconut grove above the beach. Further north is the sizeable bay of **Lo Bakao**, where there is a small resort, and near the tip of Laem Tong are three luxury resorts.

Unfortunately, the park administrators seem to be letting development on Phi Phi Don continue unchecked. Rumour has it that park officials won't dare even set foot on Ko Phi Phi for fear of being attacked by village headmen and bungalow developers profiting from tourism. Beautiful Ao Ton Sai is becoming littered, and more and more bungalows have been crowded onto this section of the island. The noise of the generators is only drowned out by the sounds of Arnold firing large weapons at his enemies during the latest Schwarzenegger epic showing at every other bungalow restaurant. The once-brilliant coral reefs around the island are suffering from anchor drag and runoff from large beach developments. The least disturbed parts of the island so far are those still belonging to the chao naam.

Phi Phi Le

พีพีเล

Phi Phi Le is almost all sheer cliffs, with a few caves and a sea lake formed by a cleft between two cliffs that allows water to enter into a bowl-shaped canyon. The so-called **Viking Cave** contains prehistoric paintings of ships (Asian junks) and is also a collection point for sea swallow nests. The swallows

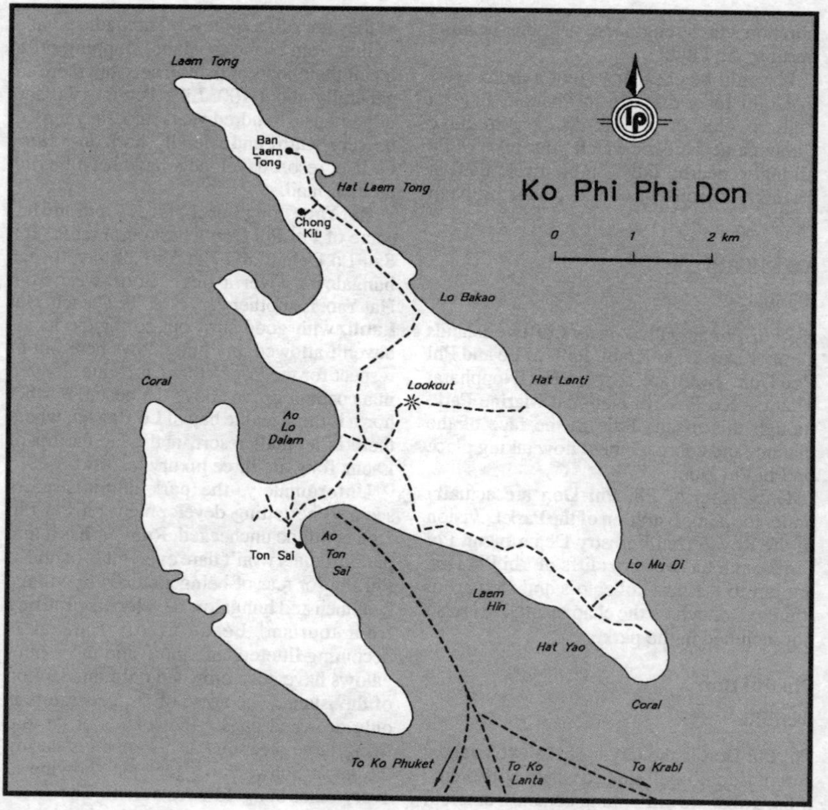

like to build their nests high up in the caves in rocky hollows which can be very difficult to reach. Agile collectors build bamboo scaffolding to get at the nests but are occasionally injured or killed in falls. People who want to collect sea swallow nests must bid for a licence in competition with other collectors which gives them a franchise to harvest the nests for four years. In one year there are only three harvests, as the birds build seasonally, and the first harvest fetches the highest prices. The collectors sell the nests to intermediaries who then sell them to Chinese restaurants in Thailand and abroad. The nests are made of saliva which the birds secrete – the saliva hardens when exposed to the air. When cooked in chicken broth, they soften and separate and look like bean thread noodles. The Chinese value the expensive bird secretions highly, believing them to be a medicinal food that imparts vigour.

No-one is allowed to stay on Phi Phi Le because of the bird-nest business, but boats can be hired from Phi Phi Don for the short jaunt over to see the caves and to do a little snorkelling at the coral reefs in Ao Ma-Ya. The usual rate for a day trip is 100B per person in a group of four or five.

Places to Stay

I'm all for boycotting travel to Ko Phi Phi until the national park comes to terms with greedy developers. On the other hand, if people don't see what's happening to Phi Phi they won't protest and the island will fall further into the iron grip of those who would turn this rare island into one big, polluted resort. What follows is a brief summary of places to stay for those who choose to go in the spirit of investigation (or for those who can ignore the obvious impact of unchecked development). If you go with the former intention, please contact one of the organisations listed under Ecology in the Facts about the Country chapter with your assessments, whether good or bad.

During the high tourist months of December to February, July and August, nearly all the accommodation on the island gets booked out. As elsewhere during these months, it's best to arrive early in the morning to stake out a room or bungalow. During the off season, rates are negotiable.

Ao Ton Sai

Tonsai Village, 50 rooms, 90 to 1500B
Phi Phi Don Resort, 38 rooms, 100 to 300B
Chao Koh Phi Phi Lodge, 400 to 500B
Pee Pee Island Cabana, 116 rooms, 600 to 1500B

Lo Dalam

Gift 2, 25 rooms, 100 to 300B
Chong Khao, 37 rooms, 100 to 300B
Krabi PP Resort, 70 rooms, 450 to 650B
Phi Phi Princess, 70 rooms, 450 to 1200B

Hat Hin Khom

Gypsy Village, 25 rooms, 350B
Pee Pee Andaman, 92 rooms, 350B
Funnyland, 21 rooms, 170 to 220B

Hat Yao

Maphrao Resort, 100 to 220B
Viking Village, 30 rooms, 70 to 120B
PP Paradise Pearl, 90 rooms, 90 to 500B
Long Beach, 60 rooms, 120B

Laem Thong

Phi Phi Palm Resort, 70 rooms, 1800 to 3900B
PP Coral Resort, 60 rooms, 1200 to 1400B
PP International Resort, 120 rooms, 850 to 3000B

Lo Bakao

Pee Pee Island Village, 60 rooms, 100 to 1500B

Getting There & Away

Ko Phi Phi is equidistant from Phuket and Krabi, but Krabi is your most economical point of departure. Until recently, boats travelled only during the dry season, from late October to May, as the seas are often too rough during the monsoons for safe navigation.

Nowadays the boat operators risk sending boats out all year round – we've received several reports of boats losing power and drifting in heavy swells during the monsoons. It all depends on the weather – some rainy season departures are quite safe, others are risky. If the weather looks chancy, keep in mind that there usually aren't enough life jackets to go around on these boats.

Another cautionary note regards the purchase of round-trip boat tickets. From Krabi there are currently two boat services and if you buy a return ticket from one company you must use that service in both directions. Neither service will recognise tickets from its competitor; not only that, they will refuse to sell you a new ticket back to Krabi if you hold a return ticket from the competitor. The advisable thing, then, is to buy one-way tickets only.

To/From Krabi From Krabi's Jao Fa pier, there are usually three boats a day leaving at 9.30 and 11.30 am and 2.30 pm. The official fare is 125B per person, but this is sometimes discounted by agents in town to as low as 90 or 100B. The trip takes about 1¾ hours on the faster boats or 2½ hours on the slower ones, to reach the public pier at Ao Ton Sai. In the reverse direction the same boats leave at 9 am, 1 and 3 pm.

The second service, operated by Pee Pee Island Cabana, leaves from a pier adjacent to the Jao Fa pier at 10 am and 1 pm for the same fare. This boat takes about 80 minutes to reach the Pee Pee Island Cabana pier.

There is talk of a new concrete pier being built at Laem Thong, the northern tip of Ko Phi Phi Don. If the pier comes about, it will probably mean the introduction of a third boat service from Krabi.

To/From Ao Nang You can also get boats from Ao Nang on the Krabi Province coast for 100B per person from October to April; there's usually only one departure a day at around 2 pm.

To/From Phuket Boat transport from Phuket's Patong Beach has been erratic lately. When they're running, boats leave Patong at 9 am, 1, 2, 3 and 4 pm for 150 to 200B per person. This trip takes 1½ hours on the fast boat, and up to three hours on the slow boat.

To/From Other Islands As Ko Lanta is becoming more touristed, there are now fairly regular boats between that island and Ko Phi Phi from October to April. Boats generally leave from the pier on Lanta Yai around 1 pm, arriving at Phi Phi Don around 3 pm. In the reverse direction the departure is usually at 11.30 pm. Passage is 125B per person (some visitors have also reported paying 150B). It's also possible to get boats to/from Ko Jam; the same approximate departure time, fare and trip duration applies.

Tours Various tour companies in Phuket offer day trips to Phi Phi, for 350 to 450B per person, that include round-trip transport, lunch and a tour. If you want to stay overnight and catch another tour boat back, you have to pay another 100B. Of course it's cheaper to book a one-way passage on the regular ferry service.

Pee Pee Islands Cabana also does package deals from Krabi or Phuket that include accommodation and a tour of Phi Phi Le.

Getting Around

Transport on the island is mostly on foot, although fishing boats can be chartered at Ao Ton Sai for short hops around Phi Phi Don and Phi Phi Le. There is an irregular boat service between Ton Sai and Hat Yao (Long Beach) for 10B per person.

KO JAM (KO PU) & KO SI BOYA

เกาะจำ(ปู)/เกาะสีบอยา

These large islands are inhabited by a small number of fishing families. At this writing there is one set of bungalows on the western side of Ko Si Boya called *Islander Hut* for 70B per night. Ko Jam's southern tip is occupied by a private residential development. *Joy Resort* on the south-western coast of Ko Jam has bungalows for 80 to 150B.

Getting There & Away

Boats to both islands leave two or three times a day from Ban Laem Kruat, a village about 30 km from Krabi, at the end of Route 4036, off Highway 4. Passage is 15B to Si Boya, 20B to Ban Ko Jam.

You can also take boats bound for Ko Lanta from Krabi's Jao Fa pier and ask to be let off at Ko Jam. There are generally two boats daily which leave at 8 am and 1 pm; the fare is 130B.

KO LANTA

เกาะลันตา

Ko Lanta (population 18,000) is a district of Krabi Province that consists of 52 islands. The island geography here is typified by stretches of mangrove interrupted by coral-rimmed beaches, rugged hills and huge umbrella trees. Twelve of the islands are inhabited and, of these, three are large enough to be worth exploring: **Ko Klang, Ko Lanta Noi** and **Ko Lanta Yai**. At present you have to get there by ferry from either Ban Hua Hin, on the mainland across from Ko Lanta Noi, or from Baw Muang, further south.

Ko Lanta Yai is the largest of the three islands – this is also where the district offices are. A private tourist information centre in **Ban Sala Dan**, at the northern tip of Lanta Yai, dispenses maps and handles enquiries. The western sides of all the islands have beaches. The best are along the south-west end of Lanta Yai, but practically the whole west coast of Lanta Yai is one long beach interrupted by the occasional stream or shell bed. There are coral reefs along parts of the western side of Lanta Yai and along the Khaw Kwang (Deer Neck) cape at its north-western tip. A hill on the cape gives a good aerial view of the island.

The people in this district are a mixture of Muslim Thais and chao náam who settled here long ago. There are now several inexpensive bungalow operations on Lanta Yai and you can camp on any of the islands – all have sources of fresh water. The village of **Ban Sangka-U** on Lanta Yai's southern tip is a traditional Muslim fishing village and the people are friendly. Ban Sala Dan at the northern end is the largest village on the island and even has a few TVs.

The little island between Ko Lanta Noi and Ko Klang has a nice beach called **Hat Thung Thale** – hire a boat from Ko Klang. Also worth exploring is Ko Ngai (Hai) – see the Trang Province section for more details as Ko Ngai is more accessible from that province.

Ko Lanta National Marine Park
อุทยานแห่งชาติทางทะเลหมู่เกาะลันตา

In 1990, 15 islands in the Lanta group (covering an area of 134 sq km) were declared part of the new Ko Lanta National Marine Park in an effort to protect the fragile coastal environment. **Ko Rok Nok** is especially beautiful, with a crescent-shaped bay featuring cliffs and a white-sand beach and a stand of banyan trees in the interior. The intact coral at **Ko Rok Nai** and limestone caves of **Ko Talang** are also worth seeing.

Ko Lanta Yai itself is only partially protected since most of the island belongs to chao náam. So far an estimated 50 bungalows have been built on lands protected by the Forestry Department – if the rangers or the villagers don't crack down soon it will become another Ko Phi Phi.

Places to Stay & Eat
Ko Lanta Outside of Ban Sala Dan, Ko Lanta doesn't have regular electric service yet. Quiet nights are still the rule at the less expensive places, while generators are buzzing at new up-market bungalows. Ko Lanta has the opportunity of becoming a model for environmentally conscious island tourism if the beach developers here will co-operate to keep the island clean and noise-free. As seems obvious elsewhere in Thailand, the national park system cannot be replied upon to protect the lands.

At the northern end of Lanta Yai near Ban Sala Dan is the *Deer Neck Cabanas*. It's actually on the south-east side of the small peninsula of the same name that juts west from the island. Nicely separated huts on a long curving beach are 80B, while bungalows with private bath reach as high as 300B. The adjacent *Khaw Kwang Beach Bungalows* is similar and costs from 60 to 600B depending on the amenities. At either place you can sometimes rent tents for as low as 50B per night.

About three km south of Ban Sala Dan along the western side of the island are four more places, *Lanta Villa*, *Lanta Royal*, *Lanta Golden Bay* and *Lanta Sea House*. All have basic huts for 80B or 150 to 300B with private bath.

About four km further south along the beach is the *Lanta Palm Beach* with similar accommodation for 80B without bath, 150B with bath. Next down the beach is the newer *Sea Gypsy Bungalows* with basic huts for 50 to 80B, followed by the *Relax Bay Tropicana* with large up-market bungalows for 600B.

Another km or two south is *Lanta Marina Hut*, a nicely designed place on shady grounds with large bungalows for 200B, with toilet inside and shower outside. They also have a few huts without toilet for 50 to 80B. Tents are also available for 30B per person. Four kms further south is a cluster of newer places similar to the Lanta Marina, including the *Coral Beach*, *Haad Beach* and *Lanta Paradise*, all with bungalows for 80B with shared bath, 100 to 200B with private bath.

Just before the road ends, about four km south of Lanta Paradise, is the *Sea Sun* with the usual 80/150B bungalows. About 2.5 km later the road ends, but a dirt track continues to Ban Sangka-U. *Waterfall Bungalows* is

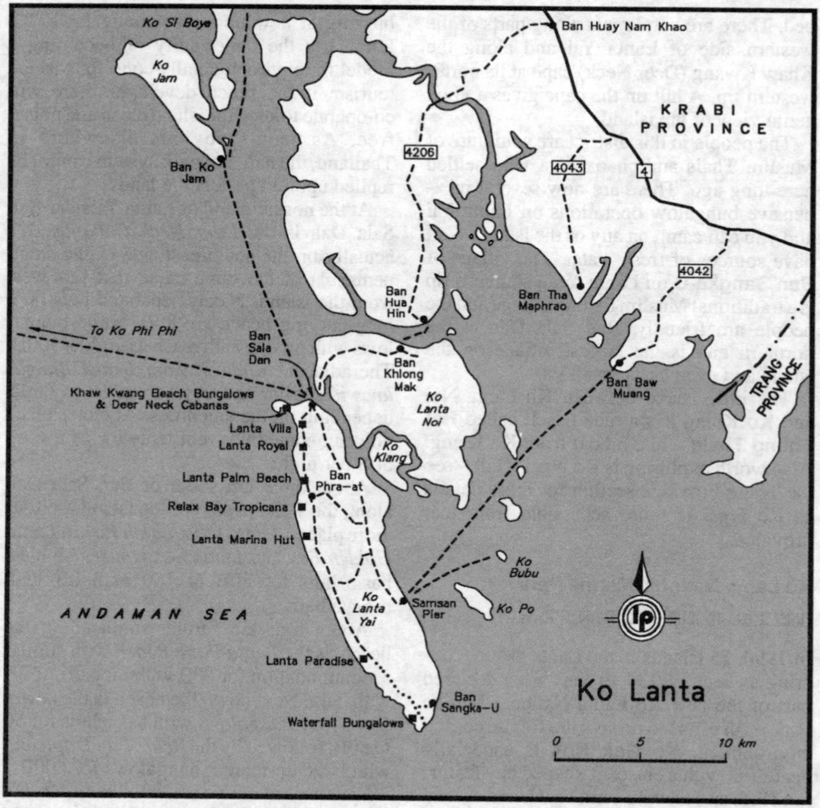

near the south-western tip of the island and costs from 250 to 500B for huts with fan and bath.

If you get tired of bungalow food there are a couple of basic places to eat in Ban Sala Dan at the northern end of Lanta Yai. One place near the pier has great khao yam and paa-thông-kõ in the mornings.

Ko Bubu This tiny island has one bungalow village with 13 huts. Rates are 100B per person in a dormitory, 200B in a bungalow with shared bath or 500B in a two-bed bungalow with private bath.

To get to Bubu from Lanta you can charter a boat from Samsan pier for 150 to 200B. From Krabi there's a daily van and express boat to Bubu for 130B per person. The other alternative is to get to Baw Muang on the mainland on your own, then charter a boat for 250B to Bubu. More information is available at the Samsan pier on Ko Lanta or from Thammachat (☎ (075) 612536), near the Jao Fa pier in Krabi.

Getting There & Away

To/From Ban Hua Hin The usual way to get to Ko Lanta is to take a songthaew (25B) from Phattana Rd in Krabi all the way to Ban Hua Hin, and then a boat (10B) across the narrow channel to Ban Khlong Mak on Ko Lanta Noi. From there, you get a motorcycle taxi (20B) across to another pier on the other side, and get another boat (5B) to Ban Sala Dan on Ko Lanta Yai. Ban Hua Hin is 26 km down Route 4206 from Ban Huay Nam Khao, which is about 44 km from Krabi along Highway 4.

If you're travelling by private car or motorcycle, the turn-off for Route 4206 is near Km 63 on Highway 4. Songthaews from Krabi (Talaat Kao junction) to Ban Hua Hin run regularly until about 2 pm. It takes about two hours because most of 4206 is unpaved (though locals say it should be paved within the next two years). Cars have to be parked near the pier in Ban Hua Hin. Motorcycles can be taken on both ferries all the way to Ko Lanta Yai.

From Ban Sala Dan on Lanta Yai you can get a motorcycle taxi to Hat Khaw Kwang for 10B, or pay 30 to 40B to other beaches. You can also hike to Khaw Kwang from Sala Dan, as it's only two km.

To/From Krabi A more direct way to reach Ko Lanta from the mainland is to take a boat from Krabi's Jao Fa pier. Boats usually depart at 10.30 am and 1.30 pm and take 1½ hours to reach Ban Sala Dan; the fare is 150B. In the reverse direction boats leave at 8 am and 3 pm.

To/From Ban Baw Muang You can also take a boat from Ban Baw Muang, which is about 35 km from Ban Huay Nam Khao at the end of Route 4042 (about 80 km in total from Krabi). The turn-off for Route 4042 is at Km 46 near the village of Sai Khao. It's 13 km from Ban Sai Khao to Ban Baw Muang on this dirt road. The boats from Ban Baw Muang are fairly large, holding up to 80 people, and they sail for an hour before reaching Samsan pier on Lanta Yai's eastern shore. The fare is only 30B.

To/From Ko Phi Phi During the dry season, October to April, there are fairly regular boats from Ko Phi Phi for about 125B per person. They take about an hour to reach Ban Sala Dan. There are also occasional boats to Lanta from the pier on Ko Jam.

Trang Province

The province of Trang has a geography similar to that of Krabi and Phang-Nga, with islands and beaches along the coast and limestone-buttressed mountains inland, but is much less frequented by tourists. Caves and waterfalls are the major attractions in the interior of the province – Trang seems to have more than its share.

Twenty km north of the capital is a 3500-rai (5.6-sq-km) provincial park, which preserves a tropical forest in its original state. In the park there are three waterfalls and government rest houses. Between Trang and Huay Yot to the north is Thale Song Hong (Sea of Two Rooms), a large lake surrounded by limestone hills. Hills in the middle of the lake nearly divide it in half, hence the name.

Music & Dance

As in other southern provinces, public holidays and temple fairs feature performances of *Manohra*, the classical southern Thai dance-drama, and nang thalung (shadow play). But because of its early role as a trade centre, Trang has a unique Indian-influenced music and dance tradition as well. *Li-khe pàa* (also called *li-khe bòk* and *li-khe ram manaa)* is a local folk opera with a story line that depicts Indian merchants taking their Thai wives back to India for a visit. It's part farce, part drama, with Thais costumed as Indians with long beards and turbans.

Traditional funerals and Buddhist ordinations often feature a musical ensemble called *kaa-law*, which consists of four or five players sitting on a small stage under a temporary coconut-leaf roof or awning. The instruments include two long Indian drums, a *pii haw* (a large oboe similar to the Indian *shahnai)* and two gongs.

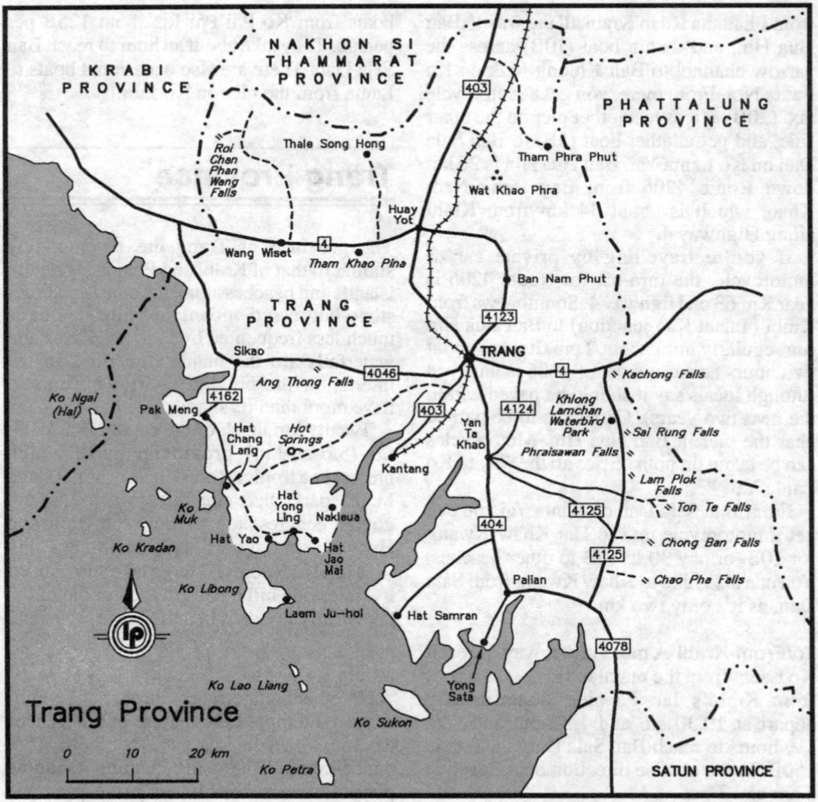

TRANG

อ.เมืองตรัง

Historically, Trang (population 47,000) has played an important role as a centre of trade since at least the 1st century AD and was especially important between the 7th and 12th centuries, when it was a sea port for ocean-going sampans sailing between Trang and the Malacca Straits. Nakhon Si Thammarat and Surat Thani were major commercial and cultural centres for the Srivijaya Empire at this time, and Trang served as a relay point for communications between the east coast of the Thai peninsula and Palembang, Sumatra. Trang was then known as Krung Thani and later as Trangkhapura (City of Waves) until the name was shortened during the early years of the Ratanakosin period.

During the Ayuthaya period, Trang was a common port of entry for seafaring Western visitors, who continued by land to Nakhon Si Thammarat or Ayuthaya. The town was then located at the mouth of the Trang River, but King Mongkut later gave orders to move the city to its present location inland because of frequent flooding. Today Trang is still an important point of exit for rubber from the province's many plantations.

One of Trang's claims to fame is that it often wins awards for 'Cleanest City in Thailand' – its main rival in this regard is Yala. One odd aspect of the city is the seeming lack of Thai Buddhist temples. Most of those living in the central business district are Chinese, so you do see a few joss houses but that's about it. Meun Ram, a Chinese temple between Sois 1 and 2, Visetkul Rd, sometimes sponsors performances of southern-Thai shadow theatre.

Trang's main attractions are the nearby beaches and islands, plus the fact that it can be reached by rail. The Vegetarian Festival is celebrated fervently in Trang in September or October. See the Phuket section for details.

Places to Stay

A number of hotels are found along the city's two main thoroughfares, Phra Ram VI Rd, Visetkul (Wisetkun) Rd and Ratchadamnoen Rd, which run from the clock tower. The *Ko Teng* (☎ 218622) on Phra Ram VI Rd has large, clean singles/doubles for a reasonable 120/180B, and a good restaurant downstairs. The management can be very helpful with enquiries on what to see and do around Trang, and they also have an information board of sorts with details on local attractions.

The *Wattana Hotel* (☎ 218184) is on the same stretch, and has recently upgraded its rooms considerably. Rates are now 160/190B with fan and bath or 350B for air-con.

Over on Ratchadamnoen Rd is the inexpensive *Petch (Phet) Hotel* (☎ 218002), with fair rooms with fan and bath for 80 to 120B. They also have a restaurant downstairs. Another inexpensive place is the *Mai Tri Hotel* on Phra Ram VI near the railway station. Basic but clean rooms are 70B.

On Visetkul Rd are the *Queen Hotel* (☎ 218522), with large clean rooms for 160B, or 260B with air-con, and the business-like *Trang Hotel* (☎ 218944), near the clock tower, with upgraded fan-cooled rooms for 300B, air-con for 700B.

The 10-storey *Thamrin* (☎ 211011; fax 218057) is an up-market place on Kantang Rd near the train and bus stations. Modern air-con rooms cost 600B standard, 900B deluxe.

Places to Eat

Plenty of good restaurants can be found in the vicinity of the hotels. Next door to the Queen Hotel is the *Phailin Restaurant*, which has a very broad selection of rice and noodle dishes. The menu has several vegetarian dishes including wûn-sên phàt jeh sài phõng kari (bean-thread noodles stir-fried with curry powder), kũaytĩaw phàt hâeng tâo-hûu (rice noodles fried with tofu), and khâo nâa kà-phrao tâo-hûu (tofu stir-fried with holy basil over rice). Or make it simple and get khâo phàt jeh, vegetarian fried rice. Another house speciality is kafae phailin, a spiced coffee made with local Khao Chong coffee.

The restaurant below the Ko Teng Hotel has good one-plate rice dishes and reputable kaeng kari kài (chicken curry), as well as ko-píi, Trang's famous Hokkien-style coffee.

Two khâo tôm places on Phra Ram VI Rd, *Khao Tom Phui* and *Khao Tom Je Uan*, serve all manner of Thai and Chinese standards in the evenings till 2 am. Phui has been honoured with the Shell Chuan Chim designation for its tôm yam (available with shrimp, fish or squid), sea bass in red sauce (plaa kraphõng náam daeng) and stir-fried greens in bean sauce (pûm pûy kha-náa fai daeng).

Ko-pĩi Shops Trang has long been famous for its coffee and ráan kafae or ráan ko-píi (coffee shops), which are easily identified by the charcoal-fired aluminium boilers with stubby smokestacks seen somewhere in the middle or back of the open-sided shops. Usually run by Hokkien Chinese, these shops serve real filtered coffee (called kafae thũng in the rest of the country) along with a variety of snacks, typically paa-thông-kõ,

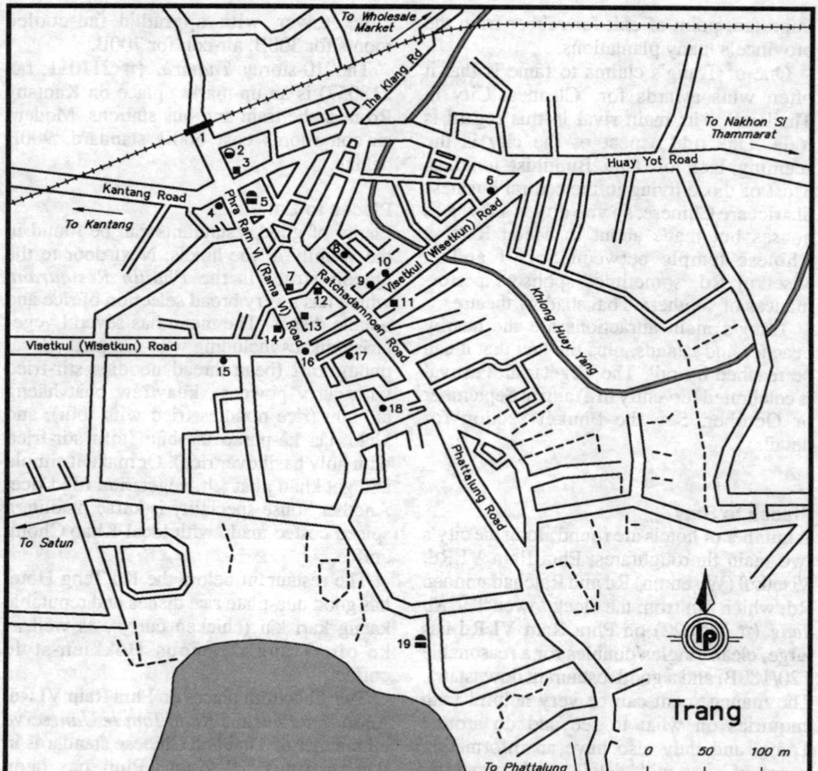

salabao (Chinese buns), khanõm jìip (dumplings), Trang-style sweets, mũu yâang (barbecued pork) and sometimes noodles and jók (thick rice soup).

When you order coffee in these places, be sure to use the Hokkien word *ko-píi* rather than the Thai *kafae*, otherwise you may end up with Nescafe or instant Khao Chong coffee – the proprietors often think this is what farangs want. Coffee is usually served with milk and sugar – ask for *ko-píi dam* for sweetened black coffee or *ko-píi dam, mâi sài náam-taan* for black coffee without sugar.

The best ráan ko-píi in town are the *Sin Jiew* (open 24 hours) on Kantang Rd near Phra Ram VI; *Bo Daeng* (open 6 am till midnight), next to a Chinese clan house and Bangkok Bank on Phra Ram VI near Kantang Rd; *Huat Ocha* (open 5 am to 5 pm) on Visetkul Rd next to Wattana School; and *Khao Ocha* (open 6 am to 8 pm) on Visetkul Rd Soi 5.

Khanõm Jiin Trang is also famous for khanõm jiin (Chinese noodles with curry). One of the best places to try it is at the tables set up at the corner of Visetkul and Phra Ram

■ PLACES TO STAY

3 Thamrin Hotel
7 Ko Teng Hotel
11 Queen Hotel
12 Phetch (Phet) Hotel
13 Wattana Hotel
14 Trang Hotel

OTHER

1 Railway Station
2 Bus Terminal
4 Motorcycle Rental
5 Post Office
6 Koh Hai Villa Office
8 Trang Rama Cinema
9 Cinema
10 Thai Military Bank
15 Thai Office
16 Clock Tower
17 Municipal Office
18 Provincial Office
19 Post Office

VI Rds. You have a choice of dousing your noodles in *náam yaa* (a spicy ground fish curry), *náam phrík* (a sweet and slightly spicy peanut sauce), or *kaeng tai plaa* (a very spicy mixture of green beans, fish, bamboo shoots and potato). To this you can add your choice of fresh grated papaya, pickled veggies, cucumber and bean sprouts – all for 5B per bowl.

Across the street from this vendor is a small night market in front of the municipal offices that also has a couple of *khanõm jiin* vendors.

Entertainment

Old Time Pub, on Kao Rd a bit east of the town centre, is a cosy, air-con place with good service and no *jii-khõ* hassles. The Relax Pub at 25/50 Huay Yot Rd is a dark, expensive place with the usual parade of Thai female singers. Underneath the Trang Rama cinema is the Boss Club, with a mix of sing-song and disco action.

Things to Buy

Trang is known for its wickerwork and, especially, mats woven of *bai toei* (pandanus leaves), which are called *sèua paa-nan*, or Panan mats. Panan mats are important bridal gifts in rural Trang, and are a common feature of rural households. The process of softening and drying the pandanus leaves before weaving takes many days. They can be purchased in Trang for about 100 to 200B.

The province also has its own distinctive cotton-weaving styles. The villages of Na Paw and Na Meun Si are the most highly regarded sources for these fabrics, especially the intricate diamond-shaped *lai lûuk kâew* pattern, once reserved for nobility.

The best place in town for good buys is the Tha Klang wholesale market along Tha Klang Rd.

Getting There & Away

Air THAI has daily flights from Bangkok (2005B), four flights weekly from Nakhon Si Thammarat (500B), two from Phuket (435B), and three from Surat Thani (495B). The Trang THAI office (☎ 218066) is at 199/2 Visetkul Rd.

Bus & Share Taxi A bus from Satun or Krabi to Trang is 30B; from Hat Yai it's 35B. A share taxi from the same cities is around 60B. Air-con buses from Krabi cost 54B and take three to four hours. From Phattalung it's 15B by bus, 20B by share taxi.

From Ban Huay Nam Khao, the junction for Highway 4 and the road to Ko Lanta, a bus to Trang is 20B.

Air-con buses to/from Bangkok are 288B (160B for an ordinary bus). The air-con buses take about 12 hours to do the route.

Train Only two trains go all the way from Bangkok to Trang, the rapid No 41, which leaves Hualamphong station at 6.30 pm, arriving in Trang at 10.10 am the next day and the express No 13, which leaves Bangkok at 5.05 pm and arrives in Trang at 7.45 am. The fare is 282B 2nd class, 135B 3rd class, not including rapid or express surcharges. You can also catch a train in Thung Song, a rail junction town in Nakhon Si Thammarat Province. From here, there are two trains daily to Trang, leaving at 9.25 am and 3.35 pm, arriving an hour and 45 minutes later.

If you want to continue on to Kantang on the coast, there is one daily ordinary train out of Trang at 5.18 pm which arrives in Kantang at 6 pm; the rapid No 41 also terminates in Kantang, arriving at 10.50 am. Trang to Kantang fare is 4B in 3rd class (5.18 pm train only) or 28B in 2nd class on the rapid No 41.

BEACHES

Trang Province has several sandy beaches and coves along the coast, especially in the Sikao and Kantang districts. From Highway 403 between Trang and Kantang is a turn-off west onto an unpaved road that leads down to the coast through some interesting Thai-Muslim villages. At the end, it splits north and south. The road south leads to Hat Yao, Hat Yong Ling and Hat Jao Mai. The road north leads to Hat Chang Lang and Hat Pak Meng.

Hat Jao Mai & Ko Libong

หาดเจ้าไหมและเกาะลิบง

Both Hat Jao Mai and Ko Libong can be found in Kantang district, about 35 km from Trang. The wide white-sand beach is five km long and gets some of Thailand's biggest surf (probably the source of the Trang's original unshortened name, City of Waves). Hat Jao Mai is backed by casuarina trees and limestone hills with caves, some of which contain prehistoric human skeletal remains. **Tham Jao Mai** is the most interesting of the caves, a large cavern with lots of stalactites and stalagmites.

This beach is part of **Hat Jao Mai National Park**, which includes Hat Chang Lang further north and the islands of Ko Muk, Ko Kradan, Ko Jao Mai, Ko Waen, Ko Cheuak, Ko Pling and Ko Meng. Camping is permitted on Jao Mai and there are a few bungalows for rent as well.

Off the coast here is **Ko Libong**, Trang's largest island. There are three fishing villages on the island, so boats from Kantang Port are easy to get for the one-hour trip. The Botanical Department maintains free shelters on Laem Ju-Hoi, a cape on the western tip of Ko Libong. On the south-western side of the island is a beach where camping is permitted.

Hat Yong Ling & Hat Yao

หาดหยงหลิง/หาดยาว

A few km north of Hat Jao Mai are these two white-sand beaches separated by limestone cliffs. There is no accommodation here as yet.

Hat Chang Lang

หาดฉางหลาง

Hat Chang Lang is part of the Hat Jao Mai National Park, and this is where the park office is located. The beach is about two km long and very flat and shallow. At the northern end is Khlong Chang Lang, a stream that empties into the sea.

Ko Muk & Ko Kradan

เกาะมุก/เกาะกระดาน

Ko Muk is nearly opposite Hat Chang Lang and can be reached by boat from Kantang or Pak Meng. The coral around Ko Muk is lively, and there are several small beaches on the island suitable for camping and swimming. The best beach, Hat Sai Yao, is on the opposite side of the island from the mainland and is nicknamed Hat Farang because it's 'owned' by a farang from Phuket.

Near the northern end is **Tham Morakot** (Emerald Cave), a beautiful limestone tunnel that can be entered by boat during low tide. At the southern end of the island is pretty Phangka Cove and the fishing village of Hua Laem.

Ko Kradan is the largest of the islands that belong to Hat Jao Mai National Park. Actually, only five of six precincts on the island belong to the park: one is devoted to coconut and rubber plantation. There are fewer white-sand beaches on Ko Kradan than on Ko Muk, but the coral reef on the side facing Ko Muk is quite good for diving.

Places to Stay & Eat *Ko Muk Resort*, facing the mainland next to the Muslim fishing village of Hua Laem, has simple but nicely designed bungalows for 125B with shared bath, 200B with bath. The beach in front tends toward mud flats during low tide; the beach in front of the nearby village is slightly better but modest dress is called for. The only telephone on the island is a radio phone in the village.

Ko Kradan Resort (☎ 211391 in Trang; 392-0635 in Bangkok) has well-appointed bungalows for 150 to 400B a night. The beach is OK, the coral is good but the food gets low marks.

Getting There & Away The easiest place to get a boat to either Ko Muk or Ko Kradan is Kantang. Songthaews or vans from Trang to Kantang leave regularly and cost 10B. Once in Kantang you must charter another songthaew to the ferry pier for 20B, where you can get a long-tail boat to Ko Muk for 20B or to Ko Kradan for 100B.

You can also get to the islands from Hat Pak Meng. There are two piers, one at the northern end of the beach and one at southern end. Boats are more frequent from the southern pier, especially during the rainy season. Boats costs 20B per person to Ko Muk, 100B to Ko Kradan. A company called First Hovercraft is starting up a hovercraft service from Hat Pak Meng to the islands off Trang but the fare hadn't been decided by the time we went to press.

Hat Pak Meng
หาดปากเมง

Thirty-nine km from Trang in Sikao district, north of Hat Jao Mai, Yao and Yong Ling, is another long, broad sand beach near the village of Ban Pak Meng. The waters are usually shallow and calm, even in the rainy season. A couple of hundred metres offshore are several limestone rock formations, including a very large one with caves. Several vendors and a couple of restaurants offer fresh seafood, and there are newish brick bungalows for rent at 200B a night.

Around the beginning of November, locals flock to Hat Pak Meng to collect *hãwy taphao*, a delicious type of clam. The tide reaches its lowest this time of year, so it's relatively easy to pick up the shells.

About halfway between Pak Meng and Trang, off Route 4046, is the 20-metre-high **Ang Thong Falls.**

Getting There & Away Take a van (20B) or songthaew (15B) to Sikao from Trang, and then a songthaew (10B) to Hat Pak Meng. There are also one or two direct vans daily to Pak Meng from town for 25B. A paved road now connects Pak Meng with the other beaches south, so if you have your own wheels there's no need to backtrack through Sikao.

Hat Samran & Ko Sukon
หาดสำราญและเกาะสุกร

Hat Samran is a beautiful and shady white-sand beach in Palian district, about 40 km south-west of Trang city. From the customs pier at nearby Yong Sata you should be able to get a boat to **Ko Sukon** (also called Ko Muu), an island populated by Thai Muslims, where there are more beaches.

Sukon Island Resort (☎ 219679 in Trang; 211460 on the island) has bungalow accommodation for 500 to 800B a night.

Ko Ngai (Hai)
เกาะไหง(ไห)

This island is actually part of Krabi Province to the north, but is most accessible from Trang. It's a fairly small island, covering about 3000 rai (4.8 sq km), but the beaches are fine white sand and the water is clear. The resorts on the island operate half-day boat tours of nearby islands, including Morakot Cave on Ko Kradan, for around 200B per person.

Places to Stay Along the east shore of Ko

Ngai are three places to stay. Near the northern end is *Koh Hai Village* (☎ 218674 in Trang) with air-con bungalows for 980B (extra bed 120B) or tents for 150B a day. Further south, towards the middle of the island, is *Koh Hai Villa* (☎ 218029 in Trang; 318-3107 in Bangkok), with less expensive fan-cooled bungalows for 300B a day and tents for 150B. At the southern end is *Ko Ngai Resort* (☎ 210317 in Trang; 316-7916 in Bangkok) where one-bed seaside huts cost 250B, two-bed rooms in large bungalows are 600 to 950B and a six-bed bungalow is 1300B. Tents are also available for 150B.

You can book any of these through the Koh Hai Villa Travel Agency in Trang, 8/19 Visetkul (Wisetkun) Rd. Each has its own office in the city, but this one is the most conveniently located if you're staying in the central business district. The Ko Teng Hotel in Trang also has contact information.

Getting There & Away Two boats a day leave the southern pier at Pak Meng for Ko Ngai at 10.30 am and 2 pm. The fare is 80B and the trip takes about 40 minutes. You can also charter a boat at the pier for 300B.

Ban Tung Laem Sai

At Ban Tung Laem Sai in Sikao district is an alternative homestay for visitors interested in ecotourism. Operated by Yat Fon, a local nonprofit organisation that promotes community development and environmental conservation, the staff can educate visitors about local mangroves, coral reefs, coastal resources and the Thai-Muslim way of life. No sunbathing or drinking is allowed in the vicinity. Contact Khun Suwit at Yat Fon, 105-107 Ban Pho Rd in Trang for reservations and transport.

WATERFALLS

Trang Province recently paved a road that runs south from Highway 4 near the Trang-Phattalung border past a number of scenic waterfalls. The waterfalls are created by the meeting of the Trang and Palian Rivers (and/or their tributaries) and the Khao Banthat Mountains. **Ton Te Falls**, 46 km from Trang, is the loftiest. It's best seen during or just after the rainy season, say from September to November, when the 320-metre vertical waterfall is at its fullest.

Chao Pha Falls in the Palian district near Laem Som has about 25 stepped falls of five to 10 metres each, with pools at every level. The semi-nomadic Sakai tribe are sometimes seen in this area.

Perhaps the most unusual waterfall in the province is **Roi Chan Phan Wang** (literally, 'hundred levels – thousand palaces'), about 30 km from Trang in Wang Wiset district in the little-explored north-west corner of the province. Surrounded by rubber groves, dozens of thin cascades of water tumble down limestone rock formations into pools below. The entire area is well shaded and a good spot for picnics. There is no public transport to the falls, however, and the road is none too good – motorcycle or jeep would be the best choice of transport.

CAVES

Tham Phra Phut, a limestone cave in the northern-eastern district of Huay Yot, contains a large Ayuthaya-period reclining Buddha. When the cave was re-discovered earlier this century, a cache of royal-class silverwork, nielloware, pottery and lacquerware was found hidden behind the image – probably stashed there during the mid-18th century Burmese invasion.

Also in this district, near the village of Ban Huay Nang, is **Tham Tra** (Seal Cave), with mysterious red seals carved into the cave walls which have yet to be explained by archaeologists. Similar symbols have been found in the nearby cave temple of **Wat Khao Phra.**

More easily visited is **Tham Khao Pina**, off Highway 4 between Krabi and Trang at Km 43, which contains a large, multi-level Buddhist shrine popular with Thai tourists. Another famous cave, **Tham Khao Chang Hai** near Na Meun Si village, Nayong district, contains large caverns with impressive interior formations.

KHLONG LAMCHAN WATERBIRD PARK

อุทยานนกน้ำลำชาน

This large swampy area in the Nayong district, east of Trang, is an important habitat for several waterbird species – similar to Thale Noi or Khukhut in Songkhla province. Accommodation is available.

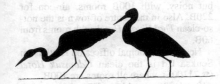

Satun Province

Satun (or Satul) is the west coast's southernmost province, bordering Malaysia. Besides crossing the Malaysian border by land or sea, the principal visitor attractions are Ko Tarutao Marine Park and Thaleban National Park. Most of the province is populated by Thai or Malay Muslims or chao náam.

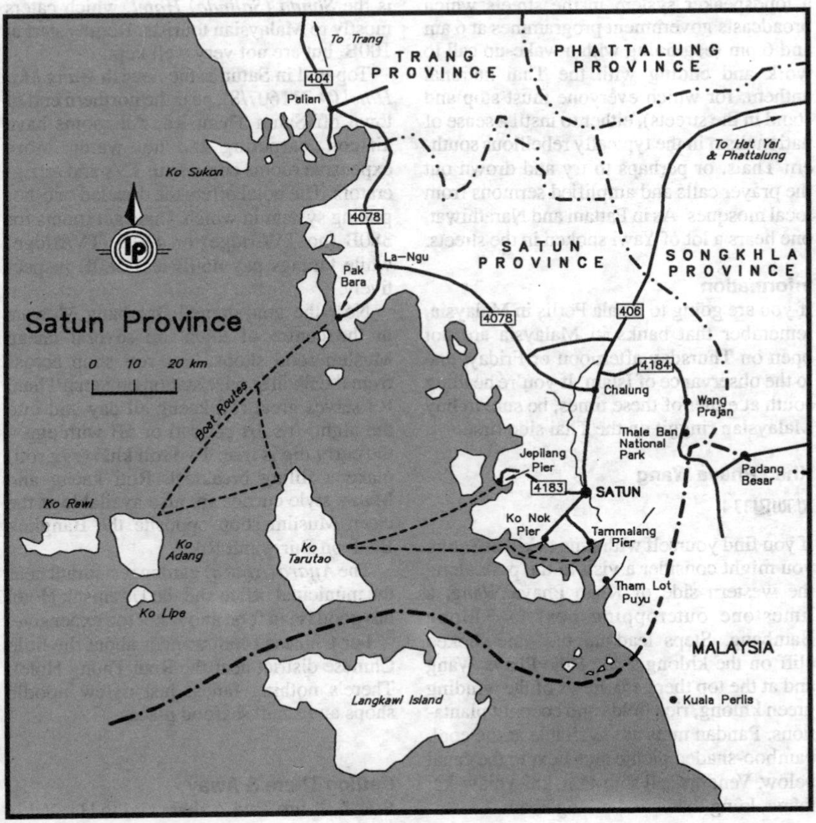

SATUN

อ.เมืองสตูล

Satun itself is not that interesting, but you may enter or leave Thailand here by boat via Kuala Perlis in Malaysia. Sixty km north of Satun is the small port of Pak Bara, the departure point for boats to Ko Tarutao.

Eighty percent of Satun's population is Muslim; in fact, throughout the entire province there are only 11 or 12 Buddhist temples, in contrast to 117 mosques. As in Thailand's other three predominantly Muslim provinces (Yala, Pattani and Narathiwat), the Thai government has installed a loudspeaker system in the streets which broadcasts government programmes at 6 am and 6 pm (beginning with a wake-up call to work and ending with the Thai national anthem, for which everyone must stop and stand in the streets), either to instil a sense of nationalism in the typically rebellious southern Thais, or perhaps to try and drown out the prayer calls and amplified sermons from local mosques. As in Pattani and Narathiwat, one hears a lot of Yawi spoken in the streets.

Information

If you are going to Kuala Perlis in Malaysia, remember that banks in Malaysia are not open on Thursday afternoon or Friday, due to the observance of Islam. If you're heading south at either of these times, be sure to buy Malaysian ringgit on the Thai side first.

Khao Phaya Wang

เขาพญาวัง

If you find yourself with time to kill in Satun, you might consider a visit to the park along the western side of Khao Phaya Wang, a limestone outcropping next to Khlong Bambang. Steps lead up the vine-choked cliff on the khlong side of the Phaya Wang and at the top there are views of the winding green khlong, rice fields and coconut plantations. Pandan mats are available at the cool, bamboo-shaded picnic area next to the canal below. Vendors sell sôm-tam, khâo niãw, kài thâwt, kûng thâwt and miang kham.

Places to Stay & Eat

The *Rian Thong Hotel* (English sign says 'Rain Tong') is at the end of Samanta Prasit Rd, next to the Rian Thong pier, an embarkation point for boats to and from Malaysia. Large, clean rooms are 100B. The *Satun Thani Hotel*, near the centre of town is OK but noisy, with 100B rooms, air-con for 220B. Also in the centre of town is the not-so-clean *Thai Niyom Hotel*, with rooms from 60B.

Near the municipal offices on Hatthakam Seuksa Rd is the clean *Udomsuk Hotel* (☎ 711006), where all rooms are 100B.

South of town a bit, on Wiset Mayura Rd, is the *Slinda (Salinda) Hotel*, which caters mostly to Malaysian tourists. Rooms start at 100B, but are not very well kept.

Top-end in Satun is the newish *Wang Mai Hotel* (☎ 711607/8), near the northern end of town off Satun Thani Rd. All rooms have air-con, carpeting and hot water; more expensive rooms come with TVs and refrigerators. The hotel offers the dreaded two-tier pricing system in which Thais get rooms for 380B (no TV/fridge) or 450B (TV/fridge) while farangs pay 460B and 580B respectively.

Near the gold-domed Bambang Mosque in the centre of town are several cheap Muslim food shops. The roti shop across from the Shell service station on Satun Thani Rd serves great roti kaeng all day and into the night. It's 3B per roti or 5B with egg – the curry dip is free. Two roti khài (egg roti) make a filling breakfast. Roti kaeng and Malay-style curries are also available at the clean Muslim shop opposite the Bangkok Bank on Buriwanit Rd.

The *Ajjara (Atjara)* garden restaurant near the municipal office and the Udomsuk Hotel has good isaan food and is not too expensive.

For Chinese food, wander about the little Chinese district near the Rian Thong Hotel. There's nothing fancy, just a few noodle shops and small seafood places.

Getting There & Away

Bus & Share Taxi A share taxi to Hat Yai is

35B. A regular government bus costs 22B. Buses to Trang are 30B, share taxis 50B.

An air-con bus from Bangkok's southern air-con bus terminal leaves once a day for Satun at 6.30 pm, and costs 355B. But this is really too long a bus trip – if you want to get to Satun from Bangkok, it would be better to take a train to Padang Besar on the Malaysian border and then a bus or taxi to Satun. Padang Besar is 60 km from Satun. See the following Train section.

A new highway between Satun and Perlis in Malaysia is in the planning stages. If the proposal is approved by the Thai and Malaysian governments, the highway would cut travel time between the two towns but it would also unfortunately mean cutting through some of southern Thailand's dwindling rainforest – many Thais are now organising to protest the proposal.

Train The only train that goes all the way to Padang Besar is the special express No 11, which leaves Hualamphong station at 3.15 pm and arrives in Padang Besar around 8 am the next day. The basic fare is 744B for 1st class, 376B for 2nd class, including the special express surcharge.

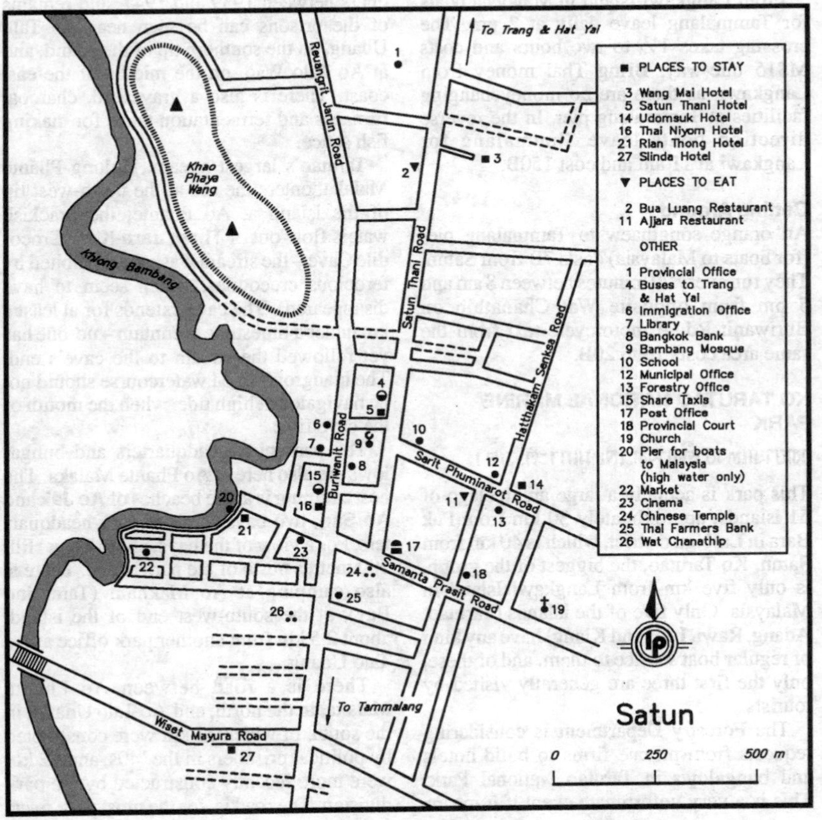

Boat From Kuala Perlis, in Malaysia, boats are M$4. Depending on the time of year and the tides, boats from Malaysia will either dock at Tammalang pier, in the estuary south of Satun, or right in Satun, on Khlong Bambang, near the Rian Thong Hotel. From Satun, the boats cost 50B from the river pier in town or 30B from Tammalang.

There's a Thai immigration post at the Tammalang pier but not at the Rian Thong pier. If you arrive at the latter by boat from Malaysia, you must go to the immigration office in town to get your passport stamped. Be sure to get an exit stamp in Perlis on the Malaysian side.

From Langkawi Island in Malaysia boats for Tammalang leave daily at 2 pm. The crossing takes 1½ to two hours and costs M$15 one-way. Bring Thai money from Langkawi, as there are no moneychanging facilities at Tammalang pier. In the reverse direction boats leave Tammalang for Langkawi at 11 am and cost 150B.

Getting Around

An orange songthaew to Tammalang pier (for boats to Malaysia) costs 7B from Satun. They run every 20 minutes between 8 am and 5 pm from opposite Wat Chanathip on Buriwanit Rd. A motorcycle taxi from the same area costs 15 to 20B.

KO TARUTAO NATIONAL MARINE PARK

อุทยานแห่งชาติทางทะเลหมู่เกาะตะรุเตา

This park is actually a large archipelago of 51 islands, approximately 30 km from Pak Bara in La-Ngu district, which is 40 km from Satun. Ko Tarutao, the biggest of the group, is only five km from Langkawi Island in Malaysia. Only five of the islands (Tarutao, Adang, Rawi, Lipe and Klang) have any kind of regular boat service to them, and of these, only the first three are generally visited by tourists.

The Forestry Department is considering requests from private firms to build hotels and bungalows in Tarutao National Park. This is a very unfortunate event if it means Ko Tarutao is going to become like Ko Phi Phi or Ko Samet, both of which are national parks that have permitted private development, with disastrous results.

Ko Tarutao

เกาะตะรุเตา

The park's namesake is about 151 sq km in size and features waterfalls, inland streams, beaches, caves and protected wildlife that includes dolphins, sea turtles and lobster. Nobody lives on this island except for employees of the Forestry Department. The island was a place of exile for political prisoners between 1939 and 1947, and remains of the prisons can be seen near Ao Talo Udang, on the southern tip of the island, and at Ao Talo Wao, on the middle of the east coast. There is also a graveyard, charcoal furnaces and fermentation tanks for making fish sauce.

Tarutao's largest stream, Khlong Phante Malaka, enters the sea at the north-west tip of the island at Ao Phante; the brackish waters flow out of **Tham Jara-Khe** (Crocodile Cave – the stream was once inhabited by ferocious crocodiles, which seem to have disappeared). The cave extends for at least a km under a limestone mountain – no-one has yet followed the stream to the cave's end. The mangrove-lined watercourse should not be navigated at high tide, when the mouth of the cave fills.

The park pier, headquarters and bungalows are also here at Ao Phante Malaka. The best camping is at the beaches of **Ao Jak** and **Ao San**, two bays south of park headquarters. For a view of the bays, climb Topu Hill, 500 metres north of the park office. There is also camping at Ao Makham (Tamarind Bay), at the south-west end of the island, about 2.5 km from another park office at Ao Talo Udang.

There is a road between Ao Phante Malaka, in the north, and Ao Talo Udang, in the south, of which 11 km were constructed by political prisoners in the '40s, and 12 km were more recently constructed by the park division. The road is, for the most part, over-

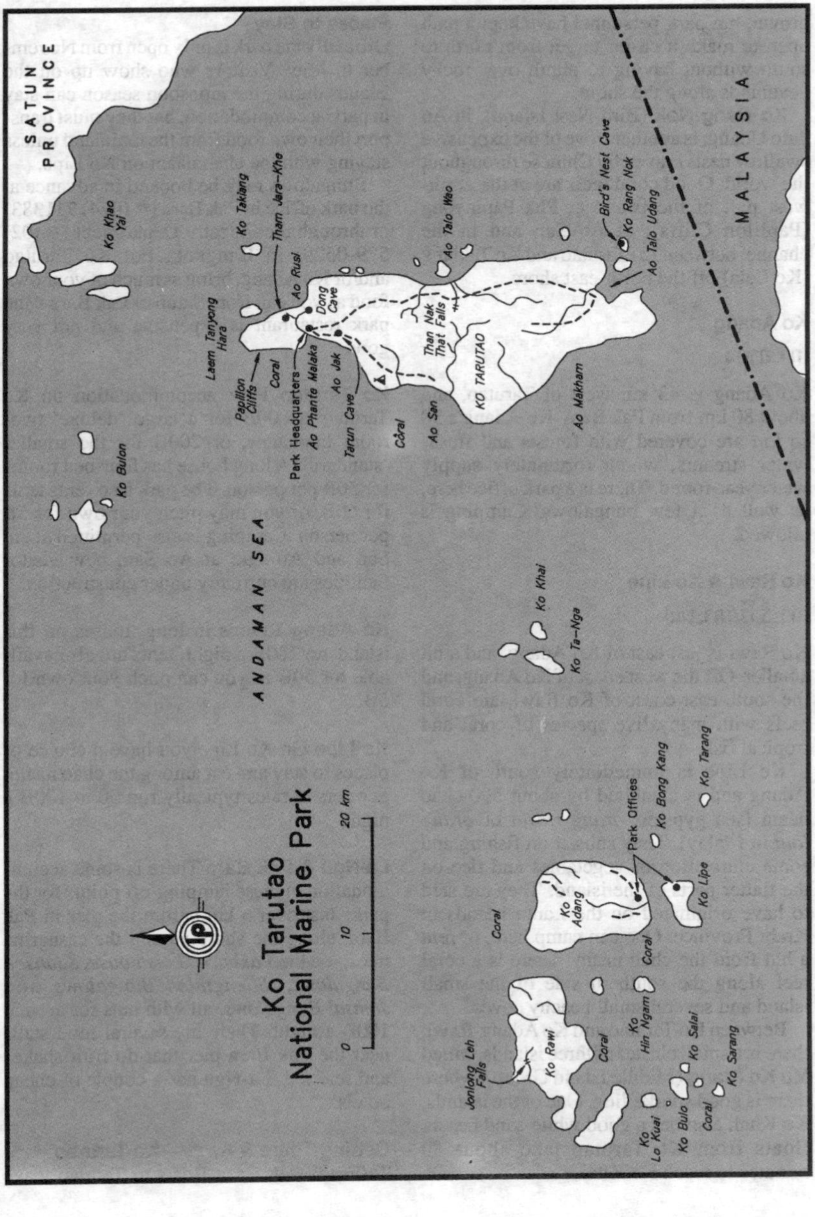
Ko Tarutao
National Marine Park
0
10
20 km
SATUN PROVINCE
ANDAMAN SEA
MALAYSIA
Ko Khao Yai
Ko Taklang
Tham Jara-Khe
Ao Rusi
Dong Cave
Laem Tanyong Hara
Papillon Cliffs
Coral
Park Headquarters
Ao Phante Malaka
Ao Jak
Tarun Cave
Ko Bulon
Coral
Ao San
Than Nak That Falls
KO TARUTAO
Ao Makham
Ao Talo Wao
Bird's Nest Cave
Ko Rang Nok
Ao Talo Udang
Ko Khai
Ko Ta-Nga
Coral
Ko Adang
Park Offices
Ko Bong Kang
Ko Tarang
Ko Lipe
Coral
Ko Hin Ngam
Ko Rawi
Coral
Jonlong Leh Falls
Ko Lo Kuai
Ko Bulo
Coral
Ko Salai
Ko Sarang

grown, but park personnel have kept a path open to make it easier to get from north to south without having to climb over rocky headlands along the shore.

Ko Rang Nok (Bird Nest Island), in Ao Talo Udang, is another trove of the expensive swallow nests craved by Chinese throughout the world. Good coral reefs are at the north-west part of the island at Pha Papinyong (Papillon Cliffs), at Ao San and in the channel between Ko Tarutao and Ko Takiang (Ko Lela) off the north-east shore.

Ko Adang

เกาะอาดัง

Ko Adang is 43 km west of Tarutao, and about 80 km from Pak Bara. Ko Adang's 30 sq km are covered with forests and fresh-water streams, which fortunately supply water year-round. There is a park office here, as well as a few bungalows. Camping is allowed.

Ko Rawi & Ko Lipe

เกาะราวี/เกาะลิเป

Ko Rawi is just east of Ko Adang, and a bit smaller. Off the west coast of Ko Adang, and the south-east coast of Ko Rawi, are coral reefs with many live species of coral and tropical fish.

Ko Lipe is immediately south of Ko Adang and is inhabited by about 500 chao náam (sea gypsies; *orang rawot* or *orang laut* in Malay). They subsist on fishing and some cultivation of vegetables and rice on the flatter parts of the island. They are said to have originated on the Lanta islands in Krabi Province. One can camp here, or rent a hut from the chao náam. There is a coral reef along the southern side of the small island and several small beachy coves.

Between Ko Tarutao and Ko Adang-Rawi, there is a small cluster of three islands, called **Mu Ko Klang** (Middle Island Group), where there is good snorkelling. One of the islands, Ko Khai, also has a good white-sand beach. Boats from Ko Tarutao take about 40 minutes to reach Ko Khai.

Places to Stay

Officially the park is only open from November to May. Visitors who show up on the islands during the monsoon season can stay in park accommodation, but they must transport their own food from the mainland unless staying with the chao náam on Ko Lipe.

Bungalows may be booked in advance at the park office in Pak Bara (☎ (074) 711383) or through the Forestry Department (☎ (02) 579-0529) in Bangkok. For Ko Tarutao and/or Ko Adang, bring as much of your own food as you can from Satun or Pak Bara – the park restaurant is expensive and not very good.

Ko Tarutao Park accommodation on Ko Tarutao is 800B for a large 'deluxe' two-room bungalow, or 200B for the smaller 'standard'. A long house has four-bed rooms for 50B per person. The park also rents tents for 60B, or you may pitch your own for 5B per person. Camping is also permitted at Ao San and Ao Jak; at Ao San, new visitor facilities are currently under construction.

Ko Adang Rooms in long houses on this island are 280B a night; tents are also available for 50B or you can pitch your own for 5B.

Ko Lipe On Ko Lipe you have a choice of places to stay and eat among the chao náam. Per person rates typically run 50 to 100B a night.

La-Ngu & Pak Bara There is some accommodation in these jumping-off points for the park. Just over a km before the pier in Pak Bara, along the shore among the casuarina trees, are the *Pakbara Guesthouse*, *Suanson Bungalows*, *Saengthien Bungalows* and *Jomsai Bungalows*, all with huts for around 100B a night. There are several food stalls near the Pak Bara pier that do fruit shakes and seafood. La-Ngu has a couple of cheap hotels.

Getting There & Away – Ko Tarutao

To/From Pak Bara Boats to Tarutao leave

regularly between November and April from the pier in Pak Bara, 65 km north of Satun and 22 km from Ko Tarutao. The rest of the year boat service is irregular since the park is supposedly closed. Satun Province officials are planning to construct a new pier in Tan Yong Po district nearer Satun that will serve tourist boats to Tarutao and other islands, possibly on a year-round basis.

For now, boats leave Pak Bara for Tarutao in season daily at 10.30 am and 2 pm. The return fare is 120B, and it takes one to two hours, depending on the boat. Food and beverages are available on the boat. Departures back to Pak Bara are at 9 am and 2 pm.

There are also occasional tour boats out to Tarutao, but these are usually several hundred baht per person, as they include a guided tour, meals, etc. Your final alternative is to charter a boat with a group of people. The cheapest are the hang yao (long-tail boats), which can take eight to 10 people out from Pak Bara's commercial pier for 500B. On holidays, boats may travel back and forth to Tarutao every hour or so to accommodate the increased traffic.

To get to Pak Bara from Satun, you must take a share taxi or bus to La-Ngu, then a songthaew on to Pak Bara. Taxis to La-Ngu leave from in front of the Thai Niyom Hotel when there are enough people to fill a taxi for 20B per person. Buses leave frequently from in front of the public library along the same road and they cost 10B. From La-Ngu, songthaew rides to Pak Bara are 7B and terminate right at the harbour.

You can also travel to La-Ngu from Trang by songthaew for 20B. From Hat Yai you would take a Satun-bound bus to the junction town of Chalung (19B, 1½ hours), which is about 15 km short of Satun, then get a songthaew north on Route 4078 for the 9B, 45 minute trip to La-Ngu. Once a day, at 7.45 am, there is a direct bus to Pak Bara from Hat Yai for 29B. In the reverse direction, it leaves Pak Bara for Hat Yai at 4.30 pm.

To/From Other Piers It is also possible to hire boats to Ko Tarutao from three different piers *(thâa reua)* on the coast near Satun. The nearest is the Ko Nok pier, three km south of Satun (40 km from Tarutao). Then there is the Tammalang pier, nine km from Satun, on the opposite side of the estuary from Ko Nok pier. Tammalang is 35 km from Tarutao. Finally there's the Jepilang pier 13 km east of Satun (30 km from Tarutao).

Getting There & Away – Adang & Lipe

From Tarutao a boat leaves daily to Ko Adang and Ko Lipe at noon, returning the next day at 9 am. Return tickets for the Tarutao-Adang boat are 250B if you stay one night only, 350B if you stay more than one night. This trip takes 2½ hours each way. As more people travel to Ko Tarutao, ticket prices will probably come down.

KO BULON LE

เกาะบุโหลนเล

Approximately 20 km west of Pak Bara is the small island group of Ko Bulon, of which the largest is Ko Bulon Le. Though considerably smaller than the major islands of Mu Ko Tarutao, Bulon Le shares many of the geographical characteristics, including sandy beaches and coral reefs.

Pansand Resort has A-frame bungalows on Bulon Le's best beach for 200B a night. Since this is the only development on the island, the only place to eat is at Pansand's restaurant – bring some food with you if you're on a tight budget. Mekong whisky seems to be at a particular premium here. More information is available from First Andaman Travel (☎ (072) 218035; fax 219513), 82-84 Visetkul Rd in Trang (opposite the Queen Hotel).

Getting There & Away

Boats to Ko Bulon Le from Pak Bara cost anywhere from 25 to 75B per person, depending on the number of passengers. The trip takes 45 minutes each way.

THALE BAN NATIONAL PARK

อุทยานแห่งชาติทะเลบัน

This 101-sq-km park on the Thai-Malaysian

border in Satun Province encompasses the best preserved section of white meranti rainforest on either side of the border. Although the forest straddles the border, the Malaysian side is becoming steadily deforested by agricultural development. The terrain is hilly, with a maximum elevation of 740 metres at Khao Chin. A number of caves and waterfalls can be visited, including Rani Falls, Yaroi Falls, Ton Pliw Falls, Chingrit Falls, Ton Din Cave and Pu Yu Tunnel Cave. Climb the limestone cliffs next to the park buildings for a view of the 100-rai lake contained by the park.

Wildlife found within park boundaries tends to be of the Sundaic variety, which includes species generally found in Peninsular Malaysia, Sumatra, Borneo, and Java. Common mammals include mouse deer, serow, various gibbons and macaques. Some of the rare bird species found here are the great argus hornbill, helmeted hornbill, masked finfoot, dusky crag martin and black Baza hawk.

Near the park office are bungalows sleeping eight to 20 people for 500 to 800B per night.

Getting There & Away

The park is about 40 km from Satun in *tambon* Khuan Sataw. Take a bus north along Highway 406 toward Hat Yai and get off at the Route 4184 junction, 19 km from Satun. From here you can catch a songthaew on its way to Wang Prajan on Route 4184. Wang Prajan is just a few km from the park entrance; you can hitch or hop on one of the infrequent songthaews from Wang Prajan into the park.

Yala Province

Yala is the most prosperous of the four predominantly Muslim provinces in southern Thailand, mainly due to income from rubber production, but also because it is the number one business and education centre for the region.

YALA

อ.เมืองยะลา

The fast-developing capital (population 65,000) is known as 'the cleanest city in Thailand' and has won awards to that effect three times in the last 25 years (its main competitor is Trang). It's a city of parks, wide boulevards and orderly traffic.

During the dry season there are nightly musical performances in Chang Phuak Park, in the south-east part of the city just before the big Lak Muang traffic circle, off Pipitpakdee Rd. The new Phrupakoi Park, just west of the làk muang (city pillar), has a big artificial lake where people can fish, go boating and eat in floating restaurants. Yala residents seem obsessed with water recreation, possibly as a consequence of living in the only land-locked province in the entire south. There is a public swimming pool in town at the Grand Palace restaurant and disco.

One of the biggest regional festivals in Thailand is held in Yala each year, during the last six days of June, to pay respect to the city guardian spirit, Jao Paw Lak Muang. Chinese New Year is also celebrated here with some zest, as there are many Chinese living in the capital. The Muslim population is settled in the rural areas of the province, for the most part, though there is a sizeable Muslim quarter near the railway station in town – you'll know it by the sheep and goats wandering in the streets and by the modern mosque – Yala's tallest building and the largest mosque in Thailand.

Wat Naa Tham

วัดหน้าถ้ำ

Outside of town, about eight km west off the Yala to Hat Yai highway, is Wat Khuhaphimuk (also called Wat Naa Tham – the Cave-Front Temple), a Srivijaya-period cave temple established around 750 AD. Inside the cave is Phra Phutthasaiyat, a long reclining Buddha image sculpted in the Srivijaya style. For Thais, this is one of the three most venerated Buddhist pilgrimage points in

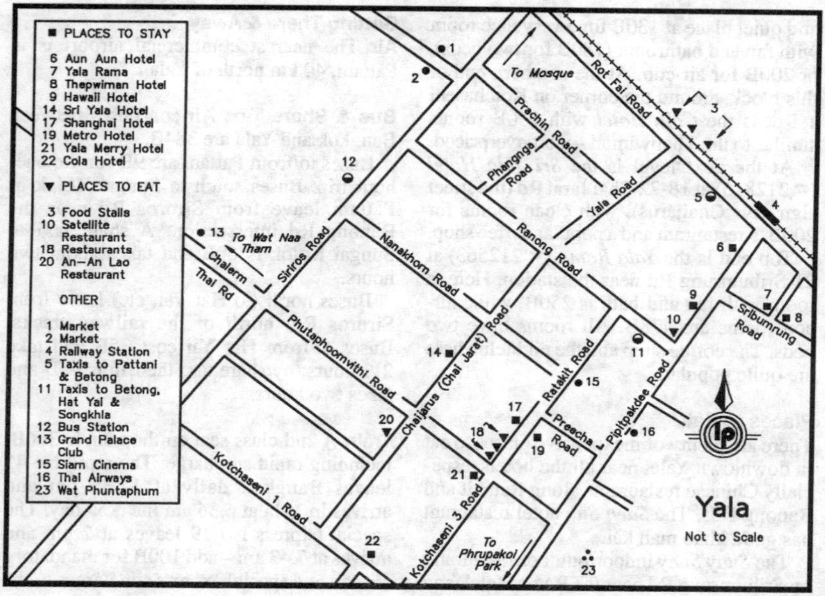

southern Thailand (the other two are Wat Boromthat in Nakhon Si Thammarat and Wat Phra That Chaiya in Surat Thani). There is a small museum in front of the cave, with artefacts of local provenance.

To get there, take a songthaew going east towards the town of Yaha or Hat Yai and ask to get off at the road to Wat Naa Tham – the fare is 3B. It's about a one-km walk to the wat from the highway.

Two km past Wat Naa Tham is **Tham Silpa**, a cave with murals from the Srivijaya era. A monk from Wat Naa Tham may be able to guide you there. There are several other caves in the vicinity worth exploring for their impressive stalactite and stalagmite formations.

Places to Stay

Yala has quite a few hotels at all price levels. Starting from the bottom, the *Shanghai Hotel*, *Metro Hotel* and the *Saen Suk* are all nearly identical Chinese hotels with Chinese restaurants on the ground floor. All are on the same block on Ratakit Rd, in the business district, not far from the railway station. All three have somewhat dreary rooms from 60B; the Saen Suk is a bit cleaner than the other two, and its restaurant is also better, specialising in generous plates of chicken rice (khâo man kài) for 15B.

The *Hawaii* and *Aun Aun* hotels, on Pipitpakdee Rd, are the first hotels you see as you walk into town from the railway station. The Hawaii is OK at 100B, but the Aun Aun is more economical at 60B without bath, 80 to 100B with. The manager at Aun Aun also speaks good English.

The *Thepwiman Hotel* (☎ 212400), a left turn from the station on Sribumrung (Si Bamrung) Rd, across from the Yala Rama, is the best value in this range. It's a friendly place, with clean, large rooms with fan and bath for 100B, or 200B with air-con.

The *Yala Merry* (☎ 212693), on Phutthaphumwithi and Kotchaseni 3 Rds, is a clean and quiet place at 130B for a very nice room with fan and bathroom (180B for two beds), or 200B for air-con. At the southern end of this block, around the corner on Kotchaseni 1 Rd, is the *Cola Hotel* with 180B rooms similar to the Thepwiman – a bit overpriced.

At the next level is the *Sri Yala Hotel* (☎ 212815) at 18-22 Chai Jarat Rd (the street sign says Chaijarus), with clean rooms for 200B, a restaurant and a popular coffee shop.

Top end is the *Yala Rama* (☎ 212563) at 21 Sribumrung Rd near the station. Here, a room with fan and bath is 250B, while air-con rooms are 478B. All rooms have two beds. The coffee shop and the nightclub here are quite popular.

Places to Eat

There are plenty of inexpensive places to eat in downtown Yala, near all the hotels, especially Chinese restaurants along Ratakit and Ranong Rds. The *Saen Suk* hotel restaurant has good khâo man kài.

The *Suay Suay* indoor/outdoor restaurant, on Sribumrung Rd near the Rama Hotel, and the big *Satellite* restaurant on the corner of Pipitpakdee and Ranong Rds specialise in steamed cockles.

On Kotchaseni 2 Rd, a couple of blocks down the street from Sri Yala Hotel, is the *An An Lao Restaurant*, a large garden restaurant specialising in kài betong, quite good and reasonably priced. The *Grand Palace Club*, at the end of Phutthaphumwithi Rd, in the opposite direction from Wat Phuthaphum, serves fancy Thai and Chinese food at fancy prices.

The day market on Siroros (Sirorot) Rd has a good selection of fresh fruit. The Muslim food stalls nearby serve roti kaeng in the early morning – a cheap and filling breakfast.

Entertainment

In addition to the popular hotel coffee shop/nightclubs, you could look in at Wild West, an old-west theme pub at the corner of Rot Fai and Pipitpakdee Rd near the railway station. The Wild West has live music in the evenings.

Getting There & Away

Air The nearest commercial airport is in Pattani, 40 km north of Yala.

Bus & Share Taxi Air-con buses between Bangkok and Yala are 384B.

Buses to/from Pattani are 9B for the one-hour trip. Buses south to Sungai Kolok or Pattani leave from Siroros Rd near the Ranong Rd intersection. A share taxi to Sungai Kolok is 60B and takes about two hours.

Buses north (to Hat Yai, etc) leave from Siroros Rd, north of the railway tracks. Buses to/from Hat Yai cost 35B and take 2½ hours; by share taxi the trip is 60B and takes two hours.

Train A 2nd-class seat on the train is 366B, including rapid surcharge. The rapid No 45 leaves Bangkok daily at 12.35 pm and arrives in Yala at 6.36 am the next day. The special express No 19 leaves at 2 pm and arrives at 7.43 am – add 100B for mandatory air-con and special express surcharges to the above fare.

From Hat Yai, ordinary trains are 23B 3rd class, and take 2½ hours. From Sungai Kolok, at the Malaysian border, trains are 22B for a 2½-hour trip.

BAN SAKAI

บ.ซาไก

The well-known village of Ban Sakai is in Tharato district, about 80 km south of Yala on the way to Betong. Ban Sakai is the home of some of Thailand's last remaining Sakai tribes, called 'Ngaw' by Thais because their frizzy heads and dark complexions remind Thais of the outer skin of the rambutan fruit (*ngáw* in Thai).

Anthropologists speculate that the Sakai are the direct descendants of a Proto-Malay race that once inhabited the entire Thai-Malay peninsula and beyond (also called Negritos, 'an aboriginal jungle race allied to negroid pygmies found in the Philippines, New Guinea and parts of Africa', according to George McFarland). It is maintained that they were subjugated by technologically more advanced Austro-Thai cultures from the north. At any rate, the peaceful, short-statured Sakai still lead a traditional village life of hunting and gathering, practice very little agriculture and express themselves through their own unique language, music and dance. Recently a development project has got the Sakai involved in tending rubber plantations.

Also in Tharato district is **Tharato Falls**, which is now a national park.

BETONG

เบตง

Betong is 140 km south-west of Yala on the Malaysian border and is Thailand's southernmost point. The area surrounding Betong is mountainous and jungle-foliated; morning fog is not uncommon in the district. Three km north of town is a pleasant hot springs.

Until recently the Communist Party of Malaysia had its hidden headquarters in the Betong vicinity. In December 1989 the CPM finally laid down arms; many guerrillas were given minor land grants in the area by the Thai government in return for their capitulation. Others – mainly Chinese – have blended into the Betong woodwork and now make their way as pedlars, Chinese-language tutors, odd-job labourers, rubber tappers and tailors. A number of former CPM members live in nearby 'Peace Village' and regale visiting journalists with tales of jungle life, how they once lived on elephant, tiger and bear meat.

The Pattani United Liberation Organisation (PULO), Thai-Muslim separatists who want Yala and other Muslim provinces to secede from Thailand, still have minor forces in this area but the word is that they, too, will soon give up the fight.

Malaysians are allowed to cross the border at Betong, so the little town is often crowded on weekends as they come across to shop for cheaper Thai merchandise including, for the Malay men, Thai women. Many townspeople speak English and Chinese as well as Thai and Malay.

Places to Stay

Most hotels in Betong are in the 150 to 200B range for basic rooms – Malaysian price levels – eg the *Cathay*, *Fortuna*, *Khong Kha*, *Thai*, *King's*, *Venus* and *My House*. Payment in Malaysian ringgit is as acceptable as baht at most hotels. One of the hassles for single male visitors is constantly being approached by pimps at many of the hotels.

The *Betong Hotel*, 13/6 Sarit Det Rd, is OK for 100 to 150B. *Si Betong* has two branches, one on Chaiya Chaowalit Rd that's primarily a brothel, and a better one on Sukayang Rd. Both cost 150B for fan-cooled rooms is 80 to 120B; *Si Betong 1* (Sukayang Rd) also has some air-con rooms for 280B.

The best budget bet is *Fa Un Rong Hotel* on Jantharothai Rd for 90B. Another decent place to stay is the *Si Charoen (Sea World Long) Hotel* at 17 Soi Praphan Phesat, where good rooms with a bit of a view cost 150B with fan and bath, 220 to 280B with air-con. The hotel's business card is written in Chinese and prices are quoted in Malaysian currency. The town's first luxury hotel, the 130-room *Betong Grand*, is scheduled to go up by the beginning of 1993.

Betong has more Muslim and Chinese restaurants than Thai. The town is famous for kài betong, the tasty local chicken, and also roasted or fried mountain frogs, which are said to be even more delicious than the mountain frogs of Mae Hong Son.

Getting There & Away

A share taxi to Betong from Yala is 70B; bus is 31B.

RAMAN

รามัน

Twenty-five km south-east of Yala by road or train, Raman is well known as a centre for the Malay-Indonesian martial art of *silat*. Two very famous teachers of silat reside here, Hajisa Haji Sama-ae and Je Wae. If you're interested in pure Thai-Muslim culture, this is the place.

Pattani Province

PATTANI

อ.เมืองปัตตานี

The provincial capital of Pattani (population 38,000) provides a heavy contrast with Yala. In spite of its basic function as a trading post operated by the Chinese for the benefit (or exploitation, depending on your perspective) of the surrounding Muslim villages, the town has a more Muslim character than Yala. In the streets, you are more likely to hear Yawi, the traditional language of Java, Sumatra and the Malay peninsula (which when written uses the classic Arabic script plus five more letters), than any Thai dialect. The markets are visually quite similar to markets in Kota Baru in Malaysia. The town as a whole is as dirty as Yala is clean.

Pattani was until rather recently the centre of an independent principality that included Yala and Narathiwat. It was also one of the earliest kingdoms in Thailand to host international trade; the Portuguese established a trading post here in 1516, the Japanese in 1605, the Dutch in 1609 and the British in 1612. During WW II, Japanese troops landed in Pattani to launch attacks on Malaya and Singapore.

Orientation & Information

The centre of this mostly concrete town is at the intersection of Naklua/Yarang Rd, the north-south road between Yala and Pattani harbour, and Ramkomud Rd, which runs east-west between Songkhla and Narathiwat. Inter-city buses and taxis stop at this intersection. Ramkomud Rd becomes Rudee Rd after crossing Yarang Rd and it is along Rudee Rd that you can see what is left of old Pattani architecture – the Sino-Portuguese style that was once so prevalent in southern Thailand. The THAI office (☎ 349149) is at 9 Preeda Rd.

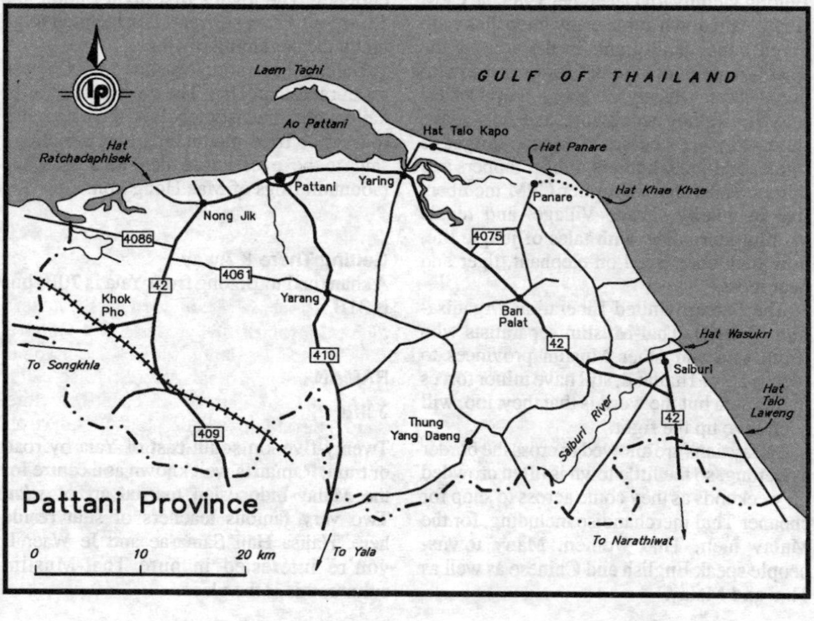

Mosques

Thailand's second-largest mosque is the **Matsayit Klang**, a traditional structure of green hue, probably still the south's most important mosque. It was built in the early '60s.

The oldest mosque in Pattani is the **Matsayit Kreu-Se**, built in 1578 by an immigrant Chinese named Lim To Khieng who had married a Pattani woman and converted to Islam. Actually, neither To Khieng, nor anyone else, ever completed the construction of the mosque.

The story goes that his sister, Lim Ko Niaw, sailed from China on a sampan to try and persuade her brother to abandon Islam and return to his homeland. To demonstrate the strength of his faith, he began building the Matsayit Kreu-Se. His sister then put a Chinese curse on the mosque, saying it would never be completed. Then, in a final attempt to dissuade To Khieng, she hanged herself from a nearby cashew-nut tree. In his grief, Khieng was unable to complete the mosque, and to this day it remains unfinished – supposedly every time someone tries to work on it, lightning strikes.

The brick, Arab-style building has been left in its original semi-completed, semi-ruined form, but the faithful keep up the surrounding grounds. The mosque is in Ban Kreu-Se, about seven km east of Pattani, off Highway 42.

The tree that Ko Niaw hanged herself from has been enshrined at the San Jao Leng Ju Kieng (or San Jao Lim Ko Niaw), the site of an important Chinese-Muslim festival in late February or early March. During the festival a wooden image of Lim Ko Niaw is carried through the streets; additional rites includes fire-walking and seven days of vegetarianism. The shrine is in the northern end of town towards the harbour.

Another festival fervently celebrated in Pattani is Hari Rayo, the Muslim month of fasting during the 10th lunar month.

Batik

Thai Muslims in southern Thailand have their own traditional batik methods that are similar but not identical to the batik of north-east Malaysia. The best place to shop for local batik is at the Palat Market *(talàat nát paalát)*, which is off Highway 42 between Pattani and Saiburi in Ban Palat. The market is held all day Wednesdays and Sundays only. If you can't make it to this market, the shops of Muslim Phanit and Nadi Brothers on Rudee Rd sell local and Malaysian batik at perhaps slightly higher prices.

Beaches

The only beach near town is at **Laem Tachi**, a cape that juts out over the northern end of Ao Pattani. You must take a boat taxi to get there, either from the Pattani pier or from Yari district at the mouth of the Pattani River. This white-sand beach is about 11 km long, but is sometimes marred by refuse from Ao Pattani, depending on the time of year and the tides.

Hat Ratchadaphisek (or Hat Sai Maw) is about 15 km west of Pattani. It's a relaxing spot, with lots of sea pines for shade, but the water is a bit on the murky side. Then there's **Hat Talo Kapo**, 14 km east of Pattani, near Yaring district, a pretty beach that's also a harbour for *kaw-lae*, the traditional fishing boats of southern Thailand. A string of vendors at Talo Kapo sell fresh seafood; during the week it's practically deserted.

Other beaches can be found south-east of Pattani, on the way to Narathiwat, especially in the Panare and Saiburi districts where there are km of virtually deserted beach. **Hat Chala Lai** is a broad white-sand beach 43 km south-east of Pattani, near Panare. Eight km further on toward Narathiwat is **Hat Khae Khae**, a pretty beach studded with boulders. Three km north of Panare is **Hat Panare**, which is another colourful kaw-lae harbour.

Near Saiburi is **Hat Wasukri**, also called Chaihat Ban Patatimaw, a beautiful white-sand beach with shade. It's 53 km from Pattani. Some private bungalows here rent for 200B, but this may be negotiable when occupancy is low. Further south still, a few km before you reach the Narathiwat provincial border, is **Hat Talo Laweng**, possibly Pattani Province's prettiest beach.

A good place to watch the building of

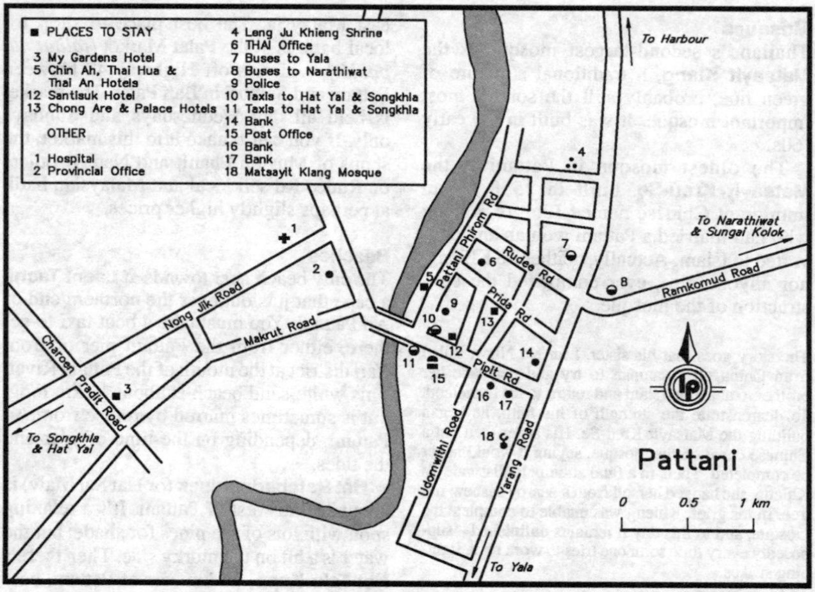

kaw-lae is in the village of Pase Yawo (Ya-Waw), near the mouth of the Saiburi River. It's a tradition that is slowly dying out as the kaw-lae is replaced by long-tail boats with auto engines.

Places to Stay

The *Chong Are (Jong Ah) Hotel* is a Chinese place on Prida Rd with rooms for 70B without a bath, 100 to 150B with. Attached to the Chong Are, with an entrance around the corner, is the *Palace* (☎ 349171), a decent place whose rooms are 120B with fan and bath, 180B with two beds, or 200B with air-con.

The *Santisuk* (☎ 349122), at 1/16 Pipit Rd, has OK rooms for 80B without a bath, 130 with private bath and 200B with air-con. As in Yala, Narathiwat, Satun and Trang, all street signs are in tortured English transliterations of Thai (better than no transliterations at all, for those who can't read Thai).

Cheaper, basic Chinese hotels can be found on Pattani Phirom Rd, including the *Chin Ah*, for 80B up, the *Thai Hua*, for 60 to 80B, and the *Thai An*, for 70 to 100B.

My Garden, about a km outside town, has been recommended as a good-value middle-range hotel – 180 to 250B for a large two-bed room with fan and bath, 280 to 330B for air-con, 440B with TV. The disco is very popular on weekends. Samlor or songthaew drivers may know it by its former name, the Dina.

Getting There & Away

Pattani is only 40 km from Yala. Share taxis are 18B and take about half an hour; buses cost only 9B but take around an hour. From Narathiwat, a taxi is 35B, bus 24B. From Hat Yai ordinary buses are 26B, air-con 35B.

There are also boats between Songkhla and Pattani – the fare depends on the size of the boat.

Getting Around

Songthaews go anywhere in town for 4B per person.

Narathiwat Province

NARATHIWAT

อ.เมืองนราธิวาส

Narathiwat (population 38,000) is a pleasant, even-tempered little town, one of Thailand's smallest provincial capitals, with a character all of its own. Many of the buildings are old wooden structures, a hundred or more years old. The local businesses seem to be owned by both the Muslims and the Chinese, and nights are particularly peaceful because of the relative absence of male drinking sessions typical of most upcountry towns in Thailand. The town is right on the sea, and some of the prettiest beaches on southern Thailand's east coast are just outside town.

Hat Narathat

หาดนราทัศน์

Just north of town is a small Thai-Muslim fishing village at the mouth of the Bang Nara River, lined with the large painted fishing boats called *reua kaw-lae* which are peculiar to Narathiwat and Pattani. Near the fishing village is Hat Narathat, a sandy beach, four to five km long, which serves as a kind of public park for locals, with outdoor seafood restaurants, tables and umbrellas, etc. The constant breeze here is excellent for windsurfing, a favourite sport of Narathiwat citizens as well as visiting Malaysians. The beach is only two km north of the town centre – you can easily walk there or take a samlor.

Almost the entire coast between Narathiwat and Malaysia, 40 km south, is sandy beach.

Taksin Palace

พระตำหนักทักษิณ

About seven km south of town is Tanyongmat Hill, where Taksin Palace (Phra Taksin Ratchaniwet) is located. The royal couple stay here for about two months between August and October every year. When they're not in residence, the palace is open to the public daily from 8.30 am to noon and 1 to 4.30 pm. The buildings themselves are not that special, but there are gardens with the Bangsuriya palm, a rare fan-like palm named after the embroidered sunshades used by monks and royalty as a sign of rank. A small zoo and a ceramics workshop are also on the grounds, and in front is Ao Manao, a pretty, curved bay lined with sea pines. A songthaew from the town to the palace area is 7B.

Wat Khao Kong

วัดเขากง

The tallest seated-Buddha image in Thailand is at Wat Khao Kong, six km south-west on the way to the railway station in Tanyongmat. Called Phra Phuttha Taksin Mingmongkon, the image is 25 metres high and made of bronze. The wat itself isn't much to see. A songthaew to Wat Khao Kong is 5B from the Narathiwat.

Wadin Husen Mosque

มัสยิดวาดินฮูเซ็น

One of the most interesting mosques in Thailand, the Wadin Husen was built in 1769 and mixes Thai, Chinese and Malay architectural styles to good effect. It's in the village of Lubosawo in Bajo (Ba-Jaw) district, about 15 km north-west of Narathiwat off Highway 42, about 8B by songthaew.

Wat Chonthara Sing-He

วัดชลธาราสิงเห

During the British colonisation of Malaysia (then called Malaya), the Brits tried to claim Narathiwat as part of their Malayan Empire. The Thais constructed Wat Chonthara Sing-He (also known as Wat Phitak Phaendin Thai) in Tak Bai district near the Malayan border to prove that Narathiwat was indeed

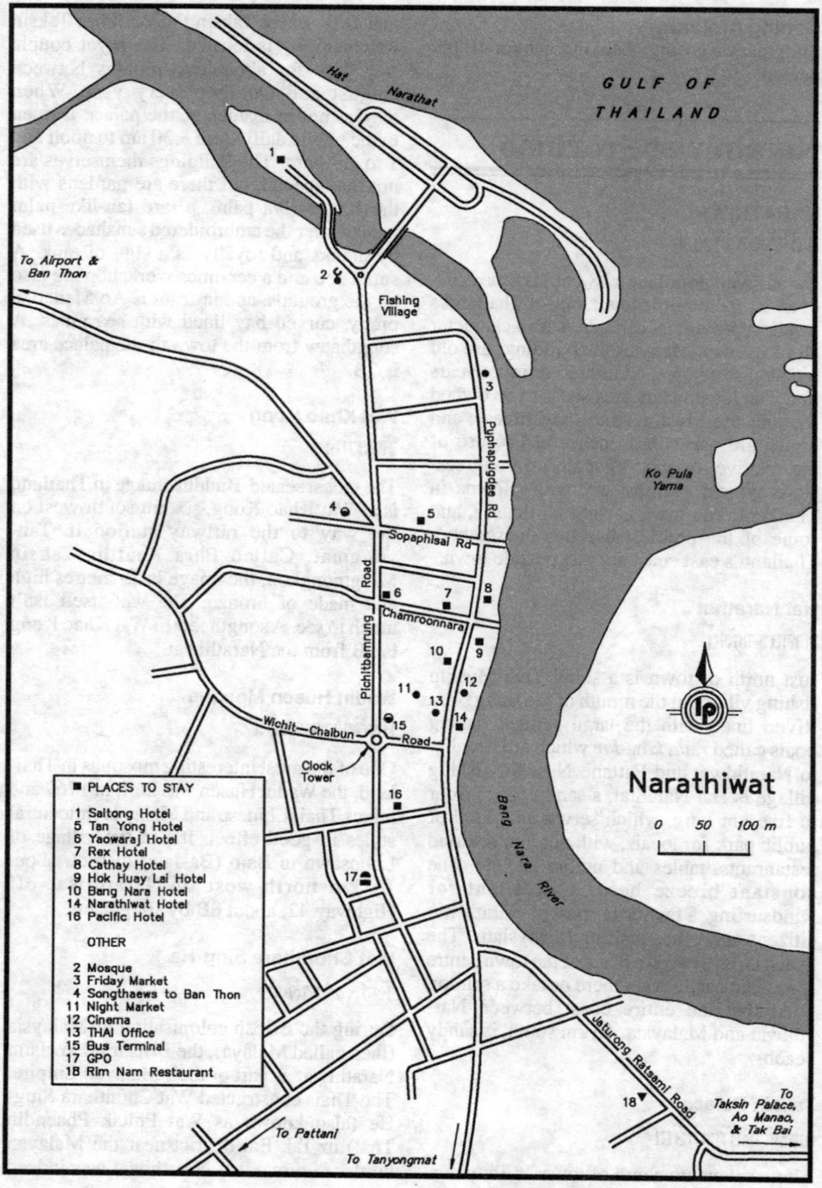
GULF OF THAILAND
Hat Narathat
To Airport & Ban Thon
Fishing Village
Puphapugdee Rd
Ko Pula Yama
Sopaphisai Rd
Pichitbamrung Road
Chamroonnara
Wichit Chaibun Road
Clock Tower
Narathiwat
0 50 100 m
Bang Nara River
Jaturong Ratsami Road
To Taksin Palace, Ao Manao, & Tak Bai
To Pattani
To Tanyongmat
PLACES TO STAY
1 Saitong Hotel
5 Tan Yong Hotel
6 Yaowaraj Hotel
7 Rex Hotel
8 Cathay Hotel
9 Hok Huay Lai Hotel
10 Bang Nara Hotel
14 Narathiwat Hotel
16 Pacific Hotel
OTHER
2 Mosque
3 Friday Market
4 Songthaews to Ban Thon
11 Night Market
12 Cinema
13 THAI Office
15 Bus Terminal
17 GPO
18 Rim Nam Restaurant

part of Siam, and as a result the British relinquished their claim.

Today it's most notable because of the genuine southern-Thai architecture, rarely seen in a Buddhist temple – sort of the Thai-Buddhist equivalent of the Wadin Husen Mosque. A wooden wihaan here very much resembles a Sumatran-style mosque. An 1873 wihaan on the grounds contains a reclining Buddha decorated with Chinese ceramics from the Song Dynasty. Another wihaan on the spacious grounds contains murals painted by a famous Songkhla monk during the reign of King Mongkut. The murals are religious in message but also depict traditional southern-Thai life. There is also a larger, typical Thai wihaan.

Wat Chon is 34 km south-east of Narathiwat in Tak Bai. It's probably not worth a trip from Narathiwat just to see this 100-year old temple unless you're a real temple freak, but if you're killing time in Tak Bai or Sungai Kolok this is one of the prime local sights. It's next to the river and the quiet, expansive grounds provide a retreat from the busy border atmosphere.

To get there from Narathiwat, take a bus or songthaew bound for Ban Taba and get off in Tak Bai. The wat is on the river about 500 metres from the main Tak Bai intersection.

Narathiwat Fair
งานนราธิวาส

Every year, during the third week of September is the Narathiwat Fair, which features kaw-lae boat racing, a singing dove contest judged by the Queen, handicrafts displays and silat martial arts exhibitions. Other highlights include performances of the local dance forms, *ram sam pen* and *ram ngeng*.

Places to Stay
The cheapest places to stay are all on Puphapugdee (Phupha Phakdi) Rd along the Bang Nara River. The best deal is the *Narathiwat Hotel* (☎ 511063), a funky wooden building that's quiet, breezy, clean and comfortable. Rooms on the water-front cost 80B with shared bath. Mosquitoes could be a problem – don't forget your repellent or mossie coils. Another OK place, across the street and next to the Si Ayuthaya Bank, is the *Bang Nara Hotel* – friendly staff and large, clean rooms for 70B with shared bathroom. Also on this road facing the river is *Hok Uay Lai Hotel*, similar to the Bang Nara. A last resort is the *Cathay Hotel*, with rooms for 80B and 100B, but they're not so special (hard beds); the owner speaks good English, however.

The *Rex Hotel* (☎ 511134), at 6/1-3 Chamroonnara Rd, is a fair place with 130B rooms. Similar rooms for 120B, but not quite as quiet, are at the *Yaowaraj Hotel* on the corner of Chamroonnara and Pichitbamrung Rds.

Near Hat Narathat, on a little island in the Bang Nara River, is the *Saitong Hotel*. Rather ordinary rooms with fan and bath are 100B, newer rooms are 150 to 200B. You can stay right on Hat Narathat at the *Municipal Bungalows* (☎ 511048) for 400B.

The new *Pacific Hotel* costs 250B for large, clean rooms with fan and bath – this price may be negotiable. Top end is the *Tan Yong Hotel* (☎ 511148), on Sophapisai Rd, with air-con rooms from 550B. Most of the guests are Malaysians and Thai government officials.

Places to Stay – out of town
Ten km south of Narathiwat, towards Tak Bai, is *Thanon Resort*, a quiet beach place with bungalows for 170B with fan and bath. The staff will provide free transport to and from town.

Places to Eat
For eating, the night market off Chamroonnara Rd behind the Bang Nara Hotel is good. There are also several inexpensive places along Chamroonnara Rd, especially the khâo kaeng place next to the Yaowaraj Hotel, for curries. *Dii Den (Li Ming)* beneath the Rex Hotel has great kài tũn yaa jiin (chicken stewed in Chinese herbs) and noodle dishes.

Along Wichit Chaibun Rd west of Puphapugdee Rd are several inexpensive

Muslim food shops. The *Rim Nam* restaurant, on Jaturong Ratsami Rd a couple of km south of town, has good seafood and curries.

Getting There & Away

Air THAI has three flights weekly between Narathiwat and Hat Yai, connecting with flights to Bangkok. The fare to Hat Yai is 420B, through to Bangkok it's 2620B. Their office (☎ 511161) is at 322-5 Puphapugdee (Phupha Phakdi) Rd; a THAI van between Nara Airport and the THAI office costs 30B per person.

Bus & Taxi Share taxis between Yala and Narathiwat are 50B, buses 30B (with a change in Pattani). Buses cost 24B from Pattani. From Sungai Kolok, buses are 15B, share taxis 30B. To/from Tak Bai, the other border crossing, is 10B by songthaew, 20B by taxi.

Air-con minivans to Hat Yai leave several times a day from opposite the Rex Hotel for 100B per person.

It's best not to travel around Narathiwat Province at night, because that's when the Muslim separatist guerrillas go around shooting up trucks and buses. In early 1989 a truck was hit by automatic weapons fire on Highway 42 between the capital and Bajo, wounding four people. A splinter group of the PULO took credit.

Train The train costs 13B for 3rd-class seats to Tanyongmat, 20 km west of Narathiwat, then it's either a 15B taxi to Narathiwat, or 8B by songthaew.

SUNGAI KOLOK & BAN TABA

These small towns in the south-east of Narathiwat Province are departure points for the east coast of Malaysia. There is a fair batik (Thai: *paa-té)* cottage industry in this district.

Be prepared for culture shock coming from Malaysia, warned one traveller. Not only are most signs in Thai script, but fewer people speak English in Thailand.

Sungai Kolok
สุไหงโก-ลก

The Thai government once planned to move the border crossing from Sungai Kolok to Ban Taba in Tak Bai district, which is on the coast 32 km east. The Taba crossing is now open and is a shorter and quicker route to Kota Baru, the first Malaysian town of any size, but it looks like Sungai Kolok will remain open as well for a long time. They're even building new hotels in Sungai Kolok and have established a TAT office next to the immigration post.

The border is open from 5 am to 5 pm (6 am to 6 pm Malaysian time). On slow days they may close the border as early as 4.30 pm.

Ban Taba
บ้านตาบา

Ban Taba, five km south of bustling Tak Bai, is just a blip of a town with only one bank and a couple of hotels. You can change money at street vendors by the ferry on the Thai side.

A ferry across the river into Malaysia is 5B. The border crossing here is open the same hours as in Sungai Kolok. From the Malaysian side you can get buses direct to Kota Baru for M$1.40.

Places to Stay & Eat – Sungai Kolok

The Tourist Business Association brochure says there are 60 hotels in Sungai Kolok, but we only found 39. The main reason Sungai Kolok has so many hotels is to accommodate the weekend trips of Malaysian males. Of these cheaper hotels, only a handful are under 100B and they're mainly for those only crossing for a couple of hours. So if you have to spend the night here it's best to pay a little more and get away from the short-time trade.

Most places in Sungai Kolok will take Malaysian ringgit as well as Thai baht for food or accommodation.

The most reasonably priced places are along Charoenkhet Rd. Here you can find the fairly clean *Thailiang Hotel* for 80B, the *Savoy Hotel* for 100B, and the *Asia Hotel* for 150B, or 200 to 250B with air-con. The *Pimarn Hotel* is also quite good at 140B with fan and bath, 230B with air-con.

Over on the corner of Arifmankha and Waman Amnoey Rds is the pleasant *Valentine Hotel*, 180B with fan, 280B with air-con. There's a coffee shop downstairs.

Other fairly decent hotels in the 100 to 150B range include the *Star Hotel* at 20 Saritwong Rd, the *An An Hotel* at 183/1-2 Prachawiwat Rd, the *Taksin 2* at 4 Prachasamran Rd, the *San Sabai 2* at 38 Waman Amnoey Rd, the *San Sabai 1* at 32/34 Bussayapan Rd and the *Nam Thai 2* at Soi Phuthon, Charoenkhet Rd. Some of these hotels also offer air-con rooms for 200 to 350B.

Top-end hotels in Sungai Kolok include:

Genting, Asia 18 Rd, from 500B
Grand Garden, 104 Arifmankha Rd, from 435B (☎ 611389)
Inter Hotel, Prachawiwat Rd, from 396B
Merlin Hotel, 40 Charoenkhet Rd, from 350B (☎ 611003)
Plaza Hotel, off Bussayapan Rd, from 370B
Tara Regent Hotel, Soi Phuthon, Charoenkhet Rd, from 370B (☎ 611401)

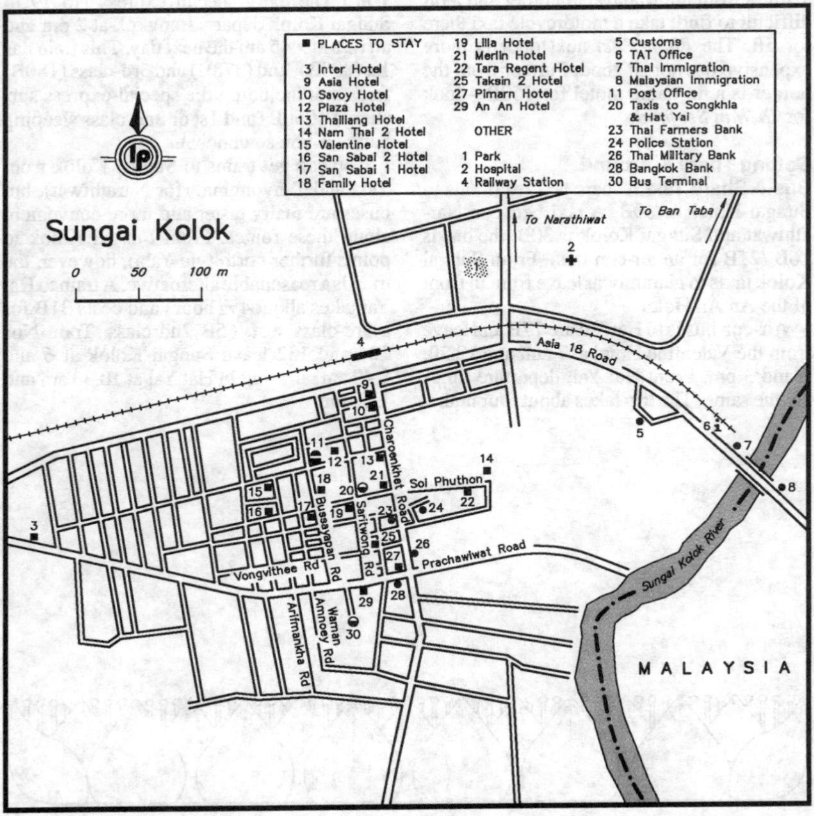

The town has plenty of food stalls selling Thai, Chinese and Malaysian food. The *Siam* restaurant next to the Merlin is good for Thai food, and the *Bak Mui* near the Tara Regent for Chinese. For an economical and delicious breakfast very early in the morning, try coffee and doughnuts at the station buffet. Some of the Malay shops also do roti kaeng (Malay: roti chanai), flat bread with curry dip, in the mornings.

Places to Stay – Ban Taba

Masya (☎ 581123) has good rooms for 220B with fan and bath, 270B with air-con or 350B with air-con and TV. It's set back off the road leading from the Malaysian border and a bit difficult to find; take a motorcycle taxi there for 5B. The *Phan Phet* next door is more expensive but not as good. Further from the border is a no-name motel for 150B – look for *Ta Wan Seafood*.

Getting There & Around

Bus & Share Taxi A share taxi from Yala to Sungai Kolok is 60B. A taxi between Narathiwat and Sungai Kolok is 30B, the bus is 16B (21B for an air-con bus). From Sungai Kolok taxis to Narathiwat leave from in front of the An An Hotel.

Air-con buses to Hat Yai are 77B and leave from the Valentine Hotel at 7 am, and 12.30, 1 and 3 pm. From Hat Yai, departure times are the same. The trip takes about four hours.

The border is about a km from the centre of Sungai Kolok or the railway station. Transport around town is by motorcycle taxi – it's 10B for a ride to the border. Coming from Malaysia, just follow the old railway tracks to your right, or, for the town, turn left at the first junction and head for the high-rises.

From Rantau Panjang (Malaysian side), a share taxi to Kota Baru costs M$3.50 per person (M$14 to charter the whole car) and takes about an hour. The regular yellow-and-orange bus to KB costs M$2.20.

Train The daily special express No 19 to Sungai Kolok departs Bangkok at 2 pm and arrives at 9.45 am the next day. This train has 1st (808B), 2nd (378B) and 3rd-class (180B) fares, not including the special-express surcharge of 50B (and 1st or 2nd-class sleeping berths if you so choose).

You can get trains to Sungai Kolok from Yala and Tanyongmat (for Narathiwat), but buses are really faster and more convenient along these routes. From Sungai Kolok to points further north (via Yala), however, the train is a reasonable alternative. A train to Hat Yai takes about 4½ hours and costs 31B for a 3rd-class seat, 65B 2nd class. Train Nos 124 and 132 leave Sungai Kolok at 6 and 8.40 am, arriving in Hat Yai at 10.33 am and 1.12 pm.

Glossary

ajaan – respectful title for teacher, from the Sanskrit term *acharya*
aahãan – food
aahãan pàa – jungle food
ao – bay or gulf
amphoe – district; next subdivision down from province, sometimes spelt *amphur*
amphoe muang – provincial capital

bâan – house or village; often spelt *ban*
bai toey – pandanus leaf
bàw náam ráwn – hot springs
bhikku – Buddhist monk in Pali; Thai pronunciation *phík-khù*
bòt – central sanctuary or chapel in a Thai temple; from Pali *uposatha*

chaa – tea
chaihàat – beach; also spelt *hat*
chao le (chao náam) – sea gypsies
chedi – stupa; monument erected to house a Buddha relic; called *pagoda* in Burma, *dagoba* in Sri Lanka, *cetiya* in India

dhammachakka – Buddhist wheel of law
doi – peak, as in mountain

farang – foreigner of European descent
hang yao – long-tailed boat

hàat – beach; short for *chaihaat*; also *hat*
hãw trai – a Tripitaka (Buddhist scripture) library
hĩn – stone

isãan – general term for north-east Thailand, from the Sanskrit name for the mediaeval kingdom *Isana*, which encompassed parts of Cambodia and north-east Thailand

jangwàat – province
Jataka – life-stories of the Buddha
jiin – Chinese
jii-khõh – Thai hoodlum

kâew – also spelt *keo*; crystal, jewel, glass, or gem
kafae thũng – filtered coffee; sometimes called *ko-píi* in southern Thailand
kàp klâem – drinking food
ka-toey – Thai transvestite
kaw lae – traditional fishing boats of southern Thailand
khaen – reed instrument common in north-east Thailand
khlong – canal
ko – island; also spelt *koh*; pronounced *kàw*
khão – hill or mountain
khon – masked dance-drama based on stories from the Ramakien
khon isãan – the people of north-east Thailand
klawng – Thai drums
kuay haeng – Chinese-style work shirt
kuti – meditation hut

lâap – spicy mint salad with mint leaves
lãem – cape (in the geographical sense)
lakhon – classical Thai dance-drama
làk muang – city pillar/phallus
lâo khão – white liquor
lâo thèuan – jungle liquor
lí-khe – Thai folk dance-drama
longyi – Burmese sarong

mâe chii – Thai Buddhist nun
mâe náam – river; literally 'mother water'
Maha That – literally 'great element', from the Sanskrit-Pali *mahadhatu*; common name for temples which contain Buddha relics
mát-mii – tie-dye silk method
mâw hâwm – Thai work shirt
mãwn khwan – triangular-shaped pillow popular in the north and north-east
metta – Buddhist practice of loving kindness
mondòp – small square building in a *wat* complex generally used by lay people, as opposed to monks; from the Sanskrit *mandapa*
muang – city; pronounced *meu-ang*
muay Thai – Thai boxing

naga – dragon-headed serpent
nakhon – city; from Sanskrit-Pali *nagara*; also spelt *nakhorn*
náam – water
náam phrík – chilli sauce
náam plaa – fish sauce
náam tòk – waterfall
nãng – Thai shadow play
ngaan wát – temple fair
noeng khão – hill
ngôp – traditional Khmer rice farmer's hat

pàak náam – estuary
pàk tâi – southern Thai
paa-té – batik
paa-thông-kõ – Chinese 'doughnut', a common breakfast food
phâakhamãa – piece of cotton cloth worn as a wraparound by men
phâasîn – same as above for women
pìi-phâat – classical Thai orchestra
phrá – monk or Buddha image; an honorific term from the Pali *vara*, 'excellent'
phrá phum – earth spirits
phuu khão – 'mountain' in Central Thai
ponglang – north-east Thai marimba made of short logs
prang – Khmer-style tower on temples
prasat – small ornate building with a cruciform ground plan and needle-like spire, used for religious purposes, located on wat grounds. From the Sanskrit term *prasada*.

rai – one *rai* is equal to 1600 square metres
reua hang yao – long-tail taxi boat
reuan thãew – long-house
reu-sĩi – a Hindu *rishi* or 'sage'
rót thammada – ordinary bus (non air-con) or ordinary train (not rapid or express)
roti – round flatbread, common street food; also found in Muslim restaurants

sãalaa (sala) – an open-sided, covered meeting hall or resting place; from the Portuguese *sala* or 'room'
sala klang – provincial office
samlor – three-wheeled pedicab
sẽma – boundary stones used to consecrate ground used for monastic ordinations; from the Sanskrit-Pali *sima*
serow – Asian mountain goat
sêua mâw hâwm – blue cotton farmer's shirt
soi – lane or small street
sõngkhran – Thai new year, held in mid-April
sôm-tam – green papaya salad
sõngthãew – literally 'two rows'; common name for small pick-up trucks with two benches in the back, used as buses/taxis
susãan – cemetery

talàat nàam – floating market
tambon – 'precinct', next subdivision below *amphoe*; also spelled *tambol*
thâat – four-sided, curvilinear Buddhist reliquary, common in north-east Thailand; also spelt *that*
thale sàap – inland sea or large lake
thêp – angel or divine being; from Sanskrit *deva*
thewada – a kind of angel
thudong – monks who have taken ascetic vows
tripitaka – Theravada Buddhist scriptures
tuk-tuk – motorised *samlor*

vipassana – Buddhist insight meditation

wang – palace
wai – palms-together Thai greeting
wát – temple-monastery; from Pali *avasa*, monk's dwelling
wíhãan – counterpart to *bòt* in Thai temple, containing Buddha images but not circumscribed by *sema* stones. Also spelt *wihan* or *viharn*; from Sanskrit *vihara*

yaa dong – herbal liquor; also the herbs inserted in *lao khao*
yam – Thai-style salad; usually made with meat or seafood.

Index

ABBREVIATIONS

NP – National Park
WS – Wildlife Sanctuary
MP – Marine Park

MAPS

Airfares 132
Ayuthaya 222

Bangkok, Greater 148-149
  Banglamphu 180
  Central Bangkok 154-155
  Chinatown – Pahurat 170
  Khao San Road Area 182
  Ko Ratanakosin 164
  Soi Ngam Duphli 186
  Thonburi Canals 176
  Siam Square – Pratunam 190
Buriram 423

Central Thailand 220
Chanthaburi 272
Chiang Khan 448
Chiang Khong 391
Chiang Mai 288-289
  Tha Phae Gate Area 301
  Around Chiang Mai 313
Chiang Rai 374
Chiang Saen 389
Chonburi to Chanthaburi 255
Chumphon 495
Chumphon Province 493

Fang 316

Golden Triangle 381

Hat Yai 563
Hellfire Pass 250
Hua Hin 483

Kanchanaburi 238
Kanchanaburi Province 237
Karon Yai & Kata 517
Khao Phra Wihaan 470-471
Khao Yai NP 418
Khon Kaen 425
Ko Chang 279
Ko Lanta 584
Ko Pha-Ngan 541
Ko Phi Phi 580
Ko Samet 267
Ko Samui 528
Ko Tao 547

Ko Tarutao National MP 597
Krabi 572
  Around Krabi 575
Krabi Province 570

Lampang 329
Lamphun 327
Loei 443
Loei Province 442
Lopburi 227

Mae Hong Son 365
Mae Hong Son Province 361
Mae Sai 385
Mae Sariang 362
Mae Sot 355
Mukdahan 458

Na Thon 531
Nai Han & Rawai 519
Nakhon Pathom 234
Nakhon Phanom 451
Nakhon Ratchasima 410-411
  Around Nakhon Ratchasima 414
Nakhon Si Thammarat 548
Nan 402
Nan Province 398
Narathiwat 608
National Parks 25
Nong Khai, Central 435
Nong Khai & Udon Thani, Around 432
North-Eastern Thailand 408
Northern Thailand 285

Old Kamphaeng Phet 334

Pai 371
Patong 515
Pattani 606
Pattani Province 604
Pattaya Area 259
  Jomtien Beach 263
  Naklua 262
  Pattaya 260
Phattalung 555

Phetburi 476
Phimai 415
Phitsanulok 336
Phrae 394
Phu Hin Rong Kla NP 342
Phuket 508
Phuket Province 506
Prachuap Khiri Khan 489
Prachuap Khiri Khan Province 481
Prasat Phanom Rung 420

Ranong 499
Ranong Province 497
Roi Et 427

Sakhon Nakhon 455
Satun 595
Satun Province 593
Si Racha 256
Si Satchanalai – Chaliang 350
Similan Islands 503
Songkhla 558
Southern Thailand 474
Sukhothai, New 346
Sukhothai, Old 345
Sungai Kolok 611
Surat Thani/Ban Don 524
Si Saket & Ubon, Around 468

Tak & Mae Sot, Around 353
Thailand 12-13
  Provinces 34-35
  Railways 136
That Phanom 453
Trang 588
Trang Province 586
Trat 275
Trat Province 274

Ubon Ratchathani 460
Udon Thani, Central 429

Wat Phra That Lampang Luang 331

Yala 601

TEXT

Map references are in **bold** type.

Accommodation 107-108
AIDS 92
Air Travel
  To/From Thailand 126-129
  Within Thailand 132-133
Airports
  Bangkok International 127, 144
  Chiang Mai 127-128
  Hat Yai 127
Ancient City (Muang Boran) 172-173
Ang Thong 231
Ang Thong National MP 530
Ang Thong Province 231-232
Ao Bang Tao 521
Ao Khanom 553-554
Ao Nang 575-577
Ao Phang-Nga 504-505
Ao Phang-Nga National MP 31-32
Ao Takiap 482
Architecture 42-47
Art Styles, Thai 42-47
Ayuthaya 219-226, **222**
Ayuthaya Province 219-226

Ban Chiang 432-433
Ban Don 523-527, **524**
Ban Phe 265
Ban Pheu 433
Ban Sakai 602-603
Ban Sangka-U 583
Ban Taba 610-612
Bang Pa In 226
Bang Saphan 491-492
Bangkok 147-218, **148-149, 154-155, 164, 180, 182, 186, 190**
  Ancient City (Muang Boran) 172-173
  Bookshops 153
  Chinatown (Sampeng) 168-171, **170**
  Churches 163
  Cooking Schools, Thai 179
  Cultural Centres 151-152
  Department Stores 211
  Dusit Zoo 171-172
  Embassies & Consulates 150-151
  Emerald Buddha 158
  Entertainment 205-209
  Future Traffic Alternatives 216
  Galleries 168
  Getting Around 214-218

Bangkok *cont*
  Getting There & Away 212-214
  Grand Palace 158-159
  Jim Thompson's House 167
  Lak Muang (City Pillar) 161-162
  Libraries 153-156
  Lumphini Park 173
  Maps 156-157
  Markets 173-174, 210-211
  Medical Services 157
  Meditation Study 178-179
  Money 149-150
  Monk's Bowl Village 173
  National Museum 166
  Pahurat 169, **170**
  Palaces 167
  Places to Eat 196-205
  Places to Stay 179-196
  Post 150
  Religious Services 152
  River Trips 175-177, **176**
  Royal Barges 166-167
  Sanam Luang 173
  Shopping 210-212
  Shopping Centres 211
  Snake Farm (Queen Saovabha Memorial Institute) 172
  Temples 162, 163
  Tourist Offices 149
  Tourist Police 157
  Travel Agencies 152-153
  Walking Tours 163-166, 169-171
  Wats 158-162, 178-179
Bargaining 73
Batik 605
Baw Sang 313
Betong 603-604
Beung Kan 441
Bicycling 143
Bo Rai 274
Books 81-83
  Hill Tribes 81
  History 82
Bookshops 82-83, 153
  Buddhist 59-60
Buddhism 54, 55-60, 179
Buriram 422-424, **423**
Buriram Province 419-424
Burmese Refugee Camps 358
Bus Travel 129-131, 133-136, 144, 146

Car Travel 140-142
  Rental 141, 218
  Road Rules 140-141

Central Thailand 219-284, **220**
Cha-am 479-480
Chachoengsao 233
Chachoengsao Province 233
Chaiya 522-523
Chaloem Ratanakosin NP 250
Chanthaburi 271-273, **255, 272**
Chanthaburi Province 271-273
Chao Pha Falls 592
Chiang Dao 316
Chiang Khan 446-448, **448**
Chiang Khong 391-392, **391**
Chiang Mai 286-312, **288-289, 301, 313**
  Entertainment 307-308
  Getting There & Away 309-311
  Information 290-292
  Places to Eat 303-307
  Places to Stay 297-303
  Shopping 308-309
Chiang Mai Province 286-319
Chiang Rai 372-380, **374**
Chiang Rai Province 372-392
Chiang Saen 387-389, **389**
Chom Thong 314-316
Chonburi Province 255-265, **255**
Chong Mek 466-467
Chumphon 492-496, **495**
Chumphon Province 492-496, **493**
Climate 19-20
Consulates 69-70
Costs 72-73
Credit Cards 71-72, 99
Customs 70

Damnoen Saduak Floating Market 174, 236
Dan Kwian 414-415
Dan Sai 446
Dan Singkhon 491
Dance-Drama, Thai 48-51, 207, 208
Dangers & Annoyances 98-103, 128, 135, 157, 297, 319, 529
  Assault 99
  Druggings 99
  Drugs 103
  Insurgent Activity 101-103
  Scams 100
  Touts 99-101
Death Railway Bridge 239-240
Dengue Fever 94
Departure Tax 129
Diving 104-105, 494, 502, 509, 514, 520, 530, 576
Doi Ang Khang 316

Doi Inthanon NP 25, 315
Doi Khuntan NP 26
Doi Phu Kha NP 405
Doi Suthep 312-313
Doi Suthep/Doi Pui NP 26, 312-313
Doi Tung 386-387
Don Chedi 232-233
Drinks 117-120
  Drinks Listing 118-120
Drugs 103

Ecology 20-24
Economy 37-41
Electricity 80
Elephants 314, 332
Embassies 69-70
Emerald Buddha 158, 373
Entertainment 120-122
Erawan Falls NP 28, 247-248
Etiquette 54-55

Fake Goods 124-125
Fang 316-318, **316**
Festivals 75-77
Floating Markets 173-174, 236
Flora & Fauna 20-21
Food 108-117
  Food List 111-117

Geography 19
Getting Around 311-312
Golden Triangle 38-39, 383, 390, **381**
Golf 105
Government 33-37
Grand Palace 157, 158-159

Hang Dong 314
Hat Bang Sak 501-502
Hat Bang Ben 500
Hat Jao Mai 590
Hat Jao Mai NP 590
Hat Khao Lak 501-502
Hat Lek 274, 277
Hat Nai Yang NP 32
Hat Noppharat Thara 574-576
Hat Noppharat Thara – Ko Phi Phi National MP 569
Hat Sa Bua 552-553
Hat Sichon 553
Hat Yai 561-569, **563**
Health 85-98
  Counselling Services 98
  Hospitals & Clinics 97-98, 157
  Medical Problems & Treatment 87-96
  Predeparture Preparations 85-86
Hellfire Pass 250-251, **250**
Hepatitis 89-90
Hill Tribes 284, 319, 326
  Books 81
Hill-Tribe Crafts 124
Hill-Tribe Treks 319-326
Hin Ngam 553
History 10-19
  Ayuthaya Period 14-15
  Dvaravati Period 11
  February 1991 Coup 18
  Lan Na Thai Period 14
  Sukhothai Period 14
Hitching 143
Holidays 75-77
Hospitals 97-98, 157, 292
Htin 399
Hua Hin 481-488, **483**
Hua Hin Railway Hotel 485
Huay Kha Khaeng WS 28
Huay Khamin Falls 248

Isthmus of Kra 500

Jim Thompson's House 157, 167

Kaeng Krachan NP 29-30, 478-479
Kamala 520-521
Kamphaeng Phet 333-335, **334**
Kamphaeng Phet Province 333-335
Kanchanaburi 237-247, **238**
Kanchanaburi Province 236-255, **237**
Karon 516-518, **517**
Kata 518, **517**
Khamu 400
Khao Chamao – Khao Wong NP 30, 266
Khao Khitchakut NP 272
Khao Laem Ya – Mu Ko Samet National MP 30-31
Khao Luang Caves 477
Khao Luang NP 548
Khao Phanom Bencha NP 578-579
Khao Phra Taew NP 509
Khao Phra Wihaan 469-472, **470-471**
Khao Sabap NP 273
Khao Sam Roi Yot NP 30, 488
Khao Saming 274
Khao Sok NP 31, 527-528
Khao Yai NP 29, 417-419, **418**
Khlong Lamchan Waterbird Park 593
Khon Kaen 424-426, **425**
Khon Kaen Province 424-428
Khong Jiam 466
Khukhut Waterbird Sanctuary 561
Khuraburi 501
Ko Adang 598
Ko Bubu 585
Ko Bulon Le 599
Ko Chang National MP 31, 278-283, **279**
Ko Jam (Ko Pu) 582
Ko Kradan 590-591
Ko Laan 259
Ko Lanta 582-585, **584**
Ko Lanta National MP 583
Ko Libong 590-591
Ko Lipe 598
Ko Muk 590-591
Ko Pha-Ngan 540-546, **541**
  Beaches 542-544
Ko Phi Phi 579-582
Ko Rawi 598
Ko Samet 266-271, **267**
Ko Samui 523, 528-540, **528**
  Beaches 532-538
Ko Si Boya 582
Ko Si Chang 257-258
Ko Tao 546-547, **547**
Ko Tarutao 596-598
Ko Tarutao National MP 32-33, 596-599, **597**
Ko Yo 560
Kok River 318
Krabi 569, **572, 574**
Krabi Province 569-585, **570, 575**

La-Ngu 598
Laem Ngop 276
Laem Singh 520-521
Laem Son NP 500-501
Laem Talumpuk 552
Lampang 328-331, **329**
Lampang Province 328-333
Lamphun 326-328, **327**
Lamphun Province 326-328
Language 60-67
  Language List 63-67
  Thai Study 60, 105-106
Laundry 80-81
Li-khe 50
Literature, Thai 51
Loei 442-444, **443**
Loei Province 441-450, **442**
Lom Sak 450
Lopburi 226-231, **227**
Lopburi Province 226-231

Mabri Hill Tribe 397
Mae Aw 368

Mae Hong Son 364-368, **365**
Mae Hong Son Province 360-372, **361**
Mae Klong River 243
Mae La-Na 368
Mae Sai 383-386, **385**
Mae Salong (Santikhiri) 380-383
Mae Sariang 360-364, **362**
Mae Sot 354-358, **353, 355**
Mai Khao 521-522
Malaria 91-94, 268, 276
Maps 83, 156-157
Martial Arts 53, 106-107
Massage 97, 209, 330, 370
  Study 296
Media 83-85
  Newspapers 83-84
  Radio 84
  Television 84-85
Medical Kit 85-86
Medicine
  Traditional Thai 96
Meditation Study 59, 106, 178-179
Monarchy 36-37, 54
Money 70-74
  Bargaining 73
  Costs 72-73
  Credit Cards 71-72, 99
  Currency 70-71
  Exchange Rates 71
  Safety Deposit Boxes 72
  Tipping 73
Motorbike Travel 140-142
  Rental 141, 218
Muay Thai, See Thai Boxing
Mukdahan 458-459, **458**
Mukdahan Province 457-459
Music 47-48, 407, 585

Na Thon 530-532, **531**
Nai Han 518-520, **519**
Nai Yang 521-522
Nakhon Pathom 234, **234**
Nakhon Pathom Province 234-236
Nakhon Phanom 450-542, **451**
Nakhon Phanom Province 450-454
Nakhon Ratchasima 409-414, **410-411, 414**
Nakhon Ratchasima Province 409-419
Nakhon Sawan 333
Nakhon Sawan Province 333
Nakhon Si Thammarat 548-552, **459**
Nakhon Si Thammarat Province 547-553
Nam Nao NP 27
Nan 399-405, **402**
Nan Province 397-406, **398**
Narathiwat 607-610, **608**
Narathiwat Province 607-612
National Parks & Wildlife Sanctuaries 24-33, **25**
  Accommodation 108
  Ang Thong National MP 530
  Ao Phang-Nga National MP 31-32
  Chaloem Ratanakosin NP 250
  Doi Inthanon NP 25, 315
  Doi Khuntan NP 26
  Doi Phu Kha NP 405
  Doi Suthep/Doi Pui NP 26, 312-313
  Erawan Falls NP 28, 247-248
  Hat Jao Mai NP 590
  Hat Nai Yang NP 32
  Hat Noppharat Thara – Ko Phi Phi National MP 32, 569
  Huay Kha Khaeng WS 28
  Kaeng Krachan NP 29-30, 478-479
  Khao Chamao – Khao Wong NP 30, 266
  Khao Khitchakut NP 272
  Khao Laem Ya – Mu Ko Samet National MP 30-31
  Khao Luang NP 548
  Khao Phanom Bencha NP 578-579
  Khao Phra Taew NP 509
  Khao Sabap NP 272
  Khao Sam Roi Yot NP 30, 488
  Khao Sok NP 31, 527-528
  Khao Yai NP 29, 417-419
  Khlong Lamchan Waterbird Park 593
  Khukhut Waterbird Sanctuary 561
  Ko Chang National MP 31, 278-283
  Ko Lanta National MP 583
  Ko Tarutao National MP 32-33, 596-599, **597**
  Laem Son NP 500-501
  Nam Nao NP 27
  Phu Hin Rong Kla NP 341-343, **342**
  Phu Kradung NP 27-28, 444
  Phu Luang NP 445
  Phu Pha Thoep NP 458-459
  Phu Phaan NP 456
  Phu Reua NP 445
  Ram Khamhaeng NP 26
  Sai Yok NP 28
  Si Nakharin NP 28
National Parks & Wildlife Sanctuaries *cont*
  Similan Islands NP 502-504
  Surin Islands NP 502
  Thai Muang Beach NP 501
  Thale Ban NP 33, 599-600
  Thale Noi Waterbird Sanctuary 555-556
  Than Bokkharani NP 577-578
  Thung Salaeng Luang NP 26-27
  Thung Yai Naresuan WS 28
Nong Khai 433-438, **432**
Nong Khai Province 433-441, **435**
North-East Thailand 407-472, **408**
Northern Thailand 284-406, **285**

Opium 38-39
Orient Express 130

Pai 370-372, **371**
Pai River 368
Painting 47
Pak Bara 599
Pak Chom 446
Pak Thong Chai 414
Pasang 328
Patong 514-516, **515**
Pattani 604-607, **606**
Pattani Province 604-607, **604**
Pattaya 258-265, **259, 260**
Payathonzu 254-255
Pha Taem 467
Phae Muang Phii 396
Phang-Nga 504-505
Phang-Nga Province 501-505
Phattalung 553-556, **555**
Phattalung Province 553-556
Phetburi 475-478, **476**
Phetburi Province 475-480
Phi Phi Don 579, **580**
Phi Phi Le 579-580
Phibun Mangsahan 466
Phimai 415-416, **415**
Phitsanulok 335-341, **336**
Phitsanulok Province 335-343
Photography 85
Phra Pathom Chedi 234
Phrae 393-397, **394**
Phrae Province 392-397
Phu Hin Rong Kla NP 341-343, **342**
Phu Kradung NP 27-28, 444
Phu Luang NP 445
Phu Pha Thoep NP 458-459
Phu Phaan NP 456
Phu Phra Bat Historical Park 433

Phu Reua NP 445
Phuket 507-514, **508**
Phuket Province 505-522, **506**
  Beaches 514-522
Phun Phin 524, 525
Prachuap Khiri Khan 488-491, **489**
Prachuap Khiri Khan Province 481-492, **481**
Prang Sam Yot 229
Prasat Hin Khao Phanom Rung Historical Park 419- 422
Prasat Muang Singh Historical Park 248-249
Prasat Muang Tam 422
Prasat Phanomwan 416-417
Prostitution 121

Radio 84
Raft Trips 243, 368
Rail Passes 136-137
Ram Khamhaeng NP 26
Raman 603
Ranong 496-500, **499**
Ranong Province 496-501, **497**
Ratchaburi 236
Ratchaburi Province 236
Rawai 520, **519**
Rayong 265-266
Rayong Province 265-271
Renu Nakhon 452-453
River Trips 175-177, 318-319, 390
Roi Et 426-428, **427**
Roi Et Province 424-428

Sai Yok Falls 248
Sai Yok NP 28
Sakon Nakhon 455-457, **455**
Sakon Nakhon Province 454-457
San Kamphaeng 313
Sangkhlaburi 252
Sangkhom 440-441
Sao Din 406
Saraburi 231-232
Saraburi Province 231-232
Satun 594-596, **595**
Satun Province 593-600, **593**
Sawankhalok 350
Sawankhalok Kilns 349-350
Sculpture 42-46, 421
Sea Travel 131, 143
Shadow Puppetry 550
Shopping 82, 122-125, 169, 210, 308-309, 404, 425-426, 428, 431, 437, 465, 566, 589
  Antiques 70, 123, 211, 309
  Bronzeware 212
  Ceramics 124, 308, 414
Shopping *cont*
  Clothing 123, 309, 437
  Department Stores 211, 309
  Fake Goods 124-125
  Furniture 124
  Gems 211-212
  Handicrafts 212, 308, 309, 392, 404, 423, 428
  Hill-Tribe Crafts 124
  Jewellery 123-124, 211-212, 309
  Pirated Goods 124-125
  Shopping Centres 211
  Textiles 122-123, 308, 404, 425
Si Chiangmai 439-440
Si Nakharin NP 28
Si Racha 255-257, **256**
Si Saket 469-472, **468**
Si Satchanalai – Chaliang Historical Park 348-351, **350**
Similan Islands NP 502-504, **503**
Snorkelling 104-105, 501, 503, 518, 520, 540, 576, 598
Songkhla 556-560, **558**
Songkhla Province 556-569
Songthaews 146
Sop Ruak 390-391
Soppong 368
Southern Thailand 473-612, **474**
Spirit Houses 51
Sport 51-54
Sports Clubs 177-178
Sukhothai 343-348, **345, 346**
Sukhothai Province 343-351
Sungai Kolok 610-612, **611**
Suphanburi 232-233
Suphanburi Province 232-233
Surat Thani 523-527, **524**
Surat Thani Province 522-543
Surin 467-469
Surin Province 467-469
Surin (Phuket) 521
Surin Islands NP 502
Surin Province 467-472

Tak 352-354, **353**
Tak Province 352-360
Takraw (Siamese Football) 53
Takua Pa 501
Telephones 79-80
Television 84-85
Temple of the Big Buddha 530
Temple of the Emerald Buddha 158
Tha Bo 438-439
Tha Khaek 452
Tha Li District 449-450
Tha Ton 316-318
Thai Boxing 51-53, 106, 208, 530
Thai Lü 397
Thai Muang 501
Thai Muang Beach NP 501
Thale Ban NP 33, 599-600
Thale Noi Waterbird Sanctuary 554-555
Tham Luang 386
Tham Malai 554
Than Bokkharani NP 577-578
Thap Lamu 501
Thap Sakae 491-492
That Phanom 452-454, **453**
Theatre 48-51
Thong Sala 541-542
Three Pagodas Pass 251-252, 254-255
Thung Kwian Forest Market 332-333
Thung Salaeng Luang NP 26-27
Thung Yai Naresuan WS 28
Time 80
Tipping 73
Ton Nga Chang Falls 569
Tourism 41
  Tourism & the Environment 22-23
Tourist Offices 74-75
  Local 74-75
  Overseas 75
Train Travel 130-131, 136-140, 144-145
  Rail Passes 136-137
Trang 586-590, **588**
Trang Province 585-593, **586**
  Beaches 590-592
  Caves 592
  Waterfalls 592
Trat 275-277, **275**
Trat Province 273-283, **274**
Trekking 319-325, 364, 376, 382, 405
Tuk-Tuks 146, 216

Ubon Ratchathani 459-466, **460**
Ubon Ratchathani Province 459-467
Udon Thani 428-432, **429, 432**
Udon Thani Province 428-433
Um Phang 358-359
Uttaradit 351-352
Uttaradit Province 351-352

Vegetarian Festival 509-510, 587
Visas 68-70

Waley 358

Wat Paa Nanachat Beung Wai 462-463
Wat Phra That Lampang Luang 331, **331**
Wat Suan Mokkhaphalaram 522
Wat U Mong 293-294
Weights & Measures 81
Women Travellers 98
Women's Health 96-97
Working Holidays 68
Yala 600-602, **601**
Yala Province 600-603
Yasothon 457-458
Yasothon Province 457-459
Young Elephant Training Centre 332

Thanks

Thanks to all the following travellers and others (apologies if we've misspelt your name) who took time to write to us about their experiences of Thailand:

Gittan (S), Dr M Abernethy (UK), Vic Adams (UK), Rachel Adler (UK), Tommy Aerts (B), Kamran Ahmad (UK), W Aldred (UK), Patsy Alexander (AUS), Rob Allen (UK), A Anamnart (T), K & L Andersson (S), Jonas Andreasson (S), Niyana Angkawut (T), M Anstis (UK), G J Arthur, Marco Aruga (I), David Ashford (UK), Neville Ashmore (UK), S Audin, Christa Auerbach, Belinda Austin (NZ), Stephen Backes (UK), Andrew Bacon (UK), G & B Baeck (B), Cynthia Balaberda (C), Mark Balla (AUS), Joy Bannett (USA), Sandra Bao, Putnam Barber (USA), Jane Barnacle (AUS), R Barrett (UK), Dr W R J Barron (UK), Dr W R J Barron (UK), Dione Bartels (AUS), Magda Bartosch (UK), Annette Baston, Mark Bateman (UK), Merv Bayer (NZ), K B Bayley (AUS), Sue Beardmore, Lt Col T R Beaton (AUS), Peregrine Beckman, Bella Belew (USA), Richard Bell (UK), David Bellis (UK), Peter Bennett (AUS), John Benson, Prema Besse (CH), Michael Billos (S), Lars Bindholt (DK), Per Birk (DK), David Blake, Guy Blakesley (UK), Fritz Blatter (USA), Richard Blitstein, Mark Blum (USA), Andris Blums (AUS), Paul Bodington (AUS), Luen de Boer (NL), Jim Boland (USA), Bruce Bonnell (USA), H van den Boogaard (NL), Ken Boom (USA), Bruno Bosch (B), DC Boyall (AUS), Catherine Brahams (UK), France Brassard (C), Gary Bray (USA), Nancy Robinson Breuer (USA), Noel Brewer (USA), Ian Bridle, Silke & Eckart Broedermann (D), Marion Broek (NL), Vaisey Bromley (UK), David Brown, Catherine Bryant (UK), Jamie Buckner (USA), Lydiya Burfield (UK), Peter Burgess, Glen Burns (AUS), Helen Butt (UK), Tony Cabasco (USA), Peter Callaghan (AUS), Lisa & Simon Capes (UK), Margaretha Carlsson (S), Katy Carmichael (UK), Douglas Casey (UK), Eugene Casey, Robin Chakrabarti (UK), Denise Chalk (UK), Kevin Chambers (USA), Jeanne Anne Chapman (USA), Isabelle Chenu (F), Robert Cherubin (USA), Nancy Chodosh, Cathy Clark (USA), David Clayton (AUS), Jem Cloof (D), Jane Coloccia (USA), Paul Considine (AUS), Neville & Ola Cook (AUS), Joop/Rose Cornelissen (NL), Ronald Cox (UK), Alice Craje (NL), Nick Crivich (UK), Philip Crohn (AUS), Rob Crow-Mains (UK), Lucy Curry (UK), Ernest & Martha D'Ambrosio (USA), Roger Daniels (UK), Jay Davidson (USA), Ivor Davies (AUS), Luc de Noyette (B), Carmine de Stefano, Peter de Waal (AUS), Dr Colin De'ath, Marc Dehossay (B), Suzy Delowe (Isr), Lothar Deutsch, Andie Devaux (CH), Scott Devine, Petra Dey (NL), Andrew Dickinson (AUS), Digby (AUS), Andrew J Dikinson (AUS), Gary Dixon, Martin Donenfeld (USA), Christiane Doring-Saad (Isr), A J Dougherty (USA), Miss J Drake (UK), Paul Drymalski (F), Rick Dubbledam (NL), E Duffy (UK), Steve Dumire (UK), Linda Dupont (C), Hans Durrer, Andrew Dyson (UK), Dr John Eggleton (UK), Tony van Eijden (NL), Peter Ellemann (UK), Andrew Elliot (UK), Julie Ellis, Janet Esposito (USA), Wichit Eungsuwanpanich (T), Matthew Evans (UK), Peter Evans, Randy Everette (USA), Igor Fabjan (Yu), G Fardell (AUS), Tim Farson, Jan Feld (D), Eric Filippino (USA), Ulrike Findeisen (D), Barbara Fitzgibbon (IRL), Flax (USA), Anthony Fleming (UK), Robert Fleming, J I C Flint (UK), Eric Forday (AUS), Richard Forrest (UK), Meg Foster (USA), Inge Fowlie (C), Annie Fox (USA), Brian Frisby (UK), Mark J Fromm, Robert Frost (UK), Robert Furrer (USA), Steve Gabell (AUS), Robert Gabriel, Pernille Gad (DK), David & Mandy Galbraith (AUS), Philip Game (AUS), Andrew Gardner (UK), Christina Gasser (CH), Marc Gautering (B), Maryann Gebauer (C), Margot Gerster (CH), Mark Gluckman (USA), Heng Golf (T), Gillian Good (AUS), Susie Gorney (UK), Corine Goubert (USA), Frank Graetz (NL), Mark Gray (AUS), Linda Greenwood (C), Stuart Greif (NZ), John Grindley, Edward Gronowetter, Maxi Gruchot (D), Stephen Guise, Joe Gumino (USA), Mr C Gwenlan (UK), Nancy Haldeman (USA), Debbie Hall (AUS), Paul Hamilton (UK), Ian Hammond (UK), Steve Hammonds (UK), Randy Hanley (USA), Jane Harland (UK), Amanda Harlow (UK), Lewis Harper (USA), Paul Harris (UK), Kate Harris (UK), Fred Harris (USA), Don Harrison (AUS), Sarah Harvey (AUS), Gili Haskin, Chris Hayward, Kevin Taylor Hebron (AUS), Fionna Heiton (UK), Alison Henderson (AUS), John Herbert (C), Alan Hickey, Glen Hill, Vicki Hinchcliffe (AUS), Julia Hobday (UK), Hartley Hobson (USA), Bernie Hodges, Janet Hodgson (UK), H P P Hoedmaker (NL), Gunter Hoffman (S), Roger Holdsworth (AUS), Ian Hollingsworth (UK), Ronald Hoppen (UK), Kristina Horlin (I), Janyk Houle, S G Howe (T), John Howes (J), Zack Huchulak (C), Wendy & Brian Hughes (UK), Samuel Hunter (UK), Harry Hunter (USA), Russell Huntingdon (AUS), Janette Huston (AUS), Ian Hutchings (UK), Steve Hutton, Patricia Hynes (AUS), Julia Ibbotson (UK), Valby Langgade Icksine (DK), Mariana Jacobs, Sompong Jaidee (T), Ajay Jani (USA), Erica Janssen (NL), Jape Chamnan Jantawan (T), Richard Jenkins (USA), K Jensen (DK), Natakan Jiwasamonaikum, Janet Johnson (NZ), Rev Kenneth Johnson, Robert Johnson (USA), Katherine Johnston (C), Guy Jones (UK), reg Kamm, A Karp, Mrs Keipers (D), Roy Kellett (UK), Peter Kerby (N), Kriangsak Ketkaew (T), Su-Ling Khoo (UK), Astrid Kierid (NL), Kalervo Kiianmaa (Fin), Julie King (UK), Charles King (UK), Lud Klaauw (NL), Maria & Mark Klein (USA), Susan Kleinig (AUS), Gobert Jan Knotter (NL), Oliver Koehler, Ralf Kohl, Marcus Kohler (UK), Willem Kox (NL), Toni Kram (AUS), Meredith Krashes,

Ittipol Krisanasuwan (T), Marion Kruger (AUS), Karin Lakerveld (NL), D L Lambert (UK), Harry Lang (AUS), H A Lang (AUS), Olav Langas (N), Susan Langridge (UK), M T Lansdown (UK), Richard Laprise (C), Michael Larsen (USA), Gert Larsson (S), Donna Lau (USA), Urs Laubli (CH), Robert Lavicka (NL), Andre Lavoie (USA), Robyn Lee (AUS), Miss Cheech Leech (UK), Elizabeth Leicester, Keneth Levine (USA), Yossy Levy (Isr), Hermes D Liberty (C), Hermes Liberty (C), Caroline Lingmerth (S), Marcel Lisi (USA), Ron Lister (AUS), B Livett, Dee Loader-Oliver (AUS), James Loutit (C), Elisa & Pietro Luka (I), Susan Lupton (UK), Max Lyons (USA), Jill Maben (UK), Laurelle MacDonald (AUS), Sean Macfarlane (AUS), Jesper Nymann Madsen (DK), Pierre Maessen (B), Donna Magensen (DK), Dave Maltz (USA), Sarah Mander, Frances Mantak, Mario Maric (S), Steven Maron (USA), Robert Marseille (USA), Harvey Marshall (USA), LW Martin (AUS), Inge Martin (S), Steve Martin, Lisa Martin, Michel Martineau (C), Keith Matthews (NZ), Jo Matthews (UK), Stephen Matthews (AUS), Bronwyn Mauldin (USA), Marlon Maus (USA), Peter May (UK), Beth Mayer (USA), Kevin Mayo (AUS), Ralph McArthur (NZ), Vanessa McGrady (USA), Glennis McGregor (C), Mark McHarry (USA), Carolyn McLeod (AUS), Nopawan McLeod (AUS), Bob McMeechan (UK), Frederico Medici (I), Joe Meline, Jim Mellefont (AUS), Jean & Mel Merzon (USA), Marietta Meyer (CH), David Meyerson (USA), Daniel Mezger (USA), Michael Michiel (C), Stephen Millar (AUS), Sian Miller (UK), Debbie Mills (AUS), Celia Minoughan (UK), Jakob Modeer (S), Johan Molenaar (NL), Enzo & Teresa Montalto (D), Bruce Moore, E P Morkel (D), John Morrow (NZ), R D Morton (UK), Susan Morton, Damian Mottram (UK), Nick Mullan (UK), Eban Murray (UK), Marcia Muszyrska, Kristie Neilson (UK), Chris Newton (UK), Wayne & Clair Nichols (UK), Wolfgang Niegl (D), Anne Nimcharoen (T), Mr Noon (T), Vicky Norman (UK), Jan Norton (AUS), Tom Nowak (C), Mary O'Connor (AUS), Ms M O'Sullivan (AUS), Jan Ochi (AUS), Brett Oglivie (UK), Mio Okahara (Jap), Annette Oliveira (USA), Stewart Olney, Olov & Tukkata (T), Larry Otto (C), Pinit Ounope (T), R S J Paauwe (NL), Todd Paddock (USA), Mrs Paffenbarger (USA), Julian Page (UK), Gabriella Paradisi (I), Cheryl Parsons (UK), Leo Pascalis, Briony Patten (UK), Jenny Peacock, Eddy Pearce (UK), Bill & Robin Pennington (AUS), Jean-Paul Penrose (UK), Patrick Percy (USA), A K Perkins (NZ), Chuck Perlee (USA), Magnus Perlestam (S), Toby Petersen (USA), John Petit, D H Phillips, D Phillips, Hywel Phillips, Naphaporn Phiroe (T), Eva Pichler (A), Cecilia & Paolo Pignatti (I), John Pigou (DK), C J Pilc (UK), Miriam Pinchok (USA), Frank & Joanne Pinelli (USA), Gary & Mary Pinkus (USA), Klaus Plitzner (A), Helena Plummer, Christina Podolinsky (AUS), Porn (T), Mr Philippe Poza (F), Massimo Pratelli (I), Matthew Price (UK), Luida M Pszan (UK), Virat Puangmalai (T), Paul Purcell (AUS), Agnes Radvanyi, Charles Raincock (UK), Juliet Randell (UK), Colleen Ranta, Rex Rattur, Tony Reed, Ray Reffold, Stephen Reid (NZ), Debbie Reiskind (C), Fred Remers (NL), Lisa Renkin (AUS), M Reynolds (UK), Sanne Reys (NL), Peter Ribbans (UK), Julia Richards (USA), Brian Richards (USA), Steven Ridley (AUS), Jose Rigau, Lance Robert (USA), Ian Robinson (USA), Richard Robinson (C), Matt Robson (UK), Bruce Roby (USA), Sarah Rooney, Aura Rose (C), Cristina & Luca Rosso (D), Dr Rouset (USA), Barbara & David Rout (AUS), David Rowley (UK), Karin Ruscher (D), Beverly G Russell (USA), Dr Darren Russell (AUS), Beverly G Russell (USA), W Ruttkowski, Noel Ryan (IRL), Moti Sabag (Isr), Wolfgang Sackenheim, Anne Marie Saget (F), Paul F Samuelson (USA), Doug Sanders, Ross Sanford (UK), Verasak Sangsawad (THAI), P Sapachai (T), Alessandro Saragosa (I), Josh Sarnoff (USA), C T Sartain (USA), Stewart Saunders (AUS), Brian Savage, Shane L Scahill (NZ), Maignt Schilter (CH), Thomas Schmidt (USA), Leon Sebek (C), Leon Sebek (C),Suksom Senajai (T), Olarn Seriniyom (T), Michael Shelly (AUS), Lucile Shelton (AUS), Richard Sherry (C), Kate Shew (AUS), Susie Siedentop (USA), Frank Sierowski (UK), Lorens Simonsen (DK), Kathy Simpson, Kathy Simpson (AUS), Danny Simpson (UK), Francois & Sin, Jim Sinfield (UK), Mr Jerry D Singer (UK), Tara Singh (USA), Vidar Skripeland (AUS), Diane Smith (C), Andrew Smith (C), Stephen F Smith (NZ), Mrs Pat Smith (AUS), Neil Smulowitz (Isr), Jonathon Soll (USA), J R Somerville (UK), Carolyn Spicer (UK), Philip Stahl (USA), Tony Stanbridge, Julie Stapleton, Ben Steeman (NL), Carl Stein (USA), Roger Stemhell, Rachel Stephens, Susanne Stevens, Robb Stewart (C), Victoria Stickland (UK), Anette Stieber (IRL), Ruth Stiles (USA), Victoria Stone (UK), Susan Strehlow (AUS), Noelle & Bob Stuart (AUS), Julia Stubbings (UK), Lisa Studdart (AUS), Summer (AUS), Rolf Svenstrom (S), Damian Joseph Sykes (AUS), Jonathon Sykes (UK), Randi Sylke (UK), Scott Takushi (USA), Joseph A Tantet (USA), Gail Taveepanichpan (T), Harold Taw (USA), S Tay (AUS), Dale & Diane Tayln (AUS), Steve Taylor (UK), Catherine Taylor (AUS), Patrick Teeuwisse (NL), Teodori (I), Fenella Thomas (AUS), Gabrielle Thon (A), JR Tippett, Aerts Tommy (B), John Tormey (USA), Tom Tornow, Collette Trudel, Richard Tucker (NL), Richard/Marijke Tucker (UK), Wendy Turnbull (AUS), David Tyler, Dave Underwood (AUS), Simon Vallings (NZ), Rosamund Vallings (NZ), Math van den Hoef (NL), Peter van der Kuil (NL), Dr Hajonides van der Meulen (NL), Bram van der Waals (NL), Henry van Gael (B), Jon van Housen (USA), Arnoud van Soest (NL), Golda van Veen (NL), S A Op het Veld (NL), Adriaan Verhage (NL), Marijke Verhoeff (NL), Sorapon Viboolbuntitgit (T), Antonio Vivaldi

(I), Margaret Wade (USA), Michael Wadman (USA), Michael Walker, Melissa Wall (USA), Mike Walmsley (UK), Peter Walsh (UK), Denise Warner (AUS), Hugh Waters, David Watkins (AUS), David Wayte (UK), Stephen Weaver, Duncan Webb, Ram Weinberger (Isr), Janet Wells (USA), G J Westenbunk (NL), Sue Wheat (UK), Paul Wheaton (UK), Jez Wicken (UK), Scarlett vanden Wijngaard (NL), Alan Wild (AUS), Jan Wilkman, Bob Williams (USA), Sheila Williamson, Els Wilschut (NL), Mrs M Wise (UK), Rebecca Woodgate (UK), Nicholas Woodward (UK), James Wright (UK), Sandy Wright (C), John Yonge (UK), Mr Prawithaya Zinprazonc (T), Thomas Zumbroich (USA)

A – Austria, AUS – Australia, B – Belgium, Bra – Brazil, BRU – Brunei, C – Canada, CH – Switzerland, Chi – China, CR – Costa Rica, CS – Czechoslovakia, CY – Cyprus, D – Germany, DK – Denmark, F – France, Fij – Fiji, Fin – Finland, G – Greece, H – Hungary, HK – Hong Kong, IND – India, Indo – Indonesia, IRL – Ireland, Isr – Israel, I – Italy, J – Japan, Jor – Jordan, Kor – Korea, L – Luxembourg, M – Malaysia, N – Norway, NL – Netherlands, NZ – New Zealand, PL – Poland, P – Portugal, Phl – Philippines, PNG – Papua New Guinea, Sin – Singapore, SA – South Africa, SL – Sri Lanka, Sp – Spain, S – Sweden, Tai – Taiwan, T – Thailand, Tur – Turkey, UK – United Kingdom, USA – United States of America, Yu – Yugoslavia, Z – Zimbabwe

Keep in touch!

We love hearing from you and think you'd like to hear from us.

The Lonely Planet Newsletter covers the when, where, how and what of travel. (AND it's free!)

***When**...is the right time to see reindeer in Finland?*
***Where**...can you hear the best palm-wine music in Ghana?*
***How**...do you get from Asunción to Areguá by steam train?*
***What**...should you leave behind to avoid hassles with customs in Iran?*

To join our mailing list just contact us at any of our offices. (details below)

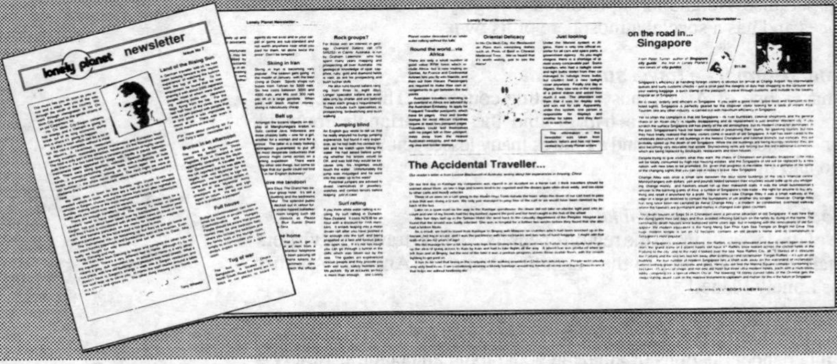

Every issue includes:

- *a letter from Lonely Planet founders Tony and Maureen Wheeler*
- *travel diary from a Lonely Planet author - find out what it's really like out on the road*
- *feature article on an important and topical travel issue*
- *a selection of recent letters from our readers*
- *the latest travel news from all over the world*
- *details on Lonely Planet's new and forthcoming releases*

Also available Lonely Planet T-shirts. 100% heavy weight cotton (S, M, L, XL)

lonely planet

LONELY PLANET PUBLICATIONS

Australia: PO Box 617, Hawthorn, 3122, Victoria (tel: 03-819 1877)
USA: Embarcadero West, 155 Filbert Street, Suite 251, Oakland, CA 94607 (tel: 510-893 8555)
UK: Devonshire House, 12 Barley Mow Passage, Chiswick, London W4 4PH (tel: 081-742 3161)

Guides to South-East Asia

South-East Asia on a shoestring
The well-known 'yellow bible' for travellers in South-East Asia covers Brunei, Burma (Myanmar), Cambodia, Hong Kong, Indonesia, Laos, Macau, Malaysia, the Philippines, Singapore, Thailand and Vietnam.

Bali & Lombok - a travel survival kit
This guide will help travellers to experience the real magic of Bali's tropical paradise. Neighbouring Lombok is largely untouched by outside influences and has a special atmosphere of its own.

Myanmar (Burma) - a travel survival kit
Myanmar is one of Asia's most interesting countries. This book shows how to make the most of a trip around the main triangle route of Yangon–Mandalay–Bagan, and explores many lesser-known places such as Bago and Inle Lake.

Cambodia - a travel survival kit
As one of the last nations in the region opens its doors to travellers, visitors will again make their way to the magnificent ruins of Angkor. Another first for Lonely Planet!

Malaysia, Singapore & Brunei - a travel survival kit
Three independent nations of amazing geographic and cultural variety – from the national parks, beaches, jungles and rivers of Malaysia, tiny oil-rich Brunei and the urban prosperity and diversity of Singapore.

Philippines - a travel survival kit
The friendly Filipinos, colourful festivals, and superb natural scenery make the Philippines one of the most interesting countries in South-East Asia for adventurous travellers and sun- seekers alike.

Indonesia - a travel survival kit
Some of the most remarkable sights and sounds in South-East Asia can be found amongst the 7000 islands of Indonesia – this book covers the entire archipelago in detail.

Hong Kong, Macau & Canton - a travel survival kit
A comprehensive guide to three fascinating cities linked by history, culture and geography.

Vietnam, Laos & Cambodia - a travel survival kit
This comprehensive guidebook has all the information you'll need on this most beautiful region of Asia – finally opening its doors to the world.

Singapore - city guide
Singapore offers a taste of the great Asian cultures in a small, accessible package. This compact guide will help travellers discover the very best that this city of contrasts can offer.

Bangkok - city guide

Bangkok has something for everyone: temples, museums and historic sites; an endless variety of good restaurants, clubs, international culture and social events; a modern art institute; and great shopping oppurtunities. This pocket guide offers you the assurance that you will never be lost...or lost for things to do in this fascinating city!

Also available:

Thai phrasebook, ***Thai Hill Tribes*** phrasebook, ***Burmese*** phrasebook, ***Pilipino*** phrasebook, ***Indonesian*** phrasebook, ***Papua New Guinea Pidgin*** phrasebook, ***Mandarin Chinese*** phrasebook and ***Vietnamese*** phrasebook.

Lonely Planet Guidebooks

Lonely Planet guidebooks cover every accessible part of Asia as well as Australia, the Pacific, South America, Africa, the Middle East, Europe and parts of North America. There are five series: *travel survival kits*, covering a country for a range of budgets; *shoestring guides* with compact information for low-budget travel in a major region; *walking guides*; *city guides* and *phrasebooks*.

Australia & the Pacific
Australia
Bushwalking in Australia
Islands of Australia's Great Barrier Reef
Fiji
Melbourne city guide
Micronesia
New Caledonia
New Zealand
Tramping in New Zealand
Papua New Guinea
Papua New Guinea phrasebook
Rarotonga & the Cook Islands
Samoa
Solomon Islands
Sydney city guide
Tahiti & French Polynesia
Tonga
Vanuatu

South-East Asia
Bali & Lombok
Bangkok city guide
Myanmar (Burma)
Burmese phrasebook
Cambodia
Indonesia
Indonesia phrasebook
Malaysia, Singapore & Brunei
Philippines
Pilipino phrasebook
Singapore city guide
South-East Asia on a shoestring
Thailand
Thai phrasebook
Vietnam, Laos & Cambodia
Vietnamese phrasebook

North-East Asia
China
Mandarin Chinese phrasebook
Hong Kong, Macau & Canton
Japan
Japanese phrasebook
Korea
Korean phrasebook
Mongolia
North-East Asia on a shoestring
Taiwan
Tibet
Tibet phrasebook
Tokyo city guide

West Asia
Trekking in Turkey
Turkey
Turkish phrasebook
West Asia on a shoestring

Middle East
Arab Gulf States
Egypt & the Sudan
Egyptian Arabic phrasebook
Iran
Israel
Jordan & Syria
Yemen

Indian Ocean
Madagascar & Comoros
Maldives & Islands of the East Indian Ocean
Mauritius, Réunion & Seychelles

Mail Order

Lonely Planet guidebooks are distributed worldwide. They are also available by mail order from Lonely Planet, so if you have difficulty finding a title please write to us. US and Canadian residents should write to Embarcadero West, 155 Filbert St, Suite 251, Oakland CA 94607, USA; European residents should write to Devonshire House, 12 Barley Mow Passage, Chiswick, London W4 4PH; and residents of other countries to PO Box 617, Hawthorn, Victoria 3122, Australia.

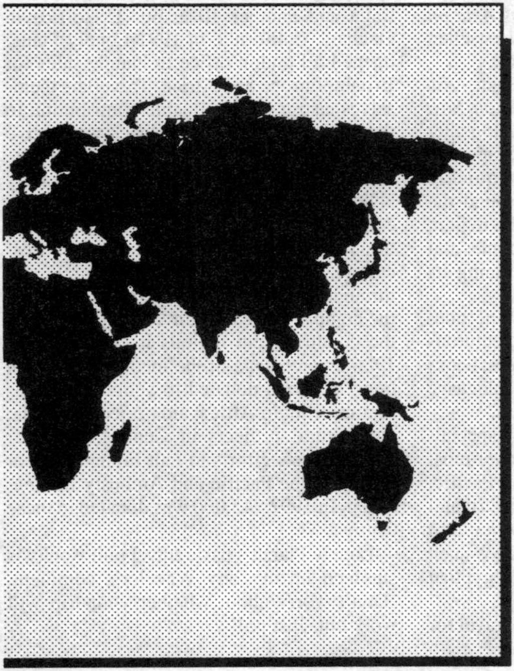

Indian Subcontinent

Bangladesh
India
Hindi/Urdu phrasebook
Trekking in the Indian Himalaya
Karakoram Highway
Kashmir, Ladakh & Zanskar
Nepal
Trekking in the Nepal Himalaya
Nepal phrasebook
Pakistan
Sri Lanka
Sri Lanka phrasebook

Africa

Africa on a shoestring
Central Africa
East Africa
Kenya
Swahili phrasebook
Morocco, Algeria & Tunisia
Moroccan Arabic phrasebook
South Africa, Lesotho & Swaziland
Zimbabwe, Botswana & Namibia
West Africa
Mexico
Baja California
Mexico

Central America

Central America on a shoestring
Costa Rica
La Ruta Maya

North America

Alaska
Canada
Hawaii

South America

Argentina, Uruguay & Paraguay
Bolivia
Brazil
Brazilian phrasebook
Chile & Easter Island
Colombia
Ecuador & the Galápagos Islands
Latin American Spanish phrasebook
Peru
Quechua phrasebook
South America on a shoestring
Trekking in the Patagonian Andes

Europe

Eastern Europe on a shoestring
Eastern Europe phrasebook
Finland
Iceland, Greenland & the Faroe Islands
Mediterranean Europe on a shoestring
Mediterranean Europe phrasebook
Poland
Scandinavian & Baltic Europe on a shoestring
Scandinavian Europe phrasebook
Trekking in Spain
Trekking in Greece
USSR
Russian phrasebook
Western Europe on a shoestring
Western Europe phrasebook

The Lonely Planet Story

Lonely Planet published its first book in 1973 in response to the numerous 'How did you do it?' questions Maureen and Tony Wheeler were asked after driving, bussing, hitching, sailing and railing their way from England to Australia.

Written at a kitchen table and hand collated, trimmed and stapled, *Across Asia on the Cheap* became an instant local bestseller, inspiring thoughts of another book.

Eighteen months in South-East Asia resulted in their second guide, *South-East Asia on a shoestring*, which they put together in a backstreet Chinese hotel in Singapore in 1975. The 'yellow bible' as it quickly became known to backpackers around the world, soon became *the* guide to the region. It has sold well over half a million copies and is now in its 7th edition, still retaining its familiar yellow cover.

Today there are over 100 Lonely Planet titles – books that have that same adventurous approach to travel as those early guides; books that 'assume you know how to get your luggage off the carousel' as one reviewer put it.

Although Lonely Planet initially specialised in guides to Asia, they now cover most regions of the world, including the Pacific, South America, Africa, the Middle East and Europe. The list of *walking guides* and *phrasebooks* (for 'unusual' languages such as Quechua, Swahili, Nepalese and Egyptian Arabic) is also growing rapidly.

The emphasis continues to be on travel for independent travellers. Tony and Maureen still travel for several months of each year and play an active part in the writing, updating and quality control of Lonely Planet's guides.

They have been joined by over 50 authors, 48 staff – mainly editors, cartographers, & designers – at our office in Melbourne, Australia and another 10 at our US office in Oakland, California. In 1991 Lonely Planet opened a London office to handle sales for Britain, Europe and Africa. Travellers themselves also make a valuable contribution to the guides through the feedback we receive in thousands of letters each year.

The people at Lonely Planet strongly believe that travellers can make a positive contribution to the countries they visit, both through their appreciation of the countries' culture, wildlife and natural features, and through the money they spend. In addition, the company makes a direct contribution to the countries and regions it covers. Since 1986 a percentage of the income from each book has been donated to ventures such as famine relief in Africa; aid projects in India; agricultural projects in Central America; Greenpeace's efforts to halt French nuclear testing in the Pacific and Amnesty International. In 1992 $45,000 was donated to these causes.

Lonely Planet's basic travel philosophy is summed up in Tony Wheeler's comment, 'Don't worry about whether your trip will work out. Just go!'